Nineteenth-Century Literature Criticism

Guide to Gale Literary Criticism Series

For criticism on	Consult these Gale series
Authors now living or who died after December 31, 1999	*CONTEMPORARY LITERARY CRITICISM (CLC)*
Authors who died between 1900 and 1999	*TWENTIETH-CENTURY LITERARY CRITICISM (TCLC)*
Authors who died between 1800 and 1899	*NINETEENTH-CENTURY LITERATURE CRITICISM (NCLC)*
Authors who died between 1400 and 1799	*LITERATURE CRITICISM FROM 1400 TO 1800 (LC)* *SHAKESPEAREAN CRITICISM (SC)*
Authors who died before 1400	*CLASSICAL AND MEDIEVAL LITERATURE CRITICISM (CMLC)*
Authors of books for children and young adults	*CHILDREN'S LITERATURE REVIEW (CLR)*
Dramatists	*DRAMA CRITICISM (DC)*
Poets	*POETRY CRITICISM (PC)*
Short story writers	*SHORT STORY CRITICISM (SSC)*
Black writers of the past two hundred years	*BLACK LITERATURE CRITICISM (BLC)* *BLACK LITERATURE CRITICISM SUPPLEMENT (BLCS)*
Hispanic writers of the late nineteenth and twentieth centuries	*HISPANIC LITERATURE CRITICISM (HLC)* *HISPANIC LITERATURE CRITICISM SUPPLEMENT (HLCS)*
Native North American writers and orators of the eighteenth, nineteenth, and twentieth centuries	*NATIVE NORTH AMERICAN LITERATURE (NNAL)*
Major authors from the Renaissance to the present	*WORLD LITERATURE CRITICISM, 1500 TO THE PRESENT (WLC)* *WORLD LITERATURE CRITICISM SUPPLEMENT (WLCS)*

ISSN 0732-1864

Volume 102

Nineteenth-Century Literature Criticism

Excerpts from Criticism of the
Works of Novelists, Philosophers, and Other
Creative Writers Who Died between 1800
and 1899, from the First Published Critical
Appraisals to Current Evaluations

<mark>**Jessica Menzo**
Russel Whitaker
Associate Editors</mark>

GALE GROUP

™

THOMSON LEARNING

Detroit • New York • San Diego • San Francisco
Boston • New Haven, Conn. • Waterville, Maine
London • Munich

STAFF

Janet Witalec, Lynn M. Zott, *Managing Editors, Literature Product*
Kathy D. Darrow, Ellen McGeagh, *Content-Product Liaisons*
Mark W. Scott, *Publisher, Literature Product*

Jessica Menzo, Russel Whitaker, *Associate Editors*
Maikue Vang, *Assistant Editor*
Jenny Cromie, Mary Ruby, *Technical Training Specialists*
Deborah J. Morad, Joyce Nakamura, Kathleen Lopez Nolan, *Managing Editors, Literature Content*
Susan M. Trosky, *Director, Literature Content*

Maria L. Franklin, *Permissions Manager*
Debra Freitas, Shalice Shah-Caldwell, *Permissions Associates*

Victoria B. Cariappa, *Research Manager*
Sarah Genik, *Project Coordinator*
Tamara C. Nott, Tracie A. Richardson, *Research Associates*
Nicodemus Ford, *Research Assistant*
Michelle Campbell, *Administrative Specialist*

Dorothy Maki, *Manufacturing Manager*
Stacy L. Melson, *Buyer*

Mary Beth Trimper, *Composition and Prepress Manager*
Carolyn Roney, *Composition Specialist*

Randy Bassett, *Imaging Supervisor*
Robert Duncan, Dan Newell, Luke Rademacher, *Imaging Specialists*
Pamela A. Reed, *Imaging Coordinator*
Kelly A. Quin, *Editor, Imaging and Multimedia Content*
Michael Logusz, *Graphic Artist*

Library of Congress Catalog Card Number
ISBN 0-7876-5234-2
ISSN 0732-1864
Printed in the United States of America

10 9 8 7 6 5 4 3 2 1

Contents

Preface vii

Acknowledgments xi

Literary Criticism Series Advisory Board xiii

Preface

Since its inception in 1981, *Nineteeth-Century Literature Criticism* (*NCLC*) has been a valuable resource for students and librarians seeking critical commentary on writers of this transitional period in world history. Designated an "Outstanding Reference Source" by the American Library Association with the publication of is first volume, *NCLC* has since been purchased by over 6,000 school, public, and university libraries. The series has covered more than 300 authors representing 29 nationalities and over 17,000 titles. No other reference source has surveyed the critical reaction to nineteenth-century authors and literature as thoroughly as *NCLC*.

Scope of the Series

NCLC is designed to introduce students and advanced readers to the authors of the nineteenth century and to the most significant interpretations of these authors' works. The great poets, novelists, short story writers, playwrights, and philosophers of this period are frequently studied in high school and college literature courses. By organizing and reprinting commentary written on these authors, *NCLC* helps students develop valuable insight into literary history, promotes a better understanding of the texts, and sparks ideas for papers and assignments. Each entry in *NCLC* presents a comprehensive survey of an author's career or an individual work of literature and provides the user with a multiplicity of interpretations and assessments. Such variety allows students to pursue their own interests; furthermore, it fosters an awareness that literature is dynamic and responsive to many different opinions.

Every fourth volume of *NCLC* is devoted to literary topics that cannot be covered under the author approach used in the rest of the series. Such topics include literary movements, prominent themes in nineteenth-century literature, literary reaction to political and historical events, significant eras in literary history, prominent literary anniversaries, and the literatures of cultures that are often overlooked by English-speaking readers.

NCLC continues the survey of criticism of world literature begun by Gale's *Contemporary Literary Criticism* (*CLC*) and *Twentieth-Century Literary Criticism* (*TCLC*).

Organization of the Book

An *NCLC* entry consists of the following elements:

- The **Author Heading** cites the name under which the author most commonly wrote, followed by birth and death dates. Also located here are any name variations under which an author wrote, including transliterated forms for authors whose native languages use nonroman alphabets. If the author wrote consistently under a pseudonym, the pseudonym will be listed in the author heading and the author's actual name given in parenthesis on the first line of the biographical and critical information. Uncertain birth or death dates are indicated by question marks. Single-work entries are preceded by a heading that consists of the most common form of the title in English translation (if applicable) and the original date of composition.

- The **Introduction** contains background information that introduces the reader to the author, work, or topic that is the subject of the entry.

- A **Portrait of the Author** is included when available.

- The list of **Principal Works** is ordered chronologically by date of first publication and lists the most important works by the author. The genre and publication date of each work is given. In the case of foreign authors whose works have been translated into English, the list will focus primarily on twentieth-century translations, selecting those works most commonly considered the best by critics. Unless otherwise indicated, dramas are dated by first performance, not first publication. Lists of **Representative Works** by different authors appear with topic entries.

- Reprinted **Criticism** is arranged chronologically in each entry to provide a useful perspective on changes in critical evaluation over time. The critic's name and the date of composition or publication of the critical work are given at the beginning of each piece of criticism. Unsigned criticism is preceded by the title of the source in which it appeared. All titles by the author featured in the text are printed in boldface type. Footnotes are reprinted at the end of each essay or excerpt. In the case of excerpted criticism, only those footnotes that pertain to the excerpted texts are included. Criticism in topic entries is arranged chronologically under a variety of subheadings to facilitate the study of different aspects of the topic.

- A complete **Bibliographical Citation** of the original essay or book precedes each piece of criticism.

- Critical essays are prefaced by brief **Annotations** explicating each piece.

- An annotated bibliography of **Further Reading** appears at the end of each entry and suggests resources for additional study. In some cases, significant essays for which the editors could not obtain reprint rights are included here. Boxed material following the further reading list provides references to other biographical and critical sources on the author in series published by Gale.

Indexes

Each volume of *NCLC* contains a **Cumulative Author Index** listing all authors who have appeared in a wide variety of reference sources published by the Gale Group, including *NCLC*. A complete list of these sources is found facing the first page of the Author Index. The index also includes birth and death dates and cross references between pseudonyms and actual names.

A **Cumulative Nationality Index** lists all authors featured in *NCLC* by nationality, followed by the number of the *NCLC* volume in which their entry appears.

A **Cumulative Topic Index** lists the literary themes and topics treated in the series as well as in *Classical and Medieval Literature Criticism, Literature Criticism from 1400 to 1800, Twentieth-Century Literary Criticism,* and the *Contemporary Literary Criticism* Yearbook, which was discontinued in 1998.

An alphabetical **Title Index** accompanies each volume of *NCLC*, with the exception of the Topics volumes. Listings of titles by authors covered in the given volume are followed by the author's name and the corresponding page numbers where the titles are discussed. English translations of foreign titles and variations of titles are cross-referenced to the title under which a work was originally published. Titles of novels, dramas, nonfiction books, and poetry, short story, or essay collections are printed in italics, while individual poems, short stories, and essays are printed in roman type within quotation marks.

In response to numerous suggestions from librarians, Gale also produces an annual paperbound edition of the *NCLC* cumulative title index. This annual cumulation, which alphabetically lists all titles reviewed in the series, is available to all customers. Additional copies of this index are available upon request. Librarians and patrons will welcome this separate index; it saves shelf space, is easy to use, and is recyclable upon receipt of the next edition.

Citing *Nineteenth-Century Literature Criticism*

When writing papers, students who quote directly from any volume in the Literary Criticism Series may use the following general format to footnote reprinted criticism. The first example pertains to material drawn from periodicals, the second to material reprinted from books.

Kim McQuaid, "William Apes, Pequot: An Indian Reformer in the Jackson Era," *The New England Quarterly,* 50 (December 1977): 605-25; excerpted and reprinted in *Nineteenth-Century Literature Criticism,* vol. 73, ed. Janet Witalec (Farmington Hills, Mich.: The Gale Group, 1999), 3-4.

Richard Harter Fogle, *The Imagery of Keats and Shelley: A Comparative Study* (Archon Books, 1949), 211-51; excerpted and reprinted in *Nineteenth-Century Literature Criticism,* vol. 73, ed. Janet Witalec (Farmington Hills, Mich.: The Gale Group, 1999), 157-69.

Suggestions are Welcome

Readers who wish to suggest new features, topics, or authors to appear in future volumes, or who have other suggestions or comments are cordially invited to call, write, or fax the Managing Editor:

Managing Editor, Literary Criticism Series
The Gale Group
27500 Drake Road
Farmington Hills, MI 48331-3535
1-800-347-4253 (GALE)
Fax: 248-699-8054

Acknowledgments

The editors wish to thank the copyright holders of the excerpted criticism included in this volume and the permissions managers of many book and magazine publishing companies for assisting us in securing reproduction rights. We are also grateful to the staffs of the Detroit Public Library, the Library of Congress, the University of Detroit Mercy Library, Wayne State University Purdy/Kresge Library Complex, and the University of Michigan Libraries for making their resources available to us. Following is a list of the copyright holders who have granted us permission to reproduce material in this volume of *NCLC*. Every effort has been made to trace copyright, but if omissions have been made, please let us know.

COPYRIGHTED EXCERPTS IN *NCLC*, VOLUME 102, WERE REPRODUCED FROM THE FOLLOWING PERIODICALS:

The American Imago, v. 36, Summer, 1979. © 1979 The Johns Hopkins University Press. Reproduced by permission.—*Brontë Society Transactions,* v. 20, 1991. Reproduced by permission.—*Connecticut Review,* v. 14, Fall, 1992 for "Narrative Experience as a Means to Maturity in Anne Brontë's Victorian Novel 'The Tenant of Wildfell Hall,'" by Edith A. Kostka. Copyright © 1992 Board of Trustees, Connecticut State University. Reproduced by permission of the author.—*ELH,* v. 51, Winter, 1984. © 1984 The Johns Hopkins University Press. Reproduced by permission.—*English Studies,* v. 63, June 1982 for "The Question of Credibility in Anne Brontë's 'The Tenant of Wildfell Hall'" by Arlene M. Jackson. © The English Association 1982. Reproduced by permission of the publisher and the author.—*Forum for Modern Language Studies,* v. 18, October, 1982 for "A Suitable Case of Treatment: Ideological Confusion in Vigny's 'Cinq-Mars'" by Keith Wren; v. 22, October, 1986 for "Truth and Humanity in Grillparzer's 'Weh Dem, Der Lugt!'" by Ian F. Roe. Both reproduced by permission of the publisher and the respective authors.—*French Forum,* v. 18, May, 1993. Reproduced by permission.—*The French Review,* v. 56, February, 1983; v. 60, December, 1986. Copyright 1983, 1986 by the American Association of Teachers of French. Both reproduced by permission.—*French Studies Bulletin,* Autumn, 1989. Reproduced by permission.—*German Quarterly,* v. 54, 1980. Copyright © 1980 by the American Association of Teachers of German. Reproduced by permission.—*The Germanic Review,* v. 56, Fall, 1981 for "'Der Arme Spielmann' and the Role of Compromise in Grillparzer's Work" by Ian F. Roe. Reproduced by permission of the author.—*Hispanofila,* v. 27, September, 1983; v. 31, May, 1988. Both reproduced by permission.—*Hypatia: A Journal of Feminist Philosophy,* v. 9, Summer, 1994. Reproduced by permission.—*Kentucky Romance Quarterly,* v. 20, 1973. Copyright © 1973 Helen Dwight Reid Educational Foundation. Reproduced with permission of the Helen Dwight Reid Educational Foundation, published by Heldref Publications, 1319 18th Street, NW, Washington, DC 20036-1802.—*Language Quarterly,* v. 29, Winter, 1991. Reproduced by permission.—*The Michigan Academician,* v. 28, March, 1996. Copyright © The Michigan Academy of Science, Arts, and Letters, 1996. Reproduced by permission of the publisher.—*Modern Language Quarterly,* v. 43, December, 1982. Copyright © 1982 by Duke University Press, Durham, NC. Reproduced by permission.—*Modern Language Review,* v. 75, 1980; v. 88, October, 1993. © Modern Humanities Research Association 1980, 1993. Both reproduced by permission of the publisher.—*Nineteenth-Century French Studies,* v. 8, Fall, 1979; v. 20, Spring-Summer, 1992. © 1979, 1992 by *Nineteenth-Century French Studies.* Both reproduced by permission.—*Nineteenth-Century Literature,* v. 53, June, 1998 for "Feminism and the Public Sphere in Anne Brontë's 'The Tenant of Wildfell Hall'" by Rachel K. Carnell. Copyright © 1998 by The Regents of the University of California. Reproduced by permission of the publisher and the author.—*Studies in English Literature, 1500-1900,* v. 39, 1999. ©1999 The Johns Hopkins University Press. Reproduced by permission.—*Theatre Journal,* v. 34, March, 1982. © 1982, University and College Theatre Association of the American Theatre Association. Reproduced by permission of The Johns Hopkins University Press.—*University of Toronto Quarterly,* v. 32, April, 1963. © University of Toronto Press 1963. Reproduced by permission of University of Toronto Press Incorporated.—*The Victorian Newsletter,* v. 87, Spring, 1995 for "'A Frame Perfect and Glorious': Narrative Structure in Anne Brontë's 'The Tenant of Wildfell Hall'" by Elizabeth Signorotti. Reproduced by permission of *The Victorian Newsletter* and the author.—*Women's Studies,* v. 20, 1992. © 1992 Gordon and Breach Science Publishers. Reproduced by permission.

COPYRIGHTED EXCERPTS IN *NCLC*, VOLUME 102, WERE REPRODUCED FROM THE FOLLOWING BOOKS:

Bell, Susan Groag. From "The Feminization of John Stuart Mill," in *Revealing Lives: Autobiography, Biography and Gender.* Edited by Susan Groag Bell and Marilyn Yalom. State University of New York Press, 1990. Copyright © 1990 by

State University of New York Press. All rights reserved. Reproduced by permission.—Buss, Robin. From *Vigny: Chatterton.* Grant & Cutler Ltd., 1984. Copyright © 1984 by Grant & Cutler Ltd. All rights reserved. Reproduced by permission.—Ireson, J.C. From "Poetry," in *The French Romantics.* Edited by D.G. Charlton. Cambridge University Press, 1984. Copyright © 1984 by Cambridge University Press. All rights reserved. Reproduced with permission of Cambridge University Press and the author.—Langland, Elizabeth. From "The Voicing of Feminine Desire in Anne Brontë's 'The Tenant of Wildfell Hall,'" in *Gender and Discourse in Victorian Literature and Art.* Edited by Antony H. Harrison and Beverly Taylor. Northern Illinois University Press, 1992. © 1992 by Northern Illinois University Press. Reproduced by permission.—Mayberry, Robert, and Nancy K. From "Histories, Essays, and Miscellaneous Writings," in *Francisco Martinez de la Rosa.* Twayne Publishers, 1988. Copyright © 1988 by Twayne Publishers. All rights reserved. Reproduced by permission.—Mullen, W. N. B. From an introduction to *Grillparzer's Aesthetic Theory: A Study with Special Reference to His Conception of the Drama "Eine Gegenrawart."* Akademischer Verlag Hans-Dieter Heinz, 1979. Copyright © 1979 by Akademischer Verlag Hans-Dieter Heinz. All rights reserved. Reproduced by permission.—Reeve, William C. From *Grillparzer's "Libussa": The Tragedy of Separation.* McGill-Queen's University Press, 1999. Copyright © 1999 by McGill-Queen's University Press. All rights reserved. Reproduced by permission.—Rossi, Alice S. From *Essays on Sex Equality.* University of Chicago Press, 1970. Copyright © 1970 by University of Chicago Press. All rights reserved. Reproduced by permission.—Sarojini. From "Better Deal for the Better Half: Mill and Harriet Taylor on the Subjection of Women," in *Women's Writing: Text and Context.* Edited by Jasbir Jain. Rawat Publications, 1996. Copyright © 1996 by Rawat Publications. All rights reserved. Reproduced by permission.—Thompson, Bruce. From "Die Ahnfrau," in *A Sense of Irony: An Examination of the Tragedies of Franz Grillparzer.* Herbert Lang Bern, 1976. Copyright © 1976 by Herber Lang Bern. All rights reserved. Reproduced by permission.—Thompson, Bruce. From *Franz Grillparzer.* Twayne Publishers, 1981. Copyright © 1981 by Twayne Publishers. All rights reserved. Reproduced by permission.—Wells, George A. From *The Plays of Grillparzer.* Pergamon Press, 1969. Copyright © 1969 by Pergamon Press. All rights reserved. Reproduced by permission.—Yates, W.E. From "Ambition," in *Grillparzer: A Critical Introduction.* Cambridge University Press, 1972. Copyright © 1972 by Cambridge University Press. All rights reserved. Reproduced by permission of Cambridge University Press and the author.—Zerilli, Linda M.G. From "Constructing 'Harriet Taylor': Another Look at J. S. Mill's Autobiography," in *Constructions of the Self.* Edited by George Levine. Rutgers University Press, 1992. Copyright © 1992 by Rutgers University Press. All rights reserved. Reproduced by permission of Rutgers, The State University.

PHOTOGRAPHS AND ILLUSTRATIONS APPEARING IN *NCLC*, VOLUME 102, WERE RECEIVED FROM THEFOLLOWING SOURCES:

Brontë, Anne, from a drawing by Charlotte Brontë in the possession of the Rev. A. B. Nicholls, 1859, photograph. Corbis-Bettmann. Reproduced by permission.—Francisco de Paula with Martinez de la Rosa, painting. © Archivo Iconografico, S.A./Corbis. Reproduced by permission.—Grillparzer, Franz, engraving. The Library of Congress.—"John Stuart Mill," painting by George F. Watts. The Library of Congress. —Mill, Harriet Taylor, photograph.—Title page from *Konig Ottokars Gluck und Ende,* written by Franz Grillparzer, photograph. Special Collections Library, University of Michigan. Reproduced by permission.—Title page from *Poetica Espanola,* written by D. Francisco Martinez de la Rosa, photograph. Special Collections Library, University of Michigan. Reproduced by permission.—Title page from *Sappho,* written by Franz Grillparzer, photograph. Special Collections Library, University of Michigan. Reproduced by permission.—Vigny, Alfred, Comte de, engraving after a painting. The Library of Congress.

Literary Criticism Series Advisory Board

The members of the Gale Group Literary Criticism Series Advisory Board—reference librarians and subject specialists from public, academic, and school library systems—represent a cross-section of our customer base and offer a variety of informed perspectives on both the presentation and content of our literature criticism products. Advisory board members assess and define such quality issues as the relevance, currency, and usefulness of the author coverage, critical content, and literary topics included in our series; evaluate the layout, presentation, and general quality of our printed volumes; provide feedback on the criteria used for selecting authors and topics covered in our series; provide suggestions for potential enhancements to our series; identify any gaps in our coverage of authors or literary topics, recommending authors or topics for inclusion; analyze the appropriateness of our content and presentation for various user audiences, such as high school students, undergraduates, graduate students, librarians, and educators; and offer feedback on any proposed changes/enhancements to our series. We wish to thank the following advisors for their advice throughout the year.

The Tenant of Wildfell Hall

Anne Brontë

The following entry presents criticism of Brontë's novel *The Tenant of Wildfell Hall* (1848). For discussion of her complete career, see *NCLC*, Volume 4; for criticism devoted to her novel *Agnes Grey,* see *NCLC*, Volume 71.

INTRODUCTION

Brontë's second and final novel, *The Tenant of Wildfell Hall*, details the departure of its heroine, Helen Huntingdon, from a disastrous marriage and into an uncertain life in provincial England. Both a love story and a novel of psychological growth, the work was considered scandalous and immoral by Victorian critics, particularly in its representation of the debauched behavior of its antagonist, Arthur Huntingdon. Composed with an exacting verisimilitude, and incorporating Brontë's personal experience of her brother Branwell's steady decline into madness, *The Tenant of Wildfell Hall* presents a tacit critique of the inequities between women and men in marriage, and serves Brontë's purpose of moral instruction by urging young women to use prudence in selecting a mate. Though the novel is perhaps flawed by moments of melodrama, and by what some consider an awkward narrative structure, most critics view *The Tenant of Wildfell Hall* as a significant and somewhat unconventional statement on Victorian morals and an enduring example of nineteenth-century literary craftsmanship by a frequently underrated novelist.

PLOT AND MAJOR CHARACTERS

The Tenant of Wildfell Hall opens with the narration of Gilbert Markham, a gentleman farmer of Yorkshire, England. Markham's tale, which takes the form of an extended series of letters to his friend Halford, begins in 1827. Gilbert recalls how he met and subsequently fell in love with a young woman, Helen, who had recently moved with her son to the neighboring estate of Wildfell Hall. Initially greeted with a strange coldness by the woman, Gilbert suspects that she and the man who accompanied her to Yorkshire, Frederick Lawrence, are lovers. Later, in a fit of misinformed frustration, Gilbert attacks Frederick before learning that he is in fact Helen's brother. Finding it difficult to explain herself to Gilbert, but wanting him to understand her stern behavior, Helen later gives him her faded journal, the pages of which form the central portion of the novel. The first entry in the diary, dated June 1, 1821, reveals some of Helen's thoughts about her paint-

ing. In the ensuing pages, Gilbert learns how Helen met and married a man named Arthur Huntingdon. Preferring the attractive and boisterous Arthur to any other suitors offered by her relatives, Helen chose him, despite protest. However, after the wedding she realizes that her husband's excessive indulgence in alcohol and gambling leave him little time for her. Arthur's debauched behavior repulses Helen, but endears him to a small sect of "gentleman" revelers, for whom he is the jovial leader. Sometime later, a spasm of rage prompts Arthur to destroy a number of Helen's paintings. She suffers this and other indignities without taking concrete action until she discovers a clandestine affair between Arthur and the governess he has hired and installed in their household, ostensibly for the purpose of educating their son. Taking the boy with her, Helen leaves, fleeing to Wildfell Hall. The journal ends, and Gilbert, having realized his mistake in judging Helen, apologizes for his immature behavior. Soon, the two reveal their love for one another. Helen, still married to Arthur, learns that her husband is gravely ill and hurries back to London in order to look after him. Unremorseful on his deathbed, Arthur Huntingdon eventually dies, allowing Gilbert and Helen to marry.

MAJOR THEMES

Brontë stated in the preface to the second edition of *The Tenant of Wildfell Hall* that her purpose in writing the novel was to tell the truth and to convey a moral idea. Thus, she hoped to caution those who might make mistakes in marriage similar to those of Helen Huntingdon. Indeed, most critics take Brontë at her word, viewing the work as a critique of marriage in Victorian England, an institution that, in cases such as the one illustrated in the novel, left little recourse for women. A minor theme related to Brontë's analysis of marriage encompasses the work's implied attack on the rakish, Regency-era morals of many of the male figures in the novel—led by Arthur Huntingdon. These men drink, gamble, and carouse with little regard for the consequences, while their solidly moral, Victorian spouses are required to abide, and even atone for, their degradations. The status of Helen as a female artist provides another theme in the work, as her struggle to support herself through painting is thwarted by an unappreciative, male-dominated society personified in Arthur. Additional themes related to the dynamics of gender also resonate in the work, though most critics agree that Brontë's heroine and novel depict a traditionally Christian/moral worldview rather than an overtly feminist one.

CRITICAL RECEPTION

Negative critical appraisals of *The Tenant of Wildfell* at the time of its publication were conditioned both by the supposedly immoral subject matter described in the novel, and by the condescending and dismissive attitude to the work taken by Anne Brontë's elder sister Charlotte, whose disparaging remarks continued to mar its reputation for decades. Criticism of the work's narrative form, which has been described as cumbersome and disjointed, originated with George Moore's 1924 evaluation. Otherwise a champion of Brontë's works, Moore observed that the novel was irretrievably divided by Brontë's use of a complicated epistolary structure, and felt that the story would have been better told without this clumsy narrative apparatus. Many subsequent commentators have echoed this criticism. However, more recently, a few scholars have begun to view the benefits of Brontë's narrative technique, particularly as it focuses on the psychological development of Helen Huntingdon in the crucial midsection of the novel. Indeed, Edith A. Kostka has praised its "ingenious design" in delineating Helen's character. And, while a few critics have viewed Arthur as the most compelling character in the book, the majority of late twentieth-century commentators have highlighted the significance of Helen, studying her as its central figure. A complementary line of inquiry has focused on the novel's feminist themes. Several scholars have studied issues related to the gendered enclosure and appropriation of Helen's narrative by Gilbert Markham's male discourse, which surrounds and comments upon her journal entries. Helen's occupation as a female artist has also been deemed significant by several critics, who have concentrated on her status as a marginalized figure in Victorian society. Additionally, the motif of Helen's socially and ideologically transgressive desire in the novel has been highlighted. Other scholars have challenged the view that *The Tenant of Wildfell Hall* should be read as a feminist or proto-feminist work, and have argued that the work fails to adequately challenge Victorian domestic ideology and its assumptions concerning the proper roles of men and women.

PRINCIPAL WORKS

Poems by Currer, Ellis and Acton Bell [as Acton Bell, with Currer and Ellis Bell (pseudonyms of Charlotte and Emily Brontë)] (poetry) 1846

Agnes Grey: An Autobiography [as Acton Bell] (novel) 1847

The Tenant of Wildfell Hall [as Acton Bell] (novel) 1848

*The Brontë's Life and Letters (letters) 1908

The Complete Poems of Anne Brontë (poetry) 1920

*This work includes letters written by Charlotte, Emily, and Anne Brontë.

CRITICISM

Rambler (review date 1848)

SOURCE: "Mr. Bell's New Novel," in *Rambler*, Vol. 3, September, 1848, pp. 65-66.

[*In the following anonymous review, the critic compares* The Tenant of Wildfell Hall *to* Jane Eyre, *claiming that the two were written by the same author, and that both are deplorable in nature.*]

The names of Acton Bell, Currer Bell, and Ellis Bell, are now pretty generally recognised as mere *noms de guerre* in the literary world. The novels lately published by these supposed individuals, or at least those which have the names of the first two of the three, are too palpably the work of one hand to deceive even the unpractised critic; while few people would doubt that that hand belonged to a woman, and, as we suspect, a Yorkshirewoman. *Jane Eyre* is the best known of all the tales bearing the *Bell* designation; and the last that has come forth from the same source is the story whose title is **The Tenant of Wildfell Hall.** These two are, indeed, so strikingly alike in sentiment, style, and general modes of thought, that the criticisms which apply to one of them are almost equally applicable to the other.

That the author is a clever and vigorous writer, the popularity of *Jane Eyre* is a fair proof. She has also a certain marked tone of mind, which has impressed itself upon her books, and rendered them more individual and characteristic than the ordinary run even of clever novels. And for the sake of the morals of the novel-reading public, we hope that this their peculiar feature has been the real cause of their attractiveness to many readers; and not that truly offensive and sensual spirit which is painfully prominent both in *Jane Eyre* and in the tale now before us. We should be sorry to believe that sympathy with the authoress's personages, or approval of her principles, had any thing to do with the interest which her books are calculated to excite in those who are wearied with the cloying monotonousnesses of the average run of novels, and who are fascinated with every thing and any thing that is new.

Jane Eyre is, indeed, one of the coarsest books which we ever perused. It is not that the *professed* sentiments of the writer are absolutely wrong or forbidding, or that the odd sort of religious notions which she puts forward are much worse than is usual in popular tales. It is rather that there is a certain perpetual *tendency* to relapse into that class of ideas, expressions, and circumstances, which is most connected with the grosser and more animal portion of our nature; and that the detestable morality of the most prominent character in the story is accompanied with every sort of palliation short of unblushing justification. The heroine, who tells the story, and who certainly is made to paint herself and her companions with very considerable force and skill, is as utterly unattractive and unfeminine a specimen of her sex as the pen of novelist ever drew.

The Tenant of Wildfell Hall is also a species of autobiography. One third of the story is told by the hero, a kind of gentleman farmer, whose morals, religion, cultivation, and talents, are about on a par with those of Jane Eyre herself; and the other two thirds consist of the diary of the lady with whom he falls in love, not knowing that, though living in solitude, she is really married to a living husband. Throughout the whole book, there does not appear a single character who has the power to interest the sympathies of the reader. All are commonplace, vulgar, rough, brusque-mannered personages, whatever their supposed station in life; while the scenes which the heroine relates in her diary are of the most disgusting and revolting species. She is married to a man of family and fortune, to whom she chose to link herself against the wishes of her friends, and who speedily turns out a sensual brute of the most intolerable kind, and treats her with every indignity, insult, and ill-usage which can be conceived, short of actual personal violence. Her diary is the record of what she endured at his hands, and details with offensive minuteness the disgusting scenes of debauchery, blasphemy, and profaneness, in which, with a herd of boon companions, he delighted to spend his days. By and by, of course, he dies, and the authoress gives us one of those pictures of a death-bed which are neither edifying, nor true to life, nor full of warning to the careless and profligate. In the end, the hero and heroine marry, after a courtship conducted with that peculiar bluntness and roughness of conduct and language which is the characteristic of all this writer's creations.

Nevertheless, on the whole, we should say that *The Tenant of Wildfell Hall* is not so *bad* a book as *Jane Eyre*. There is not such a palpable blinking of the abominable nature of the morality of its most prominent characters. The hero and heroine are people of decent intentions; and though the same offensive element of interest (so to call it) occurs in both of the tales, and in each our sympathies are unwittingly engaged for an attachment formed by a married person before death had dissolved the first contracted bond; yet the subject of this second passion in the last published story is more conscious of its real nature than in its predecessor. The religious sentiments which the authoress puts into the mouth of her heroines are either false and bad, or so vague and unmeaning as to add to the unreality of the scenes, without in any way redeeming their blots, as uncalled-for and unhealthy representations of the viler phases of human life. In a word, unless our authoress can contrive to refine and elevate her general notions of all human and divine things, we shall be glad to learn that she is not intending to add another work to those which have already been produced by her pen. . . .

Arlene M. Jackson (essay date 1982)

SOURCE: "The Question of Credibility in Anne Brontë's *The Tenant of Wildfell Hall*," in *English Studies*, Vol. 63, No. 3, June, 1982, pp. 198-206.

[*In the following essay, Jackson asserts that* The Tenant of Wildfell Hall, *despite the flaw of its somewhat burdensome narrative structure, avoids melodrama by counterbalancing Helen Huntingdon's psychological realism with the debauched behavior of her husband Arthur.*]

Author of *Agnes Grey* (1847) and *The Tenant of Wildfell Hall* (1848), Anne Brontë is the least known of the Brontë family, but seems ready for rediscovery in this period of new interest in minor and neglected women writers. Measured against her sisters, Anne becomes the inferior artist, either because her novels lack the passion of a *Jane Eyre* or *Villette,* or the 'other world' drama of a *Wuthering Heights*. Without the searing intensity of Charlotte or the dramatic inventiveness of Emily, however, Anne demonstrates through her writing that she has a conscious, perceptive control of her fictional materials. This control gives Anne Brontë a claim to artistic merit in her own right.

George Moore once labeled *Agnes Grey* the most 'perfect prose narrative in English letters',[1] but this judgment today is assuredly a minority opinion, as it certainly was in its own time. But even if *Agnes Grey* is 'perfect' in recreating the moral realism which seems to have been its aim, *The Tenant of Wildfell Hall* is the work showing greater artistry, based on a greater understanding of character psychology. Though at times the novel seems to be a replay of the traditional morality theme, complete with moral hierarchies and voiced reminders of eternal damnation for the unrepentant,[2] it possesses a moral realism which goes beyond the earnestness of content present in the earlier *Agnes Grey.* Even more important, its greater understanding of character psychology is intrinsically related to narrative technique, particularly in the choice of 'storyteller' and in the structuring of plot materials. Both point of view and plot organization, in fact, are used to increase the novel's credibility.

At first, the narrative structure seems extraordinarily cumbersome for what is basically an uncomplicated story. The novel consists of two letters, the first covering an initial 'explanation' as well as Chapter One, the second comprising the remainder of the two volume work.[3] Within the long second letter is a journal covering six years, letters within letters, and finally the information that the entire story is being told from a retrospective view some twenty to twenty-six years after the events described. Cumbersome though this organization may be, some interesting effects do accrue from this manner of structuring plot materials.

The 'explanation' conveys the information, in the voice of gentleman farmer Gilbert Markham, that he has been asked by his friend Jack Halford to give him some information regarding his past life. Markham had not done so at the time and now wishes to atone for his delay by giving 'a full and faithful account of certain circumstances connected with the most important event of my life . . .'[4] Chapter One then relates how Gilbert meets and falls in love with Helen 'Graham', a woman who has moved into a neighboring estate with her young son, and who has taken up painting as a means of financial support. When

Gilbert professes his love, Helen coldly rebuffs him. When he confronts her with what he believes is evidence that she has compromised her reputation by a clandestine affair with a neighbor (Frederick Lawrence), Helen sends Gilbert off with a journal that she claims will explain her actions. Thus ends the early, 'framework' section of the narrative.

The journal recounts how Helen 'Graham' fell in love with and married Arthur Huntingdon some few years earlier. (The time span seems much greater, primarily because of the contrast between the youthful, headstrong, and naïve young woman narrating this part of the journal, and the mysterious woman Gilbert Markham knows, but not more than six or seven years have elapsed between these two stages of Helen's life).

As the journal reveals, Arthur Huntingdon turns out to be a classic case of Victorian debauchery[5]—a drunkard who verbally abuses his wife, who prefers the companionship of fellow or even potential debauchees, who prefers to spend more time in London than with his wife on their country estate, and who feels it is his right to have affairs with whatever pretty women come his way. The story of Huntingdon's increasing lack of self-control as he declines into greater dissipation is extraordinarily well done. We hear of his going off to London, even in the very early days of the marriage, and we are kept in Helen's position—not knowing really what it is that Arthur does in London, but gradually coming to believe that it is anything but gentlemanly. By keeping the reader restricted to the diarist's point of view, Anne Brontë makes us believe it is debauchery so great it cannot be described. From the comments later dropped by Huntingdon's 'friends', who visit his country estate, we are given support for our belief.

Huntingdon not only leads a dissolute life but is also the leader of his set, and therefore is responsible for drawing others into his debauchery. Helen's realization of this, the confrontations between Arthur and Helen, her refusal to sleep with him, his affair with two women (his young son's governess as well as the wife of one of his 'friends') all have considerable shock value. Finally, her suffering is so great that Helen leaves with her child, and with the secret assistance of her brother (the Frederick Lawrence whom Gilbert had thought of as Helen's secret lover), has taken an assumed name and hidden her residence from her angered husband. Here the journal ends. Gilbert Markham is deeply shocked at the experiences Helen has lived through, but her revelations have only made him love her all the more.

The materials following the journal comprise the final section of the novel's framework. Gilbert and Helen admit their love for each other, but both respect her married position (though Gilbert had just been at the point of trying to convince Helen that her marriage to such a scoundrel could not really be considered as a marriage). Gilbert maintains that he will wait for her to be free. Soon after, Helen hears her husband is grievously ill, and she returns to nurse him through his illness. After word of Arthur Huntingdon's death, Gilbert hears nothing from Helen, but does not, himself, correspond with her. Hearing rumours of her approaching marriage, Gilbert is devastated but travels to her estate to discover the truth. The truth, he soon finds out, is that her brother is to be married to a young protégée of Helen's. After one or two false starts, Gilbert proposes to Helen and they marry. Gilbert closes his narrative, revealing that his listener has been his brother-in-law, and that he and Helen have been happily married for some twenty years.

Though the novel ends as a conventional pre-1880 Victorian novel usually does, with troubles resolved and marriage part of that resolution and reward for persevering through trial, *The Tenant of Wildfell Hall* is quite unconventional in its allowing the sinner to remain unrepentant, even on his deathbed, and its revealing a marital discord full of suffering, agony, and even ugliness. As Derek Stanford points out, Anne Brontë 'exploded' the myth of marriage and the 'semi-sacrosanct' belief in 'the notion of conjugal obedience' that a wife owed her husband. 'The novel shows how continued intimacy with a worthless husband one has come to despise is a most contagious form of degradation'.[6]

These are strong issues for a novel of 1849, and their handling must cope with the danger of letting materials outrun the author's control. Arthur Huntingdon's story poses the particular danger of passing from strong drama into sheer melodrama—a story of a debauched Victorian 'gentleman' as told by his naïve, excitable, uninformed wife. Such a story, of course, would have a certain charm all its own—but it would not be Anne Brontë's story. As it is, Arthur's story is so strong that it is sometimes considered the most important, most realistic, the most dramatic—in short, the best part of the novel.[7] Another potential problem for Miss Brontë's text is the inadequacy of Gilbert Markham—shallow, petulant, certainly not worthy of Helen Huntingdon's love and a puzzling choice as her marriage partner. Helen herself seems to pale before Arthur's excesses, and thus the novel's characterization runs the risk of disproportionately favoring Arthur and, what would be ironic but not unusual in fiction, favoring the 'sinner theme'. The dissolute character, because of the inherent excitement of his life, often threatens the balance of characterization in fiction or drama. With such a character in this narrative, Helen Huntingdon runs the risk of becoming a mere storyteller, an observer-participant whose own story is subordinate to what she observes of her husband's gradual disintegration.

Other problems exist, as well. Does Helen, because of her inexperience of the world, make Arthur out to be worse than he actually is? Would a man of the world understand Arthur and forgive him his 'lapses'? Anne Brontë consciously controls Arthur's story, however, and keeps it within the realistic sphere by means of both internal (within the journal) and external (within the framework) sections of her narrative. In a matter-of-fact manner, Helen recounts in her journal how some of Arthur's companions leave him or at least make revealing comments on the dissipation of his life. A second way in which the reader becomes convinced of the journal's accuracy occurs through the medium of the journal itself. Helen's early view of Arthur and her marriage are defined, committed through the language on the journal's pages, as she then perceives things. Through the retrospect of a calmer time, with its chronological and psychological maturity, Helen has the possibility of measuring the journal's early information against later perceptions. The older and wiser Helen, we are to understand, has changed nothing in the journal, nor warns Gilbert of any problems in its 'reading' of her marital experiences.

The dissipation of Arthur Huntingdon is sufficiently heinous that it calls for even more measures insuring credibility to the story, thus further removing it from melodrama. Though Gilbert Markham is not very worldly-wise, his basically good nature, his own adherence to truth, and his respect for Helen's truthfulness make him a relatively knowledgeable and objective observer. Gilbert's acceptance of Helen's story with no reservation or doubt of its accuracy is a means through which Anne Brontë increases credibility.[8]

Having Gilbert (a male voice) convey Helen's story to his brother-in-law (a male audience), and then having Gilbert indicate Halford's acceptance of Helen's story are fairly subtle touches in what first seems a heavy-handed use of the epistolary technique. Stereotyped roles of male and female seem to be used here to good effect, though not without some irony. (Helen, for instance, is not prone to hysterics or exaggeration, and neither is Gilbert a paragon of 'masculine' virtues of objectivity, wisdom, and silent strength). Yet if such stereotyped roles could be expected, as they certainly would be by part of the Victorian audience, they would only increase the credibility, the audience's impulse to accept Helen's account as truthful, since Gilbert accepts it as such.

Though Gilbert Markham matures almost too rapidly after reading the journal, his change is believable, and it is primarily the journal itself that accounts for the change. Earlier, Gilbert had been seen as self-centered and petulant, but certainly not beyond the capacity to change. Family and friends in his narrow world of farm and village all treat him as a 'star' figure. He is a first-born son and an eligible bachelor in a village beset with hopeful maidens, and self-centeredness seems an ordinary result of such attentions—yet his is a good nature, capable of feeling shame as well as expressing generosity.

At first, after reading the journal, Gilbert is disappointed that Helen's account stopped just short of giving her initial opinion of him (an unfavorable one, he is sure). But then he quickly comments: 'I could readily forgive her prejudice against me, and her hard thoughts of our sex in general, when I saw to what brilliant specimens her experience had been limited' (III, 130-1). Again, however,

Gilbert reverts to thinking of himself: 'If, at first, her opinion of me had been lower than I deserved I was convinced that now my deserts were lower than her opinion . . .' But then he cannot resist thinking: 'I would have given much to have seen it all—to have witnessed the gradual change, and watched the progress of her esteem and friendship for me . . . but no, I had no right to see it: all this was too sacred for any eyes but her own, and she had done well to keep it from me' (III, 131-2). Gilbert thus reveals certain signs of maturity, an honest struggle to be fair and compassionate, but cannot help interpreting Helen's experiences as they affect himself.

Gilbert's letter continues this struggle, as he then confesses to his correspondent Halford that he took pleasure in watching Helen's love for Huntingdon disappear:

> not that I was at all insensible to Mrs. Huntingdon's wrongs or unmoved by her sufferings, but I must confess, I felt a kind of selfish gratification in watching her husband's gradual decline in her good graces, and seeing how completely he extinguished all her affection at last. The effect of the whole, however, in spite of all my sympathy for her, and my fury against him, was to relieve my mind of an intolerable burden and fill my heart with joy, as if some friend had roused me from a dreadful nightmare
>
> (III, 133-4).

The journal allows Gilbert to respond in private, to turn over his responses and discover their origin and meaning. With Halford as the recipient of his letter (which traces the responses) Gilbert is aware that someone else is passing judgment on his actions, or that at least someone else is aware that there are actions to be judged. The fact that Gilbert does reveal so much of himself to Halford ought to make the novel's audience aware that his is a public confession, and one that also reveals his essential honesty and generous nature.

From this point to the novel's end, Gilbert rises in our estimation. He sees the shallowness of his village companions, though he is a bit too quick and even snobbish in turning away from them. Yet, in juxtaposition to Helen and her experiences, their lives seem silly and selfish, as was his own. Later, he becomes a friend of Frederick Lawrence and confesses to his own boorish and unpleasant attitudes toward him earlier, when Gilbert had physically attacked him in his frustration over believing Lawrence and Helen were in love with one another. Again, he shows signs of selfishness as he is tempted to try to convince Helen she might love him in freedom, since her marriage would not be recognized as such by 'Heaven'. Yet, Gilbert immediately asks her forgiveness for his suggestion. Arthur Huntingdon and Gilbert Markham are pointed contrasts, though Gilbert is not so perfect that he is idealized. Gilbert's self-centeredness and petulance are never completely eradicated, but when he recognizes his faults, he readily admits them and he feels ashamed or asks Helen's forgiveness. Gilbert is considerably matured over the course of his love for Helen Huntingdon and ends the novel by becoming not an ideal but a believable marriage partner.

Though Gilbert's characterization has some nice touches, and Arthur Huntingdon's presentation makes him a strong dramatic figure, Helen Huntingdon is the most psychologically interesting and important character. In a very real sense, Helen's own story (and not the story of Arthur's dissipation she recounts in her journal) is the novel's *raison d'être,* yet it is often overlooked because of Arthur's more dominant and dramatic story. The novel's framework and its journal sections, in fact provide a special kind of insight into Helen Huntingdon's psyche as it reacts to the stress of an unhappy marriage. This insight includes not only immediate stress but also the effect of stress felt over several years.

Because of the novel's organization, the older Helen is presented first, and she is clearly presented as a psychologically distressed and troubled woman. In three early episodes in the framework section, the reader sees the externals of Helen as Gilbert Markham does, though the astute reader might suspect that the author is being ironic when she has Gilbert declare to himself that he would not care to know such a woman. This, at least, is his initial reaction when he catches his first glimpse of 'Mrs. Graham's' face during a church service. But this brief reference to a cold, hard, severe face gives special insight into the effects of distress, and should not be dismissed merely as an ironic handling of the 'reluctant lover' theme, as it appears on the surface.

A second episode occurs when Gilbert tries to befriend 'Mrs. Graham's' young son, Arthur, only to have the mother grab her child away from him, an impulsive action born of paranoia about her son's safety. Again, Gilbert notes a look of 'repellent scorn' on Helen's face—'it seemed like the natural expression of the face . . .' (I, 37-8).

Finally, in the third episode, Helen warms toward Gilbert, enough at any rate that he believes he has fallen in love with her. At this point, to explain her sternness and inaccessibility, she gives to Gilbert the journal detailing her marriage to Arthur Huntingdon. What these three episodes do, then, is delineate an apparently cold, stern woman—an effect whose cause waits to be revealed. As much as Anne Brontë tries to provoke suspense in the reader by using Gilbert's curiosity as a lead, her main emphasis in this framing section is clearly on Helen's pain and suffering, marked by agitation, disdain, and the pinched, dry features she first presents for public view. The framing section with its gradual unfolding of 'Mrs. Graham' to an unsuspecting Gilbert prepares the reader to discover the psychological causation of her cold, scornful demeanor and her mysterious life-style as well, surely, as to discover the 'facts' of her story.

As mentioned earlier, Arthur's story is prominent because it is dramatic, obvious yet fascinating in its grandiose way. Its moral function is clear: beware of an undisciplined life—with its neglect of duties, it leads to great tragedies. But, more than this, Anne Brontë also answers a question that other novels of her time do not ask: what happens to a marriage and to the innocent partner when one partner (specifically, the male) leads a solipsistic life, where personal pleasures are seen as deserved, where maleness and the role of husband is tied to the freedom to do as one wants, and femaleness and the role of wife is linked to providing service and pleasure not necessarily sexual, but including daily praise and ego-boosting and, quite simply, constant attention.

Neither Charlotte nor Emily deal with the female half of an unhappy marriage, particularly marriage with such a one as an Arthur Huntingdon. Both sisters, however, indicate they are well aware of long-suffering wives in the admittedly quite different situation surrounding Isabella Linton as Heathcliff's wife, and the potential awaiting Jane if she were to marry either Rochester (as bigamist) or St. John Rivers (as missionary). Neither author handles the issue as Anne Brontë does: she concentrates her energies on Helen's story, and through the means of framework and journal, we are able to study causation and development of stress. Significantly, the journal allows the subject to comment on and analyze the reactions and changes in her own personality.

The journal details a young Helen—an impulsive, headstrong girl who decides on Arthur as a husband because she is genuinely attracted to him and because, in contrast to the suitors her aunt encourages, Arthur appears more attractive. Clearly, Helen responds to Arthur's sexual charm—but it is real, and the journal makes the reader understand that Helen has physical desires that older people are not taking into account in their very Victorian way of managing her future. This physical attraction seems also to be recognized by Helen herself in the first part of her journal.

Helen is married in December of 1821, but as early as two months before her marriage, her fears reveal she has already gained some unpleasant knowledge about Arthur's less-than-generous instincts. Her response to their wedding trip continues to demonstrate the unhappy realization of the kind of marriage she has made: 'When I had expressed a particular interest in anything that I saw or desired to see, it had been displeasing to him in as much as it proved that I could take delight in anything disconnected with himself' (II, 69).

By February of 1822, Helen admits that if she had known earlier what she now realizes, she would not have fallen in love with Arthur and would not, therefore, have married him. At first, such a comment seems naïve, but then she continues to clarify her point: Helen admits she still loves Arthur, but sees he is not the person she ought to have married, since he will not share with her *his* life, nor does he show any sympathetic concern for *her* own needs. Later she discovers all too well why he cannot let her into his world. These early distinctions and understandings, however, demonstrate how rapidly Helen Huntingdon has matured over approximately a four month period.

Helen's journal insights into the early months of her marriage continue until the Fall of 1824 and reveal how rapidly she continues to mature—but most of the changes are caused by unpleasant experiences. She and Arthur, as she painfully realizes, have two very different ideas of what marriage and love are. Anne Brontë's point here is not as simplistic as it might appear on the surface. This is no sentimental treatment of a wronged, long-suffering wife. While this section of the journal traces Arthur's increasing debauchery and neglect of Helen, it also traces the gradual hardening of Helen's personality. She describes, for instance, how she starts to nag Arthur, and how nagging turns into lecturing. She begins to manifest a superior attitude, a moral righteousness that increasingly alienates what remains of Arthur's good intentions. Helen is aware of how she is changing, but cannot stop herself; when she feels how much Arthur has wronged her, she 'was determined he should feel it too' (II, 178). Helpless to change the situation for the better, she decides to strike back. Again, the journal reveals she is well aware of how much the situation is changing her own personality.

The breakdown in communications becomes complete when Helen discovers Arthur has arranged a lover's tryst with Annabella Lowborough, one of their Autumn house guests, and the wife of one of Arthur's 'friends'. After this event, and in the last months of her life with Arthur Huntingdon, Helen becomes very cold towards him and reveals he is not allowed into her bedroom. Her love is now 'crushed and withered' (II, 333), but so is her personality. More suffering occurs when Arthur tries to interfere with the education of his son, and Helen becomes deeply worried over the effect of Arthur's example on the child. Plans to leave Arthur are made and abandoned because he discovers and destroys the paintings Helen has carefully worked on—paintings which were to be sold as a means of financial support in her future refuge. In one of his drunken fits, finally, Arthur offers his wife to the highest bidder among his friends. After Helen discovers that the governess Arthur has installed in their home for the ostensible purpose of educating their son is actually his mistress, her desperation becomes so great that she takes her child and leaves Arthur: 'My heart is too thoroughly dried to be broken in a hurry, and I mean to live as long as I can' (III, 39). After some six years of marriage, Helen cries: 'Thank Heaven, I am free and safe at last' (III, 114).

Admittedly, there are some melodramatic touches here as Hargrave offers his assistance in Helen's escape plans, but then reveals he desires her to be his mistress, and as Helen discovers the depravity of Arthur's friends, and his own outrageous actions. These actions become more outrageous, systematically following one another so that the reader shares Helen's growing pain and the hardening of her heart towards Arthur. And there are other important insights into Helen's reactions as well: she admits that she has 'unamiable feelings against my fellow-mortals—the male part of them especially' (III, 75). She perceives that men are free, where women are not, and the bitterness of this perception finally leads her to give succinct advice to her young friend Esther Hargrave: '[You] must, indeed, be careful whom you marry—or rather, you must avoid it altogether' (III, 85).

The misogamist theme here is clearly Helen's own, and not Anne Brontë's. Esther Hargrave eventually marries Helen's brother Frederick Lawrence; Lord Lowborough divorces the unfaithful Annabella and remarries; Mary Millward marries Richard Wilson; Hattersley reforms and realizes his wife loves him. All these turn out to be happy marriages. Helen herself does believe such happiness is possible when she defines for the Victorian audience what marriage ought to be: 'The greatest worldly distinctions and discrepancies of rank, birth, and fortune are as dust in the balance compared with the unity of accordant thoughts and feelings, and truly loving, sympathizing hearts and souls' (III, 333).

This recognition explains why Helen loves and marries Gilbert, a man who on the surface seems shallow and all too prone to faults of pride and petulance, yet who is basically good and, significantly, recognizes and respects Helen's 'personhood'. After that year of waiting, between Arthur's death and Gilbert's proposal, Helen is still reserved and even distant, again a sign of Anne Brontë's understanding the character she has created. And though Gilbert twenty years after these events tells Halford of his happiness in marriage, we really hear nothing of the later Helen—rightly so, I believe, since this 'shadow' future suggests that Helen has been irrevocably touched by the sufferings of her earlier life. Even so many years of marital happiness with Gilbert seem not quite enough to right the past wrongs done to Helen's psychic life.

Anne Brontë's understanding of psychological stress and its long term effects, as well as a certain understanding of women's vulnerable position in marriage, emerges through her creation of Helen Huntingdon. The drama of Arthur's debauchery is counterpointed, not so much by the moral earnestness of Brontë's theme, but by the psychological realism of Helen Huntingdon. The framework device utilizing the male voice of Gilbert Markham and the male reader-listener in Halford, as well as Helen's acceptance of her journal's accuracy, even with the advantage of retrospective judgment—all these show considerable control of her materials. Though the journal and letter devices are not very subtle means of story-telling, Anne Brontë's handling of her narrative does increase the credibility of both the male and female characters. A potential Victorian melodrama thus becomes a perceptive and realistic reading of men, women, and marriage.

Notes

1. As quoted in Derek Stanford, *Anne Brontë: Her Life and Work,* by Derek Stanford and Ada Harrison (New York: 1959), p. 227.

2. Inga-Stina Ewbank, *Their Proper Sphere*: A Study of the Brontë Sisters as Early-Victorian Female Novelists (Cambridge: 1968), pp. 73-4.

3. Significant changes occur between the first and second editions of the novel. The first omits a Preface, in which Anne Brontë presents her claim for realism: 'My object in writing . . . was not simply to amuse the Reader; neither was it to gratify my own taste, nor yet to ingratiate myself with the Press and the Public: I wished to tell the truth . . .' (Second Edition)

Though the second edition contains this Preface, it omits the 'Explanation' and, instead, opens immediately with Chapter one, thus depriving the reader of knowing why the material is presented. See G. D. Hargreaves, 'Incomplete Texts of *The Tenant of Wildfell Hall*', *Brontë Society Transactions* (1972), pp. 113-17.

4. *The Tenant of Wildfell Hall,* 3 Vols. (London: 1848), pp. 1-4.

5. Arthur Huntingdon is usually considered to have been based on Branwell Brontë. See Stanford, pp. 223-4.

6. Stanford, p. 232.

7. W. A. Craik, *The Brontë Novels* (London: 1971), p. 232.

8. Craik briefly treats the issue of Gilbert's contribution to the novel's credibility. See p. 231.

Juliet McMaster (essay date 1982)

SOURCE: "'Imbecile Laughter' and 'Desperate Earnest' in *The Tenant of Wildfell Hall*," in *Modern Language Quarterly,* Vol. 43, No. 4, December, 1982, pp. 352-68.

[*In the following essay, McMaster contrasts the Regency-era rakishness of the male characters with the Victorian morality of the females in* The Tenant of Wildfell Hall, *finding in the struggle of these opposites the thematic and structural pattern of the novel.*]

"You must go back with me to the autumn of 1827," Gilbert Markham begins the first chapter of **The Tenant of Wildfell Hall.**[1] The last words of the novel are likewise a date, a much later one, "*June 10th, 1847*" (p. 490)—the very year in which Anne Brontë was writing the novel.[2] In the internal story of Helen Huntingdon's marriage we also have dates and anniversaries carefully recorded, beginning with the journal entry for June 1, 1821, the year after George IV had become king.[3]

This prominence of time and dating signals that Anne Brontë is offering us, among other things, a period commentary, a Victorian view of certain dominant manners and mores of the preceding generation. Gilbert Markham's standpoint is that of the respectable Victorian husband, father, and landowner, looking back in 1847 on the wild days of his Georgian youth. The Victorians were fond of

defining themselves by contrasting their values with those of the Regency and George IV. Thackeray, perhaps, did it most memorably, in his lecture on George IV, which he delivered to a very respectable Victorian audience in 1860:

> He is dead but thirty years, and one asks how a great society could have tolerated him? Would we bear him now? In this quarter of a century, what a silent revolution has been working! how it has separated us from old times and manners! How it has changed men themselves! I can see old gentlemen now among us, of perfect good breeding, of quiet lives, with venerable grey heads, fondling their grandchildren; and look at them, and wonder at what they were once. [And here Thackeray probably looked knowingly at certain members of his audience.] That gentleman of the grand old school, when he was in the 10th Hussars, and dined at the prince's table, would fall under it night after night. Night after night, that gentleman sat at Brookes's or Raggett's over the dice. If, in the petulance of play or drink, that gentleman spoke a sharp word to his neighbour, he and the other would infallibly go out and try to shoot each other the next morning. . . . That gentleman, so exquisitely polite with ladies in a drawing-room, so loftily courteous, if he talked now as he used among men in his youth, would swear so as to make your hair stand on end.[4]

Drunkenness, gambling, dueling, and swearing[5] are likewise the major sins castigated in Arthur Huntingdon and his boon companions. What amazed Thackeray was the change that had occurred both in behavior and in moral principle, a change that constituted the "silent revolution." No doubt there were drinkers and gamblers among the Victorians; but the difference was that their rowdy behavior was no longer considered right and proper, manly and admirable, as it had been in the past.

Anne Brontë too explores the extraordinary change in moral fashion according to which the rakes could take pride in their rakishness. In the story of Helen's first marriage, which is set in time before the first part of Gilbert Markham's narrative, we have her commentary on the masculine ethos of the Regency. The men drink and wench and swear, not out of simple inclination, but out of a sense of social obligation. Walter Hargrave, for instance, though "no reckless spendthrift, and no abandoned sensualist," feels obliged "to go to a certain length in youthful indulgences—not so much [to] gratify his own tastes as to maintain his reputation as a man of fashion in the world, and a respectable fellow among his own lawless companions" (p. 243). How the connotations of the word *respectable* were to change in the next thirty years! When Lord Lowborough leaves the convivial gentlemen at their after-dinner celebrations before he is blind drunk, his wife is quite ashamed of him. "What *can* induce you to come so soon?" she demands when he joins the women in the drawing room. "It looks so silly to be always dangling after the women," she taunts him, and declares, "At least . . . I know the value of a warm heart and a bold, manly spirit!" (p. 282). Even in the less rakish society of Linden Grange, Mrs. Graham is laughed to scorn when she tries to wean her five-year-old son from his taste for wine and spirits.

"The poor child will be the veriest milksop that ever was sopped!" warns Mrs. Markham (p. 54). And she adds: "Well, but you will treat him like a girl—you'll spoil his spirit, and make a mere Miss Nancy of him" (p. 55).[6]

Of course a little *girl* would not have been encouraged, even by Arthur Huntingdon, to tipple spirits or to shoot off volleys of oaths. And as Anne Brontë examines the difference between Regency and Victorian mores, so she explores the huge discrepancy between the moral standards for women and men. She uses the standard Victorian commentary on the excesses of the previous generation as a paradigm for the relationship between the sexes. For men and women are trained to be almost different species. The men are rakish and Regency; the ladies are staid and Victorian. If it is a point of honor with the men to live high and take no thought for the morrow, it is equally incumbent on the women to specialize in morality, in order to make up for the sins of their fathers, husbands, and sons. Helen comes to like this conventional distinction as little as her author,[7] and firmly resists her son's absorption into the male world. Appropriately, it is this issue that finally causes the absolute rupture of the Huntingdon marriage. She cannot bear to see the moral gulf grow between herself and her son as he is instructed in what to her are "embryo vices" and "evil habits," but to her husband and his friends are the proper male amusements that will "make a man of him" (p. 356).

At the outset, however, Helen is prepared to enter with zeal into her role as the good angel, the woman specializing in goodness. It is her hubris, her special arrogance, to suppose that she can be good enough for two, reform the rake, and save the sinner's soul. She is too womanly, as Arthur is too manly. "There *is* essential goodness in him;—and what delight to unfold it!" she tells herself, when she is first falling in love with him. "If he has wandered, what bliss to recall him! If he is now exposed to the baneful influence of corrupting and wicked companions, what glory to deliver him from them!—Oh! if I could but believe that Heaven has designed me for this!" (p. 168). It is the insidious temptation to play saint, and almost as reprehensible in its way as Huntingdon's opposite role of Mephistophilis to Lord Lowborough. The courting Arthur himself is delighted to call her his good angel, and knows how to control his women by nicely calculated shows of reformation. "He always listens attentively now, when I speak seriously to him . . . , and sometimes he says that if he had me always by his side he should never do or say a wicked thing, and that a little daily talk with me would make him quite a saint," the infatuated Helen records proudly (p. 166). In her hour of awakening she recognizes her folly and arrogance: "Fool that I was to dream that I had strength and purity enough to save myself and him!" she reproaches herself (p. 274). At this stage Arthur changes his tactics. He still expects the woman to bear his moral burden; but whereas initially it was her job to reform him, now it is her fault that he is unreformed. His immoderate drinking, he says, is caused by her "unnatural, unwomanly conduct." But Helen will no longer settle for the impos-

sible role of saint: "he may drink himself dead, but it is NOT my fault!" she declares (p. 330).

The enormous gulf in interests and values that separates men and women in the Huntingdon world is nicely dramatized in a little scene with Hattersley, a rake who does turn out to be reformable. Helen and Milicent have settled to their ladies' amusements in the library, "and between our books, our children, and each other," says Helen, "we expected to make out a very agreeable morning." Into this female sanctum penetrates Hattersley, "redolent of the stables, where he had been regaling himself with the company of his fellow-creatures, the horses," remarks Helen with asperity. He romps with his little daughter until, inevitably, she gets hurt; then he tosses her to her mother, "bidding her 'make all straight'" (p. 296)—the woman's usual task. He proceeds to exert his social talents to amuse the ladies, and fails signally. His interests and values barely intersect with theirs. He scarcely talks the same language.

> "Deuced bad weather this!" he began. "There'll be no shooting to-day, I guess." Then, suddenly lifting up his voice, he regaled us with a few bars of a rollicking song, which abruptly ceasing, he finished the tune with a whistle, and then continued,—"I say, Mrs Huntingdon, what a fine stud your husband has!—not large but good . . . upon my word, Black Bess, and Grey Tom, and that young Nimrod are the finest animals I've seen for many a day!" Then followed a particular discussion of their various merits, succeeded by a sketch of the great things *he* intended to do in the horse-jockey line when his old governor thought proper to quit the stage—"Not that I wish him to close his accounts," added he; "the old trojan is welcome to keep his books open as long as he pleases for me."
>
> "I hope so, *indeed,* Mr Hattersley!"
>
>   (p. 297)

Cutting across the sporting interests, the slang, and the cultivated casualness of the male is the stringently moral disapprobation of the lady.

Winifred Gérin has commented that in setting her story in the 1820s Anne Brontë "rendered more credible the 'Regency' manners of her gentlemen. For they are nothing less than a set of Regency rakes. . . . Very far off, yet, is the Victorian convention of morality, even of decorum, in this quite uninhibited society."[8] But it is not so far off after all; it is right there in the person of Helen Huntingdon, not to say in her author and her contemporary readers. As observer of the masculine regime at Grassdale, Helen provides the piquant viewpoint of the disapproving outsider. Her vision is the sharper for being hostile, and she can furnish details of debauchery not available to the participants. She is like a sober nondrinker among the drunks at a boozy party, with an embarrassing clarity of vision. In fact she often *is* a sober nondrinker among drunks.

One aspect of Anne Brontë's vision of the disastrous divergence between the male and the female is her alignment of fun and laughter with the men, moral earnestness and tears with the women. (The woman who partakes in the men's devil-may-care attitudes, like Annabella, and the man who disapproves of them, like Lowborough, are considered embarrassments by their own sex.)[9] The men are supposed to have a monopoly on gaiety, as the women on seriousness. There is a certain appropriateness in the facts that the monarch in the Victorian era was not only a woman, but also one who was characteristically "not amused." These were sexual characteristics that Thackeray, who was recognized in the Brontë household as a brilliant social commentator, had also noted. We may recall the memorable scene in *Vanity Fair* in which Becky Sharp, pretending to love everything Indian in order to captivate Jos Sedley, swallows fiery curry and chili and then gasps, "Water! for Heaven's sake, water!" Jos and his father think the joke capital and roar with laughter. But, Thackeray tells us, "The ladies only smiled a little. They thought poor Rebecca suffered too much" (chap. 3). There are several parallel scenes in *The Tenant,* where what is a huge joke to the men leaves the ladies unsmiling. Hargrave relates an anecdote of escaping from his rowdy companions through the pantry, to the comic bewilderment of the butler: "Mr Hargrave laughed, and so did his cousin; but his sister and I remained silent and grave," records Helen (p. 284). As the rift between Helen and her husband widens, her seriousness turns to a dour joylessness that begins to alienate her child. When little Arthur tipples and swears, to the loud amusement of his father and his cronies, he is sobered by her disapproving gaze. "Mamma, why don't *you* laugh?" he asks her. "Make her laugh, papa—she never will" (p. 356).

The imagery of laughter, smiles, and tears forms a consistent pattern in the novel by which Anne Brontë articulates her moral theme and develops her characters and their relations with one another. One of the great virtues of *The Tenant* is its highly dramatic quality, and the vivid development of scenes through dialogue. And the dialogue gains in force by the meticulous recording of tones of voice, facial expression, and the accompaniments of smiles, sighs, tears, and laughter. We come to get the feel of a character not only by his or her words, but by the style in which they are delivered. And the style is always significant.

From the outset Arthur Huntingdon is characterized by his smiles and laughter. Our initial image of him is as painted by Helen in the first glow of her love: "The bright, blue eyes regarded the spectator with a kind of lurking drollery—you almost expected to see them wink; the lips—a little too voluptuously full—seemed ready to break into a smile . . ." (pp. 70-71). The love of the artist, as well as the character of the subject, is painted into this image; and Helen is susceptible not only to Arthur's handsome person but also to his fund of joy and good spirits. "I cannot believe there is any harm in those laughing blue eyes," she admits (p. 154). The progressive deterioration of their love is marked by Helen's learning to be pained by, and finally to hate, "that same blithe, roguish twinkle of the eyes I once so loved to see, and that low, joyous laugh it used to warm my heart to hear" (p. 279). His attractive smile and

laughter are early connected with pain and humiliation for her. He abducts her embarrassingly telltale portrait of himself "with a delighted chuckle" (p. 171) and peruses it "complacently smiling to himself" (p. 172); and she finds she can be "tyrannized over by those bright, laughing eyes" (p. 173). Presently she is pained to hear him "laughing immoderately" at the tale of Lowborough's ruin and degradation (p. 205).

The laughter becomes in fact a sign of sadism.[10] Though Arthur does not abuse Helen physically, he clearly derives pleasure from inflicting humiliation and psychological pain in a sexual context.[11] One of his chief amusements is to tell her of his previous amours and, when she reacts, to laugh "till the tears run down his cheeks" (p. 221). This amusement becomes more sinister when he watches her responses to his *current* amours. His wife's knowledge of his affair with Annabella clearly adds spice to it for him. The couple are indiscreet, and almost flaunt their affair before the abused wife. When Helen gives way to her anger and makes a scene, she says, "Arthur's low laugh recalled me to myself. I checked the half-uttered invective, and scornfully turned away, regretting that I had given him so much amusement" (p. 324). When Annabella departs, Arthur's next enjoyment is to show her passionate love letters to his wife. "He gave a slight titter on seeing me change colour," she says (p. 332). The intensely accurate rendering of that "slight titter" economically conveys a great deal about Arthur's psychology and the state of their marriage. Arthur has become a specialist in sexual humiliation.

Arthur's laughter and cheerfulness, originally so attractive, become the marks of a congenital inability to be serious about anything. His good cheer and high spirits themselves are not attached to any real cause; and increasingly we see him as incapable of being moved to anything *but* laughter, in any situation. A typical early exchange between him and Helen is on Annabella's campaign to catch Lord Lowborough. When Helen urges Arthur to warn his friend, he responds:

> "What, and spoil all her plans and prospects, poor girl? No, no; that would be a breach of confidence, wouldn't it, Helen? Ha, ha! Besides, it would break his heart." And he laughed again.
>
> "Well, Mr Huntingdon, I don't know what you see so amazingly diverting in this matter; *I* see nothing to laugh at."
>
> "I'm laughing at *you,* just now, love," said he, redoubling his cachinnations.
>
> (p. 211)

An unscrupulous woman's maneuvers, a friend's broken heart, his fiancée's distress—everything equally moves him to mindless giggles. He apparently feels hardly anything deserving the name of an emotion, and would be incapable of expressing it if he did. Occasionally circumstances call for some show of feeling, and then he has *more* fun, by putting on an act. When Helen has caught him kissing Annabella's hand, he does a piece of clowning for her benefit: throwing himself on his knees, "with clasped hands uplifted in mock humiliation, he continued imploringly—'Forgive me, Helen!—dear Helen, forgive me, and I'll *never* do it again!' and burying his face in his handkerchief, he affected to sob aloud" (p. 246). Because he has no feeling himself, he cannot credit it in others. Helen's intense religious conviction is for him a point of style: "Now I like a woman to be religious," he says, "and I think your piety one of your greatest charms, but . . . it may be carried too far" (p. 217). So also for her moral outbursts. After one of his debauches in town, when she implores him with tears to reform, he takes her demonstration too as an act, a "game" (p. 269), and delivers a cutting speech well calculated to dry her eyes.

> "A burst of passion is a fine, rousing thing upon occasion, Helen, and a flood of tears is marvellously affecting, but, when indulged too often, they are both deuced plaguy things for spoiling one's beauty and tiring out one's friends."
>
> Thenceforth, I restrained my tears and passions as much as I could.
>
> (p. 271)

After the elegant manner of the Regency, Arthur habitually converts matters of principle into matters of style; and the woman's genuine moral concern is turned by the man into an inappropriate piece of affectation.

It is characteristic of Arthur that in the great drunken scene, after he has summoned the "lads" to "a regular jollification" (p. 282) in the ladies' absence, his state of drunkenness takes the form of an inability to do anything but laugh. While Lord Lowborough, "in desperate earnest," struggles with a brawling Hattersley, and even Helen takes action in the scene by furnishing Lowborough with a candle to burn his assailant, Arthur lies back in his chair laughing helplessly. "'I can't do anything else if my life depended on it! . . . Oh, ho!' and leaning back in his seat, he clapped his hands on his sides and groaned aloud" (p. 288). Presently even Hattersley is infuriated by his "imbecile laughter," and proceeds to throw things at him. But Arthur "still sat collapsed and quaking with feeble laughter, with the tears running down his face; a deplorable spectacle indeed," comments Helen (p. 290).

His laughter is indeed imbecile—mindless, inappropriate, irresponsible. And when it comes to a significant issue, when his life *does* depend upon it, he cannot take any action but frivolous laughter, and he is damned. Perhaps one aspect of **The Tenant** that has put off readers is its author's readiness to be explicit about life after death. The average reader opens a novel in the expectation that it will deal with the here and now, and is apt to be embarrassed if he finds it deals also with the hereafter. But this book needs to be read not only as a novel but as a spiritual drama of the progress of the soul, like *Everyman, Doctor Faustus,* and *The Pilgrim's Progress.* Arthur, like Faustus, must be damned because he refuses to believe in the es-

sentially serious concepts of heaven and hell. "I think hell's a fable," Marlowe's Faustus glibly tells Mephistophilis, who grimly replies, "Ay, think so still, till experience change thy mind." Similarly, Arthur, even when he has some qualms about death and the possibility of hell, asserts, "Oh, it's all a fable"; and in response to Helen's urgent promptings—"Are you sure, Arthur? Are you *quite* sure?"—he can only reply facetiously, "It would be rather awkward, to be sure" (p. 446). He too must go to hell, where experience will change his mind. But because of Anne Brontë's merciful theology, he will only do *time* in hell, not eternity.

If Arthur is all frivolous laughter, at least up to his death scene, Helen is on the other hand committed to seriousness and inclined to tears. Her upbringing with her heavily moral aunt has made her, in fact, too serious, and we are shown how the cramping of her nature makes her particularly susceptible to Arthur's charms: she craves joy, and at the outset he represents joy to her. But soon she has some prophetic worries about their marriage: "I do wish he would *sometimes* be serious," she writes in the last diary entry before the wedding. "I cannot get him to write or speak in real, solid earnest. I don't much mind it *now*; but if it be always so, what shall I do with the serious part of myself?" (p. 214).

Although Helen's earnestness and moral seriousness are by and large endorsed, and we are expected to disapprove along with her of the irresponsible indulgences of her husband, there is also a keen observation of *her* moral and psychological deterioration during her marriage. From the eager idealism of her first diary entries to the bitter strictures of the last, we are invited to watch the increasing embitterment of a potentially happy nature. When Arthur's blatant intrigue with Annabella tempts her to encourage Hargrave's advances, she is horrified at her own impulse: "then I hate [Arthur] tenfold more than ever, for having brought me to this! . . . Instead of being humbled and purified by my afflictions, I feel that they are turning my nature into gall" (p. 323). Things between husband and wife have now reached such a pass that they can only aggravate every unpleasant tendency in each other: his enjoyment of her discomfiture makes her the more disapproving, gloomy, and bitter. Their child suffers doubly from his father's indulgences and his mother's habitual disapproval of them. "I am too grave to minister to his amusements and enter into his infantile sports as . . . a mother ought to do," she admits, "and often his bursts of gleeful merriment trouble and alarm me; I see in them his father's spirit and temperament, and I tremble for the consequences; and, too often, damp the innocent mirth I ought to share" (p. 334). She becomes the "cross mamma" (p. 356) who will not laugh; and Arthur is almost right in his claim that she is unfit to care for the child, because "I should freeze all the sunshine out of his heart, and make him as gloomy an ascetic as myself" (p. 387). Although she continues rigorously to do her duty, she is almost incapacitated as a moral agent. Just as Arthur's cheerful irresponsibility can be finally damnable, so Helen's moral earnestness can be crippling, morally debilitating. Although in context the phrase "in desperate earnest" is applied to Lowborough (p. 288), it has a large resonance in the book as a whole. It is good, compared with Arthur's irresponsible cachinnations, to be in earnest; but desperate earnest, earnestness taken to an extreme, can become a form of spiritual sin.

So much for the Huntingdon marriage. It is a union of opposites, and it is a disaster. The husband is Regency, stylish, irresponsible, and characterized by laughter; the wife is Victorian, dour, morally earnest, easily moved to disapproval and tears. And the opposites, instead of modifying one another, aggravate the worst tendencies in each. The record of the marriage is a record of progressive degeneration, both of the relationship and of the two individuals who constitute it.

It will be seen from what I have said that I am far from agreeing with George Moore and his followers,[12] who argue that the introduction of the diary was an artistic mistake and that Helen should have told Gilbert about her marriage in a tender interview. Not only are such critics ready to throw out half the novel, and the better half, but they miss the fine art by which a deteriorating relationship is recorded with dramatic immediacy. Helen's diary, written in stages of experience only as she reaches them, can adequately convey the pain, the pathos, and the bitterness of a strong love going sour.

As Helen's diary records the destruction of opposites, the story of Gilbert Markham serves to restore our faith in the possibility of a relationship between a man and a woman that is one of equals who are capable of mutual accommodation and beneficial modification.

When Gilbert meets Helen Graham, she is almost at her embittered worst. In escaping with her son from Arthur she has begun her cure, but her wounds are still raw. Hard and easily offended, she is that stern exaggeration of herself that her marriage has developed. Her face, as Gilbert examines it in church, is an antithesis of the portrait of her young husband: "the lips, though finely formed, were a little too thin, a little too firmly compressed" (p. 41). No glib smiles will be forthcoming from that countenance. "Everybody laughed," we hear of one characteristic exchange in the Linden Grange company, "except the young widow and her son" (p. 54). In fact this relationship too is to be developed through the imagery of smiles that are to be carefully differentiated in their quality from Arthur's.

Conscious of his role as the "beau of the parish" (p. 400), Gilbert approaches the attractive young widow (as he thinks her) with the same kind of breezy assurance Arthur had shown, fixing her with a quizzical stare in church; and she freezes him off. (At a second reading the opening of the novel has a special piquancy for the reader, who knows, as Gilbert does not, what Helen's experience has been, and how her response to him is determined by it.) Gilbert perseveres in his standard charm routine: "I smiled.—There was something either in that smile or the

recollections it awakened that was particularly displeasing to her, for she suddenly assumed again that proud, chilly look . . ." (p. 48). He does not know how little his smiling will recommend him to her, but the reader does.

The difference between Gilbert and Arthur is that Gilbert can recognize her responses and is willing to adapt himself. When he discovers that Helen thinks him "an impudent puppy" (p. 41), he is moved to do something to win her esteem. He learns and changes under the influence of a serious and intelligent woman. If he is at the outset something of the "beau," "an impudent puppy," "a fop" (p. 58), an "empty-headed coxcomb" (p. 92)—the standard Regency male, in fact—his love for Helen educates and sensitizes him.

His development is marked partly by the change of his affections from Eliza Millward to Helen. Eliza—lively, attractive, and utterly frivolous—represents for Gilbert, on a small scale, what Arthur was for Helen. In contrast to Helen's impenetrable gravity in church, Eliza's countenance shows her ready for a little flirtation: "she glanced at me, simpered a little, and blushed,—modestly looked at her prayer-book, and endeavoured to compose her features" (p. 41). Arthur's behavior in church had been very similar (p. 192). Eliza subdues Gilbert with "one of her softest smiles" (p. 50) and insists that he "be very good and amusing" (p. 49)—goodness and amusement being equated for her, as they are for the Regency beau. Presently, however, he finds her "frivolous, and even a little insipid, compared with the more mature and earnest Mrs Graham" (p. 73). Like Arthur's sadistic mirth, Eliza's smiles and laughter turn nasty. She tells Gilbert bad news while "smiling with delight" at his emotion, and, enjoying his discomfiture, "broke out into a long shrill laugh" (p. 463). Anne Brontë expects her reader to recognize the parallels, though her narrator cannot.

Fergus, Gilbert's younger brother, whom some critics have found rather tiresome,[13] is another minor character who seems to reiterate the novel's themes and remind us of the hero's education. When we meet Fergus, he is a facetious young fellow much given to badger-baiting and pointless bursts of laughter; and Gilbert, who sees in him a stage he has passed, is frequently exasperated by him. At the end of the novel, following in Gilbert's footsteps, Fergus is worthy to take over Linden Grange, because he has "lately fallen in love with . . . a lady whose superiority had roused his latent virtues" (p. 490). His development is an epitome of Gilbert's.

Gilbert's moral progress includes not only the curbing of his tendency to frivolity, a growing ability to recognize and properly revere what is good and beautiful, but a regulation of his passionate nature. For Gilbert, though much more moral than Arthur, is not the St. John Rivers to Arthur's Mr. Rochester, all cold reason against fire and passion. Despite some appearances to the contrary, it is Arthur who emerges as the passionless figure. Gilbert, on the other hand, is tempestuous and genuinely impulsive, swung this way and that by his feelings. His love for Helen once seriously roused, he tends to be violent about it. When he sees her, as he thinks, giving her favors to another man (who eventually turns out to be her brother), he rushes away and hurls himself to the ground "like a passionate child . . . in a paroxysm of anger and despair" (p. 125); and when he meets his supposed rival, he smashes him over the head with his riding whip (p. 134). Clearly we are not meant to approve of such behavior, though Gilbert's passion makes him a more sympathetic character than Arthur with his pointless laughter. But Anne Brontë takes pains to show his growing ability, not to cease to feel strongly, but to regulate the manifestations of his feelings. His alertness to the feelings of others makes him able to restrain his own. A late scene shows him again with Lawrence, and desperate for news of Helen. He snatches her letter from her brother's hand; but then, he records, "Recollecting myself, however, the minute after, I offered to restore it" (p. 428). It is a small touch, but one of the many unobtrusive demonstrations of Gilbert's development. When, as the mature narrator, he speaks of his youth before he knew Helen, he refers to it as the time when "I . . . had not acquired half the rule over my own spirit, that I now possess" (p. 35).

Does Helen Huntingdon, then, have it all her own way—leaving and morally triumphing over a husband who will not adapt to her high standards, and marrying instead a pliant man who does? No, it is not only Gilbert who has to adapt in the Markham marriage. For one thing, she has to learn to cast off her severity and gloom. When Gilbert first meets her, he says, she is "too hard, too sharp, too bitter for my taste" (p. 65). But as she sees he is wounded by her sharpness, she learns gradually to ameliorate it. At one point, after an angry rejoinder to a question of his, Gilbert notes that she was "attempting to cover the tartness of her rebuke with a smile" (p. 71)—a characteristic notation on their relationship at this point. Here the smiling is still an effort, as though it would crack the face of one who has trained herself to maintain a stony expression. Presently the smile comes more naturally. There is a poignant little scene marking a threshold of consciousness in their love, when Gilbert watches her sketch.

> She did not talk much; but I stood and watched the progress of her pencil: it was a pleasure to behold it so dexterously guided by those fair and graceful fingers. But erelong their dexterity became impaired, they began to hesitate, to tremble slightly, and make false strokes, and then suddenly came to a pause, while their owner laughingly raised her face to mine, and told me that her sketch did not profit by my superintendence.
>
> (pp. 74-75)[14]

Laughter at last! And it is both a sign of conscious love and a manifestation of reawakening gladness in a life in which laughter had become horrible. Now the smiles are more frequent. She accepts Gilbert's gift of a copy of *Marmion* "with a most angelic smile" (p. 95) and greets him with a "countenance radiant with smiles" (p. 109). When Arthur is dead, and the chief obstacle between her

and Gilbert has been removed, she is able to receive him "with a dawning smile" (p. 481) and to look upon him as her betrothed "with a smile of ineffable tenderness" (p. 486). The bitter resistance to smiles and laughter that her first marriage had induced has been dispelled. "Why, then, methinks 'tis time to smile again," she might say, with Shakespeare's Olivia.

As her love for Gilbert mitigates her dour seriousness, so it also induces her to ease her posture of embattled righteousness. At one point, after she has returned to Grassdale Manor to nurse the ailing Arthur, she writes to her brother: "I find myself in rather a singular position: I am exerting my utmost endeavours to promote the recovery and reformation of my husband, and if I succeed what shall I do? My duty, of course,—but how?" (p. 435). Anne Brontë never disapproved of anyone who could stick to duty, but she knew that a woman for whom "My duty, of course" was the automatic answer to all questions was a limited being. In the central story of the Huntingdon marriage, Helen is the outraged wife contemplating her husband's adulterous love affair. In the frame story of Gilbert Markham, she becomes the errant wife who is succumbing to a love for a handsome young farmer—a role not nearly so conducive to moral dignity.

When Gilbert has read her diary, and so knows she is a married woman, the two have an impassioned interview in which they face the terrible obstacle to their love. Helen is if anything the more passionate of the two, but when he pleads his cause she appeals to him, "Instead of acting like a true friend . . . and helping me with all your might—or rather taking your own part in the struggle of right against passion—you leave all the burden to me" (p. 406). It is the first time Helen has admitted to an agonizing conflict of right against passion. She has been perfectly immune to Hargrave's advances. But "My duty, of course" is not a formula that will work in this instance. And her exhortation to Gilbert to share the burden of resistance to temptation (to which he responds nobly) is not only an admission of her own moral inadequacy but a necessary appeal for equal responsibility. This union is not to be one where the woman automatically shoulders a moral burden for two.

Helen must come to terms with her status as a fallible human being in the final proposal scene. Here it is Gilbert who is the proudly scrupulous one, and she who must overcome her moral pride to woo him. She practically does the proposing, and is even caught out in some sly intriguing to get little Arthur out of the way while she does it (p. 487). Gilbert has the salutary effect of making her get off her moral high horse.

When Helen was summoned back to the side of her reprobate husband, her brother piously announced, "Nothing persuaded her but her own sense of duty." Gilbert's swift response to this assurance is "Humbug!" (p. 427). We are not to suppose that Helen's finely developed sense of duty is indeed humbug, but rather that in her marriage to Gilbert she will not have the inalienable right to play the good angel to the husband as reprobate. There is to be some communication of values between husband and wife, some sharing of responsibility as well as some sharing of laughter. So much is confirmed by the memorable image of the Christmas rose which Helen gives to Gilbert at their betrothal, and which is the emblem of their love. Combining the most joyous elements of winter and summer, the Christmas rose also symbolizes an achieved union of delight and pain, passion and duty. The mature Gilbert, considering his development after years of marriage to Helen, can say with a well-based confidence, "I have learned to be merry and wise, . . . and I can afford to laugh" (p. 458). It is a propitious conclusion.

In *The Tenant of Wildfell Hall* Anne Brontë has produced a novel of great power and subtlety. The story-within-a-story, which incorporates a change in period as well as a change from male to female narrator, allows both for a period commentary and an exploration of society's unequal expectations of men and women. In the internal story of a failed marriage the dichotomies between the male and female worlds are exaggerated and never resolved, while in the frame story of the second courtship and marriage we are offered the possibility of accommodation and reconciliation. This structural and thematic pattern is supported at the dramatic level by the vivid delineation of irresponsible laughter and moral seriousness in the sayings and doings of the characters. The two marriages of Helen Huntingdon represent both society's emergent sense of moral urgency, which is to displace the Regency ethos of fun and frivolity, and the individual's attainment of social and psychological fulfillment.[15] If the woman has to learn to exceed her stereotype of good angel and to partake of joy and pleasure, so the man must learn—and earlier in the Victorian era than we thought—the importance of being earnest.

Notes

1. Anne Brontë, *The Tenant of Wildfell Hall,* ed. G. D. Hargreaves, introd. Winifred Gérin (Harmondsworth, Eng.: Penguin Books, 1979), p. 35. The Penguin text restores the prefatory address to Halford and other passages that were excised from the 1854 and many subsequent editions.

2. See F. B. Pinion, *A Brontë Companion* (London: Macmillan, 1975), p. 246: "She was busy at [*The Tenant of Wildfell Hall*] in the summer of 1847, and this is the time when she imagines it to have been concluded by Gilbert Markham."

3. I do not take time here to make again a case for *The Tenant of Wildfell Hall* as a major and unjustly neglected novel; this has been argued before (though not yet so as to convince many critics), notably by George Moore, *Conversations in Ebury Street* (New York: Boni and Liveright, 1924), pp. 252-57; Ada Harrison and Derek Stanford, *Anne Brontë: Her Life and Work* (London: Methuen, 1959), pp. 236-45; and A. Craig Bell, *Anne Brontë: "The Tenant of Wildfell Hall": A Study and Reappraisal* (Ilkley, Eng.: Emeril

Publications, 1974). Pinion states that "there can be little doubt that, had *The Tenant of Wildfell Hall* received more critical attention, its merits would be more widely recognized" (p. 258). Lewis K. Tiffany has shown how Charlotte Brontë's dislike of *The Tenant,* which was largely a result of her personal feelings in recognizing a depiction of Branwell's degeneration, has adversely affected the novel's literary reputation ("Charlotte and Anne's Literary Reputation," *Brontë Society Transactions,* 16, no. 4 [1974], 284-87). I proceed on the assumption that *The Tenant* is a fine and important Victorian novel that deserves serious critical attention as a work of fiction, and apart from biographical considerations.

4. *The Four Georges* (1860), in *The Oxford Thackeray,* ed. George Saintsbury, 17 vols. (London: Oxford University Press, 1908), XIII, 792.

5. Much of the swearing was bowdlerized in the 1854 and subsequent editions, as Hargreaves points out in his "Note on the Text" (p. 19). The Victorian editor was reluctant to let Anne Brontë make her point about the habitual profanity of men of fashion.

6. Compare the masculine ethos of Thomas Hughes's *Tom Brown's Schooldays* (1857), where Tom, born in the 1820s, is similarly proved to be a manly little fellow when he shows his "inaptitude for female guidance" and casts off the "petticoat government" of his nurse, Charity Lamb (see chaps. 2 and 3).

7. Anne Brontë was to have further proof of the different sets of standards applied to men and women in the critical reception of *The Tenant.* The reviewer for *Sharpe's London Magazine* (August 1848, pp. 181-84) was fairly typical in being shocked at the book's "disgustingly truthful minuteness," "the revolting details of such evil revelry," and was emphatic in refusing to "believe any woman could have written such a work." The novel, he said, was "unfit for the perusal of . . . girls" (*The Brontës: The Critical Heritage,* ed. Miriam Allott [London: Routledge & Kegan Paul, 1974], pp. 264-65). It was in answer to such objections that Anne Brontë bravely wrote in her preface to the second edition (July 1848), "All novels are or should be written for both men and women to read, and I am at a loss to conceive how a man should permit himself to write anything that would be really disgraceful to a woman, or why a woman should be censured for writing anything that would be proper and becoming for a man" (p. 31).

8. *Anne Brontë* (London: Thomas Nelson and Sons, 1959), p. 246.

9. Anne Brontë does not take her feminism so far as to approve of the woman who becomes mannish. Annabella's values are very much like those of the men: she "amuses herself with the lively Huntingdon" (p. 178) and can joke about her affair with Arthur to his wife (pp. 324, 327). She is also, like Arthur, apt to suppose that displays of emotion must be affected.

Weeping, she says, is woman's "grand resource . . . but doesn't it make your eyes smart?" (p. 250). She reaps her appropriate reward. After bearing Arthur's illegitimate child, "a little girl . . . with blue eyes and light auburn hair" (p. 354) that Lord Lowborough knows is not his, she takes off with another gallant, and finally sinks "in penury, neglect, and utter wretchedness" (p. 460). Her husband, however, whom her fortune had redeemed from financial ruin, lives to marry again and live respectably, presumably on Annabella's money. Anne Brontë was apparently not moved by the injustice of the husband's taking full possession of his wife's fortune. The Married Women's Property Acts were not passed until 1870 and 1882.

10. Robert Barnard calls Huntingdon "a drunken sadist," though he does not develop the point ("Anne Brontë: The Unknown Sister," *Edda* [*Scandinavian Journal of Literary Research*], [1978], p. 37).

11. Janet Kunert has explored the husband's deliberate humiliation of the wife, with the appropriate punishment of dying of "mortification," in "Borrowed Beauty and Bathos: Anne Brontë, George Eliot, and 'Mortification,'" *RS* [*Research Studies*], 46 (1978), 237-47.

12. According to Moore, "Anne broke down in the middle of her story. . . . An accident would have saved her; almost any man of letters would have laid his hand upon her arm and said: You must not let your heroine give her diary to the young farmer. . . . Your heroine must tell the young farmer her story, and an entrancing scene you will make of the telling" (pp. 253-54). I suspect that Anne Brontë would have told the "man of letters" to mind his own business, and quite rightly. Gérin, however, after quoting this passage in her introduction to the Penguin edition, exclaims, "How right was Moore!" (p. 14). Melvin R. Watson similarly wishes that Anne Brontë had "been able to reduce Helen's account of her trials to a chapter or two" ("Form and Substance in the Brontë Novels," in *From Jane Austen to Joseph Conrad: Essays Collected in Memory of James T. Hillhouse,* ed. Robert C. Rathburn and Martin Steinmann, Jr. [Minneapolis: University of Minnesota Press, 1958], p. 109).

13. A. Craig Bell, the most outspoken admirer of this novel, finds Fergus to be one of the few failings in the book: "Why Anne Brontë ever had the idea of creating this teen-age hobbledehoy and would-be wit must remain conjectural" (pp. 15-16). I present a conjecture.

14. There is not space in this paper to discuss the significance of Helen's role as a painter, though it is a subject that can profitably be pursued, as Sandra M. Gilbert and Susan Gubar have made clear (*The Madwoman in the Attic: The Woman Writer and the Nineteenth-Century Literary Imagination* [New Ha-

ven and London: Yale University Press, 1979], pp. 81-82). It is part of the feminist theme of the novel that Helen and Gilbert should develop their love while they are mutually pursuing their professions of artist and farmer in the pleasant countryside.

15. As my argument should have made clear, I differ from Terry Eagleton, who finds that "the protagonists are too abstractly individuated, too internally unpressured by the strains and frictions of their social worlds. It is for this reason that the union of Helen and Gilbert can articulate nothing of that questioning sense of fundamental values, and of the social tissue in which they are embedded, which communicates itself so powerfully in the coming together of Hareton and Catherine" (*Myths of Power: A Marxist Study of the Brontës* [London: Macmillan, 1975], p. 137).

Jan B. Gordon (essay date 1984)

SOURCE: "Gossip, Diary, Letter, Text: Anne Brontë's Narrative *Tenant* and the Problematic of the Gothic Sequel," in *ELH,* Vol. 51, No. 4, Winter, 1984, pp. 719-45.

[*In the following essay, Gordon studies gossip and narrative enclosure in* The Tenant of Wildfell Hall, *as well as the relationship between Anne Brontë's novel and his sister Emily's* Wuthering Heights.]

> The frame, however, is handsome enough; it will serve for another painting. The picture itself I have not destroyed, as I had first intended; I have put it aside. . . .
>
> (*The Tenant of Wildfell Hall,* 398)[1]

Anne Brontë's *The Tenant of Wildfell Hall* quickly calls attention to itself as the longest single-narrative, enclosing epistolary novel of the nineteenth century. Beginning "dear Halford," it concludes four hundred and fifty pages later with a "Till then, farewell, Gilbert Markham." It is not the characters of the individual subjects of the novel nor the contents of Markham's narrative that shape the meaning of *The Tenant of Wildfell Hall,* but rather the relative dispensation of alternative narratives competing for our attention and hence for a textual priority. Each mode of discourse must confront the recognition that in any scheme of recovery, "voice" is a privileged aspect of language, that the intrusion of the "otherness" of the listener is a necessary constitution of meaning. The engagement of a narratee is achieved by sublating a variety of second- or third-hand discourse: community gossip; the narrator's own source, a "faded old journal" (*TWH,* 34); the incomplete manuscript of Helen Huntington's diary, given to the narrator because she cannot *speak* her story; a cluster of failed correspondence between Gilbert and Helen; and finally, a sort of running commentary on another and historically prior text, Helen's exegesis of the Bible, which serves to foreground all the other narratives. Each of the enclosed varieties of discourse appears as a supplement, an attempt to amend or correct either the inadequacy or the social threat posed by another "version" of the same events. Rather than seeking to establish their primacy or priority by creating a discontinuity among narratives that would furnish a ground for deconstruction,[2] however, Anne Brontë's narrator presents the reader with another situation: a world of proliferating "texts" which cannot be contained, except by a desperate and arbitrary act of enclosure.[3] The formal rivalry between narratives has its genetic parallel in the way *The Tenant of Wildfell Hall* encloses its originary, *Wuthering Heights,* as it strives to supplant it. This structural belatedness is paralleled by a historical belatedness—a nineteenth-century epistolary novel.

The enclosing letter to Halford with which Gilbert Markham opens and closes his narrative occupies a curious structural position, partially inside and partially outside the body of *The Tenant of Wildfell Hall.* For the novel makes a clear distinction between its temporal, chronological "beginning" (chapter 1) and its narrative commencement in front of the first chapter. Formal priority is chronologically posterior, a relationship that holds throughout the novel, an inversion that points to the necessary belatedness of the novel as a form. It is always attempting to recover a prior text; hence it opens with six paragraphs, not part of any chapter, to Markham's friend, Halford, sandwiched between Anne Brontë's "Preface to the Second Edition" and the actual commencement in chapter 2 of the events that the novel purports to describe. This enclosed, "framed" nature of the narrative points to its provisionality, an arbitrariness that separates the beginning of the novel from the commencement of the act of writing:

> I have not my memory alone to depend upon; in order that your credulity may not be too severely taxed in following me through the minute details of my narrative.—To begin then, at once, with Chapter First, for its shall be a tale of many chapters.
>
> (*TWH,* 34)

And then begins the narrative *per se:* "You must go back with me to the autumn of 1827" (*TWH,* 35). Anne Brontë, by the framing device of the letter, suggests a feature of writing to which the characters of *The Tenant of Wildfell Hall* continually defer: that writing is always belated, always attempting to "recover" and bring into the present what remains forever lodged in the past. The vestige of this urge to recovery is a kind of narrative residue, a beginning before the beginning. It is a narrative device common to Gothic fiction with its plethora of found letters, scraps of documents in attics, texts as clues to a prior and whole truth which must somehow be pieced together. It is the formal corollary to the structures of the *ruin* and the *monstrous* which seem to belong to the beginning before the beginning.[4] Stated in another way, the dialectic that Gilbert's letter enacts depends upon the way it flamboyantly plays on a temporal distance between the world it creates and the world in which the apparatus of invention is constructed.

Chapter 1 begins with a discussion of Gilbert's prospects. His father's deathbed wish is that the "paternal lands" be "transmit[ted]" (*TWH,* 35) to his own grandchildren, in-

tact and unentailed, through the mediation of his son and our narrator, Gilbert Markham. The novel begins, then, with the death of paternity—a theme that continues throughout—and the gesture of transmission, that maintenance of property from one generation to the next that made the Victorian will such an instrument of social control and order.[5] In fact, the setting of the first chapter is almost entirely devoted to ritual images of Victorian order: afternoon tea; visits by the curate, Millward; Guy Fawkes Day parties (which use a celebration to control the memory of subversion); knitting projects; and plans for a spring outing. Social order is a function of rituals whose meanings are communally shared and hence capable of being transmitted, more or less intact, to others. Stability is a function of the transactional nature of human discourse. But this seemingly endless round of trivial socialization is interrupted by the announcement that there is a new arrival in the neighborhood; like Heathcliff before her, she is dressed in black, and has recently moved into Wildfell Hall, now lapsing into the run-down condition of abandonment that characterizes the ruin:

> 'Well,' resumed Rose; 'I was going to tell you an important Piece of news I heard there—I've been bursting with it ever since. You know it was reported a month ago, that somebody was going to take Wildfell Hall— and—what do you think? It has actually been inhabited above a week!—and we never knew!'
>
> 'Impossible!' cried my mother.
>
> 'Preposterous!!!' shrieked Fergus.
>
> 'It has indeed!—and by a single lady!'
>
> 'Good gracious, my dear! The place is in ruins!'
>
> (*TWH,* 37)

The woman is single with a child, did not attend Sunday church services, and is clearly a tenant rather than an owner of property, all of which serves to establish Mrs. Graham's subversiveness in Linden-Car.

But perhaps the most pointed signifier of her role as a potentially disruptive outsider in the community is the speech that relates her intrusion, for it is the first of many instances in which the force of gossip makes itself felt. In fact, the first ten chapters of the novel are really nothing more than the attempt of gossip to come to terms with meaning. Almost everyone in Linden-Car speculates about the past of the mysterious Mrs. Graham, and, although at the outset, only Mrs. Wilson is labelled "a tattling old gossip" (*TWH,* 43), eventually almost all of the characters come to participate at one time or another in that mode of discourse. There is the suspicion that Mrs. Graham is linked with some scandal, that she is poverty-stricken, that she is unsociable. All of these reports are incomplete and inadequate, not because of the inscrutability of their object, but because of the nature of the discourse.

As Heidegger understood, gossip, like the nineteenth-century novel itself, circulates, floating about the culture as *Geschwätz,* a kind of metalanguage.[6] And, as a metalanguage, it has a number of features that particularly endear it to the residents of Linden-Car. In *The Tenant of Wildfell Hall,* as with the arena of most gossip, "overheard language" has no authorship that can be readily identified. It is a speculative language thrown out at that which is only incompletely understood, and its origins can never be traced or determined. Whenever anyone in the novel attempts to identify the source of a given rumor, it seems to recede into the folds of progressive narrative enclosure:

> 'Well, tell me then,' I answered, in a lower tone; 'what is it you mean? I hate enigmas.'
>
> 'Well, you know, I don't vouch for the truth of it—indeed far from it—but haven't you heard—'
>
> 'I've heard nothing, except from you.'
>
> 'You must be wilfully deaf then; for anyone will tell you that—but I shall only anger you by repeating it, I see; so I had better hold my tongue.'
>
> She closed her lips and folded her hands before her with an air of injured weakness.
>
> 'If you had wished not to anger me, you should have held your tongue from the beginning; or else spoken out plainly and honestly all you had to say.'
>
> (*TWH,* 98)

The author of gossip tends to be an anonymously democratic "anyone" who cannot be identified as an origin and hence held responsible. All who participate in gossip are mediators, who invariably heard it from someone else. And it is potent in shaping reputations and responses to people or events in direct proportion to the dilution of its author(itative) base. Because it is essentially a speech-act, gossip can never be "recovered" in either sense in which we typically use that word—recaptured in its original form or covered over and stopped. As many Victorians must have understood, gossip is a deployment of discourse that is forever enlarging and expanding the field of its domain. As the volume of gossip in *The Tenant of Wildfell Hall* increases, it begins to affect almost everyone; people seem to live as if they were always being talked about. To fear gossip is to fear that one is becoming a character, an "other," in someone else's fiction:

> The pair had now approached within a few paces of us. Our arbour was set snugly back in a corner, before which the avenue, at its termination, turned off into the more airy walk along the bottom of the garden. As they approached this, I saw, by the aspect of Jane Wilson, that she was directing her companion's attention to us; and, as well, by her cold sarcastic smile, as by *the few isolated words of her discourse* that reached me, I knew full well that she was impressing him with the idea that we were strongly attached to each other.
>
> (*TWH,* 105; my italics)

Gossip, by its very nature, is isolated and unenclosed, which has the effect of tempting closure. "Anyone" can become a collective participant in a depersonalized speech-act, can in fact become an author, merely by supplement-

ing a prior version. The widow Graham constantly seeks to remove herself from the range of what she calls "small talk"—the various "spicy piece[s] of scandal" (*TWH,* 103) that engage the narrative powers of the community. But the greater her distance, the more quickly the range of gossip is enlarged. It is as if language takes the place of the object of discourse and is itself "passed along." Gossip presents the illusion of transaction.

In one sense, gossip represents a kind of collective conspiracy to gain access to that which is spatially or socially hidden, and tends to be subversive precisely because it challenges our private spaces, because it treats history as a kind of property. The lower classes tend to gossip about the upper classes, but not vice versa, a feature of gossip which enabled Nelly Dean to be such a complex narrator in *Wuthering Heights,* gradually supplanting Lockwood. If the love of Heathcliff and Cathy represented unmediated desire, then Nelly Dean's narrative, tainted with the envy of a servant's gossip, represents mediation passing itself off as direct knowledge.

Forever seeking to establish its authenticity, gossip in *The Tenant of Wildfell Hall* threatens cultural values as it establishes its textuality. First of all, gossip can be directed. If the mere spatial contiguity of any two people of the opposite sex gives rise to the speculation that is gossip, then characters can effect, even initiate gossip by manipulating proxemics. Its apparently random circulation may not be so random after all. Late in the novel, Arthur Huntington refuses to accede to his wife's request for an end to their marriage on the grounds that such an estrangement would make him "the talk of the country" (*TWH,* 315)—a marvelous euphemism for gossip. Ralph Hargrave, who wishes to accompany Helen and her child as a guardian, attempts to convince her of his worth as protector and lover. In the process of kneeling before her, he notices that there is a witness:

> 'That is Grimsby,' said he, deliberately. 'He will report what he has seen to Huntington and all the rest, with such embellishments as he thinks proper. He has no love for you, Mrs. Huntington—no reverence for your sex—no belief in virtue—no admiration for its image. He will give such a version of this story as will leave no doubt at all, about your character, in the minds of those who hear it.'
>
> (*TWH,* 363)

Has her husband used a common friend to manipulate his wife into a compromising position in order to feed gossip? In that case gossip would have a beginning and an end, in the sense that it could be purposive, used for directed revenge.

Gossip always attempts to be what it is not by incorporating the patterns of relatedness appropriate to the novel; i.e., it creates plots where none exist. One of the most remarkable accomplishments of gossip in Anne Brontë's novel occurs when the community becomes aware of the frequent conversations between Frederick Lawrence, a familiar bachelor in the neighborhood, and the dark Helen Graham. Searching for clues to her past life, the Millward girls spread the story that Frederick Lawrence is her secret lover, a revelation that tempts Gilbert Markham into an assault. As it turns out, of course, Frederick and Helen are not lovers, but brother and sister. In generating lovers out of a relationship of consanguinity, gossip conspires to create the disappearance of difference that is incest. Hence it is not only that gossip obscures sources or "versions" of a story as well as the authors of a story, but also that it blurs the internal relationships of its objects.[7] In a novel filled with references to the "value" and "investment" of a good marriage, to the transactional and contractual nature of the marriage "bond," gossip always appears as a threat to value: it either "speculates" or exaggerates by "inflating" (*TWH*, 415). In short, gossip devalues because it has nothing standing behind it. Lacking the authenticity of a definable source, it is simultaneously financially, theologically, and narratively unredeemable:

> 'And who gave you this piece of intelligence, Miss Eliza?' said I, interrupting my sister's exclamations.
>
> 'I had it from a very authentic source, sir.'
>
> 'From whom, may I ask?'
>
> 'From one of the servants at Woodford.'
>
> 'Oh! I was not aware that you were on such intimate terms with Mr. Lawrence's household.'
>
> 'It was not from the man himself, that I heard it; but he told it in confidence to our maid Sarah, and Sarah told it to me.'
>
> (*TWH*, 425-26)

Gilbert Markham's attempts to discover who Helen Graham is must initially discount the community's gossip. In order somehow to get behind the collective speech attempting to establish its dominance, Gilbert resorts to the expediency of using the text as a pre-text. In order to prevent other churchgoers from guessing at his admiration of Mrs. Graham's beauty, he somewhat sacrilegiously hides his own blushing face behind the prayer book at church (*TWH*, 41), even as the Rev. Millward is conducting a commentary. Later, on an outing, he encounters the elusive widow, sketch-book in hand, "absorbed in the exercise of her favorite art" (*TWH*, 74), drawing copies from nature. Gilbert takes the opportunity to question her about life at the lonely and desolate habitation, and her response makes the role of the book as a potential instrument of repression obvious:

> 'On winter evenings, when Arthur is in bed, and I am sitting there alone, hearing the bleak wind moaning round me and howling through the ruinous old chambers, no books or occupations can repress the dismal thoughts and apprehensions that come crowding in. . . .'
>
> (*TWH*, 76)

The course of their friendship is initially defined in terms of the exchange of books:

> So we talked about painting, poetry, and music, theology, geology, and philosophy: once or twice I lent her a book, and once she lent me one in return: I met her in her walks as often as I could; I came to her house as often as I dared. My first pretext for invading the sanctum was to bring Arthur a little waddling puppy of which Sancho was the father, and which delighted the child beyond all expression. . . . My second was to bring him a book which, knowing his mother's particularity, I had carefully selected, and which I submitted for her approbation before presenting it to him.
>
> (*TWH*, 93)

Quite literally, Gilbert's knowledge of Helen, apart from that revealed by gossip, is derived entirely from their exchange of books: "She called me Gilbert, by my express desire, and I called her Helen, for I had seen that name written in her books" (*TWH*, 113). Any transgression of the highly limited nature of their friendship is measured in terms of a violation in the conditions of their book-loan agreement. Knowing that Helen Graham would like to be entertained by reading Scott's *Marmion*, Gilbert orders a copy from a London publisher, only to discover on presenting it to her that she demands to pay him for it:

> 'I'm sorry to offend you, Mr. Markham,' said she, 'but unless I pay for the book, I cannot take it.' And she laid it on the table.
>
> 'Why cannot you?'
>
> 'Because—' She paused, and looked at the carpet.
>
> 'Why cannot you?' I repeated, with a degree of irascibility that roused her to lift her eyes, and look me steadily in the face.
>
> 'Because I don't like to put myself under obligations that I can never repay—I am obliged to you, already, for your kindness to my son; but his grateful affection, and your own good feeling must reward you for that.'
>
> (*TWH*, 94)

The attempt to use books to get behind the community's gossip, as it turns out, has severe limitations. For instead of using the contents of the book to reveal more about herself, Helen Huntington deflects the status of the book from *clue* to *occasion* of exchange. Using the economic imagery of indebtedness and redemption in keeping with her religious convictions, Helen always demands the "exchange" of discourse: "I hate talking where there is no exchange of ideas or sentiment, and no good given or received" (*TWH*, 104). She wants a world where obligations and duties are faithfully recognized and discharged, as opposed to the world of "small talk" that achieves the opposite, inflationary effect.

Although Gilbert Markham is relatively immune from gossip, he does fall victim to the assumption that every text exchanged is a representation of love exchanged. One day, visiting Helen's parlor whose "limited but choice collection of books was almost as familiar to me as my own" (*TWH*, 143), he discovers an intruder among the volumes. There is an edition of Sir Humphrey Davy's *Last Days of a Philosopher* on whose fly leaf Frederick Lawrence's name appears. Although texts have a specificity that gossip does not have, Gilbert is plunged into the same speculation about their relationship as the rest of the community is. Demanding an explanation, he gets another text:

> She did not speak, but flew to her desk, snatching thence what seemed a thick album or manuscript volume, hastily tore away a few leaves from the end, and thrust the rest into my hand, saying, 'You needn't read it all; but take it home with you,'—
>
> (*TWH*, 146)

Gilbert rushes home in accordance with her instructions, and discovers, in the process of reading it, the contraceptive to the community's gossip, except that its unfinished nature—unfinished at precisely the point of engaging his own "otherness"—tends to make him an object of gossip. He encloses it within his own narrative, repressing in the process the progressive failure of marriage and the subversion that it represents:

> I have it now before me; and though you could not, of course peruse it with half the interest that I did, I know you would not be satisfied with an abbreviation of its contents, and you shall have the whole, save, perhaps *a few passages here and there of merely temporal interest to the writer,* or such as would serve to encumber the story rather than elucidate it. It begins somewhat abruptly, thus—but we will reserve its commencement for another chapter, and call it,—
>
> (*TWH*, 147; my italics)

The process of enclosing one narrative within another serves to deflect the act of recovery, because the text now occupies a different disposition in the field of discourse. Helen retains a "few pages from the end" at her end of the narrative transaction and Gilbert selectively edits what remains. Hence her attempt to use the private confessional form to combat the metalanguage of the community is only partially successful, because the diary has some of the limitations of gossip: once exchanged, it tends to be replicated in successive versions; in the process of disclosure, the private world becomes public, making for more or less equal access; and finally, the diary, once having gone from her hands, cannot return to her in the same way. It suddenly has a "currency," an exchange value that is quite different from its value as self-reflection *for her.*

In a society where gossip seems to determine relationships, Helen Huntington's diary/ms. is an attempt to set the record straight, but it leaves gaps in testament and chronology that cry out for closure much as does gossip. Hers is a language that reveals its necessary incompleteness and hence its inadequacy at every turn. The dilemma of textuality, succinctly stated, is this: in their belatedness, texts are necessarily incomplete agents of recovery. Gossip has all the power of speaking as opposed to writing: it is democratic, spontaneous, all-encompassing in the sense of participating in that which it purports to describe. But it has no author(ity) which might give it a basis in transac-

tion. It cannot be bequeathed or inherited *as is.* Texts, on the other hand, can be "passed on," incorporated within other discourse which gives them form. Texts have a repository, either in other texts or in libraries, which means that they can be put aside in ways that gossip cannot. The community's gossip serves to give Helen Huntington a past which her diary/ms. attempts to counteract. When she gives her diary to Gilbert Markham and he "frames" it within his enclosing letter (novel) to Halford to create the layered narrative that is *The Tenant of Wildfell Hall,* his object, to borrow from the language of psychoanalysis,[8] is to make her past definitively past, so that he might marry her. Her object had been to make present her past. Hence, his narrative can never enclose her intentionality.[9]

But even were that problem solvable by accommodating intentionality in the doubtful way in which E. D. Hirsch recommends,[10] there is something in the very composition of her diary/ms. that prevents it from ever severing itself from gossip. The burden of the scriptural passages she incessantly cites—and often misinterprets—is that life on earth is a kind of endless preparation for a glorious afterlife. Hence the suffering on earth that her diary details is necessary in order for the sequel to be enacted. Arthur Huntington's agony and the genuine physical horror of a life of *delirium tremens* is less threatening to Helen than is his refusal to live within the dialectic of constant preparation. When Huntington's guest, Hattersley, promises to make amends for a life of profligacy, Helen replies:

> you *cannot* make amends for the past by doing your duty for the future, in as much as your duty is only what you owe to your maker, and you cannot do *more* than fulfil it—another must make amends for your past delinquencies.
>
> (*TWH*, 385)

Her diary, by self-consciously omitting the final three pages, postpones the ending, becoming in the process an exercise synchronous with her theological condition: it is always in preparation, desperately seeking a narratee to complete the necessary fiction of a bond, a covenant between texts and their recipients.[11]

In *The Tenant of Wildfell Hall,* the composition of Helen's diary/ms. takes up an enormous amount of space. As her marriage fails and Arthur's drunken bouts increase in frequency, she seeks recourse in writing. It would seem that private writing not only provides a refuge against that other public language, gossip, but becomes her only joy, as it must have indeed been for the Brontës:

> I have found relief in describing the very circumstances that have destroyed my peace, as well as the little trivial details attendant upon their discovery. No sleep I could have got this night would have done so much towards composing my mind, and *preparing me* to meet the trials of the day—I fancy so, at least;—and yet when I cease writing, I find my head aches terribly. . . .
>
> (*TWH*, 317; my italics)

Her own text becomes a structural and thematic companion to the other text, an indispensable aide in preparation. The progressive life of debauchery led by Arthur Huntington and his assorted household guests—Grimsby, the Hattersleys, Lord and Lady Lowborough—is always seen as a conspiracy against both texts: "none of our gentlemen had the smallest pretensions to a literary taste" (*TWH*, 359). Helen finds herself spending ever larger amounts of time in that repository of Victorian repression, the library. It is not only that her husband, Arthur, hurls books at the dog (in distinction to her future second husband, Gilbert Markham, who brought books and dogs), but that his role as the demon of the anti-text prompts him to invade the privacy of her diary:

> Jan. 10th, 1827. While writing the above, yesterday evening, I sat in the drawing-room. Mr. Huntington was present, but as I thought, asleep on the sofa behind me. He had risen, however, unknown to me, and, actuated by some base spirit of curiosity, been looking over my shoulder for I know not how long; for when I had laid aside my pen, and was about to close the book, he suddenly placed his hand upon it, and saying—'With your leave, my dear, I'll have a look at this,' forcibly wrested it from me. . . .
>
> (*TWH*, 370)

Given such a history of textual predation, her sudden offer of it to Gilbert Markham as an explanation of her past and an attempt to put an end to gossip represents an astonishing urge to go public. But, of course, she does not give him all of the diary. Her private manuscript from which she has torn away pages at the end, concludes thusly, as Gilbert relates in his enclosing epistle to Halford:

> November 3rd—I have made some further acquaintance with my neighbors. The fine gentleman and beau of the parish and its vicinity (in his own estimation, at least) is a young. . . .
>
>   . . . . .
>
> Here it ended. The rest was torn away. How cruel—just when she was going to mention me! for I could not doubt it *was* your humble servant she was about to mention, though not very favorably of course—I could tell that, as well by those few words as by the recollection of her whole aspect and demeanor towards me. . . .
>
> (*TWH*, 400)

Helen's manuscript, because it is unfinished (and it is unfinished because it has been given to Gilbert) can never enact the otherness of its recipient. Instead, the gift of her private history to Gilbert displaces his role *in* the diary, and creates once again the idle speculation that is gossip. Was she about to talk about me, or someone else? Was she to mention me favorably or not? The very fact that he has the diary ironically prevents him from knowing the crucial detail of her history—his role in it: "I had no right to see it: all this was too sacred for any eyes but her own" (*TWH*, 401). Its failure to enact his otherness, ironically, becomes the ground for its sacredness.

What is really being engaged here is the potential paradox involved in the stance of a narrator who is suddenly an owner of someone else's private narration. The framing device must stabilize the incommensurable relation between an author conceived of as somehow outside his creation and a privileged but fictitious consciousness within that imagined world. Gilbert's role as an owner, in the bourgeois sense at least, succumbs to a logic of inertia and permanence, whereas his own narration to Halford is rooted in change. In *The Tenant of Wildfell Hall* Gilbert Markham's narrative letter to Halford, as a belated response to Halford's request for a renewal of correspondence, constitutes potential exchange as the basis for textuality. The novel itself, as we read, is the record of a private text entering the public, novelistic domain—which it can do only when it is resubmerged within Gilbert's enclosing narrative to his friend, Halford. Otherwise, Helen's diary/ms. in its drawer in the library remains a potential source of violence, either from her husband or the community.

The recovered text tends to transform reality itself into a kind of lost or fallen text, the ironic result of a reading which surrenders to the centripetal powers of an enclosing fiction. This transformation also effects a kind of currency or exchange value in Helen Huntington's diary. The fallen woman and the fallen world can be redeemed only by a narrative transaction, by creating a text that makes room for the intrusion of the other. Helen's creation, unlike that of the God she worships, can no longer be indifferent or neutral as soon as it is part of a narrative contract that includes Gilbert as a party. Her history must be made eligible for a narrative consumption, in order that the private history which had been such a threat to community stability might become part of the community's collective fiction. That is surely part of the socialization of Helen Huntington, part of her eventual acceptance within that other of society's exchange contracts—remarriage. The passing on of her diary to Gilbert, along with its subsequent resubmergence within his own epistolary novel, paves the way for discourse based on exchange because it recognizes the arbitrary nature of beginnings and endings. Gossip can never be so exchanged, because each speaker adds to the whole; it is discourse as perpetual supplement, in the same way that Helen's unenclosed diary could be said to be discourse in perpetual preparation.

And yet, neither Gilbert nor Helen immediately recognizes that the framed enclosure will ensure the contractual nature of both their lives and their discourse. Dispossessed of her private diary and still the object of speculation, Helen Huntington at last wishes to put an end to their relationship, by elevating it to the level of "a spiritual intercourse without hope or prospect of anything further" (*TWH*, 408). This radical act seeks to replace the world of perpetual beginnings and perpetual supplements with the heady realm of pure spirit. Such is a peculiar affection, somewhat like that of Cathy and Heathcliff, unmediated, but infinitely distant. Resigned to that end, Gilbert Markham proposes a discourse appropriate to such an agreement: "'Is it a crime to exchange our thoughts by let-ter? May not kindred spirits meet and mingle in commun-ion, whatever be the fate and circumstances of their earthly tenements?'" (*TWH,* 408). As community gossip had ear-lier transformed a brother and sister into lovers, so Helen Huntington consents to use the discourse of the letter in order that she might convert a relationship of lovers to one of brother and sister: *kin*dred spirits. As if to make that change more obvious to poor Gilbert, she requests that they communicate to each other only through her brother, Frederick Lawrence, as she wishes that her "new abode should be unknown to you as to the rest of the world" (*TWH,* 408). The letters, like gossip, will have no point of origin, and in an attempt to avoid rumor, she embargoes all exchange of letters for six months, cautioning him to "maintain a correspondence all thought, all spirit, such as disembodied souls or unimpassioned friends might hold" (*TWH,* 409). Her wish for disembodied discourse is the antipode of enclosed discourse, and exchange is reduced to a mere vehicularity as letters float about the country-side—often delayed or undelivered. The lovers are asking the letter to be pure spirit, a task for which it is hopelessly inadequate.

The last quarter of the novel is filled with the intermittent and irregular news of Helen Huntington ministering to her husband in his terminal illness at Grassdale, repeated through the agency of Frederick Lawrence's selective nar-ration of her letters. In one sense, the letters have no ob-ject; because she is writing to her brother, who agrees to relay any important news to Gilbert, Helen Huntington cannot use the mode of discourse appropriate to lovers. In an attempt to escape community conjecture about her whereabouts, she is forced to strip her language of its specificity. But the more she "purifies" her language through incompleteness, the more she erases any trace of a narratee, the more Gilbert Markham must treat her letters as fallen texts which he must somehow enclose, as he looks for clues of his own presence:

> 'May I keep this letter, Lawrence?—you see she has never once mentioned me throughout—or made the most distant allusion to me; therefore, there can be no impropriety or harm in it.'
>
> 'And, therefore, why should you wish to keep it?'
>
> 'Were not these characters written by her hand? And were not those words conceived in her mind, and many of them spoken by her lips?'
>
> 'Well,' said he. And so I kept it; otherwise, Halford, you could never have become so thoroughly acquainted with its contents.'
>
> (*TWH,* 435-36)

Gilbert Markham is almost forced into a kind of nominal-ism—the word *is* Helen—in order to enclose discourse. His problem is that the letter participates in a modality of time, and hence meaning is partially a function of fre-quency. To create unexplained gaps in the frequency is to add to or subtract from meaning, and these gaps must oc-

cur because the agent of conveyance is not disinterested in the same way that she desires language to be. The ex-change value of a letter is not what is said, but the occasion(s) of its delivery. Intentionality is a function nei-ther of narrative subject nor narratee, nor its formal con-struction, nor its contents, but of something "outside" the letter.[12] Helen's letters act as social signifiers not because their contents are lacking, but because their real function (as reminders of her presence) is less dependent on the knowledge or non-knowledge of their contents than Gil-bert believes.

Gilbert Markham, like so many lovers, must resort to at-tempting to recover the *occasion* of the letter's composi-tion, since he receives only mediated contents. And the re-sult is collapse back into speculation and gossip. After Arthur Huntington's death, there is an interruption in the regular flow of letters, and Gilbert comes to blame his old adversary, Frederick Lawrence, for perhaps plotting to in-tercept his epistles to Helen: "I would wait, and see if she would notice me—which of course she would not, unless by some kind of message entrusted to her brother, that, in all probability he would not deliver . . ." (*TWH,* 456). When the hiatus in the exchange of letters continues, he decides not to write, but to wait for news. And he discov-ers that Lawrence does not positively withhold communi-cation, but confines himself to a literal interpretation of Markham's enquiries that again leaves no room for his own inclusion in her discourse:

> Ten weeks was long to wait in such a miserable state of uncertainty, but courage! it must be endured;—and meantime I would continue to see Lawrence now and then, though not so often as before, and I would still pursue my habitual enquiries after his sister—if he had lately heard from her, and how she was, but nothing more.
>
> I did so, and the answers I received were always pro-vokingly limited to the letter of the enquiry: She was much as usual: She made no complaints, but the tone of her last letter evinced great depression of mind:—She said she was better:—and finally;—She said she was well. . . .
>
> (*TWH,* 456-57)

The problem with the letter is always the same for Gilbert. Does she not mention me because she does not want her brother to know? Or, does the authority for my omission rest with him? The problematic of the letter is how to raise it from a residue of distant desire to a cipher of spiritual presence, given the conditions of its mediated vehicularity.

Throughout *The Tenant of Wildfell Hall* there is the re-current suspicion that writing can be justified only if raised to some spiritual level. Otherwise it continues to exist as "re-crimination," the repetitive enlargement of plots and suspicion that moves discourse closer to gossip with all of its threat to human relationships. And the solution that the novel somewhat conservatively proposes is that of valoriz-ing writing by exchange, which encloses and supplants other types of discourse, in the process making distinctions among them. Figuratively speaking, Gilbert Markham must get hold of all her writings—diary as well as letters—because only then can the unfinished, mediated status that always threatens to turn her life into gossip be put to an end. Gilbert must himself write the textual supplement to her life's diary—which cannot accommodate the otherness of the listener—and pass it on in order to prevent it from lapsing back into speech or gossip. Without that transactional frame, Anne Brontë's novel threatens to revert to the world of the narrative fragment, Gothic monsters, incestuous relationships, and, of course, whispered gossip—all of which call out for the completion of a closure that will restore differentiation. And in fact, as soon as Gilbert Markham's frame encloses all the other more subversive varieties of discourse, he marries Helen and the community's gossip vanishes. This takes place contemporaneously with the settlement of the dead father's farm upon Gilbert's brother Fergus, thus maintaining a legacy and keeping it from falling into other hands. The restoration of the narrative frame takes place at the same time as the investiture of the paternal lands, falling into disrepair during the plague of gossip. Just as the Victorian novel used a finalizing marriage, the fairy-tale ending, as an antidote to the threat of less socially acceptable forms of intercourse that threatened it, so *The Tenant of Wildfell Hall* equates a sort of narrative contract—the give-and-be-given of discourse—with the marital bond: both keep other monstrous plots at bay.[13] The burden of my argument, in contradistinction to the thrust of much post-structuralist thought—is that the framed discourse that encloses more free-floating, incomplete, or discontinuous discourse in Gothic structures is not a formal component of the radical thematics of the mode, but rather serves to restrain and repress. The salvation of texts by arbitrary supplements, the recovery of subversive discourse, does for "fallen" writing what the Rev. Brontë's sermons did for the unregenerate soul: they define an ending that restores the fiction of a distinction between the elect and the babble of tongues. Closure restores metaphor—and hence likeness and difference—at the cost of containing a crisis in discourse.[14]

Almost. There is a curious way in which Anne Brontë's novel by itself serving as a kind of supplement to *Wuthering Heights,* makes problematic the strategy of enclosure by belatedness. Not only does Anne Brontë's novel repeat its predecessor's initials and amplify its aspirant *h*'s of names and its climatic conditions, but there is something in the circumstances of its genesis that suggests more than the normal anxiety of sisterly influence.[15] In her "Preface to the Second Edition," Anne Brontë betrays the fact that the struggle for primacy between gossip, letter, and textuality may well have been a feature of the novel's very composition. Largely because of the popular commercial success of *Jane Eyre,* Newby attempted to capitalize on the gossip among publishers and some readers that all three "Bells" were one and the same person.[16] As if answering these charges, "The Preface" commences as a kind of letter to those who would discredit the novel's authenticity. But, like Helen Huntington's private letters to Gilbert Markham, it is a letter that must remain anonymous in two senses: it has a generalized rather than a specific object of address, and she must set herself apart from her sisters while simultaneously withholding revelation of her true identity:

> Respecting the author's identity, I would have it to be distinctly understood that Acton Bell is neither Currer nor Ellis Bell, and therefore let not his thoughts be attributed to them. As to whether the name be real or fictitious, it cannot greatly signify to those who know him only by his works.
>
> ("The Preface to the Second Edition," *TWH,* 31)

In this remarkable paragraph, Anne Brontë says, in effect, "I am different from them, but you cannot know how because I am also different from my writing." In other words, the maintenance of her self as a narrative object is dependent upon the erasure of self as a narrative subject. Just as all the eponymous narratives within the novel threaten to collapse into one another, so Anne Brontë senses the pressure of publisher's gossip that threatens to create a univocity out of their separate and diverse achievements. Gossip threatens to turn a relationship of consanguinity into one of contractual identity (the three Brontë sisters are really one person) much as village gossip turns Lawrence and Helen (brother and sister) into one (lovers) or does the same thing later by erroneously replacing the news of Lawrence's upcoming betrothal by the false rumor of Helen's. The novel's genesis participates in the same crisis of discourse that it describes.

And in fact, *The Tenant of Wildfell Hall* is always on the verge of collapsing back into its originary, *Wuthering Heights.* Both novels make use of the crossed marital lines of two neighboring families: Helen's son, Arthur Huntington, marries her own namesake, Helen Hattersley, repeating in the second generation the names but not the facts of the first marriage—Arthur (Huntington) and Helen (Graham). Like the second Cathy and Hareton Earnshaw in *Wuthering Heights,* it is a repetition of the form of the earlier marriage, suggesting that a passing beyond the passionate hell of the first is necessary to a second generation's salvation. Both novels make abundant use of the servant figure, as Rachel and Nelly Dean echo one another in their manipulative faithfulness. In both *Wuthering Heights* and *The Tenant of Wildfell Hall* the puritanical hypocrisy of those who believe in the literal truth of the Text, transmittable of course only by memorization, Joseph and Rev. Millward, respectively, is posed against the possibility of other, more subversive texts. And both novels early on raise the possibility of incest as an explanation of obscured or absent origins: in *The Tenant of Wildfell Hall* by the gossip-created union of Frederick and Helen; and in *Wuthering Heights* by Heathcliff's obscure origins when he is adopted by the elder Earnshaw, by the fact that he and Cathy wear each other's clothes as children, and that as adults they define their love in terms of identity as in Cathy's infamous "I *am* Heathcliff."

But surely the area where resemblance between *Wuthering Heights* and its supplement, *The Tenant of Wildfell Hall,* is most acute lies in their exploration of the problematic of textuality itself. That Anne Brontë, like Emily before her, used the framed narrative to raise a fallen metaphor is intriguing. Just as the urbane Lockwood, forced to seek refuge at *Wuthering Heights* during a storm, uses the first Cathy's diary as a source for his own biased narrative, so Gilbert Markham is handed Helen's diary as a refuge against the storm of community gossip, a clarification of a legend. The texts of both novels come to have the structural features of the Gothic house—that "penetralium" that J. Hillis Miller first noticed: one text lies enclosed by another, then another, as the boundaries between narratives are blurred.[17] The whole question of belatedness and priority threatens to collapse all the narratives back into a single narrative in much the same way that genealogy threatens to collapse back into the disappearance of difference that produces the monstrous, the ruin, or the fragment—the ontic status of lacking paternity or succession.

One way of thinking about *Wuthering Heights* is to envision the novel as a struggle for supremacy between and among competing texts. There is of course Joseph's Text that on a fateful day he finds rejected by two children who, in refusing to memorize, flee to a different world, that of Thrushcross Grange. There, they are introduced to Edgar Linton whose virtual emblem is the library that provides him with an uninterrupted flow of textuality forever distancing his response to the passions. Nelly Dean's self-serving gossip is the mode of speech appropriate to outsiders, as is Lockwood's speculation; the former is an outsider by virtue of class, the latter, as a result of geography. There is Cathy's diary in its repository, the private closet, like Helen Huntington's in its drawer, increasingly vulnerable to being transformed into a "source" by Lockwood. And finally there is the culminating text on the novel's last page, the one read by the second Cathy to the illiterate Hareton Earnshaw: the emblem of writing—probably the novel we read, *Wuthering Heights*—itself being transformed into speech, a replication of the act that the novel phonetically attempts by its use of the Yorkshire dialect. In reading to her husband the second Cathy is doing what the first Cathy could never do for Heathcliff, committed as she was to the authorship of her private, closet diary: transforming private discourse into speech by a gesture of transaction, enacting the inheritance of literacy by those less fortunate. An added side benefit is the repression of all the earlier violence by this last, best text which combines the belatedness of textuality with the spontaneous presence of speech.

Similarly, the question posed by the narrative structure of *The Tenant of Wildfell Hall* is how a textuality inclusive of the varieties of discourse which comprise it is to be transmitted without threat. What is the process by which the proliferation of discourse is prevented from being subversive to a culture? Gossip, Helen's increasingly vulnerable diary, and the curiously mediated letters whose contents Frederick Lawrence orally edits—all equate the *process* of literary production with the product itself. They make no distinction between production and consumption since they are all part of what might be called "folk dis-

course." As a result of that equation, none of the forms of latent communication that float about the novel can ever enter the domain of a possible consumption; they can never be appropriated by an "other" and used for the same purpose as that which initiated them. In much the same way that gossip can never be "used up," so it is with Helen's private, unfinished diary or the flow of the mediated, yet "pure speech" letters from Grassdale. The novel in one sense traces that gesture by which an audience is defined and a narratee is given a fixed address, thereby enabling threatening discourse to be coopted.[18] Gilbert Markham's extraordinarily long cover letter, however, does for *The Tenant of Wildfell Hall* what the second Cathy's reading does for Hareton Earnshaw in *Wuthering Heights*: it enables narrative once again to become an instructional device, to be legitimized within a corpus. This saving of the text (to borrow from Derrida through the mediation of Geoffrey Hartman[19]) by an act of supplementary enclosure would hint at another problem for the student of Victorian discourse: what are the implications of this salvational gesture for the history of the novel? Formally, the process of "passing on"—the logical succession in textuality—is obviously related to the restoration and revaluation of writing-as-containment. It restores a lineage of sorts to forms of writing and speech which seemed increasingly discontinuous from an originating authority. In both Emily and Anne Brontë's novels the suggestion is always present that the gradual disappearance of religious orthodoxy, with its emphasis upon the primacy of a single, authoritative text, is responsible for the proliferation of texts and tongues.[20] The church at Gimmerton Slough has fallen into disrepair at the conclusion of *Wuthering Heights,* and in *The Tenant of Wildfell Hall,* the hypocritical Rev. Millward has died, his living having passed into the hands of his milder scholarly successor, Richard Wilson, himself a devotee of classical texts.

The immense popularity of the Gothic mode in the late eighteenth and early nineteenth centuries in effect created a world of fragmentary texts, incomplete manuscripts, unfinished diaries—all traces of decentered writing. Its equivalent in the so-called mainstream Victorian novel would have been the proliferation of the orphan, who, having no genealogical lineage, was the perfect emblem of discontinuous discourse—the gossip, diaries, partial letters, and other fragments of floating writing or speech to which the frame restores historicity.[21]

There is abundant evidence that for all the Brontës, writing itself was a kind of conspiracy against the dictates of another, prior text. Writing was simultaneously pleasurable and an activity to be kept secret, as the existence of the Angria legend and its later successor, the Gondal poems, attests. The publication of first *Wuthering Heights* and then, in July, 1848, *The Tenant of Wildfell Hall,* with the advertisement implying that all the Bells were one and the same, prompted the notorious ride to London in the same month, and the disclosure of their true identities to the publisher.[22] In that crucial period, sometime between 1846 and 1848 the close relationship between Anne and Emily

Brontë which Ellen Nussey had termed "like twins" in 1833,[23] clearly underwent a sea change. In June of 1845 Anne had given up her employment and returned to Haworth, resuming a life she had known six years earlier in the Brontë household. But something had clearly changed, and Anne Brontë's poem **"Self-Communion"** is almost certainly a partial record of the disappearance of the "genial bliss that could not cloy" (*Poems,* **"Self-Communion,"** 1. 179) but apparent did. In that lengthy poem, Anne catalogued the causes of the "jarring discords" that came between the sisters:

> But this was nothing to the woe
> With which another truth was learned:—
> That I must check, or nurse apart
> Full many an impulse of the heart
> And many a darling thought:
> What my soul worshipped, sought, and prized,
> Were slighted, questioned, or despised;—
> This pained me more than aught.

> **(*Poems,* "Self-Communion," ll. 188-195)**

In imagery that seems partly derivative of one of the famous scenes in *Wuthering Heights,* the speaker describes a separation:

> I saw that they were sundered now
> The trees that at the root were one:
> They yet might mingle leaf and bough,
> But the stem must stand alone.

> (204-7)

The destruction of the Gondal saga (December 1846?) and with it, the virtual cessation of communal projects between Emily and Anne, plus the gradual but discernible replacement of an editorial "our" in the pre-1846 poems with the emergence of first person singular possessive pronouns in the later poems by Anne—all would suggest that the public disclosure of separate identities by the Brontë sisters was but the making public of what had already happened in private: a rift. The publication of *Wuthering Heights* had been a betrayal of the private, albeit communally shared imaginative world of the Brontës. **The Tenant of Wildfell Hall** was a belated attempt to domesticate the damage. Like all enclosures, it has not been entirely successful because of a perceived distance between the supplement and its originary. Hence, the disparagement of even Charlotte Brontë, on grounds of its historical displacement, of Anne's quietness:

> Anne's character was milder and more subdued. . . .
> She wanted the power, the fire, the originality of her sister, but was well endowed with quiet virtues of her own.[24]

The Tenant of Wildfell Hall supplements and encloses *Wuthering Heights* partially, of course, by parodying it.[25] It does in one sense what sequels always do to the Gothic impulse, from Hogg's *The Confessions of a Justified Sinner,* which supplants and justifies the "found" manuscript which is its originary, "The Private Memories and Confes-

sions of a Sinner," to the celluloid *Jaws II,* which supplants and justifies an early version by "passing it on." It contains potentially independent, straying texts by keeping them within the same generic family. The very book we read, Anne Brontë's **The Tenant of Wildfell Hall,** simultaneously enacts a transformation in the reader, in the narratee, Halford (who, as part of the "exchange" marries Markham's sister, Rose), and in the new Mrs. Markham all by calling attention to itself as a framed narrative. The belated, embodied nature of narrative has finally triumphed, enclosing those forms of speech and writing whose pretense to a counterfeit currency threatened the framing sequel. Enclosure does for Mrs. Huntington's past what **The Tenant of Wildfell Hall** does for *Wuthering Heights*: by giving it a new name, it reestablishes for it a rightful place within a family. Contrary to Benveniste's assertion that narrative erases or conceals signs of the narrator, Anne Brontë's use of Gilbert Markham's enclosing cover letter allows for the reintrusion of the narrator, whose role had been threatened by a range of anonymous, floating discourse.[26] Narrative enclosure is part of a process of extension without subversion, a reminder of the importance of "our contract" (*TWH,* 111) in controlling the inflation of orality—gossip.

The impulse to "enclose" sweeps all before it, including the wind and the weather that swirl about Wildfell Hall and its environs. At the beginning of Anne Brontë's novel, nature itself is part of the imperfection of the fragmented, fallen world. Wildfell Hall is shielded from the war of wind and weather only by a group of Scotch firs, "themselves half-blighted with storms" (*TWH,* 45). It is clearly an environment of incomplete closure where "the close green wall of privet, that had bordered the principal walk, were two-thirds withered away" (*TWH,* 46). By the time we reach the novel's end, however, a marvelous image of the conservative powers of enclosure appears. Helen Huntington wishes for her future husband, Gilbert, to be accepted by her aging aunt, now, like Helen, a widow. He must agree to the aunt's residence at the Staningley household, which has passed into Helen's inheritance. The aunt's avocation is the gentle nurturing of flowers out of season, a pastime made possible by the existence of an indoor *conservatory* to which Gilbert must pay homage. It is a fitting supplement to the bluebells in the gentle breeze which blows on the last page of *Wuthering Heights.* This arrangement enables three generations to live under one roof, much as Gilbert Markham's framing letter to Halford, a letter outside the novel's first chapter, enables discontinuous narrative to become suddenly continuous. The domestication of potentially anarchic nature, the nurture of roses in winter, is achieved by the same gesture that brings the civilizing influence of inheritance, marriage, the enclosure of unfinished texts, and the containment of the narrative rivalry that was part of the publication history of Anne Brontë's novel. Only then, safely passed on, is the fiction of the family and the family of fictions secure against those forces which would confuse narrative or generational lines.

Notes

1. All citations from *The Tenant of Wildfell Hall,* here-after referred to as *TWH,* are taken from the Penguin edition, introduced by Winifred Gerin and edited by G. D. Hargreaves (Hammondsworth: Penguin, 1979).

   All citations from the poetry of Anne Brontë, hereafter referred to as *Poems,* are from Edward Chitham, *The Poems of Anne Brontë, A New Text and Commentary* (London: Macmillan, 1979).

2. In order to avoid the abyss of so much deconstructive criticism—the conviction that everything is literature, text, or writing—it may be appropriate to reread the portion in *Of Grammatology* where Derrida himself warns against mistaking writing (as archewriting) for the colloquial meaning of writing. Since the notion of the "trace" is anterior to any experience of "presence," the trace or writing is not something which can be present in all discourse. A great many deconstructive critics, I feel, make an illicit application of the Derridean notion of *ecriture,* blurring distinctions between terms. The burden of the present essay moves in another direction: that in such a blurring of boundaries, deconstructive criticism, like much random discourse in the Gothic novel, is seen as being more threatening than in fact it may be. One critic who does see the dangers of this misunderstanding is Rodolphe Gasché, "Deconstruction as Criticism," *Glyph* 6 (1979): 177-215.

3. The "oversaturation" of texts is the subject of a marvelous study that needs to be published in an easily accessible format: M. Kajman, *Corps et Ecriture dans Les Lois de l'hôspitalité* (Diplôme d'études superieures, Université de Lille III, June, 1971, under the direction of A. Nicolas). Although Kajman sees this proliferation of texts within the framework of a discontinuity apropos of modernism, I see such a discontinuity only with a preliminary image, not the text. What *The Tenant of Wildfell Hall* does is to play with the notion of narrative insurrection, which threatens different communities with a kind of polytheism of discourse that must be contained in order to restore stability.

4. See my own "Narrative Enclosure as Textual Ruin: An Archaeology of Gothic Consciousness," forthcoming in *Dickens Studies Annual: Essays on Victorian Fiction,* 11, edited by Michael Timko, Fred Kaplan, and Edward Guiliano.

5. The idea of the reading of a will, with which so many of the novels of Dickens and George Eliot reach a narrative climax, as a sort of textual *post facto* contraceptive, is intriguing. Even if one could not in fact "author" one's own life, as did so many Victorian autobiographers, there was an opportunity through writing at the last moment of consciousness to reshape one's family by making textual changes: excluding a wayward son here, admitting to an illegitimacy there. Such an event occurs in *The Tenant of Wildfell Hall* when, toward the novel's end, Helen is informed that her uncle has bequeathed to her his property at Staningley, giving her the "absent" father she never had.

6. One of the features that Heidegger touches upon in *Sein und Zeit* is the ability of gossip to distort temporality. There is always a tendency to associate "versions" or "accounts" of a story with the temporality in which it dwells. Gossip is always either very far behind what we have already heard or very far ahead of it, but it always pretends to be *in it.* See Martin Heidegger, *Sein und Zeit* (Tubingen, Max Niemayer Verlag, 1967), 322-46.

   As it actually functions in the novel, gossip exhibits some of the features of contemporary "reader-response" criticism. By locating meaning entirely within the collective "history" of the recipients' encounter, it confuses a personal "case history" with the history of the text.

7. Tony Tanner, *Adultery in the Novel* (Baltimore: Johns Hopkins Univ. Press, 1979) argues that many of the great nineteenth-century novels broach the incest motif as a way of avoiding the possibility of adultery. Anne Brontë, however, uses the incest motif in an entirely different way: not so much as a moral safety net, but as a way of talking about the relationship between the "plots" of gossip and family "conspiracies." Why do the village gossips who are very familiar with Frederick Lawrence (he attends all the social functions of the community) not know that he has a sister, thereby mistaking Helen as his lover? Being an eligible bachelor, he is so visible that everyone should know everything about him, obviating the necessity for gossip.

8. Peter Brooks, "Narrative Transaction and Transference (*Unburying Le Colonel Chabert*)," *Novel* 15. 2 (Winter, 1982): 101-10, sees the process of narrative enclosure entirely within the psychoanalytic nomenclature of transaction and transference in a splendid essay. Its limitations lie in that, because he must see the "frame" as Freud's "real life," which enables a buried story to be told, he cannot see that transaction takes place at the expense of suppression, that the frame is a part of a politics of the sequence.

9. Gerard Genette, "Discours du récit," in *Figures III* (Paris: Editions du Seuil, 1973).

10. E. D. Hirsch, *Validity in Interpretation* (New Haven: Yale Univ. Press, 1967), particularly chapters 1, 2, and 4. A tenuous distinction between "understanding" and "explication" is crucial to Hirsch's endorsement of an identity between meaning and author's intention. Neither gossip nor Helen's curious diaries and letters enable such an abstraction to be made.

11. Gerald Prince, "Introduction a l'étude du narrataire," *Poétique* 14 (1973). I am indebted here to Julia Kristeva, "Le texte clos" in *Recherches pour une se-*

manalyse (Paris: Editions du Seuil, 1969), 52-81. In pleading to replace distinctions of genre with what she calls a typology of textuality, Kristeva wishes to show that narrative is in effect an *operation,* and that the narrative contract is an attempt to circumscribe the nature of that *operation.* Her thought in many ways lies behind its reformulation in Prince.

12. Barbara Johnson, "The Frame of Reference," in *The Critical Difference* (Baltimore: Johns Hopkins Univ. Press, 1980), 110-46. "Everyone who has held the letter—or even beheld it—including the narrator, has ended up having the letter addressed to him as its destination. . . . The reader is comprehended by the letter" (142). In willfully ceasing to be "private," Helen's letters become discourse conditioned by the fact that they must always be forwarded. Their alleged spirituality, like Gilbert's earlier description of her diary as sacred, is a function of the letter's failure to accomodate his otherness.

13. Helen's last attempt at reforming Arthur Huntington suggests her fear of speech rather than writing. She almost forces him to *sign* an agreement, a contract, to leave little Arthur in the exclusive care of his mother: "I must have a written agreement, and you must sign it in presence of a witness" (*TWH,* 431).

14. For a discussion of this way in which closure signifies a crisis in discourse, see Timothy J. Reiss, *The Discourse of Modernism* (Ithaca: Cornell Univ. Press, 1982), 351-85.

15. The interaction between the three Brontë sisters has never really been studied in detail, except for the cursory attention given the subject in Winifred Gerin's biographies. What may be at stake is the whole question of the "disciple" and its implications for the process of the sequel. A book that deserves to be better known than it is discusses rivalry and the question of the disciple: Francois Roustang, *Un Destin si funeste* (Paris: Minuit, 1976), 53: 'Mes disciples, ceux qui retiennent mes paroles et les repandent me libèrent de la parole solitaire, la transforment en science et en principe de communication.' Roustang relates the question of the disciple to the public projection of an artist's work, to the whole question of "succession."

16. Tom Winnifrith, *The Brontës and Their Background* (London: Macmillan, 1973), 113.

17. J. Hillis Miller, "Emily Brontë" in *The Disappearance of God: Five Nineteenth-Century Writers* (Cambridge, Mass: Harvard Univ. Press, 1976).

18. The work that best defines the process by which a novel enters a "familiar order of things" with its own laws of production and consumption is Pierre Macherey, *Pour une théorie de la production littéraire* (Paris, 1966), 265-67.

19. Geoffrey Hartman, *Saving the Text: Literature/ Derrida/Philosophy* (Baltimore: The Johns Hopkins Univ. Press, 1981). In this essay on Derrida's *Glas,* Hartman does begin to discuss the dialectic involved in the process of mediation. The question to be posed, however, remains: "Saved from what?" If Anne Brontë's novel were seen as a "model" text, then the condition of damnation would be discourse which circulates as *potential* speech, threatening the "novelistic plot" with another, more political plot in which everyone were a potential victim. The novel in its belatedness would be an attempt to control plots, which gossip, mediated letters, and seized diaries could never do.

20. I am here applying the same argument to the prospect of a typology of textuality of the nineteenth century as Walter J. Ong, S. J. does to the "reduction" of the linguistic order to a visual image in *Ramus, Method, and the Decay of Dialogue* (Cambridge: Harvard Univ. Press, 1958).

21. J. Hillis Miller, *The Form of Victorian Fiction* (Notre Dame and London: Notre Dame Univ. Press, 1968), 29-50.

22. The hasty trip made by Anne and Charlotte Brontë to the offices of Smith, Elder to reveal their true identities was prompted by Newby's boast to Harper's of New York that *The Tenant of Wildfell Hall* was by Currer Bell (arousing the suspicion that Currer Bell had gone behind Smith, Elder's back and given "his" new book to another publisher). The fact that the trip to London—a trip made because, in the words of Charlotte, "mystery is irksome"—was regarded by Emily as a betrayal is suggested in a later letter of Charlotte's. It is in part an apology written *after* she and Anne returned to Haworth: "Permit me to caution you not to speak of my sister when you write to me. I mean, do not use the word in the plural. Ellis Bell will not endure to be alluded to under any other appellation than the nom de plume. I committed a grand error in betraying her identity to you and Mr. Smith. (CB to WSW, July 31, 1848, in T. J. Wise and J. A. Symington, *The Brontës: Their Lives, Friendships, and Correspondence* [Oxford, Shakespeare Head Press, 1932], 11:240-43).

23. Elizabeth Nussey, "Reminiscences of Charlotte Brontë," *Scribner's Monthly,* May, 1871.

24. Charlotte Brontë, "Biographical Notice of Ellis and Acton Bell," prefaced to *Wuthering Heights* and *Agnes Gray.* Shortly before she wrote the biographical note, Charlotte Brontë was to write to the publishers that *TWH* "hardly appears to be desirable to preserve" (in *Wise and Symington,* 3:156). Her negative assessment which has unfortunately plagued Anne Brontë's achievement even now, may well be evidence that all three sisters had fallen into discord, as their separate achievements came to be known.

25. One of the few critics to observe *Wuthering Heights* and *The Tenant of Wildfell Hall* in terms of the latter's supplementary status is Edward Chitham, *The*

Poems of Anne Brontë: A New Text and Commentary (London, Macmillan, 1979), 8, who calls it "parodic."

26. My argument here is precisely opposite to that elaborated by E. Benveniste, *Problemes de linguistique generale,* vol. 1 (Paris, 1966), 237-50. For Benveniste, in narrative as opposed to discourse the specific modality of its enunciation is to erase or conceal the signs of the narrator in the narrative proposition. My point is that the "frame" allows the reintrusion of the specific signs of the narrator that "floating" discourse had threatened to obliterate.

Lori A. Paige (essay date 1991)

SOURCE: "Helen's Diary Freshly Considered," in *Brontë Society Transactions,* Vol. 20, No. 4, 1991, pp. 225-27.

[*In the following essay, Paige maintains that the complex narrative of* The Tenant of Wildfell Hall *does not mar the integrity of the novel, but rather serves to further Brontë's stated purpose of examining the institution of marriage in Victorian England.*]

In her second novel,[1] Anne Brontë attempts a more complicated structure than the simple autobiographical mode she utilized in *Agnes Grey.* As anyone who has attempted even a cursory reading of Anne Brontë criticism knows rather too well, the diary device she chose is generally disparaged as a flaw that comes close to ruining the entire novel. George Moore's 1924 pronouncement that the diary cleaved the story into disjointed halves has been endlessly parroted by every subsequent study of the novel; even Winifred Gérin lends her wholehearted concurrence in her Penguin introduction to the novel (14). Interestingly, no one has stopped to consider that Moore's statement, at its most literal level, is erroneous. In fact, *The Tenant of Wildfell Hall* is divided not into halves, but consciously into thirds. Understanding this arrangement is, moreover, essential to comprehending Anne Brontë's ultimate purpose as the author of this highly serious novel.

The three sections of *The Tenant of Wildfell Hall* are easily delineated. The first consists of Gilbert Markham's first-person narrative, which is enclosed within a series of letters to his brother-in-law, Jack Halford. The second, and longest, presents Helen's diary from June 1, 1821 to November 3, 1827. The third incorporates first-person commentaries from both Gilbert's letters and Helen's letters to her own brother, Frederick, after her return to Grassdale a year later. It should be obvious, especially from these stark descriptions, that the novel's narrative stance shifts in direct correspondence to the development of the love relationship. That is, the first-person voice begins with Gilbert, whose persistence initiates the relationship, switches to Helen, as she responds to him only gradually, and finally yields to a mixture of the two voices once a communion of souls is established. In each case, the narrative stance reflects the status of the couple who stand at the novel's centre; quite properly, too, the still-married Helen assumes her remotest textual position—that of a voice within the diary only—once the possibility of a second, and potentially bigamous, romantic alliance becomes apparent.

Gérin's introduction further faults the device of the diary because it supposedly alienates the reader at the story's most emotional moments. We, as readers, should be experiencing Helen's disastrous humiliation "in the heat of action, in the palpitating moments of hurt and disillusion, at the height of anger and recrimination" (14). However, careful consideration should reveal that the diary really functions in exactly the opposite manner. Because Helen has set down each detail of her married life at the very time of the incident (no entry occurs more than two days after the event described), her recounting cannot be (and has not been) subject to critical disbelief or accusations of exaggeration in retrospect. Surely Moore's alternative—having Helen present her story verbally—would have allowed her tale no such impunity. That we accept Helen's fidelity to details which are in some cases six years old is essential to Anne Brontë's stated object of "tell[ing] the truth" (Preface, 29). Elsewhere, certainly, Helen's aims stand unequivocally for Anne Brontë's.[2]

Helen is not the only diary-keeper in the novel, of course. Gilbert is Helen's moral equal, and he is given to the same self-scrutinizing pastime. His own depictions of past events are, he assures Halford, truthful to the last degree because they too are based on a "certain faded old journal" which he refers to so that Halford's "credulity may not be too severely taxed" in reading these "minute details" concerning events long past (34). Of course, Gilbert has certainly had his detractors in the recent (and supposedly enlightened) "reassessments" of Anne Brontë's works; P. J. M. Scott, for example, suggests that once we begin wondering why Gilbert is writing of these events at all, we will recoil with "shock" upon realizing that "the undertaking is mere self-indulgence . . . he has no better motive than beguiling time."[3] He also questions Halford's worthiness as a recipient of the tale, never realizing that Halford is, in fact, the ideal reader of so morally instructive a document. *The Tenant of Wildfell Hall* is an examination of marital values in an intensely patriarchal society, and Halford, like Gilbert, has the sort of equal marriage which would allow him to appreciate the lesson.

Lastly, and perhaps more importantly, the device of the diary is defensible in the larger context of the written word's role in the novel. Gilbert Markham's letters are intended to enlighten as well as entertain Halford, and Anne Brontë's own Preface has already admitted the novel's similar didactic function. It is neither arbitrary nor unwarranted, then, for Helen's efforts at informing and instructing Gilbert to climax in the giving of a written text for him to study. The giving of a book also plays into an established system of imagery: Gilbert has already presented Helen with an edition of *Marmion* as a gesture of affection (91), while her former husband, significantly, never allowed her to read unmolested (221).

Gilbert's gift, then, represents an important gesture towards relaxing the rigid gender distinctions ingrained in their contemporaries. A typical hierarchical relationship between a man and a woman is that of Richard Wilson and Mary Millward: Wilson sits reading a pocket-sized Classic, while his fiancée regards him with awe and rapture (89). Indeed, even Gilbert initially considers it proper for him to sit and read, ignoring the trivial conversation of the women during Helen's first visit (52). Still, by the end of the novel a shift in values has begun, if not at a societal level then at least in the individual consciences of men like Gilbert, Frederick, and Halford. Mrs. Markham's original prescription for ideal wifely behavior (78) is ultimately adopted by neither of her married children: Gilbert lives up to his desire to "find more pleasure in making my wife happy" than in being slavishly ministered to (see, e.g., 119, "I want to see you comfortable before I go"), and Rose's marriage to Halford, he jokingly reveals, is far from subservient ("Is it so, Halford?" etc., 79). Whereas a more naïve Helen once believed it was both her duty and her "delight" to "please" Arthur (216), she, like the novel's second group of brides, will now marry "to please [her]self alone" (486). As the example of Ralph Hattersley attests, men too can find a more equal match a greater source of happiness (385). The regeneration of male-female relations is further reinforced by a series of botanical and agricultural images (culminating, of course, in the offering of the "winter rose," 484) as Helen recovers from her shattering Grassdale ordeal and begins, almost literally, to bloom again. The new marriage takes place not in the barren month of December, in which the doomed marriage both began and ended, but in late summer, after a season of growth and ripening. The lessons implicit in Helen's makeshift textbook on marital relations have begun to be disseminated.

Notes

1. All references to the text are to *The Tenant of Wildfell Hall,* ed. G. D. Hargreaves, introduction by Winifred Gérin. Harmondsworth: Penguin Books, 1979.

2. For example, her explanation to the Markhams concerning her efforts to steer young Arthur from the "snares" of corruption (54-56) echo precisely the Preface's refusal to "cover" these same types of "snares and pitfalls . . . with branches and flowers" (30).

3. P. J. M. Scott, *Anne Brontë: A New Critical Assessment.* (London: Vision and Barnes, 1983) III. Further negative commentary on Gilbert's character can also be found in Terry Eagleton, *Myths of Power* (London: Macmillan, 1975) 130-135.

Edith A. Kostka (essay date 1992)

SOURCE: "Narrative Experience as a Means to Maturity in Anne Brontë's Victorian Novel *The Tenant of Wildfell Hall,*" in *Connecticut Review,* Vol. 14, No. 2, Fall, 1992, pp. 41-47.

[In the following essay, Kostka considers Gilbert Markham's reading of Helen Huntingdon's diary as the act of an inexperienced male achieving maturity via female writing.]

One of the pleasures of studying literature is the unexpected encounter with ingenious design. Anne Brontë's *The Tenant of Wildfell Hall* is a case in point. At first *Tenant* appears to be a Brontëan version of the male "Bildungsroman" which traditionally catalogues the progress of a young man's development. But Brontë effects a subtle turn as she shifts her narrative from the focus of an immature youth who has yet to gain knowledge of the ways of the world, to that of a woman who has already learned the painful lessons such worldly knowledge entails.

At play in this Brontëan shift are two notable issues. In her depiction of Helen Huntingdon as a beleaguered wife subject to the caprices of a profligate husband, Brontë dramatizes the inequities inherent in the Victorian marriage system. The reader observes Helen's frustration and her lack of legal recourse as her husband relinquishes temperance and reason to alcohol, gambling and infidelity. Social convention grinds Helen into social stasis. Because Helen survives her difficulties with a degree of dignity and self-containment, Brontë seems to portray the woman as an individual mature in her approach to the problems of life. Adversity provides her with the wisdom to assess issues intelligently, and the understanding to see situations as they truly are, often arbitrary, and generally tilted to male advantage. Helen's process of development, in turn, formulates the foundation of the second issue of importance to Brontë, the nature of maturity in terms of gender.

In a world governed by men, to be a woman was to be a silent partner in a social contract. Men wrote the laws, formulated conventions and established the rules of conduct. Women were passive participants who read the laws, suffered the conventions and followed the rules. Helen Huntingdon assumes her place in this construct where her husband automatically possesses ascendency over herself and her child. When his plunge into degradation overwhelms her spirit, Helen defies law and flees an insupportable situation. Because she keeps a journal, her experience formulates the fabric of narrative which allows the young protagonist Gilbert Markham to share her experience, and develop a sense of both compassion and comprehension of the difficult burden Helen in particular, and Victorian women in general, had to suffer within the social order. Thus, what Brontë demonstrates in her narrative experiment is that the simple act of reading has within its nature the means to change youthful indifference into responsible, aware adulthood.

Tenant begins as a framed tale that opens with a letter from Gilbert to his brother-in-law who has requested the return favor of a story. Dated June 10, 1847, Gilbert's letter conveys his intention: "I am alone in my library, and have been looking over certain musty old letters and papers, and musings on past times; so that I am now in a very proper frame of mind for amusing you with an old-world story" (34). What follows is Gilbert's rather lengthy letter which constitutes the first half of Brontë's text.

Because Brontë opens the novel with male discourse, she provides her readers with a conventional device that seems to suggest the rightly ordered world of male superiority.

But a surprise awaits her readers. As Gilbert's letter progresses, certain personal characteristics reveal him to be an underdeveloped, incomplete young man. In his first encounter with the mysterious Helen, she rebuffs him for chatting with her young son whom she fiercely guards, and Gilbert smarts under the rejection. Returning home he chafes in frustration and notes, "I only stayed to put away my gun and powder-horn, and give some requisite directions to one of the farming-men, and then repaired to the vicarage, to solace my spirit and soothe my ruffled temper with the company and conversation of Eliza Millward" (48). Rejected by one woman, Gilbert seeks solace and renewed confidence in the company of the village coquette with whom he carries on a superficial flirtation. Not encumbered by any family responsibilities, he has earlier confessed to his brother-in-law that he has no particular plans or designs for his life, and once the family estate falls to his purview as eldest son he resolves as his highest ambition ". . . to walk through the world, looking neither to the right hand nor to the left, and to transmit the parental acres to my children, in at least, as flourishing condition as he [Gilbert's father] left them to me" (35). Such a lack of enterprise and initiative places Gilbert in a position inferior to that of Helen Huntingdon who has faced difficulties boldly and seized opportunity to better her life and that of her child. To underscore the contrast between the young Helen and the young Gilbert, Brontë establishes strong differences in their respective approaches to life. In Brontë's view, Helen is always mature in assessment, word and deed, while Gilbert must acquire such maturity by means of reading the young woman's narrative.

Gilbert's first notice of Helen occurs on a Sunday morning when she takes her place in the Wildfell pew which has long been unoccupied. Compelled to stare at her silent beauty, Gilbert makes uneasy eye contact with her: "Just then, she happened to raise her eyes, and they met mine; I did not choose to withdraw my gaze, and she turned again to her book, but with a momentary, indefinable expression of quiet scorn, that was inexpressibly provoking to me" (45). What grows obvious to the reader in this scene is that Gilbert senses but is not consciously aware of the disparity that separates him from Helen. While she is thoughtful and suitably reverent within the confines of the church, he muses upon her beauty and mystery, and stares impolitely at her in childish infatuation. What grows even more obvious to the reader is Gilbert's shallowness as he recounts his opinion of the village flirt:

> Now, Halford, before I close this letter, I'll tell you who Eliza Millward was; she was the vicar's younger daughter, and a very engaging little creature, for whom I felt no small degree of partiality;—and she knew it, though I had never come to any direct explanation of so doing, for my mother, who maintained there was no one good enough for me, within twenty miles round, could not bear the thought of my marrying that insignificant little thing, who, in addition to her numerous other disqualifications, had not twenty pounds to call her own.

(41-42)

Not only does Gilbert lack the personal presence that would have accorded him a look of friendliness from Helen, but he also lacks an inner presence that would have allowed him to judge a fellow human being with compassionate objectivity. Rather than assess the ingenuous Eliza for her freshness and youth, he parrots his mother's disapproving opinion and recalls the fact that the young girl possesses neither wealth nor position. In contrast to Helen, about whom he knows nothing, young Eliza Millward pales both as a friend and as a woman, and in this shallow formulation of opinion, Brontë underscores Gilbert's lack of adult comprehension, and his failure to appreciate the young Eliza as a human being of worth who may possess talents and mysteries of her own. What Brontë demonstrates is that Gilbert dismisses the young girl as "an insignificant little thing" who is useful to him for an occasional diversion, but who is not good enough to marry since she "had not twenty pounds to call her own." Thus, she is disqualified by Gilbert not only for lack of money, but also because she does not meet his mother's standards, which further suggests his dependency upon a parental figure. By contrast, Helen reveals no such dependency, and makes decisions and takes action based upon her own assessments and experience.

As if to deepen the issue of female disqualification, Brontë depicts Eliza's sister, whom Gilbert describes to Halford:

> Her sister, Mary, was several years older, several inches taller, and of a larger, coarser build—a plain, quiet, sensible girl, who had patiently nursed their mother through her last long, tedious illness, and been the housekeeper and family drudge from thence to the present time. She was trusted and valued by her father, loved and courted by all dogs, cats, children, and poor people, and slighted and neglected by everybody else.

(42)

One of the indications of Gilbert's lack of maturity rests in the responsibilities he fails to undertake. Not only does he not resist the sovereignty of his mother, nor her mean-spirited opinions, but he never undertakes to ease the condition of Eliza's sister Mary. Because she possesses less flash than Eliza, he shuns her not only from his little social orbit, but also from his narrative. In his self-serving interest in pursuing Helen Huntingdon, he fails to accord basic human civility to women whom he considers social inferiors. In his relation to these and other minor characters in the novel, Brontë portrays Gilbert as a character who lacks depth and purpose, and who, although of marriageable age, is not constructed of marriageable material.

For Brontë, clear judgment and generosity to other persons seem to be the characteristics of adulthood. In both Gilbert's and Helen's narratives, scenes occur in which young marriageable people explain their understanding of a future married life. What seems important to Brontë is that the young women in the novel wistfully hope their husbands will be handsome and caring and provide them with loving married lives, while the young men in the novel fail in fulfilling these desires. Thus it appears that the so-

Anne Bronte, 1820–1849.

cial signposts of the novel, those guidelines that direct young people into marriage, cross signals. Not only does Brontë depict the psychological and social violations Arthur Huntingdon inflicts upon Helen, but she details similar abuses within the marriages of the marginal characters as well. By signaling the reader to expect conformity and then delivering non-conformity, Brontë dramatizes the institution of marriage, not as a condition of interpersonal harmony, but rather as an arena for gender atrocity.

By centering the major moral dilemma within the framework of Helen's journal, Brontë restructures the cross-switches along the gender track. Female narrative assumes a predominant position in relation to male narrative because it is in the female narrative that Brontë establishes her model for maturity. Sweeping along its dynamic path, Gilbert's text takes the reader to the juncture where the young protagonist presses Helen for information about her background. How is it that she has come to live in isolation upon the moors in the shadowy world of Wildfell Hall? Where is the never-mentioned father of her child? And what financial means sustain her as she hides from the world incognito and afraid? Pitched with emotion, Helen responds to Gilbert in order to relieve the tension that has come between them as a result of the unanswered questions that surround her. Her response, however, does

not come in the conventional form of spoken dialogue, but rather assumes a more powerful medium:

> Her cheeks burned and her whole frame trembled, now, with excess of agitation. She did not speak, but flew to her desk, and snatching thence what seemed a thick album or manuscript volume, hastily tore away a few leaves from the end, and thrust the rest into my hand, saying, 'You needn't read it all; but take it home with you,'—and hurried from the room.
>
> (146)

It is upon this scene that the novel turns and that Brontë begins her redefinition of gender maturity and its relation to gender experience. Struck by the highly charged emotional pitch of the moment, and by the deeper mystery hidden within the pages of Helen's journal, Gilbert returns home to the solitude of his bedchamber (where a new birth is about to occur) and undergoes the transformation from character-as-protagonist to character-as-reader:

> Panting with eagerness, and struggling to suppress my hopes, I hurried home, and rushed upstairs to my room,—having first provided myself with a candle, though it was scarcely twilight yet,—then, shut and bolted the door, determined to tolerate no interruption, and sitting down before the table, opened out my prize and delivered myself up to its perusal—first, hastily turning over the leaves and snatching a sentence here and there, and then, setting myself steadily to read it through.
>
> (147)

Youthful, irresponsible Gilbert, sheltered by the largess of family and financial security, untempered and untried, begins the process of growing up. What sets the maturing process in motion is the revelation acquired by means of the act of reading. Self-absorbed and self-contained, Gilbert pores over the pages of a narrative written by a woman, and the boy who fumbles through the pages laden with female suffering and pain emerges as a man who sees with clearer vision, newly self-possessed and self-assured, and newly able to be an individual equal to the maturity of Helen Huntingdon Graham. Thus, Brontë seems to offer an alternative to the process of maturity, which in Victorian society centered on a model in which men became adults by the acquisition of property and money. By contrast, she seems to suggest that maturity occurs by means of the common sense to learn from the lessons of experience, and she further seems to suggest that those lessons of experience can occur to women, and can be conveyed through the medium of women's writing. To dramatize her point, she creates the situation where Gilbert isolates himself from all distractions in order to experience the full import of Helen's words.

Assertive and self-possessed, Helen's journal first recounts happy days with her aunt and uncle who are charged to provide her with a comfortable home and opportunities to meet marriageable young men. But her happiness is clouded by a sober warning from her aunt, who seems to anticipate future events:

'If you should marry the handsomest, and most accomplished and superficially agreeable man in the world,
you little know the misery that would overwhelm you,
if, after all, you should find him to be a worthless reprobate, or even an impracticable fool.'

(150)

What follows in Helen's journal is the story of her encounter and infatuation with a free-spirited, smoothly man-
nered young man whom she subsequently marries. But
marriage proves to be a deadly business as Arthur Huntingdon removes Helen from her family and friends in
London and takes her to his estate deep in the country.
Even in the early weeks of their marriage, Helen begins to
suffer the bitterness of her mistake:

I am married now, and settled down as Mrs. Huntingdon of Grass-dale Manor. I have had eight weeks experience of matrimony. And do I regret the step I have
taken?—No—though I must confess, in my secret heart,
that Arthur is not what I thought him at first, and if I
had known him in the beginning as thoroughly as I do
now, I probably never should have loved him, and if I
had loved him first, and then made the discovery, I fear
I should have thought it my duty not to have married
him.

(215)

What is significant in this passage is that Helen admits
that her experience with unhappiness has opened her eyes
to the depth of her mistake. This unhappiness deepens as
her married life continues and Arthur slips steadfastly into
habits and vices that repulse the young wife. Even after
she has a child, Arthur shows little sign of improvement,
and instead attempts to corrupt the child with his intemperance and profligacy:

Another year is past; and I am weary of this life. And
yet, I cannot wish to leave it: whatever afflictions assail
me here, I cannot wish to go and leave my darling in
this dark and wicked world alone, without a friend to
guide him through its weary mazes, to warn him of its
thousand snares, and guard him from the perils that beset him on every hand.

(334)

What Brontë drives home in this depiction of Helen's
marriage is that the young wife is both victim and prisoner
of her husband. Despite Helen's high-minded moral conduct, she cannot remove her son from the home of such an
unprepossessing father. Were she to do so, she would be
violating the laws and conventions that place a wife and
child under the legal aegis of a husband. While this condition may have served to protect families whose husbands
and fathers were fundamentally good, moral beings, it also
served to impose cruelty and suffering upon family members whose men were morally bankrupt.

As if to emphasize the injustice of such a patriarchal system, Brontë compresses the suffocation Helen endures as
Arthur slips more and more deeply into the degradation
and self-destruction of alcohol and gambling addiction and
subsequently attempts to take the child with him in his
plunge:

So the little fellow came down every evening, in spite
of his cross mamma, and learnt to tipple wine like
papa, to swear like Mr. Hattersley, and to have his own
way like a man, and sent mamma to the devil when she
tried to prevent him. To see such things done with the
roguish naivete of that pretty little child and hear such
things spoken by that small infantile voice, was as peculiarly piquant and irresistibly droll to them as it was
inexpressibly distressing and painful to me; and when
he had set the table in a roar, he would look round de-
lightedly upon them all, and add his shrill laugh to
theirs.

(356)

No longer able to endure the categorical demoralization of
her child, Helen recounts her resolve to escape Grass-dale
and to take her child with her. Assisted by her brother, she
makes good her escape to take residence at Wildfell Hall
where she assumes the name Helen Graham.

Helen's journal details experiences that Gilbert has not
suffered. Her narrative depicts events in the world at large
of which he has appeared to be unaware. His childish need
to salve injured pride is replaced by the adult assessment
of Helen and her early treatment of him. He responds to
the mystery of what she may have written of him in those
final missing pages:

Here it ended. The rest was torn away. How cruel—just
when she was going to mention me! for I could not
doubt it was your humble servant she was about to
mention, though not very favorably of course—I could
tell that, as well by those few words as by the recollection of her whole aspect and demeanor towards me in
the commencement of our acquaintance. Well! I could
readily forgive her prejudice against me, and her hard
thoughts of our sex in general, when I saw to what
brilliant specimens her experience had been limited.

(401)

To employ a journal as a device for shared experience underscores the power of the printed word and its effects
upon the reader. Not only does Gilbert feel the indignation
and suffocation Helen feels, he also undergoes a transformation that is effected through several dimensions. Reading forces him into solitude where he shuts himself from
the world, not unlike an embryo that is about to undergo
the change into adulthood. Wrapped in the cocoon-like security of his bedchamber, he shuts his door as his mind
opens to the thoughts and feelings of another human being. Solitude becomes populated by visions and images
that are charged with emotion. Gilbert not only sympa-
thizes, he empathizes, and thus lives within his own imagination the suffering and indignation suffered by Helen.
Her need to face life with courage becomes an experience
that Gilbert not only observes, but comes to adopt. In addition, in his empathy and absorption, Gilbert encounters a
dimension which provides him not only with change, but
also with a new vision and a freshly acquired maturity.

Time is the dimension that unleashes the forces of change
for Gilbert. The "now" of the novel is 1847. Gilbert's
story begins in 1827, at a time when he has little knowl-

edge of the world and halfheartedly embraces the precepts of the male master code. It is 1827 when Helen hands him her journal. Her experience at this point eclipses his because it has evolved over time. Her narrative, a deeper retrospection than his, begins in 1821. Like her existence at Wildfell Hall, Helen's narrative becomes isolated in time. This isolation comes to an end through Gilbert's reading, which in turn brings an end to his immature perceptions and assumptions.

When Gilbert finishes his final letter to his brother-in-law Halford, the time of his narrative of village life is the same as the time of Helen's exile. Brontë signifies the parity of Gilbert's maturity level when she permits him to finish both narratives in the final chapters. Conflation at this point makes sense because ultimately the couple will wed. Brontë follows convention in this respect since the major violation in the novel, according to the Victorian standard, is not that of the dissolute immoral husband against his wife, but the criminal act of the wife against the husband.

Brontë deflects the impact of Helen's action with Huntingdon's miserable death. When Helen accepts Gilbert at the close of the 1827 story, Brontë establishes the notion that it is not marriage to which she so vehemently objects, but rather the unfair code that ties a moral woman to an immoral man and then judges the man to be socially and emotionally superior by virtue of gender.

In the final chapter, the events of 1827 come to a close and Gilbert ends his 1847 letter. Twenty years have passed and time has proven that experience clarifies perceptions and enables an inexperienced youth to acquire maturity. In his closing words to his brother-in-law, Gilbert writes: "As for myself, I need not tell you how happily my Helen and I have lived together, and how blessed we still are in each other's society, and in the promising young scions that are growing up about us" (490). By means of experience, the young man who was going to "walk through the world, looking neither to the right hand nor to the left," has found his focus and his future.

Since many nineteenth-century novels were written, published and read by male readers, *Tenant* seems to offer no breach of the gender contract in its early pages. When Gilbert begins his narrative, he appears to be self-composed in his position of time present, and promises to recount a retrospective that signals his role as self-assured male within the social order. What surprises the reader is the progress of the narrative, which reveals Gilbert's early immaturity and irresponsibility. He is not subsequently catapulted into maturity because he has encountered and vanquished adversity, but because he has read the journal of someone who has already experienced such dragon-slaying. Gilbert does not develop as a human being because he has embraced human courage, but rather because he has undertaken the reading act. What has launched him into adulthood has not been the experience of male order and reason, but rather the reading of male disorder and unreason as written by a woman.

Work Cited

Brontë, Anne. *The Tenant of Wildfell Hall.* Ed. G. D. Hargreaves. New York: Viking, 1979.

Elizabeth Langland (essay date 1992)

SOURCE: "The Voicing of Feminine Desire in Anne Brontë's *The Tenant of Wildfell Hall,*" in *Gender and Discourse in Victorian Literature and Art,* edited by Antony H. Harrison and Beverly Taylor, Northern Illinois University Press, 1992, pp. 111-23.

[*In the following essay, Langland offers a feminist/post-structuralist analysis of* The Tenant of Wildfell Hall *as a Victorian narrative of transgressive feminine desire.*]

Because of its radical and indecorous subject matter—a woman's flight from her abusive husband—Anne Brontë's *The Tenant of Wildfell Hall* shocked contemporary audiences. Yet the very indecorousness of the subject may seem to be undermined by the propriety of the form this narrative takes: the woman's story is enclosed within and authorized by a respectable man's narrative. Within the discourse of traditional analysis we would speak of the "nested" narratives of Anne Brontë's novel, one story enclosed within another. In this case, the woman's story, in the form of a diary, is "nested" within the man's narrative. The critical language we are employing here already suggests certain conclusions about priority and hierarchy. The woman's story must, it seems, be subsumed within the man's account, which is prior and originary. The presentation of her version of events depends upon his representation. Within a traditional narrative analysis, then, Brontë's *Tenant* may tell an untraditional tale of a fallen woman redeemed, but it tells it in such a way that reaffirms the patriarchal status quo of masculine priority and privilege, of women's subordination and dependency. The radical subject is defused by the form. But such a traditional analysis that speaks of nested narratives is already contaminated by the patriarchal ideology of prior and latter and so cannot effectively question what I wish to question here: the transgressive nature of narrative exchange.

Following Roland Barthes I propose that we recognize "[a]t the origin of Narrative, desire," because at the heart of narrative operates an economic system, an exchange. To Barthes, "[t]his is the question raised, perhaps, by every narrative. *What should the narrative be exchanged for? What is the narrative 'worth'?*" In this analysis of "Sarrasine," the exchange is a "night of love for a good story." Thus "the two parts of the text are not detached from one another according to the so-called principle of 'nested narratives.' . . . Narrative is determined not by a desire to narrate but by a desire to exchange: it is a *medium of exchange,* an agent, a currency, a gold standard."[1]

I wish to examine Anne Brontë's *The Tenant of Wildfell Hall* in the light of narrative as exchange—of narrative within a narrative not as hierarchical or detachable parts but as interacting functions within a transgressive economy that allows for the paradoxic voicing of feminine desire. Articulating this process will be the focus of my essay. I also suggest here (to indicate implications of this analysis) that such narrative exchanges are common in Victorian stories of transgression, as in Barthes's example, Balzac's "Sarrasine" (the castrati as man/woman); in Emily Brontë's *Wuthering Heights* (the self as Other—"I am Heathcliff"); in Mary Shelley's *Frankenstein* (the human as monster); and in Joseph Conrad's *Heart of Darkness* (the civilized man as savage).

The ideas of feminine voice and feminine desire in Victorian England were oxymorons, in Roland Barthes's coinage, *paradoxisms,* a joining of two antithetical terms, a "passage through the wall of the Antithesis."[2] The patriarchal discourse of Victorianism coded terms such as masculine/feminine, desire/repletion, speech/silence as opposites, as paradigmatic poles marked by the slash. Thus the feminine view, which was repressed, could have no voice, and passion, or desire, was the province of the masculine, a function of what Barthes calls the symbolic code.

Barthes elaborates, "The antithesis is a wall without a doorway. Leaping this wall is a transgression. . . . Anything that draws these two antipathetic sides together is rightly scandalous (the most blatant scandal: that of form)."[3] Barthes's formulation suggests the immense difficulty confronting the Victorian writer who wished to give voice to feminine desire. This transgressive act at its most blatantly scandalous depends on formal juxtaposition: something that "draws these two antipathetic sides together." I propose that we examine the transgressive possibilities inherent in the symbolic code itself and, further, that we look at the narrative within the narrative as a mode of juxtaposition, both of meanings and of focus.

In Brontë's **The Tenant of Wildfell Hall** the subject is transgression—a woman's illegal flight from her husband.[4] Brontë uses the transgressive possibilities of narrative exchange to *write* her transgressive story, a story of female desire, and she uses the transgressive possibilities of the symbolic code to *rewrite* her transgression or "fall" as her triumph. A brief summary of the novel's plot will focus the central issues. A young and idealistic woman marries a man whose character is already in need of reformation. Believing herself called to this task, she begins optimistically only to discover that she is powerless to effect any changes that cannot be wrought by the force of moral suasion. She has no social or legal leverage. Ultimately, finding her son and herself sinking into the corruption generated by her husband, she plans to flee, only to be defeated on a first attempt when her husband, discerning her intention, confiscates all her property. Prompted by her husband's introduction of his mistress into the house as his son's governess, she succeeds at a second attempt, but she must carefully guard her identity from her inquisitive neighbors or she may be betrayed to her husband and forced to return.

These events, at the heart of the novel, are told only retrospectively. The novel is, in fact, doubly retrospective—

Helen's narrative is nested within Gilbert's narrative, which is, in turn, a story told to his friend Halford. The novel opens in 1847 when Gilbert commences his correspondence with Halford. He has felt that he owes Halford a return for an earlier confidence and will now make good his "debt" with an "old-world story . . . a full and faithful account of certain circumstances connected with the most important event of my life."[5] Gilbert's narrative itself begins twenty years earlier, in the autumn of 1827, with the arrival of a new tenant at Wildfell Hall. Helen Graham, the mysterious tenant, is that woman who has transgressed Victorian social convention by leaving her husband, and her story—incorporated through her diary—begins on 1 June 1821. Brontë anticipates Barthes by having Gilbert define narrative exchange as economic exchange. He writes to Halford: "If the coin suits you, tell me so, and I'll send you the rest at my leisure: if you would rather remain my creditor than stuff your purse with such ungainly heavy pieces . . . I'll . . . willingly keep the treasure to myself" (44). The monetary metaphors underline the novel's implicit insistence that one does not narrate simply because of a desire to narrate: narration enacts an exchange and a gain or loss.

Traditional literary criticism has faulted Brontë's **Tenant** for its clumsy device of Helen Graham's interpolated diary. George Moore, otherwise ardently enthusiastic over Brontë's talents, instigated criticism of her artistic "breakdown" in the middle of the novel. Moore regretted not the interpolated tale but the manner of exchange. He complained, "You must not let your heroine give her diary to the young farmer . . . your heroine must tell the young farmer her story" to "preserve the atmosphere of a passionate and original love story."[6] This distinction in the mode of exchange, telling versus writing, raises a question Barthes does not discuss, and it encourages further reflection. Were the heroine merely to speak her tale, then one kind of economic exchange would be confirmed: her story for his chivalric allegiance, something he is struggling to preserve in the face of society's calumny. Such a "telling" would preserve the atmosphere of "a passionate and original love story," as George Moore saw, but that story would be the traditional one of a male subject's reaffirmation of his desire for a woman as object. That is not the story Brontë wanted to write. Helen's diary spans one-half of the novel, and it confirms another kind of economic exchange: her story for the right to fulfill her polymorphous desire—to restore her reputation, to punish with impunity her husband, and to marry a man who consents to be the object of her beneficence and affection.

Gilbert Markham opens his narrative with the arrival of Helen Graham at Wildfell Hall. She is immediately put into circulation as an object of community gossip, speculation, and horror that a "single lady" has let a "place . . . in ruins" (37). The community reads her character through this behavior, concluding she must be a "witch," a decoding that follows from an initial suspicion that she cannot be a "respectable female" (38, 39). Such suspicions unleash a barrage of one-way exchanges in the form of "pastoral advice" or "useful advice" (38, 39) as community members seek to circumscribe her within the usual sexual economies, to regulate "the apparent, or non-apparent circumstances, and probable, or improbable history of the mysterious lady" (39). The explicit oppositions in this passage emphasize the binaries that undergird Brontë's story from the outset, the excesses of which disrupt the seemingly simple love story of a young farmer and beautiful stranger. As we have seen in Barthes's formulation, this is a function of antitheses or the symbolic code, which both separates and joins and thus allows for the transgression as well as the conservation of oppositions.

Is Helen Graham a witch-devil or an angel? Is she a wife or a widow, amiable or ill-tempered? Is she pure or corrupt, a saint or a sinner, faithful or fallen? Her identity is made more problematic because her decorous appearance and religious devotion coexist with her claims that she has no use for "such things that every lady ought to be familiar with" and "what every respectable female ought to know" (39). Although civilized in manner, she appears to "wholly disregard the common observances of civilized life" (51).

It is immediately plain that Brontë is not giving us the traditional generic domestic comedy, that is, the story of a woman who focuses on making herself into a desirable object for a suitable man. That story is circumvented at the outset with Helen Graham's ambiguous status as widow/wife, and yet the pressure of that traditional narrative is such, and the cultural expectations for beautiful women are such, that Gilbert's story strives to become that narrative as he falls out of love with Eliza Millward and into love with Helen Graham and begins to write himself into the narrative as the rescuing figure of the maligned and misunderstood lady. Significantly, Gilbert's narrative at first tends to assign similar traits to Eliza and Helen despite their manifest differences. For example, Gilbert describes Eliza Millward as a woman whose "chief attraction" (like Helen's) lay in her eyes: "the expression various, and ever changing but always either preternaturally—I had almost said *diabolically*—wicked, or irresistibly bewitching—often both" (42). This assignment of traits aligns Eliza paradigmatically with Helen (she is already syntagmatically aligned since she is another love interest of Gilbert's), and the effect is to domesticate Helen and her true strangeness because we rapidly perceive that Eliza is a very ordinary young woman who does desire only to become the object of some man's affection. Thus, at this early point, Gilbert's narrative strives to interpret Helen Graham as it does Eliza Millward—as just another woman whose life could be fulfilled by connection with his.

By initially making Helen Graham an object of Gilbert's narrative and not the subject of her own, the text enacts what it also presents thematically: women's objectification and marginalization within patriarchal culture. Specific comments underscore our perception of this process. Helen Graham is criticized for making a "milksop," not a "man,"

of her little boy, who is supposed to "learn to be ashamed" of being "always tied to his mother's apron string" (52). Helen's energetic defense insists, "I trust my son will never be ashamed to love his mother," and "I am to send him to school, I suppose, to learn to despise his mother's authority and affection!" (55).

Women are paradigmatically all linked and consequently all marginalized by obsessive attention to men and their needs. Gilbert's sister complains, "I'm told I ought not to think of myself." She quotes her mother's words: "You know, Rose, in all household matters, we have only two things to consider, first, what's proper to be done, and secondly, what's most agreeable to the gentlemen of the house—anything will do for the ladies'" (78). Mrs. Markham sums up the duties of husband and wife: "you must fall each into your proper place. You'll do your business, and she, if she's worthy of you, will do hers; but it's your business to please yourself, and hers to please you" (79).

Gilbert Markham is suddenly and surprisingly enabled to articulate this process and his own benefits: "Perhaps, too, I was a little spoiled by my mother and sister, and some other ladies of my acquaintance" (5). He achieves this unusual self-knowledge partly to prepare for his ceding the position of subject to Helen and thereby crediting her story and the possibility of her desire. He tells his mother, "[W]hen I marry, I shall expect to find more pleasure in making my wife happy and comfortable, than in being made so by her: I would rather give than receive" (79).

We are also prepared for the narrative's change of focus by the extent of Helen Graham's difference from the women around her. A professional painter who supports herself and her son, she "cannot afford to paint for [her] own amusement" (69). She does not allow her painting to be interrupted by casual social calls, objects to Gilbert's "superintendence" of her progress on a sketch and to being the object of his appreciative gaze, and manifests an "evident desire to be rid of [Gilbert]" (89). A visit he pays her provokes his recognition, "I do not think Mrs. Graham was particularly delighted to see us," an indirect confession of his initial failure to accord primacy to her as desiring subject instead of desired object.

These thematic shifts anticipate and prepare for the narrative exchange that is about to take place as Gilbert cedes the story to Helen. In fact, such shifts proliferate just prior to the commencement of Helen's diary narrative. Gilbert begins to change his orientation toward Helen, focusing less on how she meets his desire and more on how he might meet hers. He confesses that his early behavior toward her made him "the more dissatisfied with myself for having so unfavourably impressed her, and the more desirous to vindicate my character and disposition in her eyes, and if possible, to win her esteem" (85).

Yet at the same time that Gilbert expresses dissatisfaction with his early behavior, he embroils himself in an embarrassing misunderstanding with Mr. Lawrence, whom he imagines to be another would-be lover of Helen because he is blind to the truth that Lawrence is, in fact, her brother. Markham here enacts a charade of the jealous lover—a charade marked by insults and, finally, by a physical assault on Lawrence. It is his nadir, the moment when he privileges the community voices and the "evidence of [his] senses" (145) over Helen's authority to speak her story. Although Gilbert Markham pretends to disregard the storm of rumor surrounding Helen Graham that the community circulates—characterized as "shaky reports," "idle slander," "mysterious reports," "talk," "the poison of detracting tongues," a "spicy piece of scandal," "the calumnies of malicious tongues," "vile constructions," "lying inventions," "babbling fiends" (96, 97, 102, 103, 120, 123, 124)—his behavior reveals that he accords rumor great authority. When he adds what he calls "the evidence of my senses," he feels his position is unassailable just at the point where it is most vulnerable. We, as readers, appreciate the limitation of Gilbert's perspective, the ways he, in focalizing events and other characters, has generated a cloud of misapprehension shaped by his own needs, fears, and desires. At this point his narrative is bankrupt, unable to provide answers to the questions generated by the text's hermeneutic code. Helen's voice intervenes at this point, with greater narrative authority, to silence the other proliferating voices. Her narrative must redeem Gilbert's and provide those answers, the final signifieds of the text's multiplying signifiers: the promise that the classic novel holds out.

I mentioned earlier that narratives of transgression often depend on narrative exchange. Whether we are dealing with the young lady in "Sarrasine," or Lockwood in *Wuthering Heights,* or Victor Frankenstein in *Frankenstein,* or the unnamed fellow in *Heart of Darkness,* or Gilbert in **The Tenant of Wildfell Hall,** the focalizer of events confronts an enigma born of a transgression of antitheses, and his explanatory power is momentarily exhausted. Answers to the enigma depend on a new viewpoint, a new focus—in this case, a new narrator or focalizer. I use the term "focalizer" deliberately to allow us to distinguish between the one who narrates and the one who sees or focuses the events.[7] But the relationship between the two focalizers is always problematic because they offer competing narratives; each claims authority to tell the story, and the two versions cannot be simply supplementary. The relationship between the two focalizers may also become problematic because one of the narrators may become the focalizer of both narratives, which is what I believe happens in **The Tenant of Wildfell Hall,** and this collapse generates a narrative transgression—a confusion of outside and inside, primary and secondary, subject and object. Although Helen's story is enclosed within Gilbert's story and might seem, therefore, to be part of his, nonetheless, by providing the answers we and Gilbert seek, it subordinates his narrative to hers. Helen's narrative rewrites Gilbert's, stabilizing it within a particular hermeneutic pattern. Thus, it is her story but also his story, a conflation that Brontë plays upon after Helen's diary concludes and Markham resumes; it becomes impossible at times to distinguish which

one is the focalizer of events, a process to be examined after we explore the operation of the symbolic code in Helen's story.

Helen's narrative fully focalizes the "paradoxism" of feminine desire. Her diary, first of all, records the story of a young woman's falling in love and concomitant distraction and alienation from her common pursuits and ordered life. That is, hers is an often told tale of a young woman's newly aroused desire for a young man: "All my former occupations seem so tedious and dull. . . . I cannot enjoy my music. . . . I cannot enjoy my walks. . . . I cannot enjoy my books. . . . My drawing suits me best. . . . But then, there is one face I am alway trying to paint or to sketch" (148). Helen's painting becomes an eloquent voice of her desire for Huntingdon because it reveals to him what her words deny. Indeed, Huntingdon pinpoints the connection between images and words, between hasty tracings and postscripts: "I perceive, the backs of young ladies' drawings, like the post-scripts of their letters, are the most important and interesting part of the concern" (172). And, as he reads the message of her desire in her sketch, Helen is mortified: "So then! . . . he despises me, because he knows I love him" (172). This recognition underscores a significant pattern already in place, that a young woman must disguise her physical desire for a man because expression of such desire only kindles contempt within a patriarchy.

Thus, Helen's perception initiates a process, first of dissembling her desire and then, more significantly, of coding a physical urge as a spiritual need. In the first move, the desire becomes a subterranean force, something not openly expressed; in the second move, the desire is no longer recognized or accepted for what it is. A woman sublimates her physical desire for a man; it becomes a need to reform him spiritually. So, women's physical desires, because illicit, are often encoded in literature as spiritual ones. The legion of female saviors in Victorian fiction testifies to this rewriting. Charlotte Brontë's Jane Eyre is to guide and protect a reformed Rochester; George Eliot's Dorothea Brooke and Mary Garth are to give a social focus to the self-indulgent desires of Will Ladislaw and Fred Vincy. Anne Brontë allows her heroine to be more vocal and articulate about her sublimated desire. In justifying her marriage to Huntingdon, Helen argues, "I will save him from" his evil companions, "I would willingly risk my happiness for the chance of securing his," and, finally, "If he has done amiss, I shall consider my life well spent in saving him from the consequences of his early errors" (167). She sighs, "Oh! if I could but believe that Heaven has designed me for this!" (168). Helen is so indoctrinated by this myth that, when she believes Huntingdon has committed adultery with Annabella Wilmot, she claims, "It is not my loss, nor her triumph that I deplore so greatly as the wreck of my fond hopes for his advantage" (178). The failure of this rosy scenario is anticipated in her aunt's summation: "Do you imagine your merry, thoughtless profligate would allow himself to be guided by a young girl like you?" (165). That, of course, is precisely the Victorian myth and ideology. While Helen quietly gloats, "[A]n inward instinct . . . assures me I am right. There *is* essential goodness in him;—and what delight to unfold it!" (168), we are already apprised of her mistaken apprehension by the retrospective structure of the narrative that testifies to the fiction she is projecting.

What does it mean, then, that Brontë's Helen fails in her efforts at spiritual reform? And not only does she fail, but Huntingdon also succeeds to an extent in corrupting her. Such failure and reversal inevitably shift attention from the spiritual realm back to the physical one, in the traditional antithesis of body and soul. Not surprisingly, reviewers of *Tenant* were outraged because the novel concentrated so heavily on sensual indulgences and abuses. Perhaps more threatening, however, *Tenant* explodes the myth of woman's redemptive spirituality and insight, and it opens the door to the unthinkable transgression, feminine desire. The force of Helen's love is now channeled into hatred; a desire to redeem becomes a desire to punish. Helen admits, "I hate him tenfold more than ever, for having brought me to this! . . . Instead of being humbled and purified by my afflictions, I feel that they are turning my nature into gall" (323).

Again, Barthes's symbolic code helps to articulate the process. The symbolic code represents meaning as difference through antithesis that appears inevitable. And, as we have seen, "every joining of two antithetical terms . . . every passage through the wall of Antithesis . . . constitutes a transgression."[8] Brontë insistently deploys such oppositions as love/hate, redemption/punishment, saint/sinner, angel/devil, female/male to set up the conditions for transgression. At this point the text works to privilege and to legitimate one binary term over another. But, inevitably, due to the operation of the symbolic code, the text also becomes the site for exposure, multivalence, and reversibility. The pivotal event is Helen's return to nurse her injured husband. Does she return to redeem or to punish? Does she go out of love or out of hatred? Is she a ministering angel or a vengeful devil? Is she a holy saint or a common sinner?

In returning to Huntingdon, Helen passes through the wall of antithesis to transgress and to collapse differences that were seemingly inviolable. Huntingdon ejaculates at her return, "Devil take her," even as Markham extols the man's good fortune to have "such an angel by his side" (428, 444). Huntingdon perceives his returned wife as a "fancy" or "mania" that would "kill" him. Helen insists his mania is the "truth." She asserts she has come "to take care" of him, to "save" him. He answers, "[D]on't torment me now!" He interprets her behavior as "an act of Christian charity, whereby you hope to gain a higher seat in heaven for yourself, and scoop a deeper pit in hell for me." She states she has come to offer him "comfort and assistance," while he accuses her of a desire to overwhelm him "with remorse and confusion" (430). Huntingdon recognizes her act as "sweet revenge," made sweeter because "it's all in the way of duty" (433). He complains that she wants to

"scare [him] to death"; she responds that she does not want to "lull [him] to false security" (434). Helen characterizes herself as his "kind nurse," while Huntingdon regrets that he has been abandoned to the "mercy of a harsh, exacting, cold-hearted woman" (439, 445). He is the object of her "solicitude"; she is no longer the object of his cruelty. Save/kill, care for/torment, angel/devil, truth/fancy, duty/revenge, kind/harsh, lull/scare, heaven/hell, higher seat/deeper pit—the signifers slide, distinctions collapse, meaning erodes. Feminine desire expresses itself in the resulting vacuum of meaning. In the novel's hermeneutic, the fallen woman of Victorian life becomes the paragon, the exemplum, and revenge becomes a fine duty.

At the point that Helen returns to Huntingdon's bedside, Gilbert Markham has resumed the narration, but he has not assumed the authority to focus the bedside events. His narrative contains frequent letters from Helen, and she is as often the focalizer of the events as he is; indeed, it is often impossible to distinguish who is the focalizer. Gilbert's perspectives merge with Helen's as he incorporates her letters into his narrative—sometimes the literal words, sometimes a paraphrase—until the reader cannot distinguish between them. One narrative transgresses the other, distinctions between narrators collapse. For example, in chapter 49 Gilbert Markham writes, "The next [letter] was still more distressing in the tenor of its contents. The sufferer was fast approaching dissolution" (449). Theoretically, he is summarizing. But suddenly, we are in the midst of a scene between Helen and Huntingdon in which present tense mixes with past to convey immediacy: "'If I try,' said his afflicted wife, 'to divert him from these things . . . , it is no better'.—'Worse and worse!' he groans. . . . 'And yet he clings to me with unrelenting pertinacity'" (450). We are then immediately immersed in dialogue.

> "Stay with me, Helen. . . . But death *will* come. . . . Oh, if I *could* believe there was nothing after!"
>
> "Don't try to believe it. . . . If you *sincerely* repent—"
>
> "I *can't* repent; I only fear."
>
> "You only regret the past for its consequences to yourself?"
>
> "Just so—except that I'm sorry to have wronged you, Nell, because you're so good to me."
>
> (450)

The "afflicted wife" of Gilbert's narrative merges with the "I" of Helen's reportage and the "you" of the dialogue. The shifting persons stabilize in the "I" of the scene's final sentence, which also stabilizes the meaning: "I have said enough, I think, to convince you that I did well to go to him" (451). The narrative exchange and transgression allow for Helen's behavior here to signify duty instead of willfulness or perversity, to signify her elevation from fallen woman to paragon. Gilbert anticipates this closure: "I see that she was actuated by the best and noblest motives in what she has done" (435). He rejoices: "It was now in my power to clear her name from every foul aspersion. The Millwards and the Wilsons should see, with their own eyes, the bright sun bursting from the cloud—and they should be scorched and dazzled by its beams" (440). His story has, in fact, become her story.

Through the transgressive possibilities of the symbolic code and antithesis, Helen's desire to punish has been enacted as a wish to succor, and, through narrative exchange and transgression, the enigma surrounding her life has been, seemingly, penetrated, and Gilbert's resumed narrative now, seemingly, conveys the "truth." The meaning of Helen's behavior—as triumph rather than fall—is therefore stabilized by Gilbert's narrative. Although it may seem strange to speak of a novel that imbeds a woman's story within a man's as "giving voice" to a woman's desire, we can now appreciate the techniques through which Brontë enacts this process.

Yet a final, difficult aspect of the expression of feminine desire in this text remains unexplored: the representation of courtship and marriage between Gilbert and Helen. As we saw earlier, Gilbert's narrative at first strives to become the traditional story of a male subject's desire for the female as object. That narrative movement is thwarted when Helen becomes the speaking subject of the diary portion of the novel, but it could easily reassert itself as Gilbert regains narrative control in the novel's concluding pages. Indeed, many critics have been dissatisfied with women's novels that must, it appears, conclude with the traditional wedding bells reaffirming the status quo. To what extent, we must ask, does Brontë elude that resolution in *The Tenant of Wildfell Hall*?

Clearly we hear wedding bells, but the status quo is destabilized by certain subversive tendencies in the narrative. Huntingdon's death, which allows the meaning of Helen's behavior to be stabilized, radically destabilizes the relationship between Helen and Gilbert, which had been, perforce, limited to "friendship." She is now capable of becoming an object of courtship, but Huntingdon's death has altered the relationship in a more significant manner by making her a wealthy widow, as Gilbert realizes: "there was a wide distinction between the rank and circumstances of Mrs Huntingdon, the lady of Grass-dale Manor, and those of Mrs Graham the artist, the tenant of Wildfell Hall" (454). The class distinction supersedes the gender difference and subverts the gender hierarchy. Gilbert becomes silent, submissive, passive, and acquiescent. He resolves to wait several months and then "send her a letter modestly reminding her of her former permission to write to her" (456). Only his receiving news that Helen is about to remarry goads him out of his passivity.

Again, Gilbert enacts the part of an ardent suitor, determined to save Helen from a bad marriage, but, as he takes on this more active role, we are reimmersed in the world of antitheses. He imagines himself in the role of heroic savior even as he recognizes he might pass "for a madman or an impertinent fool" (465). He goes to her, "winged by this hope, and goaded by these fears" (466). When he dis-

covers he has been mistaken in his information, he resolves to find Helen and speak to her. He seeks her at Grass-dale Manor (Huntingdon's estate) and is impressed by the "park as beautiful now, in its wintry garb, as it could be in its summer glory" (472). He discovers that Helen has removed to Staningly, her uncle's estate, and that she has become even more remote from him through inheriting this property as well. He now feels himself to be, indeed, on a madman's or fool's errand and resolves to return home without seeing Helen. Their fortuitous encounter leaves him silent and forces upon her the role of suitor. She must propose to him and so transgress the boundaries of the masculine and feminine. She plucks a winter rose—a paradoxism particularly within a literary economy that metaphorically aligns the rose with youth and innocence, not with age and experience—and says, "This rose is not so fragrant as a summer flower, but it has stood through hardships none of *them* could bear. . . . It is still fresh and blooming as a flower can be, with the cold snow even now on its petals—Will you have it?" (484). The paradoxism of a winter rose, the transgression of customary antithesis, prepares for the paradoxism of the assertive woman expressing feminine desire.

In addition, although Gilbert is narrating, Helen is the focalizer of the scene. Gilbert, here a very diffident suitor, hesitates to understand the meaning of the rose, and Helen snatches it back. Finally she is forced to explain, "The rose I gave you was an emblem of my heart," but he is so backward that he must ask, "Would you give me your hand too, if I asked it?" (485). Though he still worries, "But if you *should* repent!" she utters definitive words, "It would be your fault . . . I never shall, unless you bitterly disappoint me" (486). She has focalized the meaning of this event. Her wishes dominate; he is *subject to* her desire, and he is the *object of* her desire.

At the same time that Helen expresses her desire, she closes off the meaning of this story and proleptically concludes all subsequent ones; if she repents, it will be his fault. Gilbert writes his story as her story. She has been defined—and now predefines herself—as the paragon, an exemplar among women. Whereas the angel could only fall in the previous narrative controlled by Victorian ideology, here only Gilbert can fall. However, a tension underlies this resolution. Because the expression of feminine desire depends on transgression and exchange, the stabilization of the narrative in closure seems simultaneously to close off the space for that expression. Not surprisingly, Brontë destabilizes her conclusion by focusing on exchange: Gilbert exchanges the final installment of his narrative with Halford, and he simultaneously anticipates the exchange of Halford's visit.

It is appropriate in a world of antitheses and in the context of their transgression that the ending of the narrative should be just such an advent. Gilbert writes, "We are just now looking forward to the advent of you and Rose, for the time of your annual visit draws nigh, when you must leave your dusty, smoky, noisy, toiling, striving city for a season of invigorating relaxation and social retirement with us" (490). The implied antithesis of country and city gives way to the explicit paradoxisms of "invigorating relaxation" and "social retirement" in the last line of the novel. And "this passage through the world of Antithesis," by keeping open the possibility for transgression, also keeps open a possible space for feminine desire.[9] If this seems a fragile and tentative resolution—one threatening to reassert the status quo—it is also a radically important one in refusing to postulate an essential female desire existing outside of and independent of the discursive practices that construct women's lives.

Notes

1. Roland Barthes, *S/Z: An Essay,* trans. Richard Miller (New York: Hill and Wang, 1974), 88, 89, 90.

2. Barthes, *S/Z,* 27.

3. Barthes, *S/Z,* 65.

4. Only recently has Anne Brontë's *The Tenant of Wildfell Hall* begun to receive the attention it deserves. The reasons for the neglect are many. See my *Anne Brontë: The Other One* (London: Macmillan, 1989).

5. Anne Brontë, *The Tenant of Wildfell Hall* (Harmondsworth: Penguin, 1979), 34. All further references are from this edition and are cited parenthetically in the text by page number.

6. George Moore, *Conversations in Ebury Street* (New York: Boni and Liveright, 1924), 254. On the subject of narrative infelicities in Brontë's *Tenant,* Moore is joined by other, later critics, notably Winifred Gérin, "Introduction," *The Tenant of Wildfell Hall,* 14. However, some fine recent articles have attempted to do more justice to the narrative structure of the novel, particularly as it revises Emily's *Wuthering Heights.* See Jan Gordon, "Gossip, Diary, Letter, Text: Anne Brontë's Narrative Tenant and the Problematic of the Gothic Sequel," *ELH* 5 (1984): 719-45; and Naomi Jacobs, "Gender and Layered Narrative in *Wuthering Heights* and *The Tenant of Wildfell Hall," Journal of Narrative Technique* 16 (Autumn 1986): 204-19.

7. Gerard Genette, *Narrative Discourse: An Essay in Method,* trans. Jane E. Lewin (Ithaca: Cornell University Press, 1980), 194-211.

8. Barthes, *S/Z,* 26-27.

9. Barthes, *S/Z,* 27.

Marianne Thormählen (essay date 1993)

SOURCE: "The Villain of *Wildfell Hall*: Aspects and Prospects of Arthur Huntingdon," in *Modern Language Review,* Vol. 88, No. 4, October, 1993, pp. 831-41.

[*In the following essay, Thormählen argues against traditional, biographically motivated estimates of Arthur Huntingdon by examining the character in cultural context,* *particularly in relation to contemporary texts on alcoholism and phrenology, as well as Victorian notions of Christian salvation.*]

With foreheads villainous low

(*The Tempest,* IV. 1. 249)

Anne Brontë's second novel has traditionally been contemplated against the background of events and circumstances in the author's life.[1] More recently, narratological aspects have been discussed by critics influenced by new developments in critical theory.[2] Other dimensions in the book have not yet received the attention they deserve, though, and the result is an incomplete appreciation of Anne Brontë the artist. A consideration of her 'villain' against the background of early-nineteenth-century theology, social developments, and science suggests that historical contextualization along these lines may be one fruitful approach to this underrated novelist.[3]

W. A. Craik argued that Arthur Huntingdon is the most important character in *The Tenant of Wildfell Hall* (henceforth referred to as *Wildfell Hall*) and that he 'decrees the rest of the characters and events'.[4] Even readers who do not go along with this contention must admit that his rake's progress from genial *bon viveur* to terminal patient is central to the development of the story. When the reader first meets him, in the diary of eighteen-year-old Helen, he is 'laughing to himself' over Helen's exasperation with a dull, middle-aged suitor. Arthur Huntingdon's merry temper is one of his chief attractions for Helen. Warned by her aunt after their first encounter, she refuses, all teenager, to 'believe there is any harm in those laughing blue eyes' (p. 154). Even the 'freedom' in his manner which, as she knows, goes too far does not prevent her from being amused by his sallies.

Before they are married, however, Helen has already realized that her Arthur's jocularity can be gross and cruel, and that it is not balanced by even an occasional hint of gravity. Her qualms, summed up in the uneasy question 'What shall I do with the serious part of myself?' (p. 214), soon prove justified: throughout the years of their disintegrating marriage, the girl whose 'serious part' was always much in evidence becomes hardened and embittered while her husband carries on laughing—often in delight at tormenting her and always during his orgies, up to the point where, incapably drunk, he is 'no longer laughing [. . .] but sick and stupid' (p. 291).

The sombre Lord Lowborough is in complete contrast to him. Thin, pale, dour, and gloomy, he is addicted to gambling, drinking, and laudanum in turn, his reformation coinciding with the early stages of Arthur Huntingdon's ruin. His spectre-at-the-feast physiognomy is totally unlike his crony's ruddy good looks. Both men have been held to be to some extent modelled on Branwell Brontë,[5] but they bear far stronger resemblances to two types of drunkards outlined in Robert Macnish's *The Anatomy of Drunkenness,* a popular treatise that went into a number of editions in the early nineteenth century:

Some are drunkards by choice, and others by necessity. [. . .] The former have an innate and constitutional fondness for liquor, and drink *con amore*. Such men are usually of a sanguineous temperament, of coarse unintellectual minds, and of low and animal propensities. They have [. . .] a flow of animal spirits which other people are without. They delight in the roar and riot of drinking clubs. [. . .]

The drunkard by necessity was never meant by nature to be dissipated. He is perhaps a person of amiable dispositions, whom misfortune has overtaken, and who, instead of bearing up manfully against it, endeavours to drown his sorrows in liquor. It is an excess of sensibility, a partial mental weakness, an absolute misery of the heart, which drives him on.

Macnish's description of the typical 'sanguineous drunkard' is very similar to his portrayal of the drunkard by choice:

Persons of this stamp have usually a ruddy complexion, thick neck, small head, and strong muscular fibre. Their intellect is in general *mediocre* [. . .]. In such people, the animal propensities prevail over the moral and intellectual ones. They are prone to combativeness and sensuality, and are either very good-natured or extremely quarrelsome. [. . .] They are talkative from the beginning, and, during confirmed intoxication, perfectly obstreperous. It is men of this class who are the heroes of all drunken companies, the patrons of masonic lodges, the presidents and getters-up of jovial meetings.[6]

The conclusion of this description might be compared with the passage in *Wildfell Hall* where Arthur Huntingdon relates the dismay of his fellow revellers at his impending marriage:

They say there'll be no more fun now, no more merry days and glorious nights—and all my fault—I am the first to break up the jovial band. [. . .] I was the very life and prop of the community, they do me the honour to say.

(p. 197)

Another telling passage is Helen's cheerful admission to her aunt before her engagement that 'he is of a sanguine temperament, and a gay, thoughtless temper' (p. 165). Arthur Huntingdon's high colour was one of the qualities that made timid Milicent Hargrave wonder at Helen's choice: 'But don't you think Mr Huntingdon's face is too red?' (p. 195).

What evidence there is that Anne Brontë read contemporary works on drinking and drunkenness is circumstantial at best, but it is a reasonable assumption. The early nineteenth century was a time when alcohol abuse became a hotly debated issue. The Temperance Movement spread over Britain; in Haworth, the Rev. Patrick Brontë and his son Branwell were at one time President and Secretary, respectively, of the local Temperance Society.[7] Helen's discussions with the Markhams and with the Rev. Millward reflect the current disputes about the merits and perils of drinking alcoholic beverages, for children as well as for adults.[8]

Helen's method of weaning her little boy off the varieties of alcohol his father had taught 'the little toper' to imbibe was one recommended by several writers on drunkenness in the 1820s and 1830s. She had 'surreptitiously introduced a small quantity of tartar-emetic' in the glasses of wine, brandy, and gin she continued to give him, 'just enough to produce inevitable nausea and depression without positive sickness' (p. 375). This remedy, originally tested and proposed by an American physician, was advocated by Macnish and other writers on the properties, effects, and dangers of alcohol.[9]

In addition to Arthur Huntingdon's jollity, his handsome appearance appeals strongly to Helen. She is not alone in finding him physically attractive; the seasoned flirt and, in due course, faithless wife Annabella Wilmot/Lady Lowborough is similarly affected from the outset. After the tête-à-tête in front of the Van Dyck (pp. 163-64), when Huntingdon ardently presses Helen's hand and tries to 'extort a confession of attachment' from her, Helen's aunt tells her she is not 'fit to be seen' with her 'shocking colour' and eyes that lack their 'natural expression'. Later, though she knows it was improper to let Huntingdon kiss her before their engagement was duly settled, she pleads that she 'could not help it' and bursts into tears due to 'the general tumultuous excitement of [her] feelings' (p. 185). Scenes such as these express as strong a physical attraction on the part of a young girl as one can expect to find articulated in an early Victorian novel, and P. J. M. Scott's complaint that there is a lack of 'erotic charge' in the book seems unjustified.[10]

A man able to make intelligent and beautiful young women commit indiscretions and, in the case of Annabella, adultery, must possess sensual magnetism as well as good looks. Few people, today or in the nineteenth century, would dispute that both qualities can coexist with high moral standards and intellectual interests, but in Arthur Huntingdon's case they do not. A few months after their wedding, his wife calls him 'sensual', and it is not a term of approbation in the context (p. 221). They still have not been married a year when she describes him as incapable of engaging in any occupation beyond mere physical pursuits (p. 238). After two years of matrimony, she supplies the following picture of the man whose faults she was so sure she could remedy by placing her 'sense' and 'principle' at his service:

Arthur is not what is commonly called a *bad* man: he has many good qualities; but he is a man without self-restraint or lofty aspirations—a lover of pleasure, given up to animal enjoyments: he is not a bad husband, but his notions of matrimonial duties and comforts are not my notions.

(p. 256)

Long before Helen comes to deliver this sombre judgement, the true character of Arthur Huntingdon was revealed in a scene which will have struck many nineteenth-century readers as ominous indeed. The newly-weds have just walked back from Sunday service in church, and Arthur Huntingdon vents his displeasure at his bride's total concentration on her worship, to the exclusion of all else, himself as well.[11] Helen is shocked at his insistence that her 'earthly lord' should take precedence over her Maker and vigorously resists the idea. Realizing that he will not be able to persuade her to come round to his way of thinking, he takes off his hat and conducts a chilling demonstration:

> 'But look here, Helen—what can a man do with such a head as this?'
>
> The head looked right enough, but when he placed my hand on the top of it, it sunk in a bed of curls, rather alarmingly low, especially in the middle.
>
> 'You see I was not made to be a saint,' said he, laughing. 'If God meant me to be religious, why didn't He give me a proper organ of veneration?'
>
> (p. 218)

Huntingdon's remark concerning his deficient 'organ of veneration' is, of course, a reference to phrenology, as several commentators have noted in passing. However, its implications, and the portent of the entire passage, deserve more attention than they have so far received.

Helen's hand sinking 'rather alarmingly low, especially in the middle' does not only signal an undeveloped capacity for religious worship (phrenologists located the organ of veneration on the crown, as Arthur Huntingdon knew).[12] According to the man who emerged as Britain's leading exponent of phrenology in the early nineteenth century, George Combe, a skull that 'dipped' in the middle of the crown denoted a want of firmness of character, a fault which Huntingdon possesses in an extreme degree.[13] To make matters worse, Combe decreed:

> The coronal region of the brain is the seat of the moral sentiments; and its size may be estimated by the extent of elevation and expansion of the head above the organs of Causality in the forehead, and of Cautiousness in the middle of the parietal bones. When the whole region of the brain rising above these organs is shallow and narrow, the moral feelings will be weakly manifested.[14]

That Charlotte Brontë drew on the tenets of phrenology in her novels is well known.[15] It seems natural to assume that this interest extended to other members of the family, too. Charlotte, at least, seems to have read up on the subject; the comparison between the skull of a girl pupil in *The Professor* and that of the vicious Pope Alexander VI suggests as much.[16]

Nobody who had any knowledge of phrenology could fail to grasp the implications of this seemingly undramatic little scene. The notion that a low forehead signalled 'a mind in which the lower propensities are the ruling springs of action' (Combe, *Phrenology*, 1, 146) would be familiar even to those who had not actually studied the new 'science'. It is significant that Gilbert Markham, contem-

plating a portrait of Arthur Huntingdon without knowing who the man was or anything about him, immediately noticed the 'lurking drollery' of the blue eyes and saw that 'the bright chestnut hair [. . .] trespassed too much upon the forehead, and seemed to intimate that the owner thereof was prouder of his beauty than his intellect—as perhaps, he had reason to be;—and yet he looked no fool' (p. 71).[17] When Helen discovers what her husband's shock of hair has hidden, she—who had once innocently boasted to her aunt of being 'an excellent physiognomist' (p. 154)—must have been dismayed (as the word 'alarmingly' implies). Even so, she is not lost for an answer to Arthur's question, 'If God meant me to be religious, why didn't He give me a proper organ of veneration?'

> 'You are like the servant,' I replied, 'who instead of employing his one talent in his master's service, restored it to him unimproved. [. . .] Of him, to whom less is given, less will be required; but our utmost exertions are required of us all. You are not without the capacity of veneration, and faith and hope, and conscience and reason, and every other requisite to a Christian's character, if you choose to employ them; but all our talents increase in the using, and every faculty, both good and bad, strengthens by exercise; therefore, if you choose to use the bad—or those which tend to evil till they become your masters—and neglect the good till they dwindle away, you have only yourself to blame.'

This answer, strange as it may sound from a teenage bride, contains a message with important bearings on the issue of Arthur Huntingdon's ultimate fate (discussed below). Helen does not for one moment dispute her husband's affirmation that his disposition is not that of a devout Christian; she has always been aware that he is 'neither a sage nor a saint' (p. 154). All that matters, in her view, is that Arthur should serve God to the best of his ability, and she makes it perfectly plain that he must *choose* to do so.

Shortly before Anne Brontë wrote this passage, a book had been published whose express purpose was to reconcile the tenets of phrenology with the 'Universalist' notion that all human beings may be saved, regardless of their individual predispositions. In her *Phrenology Considered in a Religious Light,* Mrs John Pugh maintains that while people with the 'right' constitution may be more naturally apt to become good Christians, those less well endowed are certainly not excluded from salvation (pp. 79-84).[18] Helen's argument that 'of him, to whom less is given, less will be required' is paralleled in Mrs Pugh's book, which distinguishes between 'natural inability' (a blind man, for instance, cannot be expected to see) and 'moral inability', 'that which a man would not do if he could' (pp. 89-98). An even more striking resemblance to the *Wildfell Hall* locus is found in a passage where Mrs Pugh quotes Luke 14. 48: 'Where much is given, much shall be required' (pp. 166-67). Drawing on George Combe's brother Andrew's *Physiology,* Mrs Pugh also emphasizes that moral and religious feelings which we 'wish to strengthen [. . .] must be [. . .] exercised', words seemingly echoed by Helen ('every faculty [. . .] strengthens by exercise').

The continued discussion of the young Huntingdons contains further obvious parallels to Mrs Pugh's tract. Arthur rejects the notion of enjoyment deferred: 'I'll sit down and satisfy my cravings today, and leave to-morrow to shift for itself' (p. 219). Helen tries to persuade him that moderation will enable him to enjoy both today *and* tomorrow. When Arthur replies, 'Our friend Solomon says,—"There is nothing better for a man than to eat and to drink, and to be merry,"' his wife counters:

> 'And again [. . .] he says, "Rejoice, O young man, in thy youth, and walk in the ways of thine heart and in the sight of thine eyes; but know thou that, for all these things, God will bring thee into judgment."'

Correspondingly, Mrs Pugh's Chapter/Letter 11 on 'Liberty or Freedom' makes the point that while animal, lower propensities are not in themselves sinful, indulging in them is. Actions are not irresistible; we can choose (a word also much used in Helen's discourse) to refrain from yielding to temptation. Mrs Pugh also quotes 'Dr. Watt' as having said that 'Man is free [. . .] to keep himself sober, or to make himself drunk. In all these things he may choose or refuse what he pleases' (p. 118).[19] A few pages later, Mrs Pugh, like Helen, invokes Ecclesiastes 11.9, 'Rejoice, O young man, in thy youth' (she reproduces the entire verse).

Anne Brontë may not have read Mrs Pugh's book, though it seems likely that she did. What these similarities prove beyond doubt, however, is that the subject of a human being's congenital constitution as related to his capacity to work out his salvation was one that engaged the minds of Christians at the time when *Wildfell Hall* was written. Obviously, too, Helen Huntingdon's views on that subject were not unorthodox in the sense that they could not be voiced by a Christian woman to whom the hope of eternal bliss was the most fundamental concern of her earthly existence.

That circumstance lends another important dimension to the scene between Helen and Arthur on their way home from morning service in Chapter 23 of *Wildfell Hall*. Arthur Huntingdon, 'no fool', though not an intelligent man, realizes that he is powerless to control, or even touch, the core of his young wife's nature and personality. Commentators on the relationship between man and woman as outlined by Anne Brontë, especially as regards the former's tyranny, have focused on material issues, and they are certainly important; but Huntingdon's failure to subjugate his wife completely is arguably an even more vital concern in *Wildfell Hall*. It has been pointed out that his ruin is hastened by his union with Helen, and it is surely true.[20] However, the factor that accelerates his downfall is not any lack of devotion, support, or dedication to his welfare on her part (she evinces them all) but the inviolability of her spirit. Try as he might, and he adopts all the means at his disposal, he never gains total dominance over the girl he surely married for love. If he had, or could have deluded himself that he had, the restlessness that drives him to drink and dissipation might never have grown so strong.

He might perhaps have ended up like Helen's uncle ('a worthless old fellow enough, in himself, I dare say'),[21] a gout-ridden, essentially superficial, but jovial country gentleman. Helen's refusal to grant her husband his conjugal rights has often been commented on, and such a step is indeed remarkable in an early Victorian novel. Still, her locking her door at one point during their first quarrel is a transient gesture and, as she announces, more a token of displeasure than anything else. (Her qualifying statement is as tactless as it is realistic: 'I don't want to see your face or hear your voice again till morning' (p. 223).) When she decrees that they will 'henceforth [be] husband and wife only in the name' (p. 315)—and she makes her point very explicitly—Arthur Huntingdon is involved in a passionate affair with Annabella Lowborough. His surly reply, a repeated 'Very good', expresses neither surprise nor outrage. The possession of her body is of no great interest to him at this point; what irks him from first to last is his inability to take possession of her soul.

The pattern of the Huntingdon marriage establishes itself at an early stage: the husband takes himself off to London, to his friends, or to the Continent for months at a time, only returning when ill health forces him to discontinue his excesses and he needs his wife's nursing. The only time when he enjoys staying at home is when his boon companions come for prolonged visits. At these times, he can indulge in his favourite pastime without having to go away, Helen's humiliation and anguish adding to his pleasure.

Gradually, Arthur Huntingdon acquires downright fiendish traits, and his actively corrupting influence becomes more and more accentuated. There is a marked difference, too, between the roisterer who boasts of not being 'a tippler' (p. 207), for thoroughly ignoble if convincing-sounding reasons, and the nervous wreck of a man who swears at luckless servants and deliberately inflicts pain on his dog: archetypal examples of ungentlemanly behaviour. Finally, towards the end of the novel, he loses all capacity to enjoy himself and deprave others.

In the early and mid-nineteenth century, writers of treatises on alcohol and alcohol abuse agreed that drinking affected the imbiber's mind and temper, destroying moral principles and intellectual faculties by degrees. The progress of Arthur Huntingdon, who did not have much in the way of either to start with, conforms to the patterns they drew up in every particular.[22] Huntingdon's last illness also illustrates their conviction that a drunkard may succumb to disorders which a non-alcoholic might have shaken off. For example, one of them pointed out:

> Intoxicating drinks have the property of producing, in a certain degree, a state of *morbid predisposition*; which places the system in a state of liability to disease, from very slight causes; besides the same causes, operate powerfully, in resisting the ordinary effect of remedies, which under more favourable circumstances, would be sure to effect a cure.[23]

This is exactly what happens in Huntingdon's case. His original injury would not have been serious in a 'man of temperate habits', according to his physician (p. 428), and his relapse is entirely due to his having poured a great quantity of strong wine down his throat in a fit of exasperation at Helen's attempts to limit his intake of alcohol (p. 445). As anyone with experience of looking after alcoholics could have told her, he was bound to discover that she had 'mingled his wine with water'; and his reaction ('To be treated like a baby or a fool [is] enough to put any man past his patience') is only what one might expect.

The result of Huntingdon's defiant gesture is 'internal inflammation', followed by 'mortification' (gangrene), two pathological states associated with alcohol not only in contemporary works on drinking but also in the medical bible of Haworth Parsonage, Graham's *Modern Domestic Medicine*. This manual would have informed Anne Brontë that 'when mortification is the consequence of inflammation, there is excessive, acute, and constant pain; great anxiety; often delirium, followed by a sudden cessation of every inflammatory symptom' (p. 422). What the wretched Arthur Huntingdon interprets as the passing of the 'crisis'—a 'sudden cessation of pain' (*Wildfell Hall*, p. 449)—is precisely this 'cessation of every inflammatory symptom'. In cases like his ('those who have lived luxuriously' (Graham, p. 424)) the outcome would be likely to be fatal.

The wreck of Arthur Huntingdon's body may hence be termed a textbook case. What of his soul, then, for which he feared so desperately at the end?

To an age as intensely concerned with eschatology as the Victorian, no query was more pressing than 'Who shall be saved?'. The Brontë family were not alone in studying, discussing, and rejecting various theories of salvation and damnation expressed by Presbyterians, Nonconformists, and Catholics, as well as by Anglican divines.[24] The orthodox position, articulated by such churchmen as Isaac Watts, John Buckworth, and G. W. Woodhouse, all thoroughly familiar to the Brontës, was clear: the wicked were destined for everlasting torment in Hell.[25]

On two occasions, Helen expresses the belief that there is no such thing as ultimate damnation, and that a period in purgatorial flames will purify the sinner's soul, fitting him for salvation at last. As Inga-Stina Ewbank observes,[26] 'the wheel [comes] full circle' when the newly-widowed Helen resorts to the same 'blessed confidence' (p. 452) that the eighteen-year-old enthusiast had expressed to her disapproving aunt: the purging fires will retain the impure soul only until it has 'paid the uttermost farthing' (p. 191).

Young Helen's idea that the only major difficulty consists in the meaning of the Greek word that is translated as 'eternal' shows how aware Anne Brontë was of the contemporary eschatological debate. The interpretation of αἰώνιος was at the heart of it, and better classical scholars than Helen ('I don't know the Greek' (p. 192)) had resisted the translation 'everlasting'.[27]

Those who argued that the doctrine of eternal perdition was untrue (among them F. D. Maurice, who has been regarded as an influence on Emily Brontë)[28] had a better stay

and prop than merely uncertainty about the meaning of a Greek word. As Thomas Erskine of Linlathen said, 'Christ is laid down at every door'; what he meant was that the Saviour died for all men.[29] A similar conviction was expressed by the Scots minister John McLeod Campbell, who was the focus of a much-publicized dispute in consequence of having maintained that Christ atoned for the sins of the *whole* world.[30] The Campbell case was attended by numerous *pro* and *contra* declarations, among them the supportive outburst of one Rev. Robert Story: 'Now, no truth is more clearly revealed in Scripture, than that God does not hate any of the sons of men [. . .] to ATTRIBUTE such a sentiment to God is BLASPHEMY'.[31] Anne Brontë may never have heard of the Campbell row, and never have read a word of Erskine or Maurice; there are no striking resemblances, as there were in the case of Mrs Pugh's book. Undoubtedly, however, the current theological debate was thoroughly familiar to her. She polemized against the Calvinist doctrine of predestination in her poem 'A Word to the Calvinists', whose last five stanzas articulate a strong belief (identical with that of Helen Huntingdon) in the ultimate redemption of all through Christ;[32] on some occasions, she was in contact with clergymen outside the Anglican church who encouraged such beliefs;[33] she belonged to a family whose members cared intensely about religious issues and were used to discussing and reading about them from a variety of standpoints; she worked as a governess for five years in the home of a clergyman whose library contained large quantities of devotional literature.

One may wonder why Helen does not soothe her suffering husband by telling him at length about her 'blessed confidence'. Only once does she utter something of the kind: when Huntingdon imagines her as an 'immaculate angel' untouched by the spectacle of him 'howling in hellfire', she answers:

> 'If so, it will be because of the great gulf over which I cannot pass; and if I *could* look complacently on in such a case, it would be only from the assurance that you were being purified from your sins, and fitted to enjoy the happiness I felt.'
>
> (p. 446)

The repeated 'ifs', the subjunctive mood, and the swift move to the question 'But are you *determined* [. . .] that I shall not meet you in heaven?' combine to make this conditional comfort, and it does not afford the dying man any consolation. Is Helen being deliberately cruel, then, in withholding her belief in universal pardon from him at a point where it might set his terrified mind at rest? On the contrary, she is, as always, true to her principles. As a girl, explaining her contention to her aunt, she had said:

> 'And as for the danger of the belief, I would not publish it abroad, if I thought any poor wretch would be likely to presume upon it to his own destruction, but it is a glorious thought to cherish in one's own heart.'
>
> (p. 192)

After Huntingdon's death, she writes to her brother:

'How could I endure to think that that poor trembling soul was hurried away to everlasting torment? it would drive me mad! But thank God I have hope—not only from a vague dependence on the possibility that penitence and pardon might have reached him at the last, but from the blessed confidence that, through whatever purging fires the erring spirit may be doomed to pass—whatever fate awaits it, still, it is not lost, and God, who hateth nothing that He hath made, *will* bless it in the end!'

(p. 452)

On both occasions, Helen makes it clear that her belief is a source of *personal* comfort to her. Throughout those hours and days of horror at her husband's deathbed, she keeps urging him to repent and pray. Here, she acts in perfect conformity with the teachings of the Anglican Church to which she belongs. Reassuring him by seeming to promise him eventual bliss in any case (not that he seems to hanker after it) would indeed have rendered him 'likely to presume upon it to his own destruction'. To the very end, she must do her utmost to persuade him actively to seek God's help and forgiveness. Consequently, the notion of universal salvation as it is voiced in *Wildfell Hall* is a 'glorious thought' rather than a doctrine. Like her heroine, Anne Brontë made sure no 'poor wretch' is diverted from the orthodox teachings of the Church in consequence of the 'hope long nursed by [her]' ('A Word to the Calvinists', l. 30).

Vanity induced the inexperienced Helen to marry a man in the belief that she could change and save him, and she pays dearly for her error. In the course of her marriage her pride suffers one mortification after another, its final collapse occurring when she tries to restrain Huntingdon from drinking too much by reminding him that the effects would lessen his appeal to his mistress (pp. 330-31).

Marriage to Arthur Huntingdon threatens to break Helen's spirit and undermine her integrity, but in the end it does neither. She retains her spiritual strength without the vanity that might make her liable to misuse it. Confronted by that strength, Arthur Huntingdon changes in the opposite direction to the one fondly expected by the young Helen. The irresponsible but not unlovable scamp becomes an agent of evil. Ultimately, though, he proves an ineffectual one: he does not manage to destroy his son; also, Lowborough and Hattersley reform independently of him and he is powerless to drag them down with him.

In one sense at least, the villain of *Wildfell Hall* resembles Heathcliff: once he has burnt himself out, his influence vanishes. His actions crowded out everything else from the centre of the stage while he lived, but they leave no lasting effects. In Emily Brontë's novel, the scions of the old families, their blood unmixed with Heathcliff's, unite Wuthering Heights and Thrushcross Grange; in Anne's, Grass-dale Manor is in due course taken over by the children of two *roués*, one saved and one perished, and the sins of their fathers do not detract from their married happiness. Helen goes on to marry a man who has to suffer

the loss of *his* vanity first, a man who loves and benefits from her spiritual force rather than wishing to conquer it—but that is a different story.

In her preface to the second edition of *Wildfell Hall*, Anne Brontë pleaded unconditional allegiance to 'the truth', which 'conveys its own moral' (p. 29). She also expressed her desire to warn rash youths and prevent thoughtless girls from misguided actions. This attitude on her part does not mean that she was incapable of, and uninterested in, combining moral and artistic integrity. Both are guided and supported by a passion for truth, in her case as in that of any serious artist. Regardless of changing fashions in the arts, insincerity was and is always the most damning criticism that a work of art can suffer.

It is natural that biographical factors should feature in analyses of the works of the Brontës, but in respect of *Wildfell Hall* such considerations have not always been applied with due circumspection. The tragic story of Branwell Brontë is a case in point. Arthur Huntingdon's deathbed cannot very well be patterned on his, as he was still alive when the novel was written,[34] nor did his family foresee his imminent demise even when Anne wrote the preface to the second edition. Another example of misguided biographical speculation is the alleged liaison between Branwell and his employer's wife, Mrs Robinson, often commented on in connection with the affair of Arthur Huntingdon and Lady Lowborough. Post-1950s research has suggested that the former entanglement might have been a self-protective fiction on Branwell's part.[35]

Anne Brontë was clearly capable of fusing her own experiences with her comprehensive reading and profound contemplation of issues that engaged many educated, open-minded early Victorians. She '[wanted] noe Judgment, nor [she] spare[d] noe paines'; and her marvellous gift for story-telling,[36] her vigorous handling of language and style, her never-slackening concentration, and her quiet humour ensure that the reader keeps turning the pages: the first obligation of any novelist.

Notes

1. See, for instance, Winifred Gérin's introduction to G. D. Hargreaves's edition of *The Tenant of Wildfell Hall* (Harmondsworth: Penguin, 1979), p. 7, and Gérin's *Branwell Brontë* (London: Nelson, 1961), p. 317. All references to the novel in this article are to Hargreaves's edition.

2. See N. M. Jacobs, 'Gender and Layered Narrative in *Wuthering Heights* and *The Tenant of Wildfell Hall*', *Journal of Narrative Technique*, 16.3 (Fall 1986), 204-19, and Jan B. Gordon, 'Gossip, Diary, Letter, Text: Anne Brontë's Narrative *Tenant* and the Problematic of the Gothic Sequel', *ELH*, 5 (1984), 719-45. (The usefulness of the latter article, which makes some perceptive statements on the nature of gossip, is severely marred by wearisome jargon and a number of inaccuracies. Thus, for instance, the heroine's

married name is consistently misspelt; the overbearing and portentous vicar is referred to as 'the curate, Millward'; Gordon has not seen that Gilbert Markham writes more than one letter to Halford; and the person who blushes in church on page 41 (Penguin edition) is not Gilbert but Eliza Millward.)

3. A. Craig Bell, 'Anne Brontë: A Re-Appraisal', *Quarterly Review,* 304 (1966), 315-21, is a gallant exception to the somewhat patronizing attitude usually evinced towards the novelist Anne Brontë. See also Elizabeth Langland's recent study, *Anne Brontë: The Other One* (London: Macmillan, 1989).

4. *The Brontë Novels* (London: Methuen, 1968), p. 230, and Juliet McMaster, "Imbecile Laughter' and 'Desperate Earnest' in *The Tenant of Wildfell Hall'*, *Modern Language Quarterly,* 43.4 (December 1982), 352-68.

5. Winifred Gérin decisively refuted the traditional idea that the portrayal of Huntingdon owes a good deal to Branwell Brontë; see her *Anne Brontë* (London: Nelson, 1959), pp. 255-57. She was followed by Craig Bell, who concluded that a weak character was the only point the two men had in common (p. 318). (One purely physical resemblance might be noted, though: like Branwell Brontë, Arthur Huntingdon had masses of red hair.)

6. Fifth edn (Glasgow, 1832), pp. 26-27, 51-52.

7. See, for instance, Wade Hustwick, 'Branwell Brontë and Freemasonry: What the Records of his Lodge Reveal', *Brontë Society Transactions,* 13 (1956), 19-23 (p. 21), and Lilian Lewis Shiman, *Crusade against Drink in Victorian England* (London: Macmillan, 1988), p. 48.

8. See *Wildfell Hall*, pp. 53-54, 63-65. The notion that it might be unhealthy to *abstain* from alcohol sounds odd to our ears today, but in the early decades of the nineteenth century teetotalism was widely felt to be positively dangerous. To many, 'temperance' simply meant drinking in moderation, and even among the men of the Temperance Movement there were many who held that the only danger came from ardent spirits (see the distinction between 'temperance' and 'abstinence' in *Wildfell Hall* (p. 64)). An excellent book on the subject of temperance in nineteenth-century England is Brian Harrison's *Drink and the Victorians: The Temperance Question in England 1815-1872* (London: Faber, 1971). Its chapter on the 1820s has been especially useful to me.

9. See Macnish, pp. 212-14, and Ralph Barnes Grindrod, *Bacchus: An Essay on the Nature, Causes, Effects, and Cure, of Intemperance* (London: J. Pasco, 1839), p. 387.

10. *Anne Brontë: A New Critical Assessment* (London: Vision Press; Totowa, NJ: Barnes & Noble, 1983), pp. 86-87. Perhaps the most 'erotically charged' scene in *Wildfell Hall* is the remarkable chess game played by Helen and Walter Hargrave; see pp. 309-11.

11. *Wildfell Hall* is full of parallels that also embody contrasts. One of them is the behaviour in church of Arthur Huntingdon and Gilbert Markham respectively. The former wants to play the fool during the service, preferably engaging Helen in his irreverent conduct; the latter stares at her in church the first time he sees her and deliberately does not look away when her eyes happen to meet his. Besides, he is vain enough to be gratified at a later date when she admits to having noticed him at the time. Gilbert, however, has the decency to be ashamed of his 'very improper thoughts' and blameworthy behaviour (p. 41).

12. Replicas of nineteenth-century phrenological model skulls can still be bought in Britain, or could until recently; the one in my home shows the organ of veneration on the crown, slightly to the left-hand side. See also the illustration in Roger Cooter, *The Cultural Meaning of Popular Science: Phrenology and the Organization of Consent in Nineteenth-Century Britain* (Cambridge: Cambridge University Press, 1984), p. 30.

13. See Combe's *The Constitution of Man,* 4th edn (Edinburgh, 1836), p. 51.

14. *A System of Phrenology,* 5th edn, 2 vols (Edinburgh: MacLachlan, Stewart, 1843), 1, 141.

15. Two scholarly articles on the subject have been published, Wilfred M. Senseman's 'Charlotte Brontë's Use of Physiognomy and Phrenology', *Brontë Society Transactions,* 12 (1967), 286-89, a recapitulation and part-reproduction of an article in *Papers of the Michigan Academy of Science, Arts, and Letters,* 38 (1953), and Ian Jack, 'Physiognomy, Phrenology and Characterisation in the Novels of Charlotte Brontë', *Brontë Society Transactions,* 15 (1970), 377-91. The latter especially is a thorough and well-argued survey, but neither scholar appears to have studied early-nineteenth-century works on phrenology in any depth.

16. Alexander VI was one of the phrenology pioneer Johann Gaspar Spurzheim's most memorable examples; his skull was one whose 'sincipital (or coronal) region [was] exceedingly low, particularly at the organs of Benevolence, Veneration, and Conscientiousness'. Nobody who has seen the drawing of it in Combe, *The Constitution of Man,* p. 41, is likely to forget it.

17. In other words, he is struck by precisely those two qualities—a merry disposition and a handsome appearance—that made the artist fall in love with the object.

18. *Or, Thoughts and Readings Consequent on the Perusal of 'Combe's Constitution of Man'* (London: Ward, 1846).

19. This will probably be either Dr Robert Watt, a celebrated physician who wrote several works dealing

with various aspects of human behaviour, or (rather more likely, especially in view of other references in Mrs Pugh's book) Isaac Watts (an honorary D.D.), hymn-writer and composer of a number of religious works. The latter was well known to the Brontës from girlhood.

20. Most recently by Langland, *Anne Brontë*, p. 143.

21. Gilbert Markham's estimate (p. 457) and undoubtedly accurate; see pp. 148, 150, 153-55, 192, 275, and 399. Many contemporary works on the effects of drink mention gout as a typical drunkard's disorder, including Thomas John Graham's *Modern Domestic Medicine*, so often consulted by the Rev. Patrick Brontë (the copy in the Brontë Museum is full of notes made by him); see 2nd edn (London, 1827), p. 315.

22. See, for instance, Grindrod, pp. 134-50, and the Wesleyan minister, G. B. Macdonald, *An Apology for the Disuse of Alcoholic Drinks, In a Letter to a Friend* (London, 1841). Macdonald recapitulated the findings of the 1834 Select Commission of the House of Commons in this respect; their *Report* is stern stuff.

23. Thomas Beaumont, Surgeon, *An Essay on the Nature and Properties of Alcoholic Drinks* (London: Simpkin, Marshall, 1838), p. 28.

24. Valuable insights in these matters are supplied by Geoffrey Rowell, *Hell and the Victorians: A Study of Nineteenth-Century Theological Controversies Concerning Eternal Punishment and the Future Life* (Oxford: Clarendon Press, 1974). Tom Winnifrith devotes an informative chapter to the Brontës and their views on 'Heaven and Hell' in *The Brontës and Their Background: Romance and Reality* (London: Macmillan, 1973).

25. Books by all three belonged to the Brontës' own 'library' (see, for instance, J. Alex Symington, *Catalogue of the Museum and Library of the Brontës Society* (Haworth: [n. pub.], 1927)). Incidentally, the Rev. Patrick Brontë had been Mr Buckworth's curate (see, for example, Annette B. Hopkins, *The Father of the Brontës* (Baltimore, MD: Johns Hopkins University Press, 1958), pp. 28-30).

26. In *Their Proper Sphere: A Study of the Brontë Sisters as Early-Victorian Female Novelists* (Gothenburg: Kvinnohistoriskt Arkiv, 4; London: Edward Arnold, 1966), p. 78. Ewbank's discussion of the 'tightly-woven tissue of religious references' (*Their Proper Sphere*, pp. 75-79), is both careful and illuminating.

27. See, for instance, Rowell, *Hell and the Victorians*, pp. 44, 73, 93, and 110.

28. See Eanne Oram, 'Emily and F. D. Maurice: Some Parallels of Thought', *Brontë Society Transactions*, 13 (1957), 131-40. (Winnifrith has criticized Oram's argumentation in vigorous terms; see *The Brontës and Their Background*, p. 29.)

29. See, for example, John Tulloch, *Movements of Religious Thought in Britain during the Nineteenth Century* (London: Longman, 1885), p. 142.

30. The controversy can be studied in *The Whole Proceedings before the Presbytery of Dumbarton, and Synod of Glasgow and Ayr, in the Case of the Rev. John McLeod Campbell* (Greenock: Lusk, 1831); the volume was also published in Edinburgh, London, and Dublin. Among the biblical instances quoted in support of his views, Campbell, like Helen in *Wildfell Hall,* p. 191, referred to Hebrews 2. 9.

31. *The Whole Proceedings,* p. 95. See *Wildfell Hall*, p. 452: 'God, who hateth nothing that He hath made, *will* bless it in the end!'

32. The relevance of this poem to *Wildfell Hall* has been noted by several scholars, among them Ewbank (*Their Proper Sphere,* pp. 77-78) and Edward Chitham in his edition of *The Poems of Anne Brontë: A New Text and Commentary* (London: Macmillan, 1979), p. 176.

33. Such as the Moravian Bishop James La Trobe and, shortly before her death, the Universalist Dr J. H. Thom; see Gérin, *Anne Brontë,* pp. 99-101, and Edward Chitham, *A Life of Anne Brontë* (Oxford: Blackwell, 1991), pp. 54-55, 175.

34. See Gérin's introduction to *The Tenant of Wildfell Hall:* 'It was not Branwell's exact story that she could write, but she could and did depict from first-hand knowledge the awful sufferings of a drunkard's death' (p. 12).

35. See Daphne du Maurier, *The Infernal World of Branwell Brontë* (London: Gollancz, 1960), Chapters 13-16. Du Maurier's scepticism in the face of the Mrs Robinson tale has been echoed by other biographers such as Maureen Peters, *An Enigma of Brontës* (New York: St Martin's Press, 1974), pp. 110-12; see also Joan Rees, *Profligate Son: Branwell Brontë and His Sisters* (London: Hale, 1986), pp. 115-36. (Chitham, however, has reconsidered the evidence presented by du Maurier and favours the traditional notion of an emotional entanglement between Branwell and his employer's wife; see *A Life of Anne Brontë,* pp. 115, 120-22, 137-38).

36. Rightly stressed by Gérin in her introduction to the Penguin edition; see p. 18.

Elizabeth Signorotti (essay date 1995)

SOURCE: "'A Frame Perfect and Glorious': Narrative Structure in Anne Brontë's *The Tenant of Wildfell Hall*," in *Victorian Newsletter*, Vol. 87, Spring, 1995, pp. 20-25.

[*In the following essay, Signorotti details Brontë's analysis of Victorian gender roles in* The Tenant of Wildfell Hall, *beginning with Gilbert's narrative "appropriation" of Helen's story and concluding with the feasibility of their marriage.*]

Early criticism of Anne Brontë's *The Tenant of Wildfell Hall* focused as much, if not more, on the mysterious identity of the author Acton Bell, as on the text itself. Several contemporary critics argued that Acton Bell was simply another *nom de plume* for the more popular Currer Bell, while others speculated solely on the gender of *The Tenant*'s author. In a particularly acerbic review in *Sharpe's London Magazine,* the anonymous reviewer decided that the "bold coarseness" and "reckless freedom of language" clearly indicated that a man took part in the writing. On the other hand, the reviewer asserted, only a woman's mind could invent such "contemptibly weak, at once disgusting and ridiculous" male characters, or the "thousand trifles" included in the text. The reviewer finally concluded that a woman, "assisted by her husband, or some other male friend," produced the book.[1] Commentary on the text itself was about as favorable as that on the author. *Sharpe's* reviewer wrote that *The Tenant of Wildfell Hall* was unfit for mention in the magazine. Nonetheless, it had to be mentioned by way of warning to readers at large, "especially . . . lady-readers, against being induced to peruse it." The story itself was described as "revolting," "coarse," and "disgusting," and showed a "perverted taste and an absence of mental refinement . . . together with a total ignorance of the usages of good society." Decidedly, Anne Brontë's second novel was not well received.

Now that the mystery of identity and gender has been solved, critics are more apt to discuss aspects of the novel than of the novelist. Although Anne Brontë's works continue to be overshadowed by the more popular works of her sisters Charlotte and Emily, recent critics have attempted to salvage *The Tenant of Wildfell Hall* through serious, thoughtful explication. Current approaches to the novel are varied, but most prevalent is the discussion of narrative technique—especially the framing of Helen Huntingdon's diary within Gilbert Markham's narrative—and its implications for the novel as a whole.

In their recent discussions of the significance of Markham's enclosing Helen's diary within his own narrative framework, Juliet McMaster, N. M. Jacobs, and Jan B. Gordon have all reached similar conclusions.[2] Although each approaches Markham's narrative enclosure from a different perspective, all three agree that his incorporation of Helen's diary reflects an equal shouldering of Helen's burdens, an equality of consciousness, and a "possibility of accommodation and reconciliation" that contrasts with Helen's first failed marriage to Arthur Huntingdon (McMaster 368). In short, each argues that Markham's narrative enclosure legitimizes Helen, redeems her, and places her on equal footing with him in their subsequent marriage. While this is a possible interpretation of Markham's incorporation of Helen's narrative, one cannot ignore the evidence within the text that points to an opposite conclusion: Markham's appropriation and editing of Helen's history reflects an attempt to contain and control her. In a society where possession of knowledge equals power, Markham's revealing epistle to Halford further reflects the means by which Victorian men maintained power over women.

Markham begins his letter to Halford by reminding him of their last visit together. At that time, Halford had shared with Markham an "interesting account of the most remarkable occurrences of [his] early life." Halford requested the "smallest return" of confidence from Markham, and now, some time later, Markham is willing to oblige. "It is a soaking and rainy day," he writes, "the family are absent on a visit, I am alone in my library, and have been looking over certain musty old letters and papers, and musing on past times; so that I am now in a very proper frame of mind for amusing you with an old-world story" (34). Markham's letter, then, becomes repayment of a debt owed to Halford. As an "unparalleled proof of friendly confidence," his private exchange of knowledge about his wife provides bargaining power with Halford and represents the basis of their male friendship. Having withdrawn his "well-roasted feet from the hobs," he begins to write Halford a story from *his* past, using as a guide a "certain faded old journal of [his]" (34). Ironically, 250 pages of *his* story happen to be copied from his wife's diary, a diary in which his name is never mentioned. This might explain why he has waited until "the family are absent" to "amuse" his old friend, or, as Markham terms him, the "old boy."

While professing to give a "full and faithful account" (35) of the circumstances under which he first met the mysterious, and presumably widowed, tenant of Wildfell Hall, Markham unwittingly reveals himself as a selfish, manipulative boy who hungers for conquest. In his narrative, which comprised the first hundred pages of the text, he recounts his unfavorable first impressions of Helen Huntingdon. While gazing on her during a church service, he confesses that her hollow cheeks and thin, firmly compressed lips "betokened . . . no very soft or amiable temper" and that he would rather admire her from afar than to "be partner of her home" (41). Helen's appearance and temperament defy the idealized image of the soft and amiable Victorian woman epitomized by Eliza Millward in the novel. When Helen returns Markham's stare with an "indefinable expression of quiet scorn," he characteristically remarks, "She thinks me an impudent puppy. . . . Humph!—she shall change her mind before long, if I think it worthwhile" (41). Helen's scornful, bold, and indifferent attitude sparks Markham's interest. She becomes a challenge to him and a threat to his masculine dominance over more amiable, "kitten-like" women such as Eliza Millward (42). In his eyes Helen becomes something to be tamed.

Before long, Markham does think it worthwhile to change Helen's mind about him. Having failed in several attempts to secure her attention all to himself, he uses her interest in literature to begin what Gordon terms their "book-loan agreement" (726). Markham's ingratiating loan initiates the exchange of books as the basis for his and Helen's growing friendship. After several book exchanges, Markham "experiments" (92) by making an outright gift of Sir Walter Scott's *Marmion,* asserting his right to provide for Helen and attempting to place himself in a dominant position over her. Helen, however, refuses to accept the book unless she pays him for it, thereby reasserting her equality with him.

Markham's ongoing "experiments" serve to establish himself, however, as Helen's trustworthy friend, a position he plans to use later to his advantage. "Let me first establish my position as a friend [he muses],—the patron and playfellow of her son, the sober, solid, plain-dealing friend of herself, and then, when I have made myself fairly necessary to her comfort and enjoyment in life (as I believe I can), we'll see what next may be effected" (93). When he and Helen are on more friendly terms, he duplicitously assures her that he "shall build no hopes upon" their friendship growing into anything more intimate, even though he admits to Halford on the bottom of the same page his "conflicting hopes and fears" (95). Essentially, Markham hopes that establishing himself as Helen's "patron" and becoming "necessary to her comfort" will place him in a position to control and enable him to disarm and conquer her. Markham continues with his "experiments" until finally he thinks his "hour of victory was come" (110). To his dismay, his excitement is quelled during an incident when Helen snatches her hand from his, thus restoring to her control over their relationship. Clearly, Markham (which sounds suspiciously like marksman) is interested only in the conquest, the hunting down, of Helen Huntingdon. Through tactics such as these, he subversively manipulates Helen's emotions and at certain junctures in their friendship gains power over her. Ultimately, though, in their mutual struggle for power Helen will remain the dominant partner.

As Helen's and Markham's friendship grows, so does the community gossip about the dubious circumstances and past of the tenant of Wildfell Hall. Throughout Helen's residence at Wildfell Hall, Markham ignores and denies the possibility of any truth in community speculation. However, when he spies in Helen's library a book with Frederick Lawrence's name inscribed on the flyleaf, he immediately suspects that Frederick is her lover, as the gossip implies. For Markham, Helen's possession of the book from another man violates the conditions of their book-exchange agreement, and he concludes that she has been encouraging the advances of another book giver and patron. He confronts her with this breach of trust, and thinks to himself as he eyes her angrily, "I can crush that bold spirit. . . . But while I secretly exulted in my power, I felt disposed to dally with my victim like a cat" (143). Neither the reader nor Markham knows at this point that Helen remains married to Arthur Huntingdon or that Frederick Lawrence is her brother, not her lover. What is clear, however, is the sadistically predatory nature of Markham's desire to conquer and control Helen.

In an attempt to explain her confusing situation, Helen, in accordance with their book-exchange agreement, tears out the final pages of her diary and "thrusts" (146) it into Markham's hands.[3] She tells him, "Bring it back when you have read it; and don't breathe a word of what it tells you to any living being—I trust your honour" (146). Markham now has his "prize" (147)—knowledge about Helen's secret past—one, he assumes, that empowers him to control her. At his fingertips he now possesses information about

Helen that serves as a bargaining tool to maintain her "friendship" and to repay his debt to Halford. Before Markham begins transcribing Helen's diary, he tells Halford "I know you would not be satisfied with an abbreviation of its contents, and you shall have the whole, save, perhaps a few passages here and there" (147). Evidently, he delivers his own edited version of Helen's life—minus the final pages that she has withheld—and we are reminded of his falsely promising a "full and faithful account" at the beginning of his letter. Markham is as little interested in remaining faithful to Helen's diary as he is in remaining faithful to her as a friend. His interest in her and her diary stems less from his affection for her than from his predatory desire to master and manipulate her-story at any cost.

Positioned immediately before Helen's diary, Markham's opening narrative serves in part to provide a background and a framework to Helen's text. But it does more than that. When Markham's narrative is interrupted by Helen's lengthy account of her first marriage, the reader is forced to draw comparisons between important aspects of the two narratives, particularly between the two courtships of Helen that occur in each narrative. Helen's diary recounts specific examples of Arthur Huntingdon's behavior that compare almost identically with examples of Markham's behavior. And Markham's account—albeit unwittingly—further reveals the close parallels between himself and the men described in Helen's story, particularly between himself and Arthur.

Both Arthur and Markham first meet Helen while on hunting expeditions. Again, this suggests the hunting down of Helen—and of women in general, Brontë implies—by typical Victorian men attempting to master women as they master birds in the bush. As Helen recounts the development of her relationship with Arthur, we notice further parallels between him and Markham. Markham's stealing a kiss from Eliza Millward mirrors Arthur's stealing a kiss from Helen. Similarly, during his perusal of Helen's sketches, Arthur turns one over and discovers that Helen has attempted to draw his portrait. This gives him a certain power over her because her private affection for him becomes public: he knows her feelings for him (while his own remain private) and can use them to his advantage. In a parallel scene, on his first visit to Helen's studio Markham impudently moves a painting leaning in a corner against the wall, discovers beneath it another painting facing the wall, turns the latter over, and finds a portrait of Arthur Huntingdon. Helen snatches the painting from Markham, returns it to its "dark corner," and harshly scolds him for his trespass. Helen reacts similarly to Arthur's trespass by snatching the sketch, tearing it, and throwing it in the fire. When Helen writes of Arthur's passionate outbursts, during which he violently attacks their dog, we are further reminded of Markham's brutal attack on Helen's brother, Frederick. Most important, just as Helen learns that she cannot trust Arthur's word, we learn that she cannot trust Markham's. He patently ignores her directions to keep her diary a private affair. She says, "don't breathe a word of what it tells you to any living being—I trust your honour'" (146), and again in a letter to Frederick she writes, "he [Markham] will know that I should wish but little to be said on the subject" (437). These incidents emphasize the ties between Markham and Huntingdon, which are further emphasized by Markham's "old boy" ties to Halford and the male complicity they represent.

Through Helen's interpolated diary, she chronicles in minute detail the raucous, drunken behavior of Arthur and his "boon companions" and the traits that tie them together. Arthur and his friends are portrayed as a wild, roving gang—a club of good old boys—who brag about preying on weaker animals (birds), weaker men (Lord Lowborough), and in particular the "weaker sex." They are a drinking, swearing, violent group whose lives revolve around destroying themselves (by drinking and whoring), each other (by encouraging adultery and other forms of vice), and the women in their lives (by abusing them emotionally). All of this falls under the guise of "sowing wild oats." Mr. Hattersley best sums up their code of conduct when he tells Lord Lowborough, who has just discovered that his wife and Huntingdon have been having an affair for over two years, "'I know what it is you want, to make matters straight: it's just to exchange a shot with him, and then you'll feel yourself all right again'" (350). But a shoot-out is not what Lowborough wants, which, in their eyes, makes him less a "man" than the other boon companions. He feels betrayed and injured, not only by Huntingdon's and Annabella's affair, but also by the fact that the old boy network conspired against him. He has been shot *at* and visibly hit. Everyone in the "club" except Lowborough knew about and helped to conceal the affair from him. Through collusion, Arthur and his gang kept Lowborough a trusting, cuckolded fool. Their secret knowledge about him served as a source of power over him. This group conspiracy epitomizes what Helen—who, like all the women in her society, lives in relative isolation compared to the group orientation of men—must confront when dealing with her husband.

In *The Tenant of Wildfell Hall* women are perceived as threats to male bonding activities—such as romps among the birds, bouts with the bottle, and romps with other women—and the old boys deal with that threat by making women the objects of their laughter. The old boy network operating in *The Tenant of Wildfell Hall* gains ammunition to control women by violating their privacy. Helen's aunt, speaking from experience, tries to warn her to "'keep guard over your eyes and ears as the inlets of your heart, and over your lips as the outlet, lest they betray you in a moment of unwariness'" (150). Helen learns this first-hand when Huntingdon repeatedly humiliates her in front of his companions by exposing private aspects of her life. In a typical assault on Helen, Huntingdon blames her for Hargraves unsavory advances toward her. Her obvious anger at the network's misinterpreting her participation in the scene prompts Hattersley's excited comment, "'She's hit!'" (365), implying that Helen is little more than an animal for their sport. By garnering knowledge about their wives, the boys can later use it (by threatening to expose them) to maintain power and control over them. Helen soon recognizes the hopelessness of her situation, and to undermine Arthur's power over her she begins to repress all emotion and to confide in only one thing—her diary. Arthur's eventual confiscation of her diary represents the climax of the power struggle between them. He "forcibly wrest[s]" her diary from her, procuring a powerful weapon against her because of the painful confessions it contains. In one act, Arthur physically and emotionally disarms his wife.

Like Arthur, Markham is a typical member in the boy's club and his participation is blatantly exposed by the narrative structure of the novel: Markham breaches his wife's trust, appropriates her history, makes light of her previous marriage, and boasts of her pain in his letter to Halford, "old boy." In his opening narrative, Markham attempts to impress upon Halford his initial power struggle with Helen and his eventual victory over her through the control he supposedly gains by marrying her. But Brontë suggests that following Arthur's death the power structure is reversed in Markham's courtship of and marriage to Helen. Markham may be disclosing to Halford his wife's intimate secrets, but this knowledge was voluntarily "thrust" into his hands by Helen (asserting *her* right to give), not "wrested" from her. In fact, Markham does not even possess Helen's whole story, for she has withheld the diary's final pages from him. Helen's voluntary surrender of the diary, its incompleteness, and the twenty-year gap in time prior to its disclosure, have a disempowering effect on Markham's appropriation of his wife's secrets and on the value of the diary. It no longer poses a threat to Helen's independence, nor can its contents any longer be used to control her. In effect, Markham is trying to pay off his debt to Halford with valueless money.

By so closely aligning Arthur Huntingdon and Gilbert Markham, Brontë shifts our focus from Markham—who, like Arthur and his boon companions, is a static character—to Helen's progress and the changing circumstances of her life. While some critics have argued that Markham matures by the end of the novel, the text itself does not sufficiently support this contention.[4] The Markham of forty-four differs very little from the Markham of twenty-four: whether a young boy or an "old boy," he still remains a boy (which—with the possible exception of Lawrence—appears to be true of all the men in the novel). What has changed during that time, however, is Helen Graham Huntingdon's attitude and behavior. Markham's letter, while attempting to do just the opposite, alerts the reader to a reversal in Helen's situation from her early days (depicted in her diary) to her present (depicted in Markham's text). Whereas she was powerless and contained in her first marriage, Markham's narrative shows that in their marriage Helen has become stronger, powerful, and uncontainable.

In her first marriage, Helen's inability to sketch or paint Arthur to her satisfaction suggests her inability to contain him. After their initial introduction, Helen begins the first of many attempts to sketch him: "there is one face I am always trying to paint or to sketch," she says, "and always without success; and that vexes me" (148). At one point she describes a "complete miniature portrait" of Arthur, which she had "sketched with such tolerable success, as to be induced to colour it with great pains and care" (176). Helen's attempts to frame and contain Arthur prove fruitless, however. Later she comments on another attempt to paint him: "how widely different had been my feelings in painting that portrait to what they now were in looking upon it! How I had studied and toiled to produce something, as I thought, worthy of the original! what mingled pleasure and dissatisfaction I had in the result of my labours!" (398). She simply cannot "capture" Arthur on her canvas just as she cannot control his debauchery. Indeed, Arthur controls Helen and finally uses his power to deprive her of her painting supplies (by which she could support herself), her valuable jewelry, and household funds. Yet, she thinks, the portrait's "frame . . . is handsome enough; it will serve for another painting" (398). For Markham's, perhaps?

Once Helen leaves Wildfell Hall, she forbids Markham's writing to her before six months elapse, placing him in a traditionally female (passive) position. Helen controls their dialogue, reversing the typical position of Victorian women.[5] Moreover, after Helen's departure Markham becomes a source of amusement for the women in Linden-Car. He nurses his emotions for Helen, mopes about town because of her absence, and finds himself the object of *women's* laughter. Humiliated, he responds to those jesting, "'You were laughing . . . and I don't like to be laughed at'" (464). Now he knows how Helen felt at the mercy of Huntingdon and his boon companions.

Helen's economic situation is also reversed after leaving Wildfell Hall. While in residence, she is literally "in ruins" (37) and supporting herself and her son by selling her paintings. Because of her ruined condition, Markham feels safe in pursuing her and potentially elevating her to his social level. By the end of the novel, however, not only her financial situation but also her marital situation are reversed. Arthur is dead and Helen is rich. In addition, Helen's uncle has recently left her a huge property settlement that increases her wealth and subverts the patriarchal tradition of passing wealth from male to male (the uncle gives only a pittance to his nephew). Markham's discovery of Helen's good fortune dismays him because, as he is only a gentleman farmer, he now "saw the folly of the hopes [he] had cherished" (482). Surprisingly, though, *she* proposes marriage to *him*. In her proposal she offers him a Christmas rose, plucked from the frigid winter air and symbolic of her ability to bloom in rough weather outside the greenhouse, a common Victorian metaphor for protected women.[6] Helen, now rich, now single, says to Markham, "'my marriage is to please myself alone'" (486). We believe her.

Markham marries up the social ladder. He marries a woman older, more experienced, and richer than he. He moves into Helen's home (a home complete with a greenhouse owned and controlled by Helen) and into Helen's

world, and in doing so he turns over the family farm to his younger brother. Markham comes to his marriage propertyless and powerless. To emphasize his dependence, Brontë goes so far as to suggest that Helen may have made legal arrangements to entail her property (471, 488). Either way, Markham's social elevation through a woman's condescension places him in an uncomfortable, traditionally female position. Elaine Showalter sums up this reversal of traditional gender roles in nineteenth-century women's novels, where men "must learn how it feels to be helpless and to be forced unwillingly into dependency. Only then can they understand that women need love but hate to be weak. . . . The 'woman's man' must find out how it feels to be a woman" (152). Markham is not forced into dependency, but we can hear his nervous uncomfortable laughter when he writes Halford, "I can afford to laugh at both Lawrence and you" (15). Maybe he can, but he also seems to be worrying about who laughs at him.

After his twenty years of silence we find Markham home alone writing his letter to Halford while Helen is away "visiting." This too reverses the pattern of Helen's previous marriage, in which she remained tethered to the home writing letters to Millicent while Arthur was out carousing. Indeed, the traditional male/female power structure has been reversed in Helen's marriage to Markham. His only means of recovering any power is to appropriate Helen's history and make it his own. In his narrative he incorporates Helen's past, edits it, calls it his own, then pays a debt with it. This attempt to frame her in his text is reminiscent of Helen's failed attempts to frame Arthur. But the secrets in the journal have ceased to be a controlling factor in Helen's life, so Markham's attempt to frame her similarly fails. Keeping his wife in her place by appropriating her private history becomes vitally important for Markham, just as the appropriation of women's secrets—and the power derived from that knowledge—was essential to the survival of Victorian boy's clubs. But in Markham's letter to Halford, we witness the ebbing power of the old boy network over women like Helen Huntingdon.

The reversal of power structures is not unique to Helen's and Markham's marriage. Brontë also implies that similar reversal takes place in Rose Markham's and Halford's marriage. In an argument with her mother on womanly and wifely duties, Rose pointedly rejects the notion that men's needs must come first. She discards her mother's belief that "what's proper to be done . . . [is] what's most agreeable to the gentleman of the house—anything will do for the ladies" (78). Mrs. Markham responds that all "any woman can expect from any man" is that "he be steady and punctual, seldom [find] fault without reason, always [do] justice to . . . good dinners, and hardly ever [spoil dinners] . . . by delay" (79). After Markham related this argument to Halford, he asks him, "'is it so, Halford? Is that the extent of *your* domestic virtues; and does your happy wife exact no more?'" (79) The ironic tone of this remark suggests that Rose exacts much from Halford. One suspects that not just Helen but Rose, too, is the dominant partner. In drawing the parallel, Brontë suggests that not only Helen but also other women of her generation have it within their power to reject traditional gender roles and establish new ones.

The twenty-year gap from the end of Helen's diary to Markham's letter to Halford requires explanation. Why the long silence? Why do we hear nothing of Helen after the wedding? And why the hasty close to his letter (perhaps he hears her returning)? By leaving this huge gap in the text, Brontë provides us with a particularly rich opportunity "to bring into play our own faculty for establishing connections—for filling in the gaps by the text itself" (Iser 280). During this twenty-year gap, we can imagine that Helen has learned from her previous marriage to Huntingdon and refuses to be victimized by male dominance again. Now having a better understanding of the power relationships between men and women—especially between husband and wife—Helen assumes the right to dictate not only the course of her life but Markham's life as well. She has found a painting to fit her own frame—Markham's—and has finally achieved not only independence but dominance.

In 1969, Hazel Mews pondered the feasibility of Helen's and Markham's marriage. Anne Brontë, she wrote in *Frail Vessels,* "realizes, subconsciously perhaps, that such a marriage depends upon . . . the view of it taken by the husband—his is the accepted position of dominance in marriage and unless he, as the acknowledged holder of power, is willing to abrogate it, there will be a gradual slipping back to the accepted view; it is, therefore, essential that Gilbert Markham hold progressive views" (139). But if he wishes to remain with Helen, Markham really has no choice other than to adjust his views. For with or without his permission, the tenant of Wildfell Hall has reached the point where she can stand on her own.

Notes

1. Other reviewers similarly attacked Brontë. See especially the unsigned reviews in *Rambler* ("Mr. Bell's New Novel," Sept. 1848) and *Fraser's Magazine* (April 1849). The *Rambler* reviewer was particularly distressed by the "offensive minuteness [of] the disgusting scenes of debauchery," but begrudgingly allowed that "on the whole . . . *The Tenant of Wildfell Hall* is not so *bad* a book as *Jane Eyre*." The *Fraser's Magazine* reviewer concluded that Acton Bell must have been a woman because "the very coarseness and vulgarity [of the novel] is just such as a woman, trying to write like a man, would invent,—second-hand and clumsy, and not such as men do use." All contemporary reviews cited here are from Allott.

2. In addition to McMasters, Jacobs, and Gordon, see Langland, where she argues that "Gilbert's recounting [of Helen's diary] . . . is an attempt to stop the free flow of oral exchange [and to] justify his version of events" (121).

3. The exchange of books as an exchange of trust is significant in understanding the importance of Helen's relinquishing her diary to Markham and his subsequent violation of that trust when he turns the diary over to Halford. Helen's surrendering her diary—as opposed to her telling her story—is not "an error in the author's technical skill," as George Moore felt, and as Winifred Gerin states in her introduction to the novel. The surrender of the diary, and Markham's later appropriation of it, are perhaps the most revealing of narrative device in understanding Helen's and Markham's relationship.

4. See, for example, Jacobs or Mink. Mink argues that "after the final maturation of the characters [including Markham]" takes place, Helen and Markham "enter into a happy marriage" (13, 15).

5. For a brief discussion of the Victorian woman's necessary subservience and submissiveness to men, see Altick and Houghton (341-53).

6. On a similar note, Hazel Mews states that in *The Tenant of Wildfell Hall* "a woman, tenderly nurtured, has stepped outside the confines of her usual sheltered experience and faces a chaos from which there appears no protection and no escape" (136).

Works Cited

Altick, Richard D. "The Weaker Sex." *Victorian People and Ideas.* Ed. Richard D. Altick. New York: W. W. Norton, 1973.

Brontë, Anne. *The Tenant of Wildfell Hall.* Ed. G. D. Hargreaves; intro. Winifred Gerin. Harmondsworth: Penguin, 1979.

The Brontës: The Critical Heritage. Ed. Miriam Allott. London & Boston: Routledge and Kegan Paul, 1974.

Gordon, Jan B. "Gossip, Diary, Letter, Text: Anne Brontë's Narrative *Tenant* and the Problematic of the Gothic Sequel." *ELH* (Winter 1984): 719-45.

Houghton, Walter E. *The Victorian Frame of Mind 1830-1870.* New Haven & London: Yale UP, 1957.

Iser, Wolfgang. *The Implied Reader: Patterns of Communication in Prose Fiction from Bunyan to Beckett.* Baltimore: Johns Hopkins UP, 1974.

Jacobs, N. M. "Gender and Layered Narrative in *Wuthering Heights* and *The Tenant of Wildfell Hall.*" *Journal of Narrative Technique* (Fall 1986): 204-19.

Langland, Elizabeth. *Anne Brontë: The Other One.* London: Macmillan Education, 1989.

McMaster, Juliet. "'Imbecile Laughter' and 'Desperate Earnest' in *The Tenant of Wildfell Hall.*" *Modern Language Quarterly* (Dec. 1982): 352-68.

Mews, Hazel. *Frail Vessels: Woman's Role in Women's Novels from Fanny Burney to George Eliot.* London: U of London P, 1969.

Mink, JoAnna Stephens. "The Emergence of Woman as Hero in the Nineteenth Century." *Heroines of Popular*

Culture. Ed. Pat Browne. Bowling Green, OH: Bowling Green State UP,. 5-22.

"Mr Bell's New Novel." *Rambler* (Sept. 1848) in *The Brontës: The Critical Heritage.* Ed. Miriam Allott. London & Boston: Routledge and Kegan Paul, 1974.

"Review." *Fraser's Magazine* (April 1849): in *The Brontës: The Critical Heritage.* Ed. Miriam Allott. London & Boston: Routledge and Kegan Paul, 1974.

Showalter, Elaine. *A Literature of Their Own: British Women Novelists from Brontë to Lessing.* Princeton, NJ: Princeton UP, 1977.

Alisa M. Clapp (essay date 1996)

SOURCE: "The Tenant of Patriarchal Culture: Anne Brontë's Problematic Female Artist," in *Michigan Academician,* Vol. 28, No. 2, March, 1996, pp. 113-22.

[*In the following essay, Clapp evaluates Helen Huntingdon as a marginalized, and hence paradigmatic, Victorian female artist.*]

Unlike many writers in history, Anne Brontë has had the misfortune not to be unknown by literary critics but to be ignored. We know that she was the youngest sister of Charlotte and Emily, and even that she was a writer, but we rarely look at what she wrote. Even scholarship devoted to "the Brontë sisters" often fails to include the work of the youngest.[1]

Scholars suggest that much of Anne Brontë's obscurity derives from Charlotte herself, whose written "apologies" for Anne's novels and her obstruction of a reprint edition of *The Tenant of Wildfell Hall* hurt Anne's reputation both then and now. Many Brontë biographers followed Charlotte's lead in pronouncing Anne's work to be inconsequential, including Elizabeth Gaskell, Margaret Lane, and Fannie Elizabeth Ratchford who brought the Brontë juvenile literary works to light.[2] Anne Brontë scholars of this century—Will Hale, Ada Harrison and Derek Stanford—have revived interest in her work so that it could be re-evaluated, but the result has usually been criticism that compares her work to her sisters'. Other Anne Brontë criticism tends either to interpret her novels merely biographically (e.g., Winifred Gérin) or judgmentally (e.g., P. J. M. Scott).[3]

Yet in this age of textual recovery, criticism would profit greatly by re-examining Anne Brontë's two novels.[4] Her second novel, *The Tenant of Wildfell Hall* (1848), is an astonishingly feminist novel, with few counterparts in nineteenth-century literature. After all, what other Victorian novel actually recounts an oppressed wife's escape—not through death or suicide, the closure that many feminist writers use—but by defying her husband, packing her bags, and leaving? As May Sinclair has written, "the slam-ming of [Helen's] bedroom door" against her husband resounded throughout the novel and, as others add, "throughout Victorian England."[5]

Unfortunately, that reverberation was too often muffled by the shouts and swearing of Arthur Huntingdon, which attracted many nineteenth-century critics' negative comments.[6] But twentieth-century scholars have been deaf to this slamming door as well. Though critics have begun to examine Helen Huntingdon's marital struggles,[7] little has been written about her artistic struggles.[8] It is her art that betrays her attraction to Arthur Huntingdon, reflects her frustrations during her marriage, and provides financial freedom so she may eventually leave Arthur.

Helen's "art" is the form of aesthetic self-expression—the music, the journal-writing, and the painting—in which she is engaged. The struggle she faces, however, is that her society fails to respect these forms of self-expression as "true art." Indeed, art by women was often evaluated by different standards than art by men. While male art was typically valued in aesthetic or financial terms—both relying on audience appreciation—women's art was often valued only in terms relating back to the artist as a person, as merely self-expressive of the artist's emotions or as highlighting only the artist's sexual attributes which could lead, ironically, to financial security in marriage.[9] Helen experiences the full range of these values: men trivialize her musical and literary self-expression and emphasizes its marginal, stereotypical nature. They also re-appropriate her private moments of music and painting to private, sexual displays on their own behalf. However, Helen successfully enters the realm of male artistry when she sells her paintings as aesthetic items and receives a financial reward which procures her freedom from her husband. If all of her artistic struggles are not completely successful by the world's standards, still, her artistic endeavors become a vital form of self-expression for her. The novel in many ways, then, mirrors the unstable nature of women's art of which Anne Brontë's own artistic marginalization is a symptom.

The narrative of *The Tenant* is divided into three parts. The first and third are told by Gilbert Markham, gentleman farmer, who falls in love with the beautiful young new tenant of Wildfell Hall, Helen. When rumors fly about her past, however, Helen gives Markham her diary to explain her story. This forms the middle portion of the novel—detailing her marriage to the rake, Arthur Huntingdon, who eventually falls back into his old habits of drinking, carousing, and womanizing. Helen leaves him, but then Arthur sickens and Helen feels it her duty to nurse him. She describes his gradual death through letters to her brother back at Wildfell Hall. In the concluding section, through Markham's eyes again, we are told of his and Helen's espousal and marriage.

This story-within-a-story structure has frequently been the focus of critical attention.[10] George Moore, Anne Brontë's earliest champion, criticized this structure by suggesting that the middle portion would have been even more powerful had Helen *told* Markham her painful story:

the presence of your heroine, her voice, her gestures, the questions that would arise and the answers that would be given to them, would preserve the atmosphere of a passionate and original love story."[11]

Yet this typical Victorian response represents the entire problem that Brontë is confronting; it implies that a woman artist must be defined by her physical presence, and then her chosen art form, her diary, is reduced to a conventional love story.

One of Helen's first aesthetic experiences is to witness how a woman's musical art is used and perceived as sexual luring as in the case of the caprices of Annabella Wilmot when she is at the piano with Huntingdon. Annabella who "never likes to waste her musical efforts on ladies' ears alone" (180) complies when Huntingdon flirtatiously requests her to sing during a musical soiree: "She exultantly seated herself at the piano, and favoured [Arthur] with two of his favourite songs, in such superior style . . . that [his] eye and brow lighted up with keen enthusiasm" (181). So Arthur is charmed with her singing in sexual, not artistic, terms. Annabella is conscious of the situation and offers her music as if it were kisses: "What shall I give you next?" she asks another man in the room (181).

Music forms the back-drop to Arthur and Annabella's affair; on several occasions, Helen catches her husband "[hanging] over the instrument" as Annabella sings (242) and "ardently [pressing] the unresisting hand to his lips" as Annabella sits at the piano (245). Music-making now proves to be a superficial entertainment and a seductive game of power where attention is focused on the artist, not the art.

Helen witnesses and understands this model of seductive art, yet resists it. She plays the piano for herself and her female friends, but avoids being seen by men. She leaves the piano as soon as the men enter the room. After all, her visibility before the male gaze could provoke the same sexual feelings as Annabella arouses in her male voyeurs. However, Helen does allow music to be the backdrop for her own display of passion when she is overcome during Miss Wilmot's sad air, "Farewell to thee!"[12] Applying the words of the song to her own situation with Huntingdon, Helen cannot hold back her tears and hides her face in the sofa-pillow (181-2). By now Huntingdon interprets Helen's emotive expression as seduction. Hearing her sob, he follows her out of the room and flirts with her. He is forced to propose to her when her aunt discovers them. What is so disturbing is how well Arthur has read Helen. He does not respect her private outpouring of emotion but egotistically assumes that she is crying only to charm him.

As Huntingdon's wife, Helen continues with her music; however, its value is, if not seductive, still to humor the male auditor rather than personally fulfilling as she enjoyed it before: "I play and sing to him for hours together . . . I fear I am spoiling him; but this once, I will forgive him . . ." (237). Her artistic self-expression becomes slave to what her husband wants. She also learns to keep her

deeper passionate response to music in check. When Huntingdon's next mistress, Miss Meyers, appears as governess, Helen describes her singing: "She had a fine voice, and could sing like a nightingale . . . [but] there was a look of guile and subtlety in her face, a sound of it in her voice" (388). But rather than allow her jealousy to be a response to the beautiful music and arouse Huntingdon's egotism, Helen has learned to temper her emotions and recognize the guile associated with music. She may not be playing the piano any more but she has learned how to play gender politics. She must learn to conceal her vulnerable, emotive outpouring.

Through her journal-writing, Helen attempts emotive art once again, exulting in the privacy of such expression: "This paper will serve instead of a confidential friend into whose ear I might pour forth the overflowings of my heart" (169). On various occasions she finds comfort in her written outpourings; before leaving Huntingdon, she writes: "I have found relief in describing the very circumstances that have destroyed my peace, as well as the little trivial details attendant upon their discovery" (317). The last clause is vital to her conception of self-expression: unlike Moore, who defined feminine aesthetic expression in terms of drama and passion, she considers even the mundane occurrences in a woman's life to be worthy of language.[13] Brontë thus redefines "art" to include the ordinary, daily expressions of life.

Yet even personal self-expression can come under a man's scrutiny, and its written form makes it even more vulnerable than temporal speech. About to leave Arthur the following day, Helen must stand by as he discovers her journal, reads of her plans, and tears her painting supplies— her means of support—to shreds. He articulates the "danger" of women's writing:

> "It's well these women must be blabbing—if they haven't a friend to talk to, they must whisper their secrets to the fishes, or write them on the sand or something; and it's well too I wasn't overfull to-night . . . or I might have lacked the sense or the power to carry my point like a man, as I have done"
>
> (372-3).

Speaking in terms as if of a gendered power struggle, Huntingdon belittles woman's self-expression as instinctive, irrational, and incriminating. Yet it is threatening enough that the man must exercise his power to extinguish it. Revoking her self-definition of "free woman" and substituting his own label of "wife"—an act condoned by society—Arthur successfully obliterates her as a person with self-expression and free agency. It is a violation of her innermost secrets, little less than rape.

If Helen does eventually escape from Arthur's home and domination and continue to write her own story, the success of this accomplishment is diminished by a second violation of her diary. When Markham reads her diary, he alters it when copying it down in his narrative. As he says, he has omitted "a few passages here and there of merely temporal interest to the writer, or such as would serve to encumber the story rather than elucidate it" (147). So even those journal entries which are available to us have been tampered with by a male editor.[14]

Markham's desire to control Helen through her writing becomes more obvious in his obsessive attempts to possess the letters she later writes to her brother Lawrence. Asking to keep a letter, he says "Were not these characters written by her hand? and were not these words conceived in her mind . . . ?" (436). Markham thus conflates Helen's texts with her sexual identity and fails to see their aesthetic value. To possess them is to possess her.

But this is not the last word on the subject. Helen *has* first controlled her own diary since she consents to make it public this time. Further, before giving it to Markham, she "hastily tore away a few leaves from the end," deleting those pages which chronicle their acquaintance (146). Not giving him the satisfaction of knowing her true feelings for him, as she had done with Arthur, Helen keeps Markham's egotism in check. When completing her diary, he fumes that she has torn away those pages discussing her feelings about him:

> How cruel—just when she was going to mention me!
> . . . I would have given much to have seen it all—to
> have witnessed the gradual change, and watched the
> progress of her esteem and friendship for me . . . but
> no, I had no right to see it . . .
>
> (401)

Markham can only half-heartedly recognize Helen's protection of her privacy. He therefore attempts to "write" himself back into the story; indeed, the last glimpse of Helen is through his eyes, as his wife. Helen the artist has once again been reduced to conventional status as wife. However, her writing cannot be totally controlled as she will always possess those ripped pages.[15]

Helen is learning the sexual power play inherent in women's art, of when to hide and when to publicize art. She is therefore able to adapt her own chosen art form—painting—by both revealing conventional paintings on one side and concealing self-expressive art on the back. She succeeds in producing art that is expressive as well as aesthetically pleasing and thus economically valuable. Yet this is not without struggle in a patriarchal society which defines her art, again, as simple and sexual. Early in the novel, she is working on a painting of "an amorous pair of turtle doves" with a young girl kneeling below (175), a simple, natural subject encouraged by society.[16] As Huntingdon notes, gazing at it: "a very fitting study for a young lady . . . girlhood just ripening into womanhood . . . she's thinking there will come a time when she will be wooed and won like that pretty hen-dove . . ." (175). He immediately trivializes the art work into something fitting for a young woman to draw—a scene of love. He also glories in the sexual implications of the scene, viewing art much as he does Annabella's music—a spring-board merely for his own wooing.

No doubt unsatisfied with the socially approved yet shallow subject matter of her paintings, Helen paints those things which truly inspire her imagination, specifically portraits of Arthur, on the back: "there is one face I am always trying to paint or to sketch, and always without success; and that vexes me" (148). Her art becomes an emotional outlet as well as an aesthetic challenge. In the *Madwoman in the Attic,* Gilbert and Gubar revel in this "wonderfully useful paradigm of the female artist" (81). Since "she draws on the backs of her paintings, she must make the paintings themselves work as public masks to hide her private dreams . . . Thus she produces a public art which she herself rejects as inadequate but which she secretly uses to discover a new aesthetic space for herself" (81). Indeed, these portraits of Arthur are the more challenging type of art form—over birds and trees, for instance—and the more rebellious since she is putting her innermost desires in tangible form in a most unladylike manner.

Like her outpouring of feelings during Annabella's song, however, Helen's feelings are also discovered by Arthur when he turns her paintings over (171). Arthur gloats over his discovery: "I perceive, the backs of young ladies' drawings, like the post-scripts of their letters, are the most important and interesting part of the concern" (172). Again he makes light of Helen's art, putting it in terms of a supposed cliché about women. Then, having the "audacity to put his arm round my neck and kiss me," Arthur betrays that his real interest is not in the art, but the sexuality of the artist and her secret feelings about himself (173). Helen must burn her art in order to deflate his ego: "To show him how I valued it [the portrait], I tore it in two, and threw it into the fire. He was not prepared for this. His merriment suddenly ceasing, he stared in mute amazement at the consuming treasure" (177). But, ultimately, like her earlier self-expression in the music room, Helen has betrayed her true feelings and cannot retract them.

Helen later seeks to turn her art into money in order to escape from Huntingdon. Her plan is to sell her paintings in order to become self-sufficient: "the palette and the easel, my darling playmates once, must be my sober toil-fellows now" (358). The catch is that she cannot take personal credit for the art but, rather, sells them under an assumed name to elude Arthur.[17] Seeking financial security and not fame, however, Helen transforms a position of anonymity and an art constructed as mere feminine pastime into financial power: "Brilliant success, of course, I did not look for, but some degree of security from positive failure was indispensable—I must not take my son to starve" (358).[18]

What is so disturbing about her renewed interest in painting, nevertheless, is the response this elicits from other men, as they translate its financial power back into sexual allurement. Mr. Hargrave, for instance, steals in when she is working at her easel and takes the occasion to declare his love to her, entreating her to run away with him. His passions aroused, a literal rape might have occurred had Helen not protected herself, ironically, with a tool of her art—her palette-knife. Markham, also, sees her art as merely the context for love-making. His conflation of the painting with the painter is clear: as Helen paints one day on the cliffs, Markham "could not help stealing a glance, now and then, from the splendid view at our feet to the elegant white hand that held the pencil, and the graceful neck and glossy raven curls that drooped over the paper" (88). Thus, to all three men, the image of the artist is more alluring than the art which she creates; the artist becomes the art. It is astonishing that, despite the obstacles, Helen is able to find both personal and material fulfillment in her painting and ultimately self-sufficiency and freedom from the male gaze.

This is especially true in the case of those emblems of true self-expression—her portraits of Huntingdon—over which she has ultimate victory. She burns one in front of Huntingdon's face and, finding another one after she has escaped, she keeps the frame to sell and muses on the picture itself:

> I have put it aside; not, I think, from any lurking tenderness for the memory of past affection, not yet to remind me of my former folly, but chiefly that I may compare my son's features and countenance with this, as he grows up, and thus be enabled to judge how much or how little he resembles his father. . . .
>
> (398)

Not bound to Huntingdon emotionally or financially, Helen extols this freedom evident in her decisions about the painting. She will disclose this emblem of hidden self-expression, utilize the picture in her role as mother, and even sell its parts for financial gain. Helen's artistic independence from the man in the painting is symbolically complete.

In the end, Helen has achieved personal and material self-fulfillment, yet it is not from her art as much as from her new marriage; Brontë's nod to the happy ending problematizes woman's artistic endeavor. So does Helen's rescue of her ultimate creation, her son, since many of her artistic endeavors are eclipsed or justified by her conventional motherly duties. Helen will never enter the professional male world of art again, and the one time she ventures, Brontë justifies it as an outgrowth of her maternal role.

Ultimately, then, what does Helen achieve as an artist? She learns the necessity of controlling her expressions, and of concealing them as well. Yet she also learns to fight for them and to reclaim them. She possesses the missing pages which leave Markham's reconstruction of her story permanently incomplete. She has the final victory over Huntingdon's portraits, retaining them even after their original is dead. Her transformation of art into financial security allows her a freedom most nineteenth-century heroines never find. Finally, she has redefined artistic self-expression to include the ordinary and the feminine, an impressive feat.

Helen partially reclaims her emotive art from the patriarchal world and, moreover, becomes a paradigm by which to understand other women artists' struggles. For instance,

Brontë herself attempted to find both personal and financial fulfillment from her art. Like Helen, she also hid her art, behind a male pseudonym, but she was ultimately forced to use her own surname in order to distinguish Currer (her sister, Charlotte Brontë) and Acton Bell (her own pseudonym) for the critics. Condemned by people of the mid-nineteenth century as too harsh and "immoral" for a lady novelist, Anne Brontë, even in this century, is still judged in relation to her sex. Now she is considered too "moral,"[19] a criticism often made of nineteenth-century women writers.[20]

Anne Brontë the novelist faced and continues to face an artistic double standard. Thus, Helen's confrontations with patriarchy are relevant to those of many actual Victorian women artists. Their victories are as problematic as their struggles. In many ways, the woman artist becomes merely a tenant, lodging only temporarily in a world of patriarchal language and art.

Notes

1. One such omission, among many examples, is *The Brontës: A Collection of Critical Essays* (Englewood Cliffs, NJ: Prentice-Hall, 1970), edited by Ian Gregor, which contains no essays on Anne Brontë's works.

2. See Elizabeth Gaskell, *The Life of Charlotte Brontë*, 1857; Margaret Lane, *The Brontë Story: A Reconsideration of Gaskell's Life of Charlotte Brontë* (Melbourne: William Heinemann, 1953); and Fannie Elizabeth Ratchford, *The Brontës' Web of Childhood* (New York: Russell and Russell, 1964).

3. See Will Hale, *Anne Brontë: Her Life and Writings* (Bloomington: Indiana University Press, 1929); Ada Harrison and Derek Stanford, *Anne Brontë: Her Life and Work* (New York: John Day, 1959); Winifred Gérin, *Anne Brontë* (London: Thomas Nelson, 1959); P. J. M. Scott, *Anne Brontë: A New Critical Assessment* (Totowa, New York: Barnes and Noble, 1983).

4. Fortunately, a few critical approaches have appeared. See, for example, Juliet McMaster, "'Imbecile Laughter' and 'Desperate Earnest' in *The Tenant of Wildfell Hall*," *Modern Language Quarterly* 43.4 (Dec. 1982): 352-70; and Marianne Thormählen, "The Villain of Wildfell Hall: Aspects and Prospects of Arthur Huntingdon," *Modern Language Quarterly* 88.4 (Oct. 1993): 831-41, which historically contextualize Arthur Huntingdon. Jan B. Gordon, "Gossip, Diary, Letter, Text: Anne Brontë's Narrative *Tenant* and the Problematic of the Gothic Sequel," *Journal of English Literary History* 51.4 (Winter 1984): 719-45; and N. M. Jacobs, "Gender and Layered Narrative in Wuthering Heights and *The Tenant of Wildfell Hall*," *The Journal of Narrative Technique* 16.3 (Fall 1986): 204-19, consider the multiple narrators and narratives of the novel.

5. May Sinclair, *The Three Brontës* (Port Washington, New York: Kennikat, 1939 & 1967), 48. For the sec-

ond quote, see the Penguin edition of *The Tenant of Wildfell Hall,* edited by G. D. Hargreaves and introduced by Winifred Gérin; the cover goes on to call the novel "the first sustained feminist novel." All references to *The Tenant of Wildfell Hall* will be to this edition (Harmondsworth, England: Penguin, 1979).

6. Undergoing a second edition within a month after its publication, *The Tenant of Wildfell Hall* was extremely popular but as a *succes de scandale;* most critics were quick to fault its coarse depictions of Huntingdon's carousing and swearing. A typical review, from Sharpe's *London Magazine* (Vol. VII, September 1848), reads: "So revolting are many of the scenes, so coarse and disgusting the language put into the mouths of some of the characters . . . that our object in the present paper is to warn our readers, and more especially our lady-readers, against being induced to peruse it, either by the powerful interest of the story, or the talent with which it is written" (quoted in Tom Winnifrith, *The Brontës and their Background: Romance and Reality,* New York: Barnes and Noble, 1973, 118).

7. See Edith A. Kostka, "Narrative Experience as a Means to Maturity in Anne Brontë's Victorian Novel *The Tenant of Wildfell Hall,*" *Connecticut Review* 14.2 (Fall 1992): 41-47, and Elizabeth Langland, *Anne Brontë: The Other One* (Totowa, NJ: Barnes and Noble, 1989) for some feminist approaches which consider Helen's marital struggles.

8. For some brief discussions of the female artist in Anne Brontë's work, see Gilbert and Gubar's *The Madwoman in the Attic: The Woman Writer and the Nineteenth-Century Literary Imagination* (New Haven: Yale UP, 1984) 80-2; and Jane Sellars' "Art and the Artist as Heroine in the Novels of Charlotte, Emily and Anne Brontë," *Brontë Society Transactions* 20.2 (1990): 70-74.

9. As Rozsika Parker and Griselda Pollock write, in *Old Mistresses: Women, Art and Ideology* (NY: Pantheon, 1981): "Victorian writers found a way of recognizing women's art compatible with their bourgeois patriarchal ideology. They contained women's activities, imposing their own limiting definitions and notions of a separate sphere . . . [which] precipitated women artists into historical oblivion . . ."(12). See also 8, 54, 83, 99, & 116 for discussions of the artistic double standard in nineteenth-century ideology. I am grateful to Rosalie Riegle who urged me to reevaluate women's art along these lines.

10. For instance, Inga-Stina Ewbank argues that "the frame fails to support the powerful middle portion. The Helen that paints pictures . . . has lost the stature of Helen, the wife of Arthur Huntingdon" (*Their Proper Sphere,* Cambridge: Harvard UP, 1966), 84, while Phyllis Bentley writes that "Helen's diary . . . proves less interesting than Gilbert Markham's ac-

count of his love for the mysterious new 'tenant'" (*The Brontë Sisters,* London: Longmans, Green, 1959), 37. The debate continues in a recent article, where Lori A. Paige argues that "the device of the diary is defensible in the larger context of the written word's role in the novel" (226). See "Helen's Diary Freshly Considered," *Brontë Society Transactions* 20:4 (1991), 224-7.

11. *Conversations on Ebury Street* (NY: Boni and Liveright, 1924), 254. Moore refers to Anne Brontë as a "sort of literary Cinderella" who, had she "lived ten years longer . . . would have taken a place beside Jane Austen, perhaps even higher" (253-60).

12. This poem was written by Brontë herself, though not published until 1920. Brontë thus concealed her poetry within a more traditional literary form for women—the novel—while still making it public, much as Helen later does with her painting.

13. As Langland argues, Helen is well aware of the aesthetic subjectivity of her diary entries. Of this moment Langland writes, "It is a telling moment. Helen describes the 'very circumstances', really a process of interpreting and fixing those circumstances in an interpretative framework; she amasses 'trivial details' to lend conviction to the interpretation" (125).

14. Langland points out that Gilbert edits Helen's account in another way, reinterpreting "the Fallen Woman and runaway wife of Victorian convention as the model of excellent womanhood that the novel proposes" (123). She praises how "Gilbert's perspectives merge with Helen's as he incorporates her letters into his narrative—sometimes the literal words, sometimes a paraphrase—until the reader cannot distinguish between them" (135). However, she does not comment on the power that Gilbert holds in this act of interpretation and editing.

15. Not recognizing the power in this moment of incompleteness, Jan B. Gordon argues that Helen's fragmented diary, among other "failed" writings, suggests "a world of proliferating 'texts' which cannot be contained, except by a desperate and arbitrary act of enclosure" (719-20).

16. Parker and Pollock discuss the popularity of nature subjects for amateur women artists in which "[p]aintings of flowers and the women who painted them became mere reflections of each other. Fused into the prevailing notion of femininity, the painting becomes solely an extension of womanliness and the artist becomes a woman only fulfilling her nature" (58).

17. See Gilbert and Gubar, 81.

18. Sellars discusses some of the struggles of actual nineteenth-century women artists who, like Helen, tried to sell their paintings for money (71).

19. Consider merely the titles of the following approaches to Anne Brontë which emphasize only the

moral issues of *The Tenant*: "Anne Brontë: The Woman Writer as Moralist" in *Their Proper Sphere* by Inga-Stina Ewbank (1966); "Moralising in 'Wildfell Hall'" in *Emily and Anne Brontë* by W. H. Stevenson (1968); and "*The Tenant of Wildfell Hall*: Morality as Art" by T. K. Meier (1973).

20. Elaine Showalter (*A Literature of Their Own: British Women Novelists From Brontë to Lessing,* Princeton, NJ: Princeton UP, 1977, 10-11) and Nina Baym (*Woman's Fiction: A Guide to Novels by and about Women, 1820-70,* 2nd ed. Urbana: U of Illinois P, 1993, 14-15) remind us of the bias which has existed against "female" literary characteristics, such as moral-religious themes.

Rachel K. Carnell (essay date 1998)

SOURCE: "Feminism and the Public Sphere in Anne Brontë's *The Tenant of Wildfell Hall*," in *Nineteenth Century Literature,* Vol. 53, No. 1, June, 1998, pp. 1-24.

[*In the following essay, Carnell claims that* The Tenant of Wildfell Hall *does not challenge the traditional Victorian separation of men and women into public and domestic spheres.*]

The narrative structure of Anne Brontë's **The Tenant of Wildfell Hall** (1848) has traditionally been criticized as a "clumsy" rupture in what might have been "a passionate and original love story."[1] By embedding Helen Graham's diary into an extended letter between her second husband and his brother-in-law, Brontë has presumably prevented a more natural scene of seduction in which Helen could have gradually revealed her story to Gilbert Markham face to face. This somewhat awkward split narrative has recently been reappraised as not a defect after all but rather as a conscious commentary on the intractable cultural rift between public and private spheres. It is not surprising that critics who analyze Brontë's **Tenant** in these terms typically depend on a traditional definition of Victorian separate spheres, a definition that limits our understanding of Brontë's actual critique of the nineteenth-century public sphere.

Most recent critics who discuss Brontë's analysis of Victorian gender roles refer to the stereotypical distinction between a female domestic sphere and a male public sphere. N. M. Jacobs describes the narrative structure of **The Tenant of Wildfell Hall** as one that "replicates a cultural split between male and female spheres that is shown to be at least one source of the tragedy at the center of the fictional world."[2] Linda M. Shires ties this critique more broadly to representations of maenads, or monstrous women—images that were viewed with particular horror in the decades following the French Revolution. She concludes that the demonized representations of women, despite the horror they induced, brought a challenge to the traditional split between the separate spheres: "so increasing her influence and decreasing his in the public sphere."[3]

In a somewhat related move, Elizabeth Langland sees Helen's narrative as transgressive, refuting the idea of "an essential female desire existing outside of and independent of the discursive practices that construct women's lives."[4] To see Helen's inner diary as subordinated to Gilbert Markham's outer frame thus indicates that our thinking "is already contaminated by the patriarchal ideology of prior and latter" (p. 111). As appealing as we may find such a Barthesian concept of transgressive narrativity, however, it is difficult to deny the fact that Anne Brontë did sandwich Helen's narrative within the confines of the correspondence between her husband and her brother-in-law. We also need to recognize that viewing the narrative as a binary choice between patriarchalism and transgression—or even between public and private—situates the text within a peculiarly modern dichotomy.

We twentieth-century feminist critics are at a disadvantage in understanding Victorian modes of feminism or protofeminism because we have inherited a binary definition of gender roles that tends to simplify history. The very terms "public" and "private" have evolved dramatically in their usage and meaning over the past several hundred years, so that a simple binary retrospective—male means public, female means private—is not necessarily adequate to describe Brontë's project. In *The Structural Transformation of the Public Sphere* (1962) Jürgen Habermas suggests that there has always been a complex, contrapuntal relationship among the political realm, the public realm of debate and exchange, the private realm of economic exchange, and, finally, the domestic household. All of these realms are richly and symbolically interconnected, and their relationships to each other have never been stable or transhistorical but have evolved continuously from the mid seventeenth through the twentieth centuries.[5] Habermas's analysis of the evolution of the terms "public" and "private" helps to illuminate the rich complexity of ideological threads that Brontë weaves into her bipartite but nonbinary narrative, even as her text helps to interrogate the ideal that Habermas describes.

Habermas analyzes, in particular, the eighteenth-century ideal of the public sphere: a meeting of minds in which men (and a few exceptional literary women) disregarded certain differences of rank or self-interest in order to discuss larger issues of the public good. According to Habermas's model, this consensual interest in the public good deteriorated by the mid nineteenth century as Luddite and Chartist uprisings challenged the narrow definition of "public" that had traditionally been intended by the educated, bourgeois men who had first described the public sphere.[6] Although much has been made of Brontë's challenge in **Tenant** to the rigid, gendered norms of the Victorian age, little has been made of her interest in the proper education of sons or in the cultivation of more rational debate among the landed bourgeois men who descend on the secluded country estates where most of the novel's action takes place. Brontë's interest in the public good does not preclude her interest in challenging the traditional separate spheres, but the novel's resolution ultimately concerns the good of the whole over the good of particular oppressed social groups, such as women. Beneath Brontë's concern about gender roles, I will argue, there lurks a reluctance to address the Chartist-influenced class challenges to an older version of the public good. In harkening back to an eighteenth-century model of the public sphere, Anne Brontë espouses not a twentieth-century-style challenge to the Victorian model of separate spheres, but a nineteenth-century-style nostalgia for the classical liberal model of bourgeois public debate. At the same time, however, the awkward rupture in Brontë's narrative represents the inherent contradictions between the different levels of discourse—literary, political scientific—within the public sphere itself and the complex ways in which these levels are both accorded and denied cultural power.

· · · · ·

As Habermas explains, the original concept of rational public debate in Britain arose during the eighteenth century among educated men who gathered in coffee houses to critique government actions and protest against any perceived abuses of power. In this model, "private" does not mean "domestic" but rather the private economic individuals who banded together to protect common interests and who joined together regardless of relative distinctions of rank or wealth under the leveling concept of reason (see *Structural Transformation,* pp. 28-37). Reason became the grounding point for political opposition during the Enlightenment; however, the ability of rational men to connect with each other intellectually or politically depended not merely on their perception of each other as equally rational creatures but on their perception of shared humanism. We must consider, then, that as much as Brontë's novel is about the way patriarchal culture encourages men to become domestic tyrants, it is also about the fragile and frequently ruptured connection between Gilbert Markham and Frederick Lawrence, educated and propertied neighbors who cannot manage to find or sustain mutual trust. Although the inner narrative of Helen's diary provides an incisive critique of stereotypically male behavior (as Jacobs and Langland argue), Helen's story is nevertheless narratively enclosed within Markham's description of his efforts to reach a harmonious relationship with his two brothers-in-law, Lawrence and Halford. As much as we may like to interpret Helen's role as "focalizer" of the narrative (to use Langland's term), the novel in fact ends with Gilbert's final letter to Rose's husband, which includes an invitation to leave the city for a period of quiet peace and reflection at home.

At this point Helen's voice has dropped out of the narrative entirely. Although the estate where Helen and Gilbert live was brought to the marriage by her inheritance, Helen remains an invisible, humanizing backdrop to a pastoral or Shaftesbury-style interlude in which "toiling, striving" city men might visit the country to engage in philosophical dialogues about beauty or moral worth. Halford and Markham will continue to reflect on what has become Helen and Gilbert's familiar topic of conversation, "the promising young scions that are growing up about us," or

the male future of the educated public sphere.[7] Certainly we must acknowledge the possibility for transgressive irony in this male-centered ending to a powerful woman's story, and yet we must remember that the proper raising of her son has always been one of Helen's main concerns: her unconventional attitude toward young Arthur's upbringing is partly what forces her to be an object of scrutiny from the time of her arrival at Wildfell Hall. To appreciate more fully Brontë's critique of the masculine public sphere, therefore, we must first clarify women's role in relation to it.

In Habermas's analysis the domestic sphere was not simply a separate female sphere defined in opposition to a public sphere of economic and political activity but also the humanizing linchpin on which both the private economic sphere and the public sphere of oppositional political debate relied. In *Structural Transformation* he describes

> a public consisting of private persons whose autonomy based on ownership of private property wanted to see itself represented as such in the sphere of the bourgeois family and actualized inside the person as love, freedom, and cultivation—in a word, as humanity.

(p. 55)

Of course, autonomy is designated for male property owners only; their wives and families provide the support and nurturing that humanizes them. As Habermas points out, "women and dependents were factually and legally excluded from the political public sphere" (p. 56). At the same time, however, there was a parallel sphere of literary discourse and debate in which, Habermas argues, "female readers as well as apprentices and servants often took a more active part . . . than the owners of private property and family heads themselves" (p. 56).[8] This so-called "literary public sphere," then, seems potentially to be the province of women: when he turns to Samuel Richardson as an ideal participant in the literary public sphere, Habermas codes him in traditionally feminine imagery (tears) as he describes how "Richardson wept over the actors in his novels as much as his readers did" (p. 50). Casting the literary public sphere as potentially female, however, generates some confusion as to whether this sphere was perceived as an integral part of rational political debate or whether it was merely a tangential stepsister to a fraternal sphere of political discourse, responsible for humanizing the fraternity of brothers actively involved in public affairs.

Part of the difficulty in understanding Habermas's references to the literary public sphere is that he does not consistently develop or maintain the distinction between the literary and political public spheres in his analysis.[9] Nor does he acknowledge the significant presence of female novelists in eighteenth-century Britain or their potential effect on the political weight of the literary realm. Yet writers such as Aphra Behn, Delarivier Manley, Eliza Haywood, and Mary Wollstonecraft, who wrote and openly published under their own names, certainly must be considered participants in the literary public sphere. As such, these eighteenth-century women may have felt slightly more welcome entering the Enlightenment public sphere than did Charlotte, Emily, and Anne Brontë when, a century later, they entered the more rigidly gendered publishing world under the pseudonyms Currer, Ellis, and Acton Bell. At the same time, however, even those eighteenth-century women who publicly dared to voice political opinions recognized themselves as exceptional, breaking rather than defining a norm. By defining themselves as exceptional women they managed to call attention to their difference as women even as they asserted the same rights as men to a public voice. For example, in the preface to her comedy *The Lucky Chance* (1686) Aphra Behn protests against her work being judged by different standards than those applied to male playwrights simply because she is a woman. In her periodical *The Female Spectator* (1740-44) Eliza Haywood insists that her anecdotes of domestic life are more significantly political than legislative disputes, which she likens to "the Knots Children tye at School in Packthread."[10] Yet while she claims political relevance for amatory narratives otherwise coded as female, Haywood also warns in her 1756 conduct book *The Wife* that it was only the rare woman who would be rational enough and informed enough to overshadow her husband in debate: "there are so few women qualified to think on those affairs."[11] Haywood believes that even a well-informed and rational wife should guard against transgressing the "bounds of her own sphere: the unmarried, however, are at liberty to act as they please" (*The Wife*, p. 21). Although she does not necessarily invite every woman to participate in public political debate (as she herself attempts to do in her two periodicals), Haywood refuses to allow the public sphere to be defined through a wholly masculine paradigm.

Behn and Haywood insisted on the political import of their work by acknowledging themselves as women but gendering their literary talents as more rational than those of men. A century later, however, women's voices within the literary public sphere would not reflect so much confidence. While Behn and Haywood had insisted on a place for their female voices within an otherwise universally masculine paradigm for public discourse, Victorian women seemed to face the risk that in defining their voices as female they would be excluded altogether from public debate. The obsession in early critical reviews of the Brontës' work with the sex of the authors or with the appropriateness of the subject matter for female readers underscores the Victorian obsession with judging all behavior through a rigid lens of gender.[12] Moreover, female authors in the nineteenth century did not demonstrate the same confidence as had their literary predecessors that they could maintain their identity as women while appropriating norms of male discourse in their literary endeavors. If they wanted to address questions of general political interest, Victorian women were encouraged to disguise their broad philosophizing with comments on particular details. Sarah Stickney Ellis explains in her 1843 conduct book *The Wives of England*: "The excellence of woman as regards her conversation, consists rather of quick, and delicate, and sometimes playful turns of thought."[13]

Nancy Armstrong further elucidates the increasing rigidity of the nineteenth-century version of separate spheres by suggesting that the novel itself played a role in transforming other sorts of political difference, such as class difference, first into gender difference and then into personality difference: "As gender came to mark the most important difference among individuals, men were still men and women still women, of course, but the difference between male and female was understood in terms of their respective qualities of mind."[14] For Armstrong, who analyzes the novels of Charlotte and Emily but not Anne Brontë, the Brontës' fiction turns "the materials of history into a representation of consciousness" (p. 204). Such an interpretation helps us to understand why gender difference came to be privileged above all other cultural differences by the nineteenth century and why it was so difficult for nineteenth-century women novelists to acknowledge the political implications of what they were doing. Armstrong's analysis of the two older Brontë sisters, however, does not fully explain the political critique implicit in Anne Brontë's fiction.

Inasmuch as her work fits into the dominant Victorian construction of gender difference, it makes sense that Anne Brontë would have made a fairly modest claim for what we perceive in retrospect as a daring novel: "if I have warned one rash youth from following in their steps, or prevented one thoughtless girl from falling into the very natural error of my heroine, the book has not been written in vain."[15] Rather than asserting, as did Eliza Haywood, that her particular domestic anecdotes are more political than a newspaper or periodical, Brontë claims merely that she speaks the truth with the modest hope of saving one soul. Brontë herself, therefore, seems to be following a Habermasian model of affective, nurturing humanism. Yet she allows her heroine, Helen Huntingdon, to speak out in the manner of the exceptional eighteenth-century woman writer and to make broad claims about nature, culture, and education: Helen thus emblemizes the rationality of the public sphere. Although Brontë skirts class issues that would threaten the unity of the public sphere, she does not translate political (or class) difference into gender difference as such but rather demonstrates how individual desires should be secondary to one's role as political creature concerned with the larger public good. Even if Helen Huntingdon describes "the unity of accordant thoughts and feelings" between herself and Markham (*Tenant*, p. 487), her more central concern, after all, is how to raise her son into a model public citizen.

In her impassioned and articulate speeches against drinking, against boarding-school education, and against the irrational differences in the education of girls and boys, Helen Huntingdon enacts the sort of *"talking on a large scale"* that Victorian conduct books such as Sarah Ellis's *The Wives of England* would prohibit (p. 103). Helen's voice is rational, confident, and self-sufficient at this point in the narrative—and by the norms of the day, her discourse would certainly be deemed masculine. Furthermore, such issues also define the domain of the public good and concern the responsible rearing of future generations more than do most of the conversations between Markham and Lawrence. For example, when explaining why she has taught her son to detest the taste of wine, Helen suggests that she is speaking universally of men and of virtue:

> "It is all very well to talk about noble resistance, and trials of virtue; but for fifty—or five hundred men that have yielded to temptation, shew me one that has had virtue to resist. And why should I take it for granted that my son will be one in a thousand?—and not rather prepare for the worst, and suppose he will be like . . . the rest of mankind, unless I take care to prevent it?"
>
> (pp. 27-28)

Helen's "talking on a large scale" here about ways to render virtuous one man among five hundred is, in one respect, a modest claim for raising her own son. Her use of probability and numbers, however, broadens her assertion: if taken one by one, any one man—hence potentially the majority among five hundred—could eventually become more virtuous and more rational, the very qualities necessary to the ideal public citizen. Thus Helen's voice provides not merely a woman's humanizing influence on the male child she is raising but also a rational critique that belongs squarely in the discourses and debate of the bourgeois public sphere.

Through her position as a professional painter, Helen also participates, as an exceptional woman, in an aesthetic realm that serves an obvious parallel for the literary public sphere. Her impeccable taste is something that she and Gilbert share: they rarely discuss her paintings, but he immediately approves of them with a smile that indicates that they see eye-to-eye on the important matter of aesthetic judgment. And as such, according to eighteenth-century aesthetic theory, Helen was helping to promulgate the ideal of a shared appreciation of beauty, an ideal that exemplifies the eighteenth-century public sphere ideal of shared, universal (or educated) understanding, so crucial to Edmund Burke's ideal of universal understanding.[16] Exceptionally literate and artistic, Helen challenges the separate gendered spheres by offering herself as one of the rare enlightened women who could claim a voice in public debate. Moreover, if we consider Helen as emblematically participating in the literary public sphere through her position as professional painter, we realize that this sphere was not merely a sphere of humanizing affect, as Habermas suggests, but in fact derived its cultural power from its rational and professional control of aesthetic mores. In this way, Brontë clearly understood—as her eighteenth-century literary predecessors, both male and female, knew quite well—that the literary public sphere located its cultural power in its simultaneous appropriation of both nurturing (traditionally female) imagery and rational (traditionally male) discourse. We return to Habermas's image of Richardson weeping over his own novels, and to Armstrong's

assertion that "the modern individual was first and foremost a woman" (p. 8). But once the public sphere has defined itself as speaking in the voice of the rational yet empathetic male, how feasible was it for women to maintain their identities as women and continue to speak in a public voice? The nineteenth-century tendency for women writers to adopt male pseudonyms suggests the difficulty that women experienced in maintaining their separate identities as they introduced their texts into the public sphere: the disappearance of Helen Huntingdon's voice at the end of Brontë's novel only underscores the difficulty facing women who wanted to contribute to the public good.

Brontë struggles, as did Haywood, with the dilemma of whether participation in the public sphere is appropriate for all women or merely for some exceptionally rational women. Almost all of the other female characters in the novel prove that Helen's experience is not necessarily being touted as a universal model for women. Rose Markham, Eliza and Mary Millward, Milicent Hattersley, and Frederick's own mother are all described as pleasant and faithful but unable to speak rationally in philosophical terms. They are not denigrated for their adherence to traditional female roles, but it is clear that they will never transcend them. After Helen has intervened to resolve their marital misunderstanding, Milicent is described as joyful to be Hattersley's "happy little wife" (p. 466). Mary Millward happily gives up her status as old maid to marry a clergyman. Rose Markham, who once protests her mother's view that her role should be to make her brother's life more convenient and comfortable, presumably goes on to play just such a role for the man who will become Gilbert's primary confidant in telling his and Helen's story. Only the second wife of Lord Lowborough is granted the highest encomium of the rational public sphere, "genuine good sense" (p. 465), but unlike Helen, she is never seen discussing matters of art or taste; her talents are restricted to becoming "an excellent mother to the children, and an invaluable wife to his lordship" (p. 465). Thus Brontë distances the literary public sphere from the traditionally female domestic sphere and so distinguishes literary women from ordinary women, focusing more on the difference between women rather than on the difference between a male and female voice in the public sphere.

Just as Mary Wollstonecraft struggles in *A Vindication of the Rights of Woman* (1792) between suggesting on the one hand that women need to be educated to perform their civic duty as rational wives and mothers and on the other hand that some women of the upper ranks might participate in aspects of professional life currently limited to men,[17] so does Helen Huntingdon struggle at first between her position as professional painter and wage earner and her duty to raise her son to be a model citizen. Rather than promulgate Wollstonecraft's more radical social views, however, Brontë ultimately channels Helen's rational and aesthetic talents back to the household, where they will be used to humanize husband and son for the good of the public sphere. Giving up her career as a professional painter, Helen emblematically removes a woman's voice from the literary public sphere at a moment in history when previously universalizing discourses of reason were being challenged by both the working class and the increasingly specialized discourses of professional scientists. By silencing Helen at the end of the narrative, Brontë once again demonstrates her uncertainty as to whether the literary public sphere, which she clearly aligns with the (rationally) feminine, could be the province of ordinary women. In focusing on a woman whose ideas triumph at the cost of their being articulated through her husband's voice, Brontë suggests that the public good itself is more crucial than whether or not women receive due credit for contributing to it. And by ending the novel with Gilbert's voice rather than Helen's, Brontë draws our attention to the central, but critically overlooked, relationship between Gilbert Markham and Frederick Lawrence, a relationship that evokes an eighteenth-century model of rational discourse and humanistic exchange only through its marked failure to achieve either.

. . . . .

The outer layer of Brontë's narrative frame, Markham's letter to his brother-in-law, is an attempt to breach an emotional gap occasioned by Markham's earlier refusal to match Halford's narrative with a similar one of his own, a gap in the affective humanism that Habermas describes as essential to rational connection in the public sphere. Markham's recognition of this breach is described in purely affective terms in his description of Halford's disappointment: "your face was overshadowed with a cloud which darkened it to the end of our interview, and, for what I know, darkens it still" (p. 5). The outer narrative begins, therefore, with an acknowledgment of the importance of affective connection between property-owning men. And while much of the suspense of Markham's story derives from the mystery of Helen Graham, narrative interest is also built up around the complex relationship between Markham and Lawrence. Markham suggests to Halford that he and Lawrence are "on tolerably intimate terms," although he also indicates that the other man is "too cold, and shy, and self-contained, to obtain my cordial sympathies" (p. 35). Lawrence apparently admires candor without coarseness, but he is too reserved to emulate it himself. Markham describes their "intimacy" as "rather a mutual predilection than a deep and solid friendship" (p. 36), such as he will later acknowledge between Halford and himself. According to an eighteenth-century Habermasian paradigm, these men should find much in common and should view each other as equal through their mutual rationality, despite Lawrence's somewhat more elevated wealth and status. But the link between Markham and Lawrence simply does not exist; one of the puzzles that the narrative explores is why two otherwise similar, rational men cannot manage to trust each other.

As Habermas would observe, without the trust or faith in another man's humanity a rational bond means little. We assume, according to Habermas's model, that the humanizing influence of a woman might help nurture such trust. Brontë shows, however, that one effect that women may

have on men is to provoke their jealousy, rather than encouraging their humanism: Markham assumes that Lawrence is his rival for Helen Huntingdon's affections, and so he brutally and fiendishly attacks his friend with the metal end of a riding whip, nearly taking the other man's life. We may try to salvage Habermas's theory by suggesting that if not the influence of women as love objects, then the feminizing influence of the literary public sphere—in this case represented by Helen's diary—will enable men to cultivate enough humanism to bond rationally. Helen's diary seems to have so powerful an effect on Gilbert that, after reading it, he remembers his duty to apologize to Frederick Lawrence, even if the apology itself seems awkward and reluctantly given. Yet merely reading Helen's narrative does not suffice to reform Gilbert. While he treats Frederick Lawrence more appropriately after understanding Helen's story, Gilbert Markham still seems unable to forge a bond of friendship: he never becomes enough of a confidant for Lawrence to confide his own wedding plans to him; nor does Markham trust that his professed friend would actually encourage the union between himself and the more affluent Lawrence family. Brontë suggests, in other words, that the bond that Habermas envisions as an ideal—the bonding of men through humanistic reason despite slight differences in rank—does not occur by a mere act of reading.

Whereas the literary public sphere has a potentially humanizing influence, Brontë recognizes that literature in and of itself does not guarantee affective humanism. One of Gilbert's original impulses to attack Lawrence was that he had seen Lawrence's name written in a book in Helen's possession. Gilbert also tries to use the gift of Scott's *Marmion* to manipulate Helen into his favor; she must insist on purchasing it from him to deflect his ploy. As a consequence, books in the hands of men risk being employed in less than humanistic ways. To prevent the misuse of literature, it seems, women must first teach men how to read. Markham reads Helen's diary and at first assumes that her unhappiness with her husband legitimizes his own right to pursue her, thereby aligning him with the other men in her narrative who have similarly tried to abuse her vulnerable position. Helen herself is forced to explain to Gilbert that their mutual recognition of passion does not imply that they may consummate it but rather that they must forever part. Subsequently, on the verge of their engagement, when Helen hands Gilbert the fairly transparent emblem of her love, the Christmas rose, he proves an inept reader. He pauses at first, "absorbed in thinking what might be the meaning of her words" (p. 492). When she finally spells out to him what the rose represents, he still does not quite fathom that this is an invitation for him to propose to her. She at last has to prompt him by asking "Have I not said enough?" and softening her words "with a most enchanting smile" (p. 493).

This romantic denouement significantly revises that eighteenth-century novel of abduction that is most directly echoed by Helen's inner narrative of oppression and imprisonment—Richardson's *Clarissa* (1747-48). It is this particular text, the most tragic of Richardson's novels, to which Habermas probably refers when he describes the affective humanism generated by Richardson and his readers weeping together.[18] Brontë, however, revises the notion that women must die tragically to generate feelings of humanity within the reading public. Instead, she suggests how women may inspire affective humanism through timely hermeneutic intervention. Helen escapes Clarissa's fate in part because she is able to teach Gilbert the one thing that Clarissa never manages to teach Lovelace: how to read his moral obligation from her narrative of distress. Accordingly, even as she demonstrates a certain romantic hope in the humanizing capacity of literature, Brontë underscores the need for women to be ever vigilant in instructing men how to read as enlightened humanists.

Gilbert Markham's somewhat uncertain capacity as reader casts doubt on Brontë's wisdom in having such an exceptionally rational woman as Helen Huntingdon renounce her professional position in order to become his wife. Helen will undoubtedly teach Gilbert and their sons to be rational and humane participants in the world of public affairs, but, having seen Helen's superior reason in action, readers may find it unfortunate that she must subordinate her role in the aesthetic public sphere in order to become helpmeet and nurturer of a husband and sons whose role in public life has yet to be proven. Then again, inasmuch as her husband and sons, unlike Helen herself, are endowed with the privileges of gender that will allow them full participation in the public realm of debate and critique, Helen does the greater public a favor by teaching these men to be more rational and insightful readers than they otherwise would be. Certainly the very fact that Markham manages to pen the extended letter to Halford that comprises the outer narrative of Brontë's novel indicates that over the years he has learned to nurture a bond of affective humanism with Rose's husband through rational, epistolary exchange, a bond such as was impossible for him to achieve with Frederick Lawrence in the period before Helen's affecting influence had taken its full effect. There is no doubt that Helen has improved her husband's ability to bond rationally and sensitively with other men and so, presumably, to be a better participant in the public sphere; however, she has done so through a traditionally feminine act of self-sacrifice.

By the end of the novel it is clear that Brontë does not envision a world in which the gendered norms of the separate spheres are radically altered; she concludes by making even the most literate of her female characters the helpmeet and nurturer of her husband, the provider of the rational humanism and sensitivity that will enable him to be a moral participant in the public sphere. Brontë also seems to accept without challenge that the public sphere should be bourgeois rather than more economically leveling. When Gilbert and Helen are finally reunited, Helen makes a plea for true love that perfectly mirrors a traditional public-sphere belief in the subordination of wealth to an ideal of affective humanism: "the greatest worldly distinctions and discrepancies of rank, birth, and fortune are as

dust in the balance compared with the unity of accordant thoughts and feelings, and truly loving, sympathizing hearts and souls" (p. 494). For all the democratic appearances of this speech, however, we must remember that the differences in rank discussed here are only gradations within the landed, educated classes. Markham has already described himself to Halford not as an upstart but as a dutiful son of a property owner who has chosen to follow his deceased father's advice "and to transmit the paternal acres to my children in, at least, as flourishing a condition as he left them to me" (p. 7).

When, once he is married, Gilbert finally has the urge to share some of his vastly increased holdings, his impulse is to give the family farm to his brother, Fergus; never does any thought occur of sharing it with his sister or with any of the laboring families who actually work the soil. Yet it is not in his brother alone that Gilbert places his faith for the future, but also in the humanizing influence of Fergus's new love interest: "I bequeathed the farm to Fergus, with better hopes of its prosperity than I should have had a year ago . . . for he had lately fallen in love with the vicar of L——'s eldest daughter" (p. 497). Brontë thus concludes the novel by reinforcing the humanizing ideal of a woman's influence on men as well as the ideal of the benevolent, rational landlord, crucial to the stability of the bourgeois public sphere. At a moment in history when the rational, bourgeois sphere was beginning to be challenged by the demands of the working class and women for inclusion within the public realm of rational debate, Brontë seems to accept the class-based and gender-based norms of the Enlightenment public sphere. The ambivalence of her bipartite narrative, similar to the ambivalence evident in the oddly mythic final paragraphs of Charlotte Brontë's *Shirley* (1849), marks Anne Brontë's reluctance to repudiate the educated, bourgeois sphere in which she was raised.[19]

This is not to suggest that, according to some ex-post-facto paradigm of progressive ideology, Brontë should have written her novel differently. But if we are to understand how her ideas fit into the evolution of feminist thought, we need to put her novel into an appropriate historical context. Linda M. Shires argues that we need to place Brontë into a historical continuum of feminist thinking: somewhere after Wollstonecraft, whose ideas she would have viewed with unease, but before the "revitalized English feminism" of the 1850s, which Shires describes as "just around the corner" (p. 162). It is difficult to be certain exactly what Brontë derived from Wollstonecraft—whose works she would not necessarily have read, although she certainly shared her interest in rational feminism[20]—or what she contributed to the next wave of feminists, presumably including Harriet Taylor Mill (although Shires never specifies particular names). Unlike Mary Wollstonecraft (writing in 1792), Brontë never suggests a parallel between the idle rich and mentally idle women.[21] Unlike Mill (writing in 1851), Brontë articulates no parallel between class movements and the women's movement, nor does she demand anything like suffrage for women.[22] In "Enfranchisement of Women" Mill herself in fact casts doubt on the feminist credentials of her contemporary female novelists when she inveighs against "the literary class of women . . . [who] are ostentatious in disclaiming the desire for equality or citizenship" (p. 119).

Obviously the example of Helen Huntingdon as exceptional woman provides a powerful example of independence and autonomy, and yet it is misleading merely to place Anne Brontë within some artificial continuum of emergent feminists, as if these voices existed in isolation from attitudes toward liberal political theory and the public sphere. Rather than demand a separate platform of rights for women, Brontë ultimately sought wholeness and integration between the sexes through an eighteenth-century ideal of the public good in which most women might participate indirectly as instructors and nurturers of their husbands and sons. Through the example of Helen Huntingdon, Brontë shows us how women might need to give up their own direct participation in the literary (or aesthetic) public sphere in order to help the men in their lives learn to participate more effectively in the broader political public sphere, even as the abrupt silencing of Helen's voice serves to remind us of the self-sacrifice that women may have had to make in order to help men to achieve the mythic paradigm of universal sympathy and rationality. Brontë offers this vision just at a moment when the natural wholeness or universality of the eighteenth-century conception of the public sphere was radically being called into question, following the French Revolution and the years of labor unrest in the early nineteenth century.

. . . . .

Even as the educated bourgeois and landed classes were working out their vision of shared humanity, focusing on the presumably universalizing power of reason and the humanizing power of affective humanism, other segments of the population were also beginning to articulate their own version of rational humanism. E. P. Thompson insists that by 1820 it would have been a mistake to see "a single, undifferentiated 'reading public'"; instead he describes "several different 'publics,'" including "the commercial public," other "more-or-less organised publics, around the Churches or the Mechanic's Institutes," and then "the active, Radical public," which was starting to organize its demands for workers' rights.[23] Although Habermas does not refer specifically to these alternative public spheres, he does describe a shift in the different conception of citizen and humanity that emerged in Britain by the 1830s and 1840s, in which the idea of the public came to suggest a broader segment of the population. In this mid-nineteenth-century movement of expanding demands for suffrage and workers' rights even liberal thinkers such as John Stuart Mill, spouse of Harriet Taylor, would refer to the "yoke of public opinion" rather than the power of rational opposition inherent in public debate (quoted in Habermas, p. 133). Habermas explains how the eighteenth-century "model of a public sphere . . . claimed the convergence of public opinion with reason . . . to be objectively pos-

sible (through reliance on an order of nature or, what amounted to the same, an organization of society strictly oriented to the general interest)" (pp. 130-31). By the mid nineteenth century

> The public was expanded, informally at first, by the proliferation of press and propaganda; along with its social exclusiveness it also lost the coherence afforded by the institutions of sociability and a relatively high level of education. Conflicts hitherto pushed aside into the private sphere now emerged in public. . . . Laws passed under the "pressure of the street" could hardly be understood any longer as embodying the reasonable consensus of publicly debating private persons. They corresponded more or less overtly to the compromise between competing private interests.
>
> (pp. 131-32)

By the 1840s the old-boys' club of rational debate between bourgeois men was ruptured; the masses of the public, with their economic and political demands—including those of the Luddites and the Chartists—changed the shape of public opposition forever.

An aspect of the evolving public sphere or spheres to which neither Thompson nor Habermas refers is the increasing tendency to use a specific subcategory of reason—scientific expertise—to create a hierarchy among rational, educated persons just at the moment when broader segments of the population were beginning to claim their rational voice. Judith Newton describes how during the 1830s and 1840s "scientific organizations such as the Royal Society, the Statistical Society, and the Political Economy Club . . . helped establish the social value of a specific expertise." Newton pointedly observes that once feminists such as Mary Wollstonecraft and Harriet Martineau had claimed the category of "rational individual" for women as well as men, periodical writers increasingly ceded cultural authority to a more exclusive category, "that pertaining to 'men of science.'"[24]

Newton's analysis helps us to understand that even as Anne Brontë was participating in a tradition of rational debate about the larger public good, her position as female novelist was diminishing in cultural authority vis-à-vis more scientifically trained writers. Her decision to have her heroine become a professional painter accords the inner narrative some of the cultural authority of a professional, albeit not that of a scientist. The language of Brontë's preface to the second edition of the novel, however, employs a certain discourse of scientific authority. She describes her aim as not "to ingratiate myself with the Press and the Public" but rather "to tell the truth" (p. xxxvii). Here the word "truth" is accorded a moral significance for "those who are able to receive it," yet her language simultaneously echoes the scientific impulse of separating truth from superstition as well as the utilitarian impulse of putting her own talents "to their greatest use" (p. xxxix) as she endeavors to benefit the greater "Public" in her hopes of steering even "one rash youth" (p. xxxviii) from following the path of error and alcoholism. However, to suggest that Brontë ever intended to privilege professionalism or utilitarianism over traditional Christian morality would be to misunderstand her insistence that whatever truth she tells will be effected by "the help of God" (p. xxxix). Her religious faith, then, becomes part of her impulse for integrating the idea of the greater public good with the wholeness of humanity.

Insofar as Helen's diary identifies her with the pragmatic and the professional, the disappearance of Helen's voice by the end of Gilbert Markham's concluding section suggests Brontë's reluctance to challenge the wholeness of the public sphere by the potentially fragmenting influence of either scientists, professionals, women, or the lower classes. Helen represents a woman who, within the confines of her inner narrative, refuses the gender role dictated to her by her culture, insists on her status as a professional painter, pursues an affective and humanistic bond between herself and her loyal servant Rachel, and challenges the economic subordination of wives. And yet, rather than allow Helen to transgress fully the bounds of the status quo, Brontë has her heroine turn from the cacophony of an increasingly fragmented public discourse to a nostalgic vision of domestic harmony within the Enlightenment public sphere. It is possible to argue that the final suppression of Helen's voice marks the underlying tragedy behind the romantic conclusion of the novel, but it would be implausible to claim that Brontë intended her poignant denouement—in which Gilbert must once again learn from Helen the power of humility so necessary to the wholeness of affective humanism—as merely ironic. Brontë, of course, does challenge marriage laws and cultural injunctions that require a woman to stay with an abusive husband, just as she criticizes the norms of the separate spheres that prevent women from raising their male children virtuously. And yet, the overall criticism of society effected by her bipartite narrative concerns the loss of such rational exchange and debate that once defined the ideal of public good—and (theoretically at least) allowed men and women to work together, in their separate spheres, for the good of the family, the state, and the country. Brontë challenges the Victorian gender roles but only within a nostalgic plea to return to the Enlightenment ideal of the public sphere.

Given that many feminists today have not yet determined whether it is more to women's advantage to press for special rights based on difference or to continue to have faith in the sameness claims of classical liberalism, we need not blame Anne Brontë for her double-edged message to women.[25] As tempting as it is to privilege the "clumsy" inner narrative that George Moore so wished had been turned into a romantic dialogue, it ultimately remains impossible to determine whether it is Helen or her future husband who claims the most powerful narrative position. And yet it is precisely through this structural indeterminacy that Brontë articulates the struggle between men and women as they mutually seek the public good. Refusing both the sameness of parallel experiences and the difference of separate interests, Brontë weaves a bipartite narrative whose center neither wholly cleaves nor wholly holds.

Notes

1. Citing the above passage from George Moore, *Conversations in Ebury Street* (London: William Heinemann, 1930), p. 216, Winifred Gérin employs the term "clumsy" in her introduction to the Penguin edition (see Anne Brontë, *The Tenant of Wildfell Hall*, ed. G. D. Hargreaves [Harmondsworth: Penguin, 1979], p. 13).

2. "Gender and Layered Narrative in *Wuthering Heights* and *The Tenant of Wildfell Hall*," *Journal of Narrative Technique*, 16 (1986), 204.

3. Linda M. Shires, "Of Maenads, Mothers, and Feminized Males: Victorian Readings of the French Revolution," in *Rewriting the Victorians: Theory, History, and the Politics of Gender*, ed. Shires (New York: Routledge, 1992), p. 157.

4. "The Voicing of Feminine Desire in Anne Brontë's *The Tenant of Wildfell Hall*," in *Gender and Discourse in Victorian Literature and Art*, ed. Antony H. Harrison and Beverly Taylor (DeKalb: Northern Illinois Univ. Press, 1992), p. 122.

5. Susan Dwyer Amussen's excellent work on social and political systems in the sixteenth and seventeenth centuries supplements many of Habermas's claims about the historical relations between public and private. In explaining the assumed relation between family and state, typical of early modern thought, she explains: "At the very least, the analogy means that it is inappropriate to dismiss what happened in the family as 'private'; the dichotomy so familiar to us today between private and public is necessarily false when applied to the experience of early modern England" (Amussen, *An Ordered Society: Gender and Class in Early Modern England* [Oxford: Basil Blackwell, 1988], p. 2).

6. See *The Structural Transformation of the Public Sphere: An Inquiry into a Category of Bourgeois Society*, trans. Thomas Burger (Cambridge, Mass.: MIT Press, 1989), p. 140. Much effort has been expended in attempting to demonstrate that the claims for the universality of the public sphere help to obscure that its major participants are propertied and male. For example, Michael Warner explains how "the bourgeois public sphere has been structured from the outset by a logic of abstraction that provides a privilege for unmarked identities: the male, the white, the middle class, the normal" ("The Mass Public and the Mass Subject," in *Habermas and the Public Sphere*, ed. Craig Calhoun [Cambridge, Mass.: MIT Press, 1992], p. 383). While this analysis is certainly apt, it is also the case that Habermas fully acknowledges the male and bourgeois face of the public sphere: he specifically analyzes the exclusion of women from all but the literary public sphere (p. 56), and he specifically addresses the narrow strata of bourgeoisie that was originally included in the idea of the public. His analysis of the fragmentation of the idea of the

public as greater demands were made by the working class is an excellent case in point.

7. Anne Brontë, *The Tenant of Wildfell Hall,* ed. Herbert Rosengarten (Oxford: Clarendon Press, 1992), p. 498. Further references are to this edition and are included in the text.

8. Of course, the participation of women as readers and occasionally as writers in the literary public sphere did not amount to any sort of universal ideal. After the Parliamentary Revolution of 1688, early English feminist writers Mary Astell and Margaret Cavendish, both staunch Tories, expressed serious reservations about the advantages to women of power being shared between men rather than concentrated in the single person of the king (see Catherine Gallagher, "Embracing the Absolute: The Politics of the Female Subject in Seventeenth-Century England," *Genders,* 1 [1988], 24-39; and Ruth Perry, "Mary Astell and the Feminist Critique of Possessive Individualism," *Eighteenth-Century Studies,* 23 [1990], 444-57). Carole Pateman has likewise argued that the bourgeois public sphere depended on a perception that the household was separate from and irrelevant to political matters (see *The Sexual Contract* [Stanford: Stanford Univ. Press, 1988], p. 3). However, just as viewing the bourgeois as "homme" obscured his economic position of property owner, so woman's humanizing influence on the male participants in public-sphere debates obscured her actual political disempowerment. The occasional and exceptionally literate woman might enter the realm of public debate through publication of novels or periodicals, further blurring most women's routine exclusion from the political public sphere.

9. See Elizabeth Heckendorn Cook, *Epistolary Bodies: Gender and Genre in the Eighteenth-Century Republic of Letters* (Stanford: Stanford Univ. Press, 1996), p. 11.

10. *The Female Spectator,* 4 vols. (London: T. Gardner, 1745), II, 124.

11. *The Wife* (London: T. Gardner, 1756), p. 19.

12. See *The Brontës: The Critical Heritage,* ed. Miriam Allott (London: Routledge and Kegan Paul, 1974), pp. 249-65.

13. *The Wives of England: Their Relative Duties, Domestic Influence, and Social Obligations* (London: Fisher, Son, and Co., [1843]), p. 102.

14. *Desire and Domestic Fiction: A Political History of the Novel* (New York: Oxford Univ. Press, 1987), p. 4.

15. "Preface to the Second Edition" (*Tenant,* p. xxxviii).

16. Burke states that "it is probable that the standard both of reason and Taste is the same in all human creatures" (*A Philosophical Enquiry into the Origin of our Ideas of the Sublime and Beautiful,* 2d ed. [1759], ed. J. T. Boulton [London: Routledge and Kegan Paul, 1958], p. 11). See Terry Eagleton, *The Ideology of the Aesthetic* (Oxford: Basil Blackwell, 1990), for a useful discussion of the progressive and reactionary uses of this type of universalizing claim.

17. Joan B. Landes describes Wollstonecraft as "shar-[ing] the implicitly masculinist values of the bourgeois public sphere" (*Women and the Public Sphere in the Age of the French Revolution* [Ithaca: Cornell Univ. Press, 1988], p. 135). But Wollstonecraft also offers more radical possibilities for certain literate women. Compare, for example, the many chapters in *A Vindication* in which she cajoles women to be more modest and virtuous and better educated for motherhood to her suggestions in chapter 9 that certain upperclass women might in fact enter business or the medical professions (see *A Vindication of the Rights of Woman,* ed. Miriam Brody [Harmondsworth: Penguin, 1992], pp. 266-67).

18. For further analysis of the connection between literary and political public spheres in Richardson, see my "Clarissa's Treasonable Correspondence: Gender, Epistolary Politics, and the Public Sphere," *Eighteenth-Century Fiction,* 10 (1998), 269-86.

19. Susan Zlotnick explains how Charlotte Brontë "places her own 'private judgment,' her sense of what a happy ending is—the progress of industrial capitalism—in a nostalgic narrative that laments change while, at the same time, she embeds the text's real tragedy—the lack of progress—in a traditional happy ending of love and marriage" ("Luddism, Medievalism and Women's History in *Shirley*: Charlotte Brontë's Revisionist Tactics," *Novel,* 24 [1991], 294).

20. See Elizabeth Langland, *Anne Brontë: The Other One* (Totowa, N.J.: Barnes and Noble, 1989), p. 39.

21. Wollstonecraft sets up the parallel in comments such as: "it is in the most polished society that noisome reptiles and venomous serpents lurk under the rank herbage; and there is voluptuousness pampered by the still sultry air, which relaxes every good disposition before it ripens into virtue" (*A Vindication,* p. 257).

22. Mill writes, for example: "The Chartist who denies the suffrage to women, is a Chartist only because he is not a lord" ("Enfranchisement of Women" [1851], in John Stuart Mill and Harriet Taylor Mill, *Essays on Sex Equality,* ed. Alice S. Rossi [Chicago: Univ. of Chicago Press, 1970], pp. 96-97).

23. *The Making of the English Working Class* (New York: Random House, 1963), p. 719.

24. Judith Newton, "Engendering History for the Middle Class: Sex and Political Economy in the *Edinburgh Review,*" in *Rewriting the Victorians,* p. 7.

25. Compare the general strategies of, for example, Catharine A. MacKinnon in *Toward a Feminist Theory*

of the State (Cambridge, Mass.: Harvard Univ. Press, 1989), and Elizabeth Fox-Genovese in *Feminism Without Illusions: A Critique of Individualism* (Chapel Hill: Univ. of North Carolina Press, 1991).

Tess O'Toole (essay date 1999)

SOURCE: "Siblings and Suitors in the Narrative Architecture of *The Tenant of Wildfell Hall*," in *SEL: Studies in English Literature, 1500-1900,* Vol. 39, No. 4, 1999, pp. 715-31.

[*In the following essay, O'Toole proposes that the narrative construction of* The Tenant of Wildfell Hall *serves to reinforce the novel's thematic tension between two forms of domesticity—marital and sibling.*]

Anne Brontë's **The Tenant of Wildfell Hall** has been singled out most frequently for two elements: (1) its unusually complicated framing device (Gilbert Markham's epistolary account of his relationship with Helen Huntingdon surrounds her much lengthier diary account of her first marriage and flight from her husband) and (2) its strikingly frank and detailed description of a woman's experience in an abusive marriage. These two features of the text, one formal and one thematic, are intertwined in the experience of reading the novel. For, in proceeding through the multilayered narrative and remaining for a surprisingly protracted time in Helen's painful account of her nightmarish marriage, the reader experiences a sensation that might be labeled narrative claustrophobia. The text thus produces an effect on the reader that mimics the entrapment Helen experiences in her marriage.

"The book is painful," Charles Kingsley declared in his unsigned review in *Fraser's Magazine,* sounding a note that would be echoed by many contemporary critics. A notice in the *North American Review* complained that the reader "is confined to a narrow space of life, and held down, as it were, by main force, to witness the wolfish side of [Huntingdon's] nature literally and logically set forth."[1] This language invokes the claustrophobic sensation that I have suggested is exacerbated by the narrative form. The reader's discomfort is likely to extend beyond Helen's diary account of her hellish first marriage, however. The events recounted in the framing narrative—Helen's courtship by and eventual marriage to Gilbert Markham—purportedly provide a happy ending for Helen, released from her disastrous first marriage and free to choose a better mate. But Gilbert is an oddly unsuitable partner for Helen. Though it may be tempting to read the events in the framing narrative as representing a recovery from the events recounted in the embedded one, such a meliorist view is challenged by the fact that the framing narrative finds Helen remarried to a man who, while not the rake that Arthur Huntingdon was, is capable, like Arthur, of violence and cowardice (as evidenced by his vicious attack on Frederick Lawrence, which he does not publicly

acknowledge). Gilbert, like Arthur, has been spoiled by his mother and has an inflated ego, and he subscribes to all the standard Victorian stereotypes about female nature and female merit (as evidenced by his behavior toward and descriptions of both the "demon" Eliza Millward, his first flame, and the "angel" Helen).

Gilbert's shortcomings become less critical, however, when attention is shifted from the relationship he describes in his letters to Halford to the one whose forging Helen narrates in her diary—the relationship with her brother Frederick, whom Gilbert perceives as his antagonist and who is his opposite in character. The formal displacement that occurs when Helen's narrative undermines Gilbert's, exceeding it in both length and power, is thus echoed in a displacement of the exogamous romantic plot articulated in his account by the endogamous brother-sister plot contained within hers. The architecture of Brontë's narrative calls attention to alternate forms of domestic containment, one deriving from courtship and marriage, the other from the natal family. Rather than representing these two forms of domesticity as continuous or overlapping, as nineteenth-century novels of family life commonly do, **The Tenant of Wildfell Hall** stresses their disjunctions, an approach that is complemented by the narrative format.

I

Treatments of **Tenant** as domestic fiction have tended to focus on marital relationships, and hence, when examining the relationship of the framing to the framed narrative, to focus on the differences between Gilbert and Arthur as spouses. The critics I will discuss below, for instance, have suggested that the agenda Helen pursues unsuccessfully in her first marriage, an agenda consistent with prevailing domestic ideology, is realized in her second. It must be acknowledged, however, that the novel's relationship to domestic ideology is an unusually vexed one. In presenting Helen's attraction to her first husband, Brontë daringly implies that her heroine's culturally sanctioned role as the would-be reformer of a sinful man serves as a cover for her sexual attraction to him, but a hellish marriage punishes Helen for succumbing to her desire for Arthur. The novel makes a heroine out of a woman who runs away from her husband; but this transgressive act is sanctioned by a conservative motive: Helen wants to save her son from his father's corrupting influence. The more subversive kind of rebellion enacted by Arthur's mistress, Annabella—a rebellion that does not have a selfless motivation—is severely punished by her society and by the text: "she [sinks], at length, in difficulty and debt, disgrace and misery; and die[s] at last . . . in penury, neglect and utter wretchedness."[2] But if Annabella's fate suggests that the novel's critique of domestic ideology has its limits, her role in Brontë's treatment of domestic reform also indicates the limited efficacy of that ideology.

Helen displays the ironic naïveté of a young woman who, subscribing to the ideas about woman's moral influence articulated by Sarah Ellis and others, ardently believes that as her husband's "angel monitress" she can redeem him. While Helen's surveillance of her home and husband accords with the function of the domestic woman posited by Nancy Armstrong in *Desire and Domestic Fiction,* Helen is not nearly so effective as that powerful creature. The futility of her efforts are underscored by Annabella; while Arthur finds his wife's moralizing tedious, he can be kept in line by his mistress's strategy, which depends on his physical desire for her. Annabella's brand of sexual management, ironically, has more pragmatic reach than domestic authority. In this way, Brontë's novel exposes rather than reproduces the myth of power embedded in cultural constructions of the domestic woman.[3] Helen's friend Millicent may be criticized for failing to provide the sort of moral management her husband needs, but the example of Helen and Arthur suggests that there is a problem with the entire notion of the wife as agent of reform.

The authorial preface to the second edition reiterates on a figural level Helen's frustrated efforts at domestic purification. Just before asserting, "if I can gain the public ear at all, I would rather whisper a few wholesome truths therein than much soft nonsense," Brontë compares herself to a cleaning woman who, "undertak[ing] the cleansing of a careless bachelor's apartment will be liable to more abuse for the dust she raises, than commendation for the clearance she effects" (p. 3). If her commitment to acknowledging unpleasant truths links her to Helen, so too does this indication of the limits of her own success, since Helen's wifely attempts at cleaning up Arthur's act are met with obdurate resistance.

This essay stresses the novel's ambivalent relationship to domestic ideology because some of the best readings of this novel become entwined with it when treating the relationship between Helen's and Gilbert's narratives. Inspired by Brontë's eloquent and compelling defense of a wronged woman, and her invention of a heroine who heroically fights back, N. M. Jacobs, Linda Shires, and Elizabeth Langland have all provided insightful readings of *Tenant* as a protofeminist text. Each of these critics, however, credits Brontë's heroine with the successful moral education of her second husband, maintaining that Gilbert is reformed by his exposure to Helen's text and that their union redeems Helen's disastrous first marriage; in so doing, they risk reinscribing the domestic ideology that it is a part of the novel's accomplishment to problematize.[4] Moreover, each has at some point to ignore, minimize, or recast elements in Gilbert's narrative that qualify a positive account of Helen's second marriage. It is my contention that these elements are linked to a narrative strategy that contrasts Gilbert the suitor, would-be hero of the framing narrative, and Frederick the brother, hero of the framed narrative. The strategy behind the narrative layering is not to show Gilbert's reform and to celebrate a restored conjugal ideal, but to juxtapose siblings and suitors, to poise natal domesticity against nuptial domesticity.

In "Gender and Layered Narrative in *Wuthering Heights* and *The Tenant of Wildfell Hall,*" Jacobs initially seems set to view Gilbert's framing narrative as part of a continuing critique of the domestic, rather than as the site of its recuperation. She notes that the enclosure of Helen's diary narrative within Gilbert's epistolary one mimics not just the division of male and female into separate spheres but also the law of couverture. The fact that Helen's diary has become her husband's possession and that he has the power to bargain with it in a bid to recover his friend's favor reinforces this point, but Jacobs does not pursue that tack. Instead, she sees the relationship between Helen's story and Gilbert's as one that works not to contain *her* but to educate *him*. According to Jacobs, the "effect on Gilbert of reading this document—of being admitted into the reality hidden within and behind the conventional consciousness in which he participates—is revolutionary, and absolutely instrumental to the partnership of equals their marriage will become. Its revelations force him outside the restricted boundaries of an ego that defines itself through its difference from and superiority to someone else."[5]

If this were the case, however, then the access to Helen's consciousness which Gilbert's reading of her diary gives him should have altered his behavior and assumptions. Jacobs, however, provides no evidence in support of Gilbert's moral growth. And far from demonstrating any such alteration, Brontë's novel shows us that in the events following upon his reading of the diary, Gilbert is as egotistical and as sexist as he appears in the opening chapters. His immediate response when he has concluded the account of Helen's harrowing domestic drama is pique that the pages detailing her initial impressions of him have been ripped out. While the diary might have restored Helen to his good graces, rendering her once again *"all I wished to think her . . .* her character shone bright, and clear, and stainless as that sun I could not bear to look on" (p. 382, my emphasis), it has not touched his tendency to demonize all attractive women who are not the exalted Helen, as his continued shabby treatment and vilification of Eliza make clear. His unreasonable resentment of Frederick continues, and his egotism is still intact; his pride almost leads him to lose Helen, as he refuses to make himself vulnerable to learn whether she still loves him. Most disturbing, the violence he exhibited in his attack on Frederick is still manifest in his behavior toward Eliza, the former object of his sexual interest; when she says something that angers him, he responds: "I seized her arm and gave it, I think, a pretty severe squeeze, for she shrank into herself with a faint cry of pain or terror" (p. 444). Thus, there does not seem to be any significant revision in Gilbert's character that would encourage us to disagree with Helen's aunt when she says, "Could [Helen] have been contented to remain single, I own I should have been better satisfied" (p. 470). The absence of growth on Gilbert's part was commented upon by Kingsley, who questioned Brontë's agenda: "If the author had intended to work the noble old Cymon and Iphigenia myths, she ought to have let us see the gradual growth of the clown's mind under the influence of the accomplished woman, and this is just what she has not done."[6] Precisely. We can only assume that Brontë knew what she was about when she chose to include details suggesting Gilbert's persistent limitations.

While Shires concedes those limitations, she maintains that Gilbert and his correspondent Jack Halford are both educated by their reading of Helen's diary: "[The novel] counsels an inscribed male friend that what he may perceive as overly independent female behavior is a strong woman's only way to maintain integrity in a world where aristocratic male dominance can easily slip into abusiveness. It is important that the text addresses a man, for the counterhegemonic project of the text is not merely to expose a bad marriage but to teach patriarchy the value of female rebellion."[7] Like Shires, Langland views the framing male narrative as one that serves a feminist agenda, though in different terms. Writing in part in response to Jacobs's description of the relationship between Gilbert's narrative and Helen's as one of enclosure, Langland argues in "The Voicing of Female Desire in . . . *The Tenant of Wildfell Hall*" that "[a] traditional analysis that speaks of nested narratives is already contaminated by the patriarchal ideology of prior and latter and so cannot effectively question what I wish to question . . . the transgressive nature of narrative exchange." Thus she proposes viewing the "narrative within a narrative not as hierarchical or detachable parts, but as interacting functions within a transgressive economy that allows for the paradoxic voicing of feminine desire."[8] Central to her argument is the fact that the text as a whole is structured around an exchange of letters, and that the epistolary exchange is the prelude for an exchange of visits (Halford and Rose to Gilbert and Helen). She argues that an exchange structure is inherently destabilizing and thus can serve a feminist agenda. She does not allow the gender implications built into this particular exchange to give her pause.[9] However, it is surely not irrelevant that the exchange of letters is an exchange between two men, nor that the material exchanged is a woman's story, though this is a point Langland's reading must ignore. It strikes the reader as curious at best that Gilbert would transcribe for another man the contents of his wife's intimate diary, and disturbing at worst that Helen's hellish experience is used for a homosocial end.

The transaction between Gilbert and Halford accords with the model outlined by Eve Kosofsky Sedgwick in *Between Men,* which describes how women are used as instruments with which those economic and affective bonds between men that structure society are forged.[10] Gilbert's revelation of Helen's story to Halford is an act of debt paying. He has fallen out of Halford's favor because he did not respond to his friend's sharing of confidences with equal candor; the story he is telling him now, which is actually his wife's story, will acquit his debt. He instructs Halford: "If the coin suits you, tell me so, and I'll send you the rest at my leisure: if you would rather remain my creditor than stuff your purse with such ungainly heavy pieces,—tell me still, and I'll pardon your bad taste, and willingly keep the treasure to myself" (p. 18). The exchange between Gilbert and Halford is not only an economic one, it is also an emotional one, geared toward a restoration of affection. It is clear that Halford has replaced the women in Gilbert's life for the top spot in his affections. Halford is Gilbert's

brother-in-law, and he has taken his sister's place in his affections. When in Gilbert's account he first refers to his sister Rose, he pauses to comment: "Nothing told me then, that she, a few years hence, would be the wife of one—entirely unknown to me as yet, but destined hereafter to become a closer friend than even herself" (p. 10). More intriguingly, Markham refers to his marriage to Helen Huntingdon as "the most important event of my life—previous to my acquaintance with Jack Halford at least" (p. 8). The story wins Gilbert his friend's love again, renewing the affective bond between the two men that was in danger of dissolving: "I perceive, with joy, my most valued friend, that the cloud of your displeasure has past away; the light of your countenance blesses me once more" (p. 19).

At one point Gilbert contrasts his warm friendship with Halford to his inability to feel that same kind of bond with Frederick Lawrence, Helen's brother: "[U]pon the whole, our intimacy was rather a mutual predilection than a deep and solid friendship, such as since has arisen between myself and you, Halford" (p. 36). His jealousy of Frederick, whom he mistakenly assumes to be Helen's lover, leads to Gilbert's resentment of him and to his violent attack on him. But even after he learns of Frederick's kinship with Helen and of how instrumental he has been in Helen's escape from Huntingdon, Gilbert is unable to forge a connection with him or even to appreciate his merit. The antipathy between the two, much more virulent on Gilbert's side, is significant, for Frederick is a man who will not engage in the sort of transactions over women that Gilbert wishes him to conduct. Frederick, while placing no impediments between Gilbert and his sister, is not willing to play the active role of go-between that Gilbert expects him to play. Gilbert resents Frederick and even considers him morally culpable for not intervening with his sister on his behalf: "[H]e *had* wronged us . . . He had not attempted to check the course of our love by actually damming up the streams in their passage, but he had passively watched the two currents wandering through life's arid wilderness, declining to clear away the obstructions that divided them, and secretly hoping that both would lose themselves in the sand before they could be joined in one" (p. 450). Though Helen sees her relationship to her brother as an end in itself, Gilbert wants the brother to serve as their mediator, to channel the passion whose object and destination is himself.

Such a structure of channeling and mediation is embodied in the novel by gossip, whose central and suspect role in this novel has been elucidated by Jan Gordon: "[G]ossip always appears as a threat to value: it either 'speculates' or exaggerates by 'inflating' . . . In short gossip devalues because it has nothing standing behind it. Lacking the authenticity of a definable source, it is simultaneously financially, theologically, and narratively unredeemable."[11] (It is in fact gossip, with Frederick as its unwitting subject, that brings Gilbert and Helen together; gossip's misconstrual of Frederick's wedding as Helen's causes Gilbert to rush to the scene, a trip which ends in his engagement to

Helen.) Gilbert implicitly links Frederick's refusal to play go-between with his refusal to gossip when he complains to Halford that "[h]e provoked me at times . . . by his evident reluctance to talk to me about his sister" (p. 397). When Helen, on the verge of rejoining her husband, had suggested to Gilbert that he might know of her through her brother, she had specified: "I did not mean that Frederick should be the means of transmitting messages between us, only that each might know, through him, of the other's welfare" (p. 386). In her formulation of the triangle, Frederick is less a mediating term than an apex. Gilbert's contrasting expectation that Frederick will serve as an intermediary is thwarted by the literalism and lack of expansiveness with which Frederick imparts news of Helen: "I would still pursue my habitual enquiries after his sister—if he had lately heard from her, and how she was, but nothing more. I did so, and the answers I received were always provokingly limited to the letter of the enquiry" (p. 436). Significantly, Frederick is a character who resists transmitting gossip. He does not, for example, let the community know it was Gilbert who attacked him. He is most reluctant to gossip about women, a reluctance that baffles and aggravates Gilbert.

Gilbert's conversation with Frederick about Jane Wilson is especially revealing in this regard. His narrative has painted Jane as a social climber who wished to ensnare Frederick. Gilbert takes it upon himself to warn Frederick of the danger Gilbert believes he faces from this predatory woman. Frederick checks Gilbert's desire to gossip about the woman and to slander her: "'I never told you, Markham, that I intended to marry Miss Wilson' . . . 'No, but whether you do or not, she intends to marry you.' 'Did she tell you so?' 'No, but—' 'Then you have no right to make such an assertion respecting her'" (p. 401). As Gilbert continues to press his point, Frederick, who is not interested in Jane, responds with gentle sarcasm to Gilbert's diatribe. While Gilbert is miffed by Frederick's refusal to join him in maligning Jane's character, to engage in this particular kind of male bonding, he comforts himself by reflecting: "I believe . . . that he soon learned to contemplate with secret amazement his former predilection, and to congratulate himself on the lucky escape he had made; but he never confessed it to me . . . As for Jane Wilson . . . [h]ad I done wrong to blight her cherished hopes? I think not; and certainly my conscience has never accused me, from that day to this" (p. 402). The assumption of his own correct insight into Frederick's attitude, steadfastly maintained in the face of a lack of evidence, and the callous indifference toward the unhappy Jane Wilson are both powerful indicators of Gilbert's self-satisfied nature and the limits of his imagination and his empathy. Significantly, this smug reflection is made by the older Gilbert who has been married to Helen for many years; it thus cautions us not to assume too much about Gilbert's improvement under Helen's tutelage.

Frederick's refusal to gossip about women is in contrast not only to Gilbert's eagerness to gossip about Jane Wilson, but also to Gilbert's sharing of his wife's intimate di-

ary with his male friend. As we have seen, attempts to read Helen's second marriage as an event which redeems the domestic ideal compromised by her first marriage must ignore evidence about Gilbert's shortcomings and the troubling implications of his transfer of the contents of her diary to his friend. It is significant that many of Gilbert's flaws are made visible through interactions with Helen's brother Frederick; this fact should encourage us to think further about the latter's role. For all the famous violence of the domestic scenes in this novel, the most violent moment in the novel is the one in which Gilbert attacks Frederick:

> I had seized my whip by the small end, and—swift and sudden as a flash of lightning—brought the other down upon his head. It was not without a feeling of strange satisfaction that I beheld the instant, deadly pallor that overspread his face, and the few red drops that trickled down his forehead, while he reeled a moment in his saddle, and then fell backward to the ground . . . Had I killed him? . . . [N]o; he moved his eyelids and uttered a slight groan. I breathed again—he was only stunned by the fall. It served him right—it would teach him better manners in future. Should I help him to his horse? No. For any other combination of offenses I would; but his were too unpardonable.
>
> (p. 109)

Gilbert's physical attack on Frederick makes particularly vivid and concrete an opposition between Helen's suitor and her brother that is visible throughout the novel, yet Frederick's importance has been largely overlooked by critics.[12]

Frederick plays an instrumental role in the recuperation of Helen's unhappy history; it is he, not Gilbert, who redeems Helen's faith in humanity after her disillusioning experience with Arthur. She writes in her diary: "I was beginning insensibly to cherish very unamiable feelings against my fellow mortals—the male part of them especially; but it is a comfort to see that there is at least one among them worthy to be trusted and esteemed" (p. 356). Curiously, Frederick is exactly the sort of man the reader who wants a happier, more appropriate second marriage for Helen would expect her to marry. He, not Gilbert, is the gentle, sensitive, and supportive male that Helen has sought. If we are to look for an optimistic, meliorist plot in the novel, it is more likely to be found in the brother-sister relationship than in the husband-wife one. The opportunity for revision and recuperation lies not in the undeniably disappointing Gilbert, so curiously less mature than his bride, but in the brother. Improvement is effected not so much by Gilbert as a replacement for Helen's first husband as it is by her brother as a replacement for her father.[13] Juliet McMaster notes a pattern of generational improvement in the novel's juxtaposition of characters who embody Regency values with those who embody Victorian values.[14] She discusses this distinction primarily with reference to the replacement of the dissolute Arthur, with his aristocratic associations, by the gentleman farmer Gilbert (elevated to the squirearchy by his marriage to the newly propertied Helen). But that pattern is most marked in the contrast between Helen's irresponsible father and his virtuous son.[15] The framing story is the wrong place to look for a positive alternative to Helen's marriage with Arthur; we must look instead to her diary, to the account of her relationship with Frederick. By shifting attention from the suitor to the brother, we can account for the dissatisfactions of the courtship narrative while revealing Brontë's display of alternate forms of domestic containment. It is Helen's growing relationship with her brother, rather than the burgeoning relationship with Gilbert, that receives the privileged place in her diary after she leaves her husband. The containment of the brother-sister plot within the embedded narrative reflects the turn inward, toward the natal family. The claustrophobic narrative structure, originally linked to an imprisoning marriage, finds an alternate thematic corollary in a potentially incestuous relationship.

II

Poised between Helen's first marriage and her second is the relationship she forges with her brother during her exile. As the person to whom Helen turns for help when she makes her escape, Frederick serves as a buffer between her and the world during her period of disguise. Helen and Frederick's relationship is peculiar for a brother-sister one because they have been raised having only minimal contact with each other. Helen's father, an alcoholic with no interest in daughters, abnegated his responsibility toward her, turning her over to relatives after the death of his wife, while keeping charge of his son. Helen's flight from her husband provides the occasion for building a relationship with her brother that they have thus far not enjoyed. Becoming better acquainted as adults, their relationship is in some ways structurally closer to a courtship relationship than to a brother-sister one. The townspeople, ignorant of Helen's true identity, construe their relationship as a sexual one, and Gilbert sees him as a romantic rival, suggesting, perhaps, the novel's own flirtation with an incest motif. Helen, after all, is fixated on her son's resemblance to the brother she loves. She reconceives her son as the progeny not of her husband Arthur but of her brother Frederick; she says to him: "He is like you, Frederick . . . in some of his moods: I sometimes think he resembles you more than his father; and I am glad of it" (p. 357). Helen's flight from her husband's to her brother's house is followed, then, by the realignment of her son's lineage in relation to her natal family. Previously, the son's physical likeness to his father was stressed, and Helen has kept Arthur senior's portrait (which had symbolized her physical desire for him) in order to compare the child to it as he grows. In raising her son, she seeks to instill the character she would create into the body she desired. Finding the embodiment of manly virtue in her brother, she redesignates her son's person as "like Frederick's."

Rather than exploring sexual overtones in the sibling relationship, however, Brontë's novel foregrounds its relationship to domestic reform; Frederick's virtue compensates for their father's neglectful treatment of Helen, and their

comfortable relationship, defined by mutual respect, contrasts with Helen's problematic relationships with her husband and her suitor. The implication that the brother-sister relationship has the potential to redeem a compromised domestic sphere bears some resemblance to Jane Austen's employment of the sibling model of relationships as described by Glenda A. Hudson in *Sibling Love and Incest in Jane Austen's Fiction*. Emphasizing the nonsalacious nature of Austen's treatment of incestuous relationships— "In her novels, the in-family marriages between the cousins and in-laws are successful because they do not grow out of sexual longing but are rooted in a deeper, more abiding domestic love which merges spiritual, intellectual and physical affinities"—Hudson argues that for Austen, "the incestuous marriages of Fanny and Edmund, Emma and Knightley, and Elinor and Edward Ferrars are therapeutic and restorative; the endogamous unions safeguard the family circle and its values . . . Incest in Austen's novels creates a loving and enclosed family circle."[16] The idea of closing family ranks for protective and restorative purposes can be applied to Helen's turn to her brother.[17] Unlike what we would find in an Austen novel, however, no warm relationship is effected between Frederick and Gilbert through the latter's marriage to Frederick's sister. The brother-in-law whose visit Gilbert eagerly anticipates at the end of the novel is Jack Halford, not Frederick Lawrence. The alternate domestic relationships of siblings and spouses remain quite distinct in Helen's experience, rather than the former fostering marital exchange.

The endogamous quality of the brother-sister relationship is exaggerated in the case of Helen and Frederick: formed during her time in hiding, it is necessarily an insular one which cannot incorporate outsiders. And it coexists with a regressive project in which Helen engages upon her flight from her marital home, for Helen's retreat from her husband is followed by a return to her natal family origins, symbolized by her adoption of her mother's maiden name as her alias and her return to the home in which her mother died. Wildfell Hall, though "no[t] yet quite sunk into decay," is a previous family home that has been exchanged for a more up-to-date one, so she is not only symbolically returning to her family, but returning to a prior stage in the family history (p. 355).

Together, Helen and Frederick revise their family history. Enjoying frequent contact with her brother, Helen reconstructs the family life she was denied as a child. Frederick's supportive and responsible fraternal behavior compensates for the poor behavior of Helen's father. The contrast between Helen's relationship with her father and the relationship she enjoys with her brother bears out claims made by Joseph P. Boone and Deborah E. Nord about Victorian brother-sister plots. They argue that the "[sister's] investment in the brother figure . . . originates as a means to combat her own devaluation within the family and society," frequently making up for paternal neglect in particular. They also note that the brother-sister relationship might be used to circumvent problems inherent in a conjugal relationship: "[I]n some cases, the sibling ideal becomes a utopian basis for figuring heterosexual relationships not based on traditional conceptions of gender polarity as the basis of romantic attraction. Theoretically, at least, the idealized union of brother and sister rests on a more egalitarian, less threatening mode of male-female relationship, precisely because the bond is one in which gender difference is rendered secondary to the tie of blood-likeness, familiarity and friendship."[18] While one might question the assumption that there is something more inherently benign about brother-sister relations than other male-female ones, Helen and Frederick's relationship does seem intended to provide an alternative to the violence and power plays that contaminate the conjugal relationship. Frederick gives her both emotional and practical support and appears to be the only male in the novel who embodies the virtues she seeks in a mate.

Contrary to the case of the brothers and sisters Boone and Nord describe, however, the intimacy of Frederick and Helen is not born and nurtured in the nursery; it is not itself, therefore, cultivated by domestic arrangements. It is, we must suspect, precisely because Frederick and Helen have not been raised together that their sibling relationship presents a strong contrast to the others in the novel, such as that between Gilbert and his sister Rose, who complains of the favoritism with which the sons of the family are treated, and that of Esther Hargrave and her brother, who attempts to pressure her into an unsuitable match. The problem of triangulation within the nuclear family is called to our attention from the first page, when Gilbert commences his account of himself with reference to the competing agendas his mother and father had regarding their son; this is swiftly followed by an exposure to the sibling rivalry between Gilbert and his younger brother as well as that between Rose and her brothers. (The fact that Helen's son is conceived alternately as an improved version of her husband and a younger version of her brother suggests that her family will not be exempt from the kind of triangulation that plagues the Markham family.) Because Helen and Frederick come together as adults, there is no parental mediation to promote rivalry or jealousy. Moreover, due to the early death of his mother, Frederick has not been spoiled by maternal indulgence in the way that both Arthur and Gilbert are said to have been. Thus, their exemplary sibling relationship is also exceptional. While Helen and Frederick's relationship seems to present a model for domestic relations, it is a somewhat utopian one, and its strength, paradoxically, derives from the absence of domestic structures in its formation. Therefore, that model is unable to provide the basis for its own reproduction.

In this respect, Brontë's treatment of the brother-sister motif differs from that of many other nineteenth-century novelists who privilege sibling bonds. Austen and Charles Dickens, for example, both use the sibling relationship as a model for the marital one by having the spouse metonymically connected to the brother (either by being him, as in *Mansfield Park,* or by having a special connection to him, as in *Dombey and Son*). In *Tenant,* this approach is visible only on the margins of the central plot, as, for ex-

ample, when Helen arranges for Frederick's marriage to Esther Hargrave, the young woman whom she has called her "sister in heart and affection" (p. 338). The marriage of Arthur Jr. and Helen Hattersly, a second "Helen and Arthur" marriage, is also a sort of fraternal/sororal match, since their mothers' closeness has caused them often to play and take lessons together from childhood, as siblings would do. Gilbert and Helen's marriage, however, does not adhere to the sibling paradigm. In the central plot, Brontë keeps the suitor and the brother steadfastly segregated: they are antithetical types and are, consequently, antipathetic to each other. Moreover, Gilbert is rendered analogous not to Helen's brother, but to her son. Using his friendship with little Arthur as a way of accessing the mother, the petulant and immature Gilbert is, as Shires describes him, the "boy child who wants to take possession of the mother."[19] It is Frederick, not Gilbert, whom Helen perceives as Arthur's ideal imaginary parent. This fact reinforces the extent to which Frederick appears to be Helen's only male equal in the novel as well as the only exemplar of manly domestic virtue. Though it is incest that is traditionally associated with the disruption of normal generational sequence,[20] Brontë reverses this association by figuring generational imbalance in the exogamous relationship.

Brontë's treatment of the sibling motif contrasts not only with Dickens's and Austen's, but, closer to home, with her own sister's. Numerous critics have traced the lines of kinship between *Tenant* and *Wuthering Heights,* which contains the more famous representation of sibling love.[21] Paradoxically, while the incest motif appears less transgressive in *Tenant* than in *Wuthering Heights*—it is where family values are housed—it is less translatable into the social sphere. In Emily Brontë's novel (as in Charlotte Brontë's *Jane Eyre*), the notion of kinship is used to figure the romantic love whose promise is a cornerstone of the domestic ideal. In *Desire and Domestic Fiction,* Armstrong alludes to the strategy behind the kind of romantic identification often associated with incest in the novels of the other Brontë sisters: "In the face of the essential incompatibility of the social roles they attempt to couple, [Emily and Charlotte Brontë] endow their lovers with absolute identity on an entirely different ontological plane." Working against a critical tradition that "has turned the Brontës' novels into sublimating strategies that conceal forbidden desires, including incest," Armstrong associates Emily and Charlotte Brontë's fiction with a development whereby "sexuality . . . become[s] the instrument of, and not the resistance to, conventional morality."[22] It is not surprising that Armstrong's account does not include Anne Brontë, for, unlike Emily and Charlotte, Anne seems to juxtapose rather than to collapse kinship relations and sexual ones in *Tenant.*[23] This makes *Tenant* a most unusual example of nineteenth-century domestic fiction, a fact that may account for the relative marginalization of Anne's masterpiece within the Brontë corpus.

Helen's relationship to her brother Frederick cannot ultimately solve the problems or contradictions that cluster around the concept of the domestic, for it apparently cannot be brought to bear on other familial relationships, or on anything outside its own circuit. While in *Wuthering Heights* the incestuous longing of Cathy and Heathcliff is replaced by the more socially acceptable (but, as William Goetz points out, sanguinally more affined[24]) marriage of Catherine and Hareton, in *Tenant,* the sibling relationship seems to exist as an end in itself. The sense of narrative claustrophobia described above is the formal corollary of this self-containment. Helen and Frederick's relationship remains insular, and it remains locked within the field of Helen's diary.

Helen's narrative itself is "locked," for, once her diary is turned over to Gilbert, she never again narrates.[25] This means that we have only his word for the success of their marriage. That he is satisfied is clear, but the reader has no firsthand access to Helen's subsequent experience. It also means that in Helen's diary the strongest affective relationship with a man that she describes after leaving Arthur is with her brother, in keeping with Brontë's use of the brother-sister plot to cast a dubious light on Gilbert and his courtship. It is no doubt because the novel privileges Helen's relationship to her brother, the record of which is confined to the embedded narrative, that Gilbert's framing narrative strikes many readers as perfunctory.

But it is more than perfunctory; it is part of a sustained critique of marital domesticity and part of an oppositional structure that segregates the nuptial and the natal forms of domestic containment. *Tenant* is distinctive in its brilliant use of compartmentalized narratives to reflect this thematic opposition. It is even more distinctive in its refusal to reconcile sexual and kinship relations, and in its willingness to sustain the resulting note of unease.

Notes

1. Qtd. in Miriam Allott, *The Brontës: The Critical Heritage* (London and Boston: Routledge and Kegan Paul, 1974), pp. 272, 262.

2. Anne Brontë, *The Tenant of Wildfell Hall,* ed. Herbert Rosengarten (New York: Oxford Univ. Press, 1993), p. 439. All subsequent citations to this novel refer to this edition and are indicated parenthetically in the text.

3. Others have commented on the novel's ironic stance toward the notion of the woman's role as "angel monitress," particularly Maria H. Frawley, who in *Anne Brontë* (New York: Twayne, 1996), argues that Brontë "challenges the domestic ideology that encouraged women to construct themselves as ethereal agents of morality and virtue" (pp. 133-4). Though Elizabeth Langland, in *Anne Brontë: The Other One* (London: Macmillan, 1989), shows with respect to Helen and Arthur that *Tenant* "explodes [the] myth" that women "can serve as redemptive angels to . . . men," she maintains that Helen's diary "serves a . . . vital function in *educating* Gilbert" and that the "Gilbert who marries Helen must accede to . . . the probity of her 'harshness' in correcting [male] weak-

ness," thus suggesting that Helen's reforming mission is realized with her second husband (pp. 141, 134).

4. In a footnote to "Acts of Custody and Incarceration in *Wuthering Heights* and *The Tenant of Wildfell Hall,*" *Novel* 30, 1 (Fall 1996): 32-55, Laura Berry comments, in a similar vein to mine: "Gilbert Markham's likeness to Arthur Huntingdon is often elided in order to read into Brontë's ending a conditional conjugal equality, and thus to make Anne Brontë's novel a proto-feminist one. This understandable gesture . . . does not always do justice to the complexity of the narrative" (p. 45 n. 19). Berry, however, does not address the role of Frederick and the sibling relationship, arguing rather that Brontë "abandon[s] hope in marital pedagogy in favour of child training" (p. 47).

5. N. M. Jacobs, "Gender and Layered Narrative in *Wuthering Heights* and *The Tenant of Wildfell Hall,*" [*Journal of Narrative Technique*] 16, 3 (Fall 1986): 204-19, 213.

6. Qtd. in Allott, p. 272.

7. Linda Shires, "Of Maenads, Mothers, and Feminized Males: Victorian Readings of the French Revolution," in *Rewriting the Victorians: Theory, History, and the Politics of Gender,* ed. Shires (New York and London: Routledge, 1992), pp. 147-65, 160. Shires explicitly acknowledges her own motivation in putting the slant she does on the novel: "Although [the text] can be read as shutting down women's independent voices and actions, [it] should be read primarily as instrumental in enabling and promoting the next wave of revolutionary English feminism" (p. 162). What I am underscoring is the connection between this act of recuperating the text for and as a feminist history and a view of recuperation as what is at stake in the novel's double marriage plot, since readings such as Shires's and Jacobs's imply that Helen's second marriage, in contrast to her disastrous first one, is benign.

8. Langland, "The Voicing of Female Desire in Anne Brontë's *The Tenant of Wildfell Hall,*" in *Gender and Discourse in Victorian Literature and Art,* ed. Antony H. Harrison and Beverly Taylor (Dekalb: Northern Illinois Univ. Press, 1992), pp. 111-23, 111, 112.

9. Langland does, however, argue in her essay that Helen controls Gilbert's narrative to Halford, that her diary "redeem[s]" his "bankrupt" narrative (p. 116).

10. Eve Kosofsky Sedgwick, *Between Men: English Literature and Male Homosocial Desire* (New York: Columbia Univ. Press, 1985).

11. Jan B. Gordon, "Gossip, Diary, Letter, Text: Anne Brontë's Narrative *Tenant* and the Problematic of the Gothic Sequel," *ELH* 51, 4 (Winter 1984): 719-45, 725.

12. For example, though Langland is interested in the way the novel "critiques the conventional manly ideal

[and] criticizes male indulgence," she does not consider how the exemplary Frederick factors into the novel's representation of male character (*Anne Brontë*, p. 137). Of Gilbert's attack on Frederick she says: "Thematically and structurally in the novel, this episode develops the insidious effects of an indulgence that leads to masculine arrogance and abuse of power," without commenting on the juxtaposition of these sharply contrasting specimens of manhood or noting that their opposition factors into the thematic and structural organization of the novel as a whole (p. 133). Langland's approach is typical in seeming to view Frederick's role in the novel as incidental. Shires notes that "[i]deologically, this text, like *Jane Eyre,* promotes gender and class equality which it figures in heterosexual marriage. Yet nearly every man in the book is susceptible to appearances, sentimental romanticizing, cant, or corruption" (p. 161); she does not consider the counterexample offered by Frederick, focusing instead on Helen's two husbands.

13. If, as has sometimes been suggested, the original of the alcoholic Arthur is Branwell Brontë, then Anne Brontë, in substituting Frederick for Arthur, might be imagining for herself an improved brother. On Anne's relationship to Branwell and her desire to rescue him, see Langland's *Anne Brontë*, pp. 16-8; for the possible influence of Branwell's character and history on *Tenant,* see Edward Chitham, *A Life of Anne Brontë* (Oxford and Cambridge MA: Basil Blackwell, 1991), pp. 137, 143, 146, and 148-50.

14. Juliet McMaster, "'Imbecile Laughter' and 'Desperate Earnest' in *The Tenant of Wildfell Hall,*" [*Modern Language Quarterly*] 43, 4 (December 1982): 352-68.

15. This pattern is iterated in Helen's attempt to make Arthur Jr. a better man than the father he risks resembling. Again, improvement is sought within the natal family.

16. Glenda Hudson, *Sibling Love and Incest in Jane Austen's Fiction* (London: Macmillan, 1992), pp. 25, 35.

17. Tony Tanner, *Adultery in the Novel: Contract and Transgression* (Baltimore: Johns Hopkins Univ. Press, 1979), acknowledges the function of incest in maintaining family values when he remarks, apropos of the ending of *The Mill on the Floss:* "There are cases when the bourgeois novel avoids adultery only by permitting or even pursuing something that is very close to incest" (p. 72).

18. Joseph P. Boone and Deborah E. Nord, "Brother and Sister: The Seductions of Siblinghood in Dickens, Eliot and Brontë," [*Western Humanities Review*] 46, 2 (Summer 1992): 164-88, 167, 165.

19. Shires, p. 162.

20. Marc Shell, *The End of Kinship: "Measure for Measure," Incest, and the Ideal of Universal Siblinghood* (Stanford: Stanford Univ. Press, 1988), p. 40.

21. Jacobs, for example, stresses the similar use of narrative layering in the two novels and what she calls "narrative cross dressing" in both. Other accounts suggest that a Bloomian rivalry is played out in the siblings' novels. Chitham suggests that "Anne's artistic and moral challenge to the content of her sisters' novels comes in *Wildfell Hall,*" noting, for instance, that she "parodied Emily's scenes of violence" and arguing that "[a]s *Wildfell Hall* developed from common ground with Emily, Anne used her story to show how very different was her 'moral' view from Emily's 'poetic' one. This argument, involving matters of realism, morality, and indeed differing world views, began to pervade [*Tenant,* which] does, finally, become Anne's considered 'answer' to *Wuthering Heights*" (pp. 134, 145, 142). Gordon discusses *Tenant* as a novel which "encloses . . . *Wuthering Heights,* as it strives to supplant it" (p. 720). Gordon also suggests that the labyrinthine narrative format of both novels can be related to their shared interest in a potentially incestuous relationship when he comments that in both *Wuthering Heights* and *The Tenant of Wildfell Hall* "[t]he whole question of belatedness and priority threatens to collapse all the narratives back into a single narrative in much the same way that genealogy threatens to collapse back into the disappearance of difference that produces the monstrous, the ruin, or the fragment—the ontic status of lacking paternity or succession" (p. 737).

22. Nancy Armstrong, *Desire and Domestic Fiction: A Political History of the Novel* (New York: Oxford Univ. Press, 1987), pp. 197, 187, 199.

23. When Armstrong asserts that "the Brontës . . . had more to do with formulating universal forms of subjectivity than any other novelists" and that "the Brontës have come to be known for a literary language that allows emotion to overpower convention and become a value in its own right, blotting out all features of political person, place, and event," her "Brontës" refers to Emily and Charlotte (pp. 187, 197). Anne is the odd sister out, as she is in Charlotte's biographical notice that accompanied the reissue of *Wuthering Heights.* While Emily appears as the genius championed by her famous sister, Anne's efforts are dismissed: "I cannot wonder [at the unfavorable reception of *The Tenant of Wildfell Hall*]. The choice of subject was an entire mistake. Nothing less congruous with the writer's nature could be conceived . . . She was a very sincere and practical Christian, but the tinge of religious melancholy communicated a sad shade to her brief, blameless life" ([Charlotte Brontë], "Biographical Notice of Ellis and Acton Bell," in *Wuthering Heights,* ed. David Daiches [New York: Penguin, 1985], p. 34).

24. William Goetz, "Genealogy and Incest in *Wuthering Heights,*" [*Studies in the Novel*] 14, 4 (Winter 1982): 359-76.

25. For a contrasting point of view, see Langland's claim in "The Voicing of Female Desire" that Helen's voice

is present in Gilbert's narrative, that she is the focalizer of his account of Huntingdon's death (pp. 119-20).

FURTHER READING

Criticism

Alexander, Christine. "Milestones in Brontë Textual Scholarship." *Text: An Interdisciplinary Annual of Textual Studies* 9 (1996): 353-68.

Details the early publication history of *The Tenant of Wildfell Hall.*

Berg, Margaret Mary. "*The Tenant of Wildfell Hall*: Anne Brontë's *Jane Eyre.*" *Victorian Newsletter* 71 (Spring 1987): 10-15.

Observes resemblances between *The Tenant of Wildfell Hall* and Charlotte Brontë's *Jane Eyre,* arguing that Anne Brontë's novel contains implicit criticism of Charlotte's view of morality.

Berry, Laura C. "Acts of Custody and Incarceration in *Wuthering Heights* and *The Tenant of Wildfell Hall.*" *Novel: A Forum on Fiction* 30, No. 1 (Fall 1996): 32-55.

Investigates themes of child custody and domestic enclosure in *The Tenant of Wildfell Hall* and Emily Brontë's *Wuthering Heights.*

Brontë, Anne. "Preface to the Second Edition." In *The Tenant of Wildfell Hall,* by Anne Brontë, pp. xi-xiii. New York: The Modern Library, 1997.

Reprint of Brontë's 1848 preface to *The Tenant of Wildfell Hall* in which she responds to vehement criticism of the novel's first edition.

Ewbank, Inga-Stina. "*The Tenant of Wildfell Hall* and *Women Beware Women.*" *Notes and Queries* 10, No. 2 (December 1963): 449-50.

Suggests the play-like qualities of *The Tenant of Wildfell Hall,* noting a shared structural device in the novel and Thomas Middleton's Jacobean drama *Women Beware Women.*

Gay, Penny. "Anne Brontë and the Forms of Romantic Comedy." *Brontë Society Transactions* 23, No. 1 (April 1998): 54-62.

Studies the influence of Jane Austen's novels on *The Tenant of Wildfell Hall.*

Gruner, Elisabeth Rose. "Plotting the Mother: Caroline Norton, Helen Huntingdon, and Isabel Vane." *Tulsa Studies in Women's Literature* 16, No. 2 (Fall 1997): 303-25.

Examines the struggles of motherhood embodied by Helen Huntingdon and several other fictional and historical Victorian women.

Jacobs, N. M. "Gender and Layered Narrative in *Wuthering Heights* and *The Tenant of Wildfell Hall.*" *Journal of Narrative Technique* 16, No. 3 (Fall 1986): 204-19.

Discusses similarities of narrative structure, and a shared critique of gender ideology, in *The Tenant of Wildfell Hall* and *Wuthering Heights.*

Mink, JoAnna Stephens. "The Emergence of Woman as Hero in the Nineteenth Century." In *Heroines of Popular Culture,* edited by Pat Browne, pp. 5-22. Bowling Green, Ohio: Bowling Green State University Popular Press, 1987.

Survey of Victorian heroines that mentions the significance of *The Tenant of Wildfell Hall* for its depiction of a self-supporting female artist.

Additional coverage of Brontë's life and career is contained in the following sources published by the Gale Group: *Dictionary of Literary Biography,* **Vols. 21 and 199;** *DISCovering Authors 3.0.*

Franz Grillparzer
1791-1872

Austrian playwright, novella writer, poet, and critic.

For further information on Grillparzer's life and career, see *NCLC*, Volume 1.

INTRODUCTION

Perhaps the most recognizable Austrian literary figure of the nineteenth century, Grillparzer is admired by critics for the intricate character studies found in his dramas, for his psychologically complex novellas, and for the critical and philosophical views he expressed in his essays. His style encompasses the influence of the classicism of ancient Greek tragedy, the neo-classicism of eighteenth-century Enlightenment authors, and the Romanticism of nineteenth-century German writers Johann Wolfgang von Goethe and Friedrich Schiller. Grillparzer's works also reflect his interest in the historical dramas and the tragedies of William Shakespeare, of the Spanish dramatists Lope de Vega and Pedro Calderón, and of the popular Viennese theater known as *Volksstueck*. His rich and varied oeuvre is widely studied today and there is new interest on the part of critics in Grillparzer's political and aesthetic ideas.

BIOGRAPHICAL INFORMATION

Grillparzer was born in Vienna in 1791 to Wenzel Grillparzer, a court lawyer, and Anna Franzisca Sonnleithner. The Grillparzers were involved in the rich musical culture of Vienna, and young Grillparzer shared a lifelong friendship with Ludwig van Beethoven, even writing a libretto for Beethoven's opera *Melusine* at the composer's request. Following the family tradition, young Grillparzer studied law at the University of Vienna from 1807 to 1811. All the while, he was keenly interested in literature and composed his first drama, *Blanka von Kastilien,* in 1809. In 1814, after brief assignments as a private tutor for an aristocratic family and as an unpaid probationer in the court library, he became an administrator at the Imperial Archives. He was appointed director in 1832 and worked there until his retirement in 1856. In the meantime, Grillparzer was arrested in 1826 as a member of Ludlamshöhle, a writers' and artists' club whose members were falsely suspected of secretly promoting subversive ideas. Even though the charges were dropped, the incident left a strong impression on Grillparzer. In his later works, he would often incorporate the theme of the rights of the individual versus an arbitrary and repressive government. After this unpleasant event, Grillparzer traveled to Germany, where he vis-

ited writers Ludwig Tieck, Georg Wilhelm Friedrich Hegel, and Goethe. In 1836 Grillparzer traveled to France and London—meeting Alexandre Dumas, Ludwig Börne, and Heinrich Heine in Paris, and Edward Bulwer-Lytton in London. While he suffered from lack of critical appreciation for his dramas throughout his career, Grillparzer fell into a deep depression and isolation toward the end of his life. His creativity grew dimmer and he never submitted any of his later dramas for theatrical production. He was, however, appointed a member of the newly-founded Austrian Academy of Science in 1847; was named Hofrat (privy councilor) on his retirement from the Imperial Archives; received honorary doctorates from the Universities of Vienna and Leipzig in 1859; and was appointed a member of the Upper House by Emperor Franz Joseph in 1861. He died at the age of eighty-one, in 1872.

MAJOR WORKS

Grillparzer's first produced play, the popular *Die Ahnfrau* (1817; *The Ancestress*), was dismissed by critics as merely a fashionable "fate-tragedy" and Grillparzer, who always aspired to the highest poetic ideals, struggled during his entire career to shake off the label of sensationalism. His second play, *Sappho,* (1818) exhibits the stylistic traits that would characterize the rest of his works: classical blank verse form, serious subject matter derived from ancient or recent history, attention to the unities of time, place, and action, and emphasis on psychological motivation. Critics reacted more favorably to *Sappho* and later plays, but none ever equaled the popularity of *The Ancestress.* In his Greek trilogy, *Das goldene Vliess* (1821; *The Golden Fleece*), Grillparzer juxtaposes two cultures, Greek and barbarian. The censorship imposed by Prince Metternich during his rule, which intervened especially in the productions of historical tragedies such as *König Ottokars Glück and Ende* (1825; *King Ottocar: His Rise and Fall*) further hindered Grillparzer's career. However, he continued to write about historical themes and the role of the individual in history in such plays as *Ein treuer Diener seines Herrn* (1828; *A Faithful Servant of His Master*), *Ein Bruderzwist in Habsburg* (1872; *Family Strife in Habsburg*), *Die Jüdin von Toledo* (1872; *The Jewess of Toledo*) and *Libussa,* (1874). In 1838, broken by Vienna's resounding rejection of his one comedy, *Weh dem, der lügt!* (*Thou Shalt Not Lie*), Grillparzer retreated from the theater, neither publishing nor producing another drama, though he continued to write for another thirty years.

CRITICAL RECEPTION

The critical recognition Grillparzer craved did not come until after his death. While today he is remembered chiefly for his classical and historical plays, which achieve tragic power through precise definition of character, Grillparzer also made other important contributions to literature, as critics point out. The maligned *Thou Shalt Not Lie* is now acclaimed as one of the best examples of high comedy in German. Three of the dramas he wrote but originally withheld from the public—*Libussa, Family Strife in Habsburg,* and *The Jewess of Toledo*—have received intense critical attention as a result of his treatment of such unusual themes as matriarchy and the role of the outsider in society. The poems collected in *Tristia ex ponto* (1835) and a series of epigrams discovered posthumously are also admired for the depth of despair they reveal in Grillparzer. And two of his novellas, *Der arme Spielmann* (1848; *The Poor Fiddler*) and *Der Kloser bei Sendomir* (1827; *The Monastery in Sendomir*) have received increased critical attention over the last twenty years because of Grillparzer's playful use of narration and his philosophic themes.

PRINCIPAL WORKS

Blanka von Kastilien (play) 1809
Die Ahnfrau [*The Ancestress,* 1938] (play) 1817
Sappho [*Sappho,* 1820] (play) 1818

†*Das goldene Vliess* [*The Golden Fleece,* 1942] (play) 1821
König Ottokars Glück und Ende [*King Ottocar: His Rise and Fall,* 1938] (play) 1825
Das Kloster bei Sendomir (novella) 1827
Ein treuer Diener seines Herrn [*A Faithful Servant of His Master,* 1941] (play) 1828
Des Meeres und der Liebe Wellen [*Hero and Leander,* 1938] (play) 1831
Der Traum ein Leben [*A Dream Is Life,* 1946] (play) 1834
Tristia ex Ponto (poetry) 1835
Weh dem, der lügt! [*Thou Shalt Not Lie,* 1939] (play) 1838
Der arme Spielmann [*The Poor Fiddler,* 1967] (novella) 1848
Ein Bruderzwist in Habsburg [*Family Strife in Habsburg,* 1940] (play) 1872
Die Jüdin von Toledo [*The Jewess of Toledo,* 1913] (play) 1872
Libussa [*Libussa,* 1941] (play) 1874
Sämtliche Werke. 42 vols. (play, novellas, poetry, essays, and criticism) 1909-48

*This is the date of composition.

†This trilogy includes *Das Gastfreund, Die Argonauten,* and *Medea.*

CRITICISM

Gustav Pollak (essay date 1907)

SOURCE: "Grillparzer's Early Years," in *Franz Grillparzer and the Austrian Drama,* Dodd, Mead, and Company, 1907, pp. 30-40.

[*In the following excerpt, Pollak relates relevant facts regarding Grillparzer's early life and first compositions.*]

Franz Grillparzer was born in Vienna on the 15th of January, 1791, and died there on the 21st of January, 1872. Fame came to him at the very beginning of his career, yet his long life, consistently devoted to high ideals, brought him disappointments such as have fallen to the lot of few writers of his intellect and character. Prof. August Sauer has prefaced his standard biography of the poet by a telling characterization of the attitude of the world toward him during his lifetime and since his death:

> Born in a land which from time immemorial has cultivated German poetry and song, but which in the march of centuries had become completely estranged from the progress of German thought; reared during a time of political stress, when the foundations of law and morality, of hereditary privileges and acquired rights were crumbling; meeting with many obstacles during the period of his youthful development, yet preserving his own individuality in spite of conflicting influences, the poet appeared before the public, at the age of twenty-six, with a work of rare maturity and power, and be-

came at one bound the literary celebrity of his day, both in his native country and the greater German fatherland. But not for long did the favor of the fickle public remain true to him. The theatres of Germany soon closed their doors to the Austrian, and even in his own country he found it difficult to make his way. Roughly handled by shallow and thoughtless critics; forced to defend his intellectual treasures against a stupidly insolent and tyrannical censorship; enduring the tortures of a melancholy temperament, he shrank from the world more and more, and finally lapsed into complete silence after his profoundest and most characteristic work had met with a bare *succès d'estime,* and a remarkable creation, revealing the humorous side of his genius, had been hooted down by the public of the very theatre which had witnessed his first triumph. And while, dejected and embittered, he gave himself up to his favorite studies—becoming, in his seclusion, a mere myth to his contemporaries—a theatre director of unusual energy and intelligence succeeded in winning back for the Vienna Burgtheater play after play from the literary legacy of the still living writer. The author witnessed the belated flowering of his fame with indifference, almost with disgust; but the homage paid him by his native city extended beyond its bounds, and the remarkable celebration of his eightieth birthday awakened all Germany from her apathetic attitude of so many years. A year later his funeral gave rise to a demonstration such as no German poet since Klopstock had evoked. The honors paid to his memory in Austria were such as had hitherto been reserved only for the most distinguished and popular of her military heroes, like Radetzky and Hess. The enthusiasm thus engendered affected most deeply the rising generation, and the year of his death marked the resurrection of his works. With a surprise akin to awe Germany beheld a half-forgotten poet rise from the shades of the past, her literary possessions being as it were suddenly enriched by the discovery of a national classic. Since then the personality of the poet has aroused growing interest, and the researches of posterity have disclosed the powers of a poet as gifted as he was unfortunate, whose life is thrown into relief by the background of a singular historical epoch now practically closed forever.

United Germany is beginning to atone for the indifference with which down to 1870 Berlin, and not Berlin alone among the great centres of thought, regarded the intellectual life of Vienna. More than any other of Austria's men of genius, has Grillparzer suffered from the wilful neglect of the literary historians of Germany. During a long period, not only critics of the stamp of Wolfgang Menzel—whose littleness has escaped oblivion only because he dared to attack the great—but writers like Gervinus and Julian Schmidt utterly failed to grasp the significance of the Austrian dramatist. Within recent years, however, there has grown up in Germany a Grillparzer literature inferior in volume and minuteness of critical research only to that which gathers steadily around the names of Goethe, Schiller, Lessing and Heine. Grillparzer's bitter remark to Beethoven: "Foreign literary men have a prejudice against anything that comes from Austria; in Germany there exists a veritable conspiracy against Austrian writers" fortunately finds no echo in the Germany of to-day. All German-speaking countries joined Austria in celebrating the centenary of Grillparzer's birth, in January, 1891, when fifty-five theatres, from Bukowina to the Baltic Provinces, performed his plays.

International fairmindedness has always been slow in making its way into literature. Certainly no German has as yet written a history of German literature that does full justice to Austrian dramatists—a history such as an enlightened foreigner, like Taine, might have produced. Had the brilliant Frenchman chosen to place before the world a picture of what is best and most enduring in the German drama, we should, in all probability, possess a fairer estimate of the achievements of Grillparzer than has until recent times been obtainable from any German source. Whatever the defects of his method, Taine, who pleaded so eloquently for the hospitable interchange of ideas in the realm of literature, who in his "History of English Literature" welcomed the fact that "the French are beginning to comprehend the gravity of the Puritans," and who hoped that "perhaps the English will end by comprehending the gayety of Voltaire"—the French critic, in comparing Grillparzer with Goethe, Schiller and the very few other German dramatists with whose genius his may fitly be compared, would have made adequate allowance for those natural, political and social characteristics of the country of his birth that made the Austrian poet what he was. The Germans too long refused in his case to heed Goethe's injunction to go into the poet's land in order to understand the poet:

> Wer den Dichter will verstehen
> Muss in Dichter's Lande gehen.

In an oft-quoted distich Grillparzer wrote: "If you look at the country around you from the heights of the Kahlenberg you will understand what I have written and what I am," and but a short time before his death he said: "I am not a German, but an Austrian, of Lower Austria, and above all am I a Viennese." And indeed it is easy to recognize in him the virtues and defects of the typical Viennese, and to trace in his character and his writings the influence of his surroundings during that eventful period of Austrian history that lies between his birth and his death—a period which includes the wars against revolutionary France, Austria's humiliation by Bonaparte, the deadening régime of Metternich, the liberal spring-tide of 1848, the reactionary gloom of the following years, and the catastrophe of Sadowa, which led in 1867, five years before the poet's death, to the transformation of the Hapsburg monarchy into the constitutional dual empire of to-day.

Grillparzer's life nearly equalled in length that of Goethe, but it was as full of sad unrest as Goethe's was of serene repose. "Grillparzer," says his French biographer, Prof. Auguste Ehrhard, "never knew that quiet and smiling happiness which the Weimar poet owed to his good fortune, to the advantages of a genius always sure of itself, to the balance and harmony of his varied endowments, and also, as we must remember, to his indifference to the political destinies of his country. The Austrian poet lacked these essentials for the enjoyment of life. He experienced bitter disappointments, which all the splendor of his fame could not efface, and his patriotic heart suffered in every crisis through which his country passed."

Grillparzer has revealed his inner life in a remarkable autobiography, which he wrote in 1853, to conform with a usage of the Vienna Academy of Sciences requiring its members to furnish a sketch of their lives. Unfortunately, his recollections close with the year 1836. There is, however, much valuable autobiographic material in fragmentary jottings and in diaries of his travels in Italy, in 1819; in Germany, in 1826; in France and England, in 1836, and in Greece, in 1843. His **"Recollections of the Year 1848"** complete the direct record of his life.

He was the son of a cultured lawyer of high character, but somewhat stern disposition, who reminds us in some of his traits of the old Councillor Goethe. The boy inherited from his father the clearness of intellect which was one of his most striking characteristics. The early education he received was desultory, and tended to the suppression of his romantic and artistic instincts. There was little intimacy between father and son. The mother, impressionable and affectionate as she was, entirely lacked the reposeful charm of "Frau Aja," who presided over young Goethe's home. She came of a musical family and was herself passionately fond of music. Haydn and Mozart had frequented the house of her father, Christopher Sonnleithner. He and his two sons were well known in the musical and theatrical circles of Vienna. Franz inherited his mother's musical talent, which afterward proved his chief solace, but, unfortunately, along with it, the tendency to melancholy which brooded over his whole life.

He was the oldest of four sons. He differed from his brothers so radically in character and tastes that he grew up, as he wrote, "in complete isolation." All his brothers proved a source of constant care to him. One of them drowned himself at the age of seventeen, another became insane. The brothers passed the years of their childhood in a gloomy dwelling with enormous rooms, into which a ray of sunshine rarely penetrated.

Franz was an omnivorous reader from a very early age. A story of the martyrdom of the saints, which fell into his hands at a country place, awakened in him the desire to become a priest and rival their heroism in suffering. "When I returned to town," he relates, "I got myself a priestly robe made of yellow paper, and read mass, my oldest brother gladly acting as my assistant. I preached leaning over the back of a chair, our old cook, who listened very devoutly to my nonsense, being my only audience. She was also the only listener I had when I played on the piano, but she cared for one piece only, which she asked me to play again and again. At that time the execution of Louis XVI. was still fresh in everybody's mind. Among other exercises I played a march, which I was told had been performed at the execution, and in the second part of

which there was a run of an octave, played with one finger, that was supposed to express the drop of the guillotine's knife. The old woman always wept copiously when I reached that passage, and could not hear it often enough."

The children received scarcely any religious instruction. "My father," he wrote, "had been reared in the period of Joseph II. and did not think much of religious exercises. My mother attended mass every Sunday; she was followed by a man-servant, who carried her prayer book; but we children never entered church. I remember that later on, at the gymnasium, where every schoolday began with mass, I, in my savage ignorance, had to watch my comrades in order to know when to rise, to kneel, or to beat the breast."

Young Grillparzer shared Goethe's early and intense interest in the theatre. He and his brothers acted in romantic plays improvised by him, and manufactured their own knightly armor and the stage settings. He was inspired by a dramatic library which he found among his father's books, and which included "Hamlet" and "King Lear," but none of the plays of Schiller and Goethe. Lessing's "Nathan der Weise" he did not find to his liking. Among other books which fascinated him were translations of Cook's "Voyages," Buffon's "Natural History" and, above all, Guthrie and Gray's "Universal History," which he "devoured rather than read." The first German poets he became acquainted with were Gessner and Ewald Kleist. When at last a volume of Goethe fell into his hands, he was charmed with the hero of "Götz von Berlichingen," but did not much care for the other characters. Nor did he fully appreciate Schiller's plays. He read "Wallenstein's Lager" eagerly, but the "Piccolomini" he found dull, because of the long speeches. He preferred a translation of Gozzi's "Raven" to all the dramas of Goethe, Schiller and Shakespeare. The boy became early aware that he was hampered in his dramatic recitations by a lisp, an inherited defect which he later overcame by imitating the example of Demosthenes.

Neither at the gymnasium nor at the university was Grillparzer remarkable for scholarship or application, but he soon became known among his fellow-students and to some of his professors for his literary gifts. His father discouraged the youthful author, although he took a certain pride in his talent. He generally wound up his criticism of his son's productions by predicting that he would die a pauper's death. "My father's displeasure," wrote Grillparzer, "reached its height at the time of the first occupation of Vienna by the French, after our disastrous campaign. My patriotic ardor, stimulated by my father's own attitude, prompted me to ridicule the absurd measures of the government in a wretched song. When I read it to him he turned pale with fright, represented to me that I ran the risk of imperilling my future by such verses, and implored me not to show them to any one, though he did not tell me to destroy them, which fact, as I thought, proved that he was not altogether displeased with them." In some unexplained way the poem had already fallen into strange hands, for the next day his father returned in dismay from the restaurant where he occasionally took a glass of beer in the evening, and told the boy that the poem had been read aloud by one of the guests and met with general approval. "The doggerel," wrote Grillparzer, "went the rounds of the city, in spite or rather because of its uncouth plainness of speech, but fortunately no one guessed the name of the author." The verses, entitled **"Schlecht und Recht"** (**"Wrong and Right"**), are included in Grillparzer's collected poems, and testify alike to his fervent patriotism and a skill in versification remarkable in a boy of fourteen.

Under the influence of Schiller's "Don Carlos," Grillparzer began, at the age of sixteen, a drama, **Blanka von Kastilien,** which he finished two years later. It deals with the fate of the queen of Pedro the Cruel, and is chiefly interesting as foreshadowing certain psychological problems which he introduced in later dramas. **Blanka** resembles "Don Carlos" in being far too long to be performed in one evening. Though not without dramatic promise, it is crude and prosy. Grillparzer's early power of self-analysis is shown in his own condemnation of the play, in 1808, as one that could never be acted. His mind was occupied with half-a-dozen ambitious dramatic schemes, but he finished only, in 1811, a little comedy, **Wer ist schuldig?** (**Who is Guilty?**), which reminds one of Körner's one-act plays.

Grillparzer, like Goethe, studied law to please his father, but like him, also, he derived the principal inspiration of his college years from contact with gifted fellow-students. Kant's philosophy was the subject of heated discussion at social gatherings in their rooms. One of his closest friends, Altmütter, who afterwards became professor of chemistry in the Vienna Institute of Technology, anticipated, according to Grillparzer, Sir Humphry Davy in a discovery concerning the nature of alkalies. "Altmütter and I," wrote Grillparzer in his autobiography, "were among the very laziest students, and really cared only for discussions. We loved to stroll among the beautiful surroundings of Vienna, indulging in the most extravagant plans for the future. Thus we stood one day upon the heights of the Kahlenberg, behind us the pedestal of some lost statue. We mounted the altar-like block with a feeling of almost godlike importance, and, embracing each other, looked out upon the vast panorama spread before us. Unnoticed by us, an elderly gentleman, evidently a North German, had climbed the height, and standing near us, regarded us with astonishment. 'Yes,' said Altmütter to him, as we descended, 'do not wonder. This one—pointing to me—will raise a temple, and I shall tear one down.' As for the latter, he meant Lavoisier's system of chemistry. The gentleman probably thought he had two lunatics before him."

At the age of fifteen Grillparzer experienced the first pangs of love. The object of his devotion was an actress at one of the minor theatres, of the same age as himself. He had an exalted idea of both her person and her accomplishments, and when he learned that her character was not above reproach, and saw her at the theatre in a box, in the company of an old man, he was so greatly shocked that he became ill. He saw and heard around him at an early day much that was objectionable, but "an innate sense of shame," he wrote, "preserved me from following the bad example given me by my comrades. This—shall I call it sense of honor?—was so strong in me that it did not even permit me to cut my lessons at school. To the best of my knowledge, I have never missed a lecture." Another youthful love episode is worth recording.

"Several years afterwards," he relates, "I fell in love with a singer, who, as Cherubin in Mozart's 'Figaro,' in all the charm of her youthful beauty, and transfigured by the glorious music, took complete possession of my imagination. I wrote a poem to her which may be called good, although its passionate fervor bordered somewhat on the insane, or even on the immoral. However, it never entered my mind to approach her in person. I was at that time in the poorest circumstances, as was evidenced by my wardrobe, while the object of my passion was decked in silk and gold, the daily gifts of her numerous admirers. Nor could I assume that the charms of my person might predispose her in my favor. I therefore locked up my verses with a keen feeling of my humbleness, and nothing in the world could have tempted me to speak of my sentiments to any one. Long after, I met a young and wealthy man, who had been during the period of my Cherubin frenzy one of the favored admirers of my heroine, that is to say, one of those who paid her tribute in solid coin. We talked of poetry, and he remarked how queer it was that poets whose first productions manifested decided talent so often disappeared from public view forever. Thus he remembered to have seen—he did not know in what way—at the time of his acquaintanceship with that singer, a poem professing the most ardent love for her in the most beautiful verses. The girl became almost frantic on reading them, and used every effort to find out who the author was, declaring that if she succeeded she would dismiss all her admirers, in order to grant to the unknown poet the favor he craved in such beautiful language. This declaration, he said, almost caused a rupture between them. At the present day, he went on to say, there was not a poet before the public able to write such verses. I asked him to show me the poem, and sure enough it was my own. In a manner unaccountable to me it had found its way to her, and while I was consumed with hopeless longing, the beautiful object of my desires awaited with impatience an opportunity of meeting me. But such has been my fate throughout life—want of confidence in myself whenever I was undecided how to act, alternating with haughty pride whenever I was disparaged or compared with some one else to my disadvantage." The poem, under the title **"Cherubin,"** has a place in the collected works, and is indeed remarkable for its glowing passion, unreservedly, though not indelicately, expressed.

The growing ill-health of his father awoke the young student from his life of careless ease. In his melancholy mood he took up once more the study of music, which he had neglected for years. But he had forgotten all he ever knew, and nothing remained but the ability to improvise. "Often," he wrote, "I placed a copper engraving upon the music stand before me and played what the subject suggested, as though it were a musical composition. I remember that later on, while I was a tutor in the house of a noble family, the violin teacher of the young count, a musician of high standing, listened to me behind the door for a quarter of an hour at a time, and on entering the room could not praise me enough. The count's possessions included only an old piano without strings; nevertheless, I often played upon it for half a day, without intermission, and regardless of the absence of sound. Later on, when I devoted myself to poetry, the gift of musical improvisation gradually diminished, particularly after I took lessons in counterpoint, in order to systematize my thoughts. My progress and development become more satisfactory, but I lost inspiration, and now I know but little more than when my fondness for music first awoke. I had always this strange peculiarity, that in passing from one subject to another, I lost my fondness for the former, and with it whatever ability for it I possessed, and what skill in it I had acquired. I have cultivated whatever a man can do. Dancing, hunting, riding, fencing, drawing, swimming—there was nothing too difficult for me. Yes, I may say that, with the exception of hunting, I cultivated everything with decided talent, and yet I have been weaned from all these things. Thus I was one of the best, or at least one of the most elegant, of swimmers, but if I were thrown into the water to-day, I should certainly drown. Inspiration has been my deity, and thus it will always be."

During his father's illness he set to music a number of songs, among them Goethe's "König von Thule," which the sufferer never tired of hearing. The father's decline was rapid. His illness was the result of his patriotic sorrow over the political misfortunes of Austria, which the son also keenly felt. The young man enrolled himself in the student corps which in 1809 was organized to defend the city against the French invaders. Grillparzer's father was financially ruined by the social disorganization following the military disasters, and the national downfall broke his heart. After he read the provisions of the humiliating peace of Pressburg, he was a changed man. "When, impelled by a presentiment of his approaching end, I sank on my knees at his bedside and, weeping, kissed his hand, he said: 'It is now too late,' doubtless wishing to convey to me that he was not fully satisfied with my character and my doings." "I never really loved my father," adds Grillparzer, "he was too forbidding in manner. Just as he most rigidly suppressed his own emotions, so he made it almost impossible for any one to approach him with any display of sentiment. Only later on, when I learned to appreciate the motives of some of his actions, and when I rejoiced in the reputation—which lives on to this day—of his almost incredible honesty, and was thereby inspired to emulate, however feebly, his own example, only then did I pay to his memory the debt incurred during his life-time."

The death of the father left the family almost absolutely without means. Two of the sons earned a living by giving music lessons, and Franz, who was then in his eighteenth

year, and had still two years of law study before him, acted as tutor to two young noblemen, and was thus enabled to contribute to the support of his mother. He bethought himself of his tragedy ***Blanka von Kastilien,*** and offered it to the secretary of the Burgtheater, Herr Sonnleithner, his mother's brother. The play was returned to him with the curt remark that it was unfit for performance, and the young author, remembering his father's prophecy, resolved to renounce forever all dreams of a literary career. Meantime, he had lost his pupils, but one of his former professors offered him a position as tutor in jurisprudence to the nephew of a wealthy count. The young man had another teacher for his general studies, and Grillparzer was only required to give him a few hours of special instruction daily.

> I got into a queer family," he writes in his autobiography. "The young count, of about my own age, who is still living, will not think ill of me if I say in this place that our studies, probably as much through my fault as through his own, amounted to very little. The old uncle was a veritable caricature, frightfully ignorant and arrogant, self-willed, stingy, and bigoted. Having formerly been ambassador at one of the more important German courts and imperial commissary at Ratisbon, he loved to talk of his missions. I have called him stingy, but he was not so in regard to two matters—his stable and the kitchen. In the former he kept a number of magnificent steeds, which, from excessive care for them, he hardly ever used. Over the kitchen presided alternately two cooks of the first quality, a German and a Frenchman. I won the count's favor through my appetite, then highly developed. Every day, between eleven and twelve o'clock, he entered my room in his soiled dressing-gown, in order to read to me the menu and to lay out a sort of plan of campaign—how much was to be eaten of one dish and how little of another, in order to leave room for the next and more tempting course. I was on the road to becoming an epicure in this house, although finally only too glad to return to my mother's simple fare. In spite of all the favor I gained in this way, I was considered by the count a Jacobin, which title he applied to anybody who had opinions different from his own. His wife—we called her the princess because she came of a princely family—passed her time in devotional exercises, and drove to church every day as many times as her husband permitted her to hitch up, in due rotation, the splendid show horses.

Grillparzer enjoyed, on the whole, his leisurely employment. He made abundant use of the library, particularly rich in English books, which the count's grandfather had brought from London, where he had been ambassador. No one else in the house ever looked at a book, and the only difficulty in using the library to his heart's content lay in turning the rusty key of the library room. Grillparzer's first care was to perfect his knowledge of English, which he had some time before begun to study by himself, in order to be able to read Shakespeare in the original. In the summer he went with the family to their estates in Moravia. The other tutor having been dismissed, he had to take entire charge of his pupil. He accompanied him daily to church and took along with him the "Vicar of Wakefield," which the family, from the name of "Vicar" on the title-page, supposed to be a devotional book of some sort. In the winter he returned with the young count to the city and continued as his tutor, although he had found, in February, 1813, an unsalaried position in the imperial library of Vienna. During the following summer months, when the library was closed, Grillparzer again joined his pupil at a castle of the family in Moravia. Nearby there was a famous shrine, Maria Stip, much frequented by pious pilgrims. He was compelled to accompany the countess on one of her visits to the church, and caught a chill there. The count's surgeon, suspecting a contagious disease, advised that the patient be isolated, and had him sent to a lonely hut near Maria Stip, where the village barber used to cup those of the pilgrims who required his attention. For a time the surgeon came to see Grillparzer, but soon his visits ceased, and he was left in charge of the village barber. His illness grew desperate and he himself believed that his end was near. When he finally recovered and was able to journey home he heard of the battle of Leipsic. The noble family had fled from the estate. His money was gone; he had seen during his illness a woman open the drawer in which it lay, but thought he was dreaming. He borrowed, however, enough for the trip, which was retarded by the confusion into which the country had been thrown. "No postmaster, no postilion, no innkeeper or waiter was to be found. Everybody was in the streets. The newspapers were read aloud publicly, people embraced, rejoiced, wept, the millennium seemed to have arrived."

On his return to Vienna he made the impression of one returned from the dead. When he called on the family of his pupil he discovered "not a trace of shame or repentance on their aristocratic faces, although there was a certain embarrassment in their manner." They had engaged a tutor for the young count, but were willing to have Grillparzer continue his special instruction. He resumed his task, devoting himself at the same time heart and soul to the study of languages in the imperial library, where his official duties were of the lightest. The condition of things there was characteristic of the easy-going ways of Viennese officialdom.

> The employees, mostly good-natured persons, conducted themselves pretty much as might old invalid soldiers in an armory; they preserved what they found on hand, showed rare things to visitors, used the slim appropriations for the purchase of all imaginable editions of the classics and kept away, as far as possible, all forbidden, that is to say, all modern, books. Systematic library work was out of the question. All this suited me perfectly. My first care was to add to my knowledge of Greek, which I and my colleague Eichenfeld studied diligently. In order to be undisturbed, we went into the manuscript room of the library, and there, surrounded by all the necessary material, we read the Greek writers. This lasted for some time, until the first custodian of the institution, an intolerable ignoramus, himself without the ability or desire to use a manuscript, got wind of our doings and, impelled by envy at the thought of our possibly editing a manuscript—a thing he could not dream of doing—forbade us from entering the manuscript room.

I had in the meantime also devoted myself to another language, the study of which I had begun some time previously, and which was to have the most important influence on my future career. I had always had a conviction that a poet could not be translated into another language. In spite of my bad memory, I had therefore acquired, in addition to the two ancient languages and the indispensable French, a knowledge of Italian and English; and at a very early age, attracted by Bertuch's translation of Don Quixote and his remarks about Spanish poets, I had begun the study of Spanish. I had stumbled upon a very ancient Spanish grammar, so ancient as to antedate Lope de Vega and Calderon and to compel me later on to unlearn and modify the rules thus acquired. Owing to lack of money, I was without a dictionary until I picked up at a second-hand bookshop a volume of Sobrino, which it is true was minus the entire letter A, but which on that account was offered for one florin in paper money. This was scarcely a sufficient equipment for the serious study of the language. About that time there appeared Schlegel's translation of some of the plays of Calderon, among which his 'Devotion at the Cross' chiefly attracted me. However admirable I considered Schlegel's translation of Shakespeare, that of Calderon's plays appeared to me entirely inadequate. That a writer who in his imaginative flights soared almost beyond the reach of poesy could not have indulged in such stiff and awkward phrases, was perfectly clear to me. Armed with all the resources of the imperial library, I threw myself with ardor into the study of Spanish, and attacked it where the difficulties were greatest, that is to say, in the plays of Calderon. In order not to pass lightly over obstacles, and to force myself to look up every new word in the dictionary, I resolved to translate the play I had chosen, 'La vida es sueño,' rendering it, passage for passage, at once into German verse and even, following the original, into rhyme. How much time I consumed in this tedious labor I do not know; at all events I did not get beyond half of the first act; but that sufficed, as the only object of my translation was the study of the language.

It so happened that this very play of Calderon's was then about to be performed in Vienna, and when Grillparzer mentioned to a friend that he had himself tried his hand at translating it, he was induced by him to lend him the manuscript, and, finally, to allow the *Modenzeitung,* an influential literary journal, to print it. Grillparzer's translation appeared the day after the first performance of Calderon's play, and was lauded to the skies by the editor of the *Modenzeitung,* to the disparagement of the other translation. The author of the latter was "Karl August West," the pseudonym of Joseph Schreyvogel, the able secretary and artistic manager of the imperial theatre at Vienna. Schreyvogel, who knew Grillparzer's family, but had never met Franz, was deeply chagrined at the thought that the young man should lend himself to a malicious personal attack on him. When he learned that the translator was entirely guiltless of any such purpose, he expressed a desire to make his acquaintance, and from their first meeting dated the beginning of the close relations between Grillparzer and Schreyvogel which ended only with the death of the latter.

George A. Wells (essay date 1969)

SOURCE: "The Greek Tragedies," in *The Plays of Grillparzer,* Pergamon Press, 1969, pp. 33-82.

[*In the following excerpt, Wells discusses Grillparzer's three Greek tragedies—*Sappho, Das goldene Vliess, *and* Des Meeres und der Liebe Wellen—*noting that they all share the theme of love and that in each Grillparzer concentrated on preserving unity of time, place, and action.*]

1. SAPPHO (1818)

In the draft of a letter to Müllner of 1818, Grillparzer confessed to being somewhat ashamed of what he called the "tolles Treiben" in **Die Ahnfrau,** and was anxious to show that he could write a play without bangs and ghosts. He added that when he came across the story of Sappho, he realized at once that he had found the material he needed for a calm play with a simple plot (III, 1. 97).

The simplicity of the material enabled him to keep the three unities. This is in fact the only play of his which keeps the unity of place; as a result, direct action is curtailed and messengers are brought on to narrate what has happened. Thus, in the first scene, Rhamnes tells the slave-girls what Sappho has achieved during her absence. The way Sappho and Phaon became acquainted is conveyed entirely by Phaon's narrative (I, 3); Eucharis narrates what happened at the banquet (between Acts I and II) at which Melitta and Phaon first become conscious of each other and which serves, as Grillparzer said, "sie in jenen Zustand des Berührtseyns zu bringen, das der Liebe den Weg bereitet" (*ibid.,* p. 101). Eucharis also narrates Melitta's ablutions (II, 3), the return of Melitta and Phaon as captives (V, 1) and—most important of all—Sappho's august behaviour (V, 5) before her final entry. Since Grillparzer prefers direct action to narrative, he does not, in his later plays, keep the unity of place, which has messengers' reports as a natural concomitant. Even in **Sappho** a great deal is directly enacted: e.g. the scene culminating in Phaon kissing Melitta, which is witnessed by Sappho, who tries to convince herself that nevertheless all is well; also the scenes where Phaon speaks Melitta's name in his dream, and Sappho, although she still resists the obvious inference, decides to question the girl; when she does so, her anger is thoroughly aroused, and she draws her knife. All these scenes bring direct and swift action.

Grillparzer did not find it easy to make his material into a convincing tragedy. In antiquity Sappho's story had been the theme of comedies. It was the comic poets who linked her with Phaon, who is not mentioned in any of her extant poems. In these comedies he is an ugly old ferryman, rejuvenated by magic ointment, supplied by Aphrodite, and then in consequence pestered by women, of whom Sappho is one. Because of her age her advances evoke no response, so she throws herself from the rock at the end of the isle of Leucas. Tradition prescribed such behaviour to cure the pangs of unrequited love; the victim jumped in, was taken from the water, and could go on repeating the jump until well and truly "cooled off" in every respect.

Grillparzer had to avoid what Carlyle called "the ridicule that lies within a single step of Sappho's tragic situation" ([Carlyle, *Critical and Miscellaneous Essays,*] p. 332). An oldish woman pursuing a young man could well be represented as ridiculous. Grillparzer himself seems to have felt that such material is repulsive rather than comic:

> Sappho ist in der Katastrophe [viz. Act IV] ein verliebtes, eifersüchtiges, in der Leidenschaft sich vergessendes Weib; ein Weib, das einen *jüngern* Mann liebt. In der gewöhnlichen Welt ist ein solches Weib ein ekelhafter Gegenstand.
>
> (III, 1, 99)

Scherer asserts that the comic element shows through the action of Grillparzer's play, and also that "die Gestalt der Sappho im Ganzen hat etwas unwillkürlich zur Parodie Herausforderndes" ([Scherer, *Vorträge und Aufsätze zur Gesch. des geistigen Lebens in Deutschland und Österreich,*] p. 234). He is thinking in particular of her suicidal leap from the rock, and says we do not feel that her passion was so great that she cannot go on living. But we must ask whether it is her passion for Phaon that in fact motivates her suicide, or whether the text gives other reasons for her behaviour. As Rippman notes, most critics have found the final tragic outcome unconvincing. He himself asserts that we "cannot but feel that death is the true ending" ([Rippmann, *Sappho,*] p. xii). But the question is: what is the basis for this feeling, if in fact we have it?

From what we are told in Act I it seems that Sappho felt desperately in need of a partner. Her relationship with Phaon was begun at the Olympic festival entirely on her initiative. He was standing "schamentgeistert" in her presence, and she bade him follow her (l. 253). He is still bewildered when they arrive in Lesbos at the beginning of the play (ll. 317-18). Her view of him then is naïvely ideal—she even recommends him to her people as an accomplished poet (l. 77)! From the first she is unsure of his affection. She warns him that she will be capable of any unreasonable behaviour if he becomes indifferent to her (ll. 123-7). And when he expresses his ecstatic feelings, she replies that he may one day view her more realistically and therefore less favourably (ll. 202-3). The basis for her fears is that she has become embittered by painful disappointments in friendship and love, and also by the early death of her family (ll. 113-22), whereas Phaon is young and a complete stranger to the cynicism born of disappointment. It is surely because of her loneliness and unhappiness that she was drawn to him in the first place, and thus deludes herself into thinking that his admiration of her is love. She expressly contrasts her own bitterness with his "Lebenslust" and "Lust an dem, was ist" (ll. 265, 267), and a little later she elaborates this contrast (ll. 370-92) and designates it as the "gulf" which divides them (l. 394). She begs the gods to give her back the outlook of her youth (ll. 380-7) and so bring her into harmony with him. But it is obviously impossible for her to become young again, "mit runden Kinderwangen", as she charmingly puts it, and the relationship is soon terminated. But this hardly gives her a motive for suicide. It would be unconvincing if she were finally to think that she cannot live without this callow youth who lacks intellectual interests and never loved her anyway. It is quite plausible that, in her state of lonely unhappiness, she should have fallen in love with him; but by the end of the play she has realized that he could never have understood her (l. 1962) and that they had better part. Nor is she represented as killing herself because, in the grief of her recent disappointment, she despairs of finding any suitable partner, yet feels she cannot live without one.

We must look for other clues. After she has spoken of the difference in age and outlook between herself and Phaon and called it the "gulf" which lies between them, she immediately goes on to describe this gulf in very different terms, and it is not easy to see the connection between her two interpretations of it. The second of these is that in pursuing her literary ambitions she has become cut off from normal warm human contacts:

> Weh Dem, den aus der Seinen stillem Kreise
> Des Ruhms, der Ehrsucht eitler Schatten lockt.

> (ll. 398-9)

She goes on to liken such a person to a mariner sailing through rough seas in a light boat. He has no green fields nor flowers, nor any living thing around him, but only the grey limitless expanses of the sea. The coast which harbours his loved ones he only sees afar off, and their cries are drowned by the roar of the waves. When he does finally return, the flowers are dead, and all life and warmth has gone. Although this whole extended simile expresses the lot of anyone who neglects those closest to him in his pursuit of his ambition, Sappho is, of course, thinking primarily of literary ambition and fame. She has just won a laurel wreath at the Olympic competition, but this success seems to her as barren as the laurel leaves. In an earlier scene she had made similar remarks:

> Umsonst nicht hat zum Schmuck der Musen Chor
> Den unfruchtbaren Lorbeer sich erwählt,
> Kalt, frucht- und duftlos drücket er das Haupt
> Dem er Ersatz versprach für manches Opfer.

> (ll. 271-4)

It is not that she has been unhappy all her life; her single-minded devotion to literary composition has brought her "des Vollbringens Wahnsinnglühende Lust" (l. 50). But she wants the warmth of family life instead, and fears that, like the mariner in her image, she will find only desolation on returning to land. In sum, then, the gulf between herself and Phaon exists (1) because of her maturity and bitterness of outlook and (2) because she has pursued her (literary) ambition instead of cultivating human relationships. She feels strongly that to devote herself further to literature would be incompatible with marriage, and so she proposes now to live a simple unpretentious life with Phaon and renounce all her ambition. She says to her people:

> An seiner Seite werd' ich unter euch
> Ein einfach stilles Hirtenleben führen.

> (ll. 93-4)

She will not give up her art altogether, but will

> Zum Preise nur von häuslich stillen Freuden
> Die Töne wecken dieses Saitenspiels.

So at this stage she believes that she can reconcile art and life (cf. ll. 280-3), although only by restricting her art drastically.

The view of poetry which she takes in Act I (clear from the passage where she specifies the dire consequences of ambition) is due partly to the fact that she is full of her love and of the married happiness that she thinks awaits her. When her relationship with Phaon has gone badly wrong, she exaggerates in the opposite direction. Instead of the argument of Act I (that devotion to literary ambition has brought her barren recompense) she says in Act IV that she was happy enough in the "meadows of poetry" until Phaon destroyed her composure. Here, it is poetry that is associated with flowers and fields, and the laurel wreath is designated not "dürr", but "heiter" (ll. 1272 ff.).

Grillparzer's comments on the play give some guidance as to how Sappho's position as an artist is related to her personal tragedy, although they do not appear completely consistent. Sometimes he suggests that her tragedy is due to her personal character, while on other occasions he derives it from the fact that she is an artist. The former view is stated in his autobiography, where he says it was not his intention to stress the poetess in Sappho:

> Ich war nämlich immer ein Feind der Künstlerdramen.
> Künstler sind gewohnt, die Leidenschaft als einen Stoff
> zu behandeln. Dadurch wird auch die wirkliche Liebe
> für sie mehr eine Sache der Imagination als der tiefen
> Empfindung. Ich wollte aber Sappho einer wahren
> Leidenschaft, und nicht einer Verirrung der Phantasie
> zum Opfer werden lassen.

> (I, 16, 130-1)

He specifies how the tragedy is derived from Sappho's character in the draft of the letter to Müllner, saying that she is:

> ein Charakter, der Sammelplatz glühender Leidenschaften, über die aber eine *erworbene* Ruhe, die schöne Frucht höherer Geistesbildung, den Szepter führt, bis die angeschmiedeten Sklaven [viz. her passions] die Ketten brechen und dastehen und Wuth schnauben.

> (III, 1, 97)

The text certainly confirms this view of Sappho's character. She warns Phaon in Act I:

> Du kennst noch nicht die Unermeßlichkeit,
> Die auf und nieder wogt in dieser Brust.

> (ll. 126-7)

In conversation with Melitta a little later she confesses to such unpleasant traits as "der Stolz, die Ehrbegier, des Zornes Stachel" (l. 350), and it is clear that she has been quick-tempered and hurtful to the girl on occasions (ll. 359-60). Melitta herself concedes that her mistress is "heftig manchmal, rasch und bitter" (l. 671). And in Act IV, when Phaon and Melitta have aroused Sappho's rage, she begs the gods to protect her from the violence of her own passions:

> Beschützt mich, Götter, schützt mich vor mir selber!
> Des Innern düstre Geister wachen auf
> Und rütteln an des Kerkers Eisenstäben!
>
> (ll. 1219-22)

This image is exactly how Grillparzer expresses himself in the letter to Müllner, where he speaks of her "enchained" passions bursting their bonds. Sappho, then, reaches a tragic situation because she is an unbalanced woman, easily led astray by rage and jealousy.

However, Grillparzer added to the words last quoted from the letter to Müllner:

> Dazu [viz. in addition to Sappho's character] gesellte sich, sobald das Wort: *Dichterin* einmal ausgesprochen war, natürlich auf der Stelle der Kontrast zwischen Kunst und Leben (wenn die Ahnfrau unwillkürlich gewissermaβen eine Paraphrase des berüchtigten d'Alembert'schen malheur d'être geworden ist, so dürfte wohl die Sappho ein in eben dem Sinne wahres malheur d'être poète in sich fassen).

He goes on to say that Phaon and Melitta represent life ("haben die Parthie des Lebens"), and that he was trying to depict "nicht die Miβgunst, das Ankämpfen des Lebens gegen die Kunst, . . . wie in Corregio oder Tasso, sondern die natürliche Scheidewand, die zwischen beiden befestigt ist". We have seen that one reason given in the text to explain the existence of this "natural barrier" is that devotion to art cuts the poet off from family life. But Sappho is prepared to abandon (or at any rate drastically restrict) her art in order to devote herself to her husband, and there is nothing in the text to suggest that she would have been incapable of finding happiness in this way if she had been given the chance. It seems that we must look for another reason for the poet's unhappiness—one that also links up with Sappho's character as an unbalanced woman.

Douglas Yates has made some helpful suggestions on this head ([Yates, *Grillparzer: A Critical Biography,*] pp. 35-6). He shows it was Grillparzer's opinion that the artist has violent passions of which he easily loses control. Thus Grillparzer once observed that he himself had strong passions, and that the dramatist must have them (and try to control them in his life) in order to depict them in his plays. Yates also points to a passage in the letter to Müllner that supports this interpretation. Grillparzer there says that Sappho has a "Kraft" (as a poetess) "die mit unter die erregenden Kräfte des Sturms [der Leidenschaft] selber gehört". This clearly implies that her nature as a poetess is partly responsible for her passionate outburst in Act IV, where her "erworbene Ruhe" vanishes and gives way to "Wut".

Yates' theory enables us to understand the basis of Sappho's behaviour up to the beginning of Act V. But at the end of this final Act, she adopts a new and unexpected attitude, claiming to have "found herself" (l. 1960). What exactly does this mean? Yates thinks that the idea is that the artist is something priestly, even divine, not to be sullied by contact with what is merely human; and that she is now conscious of having betrayed her art by wanting to marry and enjoy life. As Yates himself is aware, this is very different from the theory that the artist is an uncontrolled person who cannot cope with life because of his passions.

Now is it in fact the case that Sappho thinks, in Act V or elsewhere, that she has betrayed her art? She does seem to express this idea in Act III, when her relationship with Phaon has begun to deteriorate radically. In this Act she has (like the priest in Act IV of *Des Meeres und der Liebe Wellen*) a number of monologues in which she resists believing something that she knows at heart to be true. When finally she can no longer resist the conviction that Phaon has betrayed her, she denounces herself for renouncing her art and seeking happiness with a mere mortal:

> O Törin! Warum stieg ich von den Höhn,
> Die Lorbeer krönt, wo Aganippe rauscht,
> Mit Sternenklang sich Musenchöre gatten,
> Hernieder in das engbegrenzte Tal,
> Wo Armut herrscht und Treubruch und Verbrechen?
> Dort oben war mein Platz, dort an den Wolken,
> Hier ist kein Ort für mich, als nur das Grab.
> Wen Götter sich zum Eigentum erlesen,
> Geselle sich zu Erdenbürgern nicht,
> Der Menschen und der Überird'schen Los
> Es mischt sich nimmer in demselben Becher.
>
> (ll. 942-52)

In what follows she certainly does not act on this conviction that she has kinship with the gods and not with man; for instead of transcending her own all-too-human nature, she goes on to reveal jealousy and vindictiveness in her resolve to summon Melitta in order to see why such an empty-headed girl could have impressed Phaon (ll. 963 ff.). When the girl comes, Sappho even draws a dagger on her. Then in Act IV she reaches her lowest moral level. In her opening monologue she convinces herself that ingratitude is a worse crime than murder. The implication is that Phaon (guilty of ingratitude to her) is worse than she (a potential murderess in her behaviour towards Melitta). She decides to take vengeance on Melitta by banishing her to Chios where she will suffer the pangs of unrequited love (ll. 1239-41). In scene 2 she continues to vent her fury at Phaon's ingratitude and orders Rhamnes to remove Melitta by trickery or by actual violence if necessary (l. 1322). When Phaon foils this scheme and himself takes flight with the girl, Sappho breathes "nur Wut und Rache!" (l. 1531), and is so utterly exhausted by the emotional turmoil into which she has been thrown that she sinks into Eucharis' arms at the end of Act IV. However, when the two fugitives are brought back and she is confronted with them, she is unable to take a firm attitude—not only because of her exhaustion, but also because by now she has begun to be conscious of having behaved wrongly to Phaon. It is surely for this reason that she cries (when the couple are announced) "Wer rettet mich vor seinem Anblick?" (l. 1592) and averts her eyes (l. 1703) when he tells her she is unworthy of her art. Admittedly, she never expressly says she has done wrong to Phaon; but it is difficult to explain these words and gestures without assuming consciousness of guilt as their basis.

As for Phaon, his attitude to her here, in the first half of Act V, scene 3, is as negative as it was at the end of Act III (the dagger scene). There he said:

> Und wenn mir je ein Bild verflossner Tage
> In süßer Wehmut vor die Seele tritt,
> Soll schnell ein Blick auf diesen Stahl mich heilen!

And here:

> Wie anders malt' ich mir, ich blöder Tor
> Einst Sapphon aus, in frühern, schönern Tagen!
>
> (ll. 1695-6)

His attitude is intelligible enough. As Grillparzer himself said, Sappho's jealous behaviour "macht ihn durch die bei Menschen so gewöhnliche Verwechslung glauben, weil er Sapphon Unrecht thun sieht, sie sey von jeher gegen ihn im Unrecht gewesen" (III, 1, 100). Yet immediately after this, he appeals to her better nature, saying that as an artist she is only soiling herself by contact with mere humans:

> Mit Höhern, Sappho, halte du Gemeinschaft,
> Man steigt nicht ungestraft vom Göttermahle
> Herunter in den Kreis der Sterblichen.
> Der Arm, in dem die goldne Leier ruhte,
> Er ist geweiht, er fasse Niedres nicht!
>
> (ll. 1726-30)

O. E. Lessing has found this a very ill-motivated change of attitude and has said that "das ganze Intrigenspiel war offenbar nicht geeignet, jene Erkenntnis [that Sappho is semi-divine] in Phaon wachzurufen" ([Lessing, *Grillparzer und das Neue Drama*,] pp. 19–20). But this verdict seems unnecessarily harsh. Phaon has repeatedly regarded Sappho as great and god-like. This is how he thought of her before they ever met (ll. 162-201), and this was still his attitude at the beginning of the play, where his own feeling of insignificance is brought out not only by his words of deference, but also (in Grillparzer's usual way) by the visible contrast between "Sappho, köstlich gekleidet" and Phaon, "ihr zur Seite in einfacher Kleidung" (directions for their entry in I, 2). In the present context he is replying to Sappho's charge that his love for her was a sham (l. 1723). He explains that he loved her genuinely, but as something divine, and that only when he met Melitta did he learn to distinguish these feelings from warm human love. As he himself says, these reflections have brought him to his senses (ll. 1740-1), and so instead of continuing to abuse Sappho as a "gifterfüllte Schlange" who ought to

destroy her lyre because she is unworthy of it (ll. 1685-7), he begs her not to desecrate the sacred arm in which she holds the instrument, as she would do if she turned to earthly love.

Although, as we saw, she had herself, on a previous occasion, argued that she has kinship with the gods rather than with men, here she expressly rejects Phaon's argument, saying in an aside that to renounce love is too high a price to pay for greatness as an artist (ll. 1731-2). However, Phaon reiterates his point at the end of this scene (V, 3):

> Den Menschen Liebe und den Göttern Ehrfurcht,
> Gib uns, was unser, und nimm hin, was dein!
> Bedenke, was du tust, und wer du bist!

All these words bring home to her that her violent and unreasonable behaviour is not what one is entitled to expect of someone of her exalted calling. We saw already that her inability to look Phaon in the face, and also the way she listens silently to his long indictment of her, imply that she is conscious of having done wrong. And after these final words of Phaon, the stage directions indicate that she retires in confusion. When she returns she appears to have taken these words to heart and to agree that her place is among the gods, not with man.

During her absence from the stage, Rhamnes lauds her character. In Act IV she has behaved in a thoroughly unworthy manner, and Grillparzer realized that it would be necessary to restore the audience's sympathy for her. So he makes Rhamnes bring out her sterling qualities in nearly a hundred lines of verse (ll. 1812-92). We can see now one of the reasons why Grillparzer did not take Müllner's advice and delete the first Act of the play, in which (as Müllner complained) there is little action. Grillparzer replied that it was "durchaus notwending, sie noch vor dem Sturm der Leidenschaften so zu zeigen, wie sie in ihrem gewöhnlichen Zustande war, damit der Zuschauer die Arme bemitleide, statt sie zu verabscheuen". If Act I were cut, we should see little but the unpleasant side of her character, and Rhamnes' account of her exalted nature would then strike us as very unconvincing. Even as it now stands, some critics have found it not altogether easy to accept, particularly as it is made to throw Phaon and Melitta into such confusion. O. E. Lessing, for instance, notes that Phaon does not deserve the curses that Rhamnes pours upon him; that if he has behaved badly to Sappho, so has she to him, and that one would expect him to answer Rhamnes by pointing this out. Lessing believes that it is only because Grillparzer's purpose is to elevate her into an august figure that Phaon (implausibly) makes no effective reply and is made to regard himself as small beside the great Sappho. But we have already seen that, a little earlier, he had reverted to his initial elevated view of her, and it is really not at all implausible that he should accept this view now, when Rhamnes presses it upon him so forcibly.

Eucharis next reports that Sappho has assumed a statuesque appearance—"im Kreis von Marmorbildern, fast als ihresgleichen" (l. 1907); that she has taken up her lyre, donned her laurel wreath and purple robe, and looks completely transfigured:

> Wer sie jetzt sah, zum erstenmale sah, . . .
> Als Überird'sche hätt' er sie begrüßt.

There is a close correspondence between this description and the one that Phaon gives of her in Act I, when he tells how sublime she appeared when he first saw her (ll. 222-35). The earlier description prepares us for the later, and this also helps us to understand why Grillparzer declined to cut the first Act.

After Eucharis' long description, Sappho herself appears in this full regalia and announces that she has discovered her true being. In the ensuing monologue she thanks the gods for their many gifts to her. They have given her poetic capacity, fame, and even a taste of the joys of life. She argues that she has completed the task assigned to her in this world (written poetry which will bring her immortal fame), and asks them on that account not to refuse her "den letzten Lohn", that is, to remove her from this life. There is no suggestion that she feels any guilt. She does not, for instance, argue that she has sinned against the gods by wishing to renounce her art in favour of married life, and should therefore be punished by them with death.[1] She is asking them not for punishment but for further "Lohn" in addition to blessings already bestowed. This reward is to consist in allowing her to die before she becomes old and is mocked by fools who deem themselves wise, and by the enemies of the gods. She certainly stresses that she belongs to the gods (l. 2004), and that it would be inappropriate for anything divine to suffer weakness and sickness. When she cries to them:

> Erspart mir dieses Ringens blut'ge Qual.
> Zu schwach fühl' ich mich, länger noch zu kämpfen

she does not expressly say against whom this struggle would have to be fought, were her life to continue. The idea seems to be that she would have to fight it against her own passionate nature; for immediately afterwards she repeats (l. 2025) what Phaon had said to her "Den Menschen Liebe und den Göttern Ehrfurcht!" and she must surely have in mind the context in which this was said, namely Phaon's rebuke of her uncontrolled behaviour—a rebuke which included the injunction: "Bedenke, was du tust und wer du bist!"

In her final monologue she never once expresses her feelings of guilt towards Phaon and Melitta. It is clear enough from her behaviour earlier in Act V that she has such feelings, and I think Grillparzer's reason for not making her allude to them here in the monologue which motivates her suicide was that he wished to avoid any suggestion that she dies in order to atone for her behaviour towards the couple. They are too insignificant to be the cause of her death, and so she is made to tell Phaon that he could never understand her and that they must go their separate ways (l. 1962). Phaon and Melitta are not the real causes of her

death, but through them she has become aware that she can no longer be certain that she will always be able to control her passionate nature, and that she would be a very unworthy ambassador of the gods if she went on living. Her recent experiences, which we have witnessed in the play, are certainly such as to provide a genuine basis for such fears. This interpretation of her final state of mind seems to me to be more in harmony with her last words than the view that she regards her death as a punishment for betraying her art, or as a relief from unrequited love.[2]

Sappho is the first of Grillparzer's plays with a final Act in which the principal character adopts a new, unexpectedly calm attitude. In Sappho's case this is not exactly the dispassionate review of previous aberrations that it is with Medea, with Ottokar, and with the king in *Die Jüdin* (see below, pp. 158-9). Sappho's final criticism of her own behaviour is implicit, not directly stated; and she is really more concerned with the transgressions she would commit in the future, if she were to live on, than with her past.

As Grillparzer's second published play, *Sappho,* is a notable improvement on *Die Ahnfrau* in that it has none of the artificial motivation that disfigures the earlier work. But it still has many repetitions, neat antitheses and other features which O. E. Lessing has said are "im Ton der Übertreibungen jugendlicher Schillerepigonen" ([*Grillparzer und das Neue Drama,*] p. 12). As an example he refers to the following passage, where Sappho can no longer doubt that Phaon is in love with Melitta:

> Sie schwebt vor seiner schamentblößten Stirn,
> In ihre Hülle kleiden sich die Träume,
> Die schmeichelnd sich des Falschen Lager nahn.
> Sappho verschmäht, um ihrer Sklavin willen?
> Verschmähet! Wer? Beim Himmel! und von wem?
> Bin ich dieselbe Sappho denn nicht mehr,
> Die Könige zu ihren Füßen sah
> Und, spielend mit der dargebotnen Krone,
> Die Stolzen sah und hörte, und—entließ;
> Dieselbe Sappho, die ganz Griechenland
> Mit lautem Jubel als sein Kleinod grüßte?

This outburst is, however, not just empty rhetoric. Sappho is not only jealous of Melitta but is also beginning to realize that Phaon is something of a nonentity. This is clearly conveyed by her question "Verschmähet! Wer? Beim Himmel! und von wem?" and by the contrast with the royal suitors that follows. I can only endorse the judgement of Scherer that "Leere Rhetorik, welche aus dem Rahmen der Situation heraustritt, um einem lyrischen Gelüste des Dichters zu fröhnen, überhaupt jene beliebten Kraftstellen, in denen ein Poet seine Figuren als Sprachrohr für seine eigenen Angelegenheiten mißbraucht, werden sich bei Grillparzer kaum finden" ([*Vorträge und Afsätze zur Gesch. des geistigen Lebens in Deutschland und Österreich,*] p. 218)

2. *Das goldene Vließ* (1821)

A trilogy is not what one would have expected from Grillparzer, who disliked plays where understanding what is happening at one point presupposes memory of many previous details. This approach, he thought, was epic and suited to a reader who can pause to correlate passages, rather than dramatic, which means suited to the stage. Thus in his autobiography he was critical of his decision to write *Das goldene Vließ* as a trilogy:

> Das Drama ist eine Gegenwart, es muß alles was zur Handlung gehört in sich enthalten. Die Beziehung eines Teils auf den andern gibt dem Ganzen etwas Episches, wodurch es vielleicht an Großartigkeit gewinnt, aber an Wirklichkeit und Prägnanz verliert.
>
> (I, 16, 135)

The only acceptable type of trilogy, he adds, is Aeschylus' three independent plays linked only by their common theme, where "der durchgehende Faden verknüpft, ohne zu bedingen"—in contrast to Schiller's *Wallenstein* trilogy, which is completely epic: "Das Lager ist völlig überflüssig, und die Piccolomini sind nur etwas, weil Wallensteins Tod darauf folgt." Grillparzer's trilogy lies between these two extremes. The action of each of the first two plays is complete in itself and not merely an exposition to the third. But the third is by far the most effective, for the same reason that, in Goethe's judgement, *Wallensteins Tod* is superior to *die Piccolomini,* namely (as he wrote to Schiller, 9 March 1799): "Die Welt ist gegeben in der das alles geschieht, die Gesetze sind aufgestellt nach denen man urteilt, der Strom des Interesses, der Leidenschaft, findet sein Bette schon gegraben, in dem er hinabrollen kann."

The final play is not completely independent of the others but most of the preceding action is summarized in it (e.g. Jason's long account in Act I of how he came to woo Medea). It is independent enough to be played separately, and is the only part of the trilogy still regularly performed. Its portrayal of how bright hopes can end in disillusion is (particularly in the two opening Acts) among Grillparzer's most powerful and moving essays in pessimism. By the time its action commences, all joy has long since vanished from the lives of Medea, Gora and Jason. And by the end Kreusa, the one adult character with no trace of ruthlessness, is brutally murdered, leaving her father, the king, heartbroken.

Many of the events presupposed in Euripides' *Medea* are enacted in the first two plays of Grillparzer's trilogy. This is partly because the modern dramatist could not assume that his audience was acquainted with the details of the legend. But it is partly, as Scherer noted, "dem Geiste des modernen Dramas gemäß" ([*Vorträge und Afsätze zur Gesch. des geistigen Lebens in Deutschland und Österreich,*] p. 236). Whereas a Greek tragedy concentrates on the final catastrophe of a series, modern tragedies begin at the beginning, with no trace of gloom in Act I, although there are of course exceptions. Schiller said (in a letter to Goethe of 26 April 1799) that the historical material for his *Maria Stuart* lent itself to what he called "the Euripidean method" of starting after a catastrophe. And in Schiller's play, Maria has in fact been imprisoned, tried and con-

demned before the curtain rises. However, it is usual in modern drama to begin before gloom and disaster, and to achieve this with the Medea legend Grillparzer had to write a trilogy.

There is a third reason why he enacts the whole story and not just the end. In barbarian Colchis, Jason found Medea radiant and beautiful "Im Abstich ihrer nächtlichen Umgebung" (*Medea*, 1. 457). But against a Greek background she seems sombre, even sinister. Grillparzer wished to show not merely this common source of human unhappiness—that the girl who thrills the youth is repulsive to the man, so that the end of the romance is anything but romantic—but something even more general; namely that the ambition which drives on the young brings disillusionment when it is fulfilled. And so he wrote of his trilogy: "Das ganze ist die große Tragödie des Lebens, daß der Mensch in seiner Jugend sucht, was er im Alter nicht brauchen kann."[3] And he made Jason come to realize the truth of this, saying:

> Ein Jüngling war ich, ein verwegner Tor:
> Der Mann verwirft was Knaben wohlgefällt.
>
> (*Medea,* ll. 1471-2)

All this can only be brought home if we actually see Jason and Medea full of confidence and vigour, and witness their gradual disillusionment, and this cannot be put before our eyes in a single play.

As the curtain rises on the first play, the one-act tragedy *Der Gastfreund,* the setting leaves no doubt that the scene is barbarian territory. The stage directions read:

> Kolchis. Wilde Gegend mit Felsen und Bäumen, im Hintergrunde das Meer. Am Gestade desselben ein Altar, von unbehauenen Steinen zusammengefügt, auf dem die kolossale Bildsäule eines nackten bärtigen Mannes steht, der in seiner Rechten eine Keule, um die Schultern ein Widderfell trägt.

The barbarism suggested by the unhewn stones, the colossal size of the statue, and the wild landscape is reinforced by the sight of Medea, bow in hand, having just shot an arrow. Later this gesture is contrasted with one which represents civilization, namely playing the lyre. When at the beginning of Act II of *Medea* she tries to learn Greek manners, she handles the instrument clumsily and complains:

> Nur an den Wurfspieß ist die Hand gewöhnt
> Und an des Weidwerks ernstlich rauh Geschäft.

Grillparzer makes the whole tragedy depend on the incompatibility between barbarism and civilization. The way the Greeks mistrust all barbarians is repeatedly stressed. To Milo Medea is "eine Barbarin, und eine Zauberin dazu", and "ein furchtbar Weib mit ihren dunkeln Augen!" (*Die Argonauten,* ll. 1101-3). Even the kind and gentle Kreusa is at first ready to believe, merely on hearsay, that she is "Ein gräßlich Weib, giftmischend, vatermörd'risch"

(*Medea,* l. 330). And neither Medea nor Jason will ever forget the scorn with which she was treated on her arrival in Greece (*Medea,* ll. 251-5). But in fact Medea has none of the repulsive qualities associated with the word "barbarian". She has none of her father's covetousness and treacherousness. She is pathetically moved when Kreusa, realizing the wrong she has done her, begs her forgiveness: kindness and consideration are qualities that Medea has hardly experienced before, and the way she values them brings out her basic nobility of character (*Medea,* ll. 370-6). But she can never acquire the appearance or accomplishments of a Greek, however hard she tries, and so Jason cannot rid himself of the horror he has come to feel for this alien woman. Back in Greece, her dark eyes, which Milo had found so horrible from the first, constantly put him in mind of the serpent which guarded the fleece in Colchis, and he confesses to the king: "Und nur mit Schaudern nenn' ich sie mein Weib" (*Medea,* l. 475). We can see, then, why Grillparzer maintained that his purpose was to make the first two plays of the trilogy "so barbarisch und romantisch . . . als möglich, gerade um den Unterschied zwischen Kolchis und Griechenland herauszuheben, auf den alles ankam." And again: "Ich hatte bei der . . . Vermengung des Romantischen mit dem Klassichen nicht eine läppische Nachäfferei Shakespeares . . . im Sinne, sondern die möglichste Unterscheidung von Kolchis und Griechenland, welcher Unterschied die Grundlage der Tragik in diesem Stück ausmacht" (I, 16, 136; 159). He adds that one method he adopted to bring out the contrast was the use of free verse when the action takes place in Colchis and iambics when it is in Greece, "gleichsam als verschiedene Sprachen, hier und dort".

A good example of what he means by "das Romantische" is the stage-setting of the final Act of *Die Argonauten.* Jason and Medea stand in a cave which has "in der Felsenwand des Hintergrundes ein großes verschlossenes Tor". When Jason strikes this with his sword, "die Pforten springen auf und zeigen eine innere schmälere Höhle, seltsam beleuchtet. Im Hintergrunde ein Baum, an ihm hängt hellglänzend das goldene Vließ. Um Baum und Vließ windet sich eine ungeheure Schlange, die beim Aufspringen der Pforte ihr in dem Laub verborgenes Haupt hervorstreckt und züngelnd vor sich hin blickt." The whole incident, culminating in Jason's capture of the fleece, is not only important for the action, but brings out the horror that all the Greeks feel for barbarian magic. And the serpent's eyes, as we saw, leave an indelible impression on Jason's mind, and forever remind him that his dark-eyed wife is a barbarian.

The principal function of the first play is to establish the fleece as a symbol. Grillparzer said he intended it to be "ein sinnliches Zeichen des ungerechten Gutes, eine Art Nibelungenhort" (I, 16, 134). It seems to confer power and victory, but there is a curse on it. Phryxus steals it, Aietes murders him for it, Jason then Pelias and Medea acquire it, Kreon seeks it—and they are all ruined. Not that it has any supernatural power. As with the picture of Rahel in *Die Jüdin,* there is no magical hocus-pocus: the fleece is

simply an outward and visible sign of ill-gotten gain, and shows the evil consequences of wealth so acquired. To illustrate this, Grillparzer quoted the words Octavio speaks at the end of *Die Piccolomini:*

> Das eben ist der Fluch der bösen Tat,
> Daß sie fortzeugend Böses muß gebären.[4]

An evil deed, then, brings misfortune, and this in turn motivates further crimes.

In the second play, ***Die Argonauten,*** Jason comes to Colchis to avenge Phryxus and regain the fleece—but not for the sake of justice. Like Phryxus, he is persecuted by his family, and leaves Greece because this is the only way he can achieve fame and power, for which he is glad to risk his life:

> Ruhmvoller Tod für ruhmentblößtes Leben,
> Mag's tadeln wer da will, mich lockt der Tausch!

(ll. 303-4)

When he left, he was indifferent to all else. As he tells Kreusa on his return:

> Ich hatte da kein Aug für deine Tränen
> Denn nur nach Taten dürstete mein Herz.

(*Medea,* ll. 867-8)

At his first meeting with Medea, he expresses in long speeches his amazement at finding such beauty in barbarian Colchis, while the turmoil she feels prevents her from uttering anything but interjections. When armed Colchians enter, led by her brother Absyrtus, she restrains them with a gesture of her arm, thus allowing Jason to escape. At the beginning of Act II, the change that has come upon her as a result of meeting him is indicated by her friendliness and warmth to Peritta, whom she had previously scornfully repudiated as a slave of passion. (This is similar to the way Grillparzer brings out the effect on Hero of the meeting with Leander by her change of attitude to Ianthe.) At their second meeting she again saves his life by warning him not to drink the poisoned cup, and then in Act III he urges her to betray her own people and follow him. For nearly 200 lines he has all the coherent speeches, and she replies with interjections, silence or tears. It is not that he is deeply in love, but he wants to enjoy the consciousness of his power by compelling her to admit her feelings. When he fails, he turns away enraged, but she then turns her face to him, stretches out her arm, and cries the one word "Jason" (l. 1327). It is enough to show that she loves him. When in the final play he recalls this incident, he says: "Und nur ihr Tun, ihr Wort verriet mir nichts" (l. 463). Here, then, the strongest emotion is expressed not with declamation but, as in real life, with broken phrases, and we find the same in most of Grillparzer's plays. Ottokar, for instance, is usually voluble enough, but when he learns that Rudolf has been elected emperor, the great shock he feels is conveyed by making him falter in the instructions he had been giving with his habitual confidence. Rudolf II of *Ein Brud-*

erzwist says practically nothing when he is really angry in Acts I and IV, but bangs on the floor with his stick or makes some other gesture.

Jason's emotion is not nearly as strong as Medea's and, so he can speak at length while she is silent. He sees that she loves him, and the very fact that she will not admit it in so many words angers him, and (as he concedes in retrospect, *Medea*, ll. 465-7) increases his determination to press her to a declaration. His relentlessness is brought out when he cries: "Du weinst! Umsonst; ich kenne Mitleid nicht" (l. 1264). Another motive for the ruthless pressure he brings to bear on her is revealed when he says to his companions:

> Sie kennt das Vlieβ, den Ort, der es verbirgt
> Mit ihr vollbringen wir's und dann zu Schiff.
>
> (ll. 1393-4)

Having claimed her as his bride, he immediately says he cares for nothing but the fleece (l. 1429). In the next Act, she threatens to kill herself if he continues his quest for it, but he merely retorts: "Beweinen kann ich dich, rückke-hren nicht" (l. 1503). Her unwillingness to help him is due partly to her conviction that she can only atone for her family's treacherous acquisition of the fleece by leaving it alone; and partly to her consciousness of how much unhappiness its possession has caused. But he is set solely on fame and glory—an attitude not infrequently taken by Grillparzer's heroes. His Sappho says despairingly of the male in general:

> Nach außen geht sein rastlos wildes Streben
> Und findet er die Lieb', bückt er sich wohl,
> Das holde Blümchen von dem Grund zu lesen,
> Besieht es, freut sich sein und steckt's dann kalt
> Zu andern Siegeszeichen auf den Helm.
>
> (ll. 820-4)

This is exactly what Jason does. In retrospect he says:

> Auf Kampf gestellt rang ich mit ihr, und wie
> Ein Abenteuer trieb ich meine Liebe.
>
> (*Medea*, ll. 466-7)

The third play begins a month after Jason and Medea's arrival in Greece, following four years at sea, during which two sons have been born to them. All that has happened in this interval is communicated by two sets of narratives—Gora's at the beginning of the first Act and Jason's at the end, which acquaints us with details omitted in Gora's briefer sketch. Both speak not simply to inform the audience, but for purposes of their own. Jason is concerned to convince the king (who interrogates him curtly and with hostile aloofness) that he is innocent, and his long speeches are punctuated only by short comments or questions from Kreon. Gora tells us less because she is addressing Medea to whom the facts are already known. While Medea is anxious to bury her past for Jason's sake, Gora reminds her of what she considers to be her guilt in deserting her

country and causing, even if unwittingly, the deaths of her brother and father. Gora speaks partly from resentment—she accuses Medea of having enticed her away from her native land into slavery in Greece—and partly from motives of religious hope: to her, the change for the worse in Medea's fortunes is proof "Daβ Götter sind, und daβ Vergeltung ist". And this means that Jason, the chief criminal, will in turn be punished (ll. 36-7). It also means that Medea must on no account attempt to put her own actions, which have had such dire consequences, out of her mind, for this would be tantamount to denying the justice of the gods. And so Gora keeps referring to what Medea is trying to put aside. Gora's preoccupation with the gods here is not a pretext for enabling her to tell us what we need to know, but is an attitude she constantly takes, and underlies the different advice she gives Medea throughout this final play.

Another important matter to which Gora alludes is that Pelias died in mysterious circumstances, "man weiβ nicht wie" (l. 80). In Grillparzer's trilogy there is no proof that Medea murdered him or committed any atrocity prior to her killing of her own children; whereas Euripides' Medea murders both her brother and Pelias, and is held in dread even by her nurse. The reason why Grillparzer mitigates her guilt is obvious enough; to keep her as the half-demented barbarian of the legend would indeed have made it easy to motivate her child-murder, but she would then have forfeited the sympathy of a modern audience.

Jason is loathed and shunned on his return to Greece because of his barbarian wife, because the Greeks could believe only the worst of a barbarian and of the man who could marry her. Gora tells her:

> Ein Greuel ist die Kolcherin dem Volke.
> Ein Schrecken die Vertraute dunkler Mächte. . . .
> Sie hassen ihn um dein, um seinetwillen.

So we can see why Medea, in the opening scene, tries quite literally to bury her past by placing her magic tools in a box and interring it, saying:

> Die Zeit der Nacht, der Zauber ist vorbei
> Und was geschieht, ob Schlimmes oder Gutes,
> Es muβ geschehen am offnen Strahl des Lichts.

Her magic things are associated with night because they are instruments of death which must be banished "aus des heitern Lebens Nähe" to which she now turns (ll. 9-10). She buries them "vor Tagesanbruch" and cries: "Der Tag bricht an—mit ihm ein neues Leben!" (l. 137). As at the beginning of *Des Meeres und der Liebe Wellen*, where Hero's happiness and confidence are brought out by the brightness of the morning sunlight, the emotions of the heroine are made clear not only by her words but by the whole situation in which we see her.

Medea buries the fleece together with her magic tools, and her address to it tells us what it has come to stand for in her mind:

Du Zeuge von der Meinen Untergang,
Bespritzt mit meines Vaters, Bruders Blut,
Du Denkmal von Medeens Schmach und Schuld!

It is for Jason's sake that she is putting away her past, not, as Gora supposes, in order to wipe out this consciousness of guilt. When Gora tells her to face the facts instead of burying them she counters with:

Geschehen ist, was nie geschehen sollte,
Und ich bewein's und bittrer, als du denkst,
Doch soll ich drum, ich selbst, mich selbst
    vernichten?
Klar sei der Mensch und einig mit der Welt!

(ll. 117-20)

"Welt" here means "environment", and to be at one with her Greek surroundings she must bury her Colchian past.

This reply to Gora also makes it clear that, although she regrets what has happened, she does not regard herself as morally guilty in Gora's sense. Gora's reiterated statements of Medea's guilt serve to remind us of how much she has sacrificed to Jason, how much grief her love for him has brought to herself and others. This needs to be emphasized so that we see the powerful motive for vengeance she will have when he deserts her. Some commentators, however, have accepted Gora's statements as the view which the dramatist is urging us to take. They are anxious to stamp some of Medea's early actions as sinful, feeling that they can thereby make her final tragedy acceptable as a just punishment.[5] But as she herself says, she did not kill her father, nor did her brother fall "durch mich" (ll. 333-4). The crucial action from which these and other catastrophes stem is that she loved and followed Jason; and Grillparzer impresses upon us that she was driven to this by overpowering emotions, which bewildered her as much as her family, which were not under the jurisdiction of her will and therefore are not open to moral censure—quite apart from the fact that following the man one loves is not, in normal circumstances, a crime. Even Jason, ruthless opportunist that he is, can be convicted of little outright villainy. He himself gives the best statement of the nature of his guilt:

Ich habe nichts getan was schlimm an sich,
Doch viel gewollt, gemöcht, gewünscht, getrachtet;
Still zugesehen, wenn es andre taten;
Hier Übles nicht gewollt, doch zugegriffen.

(ll. 765-8)

If Medea's situation in the final play were something for which we could blame her, Grillparzer would not be prompting us to pessimistic reflections, showing in accordance with his theory how the finest characters must come to grief and tragedy; he would merely be demonstrating that certain moral shortcomings are apt to have painful consequences, and this, however adequate to a Gottsched, is much too trite for a Grillparzer.

Medea's nobility of character is at its clearest in this opening Act. Her calm acceptance of all the misfortune that has befallen herself and Jason is expressed by her line: "Laβ

uns die Götter bitten um ein einfach Herz" (l. 86). To this, Gora replies: "Ha! Und dein Gemahl?"—knowing that, whatever Medea may do, Jason is incapable of such humility. Later, when Kreusa bids him bear his lot with "Ein einfach Herz und einen stillen Sinn" (l. 829), he can only helplessly contrast the promise of his youth with the bleak grimness of his present. Such contrasts repeatedly occur in order to bring out the tragedy of lives which had begun so auspiciously. A fine example is the short monologue which Jason begins by flinging himself despairing on a bench and crying, as he beats his breast: "Zerspreng' dein Haus und mach' dir brechend Luft!" He does not lecture on despair in the abstract, but expresses his feelings by addressing the walls of Corinth, visible in the background. This town, which harboured him as a youth, seems now so inaccessible:

Da liegen sie, die Türme von Korinth,
Am Meeresufer üppig hingelagert,
Die Wiege meiner goldnen Jugendzeit!
Dieselben, von derselben Sonn' erleuchtet,
Nur ich ein andrer, ich in mir verwandelt.
Ihr Götter! warum war so schön mein Morgen,
Wenn Ihr den Abend mir so schwarz bestimmt—
O wär'es Nacht!

(ll. 203-11)

Again, ideas and emotions are expressed vividly and with immediacy by being linked with something we can actually see on the stage.

Soon after this we see Jason and Medea alone for the first time in this final play, and their conversation tells us what their relationship has become. We have seen how much Medea is prepared to do for his sake. For instance, when he had complained that her red veil is Colchian rather than Greek dress, she expressed her complaisance to his will by silently handing it to Gora. (The magic veil, which, for him, represented barbarism and which he had taken from her in Colchis when he claimed her as Greek, she had already buried, earlier in the scene.) But the conversation she now has with Jason shows that she fears he will repudiate her; and the slightest thing makes her suspicious and resentful. This resentment gradually gains the upper hand, and in Act II we see that she knows at heart that Gora is right, that Jason has not the strength of character to accept misfortune with quiet resignation. She indicts his ruthless egoism, saying:

Nur Er ist da, Er in der weiten Welt
Und alles Andre nichts als Stoff zu Taten. . . .
Lockt's ihn nach Ruhm, so schlägt er einen tot,
Will er ein Weib, so holt er eine sich,
Was auch darüber bricht, was kümmert's ihn!

(ll. 630-6)

The speech culminates in the terrible line "Ich könnt' ihn sterben sehn und lachen drob." Aietes had foretold that Jason would despise her "wenn gestillt die Begier" (*Die Argonauten,* ll. 1372-4). At the beginning of the third play he is still determined to stand by her, although she is nothing but a burden to him (ll. 552-4). She for her part tries desperately to suppress her fierce resentment and to do everything to please him. In Act I he had complained of her barbarian dress. At the beginning of Act II she appears "griechisch gekleidet" and learning the lyre. But then Kreusa tells her the words of the prayer that, as a boy, he used to sing to the gods:

> Wölbt meine Brust
> Daß den Männern
> Ich obsiege
> Und den zierlichen
> Mädchen auch.

Medea is naturally put in mind of his selfishness, and although she makes a tremendous effort to forget the wrongs he has done her, she fails and cries "Doch das vergißt sich nicht" (l. 699).

Grillparzer has produced nothing so overpoweringly pessimistic as these first two Acts of **Medea.** The spouses have come to hate each other, although they feel they must stay together. Kreusa, horrified at their mutual hatred, asks: "Wer sagte mir denn, Gatten liebten sich?" (l. 721). Jason points the pessimistic moral when he observes, not merely that their relationship has failed to stand the test of misfortune, but the more general truth that man is worsened, not purified, by hardship and deprivation:

> Es ist des Unglücks eigentlichstes Unglück,
> Daß selten drin der Mensch sich rein bewahrt.

> (ll. 757-8)

We are reminded of Octavio's words about "der Fluch der bösen Tat" (see above, p. 51).

Jason goes on to exchange reminiscences with Kreusa about their happy youth. When Medea enters, she tries to attract his attention to tell him that she has learned a Greek song—a good example of her determination to assume Greek manners for his sake. What follows is a fine illustration of how Grillparzer conveys the most powerful emotions by gesture rather than by word. Jason is so absorbed in his conversation with Kreusa that Medea has to say three times "Jason, ich weiß ein Lied" before she is even heard. And then it is Kreusa who notices her and brings him to let her perform the song. He is cruelly contemptuous, and says she would do better at throwing a spear or hissing at a snake. Naturally, her confidence sinks, and so she bungles the complicated and difficult task which she had only just begun to master. Then she drops the lyre and covers her eyes with her hands to express her shame and despair. Jason tells Kreusa, a decent civilized Greek, to sing the song. But when Kreusa makes to pick up the lyre, Medea fends her off with one hand and takes it herself with the other. When Jason advances on her to retrieve it, she breaks it, shows him the broken pieces, and then throws them at Kreusa's feet. Kreusa recoils in horror at this barbarous action and cries "tot", referring of course to the lyre. Medea looks round quickly and says "Wer?—Ich lebe—lebe." And the stage directions indicate an attitude

of pride and defiance. "Sie steht da hoch emporgehoben vor sich hinstarrend." The incident is closed, for there follows "von außen ein Trompetenstoß", distracting attention and preparing the arrival of the herald with his sentence of banishment. Both Medea and Kreusa have said little, but their powerful emotions have been very clearly conveyed.

By this time Jason has lost all initiative. Whereas he had earlier told the king he would stand by Medea, he now acquiesces in the king's plan that she should be banished and he wed Kreusa. Kreon is acting justly, according to his lights.[6] The herald's evidence (ll. 960-1005) can only confirm his opinion that Jason is innocent of Pelias' murder, while giving him good grounds for thinking that the real culprit was Medea. Thus to repudiate her will not be an injustice, while to make Jason his son and heir will protect him from the sentence of banishment which has been decreed against both Jason and Medea. Medea pleads to remain, yet cannot suppress her resentment, and she expresses these conflicting emotions when she says to Jason: "Verhaßter komm! Komm mein Gemahl!" (l. 1110). It is the same alternation between hatred and dependence that Bancbanus shows towards Otto at the end of **Ein treuer Diener,** and is expressed in the same way. We shall again meet this way of expressing an alternation between contrary emotions in Act III of **Des Meeres und der Liebe Wellen,** where Hero fiercely accuses Leander of selfishly taking risks that will jeopardize her life as well as his, and then changes her tone as her love for him begins to outweigh this resentment:

> Entsetzlicher! Verruchter!
> Was kommst du her? nichts denkend als dich selbst
>   . . .
> Und du—Entsetzlich Bild—Leander, O!

By the end of the second Act Medea's hatred has obliterated the contrary emotion that had held it in check. She tears the Greek coat that Kreusa had given her, and says to Jason:

> Sieh! Wie ich diesen Mantel durch hier reiße
> Und einen Teil an meinen Busen drücke,
> Den andern hin dir werfe vor die Füße,
> Also zerreiß' ich meine Liebe, unsern Bund.

> (ll. 1125-8)

Such an explanation of what a gesture represents is not infrequent. In the second play, when Jason claims Medea as his bride, he gives visible expression to this by taking her magic veil from her, stripping her of this barbaric accessory in order to make her a Greek. He says:

> Und wie ich diesen Schleier von dir reiße,
> Durchwoben mit der Unterird's chen Zeichen,
> So reiß' ich dich von allen Banden los,
> Die dich geknüpft an dieses Landes Frevel.

> (ll. 1402-5)

The Act finishes with Kreon's refusal of her plea at least to be allowed to take her children into banishment. Again, it is Kreon who decides what is to happen, and Jason simply follows his initiative. Only Kreusa feels misgiving at this treatment of Medea, and asks: "Ich sinne nur, ob recht ist, was wir tun."

At the beginning of Act III Gora urges her mistress to avenge herself on Jason, and reminds her that her betrayal of her family and country for this hated Greek brought her father to his grave:

> Du hast wohl gehört, dir ward wohl Kunde . . .
>
> . . . . .
>
> Daß er den Schmerz anfassend wie ein Schwert,
> Gen sich selber wütend, den Tod sich gab.

But Medea is more concerned with keeping her children than with thoughts of revenge. Jason, we saw, weakly accepted the king's ruling that the children must stay in Corinth. But she contrives to speak to him in the absence of the king and he gives in to her to the extent of agreeing that one of the children shall be allowed to go with her. Nowhere is Jason's injustice clearer than at this interview. He cannot deny that he urged her to murder his uncle (ll. 1082-1105, 1434-41), but there is no proof that she actually did so. Yet he acquiesces in her sentence of banishment for this crime in order to be rid of her. And this is the man for whom she has given up everything! Jason is by now completely broken. He shows no joy at the prospect of marriage with Kreusa—not only when he speaks of his future to Medea, to whom he might be expected to minimize his happiness with her rival, but even in conversation with Kreon, her father (ll. 1324-42). He can only grieve at his loss of fame and power:

> Ich bin nicht der ich war, die Kraft ist mir gebrochen,
> Und in der Brust erstorben mir der Mut.
>
> (ll. 1523-4)

His feeling of impotence and inability to take effective action is brought out by his declaration, repeated at every new development, that all has been willed by the gods.

Prior to their death in Act IV the children make three appearances. In Act I they bring out the mutual hatred of Greeks and barbarians. One of the boys asks his father whether he is a Greek, saying that, according to Gora, these are "betrügerische Leut' und feig" (l. 217). Later in Act I, Jason stands with them to plead for asylum in Corinth, and they immediately win both Kreon's and Kreusa's affection. Hence Kreon's later insistence that they should remain in Corinth and not accompany their barbarian mother into banishment. He has not merely taken a fancy to the children, but feels he must not entrust them to someone who, he believes, has committed a foul murder. They are at once drawn to the gentle Kreusa and cling to her when Medea calls them (ll. 353-6). Medea truly loves them, and is not a harsh mother—she was tactful and conciliatory to them when they taunted Jason for being a Greek (ll. 218-22). But she has none of Kreusa's sweetness, and gentleness, and this has fatal consequences. From the end of Act II, where Kreon banishes her, she repeat-

edly says she will go if she may take her children with her. After Jason has conceded that one of the two shall accompany her, they are brought on to the stage for the third time to see which of them will choose to follow their mother. Medea's desperation leads her to speak roughly to them, and this makes them flee to Kreusa. They do not really positively reject Medea, but are frightened—both of her manner and (as they reveal in the following Act, ll. 2042-3) of another long voyage in a ship "wo es schwindlicht ist und schwül", which they know awaits them if they accompany her (l. 1653). But here in Act III they are silent, and their behaviour naturally makes Medea think that her own—all that she has left—has turned against her. This provokes her cry:

> Wer gibt mir einen Dolch?
> Einen Dolch für mich und sie!
>
> (ll. 1697-8)

The rest of the play is not so powerfully effective. Act IV is concerned mainly with the further motivation of Medea's murder of the children, and Act V with exonerating her and ensuring that we continue to sympathize with her. As Grillparzer himself noted, this murder is the one thing that modern audiences know of Medea, and so it must form the culmination of the play. The deed is done at the end of the only long monologue of the final play (in contrast to *Sappho,* the fleece-trilogy already shows the tendency of the mature Grillparzer to restrict the length and number of the monologues). This one not only makes Medea's motives clear but also creates a sense of suspense. The catastrophe of a play entitled *Medea* cannot come as a surprise, so while we are looking onwards, to the murder, she keeps us in suspense by reviewing her past.

The weakness of Act IV is that Grillparzer does not succeed in motivating the murder very convincingly, although the effect of this failure is not as serious as one might think; for whether the children die or not makes no difference to the tragedies of the lives of Medea and Jason. Both were so full of hope and strength, but both are now so completely broken in will and embittered that any future happiness is out of the question for either of them. If we recall Grillparzer's statement that the whole trilogy shows "die große Tragödie des Lebens", then we can understand that the killing of the children is not really essential to the tragic effect.

Medea is not set on murder at the beginning of Act III. All she knows at this stage is that she will not accept banishment (ll. 1281-2). She does think of murdering them as a means of avenging herself on Jason, but Gora dismisses this suggestion, saying: "Dich selber trifft deine Rache, nicht ihn" (l. 1235). Then Gora tells how the Greek heroes who accompanied Jason to Colchis have all met an untimely death—evidence, for her, of divine retribution. She mentions Hercules' death when he donned a poisoned coat prepared by his wife, and Medea's interest is visibly aroused. It is clear that she is now thinking of murdering

Jason (as she later does Kreusa, by sending a poisoned garment), not the children. But by the end of Act III the children have, she thinks, repudiated her, and this makes her think of revenge on them. She now begins to talk of hating them, as she hates their father whom they so strongly resemble (ll. 1776-83). This hatred for them is just a moment of desperate rage; her love is far stronger, but that too impels her to kill them. She knows that if she leaves them, as she must, they will be taunted as barbarians by the children of Jason and Kreusa:

> Oder der Ingrimm, am Herzen nagend,
> Macht sie arg, sich selbst ein Greuel.

(ll. 1794-5)

She knows what it is to become "sich selbst ein Greuel", and cries:

> Ich wollt' mein Vater hätte mich getötet,
> Da ich noch klein war,
> Noch nichts, wie jetzt, geduldet,
> Noch nichts gedacht—wie jetzt.

And again:

> Man hat mich bös genannt, ich war es nicht:
> Allein ich fühle, daβ man's werden kann.

(ll. 1849-50)

These lines reiterate the truth already stated by Jason that man is worsened, not purified, by oppression and misfortune. The desire to spare her children this fate alternates with the rage and resentment that her own misfortunes have made so strong in her, and which lead her to think once more of killing her children in order to take revenge on Jason who loves them (ll. 1809-14). It is already clear that she will not kill them for one single clearly stated reason, but will be impelled by a number of motives, as is so with many acts in real life.[7] Even the motives already discussed do not give her the strength to do the deed. "Dem alten Wollen fehlt die alte Kraft" (l. 1860). She means that without her magic implements, which she buried in Act I, she is powerless (ll. 1869-76). But she can easily recover the box in which she interred them: "Zwei Handvoll Erde weg—und es ist mein!" And that she fails to take the necessary action means that she lacks the will-power, not just the means, to kill. It is her horror of the fleece that deters her from excavating the box. Just as the dying Pelias could not look at it without seeing the man he had murdered, so Medea fears that the sight of it will torment her with her memories of how her brother and her father died as a result of her allegiance to Jason. In the upshot, she acquires the box, and with it the strength to kill, as a result of a series of coincidences and implausible acts by others. First, the king has found the buried box, and she admits it contains the fleece which he covets—not from personal greed, but as the token of Jason's greatness. He thinks (ll. 1366-8) that if Jason has this fleece which symbolizes and proves the success of his adventure, then he will necessarily recover his power and popularity. Once again, Kreon's be-

haviour is not rank injustice, but must look like this to Medea and further provoke her. When the box is brought, he orders her to open it, for she alone can break the magic spell that closes it. She bids him wait, and he complies, saying that she should send the fleece to Kreusa when she does eventually open the box. What basis he has for this suggestion is not clear, but it gives Medea the idea of murdering Kreusa with the lethal instruments in the box. Next, he announces that, since Medea seems calm and co-operative, he is ready to comply with Kreusa's request that she be allowed to spend an hour with her children before she departs into banishment. It is, of course, important for the plot that they should be brought into her presence, but the king's readiness to send them is hardly convincing. He has repeatedly said that he regards her as a treacherous barbarian who will stick at nothing. And he was present when she cried out for a dagger to kill them, and herself too, when they repudiated her.

But we have yet to see how she acquires the will to kill them. The king leaves in order to send them to her. She opens the box and gives Gora a vessel from it, to be handed to Kreusa as a gift. In spite of her later disclaimer (l. 2172) Gora must realize that this vessel is in fact lethal, for when she accidentally raises its lid, a flame spurts out, and she cries: "Mir ahnet Entsetzliches!" (l. 2009). Medea then covers the vessel with the fleece, and both with a coat. We think at once of the poisoned coat which killed Hercules, and in which she had earlier shown so much interest. After some hesitation, Gora does Medea's will and takes all these things to Kreusa. This is virtually an act of suicide, for she can reasonably anticipate that her part in Kreusa's murder will be punished by death. It is, however, not in itself implausible that she should give up her life. She has repeatedly said that it is meaningless; she has long since ceased to love Medea, and the two children to whom she had clung are now to be cut off from her. It is for a quite different reason that her meek compliance with Medea's will is difficult to accept. At this stage of the play she is represented as trying to restrain her mistress, and we must see how she comes to take this attitude.

At the beginning of the final play she was openly defiant and justified her refusal to help bury the magic implements by saying that she is Jason's slave, not Medea's (l. 31). She had repeatedly urged Medea to return to Colchis, and only when the Greeks banish her from Corinth does she change her counsel and urge her mistress to stay, thinking that it would be shameful to return, now that the initiative for departure has come from the Greeks. Then, at the beginning of Act IV, she again changes her advice and suggests flight. The change strikes Medea as remarkable:

> Und was hat dich denn so weich gemacht?
> Schnaubtest erst Grimm, und nun so zagend?

(ll. 1754-5)

Gora has become "weich" because the children have repudiated their mother, and because in this she sees divine vengeance, punishing Medea for abandoning her country and family. For the rest of Act IV she tries to dissuade Medea from active revenge. Yet finally she allows herself to be bullied into bringing about Kreusa's death. All this is only intelligible if we consider that Kreusa's murder is essential to the action, in that it makes Medea feel that she must kill her children (to save them from a worse fate) and so gives her the strength she hitherto lacked. She knows that the king will avenge Kreusa by torturing and killing the children as well as herself, and this forces her hand:

> Ist's nicht schon zu spät?
> Zu spät zum verzeihn?
> Hat sie nicht schon, Kreusa, das Kleid,
> Und den Becher, den flammenden Becher? . . .
>
> Sie kommen, sie töten mich!
> Schonen auch der Kleinen nicht.

(ll. 2141-8)

It is doubtless because the fleece-trilogy is an early work (Grillparzer's third published play) that it shows some artificiality of motivation. But the effect of making Medea's action dependent on factors external to her (on contingencies and on badly motivated acts by others) is not entirely negative. It does impair the inevitability of the death of the children, but it also mitigates her guilt. In *Des Meeres und der Liebe Wellen* the tragedy is caused almost exclusively by the characters. Once Hero and Leander have fallen in love, it does not need any chance happenings to kill them: their passion leads them straight to their deaths. But there the passion is love and, in the case of the priest (whose action in extinguishing the lamp is so decisive), duty. With Medea the passion is of a much uglier nature, and it would be intolerable if Grillparzer showed her murder of the children determined entirely or even principally by her lust for revenge. That outer circumstances have to be invoked to play a large part in the motivation of her deed helps to reconcile us with her.[8] This too is the function of the second scene of the fifth Act of *Medea*. Both Jason and Medea feel annihilated, all that remains for them is (as Medea urges him) "Trage . . . dulde . . . büße", and she appears as the more resolute of the two in this determination to atone.

In the first scene of Act V Gora is made to pass judgement on Kreusa, Jason and the king, and the stress thus placed on their guilt also has the effect of diminishing Medea's. Gora is even made to exaggerate the guilt of Kreusa and the king. The latter deprived Medea of her husband and children only because the evidence against her seemed so damning, and Kreusa had acquiesced for the same reason, but even then with misgivings. It is without justification when Gora asks of her: "Warum griff sie nach des Unglücks letzter Habe?" But what really matters at this stage is not whether what they had done is just but that we should be conscious of the undeniable fact that the natural effect of their deeds was to goad Medea to desperation, as if she were a hunted beast. Gora says to the two men:

> Habt ihr es nicht umstellt mit Jägernetzen
> Des schändlichen Verrats, das edle Wild,

> Bis ohne Ausweg, in Verzweiflungswut,
> Es, überspringend euer Garn, die Krone,
> Des hohen Hauptes königlichen Schmuck,
> Mißbraucht zum Werkzeug ungewohnten Mords.

(ll. 2245-50)

It is obvious that the effect is to exonerate Medea. And the final scene of the play elevates her further. It has something of the transfiguration of the heroine at the end of Euripides' play, where she appears on a chariot drawn by winged dragons, which finally rises into the air. Grillparzer gives her more than natural knowledge when he makes her tell Jason that she is not destined to fall by his hand, and that they will never again confront each other. Furthermore, her meeting with Jason here is not motivated in the ordinary sense. She seems to know where to find him.[9]

Grillparzer's trilogy ends with an allusion to the symbolism of the fleece. Medea is on her way to return it to the temple at Delphi. She shows it to Jason, saying:

> Erkennst das Zeichen du, um das du rangst?
> Das dir ein Ruhm war und ein Glück dir schien?
> Was ist der Erde Glück?—ein Schatten!
> Was ist der Erde Ruhm?—ein Traum!
> Du Armer! Der von Schatten du geträumt!
> Der Traum ist aus, allein die Nacht noch nicht.

The parallel with what Rustan says when he awakens at the end of *Der Traum ein Leben* . . . is striking. As Professor Yuill has said (56, p. xxiii)) Rustan gives the same message of resignation, but in a less sombre light, since his terrifying dream prevents him from embarking on the course that has led Medea and Jason to ruin.

3. *DES MEERES UND DER LIEBE WELLEN* (1831)

Modern writers who treat themes from classical antiquity often do so in order to write about love, and Grillparzer's plays on Greek material all depict love's first awakening in young people, although only *Des Meeres und der Liebe Wellen* is restricted to this theme. As in his two other Greek plays, the story is not about the real historical world of Athens or Sparta, but is taken from myth and legend. Free from the limitations which go with a historical setting, these plays show human emotions and problems common to all ages and special to none.

Des Meeres und der Liebe Wellen is essentially a study in a girl's growth to womanhood. All the other characters, even her partner, are less important than she. Her opening monologue, spoken on the morning of the day she is to be consecrated priestess, is a splendid piece of character-drawing. Almost her first words bring out her pride at the thought of the career which is to be initiated at the ceremony:

> Und ich bin dieses Festes Gegenstand.
> Mir wird vergönnt, die unbemerkten Tage,
> Die fernhin rollen ohne Richt und Ziel,
> Dem Dienst der hohen Himmlischen zu weihn;
> Die einzelnen, die Wiesenblümchen gleich,

Der Fuβ des Wanderers zertritt und knickt,
Zum Kranz gewunden um der Göttin Haupt,
Zu weihen und verklären. Sie und mich.

Like her uncle, she is proud of her descent from a family of priests (ll. 20-3) and very conscious of her superiority to "der Schwarm"—the common herd, who leave undone those things which they ought to have done (ll. 52-3), while she rectifies their omissions with complacency. Her playful mockery of Hymen, god of marriage (ll. 33-7), and of Amor, shows that she is glad to enter upon the celibate life of a priestess and does not regard it as a sacrifice. When Ianthe suggests that Hero, like any other girl, would have stolen a glance through the gate at the youths waiting to be admitted to the festival, she is visibly angered and tells Ianthe, not once but repeatedly, to silence her wanton tongue:

Sprich nicht und reg dich nicht'

(l. 85) . . .

Du sollst nicht reden, sag' ich, nicht ein Wort!

(l. 90)

And her uncle's suggestion that her mother will arrive "mit dem Bräut'gam an der Hand" (l. 216) provokes likewise a strong reaction. She accuses him of tactless and hurtful joking (l. 217) and turns her back on him—the strongest gesture she can make to one who (unlike the servant girls) is her superior.

Grillparzer makes her lack of interest in young men understandable enough. Those she has met have all been like her brother:

Vom gleichem Sinn und störrisch wildem Wesen.
Das ehrne Band der Roheit um die Stirn,
Je minder denkend, um so heft'ger wollend.

(ll. 308-10)

The temple, where she has spent the last eight years, has been in every respect a place of peace and refuge for her. She came to it from the rancour and discord of an unhappy home (ll. 201-4) in a society where women had duties but no rights—whereas "Im Tempel hier hat auch die Frau ein Recht" (l. 279). So for her the temple represents calm and happiness, and she is not conscious of making any sacrifice in renouncing normal life: "Hier ist kein Krieg, hier schlägt man keine Wunden" (l. 389). The sequel shows that it is otherwise.

Papst, who is well aware that Hero's experience of men and of normal life have been distasteful to her, nevertheless supposes that her readiness to renounce them is due to suppression of subconscious desire for erotic experience; that her renunciation is so emphatic as to suggest resolution of an "inner conflict" of this kind. My view is that the motives of which Grillparzer shows her conscious are adequate to explain her attitude. Papst also interprets the sharpness of her replies to Ianthe's suggestions as evidence of "subconscious fear of admitting to herself even the possibility of their partial truth", while I think that Hero's sharp manner testifies to her consciousness of her superiority over ordinary girls. He also mentions her father's reference (l. 250) to "kleinlich dunkle Zweifel", and interprets these as Hero's doubts as to her suitability for the priesthood, these being in turn interpreted as caused by subconscious desire for love that is incompatible with office. But the "Zweifel" are clearly not Hero's at all, but her mother's. The subconscious has become an unfortunate adjunct of recent literary criticism, and Papst goes so far as to distinguish, as a specifically Austrian element in Grillparzer's heritage, a "highly developed sensitivity to twilight mental states on the borderland between the conscious and the subconscious" ([Pabst, "Des Meeres und der Liebe Wellen,"] pp. 17, 29–30, 50). I do not wish to deny that much in human thought and behaviour is unconscious, nor that dramatists sometimes represent characters as impelled by motives of which they are not conscious. But it seems to me that the subconscious motives that critics sometimes discern contribute more to their own reputation for subtlety than to the elucidation of the play. I would remind the reader of Grillparzer's words quoted as the motto of this book.

Although, to my mind, Hero is not repressing any desires, she certainly does not know her potentialities. Already in this first Act Grillparzer shows that she is not really a dedicated priestess. She is represented as finding peace and calm in the practical duties of her office. We first see her as she decorates the temple with flowers, and she envisages her future days:

Einförmig still, den Wasserkrug zur Hand,
Beschäftigt, wie bisher, an den Altären;
Und fort so Tag um Tag.

(ll. 396-8)

She does not even understand her uncle's suggestion that she should become a seer and commune with the goddess by night. "Du hast mich nicht gefaβt", he says (l. 136), showing how much more her mind is on this world than is his, even though she is less worldly than the servant girls whom she had in turn professed, with haughty disdain, not to understand (l. 65). When he explains what he meant, she immediately rejects his suggestion:

Verschiednes geben Götter an Verschiedne;
Mich haben sie zur Seh'rin nicht bestimmt.
Auch ist die Nacht zu ruhn; der Tag, zu wirken,
Ich kann mich freuen nur am Strahl des Lichts.

(ll. 184-7)

How much irony there is here! She is to find in Act III that the night is not for rest, in Act IV that in her exhaustion she cannot "wirken" throughout the day, and that instead of rejoicing in it she longs for night.

In these opening incidents of Act I her character is also brought out by contrast with her parents. Her father's pride is not, like Hero's and the priest's, centred on higher things, but is that of the pompous petit-bourgeois, as is clear when he goes out of his way to mention how he is envied because of

> . . . das Amt, mit dem seit manchem Jahr
> Bekleidet das Vertraun mich unsrer Stadt.

(ll. 238-9)

Only with reluctance does he leave his wife and daughter to speak alone, since he knows that his wife would gladly persuade Hero to return home instead of becoming a priestess and filling his heart with pride. The mother is too upset to say much, and while Hero talks to her in the front of the stage, a dove which had made its nest in a bush at the back is removed by the Tempelhüter, with Hero's uncle and father watching. This brings some action into a scene which is otherwise limited to character-drawing, and this action is in turn made to effect a further portrayal of character, for the mother sees her own fate reflected in the treatment of the dove:

> Unschuldig fromme Vögel stören sie
> Und nehmen aus ihr Nest. So reißen sie
> Das Kind auch von der Mutter, Herz vom Herzen.

(ll. 338-40)

Furthermore, just before this, Hero has said that she proposes

> Hier an der Göttin Altar, meiner Frau,
> Das Rechte tun, nicht weil man mirs befahl,
> Nein, weil es recht, weil ich es so erkannt.

(ll. 333-5)

There could be no clearer illustration of her independence than the way she goes on to ignore the temple rule that "All was sich paart bleibt ferne diesem Hause" (l. 357), and to caress the dove which the others had been trying to remove. Scherer rightly stresses her independence as an important factor in motivating her death. "Sie hält von ihrem Wesen jegliche Störung fern. Sie will den eigenen Sinn bewahren, ablehnend alles Übrige. . . . Solche Unabhängigkeit kann sich nicht leidend fügen und nach thränenreichen Klagen ins Unvermeidliche schicken. Wenn sie das Unglück trifft, zerbricht sie" ([*Vorträge und Afsätze zur Gesch. des geistigen Lebens in Deutschland und Österreich*,], pp. 258–9).

When Hero leaves the stage to dress for the ceremony, the crowd of spectators gathers. It includes Naukleros, who is talkative and cheeky, and Leander, who says not a single word in this first Act. He is still suffering from what Naukleros calls "der alte Trübsinn", brought on by his mother's death. But although he does not speak in Act I, he does (urged on by Naukleros) raise his eyes from the ground at the point in the ceremony when Hero stands in front of him and speaks the formula to renounce Hymen. As their eyes meet, she is overcome with confusion, expressed by her hesitation, which she excuses by saying that she has forgotten the tongs for putting incense on the

altar fire—only to be told that she is holding them in her hand! When she begins to speak the formula, it is the wrong one, and she then clumsily puts too much incense on, making the flame surge up. It is quite natural that Leander should attract her, for he is a peaceable fellow, has been a good son to his mother, and his friend calls him "dumpfer Träumer, blöder Schlucker". Although these details are given only later, she must see from his whole appearance that he is quite unlike what she has hitherto understood a man to be. In *Das goldene Vließ* Medea's irresistible attraction to Jason is something we must accept as a datum. That in *Des Meeres und der Liebe Wellen* Grillparzer gives such clear indications of what basis Hero has for her love for Leander shows how much more the emphasis is on love here.

Act II draws Leander's character as Act I has done Hero's. He still says little, and Naukleros does nearly all the talking. He is used to Leander's gloomy silence, but learns now of its new cause. Leander's despair is expressed in the one terse line: "Ich wußt' es ja. Komm Nacht! Und so ists aus" (l. 677). When Hero enters, on her way to draw water, her song of Leda and the swan (to which she repeatedly returns even though her uncle has forbidden it to her) shows that she is not now quite uninterested in love. That such a song should rise to her lips at this juncture is as significant as Gretchen's singing of "Der König in Thule" just after the first encounter with the handsome young stranger. Leander is too shy to approach her (a touch very true to his character) and he has to be taunted by the forward and cheeky Naukleros before he can bring himself to rush forward and fling himself at her feet. Naukleros tells her, in his usual forthright manner, that her eyes have made Leander a sick man, and she reacts sharply—as she had twice done in Act I—to suggestions that she is capable of love:

> frech ist der Menge Sinn,
> Und ehrfurchtslos, und ohne Scheu und Sitte.

But when Leander raises his head and she sees that he is the youth whose eyes she had caught at the festival, she changes her tone and addresses him as "guter Jüngling". There is no further trace of anger, and at this stage she feels, if not love, then at least compassion, calling him "armer Mann" and saying: "Er ist so schön, so jugendlich, so gut." When her uncle arrives, she does not hesitate to deceive him in order to explain why she is in conversation with the two youths. He urges them to leave at once, for they have no right to stay after midday:

> Denn wenn die Sonn auf ihres Wandels Zinne
> Mit durst'gen Zügen auf die Schatten trinkt,
> Dann tönen her vom Tempel krumme Hörner
> Dem Feste Schluß, dir kündigend Gefahr.

(ll. 836-9)

The use of this striking image to state the shortening of shadows at midday is a good example of Grillparzer's manner of conveying ordinary facts. [Cf. below . . . for other examples and comment on Grillparzer's method.]

At the beginning of Act III we see how greatly Hero's mind is pre-occupied with Leander. She is unresponsive to her uncle's long speeches as he introduces her to the tower where she is to live as priestess. He is hurt by her obvious indifference to what moves him so deeply, and warns her not to be unfaithful to her charge:

> Du fändest auch in mir den Mann, der willig,
> Das eigne Blut aus diesen Adern gösse,
> Wüβte er nur einen Tropfen in der Mischung,
> Der Unrecht birgt, und Unerlaubtes hegt.

Both Hero and Leander have been, and are to be, warned repeatedly that to indulge their passion will be dangerous to themselves and others. The priest's remark in Act I about a bridegroom for her was not the tactless joking for which she took it, but a determination on his part to make quite sure that she is suited for the celibate life. Just before the consecration ceremony he said: "Wüβt' ich sie schwach, noch jetzt entlieβ' ich sie" (l. 407). Here, in Act III, he is at first reassured when she answers his reproach with an assurance that "Sammlung wird mir werden, glaube mir". He becomes ecstatic at the thought of the efficacy of "Sammlung"—but when she declares that such flights are beyond her he finds her pedestrian attitude to her exalted vocation "ärmlich", and his memory of the incident in the grove with the two youths makes him go on to warn her, saying "Den ersten Anlaβ meid!" When he has left, she voices her awareness that this single day has changed her more than whole years have done, and that whole years will not suffice to obliterate it:

> Wie vieles lehrt ein Tag, und ach, wie wenig
> Gibt und vergiβt ein Jahr.—Nun er ist fern.

When shortly afterwards Leander enters her room, she indeed again calls him "guter Jüngling", but firmly bids him go. At this stage she still feels first and foremost a priestess, and tells him how her people treat a priestess who has a lover:

> Mein Volk . . .
> Es schonet zwar das Leben der Verirrten
> Allein stöβt aus sie, und verachtet sie,
> Zugleich ihr ganzes Haus und all die Ihren.

It is thus clear that her later surrender is not due to ignorance of what is at stake. Nor do these words imply that she wishes to continue to see Leander but is afraid of the consequences, for she gives the information only in reply to his inquiry about the fate of an erring priestess, and makes it quite clear that the principal reason for her rejection of him is "weil ich nur schwach erwidre deine Meinung". Grillparzer himself noted that "nie soll Hero darauf ein besonderes Gewicht legen, daβ jenes Verhältnis verbothen, oder vielmehr strafbar sey. Es ist mehr ihr Inneres, das sich früher nicht zur Liebe hinneigte, und das nicht ohne Widerstreben nachgibt, als daβ sie ein Äuβeres fürchtete" (I, 19, 232). Thus in Act I she renounced love because she had never known it. When she comes to know it she at first resists it: she tries to dissuade Leander both

in Act II, in the grove, and here in Act III, in the tower. But these new feelings she finds so disturbing rapidly come to dominate her, and the very title of the play alludes to the change which is wrought in her. Up to Act III the sea is calm:

> Der Hellespont
> Läβt Kindern gleich die frommen Wellen spielen;
> Sie flüstern kaum, so still sind sie vergnügt
>
> (ll. 1027-9)

But the rise of a strong wind can completely transform it, as Hero's initial calm contentment with the religious life is transformed by her encounter with Leander. Both the waves of the sea and those of love can arise suddenly with destructive force to which all else must yield.

The fourth Act is the longest of all, yet contains little outer action. Hero is shown as thinking only of her love, and makes no attempt to hide evidence that incriminates her— her fatigue after the sleepless night, her change of attitude to Ianthe. She is needlessly tactless to the Tempelhüter, and actually provokes him into seeking evidence of her guilt. And he in turn influences the priest, who throughout the Act gropes his way towards the conclusion that she is guilty. Grillparzer noted, in continuation of the passage last quoted, that "Im IV Akte ist . . . keine Spur von Ängstlichkeit in Heros Wesen, obschon es ihr ziemlich nahe liegt daβ man Verdacht geschöpft habe. Sie ist schon wieder ins Gleichgewicht des Gefühls gekommen, aber eines neuen, des Gefühls als Weib." Once again we see how independent she is. To decide what is right or wrong she follows not convention nor authority, but her own feelings. In Act IV she defines duty as:

> das alles, was ein ruhig Herz,
> Im Einklang mit sich selbst und mit der Welt,
> Dem Recht genüber stellt der andern Menschen.
>
> (ll. 1732-4)

Her view of her rights and duties changes because her feelings, on which this view is based, change so drastically in the course of the play.

The priest has three important monologues in this fourth Act. They serve to show how he is gradually convinced by the mounting evidence of Hero's guilt, and also to underline that it is as custodian of the divine law that he acts to thwart the lovers. Thus he says: "In meinem Innern reget sich ein Gott" (l. 1365) and he addresses Leander in his thoughts:

> Unseliger, was strecktest du die Hand
> Nach meinem Kind, nach meiner Götter Eigen?
>
> (ll. 1517-18)

Unfortunately his behaviour in Act V suggests that his motives are not as pure and disinterested as he wishes to represent them. When Leander's body is discovered, he lies to Ianthe about Hero's relation to the youth (ll. 1910-13), even though he had earlier said

Der Tücht'ge sieht in jedem Soll ein Muβ
Und Zwang, als erste Pflicht, ist ihm die Wahrheit.

(ll. 415-16)

And he resorts to mean threats in order to ensure that the whole matter will be hushed up. It is difficult to avoid the inference that he fears Hero's transgression will be punished upon her whole family, as she herself had said would be the case. The scorn with which Ianthe treats him at the end is a just indictment of the way his concern with his own status has led him to drive Hero to her death. It is only in Act V that his behaviour appears in any way selfish, and the obtrusion of such motives comes as something of a shock after his apparent disinterestedness. It was doubtless with Act V in mind that Grillparzer said "die Figur des Priesters ist zu kurz gekommen" (II, 10, 178).

In his third monologue in Act IV he makes a final attempt to convince himself of Hero's innocence, but she herself provides the evidence of her guilt by lighting the lamp which is to guide Leander to her tower. When she falls asleep, exhausted after the day which the priest has deliberately made as tiring as possible for her, he turns to the lamp and cries: "Der Götter Sturm verlösche deine Flamme." The Tempelhüter's monologue expresses the suspense we all feel at this crucial point in the action. He asks, as the priest is about to extinguish the lamp: "Was sinnt er nur? Mir wird so bang und schwer." In Grillparzer's sources it was put out by a storm, but he changed this contingency into an action motivated primarily by impersonal devotion to religious principles. The priest's purity of motive is suggested by contrast with the Tempelhüter, who has been stung by Hero's taunts into making a damning case against her. Now that he has done so, he begins to pity her:

—Unselig Mädchen!
Erwacht sie? Nein. So warnet dich kein Traum?
Mich schaudert. Weh! Hätt' ich mein Oberkleid!

Unlike the priest, who is an educated man with his principles very much in mind, the Tempelhüter is an unsophisticated person whose actions are prompted directly by his feelings—first resentment and here sympathy. To use the monologue to voice such fears and misgivings at a crucial moment is a common dramatic device. We have only to think of Leicester's monologue as Maria Stuart is executed, or of Mirza's while Judith and Holofernes are together in the tent.[10]

Act IV consists of three scenes, and the central one takes us back to Naukleros and Leander, who are now in Abydos. This scene fills out the time interval between the first, which takes place after Leander's departure from Sestos in the morning, and the last of the Act, in which Hero falls asleep as she waits for him to return in the evening. It also shows the marked change that has come over him in consequence of the vitalizing experience of love. It is the last time we are to see him alive, and the words of the priest at the end of the previous scene as he lays the snare make us

very conscious of the peril that awaits him. It is tragically ironical that he has now lost all traces of his former melancholy. His defiance of Naukleros, who tries to restrain him, forms one of the few rhetorical, declamatory outbursts in the play:

Tor, der du bist! und denkst du den zu halten,
Den alle Götter schützen, leitet ihre Macht?
Was mir bestimmt, ich wills, ich werds erfüllen:
Kein Sterblicher hält Götterwalten auf.

His prayer to the gods is in the same style:

Poseidon, mächt'ger Gott!
Der du die Wasser legtest an die Zügel,
Den Tod mir scheuchtest von dem feuchten Mund.
Zeus, mächtig über Allen, hehr und groβ!
Und Liebesgöttin, du, die mich berief,
Den kundlos Neuen, lernend zu belehren
Die Unberichteten was dein Gebot.
Steht ihr mir bei und leitet wie bisher!

Comparable passages are spoken by Hero in Act V when she turns on her uncle and curses him loudly, instead of concealing what has happened, and then bids the dead Leander farewell. Such declamation is the more effective because restricted to points of powerful emotion, and also because the zest of the lover, the indignation of the wronged and the grief of the bereaved are of general interest. Tragedy commonly includes speeches which, even in isolation from their context, appeal because they express ideas and emotions of general interest. For maximum effectiveness each speech must be relevant to the situation in which it is made (as Grillparzer himself insisted, see above, ...) and not form an unrelated strand. But if it is of no interest in itself, but only a means of reaching a final tragic situation, we might well be bored before the end. Grillparzer makes both these points by implication when he says: "Das ist der innere Zusammenhang des Drama, daβ jede Szene ein Bedürfnis erregen, und jede eines befriedigen muβ" (II, 11, 75). And the latter end can be achieved if the scene includes passages which are relevant to a wider context than their immediate one. The following extract from Hero's farewell to Leander, for instance, expresses not merely her personal emotion, but the bewilderment universally felt at the sudden loss of one to whom one is conscious of owing much:

Nie wieder dich zu sehn, im Leben nie!
Der du einhergingst im Gewand der Nacht
Und Licht mir strahltest in die dunkle Seele,
Aufblühen machtest all, was hold und gut,
Du fort von hier an einsam dunkeln Ort,
Und nimmer sieht mein lechzend Aug' dich wieder?
Der Tag wird kommen und die stille Nacht,
Der Lenz, der Herbst, des langen Sommers Freuden,
Du aber nie, Leander, hörst du? nie!
Nie, nimmer, nimmer, nie!

When I speak of the "rhetoric" of this and other speeches in the play, I have in mind features of style and diction that are often present when a speaker expresses emotion to an audience. In real life a sincere public speaker may use expressions which would not be used in conversation, and he may employ figures of speech, repetitions, inversions, enumerations and other peculiarities as the spontaneous result of his emotional delivery. A speaker may also employ them to simulate an emotion, and in either case we may call his style "rhetorical". Now the dramatic character is a creation of the dramatist, and so his words will not normally be the spontaneous effect of emotion. We cannot suppose that Grillparzer, writing Hero's farewell to Leander, felt the full strength of emotion he represents her as feeling. Nevertheless, what she is made to say is effective because the emotion she expresses is one with which we are familiar, and in which we are ready to participate, and also because the whole play has built up this situation in which a strong expression of this emotion is appropriate. If either circumstance were altered—if the emotion were unfamiliar or appeared uncalled for—we should be conscious of the artificiality of what she says, and this would destroy all appearance of sincerity. Even when the emotion is familiar and appropriate the effect may be destroyed if the style is recognizably derived from some literary model or if a particular trick is repeated so often that we become aware of it. I indicated above (pp. 2-4) that this is sometimes the case (or has often been regarded as so, . . .) in Grillparzer's earliest plays.

Hero's death when the priest tears her from Leander's body is intelligible not only from her independence (the factor stressed by Scherer) but also from the swiftness with which one drastic change in her life has followed another. Grillparzer noted in his autobiography that one reason for concentrating the events of a play into a short period is that "die Zeit ist nicht nur die äuβere Form der Handlung: sie gehört auch unter die Motive: Empfindungen und Leidenschaften werden stärker oder schwächer durch die Zeit" (I, 16, 168). What he surely had in mind is that when events follow each other quickly the characters are forced into reactions they would not have chosen had the pace been more leisurely. In this play, Hero is unable to adjust herself to her sudden bereavement which follows so hard upon an equally drastic change from priestess to lover.

Of all Grillparzer's plays this one has perhaps suffered most from the "close analysis" that informs so much recent literary criticism. Miss Atkinson's discussion of it ([Atkinson, "Grillparzer's use of symbol and image in 'Des Meeres und der Liebe Wellen,'"] pp. 261 ff.) is a good example. In Act I Hero is seen against a background of sunlight, is said to tread a radiant path in casting aside earthly ties to become a priestess, and can find no pleasure in nocturnal vigils. Miss Atkinson infers that these details link her with sunlight so closely that later references to it may plausibly be interpreted as meaning her! Leander, on the other hand, "is immediately identified with darkness", for he is dark-skinned and depressed, and so references to shadows are likely to be really references to him. It is from these premises that Miss Atkinson comments on the four lines in which the priest explains to Naukleros and

Leander that they must depart by midday (see above, p. 74), and she argues that his image of the sun drinking the shadows is "a hint that Hero's love has the power to disperse the shadows that beset Leander" (i.e. his depression). Miss Atkinson has herself shown very clearly that some of the references to light in Act I bring out the cheerfulness, happiness and confidence the heroine feels at this stage, and that many later references to light and darkness are natural enough in a play in which lovers are prevented by guards from meeting except at night, and the catastrophe is brought about by the extinction of a light. It seems, then, unnecessary to assume the complicated symbolism that she invokes on such a flimsy basis.

Papst's interpretation of the play is likewise in part spoiled by this quest for symbols. He also will correlate two words or incidents which have some similarity (however trivial) and assign a like symbolic meaning to both. At the end of Act IV Hero loosens her shoe as she assumes a reclining posture and thereby indicates that she will not be able to remain awake for long. Papst links this with the end of Act I where, he says, "Hero, hurried off by the Priest, fumbles at her shoe, while her eyes glance over her right shoulder and alight once more on Leander" (["Des Meeres und der Liebe Wellen,"] p. 27). His argument is that in both cases her behaviour to the shoe symbolizes "a relaxation of her powers of conscious control". But in actual fact she does not "fumble at" her shoe in Act I, but merely looks over her shoulder at Leander as if she were looking at some defect in her shoe that had drawn her attention. It is difficult to avoid the conclusion that Papst has made the shoe more prominent in this incident and has made her at least touch, if not loosen it, in order to link this with the later loosening and so facilitate a common symbolic interpretation of both.

Notes

1. Yates, ([*Grillparzer: A Critical Biography,*] p. 53) however, thinks that this is her motive for suicide. But the passage he quotes in support (ll. 1995-8) does not imply that she has wronged the gods.

2. Ehrhard's discussion of the play illustrates how perplexing critics have found its ending. He declares that her suicide would be intelligible enough if it resulted from her disappointment in love, but that such a motive is nowhere suggested in her final speech, where (he alleges) she poses as a higher being who must die as a punishment for having sullied herself with what is lowly. This he finds absurd, and asks how the poet can write about love, despair, and other emotions, if he is a superior being who must never experience them. He concludes that we can only accept Sappho's suicide if we suppose that, in spite of her apparent calm, her grief at Phaon's betrayal makes continuation of life impossible for her. ([Ehrhard, *Grillparzer: le théâtre en Autriche,*] pp. 259–60)

3. Quoted by Backmann ([Backmann, "Vom Werdegang des 'Goldenen Vlieβes,'"] p. 168). Cf. I, 17, 308.

4. Quoted from Grillparzer's manuscript by Backmann (["Vom Werdegang des 'Goldenen Vlieβes,'"] p. 176). Cf. I, 17, 196 and 301.

5. For instance, Stefan Hock complains, in his otherwise excellent introduction to the play, that "sie hat die Schranken überschritten, die ihrem Wesen gesetzt sind, sie ist sich nicht treu geblieben, die Barbarin hat sich dem Griechen, die Zauberin dem Menschen verbunden. Sie hat die Heimat verlassen, ihr Magdtum preisgegeben. . . ." The moral standpoint is even clearer in the criticism of Jason that follows. "Auch er überschreitet die Schranken seiner Natur; er geht in ein Land, das ihm fremd ist und bleibt, er vermischt sich mit Greulichem, das dem Menschen stets fernbleiben soll" ([Hock, *Grillparzers Werke,*] pp. 28–9). An attitude of moral condemnation towards Medea is apparently supported by a note Grillparzer made while writing the play: "Vergiβ nie, daβ der Grundgedanke des letzten Stückes der ist, daβ Medea, nachdem sie Kolchis verlassen, tadellos seyn *will,* aber es nicht seyn kann" (I, 17, 300). But, as Backmann has observed, Grillparzer's original plan made her guilty of the murder of Pelias on her arrival in Greece, and he seems to have made this note before he abandoned this plan. Backmann also notes that Medea's estrangement from her brutal father in the first two plays places her "in jene für sie so charakteristische Mittelstellung zwischen Barbarei und Hellenentum. . . . Sie wird zu gut für Kolchis und doch nicht gut genug für Griechenland, zu einer tragischen Person gleich von vornherein" (["Vom Werdegang des 'Goldenen Vlieβes,'"] pp. 133–4, 167, 173).

6. In his "Vorarbeiten" Grillparzer wrote of Kreon's "strenge Gesetzlichkeit" and "Rechtlichkeit" (I, 17, 294 and 300). Coenan, however, finds it "impossible to detect any sense of justice" in him ([Coenan, "Grillparzer's Portraiture of Men,"] p. 20).

7. Stiefel ([Stiefel, "Grillparzer's 'Golden Vlieβ,'"] p. 40) quotes Grillparzer's note of 1820: "Medeas Gefühl gegen die Kinder muβ gemischt sein aus *Haβ* gegen den Vater, Jason, von dem sie weiβ, daβ er die Kinder liebt und ihr Tod ihm schmerzlich wird; aus *Grimm* gegen die Kinder, die sie flohen und ihren Feinden den schmerzlichen Triumph über sie verschafften; aus *Liebe* gegen eben diese Kinder, die sie nicht mutterlos unter Fremden zurücklassen will; aus *Stolz,* ihre Kinder nicht in der Gewalt ihrer Feinde zu lassen" (cf. I, 17, 306). Although he did not necessarily follow this early plan rigorously, it does show that he envisaged complex motivation of Medea's deed.

8. Backmann notes (["Vom Werdegang des 'Goldenen Vlieβes'"] p. 167) that Grillparzer was so anxious to find "äuβerer Zwang für Medeas gräβliche Tat" that he planned a scene in which she is provoked by the noise of a banquet in the palace and by shouts of "Jason hoch! Jason und Kreusa!".

9. Grillparzer noted that in her final appearance she speaks with Jason "etwa wie ein abgeschiedener Geist über das Ereignis reden könnte, etwa wie der Chor bei den Alten" (I, 17, 297).

10. Schiller, *Maria Stuart,* Act V, scene 10; Hebbel, *Judith,* Act V.

Abbreviations

DD = Das deutsche Drama von Barock bis zur Gegenwart. Interpretationen, hrsg. B. von Wiese, Bagel, Düsseldorf, 1958, Bd. I.

G = Grillparzer

GLL = German Life and Letters, New Series, Blackwell, Oxford.

JGG = Jahrbuch der Grillparzergesellschaft, Konegen, etc., Wien.

MLR = Modern Language Review, publ. by Modern Humanities Research Association.

Works Cited

ATKINSON, M. E., "G's use of symbol and image in 'Des Meeres und der Liebe Wellen'", *GLL,* IV, 1951.

ATKINSON, M. E. edn. of Tieck, *Der Blonde Eckbert,* Blackwell, Oxford, 1952.

BACKMANN, R., "Vom Werdegang des 'Goldenen Vlieβes,'" *G-studien,* ed. Kataan, Gerlach & Wiedling, Wien, 1924.

CARLYLE, T., German playwrights, *Critical and Miscellaneous Essays,* Chapman & Hall, London, 1894, vol. I.

COENAN, F. E., "G's Portraiture of Men," *Univ. of N. Carolina Studies in the Germanic Langs. and Lits.,* No. 4, Chapel Hill, 1951.

EHRHARD, A., *G: le théâtre en Autriche,* Société d'Imprimerie, Paris, 1900.

HOCK, S., *Gs Werke,* Tl. IV, Bong, Berlin, etc., n.d.

LESSING, O. E., Schillers Einfluβ auf G, *Bulletin of Univ. of Wisconsin, Philos. and Lit. Series,* LIV, 1902.

LESSING, O. E., *G und das Neue Drama,* Piper, Leipzig, 1905.

PAPST, E. E., edn. of *Der arme Spielmann,* Nelson, London, 1960.

PAPST, E. E., "G's 'Des Meeres und der Liebe Wellen'", *Studies in German Lit.,* ed. FORSTER and ROWLEY, No. 9, Arnold, London, 1967.

RANKE, L. VON, *Vom Religionsfieden bis zum dreiβigjährigen Kriege, in Sämtliche Werke,* 54–vol. edn., Duncker & Humblot, Leipzig, 1868, VII.

RIPPMANN, W., edn. of *Sappho,* MacMillan, London, 1942.

SAUER, A., "Ein treuer Diener seines Herrn," *JGG,* III, 1893.

SCHERER, W., G, in *Vorträge und Aufsätze zur Gesch. des geistigen Lebens in Deutschland und Österreich,* Weidmann, Berlin, 1874.

STIEFEL, R., "Gs 'Goldenes Vlieβ'", *Basler Studien zur deutschen Sprache und Literatur,* Hft. 21, 1959.

YATES, D., *G: a Critical Biography,* Blackwell, Oxford, 1946 (repr. 1964).

YUILL, W. E., edn. of *Der Traum ein Leben,* Nelson, London, 1955.

W. E. Yates (essay date 1972)

SOURCE: "Ambition," in *Grillparzer: A Critical Introduction,* Cambridge University Press, 1972, pp. 84-131.

[*In the following excerpt, Yates offers detailed discussions of Grillparzer's* Das Goldene Vlies, Köning Ottokar's Glück und Ende, *and* Der Traum ein Leben, *focusing on characterization and pointing out that achievement is often linked with the fulfillment of duty in Grillparzer's plays.*]

DAS GOLDENE VLIES

In the preface to **Das Goldene Vlies** which Grillparzer composed in November 1821, he wrote that it was impossible for a writer to escape the spirit of his own age; that in his age writers too rapidly lost that 'certain innocence of mind' that was essential for creative work, and turned to reflection, with the result that in the search for deeper motivation and 'higher guiding principles' they fell victim to formlessness; and that this point applied to himself in respect of his trilogy. A significant indication of the uncharacteristically 'reflective' nature of the work is that while he was still engaged on its composition Grillparzer was able to define its theme or basic idea in a generalized formula, which he borrowed—misquoting slightly—from Schiller's *Wallenstein* trilogy:

> Das eben ist der Fluch der bösen Tat,
> Daβ sie, fortzeugend, [. . .] Böses muβ gebären.[1]

He wrote these lines over his scenario for **Medea** in early October 1819, and later in the month, when he was completing **Die Argonauten,** he wrote a memorandum reminding himself that the whole work was no more than a realization, or enactment, of the idea expressed in them.

Grillparzer's concern with this idea conditioned the form of the work. In comparison with Euripides' *Medea,* which he read in 1817 and again in 1819, or, among modern treatments of the theme, with Corneille's *Médée,* one of the most striking differences lies in the breadth of the material that Grillparzer's version takes in. Euripides and Corneille both begin as Jason is about to marry Creon's daughter; Grillparzer does not reach this point until the second act of the final part of his trilogy. While his first plan was to write only a **Medea,** he conceived Medea's tragedy as the culmination of a whole series of events beginning with her father's capture of the Golden Fleece and murder of Phryxus. To dramatize the whole chain of cause and effect involved treating the story in three distinct parts: the Phryxus episode (in **Der Gastfreund**), Jason's wooing of Medea and his recapture of the Fleece (**Die Argonauten**), then the tragic finale in Greece four years later (**Medea**). In this finale we see fulfilled the revenge which Phryxus was promised by Apollo in the cryptically oracular formula 'Take victory and vengeance!' ('Nimm Sieg und Rache hin!') in the course of the vision which first inspired him to set out for Colchis. Looking back on his murder, Medea warns her father how a single commitment to evil develops into a whole chain of evil consequences from which there is no escape:

> Kein Mensch, kein Gott löset die Bande,
> Mit denen die Untat sich selber umstrickt.

(***Die Argonauten*** 131f.)[2]

The long chain-reaction of evil and suffering draws in not only the guilty but those of good will, like Aietes' son Absyrtus and Kreusa, the daughter of the King of Corinth. This presentation of the inevitability with which evil engenders evil has, as Grillparzer saw, fatalistic undertones; not in the sense of the spooky atmospheric fatalism of **Die Ahnfrau**—'There is no question of *Fate* here', he noted in anxious self-defence in the memorandum of October 1819—but in the sense that we see the main characters of the work fashioning their own fate, from which they can never extricate themselves. The idea is a recurrent one in Grillparzer. It is expressed—albeit sophistically—by Jaromir in his argument that human actions are only 'Würfe / In des Zufalls blinde Nacht'; the same image is used in **Libussa** by Wlasta: 'Der Wurf geworfen, fällt das Los—und trifft' (2287);[3] in the same play, Primislaus sees this chain of causality running throughout human history: 'Im Anfang liegt das Ende' (1435).[4] The past is irredeemable, and this Medea discovers by harsh experience. For at the beginning of the final play in the trilogy, when she is longing to adapt herself completely to the life of Jason's homeland, she buries a chest full of her magic paraphernalia, in a conscious attempt to bury her past: the past is to be 'wafted away', with Colchis and its gods (**Medea,** 49-51). Her nurse, Gora, who cannot forgive her for her desertion of Colchis, sees the growing gulf between her and Jason as a just consequence, the proof that the actions of the past live on, wreaking their own effects and ineradicable from the mind:

> Grab ein, grab ein die Zeichen deiner Tat,
> Die Tat begräbst du nicht!

(109f.)[5]

Medea faces, then, the dread possibility that the past can never be extinguished:

So wär' denn immer da, was einmal da gewesen
Und alles Gegenwart?

(113f.)[6]

At the time she disputes the idea, but later she has to acknowledge its truth: the past lives on within herself, for example, in her memory of her past position, which, she tells Kreusa, contrasting it with her present humiliation, can never be forgotten (699). And Jason too, also talking to Kreusa, dwells on the contrast between his proud position before the Argonauts set off, surrounded by the admiration of the celebrating people of Corinth, and his present position, unrecognized or ignored in the same streets (*Medea* 795-816). The only possible escape from such memories would, as he says, be to unmake the past (821ff.), which he knows to be impossible. His past—both his triumphs and his wrongs—lives on within him, and breaks his spirit, as he later admits to Medea:

. . . Erinnrung des Vergangnen
Liegt mir wie Blei auf meiner bangen Seele,
Das Aug' kann ich nicht heben und das Herz.

(1525-7)[7]

The evil of the past acts as a curse upon the future; and as though in demonstration of this theme, the action of the three parts of the trilogy is linked by curses. At the end of *Der Gastfreund,* Phryxus curses Aietes as he dies, and prays for revenge, which he associates with the Fleece for which Aietes has murdered him:

Und dieses Vlies, das jetzt in seiner Hand,
Soll niederschaun auf seiner Kinder Tod!

(491f.)[8]

One of Aietes' children, his son Absyrtus, dies in *Die Argonauten*; the other, Medea, lives on but faces at the end of the trilogy a misery which, she says, is worse than death (*Medea* 2312f.)—a state of emptiness, humiliation and shame which is the fullest realization of the second curse, that spoken over her by her father when she opts to follow Jason:

. . . Nicht sterben soll sie, leben;
Leben in Schmach und Schande; verstoβen, verflucht,
Ohne Vater, ohne Heimat, ohne Götter!

(*Die Argonauten* 1361-3)[9]

To this curse Jason refers back in the *Medea,* admitting that it seems to be working still (*Medea* 749); and when it is wholly fulfilled, Medea again recalls it as she nurses her thoughts of revenge, banished and alone, 'shunned like a beast of the wild' (2112) but, as Aietes foretold, 'not dead—alas!' ('leider nicht tot', 2114).

Throughout all these events the constant centre of interest is the fateful Fleece. In the 1819 memorandum Grillparzer observed that it stood as a symbol of the main theme, 'accompanying' the events but not causing them. In 1821, in a diary note, he called it the 'intellectual centre' of the

work, and redefined its symbolical significance: it should be seen to stand as 'a physical symbol of all that is desirable, and greedily sought, and wrongfully gained' (**T** [*Tagebücher,* numbered entries in vols. II/7–12 of Grillparzer's *Sämtliche Werke,* ed. A. Sauer and R. Backmann (Vienna, 1909–48)] 1241). And this was the conception that he adhered to in the autobiography, where the Fleece is described more succinctly as 'a physical symbol of wrongful possessions' (**SB** ['**Selbstbiographie,**' page references to vol. I/16 of Grillparzer's *Sämtliche Werke,* ed. A. Sauer and R. Backmann (Vienna, 1909–48)] 134). This is a more satisfactory formula than that of 1819; for as a symbol of the desirable material possessions which men commit evil to acquire, the Fleece clearly does provoke the events of the play, acting as a catalyst to the passions or the acquisitiveness of successive characters who are subsequently either killed or left in tragic emptiness: Aietes, Jason, Kreon. But even the later definitions are inadequate. They are not, for example, appropriate in relation to Phryxus; for while he may have done wrong in removing the Fleece from Delphi in the first place he did so not out of personal acquisitiveness, but in interpretation of a divine vision—even if there was an element of personal ambition in his attempt to fulfil the promise of 'victory and vengeance'. Even after Aietes' crime the Fleece is not merely a symbol of unjustly gained possessions; for in the course of the action it develops other, wider connotations. In the final act of *Die Argonauten,* when Jason displays it to Absyrtus, it serves as a sign of Medea's betrayal, and not only seals her estrangement from her family but contributes to the motivation of Absyrtus' suicide. And in Act IV of *Medea,* when Medea promises it to Kreon with the ominous assurance that he will receive what is his 'due' (1952), it is clearly being used as a symbol of retribution, as foreshadowed in Phryxus' curse. The Fleece itself embodies the sense of that curse: it stimulates the selfishness of mankind, it brings disaster to its wrongful holders, it is an instrument of the final tragedy, and its survival at the last will bring Medea to Delphi in search of divine judgment.

By tracing the whole history of the curse, Grillparzer laid himself open to the charge of formlessness that he levelled against himself in the unpublished preface. In his autobiography he called the trilogy a 'monstrosity' (**SB** 159); and, illustrating his point by reference to *Wallenstein,* he condemned the form of the trilogy from the dramatic point of view:

> Einmal ist die Trilogie oder überhaupt die Behandlung eines dramatischen Stoffes in mehreren Teilen für sich eine schlechte Form. Das Drama ist eine Gegenwart, es muβ alles, was zur Handlung gehört, in sich enthalten. Die Beziehung eines Teiles auf den andern gibt dem Ganzen etwas Episches, wodurch es vielleicht an Groβartigkeit gewinnt aber an Wirklichkeit und Prägnanz verliert . . .

(**SB** 135)[10]

The criteria implicit in this argument are characteristic of Grillparzer's view of drama. He recognized that in ancient Greek drama a 'predominance' of 'description and narration' over action was historically inherent in the dramatic tradition (T 2149); but the same is not true of modern treatments of ancient subjects. And while *Das Goldene Vlies* contains some impressive scenes, it would be idle to deny that by Grillparzer's own criteria his criticisms of the weakness of the trilogy form apply aptly to it. Much of the story of the first two parts is essentially epic material, and its treatment inevitably involves long passages of narrative. The principal example in *Der Gastfreund* is Phryxus' story of his bringing of the Fleece (270ff.). In *Die Argonauten* the climax of the legend, Jason's encounter with the dragon that guards the Fleece, has to take place off stage, while on stage Medea is left exclaiming in horrified suspense (1557-74); and when Jason emerges triumphant, he then rehearses his adventure in a purely narrative speech (1586-96). In relation to the tragedy of the *Medea,* all the action of these first two plays is pre-history, four years past, causally connected with the events of the *Medea* but not dramatically part of them. Its place in Euripides and in Corneille is in expository speeches, spoken by the nurse and Jason respectively, in the opening scenes. In Grillparzer's *Medea* too Jason recapitulates the story of the Argonauts to Kreon (429ff.). By the criteria of drama that is enough, and the *Medea* has taken its place in the classical repertoire of the German theatre, independent of *Der Gastfreund* and *Die Argonauten.* A mere speech of exposition does not, however, satisfy the demands of analytical 'reflection', it is not enough to develop the underlying ideas of the work. The truth is that the demands of drama and 'reflection' were by Grillparzer's standards irreconcilable, and it is his recognition of this that he expressed in his preface of 1821.

The first two plays of the trilogy are rarely performed. They include what is, dramatically, some of Grillparzer's weakest writing, and the verse reflects the lack of dramatic life: it is at times stilted, at times melodramatically exclamatory, and often artificial in the short lines used to distinguish the speech of the Colchians from that of the Greeks. Where the action does spring into dramatic life is, significantly, in the scenes between Jason and Medea in *Die Argonauten,* particularly the wooing-scene in Act III: it comes to life, that is, not in treating Jason's adventures, which are strictly epic material, but in the interplay of characters, which is the stuff of drama. The dramatic effect of the whole trilogy is founded on this interplay between the two incompatible principal figures; but Jason is too reprehensible to be a tragic hero, while Medea, however cruelly driven to her final atrocity, inevitably forfeits sympathy with her vengeful murder of Kreusa and her stabbing of her own children.

Jason's lack of moral stature is most clearly demonstrated in his wooing of Medea, which is cynically calculated as a means towards the capture of the Fleece. Even when declaring his love, he himself admits to a certain dispassionateness, a sense that he is standing outside himself, not committed but observing: 'Ich selber bin mir *Gegenstand* geworden' (*Die Argonauten* 1196).[11] It is this that justifies Medea's later charge that he made love to her to further

his ambition, that she was a mere tool, serving his selfish purpose (*Medea* 635f.), and also the repeated charges of hypocrisy that Gora levels against him in the third and fourth acts of the *Medea.* Were Medea not blinded by love, she would have recognized Jason's character from his behaviour towards her from the first. When he has declared his love for her and she tries to escape, he holds her by force, forces her on to her knees and proclaims himself her 'master' (*Die Argonauten* 1229). He then tries to bully her into an admission that she loves him, repeating over and again that she does so (1256ff.), challenging her to deny it, cajoling her into saying it herself. Later, presenting her to the Argonauts, he himself rips off her sorceress's veil, brushes aside her protests (1401-3), and at once (clearly *using* her love for his own acquisitive interests) demands that she direct him to the Fleece. Again he brushes aside all her protests; and when she threatens to kill herself, he makes it plain that the ambition to which he is committed is more important to him than her very life: 'Mein Höchstes für mein Wort und wär's dein Leben!' (1504).[12]

Once he has actually captured the Fleece, it appears, when he is challenged by Absyrtus, that he would be willing for Medea to remain in Colchis if she chose to (1703). In this same scene he also shows that he is not just boastful—this has been clear from the first—but boastful beyond his achievements. It is Medea's potion that has lulled the dragon; but it is Jason who is quick to assume the public credit: he tells Absyrtus that he is 'used to fighting dragons' (1718). When Absyrtus throws himself into the sea, Jason's complete lack of moral sense is evident in the way he at once disowns any responsibility for the incident, and blames it on Aietes:

> Die hohen Götter ruf' ich an zu Zeugen,
> Daß *du* ihn hast getötet und nicht ich!
>
> (1755f.)[13]

In the inauspicious life she shares with him in the years separating the second and third plays of the trilogy, Medea, despite her continuing love for him, learns to see through Jason's unscrupulous egoism, and she condemns it roundly to Kreusa:

> Nur *er* ist da, *er* in der weiten Welt,
> Und alles andre nichts als Stoff zu Taten.
>
> (*Medea* 630f.)[14]

Jason shows his selfishness in its worst light to Kreon. First he tries to excuse himself for ever having involved himself with Medea, arguing in self-defence that in Colchis 'the measure of all things was lost' (*Medea* 446). Later he applauds her banishment; as a punishment for her part in the death of King Pelias it is indeed, he says, mild:

> Denn wahrlich, minder schuldig doch als sie,
> Trifft mich ein härtres Los, ein schwerers.
>
> (*Medea* 1327f.)[15]

His uppermost feeling, that is, is one of self-pity; for Medea he has no consideration, but takes refuge in a piece of flagrant sophistry: 'Sie zieht hinaus in angeborne Wildnis' (1329).[16] This is sophistry because it equates two quite separate, and for Medea very different, senses of the word 'Wildnis'. In fact the island of Colchis from which she came, and in which she was a powerful princess, is very far from being comparable to the abject disgrace of banishment from Corinth, to which Medea's own word, 'Elend' (2136), implying the wretchedness of exile, is much more applicable. But Jason rejects her pleas to him and supports her banishment, with a shamelessness that Medea herself comments on (1405); he defends himself as merely shrinking back from atrocity (1410) and does not acknowledge his own role in stimulating Medea's erratic conduct—a role which in her eyes, we know, is so fundamental that he seems the 'originator and sole cause' of her deeds (1070). And when Medea charges him with his responsibility towards her, he again shakes off any blame for deserting her, just as he shook off all blame for her brother's death. The fault, he says, is her own:

> MEDEA: Mein Vaterland verließ ich, dir zu folgen.
> JASON: Dem eignen Willen folgtest du, nicht mir.
> Hätt's dich gereut, gern ließ ich dich zurück!
>
> (*Medea* 1564-6)[17]

To admit that he would have left her behind—after gaining the Fleece—is callous; to claim that it was her 'will' to follow him is dishonest, for he had to break down her resistance, and at the last she would gladly have stayed on Colchis (*Die Argonauten* 1703) were she not driven by love for Jason and had she not already irrevocably severed her links with the island by her (reluctant) assistance of him in the capture of the Fleece. To such facts Jason pays no heed: he blames her, and then proceeds to blame the Amphictyonic edict:

> Ich verlass' dich nicht,
> Ein höhrer Spruch treibt mich von dir hinweg.
>
> (*Medea* 1569f.)[18]

He uses the political edict as a shield to hide behind, a means of wriggling out from under his moral responsibility, with which Medea is confronting him.

By contrast with Jason, Medea is portrayed as having a much more acute moral awareness. One of the many notes Grillparzer made during his work on the trilogy towards the end of 1819 reads: 'Never forget that the basic thought of the last play is that after leaving Colchis Medea *wants* to be *faultless,* but cannot be.'[19] This note, while not really summarizing the 'basic thought' of the *Medea,* comes to grips with one of the most fundamental problems he faced: how to show Medea in the first two plays as being sufficiently uncivilized and as having sufficiently violent passions to motivate her murder of Kreusa and the children in the final play, while yet retaining our sympathy for her as a tragic heroine in a modern drama. He attempted to solve this difficulty by two expedients. First, he radically altered the traditional character of Medea, making her appear morally superior to the other Colchians, abandoning the gruesome legend that it was she who killed Absyrtus and then strewed the pieces of his body over the seashore to halt Aietes' pursuit, and also throwing a veil of imprecision over the details of the death of Pelias; far from being simply a barbarian sorceress, Grillparzer's Medea is wise, strong in character and outraged by her father's treatment of Phryxus. Secondly, Grillparzer emphasized as strongly as possible the general contrast between Colchis and Greece, partly by his use of different metres. From the first, as he recalled in the autobiography, he saw this contrast as being of central importance, and involving a basic contrast in atmosphere between the first two plays and the last: 'The first two parts had to be kept as barbaric and romantic as possible, precisely to bring out that difference between Colchis and Greece on which everything turned' (**SB** 136). In *Die Argonauten,* Jason makes this contrast in the wooing scene itself:

> Ich ein Hellene, du Barbarenbluts,
> Ich frei und offen, du voll Zaubertrug . . .
>
> (*Die Argonauten* 1204f.)[20]

He speaks of Greece as a land of light, in contrast to the dark of the island, and depicts it as an ideal country full of the spirit of friendship (1237-42). Medea has previously heard Phryxus too speak with pride of the beauty of Greece (*Der Gastfreund* 263); and it follows from her superiority to the other Colchians that she is drawn to it. Once she is there, however, she finds that a great gulf separates her from the Greeks; and this is brought out repeatedly in the first two acts of the *Medea.* She admits that she is not used to the customs of Greece: and it is for that reason, she says, that the Greeks despise her (*Medea* 400-3), degrading her who was by birth a princess. Both her endeavour and her failure to assimilate the culture of her adopted home are crystallized in her attempt to learn a favourite song of Jason's to sing to him. When first we see Kreusa trying to teach her to play the harp, Medea feels that it is hopeless, that what her hand is used to is not playing musical instruments but hunting with a spear (587f.). Then when she does try to sing for Jason, she has to beg for his attention with fearful insistence: 'Jason, ich weiß ein Lied';[21] when she fails, breaking down at the very beginning of the song (906f.), her tears bring out the depth of her suffering at the humiliation she is going through in Greece—a humiliation which is partly caused, as in this episode, by her own struggle to gain acceptance, but which still imposes an intolerable strain. When Jason asks Kreusa to sing instead, all Medea's self-restraint breaks, in a violent eruption of her natural feelings. She expresses her emotion in one of those highly theatrical gestures that are characteristic in Grillparzer, snatching up the lyre that symbolizes the culture of Greece, crushing it in her hands and throwing it at Kreusa's feet (*Medea* 924). It is the moment at which all that part of her character breaks out—all her 'barbarian blood'—which she has vainly sought to bury as belonging to the past.

The character in whom this past is articulated is Gora, Medea's companion since the very beginning of the trilogy. In the *Medea* the occasional use of shorter metres in scenes between Medea and Gora effectively brings out, by the contrast with the pentameters spoken by the Greeks, their strangeness in the alien land; as the work builds up towards tragedy, both the third and fourth acts begin with scenes of this kind, in which the shorter metres are used, and Medea returns to them at the climax itself at the end of Act IV. In the first of these scenes, that at the beginning of Act III, Medea, despairing, thinks of suicide, and then of dying together with her children, as a means of avenging herself on Jason (1230-4). When she thinks of killing Kreusa instead, she at once tries to resist the idea (1238-41); but Gora takes over, spurring her on to vengeance by recounting the dreadful fates of a series of other legendary heroes (1252ff.). At this stage Medea remains undecided, pinning her hopes on a last confrontation with Jason. She fails to change his attitude, but he allows her to take one of their children into exile with her. The children have been her one source of consolation from the outset of the *Medea,* and she has clung to their embrace when left alone with them (362f.); now when they are brought to her, the sight of their preference for Kreusa comes as an annihilating defeat, the ultimate, intolerable humiliation:

> Ich bin besiegt, vernichtet, zertreten,
> Sie fliehn mich, fliehn!
> Meine Kinder fliehn!
>
> (1710-12)[22]

It is this thought of the children that returns to her at the beginning of the next act, prompting on the one hand a sense of despair about her whole life (1798-1802) and on the other hand renewed thoughts of revenge, which she comes finally to contemplate with a horrible delight:

> Entsetzliches gestaltet sich in mir,
> Ich schaudre—doch ich freu' mich auch darob.
>
> (1851f.)[23]

The compound motivation for the destruction of her self-control is complete: the selfish injustice of Jason, the successive humiliations of her life in Greece, her jealousy of Kreusa, the loss of her children. But however well motivated, her actual crime cannot be seen as anything but an inhuman atrocity, which repels our sympathy. Moreover, to the last she does not repent her act, but instead laments the whole tragic sequence that is life itself:

> Nicht traur' ich, daß die Kinder nicht mehr sind.
> Ich traure, daß sie *waren* und daß *wir* sind.
>
> (2324f.)[24]

These lines sum up that recognition of 'das Nichtige des Irdischen', the emptiness of all earthly things, which in the essay **"Über das Wesen des Drama"** Grillparzer defined as belonging to the essence of tragedy.

While Medea's conception of the universal tragedy of human existence is securely founded on her experience in association with the Golden Fleece, so that her final plight may be said to embody the lesson or moral of the trilogy,

nevertheless her crime and her subsequent attitude of desolation rather than repentance together make her an unsuitable vehicle for the expression of the moral. In real life we could not stomach moralizing from a person who had committed an atrocity such as Medea's, and still less from one who remained unrepentant; and the same is true in the work of art. Yet in the final scene Grillparzer has Medea confront Jason and expound to him in a long speech the moral of the events they have lived through. This misjudgment may be attributed in part to Grillparzer's overestimation, at this stage of his career, of the moral function of tragedy: in the essay **"Über das Wesen des Drama"** one of the essential characteristics he ascribed to tragedy was that it should show that every disruption of the eternal order of right ('das ewige Recht') must be brought to nought. This moral element appears, however, to have been further inflated by a subjective element of self-recrimination; for just as Jason has been accused by Medea of making love to her out of selfish ambition, so Grillparzer accused himself (most openly in *Le poète sifflé*) of having wronged Charlotte von Paumgartten, the dedicatee of the trilogy, by deliberately holding her love and coldly observing it, exploiting it for the benefit of his art. He saw himself as having undermined her happiness, yet felt too that his ambitious artistic project—the completed trilogy—fell far short of his hopes. With all these subjective undertones, the moral takes on an accusing urgency that overrides strictly dramatic considerations, and it is hammered home as Medea tells Jason again that he is at fault for their plight (2314f.): he has deserved the unhappy lot that has now befallen him (2327), for he has overreached himself (2331) and must now bear the suffering that is the consequence (2342ff.). Her own suffering, she tells him, is still greater (2346)—a reversal of the point earlier made by him to her, and no more convincing. She is taking the Fleece back to Delphi, and there she will submit her fate to the judgment of Apollo; meanwhile she shows it to Jason as a symbol of the vanity of human desires, a symbol of the gain and the glory which he sought but which are without substance, and she reminds him that though his illusion is shattered, its consequences still face them both:

> Erkennst das Zeichen du, um das du rangst?
> Das dir ein Ruhm war und ein Glück dir schien?
> Was ist der Erde Glück?—Ein Schatten!
> Was ist der Erde Ruhm?—Ein Traum!
> Du Armer! der von Schatten du geträumt!
> Der Traum ist aus, allein die Nacht noch nicht.
>
> (2364-9)[25]

While the prospect she holds out is the dark 'night' of expiatory suffering (2373f.), this whole final scene, like the final scene in *Sappho,* is played against a sunrise, and similar objections arise: the contrast with the darkness of the previous act is at odds with the position which the central figures in fact face. Medea tells Jason that the night of their suffering is not over; and her bleak moralizing prescription, in the last lines of the play, of atonement through suffering, gives no positive hope for the future, ei-

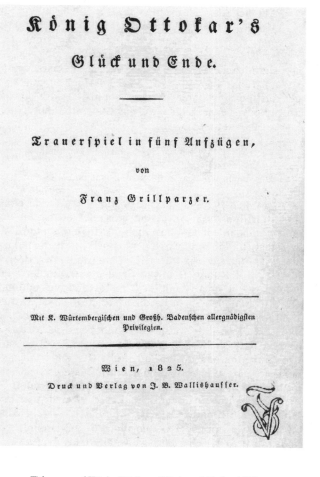

Title page of König Ottokars Glück und Ende, *1825.*

ther in practical or in moral terms, such as the sunrise behind her might suggest. If her moralizing is unacceptable, so the scenic effects accompanying it are at the least suspect.

The theme of the vanity of ambition was a rich one for Grillparzer, but he had yet to realize its full dramatic potential. He did this, abandoning the trilogy form, in two very different plays. In *König Ottokars Glück und Ende* he explored in depth a character as ambitious as Jason but portrayed with a wider humanity, the moral issues being represented in the main dramatic conflict and the whole action of the play demonstrating the consequences of Ottokar's ambition on his peoples as well as on himself and his court. In *Der Traum ein Leben* he adopted a much more stylized convention, that of the *Besserungsstück* of the Viennese popular stage, and used it to explore in the monitory dream-adventures of the central figures the potential consequences of ambition for him as an individual.

KÖNIG OTTOKARS GLÜCK UND ENDE

One of the first notes Grillparzer wrote in his diary when he was beginning work on *König Ottokars Glück und Ende* reads simply: 'Overweening pride (*Übermut*) and its

downfall. King Ottokar' (**T** 612, February 1820); and it is well known that his work on the tragedy (and on his plan for a drama *Krösus*), by absorbing his interest in the theme of the vanity of ambition, was one of the principal reasons for the long gap in his composition of *Der Traum ein Leben,* the earliest of his mature plays to be based on this theme. The actual composition of *König Ottokars Glück und Ende* in February and March 1823 was preceded by long research into the thirteenth-century background—by 'prodigious study of everything I could get hold of on Austrian and Bohemian history of that period' (**SB** 166). Aspects of the play and its genesis on which modern critics have in the main concentrated include: first, the freedom with which Grillparzer has treated his historical material;[26] secondly, the role of the Emperor, Rudolf, as the defender of the just cause of political order or of some wider standard of absolute right; thirdly, the apparently unheroic nature of Ottokar's repentance; and fourthly, the question of the extent to which Ottokar's character reflects that of Napoleon—this last being prompted by Grillparzer's admission of his interest in a 'distant similarity' between the fates of Ottokar and the Emperor of the French (**SB** 166). Particularly the first three of these approaches are suggestive and rewarding; but as a starting-point to an appreciation of the finished tragedy as a whole a further fundamental question arises: to what extent *is* it still essentially a study of the vanity of ambition, of 'overweening pride and its downfall'?

After his first defeat, Ottokar's career is seen in just such simple proverbial terms—'Pride comes before a fall'—by the mayor of Prague (2050); but the mayor is an unimaginative figure, and his trite comment is made unimaginatively. The play as a whole is not intended merely to present any such platitudinous moral. Nor is it just a single character-study, for essentially the action presents a contrast and a struggle: between Ottokar, whose goal is the imperial crown, and Rudolf von Habsburg, who is elected to that crown. In the latest Burgtheater production, which was given its première in December 1965, nearly all the loyalist cheering for the Habsburg cause was omitted. This is a case of political touchiness in modern republican Austria outweighing artistic considerations; it is not merely a sycophantic (and hence outdated) rounding-off when the play ends—and always ought to end—with cries of 'Habsburg for ever!' For Rudolf is in the play everything that Ottokar should be and is not. Ottokar is still the hero, in the sense that he is the central character: whereas Rudolf does not appear at all in the second and fourth acts, Ottokar is central in the first act in his power, in the second in his sudden discomfiture, in the third in his submission, in the fourth in his humiliation and the upsurge of his murderous rebellion, and in the fifth in his repentance and death. But when he flouts first the rights of his queen, Margarete, and then the authority of the empire, it is Rudolf's active opposition that he has to face, and it is to Rudolf's standards that his actions stand in constant contrast.

Rudolf is a pious figure, and so consistently in the right that his character can seem flat and wooden, at least on the printed page (in performance the sheer fact of physical presence always tends to lend the role substance and colour). Unlike Ottokar, he has never been exposed to the corruption of material power. His concern with the proper rights of the empire antecedes his election (375-7); and as Emperor he is able to tell Ottokar during their confrontation in the third act that he has set personal ambition behind him (1911). His conception of kingship is based on the ideal of service, and he enters battle as a crusader for a divine cause:

> Nun vor, mit Gott! und Christus sei der Schlachtruf!
>
> (2749)[27]

He himself makes explicit his exemplary stature and function:

> Was sterblich war, ich hab' es ausgezogen
> Und bin der Kaiser nur, der niemals stirbt.
>
> (1789f.)[28]

That Ottokar, like Sappho, is shown as falling short of an absolute ideal, and that this is the *moral* core of his tragedy, is in keeping with a recurrent tendency in Grillparzer's dramatic work; and since Grillparzer's choice of, and approach to, the subjects of his works was always subjective (his treatment of the motive of ambition, for example, to a significant extent reflects a critical attitude to his own aspirations as a dramatic poet), this also suggests that the absolute values which Rudolf represents and against which Ottokar offends should not necessarily be interpreted literally as being confined to the essentially imperial and religious terms in which Rudolf states them. Certainly his use of the words 'God' and 'Christ' does not imply that his representative role was conceived by Grillparzer as having an essentially religious significance.

Grillparzer's freethinking approach to religion (in any orthodox sense of the term) may be illustrated from a diary note of 1828: 'It is highly probable that there is a centre and complex of divinity, even a force which disposes and creates—to which, however, we perhaps come closer if we say "There is *no* God" than if with our human comprehension we say "There *is* a God"' (т 1681). That he was still an unbeliever nearly thirty years later is clear from his epigrams (e.g. **G** ['Gedichte,' numbered poems in vols. i/10–12 of Grillparzer's *Sämtliche Werke* ed. A. Sauer and R. Backmann (Vienna, 1909–48)] 1513). In old age he insisted in conversation that he had never been an atheist or anti-religious (*Gespr.* [numbered entries in **Grillparzers Gespräche und die Charakteristiken seiner Persönlichkeit durch die Zeitgenossen,** ed. A. Sauer (7 vols., Vienna, 1904–41)] 1201), and once he even remarked that he was actually beginning to grow religious. But even then his attitude was still very far from one of conviction: he observed that neither belief nor disbelief could be based on proof, but at least the former had the merit of being comforting (*Gespr.* 1247). And his attitude to the institution of the Christian church in particular is summed up in an epigram of 1857:

> Mit drei Ständen habe [ich] nichts zu schaffen:
> Beamte, Gelehrte und Pfaffen.
>
> (**G** 1526)[29]

The significance of the word 'God' in Grillparzer is best explained in a diary-note of 1820 (т 641). The gods of the ancients, he notes, are not to be compared with the modern divinity, because they were not supreme, but subordinate to 'the eternal Law':

> Die Götter waren nicht das Höchste; über ihnen stand
>   das ewige Recht.
> Das haben wir personifiziert und nennen es: Gott.[30]

In a way that is highly characteristic of the moral emphasis in Grillparzer's work, the idea of God means a supreme standard of law and of right. It is this *moral* standard that Rudolf I invokes, 'personified' in the name of the deity; and the same is true also of Gregor in **Weh dem, der lügt!** and of Rudolf II in the **Bruderzwist.** Rather as Goethe uses 'the clearly outlined figures and conceptions of the Christian church' in the final scene of *Faust* as a conventional structure of reference to represent wider 'poetic intentions'[31] so too Grillparzer symbolizes the idea of the highest duty (in whatever sphere) in the devotion of the two Emperors and the bishop to their Christian ideals. In Gregor's case it is an idea inherent in his episcopal office; in the case of Rudolf I (as also in the case of Rudolf II) it is inherent in his historical position as elected ruler of the Holy Roman Empire. Against Rudolf's positively conservative role as defender of the order of the empire, which he is prepared to represent against any odds (1779-84), Ottokar stands as a destructive counterpart, endangering the political continuity embodied in the house of Habsburg.

The contrast between the standards of the two rulers is made in the first act, as in successive scenes we are shown Rudolf's sympathy and obedience towards Margarete of Austria and then the brusqueness with which Ottokar treats her. The measured account that she gives to Rudolf of her marriage to Ottokar (206ff.) brings out both the pathos of her situation and her own dignity; and it is from the point when he dissolves this marriage—which, as Margarete makes clear, he does primarily so that he can remarry in the hope of an heir (256-65)—that fortune deserts Ottokar, and his star wanes as Rudolf's ascends. That in 1820 Grillparzer also used the key phrase 'the eternal Law' in relation to tragedy, when he wrote that tragedy has essentially to show that 'every offence against the eternal Law must be brought to nought' (т 639), is perhaps a suggestive pointer to the moral pattern of this play, as well as of the trilogy. Margarete is insistent that Ottokar is acting unjustly towards her (237), and she foresees his downfall:

> Er soll vor Unrecht sorglich sich bewahren;
> Denn auch das kleinste rächt sich . . .
>
> (380f.)[32]

The fact that his downfall arises directly from his repudiation of his queen (a significant reshaping of history on Grillparzer's part) concentrates our attention on the way that Ottokar is himself unknowingly sowing the seeds of his inevitable tragedy, and is doing so in the very sphere of action—a sphere in which personal and political motives intertwine—where his seeming ruthlessness has been most sharply contrasted with Rudolf's gentleness and loyalty. Ottokar protests that his dissolution of his marriage is not prompted by mere self-seeking; but clearly it *is* largely motivated in the first instance by ambition, whether that ambition be for himself or, as he claims, conceived as patriotic service of his people (508-20). The unity of motivation in Ottokar's personal and political life is suggestively underlined by the main (political) action: his unjustified pursuit of the imperial crown after Rudolf's election brings him in the final act to the scene where, in defeat, he kneels in repentant prayer by Margarete's coffin: the action has come full circle, his wrong is avenged, he has come to the truth when it is too late. Later, taking stock of his achievements, he acknowledges that his downfall is deserved:

> Ich hab' nicht gut in deiner Welt gehaust,
> Du großer Gott! . . .

He acknowledges that he has achieved not good, but the evil of destructiveness:

> . . . Wie Sturm und Ungewitter
> Bin ich gezogen über deine Fluren . . .
>
> (2825-7)[33]

He has in short been misled by his dreams of being a second Charlemagne, 'ein zweiter Karl' (1182); he has been misled, like Jason in *Das Goldene Vlies* or Rustan in *Der Traum ein Leben,* by his selfish will; and the link between his disastrous ambition and the first fateful step of faithlessness is re-established when finally, after his murder, his corpse lies beside Margarete's coffin.

It was probably not long after the première of *König Ottokars Glück und Ende* that Grillparzer wrote that Shakespeare was 'tyrannizing his mind' (T 1407); and indeed Shakespeare's influence is particularly strong on this work. One result of this is a richness and liveliness of characterization in the secondary roles, such as Grillparzer had achieved in none of his previous dramas. In its structure, moreover, *König Ottokars Glück und Ende* is essentially a history in the Shakespearian manner, and of course its subject matter is as important in the history of Austria—indeed of Germany and vast stretches of eastern and southeastern Europe—as the material of any Shakespearian history is to an English audience; for Rudolf's election as 'German King' brought the crown for the first time to the Habsburgs, who later were Emperors, with only one brief interval in the mid-eighteenth century, from 1438 onwards, and who remained the rulers of the Austrian Empire until its dissolution after the First World War.

That Grillparzer took Shakespeare as his model may also be seen in the treatment of Ottokar's decline, which is reminiscent of *King Lear,* in two scenes particularly: in the fourth act, when Ottokar finds himself deserted by all but his faithful chancellor (2261), as Lear is left with his Fool; and in the fifth act, where Lear's pathetic dependence on Albany to undo his button is matched by Ottokar's turning to his servants for a cloak, with a wild laugh that degenerates into a raucous cough: ''s ist kalt! Hat niemand einen Mantel?' (2584)[34]—a moment as succinctly revealing of the reduction of pride to abject dependence as Medea's plea 'Jason, ich weiß ein Lied'.

As a history, *König Ottokars Glück und Ende* gains much of its effect by the breadth of its canvas, with a sub-plot running parallel with the main plot. But this widening of scope does not undermine the unity of the play. Both actions start with the rejection of Margarete and lead to Ottokar's humiliation at the hands of Zawisch von Rosenberg. When he dissolves his marriage with Margarete he chooses as his new queen not Zawisch's niece Berta, as the Rosenbergs had hoped, but Kunigunde of Hungary. The Rosenbergs conspire to gain revenge. Zawisch hints at his vindictive intentions in the first act (182f.); and from then on he feeds Ottokar's ambitions, inflates his illusions, and so spurs him on to disastrous self-assertion.[35] Ottokar is in effect led on to disaster by his own self-conceit, which Zawisch sedulously cultivates. Early in Act III, for example, the chancellor frankly warns Ottokar that he is losing his war against Rudolf. Ottokar will not believe him:

> KANZLER: Herr, es steht schlimm!
> OTTOKAR: (*auf und nieder gehend*) Es steht sehr gut!
>
> (1427)[36]

The chancellor lists his evidence: disease and hunger among Ottokar's troops; armies in retreat; the enemy closing in (1428-46). And then Zawisch recharges all the king's illusions of grandeur and military superiority (1526-42). That Ottokar is completely taken in by Zawisch's plausible encouragement in spite of all the real evidence is proved by his willingness to meet Rudolf; and it is precisely here that Zawisch finally achieves his political revenge when, in one of the most visually dramatic of all Grillparzer's scenes, he cuts the ropes of the tent in which Ottokar is kneeling before Rudolf, and so exposes to the whole camp the humiliating spectacle of Ottokar in defeat. Traditionally this exposure was instigated by Rudolf. This is the case, for example, in Lope de Vega's play on the same subject, *La imperial de Otón.* When Grillparzer read this work in the early 1850s he found that the integrity of Lope's Rodulfo was compromised by precisely this motif—indeed, Lope's Otón makes the point himself, saying in the final act that the episode has revealed the Emperor as a man without honour. It is, by contrast, symptomatic of Grillparzer's exemplary characterization of Rudolf that he avoids involving him in any such trickery and transforms the episode into a climax in Zawisch's revenge. Throughout these political developments, moreover, Zawisch is gaining personal revenge by his calculated wooing of Kunigunde. With his elegance and spirit he presents an obvious contrast to Ottokar, whom the hot-blooded young queen despises as an old man; having spurned Margarete because (among other reasons) she is too old, Ottokar is now himself deceived by a girl who finds him 'as grumpy as an old man' (981).

The two plots link in the fourth act. The picture of himself kneeling before his victorious rival haunts Ottokar: 'Ich kann nicht knieen sehn!' (2454);[37] and Kunigunde taunts him with it, contrasting him with Zawisch:

> KÖNIGIN: . . . Rosenberg!
> ZAWISCH: Erlauchte Frau!
> KÖNIGIN: Habt Ihr schon je gekniet? Vor Frauen nicht—
>   vor Männern schon gekniet? Um Sold, um
>   Lohn, aus Furcht, vor Euresgleichen?
> ZAWISCH: Ich nicht.
> KÖNIGIN: Und würdet's nie?
> ZAWISCH: In meinem Leben!
> KÖNIGIN: Er aber hat's getan! vor seinem Feinde, Vor
>   jenem Mann gekniet, den er verachtet . . .
>
>   (2169-75)[38]

Here the political humiliation is being combined with sexual humiliation; and it is finally the sexual element that leads Ottokar to his last defeat. For it is Kunigunde's taunts that seduce him to make his last attempt to free himself from what she presents as his shame:

> Solang Ihr Euch nicht von der Schmach gereinigt,
> Betretet nicht als Gatte mein Gemach!
>
>   (2404f.)[39]

And so Ottokar goes to war under the pretext of salvaging his 'honour' (2407). It is a hollow pretext, for at the political level this is the very conception of honour that he has heard Rudolf condemn as vain (1893), and at the personal level, as he later admits (2672), Kunigunde has already compromised his honour with Zawisch.

Kunigunde was originally designed as a secondary figure, included because of the dramatist's need to externalize the motivation for Ottokar's rejection of Margarete: she was, that is, to be merely the 'other woman', like Melitta in *Sappho*. In fact, however, from her first entrance she stands out as a well-delineated character, spirited in manner, caustic in comment, and speaking (as Wells has observed) in a staccato style of speech which contrasts with the slower, more reflective style of Margarete and so underlines the whole contrast in character between them. The expansion of Kunigunde's role involves a considerable deepening of the psychology of the piece—for no mere 'other woman' could credibly taunt the king to the point of making him set aside all his very real scruples (2397-2400) about the ravages and dangers of the war he is being forced into unleashing; and while the play is lengthened in the process, still (as we have seen) Grillparzer maintains an intricate unity. Nor is this unity of subject-matter essentially impaired by the further subsidiary action which culminates in Ottokar's death. This is an off-shoot of the political action, in which we follow up a single example of the suspicion and injustice to which Ottokar's ambition drives him and are shown their consequence, Seyfried Merenberg's avenging of his father.

König Ottokars Glück und Ende is, as Grillparzer's contemporary Josef Karl Rosenbaum wrote in his diary, 'a masterpiece—but too long' (*Gespr.* 401/iii). It is the longest of all Grillparzer's plays, and it was quickly recognized that some cuts have to be made in the text for performance. One of the scenes most frequently omitted is the opening one of Act III, which shows the arrest of Merenberg. This action prepares the basis for the motivation of the eventual murder of Ottokar; but since we see Merenberg again as Ottokar's prisoner in Act IV, there is no need for his actual arrest to be shown. The real purpose of the scene is atmospheric: by affording a glimpse of Merenberg's life it illustrates qualities of simple peacefulness which are diametrically opposed to Ottokar's bearing and way of living but which are essentially the qualities defended by Rudolf as the leader of the Austrians. Thus the scene enlarges on, and gives background to, the central conflict; but as an atmospheric episode it is not strictly necessary to the economy of the play, and indeed its inclusion makes for a rather episodic effect. Later in the same act, the sequence including Horneck's eulogy of Austria (1665-1717) is also dispensable dramatically, though it is never omitted in any Austrian production. Apart from these two scenes, however, the process of deletion is a very difficult one, precisely because—as Fuerst rightly stresses in his analysis of the work as a stage play—the various strands of the action are so closely linked. Grillparzer was never lavish with self-praise, yet even he was satisfied with the general design of the action of *König Ottokars Glück und Ende*: 'I had to admit that the construction was excellent'. (**SB** 167); and in the late 1850s, according to Helene Lieben's account, he still regarded it as his best play (*Gespr.* 1066).

At the centre of this complex action is a complex hero. For Ottokar is not a victim of *mere* ambition; he is not merely led (as Rudolf suggests) by a 'vain craving for glory' (1893). The initial impression he makes in the first act is one of arrogance: he is inconsiderately tactless both towards his subjects (395ff.) and towards his queen (524) and heartless about one of his own kinsmen whose death has brought him more lands (668-75). As a result, when he protests that his conquests have been made not for his own sake but for that of the land he rules (497-501), and that his divorce is similarly dictated by the needs of his people and his nation (506-15, 592-5), we disbelieve it, we assume it is mere sophistic rationalization. Rationalization it is; but not sophistry, for it is a rationalization that Ottokar himself has grown to believe in; it is the belief that sustains him in his struggle, lends him his stature as a ruler and finally his Lear-like pathos in defeat. Ottokar is absolutely consistent in his conviction that his actions as a ruler are performed in the interests of his people. He believes that he has bettered the lot of his territories—a conviction that makes their defection to Rudolf all the more bitter a pill (1946f.). He believes that when first he makes peace with Rudolf it is to save the lives of innocent subjects (2390f.). When he senses that he is about to face divine judgment, he prays that at least his people be spared: 'So triff mich, aber schone meines Volks!' (2862). More-

over, the people around him know that he is no mere selfish tyrant. For Seyfried Merenberg, his eventual murderer,
he is at the outset a figure to be admired, '. . . so ein
Herr, ein Ritter, so ein König' (16);[40] he has been a model
of chivalry and honour (19f.; 2896f.). For his chancellor,
who does not escape the harshness of his temper (1234/SD
[stage direction]), his stature is nevertheless comparable to
that of the Emperor himself: 'zwei Herrn, so hoch, so
würdevoll' (1502).[41] When Rudolf is pleading for his submission, his final argument—presented not as cajoling flattery but following an earnest request that Ottokar set aside
all self-deception (1879)—takes the form of an appeal to
his real sense of duty to the country and people he rules:

> Ihr habt der Euren Vorteil stets gewollt;
> Gönnt ihnen Ruh', Ihr könnt nichts Beβres geben!
>
> (1927f.)[42]

When Ottokar is played as a wholly selfish tyrant, a brag-
gart, arrogant and cruel and nothing else (as he was in the
1965 Burgtheater production, and as he often is), these
passages make no sense; and the Ottokar of the second
half of the play seems a quite different character from the
Ottokar of the first half. Even Professor Walter Silz, who
in a perceptive analysis of Ottokar's role discounts any
view of him as a mere blustering and brutal tyrant and recounts in detail his good and admirable qualities, writes of
a 'change and break in his character' and argues that 'there
is too great a gap between the arrogant triumphator of Act
I and the crushed and contrite individual of Act v'. In performance, the danger is that Ottokar's remorse will appear
not as conscientious insight but as mere weakness. This
seems to have been the effect at the première in 1825, to
judge from Costenoble's diary-note: 'At the end the mighty
hero declines into pitiful weakness' (*Gespr.* 401/ii). Similar comments may be found among reviews of the 1965
production.

In the text, however, Ottokar is consistently portrayed as a
victim of his own self-confident enthusiasm, which has fed
his capacity for self-deception. One indicative scene fairly
early in the play is that in which news of Rudolf's election
arrives. Ottokar is boastfully planning the dispositions he
will make when he becomes Emperor:

> OTTOKAR: (*hat unterdessen den Gesandten den Brief
> gewiesen, mit dem Finger einzelne Stellen bezeichnend*)
>
> Die müssen fort—seht, der!—
>
> (*Bei der ersten Rede des Kanzlers horcht er, in der-
> selben Stellung bleibend, nach hinten hin in höchster
> Spannung. Als jener den Namen Habsburg nennt, fährt
> Ottokar zusammen; die Hand, mit der er auf den Brief
> zeigt, beginnt zu zittern; er stottert noch einige Worte.*)
>
> und der—muβ fort!
>
> (1220)[43]

In his self-confidence he cannot at first believe what he
hears: it is as though he refuses to take it in, and goes on
planning. Then his hand sinks down and he stands for a
moment, staring, fixed in the graphic posture of despon-
dency; but then he pulls himself together, strides off to his
room, and returns shortly to proclaim that on the following
day his whole court will go hunting. Leading his followers
off to prepare for the chase he displays (as Miss Margaret
Atkinson has observed) 'a noisy self-confidence which is
emblematic of his noisy self-confident way of embarking
on ambitious schemes'. Some of his 'noisiness' is, no
doubt, bravado, but at this stage his self-confidence and
his determination are still quite genuine. It is precisely his
self-confidence that leads him to defiance and, ultimately,
defeat, to the position where finally he himself is hunted
down by Rudolf's troops. Yet still, as in the scene just discussed, he clings to his illusion, he clings—against all the
evidence that he is the quarry—to the belief, or at least the
pretence, that he is the hunter:

> OTTOKAR: Wie heiβt der Ort hier?
> DIENER: Götzendorf, mein König.
> OTTOKAR: Der Bach?
> DIENER: Die Sulz.
> OTTOKAR: Ich dacht', ich wär' in Stillfried.
> DIENER: Wir ritten gestern durch in dunkler Nacht. Jetzt
>   liegt der Kaiser drinnen.
> OTTOKAR: Nun, Gott walt's!
> DIENER: Ihr solltet dort ins Haus gehn, gnäd'ger Herr!
> OTTOKAR: Und daβ mir niemand angreift, bis ich's
>   sage! Ich hab' ihn hergelockt in diese
>   Berge Mit vorgespiegelter, verstellter
>   Flucht. Dringt er nun vor: die Mitte we-
>   icht zurück, Die Flügel schließen sich—
>   dann gute Nacht, Herr Kaiser! Ich hab'
>   ihn wie die Maus im Loch! Ha, ha!
>
> (2573-83)[44]

The first sign that Ottokar is gradually developing out of
this obstinately ingrained conceit is given, in a way characteristic of Grillparzer's theatrical style, not only in words
but in symbolic action, when Ottokar kneels by Margarete's coffin (2677/SD), adopting voluntarily at last that
symbolical posture of humility which has rankled so long
as a posture of humiliation.

But that the Ottokar of the first act and the Ottokar of the
last act are one and the same character, the one the product of the other's error, is the point enforced by the construction, the beginning and ending with Margarete; and
the truest epitaph for Ottokar is spoken by his chancellor:
'O Herr! du mein verirrter, wackrer Herr!' (2956). Ottokar
is *verirrt,* he is tragically enmeshed in his own wrong; but
at heart he is *wacker,* he is a valiant and upright servant of
a 'duty' conceived in pride but conceived nonetheless as a
duty. The key to his whole character lies in his final self-
analysis (2825ff.):

> Ich hab' nicht gut in deiner Welt gehaust,
> Du groβer Gott! . . .

Here Ottokar has finally reached the point of honest self-
knowledge. He perceives that he has stormed destructively
over the lands he should have ruled in peace, and he is
full of self-reproach and self-accusation:

Wer war ich, Wurm? daß ich mich unterwand,
Den Herrn der Welten frevelnd nachzuspielen,
Durchs Böse suchend einen Weg zum Guten![45]

And now the self-accusation is at the same time a self-defence: he has done wrong, but in a good cause, the cause of the people whom he has always believed himself to be serving; his earlier protestation—'Für wen hab' ich's getan? Für euch!' (501)[46]—was not hollow. And if when these words were delivered Ottokar seemed arrogant and self-willed, that arrogance was not merely cold and careless, it was what the chancellor calls 'Raschheit' (2493)—a term used also by Rudolf (1862) and by Merenberg (2430). It was, in other words, an unpremeditating pride felt for his nation as well as for himself (cf. 498). He is not the only one of Grillparzer's characters to be both *rasch* and *wacker*, for Garceran too '. . . ist wacker, obgleich jung und rasch' (*Die Jüdin von Toledo* 238); indeed, *rasch* is the normal word used in Grillparzer's plays to refer indulgently to the impetuosity of youth: Kreon is willing to forgive Jason's actions in Colchis as those of 'ein rascher Knabe' (*Medea* 1347), and Rudolf II speaks half-affectionately of his nephew Leopold as 'ein verzogner Fant, / Hübsch wild und rasch, bei Wein und Spiel und Schmaus' (*Bruderzwist* 512f.).[47] As well as being impetuous, Ottokar is, obviously, ambitious: he longs for political greatness for himself (608-13, 683, 1182), he thinks of his territories as belonging to himself (1296, 1305). But what is equally important is that he does not recognize this ambition in himself, so that in the motivation of his actions pride and service are mingled, ambition blends with what he feels to be his sense of duty. Even at the end he wants to protest his real innocence:

Geblendet war ich, so hab' ich gefehlt!
Mit Willen hab' ich Unrecht nicht getan!

If this were hypocrisy, if this were protesting too much in the face of conscious guilt, his final admission would be a *volte-face* of character, and it is not that; it is a moment of insight, when he suddenly pierces through his own rationalizations:

Doch, einmal, ja!—und noch einmal! O Gott,
Ich hab' mit Willen Unrecht auch getan!

(2863-6)[48]

This is not pretence, nor is it a reversal of character: it is the workings of honest, bitter, self-punishing recollection. When, by contrast, Grillparzer's previous ambitious hero, Jason, takes stock of his life in the second act of *Medea,* he admits that he has forfeited his own self-respect, he admits that he has done wrong; but—lacking Ottokar's moral courage—he insists that it has happened independently of his intention (763-71). It is Ottokar's integrity that also stands out in a comparison with the Shakespearian passage which his accusing self-contradiction echoes, the scene on Bosworth Field in which Richard III is afflicted by 'coward conscience' (*Richard III* v, 3). Richard asks 'Is there a murderer here? No. Yes, I am.' But he is ready to contradict himself again as quickly and eager to acquit himself:

. . . Alas, I rather hate myself
For hateful deeds committed by myself!
I am a villain; yet I lie, I am not.

Though he then yields again to the 'thousand several tongues' of conscience, when the time for action approaches he is soon dismissing his 'babbling dreams' and decrying conscience once more as 'but a word that cowards use'. He too lacks the resolute moral courage that gives Ottokar, even in defeat, the stature of a true tragic hero.

If Ottokar's good will has often escaped critics, it is surely partly because he is presented in the framework of so extreme a contrast with the invariable goodness and rightness of his chief antagonist—a contrast that Grillparzer only heightened by such divergencies from his source-material as the association of Ottokar's decline with his repudiation of Margarete and the dissociation of the Emperor from the cutting of the tent-cords. This central contrast tends to focus our attention on the morality of Ottokar's position, as opposed to the subtleties of his motivation; and when the presentation of character is distinctively coloured by so strong a moral emphasis, the artistic danger is that to the uncommitted spectator or reader the dramatic conflict may seem slanted. Thus Silz, commenting on Rudolf's 'ideal character', argues that it is detrimental to the balance of the play because 'our interest and sympathy, contrary to the playwright's intent . . . , go with Rudolf' so that 'Rudolf . . . detracts from the hero's effect all through'. Much must depend here on the emphasis achieved by production and acting; and it is true that there have been productions of the play (Laube's revival in the late 1850s appears to have been a case in point) which have allowed Rudolf's role to seem the dominant one. In fact, Rudolf is too simple a character—pious to the point of self-righteousness—to sustain such prominence, and to accord it to him is to give too much weight to the moralistic element in the play; nevertheless, the standards he represents *are* those by which the central character comes to judge himself in the final shedding of his self-delusion.

The process of emerging from self-delusion into a fuller moral self-awareness is a recurrent pattern in Grillparzer's plays; it characterizes the development of Sappho, Rustan, Alphons and Mathias as well as Ottokar. Clearly the idea of attaining a condition of insight and certainty presupposes a moral order whose rightness—'the eternal Law'—is unchallengeable: right and wrong are open to 'recognition', and are clear, finally, to the characters themselves. Hence their ability to follow up their catastrophe with elegiac reviews of the course of events and to express their perception of 'the emptiness of all earthly things'. Formally, the result is a striking example of how the influence of Austrian and Spanish dramatic traditions seems to be superimposed on the manner of Shakespearian and classical traditions; but while a moral summary is conventional in the (indigenous) form of *Der Traum ein Leben,* it is unorthodox in tragedy.

Grillparzer's basic conception of tragedy was not unorthodox; he regarded the intention of a tragic action as being to induce in the spectator or reader the classic cathartic reaction of pity and fear:

> Das Tragische, das Aristoteles nur etwas steif mit Erweckung von Furcht und Mitleid bezeichnet, liegt darin, daß der Mensch das Nichtige des Irdischen erkennt; die Gefahren sieht, welchen der Beste ausgesetzt ist und oft unterliegt; daß er, für sich selbst fest das Rechte und Wahre hütend, den strauchelnden Mitmenschen bedaure, den fallenden nicht aufhöre zu lieben, wenn er ihn gleich straft, weil jede Störung vernichtet werden muß des ewigen Rechts. Menschenliebe, Duldsamkeit, Selbsterkenntnis, *Reinigung der Leidenschaften durch Mitleid und Furcht* wird eine solche Tragödie bewirken.
>
> (**T** 639)[49]

For this tragic effect to be achieved, it is essential that the moral emphasis—the absolute condemnation of ambition in Jason and Ottokar, or the emphatic association of love with wrongfulness and guilt in ***Des Meeres und der Liebe Wellen*** and ***Die Jüdin von Toledo***—must not become so dominant as to inhibit our 'pity' and 'love' for the chief characters. In ***Des Meeres und der Liebe Wellen,*** and also in ***Ein treuer Diener seines Herrn,*** the virtue of duty is in fact challenged by inclination and emotion that are not selfishly destructive but honest and mature; the balance of the dramatic action is evenly weighted and the implications of the tragic situation open. In ***Des Meeres und der Liebe Wellen,*** both Hero and the priest are by their own standards in the right; in ***Ein treuer Diener*** Bancbanus, a figure of unmistakable goodness of intention, is caught between two opposed claims (that of the king, who imposes his task, and that of the rebels who defy him) which are equally wrong. Both these plays move us to experience the full effect of pity and fear for the innocent victims of true tragedy. ***Die Jüdin von Toledo,*** on the other hand, presents a close parallel to ***König Ottokars Glück und Ende.*** Just as Ottokar is tragically dominated by ambition (which he rationalizes as belonging to and consistent with his duty), so Alphons is led to disaster because his moral nature is dominated by the passion of love. Like Ottokar, Alphons is a being of noble potential, capable of achieving recognition of his errors. But both figures act wrongly, and are contrasted to antagonists who act in accordance with ideals of duty; and this extreme moral contrast must tend (in varying measure, depending on the production and acting) to dull our perception of the fact that Ottokar and Alphons are each, potentially, 'der Beste'—each a good man, as Aristotle requires tragic characters to be. To this extent the effect of these particular works diverges from what is traditionally understood by the effect of tragedy, in the most exact sense of the term.[50]

Yet both plays are richly effective in other respects. ***König Ottokars Glück und Ende*** in particular is a many-sided work. It is a study of kingship, just and unjust; it is a work of patriotic imperialism, the national drama of Habsburg Austria; but above all it is a character-study in depth of the tyrant-hero on whom the separate but connected threads of the intricate action centre. We see his fateful injustice and its consequences in his relations with the two queens, with the Merenbergs, and with Rudolf. The depiction of his character is enhanced in depth and subtlety by the variety of separately developing situations in which we are shown his actions and their effects. And it is above all in the subtlety of the characterization, in which the dividing line between rightful and wrongful motivation is blurred by self-deception, so that faithlessness can seem justified and ambition selfless, that the play has outgrown the original formula—the simple action of a morality—'overweening pride and its downfall', while yet presenting in its complex unity a portrait of the disastrous consequences attendant upon one man's ambition.

Ottokar is the first of a series of great characters—the others include Bancbanus, Hero and Rudolf II—who at their various stages of moral development possess a reality and many-sided life, a life of acute feeling and revealing action, such as in English we know only, perhaps, in Shakespeare, and which is not matched in the drama of the German language. No less subtle, though using very different techniques, is Grillparzer's next study of ambition, the depiction of Rustan in ***Der Traum ein Leben.***

Der Traum ein Leben

On the manuscript of ***Der Traum ein Leben*** that Grillparzer showed to Schreyvogel in 1831, the play was designated 'Spektakelstück' (***Gespr.*** 615). This term was normally applied, pejoratively, to the kind of popular drama that depended too largely on extravagant stage effects; and though in atmospheric intensity and psychological subtlety ***Der Traum ein Leben*** wholly transcends the limitations of the popular theatre, Grillparzer's ironic use of the term testifies to his awareness of the affinities between his dream-play and the popular *Zauberstücke* of the period. The general outline of the action of the play was drawn in the first place from a short *conte* by Voltaire, *Le blanc et le noir* (1764); but the form in which the material is treated is closely related to the popular *Besserungsstücke* of the 1820s, of which Raimund's plays are the best-known examples. In these pieces the supernatural figures and magicians traditional in the *Zauberstück* use their powers to bring the central comic character to the kind of ethical regeneration that was familiar on the popular stage as the traditional ending of more realistic satirical comedy. A typical example is *Der Berggeist, oder Die drei Wünsche,* by J. A. Gleich (1819). The central figure of this piece (a role that was played by Raimund) has the symbolical name Herr von Mißmuth. Mißmuth is cured of his discontent by the beneficent mountain spirit, who grants him three wishes and fulfils them by magic; in other plays of the same type, a character's hopes and wishes are sometimes realized in a dream or dreams induced by a spirit or a magician. Mißmuth wishes for himself attractiveness to all women, enormous wealth, and phenomenal longevity; and the fulfilment of these desires brings him only trouble and unhappiness. Realizing his folly, he repents and wishes he were as he was before; and the Berggeist restores him to his former state, and spells out the moral—the common moral of the genre—that happiness lies in the virtue of modest and unquestioning acceptance of one's given lot.

The first act of **Der Traum ein Leben,** like the first act of a *Besserungsstück,* reveals the fault from which the central character suffers and will be cured by his dream. Rustan's fault is a restless ambition, a longing to escape from the constrictions of the unadventurous pastoral life he leads. This weakness is not, however, merely stated in the black and white terms of the popular stage: the exposition brings his problematic position to life by sketching in his background and his relations with other characters. Thus what we are shown at the very start, as Mirza waits for him to return from hunting, is the depth of her affection for him. She admits her anxiety about him (60f.), and though she tries to pretend to her uncle, Massud, that she has complete confidence in his valour (158ff.) her worry shows through in her anxious questioning of Massud (178) and her relief and reproaches when Rustan finally returns (411ff.). Moreover, when Massud tells Rustan openly of Mirza's love for him, Rustan lays his hand on his heart and indicates that he returns her feelings (571f.). That his ambition has gained the upper hand over this affection, and that the peace of Massud's home has been disrupted, is blamed by Mirza unequivocally on the influence of the slave Zanga (121-37) who, as the apostle of action (379f.), scorns the peacefulness of Rustan's present life (262f.) and dismisses as soft-heartedness his feelings for his relatives, which blunt his resolve to set out in pursuit of heroic adventure (344); and indeed we see the skill with which Zanga spurs Rustan's ambition, dwelling on the fact that the King of Samarkand has risen to his position from lowly rustic origins like Rustan's own (292-5), and twice suggesting that Rustan himself is a born hero and leader (296-8, 408-10). We learn too that Rustan has been goaded by the mockery of Osmin, who has a position in the Samarkand court and who has derided Rustan as a mere yokel, unfit to serve the king as a warrior and so win the hand of his daughter (519-22); Rustan bitterly acknowledges his lack of achievement so far and resolves to prove Osmin wrong (526-30). We are also shown that Rustan's resolve has a depth that both makes it distinctive and lends it its dangerous strength. His restlessness is not the negative kind of general discontent from which a stereotyped figure such as Mißmuth suffers. He experiences a genuine need for self-expression:

> Ich muß fort, ich muß hinaus,
> Muß die Flammen, die hier toben,
> Strömen in den freien Äther . . .
>
> (535-7)[51]

Like Ottokar, moreover, he sees the goal of his ambition as a noble ideal (275)—though not, even speciously, as a selfless one.

All this expository material, which gives depth to the depiction of Rustan's ambitions, is presented in language which itself enriches the whole atmosphere of the setting.

The trochaic metre, which Grillparzer chose for its liveliness (**Gespr.** 1100), does not easily conform to the natural rhythms of the German language (or of English): the consequent rearrangements of word order, omissions of unstressed syllables and endings, and the use of elliptical constructions give the verse a markedly stylized quality, and this is heightened by the shortness of the octosyllabic line, which the constant stress on the first syllable emphasizes. The metre has an unfamiliar ring, which makes it suitable for conveying the exotic flavour of mysteriously distant settings. Goethe uses it frequently in *Der westöstliche Divan*; Heine uses it in oriental ballads such as 'Der Asra'; in English we know it best as the metre of *The Song of Hiawatha*. And in the exotic atmosphere established by this rhythm Grillparzer stresses the oppressive peacefulness of Rustan's pastoral life by recurrent use of the word *still* (51, 57, 467, 533). But the first act is full of contrast and conflict too; and the language enhances the changes in mood through striking variations of pace. There is, for example, a great contrast between the leisured tone of factual narrative, as when Zanga reports on Osmin's behaviour at midday (485ff.), and his breathless description of the joys and excitement of battle, which finally breaks into free verse (362ff.), or the crisp exchanges of Rustan and Massud, where stichomythia gives expression to the tension between their opposed viewpoints (550ff.). Such contrasts in pace may be enhanced by the use of rhyme. That within Zanga's description of battle most of the lines 352-406 are rhymed emphasizes—and especially in the shorter lines of the later part of the speech (381-406)—the accelerated speed of the stirring narrative of rapid action. In complete contrast to this stand the words of the dervish's song (628-35), where the regular rhyming of alternate lines serves to emphasize, as it were to beat out, the importance of the moral teaching. It is this song that lulls Rustan to sleep; and in its insistence on the vanity of worldly ambition, it presents one aspect of the moral lesson that he learns from his dream.

The actual coming of sleep is shown by the use of allegorical figures, genii representing real life and dream life. As Rustan's dream begins, the torch of the genie of real life (who is drably clad in accordance with Rustan's view of his present existence) ignites that of the brightly clad genie of dream life and is then extinguished, the scene of the dream-action becoming visible behind transparent gauze curtains. This technique of representing the transition from waking to dreaming is strongly reminiscent of the popular stage, where simple allegorical effects were common. In *motivating* the dream, however, Grillparzer has done away with the spirits or magicians of the popular stage convention; he has transformed what were traditionally the effects of magic into the effects of a credible psychological process. Although the dervish's song in a sense anticipates the outcome of his dream, the dream is a natural one, not the product of a magic spell. We are well prepared for it; not only do we know of his confrontation with Osmin, we also learn from Massud (92f.) that at night he habitually dreams of battles, and his lively imagination is revealed in his use of colourful imagery (e.g.

243ff.). So now his dreaming imagination peoples a night-mare world with figures who have the form of characters familiar to him in his everyday life: Gülnare resembles Mirza, her father the king resembles Mirza's father Massud, Kaleb resembles the dervish, the mysterious 'man on the rock' is strikingly like Osmin. Even the demonically exaggerated tempter of the dream, who when he throws off his cloak appears to Rustan to have black wings (a detail drawn from the black servant Ebène in *Le blanc et le noir*) and snakes for hair (2515-18), appears in the form of the slave Zanga because the standards he represents are associated in Rustan's mind with Zanga's tempting tales and eager encouragement. The real-life Zanga has actively goaded Rustan into rebellion and adventure; but despite his real domination of Rustan's thoughts, he has on the whole remained aware of his position as a servant (408f.)—indeed, in his humorous inquiry to the audience about the disadvantages of love (438ff.) and later in his timorousness (2554f.) he is akin to the comic servants of popular stage tradition. But the dream-Zanga develops a manner of Mephistophelean disrespect, which shows at once in the derisive tone in which he dismisses the rejoicing enthusiasm of Rustan's first dream-monologue: 'Herr, und jetzt genug geschwärmt' (653).[52] As a projection of Rustan's own unconscious mind, what he represents is Rustan's own wrongful ambition, the selfish *will* which rejects the humble background of Mirza's true love:

> RUSTAN: Arme Mirza!
> ZANGA: Ja, weil arm,
> Hindert sie ein reiches Wollen.
>
> (724f.)[53]

As the incorporation of ambition he eggs Rustan on with his Mephistophelean blend of assistance and derision. That in the last moments of the dream Rustan finally sees him as having the appearance of a devil means that Rustan has at last perceived the true evil nature of the motivating force behind his own would-be self-advancement. For the series of adventures in Rustan's dream, ending in disaster and defeat, present the potential outcome of his own submission to the ambition which he has entertained and which his slave has encouraged. In *Melusina* the hero is warned that what dreams reveal must already be contained in the mind (246-9); so too Rustan has later to be reminded by Massud that his dream is only a development of his own motives and desires (2697-2701).

This dream sequence is presented with convincing authenticity, except for the fact that twice, contrary to the usual pattern of dreams, Rustan (the dreaming character) is briefly absent from the scene (1010-19, 1165-1200). In the final scene of the first act, his ambition overriding all moral considerations, he has spoken of the dervish with complete disrespect (627) and dismissed his song as nonsense (636); he has thoughts only for adventure, and as he falls asleep, he cries out: 'König! Zanga! Waffen! Waffen!' (638),[54] his mind racing with the ideas discussed in the previous scenes. The liveliness of his expectation contributes to the reality his dream has for him; and as the dream gets under way in the second act, it reflects his excitement. Filled with the invigorating feeling of liberty (639f.), the dream-Rustan compares his position to that of a bird venturing on flight and bursting at last into rejoicing song:

> Nicht mehr in dem Qualm der Hütte,
> Eingeengt durch Wort und Sorge,
> Durch Gebote, durch Verbote;
> Frei, mein eigner Herr und König!
> Wie der Vogel aus dem Neste,
> Nun zum erstenmal versuchend
> Die noch ungeprüften Flügel.
> Schaudernd steht er ob dem Abgrund,
> Der ihn angähnt. Wagt er's? Soll er?
> Er versucht's, er schlägt die Schwingen—
> Und es trägt ihn, und es hebt ihn.
> Weich schwimmt er in lauen Lüften,
> Steigt empor, erhebt die Stimme,
> Hört sich selbst mit eignen Ohren
> Und ist nun erst, nun geboren.
> Also fühl' ich mich im Raume . . .
>
> (657-72)[55]

Hardly are his reflections over and Zanga's plans for deception agreed than the adventures begin: the falsehood of Rustan's position is demonstrated in stage action. In a sequence that clearly draws on the opening scene of *Die Zauberflöte* (though perhaps also on a play by Lope de Vega, *Los donayres de Matico*), the King of Samarkand appears, pursued by a serpent (a traditional symbol of danger on the popular stage) and crying out for help (769f.). Confronted, after his own failure to rescue the king, by the true victor over the serpent, the mysterious figure of the courtier on the rock, Rustan finds himself mocked, laughed at as an incompetent shot (780f., 1083f.), as Osmin has laughed at him (221, 517) and shown up his real lack of achievement—humiliating details which Rustan's subconscious mind has retained and now develops in his dream. Already the dream is turning to nightmare; and again the language helps to build up the effect. The fluency and unfamiliarity of the trochaic verses are particularly suited to the swift action and strange atmosphere of the dream-world, and contribute to the sense of eeriness that pervades it. One device which is partly dictated by the demands of the short line and which is used to great effect in the dream sequence is frequent repetition, both of exclamations at moments of climax and of names: thus Zanga's name is often repeated (e.g. 985, 1143), and Rustan's especially rings out, as Stefan Hock has observed, in a whole range of urgent tones, in triumph, in warning and in threat.

But from the first the nightmare effects are directly linked to the moral issues. Thus when Zanga first advances the tempting argument that the whole apparition of the courtier on the rock was imaginary (807), what he is trying to have Rustan deny is the uncomfortable truth—which the Osmin-like courtier embodies—that Rustan is not the supreme warrior he aspires to be. Rustan has to learn that active achievement will always escape him: he was born to be a countryman, not a hero; born, as Osmin has pointed out (522), to wield a plough, and not a sword or a sceptre.

Even at the height of his dream, when he is given credit for the victory of the king's army, he himself has played no very glorious part in the battle, as Zanga recounts:

> Da sieht Rustan jenen Khan,
> Der so überstolz getan,
> Sprengt auf ihn,—zwar, wie mich dünkt,
> Ist das just der Punkt, der hinkt—
> Rustan stürzt . . .
>
>   (1183-7)[56]

Similarly, in his very first adventure, by yielding to Zanga's advice and the lure both of the king's evident wealth and of the prospect of Gülnare's hand, and denying the claim of the banished courtier to his reward for saving the king when he himself has failed to do so, Rustan is denying the truth about himself. The courtier, then, symbolizes the truth; he represents a part of Rustan's conscience, and his toneless voice (sd/1079) and deathly pallor (sd/1061), by suggesting a certain incorporeality, point to the monitory and symbolic function of his role. Himself banished from the court for his love of Gülnare (who represents the wrongful goal of Rustan's selfish ambition) and dressed in humdrum brown, he stands for the (unexciting) standards of right and responsibility which Rustan is repressing. In arguing with him, Rustan is arguing against the dictates of conscience, and knows that his opponent is in the right (1124). It is when Rustan finds himself powerless in the fight with the brown-cloaked courtier—a fight which is based on his real-life quarrel with Osmin (cf. 478f.)—that his dream turns wholly to nightmare (1136ff.); and when he is spurred on by Zanga ('Braucht den Dolch! / Braucht den Dolch!') to stab his adversary, what we are shown is how at this stage Rustan is led on by the temptations of ambition to suppress—to silence and to 'kill' within himself—the claims of responsibility and right. The bridge from which the courtier plunges to his death is seen by Rustan as a threshold to his fortune:

> Unmensch! Halt! Nicht von der Stelle!
> Diese Brücke wölbet sich
> Als des Glücks, der Hoheit Schwelle,
> Sei es dir, sei es für mich.
>
>   (1130-3)[57]

The rhyming, especially the rhyme on the word *Schwelle*, puts extra emphasis on the symbolic function of the bridge; the mortal confrontation there ('Ich oder du!', 1136) represents the fact that for a Rustan fortune *can* be attained only by overthrowing the order of truth. Just as the real-life slave, spurring his master on to try his fortune in adventure, has sought to alienate his affections from his uncle and cousin (340f.), so it is significant that in the dream-adventures the first step Zanga insists on Rustan's taking is to conceal the truth about his origins (714ff.). To this first temptation Rustan falls, and later in the same act he himself orders Zanga to throw away the knapsack which might give them both away (1022-4)—a gesture which symbolizes his determined rejection of his home background. So almost from the outset he commits himself to a deception that he never rectifies; in denying his home he is denying the truth about himself—significantly, it is with a reminder of Rustan's home and family on his lips that the courtier dies (1146-8).

The potential for good in the Rustan of real life—which lends conviction to his final repentance—is suggested by the way his dream counterpart capitulates to dishonesty only after a struggle. When the king first addresses Zanga and him, that he kneels at some distance is a sign of his indecision (842/sd). It is Zanga who first actually lies (845ff.), and Rustan tries to resist being manoeuvred into deception (859f.); the lure of the prize overcomes his scruples, but he remains conscious of the falsity of his claim (cf. 912). Later, when he is committed to his denial of the courtier's claims, he twice covers up his weakness with transparent rationalizations (1030-5, 1044-6); but when his rival confronts him again, he again acknowledges the strict demands of right before once more quietening and denying them (1124-9). Moreover, no sooner is the murder committed than Rustan regrets it (1145, 1154).

As the second act ends, however, he once more sets aside his scruples for the sake of prospective reward (1163f.), and in the third act his continued refusal to face up to the wrongful nature of his adventure—in other words, his continued silencing of the voice of truth—is given visible representation in the voiceless presence of Kaleb, the murdered man's dumb father, whose role as the voice of truth is later made explicit (1725). This old man, on whom the dreaming Rustan bestows the name of an otherwise unrelated real-life huntsman mentioned in Act I (62), corresponds to the real-life dervish in standing for the standards of right now voiceless in Rustan. It is the dervish he resembles—to the alarm of Zanga (1372) and subsequently to the horror of Rustan (2710). Kaleb only regains his voice in the last act; meanwhile his silent presence suggests that the truth is in fact nagging away at the mind of the dreaming Rustan, repressed but not conquered. This shows, too, in the way that during Acts II and III the king's questions both about Rustan's origins and about the killing of the serpent become gradually more insistent, until finally Rustan confirms that he was standing 'am Felsen' (1300). Even here his phrasing avoids the issue, for *am Felsen* is South German and Austrian for *auf dem Felsen*, and while Rustan indeed stood *am Felsen* in the standard German sense, 'beside the rock', it was the courtier who stood *am Felsen* in the sense of 'on the rock': Rustan's words take advantage of Viennese idiom to seek refuge in ambiguity, and it is left to Zanga to make the lie explicit in the following line.

Moreover, as his luck begins to change, Rustan turns against Zanga, admitting his error in following Zanga's advice (1424ff.). At this stage, as the accusation in 1435-7 makes clear, it is still only of his falsehood, not of his whole goal of fame and glory, that he repents; he has not yet perceived the essential interconnexion of end and means. Reflecting on the events at the beginning of the dream, he again distorts them by rationalization:

Nicht daβ ich den Mann erschlug!
Hab' ich ihm den Tod gegeben,
War's verteidigend mein Leben,
War's, weil jener Brücke Pfad,
Schmal und gleitend wohl genug,
Einen nur von beiden trug.
War's, weil er mit gift'gem Hohn
Lauernd seine Tat versteckte
Und die Hand erst nach dem Lohn,
Dem bereits gegebnen, streckte.
War es, weil—muβ ich's denn sagen—
Er und ich zwei Häupter tragen,
Und dies Land nur eine Kron'.

(1475-87)[58]

What, however, his image of the two heads seeking one crown truly symbolizes is the irreconcilability of conscience and falsehood. And now, indeed, his dissatisfaction comes briefly to a head; he expresses his regret that he has ever allowed himself to be led on to the false and giddy path of ambitious adventuring and acknowledges that he has sacrificed his integrity for a prize that was both superficial and insubstantial; the fame he once saw in the distance now seems an illusion:

O, hätt' ich, o hätt' ich nimmer
Dich verlassen, heimisch Dach,
Und den Taumelpfad betreten,
Dem sich Sorgen winden nach;
Hätt' ich nie des Äuβern Schimmer
Mit des Innern Wert bezahlt
Und das Gaukelbild der Hoffnung
Fern auf Nebelgrund gemalt!
Wär' ich heimisch dort geblieben,
Wo ein Richter noch das Herz,
Wo kein Trachten ohne Lieben,
Kein Versagen ohne Schmerz!

(1497-1508)[59]

Once again, the moral reflections are made to stand out by a change of pace; the rhyming of every other line gives a more measured regularity to the verse, in keeping with the pensive regret it expresses. In a popular comic *Besserungsstück* this regret at having ever left home would be the end of the dream, and Rustan would return, reconciled, to Massud's cottage. But in **Der Traum ein Leben** Rustan's self-deception is more deeply engrained, and his 'cure' is more gradual (and hence more convincing). At this stage regret is again conquered by the unscrupulousness of greed; he dismisses conscience, as represented in his mind by the shade of the murdered courtier, as a mere delusion (1516), which must not be allowed to obscure his vision of the prize that lies within his grasp (1513f.).

When, later in this act, Rustan is confronted with a new temptation, it is again given concrete form in that it is introduced by the witch-like old woman who follows Zanga into Rustan's presence (1529/SD). This grotesque figure appears only to Rustan (1608), she is only a symbol; she enters the dream as a crystallization of his feelings in the desperate situation into which his ambition has led him. Among those feelings are certainly both fear and (still) un-

principled ambition: from them grows Rustan's will to commit calculated murder, which creates its own evil opportunity. This will, then, is incorporated in the old woman, who *tempts* Rustan[60] by presenting him with the means of committing his second murder, the killing of the king. He tries to withstand the temptation (1592f.); but if the old woman seems repellent to him, she also fascinates him, and in the end, after a single brief moment of horrified hesitation (1716), he allows the king to drink the poisoned wine. Rustan himself realizes the fateful nature of this temptation; and in his lines

Sieh den Becher halb geleert,
Ganz erfüllt schon mein Geschick

(1825f.)[61]

the balanced antithesis between *geleert* and *erfüllt* brings out the essential interconnexion between the goblet and the fate he is fashioning for himself. For while the murder of the king brings him to the climax of his attainment so far, all his success is still based on evil and untruth; this, indeed, is precisely what the king has tried to make clear in his dying accusation of Rustan, which Gülnare misinterprets as a commendation (1900ff.). By the time of the episode with the old woman, the dreaming Rustan has already become aware, in his unconscious mind (which is projecting the whole dream), of the guilt of that potential self which the dream is revealing to him; this awareness shows in the old woman's criticism of his lack of moral independence (1577f.), then later the subconscious sense of guilt is given expression in the warnings and accusations of the letters (1774ff.), followed by the vision of Mirza and the dervish and the vision of the courtier; and finally the dream-Rustan is surrounded by the inescapable evidence of his evil deeds—he is shown (SD/1844) attempting to hide the instrument of his second murder (the goblet) under the symbol of his first (the cloak). The increasing sense of guilt which characterizes this whole third act coincides with and develops from the discovery on the river-bank of the body of the courtier in brown—a discovery which, in symbolical terms, signals the re-emergence from its suppression of Rustan's acknowledgment of his evil deed (the 'killing' of conscience). Finally in the fourth act Kaleb regains his voice to make explicit his accusation of Rustan as the king's murderer: the truth makes itself heard again, with a certainty that can no longer be held silent.

Still finding himself—to his desperate disappointment (SD/1939)—not king, but merely consort, Rustan has to build up his power further, and we are given a miniature type-sketch of the psychology of tyranny, as he removes his enemies from power (1949ff.) and like Ottokar (**König Ottokar** 1018f.) grows suspicious of all around him (2009ff.). Yet all the time he is only hastening his fall; and the growing sharpness of his clashes with Gülnare is enhanced by skilful use of repetition and rhyme. Thus when Karkhan is pleading with Gülnare to grant Kaleb an open trial, and Rustan demurs, she begins to insist:

GÜLNARE: Billing scheint, was sie begehren.
RUSTAN: Wär' es so, würd' ich's gewähren.
GÜLNARE: Und wenn ich's nun selber wünsche?
RUSTAN: Wünsche! Wünsche!
GÜLNARE: Und befehle.

(2053-6)[62]

After the rhymed riposte-effect, Rustan's repetition of Gülnare's 'wünsche' allows full expression of the cruel scorn in his attitude to her, showing how in his now monstrous self-seeking his pursuit of his own desires runs roughshod over the desires or wishes of all others. A more extended example of the use of rhyme to set off contrasted speeches against each other can be seen in a later exchange (2153-70) in which the same rhyme occurs nine times in eighteen lines, so that Gülnare's speech has the effect of an ironic echo of Rustan's.

As the nightmare intensifies, the moment of Rustan's waking draws near. This waking is a gradual process, and is most convincingly suggested. After the dream-Rustan has tried to explain away as nothing but a feverish fantasy (2291) the whole episode of Kaleb's accusation, there follows a moment of half-waking, an escape from the high drama of the new situation, as he hears through his sleep a clock striking in Massud's cottage (SD/2294). The clock draws him one stage further out of his now shallow sleep; and from now on actions and activities in the real world begin to impinge on the dream. First Rustan—his thoughts still centring on the real world to which he has briefly half-returned—mistakes Gülnare's servant for Mirza (2301); later the fire that the dream-Zanga ignites (2351-3) can be seen as a dream-version of the light with which Mirza is moving about in the next room in Massud's cottage (SD/2356). So also her movement seems to be reflected in the dream as the noise of pursuit (2499f.); and finally the torch of decayed wood and fungus which Rustan sees in Zanga's hand (2521-3) corresponds to the lamp carried by the real-life slave, who is moving around preparing the horses (SD/2542). And when Rustan at last awakes, it is still in confusion, his cry that he is lost ('verloren!', 2538) echoing the triumphant claim of the devilish Zanga at the end of the dream-sequence; still not fully awake, he sees in the real-life Zanga the devil of his nightmare (2544ff.), takes fright (2548) at the flashing light of Zanga's lamp, which reminds him of the flash of the sword with which the dream-Zanga has threatened him (2457f.), assumes he is being held captive in the room in which he finds himself (2562), and, when Massud and Mirza first appear, assumes they too must be their dream-equivalents (2568).

This gradualness carries much more verisimilitude than the summary magic awakenings of the *Besserungsstück* routine. Another subtle variation of the convention is the brief scene in which, as the dream-Rustan sets out on his flight from Gülnare and her forces, Mirza hears him in real life, crying out in his dream (2356), and we return briefly to Massud's cottage. This scene serves to remind the audience that the disasters overtaking the dream-Rustan *are* only a dream, and at the same time points forward to the morning and the end of the nightmare after its final episode, in which the dream-hero, exposed, pursued and surrounded, throws himself off the very bridge that was to be his threshold to fortune. The sensation of falling is a characteristic ending to nightmare; and for this reason it is important that when *Der Traum ein Leben* is produced on the stage Rustan's fall (SD/2538) should be *seen* by the audience, and not left to their imagination. But while the fall is a nightmarish effect, it is also Rustan's return—which his nightmare has impelled—to the upright standards and morality of Massud and his kind. When finally he is fully awake, he realizes that the dream has given him the self-knowledge he has hitherto lacked: his mention of dawning light ('Was verworren war, wird helle', 2636) has a figurative sense as well as describing the sunrise. He has been vouchsafed a mirror to his potential self; like the hero of any *Besserungsstück* he is cured of his discontent; and as in a *Besserungsstück* the moral teaching of the play is spelt out, affirming quiet domestic contentment and denouncing the dangerous emptiness of 'greatness' and 'fame' (2650-6). But it is important to remember that this ethical thesis is no more than a cliché of the *Besserungsstück* genre, which was taken for granted as a standard conclusion: the interest lay not in the final, often very summary, formulation of the moral, but in its illustration in the whole theatrical action of the play. This is as true of *Der Traum ein Leben* as of its equivalents on the popular stage, and the action has all the plasticity that Grillparzer consistently valued in stage works. It is characteristic that even Rustan's moral decision to renounce his ambition is not expressed in preceptive form only, but is also symbolized visually in the freeing of Zanga.

In the mood of reconciliation in which the play ends Zanga and the dervish together play the melody of the dervish's song (2707/SD), as a recapitulation of the theme of the vanity of ambition. Massud listens intently (2720f.) to the words of the song, which now take on a special sense:

. . . Schatten Worte, Wünsche, Taten;
Die Gedanken nur sind wahr.
Und die Liebe, die du fühlest,
Und das Gute, das du tust . . .

(630-3)[63]

Rustan's *Worte, Wünsche, Taten,* his self-conceit and his desires for glory and heroism, are set behind him; in his moral conversion (*das Gute*) through the insights vouchsafed him by his dream (*die Gedanken*), he has reaffirmed (2683ff.) his true love for Mirza (*die Liebe, die du fühlest*), of which his pursuit of Gülnare was a denial. Recognizing this, Massud unites the lovers. If this ending corresponds to that of innumerable popular comedies, it also corresponds to the ending of Grillparzer's own tragedy *Sappho*: 'Und nur das *Gleiche* fügt sich leicht und wohl!' (1742).[64] Similarly the whole moral tendency which the work shares with the *Besserungsstück* genre corresponds to a recurrent element in Grillparzer's work. As early as 1812 he planned to write a continuation to the first part of Goethe's *Faust*, in which Faust was to find happiness in 'self-limitation and peace of mind' (T 1083)—the very opposite, in fact, of the qualities which are generally associated with the 'Faustian' spirit. In the plays of Grillparzer's maturity, it is by self-seeking or ambition that his characters from Jason and Ottokar onwards sow the seeds of their own tragedy. By its revelations Rustan's corrective dream affords him a second chance, tragically absent in the reality of the world of Jason or of Ottokar, to realize the true happiness that lies in 'self-limitation and peace of mind' or, as Rustan formulates it, 'quiet inner peace and a heart free of guilt' (2651f.). The process of self-discovery and moral self-liberation entails the renunciation of unrealistic desires; so it does for Sappho also, and the idea is expressed again in *Libussa* in two lines which are very reminiscent of the late Goethe and which might almost serve as a motto for *Der Traum ein Leben*:

> Wer seine Schranken kennt, der ist der Freie,
> Wer frei sich wähnt, ist seines Wahnes Knecht.
>
> (*Libussa* 1185f.)[65]

Erich Hock points out, in his essay on *Der Traum ein Leben,* that a similar insight is expressed in the closing lines of the poem 'Entsagung'(G 87):

> Und in dem Abschied, vom Besitz genommen,
> Erhältst du dir das einzig deine: Dich![66]

What Rustan's dream has shown is that the power and kingship for which he has longed are properly beyond his grasp, so that he has had to jeopardize his entire *moral* self, he has had to resort to deception and wrong-doing in order to achieve them. It is in this sense that the dream-Zanga's final exclamations—'Mir! Verloren!' (2537)—seem most like a Mephistophelean claim for Rustan's lost soul, a parallel to the 'Her zu mir!'[67] at the end of the First Part of Goethe's *Faust.* For in the course of his dream Rustan's commitment to wrong has become deeper and deeper. His capitulation to Zanga's threat of betrayal (2241-54) has exemplified the difficulty of renouncing evil once one has committed oneself to it, and his repeated appeals to Zanga for help in the final scenes of the dream further reveal the dependence of the would-be hero on his supposed servant. In this respect the implications of the piece are akin to those of *Das Goldene Vlies*—the first work Grillparzer embarked on after abandoning *Der Traum ein Leben* as a fragment in 1817-18—in that the evil into which the dream-Rustan's ambition lures him develops into a whole chain of wrong-doing from which he is powerless to extricate himself.

Yet despite all the similarities of subject and implication between *Der Traum ein Leben* and others of Grillparzer's works, the final moral formula expounded by Rustan should in no way be seen as an expression of a general ideal or as a statement of a commended philosophy of life:

> Eines nur ist Glück hienieden,
> Eins: des Innern stiller Frieden
> Und die schuldbefreite Brust!

> Und die Größe ist gefährlich,
> Und der Ruhm ein leeres Spiel.
>
> (2650-4)[68]

The positive argument here amounts to little more than the truism that contentment lies in contentment; and in fact, precisely because this speech is built up of platitudes, it does not come properly to grips with the moral issues inherent in the play. There are higher things than contentment, and as Grillparzer's other plays confirm he does not condemn action, adventure, or eminence in themselves in any absolute sense; nor is their opposite, the quiet happiness of passive resignation, in any sense his consistent ideal.

The reason why Rustan's would-be-heroic adventuring leads him to disaster in his dream, and why he subsequently resigns himself to the plough—to which Osmin has alluded as a symbol of humdrum domesticity and weakness (522), but which also stands, as in *König Ottokar* (1921), for the life of peace—is to be sought in his own character. His dream reveals his unsuitability for the heroic stature to which he has aspired; his will—as Zanga scornfully observes towards the end of the dream (2438f.)—has outstripped his capability. Ambition is not disastrous, on the other hand, in such a character as Osmin, who has gained access to the court, can boast of the impression he has made there (496ff.), and can with justice scorn Rustan as an inferior. Again, for the King of Samarkand fame and worldly greatness are neither a hollow illusion, 'ein leeres Spiel', nor dangerous, either in the sense of morally corrupting or even in the literal sense (for it is only the dream-king who is killed, a piece of wishful imagination born of Rustan's ambition); yet he has risen to eminence from origins as humble as Rustan's are, and there is no suggestion that this rise was wrongful, as Rustan's is. So too in *König Ottokars Glück und Ende*, whereas it appears wrongful for Ottokar—who like Rustan lacks the self-knowledge that would teach him his innate limitations—to aspire to the imperial throne, Rudolf I, whose skill as a warrior Ottokar himself readily concedes (438f.), has the true stature of the rightful ruler, and is able to battle successfully in defence of the order of the empire. It is only those who are not born with the capacity for great achievement who must console themselves with the conception, propounded in the dervish's song, of desires and deeds as alike insubstantial, and the resignation of all 'greatness' in the name of inner contentment, 'des Innern stiller Frieden'. Such resignation is not an ideal achievement, but rather a defence: it derives from the perception of the tragedy that can ensue when the whole personality is dominated and so misled by a single motive—in Rustan's case by ambition, in other plays by love and even by excessive loyalty.

In Grillparzer's work, as the examples of *König Ottokars Glück und Ende* and *Sappho* both illustrate, positive achievement is characteristically presented in association with the idea of a supreme duty. If his works suggest a spiritual ideal, it is that state which he saw as a prerequisite for the fulfilment of his own poetic duty and which he called 'Sammlung'. This condition, . . . is not one of negative resignation, but of inspired, creative concentration—what in the late essay **'Zur Literargeschichte'** he described as 'that inner concentration . . . without which either a deed or a work is impossible'. This significant passage is highly characteristic in that it defines achievement not only in literary terms ('a work') but also in practical terms ('a deed'). So too in a letter of 1850 the idea of inspiration is related not only to artistic achievement but also to the valour of the warrior (**B** ['**Briefe,**' numbered letters and documents in vols. III/1–5 of Grillparzer's **Sämtliche Werke,** ed. A. Sauer and R. Backmann (Vienna, 1909–48)] 709); so too in **Libussa** Primislaus uses the verb 'sich sammeln' in connexion with practical ('tatenschwanger') ideas (2106-9); and so too in **Des Meeres und der Liebe Wellen,** when the priest commends 'Sammlung' to Hero, he couples with the ideal of artistic achievement the ideal of the greatness of heroic action:

> Des Helden Tat, des Sängers heilig Lied,
> Des Sehers Schaun, der Gottheit Spur und Walten,
> Die Sammlung hat's getan und hat's erkannt . . .
>
> (951-3)[69]

Notes

1. 'This is the curse of every evil deed, / That, propagating still, it brings forth evil' (Coleridge's translation). See *Wke.* I/17, 301.

2. 'No man and no god can loose the bonds in which wickedness ensnares itself.'

3. 'Once the die is cast, it cannot be undone.'

4. 'In the beginning is contained the end.'

5. 'Bury deep the tokens of your deed!—You will not bury the deed.'

6. 'So what has once been must exist for ever, and all is present?'

7. 'Memory of the past lies like lead upon my anxious soul; I cannot raise my eyes or lift up my heart.'

8. 'And that Fleece, now in his hands, shall look down on his children's death!'

9. '. . . She shall not die, but live: live in disgrace and shame—cast out, accursed, without father, without country, without gods!'

10. 'In the first place, the trilogy form, or any treatment of a dramatic subject in several parts, is inherently a bad form. Drama is an action in the present, it must contain within itself everything that is part of the action. To relate one part to another is to give the whole an epic quality, which may perhaps make it gain in grandeur but which makes it less realistic and less telling . . .'

11. 'I have become an *object* to myself.'

12. 'For my word I will stake my all—even your life!'

13. 'I call the gods on high to witness: it was *you* who killed him, and not I!'

14. 'Only *he* exists, only *he* in the whole world, and all else is merely fodder for his deeds.'

15. 'For truly, though I am less to blame than she, mine is the harsher, harder fate.'

16. 'She is going out into her native wilderness.'

17. 'I left my homeland to follow you.' 'You were following your own will, not me. Had you regretted it, I should gladly have left you behind!'

18. 'I am not deserting you: a higher judgment is driving me away from you.'

19. *Wke.* I/17, 300.

20. 'I a Greek, you of barbarian blood; I free and open, you full of treacherous magic . . .'

21. 'Jason, I know a song' (863, 874, 877).

22. 'I am defeated, annihilated, crushed—they shun me, shun me! My children shun me!'

23. 'A terrible thought is taking shape in my mind; I shudder—and yet I also rejoice at it.'

24. 'I do not grieve that the children are no more. I grieve that they ever *were,* and that *we are.*'

25. 'Do you recognize the prize for which you struggled, which meant fame to you and promised happiness? What is earthly happiness? A shadow!—What is earthly fame? A dream! You poor creature, who dreamt of shadows! The dream is over, but the night is not.'

26. For a summary of the historical background, see the edition of the play by L. H. C. Thomas (Oxford, 1953), Introduction, pp. xvi-xxii.

27. 'Advance, with God! And let Christ's name be our battle-cry!'

28. 'I have shed all that is mortal in myself, and am simply the Emperor, who never dies.'

29. 'There are three classes I have no truck with: officials, academics and clerics.'

30. 'The gods were not supreme: above them was the eternal Law. That we have personified, and we call it "God".'

31. J. P. Eckermann, *Gespräche mit Goethe in den letzten Jahren seines Lebens (1823-1832)*, entry dated 6 June 1831.

32. 'He must guard carefully against committing injustice, for even the least injustice will avenge itself . . .'

33. 'Oh Lord above, I have not lived a good life on thy earth! Like storm and tempest I have swept across thy plains . . .'

34. 'It's cold! Has no-one a cloak?'

35. See ll. 767ff., 1518ff., 2195-7.

36. Chancellor: 'The position, Sire, is grave!' Ottokar (*walking to and fro*): 'It's very good!'

37. 'I cannot bear to see anyone kneel!' He has also dwelt bitterly on the memory of his public humiliation in ll. 2283-6 and 2332f.

38. Queen: '. . . Rosenberg!' 'Your Majesty?' 'Have you ever knelt—not to a woman: have you ever knelt to a man? To your equal, for money, for reward, from fear?' 'Never.' 'And you never would?' 'Not as long as I live!' 'But *he* did! He knelt to his enemy, to the very man he despises . . .'

39. 'Until you have purged yourself of this dishonour, do not enter my room as my husband!'

40. '. . . so fine a lord, so fine a knight and king!'

41. 'Two lords so noble and so full of majesty.'

42. 'You have always worked for the good of your people: grant them peace, you can give them nothing better!'

43. Ottokar (*has meanwhile shown the letter to the messengers, pointing with one finger to particular passages*) 'They must go—look, *he* must! . . .' (*As the Chancellor first begins to speak behind him he listens tensely, without moving. When the Chancellor pronounces the name "Habsburg", Ottokar gives a start; the hand with which he is pointing to the letter begins to shake; he stammers out a few more words:*) 'And he . . . must go!'

44. 'What is this place called?' Servant: 'Götzendorf, your Majesty.' 'And the stream?' 'The Sulz.' 'I thought I was in Stillfried?' 'We rode through yesterday at dark of night. Now the Emperor is there.' 'Well, God's will be done!' 'You ought to go into the house over there, my lord.' 'And no-one is to attack until I say! I have enticed him into these mountains by feigning, pretending to retreat. Now when he thrusts forward, our centre will fall back, the flanks will close in—and then good night to the Emperor! I've got him like a mouse trapped in his hole! Ha, Ha!'

45. 'Worm that I am, who was I that I should have presumed sinfully to imitate the Lord of earth and sky, seeking through evil a way to good!'

46. 'For whom have I done it? For you!'

47. Garceran 'is gallant, although young and impetuous', Jason 'an impetuous youth', Leopold 'a spoilt coxcomb, wild and impetuous in his wining and gaming and feasting'.

48. 'I have been dazzled, that is how I have erred! I have not done wrong with intent!—Yet once—I did! And then once more! Oh God, I *have* done wrong, with intent!'

49. 'The tragic effect, which Aristotle defines somewhat rigidly as the arousing of pity and fear, lies in our recognizing the emptiness of all earthly things, in our seeing the dangers to which the best of men is exposed and often succumbs, and—while ourselves holding fast to right and truth—pitying our stumbling fellow-man and continuing to love him as he falls, though also condemning him, since every offence against the eternal Law must be brought to nought. Such a tragedy will induce love, tolerance, self-knowledge, and a purging of the passions through pity and fear.'

50. On the relation of tragic characters to the emotional effect of tragedy, see W. Macneile Dixon, *Tragedy* (London, 1924), and F. L. Lucas, *Tragedy in relation to Aristotle's 'Poetics'* (London, 1927). Lessing's comments on the unsuitability of wholly blameless characters as tragic heroes (*Hamburgische Dramaturgie*, 75. Stück) are pertinent to the role of Rudolf in *König Ottokar*.

51. 'I must away, I must escape, must let the flames that rage within me blaze into the open sky . . .'

52. 'Now sir, that's enough enthusing!'

53. 'Poor Mirza!' 'Yes, and since she's poor she inhibits richness of will-power.'

54. 'The King! Zanga! To arms, to arms!'

55. 'No longer in that stifling cottage, hemmed in by words and cares, by instructions, prohibitions—free, my own master and king! Like a bird emerging from his nest, trying out for the first time his still unproven wings: trembling he stands above a yawning abyss—dare he? Will he? He tries, beats his wings—and is borne up and lifted! Sweetly he soars in the mild breezes, climbs, and sings, hears himself with his own ears—and now for the first time is truly alive! Just like that I feel in the free air . . .'

56. 'Rustan saw the Khan who has been so overweening, charged at him—yet surely this is in fact the snag: Rustan fell . . .'

57. 'Monster, stop! Do not move! The arc of this bridge forms the threshold to fame and fortune, whether for you, whether for me!'

58. 'Not that I murdered him! If I killed him, it was in defence of my life, it was because the path across that bridge, narrow and slippery as it was, could carry only one of us. It was because with venomous scorn he lay in wait, concealed his deed, and only reached out for the reward once it was already given. It was because—if I must say it—we were two heads seeking this country's single crown.'

59. 'If only I had never left my home to tread that giddy path where cares come winding after—if only I had never paid for surface glitter with my heart's integrity and had never painted a mirage of hope in the

misty distance! If only I had stayed at home, where the heart is still the judge, where there are no aspirations without love and no failings without sorrow!'

60. Cf. ll. 1579-81: 'Ei, ich zwinge niemand, Sohn! / Bietend reich' ich meine Gaben, / Wer sie nimmt, der mag sie haben.' ('Oh, I do not force anyone, my son! I hold out my gifts as offerings: he who takes them is welcome to them.')

61. 'See the goblet now half-empty, and my fate wholly fulfilled!'

62. 'What they ask seems just and fair.' 'Were it so, then I should grant it.' 'And if I wish it now myself?' 'Wish it, wish it!' 'And command it!'

63. 'Words, desires and deeds are shadows, thoughts alone are true—and the love you feel, and the good you do . . .'

64. 'And only like and like go well together!'

65. 'The free man is the man who knows his limits; he who deludes himself that he is free is the slave of his delusion.' Cf. especially Goethe's maxim 'Niemand ist mehr Sklave, als der sich für frei hält, ohne es zu sein' ('No-one is more of a slave than he who believes he is free without being free in fact': *Die Wahlverwandtschaften*, II, ch. 5). Clearly, however, the self-limitation learnt by Rustan is much less positive than, for example, the purposive self-direction learnt by Faust in Goethe's Part Two. Cf. also p. 235, below.

66. 'And in parting from what you possess you preserve what alone is yours: yourself!'

67. Zanga: 'To me! You are lost!'—Mephistopheles: 'Hither to me!'

68. 'On this earth happiness lies in one thing, one alone: quiet inner peace and a heart free of guilt! And greatness is dangerous, and fame is hollow and vain.'

69. 'The hero's deed, the bard's sacred song, the seer's vision, the imprint and the sway of divinity—composure has wrought it or perceived it . . .'

Abbreviations

Wke.: Franz Grillparzer, *Sämtliche Werke*, ed. A. Sauer and R. Backmann (Vienna, 1909–48). All references to Grillparzer's works are to the text of this edition; the orthography has been modernized in passages quoted in the original. References to the plays follow the line numbering in this edition. SD/1529 = stage direction preceding line 1529; 1529/SD = stage direction within, or following, line 1529. Page references for the short stories refer to the text in vol. I/13 [i.e. I. Abteilung, 13. Band].

B: *Briefe*, numbered letters and documents in vols. III/1–5.

G: *Gedichte*, numbered poems in vols. I/10–12.

SB: *Selbstbiographie*, page references to vol. I/16.

T: *Tagebücher*, numbered entries in vols. II/7–12.

Gespr.: numbered entries in *Grillparzers Gespräche und die Charakteristiken seiner Persönlichkeit durch die Zeitgenossen*, ed. A. Sauer (7 vols., Vienna, 1904–41.)

No page references are given for quotations from variants to the texts of the plays (from vols. I/17–21), or for Grillparzer's essays (vols. I/13–14), notes on Spanish drama (vol. I/15), and short memoirs (vol. I/16); but the context is specified in each case.

Bruce Thompson (essay date 1976)

SOURCE: "*Die Ahnfrau*," in *A Sense of Irony: An Examination of the Tragedies of Franz Grillparzer*, Herbert Lang, 1976, pp. 19-36.

[*In the following essay, Thompson discusses Grillparzer's drama* Die Ahnfrau, *focusing on his handling of supernatural elements and observing that the actions of Grillparzer's characters stem naturally from their motives, despite the supernatural workings of the plot.*]

Since its first performance in 1817 Grillparzer's **Die Ahnfrau** has frequently been the subject of controversy, much of the argument having centred on the problem of the play's classification.[1] Initially it was regarded as a mere "Gespensterstück" and attacked as an example of romantic fate-tragedy,[2] but it was eventually recognised, for example by Jakob Minor, that although the undoubted presence of fatalistic elements placed the play within the tradition of the German fate-tragedy, one need not necessarily assume that events are brought about by the machinations of supernatural malignant forces.[3] If a fatal force exists at all in **Die Ahnfrau** it has no specific origins such as a divine figure or a curse, as was the case with Schiller's *Die Braut von Messina* and the celebrated fate-tragedy by Zacharias Werner, *Der 24. Februar*. In Grillparzer's play there is only a legend existing in the minds of the characters that the ancestress must atone for her adultery by wandering as a ghost until her descendants die out. Although Borotin is himself convinced that fate has determined to extinguish them (88-92), at various times reiterates his fatalistic feelings (e.g. 998-1006) and eventually attributes his own death at the hands of his son Jaromir to the machinations of obscure powers, there is no proof of this. For this reason it is possible to argue that the play is not a fate-tragedy at all, but a ghost story. For example Zdenko Škreb has recently asserted the links between **Die Ahnfrau** and the Vienna "Volksstück", placing it within the classification of "Räuberund Gespensterromantik".[4] Moreover because the catastrophes are not explicitly foretold, but appear to result simply from the characters of those involved, Emil Reich argued shortly before Minor's pronouncements that the play is simply a character-tragedy with the extra ingredient of some rather unfortunate coincidences.[5] Joachim Müller also argues that the catastrophes stem from guilty actions for which the characters themselves are responsible,[6] and it is true that the ancestress was killed because of her adulterous passion (488f), as also that Jaromir is a scoundrel who has deceived the family concerning his origin and identity. But for this the incestuous love between himself and Bertha, as well as his murder of Borotin, may well have been avoided. Even allowing for the fact that there at least seems to be a suggestion of powers operating beyond human control it should not be overlooked that these are embodied in human passions. For these reasons critics have claimed that Grillparzer has "internalised" or "deepened" the concept of fate,[7] and in recent years a number of critics have also paid attention to the psychological aspects of the work, concentrating on the character of Jaromir, and treating the play as though it were a projection of Grillparzer's own psychological condition.[8]

Grillparzer may himself be held partly responsible for these tendencies, for as he points out in his autobiography, the fact that the characters themselves believe that they are subject to an avenging fate provides no decisive evidence for the existence of such a force:

> Dass die Personen zufolge einer dunklen Sage eines frühen Verschuldens sich einem Verhängnis verfallen glauben, bildet so wenig ein faktisches Schicksal, als einer darum unschuldig ist, weil er sich für unschuldig ausgibt.[9]

Moreover following the adverse criticism of the play as a romantic fate-tragedy he claimed that the fate motif had been imposed upon his own original version as a result of suggestions on the part of Josef Schreyvogel, the Secretary of the Vienna Burgtheater.[10] According to Grillparzer Schreyvogel wished that the fatal theme be developed more fully, and Grillparzer felt that the subsequent alterations brought the play closer into line with the fate-tragedies of his time.

> Ich habe sogleich nach der Aufführung bemerkt, dass durch diese "tiefere Begründung" mein Stück aus einem Gespenstermärchen mit einer bedeutenden menschlichen Grundlage, sich jener Gattung genähert hatte, in der Werner und Müllner damals sich bewegten.[11]

The main alteration which Grillparzer made was to provide a link between the adultery of the ancestress and the sufferings of her descendants. At Schreyvogel's suggestion[12] he has inserted the section in which the servant relates that the son of the ancestress who inherited the title was the product of her adulterous relationship with her lover (*F* only, 513-76).[13] Consequently her sin is preserved in every succeeding generation, and the sufferings of her descendants are more easily linked with her adultery. This gives the fatal force a moral twist, for it seems that the descendants are being punished for succeeding to a title which is not legitimately theirs. The fatal force appears to operate against the later generations with greater justification, and becomes an instrument of divine punishment. But although the ultimate punishments are now more comprehensible, the play is not necessarily rendered more fa-

talistic. We may still sense the influence of higher powers, whether or not there is a reason behind the hand that strikes. Schreyvogel's alteration may affect the origin of the fatal force, but it alone does not turn the play into a fate-tragedy. Fatalistic elements which are part of the machinery of fate-tragedy are already present in Grillparzer's original version. Most obviously there is the fatal weapon, namely the dagger hanging ominously on the wall, and the eerie atmosphere of the Gothic hall, and of the dark cold night fills characters and audience alike with forebodings. We also find fatalistic thoughts voiced by Borotin, as also the latter's final conclusion that fate was responsible for his death at the hands of Jaromir (*E* 2086, *F* 2541). Moreover in both versions there is the undeniable fact that the ancestress appears as a ghost on the stage to signal approaching catastrophes which actually occur.[14] Borotin's forebodings are proved correct, and the ancestress does indeed wander as a ghost until the family is extinct, so that the existence of supernatural influence is certainly suggested. In the original version the ancestress is no less sinful, for she is found in the arms of a servant (in the final version it is a lover). Thus although there is no direct link in the first version between her "sin" and her progeny, the sin of adultery is referred to in both versions and she and her descendants are doomed, no matter the identity of the father of the child who inherits the title. Even in the first version, therefore, the fatal force has moral implications, for the descendants appear to be punished for her sins. Schreyvogel has not provided a new essential feature, he has merely developed a theme already present and made it more obvious and more comprehensible.[15] In both versions we sense the influence of fate through the atmosphere of the play, through the very nature of events, and particularly through the appearances of the ghost. If the play were a character-tragedy only, then there would be no point in introducing the legendary fatal force at all.

It thus seems that Grillparzer was not prepared, in view of the hostile reception afforded the fatalistic elements in the play, to admit that the fatal theme had already been present in his original manuscript. To deny the presence of fatalistic elements in either version is to ignore the obvious, and as has been recently pointed out, criticism which concentrates solely on the psychological or autobiographical aspects of the play tends to neglect the poetic merits and purposes of the work.[16] Our belief in the influence of supernatural forces is encouraged and the dramatic effectiveness of the work is thereby enhanced. Moreover it is clear that Grillparzer also appreciated the dramatic potential of fate from his discussion of its use by his contemporaries, which suggests that from the very beginning he intended that the fatal force should at least serve a dramatic function.[17] It is also apparent from the large number of notes and marks made by Schreyvogel on Grillparzer's manuscript that the bulk of his suggestions were concerned not with the origins of the fatal force, but with making the play more effective dramatically.[18] His success in this direction was initially not acknowledged by Grillparzer who was more preoccupied with laying the blame for the fatalistic elements on Schreyvogel's shoulders, but has subsequently been frequently recognised.[19] It is with the use of fate as a dramatic device that both Grillparzer and Schreyvogel were primarily concerned.

As we saw in the previous chapter the mere presence of a fatal force, whatever its origin, affords the dramatist ample opportunity for the creation of ironic effects, enabling the audience to anticipate impending disaster at the expense of an ignorant and unsuspecting character. In *Die Ahnfrau,* however, it is Borotin who believes that the family is doomed and in the early stages of the play the atmosphere of doom is established by the characters' own pronouncements and reactions. Borotin is convinced that the family will be extinguished (88-92) and his convictions are apparently justified by the loss of two brothers (123), his wife (131), and his son (139-59). They are substantiated by the descriptions of the history of the ancestress. Meanwhile Bertha has described the terrifying night (17-29), which contributes appropriately to the prevailing atmosphere. Because the audience's awareness of the fatal power stems originally from characters' own convictions, the audience is not placed in any position of superiority. Nor is the audience any better informed of what is to come than are the characters themselves. Only when disasters occur and we finally become aware of the whole sweep of the dramatic action can the ironic effect produced by various actions and remarks be appreciated. It is arguable, therefore, that the presence of fatalistic elements does not help to create an immediate ironic effect, and it would seem that any ironic effect produced in this play would be largely retrospective. That this is not the case, however, is due to the manner of the presentation of the fatal force, for it is the appearance of the ancestress on the stage as a ghost which affords the audience some degree of superiority and some notion of what is to come.

Although the ghost is the most obviously dramatic fatalistic element contained in the play, the ancestress cannot herself be regarded as an embodiment, or representative of fate, for we are told that she is herself doomed to wander as a ghost until the family is extinct (497-500). Thus she is as much a victim of fate as are her descendants, and she must wait with patience until the day of her deliverance. Nevertheless her appearances do have a dramatic function, for they give warning of the approach of future disasters and serve to remind us of the possible existence of the fatal force. In so doing they generate dramatic tension and help to produce a sense of irony, for whereas her warnings suggest that the disasters are avoidable provided that the characters take appropriate action, they fail to respond to her warnings correctly. We shall see that this sense of irony which derives from the dramatic use of the ghost is developed considerably by the additions made as a result of Schreyvogel's suggestions.

When the ghost makes her final appearance Borotin is confused by her resemblance to Bertha, and bids his "daughter" dispel his bad dreams with music (*E* 300 f., *F* 325f.). This reaction is clearly inappropriate, for the figure only provides fresh horror for him. Thus for the first time

the audience is in a superior position to the character, so that a degree of dramatic tension is generated, and a sense of irony produced, of which Borotin is the victim. Grillparzer dwells for some time on Borotin's confusion. Having decided that the ghost is his daughter, he tells Bertha that he is convinced that it was she whom he saw in spite of her protests to the contrary. When she claims to have been on the balcony he feels that she is mocking him:

> Schändlich!—Mädchen, höhnst du mich?

> (385)

Here his sense of mockery is indeed ironic, for it is not Bertha who is mocking him, but the appearance of the ghost. Although we are as yet ignorant of the implications of the appearance of the figure, a skilful application on the part of the producer of the stage directions describing her will make it clear to the audience that Borotin has seen a ghost, and the effect of irony will be conveyed immediately. In addition the ghost's first words "Nach Hause" strike an ominous note and may be regarded as an anticipation of the eventual fulfilment of her wishes and of the extinction of the family. This becomes particularly clear when, shortly after this episode, we are given details of the legend, so that the ghost's appearance takes on an even more ominous significance. In the final version of the play Grillparzer exploits further the similarity of Bertha's appearance to that of the ghost by having Borotin make a statement which carries a deeper significance than he himself realises. He warns Bertha that they must be careful not to emulate the ancestress, and avoid such sins themselves:

> Lass uns eignen Wertes freuen
> Und nur *eigne* Sünden scheuen.
> Lass, wenn in der Ahnen Schar
> Jemals eine Schuldge war,
> Alle andre Furcht entweichen,
> Als die Furcht, ihr je zu gleichen.

> (*F* only 580-5)

In the original version Borotin merely suggests that they should accept whatever Heaven sends them (*E* 486-91). The new lines are clearly designed to produce a further ironic effect, for whilst warning Bertha that she should not emulate the sins of the ancestress, Borotin is unaware of the fact that she has, so to speak, already "sinned". Though her relationship with Jaromir is not adulterous, it is nevertheless unwittingly incestuous, and it is arguable that the sinful blood of the ancestress does indeed live on in the veins of Borotin's daughter. Although the audience is as yet unaware of the implications of Bertha's relationship with Jaromir the ghost's appearance has already provided a warning, and an attentive spectator may already react to their similarity in appearance sufficiently to appreciate the irony of Borotin's words, which consequently may themselves function as a pointer to the future. The sudden arrival at this point of Jaromir is particularly well-timed, for it is he who is unwittingly encouraging Bertha to "sin". It is noteworthy that in the final version Grillparzer removes from this episode the concluding speech of Günther (*E* 495-508), so that Jaromir's arrival follows immediately upon Borotin's warning, and a link is suggested between the two.

The arrival of Jaromir also gives rise in itself to considerable dramatic tension, and here too a sense of irony is produced, this time by the ignorance on the part of the characters of his identity. Even before his arrival several remarks are made which, retrospectively at least, have greater significance for the audience than for the unwitting speaker. In the original version, for example, Borotin promises that he will welcome him as a son, and as Borotin sleeps, Bertha's words about their relationship may be regarded as ambiguous:

> Ich soll also ihn besitzen
> Mein ihn nennen, wirklich mein?

> (*E* 268f.)

In the final version Grillparzer has made various alterations and additions. For example Borotin now refers to his noble lineage:

> Edel nennst du sein Geschlecht,
> Edel nennt ihn seine Tat, . . .

> (*F* only 201f.)

Here he provides a good reason for welcoming Jaromir as a future son-in-law, whereas in fact the identity of his noble lineage makes this impossible. The line:

> So begrüss ich ihn als Sohn

> (*E* 187)

has been changed to:

> So kann manches noch geschehn.

> (*F* 205)

This is vaguer, but more inclusive, and could be made to refer to the murder of Borotin and all ensuing disasters, in addition to the actual relationship. However the most strikingly ironic effect is established by the joy with which he is received, for the characters assume that his new association with the house may offer some hope for the future. For example Borotin shows great enthusiasm, and even wishes he could give his life for Jaromir (!):

> Könnt ich dankbar nur mein Leben
> Für dich hin, du Guter, geben,
> Wie du deines gabst für sie!

> (*E* 596-8, *F* 678-80)

The irony of this unconscious anticipation of later developments is exploited further in the final version when Borotin forecasts that Jaromir will give his life for Bertha when she too is summoned by fate (*F* only 1150-2).

In the final version there are two large insertions during the scene of Jaromir's first appearance, the first of which develops Borotin's enthusiasm, containing words of gratitude (*F* only, 683f.) and hope (*F* only 708-12). The second, at the close of Act I, introduces a speech from Jaromir himself, in which he begs the gods of the house to accept him over its pure threshold:

> Nehmt mich auf, ihr Götter dieses Hauses,
> Nimm mich auf, du heilger Ort,
> Von dem Laster nie betreten,
> Von der Unschuld Hauch durchweht.
> Unentweihte, reine Stelle,
> Werde, wie des Tempels Schwelle,
> Mir zum heiligen Asyl!

> (*F* only, 742-8)

Schreyvogel required an ending to the Act which was dramatically effective,[20] and this is achieved by a supreme moment of dramatic irony. Jaromir unconsciously makes remarks about the house which are patently inappropriate, and expresses hopes which will be contradicted. That he should conclude with an appeal to an unknown power reinforces the ironic effect:

> Unerbittlich strenge Macht,
> Ha, nur diese, diese Nacht,
> Diese Nacht nur gönne mir,
> Harte! und dann steh ich dir!

> (*F* only 749-52)

for we are invited to believe that the inexorable power which will actually operate this night will cause him to kill Borotin, and bring about his own death too. The irony of this speech may be compared with that found in Act III when Jaromir, having been identified by Bertha as the robber, still hopes that he will be purified by his relationship with her. He talks of gaining peace and happiness (1958), and purity (1960), and addresses her as an angel of Heaven (1971-3). As they embrace he feels purged of guilt:

> Wenn dein Arm mich, Teure, hält,
> Trotz ich einer ganzen Welt.
> Meine Schuld ist ausgestrichen,
> Jubelnd bin ich mirs bewusst, . . .

> (1977-80)

when in fact the reverse is true. In the final version the ending of the third Act is similar to that of the first, for Jaromir still looks forward to a happy future:

> Mutig, Froh!—Die Zukunft lacht!
> Und gedenk: um Mitternacht!

> (2158f.)

In the original version, which consists of four Acts only, these lines occur in the middle of Act III (*E* 1716f.). Grillparzer has thus succeeded in providing similarly ironic conclusions to both Acts I and II. Clearly a knowledge of later events is required for a full appreciation of the irony of hopes expressed in the first Act, but Grillparzer has given some immediate help through his use of the technical machinery of fate-tragedy. Moreover the appearance of the ghost has given a hint that Jaromir may bring misfortune rather than the opposite, so that the audience may react already to the optimism of the characters.

When the ghost makes her second appearance we have already been fully acquainted with the details of the legend, so that the impact is all the greater. Here Jaromir is the victim, and she is trying to avert disaster for the family by encouraging him to go away (*E* 661, *F* 790 and *E* 669, *F* 798). This provides the audience with an indication that Jaromir will be somehow concerned with the eventual disasters, and his reaction, like that of Bertha before him, is recognisably inappropriate, and similarly ironic. Imagining that the ghost is Bertha herself, he greets her with enthusiasm (*E* 662, *F* 791) and even attempts to embrace her (812 S.D.). The intention of the ancestress is thus again thwarted by her own similarity to Bertha. Even after he has learnt that the figure is indeed a ghost, he is full of defiance and confidence, precisely the opposite reaction to those required by the situation. Furthermore his appeal to the real Bertha to embrace him, that they might dispel the supernatural threat (*E* 830-3, *F* 952-5), is unfortunate, for he does not realise that they are, through their love, setting the family on a course for disaster. For anyone already acquainted with the details of the plot Jaromir's reaction creates a powerful sense of tension and irony, but an uninformed spectator should also now realise something of the implications of the ghost's warnings, particularly as Grillparzer supplies a number of hints. Jaromir's hopes for the first night have already been contradicted by his hallucinations and Grillparzer also supplies words of warning from Borotin that in associating himself with the family, Jaromir, referred to occasionally as "Sohn" (e.g. *E* 898, *F* 981) and "mein Kind" (*E* 873, *F* 1005), will only go down with them (*E* 874f., *F* 1005f.), a possibility which Jaromir is boldly prepared to accept:

> Möge, was da will, geschehn,
> Ich will Euch zur Seite stehn,
> Muss es, mit euch untergehn!
>
> (*E* 880-2, *F* 1011-3)

Thus again the outcome is anticipated with an unconscious allusion to the actual situation. Jaromir is continuing blindly on his path in spite of warnings and forebodings, and is anticipating unconsciously the outcome of events. Similarly, in the final version only, Borotin describes the situation unwittingly when he reacts to the news that Jaromir has seen the ghost:

> Zählt man dich schon zu den Meinen?
>
> (978)

Consequently when Borotin gratefully welcomes Jaromir as someone who will share their joys as well as their sorrows, reversing the traditional metaphor of the rose which has thorns, his choice of image is recognisably ironic, for its more usual form would be more appropriate. Jaromir is certainly concealing a fatal thorn, and in the final version Grillparzer develops the image when Bertha refers to the thorns on which she has walked since meeting him:

> Seit ich fühlte seinen Kuss,
> Ist das Feenland verschwunden,
> Und auf Dornen tritt mein Fuss;
> Dornen, die zwar Rosen schmücken,
> Aber Dornen, Dornen doch, . . .
>
> (*F* only, 1552-6)

These words could be applied to the actual situation in a manner which she does not yet envisage, for Jaromir brings her joy as her lover, but drives her to suicide when the truth is revealed. They also provide an appropriate contradiction of Borotin's hopeful interpretation of Jaromir's arrival. Although characters commit themselves unwittingly to ironic remarks whose full significance may become apparent only later, some of these remarks provide in themselves an indication of future developments to an attentive audience. In the final version Grillparzer develops considerably the contradiction existing between the forebodings of disaster and the hopes which characters also entertain. For example, Borotin entrusts Bertha to Jaromir's care with confidence (*F* only, 1148f.), having shortly before this recalled details of the legend:

> Wenn sie wahr, die alte Sage,
> Dass der Name, den ich trage,
> Der mein Stolz war und mein Schmuck,
> Nur durch tief geheime Sünden—
> Fort, Gedanke!—Ha, und doch!
>
> (*F* only, 1104-8)

Similarly Bertha now senses that her love involves her in guilt:

> Tief im Busen scheints zu sprechen,
> Wenn mein Blick in seinem ruht:
> Deine Liebe ist Verbrechen,
> Gottverhasst ist diese Glut.
>
> (*F* only, 1563-6)

The characters thus have intimations that all is not well, but disregard them and the irony inherent in these situations is intensified by Grillparzer's additions in his final version.

The ancestress appears for the third time in Act III, to warn Jaromir not to take the dagger from the wall (*F* only, 2094). In the original version a warning is provided only by Bertha's words (*E* 1698-1703), but in the final version the ghost provides a more definite and vivid indication that the use of the dagger may be fatal to the family.[21] Grillparzer has also added other ominous touches. For example, immediately before the ghost's appearance, Bertha now says of the dagger:

> Blutges hat er schon gesehn.
> Blutges kann noch jetzt geschehn!
>
> (*F* only, 2093f.)

without yet realising just how disastrous Jaromir's use of the dagger will be. Jaromir's reaction to the ghost's appearance is again inappropriate and he also produces several significant remarks. For example he welcomes the dagger as something which he recalls from the days of his childhood (*F* only, 2104), and even senses that fate is inviting him to take it:

Sei gegrüsst, du hilfreich Werkzeug!
Lockend seh ich her dich blinken,
Und mein Schicksal scheint zu winken.
Du bist mein! Drum her zu mir!

(*F* only, 2125-8)

Jaromir thus disregards the warning again, and his words have far more sinister implications than he realises. Grillparzer has again exploited the appearance of the ghost, this time in the final version only, to create a situation whose drama and irony depend on an inappropriate reaction on the part of the victim, who then produces words which have a significance of which he is not conscious. The ancestress makes her final appearance at the close of the play when she comes to tell Jaromir that there is still time for him to fly, and thus to save himself and the family name. Again Jaromir takes her for Bertha, but although he now knows that Bertha is his sister (3220-2), he refuses to take her advice, desiring to remain at her side:

Leben, Bertha, dir zur Seite,
Oder sterben neben dir.

(3280f.)

These words are particularly poignant, for it is at this point that the ghost reveals her identity, and that Bertha's corpse is discovered. Jaromir dies in the ghost's embrace. The whole episode reflects the irony of the situation: Jaromir fulfils the fate of the family by embracing the ancestress, who resembles Bertha. This emphasises the fact that it is through his love for Bertha, the very thing which inspires Borotin and himself with hope, that the doom is eventually sealed. The ghost provides warnings to the characters, but these are either disregarded or misunderstood; Jaromir's arrival fills them with false hopes, which may be viewed ironically, for his arrival in fact heralds their doom; the series of revelations also creates an ironic effect, for these are gradual, and the full circumstances are not always known by all.

From the foregoing analysis it is clear that the introduction of the ghost onto the stage serves an important dramatic function in *Die Ahnfrau,* particularly with regard to the creation of irony. In Chapter I we have seen that a fatal force may provide the basis for an ironic effect, allowing the spectator to anticipate eventual disaster, and placing him in a superior position in relation to the ignorant and unsuspecting victim, and in *Die Ahnfrau* it is Grillparzer's particularly skilful use of his dramatic medium that produces the appropriate effect. Though we are not yet aware of the precise nature of later events, the appearances of the ghost, together with the fatalistic atmosphere and the use of various warnings and expressions of forebodings, provide the audience with appropriate indications. Thus the ironic effect depends initially on the contradiction existing between our forebodings and the failure of the characters to respond to the warnings of the ghost. The dramatic function of the ghost is to provide a hint of future disaster, and although the full implications of many of the examples of dramatic irony may only be appreciated retrospectively, the attentive audience may already gather something of their significance. The projection of the minds of the spectators forward to later events creates a sense of movement and excitement, and the ignorance, or "innocence", of the character produces tension and a sense of irony. It is not therefore the actual presence of fatalistic material which is the important factor in this play, but the manner of its presentation. It is also clear that the dramatic function served by the introduction of the ghost onto the stage is developed considerably in the final stage version of the play, apparently at the instigation of Josef Schreyvogel. Schreyvogel did not turn the play into a fate-tragedy, but developed a theme already present in Grillparzer's original manuscript. His prime concern was to capitalise on Grillparzer's use of fate as a dramatic device and to make the play more effective dramatically. In this connection it is significant that many of the alterations led to an increase in the number of remarks producing a dramatic effect which, for various reasons, could be called ironic. Such remarks depend for their effect on the contrast between the viewpoint of the audience, who respond to the indications given of approaching disasters, and that of the character concerned, who remains unconscious both of the fate which awaits him and of the significance of his remarks. Such situations are obviously theatrically effective, and it is not fortuitous that they should have been developed following suggestions by a man of the theatre.

That Grillparzer had in mind a purely dramatic, as opposed to a philosophical or moral function for the fatal force, is clear from his writings at the time on the use of fate in drama. He rejects the notion that the presence of fatalistic elements in a play necessarily implies a belief in fate on the part of the dramatist. Even though the characters themselves may express such a belief we do not have to identify with them.[22] Nevertheless he recognises that his contemporaries still sense the influence of fate on events, and it is to this vague awareness of fate ("dunkle Ahnung") that the modern dramatist may appeal:

Als Ahnung nun muss sie (die Idee des Fatums) auch sich in der Tragödie zeigen. Es müssen die Fakten gegeben sein, und dem Zuschauer überlassen werden, dabei schaudernd ein Fatum zu denken.[23]

Though we may recognise that a belief in fate is an irrational one, our imaginations may prefer in the theatre to believe in the workings of supernatural forces. Moreover in poetry the concept of fate may be used to great effect, and in contemporary tragedy it functions purely as a dramatic device ("Maschine"):

bei den Neuern wird sie—Maschine, eine schwer zu behandelnde, vorsichtig zu brauchende Maschine, . . .[24]

Grillparzer is stressing its practical usefulness in the theatre, and he goes on to criticise some of his German contemporaries for turning their tragedies into vehicles for ideas at the expense of dramatic qualities.[25]

Though Grillparzer mentions no names, a celebrated forerunner of **Die Ahnfrau,** Schiller's fate-tragedy *Die Braut von Messina,* could come within the orbit of such criticism, for the concept of fate and the problem of Man's relationship with forces greater than himself are frequently raised as ideas in this play (e.g. 11. 879-883, 929-43, 1476-8, 2267-2308), and a chorus offers periodic reflections both on the development of events and on the human condition in general. Like Grillparzer, however, Schiller also makes use of his fatalistic material, namely the oracles and dreams, to create dramatic tension and a sense of irony,[26] and many ironic remarks are also made during the succession of tragic revelations in the latter stages of the play. Here too there are similarities between *Die Braut von Messina* and **Die Ahnfrau,** for Grillparzer appears to have taken Schiller's play as his model at this point in the action.[27] Nevertheless there are two fundamental differences between the two dramatists' methods of presenting their fatalistic material. First, Grillparzer has the legend narrated at an early stage of the play (11. 108-15), so that the audience are immediately in the picture, whereas in *Die Braut von Messina* the story of the grandfather's curse upon his son's progeny is not uttered until approximately one third of the way through (11. 960-80), and the report of the dreams and oracles does not occur until 11. 1306-51. Secondly, as well as narrating the legend, Grillparzer provides us with a recurrent visual reminder of the existence of the fatal force in the figure of the ghost, whereas Schiller relies solely on the spoken word, and the sense of fatality remains a concept, existing in the minds of the characters, and established only by hearsay and by the course of events.

Grillparzer's methods in this respect may also be contrasted with those employed by Kleist in his contribution to fate-tragedy, *Die Familie Schroffenstein.* In this play it is not definitely established that a fatal force is at work, for the witch who appears in the final scene explains that the unfortunate succession of murders has been launched by an error ("ein Versehen"—1. 2705).[28] However, as I. V. Morris points out, "the many coincidences, the disguises and mistaken identities convey the impression of a mysterious, capricious power confusing the characters".[29] The confusion of the characters lasts until the solution is eventually revealed at the close. What is particularly distinctive about this technique is that the spectators remain similarly confused until the later stages of the play. Although it is possible to recognise that the characters may be in error in their attempts to analyse and explain the course of events,[30] the degree of superiority of spectator over character which is established in **Die Ahnfrau** is lacking in Kleist's play. Grillparzer affords us the pleasure of being privileged spectators. Kleist allows us to share in the confusion and mystification of his characters.

Although we have seen that Grillparzer's use of fate in **Die Ahnfrau** is a major factor in his attempts to generate tension and a sense of irony, it must be stressed that the presence of a fatal force is not vital for the creation of ironic effects such as have been described. So long as indications of future possibilities can be given to the audience at the expense of unsuspecting characters a sufficient amount of tension may be created. After writing **Die Ahnfrau** Grillparzer abandoned the form of the fate-tragedy, not only because of the controversy it had inspired, but also because he felt that he could achieve the same dramatic purposes by other means. Through his skilful use of his dramatic medium we are enabled to anticipate, for example, the downfall of Ottokar, the fatal error of Hero, the wretchedness of Jason, the frustration of Sappho's hopes. In his tragedies Grillparzer frequently places his audience in a position of relative superiority over his characters, whose errors may be anticipated or immediately recognised, or who are depicted in moments of weakness or in the grip of powerful emotions. From the analysis of his use of his fatalistic material in **Die Ahnfrau** it has been seen that Grillparzer endeavours to produce dramatic effects which may be appreciated immediately, rather than retrospectively within the context of the dramatic action as a whole, and it is his use of the ghost as a dramatic device which most obviously enables him to achieve this. It is significant that Schreyvogel, the man of the theatre, further exploited the young author's method of presenting his fatal force, and Grillparzer served a useful apprenticeship, not as a future writer of fate-tragedies, but as a dramatist who wrote for immediate stage-purposes.

Notes

1. Accounts of the furore which the play originally inspired are provided by I. V. Morris (Morris 1), H. C. Seeba (Seeba 1), and R. Bauer. For an account of the early criticism of the play see also H. M. Wolff. Details are given in the Bibliography.

2. Especially by Hebenstreit, the editor of the Wiener Modenzeitung, who condemned the play primarily as an offence against religion. For details, see Morris 1.

3. Minor, pp. 59, 75.

4. Škreb, p. 237.

5. Reich, pp. 27-49.

6. Müller 1, pp. 9-15.

7. See Müller 2, pp. 25-26.

8. Notably by W. Paulsen, who attempts to rescue the play from the stigma of fate-tragedy and to interpret it as "Erlebnisdichtung"; by E. Krispyn (Krispyn 1), who is essentially concerned with the autobiographical elements in the play; and by Seeba (Seeba 1), who interprets the play in terms of Grillparzer's "Selbstentfremdung" and of Jaromir's Oedipus complex.

9. Hanser IV, p. 79 (*Selbstbiographie*).

10. Recent critics who take account of Schreyvogel's influence on the play include Krispyn and Morris. Morris, following Grillparzer's own plea, suggests that it

is the original version which should be appreciated for its poetic merits alone, but as will be seen, it may at least be claimed that the final version is dramatically more effective.

11. Hanser IV, p. 76 (*Selbstbiographie*)

12. reported by August Sauer in his notes to the first version, Sauer-Backmann, I, i, p. 420.

13. References to *Die Ahnfrau* are to Sauer's edition. References are occasionally given to the two versions of the play printed by Sauer, the original version (Sauer, I, i, 153-256), designated by the letter E ("erste Fassung"), and the fifth or final stage version, printed in 1844 (Sauer, I, i, 9-148), designated by the letter F ("fünfte Fassung"). In contrasting the text of the original version with that of the fifth version in order to demonstrate the effect of Schreyvogel's advice, I am following the example of Krispyn.

14. That Grillparzer would not wish his ghost to be considered as a mere poetic symbol is clear from his rejection of the interpretation of the witches in *Macbeth* as extensions of the hero's own ambition. Like the ghost of Banquo they are real and to be regarded as such. Hanser IV, p. 79. This point has been made by Morris, op. cit., p. 289.

15. as recognised by Seeba, who writes: "Die publikumswirksame Moralisierung des Schicksals zum Sühnegeschehen, nicht die Schicksalsidee selbst ist es, was Grillparzer Schreyvogel hätte vorwerfen können". Seeba 1, p. 143.

16. by R. K. Angress, who claims that such criticism overlooks the play's "dichterische Aussage und Absicht", and goes on to interpret the play as an example of "Unterhaltungsliteratur".

17. Friedrich Gundolf also held that Grillparzer was using the accessories of fate primarily for technical reasons, Gundolf, p. 30, and Benno von Wiese describes the fatal force as "ein theatralischer, effektvoller Apparat", von Wiese, p. 384.

18. Morris notes, p. 291, in spite of her plea in favour of the early version, that Douglas Yates considers that the play "profited considerably in content and in form by Schreyvogel's aid and criticism", Yates 1, p. 29.

19. See for example Minor, p. 70, Ehrhard, p. 48, Yates 1, p. 29.

20. as reported by Sauer, op. cit., p. 421.

21. The appearance of the ghost at this stage was introduced at the express suggestion of Schreyvogel. Sauer, op. cit., p. 427.

22. Hanser iii, pp. 310-11. (Zweiter Brief *Über das Fatum,* 1817)

23. ibid, p. 307. (*Tagebücher* 270, 1817)

24. ibid, p. 310.

25. ibid, p. 311.

26. as recognised by Benno von Wiese, see von Wiese, p. 260.

27. as noted by G. A. Wells, Wells 1, p. 8. In Grillparzer's play the appearance of the Captain and the soldier, who provide information for the main characters, are also used to produce moments of dramatic irony, as also are the various revelations at the close of the play. These instances are also developed in the final version. See F only, 1321f., 1498.

28. H. C. Seeba concludes that this play too does not strictly belong to the category of fate-tragedy, but acknowledges the fatalistic nature of the plot, mentioning, for example, the "fatale Verwechslung" (p. 65) and "verhängnisvolle Kettenreaktion" (p. 74). Seeba 2.

29. Morris 2, p. 56.

30. as pointed out by Seeba, op. cit., p. 78.

Bibliography

1. General Works of Literary Criticism Consulted

The following lists contain only those works consulted and are not offered as a full bibliography either of Grillparzer or on the subject of irony.

ALLEMANN, B., *Ironie und Dichtung,* Pfüllingen, 1956.

BRADLEY, A. C., *Shakespearean Tragedy,* London, 1904.

BROOKE, N., *Shakespeare: King Lear,* London, 1963.

CAMPBELL, L., edition of *Sophocles' Works,* Vol. I, Oxford, 1871.

FRYE, N., *Anatomy of Criticism,* Princeton, 1957.

HELLER, E., *The Ironic German: a study of Thomas Mann,* London, 1958.

JEPSON, L., *Ethical Aspects of Tragedy,* Gainesville, Florida, 1953.

JOHNSON, S. K., "Dramatic Irony in Sophoclean Tragedy", *Classical Review,* December 1928, pp. 209-214.

JONES, J., *On Aristotle and Greek Tragedy,* London, 1962.

KITTO, H. D. F., *Greek Tragedy,* London, 1939.

KNOX, B., *"Oedipus Rex",* in *Tragic Themes in Western Literature,* ed. Cleanth Brooks, New Haven, 1955.

MORRIS, I. V., "Fate and Form in German Drama of the Age of Goethe", *Publications of the English Goethe Society,* 41, 1970-71, pp. 45-64. = *Morris 2.*

MOULTON, R. G., *The Moral System in Shakespeare,* London, 1903.

MUECKE, D. C., *The Compass of Irony,* London, 1969.

MULLER, H. J., *The Spirit of Tragedy*, New York, 1956.

NICOLL, A., *The Theatre and Dramatic Theory*, London, 1960.

PEACOCK, R., *The Art of Drama*, London, 1957.

PRAWER, S. S., *Heine: The Tragic Satyrist*, Cambridge, 1961.

RAPHAEL, D. D., *The Paradox of Tragedy*, London, 1960.

SEDGEWICK, G. G., *Of Irony. Especially in Drama*, Toronto, 1948.

SEEBA, H. C., "Der Sündenfall des Verdachts: Identitätskrise und Sprachskepsis in Kleists Familie *Schroffenstein*", *Deutsche Vierteljahrschrift*, 44, 1970, pp. 64-100. = *Seeba 2*.

SENGLE, F., *Das Deutsche Geschichtsdrama*, Stuttgart, 1952.

SHARPE, R. B., *Irony in the Drama*, Chapel Hill, 1959.

SKREB, Z., "Die deutsche sogenannte Schicksalstragödie", *Jahrbuch der Grillparzer-Gesellschaft*, 9, 1972, pp. 193-237.

STYAN, J. L., *The Elements of Drama*, Cambridge, 1963. = Styan 1.

STYAN, J. L., *Shakespeare's Stagecraft*, Cambridge, 1967. = Styan 2.

THIRLWALL, C., "On the Irony of Sophocles", *Philological Museum*, II, 1833, and *Remains, Literary and Theological*, ed. J. J. S. Perowne, London, 1878.

TYMMS, R. V., *German Romantic Literature*, London, 1955.

WELLS, G. A., "Fate-tragedy and Die Braut von Messina", *Journal of English and German Philology*, LXIV, 1965, pp. 191-212.

WIESE, B. von, *Die deutsche Tragödie von Lessing bis Hebbel*, Hamburg, 1948.

2. EDITIONS OF INDIVIDUAL WORKS BY GRILLPARZER REFERRED TO IN THE TEXT

SPALDING, K., edition of *Sappho*, Macmillan, London, 1965.

WELLS, G. A., edition of *Die Jüdin von Toledo*, Pergamon, Oxford, 1969. = *Wells 3*.

YATES, D., edition of *Des Meeres und der Liebe Wellen*, Blackwell, Oxford, 1947, reprinted 1960. = *Yates 2*.

3. WORKS OF CRITICISM RELATING TO GRILLPARZER REFERRED TO IN THE TEXT

ANGRESS, R. K., "Das Gespenst in Grillparzer's *Ahnfrau*", *German Quarterly*, 15, 1972, pp. 606-619.

ATKINSON, M. E., "Grillparzer's use of symbol and image in *Des Meeres und der Liebe Wellen*", *German Life and Letters*, N.S. IV, 1951, pp. 261-277.

BAUER, R., "*Die Ahnfrau* et la querelle de la tragédie fataliste", *Études Germaniques*, 27, 1972, pp. 165-192.

BAUMANN, G., *Franz Grillparzer: Sein Werk und das oesterreichische Wesen*, Wien & Freiburg, 1954. = *Baumann 1*.

BAUMANN, G., "*Ein Bruderzwist in Habsburg*", *Das deutsche Drama vom Barock bis zur Gegenwart. Interpretationen*, ed. B. von Wiese, Düsseldorf, 1958, Vol. 1, pp. 422-450. = *Baumann 2*.

BERIGER, L., *Grillparzers Persönlichkeit in seinem Werk*, *Wege zur Dichtung*, ed. E. Ermatinger, Vol. III, Zürich & Leipzig, 1927.

BLACKALL, E. A., "*Die Jüdin von Toledo*", *German Studies presented to W. H. Bruford*, London, 1962, pp. 193-206.

BUSCH, E., "Wesen und Ursprung von Grillparzers Idee des Tragischen", *Dichtung und Volkstum*, 40, 1939, pp. 257-276.

CYSARZ, H., "Grillparzer und das neunzehnte Jahrhundert", *Hochschulwissen*, VI, 1929, pp. 139-146, 226-232.

COWEN, R., "The tragedy of *Die Jüdin von Toledo*", *German Quarterly*, January 1964, pp. 39-53.

EHRHARD, A., *Franz Grillparzer: Sein Leben und seine Werke*. München, 1910.

FISCHER, E., "Franz Grillparzer", *Von Grillparzer zu Kafka, Sechs Essays*, Wien, 1962, pp. 9-56.

FRICKE, G., "Wesen und Wandel des Tragischen bei Grillparzer", *Studien und Interpretationen*, Frankfurt, 1956, pp. 264-284.

FÜLLEBORN, U., *Das dramatische Geschehen im Werk Franz Grillparzers*, München, 1966.

GUNDOLF, F., "Franz Grillparzer", *Jahrbuch des Freien Deutschen Hochstifts*, 1931, pp. 9-93.

HOCK, E., "*Libussa*", *Das deutsche Drama vom Barock bis zur Gegenwart. Interpretationen*, ed. B. von Wiese, Düsseldorf, 1958, Vol. I, pp. 451-474. = *Hock 1*.

HOCK, E., *Franz Grillparzer: Besinnung auf Humanität*, Hamburg, 1949. = *Hock 2*.

HOFF, H., and CERMAK, I., *Grillparzer: Versuch einer Pathographie*, Wien, 1961.

KAISER, J., *Grillparzers dramatischer Stil*, München, 1961.

KLARMANN, A. D., "Grillparzer und die Moderne", *Die Neue Rundschau*, 67, 1956, pp. 137-152.

KOCH, F., "Grillparzers Staatsdramen", *Germanisch-Romanische Monatsschrift*, 37, 1956, pp. 15-31.

KRISPYN, E., "Grillparzer and his *Ahnfrau*", *Germanic Review*, 38, 1963, pp. 209-225. = Krispyn 1.

KRISPYN, E., "Grillparzer's Tragedy *Die Jüdin von Toledo*", *Modern Language Review*, 60, 1965, pp. 405-415. = Krispyn 2.

LANGE, E., Franz Grillparzer. *Sein Leben, Dichten und Denken,* Gütersloh, 1894.

LESSING, O. E., *Grillparzer und das neue Drama,* München & Leipzig, 1905.

MATT, P. von, *Der Grundriss von Grillparzers Bühnenkunst,* Zürich, 1965.

MINOR, J., "Zur Geschichte der deutschen Schicksalstragödie und zur Grillparzers *Ahnfrau*", *Jahrbuch der Grillparzergesellschaft,* IX, 1899.

MORRIS, I. V., "The *Ahnfrau* controversy", *Modern Language Review,* LXII, 1967, pp. 284-291. = *Morris 1.*

MUELLER, J., *Grillparzers Menschenauffassung,* Weimar, 1934. = *Müller 1.*

MUELLER, J., *Franz Grillparzer,* Sammlung Metzler 31, Stuttgart, 1963. = *Müller 2.*

MUENCH, I., *Die Tragik in Drama und Persönlichkeit Franz Grillparzers, Neue Forschung* 11, Berlin, 1931.

MULHOLLAND, G. A., *A Study of Grillparzer's major dramatic works in the light of a Baroque Tradition in Viennese Popular Drama,* Diss., London, 1966.

NADLER, J., *Franz Grillparzer,* Vaduz, 1948.

NAUMANN, W., *Grillparzer: Das dichterische Werk,* Stuttgart, 1956. = *Naumann 1.*

NAUMANN, W., *"König Ottokars Glück und Ende", Das deutsche Drama vom Barock bis zur Gegenwart. Interpretationen,* ed. B. von Wiese, Düsseldorf, 1958, Vol. I, pp. 405-421. = *Naumann 2.*

PAPST, E., "Grillparzer", *German Men of Letters,* ed. A. Natan, London, 1961, pp. 99-120. = *Papst 1.*

PAPST, E., *Grillparzer: Des Meeres und der Liebe Wellen, Studies in German Literature,* ed. L. W. Forster and B. A. Rowley, N. 9, London, 1967. = Papst 2.

PAULSEN, W., *Die Ahnfrau—Zu Grillparzers früher Dramatik,* Tübingen, 1962.

PEACOCK, R., "Grillparzer" in *The Poet in the Theatre,* London, 1946, pp. 39-53.

REICH, E., *Franz Grillparzers Dramen,* Wien, 1894. 4th ed. *Grillparzers dramatisches Werk,* Wien, 1938.

SEEBA, H. C., "Das Schicksal der Grillen und Parzen. Zu Grillparzers *Ahnfrau*", *Euphorion,* 65, 1971, pp. 132-161. = Seeba 1.

STAIGER, E., *"König Ottokars Glück und Ende", Meisterwerke deutscher Sprache aus dem neunzehnten Jahrhundert,* Zürich, 1948, pp. 165-187.

STEIN, G., *The Inspiration Motif in the works of Grillparzer,* The Hague, 1955.

STERN, J. P., "Grillparzer's Vienna", *German Studies presented to W. H. Bruford,* London, 1962, pp. 176-192.

SWALES, M. W., "The Narrative Perspective in Grillparzer's *Der arme Spielmann*", *German Life and Letters,* N.S. XX, 1967, pp. 107-116.

VOLKELT, J., *Franz Grillparzer als Dichter des Tragischen,* Nördlingen, 1888.

WELLS, G. A., *The Plays of Grillparzer,* Oxford, 1969. = *Wells 1.*

WELLS, G. A., "The Problem of Right Conduct in Grillparzer's *Ein Bruderzwist in Habsburg*", *German Life and Letters,* N.S. XI, 1958, pp. 161-171.

WEISSBART, G., *Bürgerliches Lebensgefühl in Grillparzers Dramen, Mnemosyne,* Heft 3, Bonn, 1929.

WOLFF, H. M., "Zum Problem der *Ahnfrau*", *Zeitschrift für deutsche Philologie,* 62, 1937, pp. 303-317.

YATES, D., *Grillparzer: A critical Biography,* Oxford, 1946. *Yates 1.*

4. OTHER CRITICAL WORKS CONSULTED RELATING TO GRILLPARZER

ALKER, E., *Franz Grillparzer: Ein Kampf um Leben und Kunst,* Marburg, 1930.

AUERNHEIMER, R., *Franz Grillparzer: Der Dichter Oesterreichs,* Wien, 1948.

BACKMANN, R., "Grillparzer als Revolutionär", *Euphorion,* 32, 1931, pp. 476-525.

BACKMANN, R., "Grillparzer und die heutige Biedermeier-Psychose", *Jahrbuch der Grillparzer-Gesellschaft,* 33, 1935, pp. 1-32.

BIETAK, W., *Das Lebensgefühl des Biedermeier in der oesterreichischen Dichtung,* Wien, 1931.

BRINKMANN, R., *"Der arme Spielmann:* Der Einbruch der Subjektivität", *Wahrheit und Illusion,* Tübingen, 1957, pp. 87-145.

BURCKHARDT, C. J., "Franz Grillparzer" in *Gestalten und Mächte,* Zürich, 1961, pp. 475-502.

COENAN, F. E., *Grillparzer's Portraiture of Men,* Chapel Hill, 1951.

ENZINGER, M., "Franz Grillparzer und das Wiener Volkstheater", *Grillparzer-Studien,* ed. O. Katann, Wien, 1924, pp. 9-39.

FRIES, A., *Intime Beobachtungen zu Grillparzers Stil und Versbau, Germanische Studien,* Heft 18, Berlin, 1922.

FUERST, N., *Grillparzer auf der Bühne,* Wien & München, 1958.

GMUER, H., *Dramatische und theatralische Stilelemente in Grillparzers Dramen,* Diss. Zürich, 1956.

GRUBER, F. E., *Franz Grillparzer und seine Bühnenwerke: Eine Einführung, Schneiders Bühnenführer,* Berlin, 1922.

HANDL, W., *Oesterreich und der deutsche Geist: Franz Grillparzer, Die Teile der deutschen Einheit,* III, Konstanz a.B., 1915.

HOELLERER, W., "Franz Grillparzer", *Zwischen Klassik und Moderne,* Stuttgart, 1958, pp. 240-294.

HELMENSDORFER, U., *Grillparzers Bühnenkunst,* Bern, 1960.

HOHLBAUM, R., *Grillparzer,* Stuttgart, 1938.

HUBER, W., "Zur Tragik Grillparzers", *Jahrbuch der Grillparzer-Gesellschaft,* 33, 1935, pp. 33-41.

KASSNER, R., "Grillparzer", *Geistige Welten,* Frankfurt am Main, 1958, pp. 90-101.

KLAAR, A., *Grillparzer als Dramatiker,* Wien, 1891.

KOSCH, W., *Oesterreich im Dichten und Denken Grillparzers,* Wien, 1946.

LASHER-SCHLITT, D., "Grillparzers 'Hero und Leander': Eine psychologische Untersuchung", *Jahrbuch der Grillparzer-gesellschaft,* 3te. Folge, 3, 1960, pp. 106-114.

MASON, E., "A new look at Grillparzer's *Bruderzwist*", *German Life and Letters,* N.S. XXV, 1972, pp. 102-115.

MUEHLER, R., "Grillparzer und der deutsche Idealismus", *Wissenschaft und Weltbild,* I, 1948, Heft I, pp. 62-75.

NAUMANN, W., "Die Form des Dramas bei Grillparzer und Hofmannsthal", *Deutsche Vierteljahrschrift,* 33, 1959, pp. 20-37.

POLITZER, H., *Franz Grillparzer oder das abgründige Biedermeier,* Wien, 1972.

REGER, H. A., *Das Sprachbild in Grillparzers Dramen, Xerogrammatica* 2, Bonn, 1968.

REDLICH, O., *Grillparzers Verhältnis zur Geschichte,* Wien, 1901.

ROSELIED, H., "Grillparzers Weltanschauung", *Grillparzer-Studien,* ed. O. Katann, Wien, 1924, pp. 40-73.

SCHAFROTH, H. F., *Die Entscheidung bei Grillparzer,* Bern, 1971.

SCHAUM, K., "Grillparzers Drama *Ein treuer Diener seines Herrn*", *Jahrbuch der Grillparzergesellschaft,* 3te. Folge, 3, 1960, pp. 72-93.

SCHNEIDER, R., *Im Anfang liegt das Ende: Grillparzers Epilog auf die Geschichte,* Baden-Baden, 1946.

SPRENGLER, J., *Grillparzer: Der Tragiker der Schuld,* Stuttgart, 1947.

STAFANSKY, G., "Grillparzers geistige Persönlichkeit", *Festschrift für August Sauer,* Stuttgart, 1925, pp. 233-269.

STRICH, F., *Franz Grillparzers Aesthetik, Forschungen zur neueren Literaturgeschichte,* XXIX, Berlin, 1905.

STROHSCHNEIDER-KOHR, I., "*Wirklichkeit* und *Erweis*: Notizen zu einem Problem im Denken Grillparzers", *Festschrift für Hermann Kunisch,* Berlin, 1961, pp. 363-380.

VOLKELT, J., "Grillparzer als Dichter des Zwiespalts zwischen Gemüt und Leben", *Zwischen Dichtung und Philosophie,* München, 1908, pp. 162-208.

WEDEL-PARLOV, L. von, *Grillparzer,* Wertheim, 1932.

Editions and Abbreviations

Quotations from Grillparzer's works and line references are taken from the Hanser edition of *Grillparzer's Sämtliche Werke, Ausgewählte Briefe, Gespräche und Berichte,* ed. Peter Frank and Karl Pörnbacher, München, 1960. Footnote references to this edition are identified by the word Hanser, followed by the volume number and page reference. The abbreviation S.D. denotes the stage direction following the line referred to.

Reference has also been made to the standard critical edition of Grillparzer's *Sämtliche Werke, Historisch-kritische Gesamtausgabe,* ed. August Sauer and Reinhold Backmann, Wien, 1909-48. Footnote references to this edition are identified by the words Sauer-Backmann, followed by the division and volume numbers, and the page reference.

References to works by authors other than Grillparzer are taken from the following editions:

Aristotle, *Poetics* and *Rhetoric,* from the Loeb Classical Library, Heinemann, London, 1927, English translation by W. Hamilton Fyfe.

Heine, *Deutschland ein Wintermärchen,* from Heinrich Heine, *Werke,* Insel Verlag, Frankfurt, 1968, Vol. I.

Kleist, *Die Familie Schroffenstein,* from Kleist, *Sämtliche Werke und Briefe,* Carl Hanser Verlag, München, 1964, Vol. I.

Schiller, *Wallensteins Tod,* from Schiller, *Werke,* 'Nationalausgabe', Weimar 1943 etc., Vol. 8. *Die Braut von Messina,* 'Nationalausgabe', Vol. 10.

Shakespeare, *Julius Caesar,* from *The Works of Shakespeare,* ed. John Dover Wilson, Cambridge, 1949. *Macbeth,* from the Arden edition of Shakespeare's works, ed. Kenneth Muir, London, 1957 (reprinted). *King Lear,* from the Arden edition, ed. Kenneth Muir, London, 1961 (reprinted). *Othello,* from the Arden edition, ed. M. R. Ridley, London, 1962 (reprinted).

Sophocles, *Oedipus Rex,* from Sophocles, *The Theban Plays,* Penguin Books, 1947, English translation by E. F. Watling.

Wilde, *The Importance of Being Ernest,* from Oscar Wilde's *Plays, Prose writings and Poems,* Everyman's Library, London, 1966 (reprinted).

Reference has been made to a number of titles of Grillparzer's plays in an abbreviated form. These are as follows:

König Ottokars Glück und Ende is referred to as König Ottokar.

Ein treuer Diener seines Herrn is referred to as *Ein treuer Diener.*

Des Meeres und der Liebe Wellen is referred to as *Des Meeres.*

Die Jüdin von Toledo is referred to as *Die Jüdin.*

Ein Bruderzwist in Habsburg is referred to as *Ein Bruderzwist*.

Footnote references to critical works are also made in an abbreviated form, and are identified by the author's name, followed by the page reference. A full description of the relevant work will be found in the Bibliography.

A reference to a particular work by an author who has more than one of his works listed in the Bibliography will also include a number which identifies the relevant work in the Bibliography. e.g. Papst 2, p. 35 refers to E. E. Papst Grillparzer: Des Meeres und der Liebe Wellen, London, 1967. i.e. the second work by this author listed in the Bibliography.

Ursula Mahlendorf (essay date 1979)

SOURCE: "Franz Grillparzer's *The Poor Fiddler*: The Terror of Rejection," in *American Imago*, Vol. 36, No. 2, Summer, 1979, pp. 118-46.

[*In the following essay, Mahlendorf argues that the two main characters in Grillparzer's* The Poor Fiddler, *Jacob and the narrator, are actually two aspects of Grillparzer himself, and that the story was probably the author's attempt to resolve his creative dilemma of how to continue writing despite critical rejection.*]

INTRODUCTION

Grillparzer's story **The Poor Fiddler** (written from 1831-1842) portrays two artists, Jacob the fiddler, who is a total failure, and the narrator of the story, a dramatist in search of dramatic material, who lives and works in a manner entirely different from the fiddler. Narrator and fiddler are two different aspects of the author's own being. Both characters, though in different ways, are concerned with the problem of rejection. Through his two artist figures, Grillparzer compares and contrasts two different uses of art and two different media of art: in the case of the fiddler the medium of sound and in the case of the dramatist the medium of persons. The fiddler uses what he thinks of as his art as a defense against a rejecting world, a defense which works in well developed patterns and methods of pathological restriction and denial. Through the fiddler's developmental history, the reader finds out why he uses his violin to keep the world at bay. The dramatist, by comparison, is open and receptive to the world and to his material (in this case the old fiddler); he pursues it, he experiences it, and he lets it speak to him. However, the narrator does not accomplish what he sets out to do with his story—namely to show his entire creative process. Contrary to what he led us believe at the outset, the narrator does not shape the fiddler into a dramatic character nor his tale into a drama. He merely completes his report on external events and then falls silent. There is a break in the story between what the first half promises and what the second half fulfills.

The break in the story reflects Grillparzer's difficulty with his narrative, the first part of which he composed in 1831 while he completed the rest in 1842.[1] He began writing the novella when he experienced agonizing troubles with his playwriting. The novella is probably an attempt to resolve his own creative dilemma by objectifying it. The 1831 attempt seems to have been largely unsuccessful. Grillparzer had completed some ten plays during the preceding fifteen years (1816-1830). At the beginning of his career, he composed easily; after the first few plays, he encountered difficulties with writing. These difficulties were an ever increasing fear of the public's reaction to his work, paralyzing self-criticism, lack of concentration, and inability to feel empathy for his characters. During the next ten years, at the time when he was at work on the fiddler story, though repeatedly resuming dramatic work, he finished only one play, **Weh dem, der Lügt** (1837). He withdrew from theatrical production after the poor reception which this play got when it was performed in 1838. When he resumed the fiddler story in 1842, he wrote only for himself and with long intervening periods of artistic sterility. The completion of the story in 1842, while not resolving his creative dilemma, may have relieved his anxiety about it, so that during the ten years following he could finish, though not for production, the three plays of his maturity, **Libussa** (1843-45) and **Ein Bruderzwist in Habsburg** (1848), dramas of vast historical-philosophical scope and the less ambitious **Die Jüdin von Toledo** (1851). During the last twenty years of his life, he ceased writing altogether.

The fiddler's pathology would have less interest to the student of the *Künstlernovelle* and the creative process, aside from its value as a case history of schizophrenic withdrawal, oedipal problems, and sibling rivalry, if Grillparzer did not implicitly contrast the fiddler and his use of art with the artist as he appears in the work of the German Romantics, the wandering minstrel in the work of a Novalis, an Eichendorff, or an E. T. A. Hoffmann. The artist of the Romantics is childlike, devoted to art, unworldly, a seeker of the divine through beauty and love. An enthusiast for his ideals, he is estranged or even alienated from his contemporaries. The fiddler is all of this and with a vengeance! The narrator, on the other hand, has few of the characteristics of the Romantic artist of this convention. Yet he is, for Grillparzer, the genuine artist. The reasons for the fiddler's use of his art, the contrast he forms to the narrator, the possible causes for the narrator's failure with his dramatic task, the interrelationship of the two figures with each other, with their author, and with his difficulties in creating is the concern of my essay. A brief summary of the plot of the **Poor Fiddler** will furnish the background for further discussion.

THE PLOT

The story contains many Romantic elements (the outcast artist, his nightly violin playing, his unfulfilled love, *etc.*). In order to distort the Romantic ideal, Grillparzer projects these elements into a realistic lower class setting and reinforces the turn of events by his irony. Among artist novellas, *The Poor Fiddler* is so arresting because its protagonist, Jacob, possesses the singular devotion and enthusiasm for his art of the Romantic artist, the discipline in its exercise of the classic artist but so little 'talent' that he learns to play only a single simple and ordinary melody and for the rest produces screeches which cause him "sensuous enjoyment" (49)[2] but are a torment to everyone else's ears. The narrator, a dramatist and the story's other main character, finds him, the seventy year old beggar musician, at a popular festival and fair in a Viennese suburb. The narrator's curiosity is aroused by the discrepancy between the old man's devotion to his musical scores and the execrable shrieks produced by his instrument. The narrator follows him through the fair and finally accosts him to find out more about him. One third of the novella is occupied with the portrayal of the folk festival, the narrator and his relationship to his art and to the old fiddler.

A few days later at the fiddler's quarters, the old man tells the dramatist his story. He is the middle son of a former government clerk, he has had a good education but, overshadowed by more brilliant brothers and pushed too hard by an ambitious father, he never amounted to more than an unpaid copy clerk tolerated in a government office. Living abandoned in a backroom of his father's house, he heard one day a neighboring grocer's daughter, Barbara, sing a popular tune. The song moved him to such an extent that he discovered music and made violin playing the passion of his life. He visits the grocery shop to obtain the score for the song from Barbara. Because he is seen during the visit by a servant of his father's, he is expelled from home in disgrace. The father dies shortly thereafter and thus, unlike his Biblical namesake, Jacob never obtains his father's blessing. After his father's death, the grocer and his daughter befriend him, the grocer in hopes of getting a share of the fiddler's inheritance, the daughter in the knowledge that he needs care. The fiddler visits them every day, awkwardly helps in the store, and attaches himself to Barbara. When Jacob finds himself swindled out of his inheritance by a clerk of his father's, he loses their friendship, and Barbara marries a butcher. Resigning himself to its loss and to that of Barbara, he takes up a career as a street musician. After a few years, Barbara having returned to town with her butcher husband, Jacob is once again befriended by her and gives violin lessons to her now teenage son.

The story told, the fiddler resumes his fiddling and the dramatist leaves his quarters in boredom. Some eight or nine months later, a flood devastates the suburbs. When the flood has receded, the dramatist visits the fiddler again to bring him help. He finds that the old man has died of a fever contracted during the flood. He comes just in time to observe Barbara and her family bury their friend. The dramatist's curiosity now fastens on Barbara and he visits her a few days later on the pretense of wanting to buy the old man's violin. Barbara refuses to sell it and, as the dramatist leaves her and her family, she turns to him a face bathed in tears.

While the dramatist describes himself as a successful artist who is used to the applause of a large public, the beggar violinist, by contrast, is jeered and rejected by his audiences. Yet both men are devoted to the exercise of their respective arts. Hence the question arises: What is the difference between them?[3] Let us first consider the fiddler. The mere plot of the tale poses a number of questions about him. What kind of a man is he? How old was he when he discovered music? Is his encounter with Barbara a love story? Why does he devote his life to art? Is he merely a man without a musical ear? Why does the butcher's wife weep so heartbrokenly over his death? What is the meaning of his death?

Unlike most of his critics who have found the fiddler a man "with inner richness," with "the happiness of a heart free of guilt," Grillparzer was aware of the pathology of his poor fiddler. Commenting on the difference between novel and novella during the time he was at work on the *Poor Fiddler,* he wrote in his diary: "The novel deals with psychology; the novella with psychopathology."[4] My analysis of the fiddler will stress the pathological aspects because they have been ignored in the past. Grillparzer's observation of the fiddler's psychopathology depends on his acquaintance with and "immediate observation" of an old fiddler, on his own family history, and on self-observation. Hence the developmental history and the characterization of a schizophrenic person with many autistic characteristics are much in advance of the psychological theory of his age.[5]

MECHANISMS OF DENIAL

When he is first asked by the narrator, about his story, the fiddler denies having one. He portrays himself as living outside of time, in a continuum in which "Today is the same as yesterday, and tomorrow as today. As for the day after tomorrow and beyond, who can tell" (51). His days are ordered in a mechanical, fixedly pedantic way. The first three hours of the day are devoted to "practice, the middle to earning a living, and the evening to myself and God" (43). The fiddler never deviates from this routine even when it might be advantageous to him, being anxious that he might slide "into undisciplined ways, into sheer anarchy" (4). His living space is as well ordered as are his temporal routines. He shares his room with two journeymen, but neatly divides off his part from theirs by a line of chalk which he never crosses. He keeps his part of the room in immaculate order. Spatial limitation, order, and time routines protect him from outer as well as inner stimuli and help him to ward off the social world. He defends his isolation and denial of reality by rationalizations. Thus, for instance, he does not speak up to his roommates when they disturb his sleep at night. He rationalizes that it is good to be awakened when one can go back to sleep again. His denial of reality appears most obvious in his violin playing. He is so "utterly absorbed in his task" (36) that the narrator has great difficulty in "recalling him to his whereabouts" (5). When he stops fiddling, he acts as if "recovering his wits after a long trance" (37). When interrupted in his playing, he is so startled that "his knees trembled, he could hardly keep hold of the violin" (50).

Lest the reader think (as many past readers in fact did) that the fiddler's absorption, his disinterest in monetary reward, his present ascetic and seemingly self-disciplined life-style are due to his devotion to art, Grillparzer provides in his past life history further background on his sensory deprivation and denial of reality. Before taking up his musical career at over forty, the fiddler spent almost thirty years as a copy clerk in similar mechanical routines with a similar deprivation of human contact. At his father's house (and for some time at a boardinghouse), he lived in a backroom, attended by none, spoken to by none, his meals being paid for and taken at a chop-house. During the day, he worked and copied, with great pains and little success, letters and documents that were incomprehensible to him. Required to return home half an hour after office hours, he spent the evening sitting idly in his dark room "because of my eyes which were weak even then" (58). His eyesight, however, like his intelligence, is selectively poor. For instance, he sees quite well when observing Barbara or when playing his scores; he understands Latin well and uses its phrases appropriately. Not being paid for his work, he has no money to buy cakes and fruit from the tradespeople as the other clerks do. He rationalizes this deprivation by saying that he does not regard food and drink "as a source of pleasure and enjoyment" (63). Thus from the time he can remember, he was deprived of sensory experience, be it by touch, sound, sight, or taste. Over the years, he learned to deprive himself by not seeing, hearing, touching, and tasting and by shutting out the external world.

The denial of the external world is accompanied by the denial and the repression of his inner world. He neither understands nor feels his deprived condition. As copy clerk and later as a fiddler, his temper is perfectly even. He sits alone in a dark room and is "neither sad nor happy" (58); scorned and laughed at by office mates and later by audiences at fairs and on streets, he keeps his "undisturbed cheerfulness" (37). Having learned to repress feeling, whether it be anger, hostility or grief, he substitutes cheerful, self-satisfied, and ornately phrased rationalizations for feelings. Thus, after telling of his father's obviously cruel, dictatorial and unjust treatment of him, he comments "my father was not a wicked man, only violent and ambitious" (55), "he meant well" (77).

The Function of the Fiddler's Pathological Art

From the beginning of the narrator's report, we know that the fiddler's music sounds dreadful. Yet he is not tone-deaf; in fact, he thrills to sound. Moreover, the narrator and the fiddler make sure that the reader knows of the utter seriousness with which Jacob approaches music. He not only practices passages from scores of Bach, Mozart, and other masters "fantastically difficult and thick with fast runs and double stoppings" (42), every day for three hours in the morning, but he also plays improvisations for his own pleasure every night. In addition, his street performance during the day consists of pieces whose score he has practiced. Despite the many daily practice hours over some twenty years, the fiddler's skill on the violin is minimal and the narrator draws our attention to "his clumsy fingers" (42). Yet there is more to the fiddler's poor performance than a lack of motor skill. Listening to the old man practicing passages, the narrator perceives the "method in his madness" (49). The narrator's understanding of this method is worth quoting in full:

> In his conception, there was only one distinction that mattered: consonance and dissonance. The former pleased, indeed delighted him, while the latter, even if harmonically justified, he avoided so far as possible. Therefore, instead of bringing out the sense and rhythm of a piece, he emphasized and prolonged the notes and intervals which struck mellifluously upon the ear, and did not hesitate to repeat them arbitrarily, his face often expressing utter ecstasy as he did so. As he skipped over the dissonances as quickly as possible and, too conscientious to miss a single note, slowed down disproportionally in passages which were too difficult for him, it is easy to form an idea of the confusion which emerged from it all.
>
> (49-50)

The fiddler is as intolerant of disharmony in music as he is of "bad" feelings in his life. If at all possible, he represses both. He relishes harmony and uses repetition of harmonies to drown out the disharmonies of the score which he is too conscientious and obsessive to omit. Two tendencies therefore dominate his music as much as they do his life: on the one hand he represses disharmony (in feeling and sound) and, on the other, he obsessively adheres to established routine (time schedule or score or fixed environment).

He further emphasizes subjective musical routine by substituting his own invariant motions for the time values of the musical score. He attempts to keep time "not only by lifting and dropping his foot, but by a corresponding movement of his whole bowed body" (36). The motion, however, is not related to keeping time. Hence, his rhythm is reminiscent of autistic rhythmical rocking, his hand and finger motions in front of his face of autistic twiddling, the repetitiveness of each having the purpose to ward off stimuli from and contact with the external world. Even the fiddler himself is aware of this function of his playing because he says, "close to my ears the sounds I made with my fingers—they came to dwell with me in my loneliness" (59).

The fiddler has shut himself off from the external world. But that does not mean that he has developed an internal world of feeling and thought. He guards against sound becoming, let alone expressing, emotions, thoughts, symbols or ideas. In describing his reaction to music, he is aware only of sensation. When he struck the first sound on a violin, he felt "as if God's finger had touched me. The sound penetrated my inmost being and thence issued forth again" (59). It is interesting that in this synaesthesia, he transforms hearing into touch. Moreover, as the sound touches him, he becomes the instrument. A similar merger of sensations and of object, sensation and perceiver occurs when he hears Barbara sing ("the song no longer seemed to come from outside but from right inside me," p. 83). The intensity of sensation causes a loss of self but it may also lead to an expansion of self which is equivalent to a loss of self ("the air around me was as if pregnant with ecstacy" 59). The fiddler experiences sound on an infantile, almost uterine level, a level so regressed that a self is not yet differentiated from the mother or the environment. It is probably not chance that at this point, the words "pregnant" ("geschwängert") and "ecstacy" ("Trunkenheit"), appear. We encounter here a regression to a primary process so basic that sensation is not yet clearly differentiated into hearing and touch. We further encounter the protoemotions pleasure and unpleasure as bound to sensation.[6] The fiddler plays with "voluptuous insistence," with "sensual enjoyment" (46). Since the fiddler has eliminated a distinct self while playing, a transformation of sensation and protoemotion into even simple emotions, images and primitive symbolizations has become impossible. Hence the primary process remains without mediation into expressive patterns. His reaction to sound is purely instinctual. By producing sounds, he satisfies the other instincts we see him deprived of—namely hunger and touch, that is the self-preserving and the social instincts. Thus the fiddler guards against the development of an inner world by the elimination of the self through sensation, and sensation in turn helps him to avoid a self and an inner world. It becomes clear now why he needs, for such an experience of regression through his violin playing, a safe, predictable, stimulus-free, routinized, autistically closed off environment. This environment makes possible the instinctual gratification. If we translate the fiddler's extreme case, his pathological use of art, into more general terms, we might say that Grillparzer shows that art enjoyed as pure sensation has a defensive function and is regressive and conservative.

The fiddler's attachment to sensation, however, is not satisfied by any sensation. He is selective and his selection is determined by his early history. He takes up music because of his encounter with Barbara who, as we shall see shortly, represents his mother. He takes up the violin because this was the instrument the rudiments of which he was taught as a child. He plays the scores of the famous old masters because they represent the upper class among whom he grew up and among whom, even as a beggar musician, he counts himself. How much early history determines the direction of his pleasure appears from his improvisations, which the narrator describes in some detail. His improvisations consist of very elementary scale relationships of the kind which the beginning violin student learns ("the single note . . . and interval . . . a fourth . . . the two notes now successively, now as a chord, haltingly linked . . . by the intervening scale . . . the third . . . a fifth . . . always the same interval, the same notes"

46). Presumably improvisation is a measure of an artist's creativity. While a score imposes a high degree of secondary process functioning on the performing artist, improvisation because it permits the exploration of new, individual and personally felt musical relationships, presumably allows him to get in touch with his primary process. However, the primitive scale relationships which the fiddler plays in improvising are not of the primary process but rather of the secondary process as it is taught to the beginner.[7]

The fiddler's improvising is directed to self-stimulation through sound just as is his playing of scores. The choice of the sound structure (score or scale) is irrelevant to the stimulation. Since stimulation has to follow some pattern, it follows the pattern of his earlier exposure to music. The fiddler uses the secondary process structures of score and of scale in the same way an autistic child uses a fantasized machine of which he imagines himself to have become a part. Scale and score for the fiddler are part of the protective environment in which his primary process takes place. Their individual sound components produce pleasurable stimulation. By producing the stimulation, the fiddler achieves a stable state of predictable pleasurable sensory input. This stable state blocks out external as well as internal reality.

The defensive system which dominates his music informs his entire life. The fiddler not only denies reality but, selectively and with skill, he makes it serve his purposes. Readers have found him an honest and simple man but they have rarely observed that these traits are supplemented by a considerable unconscious cunning. He sees and understands, forgets and remembers, just what serves his purposes. The fiddler not only defeats his father's ambitions for him but he also foils Barbara's plans for a common future. He remains unencumbered in the pursuit of his regressed existence.[8] Even though a beggar, he earns enough of an income to maintain himself. We can see his acuity of observation and aptness in social manipulation in his dealings with the narrator. He sizes up the dramatist stranger quite correctly and manages, by a combination of surmise and flattery ("a kind gentleman and a music lover" 40), by philosophical comment and learned allusion, by humility and ingratiating politeness ("My abode will be honored to receive such a distinguished visitor" 41), to receive a continuous supply of money. His self-satisfied rationalizations about his art serve a similar purpose. By maintaining that his listeners' "taste and feeling . . . is confused and misled" (43), that it is spoilt by "a few popular hits, . . . lewd song" (42) of the other street musicians, he negates their jeering and laughter and establishes himself, his values, and his way of life, as superior and hence inviolable.

Everything in the fiddler's life and music fits into a very tight and cunningly well-knit magic cycle of pathology. *The fiddler's art is not his fiddling but the artistry of his defenses against inner and outer reality.* How necessary and how airtight this defensive system has become appears from the fact that the fiddler does not relinquish it even in his mortal illness. He goes on fiddling and hearing sound even as he dies. In his regresse sterility and with his pathological artistry, the fiddler anticipates Kafka's hunger artist and negates the romantic portrait of the artist.

DEVELOPMENT AND OEDIPAL SITUATION

The fiddler must have had a profound need for defenses to have built them as tight as he has. In the fiddler's account of his childhood, Grillparzer provides the developmental reasons for the defensive structure. But since the story is told by the fiddler, the builder of artful defenses, we must attempt to penetrate the surface screen of his chronological account to find the real story. His is the account of singular parental and fraternal rejection, a rejection which appears behind the surface of distortion and rationalization of his story, a rejection against which the old fiddler must protect himself even as he tells his story, and a rejection from which the child fled into regressed withdrawal. Jacob is the middle son of an ambitious, very influential but low-ranking government official. He cannot satisfy, in competition with his brothers, any of his father's demands upon him. The enormity of the father's demands appears precisely in the discrepancy between the smallness of a task at which Jacob fails and the momentous consequences of the failure. For instance: young Jacob is removed from school because he cannot remember one word in a Latin poem during a public examination. But his punishment by removal from school is not enough. After this one failure, the father does not allow his son to enter a trade or an apprenticeship, or even to take a paid position as a clerk (it is his father who votes against his receiving a salary at the office). Moreover the father crushes any, even the most innocuous display of initiative by massive rejection, thus acting as if initiative were rebellion. Because of a visit at the grocery store, for instance, during which he is observed by a servant, Jacob is permanently evicted from his father's house.

Despite occasional resistance to and unconscious resentment of his father's severity (understandably Jacob feels the guilt of a murderer at his father's death from a stroke), Jacob internalizes his father's demands and obeys them to the end of his days. For instance, he makes restitution for omitting the single word of the Horace poem by never again omitting what is written, thus playing every note of his scores. Or, Jacob returns to his room before nightfall, because his father had once insisted upon it. He may give his own reason for doing so—his life needs order and he likes to improvise at night—but he remains obedient. From his story, we do not know when his ego was crushed so permanently that he can only live his father's commands; we only know that it was.

A child's ego cannot be so thoroughly annihilated by one parent acting alone. What about the role of the fiddler's mother? Jacob's mother is almost entirely omitted from his childhood story. He mentions her once in passing ("—my mother was long dead—," p. 58) when speaking of the meal arrangements at his father's house. Having repressed the memory of his own mother, Jacob projects her onto Barbara and relates to her as a pre-oedipal child does to his mother. This appears in his perception of her. Once when she hits out at him, she seems enormous to him and there is "something gigantic about" her hand (84). To appreciate the degree of regression in his "courtship" relationship to Barbara, let us look closely at the visit to the grocery shop which has such fatal consequences for him. Let us remember that Jacob at that time was in his forties and Barbara about twenty. His timidity is such that he dare not approach the grocery shop for several weeks; "whenever" he came "near the grocer's shop", he "was overcome by such violent trembling that willy-nilly," he "had to turn back" (69). When he finally desperately approaches the shop one evening, peeped through a crack in the door, trembling, saw Barbara in the company of "a rough, sturdy man" (70), he was "grabbed rudely from behind and dragged forward . . . inside" (71) to be punished. The symbolism Grillparzer employs points to the pre-oedipal, even the oral period, to the context of the child's approaches to the forbidden mother, a prohibition he misunderstands (food and grocery shop, Barbara as a seller of cakes Jacob cannot buy, Jacob caught peeping, Jacob trembling at seeing, Jacob having the "painful sense of hiding something, of being in the wrong," p. 75, when visiting the grocery shop).

Jacob experiences his relationship to Barbara as an offense against his father, an offense for which Barbara's father is just about to punish him when Barbara rescues him. His own father, however, then punishes him by banishment from the family (p. 75). Jacob feels that in going to see Barbara, he has overstepped a serious paternal injunction, an injunction whose meaning he does not understand but one which he keeps to. And more than a breaking of the class barrier is at stake. He does not return to Barbara after his removal from his family even though he could hardly provoke further reprisals from his father. Figuratively, he keeps to his father's injunction to the end of his days and does not marry Barbara even when his father is dead. In his account, the fiddler strictly separates the story of his relationship to his father from that of his relationship to Barbara. If we superimpose the two relationships on each other, we understand Jacob's oedipal (or rather preoedipal) situation between father and mother. To sum up the oedipal conflict reflected in the fiddler's narration: the father interprets any action of his son as disobedience against him especially when this action has any reference to the mother. The child interprets the father's reaction to his actions as rejection and feels it so severely that it crushes him and forces him into regression and into withdrawal from human contact.

Barbara, the recipient of the mother-projection, acquiesces in her role in Jacob's life unwillingly, because she is, after all, a healthy child of the people (it is apt that she marries a butcher) and not his mother. She quickly realizes his inadequacy as a person; she objects to his "obsequiousness to customers" (82) which hides his incompetence in handling cash; she understands that he would "hardly be capable of looking after" his own affairs (87), and that he is a child whom she would need to shelter. When she offers to buy a milliner's shop with his father's inheritance and thus to provide for him, she is willing to settle for a mother's role in exchange for financial security and personal independence. Hence when Jacob loses his money, she leaves him. Being a realist, she sees that he is responsible for the loss of his inheritance ("It's your own fault" 96), that the loss reflects his unwillingness to stay with her, and that she cannot control him sufficiently to take care of him and herself. And she is not self-sacrificing enough to stay with him. Yet she never entirely loses her motherly affection for him, nor a sense of guilt for having forsaken him. The naming her own son Jacob hence is a propitiatory gesture. Moreover, she, on her return to town, gets in touch with Jacob and through the "violin lessons to their boy" (100) resumes her provident, motherly role towards him. When, after having taken care of the funeral, she refuses the narrator Jacob's violin, saying the "fiddle belongs to our Jacob" (108), her son and the fiddler have merged in her mind. Her fiercely protective gesture of the violin ("as though she were afraid of robbery" 108) is a compensation for having forsaken Jacob years earlier. Her surprising outburst of feeling, her stream of tears, is grief for a dead child, her tears are tears of regret and of old guilt.

What matters in all this to the fiddler is, however, that he is rejected by Barbara. Her rejection reflects and repeats maternal rejection. Maternal rejection complements the father's rejection. Hence the child retreats from any contact. His fear of his father (it is both fear of losing his father's protection and fear of castration, cf. his horror at "bloodshed and butchery as a calling," p. 56) first led him to fear any but the most infantile contact with his mother. Having internalized the father's injunctions too well, he cannot approach women in any other than infantile ways. Seeing Barbara (and all other women for that matter, cf. his approach to his landlady in asking for fruit, p. 50) as a mother, he cannot possibly marry her and thus "grow and multiply" as his name Jacob ironically promises. Therefore he remains at the pre-oedipal level of psychosocial development in his relationship to men and to women just as he remains at the level of his first violin lesson as an artist.

Grillparzer gives the name Jacob to the fiddler to draw attention to the importance of the parental blessing in the child's development. The biblical Jacob obtains, with his mother's help, the blessing of his father. The meaning of the paternal blessing appears to be that, by his blessing, the father encourages his son to grow. The son feels that, even if he transcends his father, he will neither lose his father's love nor be punished by him. Rather than a blessing, Grillparzer's Jacob receives a curse from his father, being called "ce gueux" (55) by him when he fails his examination. After having pronounced the curse, the father never again speaks to him and thus it becomes the prophecy which determines the course of his life. Yet Jacob waits for his blessing as long as his father is alive. This seems to be the meaning of his continued obedience to his father. Even thirty years after the father's death, he regrets that he did not attend him in his last illness because, as he says in his usually defensive manner, he could not obtain his pardon and "thank him for the indulgence" he supposedly received (p. 77—note that the German uses *Gnade*-grace for indulgence). In retrospect, therefore, Jacob almost succeeds in manufacturing a father's blessing for himself. But at the time of his father's death, he collapses "on the floor, unconscious" (77), realizing that he has lost his father's indulgence forever.

The mother figure compensates Jacob for the loss of the father's love, encouragement, and care. It is after all Barbara who gives Jacob the only gift of his life, her song, that is: his music and means of self-gratification. While the father's curse condemns him to poverty in literally everything, the mother's gift makes the poverty tolerable. In fact, once the fiddler has received the gift, there is no hope that he will relinquish the pleasure it offers him. Unwillingly and unknowingly, Barbara thus contributes to the stunting of his growth. Our interpretation is confirmed by the blessing Barbara gives Jacob as she leaves him: "Your linen is in order now. See that none of it disappears. You'll be having a hard time. She raised her hand, made the sign of the cross in the air, and cried: 'God be with you, Jacob!—For ever and ever, Amen'" (97). If we consider that a blessing is designed to further the child's productivity and fruitfulness, then Barbara's blessing discourages, admonishes him to keep to the parental order, and thus reenforces the father's injunction against growth and maturity. The mother thus becomes the collaborator in the father's oppression of the child. Kafka's letter to his father comes to mind.

THE NARRATOR'S CREATIVE PROCESS

The fiddler's story by itself would be interesting pathology, a fascinating account of what art is not and what stunts artistic development. In the counter story of the narrator, Grillparzer offers us insight into the artist's ability to delve into life, to derive substance from it, and to communicate this experience effectively. The narrator, unlike Jacob, does not live outside of time. He begins with a general evocation of the Viennese folk festival which forms the background of his meeting with the fiddler He feels the festival to be a flood of life. He explains that it is the matrix from which he, as an artist, derives his inspiration. Next, he turns to the near past and tells of his meeting the fiddler two years ago. Once he has firmly situated the reader in that time, he has the fiddler insert his story, in which time sequences are rather vague. In the somewhat too rapid concluding pages, treating of the flood of death which destroys the fiddler's life, the narrator returns to the near past of two years ago. By this ordering of time, the narrator shows himself to be in control of his material. Yet he is not obsessively controlling but rather open to the flow of life. He sees his task as an author to experience "the collective biographies of men unknown to fame" (33). He learns as a dramatist from the non-verbal communication of the common people, from their faces, from their gait, from their behavior toward each other, from their every "unpremeditated remark" (33). He feels empathy with the people because "no one can understand the lives of the famous unless he has entered into the feelings of the humble" (33). The people and the folk festival are for the dramatist what sound is for the fiddler, namely the "raw material" of his art. As the fiddler thrills to sound, the dramatist thrills to the people. There is, however, a world of difference between the fiddler and the dramatist in their respective relationships to their medium.

The most important difference between the two appears in the degree of each one's tolerance of and openness to disharmony, disorder and multiplicity. In the tumultuous flood of the festival, described at considerable length, the narrator, moved along by the crowd ("I had abandoned myself to the drifting throng" 34). In the identical situation, the old fiddler works "his way through the crowd coming to the fair, against the stream" (37); he cannot tolerate the drifting along in a stream of people. While being carried along by the crowd, however, the narrator scans the scene around him. The reader follows his glance as it gradually focuses on the old fiddler. By the wayside, he observes "a woman harpist, . . . an old cripple . . . a misshapen boy" (35-36) before his attention comes to rest on the old man. It is precisely the discrepancy between the old man's appearance and the sound of his music, a discrepancy that rapidly reveals a whole host of disharmonies, which catches the narrator's attention. The narrator, therefore, as he develops his narrative has us observe his creative process, his response to his medium, his selection of a particular part of the medium (the fiddler), and his criterion in this selection, namely the conflict in the fiddler, a conflict which he hopes to use as the basis for a play.

Once the dramatist has identified his subject and opened himself to its individual features in a lengthy paragraph which describes the fiddler in detail, he turns his attention to himself. In a short paragraph, he reports his feelings and thoughts and evaluates his impression of the fiddler. ("So the man had enjoyed a fairly good education, . . . now was a begging, itinerant musician! I was eager for an explanation" 37-38.) But because his medium is not static but has a will of his own, the dramatist, when his attention is centered on himself, loses the old fiddler as he moves away into the crowd. The narrator finds him again after a long search, quite significantly when he has almost given up searching. Moreover, he finds the fiddler in a place he has least expected him to be.

At the second encounter, the narrator moves in on his subject at once to hold it fast. He addresses the fiddler and expresses sympathy for him; he gives him money and openly states his curiosity, asking the fiddler for an explanation of the puzzling behaviour he has observed ("you go away just when . . . you could easily earn more" 39-40). The old man's explanation increases his curiosity so that he asks for permission to visit him to get to know him better. The narrator's interest in the fiddler is the interest of

the artist for his subject matter. He is friendly because he needs the cooperation of his subject. He is direct ("I am curious to know your story" 51). He does not pretend that he wants more than material for his art.

On the evening of the day he has met him, the narrator checks on the old fiddler by returning home past his house. He goes by the house in the darkness, hears the scraping of the fiddler's "improvisations" and observes the neighbor's reaction to the disturbing "music." The nature of the improvisations and the reactions of the neighbors together with his previous impressions of the old man confirm the narrator in his hunch that he has found a valuable subject. Thus the narrator checks out his subject from many sides, in several different situations, and at several different times. The entire introduction of the novella is a dissertation on the dramatist's relationship to his material. This relationship contrasts sharply with the fiddler's relationship to sound. The dramatist is capable of giving himself over to impressions and to the flow of people. From this flow, the matrix of his creativity, he selects a character who seems promising. The narrator finds the promise, the attraction, in the character's conflicts, disharmonies, and discrepancies. Once he has found a promising subject, the dramatist examines it for further detail of flawing and promise just as a sculptor might tap a block of granite for its suitability for his special purpose, that is: whether the figure he has in mind fits the grain, the flawing, the contours, the strengths and weaknesses of a particular piece of stone. Unlike the fiddler, the narrator-dramatist uses his own emotional reactions to guide him in the further exploration of his theme and subject matter. He not only tolerates the conflict he feels in the fiddler's appearance and actions, but the discovery of every new conflict stimulates him to explore further.[9]

THE NARRATOR'S PROBLEM WITH DEATH AND REJECTION

When the narrator resumes his story after the fiddler's account, we seem to encounter a very different person, who reports in a markedly different style. The narrator of the introduction to the novella interacts with his environment and with the fiddler as he observes. He also registers his own reactions, his feelings and thoughts. His attitude is reflective and analytical. His structure is complete, lengthy, subordinating. He displays his learning and his wit. He takes his time about furthering the plot. The narrator of the final pages completes the mere plot of the story in three pages. He restricts himself almost exclusively to a reportage of external detail. He does not display learning or wit. His interaction with the environment and with persons is sharply curtailed. For instance, when he approaches Barbara before the funeral, he does not get a chance to talk to her. When she answers his question the Sunday after, she turns away from him. Even more importantly, the narrator never expresses his feelings and thoughts about events. When he depicts the fiddler's funeral, he even moves from the perspective of the participant observer which he has maintained all through the story to the perspective of the all-knowing author. Thus, though walking behind the butcher's family in the funeral procession, he sees that the "husband was continually moving his lips as though in prayer" (106). The reader gets a feeling of distance from this perspective. As the narrative moves on, the sentences become very short and pithy. They report merely the external, visible details. "Thus the procession came to the cemetery. The grave was open. The children threw in the first handful of earth. Still standing, the husband did likewise. The wife knelt down and held her book close to her eyes. . . . The mourners separated and dispersed. The old fiddler was buried."

This style and manner of reporting is very effective. The reader no longer witnesses the events through the medium of the narrator's consciousness but is exposed to them directly. The narrator has lost his explanatory stance of the beginning of the story, he has been silenced, his mastery over the subject matter appears to have been shattered. The material appears to have taken on a life (or death) of its own. The nature of the flood, which leads to the fiddler's death, the curious perspective on the funeral procession, the cracked violin on the wall, the prayer of the butcher's family, Barbara's silent stream of tears, all these and many more symbols or symbolic events remain unaccounted for by him. We should remember that the dramatist earlier in the narrative promised to be on the lookout for dramatic characters (Juliets, Medeas, Didos, Achilles, and Agamemnons). The narrator succeeded in raising expectations in the reader, expectations of his mastery over a subject matter. At the end of the story, having been refused his request for the fiddler's violin and being turned out of Barbara's house by the solid front of the family against his advances, he is left with nothing. He has neither a human relationship (which finally even the fiddler did have) nor does he have the symbol of even a perverted art (the cracked violin which the butcher family keeps). Moreover, he has not yet used his poetic material to create a piece of dramatic literature (he has been on a journey instead).

The fiddler's story revolves around catastrophic rejection and defense against and avoidance of rejection. The narrator seems to be free of both. Yet, if we look at the story's ending, the situations of the two seem to be reversed. Able to overcome his regression during the flood (the proverbial emergency during which, temporarily, even the most regressed schizophrenic acts appropriately), the fiddler has saved children and his landlord's savings account (Grillparzer's irony is alive even here). As a consequence, the community accepts him and attends his funeral. Barbara and her family even grant him a kind of sanctification as they keep his violin on their wall "in symmetry with a crucifix" (108). The narrator, on the other hand, is rejected by Barbara and her family.

The fiddler's death, however, does not solve the problem of his rejection. After all, the fiddler is dead and cannot experience his acceptance. Moreover, he paid for the acceptance with his death. And personal death is feared because it is the ultimate rejection man can experience. Let us remember that the fiddler made himself dead psychically in order to survive a paternal and maternal rejection so severe that it would have killed him physically. If we take the flood as a consequence of which he dies to be the maternal element, it is maternal rejection which kills him in the end. The narrator may be rejected by the fiddler once he resumes his violin playing after telling his story. He may be rejected by Barbara and her family. But he, at least, remains alive. Though he does not succeed in his transformation of the fiddler into a dramatic character, (we might remember that the fiddler is part of the narrator's creative matrix) he, at least, survives his encounter with the maternal element.

All through the last pages of the story, something threatens the narrator. As he goes to see the fiddler after the flood, death lurks all about him The suburb is devastated The building he enters by chance on his way contains, pressed against the window screens, the dead bodies of those who desperately struggled for their lives against the flood. As he approaches the fiddler's house, the narrator assures himself that the fiddler has not died in the flood but he is worried. When he finds him dead, he seems shocked. He acts as if he has not suspected the violence and anger of the maternal element.

Because Barbara (in his and our minds) has come to represent the maternal element, it is hardly surprising that she rejects his wish to talk to her. But what, after all, has he come to find out from her when he goes to see her the Sunday after the funeral? He says that his request to Barbara to be sold the violin is only a pretext (p. 106). A pretext for what? Earlier in the story, he needed no pretext to gratify his artistic curiosity. Has he come to find out why the maternal element is deadly? Or does he want Barbara to betray the dead fiddler by selling his violin? The story's symbolism and the dramatic characters mentioned earlier (Juliet, Dido, Medea) provide an answer to the narrator's unanswered question to and about Barbara. The reader understands her grief, her loyalty, and her remorse from her silence, her tears, and her refusal to sell the violin. Barbara represents the love of Juliet who laments dead Romeo, the loyalty of Dido who mourns faithless Aeneas, and the violent anger of Medea who weeps over the children she killed. In the figure of the woman and mother, love and deadly anger are inextricably mixed. For the narrator as much as for the fiddler, the encounter with woman is threatening. At the end of the story, the narrator does not indicate what he understands about Barbara and about women. His silence seems like flight. He has found a drama he cannot master.

Inasmuch as his heroes either founder in the midst of their creative task or are incapacitated by rejection or finally are killed by the maternal element, it is small wonder that the story did little to relieve Grillparzer of his writer's cramp. And if to die a failure or to fail with his work was man's lot and if art did not help but rather endangered man, then why should he, Grillparzer, write plays!

The Interrelationship between Rejection, Denial, and Regression in Grillparzer's life

Throughout his career as a dramatist, Grillparzer was exceedingly sensitive to criticism of his work. Like any successful author (and he was successful), he had his share of trouble with critics and with censorship (this was the Metternich area and even a conservative writer could be subject to the seasonal paranoia).[10] The inability to cope with adverse public reaction and criticism led him in 1838, after the unsuccessful performance of *Weh dem, der lügt,* to withdraw from the theater for good—that is: to reject the public, which had not altogether appreciated him. For a few more years, his rejection of the public may have given him enough strength to go on writing. Why was Grillparzer so keenly sensitive to criticism? For one thing, Grillparzer intimately identified with his plays; they were himself. To have a play of his performed meant to be exhibited in public. Indeed, Grillparzer, after attending and being mortified at the performance of his first drama (a disguised oedipal drama at that),[11] never again witnessed a performance of a play of his. A negative remark about his poetic products was thus a rejection of himself as a person.[12]

Grillparzer escaped from rejection of all kinds in ways very similar to the fiddler's. Especially during the 1830s, he experienced the same mindless states of regression and denial of reality as the fiddler. Hruschka reports that during these years, Grillparzer used "to play scales on the piano for two hours or more, saying that this rested his mind."[13] In his autobiography (1851) Grillparzer, in looking back on the early thirties, recognizes his own tendency to deal with personal difficulties by denial, by forgetting, and by distracting himself much as the fiddler does. He finds that this tendency harmed him permanently. Because of its insight, the passage is worth quoting in full:

> I am in great confusion about the sequence of events. The reason is that I have, until now, always tried to forget them. Perhaps somewhat hypochondriacally, I felt pressured and hemmed in by everything so that I knew no other help but to cut off the tormenting thoughts and to begin a new train of thought. As a matter of fact that harmed me much in other ways as well. Whatever in my character was stable originally (to express myself in a Kantian manner) was thereby made diffuse, and even my memory, which was excellent in my youth, became weak and unreliable through the continuous breaking off and distraction of thought. I would advise anyone who wants to achieve something, to think through his unpleasant thoughts until he has found a resolution. Nothing is more dangerous than distraction.[14]

By creating the figure of the fiddler, Grillparzer must have hoped to overcome his own sterility as well as his own fear of rejection. But even if he saw criticism of his work as personal rejection, this would not be reason enough for him to react with such an anxiety that it finally silenced him and made him act as if his very life were threatened. Whom did the critics represent? Two facts, one in the fiddler's story and one in Grillparzer's life, supplement each other and give an answer to this question.

In 1831, Grillparzer breaks off *The Poor Fiddler* in the middle of the fiddler's first visit to Barbara and her father. The break occurs when both together criticize his fiddling (the father by calling it scraping, the daughter by her scornful smile, p. 74). Grillparzer thus breaks off his narrative when Barbara and her father (who represents her more aggressive, outrightly rejecting self) reject the fiddler and his music, that is when his character experiences the same problem which plagued him, the author. We might then say that it is the mother's criticism, her rejection, which makes the author stop his writing though it does not make the fiddler stop his fiddling.

The kind of scorn the fiddler experiences with his musical efforts with Barbara, Grillparzer experienced from his mother during his piano lessons as a child. A keen lover of music, his mother was violently critical of his playing, screaming at him and snatching his hands off the keys at every wrong note. Thus piano lessons became a torture to him as violin lessons were a torture to the fiddler. Just as Barbara awakens the fiddler's love of music while rejecting his actual playing, so Grillparzer's mother instilled in him a love of music while violently rejecting his performance and causing him intolerable fear and anxiety. It is not surprising that despite his love of music, which found expression in his improvising on the piano, Grillparzer did not pursue a musical career. When he chose an artist's career, he chose literature, the art which, in his autobiography, he described as the province of his father. Grillparzer's choice of his artistic medium, literature, and the split in the story into narrator-dramatist (father-self) and fiddler-musician (mother-self) thus derives from his early experience with father and mother and each parent's preferred art form.

The depth of Grillparzer's fear of rejection can be estimated from his early relationship to his parents. Grillparzer testifies that he was loved by both. The brilliant first born Franz was his father's favorite. Like the fiddler's father, however, Grillparzer's father was an unsociable, cold, and ambitious man. A respected, busy, yet ultimately not very successful lawyer, the father was unable to demonstrate understanding and love to the child. Nevertheless, young Grillparzer was convinced of his unconditional love. This was not true of his mother. A profoundly disturbed, moody and dissatisfied woman, she preferred her eldest to the other children, but probably was not capable of giving much love. Moreover, what love she could give was conditional on what he could do for her.

The parents were very unhappy and often quarreled. They rejected all of their younger children in various degrees. Grillparzer thus knew vicariously from the treatment of his three brothers what rejection was. Moreover, with parents as rejecting and disturbed as his, he cannot have escaped their rejection entirely. Being the most loved child, he had most to lose and hence must have felt the threat of rejection most painfully. The psychic havoc these parents wrought can be appreciated from their children's lives. Grillparzer himself never married. His second brother was severely mentally ill. His third brother, in his younger days a promising musician, spent his life as a hypochondriacal, dissatisfied, bachelor minor official and in many respects resembled the fiddler. His youngest brother gifted and musical like his brothers, drowned himself at age seventeen. At the father's death, when Grillparzer was eighteen, the mother expected him to take care of her and his brothers. He did so and was for her "son and husband," as he put it. There is no doubt that he was profoundly attached to her. She took care of household matters, but refrained from interfering in his "thoughts, feelings, work, and convictions."[15] After ten years of living with him, she committed suicide. Even during her lifetime, Grillparzer was remarkably silent about her. In his autobiography, he describes her death as due to a heart attack. None of the heroes in his plays have mothers. It seems that at least consciously, he avoided dealing with the son's relationship to his mother. The unconscious preoccupation with this theme, his fears about it, and its relationships to his creativity, dominates *The Poor Fiddler.*

The parental love which the child Grillparzer, unlike his brothers, received must have made the difference between his artistic genius and their failure. The father's and the mother's love and ambition for him must have inspired in the child the wish to excel. However, the need to perform in order to keep the mother's love, must have caused him terrifying anxiety, an anxiety which could easily lead to artistic paralysis. In any case, fear of his mother's rejection and of demands on him was greater than fear of his father's rejection. Hence, he chose an artistic career associated with his father's domain rather than with the music of his mother. Then, when he became exposed to the reaction to his plays of critics and the public, public criticism reactivated in his mind the early parental rejection, the mother's voice probably being louder than the father's. But since early parental rejection and criticism are deeply internalized, the awakening of their voices through public criticism became self-criticism and self-rejection. And self-rejection inspired by these parents could not have been an easy matter to deal with!

In writing *The Poor Fiddler* Grillparzer attempted a confrontation between his internalized mother-self, the fiddler, and his father-self, the narrator.[16] The narrator, who is the healthier part of Grillparzer's self, searches out the weaker, less developed part (the self Grillparzer would have become had he chosen the mother's art, music). The self with the greater ego-capacity (as represented by created mastery of reality, education, success, social standing) seeks the other in order to understand him, to make himself master over him, and to incorporate him or to cast him off. Yet, the mother-self is too regressed to allow assimilation through interaction or through conflict. Though the narrator perceives him as a conflicted subject, the fiddler does not lend himself to dramatic treatment. He is simply too autistic and too pathological. He is not a fit subject for drama. Hence after his first visit, the narrator leaves the fiddler to his fiddling and goes on his way. But the narrator cannot cast off the fiddler. At the end of the

narrative and at the fiddler's death, there appears behind the fiddler's figure the flood, the maternal element, a Barbara grown to mythical proportions, and rejections unto death. And we realize then that the fiddler contained death all along. In his regressed and autistic state, the fiddler was death in life all along.

Thus, from an understanding of Grillparzer's biography, we derive insight into the narrator's dilemma. The narrator experiences material destructiveness through his encounter with the fiddler and withdraws in awe. From Grillparzer's biography and from our understanding of what this story meant to him, we can also appreciate Grillparzer's courage in writing the fiddler's and the narrator's story and in finishing the novella and further plays. Sooner or later, all creative activity put Grillparzer in touch with the deadly core which the narrator discovered in the fiddler and which Grillparzer felt in himself. And because Grillparzer had so little of a blessing from his father, it is not surprising that he finally fell silent as an author.

Notes

1. The manuscript of *The Poor Fiddler* shows how difficult its writing must have been for Grillparzer. The manuscript of the working copy of the first half of the story has many breaks, the author stopping often after only a few lines. The manuscript thus gives the impression of Grillparzer's working against resistance. Halfway through the fiddler's account, the manuscript breaks off. One reason for not completing the story at this time was the state of mind in which Grillparzer found himself as a result of the harsh criticism accorded the first performance of his play *Des Meers und der Liebe Wellen* in Spring, 1831. This increased his self criticism and hence his writing problems.

2. Franz Grillparzer, *The Poor Fiddler,* translated by Alexander and Elizabeth Henderson, Frederick Ungar Publishing Co., New York, 1967. All text references will be to this translation, the page reference following the quotation in parenthesis.

3. Heinz Politzer in *Franz Grillparzer's "Der arme Spielmann,"* J. B. Metzlersche Verlagsbuchhandlung, Stuttgart, 1967 and in *Franz Grillparzer oder das abgründige Biedermeier,* Verlag Fritz Molden, Wien, München, Zürich, 1972, and John M. Ellis in *Narration in the German Novelle: Theory and Interpretation,* Cambridge University Press, Cambridge, 1974, reflect two important critical attitudes to the narrator-fiddler problem. Politzer sees, as I do, the two figures as aspects of the author, and gives an excellent analysis of the fiddler's relationship to his father. He overlooks the severity of the pathology in the portrayal of the fiddler. Furthermore, he does not consider, as I do, the creative process and its failure to be the theme of the novella. Ellis pays more attention to the narrator than do most other critics of the novella. However, he considers the relationship between narrator and fiddler from an ethical perspec-

tive, a point of view which blinds him to the theme of creation. Ellis' account, however, contains the most recent bibliography on the novella and a valuable summing up of the most important recent critical literature in German and English.

4. Grillparzer, *Sämtliche Werke,* II: 4, p. 286. Author's translation. Grillparzer seems to mean that because the novella is a shorter piece of fiction than the novel, the author depends more on the extreme states of the psyche which produce a stronger and more suggestive effect on the reader.

5. None of the fiddler's individual characteristics are obviously pathological in themselves (such as hallucinations would be). It is their interplay and the severity of the regression which constitutes the pathology. As in the second stage of chronic schizophrenia, the fiddler's symptoms seem to have achieved an equilibrium while the more glaring symptoms have disappeared.

6. Cf. Silvano Arieti: *The Intrapsychic Self: Feeling, Cognition and Creativity in Health and Mental Illness,* Basic Books, Inc., Publishers, New York, London, 1967. Arieti's distinctions are particularly helpful, as they make clear on what level the fiddler experiences music, that is sound. When the fiddler says in reference to music that he finds other musicians lacking because "they play Wolfgang Amadeus Mozart and Johann Sebastian Bach, but no one plays God" (60), he associates sound itself, the protoemotion "pleasant sensation," with God. This protoemotion of pleasure in the sensation of sound has, for the fiddler, the force of an instinct, or rather it is clearly a substitution for an instinct.

7. Much has been made of the fiddler's remark that none but himself "plays God" (p. 60), that his interest is in playing as such, in the elements of music itself, "the whole heavenly edifice" (61). The elements the fiddler refers to are, however, rudimentary secondary process structures of scale and basic harmony. He could not tolerate the disharmony inherent in new combinations of sounds which are in fact characteristic of the primary process in music, cf. Anton Ehrenzweig: *The Psychoanalysis of Artistic Vision and Hearing: An Introduction to a Theory of Unconscious Perception,* The Julian Press, Inc., New York, 1953, particularly chapter 5. The reader might also think of the quality of Adrian Leverkühn's music and his creative exploration of, for instance, glissando effects, in Thomas Mann's *Doctor Faustus* (1948).

8. Politzer gives a detailed account of the fiddler's forgetting and of the skill with which his unconscious outwits his father as well as Barbara. Politzer in his two studies on the fiddler is concerned with sibling and father relationship. Like Grillparzer himself, Politzer omits the figure of the mother and her influence on the father-son-relationship; hence he stresses somewhat different aspects of the father-son problem.

9. A number of other contrasts between fiddler and narrator: While the fiddler's sacred hours for improvisation are at night, the narrator-dramatist's hours "of special value," presumably his hours for composition, are in the morning, like Grillparzer's own. The narrator is vastly more educated and sophisticated than the fiddler, he is wealthy and successful.

10. Grillparzer's problems with critics and censors were not all imagined. To mention the most outrageous case: in 1829, Francis I, after the performance of the perfectly loyal play *Ein treuer Diener seines Herrn* offered to buy the play so that it would never be performed again. Such treatment of his loyalty must have been a fearful threat to Grillparzer.

11. Politzer, *Franz Grillparzer oder das abgründige Biedermeier,* "Ödipus in Wien," p. 58-80.

12. This sensitivity is reflected in the following excerpt from his diary of 1928: "Unqualified applause surely would have raised me into the highest poet; the continual squabbling and downgrading of the critics, however, leaves too much room for my hypochondria." *Sämtliche Werke,* Hanser edition, vol. IV, 443.

13. *Sämtliche Werke,* vol. 22, p. 64.

14. *Sämtliche Werke,* Hanser edition, vol. IV, pp. 163-164.

15. *Sämtliche Werke,* vol. XVI, 138.

16. On the father/mother-self as identifications, cf. Freud's *Group Psychology and the Analysis of the Ego,* VII, "Identification," *St. Ed.,* 18, p. 107, "identification is the earliest and original form of emotional tie . . .". In regression, "object-choice is turned back into identification—the ego assumes the characteristics of the object." The two characters, father-self and mother-self, both of which represent early internalizations, demonstrate nicely that the creative process of the author in forming his fictional characters, on the unconscious level, follows a parallel course and has a similar function as does symptom formation in pathology. For instance, the author experiences discomfort (anxiety, stress, cannot write). His psyche regresses to an earlier stage (oral-anal, cf. the oral symbolism which dominates the fiddler's account). The author then externalizes the early introjections as symptoms or characters. With respect to psychic origins, the fiddler's fiddling and Grillparzer's invention of his two characters do not differ. The purpose for which the author and the fiddler use their respective externalizations, makes one of the differences between pathology and art.

W. N. B. Mullan (essay date 1979)

SOURCE: An introduction to *Grillparzer's Aesthetic Theory: A Study with Special Reference to His Conception of the Drama* "Eine Gegenrawart," Akademischer Verlag Hans-Dieter Heinz, 1979, pp. 1-23.

[*In the following excerpt, Mullan introduces Grillparzer's ideas regarding aesthetic theory, asserting that the drama-*

tist's ideas were based on induction and his study of human psychology, rather than on philosophy.]

THE UNITY OF GRILLPARZER'S AESTHETIC THEORY

Despite his lifelong reflection on aesthetic problems Grillparzer never produced a systematic account of his conclusions. His one and only half-hearted attempt to do so in 1820-21[1] did no more than touch on the fringes of the subject and was in any case very quickly abandoned. His ideas therefore remained in a fragmentary form to the end of his days, widely scattered throughout his essays and critical writings, his diaries, conversations and letters, his autobiography, his dramatic plans and sketches and a profusion of often very witty epigrams and satires. The lack of organized presentation is due to the fact that his views were never intended for publication. Only a minute fraction of his aesthetic writings, the total volume of which is considerable, was published during his lifetime, and even if he had produced a comprehensive and carefully argued treatise it is most unlikely that his intense dislike of publicity[2] would ever have permitted him to publish it. For the most part his ideas were either written down solely for his own use or else expressed privately in conversations with friends.

But even though his theory cannot be compared either in its presentation or its pretensions with the aesthetic writings of Schiller or some of the Romantics, Grillparzer cannot on that account be dismissed as a thinker of minor significance. On the contrary, when a man of his literary talent and insight repeatedly states that poetry is the all-consuming aim and interest in his life[3]—a claim which is fully substantiated by even a little reading of his diaries—there are sound reasons for concerning oneself with his theoretical beliefs. He thought long and deeply about the problems of his art and he came to hold strong, even passionate, convictions. Moreover, since he thought through all the main general problems of aesthetics, his theory does represent a fairly comprehensive treatment of the subject. It is true that there are a number of omissions, obscurities and inconsistencies, some of the more important of which we shall have occasion to consider; indeed, it would be surprising, in view of his unsystematic approach and the fragmentary form in which his theory was left, if this were not so. But such shortcomings should not be exaggerated, for his views are broadly coherent and his theory can be pieced together to form an admirably clear, consistent and complete whole. With regard to the question of his originality opinions have differed considerably. It is, I think, difficult to accept the view that he is an outstandingly original thinker;[4] his theory reveals him rather as an eclectic,[5] though sturdily independent in his attitudes. Yet we shall see, particularly in Chapter IV, that his theory of the drama does embody some interesting and important original features.

The unity of his thought undoubtedly owes a good deal to the constancy of his views. He asserted with some pride that his opinions, once formed, hardly ever changed,[6] and

his aesthetic theory bears out the truth of this claim, for it is remarkable how little the basic ideas altered during the course of his long lifetime. This is not to say that his theory did not grow and develop through time. There are points to which he returns again and again, refining and polishing his thought, so that his ideas emerge with ever greater clarity and precision,[7] shifts of emphasis occur here and there, new terminology is introduced and new ideas are incorporated into his theory; yet the basic structure remains unimpaired. Such resistance to change must be attributed at least in part to Grillparzer's deeply conservative nature for, as he said himself, he hated all change which was not unavoidable or manifestly change for the better.[8] The most active period of his life spans the years from 1817 to about 1822. In this vital formative period he not only matured as an artist, but also laid the foundations of his aesthetic theory. His later thinking rarely deviated significantly from the broad outlines established in these early years. What Hofmannsthal says about his diaries is equally true of the greater part of his aesthetic writings—that they are "medusenhaft", one can never be sure from what period of his life a particular passage dates.[9]

GRILLPARZER'S APPROACH TO AESTHETIC THEORY

Grillparzer's general attitude towards aesthetic theory is characterized by a curious ambivalence. Despite his enduring interest in the subject he had profound misgivings about its practical value for the creative artist, and there can be little doubt that his scepticism on this score was largely responsible for his failure to produce any tightly knit aesthetic system. The explanation for his ambivalent approach must ultimately be sought in the dual nature of his own personality, for, as he tells us in his autobiography: "In mir . . . leben zwei völlig abgesonderte Wesen. Ein Dichter von der übergreifendsten, ja sich überstürzenden Phantasie und ein Verstandesmensch der kältesten und zähesten Art."[10] His intellectual curiosity prompted him to subject the phenomena of art to constant critical analysis in an effort to discover what general laws governed their nature. But at the same time his poetic instinct rejected any attempt to lay down abstract theoretical rules which the artist must obey and instead urged the claims of native inspiration as the only sure guide for the creative genius.

His scant regard for aesthetics is perhaps best illustrated by a diary entry of 1845-46[11] and an almost identical passage in his later essay *Zur Literargeschichte*.[12] Here he expresses the view that aesthetic theory is unnecessary because the correct principles which the artist needs to follow are already contained, more or less unconsciously, in his own talent. Just as one can think correctly without logic and act properly without a formal moral code, so too it is possible to appreciate, and even produce, a beautiful work of art without aesthetics. Far more important than any positive value which aesthetics may have is the damage which can be done by false theories. He reminds us that some of the greatest works of art—by which he means primarily the ancient Greek dramas—were produced *be-*

fore any literary theory existed, whereas for contemporary German literature the unfortunate influence of various misguided theories has had disastrous consequences. The more intensive the preoccupation with theoretical matters, the more empty and lifeless literature has become. The only worthwhile function he can find for aesthetics is essentially a negative one—he concedes that a proper theory could play a useful part in eliminating those misconceptions which give rise to so many totally perverse and absurd artistic productions.[13] Similar views find expression elsewhere. One of his epigrams[14] contains the following barb:

> Die Ästhetik vor allem verpön ich,
> Sie spielt ein gefährliches Spiel:
> Die gute nützt sehr wenig,
> Die schlechte schadet sehr viel.

while another[15] advises the poet thus:

> Die eine Vorschrift nenn ich, durch die du alle
>   erfüllst:
> Habe Talent, mein Lieber, und schreibe, was du willst.

Even the theories of such major figures as Aristotle and Schiller do not escape his censure. Emil Kuh recalls a conversation with him: "Auf die philosophischen Kunstbestrebungen der Deutschen liess er in einem der Gespräche harte Worte fallen. Das tauge alles nichts und sei nur zur Hälfte wahr. Für den Künstler hätte dergleichen keinen Wert. . . . Die Lehre des Aristoteles z.B. von Furcht und Mitleid, die passe, wie ein Einschnitt, auf eine ziemlich grosse Menge von Dramen, aber auf der anderen Seite lägen noch recht viele, auf welche die Lehre ganz und gar nicht passe, Wo um's Himmels Willen, fragte Grillparzer, wird mir denn der Macbeth Mitleid erregen?!";[16] and in his diary Grillparzer writes: "Wenn Schiller in seinem Aufsatze über das Pathetische meint, das Tragische liege in dem Widerstand der geistigen Kraft gegen die sinnliche Gewalt; so möchte ich wissen wo in Romeo und Julie auch nur der geringste Widerstand gegen die Empfindung geleistet wird, und doch ist Romeo und Julie im höchsten Grade tragisch. Darin soll kein Tadel gegen Schiller liegen, sondern gegen die philosophische Theorie in Kunstsachen überhaupt. Die Regel passt nie auf alle Fälle, und darum hat Schiller in den Jahren seiner Reife ausdrücklich jede Stunde bedauert, die er mit solchen Spekulationen verloren."[17]

The fact is, in Grillparzer's view, that poetry—and, we may add, art as a whole—as the highest activity of the human mind, superior to all the sciences, is ultimately not fully explicable in rational terms.[18] Any attempt to approach art as a science, as aesthetics does, is therefore absurd. Beauty is incalculable. It cannot be created by applying a formula established a priori in the way that a scientific result can be obtained. The artist cannot be sure of success until his work is finished and experience confirms that he actually has created something beautiful. If it were otherwise, if a beautiful work of art could be produced like a scientific result, the pleasure which art affords would not be significantly different from the pleasure which we derive from the contemplation of the systematically ordered structure of a branch of scientific knowledge. But we know from experience that the pleasure derived from art is in fact unique and of a far higher order than that afforded by any science.[19]

Joachim Müller asserts that Grillparzer's distrust of aesthetics grew with the years,[20] but there is no evidence to support this view. His attitude appears to have been highly sceptical from the very beginning. His earliest references to the subject, in 1817,[21] are no less hostile than his later remarks, and occasional half-hearted indications of a more favourable assessment[22] are quite unrepresentative of the general direction of his thought.

His dislike of aesthetics, derived in the first instance, as we have seen, from his instinctive belief in the supremacy of artistic inspiration over all prescriptive theory, was reinforced by a number of contributory factors. He was not, as he himself admitted, by nature of a systematic, scientific turn of mind,[23] and this characteristic can only have been accentuated by his haphazard and undisciplined education, which he describes in some detail in the *Selbstbiographie*; being largely self-taught and lacking the advantages of a rigorous formal training, he never had much respect for any strict intellectual discipline.[24] Moreover, his attitude towards aesthetics was jaundiced from the start by the contempt which, as an impressionable young student in Vienna, he felt for the professor of aesthetics at the university—unfortunately, as he explains, his low opinion of the man transferred itself to the subject as well.[25]

A further relevant consideration is the importance of the distinctive Austrian background into which he was born. It is a measure of the gulf which at that time separated the Austrian tradition from the mainstream of German culture that he knew almost nothing of the works of Goethe until his eighteenth year.[26] The intimate link between aesthetic theory and literary practice which had existed in Germany since the time of Lessing had no parallel in Austria. Here the attitude towards art had remained, as Scherer says, more "naive".[27] There was never the same concern for questions of theory as there was in Germany, and Grillparzer, who felt himself to be Austrian through and through, bears the clear imprint of his national heritage not least in this respect. It was an enduring source of comfort and pride to him that both the artists of Austria and their public had retained the sound, practical common sense which seemed to him to have been long since swept away in Germany by a flood of abstract speculation.[28]

And with this we come to a point of major significance: Grillparzer's dislike of aesthetics was above all a dislike of the contemporary speculative aesthetics which owed their development in the first instance to the German Romantics. With the Romantic movement there began in Germany the great age of speculative thought which saw the construction of a truly amazing number and variety of aesthetic systems. But with the exception of Schopenhauer's thought, some aspects of which did exert a positive influence on him, Grillparzer's reaction to these theories was almost entirely negative. He saw the great weakness of the speculative aestheticians in the predominantly deductive character of their theory. This, instead of being soundly based, like Grillparzer's own theory, upon the empirical observation of human psychology and the close analysis of individual works of art, was to a very large extent either deduced a priori from the premises of Idealist philosophy or based upon the conclusions, themselves so often highly speculative, of the currently flourishing sciences of cultural history, principally of those branches concerned with the history of thought and the history of literature. As Grillparzer ironically says in a general critical review of the aesthetic thought of the period, though with an obvious eye on A. W. Schlegel's *Vorlesungen über dramatische Kunst und Literatur* in particular: "Das Schöne war apriorisch erwiesen, die Kunstformen desgleiches so dass, wenn sie zufällig verloren gegangen wären, man sie augenblicklich aus freier Faust wieder hätte erfinden können. Grosse Schubfächer wurden gezimmert für die Hervorbringungen aller Zeiten; da mussten sie unterkriechen, und was für das eine Schubfach als Grundwahrheit galt, war für das andere grundfalsch, als ob der Unterschied zwischen Mensch und Mensch in allen Lagen und Zeiten weiss Gott wie gross wäre. Dem gesamten Altertum ward als Marionettendraht die Schicksalsidee beigegeben und Atriden und Labdakiden mussten sich abmartern, bloss um den breitgetretenen Heischesatz: dass niemand seiner Bestimmung entgehen könne, beispielsweise einzuschärfen. Der Chor war der idealisierte Zuseher, auch da wo er Mitspielender, auch da wo er Hauptperson, auch da wo er einseitiger befangen ist, als der Zuseher selbst."[29]

Art was thus subjected in these speculative systems to an abstract intellectual schematism which Grillparzer considered wholly inappropriate. The very fact that the artists who subscribed to such theories were manifestly unable to produce great works of art was in itself, he thought, ample proof of the truth of his conviction that they were irrelevant and impracticable.[30] And his antipathy was intensified by the, to him, degrading spectacle of the contemporary literary scene in Germany, where theoretical beliefs, and with them literary tastes and styles, were changing radically every few years.[31] If these fashionable speculative theories were so ephemeral, than clearly it was difficult to believe that they had much true worth.[32]

It is of course a fact that Grillparzer's lifetime coincided with one of the most intense periods of turmoil and innovation in the whole history of German culture, and it is therefore not difficult to see how he formed the view that their predilection for ineffectual speculation and for constant "progress" in art (as in everything else), regardless of its effect on the quality of production—"das Schwanken und Tappen in der Kunst", as he called it[33]—was the great national weakness of the Germans.

Among the theoretical writings of the Romantics, A. W. Schlegel's lectures were singled out for his especial scorn;

and, interestingly, it was their prominent speculative element which attracted his most scathing criticism. They are, he roundly declares, one of the most dangerous books with which the inexperienced mind can come into contact, for they combine the most accurate details with the most erroneous principles, they raise to the status of universal laws propositions which have in reality only limited validity, and they attempt to construct systems when the foundations upon which they build are still most uncertain. In short, although they contain no single sentence which is entirely wrong, they also contain none which is completely true.[34]

His most virulent attacks, however, were reserved for the speculative systems of Hegel and the Hegelians of the mid-nineteenth century, though Hegel himself, whom he met in the course of his visit to Germany in 1826, he found personally most agreeable.[35] He viewed Hegel's entire philosophical system (and not merely his aesthetics) with the critical eye of an admirer of Kant—and found it thoroughly unconvincing: "Seine Theorie möchte ich ein Postulat der theoretischen Vernunft nennen, im Gegensatz von Kants praktischen. Der Unsinn als Weg zum Sinn."[36] He condemns Hegel's philosophy, which arrogantly attempts by means of Reason alone to find a complete explanation for everything, as the most monstrous excrescence of human pride;[37] and it was with a feeling compounded of disgust and despair that he watched the formidable growth of Hegelian influence in almost every sphere of intellectual life in Germany. Most of all, however, he regretted its pernicious influence on literature. As he said in 1847 to his friend Adolf Foglar (an aspiring young dramatist to whom we owe a scrupulously accurate record of some of Grillparzer's most important conversations): "Überhaupt ekelt mich das Treiben der Deutschen an, nicht nur in der Kunst, auch in Philosophie und Politik. An alldem ist Hegel schuld, der sie wieder in die alte Gottschedsche Charnier brachte, aus welcher Goethe und Schiller sie kaum gerissen hatten. Und sie rühmen sich Goethe und Schiller überwunden zu haben! Ja wohl haben sie sie überwunden!—Und wenn man nichts tut, so muss man auch nicht schreien."[38] It was primarily to the widespread dissemination of Hegelian ideas that he attributed the destruction of the common sense of German artists and their public and the growth of that love of abstract thought which he regarded as the scourge of contemporary German literature.[39] He specifically attacks Hegelian influence on German aesthetic theory on the grounds that it has encouraged the development of an arrogant, yet barren, intellectualism, as a result of which "die Ästhetik mit ihren dürftigen Begriffsbestimmungen sich den unerklärten Wundern des menschlichen Innern, nicht etwa zu nähern—was erlaubt, ja wünschenswert wäre—sondern sie vollständig zu erreichen meint." In direct opposition to Hegel he states his own belief that "die Ästhetik wird hemmend, da sie das Zusammenspiel aller menschlichen Kräfte der Gesetzgebung einer einzelnen, der Denkkraft unterwerfen will."[40] There can be no doubt that in the excessive intellectualism which he found in Hegel and the Romantics, and which was entirely alien to his own nature, there must be sought the main reason for his complete rejection of their theories.[41]

In all probability it was Grillparzer's intense dislike of the contemporary speculative trends in aesthetics that led him to adopt the uncompromising (and surely unwarrantably harsh) view that philosophy as such is incapable of making any useful contribution at all to aesthetic theory. Even of Kant, whose theory he respects more than that of any other philosopher, he writes: "Nie hat ein Philosoph aneignender über die Vorfragen der Kunst gesprochen als er, und wenn, was er sagte, nicht künstlerisch förderlicher war, so liegt die Ursache nur darin, dass aus dem Standpunkte der Philosophie die Kunst überhaupt nicht zu fördern ist."[42] Considering the strength of his feeling on this point it is hardly surprising that his own theory is not deeply rooted in any philosophical system. It thus lacks the systematic underpinning which close adherence to a particular, tightly knit philosophy might have lent it; and in this respect it differs strikingly from the theories of the other major dramatists of the Classical and post-Classical period, such as Schiller or Hebbel. It is true that he uses a number of philosophical terms (taken chiefly from Kant) and that some of his ideas owe their origin to his study of philosophical works. But his theory is not concerned in the first instance with the philosophical aspects and problems of art; his approach to the subject is essentially psychological, and his theory is derived empirically from his insight into the psychological processes which take place in the mind of the creative artist and in the mind of the individual member of the public as he responds to a work of art.[43]

It is worth noting at this point that his preference for an aesthetic grounded in psychology rather than philosophy accords fully with his passionate belief that the science of psychology, which he knew to be still in its infancy, held out the prospect of far greater advances in human knowledge than any philosophy. As early as 1809-10 we find him writing that the very word philosophy makes him laugh, for all of our philosophy starts from hypotheses and is built up entirely by means of hypotheses, so that the results are—quite naturally—likewise mere hypotheses; and he finds the main reason for this weakness in the complete neglect of psychology, without which, he believes, no real progress in philosophy can possibly be made.[44]

The fact that Grillparzer's aesthetic is based upon the study of human psychology and the practical analysis of works of art means that his theory, unlike that of the Romantics and the Idealist philosophers, is essentially inductive in character. It is significant that he once described Friedrich Bouterwek, for many years professor of philosophy in Göttingen (where Schopenhauer was one of his students), as the best of all aestheticians and the only reliable guide in the field of aesthetic theory,[45] for Bouterwek shares with Grillparzer himself the distinction of being one of the few inductive aestheticians in this age of abstract speculation. In his interest in psychologically based aesthetics Grillparzer anticipates by a considerable number of

years the work of the new generation of inductive theorists who, following the pioneering work done by F. T. Vischer in his Ästhetik *oder Wissenschaft des Schönen* which appeared in six weighty volumes from 1846 to 1857, came to dominate the scene in the later decades of the nineteenth century. There is, however, no evidence that Grillparzer took much interest in their ideas or felt any sympathy for them. Indeed, the contrary appears to have been the case. His comments on Vischer, for example, all display the same marked disapproval as the following epigram[46] of 1859:

> Vischers Ästhetik
> Du trittst ruhig der Kritik entgegen,
> So unangreifbar ist noch keiner gewesen:
> Wer dich nicht gelesen, kann dich nicht widerlegen;
> Und wer dich widerlegen könnte, kann dich nicht
>   lesen.

It must of course be remembered that Grillparzer, by this time old and embittered, had long since withdrawn into his own shell and was no longer receptive to any new ideas, from whatever source they might come.

The inductive nature of Grillparzer's approach is clearly revealed by the thoroughly practical manner in which the detail of his theory was worked out. Whereas Schiller starts from the basis of an established philosophical system and builds his theory upon it, Grillparzer's theory is derived in a much more pragmatic way from his reflection on the numerous problems and points of interest which he encountered both in his work as a creative writer[47] and in the course of his very extensive reading—mainly of works of literature and criticism, though also of certain philosophical works. It was his custom to jot down his reactions to what he read—sometimes agreeing, sometimes disagreeing with what he found—and in this way he was able to clarify his mind with regard to a whole range of issues. For example, many of his theoretical ideas are to be found in his critical writings on Lope de Vega (which, it has been quite rightly observed, reveal at least as much about Grillparzer himself as they tell us about Lope); frequently a particular play of Lope would bring up some problem or other, and, as a result of his consideration of this particular case, he would evolve a general theoretical principle.

The strong practical bias of his working method accounts very largely for the pronounced subjectivity which Grillparzer's aesthetics displays. By far the greatest proportion of his theoretical writings is devoted to literature; and just as his creative output is made up overwhelmingly of dramatic works, so too the major part of his poetics is concerned with the drama. He said himself—and successive generations of critics have repeated it since[48]—that he was not a lyricist,[49] despite the fact that he did produce a very considerable volume of verse; moreover, his epic production is—even if only quantitatively—comparatively slight; and correspondingly, we find that he has relatively little to say about the lyric and epic forms. His dramaturgy itself shows the same subjective tendency: being, as he says, of an essentially elegiac nature,[50] he had a preference for tragedy rather than comedy; hence we find that in his theory he deals primarily with tragedy, while comedy is treated only incidentally and rather superficially.

The steadfast practicality of his approach is one of the most outstanding features of Grillparzer's entire aesthetic theory. It is certainly its greatest strength. In his dramaturgy, with which we shall be most closely concerned, this practicality manifests itself perhaps most strikingly in a deep concern for the theatrical side of the drama; for Grillparzer regarded the drama not merely, or even primarily, as literature, but as an essentially theatrical art, and he gives great prominence and much careful thought to the theatrical aspects of the genre. His dramaturgy is thus as much a guide-book to theatrical practice as it is a theory of the dramatic form. This was in itself unusual enough in an age when most dramaturgic writings tended to neglect the theatre, but it is all the more remarkable when one remembers that, unlike Lessing for example, Grillparzer never enjoyed a close working relationship with any theatre. Indeed, it was only out of politeness that he attended the rehearsals of his own plays, and even then he sat silently throughout the whole of the activities, never intervening to offer suggestions or advice, or even to correct mistakes.[51]

BACKGROUND AND INFLUENCES

The exceptional number and variety of background factors and influences which Grillparzer-criticism must take into account make him an unusually elusive figure; and this is as true of his aesthetics as of any other aspect of his work or personality. The complexity arises from two main circumstances: firstly, the particularly unsettled nature of his time, which saw the advent and eclipse in the German-speaking world of a very wide range of philosophies and cultural movements; and secondly, the fact of his Viennese birth. The importance of this latter fact can scarcely be exaggerated, for it is in the cultural tradition of his native city that Grillparzer's deepest spiritual roots lie. In the late eighteenth and early nineteenth centuries—the period of Grillparzer's youth—Austrian culture was dominated by two main currents, each of which was fundamentally in conflict with the other. These were, firstly, the specifically Austrian form of the Enlightenment known as Josephinism (so named after the enlightened Kaiser Josef II), and secondly, the older Baroque tradition which, though by now well past its peak, still survived in the flourishing Volkstheater of Vienna.

The influence of Josephinism is evident in various aspects of Grillparzer's work and thought quite apart from his aesthetic theory. It may be seen, for example, in the undeniable moralizing tendency of some of his plays, or, moving away altogether from the sphere of literature, in his religious agnosticism.[52] Its most important effect as far as his aesthetics is concerned was not to implant in his mind any particular body of ready-made theoretical ideas, but rather to endow him at an early age with a general sceptical attitude of mind which in turn powerfully affected his reaction to the theoretical ideas and artistic practices of many of the thinkers and writers with whose works he was to become acquainted in later years. In a sense, therefore, the influence of Josephinism, vital though it was, affected his thought only indirectly. It was probably within his own family circle that he first fell under the influence of Josephinism, for his father, Wenzel Grillparzer, a clear-thinking legal man by profession, was himself a staunch supporter of Josephinian ideas, and his beliefs and loyalties must certainly have influenced the development of his son's outlook.[53]

But the personal relationship which most profoundly influenced the direction of his thinking was unquestionably his acquaintance with another upholder of Josephinian ideals: Josef Schreyvogel. Schreyvogel, Grillparzer's senior by more than twenty years, was from 1814 until just before his death in 1832 Secretary of the Burgtheater and as such one of the most influential figures in contemporary Viennese theatrical circles. It was he who first encouraged Grillparzer to write, and it was he who launched him, "gleichsam als ein[en] halb Widerstrebend[en]",[54] on his public career with the successful first production of *Die Ahnfrau* in 1817. When the two men first met in 1816 they were instantly drawn to one another and quickly established a close and lasting friendship in which there was, at least in the early years, more than a little of the father-son relationship.[55] Such was Grillparzer's respect for the older man that he placed him almost on an equal footing with Lessing,[56] and there can be no doubt that in the years of contact with him Grillparzer absorbed something of his rationalistic way of thinking. But even before the beginning of their personal acquaintance Schreyvogel's influence had already been at work. His weekly literary publication, the *Sonntagsblatt,* which bore the clear imprint of his Josephinian ideas, was acknowledged by Grillparzer himself to have been a determining influence on his thought from the date of its first appearance in 1807.[57] In Schreyvogel's death Grillparzer suffered a grievous loss, for Schreyvogel stood intellectually closer to him than anyone else in his entire life either before or afterwards. There was a very large measure of agreement in their views on artistic matters, and even four years after Schreyvogel's death Grillparzer was still confiding to his diary that there was now no-one in Vienna, or indeed in the whole of Germany, with whom he felt any desire to discuss such things.[58]

It was the sceptical turn of mind which was his Josephinian heritage that made him receptive to the critical philosophy of Kant. Here again Schreyvogel, who was himself an enthusiastic admirer of the great philosopher,[59] seems to have played an important part. It was apparently his loan of a set of Kant's works in 1817[60] that prompted Grillparzer's first serious study of the Kantian system. He had of course learnt something about Kant in his university days,[61] but he was still very young at this time and his knowledge seems to have been only very superficial. Even the effect of Schreyvogel's prompting was delayed for some two years, for it was not until after the Italian journey of 1819 that his philosophical reading was begun in earnest.[62] The precise extent of Kant's influence on him is a question about which there has been a certain amount of disagreement. Störi, who carried out a special investigation of the links between the two, is of the opinion that Strich and Ehrhard overestimate it, believing that some of the ideas which they attribute to the study of Kant were in fact the result of Grillparzer's own thinking.[63] However, since one here enters the realm of speculation it is impossible to produce conclusive arguments one way or the other; the fact is that the full extent of Kantian influence simply cannot be ascertained with complete precision. This has been recognized by the majority of critics, most of whom have quite rightly been content to note the fact of Kantian influence where it is incontestable and to leave it at that. There is, however, general agreement, supported by Grillparzer's own words, that of all the philosophical influences exerted on him Kant's was the most profound. What attracted him to Kant was above all the latter's critical method and, contrasting with the arrogance of the speculative Idealists, the relative modesty of his pretensions. In Kant's "Philosophie der Bescheidenheit, die das demütige 'Ich weiss nicht' an die Spitze des Systems stellt", he applauds "die wissenschaftliche Anerkennung der menschlichen Beschränktheit",[64] and in a diary entry stimulated by his reading of Hegel he writes: "Alles was ich Philosophisches lese, vermehrt meine Achtung für Kant."[65] As far as his aesthetics is concerned the most important part of Kant's work was, as one would expect, the *Kritik der Urteilskraft.* It is impossible to say exactly when he first read this, but he was certainly familiar with it by the early months of 1821 at the latest, and probably earlier.[66] Its influence is, as we shall see, most evident in his general aesthetic theory, rather than in the particular field of his dramaturgy.

Kant of course was not the only philosopher of whom he had an extensive knowledge. Despite his generally low opinion of philosophy and philosophers he was, ironically enough, deeply interested in the subject and widely read in it, and although he never committed himself heart and soul to any one system, his wide knowledge was nevertheless not acquired in vain, for his aesthetic theory was influenced by a number of philosophers—and not only by their aesthetic thought. There is clear evidence of direct links with Schopenhauer's *Die Welt als Wille und Vorstellung* and with Bouterwek's *Ästhetik,* both of which he knew by 1820 or 1821;[67] in addition to these Strich has argued convincingly for the influence of Spinoza's *Ethics,* with which he was acquainted by 1822;[68] and, as we have already seen, the influence of Hegel—in a negative sense[69]—cannot be ignored. Of these four Schopenhauer is probably the most important though, as is the case with Kant, the exact extent of his influence has been a matter of dispute. There can, I think, be little doubt that it is grossly exaggerated by Geissler; yet Alker seems to go too far in the other direction when he expresses the view that Schopenhauer failed to make any deep impression whatever on the poet.[70] Stein probably comes closest to the truth when she

states the cautious opinion that there is "a certain, if circumscribed relationship" between the two.[71] It is beyond doubt that Grillparzer was influenced by Schopenhauer's distinction between the scientific and the contemplative views of the world—a fact which was to have the most far-reaching consequences for his aesthetics. No further direct connection of major significance over and above this point can be conclusively proved; but the similarity between the ideas of the two men is often so striking that one may well be justified in believing that Schopenhauer's influence is more considerable than the small number of Grillparzer's explicit references to him would superficially indicate. Strich, for example, argues very persuasively for Schopenhauerian influence on his negative attitude to the science of history even though no absolutely unassailable evidence of such a link can be produced.[72] But at the same time it must be acknowledged that the close proximity of their views on many points may be due quite simply to a similarity of temperament. Both were profoundly pessimistic in outlook, both painfully aware of the irrationality of the world and of the transience and mutability of all human life.

Important as all these philosophical influences are, however, their significance is overshadowed, at least as far as Grillparzer's dramaturgy is concerned, by that of the literary and theatrical influences to which he was exposed.— And with this we are led back to the matter of the popular theatrical tradition of Vienna, for the Viennese *Volksstück* was the first art-form to cast its spell over him. One of the first books he ever read was Schikaneder's libretto for Mozart's *Die Zauberflöte,*[73] and it was in the Leopoldstädter Theater that his earliest, and possibly his deepest, theatrical impressions were received.[74] It is, moreover, surely significant that his earliest dramatic fragments and his first public success were in the style of the native *Volksstück* rather than the Classical mould imported from Germany. Indeed, so powerful was the influence of this peculiarly Viennese tradition over him that Gundolf believed it was this, rather than his inborn temperament, that had drawn him to the dramatic genre;[75] and Sauer was inspired to make the amusing suggestion that Kotzebue might have given **Sappho** the title *Kuss, Rose und Dolch.*[76] Yet full recognition of his debt to the *Volkstheater* was relatively slow in coming. It was not until the publication in 1918-19 of Enzinger's history of the Viennese theatre,[77] with its enormous wealth of detail, that the true extent of its influence on him was at last revealed. With this the older view, which had seen both in his plays and in his dramaturgy a combination of Classical and Romantic elements,[78] gave way to the modern view that he in fact represents primarily a fusion of the German Classical with the Austrian Baroque tradition.[79]

Grillparzer himself was perfectly well aware of the importance of his Viennese background.[80] He knew that because of it he was not, and could not be, properly understood in the northern parts of Germany,[81] and it was always with Vienna in mind that he wrote his own plays.[82] Specifically, he was aware that he had been deeply influenced by the

Volkstheater. In 1846 he reflects in his diary: "Die Jugen-deindrücke wird man nicht los. Meinen eigenen Arbeiten merkt man an, dass ich in der Kindheit mich an den Geis-terund Feen-Märchen des Leopoldstädter Theaters ergötzt habe.["83] But his attitude to the popular stage was not un-complicated. Although he acknowledges its influence on him he refers to it more often than not in highly unflatter-ing terms: for example, he recalls in the *Selbstbiographie* that he had hesitated to write *Die Ahnfrau* partly because he had been ashamed to treat a subject which seemed fit only for the suburban theatre—it was in the suburbs of Vi-enna that the popular theatres were located—and which would therefore cause him to be identified with a class of poets whom he had always despised.[84]

He never tells us exactly what it is that he dislikes in the *Volkstheater,* but there can be little doubt that he took exception mainly to its lack of artistic form and to its crude exaggerations and extravagances, characteristic fea-tures which were bound to offend his sophisticated and sensitive taste. Only in its more refined, artistically supe-rior manifestations—such as the works of Raimund, which he greatly admired[85]—does it meet with his warm approval. In these superior productions, which achieved a measure of permanence as works of literature, he could admire the positive qualities of the tradition unmarred by the artistic deficiencies of the ephemeral, non-literary, run-of-the-mill *Volksstück.* Most notable among these qualities were a re-freshing naturalness and vividness, an unsurpassed vein of light-hearted comedy, a quite outstanding richness and va-riety of stage-spectacle and other theatrical effects—not least the use of music—and an unparalleled emphasis on action and movement.

These are, of course, all prominent characteristics of Grill-parzer's own dramatic style and they serve, together with a host of individual themes and motifs too numerous to mention,[86] to underline the closeness of his links with the *Volkstheater.* On the theoretical side, his dramaturgy re-veals a no less substantial indebtedness to the popular tra-dition. Here its influence makes itself felt mainly in the powerful emphasis which he places on the necessity for the drama to be performed on the stage and on the corre-sponding need for the poet to exploit to the full the theat-rical potential of the medium; it also makes itself apparent in his acceptance of the logical corollary of these require-ments, namely the need to please and to entertain the theatre-going public.

None of this implies, however, that he is simply one more poet in the Viennese tradition. On the contrary, the spirit of the popular theatre reappears in him in a higher and more refined form than it ever achieved even in Raimund. The measure of his refinement emerges very clearly in his dramas, especially in the plays of his maturity and above all in the three late dramas which were published posthu-mously. In them the influence of the *Volkstheater,* while still present, is much less readily apparent than in, for ex-ample, *Die Ahnfrau*—though even in this early work the crasser effects of the *Volksstück* have been toned down

considerably. While, therefore, Grillparzer represents the culmination of the long popular tradition of Vienna, at the same time he transcends it and places Austrian literature for the first time on an equal footing with the Classical masterpieces of Germany, so that his friend Bauernfeld was at least half right when he described him as the first Austrian and the last German poet.[87]

Alongside the native tradition a second major current in the Viennese literary world during the period of Grillparz-er's youth was that of German Classicism. This was the movement to which he always felt himself consciously most closely allied and which he most admired; it was also the last contemporary movement in literature with which he was in sympathy. In the work of Goethe and Schiller he saw the highest ever flowering of German liter-ary genius.[88] In everything that followed them he could see only a continuing process of decline, without however go-ing so far as to accept Gervinus' view that with Goethe German literature must be regarded as having come to an end and that German poets should therefore now stop writing![89] His earliest love was for Schiller, with whose works he was acquainted at a very early age and whose *Don Carlos* provided the model for *Blanka von Kastilien.*[90] But when, prompted by the *Sonntagsblatt,* he began the serious study of Goethe, some time in 1808 or 1809, the effect on him was so overwhelming that his admiration for Schiller temporarily cooled and was replaced by an ardent worship of Goethe.[91] Interestingly, he appears to have been particularly attracted at this time to *Tasso,* in which Goet-he's treatment of the problematic position of the artist in society—a question which was to loom so large in Grill-parzer's own life—already called forth a powerful re-sponse in the youthful poet's soul.

Nothing more effectively reveals his stubborn conserva-tism than his lifelong struggle to uphold the Classical ide-als of his youth in the face of all the changes that were taking place around him. His determination finds its most familiar expression in the often quoted lines of 1844:[92]

> Endlos ist das tolle Treiben,
> Vorwärts, vorwärts schallts durchs Land,
> Ich möcht lieber stehen bleiben
> Da, wo Goethe, Schiller stand.

And no false modesty interfered with his own assessment of the degree to which his struggle was ultimately success-ful. More than once he quite candidly states his conviction that his own works are the best that have been produced in Germany since the death of his two great predecessors.[93]

But not only his dramatic practice marks him out as a dis-ciple of the Classical school. His aesthetic theory reveals a similar enthusiasm for Classical ideals. The influence of Lessing, Goethe and Schiller, sometimes individual, some-times collective, played a major part in the formation of his views on a wide range of matters: his conviction that art must not be didactic; his conception of the drama as "eine Gegenwart"; the belief that the drama should be concerned with the creation of archetypal human characters and their passions and destinies (rather than with, for example, current social and political problems); the view that the poet using historical material is free to make any necessary alterations in historical fact in the interests of his art; and, perhaps most important of all, his repeated insistence on the importance of strict form in the drama.[94] But at the same time it would be misleading to give the impression that he is no more than an unoriginal imitator of a past literary mode. He differs markedly from the Classical writers in a number of important respects: in his greater respect for his audience, his emphasis on the theatrical aspect of the drama, and his unrelievedly pessimistic conception of tragedy.[95]

As the Classical era receded and its style and outlook were replaced by others of a very different complexion he felt himself more and more estranged from contemporary movements in literature. He has almost nothing good to say of any of the movements which followed the golden age when Goethe and Schiller worked together in Weimar. But he was aware that he was fighting a losing battle— "Ich merkte wohl, dass ich als der letzte Dichter in eine prosaische Zeit hineingekommen sei."[96] Embittered and disgusted he retreated into his own shell and lived out the rest of his life in almost complete isolation. He refers with a certain sour pride to his stubborn refusal to have anything to do with the literary cliques and coteries of the time.[97] His position is effectively summed up by a succinct epigram of 1859:[98]

> Will unsre Zeit mich bestreiten,
> Ich lass es ruhig geschehn,
> Ich komme aus andern Zeiten
> Und hoffe in andre zu gehen.

But for a full picture of the depth of his sense of alienation and the intensity of his feelings of frustration and disappointment one must turn to his essays on the contemporary state of German literature,[99] for it is there that they find their most eloquent expression.

His extreme dislike of Romanticism,[100] which unmistakably coloured his aesthetic theory, was first and foremost a dislike of German Romanticism. It was due in part, as he himself acknowledged, to the early influence of Schreyvogel who used the pages of the *Sonntagsblatt* to conduct a vigorous campaign against the Romantics.[101] But it seems not unlikely that personal dislikes and jealousies played a part too. It is certainly a fact that he felt a strong personal dislike for Friedrich Schlegel[102] and it is possible that he was irritated by the Romantics' conspicuous lack of enthusiasm for his own works. The most important implications for his aesthetics arise from his attacks on the formlessness[103] of Romantic art and on the Romantic tendency to fuse—or rather, as it seemed to him, to confuse—poetry with philosophy.[104] Important too are his rejection of the Romantics' love of the folksong,[105] indeed of the very idea of *Volkspoesie*,[106] and his refusal to share their glorification of the Middle Ages and their enthusiasm for medieval German literature.[107] He was no literary nationalist and discounted as nonsense the charge that the national culture of

medieval Germany had been stifled by the superimposed alien culture of Classical antiquity.[108] A further difference reveals itself in divergent attitudes to literary history and criticism, for while the Romantic movement lent a major impulse to these activities, Grillparzer could find only the most limited use for them.[109] His hostility to Romanticism was not, however, confined to things literary. He was equally outspoken in his criticism of Romantic music. He records, for example, how Weber's departures from traditional principles in his *Euryanthe* so offended his ear as to make him feel physically ill.[110] For him music had reached an unparalleled and unsurpassable climax of perfection in the well-ordered Classical art of Mozart. Even Beethoven, who displayed a dangerous tendency toward what seemed like formlessness, did not meet with his unqualified approval.[111]

At the same time, however, it must be said that Grillparzer's poetic practice is a good deal closer to Romanticism than his theoretical position might lead one to expect. Not only is his libretto **Melusina** clearly indebted to Weber's Romantic opera *Der Freischütz*,[112] but his plays too have been felt by most critics to reveal a definite Romantic influence. He himself refers to the Romantic character of two of his works, though in the case of **Das golden Vliess** he makes it clear that the deliberate fusion of Romantic with Classical features is not due to any reverence for Romanticism as such, but to a desire to heighten the dramatically important contrast between barbaric Colchis and civilized Greece.[113] More puzzling is the case of the other play which he describes as Romantic: **Des Meeres und der Liebe Wellen.** This, he says—and here he seems totally and inexplicably inconsistent with his theoretical position—was an attempt to unite the Romantic with the ancient (i.e. Classical) style.[114]

In complete contrast to the otherworldly Romantic "Nebler und Schwebler"[115] was the new, practically-minded generation of *Das junge Deutschland* which came to the fore in the early 1830s. But Grillparzer had no more time for them than he had for their Romantic predecessors. The principal virtue of the movement in his view was that it had acted as an effective "Pferdekur" against the "faselnd-mittelalterliche, selbsttäuschend-religiose, gestaltlos-nebelnde, Tieckisch-Menzlisch-unfähige Periode"[116] and thus finally brought the despised Romantic era to a close. But he had no patience with the crude efforts of the Young Germans to bring literature closer to reality by harnessing it in the cause of necessarily transient social and political objectives.

He gave equally short shrift to other movements in the post-Romantic period. He pours scorn on the "Ideendichter",[117] such as Hebbel, for whom art seemed to be little more than an abstract exercise in Hegelian dialectics. And although he himself stands on the threshold of nineteenth-century Realism, he is highly critical of the dull prosiness of the "Dichten des Wirklich-Wahren".[118] Freytag's *Soll und Haben* which, in the celebrated words of Julian Schmidt, portrays "das deutsche Volk . . . , wo es in seinen Tüchtigkeit zu finden ist, nämlich bei seiner Arbeit", provoked from him the caustic comment:[119]

> Dass die Poesie Arbeit,
> Ist leider eine Wahrheit,
> Doch dass die Arbeit Poesie,
> Glaub ich nun und nie.

As his sense of isolation in his own age grew, Grillparzer's reaction was increasingly to seek solace in the more congenial literature of past ages; and this had just as important consequences for his aesthetics as did his reading of more modern works. He was drawn especially to the dramatic literatures of ancient Greece, especially Euripides,[120] of the Spanish Golden Age and of Shakespeare. Instinctively he preferred the type of poetry defined in Schillerian terms as "naiv" to the "sentimentalisch" variety, and it was in these older literatures, above all in the Baroque dramas of his particular favourites, Lope de Vega and Shakespeare,[121] that he found the supreme examples of the "naive" naturalness and simplicity which he came to regard as the essential qualities of the greatest and purest poetry. Such poetry, he believed, had flourished best in earlier ages because these, being less highly cultivated, were intrinsically more poetic than his own.[122] How completely he was captivated by these older poets and how forcibly they influenced his thought and work is most eloquently revealed by his own words: "Was mein—weniger absichtliches als durch meine Natur gebotenes—Streben war, und, wie es scheint, mir nicht gelungen ist, war die Poesie dem ursprünglichen, durchaus bildlichen, die Berechtigung in der Empfindung und nicht im Gedanken suchenden der alten Dichter näher zu bringen, die neuern Dichter, so vortrefflich sie sein mögen, hatten mir immer so viel Beimischung von Prosa, so viel Lehr—und Reflexions—mässiges, dass ich eigentliche Erquickung nur in der alten Poesie fand, wo die Gestalt noch dér Gedanke und die Überzeugung der Beweis ist. Damit ist nicht jene alte Poesie gemeint, die jene Eigenschaft nur aus Unbeholfenheit und Unfähigkeit hat, wie die mittelhochdeutsche, oder dass ich mich je vom Volksliede angezogen gefunden hätte, sondern jene Dichter waren es, die mit Talent und Geist begabt, als die Spitze einer an sich poetischen Zeit jene Einheit abspiegelten mit der das Leben sie umgab, und die die neuere Zeit im Fortschritt der Entwicklung—vom Standpunkte der Prosa aus: zu ihrem Glücke—längst abgestreift hat. Die Griechen, die Spanier, Ariost und Shakespeare waren die Freunde meiner Einsamkeit und ihre Darstellungsweise mit der Auffassung der neuern Zeit in Einklang zu bringen, mein halb unbewusstes Streben."[123] It need not surprise us that he makes no mention in this context of any French writers, for although he admired the strictness of form of the Classical dramatists of the seventeenth century, there is no firm evidence that he was otherwise significantly influenced by French literature. Nor can it be conclusively shown that he owes much to the influence of French literary theoreticians: Strich's attempts to establish close links between his dramatic theory and the ideas of Corneille and Diderot, although interesting, must be regarded as essentially speculative.

Of the poets whose influence Grillparzer does acknowledge the most significant for his aesthetics (as well as his dramatic practice) were Lope de Vega and Shakespeare. We shall see in Chapter IV how his admiration for them was translated into practical terms and influenced his ideas on certain questions of dramatic form and of characterization, thus contributing to what must be regarded as the most important original aspect of his dramatic theory. Although the serious study of Shakespeare, and with it Shakespearean influence on his thinking, began as early as 1816 or 1817,[124] it was not until some years later that the influence of Lope became a major factor. The earliest references[125] to him in the diaries are dated 1824 and they make it clear that before this date Grillparzer's knowledge and understanding of him were only very superficial. In his interest in the *Siglo de Oro* Grillparzer was, of course, not alone in the early years of the nineteenth century, for Spanish literature had been discovered by the Romantics and was currently enjoying an unprecedented wave of popularity in Germany. The Romantics did not, however, share Grillparzer's keen admiration for Lope; both the Schlegels rated him far below their own idol Calderon, who was for them the greatest of the Spanish poets.[126] Grillparzer too had been attracted in the first instance to Calderon. Indeed, it was A. W. Schlegel's translation of a number of Calderon's plays, published 1803-9 under the title *Spanisches Theater,* that gave him his first real opportunity to get to know something about the Spanish drama. We know that he had read this translation by the time of his employment in the Hofbibliothek in 1813 but had serious reservations about its quality. These doubts determined him to learn the language himself in order to be able to read Calderon in the original, and it was primarily as a language exercise that he made his own translation, in 1813, of the opening scenes of *La vida es sueno*—the fateful translation which was later instrumental in bringing about the first meeting with Schreyvogel.[127]

It was not until more than ten years after the initial acquaintance with Calderon that he first turned his attention to the serious study of Lope. His first impressions were not particularly favourable. Having read twelve of the plays he compares Lope to his disadvantage with Calderon: he is frequently extravagant, on occasion even lacking in taste, and he is without Calderon's masterly skill in the art of constructing a drama.[128] But Grillparzer's resistance very quickly thawed and he is soon writing with approval of Lope's "Naturwahrheit, die man beim Calderon meistens vergeblich sucht".[129] With this the battle for recognition was over, Lope's naturalness and vitality were now apparent and Grillparzer never again doubted either the greatness of his genius or his superiority to Calderon. Calderon he describes as the Schiller of Spanish literature, while Lope is its Goethe;[130] and just as he had come to prefer Goethe to Schiller, so too he was now convinced that Lope was an essentially greater poetic talent than Calderon.

With this account of his capitulation to the poet who was to remain his favourite for life we come to the end of our review of the general background to Grillparzer's aesthetics. Clearly, any attempt to situate a writer of his complexity in the context of his cultural background and interests carries with it a real risk of making him appear to be little more than an unoriginal vehicle for the reproduction of other men's ideas. And with Grillparzer this danger has not always been avoided. Strich, for example, is not entirely blameless in this respect. It must therefore be stressed that, while one cannot reasonably claim for Grillparzer the distinction of outstanding originality, his mind and personality do nonetheless reveal an unmistakable individuality and a healthy spirit of independence which have not failed to leave their imprint on his aesthetic thought. For this reason he defies facile classification. His theory cannot be tidily labelled as the unalloyed, purely derivative product of a single cultural movement, whether it be the *Aufklärung*, Classicism, Romanticism or simply the Austrian Baroque. He was influenced in different ways and in varying degrees by all of these, and yet he remains at all times unalterably himself.

Notes

1. *SW*, [*Sämtliche Werke*] August Sauer and Reinhold Backman trans., section II, volume 7, p.329ff., especially p.343, *Tgb.* [*Tagebücher*] (diary entry) 888.

2. *SW* I, 16, p.115; *SW* II, 11, p.199, *Tgb.*4025; *Gespr.* [*Gespräche und die Charakteristiken seiner Persönlichkeit durch die Zeitgenossen*, August Sauer trans.] III, No.880, p.371.

3. *SW* II, 8, pp.289-290, *Tgb.*1614; *SW* II, 9, p.127, *Tgb.*2074; *SW* II, 10, p.49, *Tgb.*2982.

4. This is the view taken by [Oswald] Redlich, *Grillparzers Verhältnis zur Geschichte*, (1901), p.3, and by Friedrich Sengle, *Das deutsche Geschichtsdrama: Geschichte eines literarischen Mythos*, (1952) p.97.

5. Cf. F. Strich, *Franz Grillparzers Ästhetik*, (1905) p.5; Erich Weiss, *Grillparzer als Beurteiler dichterischer Werke*, (1938) pp.11-12.

6. *SW* II, 10, p.149, *Tgb.*3206; *SW* II, 8, p.300, *Tgb.*1634.

7. As we shall see, his ideas on the nature of the dramatic illusion, out of which his conception of the drama as "eine Gegenwart" eventually developed, fall into this category.

8. *SW* I, 14, p.151.

9. Hugo von Hofmannsthal, "Notizen zu einem Grillparzer-Vortrag", *Gesammelte Werke*, Prosa II, p.85.

10. *SW* I, 16, p.135.

11. *SW* II, 11, p.110, *Tgb.*3819.

12. *SW* I, 14, p.166.

13. Cf. *SW* II, 8, p.24, *Tgb.*1053.

14. *SW* I, 12/1, p.351, No.1825. Cf. *Gespr.* V, No.1149, p.50.

15. *SW* I, 12/1, p.128, No.807.

16. *Gespr.* V, No.1148, p.44.

17. *SW* II, 12, p.30, *Tgb.*4244.

18. *SW* II, 11, p.195, *Tgb.*4023. Cf. *SW* II, 7, p.314, *Tgb.*828 and *SW* I, 12/1, p.226, No.1238.

19. *SW* II, 7, pp.338-339, *Tgb.*882; *SW* II, 11, p.228, *Tgb.*4057.

20. J. Müller, *Franz Grillparzer*, (1963) p.85.

21. *SW* II, 7, pp.90-91, *Tgb.*203; *SW* I, 14, p.8.

22. Note the grudging tone of the following: "Wozu also eine Ästhetik, wenn sie weder lehren kann, wie das Schöne hervorzubringen, noch wie es mit Geschmack zu geniessen ist? Dazu, weil es die Sache eines vernünftigen Menschen ist, sich von allen seinen Handlungen und Urteilen einen Grund angeben zu können. Wenn die Ästhetik auch keine Rechnenkunst des Schönen ist, so ist sie doch die Probe der Rechnung." (*SW* II, 7, p.331, *Tgb.*873).

23. *SW* II, 7, p.295, *Tgb.*771.

24. Cf. Sauer, *Einleitung in die fünfte Ausgabe von Grillparzers Werken*, Vol. I, pp.18-19.

25. *SW* I, 16, pp.85-86.

26. *SW* I, 16, p.17; *SW* II, 7, pp.49-50, *Tgb.*92.

27. W. Scherer, *Vorträge und Aufsätze zur Geschichte des geistigen Lebens in Geschichte der Deutschland und Österreich*, (1874) p.303.

28. *SW* I, 14, p.153; *SW* I, 16, pp.160-161; *Gespr.* IV, No.1098, p.227. The important differences between the poets and public of Austria on the one hand and Germany on the other is a subject of which we shall hear more later.

29. *SW* I, 14, p.82. Cf. A. W. Schlegel, *Vorlesungen über dramatische Kunst und Literatur*, Lectures 4 and 5.

30. *Gespr.* III, No.718, p.195; *SW* II, 11, p.110, *Tgb.*3819.

31. *SW* I, 16, p.185; *SW* II, 8, p.327, *Tgb.*1679; *Gespr.* III, No.927, p.443; *Gespr.* III, No.838, pp.334-335.

32. It is possible, as E. Reich suggests, *Grillparzers Kunstphilosophie*, p.8, Anm.1, that his low opinion of speculative aesthetics also owes something to the influence of his great friend and mentor, Josef Schreyvogel, whose opinion of them was even more contemptuous than Grillparzer's.

33. *Gespr.* III, No.800, p.274. Cf. *Gespr.* III, No.927, p.443.

34. *SW* II, 7, p.128, *Tgb.*284. Cf. *SW* II, 7, p.88, *Tgb.*199.

35. *SW* I, 16, p.188. Cf. *Gespr.* II, No.459, IV, p.308, from which it appears that Hegel reciprocated the feeling.

36. *SW* II, 9, p.81, *Tgb.*2016. Cf. *SW* II, 9, p.173, *Tgb.*2179.

37. *SW* II, 12, p.40, *Tgb.*4269.

38. *Gespr.* III, No.911, p.407. Cf. *Gespr.* III, No.899, p.391.

39. *SW* I, 14, pp.140-141 and pp.164-165; *SW* II, 11, p.234, *Tgb.*4068.

40. *SW* II, 12, p.40, *Tgb.*4269.

41. Cf. W.Naumann, *Franz Grillparzer: Das dichterische Werk,* (1967) p.11.

42. *SW* I, 14, pp.81-82.

43. Cf. J. Nadler, *Franz Grillparzer,* (1948) pp.322, 335; Müller, op. cit., p.85.

44. *SW* II, 7, pp.33-34, *Tgb.*79.

45. *Gespr.* V, No.1149, p.53. F. Bouterwek's *Ästhetik,* which first appeared in 1806, was not without influence on Grillparzer's theory, as Strich in particular has shown. Grillparzer's library contained a copy of the 1815 edition of Bouterwek's work (*SW* II, 12, p.134).

46. *SW* I, 12/1, p.302, No.1604. Cf. *SW* II, 12, p.25, *Tgb.*4231 and *SW* I, 12/1, p.294, No.1560.

47. Only the creative artist, he believes, can be a truly competent judge in aesthetic matters. Thus he writes of Schreyvogel in 1832: "Insoweit man ohne ein grosses hervorbringendes Talent Kunstrichter sein kann war er es in vollem Masse." (*SW* I, 14, p.52). Cf. *SW* I, 14, p.73.

48. Naumann, for example, says bluntly: "Als Lyriker ist Grillparzer ohne Bedeutung." (Op. cit., p.12). Scherer, op. cit., p.303, makes the interesting point that he is a better lyricist in his dramas than in his lyrical poems.

49. *SW* I, 16, p.211.

50. *SW* II, 8, p.291, *Tgb.*1617.

51. *Gespr.* VI, No.1531, VII, p.278.

52. *Gespr.* VI, No.1531, IV, p.276.

53. This is to some extent confirmed by the *Selbstbiographie, SW* I, 16, p.71, where Grillparzer recalls how his father's Josephinian views affected the children's religious upbringing.

54. *SW* I, 14, p.52.

55. *SW* I, 14, p.24; *SW* I, 16, p.117; *Gespr.* II, No.55, p.24.

56. *SW* I, 14, p.51; *SW* I, 16, p.121.

57. *SW* I, 16, p.116.

58. *SW* II, 10, p.141, *Tgb.*3168.

59. Fritz Störi, *Grillparzer und Kant,* (1935) p.22.

60. A diary-entry of Schreyvogel's dated 15th March 1817 reads: "Ich habe Grillparzern die Hauptwerke von Kant gegeben. Vielleicht findet er Beruhigung darin." (*Gespr.* II, No.59, p.31).

61. *SW* I, 16, p.92.

62. *SW* I, 16, pp.158-159. Cf. Störi, op. cit., pp.22-24, for a detailed attempt to establish precise dates for the growth of Grillparzer's interest in Kant.

63. Störi, op. cit., pp.131, 180-182.

64. *SW* I, 16, p.58; *SW* I, 14, p.137.

65. *SW* II, 9, pp.78-79, *Tgb.*2010.

66. *SW* II, 7, p.323ff., *Tgb.*864. See also Störi, op. cit., p.23.

67. *SW* II, 7, p.341, *Tgb.*886; *SW* II, 7, pp.343-344, *Tgb.*889.

68. *SW* II, 8, p.3, *Tgb.*959.

69. On the other hand some early critics, notably O. E. Lessing in *Grillparzer und das neue Drama,* claimed to see positive Hegelian influence on his thinking. Their claim rests not upon anything contained in his theoretical writings but upon his actual practice in the historical dramas, in which they found evidence of the dialectical process. Their views have not, however, found general acceptance among later critics.

70. Ernst Alker, *Franz Grillparzer: Ein Kampf um Leben und Kunst,* (1930) p.15.

71. Gisela Stein, *The inspiration motif in the works of Franz Grillparzer,* (1955) p.12.

72. Strich, op. cit., pp.156-159.

73. *SW* I, 16, p.70.

74. *SW* I, 16, p.72.

75. F. Gundolf, "Franz Grillparzer", *Jahrbuch des Freien Deutschen Hochstifts,* 1931, p.12.

76. *SW* I, 1, LXXXIV.

77. M. Enzinger *Die Entwicklung des Wiener Theaters vom 16. zum 19. Jahrhundert* was followed in 1924 by the specific study, *Grillparzer und das Wiener Volkstheater,* which summarized the main findings of the larger work as far as Grillparzer was concerned.

78. Strich, op. cit., pp.130-131, 236; Reich, Grillparzers dramatisches Werk, p.359.

79. Enzinger, *Grillparzer und das Wiener Volkstheater,* pp.11-12, Alker, op. cit., p.91 and Müller, op. cit., p.89.

80. *SW* I, 12/1, p.153, No.908.

81. *Gespr.* VI, No.1539, II, p.291. Cf. *SW* I, 12/1, p.270, No.1439.

82. *Gespr.* IV, No.1098, p.227; *SW* I, 16, p.214.

83. *SW* II, 11, p.132, *Tgb.*3882.

84. *SW* I, 16, p.118. Cf. *SW* I, 14, p.124.

85. *SW* I, 14, pp.92-95.

86. For full details see Enzinger, *Die Entwicklung des Wiener Volkstheaters,* passim, and *Grillparzer und das Wiener Volkstheater.*

87. *Gespr.* I, No.2, p.27.

88. *SW* I, 13, p.113; *SW* I, 14, p.138; *SW* I, 14, p.160.

89. *SW* II, 11, p.241, *Tgb.*4077. Cf. *SW* I, 14, pp.169-170.

90. *SW* I, 16, p.91.

91. *SW* II, 7, pp.49-50, *Tgb.*92.

92. *SW* I, 12/1, p.149, No.893.

93. *SW* I, 16, p.201; *SW* I, 16, p.34; *SW* III, 3, pp.157-158.

94. All of these points will be dealt with in full later.

95. These points too will be fully examined in due course.

96. *SW* I, 16, p.127.

97. *SW* I, 16, p.159; *SW* III, 1, p.300.

98. *SW* I, 12/1, p.299, No.1590.

99. Especially Über den gegenwärtigen Zustand der dramatischen Kunst in Deutschland, *SW* I, 14, pp.72-77, pp.81-85; and Zur Literargeschichte, *SW* I, 14, pp.136-143, pp.156-170.

100. See, for example, *Gespr.* III, No.842, p.337, where he describes the Romantic period as "eine erbärmliche Zeit".

101. *SW* I, 16, p.116. Such was the extent of Schreyvogel's influence over Grillparzer's tastes that Farinelli, *Grillparzer und Lope de Vega,* p.36, goes so far as to claim that most of his literary likes and dislikes can be attributed directly to it.

102. *SW* II, 7, p.313, *Tgb.*821; *SW* II, 8, p.92, *Tgb.*1224; *SW* I, 16, p.144.

103. *SW* I, 14, p.27; *SW* II, 10, pp.179-180, *Tgb.*3248.

104. *SW* I, 14, pp.82-83; *SW* I, 14, p.162; *SW* II, 9, p.230, *Tgb.*2351; *Gespr.* I, No.13, p.269.

105. *SW* II, 11, pp.197-198, *Tgb.*4025; *SW* I, 12/1, p.165, No.960; *SW* I, 12/1, p.165, No.961.

106. *SW* I, 14, p.165; *SW* II, 9, pp.299-300, *Tgb.*2779; *SW* II, 9, p.313, *Tgb.*2822.

107. *SW* II, 11, pp.197-198, *Tgb.*4025; *SW* I, 16, p.181.

108. *SW* II, 9, p.300, *Tgb.*2780.

109. *SW* I, 14, p.156ff., Zur Literargeschichte. Cf. *Gespr.* VII, No.1740, p.143, where he dismisses literary history as having no more substance than "ein gemaltes Mittagessen".

110. *SW* II, 8, pp.128-129, *Tgb.*1315, 1316. For a detailed examination of his views on music see A. Orel, "Grillparzers Verhältnis zur Tonkunst", *Grillparzer-Studien,* ed. Katann, especially pp.283-285.

111. *SW* II, 7, p.30, *Tgb.*62; *SW* II, 9, pp.171-172, *Tgb.*2174; *SW* II, 11, p.13, *Tgb.*3618.

112. Orel, op. cit., p.293.

113. *SW* I, 16, pp.136, 159.

114. *SW* II, 10, p.178, *Tgb.*3247; *SW* I, 16, p.230.

115. *SW* I, 15, p.208, No.482.

116. *SW* II, 9, p.354, *Tgb.*2856.

117. *SW* I, 14, p.166.

118. Ibid. Cf. *SW* I, 11, p.255, No.327.

119. *SW* I, 12/1, p.268, No.1427.

120. *Gespr.* III, No.591, II, p.62.

121. The volume of the Sauer/Backmann edition devoted exclusively to his Spanish studies (*SW* I, 15) contains abstracts of the plots of literally hundreds of Lope's plays together with sometimes quite detailed comments on them. As an indication of the depth of his interest in Shakespeare we may point to his claim to have read Othello no less than thirty times (*Gespr.* V, No.1208, p.226).

122. *SW* I, 14, p.118; *SW* II, 10, p.143, *Tgb.*3173. This line of thinking finds confirmation elsewhere in his aesthetic writings. What Schiller calls "naive und sentimentalische Dichtung" Grillparzer prefers to call respectively "Anschauungs- und Empfindungspoesie". But while it is clear that he rates the "Anschauungspoesie" the more highly of the two, he accepts that it is now unhappily very much more difficult to write it, because, as he explains, "sich immer auf dem Standpunkte der Anschauung zu erhalten, wird schwer in unserer auf Untersuchung gestellten Zeit". (*SW* II, 12, p.20, *Tgb.*4216; *SW* I, 16, p.215).

123. *SW* II, 11, pp.197-198, *Tgb.*4025.

124. The first relevant diary-entry dates from 1816: *SW* II, 7, p.87, *Tgb.*193.

125. *SW* II, 8, pp.157-158, *Tgb.*1362; *SW* II, 8, pp.158-159, *Tgb.*1365.

126. A. W. Schlegel, *Vorlesungen über dramatische Kunst und Literatur,* Lecture 25, especially p.114, and Lecture 35; F. Schlegel, "Vorlesungen zur Geschichte der alten und neuen Literatur", Lecture 12, in F. Schlegel, *Kritische Schriften,* p.605ff..

127. *SW* I, 16, p.114ff.

128. *SW* II, 8, pp.157-159, *Tgb.*1362, 1363, 1365.

129. *SW* II, 8, p.164, *Tgb.*1379.

130. *SW* II, 8, p.255, *Tgb.*1570.

Renny Keelin Harrigan (essay date 1980)

SOURCE: "Woman and Artist: Grillparzer's *Sappho* Revisited," in *German Quarterly,* Vol. 54, No. 3, 1980, pp. 298-316.

[*In the following essay, Harrigan suggests that Sappho appealed to Grillparzer because he viewed her as a figure who was able to integrate her life and art into a complex whole.*]

I

Since it was first performed in 1818, the tragic fate of Grillparzer's Sappho has been interpreted primarily in two ways: either as the result of the artist's betrayal of her calling through descent into life's occasionally murky depths or as the only acceptable exit left for a jealous woman who is incidentally an artist.[1] These expositions accentuate a dualism of character which compartmentalizes Sappho into single, isolated and apparently fully contained components: successful artist or jealous woman in love. While these approaches are useful in distilling different aspects of Grillparzer's theme, they ignore the complexity and totality of the title character. The fundamental mistake of the critics is that of taking the opposition of art and life for granted and of ignoring those discordant elements in the play which don't fit their dualistic conception of Sappho's personality. Implicit in this notion is an unquestioning acceptance of the Cartesian duality between mind and body, between spirituality and sexuality, which has had a lasting impact on Western culture and literature.[2] In addition, this notion is accompanied by an uncritical acceptance of the separation between art and life as something "natural."

I hope to provide an analysis here which reaffirms the integrity of the whole person and which builds on the insights of one critic who has provided the beginnings of an alternative to the picture sketched above. George Reinhardt interprets *Sappho* on two levels—the psychological and the mythic: "Reason alone can explore the depths of Sappho's ravaged psyche. Empathy alone, aroused and assisted by the skill of a great actress, can fully appreciate Grillparzer's tragic vision of the artist as both more and less than the average mortal. By accepting the dual nature of Sappho, the passionate woman who is also an archetypal Muse, one can reconcile otherwise discordant elements of her character."[3] Reinhardt's insights into the reciprocity between Sappho's art and life are invaluable, especially since they are unique in Grillparzer criticism. But despite these insights, Reinhardt eventually reverts

back to the traditional view—which of course was that of the romantics and of Grillparzer himself—that art and life cannot be united: "The Muse exacts a harsh penalty: her own must come to know the 'malheur d'être poète'!" (p. 140). By insisting on Sappho's identity as the Muse's own, Reinhardt too ascribes her artistry to the divine realm which is far removed from everyday life: "Because Sappho is a genius her love will not be reciprocated. . . . The poet is a marked man [sic], doomed to isolation and denied human companionship" (loc. cit.). I, in contrast, tend to view Sappho's immortalization as an unsuccessful attempt by the world she leaves behind in the play, as well as by the critics, to mystify what they fail to understand about the creative process and the exceptional female in a world where only males are assumed to be subjects. Sappho's tragedy is neither the tragedy of a woman nor that of a poet. It is the tragedy of a woman-poetess who challenged both the separation of art and life and the extant male/female role models. Since both the art/life dichotomy and traditional difference between masculine and feminine roles have come to be recognized in their historic specificity and development, we should no longer interpret Sappho's death as a return to her genuine calling as a poetess, but rather as her acknowledgment of failure to achieve the unity she desired.

In contrast to previous studies, Sappho is viewed here as a multifaceted person who lives but one level of existence and who neither ascends nor descends in any real existential or psychological sense. Her art is public and lived, and it ceases to find an outlet at the end of the play. Her rejection by Melitta, the beloved child, is surely as important as her rejection by Phaon, a consideration which previous critics underestimated.[4] Sappho's death is not only a vindication of her passionate past as Reinhardt claims (p. 140), but simultaneously a denial of art—*because* it is the ultimate denial of life.

Sappho dies unable to fulfill the mandates of her calling because she has been effectively prevented from living as the result of the constellation which crystallizes in the course of the play: she is unable to fulfill herself in the private sphere because she cannot be accepted in any role except that of artist/deity by those around her. Since her public fame has become undeniable—a fact underscored by the victorious return from Olympia which opens the play—she can be henceforth ignored only as the private person who is a woman. Sappho the woman creates with all her sensibilities, but she is de-sexed by her public through the divinity they thrust upon her. Without life to draw from, she cannot create, for her poetry is nothing less than the product of the interplay between her passionate, sensitive nature and the world around her. She commits suicide because the relationship between art and life has been destroyed.

If it is Sappho's need for integrity that leads to her death, why are the critics almost unanimous in their assumption of a strict separation between the components of her life—art and reality—in which Sappho's choices are mutually

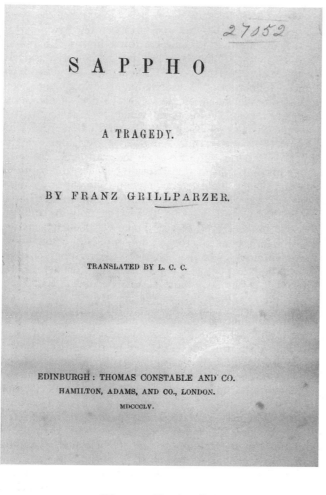

Title page of Sappho, *1818.*

exclusive? A familiar pattern can be detected which begins with the works of female artists. These women, viewed as exceptions to the rule of "human" nature, are mentally transformed into abstract notions of general "human" perfectibility by male-dominated criticism. Here, the critics have divorced Sappho's art from her person by declaring her a body-less, sex-less god. It is the only way her production as an artist can be understood and accepted. Silvia Bovenschen, commenting recently on this phenomenon, said: "Diese Argumentation—die Zahl der Kunsttheoretiker, die in diese Kerbe schlugen ist Legion—auf ihre banale Grundstruktur gebracht, heisst: Frauen sind anders, und ein Moment ihres naturgegebenen (wohlgemerkt!) Andersseins ist, dass sie zur Kunst nicht fähig sind. . . . Die spärlich gesäten weiblichen Literatur-, Kunst- und Musikproduzentinnen sind von der Kunstkritik stets als exotische Sonderfälle behandelt worden. . . ."[5] It is this type of thinking which accounts for the dualistic concept which dominates *Sappho* criticism: either Sappho is a passionate woman (and human) or a creative artist (and divine) but it is simply incomprehensible to the critics that she could be both artist and woman. Grillparzer's text is in

fact far richer than this type of reductive thinking gives it credit for, and Bovenschen suggests an approach which unlocks its insights and ambiguities: ". . . solche Ausführungen, [wie, z.B, hier die *Sappho*-Kritiker—RKH] halten Momente von Wahrheit, wenn auch in steter Verwechslung von Ursache und Wirkung. Gegen den Strich, gegen die Intention gelesen, ergeben derartige Elaborate ein unverschleiertes Bild . . . des verstellten Zugangs" (*loc. cit.*). Bovenschen's insistence on the value of reading against the grain opens the way for a reinterpretation of *Sappho* based on textual, historical and societal evidence.

II

Grillparzer's own understanding of his play changed in the course of his lifetime, which is not unusual. His lengthiest comment on Sappho is contained in the often-cited letter from 1818 to Adolf Müllner. Sappho is a character of "glühender Leidenschaften" and "*erworbene* Ruhe," but above all,

> Sappho ist Dichterin! Dass *das* hervorgehoben werde ist durchaus nötig, die Wahrscheinlichkeit der Katastrophe hängt wie ich glaube wesentlich davon ab . . . Ich . . . musste *vor* dem Sturme der Leidenschaften eine Kraft anschaulich machen, die mit unter die erregenden Kräfte des Sturmes selber gehört. Die Dichtungsgabe ist kein in der gewöhnlichen Menschennatur liegendes Ressort, sie musste daher herausgehoben werden.[6]

In Grillparzer's view, Sappho is a superior character simply because she is a poetess. Modern audiences may have trouble with this somewhat romantic definition of the artist although Sappho's critics prefer to ascribe her emotional extremes to this cause. The letter continues:

> Ferner! Sappho ist in der Katastrophe ein verliebtes, eifersüchtiges, in der Leidenschaft sich vergessendes Weib; ein Weib das einen *jüngern* Mann liebt. In der gewöhnlichen Welt: ist ein solches Weib ein ekelhafter Gegenstand. War es nicht durchaus notwendig, sie noch vor dem Sturm der Leidenschaften so zu zeigen, wie sie in ihrem gewöhnlichen Zustande war, damit der Zuschauer die Arme bemitleide, statt sie zu verabscheuen

> (*loc. cit.*).

The age disparity is Grillparzer's own invention and he ridicules it here with a vehemence which corresponds not at all to the reality in the text nor to his later utterances. Thirty years later Grillparzer wrote of the character, "Was man meiner Sappho zum Vorwurf machte, ist vielmehr ein Vorzug des Stückes—dass ich nämlich mehr das leidende Weib als ihr poetisches Element hervorhob" (p. 108). Finally, in 1866 or 1867 Grillparzer wrote to Auguste von Littrow-Bischoff of a Sappho who is fully consistent with my interpretation of the play but who completely contradicts his own understanding of the figure in the earlier letter to Müllner: Es war dem Geiste des Stückes entgegen, dass ältere oder reizlose Frauen diese Rolle spielten, weil Entsagung in der Liebe von seiten der Frau in reiferen Jahren allzu sehr in der Ordnung der Natur liegt" (p. 115).

Since assumptions about Sappho's age in the play have led to different interpretations, it is perhaps best to clarify the matter immediately from the text. Sappho once comments, "Von Mytilenes besten Bürgerinnen / Ist manche die in freudiger Erinnrung / Sich Sapphos Werk aus frühern Tagen nennt (II, vi, 749-51),[7] but this information tells more about her position in the community than her age. A better estimate of Sappho's age is contained in the latter's conversation with Melitta who at the age of either 15 or 16 has been Sappho's slave for thirteen years (III, v, 1049), since the time Sappho was "selber noch ein kindlich Wesen" (III, v, 1054). Assuming that a woman is still partially a girl from the ages of 12 to 16, Sappho is still under thirty. Grillparzer's conception of the poetess as an impassioned woman whose renunciation of love is forced upon her too early is confirmed also by Sappho's words at her death when she consecrates herself to the gods "in voller Kraft, in ihres Daseins Blüte" (V, vi, 2005). George Reinhardt sensibly concludes that Grillparzer presents "not aging but a gap in age between lover and beloved" (p. 140); I would add he presents a gap in experience as well.

The age difference was accepted and even ignored, it seems, by the Viennese public if its adulation of the 37-year-old Sophie Schroeder in the title role is any indication. The actress was constantly involved with younger men and had in fact started a relationship with a 26-year-old—Grillparzer's age at the time—shortly before opening in *Sappho*.[8] Perhaps the public tolerated more from its "exceptional" women, but the extent to which actresses were sexually and economically independent was accompanied by a lesser degree of social acceptability. The city of Vienna had been exposed to licentious activity of the European nobility during the Congress of Vienna three years before.[9] Thus the thesis might instead be advanced that Sappho's experience would actually be an exotic lure for younger males and females rather than a problem and that if in fact she becomes an "ekelhafter Gegenstand," it is only through her jealousy that she does so.

If Sappho's age is Grillparzer's innovation, his choice of a protagonist is clearly the historical Sappho:[10] both are educators of women, both are high priestesses in the cult of Aphrodite, goddess of sexuality and fertility; both are reputed to be erotic creatures, whether homo-, hetero-, or bisexual. The most important aspect of the historical Sappho for our study is her position "as a poet with an important social purpose and public function: that of instilling sensual awareness and sexual self-esteem and of facilitating role adjustment in young females coming of age in a sexually segregated society."[11] Such a view lends credence to the idea that Sappho's relationship with Melitta should be re-evaluated. After all, if Grillparzer had been interested solely in the question of art or passion why would he have gone out of his way to choose Sappho as his protagonist? And even if his age did not care to speculate about Sappho's sexuality, the fact that he chose a poet who lived with and educated only women is surely of significance.

III

Grillparzer's Sappho views her art as an integrated part of her life and in this she is similar to the historical Sappho.[12] Our first view of her is at her public and professional best—an effect calculated by Grillparzer in the above mentioned Müllner letter. Her salutation to her people gathered to welcome her home as the victorious poet of the Olympic games is couched in terms which connect her art with her role in the community: "Um euretwillen freut sich dieser Kranz, / Der nur den *Bürger* ziert, den *Dichter* drückt, / In eurer Mitte nenn ich ihn erst mein" (I, ii, 45-47). Although a distinction is made between common citizen and poet, Sappho embodies both without any contradictions here. The concrete manifestation of her poetic calling, the wreath, takes on its meaning only to the extent that she is the citizen of a community, albeit first among equals. Her art has its proper value in public service within that community which had witnessed and nourished her growth both as poet and as person. Rather than separating art and life, she sees them as interdependent and Grillparzer presents them that way in the first act.

Sappho continues this theme in the following scene with Phaon, although here she can be justly accused of exaggerating to disarm him and praise him. She lists his gifts as "Leibesschönheit," "Lebenslust," "Mut," "Stärke," "Entschlossenheit," "Lust an dem was *ist,* und Phantasie." She asserts, "Und *leben* ist ja doch des Lebens höchstes Ziel!" (I, iii, 264-70). She ascribes traditional masculine traits to Phaon here, except that fantasy, the artist's creative power, in fact belongs to Sappho. She continues by granting Phaon—through gesture if not actual word—the will to live, leaving for herself by implication the aesthetic realm: "Und ewig ist die Kunst gezwungen, / [mit ausgebreiteten Armen gegen Phaon] Zu betteln von des Lebens Überfluss" (I, iii, 276-77). Two latent problems are contained *in nuce* here. First, it will become important that Sappho alone by virtue of her position and her experience can do the bestowing; secondly, the first hint at separation of what has been a harmonious relationship for Sappho is implied by the open arms which allot life to Phaon and art or intellect to Sappho. In an attempt to create reality through the power of her words, she now aims at exaggerating the difference between herself and Phaon, thus positing the eternally masculine and the eternally feminine as antipodes. The mystifying dichotomy which Sappho hints at here is prompted by her desire to create two opposites which seek each other for completion, herself and Phaon. She also attempts with her words to alleviate Phaon's obvious discomfort with her accomplishments and her position. She implies the duplicity of her attempt with the words which conclude her speech:

> Lass uns denn trachten, mein geliebter Freund,
> Uns *beider* Kränze um die Stirn zu flechten,
> Das Leben aus der Künste Taumelkelch,
> Die Kunst zu schlürfen aus der Hand des Lebens.
>
> (I, iii, 280-83).

Thus she ends the interchange on the earlier note of unity between art and life which we expect from her.

At the Olympic games she had been one among many competing artists; here she is obviously without peer. If Sappho's description of her life and her past are to be believed, the abstract opposition of art and reality has had no place in her life up to now. The dichotomy between art and life which she forces at this point becomes a problem for Sappho only because she begins to believe it herself in the course of the play. The more difficulty she has with her new love, the more worthless the life she had formerly valued becomes (III, ii, 944) and the more extreme she believes to be her choice of either life or art (III, ii, 950-53; IV, ii, 1271-75). Such rationalizations and abstractions characterize the middle of the play; when Sappho later opts for death, it is a decision informed by her earlier experience of the reciprocity between art and life.

The demands and rewards of Sappho's art are equalled by her immersion in life. Her opening dialogue with Phaon (I, iii), with its twice repeated "Ich hab gelernt verlieren und entbehren" (I, iii, 113; 122), reveals either hard-won equilibrium or resignation which stems from the breadth of her past experiences: "So ward mirs stets im Wechseltausch des Lebens; / Ich war zufrieden, und bin hoch beglückt" (I, iii, 109-110). The personal losses she refers to in the next lines extend beyond her relatives (I, iii, 115-18) for she admits, "Der Freundschaft und der—Liebe Täuschungen / Hab ich in diesem Busen schon empfunden" (I, iii, 120-21). The pause before admitting to her sexual experience seems less a product of drama than of her momentary uncertainty about whether or not to reveal to the insecure Phaon that here too she probably overshadows him completely. Although she has not achieved a personal happiness which would preclude her search for new relationships, her experiences have not left her embittered. Quite the opposite—through experiencing life in its many guises she is able to embrace life without reservations. The "Unermesslichkeit / Die auf und nieder wog in dieser Brust" (I, iii, 126-27) remains intact, the source of life which is simultaneously the source of her art.

The ability to interact with one's environment, or in Sappho's vocabulary, to immerse oneself in life, is a necessary pre-condition for psychological and emotional growth but because of Sappho's "Unermesslichkeit," or boundless receptivity, the potential for self-dissolution is present as well. At the same time, Sappho's capacity to love is possible only through her *choosing* vulnerability, which is a necessary component of the "Unermesslichkeit" so important to her both as artist and woman. This, rather than inexperience, is what kindles Sappho's rage later. Her living at the limits is what makes it difficult for others to accept Sappho; for Sappho to live that kind of life without destroying herself proves finally impossible.

Sappho's desire for intensity is what prevents her from finding her equal among either friends, lovers or even other artists. The realization of her isolation, the enormity of which is only beginning to dawn on Sappho at the play's beginning, makes her long for a return to her innocent, pre-conscious youth. Some critics interpret Sappho's desire here to return to her childhood as evidence of her inexperience,[13] but textual evidence, as shown above, proves quite the contrary. Her wish is rather a manifestation of doubt which the exposure of self causes in any love relationship:

> Lasst mich zurückekehren in die Zeit,
> Da ich noch scheu mit runden Kinderwangen,
> Ein unbestimmt Gefühl im schweren Busen,
> Die neue Welt mit neuem Sinn betrat.
> Da Ahnung noch, kein qualendes Erkennen
> In meiner Leier goldenen Saiten spielte

> (I, v, 385-90).

To interpret these lines as the desire for youth alone is to miss their full import, for the responsibility of authentic existence is so great that even someone as dynamic as Sappho occasionally desires release from it. Sappho connects her youthful prescience here with her art. At that time she had created through the fresh appreciation of her senses for the world she was beginning to discover about her. Since then her art has become critical and conscious, no longer spontaneous and instinctive. The immediacy of experiencing life is accompanied by her longing for and appreciation of it. Life and art are repeatedly interrelated even here. Sappho's heightened awareness of isolation is the result of the constellation which opens the play: public acknowledgement of her poetic genius which will make it more and more difficult for others to accept her as a person also in need of love and companionship.

IV

The first indication we have of Sappho's complete isolation resounds in her conversation with Melitta in the first act. At this point she is secure, or blind, in her love for Phaon. In this mood she cannot perceive here the possibility of betrayal from either Melitta or Phaon. Despite Melitta's spontaneous appreciation of Phaon's beauty, the bond between her and Sappho is intact. Sappho's relationship with Melitta has generally been underestimated, starting with Grillparzer himself who debated in his letters whether he should leave Melitta "ganz aus dem Spiele" (p. 109), calling her a "dummes" (p. 109) and "albernes Mädel" (p. 114). Insofar as he perceives the unfolding of Sappho's personality as the focal point of the play, Melitta may indeed be regarded as a marginal figure; but Sappho's relationship with Melitta is unique and essential for an understanding of the play. Sappho's attempt to create a friendship between equals with Melitta is sincere, given their close relationship. Having eschewed Phaon's address of "Erhabene Frau" (I, iii, 130) in the previous scene, Sappho acts in a similar manner with Melitta here: "Nicht Sappho, die Gebietrin steht vor dir, / Die Freundin Sappho spricht mit dir Melitta" (I, v, 348-49). Sappho desires a love from both these people which includes friendship and a recognition of both individuality and differences. Sappho wishes with Melitta "In Zukunft . . . als traute Schwestern / In seiner [Phaons] Nähe leben, gleichgepaart, / Allein durch seine Liebe unterschieden" (I, v, 361-63). Her love for Melitta is distorted here by the immediacy of her interest in Phaon but Sappho's incessant talk of "him" who remains unnamed throughout the entire scene betrays above all the need to share her heady experience with her natural confidante and potential equal. The gulf which nevertheless separates the two women has already been made apparent through Sappho's role as Melitta's teacher and model in the lines opening this scene.

It is Melitta's emergence from adolescence during Sappho's absence which sets the pre-conditions for transformation of the relationship between the two. Sappho's wish is not as capricious as it seems, although the emotional history Melitta and Sappho share—ultimately that of mother and daughter—is stronger than their tentative attempts at a new beginning. The emphasis on the mother-daughter relationship is constant; "Mein Kind" is Sappho's spontaneous appellation for Melitta (I, v, 339; 425) except when calling her by name. It is also the relationship to which not only Melitta reverts when she calls Sappho "Mutter" (V, iv, 1758-60; 1774; 1785) but Sappho as well (V, vi, 2020) when she calls herself "Mutter." Although Sappho's emphasis on this aspect of their relationship is exaggerated for her own purposes when she speaks to Phaon in Act II (vi, 739-47), her inability to see Melitta as a rival is prompted by the mother's desire not to have her child hurt in an irresponsible flirtation. The intense conflict Sappho feels is confirmed by her inability to meet Melitta face to face after she has commanded her removal to Chios (IV, iii, stage directions at end) and by her bewailing the strength of their past relationship, of habit as "Ein lästig Ding" (IV, iii, 1333) shortly before this decision is made. It is the habit of the mother-child relationship which is referred to here, for this is the context in which Sappho describes her past with Melitta, from the time she purchased her as a sickly baby from the "wilde[n] Männer[n]" (III; v, 1050) who had kidnapped her: "Mich dauerte der heimatlosen Kleinen, / . . . ich bot den Preis / Und schloss dich, selber noch ein kindlich Wesen / Mit heisser Liebe an die junge Brust" (III, v, 1052-55). Through the sleepless nights which follow in nursing Melitta back to health, Sappho demonstrated a mother's need-oriented, selfless, and at times self-denying love.[14] It is the intensity of this bond which is still felt, and which prevents her from seeing Melitta as a rival even after she has witnessed the kiss (III, v, 1071-72). Grillparzer has captured here in terse dramatic language and compressed action the difficult process of a child's path to independence from its mother, a process often effected through the child's assertion of its sexuality.[15] Later adolescent attraction to the mother on the part of both boys and girls is directed toward more acceptable love objects in the course of the child's separation from the mother. The phenomenon is complicated here since mother and daughter have chosen the same man. Sappho concludes at this time with a wish for the future, that Melitta and she be sisters and equals: "Lass unsre Herzen aneinanderschlagen, / Das Auge sich ins Schwesteraug versenken / Die Worte mit dem Atem uns vermischen" (III, v, 1073-75). The words describe a highly eroticized relationship to which only Politzer alludes through his recognition of Sappho's jealousy not only of Melitta

but also of Phaon (p. 94). The exclusivity of the mother-child bond is the case in the family Freud was to describe much later, but it is unusual both for Sappho's and for Grillparzer's period.

By the middle of the play, the "Schwesteraug" of Sappho's hopes disintegrates, albeit with much hesitation and confusion, into the "Herrinaug" (III, v, 1091) of the stern and disciplinary mother. The friendship between equals is impaired by pre-established patterns of behavior—just as reframing any mother-child relationship into one in which both recognize the other as independent is not only difficult but for many impossible. To expect a new basis to emerge within the short time span of the action is unrealistic and complicated by the external pressures placed upon that relationship, namely Sappho's public position and Phaon's aggressive pursuit of Melitta. Sappho's "tragic guilt" seems to me greatest not in the betrayal of her art but in the rash attempt to kill and later to remove Melitta from Mytilene. The mother sins against the daughter. Infanticide, particularly by the mother, is an act of such enormity that it makes us shudder even in today's calloused age, when we are only beginning to understand the conflicting pressures upon maternal love and the institution of motherhood within the nuclear family.[16]

Grillparzer's age was dominated, according to Friedrich Sengle, by a mother cult in which "Liebe und Gefühl" were prized more highly than "Leistung und Autorität."[17] Thus, qualities associated with the historically feminine (and specifically maternal) were prized more highly than those associated with the historically masculine. This assignation of value was, of course, still possible in a primarily pre-industrial age. The image of woman as mother, mainstay and center of the Biedermeier hearth, was even more idealized, it seems, than it is today. The natural conclusion, then, would be that Melitta as the child and the potential friend has a special place in the play.[18] Precisely because Grillparzer chose as a protagonist Sappho, the educator of women, the center of a women's cult in honor of Aphrodite, we must pay close attention to her relationships with women. Like all other characters, Melitta has meaning only in relationship to the title character; however, she is the only one who consistently sees Sappho as a woman and an individual behind her many roles. We recognize this in the first scene: the people prepare to greet Sappho as a triumphant poet laureate, but Melitta at first seems to scoff at what she perceives as their exaggeration. She receives the announcement of Sappho's arrival with an ironic question: "Wer?—Götter!" (I, i, 7). This implies not only a more intimate relationship with Sappho than, for example, Rhamnes has, but also a healthy disrespect for any tendency to deify a woman whose humanity she knows so well. When Melitta discovers that her friend has won the poetry contest, she becomes enthusiastic, but even here she sees the person rather than the "Kranz": "Ich sehe Sappho nur! Wir wollen ihr entgegen!" (I, i, 24-25). Rhamnes immediately squelches Melitta's enthusiasm by saying, "Der *Mann* mag das Geliebte laut begrüssen, / Geschäftig für sein Wohl liebt still das *Weib*" (I, i, 38-39). Rhamnes' words here certainly imply that Melitta and Sappho's relationship is a close one; more important, however, he emphasizes how little Sappho fulfills society's expectations for women by transforming her into the man for whom Melitta, the woman, waits "geschäftig" and "still."

Melitta's special role is also evident as a mediator between Sappho and her environment, most often in explaining her to Phaon. He is incapable of comprehending Sappho as an integrated person (II, iv, 671-72; V, iv, 1776-77; 1795-98). At the conclusion of the play, Melitta is the only one of the entire assemblage who understands Sappho's pain. In a great many respects, this last act represents Melitta's coming of age; she approaches Sappho as an emotional and psychological equal even though her words are often couched in the patterns which their past history has established. Melitta's naivete and innocence are gone forever:

> Ich kann nicht leben, wenn sie mich verdammt!
> Ihr Auge war von jeher mir der Spiegel,
> Vor dem ich all mein Tun und Fühlen prüfte!
> Er zeigt mir jetzt die eigene Ungestalt!
> Was muss sie leiden, die gekränkte Frau!
>
> (V, iv, 1788-92).

Melitta assumes responsibility here at last for her own role in this particular tragedy. There is a marked difference in the Melitta here and the Melitta of the third act who is passively ready to give Sappho both Phaon's rose and her life and then just as passively allow herself to be drawn from the scene by Phaon.

V

Phaon's most important function in the play is that of catalyst, for it is difficult to see why Sappho could fall in love with him. He is certainly believable as the object of passion[19] but hardly as an appropriate consort for Sappho. The situation his appearance precipitates is extreme because it requires an end to Sappho's relationship with Melitta. If Melitta is the only one who sees Sappho as a complete person, and Sappho rejects Melitta in favor of Phaon, then in the symbolic context, this means that Sappho would have to reject the possibility of an integrated existence and accept herself as a truncated personality. Since this is humanly and psychologically impossible, Sappho chooses to die affirming her own integrity. Phaon comes to represent in essence the voice of the people which Reinhardt very correctly labels the voice of conventionality (p. 130).

We already have some idea of the conventions which govern male and female behavior from Rhamnes' comment to Melitta on the occasion of Sappho's homecoming. But such conventional expectations are complicated by Sappho's public position, hence Rhamnes' consternation when Sappho introduces Phaon as his master—and her consort (I, iv, 302). In this response, Rhamnes is not dissimilar to Phaon who had already expressed his misgivings to Sap-

pho: "Und bist du wirklich jene hohe Frau, / Wie fiel dein Auge denn auf einen Jüngling, / Der dunkel, ohne Namen, ohne Ruf, / Sich höhern Werts nicht rühmt?" (I, iii, 155-58). Both men are incapable of seeing the particular woman with human needs who is also Greece's poet laureate, and both operate from assumptions based on stereotypes of accepted behavior for a man and woman of Sappho and Phaon's respective stations.

Sappho recognizes from the start that her worldly superiority will be a problem. Only that realization could prompt her self-delusive wish to exchange the laurel wreath of fame with the myrtle wreath of domesticity (I, ii, 95). Whereas both Sappho and Phaon recognize more and more consciously their differences as the play progresses, both lovers wish to remain blind to the emotional maturity and sensitivity which mark Sappho's superiority over Phaon, a superiority which is not even diminished by her irrationality and jealousy. The desire of all lovers to shower each other with gifts poses yet another unforeseen problem since Sappho alone has the abundance from which to bestow. Her impulsive offer, "Was mein ist, ist auch dein. Wenn dus gebrauchst, / So machst du erst, dass der Besitz mich freut" (I, iv, 293-94), is deflated by Phaon's reply which clarifies how uncomfortable he feels in his position of grace: "Wie kann ich so viel Güte bezahlen? / Stets wachsend fast erdrückt mich meine Schuld!" (I, iii, 299-300). Phaon's immediate translation of Sappho's gifts into concrete money terms is the simplest way of dealing with the situation but also most unfortunate since it is doubtful whether Phaon would ever be able to repay such munificence—at least in kind. Sappho later recalls her impulses at that time as an attempt to make Phaon her equal (IV, i, 1222-30) but great inequality between two lovers places an immense burden on any relationship. Had the roles been reversed, the problem would undoubtedly have been overcome; after all, the Pygmalion myth is a popular model for male / female relationships and it does not have a female equivalent.[20]

The conventions of accepted sex role behavior are confirmed by Sappho at the start of Act III. The passage is an attempt to rationalize the kiss she has just witnessed, but it is also an expression of the problems confronting a socially prominent, successful female whose male lover is neither well known nor accomplished. Sappho ruefully questions, "Was heisst den Masstab denn für *sein* Gefühl / In *dieser* tiefbewegten Brust mich suchen?" (III, i, 809-10). The somewhat rhetorical question focuses upon the age-old problem of unequal emotional involvement. Love is a gift freely and often capriciously given; however, Sappho delineates the male role as inconstant, insistent on change and hungry for renown (III, i, 813-20) and proceeds,

> Und findet er die Lieb, bückt er sich wohl,
> Das holde Blümchen von dem Grund zu lesen
> Besieht es, freut sich sein und steckts dann kalt
> Zu andern Siegeszeichen auf den Helm
>
> (III, i, 821-24).

In this extended metaphor, the man lowers himself in order to raise the beloved one to his level; once conquered, however, the woman becomes his reflection rather than retaining any identity of her own. The image of the woman as the "holde Blümchen" evokes a picture of shyness, purity and, with the diminutive, youth in need of protection. Even less astute readers would realize that this image does not correspond to the sophisticated Sappho; in fact, the description reads as an entrance cue for someone like Melitta.

The social expectations for the female are not unknown to Sappho as the above quote from Act III details. Woman is overcome completely by the emotion of the moment. She lives in and through her relationship to the loved man:

> Er kennet nicht die stille mächtge Glut
> Die Liebe weckt in eines Weibes Busen!
> Wie all ihr Sein, ihr Denken und Begehren,
> In diesem einzgen Punkt sich einzig dreht
> . . . Das ganze Leben als ein Edelstein
> Am Halse hängt der neugebornen Liebe!
>
> (III, i, 825-34)

On the one hand, Sappho correctly identifies women's traditional susceptibility to and emphasis on need-oriented relationships. On the other, she is deluding herself if she believes that Phaon's love can become her whole life, as is so often the goal of the woman socialized to domesticity. Psychologically Sappho feels the need to camouflage what she perceives to be the unequal commitment in her own love relationship behind the guise of generalizations about female and male behavior. Although Sappho wishes indeed to immerse herself completely in her new love, she is able to do so without becoming Phaon's appendage. This combination in Sappho of self-abandonment and self-affirmation pinpoints her problem in conforming to the norm.

The dualistic conception of Sappho's personality which denies the complexity of the individual only serves to extend the conventional view which would place Sappho within the accepted norm for women. Phaon's perception of Sappho fails consistently in comprehending the whole person: he views her only as the "erhabene Frau" (I, iii, 130-31) of public office, as a "hohes Götterbild" (I, iii, 164) who will be deified by all at the play's end, and as the victorious and famed poet (I, iii, 240-48), the office which combines her many different roles.[21] Phaon's is a lone voice at the start of the play and Rhamnes' stereotypical admonition of Melitta can be dismissed as that of a loyal but obtuse bureaucrat; in any case Melitta's human view of Sappho counterbalances both male attitudes. Grillparzer himself undermines Phaon's exaggerated, idealized picture of Sappho by having him detail his own inadequacy and immaturity. Phaon constantly refers to himself in self-deprecating terms as "Hellas letzte[n] Jüngling" (I, iii, 257), a "blöde[n] Jüngling" (I, iii, 245), an "arme[n] Jüngling" (I, ii, 80) whose life before being chosen by Sappho has been one of "stille[n] Niedrigkeit" (I, iii, 133). His confusion and self-questioning, expressed in his mono-

logue at the start of Act II, are completely understandable. Rather than accept the challenge of meeting Sappho as a person, his exaggerated perception of both Sappho's grandeur and of his own lowliness serves to protect him from that encounter. Phaon's peremptory and insensitive treatment of Melitta provides the psychological counterpoint to his threatened loss of self under Sappho's beneficence and power.[22]

Phaon's evasion of this personal challenge issued by Sappho is accompanied by his rationalization that Sappho can function only as a divinity if she wishes to maintain any sort of moral integrity. He is in actual fact simply taking the escape route which Sappho had opened for him at the start through her forced description of a dichotomy between art and life which she does not accept. Phaon extends it here in the interests of his own self-preservation. At first, he defines Sappho's regained "divinity" in terms of his own subjective needs:

> Du bist mir wieder was du einst mir warst,
> Eh ich dich noch gesehen . . . Dasselbe Götterbild,
>   das ich nur irrend
> So lange für ein Menschenantlitz hielt,
> Zeig dich als Göttin! Segne, Sappho, segne!
>
> (V, iii, 1717-21).

Phaon implicitly admits his inability to deal with the complexities of Sappho as a woman, wishing for the same distance his image of her had provided him before they met. From here he proceeds to extend the image of a divine Sappho, constructed from his personal needs, to the entire community:

> Mit Höhern, Sappho, halte du Gemeinschaft,
> Man steigt nicht ungestraft vom Göttermahle
> Herunter in den Kreis der Sterblichen.
> Der Arm, in dem die goldne Leier ruhte,
> Er ist geweiht, er fasse Niedres nicht!
>
> (V, iii, 1726-30).

With these words Phaon's personal needs become the moral imperative for the whole community—except for Sappho, since for her it means exclusion from life, and thus death. With this glib mental abstraction Phaon saves himself and effectively shuts the door to Sappho's participation in the emotions and inconsistencies of a life lived rather than thought.

That other voice of conventionality, Rhamnes, concludes the play in a summation which cannot be regarded as anything but a mystifying conclusion: "Es war auf Erden ihre Heimat nicht— / Sie ist zurückgekehrt zu den Ihren!" (V, vi, 2040-41). Sappho herself provides a more plausible explanation when she says, "Ihr, die ihr Sapphon schwach gesehn, verzeiht! / Ich will mit Sapphons Schwäche euch versöhnen" (V, vi, 1973-74). These words relieve Phaon, Rhamnes and her entire people of all responsibility toward her. Only the public Sappho can henceforth be exhibited, but a Sappho in need of guidance, comfort and love must be concealed. Constant fortitude—self-motivated, self-sustaining and self-regenerating—is beyond the realm of the human and Sappho, understandably so, rejects the sterile life of a pseudo-deity. She "chooses" to die only because she has no other choice. Her death is indeed an affirmation of her whole life which is the source of her art. Art and reality have been closely related in Sappho's life but this close relation—which should not be mistaken for identity[23]—brings her into conflict with a world demanding that art and reality define their difference by total separation. Although the people's view of Sappho as a divinity renders her acceptable to them as a poet, in actual fact that vision floats free of all flesh and blood. Sappho's private view of herself is that of a still integrated personality, "voller Kraft, in ihres Daseins Blüte" (V, vi, 2005), but simply "zu schwach . . . länger noch zu kämpfen" (V, v, 2014).

Is it an accident that the two female characters express an appreciation for the totality of human existence while the two males construct an abstract compartmentalization of art and life, male and female? I think not, for Grillparzer has molded historically recognizable male and female types. Rhamnes and Phaon represent the dominant male culture which has ascribed positive value to the rational, the analytical, the objective, the instrumental. Alternatives associated with the female—intuitive, poetic, subjective, associative—have been labeled irrational or hysterical and are therefore seen as negative, both by the males in the play and by many of the critics. The dualistic conception of Sappho which is a product of this sort of thinking has dominated much of the *Sappho* criticism. In my attempt to understand Sappho's character, I hope to have shown that such abstractions are inaccurate, delusive or at best incomplete constructs which outline abstract ideas rather than doing justice to Grillparzer's representation of a character. Even though Grillparzer's criticism of his culture's dualistic evaluation of the male/female split is at best semiconscious, his text does criticize this duality precisely by presenting as his protagonist a woman who unsuccessfully attempts to hold the opposite poles of male and female, art and life together. To speak with Silvia Bovenschen, "reading against the grain" of the criticism, and to a lesser extent of the text, magnifies those aspects of Grillparzer's critique which continue to make his play so readable today.[24]

Notes

1. There is a review of the literature in Joachim Müller, *Franz Grillparzer,* 2nd ed. (Stuttgart: Metzler, 1966), pp. 25-29; and in George Reinhardt, "A Reading of Grillparzer's *Sappho,*" in *Studies in the German Drama: A Festschrift in Honor of Walter Silz,* ed. Donald H. Crosby and George C. Schoolfield (Chapel Hill: University of North Carolina, 1974), esp. pp. 125-27. Some of the critics who view Sappho as an artist are Roy Cowen, "Zur Struktur von Grillparzers *Sappho,*" *Grillparzer Forum Forchtenstein* 1 (1968), 66; on page 65 he states "die einzige mögliche Lösung" is what happens in the last act, "die Wiederherstellung des ursprünglichen Dualismus;" Michael

Ossar, "Die Künstlergestalt in Goethes *Tasso* und Grillparzers *Sappho,*" GQ 45 (1972), 6; Keith Spaulding, ed., *Sappho* by Franz Grillparzer (London: Macmillan, 1965), p. xvii; Benno von Wiese, *Deutsche Tragödie von Lessing bis Hebbel,* 2nd ed. (Hamburg: Hoffmann & Campe, 1952), pp. 395, 396.

Those who emphasize her human weaknesses are Joachim Müller, "Figur und Aktion in Grillparzers 'Sappho'-Drama," *Grillparzer Forum Forchenstein* 6 (1970), 8-43; Berndt Breitenbach, *Ethik und Ethos bei Grillparzer,* Quellen und Forschungen zur Sprache- und Kulturgeschichte der germanischen Völker," N.F. 18 (Berlin: De Gruyter, 1965), p. 142; Gert Kleinschmidt, *Illusion und Untergang: Die Liebe im Drama Franz Grillparzers* (Lahr/Schwarzenwald: Schauenbach, 1967), p. 78; Heinz Politzer, "Der unfruchtbare Lorbeer: *Sappho*" in *Franz Grillparzer oder das abgründige Biedermeier* (Vienna, Zurich, Munich: Molden, 1972), pp. 81-100.

2. This assumption is found in one very prominent work, Paul Kluckhohn, *Die Auffassung der Liebe in der Literatur des 18. Jahrhunderts und in der deutschen Romantik,* 3rd ed. (Tübingen: Niemeyer, 1966).

3. Reinhardt, p. 127. Douglas Yates is another critic who makes an attempt to view Sappho as a whole person (p. 37) but he also says, "Sappho was by her poetic nature a woman of violent passions. She was a poetess by virtue of this fact, but only when she exercised restraint over her true nature" (p. 50) in *Franz Grillparzer: A Critical Biography* I (Oxford: Blackwell, 1946).

4. Politzer, p. 97.

5. Bovenschen, "Über die Frage: gibt es eine weibliche Ästhetik?," *Ästhetik und Kommunikation,* 25 (1976), 62. Heinz Politzer says, for example, "Es ist ein Frauenschicksal, das Grillparzer hier darstellt, und ein Künstlerdrama nur insofern, als der Ruhm des Dichters [sic] dieser Frau lediglich als ein Makel oder wie ein körperliches Gebrechen anhaftet. Erst am Ende, wenn sie ihren Tod auf sich nimmt, vollendet sich diese Sappho als Dichterin [sic] und damit als tragische Figur" (p. 86).

6. All the quotations from Grillparzer's letters are taken from Karl Pörnbacher, ed., *Dichter über ihre Dichtungen: Franz Grillparzer* (Munich: Heimeran, 1970), here p. 103 ff.

7. All quotations from the play in Franz Grillparzer, *Sämtliche Werke,* ed. Peter Frank and Karl Pörnbacher, I (Munich: Hanser, 1960).

8. Schroeder later married a man twenty years her junior. See Yates, p. 45-46.

9. Friedrich Gentz' public affair with the dancer Fanny Elssler is but one example in Stella Muson, *Vienna in the Age of Metternich: 1805-1848* (Boulder, Col.: Westview, 1975), p. 222.

10. Grillparzer wrote, "Ich konnte der Versuchung nicht widerstehen, die zweite der beiden übriggebliebenen Oden Sapphos, die mir zu passen schienen, in dem Stücke, das ihren Namen führt aufzunehmen, damit man mir doch nicht sagen könnte, es sei *gar nichts von ihrem Geiste darin*" (p. 106 in Pörnbacher). For an account of the historical Sappho, see Denys L. Page, *Sappho and Alcaeus* (Oxford: Clarendon, 1955); Sarah Pomeroy, *Goddesses, Whores, Wives and Slaves: Women in Classical Antiquity* (New York: Schocken, 1975), p. 56 ff; and most recently Judith Hallett, "Sappho and her Social Context: Sense and Sensuality," *Signs: An Interdisciplinary Journal of Women's Studies,* 5 (1975), 447-64.

11. Hallett, p. 450.

12. Ossar, pp. 646-47.

13. Müller, "Figur und Aktion," p. 20; Cowen agrees with one exception: "Ihr einziger Kontakt mit dem Leben ist bisher ihre Mutterrolle gewesen, nicht nur Melitta, sondern auch der Inselbevölkerung gegenüber" (p. 67); Politzer believes her love to be reciprocated here for the first time, "zumindest für die kurzen Stunden der Reise von Olympia nach Leukas" (p. 86).

14. Both Ulrike Prokop in *Weiblicher Lebenszusammenhang: Von der Beschränktheit der Strategien und der Unangemessenheit der Wünsche* (Frankfurt: Suhrkamp, 1976), p. 67 and Adrienne Rich in *Of Woman Born: Motherhood as Experience and Institution* (New York: Norton, 1976) talk about this dual quality of maternal love.

15. Sigmund Freud would have to be called the first to discuss the eroticization of the mother-child relationship, implied through his theories of infant sexuality, oedipal conflict, and choice of the first love object. For a discussion of Freudian theory applied to mothering see Alice Balint, "Love for the Mother and Mother-Love," in Michael Balint, ed., *Primary Love and Psycho-Analytic Technique* (New York: Liveright, 1965); Nancy Chodorow, *The Reproduction of Mothering* (Berkeley, Los Angeles: University of California Press, 1978). A popular book which makes mother the culprit is Nancy Friday, *My Mother, My Self* (New York: Dell, 1977).

16. Adrienne Rich has a very interesting discussion of this phenomenon, and Michael Cacoyanis' film *Medea* (1978) also deals with it.

17. Friedrich Sengle, *Biedermeierzeit: Deutsche Literatur im Spannungsfeld zwischen Restauration und Revolution: 1815-1848* (Stuttgart: Metzler, 1971), I, 60.

18. The only article on Melitta is by Sylvia C. Harris, "The Figure of Melitta in Grillparzer's *Sappho*," *JEGP* [*Journal of English and Germanic Philology*] 60 (1961), 102-10. She sees her only as Sappho's rival.

19. Phaon's rejection of Sappho certainly causes pain as evidenced in her exchanges with Melitta (III, v) and with Phaon at the end (V, iii) and by her own non-verbal gestures: her tears (III, vi, 1180); her rigid, uncomprehending stare (III, vi, after 1161 and 1177); her inability to meet Phaon's eyes (III, v, after 1673); and her painful shudder when she finally does (III, v, middle 1708). I think that the relationship has to be put into a broader context than it usually is.

20. Politzer sees Sappho as a Pygmalion to Melitta (p. 95).

21. Norbert Griesmeyer's book, *Das Bild des Partners in Grillparzers Dramen*, Wiener Arbeiten zur deutschen Literatur (Vienna: Braumüller, 1972) is useful in analyzing the self-deception involved in Sappho's and Phaon's perceptions of one another.

22. Phaon's own self-deception is nowhere more evident than in his relationship with Melitta whom he believes he treats as an equal. This never prevents him from ordering her around and treating her in general with a callousness of which Sappho at her worst was incapable.

23. According to Reinhardt, "The poetess does not admit this distinction between art and life," p. 143.

24. Pat Russian, with whom I once spoke about many of the ideas expressed in this paper, provided one important impetus for my writing of it.

Edward McInnes (essay date 1980)

SOURCE: "Psychological Insight and Moral Awareness in Grillparzer's *Das goldene Vliess*," *Modern Language Review*, Vol. 75, No. 3, 1980, pp. 575-82.

[*In the following essay, McInnes explores the tension between analytical insight and moral concern in* Das goldene Vliess, *emphasizing that Grillparzer's imagination operated outside the conscious level of action. McInnes further suggests that Grillparzer anticipated later and more radical developments in nineteenth-century German drama.*]

The dramatic work of Grillparzer has proved notoriously difficult to relate to the wider development of German literature in the nineteenth century.[1] It is not that links with the main literary movements are hard to establish, but rather that those that present themselves seem so diverse and mutually incompatible. It was, for instance, as easy for the Naturalists to show that he was a significant forerunner of their own radical concerns as it was for Gundolf to contend with some conviction that he was a mere epigone of Weimar classicism.[2]

The difficulty which has always confronted critics seems to stem from the fact that Grillparzer's work is shaped by such diverse impulses, and embraces such seemingly discontinuous modes of awareness that its essential character is particularly hard to define. Looking back we can now see that the steady rise in Grillparzer's standing as a dramatist in the past fifty years or so coincides with the deepening critical appreciation of the power of his creative imagination to integrate divergent drives and aspirations and embody them in an original and coherent aesthetic form.³ It is also noticeable that commentators, while not denying the probing, experimental energy of his dramatic work, have tended to assume that its conception can still finally be understood in terms of the artistic and moral assumptions which he inherited from the eighteenth century. The drama as Grillparzer conceives it, they have claimed, resists the relativizing tendencies apparent in the work of contemporary and later playwrights. It still represents— and on this critics as different as Münch, von Wiese, Baumann, Kaiser, Papst, Fülleborn, and Schafroth seem to be agreed—a wholly coherent, self-sufficient, symbolic form which reflects in itself an ultimate moral universe.⁴ Though they have all recognized in their different ways Grillparzer's often radical concern to lay bare the psychological and circumstantial pressures which undermine the individual's moral freedom and distort his understanding of himself, they have none the less insisted that the controlling impetus of his imagination is to assimilate these empirical tendencies, to subdue them to a conception of destiny which claims absolute moral significance.⁵

It is within this very broad framework of agreement that commentators in recent years, however different their individual methods and preoccupations, have pursued their studies of Grillparzer's work. Although their particular conclusions have often diverged widely, many of their basic presuppositions have remained strikingly constant. In this essay I would like to look again at some of these critical assumptions by re-examining from a rather specific point of view the tension between analytical insight and moral concern which critics have generally held to be central to the conception of Grillparzer's plays. I have chosen to approach this question through a detailed discussion of *Das goldene Vliess* (1820) which seems to me to occupy a crucial, if by no means clear-cut, place in his work. The dramatist himself was in many respects uneasy about this trilogy and many of his critics seem to have shared his disquiet.⁶ Although they have normally accepted that it is a significant work they have tended in practice to play down its importance when attempting to arrive at a general estimate of Grillparzer's work as a whole.⁷

The dramatist's doubts about *Das goldene Vliess* are reflected in his apparent unease about the symbol of the Fleece and its place in the dramatic world of the trilogy. His comments on it are for the most part explanatory and defensive, as if he were intent on confining, even neutralizing, its imaginative impact. The Fleece, he insists, does not reveal the working of an impersonal fatality, it does not in itself determine the action or infringe the sovereignty of the characters as moral agents.⁸ This is all quite true, but it takes no account of the strangely disconcerting power of this symbol to evoke a sense of pervading moral

impotence which is just as averse to the clear rationalizing interpretation which Grillparzer's comments seem to imply. In the course of the trilogy, the Fleece comes to enforce more and more strongly a harshly sceptical and ironic mode of perception. It seems to focus the dramatist's will to suggest the elusiveness and ambiguity of the world which the dramatic figures claim to know and interpret. For the Fleece, as he presents it, is essentially mysterious and inaccessible. Though those who desire it may claim it is theirs by right, its origins are in fact irrecoverably lost in legend (I, 848 f.); and though they consistently try to use it as a vindication of their actions, it remains opaque to moral understanding.

This remote, impenetrable character of the Fleece is apparent right at the beginning of the trilogy. Phryxus takes the fateful step of removing it from the temple in Delphi because he believes he has been instructed to do so by a god who has appeared to him in a dream. Once he has taken the Fleece, the dramatic improvement in his fortunes convinces him that he is indeed the agent of a divinely-ordained plan (I, 807 f.). The fact that he is brought against all the odds through a terrible storm to Colchis and finds there the image of the god who appeared in his dream is for him the ultimate proof that the whole inscrutable course of events is determined by the gods. In this unquestioning belief he commits himself to Aietes, the barbarian king. 'Den Himmlischen vertrau ich mich und dir!' (I, 809).

The dramatist ironically opposes this faith of Phryxus with the equally insistent belief of Aietes that he is called by Peronto, the tribal god of Colchis, to claim the Fleece, 'das heilige Pfand des Gottes', for his people (I, 810). The god demands that he punish the Greek's terrible act of desecration and forces him to override the obligation of hospitality. He treacherously murders Phryxus and seizes the Fleece in the conviction that he is fulfilling a divinely appointed duty.

It is news of this murder and seizure of the Fleece that brings Jason and the Argonauts to Colchis. The gods, they believe, oblige them to punish the breach of the sacred law of hospitality and reclaim the Fleece for the Greeks (I, 843, 849 f.). When in the end Jason has succeeded in winning back the Fleece, he is able triumphantly to confront the stricken Aietes with the higher significance of his mission: 'Als Werkzeug einer höheren Gewalt | Steh ich vor dir' (I, 887).

In the first two parts of the trilogy, *Der Gastfreund* and *Die Argonauten*, Grillparzer sceptically questions the shared belief of the three central male figures that their actions enjoy a divine sanction by showing in each case how this belief coincides with their deepest half-hidden desires. He shows that the murderous desire of Aietes to rob the intruding Greek is there before he hears of the Fleece (I, 800 f.), and makes it clear that the conviction of Phryxus and Jason that they are chosen by the gods is bound up with a deeply resentful sense of having been cheated by life (I, 806 f., 829). The dramatist seems to be suggesting that the characters' awareness of the supernatural is psychologically conditioned, that it is part of the process through which an irrational compulsion gains control of the conscious mind and co-ordinates all the energies of the self in the pursuit of a single goal.

This subjection to the irrational is most fully explored in the presentation of Jason in *Medea,* the final part of the trilogy. Grillparzer shows that even after his return to Colchis when he is in the grip of real hardship Jason's awareness of the gods is still controlled by the pressure of his selfish will. Although, it is true, he regards the disgrace and homelessness of himself and Medea as a divinely imposed punishment (I, 898 f.), it soon becomes clear that this does not involve any profound, transforming awareness of failure. The dramatist shows rather that he is able to use this awareness as a means of asserting himself against the woman he now rejects (I, 906, 908). While still nominally accepting his guilt he is able, by substantially exonerating his own intentions, to see Medea more and more as the real source of his plight and thus as fully deserving divine punishment (I, 921, 937, 939 f., 945 f.). When Kreon finally decides to offer Jason hospitality on condition that he separates from her for good, this serves to confirm his largely inarticulate sense of what the gods in their justice must decree. It appears to him as a destiny which is imposed on Medea, a destiny not of his making and against which it is futile to protest. His readiness to see the king as the instrument of divine powers is rooted, the dramatist suggests, in a deep driving resentment of Medea which he cannot fully acknowledge.

This reiterated exposure of weakness and delusion in Grillparzer's portrayal of the male protagonists is, as it were, the effective frame within which he explores the experience of Medea which is at the very centre of his artistic concern. She appears throughout as a being who, in contrast to these male figures, is capable of confronting genuine moral crisis in herself and who (again unlike them) is driven more and more to acknowledge a world which contradicts her deepest spiritual intuitions.

Right at the beginning of the trilogy Medea is aware of a conflict between the god's demands, as her father interprets them, and her own sense of religious obligation (I, 809 f.). Though they worship the same deity and acknowledge the same loyalties, she rejects Aietes's claim that he is obliged to kill the Greek who is seeking asylum. When in the end she does yield to her father's demand for help, she does so reluctantly and in the knowledge that she is involved in a crime which will be punished (I, 814 f.). She is aware that this premonition is fulfilled when her father approaches her some time later and asks again for help against the invading Argonauts (I, 822 ff.). This renewed experience of crisis, however, is suddenly swallowed up in a quite new and shattering awareness of moral helplessness which is precipitated by her sexual encounter with Jason. In her involuntary attraction to the Greek, Medea is visited by a feeling of total inner impotence. She experiences love as a force which estranges her from herself, an-

nuls her will, and drives her into a betrayal of the ties and loyalties which have sustained her from birth and shaped her sense of her identity (I, 856 f., 868 f.). This betrayal also leads to terrible consequences which she could never have conceived: the suicide of her brother, and her rejection by her father followed also by his eventual death (I, 887, 930). In the whole process of sexual submission and guilt Medea is overcome by an annihilating sense of moral victimization. She can see no real connexion between her own conscious will and the actions she performs, or between these and the catastrophes to which they lead. She sees herself as invaded by an alien force which treacherously combines with circumstances equally beyond her control to thrust upon her a guilt too awful to bear, but which she must accept as her own.

In *Medea* it becomes clear that the experience of moral violation has undermined her spiritual existence. But it is equally apparent that what lends this experience such destructive force is the fact that it becomes for her the vehicle of a deeper sense of metaphysical horror. In this experience of moral bondage she is aware of having been abandoned by the gods and left the prey of a senseless, chaotic world (I, 892). At the beginning of *Medea,* however, Grillparzer shows that she still recoils from this recognition of lostness and fights with despairing intensity to prove she can begin life anew.

The structure of *Medea* is thus essentially analytical. The dramatist shows how she is forced by events beyond her control to face the fate she obscurely acknowledges, but which she still despairingly resists. Both the events which precipitate her final breakdown—her rejection first by Jason, then by her children—she knows in some part of herself to be inescapable. Although she insists that she can find a new beginning through Jason's love, placing in him, as Gora sees, the kind of faith she once gave the gods (I, 892), she also realizes that he is by his very nature unable to give her the love she craves (I, 912); and despite her ferocious struggle to keep her children, in whom she places her hope of an untainted future, it is clear that she also senses at the very moment of her betrayal that she could never break its strangling hold upon her (I, 951 f.).

The effect of this twofold rejection, as the dramatist makes clear, is to expose her to an irresistible despair. It finally destroys her frenzied struggle to give meaning and purpose to her life. And it is as though all the driving energy of this struggle were transformed into a violent compulsion to destroy. Helpless in its grip it seems to her deranged mind as if she were called to take upon herself the task of retribution which indifferent gods have ignored, of righting the flagrant injustice they have left unchecked (I, 948).

In revenge Medea does not seek to lessen her own suffering, but to draw Jason into the depth of her own despair. Her aim is not to kill him, but to empty his life of hope by depriving it of a future. In murdering first Kreusa, his bride-to-be, then his children, she takes from him all possibility of finding a new meaning which could redeem the guilt and misery of the past. At the same time, as Gora foresees (I, 931), she is also celebrating her own inner death, expressing in the only way open to her the totality of her own despair.

In *Das goldene Vliess* the dramatist uses the imaginative possibilities inherent in the mythical setting to embody his own individual, sceptical preoccupation. Within this setting he is able to counterpose directly the belief of the dramatic figures in the power and the ubiquity of the gods with the ironic demonstration of their ultimate elusiveness. The awareness of the supernatural, as Grillparzer portrays it here, is always essentially subjective, always ambiguously bound up with the constraints of the selfish will.

In this concern to undermine the characters' sense of the divine which plays such an important part in their understanding of themselves, the dramatist is emphasizing the isolation and weakness of the moral self. Throughout the trilogy the individual appears as imprisoned in his own subjective self-awareness, unable to perceive or respond to any order of value beyond the scope of his own pressing desires. The determining motives of the characters, Grillparzer shows, lie in a sphere of irrational compulsion which is largely inaccessible to the conscious will, but which has the power so to subdue and exploit the individual's reasoning faculties, as to leave him defenceless before it.

The persistent drive to question the standing of the characters as moral agents implies, it seems to me, a basic uncertainty about the ultimate character of the dramatic world itself. This appears as a world in which the position of all moral experience is fundamentally doubtful. This uncertainty is especially evident when we attempt to interpret the fate of Medea. While the dramatist sees the male protagonists as morally disabled by passion, he seems to show the heroine's experience of meaninglessness as stemming from a genuine metaphysical contradiction, from a discrepancy between an innate longing for moral significance and a deepening awareness of contingency in her actual existence. Her breakdown seems, that is, to presuppose a primary moral aspiration which is understandable only in metaphysical terms. But even here the sceptical, discursive drive of Grillparzer's imagination suggests the possibility of another interpretation. The persistent analysis of moral helplessness throughout the trilogy forces us to ask whether Medea's spiritual breakdown may not stem from a specific psychological weakness, from an emotional inability to withstand the tension arising out of her experience of guilt, rejection, and exile. It seems possible to see it, in other words, as a particular, psychologically-conditioned process which, however the heroine may see it, lacks all wider moral-metaphysical significance.

This impression of moral ambiguity is heightened by the dramatist's failure to put forward any positive, coherent moral principle in the trilogy. He does not seem to see either in communal life or in the sphere of close personal relationships any standard of value or ethical imperative, to which we might attribute normative significance. Certainly his sceptical, ironic mode of vision does clearly entail a powerful moral awareness. But this remains implicit and does not lead, as far as I can see, to any positive and concrete ethical assertions.

This points to a deep-lying tendency in Grillparzer's work which critics have not yet, in my view, adequately assessed. Much of its tense, sceptical energy stems from the impetus of his imagination, which is never fully conscious, to probe and even to undermine his explicit moral assumptions. I can perhaps illustrate this most clearly by looking briefly at the works of his middle period, *König Ottokars Glück und Ende* (1823) and *Des Meeres und der Liebe Wellen* (1829), in which he is most obviously concerned to show the working of a supreme moral force in a specific dramatic situation. In both these plays, in marked contrast to *Das goldene Vliess,* Grillparzer is intent on presenting a dramatic figure whose attitude to life is determined by a renewing awareness of a transcendent order of value. In both works (again in contrast to *Das goldene Vliess*) he seems concerned to realize a dramatic world which is able to reflect and sustain this personal awareness of meaning.

In *König Ottokar* Grillparzer's moral purpose is quite clear and consistent. He is concerned to represent a vision of history as the vehicle of an ultimate ethical process. He shows that decisive historical developments are determined not by impersonal forces, but by the willed actions of responsible individuals. Ottokar's failures as a ruler reflect his basic weakness as a man. In divorcing his wife he is driven by an insatiable vanity which destroys his personal happiness, causes the break-up of his kingdom, and brings him into confrontation with the Empire (I, 995 f., 976, 1019 f.).

The dramatist also makes it clear that Rudolf's selfless dedication to his vision of the divinely instituted order of the Empire is a transforming political force (I, 1021, 1039 f.). It is this vision which enables him to settle long-standing disputes, bring together people and individuals who have been at odds, and inspire them with a dynamic sense of purpose (I, 1030).

This clear moral intention, however, remains at important points in conflict with the working of Grillparzer's creative imagination. I have tried to show in detail elsewhere how in realizing the dramatic action he actually sees the central developments within the context of a wider collective situation which goes far beyond the scope of the personal responsibility of the individual figures.[9] Although he repeatedly stresses their moral independence, he actually portrays their actions as decisively modified by far-reaching historical-political processes, over which they have no control. This discrepancy is most evident in Grillparzer's presentation of Rudolf. The dramatist's concern to stress the political effectiveness of his mystical idea of the Empire is in tension with his particularizing, pragmatic view of historical causality. This seems to me symptomatic of a rift in the conception of Ottokar, with which Grillparzer himself has not come to terms. His empirical awareness always threatens to subvert his moral aim in a way which the dramatist seems unable to acknowledge.

In *Des Meeres und der Liebe Wellen* we can see a similar conflict of impulses. Here again the dramatist seems to attribute a normative moral significance to an outlook which is governed not by self-will, but by the individual's awareness of his ultimate dependence upon a universal order of being. This is focused in the notion of 'Sammlung', as this is so eloquently defined by the Priest (II, 43 ff.). This denotes an essentially visionary mode of perception, in which the human being is able to reach out beyond the limits of his own subjectivity and grasp his existence as part of a divinely ordained cosmos (see Papst, pp. 12 f.). In this state of heightened mystical responsiveness there lies, as the Priest makes clear, the possibility of an integration and fulfilment of the self which overcomes the fragmentation of ordinary, day-to-day experience and transforms every aspect of existence.

Grillparzer does not attempt, as far as I can see, to qualify critically this notion of 'Sammlung', and as Papst, in particular, has shown, it corresponds to beliefs to which the dramatist in his personal life was deeply committed (Papst, pp. 13 ff.). Yet despite this it is noticeable that critics disagree sharply about Grillparzer's presentation of the Priest and about his function in the development of the tragic action.[10] Grillparzer's own comments leave little doubt, however, that he was concerned to show the Priest's decisive intervention as motivated by a desire to protect Hero from the danger into which her relation with Leander has brought her and to win her back to the priesthood. In destroying Leander he is convinced that he is selflessly fulfilling the obligation of his office and carrying out the will of the gods (II, 58 f., 75 f.).

Grillparzer himself was aware that he had not fully succeeded in realizing this conception of the Priest (see Yates, pp. 174 f.). He sensed in particular that he had failed to bring to life the determining force of the Priest's commitment to a moral ideal. This is probably true, but it does not go far enough. The real problem, in my view, lies not in the dramatic presentation of the figure, but in the nature of the ideal he is supposed to represent. It is hard to see how his notion of 'Sammlung' could be expressed as a coherent moral attitude in the particular situation in which he is caught up. The need for quick, decisive action is necessarily in conflict with his commitment to the essentially contemplative values which represent for him man's highest spiritual achievement. It forces upon him the distorting anxieties of the committed agent which he himself knows to be hostile to his ideal aspirations (II, 43 f.).

This reveals a discrepancy in the conception of the figure of the Priest. His dedication to the ideal of 'Sammlung' has no necessary connexion with his position as custodian of the temple. Although he himself is unable to see it,

there is a split between his belief in the liberating possibilities of a mystical self-awareness and that moral-intellectual commitment to certain specific forms of religious practice which drives him to oppose Leander. It is important to note this discontinuity. For not only does it force us to see the behaviour of the Priest in a way which Grillparzer himself does not intend; it also drives us to question the relevance of the notion of 'Sammlung' to the dramatic conflict. However valid as a spiritual aim, however sincerely advocated by the Priest, are we not forced to see it in the end as an ideal relevant to the subjective aspirations of this one figure, but lacking direct influence on the actual tragic development?

I have been trying to suggest that in these two important works following *Das goldene Vliess* the dramatist has difficulty in realizing his essentially intellectual sense of moral purpose in terms of a concrete developing dramatic situation. In both works, although in rather different ways, the moral values, to which he seems to attribute normative significance, remain largely detached from a view of the dramatic action which is shaped by a determinist awareness of causal process. In the conception of both *König Ottokar* and *Des Meeres und der Liebe Wellen,* there is a deep unresolved tension with which, as far as I can see, the dramatist has not fully come to grips.

The implications of this pervading tension in Grillparzer's work are most fully revealed in the powerful late play *Ein Bruderzwist in Habsburg.* Here the playwright is attempting to evolve a form 'open' and flexible enough to embrace dramatically a basic disparity between ethical will and circumstance, tragic action and historical process. This is embedded in the opposition of two contrasting levels or kinds of dramatic development which Grillparzer ironically counterposes throughout. In the imaginative foreground there is an inter-personal sphere, in which the characters make plans, conflict with one another, and pursue their own particular objectives. But beyond this, the dramatist also evokes the shaping momentum of social-historical processes which pervade most of the European continent and which none of the dramatic figures can oversee or understand (II, 434 ff., 443 ff.). These immense processes are seen as engulfing all their lives, sweeping them along towards a cataclysm which threatens to destroy the whole fabric of civilization. The ironic impetus of Grillparzer's vision is openly apparent in his portrayal of figures like Klesel and Ferdinand who believe they can direct and manipulate events. But he also sees the withdrawn, anguished existence of Rudolf II in a similarly ironical perspective.[11] For although the Emperor's unbearable responsibility and failure lead to an awareness of self-violation which seems at times genuinely tragic, this experience is diminished and called in question by the wider historical frame. The act of impetuous anger in which he sees himself betray his God-given trust and thrust his people into destruction (II, 431 f.), appears in its historical context at the very most to hasten slightly the outbreak of this terrible war which has been coming closer and can no longer be avoided (II, 360, 399 ff., 423). The climax in the foreground inter-personal action is eclipsed by the momentum of those historical forces, on which it has only a minimal effect.

In this essay I have been suggesting that the conception of Grillparzer's drama is governed by the working of a probing, sceptical imagination which seems to operate to an unusual extent outside the control of his conscious moral awareness. I have been keen to emphasize this, because I think it can open up a way of approach which could enable us to see more clearly the deep underground affinities which link his work with the more openly radical, experimental drama of his contemporaries Grabbe and Büchner. It might also make it possible for us to assess those profound, though often obscured, impulses in his creative imagination which reach far beyond the scope of his express aesthetic-moral intentions and, so it seems to me, anticipate powerfully the main development in the German drama towards the end of the nineteenth century.

Notes

1. For a full and perceptive critical survey of these attempts see W. N. B. Mullan, 'Grillparzer and the Realist Tradition', *FMLS* [*Forum for Modern Language Studies*], 13 (1977), 122-35.

2. See, for example, O. Brahm, *Kritiken und Essays,* edited by F. Martini (1964), pp. 250 ff. and F. Gundolf, 'Franz Grillparzer', *Jahrbuch des freien deutschen Hochstifts* (1933), pp. 9-93.

3. This has been well brought out by Mullan, p. 122.

4. See, for example, J. Münch, *Die Tragik in Drama und Persönlichkeit Franz Grillparzers* (Berlin, 1931), pp. 43 ff.; B. von Wiese, *Die deutsche Tragödie von Lessing bis Hebbel,* second edition (Hamburg, 1952), pp. 385 ff.; G. Baumann, *Franz Grillparzer: Sein Werk und das österreichische Wesen* (Freiburg, 1954), pp. 51 ff.; J. Kaiser, *Grillparzers dramatischer Stil* (Munich, 1961), pp. 39 ff., 112 ff.; U. Fülleborn, *Das dramatische Geschehen im Werk Franz Grillparzers* (Munich, 1966), pp. 199 ff.; E. E. Papst, *Grillparzer: Des Meeres und der Liebe Wellen* (London, 1967), pp. 17 f., 56 ff.; H. H. Schafroth, *Die Entscheidung bei Grillparzer,* Sprache und Dichtung, 19 (Berne, 1971), pp. 51 ff. See also K. Partl, *Schillers 'Wallenstein' und Grillparzers 'König Ottokars Glück und Ende'* (Bonn, 1960), pp. 79 ff., 229 ff.

5. The implications of this are most fully explored by Kaiser, pp. 114 ff.

6. See Franz Grillparzer, *Selbstbiographien,* in *Sämtliche Werke,* edited by P. Frank and K. Pornbacher (Munich, 1960-65), IV, 88 f. and 111 f. All references to Grillparzer's works in the body of the text are to this edition. *Das goldene Vliess* and *König Ottokars Glück und Ende* are in Vol. I; *Des Meeres und der Liebe Wellen* and *Ein Bruderzwist in Habsburg* are in Vol. II; the *Selbstbiographien* and *Tagebücher* are in Vol. IV. On the problems of Grillparzer's use of the

trilogy form see U. Fülleborn, 'Zu Grillparzers "Goldenem Vliess": Der Sinn der Raum- und Zeitgestaltung', in *Jahrbuch der Grillparzer-Gesellschaft,* 12 (1976), 39-59.

7. As far as I can see only Fricke lends this work a really crucial place in his interpretation of Grillparzer's view of tragedy. See G. Fricke, '*Wesen und Wandel des Tragischen bei Franz Grillparzer*', in Fricke, *Studien und Interpretationen* (Frankfurt a.M., 1956), pp. 264-84.

8. F. Grillparzer, *Tagebücher* 1241, p. 380; *Selbstbiographien,* pp. 87 ff. On the symbol of the Fleece in the trilogy see W. E. Yates, *Grillparzer. A Critical Introduction* (Cambridge, 1972), pp. 87 f.

9. See E. McInnes, '"König Ottokar" and Grillparzer's Conception of Historical Drama', in *Essays on Grillparzer,* edited by B. Thompson and M. Ward (Hull, 1978), pp. 25-36.

10. See C. Walker, 'The Light of the Gods in "Des Meeres und der Liebe Wellen"', in Thompson and Ward, pp. 37-46.

11. I have discussed this fully in an article on 'Grabbe and the Development of Historical Drama in the Nineteenth Century', in *German Life and Letters,* 32 (1979), pp. 104-14.

Ian F. Roe (essay date 1981)

SOURCE: "*Der Arme Spielmann* and the Role of Compromise in Grillparzer's Work," *Germanic Review,* Vol. 56, No. 4, Fall, 1981, pp. 134-39.

[*In the following essay, Roe discusses Grillparzer's* Der Arme Spielmann, *as well as several other plays, in terms of the dramatist's artistic and spiritual development, noting that* Spielmann *demonstrates a more mature artistic and moral vision.*]

Grillparzer's **Der arme Spielmann** has in recent years attracted considerable critical attention, and the debate concerning Jakob's negative or positive qualities shows no sign of ending. Nevertheless, as the titles of the two most recent full studies of Grillparzer's work indicate,[1] there is still a tendency to treat his one major prose-work in isolation from the dramas or, at best, to consider its relevance in an understanding of the author himself. Such biographical links are certainly of considerable interest: the echoes of the **Selbstbiographie** are only too obvious, whilst the ambivalent attitude of the narrator to the masses and their festival reflects Grillparzer's own equivocal approach to the emergence of nationalism and liberalism in the period which culminated in the upheavals of 1848. But in addition one may seek to demonstrate that in the picture of Jakob's isolation and artistic failure, despite all his acclaimed moral standards, there are clear links with similar characters in Grillparzer's mature plays.

As early as 1822 Grillparzer had suggested in his diary that there was a delicate balance between good and bad: "die meisten Laster sind eigentlich nur der Exzeß guter Eigenschaften" (*Tgb.* [*Tagebücher*] 1202).[2] Grillparzer's early plays, however, are relatively unambiguous in their insistence on moral values—peace, purity, justice, limitation, moderation, humanity[3]—and *König Ottokars Glück und Ende,* with its specific comparison of Ottokar and Rudolf in moral terms, is the culmination of this early period. By comparison, *Ein treuer Diener seines Herrn* already reflects a more original treatment by Grillparzer of the problems inherent in ethical and moral standards. True morality must never be taken to extremes, as the King makes quite explicit:

> Doch Sitte hält ihr unverrückbar Maß
> Streng zwischen allzuwenig und zuviel.

> (11.295-6)

Bancbanus's adherence to peace and justice is certainly excessive, if ultimately to be praised. From 1830 onwards such adherence is not to be praised; Grillparzer's plays repeatedly point to the dangers inherent in "zuviel des Guten," in an "Exzeß guter Eigenschaften." Increasingly one detects a tendency to put life higher than morality, to compromise, however reluctantly, for the benefit of activity and life as a whole. To take the most obvious example at this stage, Bishop Gregor comes to realize at the end of the comedy *Weh dem, der lügt!* that his demand for absolute truth was unnatural, inhuman even, that mistakes are human and a part of life. There is no question of rejecting morality; on the contrary, the plays reveal a constant stress on the need for the ethical standards that Grillparzer drew predominantly from German Classicism, and warn the audience of the dangers of ignoring such values. But equally the dramatic works contain numerous warnings on the quite different dangers of excessive morality in the world of reality and activity. It is these dangers that are fully evidenced also in *Der arme Spielmann.*

By the standards of the society in which he moves, Jakob does indeed lead "a life of failure at every step."[4] He fails at school, at work, in love, and in music. Again and again the other characters, or where necessary the narrator, point out this failure or the inadequate nature of his successes. His handwriting is "widerlich steif" (III, 153), Barbara's song "gar nicht ausgezeichnet" (162), his music "ein höllisches Konzert" (156), whilst of Barbara we are told: "es schien fast als ob sie nie schön gewesen sein konnte" (185). After saving the children from the floods, he dies of a chill because he returns to save ledgers and money. The happiest day of his life is a kiss through a glass door. He cannot pluck up courage to see Barbara, he is over-conscientious at school and at work, he is condemned as weak, effeminate, as a child who ignores important matters.

And yet one of the clearest indications of Jakob's isolation from others also gives a first pointer to the positive side of his character. The chalk line in his room divides "Schmutz" from "Reinlichkeit," chaos from order (156). Jakob himself insists, "die Unordnung ist verwiesen" (157), order was a theme of his first conversation with the narrator: "der Mensch (muß sich) in allen Dingen eine gewisse Ordnung festsetzen, sonst gerät er ins Wilde und Unaufhaltsame" (152). Similarly he believes he could have learnt at school, "wenn man mir nur Zeit und Ordnung gegönnt hätte" (159), if he had been given time to organize each item "im Zusammenhange mit dem übrigen" (160).

This search for order is a sign of Jakob's moral fibre. He disapproves of the activities of "Nachtschwärmer," which he considers "ein widerliches Vergehen" (152), he condemns the masses for their "genossene Tanzfreuden oder sonst unordentliche Ergötzlichkeiten" (153). His music must not encourage such dubious entertainment with "unartige Lieder," instead he hopes that the effect of his music will be "Veredlung des Geschmackes der ohnehin von so vielen Seiten gestörten und irregeleiteten Zuhörerschaft" (ibid.). Jakob is normally a man of modesty, self-critical, content with his lot, but he takes a certain pride in his appearance, upholds middle-class values of cleanliness, tidiness, order, as well as morality. Above all he has a pride in his music, he does not want to be thought of as a beggar, he insists on practising in order to put on a worthy performance.

The only song he can play, however, is Barbara's song. The reason why he cannot otherwise play a recognizable melody is fascinating, and becomes clear from two descriptions of his music, the first of which is introduced as the narrator visits Jakob:

> Der Alte genoß, indem er spielte. Seine Auffassung unterschied hierbei aber schlechthin nur zweierlei, den Wohlklang und den Übelklang, von denen der erstere ihn erfreute, ja entzückte, indes er dem letztern, auch dem harmonisch begründeten, nach Möglichkeit aus dem Wege ging.

> (156-7)

Jakob distinguishes between harmony and dissonance, between good and evil notes. He lengthens, repeats the good notes; the bad notes he skips over as quickly as possible. The reason for such a musical interpretation becomes clear in Jakob's own words later:

> Die ewige Wohltat und Gnade des Tons und Klangs, seine wundertätige Übereinstimmung mit dem durstigen, zerlechzenden Ohr, daß . . . der dritte Ton zusammenstimmt mit dem ersten und der fünfte desgleichen und die Nota sensibilis hinaufsteigt, wie eine erfüllte Hoffnung, die Dissonanz herabgebeugt wird als wissentliche Bosheit oder vermessener Stolz und die Wunder der Bindung und Umkehrung, wodurch auch die Sekunde zur Gnade gelangt in den Schoß des Wohlklangs.

> (163)

Harmony is seen by Jakob in moral, even religious terms as eternal grace and goodness, dissonance however is evil arrogance. So also he praises those aspects of music which suggest order and harmony (fugue, counterpoint, canon), the learning of which in his youth Grillparzer saw in terms of order (IV, 54). Jakob stresses the purity of music which must not be sullied by common words, and again he sees this in religious terms, "wie die Kinder Gottes sich verbanden mit den Töchtern der Erde." Music is a gift from God's finger, hence he desires to play music "überhaupt," absolute music, one might say; he even hopes to play God himself.

Sadly, Jakob has drawn his theories from listening to an expert; his own musical skill and insight are not equal to such considerations. The expert has told him how even the dissonant notes of a chord are taken up into a higher totality and harmony ("wodurch auch die Sekunde zur Gnade gelangt in den Schoß des Wohlklangs"), but it is clear that in practice Jakob cannot apply this knowledge to his playing as a whole. We discover that he has no ear for music, he is amazed by Barbara's natural ability to sing without notes. If this were not disastrous enough, he tries in addition to play the most complex passages of the old masters. Here of course there is a small autobiographical touch: Bach and Mozart, the musical masters of the eighteenth century, are Jakob's idols, as they were Grillparzer's, but Jakob's inability to play such pieces is presumably also an ironic indication of Grillparzer's fear that even, as it were, with notes he had failed to emulate the *literary* greats of the eighteenth century, Goethe and Schiller.

In the rather corrupt society in which he lives, Jakob's moral concerns encourage admiration. For J. P. Stern he is a man of integrity, of "disembodied good will," Walter Höllerer sees him in terms of a "schöne Seele," according to John Ellis we should all choose to lean in the Spielmann's direction, Heinz Schafroth writes of Jakob's "seelischer Aristokratismus," Walter Silz insists on his "rare saintly spirit," whilst in 1871 Gottfried Keller had spoken of the "Gewalt der absolut reinen Seele über die Welt."[5] More recently, Robert M. Browning has argued that "the Spielmann's playing is a peculiar kind of theodicy . . . a theodicy that leaves out evil altogether." Jakob, so Browning argues, lives utterly apart, in a world before the fall from grace, which consequently cannot be understood by others: "because Jakob keeps the drink pure, he cannot pass it on to others."[6] This interpretation, concentrating almost exclusively on Jakob's ideal, saintly qualities, seems somewhat extreme and one-sided, although admittedly less so than the recent assessment by W. C. Reeve that Jakob's enjoyment of his music "rests upon a purely selfish pleasure principle."[7] It is important to see Jakob's apparently religious approach to his music in more general ethical terms. Like Goethe, Grillparzer had no orthodox Christian belief. Alfred Anzenberger, in his study of Grillparzer's religious views, insists "also war Grillparzer kein Christ," and he justifiably concludes: "er war nicht atheistisch, sondern areligiös."[8] Numerous diary entries reveal Grillparzer's scepticism towards God,[9] although he insists that God be taken seriously rather than mutilated by Strauß and the Hegelians. Grillparzer saw God as a personification of "das ewige Recht" (*Tgb.* 641), like Goethe he uses

the idea of divinity as a symbol of a higher moral order ("daß das Gute und Wahre eine objektive Geltung erhält" [*Tgb.* 3313]), and one must agree with Andreas Oplatka that "Grillparzers Blick ist grundsätzlich auf das Diesseitige gerichtet," and with Ždenko Škreb: "Das Göttliche ist für Grillparzer die Bezeichnung für die höchste Ausprägung des Menschen."[10] Like Gregor in *Weh dem, der lügt!* and like the two Rudolfs, Jakob talks in religious terms which one may justifiably transfer to a wider ethical realm.

Jakob however is applying his concern for morality to the realm of art, to the actual process of playing music, not simply to types of music. At about the time that Grillparzer wrote his first draft of the story, we find two significant entries in his diary:

> Die sogenannte moralische Ansicht ist der größte Feind der wahren Kunst, da einer der Hauptvorzüge dieser letztern gerade darin besteht, daß man durch ihr Medium auch jene Seiten der menschlichen Natur genießen kann, welche das Moralgesetz mit Recht aus dem wirklichen Leben entfernt hält.
>
> (*Tgb.* 1775 [1830])

> Die moralische Kraft gehört auch in den Kreis der Poesie, aber nicht mehr als jede andere Kraft, und nur insofern sie Kraft, Realität ist; als Negation, als Schranke liegt sie außer der Poesie.
>
> (*Tgb.* 2064 [1832])

Certainly Jakob's attempt to treat art from an ethical standpoint is doomed to failure. His attempt to play only harmonious chords, only the good notes, results not in harmony, but in cacophony. He apparently cannot come to terms in practice with what has been explained to him in theory, namely that the totality of music is composed of harmony and dissonance, that discord can also be "harmonisch begründet." Schafroth argues that Jakob's artistic incompetence is irrelevant ("auf die geistige Haltung allein kommt es an"), but E. E. Papst rightly stresses Jakob's incompetence and the need for illogicality and dissonance in art.[11] Much more vital, however, is the wider context involved; his music is a sign of his dangerously solipsistic attitude to life in general. Jost Hermand describes Jakob as "lebensuntüchtig,"[12] and he is so because he fails to realize what Rudolf II does recognize in theory—"daß Satzungen der Menschen / Ein Maß des Törichten notwendig beigemischt" (*Bruderzwist*, 2336-7)—or what Zares insists on in *Esther*: "das Schlimme will auch sein Recht" (1.277). Jakob may indeed be an "absolut reine Seele" in Keller's words, but he has no "Gewalt über die Welt" as a result; on the contrary he can only exist in total isolation from everyday affairs: misunderstood, incompetent, unpractical. In ordinary life, not just in music, Jakob fails to see the unavoidability of dissonance. Perfection in one's work is impossible, life goes on too fast; people are not perfect, the inability to see this is dangerous in the extreme. Jakob's ideal concept of order and harmony cannot be applied to real life, his ordered life is artificial, a timeless, artistic realm of his own creation. One may, as Roland Heine suggests, see Jakob's life as an artistic whole rather than an existential totality,[13] and the depiction of Jakob's pure life and art does tally with Grillparzer's distinctions between poetry and prose and his fear that contemporary poetry was tending increasingly towards prose;[14] and yet Heine's distinction becomes insignificant once one remembers that Jakob cannot play. He is incompetent at all levels, he is competent only in an artistic world of his own creation that is cacophony to everyone else. One may indeed have a certain sympathy for Jakob, who upholds the cause of morality in the midst of sordid reality, and yet Jakob is a failure in all practical senses. The narrator, who has no obvious moral code, is a successful dramatist however. It is surely therefore significant that there is a shortage, even absence in the story of most of the ethical and moral concepts used by Grillparzer in his dramatic works; the narrator has no cause to stress them, whilst Jakob takes them to extremes, so that Grillparzer is not inclined to suggest that Jakob's attitudes are the right ones. Whilst there is undoubtedly justification for Martin Swales' assertion that the narrator "dare not answer the question whether Jakob is fool or saint,"[15] one may equally argue that Jakob's moral saintliness is also his foolishness in that it allows of no compromise with reality.

The artificiality and impracticality of Jakob's sense of order is noted by almost all recent critics, whether they judge his isolation in a positive or negative light. It would seem clear, however, that the picture of Jakob is symptomatic of Grillparzer's mature work as a whole. The fact that Jakob is incompetent in art as well as in life makes him an extreme case, but he is no more "lebensuntüchtig" than many of the characters in the plays: Bishop Gregor, Rudolf II, Libussa's sisters, the Queen in *Die Jüdin von Toledo* and Alphons also at the start of the play, the priest in *Des Meeres und der Liebe Wellen.* Within our present framework it will be possible to give only a brief analysis of the situation in these plays.

A study of the first drafts and variants of *Des Meeres und der Liebe Wellen* reveals that Grillparzer originally intended a greater emphasis on the laws, customs and order of the temple. Hero attacks Leander, or men in general, for having no concept "ob Recht nun oder Unrecht," but of merely following whatever is pleasing (*HKA* I/19, 195), and her condemnation of her mother is much stronger than in the final version:

> Mit Recht bewahrt man heilige Gebräuche . . .
> Wir kannten ja die bindend strengen Pflichten,
> Als du hierher mich brachtest, halb noch Kind.
>
> (I/19,277)

Even in Act IV one might have expected a greater insistence on the principles which the priest defends, and one cannot help thinking that this had been Grillparzer's intention. Originally Hero was to be seen as much more culpable, the stress was to be on her breaking of her vows and duties and on her being punished accordingly. The priest was seen very much as the agent of divine retribution, preserving the standards of right conduct, an instru-

ment of fate that catches up with the lovers. In this role he was "herb und düster" (I/19,234), revealing "Verstandesschärfe und Kälte" (I/19,239).

In the play's final version, however, what is more important is that he is "keine moderne Humanität" (I/19,233). The priest can understand duty and responsibility, but not love and the human heart. His experience is bounded by the temple precincts. Marriage he sees as an institution which joins animals rather than human beings (364), whilst his denial of personal freedom of choice is a total rejection of the Classical insistence on "wollen" rather than "müssen." The priest is hence unable to judge people from a profound, humane viewpoint, but only in rigid moral terms. The priest's desire to see duty and responsibility in absolute terms is a dangerous one; such abstract concepts cannot cope with the complicated and exceptional aspects of life that confront them. Moral absolutes as defended by the priest destroy life instead of promoting it, as is true of Jakob's absolute moral approach to his art.

In his early work, and in his poems and diaries of the 1820s, Grillparzer had often longed for "Sammlung," for a state of complete concentration as a prerequisite for the achievement of aesthetic totality, as seen especially in the famous diary entry of 1826—"und doch ensteht nichts Großes . . . ohne Sammlung" (*Tgb.* 1413)—but also in early notes for *Des Meeres und der Liebe Wellen* (*HKA* I/19,206). In his later works there is an increasing awareness that such a state is inferior to the ordinary world of reality, however chaotic, discordant, or, in the words of Bishop Gregor, "buntverworren" this world may be. The realm of "Sammlung" is cast in its most ironic light in *Der arme Spielmann,* but its dangers are clearly seen in the portrait of the priest. He believes that only the priestly community can provide the key to full existence (11. 375-6), but in the final version the idea of "Sammlung" appears only once, and it is life and love that turn Hero and Leander into adults, whilst the priesthood is seen as the isolated and unnatural form of existence. After the completion of *Des Meeres und der Liebe Wellen,* Grillparzer makes little further use of the concept of "Sammlung," with the one admittedly important exception of the poem **"An die Sammlung"** (1833). The idea is however present in *Libussa.*

The realm of the sisters is also a haven of quiet aesthetic concentration, in which it is possible "all die bunten Kräfte / Im Mittelpunkt zu sammeln seines Wesens" (11.1146-7). Yet the sisters show the dangers of such a life; they are concerned with the spirit, with meditation, their search for totality causes them to avoid all limiting actions (11.218,440), they are above human considerations and need to remain untarnished by human affairs (11.128,439,469). Although Libussa leaves her sisters in order to enter the sphere of ordinary human activity, her first plans to found a matriarchal state that is based on instinctive humanity, on equality and complete trust in one's fellow men are still imbued with the idealism of her sisters' realm. Only through marriage to Primislaus is a more realistic and practical assessment of political problems achieved which will ensure the continued existence of the state through the turmoils of the future. In marrying Primislaus she espouses the realistic social world and turns away from the sisters' isolated realm of spiritual concentration and also away from her first impractical idealism; her final prophecy, in which she seeks to return to the earlier state she has rightly left, is now beyond her powers and she dies.

For a similar situation we may turn to *Die Jüdin von Toledo*. Like Jakob, like the priest or Libussa's sisters, Alphons has had inadequate knowledge of the totality of life. He has had no time for "des Lebens Güter" (1.180), above all no time for women:

> Daß Weiber es auch gibt, erfuhr ich erst,
> Als man mein Weib mir in der Kirche traute.

> (11.182-3; cf. also 11.354-396)

As a result he is quite at a loss when he first meets Rahel, he has no defence against her, none of the immunization which the sowing of youthful wild oats would normally have provided (11.851-3, 863-4). But on a wider plane, his lack of experience is symptomatic of his earlier failure to live a normally balanced life, which includes the more instinctive, even the more sinful aspects. Manrique testifies to the King's being without fault, "fleckenlos" (1.159), and Alphons himself agrees: "Mir selber ließ man nicht zu fehlen Zeit" (1.176). Yet Alphons is not proud of this, he realises the dangerous side of such a lack of faults:

> Bin ich nicht schlimm, so besser denn für euch.
> Obgleich der Mensch, der wirklich ohne Fehler,
> Auch ohne Vorzug wäre, fürcht ich fast. . . .
> Besiegter Fehl ist all des Menschen Tugend,
> Und wo kein Kampf, da ist auch keine Macht.

> (11.162-75)

It has been Alphons' fate to grow up as a king, but not as a human being, and his great desire is to be a man among his people (11.94-7). Man, however, needs faults to be "ein Mensch," and it is precisely through his encounter with Rahel that Alphons becomes one. As a result he is able to distinguish between his role as King and "ich, Alfonso, ich der Mensch, der Mann / In meinem Haus" (11.1519-20), between his regal life and his domestic circle, and he no longer wishes to lock himself away from the ordinary world (11.1395-1401). He now understands the difference subjectively, not simply as a result of "Bücherweisheit" (*Tgb.* 1330). Lola Montez, in the poem of that title, has a similar effect on Ludwig I of Bavaria:

> Drum kehrt euch nicht verachtend von dem Weib,
> In deren Arm ein König ward zum Mann.

> (I,311)

In the arms of his cold and frigid Queen, however, Alphons remains the child he was when he was first married to her. She is faultless to an extreme (1.184), but her ex-

cessive insistence on purity and morality is a sign of coldness and inhumanity which affects her husband adversely, as Alphons spells out to her:

> Das ist die Art der tugendhaften Weiber,
> Daß ewig sie mit ihrer Tugend zahlen.
> Bist du betrübt, so trösten sie mit Tugend,
> Und bist du froh gestimmt, ists wieder Tugend,
> Die dir zuletzt die Heiterkeit benimmt,
> Wohl gar die Sünde zeigt als einzge Rettung.

> (1499-1504)

Alphons had suggested the same at the start, as Eleonore and her ladies went off, leaving him with Rahel (335-6), and it is precisely what happens to Alphons. The Queen, in her exaggerated defence of purity and virtue, in her abhorrence of the sexual act, fails to satisfy Alphons' more sensual needs, or even his more modest desire for a happy home life; Rahel, on the other hand, is described as a ray of light and life illuminating the boredom of the court and its lifeless morality.[17] The Queen is of course "ohne Fehl," but Alphons would prefer her to have some fault which he might forgive (186), and it is for him a sign of her humanity when he detects a flaw in her, namely ordinary human jealousy:

> Wohl etwa Rachsucht gar? Nun, um so besser.
> Du fühlst dann, daß Verzeihen Menschenpflicht
> Und niemand sicher ist, auch nicht der Beste.

> (1415-7)

Forgiveness, one might say, is a human virtue practised in the recognition that one's partner is fallible, and as a result human.

In the course of the play the King acquires a full awareness of what at the beginning he can abstractly conceptualize, the need for a balanced view of life which eschews excesses and avoids meaningless absolutes. By the end of the play he has realized the need to apply both sides of his character, intellectual and sensual, to life as a whole. Man should put both "Gefühl" and "Verstand" into what he does and says (11.1366-8), previously he has had only the latter. Similarly, in a late essay "Zur Literaturgeschichte," Grillparzer ridicules any suggestion that one side of man's nature may take over the jurisdiction of the other: "der Trieb, die Neigung, das Instinktmäßige sind ebenso göttlich als die Vernunft" (III,719). Even more vital in the present context are the ideas expressed in the poem **"Lola Montez,"** written at the same time as work on *Die Jüdin von Toledo*:

> Denn harrtest du, bis aus Vernunft und Recht
> Entstünde, was das Recht und die Vernunft gebot,
> Schlimm wärs bestellt ums menschliche Geschlecht,
> Der Trieb erzeugt die Handlung, die uns not.

> (I,311)

Consequently, in pointing to Dona Clara, Alphons demands that man be inclined to virtue, that virtue be not merely "achtungswert" but also "liebenswürdig" (ll.1910-

11), which is the Classical ideal of moral beauty and a further expression of the more balanced middle way that is sought.

Unfortunately, when Alphons returns to Toledo and his duties, having by now grown tired of Rahel, the Queen's inability to think in other than absolute moral terms, her inability to understand and forgive her husband, drive Alphons once again to compare Rahel's natural instincts with the unnatural life of the court that his wife represents. His defiance, his warning that he could go back to Rahel and his refusal to part with the portrait which he had until then forgotten are not signs of Rahel's continuing hold over him, but merely part of his insistence that he now understands his position as a human being, not just as King. Bruce Thompson is perfectly justified in underlining the superficial nature of the affair with Rahel, and in asking whether her death was really necessary; but his statement that "Rahel owes her death to a misunderstanding, indeed to a 'joke' on the King's part,"[18] is a view that needs some revision: Rahel owes her death to the gulf between King and Queen, to the Queen's continued insistence on excessive and absolute morality, which causes the King to reassert his newly found independence and manhood, even if the King is also to blame for losing control of himself and rising to the Queen's bait.

In *Weh dem, der lügt!* also, the isolated and artificial pursuit of absolute morality is replaced by the realization that true morals are learned and acquired in direct confrontation with the "buntverworrene Welt." Total truth is to be found only in heaven, real life is a confusing blend of truth and lies, good and evil. However, although the ending of the comedy seems to echo Goethe's famous dictum, "es irrt der Mensch, solang' er strebt," Grillparzer is not prepared to adopt the cavalier attitude to evil that is the hallmark of *Faust*; in a diary note of 1834, he specifically criticizes new ideas of "Gut und Böse eine Art Polaritätsgegensatz" (*Tgb.* 2169), and he attacked Goethe for the laxity of his moral standpoint in *Die Wahlverwandtschaften* (*Tgb.* 3538; III,55). *Ein Bruderzwist in Habsburg* clearly presents a more problematic picture than the other plays we have considered, yet even here excessive insistence on moral values, in this case the ideals of absolute right and perfect divine order,[19] lead to a dangerous inability and refusal to come to terms with reality. Like Bancbanus in *Ein treuer Diener seines Herrn*, Rudolf II is a man not cut out for the world of politics, he is "blöd, langsam, verschlossen" (*HKA* I/21,107; he himself is conscious of his limitations, aware that he is "ein schwacher, unbegabter Mann" (ll.351,421) who is incapable of action (ll.446-7). Bancbanus, however, for all his "Borniertheit," is prepared to put his principles into practice and averts a greater tragedy as a result; by comparison, Rudolf refuses to act because his ideals cannot be realized and his inactivity produces a situation whereby men less morally equipped, less circumspect, less aware of the complexities of life, can arrogate the responsibility for action that is rightly his.

The notes for the play which appear to defend Rudolf were made during the 1820s, during a period of Grillparzer's life in which he clearly did see passivity and withdrawal as the only possible way to preserve the higher moral values of life. In this respect *Der Traum ein Leben* is very much a product of the period in which it was first planned, above all in its almost total rejection of ambition and its emphasis on peaceful withdrawal.[20] By comparison, Grillparzer's mature plays and *Der arme Spielmann* make a much more positive appeal for an understanding of mistakes and wrongs, and for the incorporation of them into a balanced view of life. The ideas of virtue, purity, truth, duty and order, which Grillparzer inherited from the Classical period, are not absolutes, and to treat them as such without an awareness of man's imperfections is to court danger and inhumanity, to banish man to a realm of artificial and potentially inhuman isolation. Grillparzer's more mature approach is expressed in the words of Zares in *Esther*:

> Niemand ist rein. Das Schlimme will auch sein Recht;
> Und wers nicht beimischt tropfenweis dem Guten,
> Den wirds gesamt aus Eimern überfluten.

> (11.277-9)

or in the words of advice to a friend reluctant to publish his work:

> Und doch soll er dran! Es ist einmal Pflicht des Menschen sich der Menschheit hinzugeben mit dem was er vermag. Im Grunde steht es auch den züchtigen Fräuleins nicht wohl zu heiraten und sich da allerhand sonst verabscheute körperliche Dinge gefallen zu lassen, aber der Mensch ist einmal nicht da um rein zu sein, sondern zu nützen, zu wirken.

> (*Tgb.* 1935)

Notes

1. Ždenko Škreb, *Grillparzer. Eine Einführung in das dramatische Werk* (Kronberg/Taunus, 1976); Bruce Thompson, *A Sense of Irony. An Examination of the Tragedies of Franz Grillparzer* (Berne, 1976).

2. Reference is made to Franz Grillparzer, *Sämtliche Werke, ausgewählte Briefe, Gespräche, Berichte*, hrsg. von Peter Frank und Karl Pörnbacher (Darmstadt, 1969), or where necessary to the *historisch-kritische Gesamtausgabe* of Sauer and Backmann (abbreviated *HKA*). Diary entries are abbreviated "*Tgb.*"

3. The presence of such often-repeated ideals leads one to question Prof. McInnes' recent assertion that the early plays lack clear moral standards ("Psychological Insight and Moral Awareness in Grillparzer's *Das Goldene Vließ*," *Modern Language Review* 75 [1980]: 575-82).

4. J. P. Stern, "Beyond the Common Indication: Grillparzer," in J. P. S., *Re-interpretations* (London, 1964), p. 66.

5. J. P. Stern, *Re-interpretations,* p. 72; Walter Höllerer, *Zwischen Klassik und Moderne* (Stuttgart, 1958), p. 257; J. M. Ellis, "Grillparzer's *Der arme Spielmann,*" *German Quarterly* 45 (1972): 678; Heinz F. Schafroth, *Die Entscheidung bei Grillparzer* (Berne, 1971), p. 67; Walter Silz, *Realism and Reality. Studies in the German Novelle of Poetic Realism* (Chapel Hill, 1954), p. 70; Gottfried Keller, conversation with Emil Kuh, 10/9/1871 (quoted in *HKA* I/22, 78).

6. Robert M. Browning, "Language and the Fall from Grace in Grillparzer's *Spielmann,*" *Seminar* 12 (1976): 224, 227.

7. W. C. Reeve, "Proportion and Disproportion in Grillparzer's *Der arme Spielmann,*" *The Germanic Review* 53 (1978): 44. According to Reeve, the more realistic form of the Novelle "provided him [Grillparzer] with the opportunity to demonstrate reluctantly the ultimate triumph of life over the ideal" (p. 48), which Reeve also sees intimated in the dramas (p. 45). For the reasons I have sought to demonstrate, one must take issue with the words "ideal" and "reluctantly."

8. Alfred Anzenberger, "Grillparzer und die Religion," (Diss., Vienna, 1948), pp. 39, 88.

9. See *Tgb.* 1680, 1681, 2803, 3288, 4073, etc.

10. Andreas Oplatka, *Aufbauform und Stilwandel in den Dramen Grillparzers* (Berne, 1970), p. 72; Ždenko Škreb, "Das Göttliche bei Grillparzer," *German Quarterly* 45 (1972): 627. For similar assessments, see also W. E. Yates, *Grillparzer. A Critical Introduction* (Cambridge, 1972), p. 202, and Schafroth, *Die Entscheidung bei Grillparzer,* pp. 55, 91.

11. Schafroth, *Die Entscheidung bei Grillparzer,* p. 110; Edmund Papst, "Grillparzers Theorie des psychologischen Realismus," *Grillparzer-Forum Forchtenstein,* (1973), pp. 15, 20.

12. Jost Hermand, *Die literarische Formenwelt des Biedermeiers* (Giessen, 1958), p. 112.

13. Roland Heine, "Ästhetische oder existentielle Integration? Ein hermeneutisches Problem des neunzehnten Jahrhunderts in Grillparzers Erzählung *Der arme Spielmann,*" *Deutsche Vierteljahresschrift* 46 (1972): 650-83.

14. See *Tgb.* 1176, 2768, 3362, 3493.

15. M. W. Swales, "The Narrative Perspective in Grillparzer's *Der arme Spielmann,*" *German Life and Letters* (New Series) 20: (1966-7): 116.

16. The same link is referred to by Karl Eibl in a recent article ("Ordnung und Ideologie im Spätwerk Grillparzers. Am Beispiel des *argumentum emblematicum* und der *Jüdin von Toledo,*" *Deutsche Vierteljahresschrift* 53 (1979): 84; unlike Eibl, however, I see no reason to distinguish between negative and positive aspects in the play and the poem respectively.

17. See 11.346-8, 511-2, 620-1, 726-7.

18. Bruce Thompson, "An Ironic Tragedy. Grillparzer's *Die Jüdin von Toledo,*" *German Life and Letters* (New Series) 25 (1971-2): 215.

19. See ll.1169-78, 1215, 1470 ("Recht"); ll.427-9, 1266-7, 1467-8 ("Ordnung").

20. Even here, one detects signs of the play's later completion, and with some justification, Mark Ward has recently underlined the way that Zanga and the Dervish go off together at the end, which he sees as "this strange rehabilitation of the vital and active forces, for all their negative potential and consequences" (Mark G. Ward, "A Note on the Figures of Zanga and the Dervish in Grillparzer's *Der Traum ein Leben,*" in *Essays on Grillparzer,* ed. Bruce Thompson and Mark Ward [Hull, 1978], p. 52). What is the merest hint in *Der Traum ein Leben* receives full treatment in the mature works. Grillparzer himself saw the play as a product of his earlier period and was annoyed to some extent by its success (report of Caroline Pichler [IV, 940]), complaining of the play's "Effektmacherei" (letter to Graf Redern, 4/11/1834).

Bruce Thompson (essay date 1981)

SOURCE: "Poetry and Prose," in *Franz Grillparzer,* Twayne Publishers, 1981, pp. 80-94.

[*In the following excerpt, Thompson presents an overview of Grillparzer's lyrical poetry, written mostly in his youth and influenced by the eighteenth-century neoclassical poets. Thompson also discusses* Das Kloster bei Sendomir *and* Der Arme Spielmann, *both of which broach the theme of the role of the artist.*]

I POETRY

It is ostensibly one of the more puzzling facts of literary history that whereas Grillparzer enjoys considerable stature as a dramatist, as a lyric poet he ranks only as a minor figure. Not that he is entirely unknown as a poet, for individual lines have become immortalized, such as "In your camp is Austria," which offered encouragement to Field-marshal Radetzky in whose imperial army Grillparzer saw the salvation of his fatherland during the troubles of 1848, and his description of Vienna as "a Capua of minds," referring to its relaxing atmosphere, so lacking in intellectual stimulus. But in both cases it is the thought behind the words that is striking, not the poetic formulation itself, and it is the reflective tone of his poems that is generally held to be the reason for their failure to achieve lasting recognition. As a poet Grillparzer has been seen as a descendant of the Rationalist tradition of the eighteenth century, writing under the influence of figures of the Enlightenment such as Christian Gellert and Martin Wieland, a tradition that strongly persisted in Austria in Grillparzer's lifetime.

The volume and range of Grillparzer's poetry is impressive. In his early period—up to the early 1820s—there are his youthful attempts at writing nature poetry such as **"Der Abend"** [**"Evening,"** 1806], reminiscent of the Anacreontic lyrics of Ewald von Kleist, and ballads which owe an obvious debt to Schiller. Further eighteenth-century influence can be detected in a leaning toward didactic poems, for example, fables such as **"Die beiden Hunde"** [**"The Two Dogs,"** 1806]. But there are also several more subjective lyrics such as **"An Ovid"** (1812), expressing his suicidal despair at being left so little time to compose poetry, and **"Abschied von Gastein"** [**"Farewell to Gastein,"** 1818], which is a moving statement on the fate of the creative artist, communicating fragments of his own joyless life to his readers.

Most of Grillparzer's subjective lyrics were written during his most fruitful period between 1820 and 1836, and provide an intimate record of his personal problems and a fascinating supplement to his diaries. **"Incubus"** (1821) is an expression of the gloom that overcame him following the failure of *Das goldene Vließ*, while **"Kaiphas, Kaiphas, Sanchedrin"** (1823) is a bitter, almost blasphemous poem comparing his failure to obtain promotion with Christ's crucifixion. **"Der Halbmond glänzet am Himmel"** [**"The Crescent Moon Shines in the Sky,"** 1827] is a statement on the contradictions in his personality and his failure to taste fully either the ordinary joys of life or success as an artist. But most of Grillparzer's confessional lyrics relate to his love life. There are attempts to capture the most striking features of the various women in his life. Kathi Fröhlich's dark eyes in **"Allgegenwart"** [**"Omnipresence,"** 1821], the latent beauty of the youthful Marie, who is likened in **"Rangstreit"** [**"Fight for Status,"** 1825] to a rose hiding its fullest bloom among a labyrinth of leaves, and the innocent charm of Heloise Hoechner in **"Begegnung"** [**"Meeting,"** 1830]. Some of these lyrics have a conciseness which belies the complexity of Grillparzer's emotional situation. For example, in **"Willst du, ich soll Hütten bauen?"** [**"Do You Want Me to Settle Down?,"** 1827] he explains his persistent refusal to commit himself to marriage in the deceptively simple terms of a desire to fulfill himself through experience in the world.

The opening stanza of **"Allgegenwart"** [**"Omnipresence"**] suggests an ability to write free rhythms with the linguistic inventiveness and spontaneous ease of the young Goethe:

> Wo ich bin, fern und nah,
> Stehen zwei Augen da,
> Dunkelhell,
> Blitzesschnell,
> Schimmernd wie Felsenquell,
> Schattenumkränzt.

> (Wherever I am, near or far away, there are two eyes, dark-bright, lightning-fast, gleaming like a mountain spring, adorned with shadows.)

But the second stanza introduces an ingenious "idea." The power of Kathi's eyes is likened to that of the sun, which for anyone who has been looking straight into it, still appears as two little black dots in the mind's eye, even when he has closed his eyes. A metaphor conceived with equal ingenuity, but more elaborately developed, is used in **"Das Spiegelbild"** [**"The Reflection"**] to represent Charlotte after Grillparzer ended his affair with her in 1821. She is seen as the still water of a well in which Grillparzer sees his reflection, and who thus contains within her the longing of his heart. Yet in the water, too, he sees the reflection of her husband, his cousin and friend, to whom she has, after all, remained faithful. How could Grillparzer have built his hopes on something so insubstantial as water?! This imagery has a clever, almost intellectual quality, and is too obviously contrived. On the other hand, when Grillparzer wrote in a simpler vein, his language could be banal, as in his final poem to Marie in 1831:

> Ich weiß ein Haar, das ist so schwarz,
> Ich weiß ein Aug, das ist so groß,
> Ich weiß ein Herz, das ist so gut,
> Und einen Mund, der spricht so süß.

> (I know hair that is so black, I know an eye that is so big, I know a heart that is so good, and a mouth that speaks so sweetly.)

This mixture of cleverness and banality partly accounts for his lack of success as a lyric-poet.

Yet during this same period Grillparzer also wrote a series of more impressive lyrics which he published in 1835 as a cycle entitled *Tristia ex Ponto*. The *Tristia* were prompted by Grillparzer's inner crisis of 1826 and represent an attempt to come to terms with the major problem, which he faced in the years immediately following, the recurrent elusiveness of artistic inspiration. The main theme of the *Tristia* is announced in the first poem, **"Böse Stunde"** [**"Evil Hour"**], in which the poet states his intention of seeking inspiration through real-life experience. Yet the experiences described in the poems which follow scarcely offer any comfort. They cause him only pain, and the prevailing mood of the cycle is one of gloom. His attempt to find some stimulus in his journey to Germany described in **"Reiselust"** [**"Desire for Travel"**] ends with the humiliating encounter with Goethe. When he turns to Marie, he tells us in **"Verwünschung"** [**"Curse"**] that he finds in her a combination of physical beauty and an evil heart, qualities possessed by the angel of death, that fill him with both ecstasy and horror:

> Und so, gemischt aus Wonne und aus Grauen,
> Stehst du, ein Todesengel, neben mir,
> Ein Engel zwar, doch auch ein Tod zu schauen,
> Und wer da lebe, der hüte sich vor dir.

> (And so, a mixture of delight and horror, you stand beside me like an angel of death, an angel indeed, yet to look at you is death, and anyone who lives near you must beware of you.)

Again we see a tendency to think out consciously the imagery of his poetry, to use his reason to convey the import of his passions.[1] That he is, on the other hand, capable of a more immediate expression of emotion can be seen in the cri-de-coeur which ends **"Noch einmal in Gastein"** [**"In Gastein again"**], in which he contrasts his broken mental state of 1831 with the optimism he felt on his visit there ten years previously:

> Nun bin ich müd, gestört, entzweit,
> Nur Mauern läßt die Bergwand mir gewahren,
> O, eine ganze Ewigkeit
> Liegt in dem Raum von zehen Jahren!

> (Now I am tired, disturbed, divided in myself. On the mountain face I can only see walls. Oh, what an eternity there is in the space of ten years!)

Similarly, in the long autobiographical poem *Jugenderinnerungen im Grünen* ["Memories of Youth in the Countryside"] in which he sums up the disappointments of his life and describes, in particular, the agonizing course of his relationship with Kathi, he can produce the spontaneous cry: "Oh blessed feeling of those early days, why were you no more than a dream?" in the midst of the more sober-sounding, carefully reasoned account. This poem provides an appropriate background to the pessimistic themes of his tragedies, conveying Grillparzer's own impression that everything that he had touched in life had gone sour, and ending on a note of despairing disillusionment. At the conclusion of the cycle, however, Grillparzer suddenly perceives the link between his unhappy experiences and the initial theme of the pursuit of artistic inspiration. In the penultimate poem **"Freundeswort"** [**"Message of a Friend"**] he tells Bauernfeld that his poetry can amount to nothing more than an outburst of pain, written with the blood of his own wounds, after which he feels in **"Schlußwort"** [**"Conclusion"**] that his despair has passed and his suffering has been put behind him like a dream. In other words, although the lesson of the *Tristia* is that experience itself will bring pain, Grillparzer's experiences have indeed brought him the desired inspiration to write. Moreover, the act of creation, the translation of his suffering into poetry, may itself bring relief. The concluding lines of the cycle represent, therefore, one of the few occasions on which Grillparzer was able to reconcile the opposing principles of art and life, and to recognize that the latter could serve the requirements of the former.

As Grillparzer grew older, his personal lyrics grew rarer, and a new form, the political poem, predominated during his final creative period. Grillparzer had already given evidence of his keen interest in contemporary affairs in a number of poems, but until the 1830s his technique had been allusive rather than explicit. As it was, the political implications of **"Campo Vaccino"** (1819) had given considerable offense, so that in the 1820s he restricted himself to a few brief poems whose political relevance was barely discernible. In **"Jagd im Winter"** [**"Winter Hunt,"** 1826], for example, he cleverly suggests that in urging the hunter to defy the cold of winter, he is really challenging poets like himself to defy the harshness of police censorship. Then in 1831 came two poems with more outspoken political sentiments, **"Klosterszene"** [**"Monastery Scene"**]

and **"Warschau"** [**"Warsaw"**]. The first, ostensibly about Charles V, contains a strong attack on the repression of freedom, which clearly refers to the contemporary situation in Austria, and which caused the poem to be banned. The second is a revolutionary poem which deplores the crushing of the Polish insurrection by Russian troops and castigates the European powers for failing to intervene. This he did not even attempt to publish.

Following his journey to France and England in 1836, he wrote a large number of political poems. Most of these remained unpublished, at least until after 1848, and although they are far less extreme than those written by many of his more radical contemporaries, they do reflect the moderate liberal views that he held during these years. Many of them are addressed to prominent political figures such as Metternich, whose financial policies he satirized in 1836 in **"Für unser Glück"** [**"For our Happiness"**], and Frederick William IV, whom he urged in 1841 in **"Warnung"** [**"Warning"**] to honor his promise to grant Prussia a constitution. Some poems provide a more extended treatment of the general political situation. **"Des Kaisers Bildsäule"** [**"The Emperor's Statue,"** 1837] presents the complaints of the statue of Joseph II against the current age, which has abandoned his reformist principles and civilized humanitarian ideals; **"Vorzeichen"** [**"Portent,"** January 1848] is an analysis of the pre-revolutionary situation in Austria, in which his hostility toward the regime is matched by his fears of the coming upheaval.

Such poems amount to a personal commentary on this momentous period in Austria's history and are primarily of historical value. Yet Grillparzer's political verses deserve a more prominent place in the literature of the Vormärz than they are usually accorded. The following stanza of **"Vorzeichen"** provides a typical example of his hard-hitting style, as he urges the members of the government to adopt further repressive measures in the face of the people's demands for reforms, only to reveal his own scorn for this policy through the ironic twist of the last line:

> Klagt euch das Denken seiner Freiheit Schranken,
> —Ruft einen Büttel, der noch engre gibt!
> Der Krone Vorrecht seien die Gedanken,
> Ein Vorrecht, das man etwa sparsam übt.

> (If you complain of [the people's] thoughts about the limitations on freedom,—send for a bailiff who will provide still harsher measures! Let thoughts be the privilege of the crown, a privilege which is exercised somewhat rarely.)

Frequently Grillparzer's verse has a distinctly witty and satirical flavor, and its lightly mocking tone bears comparison with that evoked in the political satires of Austria's foremost political poet of the time, Anastasius Grün, and of Heinrich Heine, whom Grillparzer met while in Paris in 1836.

The same kind of acumen and wit is to be found in the innumerable epigrams and aphorisms that Grillparzer penned during his later years. Many of these amount to little more than intellectual word-games or wise offerings for the *Stammbuch* ("family album") of some acquaintance or admirer, but some provide sharp comments on contemporary issues, both political and cultural. They range, for example, from his protestation in 1843 that so many of his countrymen have been spiritually enslaved through recruitment into the imperial army, to his expression of scorn for the students of 1848, who have abandoned their studies to destroy their fatherland; from his criticism of contemporary poets generally, who are pregnant with works of genius, but who rarely give birth, to specific attacks on the poets Ludwig Uhland and Ludwig Tieck, and the philosophers Schelling and Hegel. Frequently he takes refuge in sardonic wit and a half-amused, phlegmatic resignation:

> Preßfreiheit steht denn oben an,
> Wo—welch absurdes Treiben!—
> Das halbe Land nicht lesen kann,
> Das andre nicht schreiben.

> (Freedom of the Press should suit those up above, where—what absurd goings on!—half the country can't read, the other half can't write.)

On the other hand, he can also express concisely and pointedly his genuine concern at what he sees as an inexorable regression from the cultural values of the eighteenth century to a future barbarism: "Der Weg der neuen Bildung geht / Von Humanität / Durch Nationalität / Zur Bestialität" (The path of modern culture leads from humanity, through nationalism, to bestiality.)

Finally, we may mention the large number of occasional poems, whose chief merit is that they offer a record and impression of cultural life in the Vienna of the Vormärz. The least interesting commemorate births, marriages, deaths, and anniversaries of friends, relatives, and public figures. Some were to be recited or sung on public occasions, such as the opening of the new concert-hall for the Gesellschaft der Musikfreunde. Others are addressed to friends such as Schreyvogel, the Pichler family, Count Stadion, or Count Auersperg. There are also poems recording performances by Liszt, Clara Schumann, and Rossini, assessments of the work of Beethoven and Schubert, a description of Kathi Fröhlich singing, accompanied by Schubert at the piano. In that these poems are drawn from and relate essentially to Grillparzer's own experience and environment, they are truly *zeithedingt,* a quality which Ernst Alker perceives in much of Grillparzer's poetry, and to which he partly attributes Grillparzer's lack of recognition.[2] In the history of German poetry Grillparzer is an isolated figure, writing essentially of his own life and times. Though his personal lyrics occasionally possess the elegiac tone of his compatriot Lenau, and his political poetry the flavor of Heine, he is associated with no particular literary movement. He avoided the subjective extravagances of some of the early German Romantics, did not share the Romantic love for the folksong, was too moderate in his views for the majority of the political poets of the Vormärz, and apparently lacked the sensitivity to the world of nature associated with the late Romantics and the Poetic Realists.

II Das Kloster bei Sendomir

In view of the fact that Grillparzer regarded poetry so much more highly than prose, it is more surprising that he should have written creatively in prose at all, than that he should have made only two contributions to the most popular genre of the nineteenth century in Germany, the shorter prose narrative. Grillparzer's two short stories, *Das Kloster bei Sendomir* and *Der arme Spielmann,* are dissimilar in content and atmosphere, and have also had markedly contrasting receptions. The former, published in 1827, has been generally regarded as a minor work and has received scant critical attention, but the latter, published in 1847, has been the subject of numerous critical studies, and has been acclaimed as one of the masterpieces in the history of the German *Novelle*. Both works are deeply rooted in Grillparzer's personal experience, treating respectively two of the dominant passions of his life, namely, love and devotion to his art. The autobiographical element is here even more than usually prominent, and it has been seen as the principal reason for Grillparzer's retreat in these two particular cases into the more protective form of prose narrative.[3]

With the sensational and improbable character of its subject-matter, its atmosphere of tension and mystery, its lack of detailed characterization, and its violent, melodramatic conclusion, *Das Kloster bei Sendomir* [*The Monastery of Sendomir*] recalls aspects of Romantic horror literature, and Kleistian and Hoffmannesque qualities have been detected in it, both stylistic and atmospheric. Grillparzer had thus returned to the kind of material that had produced *Die Ahnfrau,* and to a genre that had really run its course. Yet it is a powerful story of dark passions and violence, treating the themes of adultery and murder, and presents a disturbing picture of an ill-fated marriage.

The story is narrated by a mysterious monk, who turns out to be the central character Starschensky, a Polish count who is lured into marrying a woman of voluptuous beauty called Elga, who accosts him at night on the streets of Warsaw. Though Elga is no prostitute in the technical sense, but the daughter of an impoverished nobleman, she ensnares Starschensky, who duly marries her and rescues her father from his precarious financial position. The couple settle down on Starschensky's estate and a daughter is born, but it is not long before their domestic harmony is disturbed. There are reports that a dark figure has been visiting the house at night, and Starschensky finds among Elga's possessions a portrait of her cousin Oginsky, which bears a strong resemblance to the child. The suspicious Starschensky returns to Warsaw, and inquiries reveal that Elga and Oginsky did indeed have a previous love affair. Later he reappears at home accompanied by a hooded figure whom he locks in a disused tower on the estate. In the final melodramatic scene Starschensky reveals to Elga that the figure is Oginsky himself, who has confessed to the paternity of the child. Oginsky flees, but Starschensky cuts Elga down with his sword and sets fire to the tower. Later he establishes a monastery near the site, becomes a monk, and does nightly penance for his monstrous crime.

Conceived as early as 1820, **Das Kloster** was based originally on Grillparzer's relationship with Charlotte, Oginsky's flight and Starschensky's violent revenge apparently representing Grillparzer's judgment on his own adultery with his cousin's wife. Yet the story was largely written in 1825, when Grillparzer had fallen under the spell of Marie and was already harboring suspicions about her character. Moreover, it is told from the viewpoint of the deceived Starschensky, rather than from that of the treacherous Oginsky, who remains a shadowy figure. Thus, as Douglas Yates has pointed out, the situation anticipates with uncanny accuracy Grillparzer's circumstances in 1826, when he felt himself betrayed by his friend Daffinger, who turned out to be the father of Marie's child.

Starschensky's story is narrated by himself, but in the third person so that he achieves a degree of objectivity about his own fate. His story is presented with sympathy, but also critically. Starschensky comes to Warsaw as an "innocent," having led a solitary existence and having had little contact with women, but this was due to his own love of independence and isolation. Thus he is particularly susceptible to Elga's charms, as she virtually seduces him into marrying her.[4] She takes the initiative in their physical relations, then tantalizes him by keeping him at a distance. When they are married, she indulges in a life of expensive pleasure-seeking. Yet Starschensky is still blissfully happy with her, blinded by passion, a victim both of his own naïveté and of this dangerously alluring creature. But though she is in some ways a forerunner of the coquettish Rahel of **Die Jüdin von Toledo,** no character in Grillparzer's work is reduced to such a level of cynical inhumanity as is Elga in the final nightmarish scene. This scene brings the work closest to some of Kleist's stories, when Starschensky threatens Elga with death, but indicates that he will spare her if she will kill the child. Elga at first protests, but soon she agrees in order to save her own life. But, before she can murder the child, Starschensky reveals that this was a trick, a test of her humanity, which she has failed, so he kills her nevertheless. In Elga the instinct for self-preservation has outweighed the instinct of maternal love; in Starschensky reason has become tainted with jealous passion, and the result is a cruelly difficult test of Elga's integrity, followed by brutal revenge. Perhaps a Kleistian Elga would have made an intuitive leap in the dark and perceived the meaning of Starschensky's test, but in Grillparzer's story there is no such salvation for the characters.

Just as Starschensky has been able to objectify his story through the medium of third-person narrative, so too has Grillparzer, through Starschensky, presented his own situation at an even greater distance. He has also exaggerated and distorted his experiences, translating his own pain, self-criticism, and, above all, his fears concerning both the nature of Marie and his own potential reaction, into a fictional situation.

III *Der arme Spielmann*

Grillparzer's second prose work, **Der arme Spielmann [The Poor Musician]**, was begun in 1831, but not completed until about 1842. It is a more mature work than **Das Kloster,** but again a major problem concerns the relationship between author and subject, and the story has alarming implications for Grillparzer's misgivings concerning the value of his own art. The most immediately striking feature of the work is the framework which has been constructed round the central story of the musician. This takes up over a third of the work and is more elaborate than that used in his previous story. Like Starschensky, the musician gives his own account of himself, though here in the more usual form of first-person narrative. Yet Grillparzer again distances himself from his subject, in this case by interposing between reader and musician a narrator, a dramatist like himself, as though to discourage any assumption that the musician is simply a projection of Grillparzer's own self.

The narrator first notices the musician playing his violin to the crowds near the Augarten on the occasion of a popular festival, and the two have a brief conversation. Later that evening he listens to him from the street below as he plays in his room in the Leopoldstadt. But the musician's story is not told until the narrator actually visits him a few days later. Through the narrator's eagerness to get to know him Grillparzer convinces us that he is a case worth investigating. The impression received is that of an eccentric curiosity, for there is a striking element of incongruity in the musician's appearance and behavior. He stands alongside a group of beggar musicians, yet his dress and manner suggest a genteel and educated background, and he is serenely oblivious to his lowly surroundings. But his music is the most remarkable aspect of him. He is engrossed in his performance, which gives him obvious pleasure, and the sheet music on the stand before him suggests a more professional approach than that taken by the majority of his kind. Indeed, he tells the narrator that he practices daily difficult compositions by the best composers. Yet what he produces is a disconnected sequence of sounds without melody or rhythm, a confusion unrecognizable as belonging to any particular piece of music and which is even painful to the ear.

Thus far the musician has remained a mystery to the narrator and it is only by having him tell his own story that he can get close to the truth about him.[5] As suggested by his appearance, the musician has indeed known better days, and his story constitutes a pathetic record of failure. Dull and painstakingly slow at his lessons, he becomes estranged from his father, who is an influential and ambitious man, and who obviously tries to forget his son's existence. He is given a menial copying job in the chancellery, and at home he leads a narrow and solitary life. When his father dies, he unexpectedly finds himself a rich man, but he imprudently entrusts his wealth to a rogue and is quickly ruined. This apparently empty and fruitless life is enriched by one engrossing experience, from which springs his passion for music. One evening he hears a girl in the courtyard below his room sing a song which entrances him, and which he finds he can play on the violin, an instrument he has not touched since childhood. The singer is a grocer's daughter, Barbara, and with timidity and embarrassment he seeks her acquaintance, initially to obtain the score of the song. She treats him with disdain, and when he visits her father's shop she ignores him. But, with the encouragement of her father, the visit is repeated, and gradually she begins to tolerate him. She even seems not to exclude the possibility of marriage when she advises him to take a shop, which she will help him run. Only when his financial ruin is discovered does she dismiss him, to marry a butcher whose proposal she had hitherto rejected. As for the musician, he is left to play his music and to give lessons to Barbara's children.

While the facts of the musician's story partly satisfy the narrator's curiosity, the story itself raises fundamental questions concerning our assessment of the man and his "music." He emerges from the story as a pathetic and occasionally absurd character, but though he is outwardly incompetent, there is no doubting either the honesty of his intentions or his moral integrity. In his office-job he works so slowly that he is thought to be lazy, yet this is because he is a perfectionist. His love for his father is such that instead of protesting against the harsh treatment that he suffers, he feels he should apologize for causing his father trouble. He allows himself to be cheated of his wealth, never imagining that not all possess the same honesty as himself. He has a decency that is occasionally misplaced or exaggerated, and that is literally too good for the world in which he lives. That his moral standards are not those of his fellowmen is suggested by the symbolic chalk line that he draws across the room to separate his own territory from that of the other lodgers. The order and cleanliness of his sector contrast with the disorder and dirt of theirs, but it is significant that whereas he observes the division, they do not. It is a one-sided and futile arrangement, from which he cannot profit in any practical sense, and there is a clear distinction between his interpretation of the situation and actuality. He is one of life's innocents, lacking the practical fiber and judgment necessary for survival.

Eventually it is his lack of judgment that leads to his death, which occurs about a year after the musician's narration of his story, and which conveniently completes the framework and rounds off the work. It is set in February 1830, at the time of Vienna's great flood, and the Leopoldstadt is a major disaster area. Fearing for the musician's welfare, the narrator returns there to offer him assistance, only to discover that he has perished. He had behaved heroically, rescuing children from the flood, but it was not this that killed him. He died of a cold caught when he had gone back in foolhardy fashion to save his landlord's tax returns. Both actions were undertaken in the same spirit of selfless generosity, but in the exercise of his virtue he failed to discriminate between a matter of life and death and a triviality.[6]

The musician's inadequacies are most cruelly exposed in his relationship with Barbara. When they first become acquainted in the chancellery, where she sells refreshments, she asks for a piece of paper on which to place her cakes, a casual request, but he goes to ridiculous lengths to please her. Instead of simply taking a piece from the office, which he dare not do, he fetches a whole quire of paper from his home a few days later, a response which is well-meaning and which serves to further the acquaintanceship, but which at face value is absurdly inappropriate. From the reader's viewpoint the relationship seems a particularly humiliating one for the musician, for Barbara scolds him incessantly for his clumsiness and general ineptitude, showing us exactly what marriage to her would have been like for him. Yet the reader can detect in Barbara signs of genuine affection for him. When they part, she is emotionally distressed, and at the close of the work she is seen weeping over his memory. Clearly she senses something of value in his nature and character, yet at the same time she is exasperated that he is so weak, gullible, impractical, and effeminate. The musician is both saint and fool, a paradox which is reflected in the ambivalence of Barbara's feelings toward him.

It is possible that Grillparzer is offering through his presentation of the musician's unhappy fate a comment on the unscrupulous harshness of his own materialistic world, and we can despair that one so pure in soul becomes an outcast and beggar. The implication is that sterner qualities are required for survival in an unsympathetic world, qualities which the musician does not possess. Yet if he did possess them, he would lose something of his essential nobility. A similarly ironic combination of nobility of character and impracticality has been observed in the portraits of Bancbanus and Bishop Gregor, but in *Der arme Spielmann* greater emphasis is placed on the hero's inadequacies. He has been justly identified as one of the first true anti-heroes of nineteenth-century literature. One incident in particular, which stands at the center of the story, suggests that the blame for his failure rests more with his own character and personality than with society. This occurs at the climax of his relationship with Barbara when he attempts to embrace her for the only time. Her response is to strike him hard on the face, but then to kiss him lightly on the cheek. She then flees from him, and as she shuts the glass door in his face, he returns her kiss by pressing his lips passionately against the glass. The emotions that prompt Barbara's contradictory actions here are clearly identifiable. The blow represents a spontaneous reaction, her genuine anger at what she regards as an impertinence. Her kiss is only a fleeting gesture of remorse, in no sense an expression of love. Yet the musician is thrown into ecstasies by the blow, and the memory of the kiss still brings tears to his eyes. His reaction is wholly inappropriate, for he invests in each of her actions a significance that is out of all proportion with reality. The gulf between reality and his own private view is symbolized by the glass which separates him and Barbara and in his ineffectual and grotesquely ridiculous attempt at a kiss. The incident both highlights his inadequacies as a man and suggests a profound division between himself and his fellow beings.

The musician's feelings for Barbara in themselves are also somewhat problematic. That this is no simple love story is suggested by the absence of any confession of love on his part. Nor is there any indication that he finds Barbara beautiful. Indeed, his colleagues find her pock-marked and generally unattractive, an opinion which he does not dispute. What does attract him is her song. It is the song that he finds beautiful, and it is his desire to possess the score of it that leads him to Barbara's home. 'It is when he finds her singing it that he attempts to embrace her; it is the song that he teaches to her elder child, that he plays after concluding his story, and that has retained its beauty for him over the years.' The song thus possesses a unique significance for him and exercises over him a frightening demonic power. On the other hand, it affords him an ecstatic pleasure and is the only piece of music that he can play with any success. Indeed, he feels divinely inspired when he first plays it; it surpasses Bach and Mozart and provides access to God. When he dies, he smiles, as though he can hear something beautiful far away. It is thus arguable that his music has brought him close to "the divine source of truth and beauty,"[7] providing his life with spiritual and aesthetic riches which it would otherwise have lacked, and which transcend the ephemeral values of reality.

Yet if the musician's ears are attuned to some loftier ideal realm, he is unable to demonstrate this, for in that it fails to communicate anything of the feeling that has inspired the performer, his music is artistically worthless. The pleasure that he finds in his song is entirely private, for both to the narrator and to Barbara it sounds just like any ordinary popular song. Moreover, although he claims to have a serious artistic mission, he is totally unsuccessful in performance. Because he lacks the ability to communicate, to "perform" the ecstasy he feels, value cannot be ascribed to it in any absolute sense.[8] *Der arme Spielmann* underlines the fact that the power of the artist's vision is without value for others if it is not translated into intelligible art. As Grillparzer himself insisted, the basis of every art is craftsmanship, and any would-be artist who does not possess this quality is an incompetent, a *Stümper* (*SB* [*Selbstbiographie*] I, 14, 73). The musician's aesthetic experience may have significance for himself, but it is for his own pleasure alone. His devotion to his art and the evidence of the ecstasy that he derives from this are indicative of the capacity of art for the enrichment of life, but in that his art takes him into a private world which he cannot share with others, it is sterile. The gulf between the musician and reality, which exists in any case because of his shortcomings as a human being, is accentuated by the privacy of his art. Thus, although he has given his own subjective account of his story, we have still not got to the bottom of the mystery, for his deepest secret, the pleasure which he takes in his music, has remained impenetrable.

It is not without significance that *Der arme Spielmann* was completed at a time when Grillparzer's doubts as to the validity of his own art had reached a critical stage. The autobiographical element in this story is strong, and in an exaggerated and distorted fashion the portrait of the musician does reflect Grillparzer's relationship with his father, with Kathi Fröhlich, his own devotion to his art, and his tortured self-doubts both as man and artist.[9] If his earlier artist-figure Sappho also expressed Grillparzer's awareness of the gulf separating the artist from life, at least the value of her art was not questioned. But the value of the musician's art *is* questioned, and precisely because, in the true sense of the word, he is no artist. At most, he can represent Grillparzer's deepest fears as to the image that he himself might present to his unappreciative public. He is a distortion of the *unsuccessful* artist, and a warning of the dangers of an oversubjective, Romantic attitude to art. But he is also a forerunner of some of the sickly and decadent artist-figures of Thomas Mann, such as Detlev Spinell of *Tristan,* who enjoys the most exquisite, but uncommunicable private aesthetic experiences. In Grillparzer's musician's devotion to his song we may see an anticipation of the exclusive aestheticism and rarefied idealism that was to become such a cult at the turn of the century.

Notes

1. In this connection comparisons have been made between Grillparzer's poetry and Byron's, which is also inspired by "a kind of passionate thinking." See W. E. Yates, *Grillparzer,* p. 156.

2. *Die deutsche Literatur im 19. Jahrhundert* (Stuttgart: Kröner, 1969), p. 174.

3. W. Paulsen, "Grillparzers Erzählkunst," *Germanic Review* 19 (1944): 59-68.

4. See R. H. Lawson, "The Starost's daughter Elga in Grillparzer's *Das Kloster bei Sendomir*," *Modern Austrian Literature* I (1968): 31-37.

5. R. Brinkmann, *"Der arme Spielmann," Wirklichkeit und Illusion* (Tübingen, 1957), pp. 87-145, argues that despite Grillparzer's attempts to provide an objective, truthful depiction of the musician, he can only achieve a subjective account, whether from the narrator's or from the musician's own perspective.

6. A point made by Benno von Wiese, *"Der arme Spielmann," Die deutsche Novelle* (Düsseldorf, 1969), I, 147.

7. E. E. Papst, ed., *Der arme Spielmann* (London, 1960), p. xxvi.

8. J. P. Stern, *Re-interpretations* (London, 1964), writes: "What emerges as the sole positive value is . . . not the art which he has so faithfully 'practised' for a lifetime. . . . What emerges at the end . . . is the intention and the pure heart alone, the disembodied good will as the absolute and only value" (p. 72).

9. As argued by Papst, *Spielmann,* p. xx.

Roger Nicholls (essay date 1982)

SOURCE: "The Hero as an Old Man: The Role of Banca-banus in Grillparzer's *Ein Treuer Diener Seines Herrn*," in *Modern Language Quarterly,* Vol. 43, No. 1, 1982, pp. 29-42.

[*In the following essay, Nicholls analyses* Ein Treuer Diener Seines Herrn *as representative of Grillparzer's propensity to portray man in all his limitations, to expose the ambiguity inherent in human life, and to show how human achievement can grow out of conflict.*]

Fundamental to the interpretation of Grillparzer's drama is recognition of the contrast between the expectation aroused by the formal language and structure of his plays and the reality of the inner action. Grillparzer's insistent emphasis on verse as the medium of his drama, his recurrent use of mythological and historical themes, and his vision of himself as the last poet in an age of prose lead us to anticipations that are not realized in practice. There was a time when Grillparzer was regarded as a third classic of German literature beside Goethe and Schiller. Later, more negatively, he was treated as an "Epigone der Klassik."[1] Both associations suggest the atmosphere of *haute tragédie* or at least an attempt to follow Goethe and Schiller in their ambition to re-create in Germany a drama that moves on the heroic scale. In fact, Grillparzer's genius lies in the presentation of man in his limitations; it is his gift to show us the doubts and ambiguities under the surface of our lives, and the conflicts within us out of which human achievements must be built.

Ein treuer Diener seines Herrn needs to be understood in this context. After the intellectualized theater of *Sappho* and *Das goldene Vliess,* Grillparzer had sought in *König Ottokars Glück und Ende* a theme of national celebration to which a diverse audience could respond at different emotional levels. The theater was to become again a focal point of society in which members of the public might unite in a communal experience. In *Ein treuer Diener,* likewise, Grillparzer looked for a subject of broad appeal in national history. The original impetus for the play came from plans to celebrate the crowning of the Empress Karoline Auguste as Queen of Hungary. But the plans could not be worked out in time, and Grillparzer's reading of Hungarian histories and chronicles led him away from national pageantry to the choice of an unexpected theme: the story of Bancbanus, an old man with many human weaknesses, who as "loyal servant" to a thirteenth-century Hungarian king is charged with the task of preserving the peace of the realm.

Grillparzer thus openly chooses a protagonist freed from the heroic inheritance of great tragedy. There is evidence enough of human frailty, it is true, in his Sappho and Medea, and much of what we appreciate in these complex and neurotic figures is the author's insight into the conflicts within human consciousness that they reveal. Yet behind the peculiarly modern feeling these heroines evoke we are aware of the significance and grandeur of the traditional themes from which their stories evolve. Again in *Ottokar,* although we may see evidence of an unexpected lack of authority and self-assurance in the rapid fall of the protagonist, he remains an imposing figure, a king who in his ambitions visibly incorporates elements of Napoleon. Bancbanus, in contrast, arouses little sense of awe. Under the colorful historical garb of his role as paladin to a medieval king, we see a fussy and pedantic man who at times even borders on the ridiculous and who is described by Grillparzer himself in his *Selbstbiographie* as "ein ziemlich borvierter alter Mann."[2] In terms of Northrop Frye's convenient categorizations, we have not only moved to the stage of "low mimetic" realism, where the hero is superior neither to other men nor to his environment and we respond only in the sense that he is one of us, but we are touching on the "ironic mode," where the protagonist is in some way inferior to us and we look down "on a scene of bondage, frustration, or absurdity."[3]

The character of Bancbanus is one of the main factors to account for the often negative tone in the secondary literature on this play. He is considered too servile and submissive, and the ideal of loyalty which he embodies too much a reflection of the limitations of the Biedermeier. Even critics who appreciate the subtleties and half shades of Grillparzer's work find Bancbanus too stiffly unaffected by feeling and passion to occupy the central role. Heinz Politzer, for instance, calls him a grey figure: "Die Gestalt Bancbanus ist grau wie ihr Haar; . . . Standhaftigkeit macht ihn zum steinernen Gast in einer Welt, die mit ihren Leidenschaften um ihn brandet. . . ."[4] Another sympathetic scholar, Urs Helmensdorfer, says of Bancbanus's central moment of choice: "Seine Loyalität grenzt ans Monströse."[5] Such judgments are understandable, yet behind them we may observe a partial unwillingness to acknowledge the significance of the choice of hero. It is no longer possible in nineteenth-century literature to seek the profound experiences associated with great tragedy. Grillparzer writes in a world deprived of heroes. We cannot anticipate the sense of horror at man's capacity for suffering that tragedy evokes or the curious consolation given us by the significance and dignity inherent in his fate. Yet if our desire for the heroic and the cathartic is not to be fully satisfied, it is still not adequate to say that all tragic force has been replaced by psychological understanding. The inadequacies Bancbanus carries with him are specifically and graphically presented, but at the same time they are also symbolic of all human weaknesses. Despite them he manages to rise to the task imposed on him; he makes of his own limitations virtues by which he can preserve the values he holds most dear. Grillparzer calls his drama a "Trauerspiel," but it is in a deeper sense a morality play. In Act I, King Andreas sets out to defend his rights in a distant land and leaves responsibility at home to his loyal councilor; in Act V, he returns to pronounce judgment on his servant's stewardship of the kingdom. Though Bancbanus is confronted with the deaths of his wife and his queen and the prospect of civil war, he saves the life of the heir to the throne and creates a situation in which peace can be restored. His virtues are not attractive ones, yet they gain from us a grudging recognition of man's determination to respond to the demands of life and to create some order in the face of chaos.

From the beginning Bancbanus's situation is a delicate one. He shares the regency with Queen Gertrude, but she, hoping to the final moment of the king's departure that he will appoint her brother Otto von Meran as co-regent with her, does not bother to conceal her contempt for the old councilor. The king angrily rebukes her and insists on her cooperation, but the seeds of disorder are clearly present. Otto's pursuit of Erny, Bancbanus's young wife, precipitates the crisis. It is a peculiarity of the drama, often criticized, that the emotional tension of Act III is centered on secondary figures: the complex and unappealing Duke Otto in his attempt to seduce Erny, the nature of Erny's resistance, and the ambivalent reactions of the queen herself. Yet this private and personal conflict leads to the national crisis of Act IV. Erny, trapped by Otto in the queen's quarters and threatened with abduction, commits suicide rather than yield. Her brother, Count Peter, and Bancbanus's brother, Count Simon, seeking revenge and fearing that the queen will succeed in helping Otto escape the country, demand that he be handed over to their authority. Bancbanus is faced with the temptation to join them and revenge himself on the unscrupulous Otto, but does not hesitate in his duty. While they assemble their forces to threaten an attack on the queen in her castle, he attempts to lead her and her son, the crown prince, as well as Otto himself, to safety. As they are escaping, the queen, mistaken for Otto with whom she has exchanged cloaks, is killed. Bancbanus brings the others away and by a dramatic turn of events gives the child into the protection of Otto, while he himself confronts Peter and Simon.

What kind of man is it who is thus able to overcome his misery at his beloved wife's death and rescue her virtual murderer in order to preserve the peace? From the beginning our feelings toward him are uncertain. The opening scene in the drama takes place in the early morning, before dawn. Bancbanus is being dressed to go to court, while outside we hear the shouts and insulting songs of the rowdies, led by Duke Otto, mocking this old man with his young and blooming wife. The servants are nervous and tense, and, though Bancbanus tries to appear calm, his own tension is revealed both by his irritation with their clumsiness and the sententious philosophy with which he tries to sustain himself. It is not necessary to accept totally the description omitted from the final version that he is a "kleine, hagere, etwas gekrümmte Figur" (I, 1318), but he is clearly an unprepossessing man, presented in unfortunate circumstances where he is by no means master of himself or the situation.

The idea of an old man with a young wife pursued by the gallants of the court suggests a comic role. And there are many occasions when Bancbanus comes close to being a comic dupe. At the beginning of Act II, at a meeting of the council after the king's departure, the queen exposes him

openly to ridicule. Bored with the legal details with which Bancbanus wrestles, she suddenly brings the meeting to a close. The councilors disappear, leaving Bancbanus, unconscious of their departure, tiresomely searching through his confused papers for the documents he needs. Again, when Otto and Gertrude prepare for festivities, Bancbanus obstinately insists on his duty, setting up his desk outside the queen's rooms to hear the complaints and petitions of the people. He is ridiculed by the courtiers, and his position seems the more ludicrous when we realize that the celebrations are only a pretext for Otto to continue his advances to Erny. But the atmosphere changes. Once the gallery gates have been opened and the people are seen to be thronging outside as they wait for their cases to be heard, matters appear in a different light. Bancbanus is no longer the heavy-footed obstacle to the youthful gaiety of the court. The festivities seem blatantly irresponsible; the courtiers, shallow and absurd. Yet the mood is strangely uncertain, and our feelings find no clear focus. Though Bancbanus's judgments on the cases he hears are vigorous and to the point, they lack the full conviction of authority. His principles of conduct are worthy but are presented so as to seem moralizing and pedantic. Above all, we feel that he is closing his eyes to the realities around him. When Erny pleads to be allowed to leave the dance, he resolutely insists on her doing her duty by remaining in attendance.

It is tempting to treat the scenes here in terms of tragicomedy. A possible parallel might be drawn with *The Wild Duck*.[6] Like Hjalmar Ekdal, Bancbanus seems in part an absurd figure, irritating in his mannerisms, self-engrossed, lacking feeling for reality. Yet both figures are treated with sympathy. In Ibsen at least comic and tragic effects are integrated. Hjalmar is never openly satirized; we cannot mock him or regard him derisively from the outside. We laugh and yet sympathize, recognizing—however unwillingly, for criticism has been slow to accept the implications—that the "life-lie" on which he builds is an essential prop if he is to maintain his existence. Bancbanus's pedantry gives him a similar hold on life. He clings to the letter of the law because it provides a stable source of conduct in the confusions of the world. Recognizing this, we may laugh at him and yet appreciate his dedication to the tasks before him, while still fearing the dangers that are building up. In the end, however, he reveals himself as a far stronger figure than Hjalmar and stronger than the figures around him. Certainly the movement of the act as a whole reverses the usual sequence of comedy. Instead of the victory of youth, traditional to comic action, and the exposure of the pretensions of age, the situation is reversed. The act which begins with the mockery of Bancbanus ends with Erny's contemptuous rejection of Otto and the latter's abysmal collapse. A tender and affectionate scene between Bancbanus and Erny seems to strengthen their relationship. Yet here too Bancbanus's weaknesses impose themselves. As a couple they seem to be more father and daughter than husband and wife. He repeatedly calls her "child," bidding her rest her head on his bosom with closed eyes, like an ostrich burying its head in the sand, as he himself says (line 868). He seems to offer her security and reassurance, but we feel uneasy at their attitudes, sensing on his part an urge to play the father, and on hers a denial of reality, a longing to remain a daughter rather than a woman, a fear perhaps of the desires that Otto may have secretly aroused in her.

The situation at the end of Act II is thus highly ambiguous. We are not sure how to respond or where the action is leading. In Act III, Bancbanus barely appears. His absence is significant for he is able to offer no protection from Otto's attempted abduction of his wife. He arrives only at the end, too late, after Erny has stabbed herself with the dagger which she had seized for protection.

In Act IV, however, we see a different side of Bancbanus. Here is his decisive moment of choice. However uncertain he may have been before in dealing with Otto's mockery, and however much he underestimated the dangers of the situation, he now acts with boldness and decision. Unexpected though the decision is, there is no suggestion of hesitation or doubt. His grief is patent enough. We see a man whose dearest tie to life has been destroyed. Yet he masters his feelings, not by yielding to anger and a natural urge for revenge, but by recognizing the duties still before him. In repudiating the attempts of Simon and Peter to embroil him in actions against the queen, he assumes control of events. It is he who takes decisive action, while Otto is in a helpless state of shock. So great is this growth of stature that Bancbanus readily carries the emotional weight of the final act. Where our attention had earlier moved to Otto, by the last scenes of the drama we are fully prepared to accept that it is Bancbanus's fate in which the moral significance of the drama is invested, and his character and actions which must be weighed in the balance.

The decision to oppose Simon and Peter is of central importance to the interpretation of the drama. It is not sufficient to imply, as do George A. Wells and Herbert W. Reichert,[7] that Grillparzer was faced with the problem of how to motivate Bancbanus's failure to avenge Erny. His refusal to take revenge arises out of his character and becomes the drama's essential theme. In the opening scene Bancbanus shows his control over his feelings. Upset though he is at the abusive behavior of Otto and his companions, he is even more indignant at his servant's wish to open the doors and attack them:

> Bist du so kriegrisch?
> Ich will dir einen Platz im Heere suchen!
> Hier wohnt der Frieden; ich bin nur sein Mietsmann,
> Sein Lehensmann, sein Gast.
> Verhüte Gott, dass er mich lärmend finde
> Und Miet und Wohnung mir auf Umzeit künde!
>
> (18-23)

Bancbanus's eloquence in the preservation of peace sustains him for a while in this scene, both in our eyes and in his own, but in Act II, under the continued provocation of Otto and Gertrude, he must keep his feelings to himself. Here he seems stolid and unimposing; we are ashamed for him in his humiliations. But his refusal to respond is a conscious and deliberate policy; he seeks at all costs to prevent a clash and avoid driving Otto to excess. Perhaps he asks too much of Erny in sending her back to the dance, but he asks it because he is himself under strain and he anticipates in his wife the same determination and control.

Bancbanus's decision after Erny's death is thus well prepared. It seems out of place to talk, as critics have done, of monstrous loyalty or degrading self-abasement in pursuit of the king's demands. Admittedly, Bancbanus's loyalty to the royal family takes some extreme forms. He is unwilling to listen to accusations which challenge or censure their behavior. But while one may understand the liberal sympathies of writers who, from the days when the play was first produced, have objected to the submissive attitude of the hero, their criticisms seem misplaced. Bancbanus's loyalty to the royal family and to his duty is the basis on which he preserves the values of his life. His bitter rejection of Simon's appeal for help in revenge expresses his deepest beliefs.

> Aufrührer! ich mit euch?—Ich bin der Mann des
>   Friedens,
> Der Hüter ich der Ruh—Mich hat mein König
> Geordnet, seinen Frieden hier zu wahren;
> Ich in den Bürgerkrieg mit euch?
> Fluch, Bürgerkrieg! Fluch dir vor allen Flüchen!
>
> (1418-22)

The contrast with Simon and Peter is most revealing. Their motives are clear and legitimate enough. They are not villains eager to find an excuse for bloodshed, but men of honor who have seen their family degraded and have reasonable cause to believe that Otto will still escape justice. Simon considers his brother old and feeble, absurdly concerned for the rights of others while unable to protect his own, and thus a source of contempt to all who love honor and courage. But he and Peter take no account of the disastrous consequences of their actions. Sustained by the righteousness of their cause, they shift the blame all too readily onto their enemies for the dangers which result. When Gertrude makes it clear to Peter that she will not hand over Otto and that any attack on him will endanger her own life and that of the heir to the throne, Peter immediately asserts that the responsibility will then be hers (1527-32). Again, after the tragic outcome of the attack, when Peter flings his dagger at what he thinks is the fleeing Otto and kills the queen, Simon refuses to accept the blame. Cursing Otto now as a "double murderer" (1660-61), he forces a fight on Otto's followers and kills one of them in his anger at learning of Otto's escape. Their attitude forces them into open rebellion when the king returns. Obliged to defend themselves, they are prepared to surrender only if the king will offer pardon in advance. Their proud insistence on their own rights and their conviction that they must uphold both their reputation for valor and family honor thus lead to violence and destruction and threaten the breakdown of the state. Only Bancbanus, in the conviction of his mission and confidence gained through the rescue of the crown prince, brings them to submit to the king's mercy.

The incalculable value of peace is a dominant motif in Grillparzer's writings. We may remember Ottokar's moving final speech in which he repents the desperate deeds of his early career. This turn in mood, so different from the Napoleonic egoism of his early life, brings him to recall how many men had been killed in the pursuit of his ambitions:

> Und keiner war von den Gebliebnen allen,
> Den seine Mutter nicht, als sie mit Schmerz geboren,
> Mit Lust gedrückt an ihre Nährerbrust,
> Der Vater nicht als seinen Stolz gesegnet
> Und aufgezogen, jahrelang gehütet.
> Wenn er am Finger sich verletzt die Haut,
> Da liefen sie herbei und bandens ein
> Und sahen zu, bis endlich es geheilt.
> Und's war ein Finger nur, die Haut am Finger!
> Ich aber hab sie schockweis hingeschleudert
> Und starrem Eisen einen Weg gebahnt
> In ihren warmen Leib.
>
> (2849-60)

Bancbanus is prepared if necessary to sacrifice revenge or justice for the sake of peace. If the death of Otto would restore Erny to him, then perhaps he would act with Peter and Simon. But the danger that Otto will escape his deserts does not move him. Whereas Simon and Peter are motivated by considerations of pride that belong to their rank and caste, Bancbanus's reaction reveals humbleness of heart, an acceptance of the limitations of his claims on the world.

In the way he ignores conventional assumptions of what is required of him and how he should react, Bancbanus reminds us of another Grillparzer peacemaker, Kaiser Rudolf in **Ein Bruderzwist in Habsburg,** whose inner doubts and desperate self-control stand in contrast to the easy self-assurance of the less than adequate men around him. Yet Bancbanus is in some ways a more ambiguous figure than Rudolf. For in acknowledging Bancbanus's achievements, we must also acknowledge his responsibility for the catastrophe. His failures are a product of his character as much as are his successes. If the accomplishment of peace arises from the modesty of his own pretensions, his acceptance of his limitations encouraged the conditions that led to disaster. When the king announces Bancbanus as his choice for regent, the old man responds with fragmentary protests: "Ach, Herr, bedenkt! . . . Ich bin ein schwacher Mann! . . . Bin alt!" (383-86). After the queen has revealed her dislike of the king's choice, Bancbanus says: "Ich sagt euchs, Herr, ich tauge nicht dafür!" (411). He seems unable to formulate the basis of his intuitive reluctance to accept the position. The king easily overrides his protests, yet we feel Bancbanus is right. In accepting the regency, he must accept partial responsibility for the tragedy.

This responsibility may be felt specifically in his relationship to Erny. His failure to aid his wife at the ball helps to bring on the disaster. In part he acts out of delicacy of feeling. Precisely because of the difference in their ages, he hesitates to play the master and exercise authority over her.

> Ich bin wohl alt genug, und du bist jung,
> Ich lebensmüd und ernst, du heiter blühend,
> Was gibt ein Recht mir, also dich zu quälen?
> Weil dus versprachst? Ei, was verspricht der Mensch!
> Weils so die Sitte will? Wer frägt nach Sitte?
>
> (823-27)

He is convinced that he must rely on her feelings and her power of decision, but thereby fails to recognize how much she needs his support. Left to herself, Erny proves too inexperienced and immature to deal with Otto's vigorous advances. Perhaps because of an almost inevitable doubt about her own feelings toward the attractive duke, she overreacts, and by asserting her scorn and contempt, she incites in Otto a violence that might not otherwise have erupted.

It might also be suggested that Bancbanus fails Otto too. By studiously ignoring Otto's insults, he simply increases the duke's sense of humiliation and self-disgust. Otto needs the guidance of someone in authority he can respect. Bancbanus is clearly incapable of providing any help. Evidence of how little he understands the problem is his suggestion of a role for Otto in leading a group of cavalry against some wandering insurgents. He fails totally to realize that, in view of their ambitions, this will seem a gratuitous insult to Otto and Gertrude, a clumsy attempt to ingratiate himself.

But Bancbanus's failure does not lie in specific omissions or decisions; it is rooted in his character. In the early scenes we feel the desperate need for someone to stand up to events and attempt to take control. Bancbanus is an official who has grown old in honorable and faithful service. He deals with his work as it occurs, case by case, trying to do his best, but leaving out of consideration the flow of emotions in the court, the incalculable changes in atmosphere which render the individual cases less important.

At the same time it must be granted that the restrictions of Bancbanus's position make it difficult to see what decisive action he can take. The situation in these early scenes is comparable to that in **Ein Bruderzwist in Habsburg,** although the political and historical setting is far less elaborate. We long for action and yet are gradually oppressed by the recognition that there is no clear path of action available. Bancbanus is an unsatisfactory leader, yet it is impossible to know what satisfactory action can be taken. Grillparzer has put great stress on the ambiguity of the conditions under which he takes over the office. The king spells out the terms in some detail. Bancbanus is invested with legal responsibility but seems to have no corresponding authority and power. The queen is regent and he is her councilor. Although the king insists that nothing can be settled without Bancbanus's agreement and he is answerable for their decisions, this assertion is modified later when the king declares that she is the ruling mind who rules through him. Bancbanus is "Reichsgehilfe," her eyes and ears, her hands and arms (381-82). How then is he to act against her? What can he do if she insists on supporting Otto's excesses?

The significance of this situation is heightened when we remember the particular structure of the drama. Acts I and V serve as a partial frame around the central action. The king's role in setting up the situation and serving as judge at the end inevitably suggests a symbolic representation of God's world. The favorite baroque theme of the ruler as God's representative standing outside the human action is not carried out here with total consistency any more than it is in other well-known German dramas. We think, for example, of the role of the Elector in *Der Prinz von Homburg* or of the Duke in *Torquato Tasso*. Nevertheless echoes of a higher authority are implicit in the king's role, particularly in the last act when he returns to his divided kingdom. The king's fear that Bancbanus may have been an "ungetreuer Knecht" (1969), together with the final assurance of his real loyalty contained in the title itself, seems a clear allusion to Christ's parable of the talents and the "good and faithful servant" of the Lord. Bancbanus thus comes to stand as a representative for man, his fate an exemplar of the human condition. His weaknesses and inevitable human failings, together with the restrictive conditions of his task, become symbolic of man's fate, "created weak but commanded to be strong." The moral of this situation does not have to be, as F. W. Kaufmann suggests, the acceptance by Bancbanus of a world which "punishes with inner destruction" the transgression of limitations, even when imposed on us against our will.[8] Instead, we may see in Bancbanus's fate an illustration of man burdened by the very nature of life with tasks that go beyond human limits. Although necessarily sharing in responsibility for the tragedy, Bancbanus nevertheless seeks to remain true to the principles of his life and finally manages to bring out of disaster a spirit of reconciliation.

The king's final judgments take fully into account the frailty of the human condition. Indeed, he acknowledges some responsibility for the situation himself, angrily accusing himself of neglect in failing to resist the mood of intransigence and immorality which was to destroy his home and happiness (1917 ff.) Such an attitude, which certainly indicates restrictions on his role as God's representative, is a characteristic turn of Grillparzer's. In *Weh dem, der lügt!* Bishop Gregor, we may recall, similarly sets the conditions of the hero's task and in the end acknowledges the limitations of his own vision. Since the king is himself largely accountable for the disasters that have occurred, he is all the more prepared to act with charity toward others who are involved. Responding to Bancbanus's pleas, he limits punishment of Peter and Simon, in effect the murderers of his wife, to banishment, while Otto too, once he has brought back the crown prince in safety, is permitted to leave the kingdom. For Otto, in fact, a checkered line of Christian grace and mercy may

be traced. Bancbanus, seeking to bring the queen and her child across the moat out of the castle, is forced to take them one by one. The queen insists that Otto must be the first to leave, even before the child:

> Dies Kind beschützt
> Schuldlosigkeit mit lilienblankem Schwert;
> Doch diesen suchen sie, und er ist schuldig.
>
> (1622-24)

Otto is allowed to escape, not in spite of but because of his guilt, and is thus granted the opportunity for atonement. Bancbanus, by giving the child into Otto's care, grants him, as he says, a last link with life and protection from despair and self-rejection (1985-86). By his rescue of the child Otto sets out on a path toward forgiveness which the king acknowledges in his final words to him: "Zieht hin mit Gott! kein Fluch sei über euch!" (2070).

A further Christian theme may be seen in Bancbanus's conflict with Peter and Simon. We have stressed to what extent his success is a victory of peace over war, of reason over passion, possibly of love over hate, certainly of humility over self-assertion and self-righteousness. The symbolic implications of this victory may be extended if we stress the associations aroused by the names of Bancbanus's opponents. We cannot help seeing here a suggestion of Christ's foremost disciple and the founder of the Church contrasted with Christ himself. In the actions of Simon and Peter after Erny's death we may see a reflection of the church militant ready to fight for its beliefs, opposed to Christ's message of peace. Such an interpretation may find support in the overtones of meaning given to the rescue of the crown prince and in the dream, envisioned in Bancbanus's final speech, of a harmonious new world to be enjoyed during his future reign.

In this context Bancbanus's humility suggests an echo of one of the most mysterious of the Christian beatitudes: "Blessed are the poor in spirit: for theirs is the kingdom of heaven." We may be reminded of the hero of *Der arme Spielmann*. The poor fiddler tells his story of failure and incompetence, even helplessness. He is simple almost to the point of being a fool; but gradually there emerges the realization that there may be another simplicity which is the expression of purity of heart. His stupidity and clumsiness may be nothing compared with his innocence and goodness. We saw Bancbanus first as an almost comic figure, ridiculed by the livelier people around him. Later his character has elements of the Christian fool. And yet the reversal of judgment which takes place in *Der arme Spielmann* never fully occurs here. Bancbanus remains in our mind as a pedantic and limited man, burdened by old age. His victory, won without passion, leaves us little feeling of Christian joy. We are left to wonder whether his achievement is a triumph of Christian humility or whether his humility is not merely an all too easy expression of his own weakness.

It may be that the conclusion of *Der arme Spielmann* is too easy, too sentimental, for us today.[9] *Ein treuer Diener* is more cautious, more subtle, more enigmatic. Yet it is a problem for drama, which traditionally paints in bold and confident colors, to leave us so uncertain in our judgment. If we assert Bancbanus's spiritual victory, insisting on the values of peace and law which he upheld,[10] then we overlook the weakness and tiresome limitations of the old man. Yet if we stress the absence of passion and the cold adherence to rules, then we ignore the elements of moral triumph.

Earlier it was suggested that the play might be considered within the bounds of tragicomedy, but this is not easy to maintain. Elements of the comic have largely disappeared by the end of the action. Moreover, the normal protagonist in tragicomedy is a man we laugh at and yet regard with a certain sympathy and even benevolence. We see in Hjalmar Ekdal's story, as we do, say, in Malvoli's or Alceste's (two often-quoted instances of tragicomic appeal), evidence of an all too human weakness which we can readily acknowledge in ourselves. Bancbanus's faults irritate us. It is difficult to break down the barriers which his weaknesses and even his virtues create. Perhaps the true clue to our sympathy lies in the poignancy of his suffering. In the heat of the action Bancbanus seems to forget his grief at the death of his wife. But when the issues are resolved and the king suggests the possibility of rewards for what he has achieved in the service of his master, we see the terrible emptiness that her loss has caused. Bancbanus's despair finds no relief in outbursts of distress, but lingers within. His life is enveloped in the sorrow and isolation that her death has brought. In the scenes immediately preceding, the drama offers conciliation. The king's son has been saved, Counts Simon and Peter pardoned, even Duke Otto allowed to go in peace. But it is a conciliation based on a shared sense of grief and suffering. Bancbanus's fate confirms this mood. His final decision to reject the king's offers and withdraw from the world of events is influenced by Otto's absolute affirmation that Erny was innocent and had never encouraged his advances. Emphasis is placed once more on the nature of a world in which innocence offers no protection. Bancbanus had sought to avoid the dangers of life through the fulfillment of daily duties, only to be engrossed in larger guilt and responsibility. But his withdrawal does not mean rejection or inner despair. The moral of the play is not like that of ***Der Traum ein Leben,*** in which a vision of the cruel world outside drives the hero to retreat to his own private corner. Bancbanus has already done what is required of him. Using all his powers in the fulfillment of his given task, he has managed to save the realm from civil war. He has known what it is to live in a threatening world and feels secure of the judgment of posterity. Thus in the midst of sadness there is consolation. In the awareness of grief we recognize the capacity of man to sustain the values by which life may still hold meaning.

Notes

1. A judgment rejected by Emil Staiger, for instance, in his influential discussion, "Grillparzer: *König Ottokars Glück und Ende,*" in *Meisterwerke deutscher Sprache aus dem neunzehnten Jahrhundert,* 2nd ed. (Zürich: Atlantis, 1948), p. 165 f.

2. Franz Grillparzer, *Sämtliche Werke,* ed. Peter Frank and Karl Pörnbacher, 4 vols. (München: Carl Hanser, 1960-65), IV, 153. *Ein treuer Diener* appears in volume 1.

3. *Anatomy of Criticism: Four Essays* (Princeton: Princeton University Press, 1957), p. 34.

4. *Grillparzer oder das abgründige Biedermeier* (Wien: Fritz Molden, 1972), p. 185.

5. *Grillparzers Bühnenkunst* (Bern: Francke, 1960), p. 60.

6. See the discussion of *The Wild Duck* in Karl S. Guthke, *Modern Tragicomedy* (New York: Random House, 1966), pp. 144-65.

7. See Wells, *The Plays of Grillparzer* (London: Pergamon, 1969), p. 23; and Reichert, "The Characterization of Bancbanus in Grillparzer's *Ein treuer Diener seines Herrn,*" SP, [*Studies in Philology*] 46 (1949), 70-78, esp. p. 74.

8. *German Dramatists of the Nineteenth Century* (Los Angeles: Lymanhouse, 1940), p. 63.

9. This view has been vigorously represented by the hero of John Irving's bestseller *The World According to Garp* (New York: E. P. Dutton, 1976), p. 88 and *passim.*

10. Cf. Benno von Wiese, *Die deutsche Tragödie von Lessing bis Hebbel* (Hamburg: Hoffmann and Campe, 1948), II, 185: ". . . der Dienst an diesen Werten ist nicht eine Pedanterie, sondern Selbsterfüllung des Ichs, das hier sich verwurzelt weiss."

Ian F. Roe (essay date 1986)

SOURCE: "Truth and Humanity in Grillparzer's *Weh Dem, Der Lügt!,*" in *Forum for Modern Language Studies,* Vol. XXII, No. 4, October, 1986, pp. 289-307.

[*In the following essay, Roe comments on Grillparzer's only comic drama, noting that in it he subjects the search for truth to comic scrutiny and ultimately advocates a balanced life that incorporates contemplation and action, striving for truth and making mistakes.*]

In the relative optimism of Grillparzer's one completed comedy, critics have more readily observed the influence of eighteenth-century ideas than in most other plays by Grillparzer. Ernst Alker's assessment in 1930—"von Klassik findet sich keine Spur"[1]—has never been wholeheartedly endorsed even by critics who have been concerned to demonstrate Grillparzer's literary and psychological distance from Weimar. Ruth Angress describes the play as "an Austrian puppet-show on Goethean themes", as Grillparzer's "Iphigenie in Vienna". Herbert Seidler sees certain parallels between Grillparzer's treatment of truth and the connotations prevalent in Classicism. Erich

Hock especially, in an article of 1954, and also W. E. Yates have pointed to the Classical concepts of "Bildung", "Tierheit", "Menschheit", "Wahrheit" which underpin two of the most important themes of Grillparzer's comedy: man's development from coarse animal to civilised human being, and the concept of truthfulness that has prompted the drawing of parallels between Grillparzer's play and Goethe's *Iphigenie*.[2] Hock, however, considers the idea of truth to be essentially religious in nature: man for Grillparzer has fallen from the complete truth that is still proved possible by the heroine of Goethe's Classical drama, hence, according to Hock, the problems of Grillparzer's play are solved not by "reine Menschlichkeit", but by God. Similarly Ulrich Fülleborn believes that only God is capable of action in the play, namely through miracles.[3] Ruth Angress also provides an essentially Christian interpretation of the play: the gulf between barbarian and civilised cultures can be overcome only through trust in God. However, much recent criticism has questioned the validity of attributing religious beliefs to Grillparzer, however much he may, like Goethe, use religious motifs in symbolic form;[4] Emil Reich, as long ago as 1901, and more recently Yates and Hans-Georg Werner have justifiably insisted on the moral content of Leon's mission. Yates, however, replaces a religious absolute with a moral one, so that Gregor is seen to represent universal good, and Seidler similarly considers Gregor to be "die reinste und edelste Form kulturvoller und bildungsgegründeter Menschlichkeit".[5] Unusual in this context is the view of Jean-Louis Bandet that the treatment of the theme of truth in the comedy is trivial, although a rather playful approach to serious themes is implied by Angress's description of the comedy as a "puppet-show", while Franz Forster appears to defuse the whole moral issue of truth and lies by claiming that they are resolved into a higher unity.[6] Most critics, however, see Gregor's affirmation of truth as a very serious ideal, whether religious or ethical, which in keeping with Grillparzer's supposedly pessimistic philosophy cannot be upheld in ordinary reality. In the real world there is no possibility of achieving pure truth except, according to Fritz Martini, in not acting or, according to Bandet, in silence. The violation of truth perpetrated by Leon means that his success is not complete (Angress), and the relative success he does enjoy is a product of the comic situation (Seidler).[7] If such a picture of the comedy implies an essential distance from Classicism despite superficial thematic links, then Bruce Thompson's affirmation of Grillparzer's more positive and liberal attitudes ironically leads to the same stress on his departure from Classical ideals. For Thompson, Gregor is a defender of absolute values that are opposed to more human values and Leon's ethically questionable methods bring success and happiness, but Grillparzer is therefore seen to be rejecting the Classical belief in the whole man.[8]

And yet one must ask whether a play that is so obviously based on Classical themes can really be as distant from the connotations of those themes as many critics have suggested or implied. Is Grillparzer's treatment of truth really "sceptical" or "trivial", as Angress and Bandet respectively have argued? Is Gregor to be admired or criticised? Is Leon unsuccessful because he fails to uphold Gregor's ideals or successful because he recognises that they cannot be upheld? What exactly does Grillparzer understand by truth? To what extent does his use of the concept in the comedy correspond to his statements on truth elsewhere? What use does Grillparzer make of Classical concepts such as those highlighted by Hock? It would appear from all these questions that a closer examination of the play's links with Classical terminology may shed some light on the significance and meaning of the comedy.

The theme of man's development from his more animal state and of his subsequent striving towards a fuller humanity constitutes a leitmotif of Classical thinking,[9] and such a contrast between "Mensch" and "Tier" is found in Grillparzer's work from an early date. According to the wanderer in "Irenens Wiederkehr",

> Das Tier in uns hat die Natur hervorgebracht,
> den Menschen schuf erst seine Göttermacht!
>
> (II,893)[10]

Faust in Grillparzer's fragment enjoys the pleasure of being "ein Mensch" amongst the animals of the forest (II,993), while Jaromir in *Die Ahnfrau* realises that he has become an animal himself in the company of the robbers (1330-31). In later works, Libussa will settle the argument between fighting rivals once "das Tier ist Mensch geworden" (696); in *Ein Bruderzwist in Habsburg,* Rudolf II sees order turning animals into men (1260, 1267) and Julius requests a fair trial for Don Cäsar,

> Daß nicht wie ein verzehrend, reißend Tier,
> Daß wie ein Mensch er aus dem Leben scheide.
>
> (2183-84)

Grillparzer, however, saw the nationalistic tendencies in the Empire involving a reversal of the development praised by Rudolf II. In the poem "Sprachenkampf" of 1849, the insistence on national languages turns men back into beasts (I,500), and the famous epigram of the same year charts man's course from "Humanität" to "Bestialität" (I,500). Elsewhere Grillparzer noted in his diary that "ohne Ahnung vom Übersinnlichen wäre der Mensch allerdings Tier" (III,1161), and he sees the newly born child in a struggle between the two sides of human behaviour: "Mensch- und Tierheit streiten, / Wem sie gehört" (I,99).[11]

It is *Das goldene Vließ* that comes closest to the comedy in its treatment of this conflict. Milo thinks the Colchians are "wilde Tiere" (*Die Argonauten,* 1650), just as Leon, more jokingly, speaks of the Germans: "Hat man nicht seine Not mit all den Tieren?" (*Weh dem, der lügt!,* 614). The Greeks are seen to be spreading "der Menschheit Samen / [. . .] in die leere Wildnis" (*Argonauten,* 835-36), and Jason wishes to give Medea the chance to prove "ob sies vermag, zu weilen unter Menschen" (*Medea,* 561).[12] Colchis is repeatedly seen as a land of coarseness and barbarity, but such a contrast of Greek and Colchian is in fact at variance with the connotations of the Classical concepts. The implication of *Iphigenie auf Tauris* is that even the barbarians are good and humane. The heroine realises "daß ich auch Menschen hier verlasse" (1524) and it is Thoas's ability to hear "die Stimme der Wahrheit und der Menschlichkeit" (1937-38) that she relies on in telling him the whole truth. In the trilogy, however, any levelling off that is apparent is not in an upward direction. Despite Grillparzer's notes envisaging an ideal picture of Greece,[13] the Greeks are in fact little or no better than the Colchians however much they may possess a veneer of culture and civilisation; hence it is ultimately the Greek king's desire to have the fleece that precipitates the final catastrophe in a chain of events initiated by Aietes's greed.

Das goldene Vließ is, however, undoubtedly an extreme example of Grillparzer's pessimism,[14] while *Iphigenie auf Tauris* may be considered as the supreme statement of Goethe's optimism. Nevertheless it is only a cynical character such as Mephistopheles who can believe that man is still basically an animal (*Faust*, 285-86), and on the whole it is more the refined type of human being that is depicted in the creative works of Goethe and Schiller; they do not portray the different stages between animal and man which are discussed in the essays of Herder and Schiller. Grillparzer's comedy shows us those stages and in the process presents a fuller and more positive treatment of the theme adumbrated in the trilogy, in which the frequent reference to "Menschen" rings hollow and ironic.

The situation at the court of Kattwald is on the surface at least a contrast between cultured Franks and the barbaric German tribe that is expressed in terms of "Menschheit" and "Tierheit". Leon, although a mere cook, considers himself to be "ein Mensch" and consequently superior to the Germans. He tells Edrita "vom Tier zum Menschen sind der Stufen viele" (688) and it is clear that in his eyes the Germans have taken very few of those steps, even though he will not class them as animals. Kattwald significantly is a man who takes an excessive delight in his food, consumes too much wine, and at the end of Act IV fumes uncontrollably as his daughter, slave and prisoner all escape. In a letter to Fichtner in 1838, Grillparzer described the Franks as "Halbtiere" (II, 1251), and Galomir in particular is seen as "tierisch, aber nicht blödsinnig" (IV,644). Man should, however, be aware of those attributes that distinguish him from the merely animal, as Leon insists to Edrita: "Ein Mensch ist um so mehr, je mehr er Mensch / Und hier herum mahnts ziemlich an die Krippe" (676-77).

In a variant reading of a scene in Act II, Leon was to say of Atalus: "er scheint mir was verwildert hier im Freien" (*HKA* I/20,277). Throughout the comedy the barbarians are described as "wild" (1320, 1474, 1602, 1669, 1762) and as "roh" (290, 949); in one instance Edrita accuses Leon of being "roh" (694). Both epithets are common in Grillparzer's writings as an indication of uncivilised, inhuman attitudes or behaviour. "Wild" is the adjective used by Melitta to describe anything of which she does not approve (*Sappho*, 648, 651, 663, 700), and by Sappho in

comparing man's "rastloses Streben" with the more circumscribed fortunes of woman (820). It is especially common in the depiction of Medea (*Medea*, 403, 571, 1306, etc., etc.) and of Rustan (*Der Traum ein Leben*, 3, 84, 102, etc., etc.). In a political context, Rudolf II sees his age in such terms of savagery (*Bruderzwist*, 321, 344, 1260, etc.) and Don Cäsar himself admits to being "wild" (1945, 2076).[15] In *Des Meeres und der Liebe Wellen*, "Roheit" is seen in the ordinary people as opposed to the isolated priestly community (309, 429). Frequently Grillparzer refers to the coarseness of modern literary productions and, increasingly from the 1830s onward, to the coarseness of society and the age. The emperor Joseph's statue looks down on "Trotz und Roheit der Menge" (I,253); an epigram of 1835, repeated ten years later, finds the Germans using "Roheit" to cover up a lack of "Hoheit" (I,417).[16]

Similarly Herder had underlined the dangers of man returning to a state of "rohe Tierheit" (XVII,138), and both "roh" and "wild" are common in Classicism as an indication of the less than human. Schiller in particular sees coarseness as a quality of animals as opposed to human beings (e.g. V,436, 821). The war in *Wallenstein* in "ein roh gewaltsam Handwerk", an age of "rohe Horden", and Max and Thekla lament the coarseness of their fate as they are caught up in the war.[17] "Wild" is used to describe the more unsavoury aspects of human behaviour in *Die Braut von Messina* and *Die Jangfrau von Orleans*, and one may also list numerous examples of its use in *Wallenstein, Wilhelm Tell,* and in poems such as "Das Lied von der Glocke" and "Würde der Frauen": "Es befehden sich im Grimme / Die Begierden wild und roh".[18] Goethe in *Die natürliche Tochter* writes of "die rohe Menge" and "das rohe Leben" (2352, 2768), the King speaks of the Duke's son's "rohes, wildes Wesen" (56); in "Ilmenau" the youthful Karl August and his friends cloak their nobility in coarseness. Goethe also makes frequent use of "roh" and "wild" as attributes of the early works and characteristics of himself and Schiller.[19]

For the Classical writer, in particular for Herder, the gradual development from animal to man is seen as "eine Bildung zur Humanität". Grillparzer also underlines the importance of "Bildung" on a number of occasions, affirming "daß der Mensch nicht von Anfang her verständig und gerecht war, sondern es erst durch die steigende Bildung geworden ist" (III,1122). However, he was not always particularly optimistic about the success of "Bildung". In 1836 he wrote in his diary "von Unsinn zu Unsinn geht der Bildungsgang der Welt" (III,802), and he feared that "die ganze Bildung der deutschen Nation in den letzten zwanzig Jahren war eine falsche" (III,715-16).[20] It is no doubt significant that Grillparzer is less optimistic than Goethe concerning the link between art and education. In 1849 he described poetry as "der Ausdruck und die Zusammenfassung der literarischen und menschlichen Bildung einer Nation" (III,283), six years later he wrote of literature as "das Organ der Bildung" (III,1010), but elsewhere he insisted that literature and education were opposed to one another (III,241, 709) and that an art-ist must forget his "Bildung" when creating his works (I,543; III,242). Although Heinz Politzer considers "Bildung" to be "dieser in Grillparzers Augen heilige und al-lumfassende Begriff", and Hock maintains that "Bildung" is "der höchste geistig-sittliche Wert" for the dramatist,[21] the term is certainly not as common, nor is it viewed in so positive a light as in the writings of the Classicists. In *Weh dem, der lügt!,* the only two references are not to "Bildung" as such, but to the less specific verb "bilden", and the education foreseen for Atalus is to equip him for a post as kitchen assistant, whilst there is no suggestion of any "Bildung" undergone by Edrita, who despite her bar-barian origins is seen to possess an instinctive goodness and humanity that is potentially comparable to Leon's and is far superior to Atalus's cultural snobbery. As Gregor suggests (290-91), the culture of the French may be no more than a superficial veneer that cloaks inner coarse-ness, and the bishop himself at times seems too concerned with externals, both in his insistence on a man carrying a mark of his trade (196) and in his hope that Leon will be ennobled by the King (1893).

Certainly there is no clear-cut equation of French and Ger-man with the concepts of "Mensch" and "Tier" respec-tively; as in *Das goldene Vließ,* Atalus, who is self-centred, snobbish and happy to stagnate, makes it apparent that cultured origins are no guarantee of "eine Bildung zur Hu-manität". On the other hand, the fact that the pessimism of the trilogy has undoubtedly been left behind is amply demonstrated by a character such as Edrita, and her ability to climb the steps "vom Tier zum Menschen" is reflected in her desire to leave her primitive surroundings and boor-ish husband-to-be, in order to enter the more cultured and ethical atmosphere of France that is symbolised in its reli-gion.[22] Despite his doubts concerning any automatic pro-cess of "Bildung", it would appear that Grillparzer wished to suggest that inner potential for development was impor-tant and that this could more readily reach fruition in a cultured and civilised environment; in this respect Leon is right to believe that Atalus "ist ein Frank und läßt sich bilden", although it becomes clear that the latter is not ex-clusively dependent on the former. The Franks are a cul-tured nation and a person in their midst is in a better posi-tion to cultivate his own humanity.[23] Leon's fear at the end of the play is that Atalus and Edrita will adopt barbaric ways if allowed or compelled to return to the Rheingau. In his letter to Fichtner in 1838, Grillparzer explained that Atalus's poor character was a result of his being in the midst of "Wilde [. . .] Halb-Tiere, die ihn verhöhnen, mißhandeln, herabsetzen". In a variant to Act II, Leon says of Atalus

> Hat erst der Mensch kein Beispiel als das seine,
> Wird er wohl ab und zu sein eignes Zerrbild.
>
> (*HKA* I/20, 277)

and the theme is retained in the play in Leon's admission that Atalus has improved since escaping "aus der wilden Fremde" (1600-602).

In a diary note of 1825, Grillparzer compared animals, which are isolated, unable to communicate and pass on in-formation and education, with human beings:

> Wodurch ist denn der Mensch, was er ist, als durch seine Gattung? Sein ganzer Bestand als Mensch liegt nicht in *einem* Individuum, nicht in tausend, sondern in der Menschheit . . . er *lebt* nur als Mensch, als Glied seiner Gattung.
>
> (IV,385)

To attack human society, which provided the foundation for such communal humanity, was thus to return to a more animal state, as Grillparzer insisted in his diary of 1844:

> Wer die Gesellschaft in ihren Grundbedingungen an-greift, schließt sich selbst von der Menschheit aus, die ihre Grundbedingungen in der Gesellschaft hat. Er macht sich selbst zum Tier und muß als Tier behandelt werden.
>
> (III,1106)

According to a diary entry of two decades earlier, one of the basic principles of a community was mutual trust, and Grillparzer had therefore felt obliged to attack Rousseau for his belief that there was such a thing as a harmless lie:

> . . . denn wenn der Mensch als Mensch eigentlich nur in Berührung mit anderen seinesgleichen, in Gesell-schaft, leben kann; jedes gesellige Verhältnis aber Ver-trauen voraussetzt, und Vertrauen ohne *Wahrheit* nicht denkbar ist, so greift jede, auch die kleinste Lüge die Grundlage aller menschlichen Zustände an, und jeder Lügner ist ein Verräter an seinem ganzen Geschlechte.
>
> (III,385)

Such strict moral views are more typical of Grillparzer's early mature work before the mid-1820s, but it was during those years that *Weh dem, der lügt!* was first planned, and Gregor still reflects the sentiments of the diary entry on Rousseau. For Gregor, lies destroy "das Vertrauen, das Mensch dem Menschen gönnt" (373). Like Franz Moser in the early play *Die Schreibfeder,* Gregor sees untruth as the prime cause of man's wickedness, and it is this message that he is preparing to put into his next sermon as the play opens:

> Denn was die menschliche Natur auch Böses kennt,
> Verkehrtes, Schlimmes, Abscheuwürdiges,
> Das Schlimmste ist das falsche Wort, die Lüge.
> Wär nur der Mensch erst wahr, er wär auch gut.
>
> (119-22)

Gregor first considers lies that are not always recognised as such—vanity, pride, false shame—before considering the worst sin of all, the deliberate lie. All the fine things in life are linked to truth, so that a lie destroys everything we cherish and in the process challenges God's creation by seeing something as false that is true (139-41). While a man who lies is worse than an animal, nature by compari-son is true by its very existence:

Wahr ist die ganze kreisende Natur:
Wahr ist der Wolf, der brüllt, eh er verschlingt,
Wahr ist der Donner, drohend wenn es blitzt,
Wahr ist die Flamme, die von fern schon sengt,
Die Wasserflut, die heulend Wirbel schlägt;
Wahr sind sie, weil sie sind, weil Dasein Wahrheit.

(146-51)

The sermon is impressive, emotive and powerful, but the insistence on truth is somewhat extreme, especially when the argument depends for its apparent logicality on a confusion between different meanings of the word "wahr": the ontological truth of nature's existence is scarcely the same as the truthfulness of human beings, but in such an intermingling of diverse connotations Grillparzer is once more following in the footsteps of the writers of Classicism.

This is nowhere more clearly seen than in Goethe's writing of the Italian period. On the one hand, *Iphigenie auf Tauris* is underpinned by a demand for absolute truth that culminates in Orest's insistence, "zwischen uns sei Wahrheit", and the heroine's call to the Gods, "verherrlicht durch mich die Wahrheit" (1080-81, 1918-19). In Italy, on the other hand, Goethe moves from praise of the ontological truth of nature's existence, "die in allen ihren Teilen wahr und konsequent ist", and which is "wie wahr, wie seiend" (*HA* XI,93, 149), to a gradual fascination with the eternal but nevertheless natural truth of the great works of art, which are "nach wahren und natürlichen Gesetzen hervorgebracht" and which represent "das innig und ewig Wahre" (XI,395,475). The letters and diaries of the Italian period, as well as the *Italienische Reise* itself, provide constant testimony to Goethe's search for truth and the belief in its importance: "es ist nichts groβ als das Wahre, und das kleinste Wahre ist groβ".[24] However, Goethe's statements of these and subsequent years reveal a considerable overlapping and confusion of ethical, ontological and aesthetic connotations of truth. The "innerliche Wahrheit und Notwendigkeit" of the "Urpflanze", the "Reinheit und Wahrheit" of light seem essentially aesthetic in their ideal quality, the truth of art is "naturgemäβ" in conforming to general laws such as are also found in nature, the truth of both nature and art in their apparently God-given "Notwendigkeit" seem to make ethical demands on man.[25] Hence although in the *Maximen und Reflexionen* there is a repeated call for man to seek and promote truth (Nos. 226, 292, 293, 319, 398, 496), it is often unclear whether the ontological truth of reality, ethical truth in man, the general truth of a work of art, or the ultimate truth of absolute knowledge is under discussion. One even finds contradictory statements; "Alle Verhältnisse der Dinge wahr. Irrtum allein in den Menschen", "Die Wahrheit gehört dem Menschen, der Irrtum der Zeit an" (Nos. 6, 1229). Ambiguity is also found in *Wilhelm Meister,* which continually praises an ill-defined but all-encompassing ideal of truth (e.g. *HA* VII,154; VIII,65, 443, 460).

For both Goethe and Schiller, the blurring of the lines dividing the various kinds of truth is a logical product of the equation, wholly or in part, of the concepts of goodness, truth and beauty.[26] If there is a greater degree of consistency in Schiller's statements on truth, it results primarily from an almost exclusive concentration on the truth of art. For Schiller, as for Goethe, true art is based on nature, but shows "wahre Natur" rather than "wirkliche Natur" (Schiller), "innere Wahrheit" rather than "Naturwirklichkeit" (Goethe), and as such it has "objektive Wahrheit" that is superior to the limited truth of historical or contemporary reality.[27] Both Goethe and Schiller stress that absolute truth cannot be achieved in this life and would overwhelm man, were he to encounter it, but that it can be reflected in veiled form in the symbolic truth of a beautiful work of art: "was wir als Schönheit hier empfunden, / Wird einst als *Wahrheit* uns entgegengehn".[28] For Goethe more than Schiller, however, truth in life and in man remained as important as the aesthetic truth of art; truth for Goethe is a reflection of general laws in nature and man, and as such more relevant to ordinary experience than it is for Schiller, who makes significantly little use of the concept in his dramatic work despite its central importance in his essays and philosophical poems. Goethe repeatedly stresses that truth is something eternal and constant—"das alte Wahre", "das ewig Wahre"—something fruitful and constructive that man must always strive for.[29]

In a diary note of 1834, Grillparzer described truth as Goethe's "eigentliche Göttin" (III,768), and Gregor insists on an absolute concept of truth such as Iphigenie defends, while his sermon presents an interlocking, even confusion, of ontological and philosophical truth such as is found in German Classicism. The insistence on absolute truth is found in Grillparzer's youthful and early mature writing, and in general the theme of truth is one that concerned him from an early age, as is evidenced by *Die Schreibfeder* and the analysis of his own untruths in the diaries of his youth (e.g. IV,230). In *Blanka von Kastilien,* reference is made to "ewge Wahrheit" (4745), and Fedriko believes "es rächt die Wahrheit ihr verletzt Gesetz" (248). There is considerable discussion of truth in the diaries of the late 1810s and early 1820s, although this mainly involves an attempt to define truth in essentially Classical terms as "naturgemäβ" (III,285) and conforming to "der Gang der Natur", to human nature in general (III,238-39, 682). The truth of art is not based on strict realism (III,71, 83), but is produced "durch den Schein" (III,223-24). In these respects, artists such as Shakespeare or Walter Scott are "wahr" in their works (III,648, 654, 671; IV,415), although Grillparzer feared that his own works were "unwahr" (III,204-205).

The libretto for the opera *Melusina* reflects this late eighteenth-century contrast of objective reality and poetic truth. Raimund laments "das Wirkliche dünkt sich allein das Wahre" (56) and it is the voice of reality that his friends wish him to heed: "laβ ihn Wahrheit ganz erreichen" (628). He, however, is convinced that Melusina is true—"was ist wahr noch, wenn nicht sie" (629)—hence he challenges his friends: "Ist sie wahr, / Fliehet Ihr! / Ist sie Lüge, / Folg ich euch" (620-23). The question as to which realm is the truth is left unanswered, however, and there is no mention of truth in the final act; nevertheless there is the insistence that Raimund's search for Melusina is causing him to lose his "Tatkraft" (815, 830), so that at the end he may be thought to be entering a realm of death and inactivity rather than one of absolute truth.

Apart from **Melusina** and the diaries, the concept of truth is not common in Grillparzer's early mature work, but is increasingly important in the 1830s and 1840s. On the one hand the diaries of these years reveal a continuing insistence on the truth of art conforming to nature and general human feelings. The truth of literature is "was man als wahr fühlt" (III,1163), "was dem empfindenden Menschen wahr ist" (III,238). The works of Shakespeare and Ferdinand Raimund have "Naturwahrheit", which is also to be sought in painting (III,283, 653, 830, 907). For Grillparzer as for Goethe, the truth of poetry lies in its symbolic quality (III,697, 226), a work of literature reveals "innere Wahrheit" (III,284), an opera has "volle Wahrheit" (IV,537-39).[30] Equally one finds in Grillparzer's writing the Classical linking of truth with beauty and goodness, as in the 1837 essay on censorship, in which "das Wahre, das Gute, das Schöne" are considered to be "die köstlichsten Güter der Menschheit" (III,1063).[31]

If there is a shift of emphasis from Classical views, then it lies in Grillparzer's insistence that art conform to general human *feelings* rather than to the more objective and all-embracing concept of human nature or humanity as a whole. Poetic truth is "in dem Kleide, der Form, der Gestalt, die sie im Gemüt annimmt" (III,226), or, to quote a much later statement, "eine Wahrheit, nicht in der Sache, sondern in den Gemütern" (III,585; cf. III,693-95). The belief that literature is based on conviction and feelings rather than objective truth is reflected in the increasing awareness that the truth of art is only "subjektive Wahrheit" (III,807), rather than the "objektive Wahrheit" claimed by Schiller. In the short scene "Le poète sifflé", Adele insists that drama is based on lies (III,39), a sentiment that is echoed in a more serious context in the essay of 1834 on the state of German literature: "das Drama lügt eine Gegenwart" (III,688).

Clearly these statements are simply a more pronounced expression of the Classical insight into the untruthfulness of literature, the occasional assertion to the contrary notwithstanding (*SW* V,594; *HA* XI,53). Of greater significance is the fact that the stress on feelings and conviction as the key to the subjective truth of literature is accompanied by an increasing emphasis on feelings and inner honesty as the most important manifestation of truth in man. If it is essential for the poet to produce something "was man als wahr fühlt", then it is also important for him to have "wahre Empfindung" (III,834), "wahres Gefühl" (III,809),[32] and equally important that these true feelings be found in man generally. Already in 1825 Grillparzer had written in his diary of his adverse reaction "sobald in Gesellschaft jemand ein unwahres Gefühl ausspricht" (IV,387) and this theme is more fully developed in the years leading up to the completion of **Weh dem, der lügt!**.

In a poem of 1831 in praise of Anastasius Grün he stresses "des Busens Wahrheit" (I,205), in a diary note of 1836 he insists that "die Wahrheit des Gefühls [. . .] geht den Menschen an und bestimmt seinen Wert" (III,286), whilst in a poem of the following year the statue of Joseph II demands "im Innern sei der Mensch sich selber wahr" (I,253). Similarly Feuchtersleben is praised for "die in unseren Zeiten [. . .] selten gewordene Wahrhaftigkeit gegen sich selbst" (IV,222; cf.I,507, 561). It is this concept of truth that finds fuller expression in the comedy, which received its ill-fated premiere in March of 1838: a play that reflects the gradual shift of emphasis in Grillparzer's understanding of the concept.

If Gregor represents a dogmatic insistence on truth which is more commensurate with Grillparzer's beliefs at the time of the play's conception, Leon by comparison reveals a somewhat ironic questioning of the value of truth. At the start of the play he is rather dubious about the efficacy of truth in securing the release of Atalus:

> Um Gottes Willen gibt man ihn nicht frei.
> Da bleibt nichts übrig, als: wir reden Wahrheit
> Und er bleibt, wo er ist.
>
> (330-32)

He sees Gregor's desire for absolute truth as something of a quirk in one who has such high standards, and takes the condition set by the bishop very much as a handicap in his venture, seeking to avoid the bishop's demand rather than face up to its implications. In pursuing what he believes to be noble intentions, Leon tells the truth in such a way that no one believes him; it is as if he enjoys the gamble of fitting in with the exaggerated terms of his mission. What he does not realise is that his whole behaviour is deceitful, for he misleads both Kattwald and, more important still, Edrita, and it is she who reprimands him:

> Hast du die Wahrheit immer auch gesprochen,
> *die Hand aufs Herz legend*
> Hier fühl ich dennoch, daß du mich getäuscht.
>
> (1137-38)

In an alternative version, Edrita was to have been even more explicit: "Es lügt der Mensch mit Worten nicht allein, / Auch mit der Tat" (II,1251). This is partly unfair to Leon, for although Edrita thinks he has deceived her, he is also attracted to her, as his actions have indeed led her to believe. Nevertheless Leon comes to realise that the letter of Gregor's command is vastly inferior to the underlying spirit of his beliefs. Leon has told the truth but has behaved deceitfully, not only in his actions but also because he hoped that the truth he uttered would be taken as a joke, as indeed it was.

Edrita finally suggests that silence is the only way to avoid lies and deception:

> Doch weiß ich ja, daß du die Wahrheit sprichst.
> So laß uns schweigen, dann sind wir am wahrsten.
>
> (1446-47)

Such a command would be in keeping with Gregor's initial distinction between man and animals, and it has led some critics, such as Politzer, Škreb, and Renate Delphendahl, to argue that truth is only possible in silence, while Bandet asserts that truth is to be found in action rather than speech.[33] Leon, it is true, becomes more reticent as the play unfolds, but this should not, as Bandet implies, involve a rejection of language.[34] Galomir is seen as the most brutish of the characters precisely because of his inability to communicate. Language for Grillparzer was one of the most important aspects of cultural development, the power to communicate meant that man could assimilate the knowledge of his contemporaries and of past generations, whereas each animal had to start from the beginning (IV,385). Just as Herder had insisted that "das sonderbare Mittel zur Bildung der Menschen ist die Sprache" (XIII,354), so Grillparzer writes "das Palladium der Geistesbildung ist die ungehinderte Mitteilung" (III,695). Leon himself shows that actions can deceive as much as words, and Kattwald and Galomir, who do not practise deceit as such, may be "wahr" in the ontological sense preached by Gregor but, like the silent but violent creatures and phenomena of nature that the bishop claims to find superior to mendacious human beings, they are not morally good, which we must assume that truth should entail. As it stands, the bishop's sermon actually reverses the normal distinction between man and animal and implies that as a consequence of language the many steps "vom Tier zum Menschen" are in a downward rather than an upward direction. The action of the comedy shows the bishop to have been misguided in his denunciation of man, and the supreme confirmation of Leon's awareness of his moral and human responsibility is his *telling* of the truth to the ferryman, because of the conviction that it is the only thing to do. Cunning and deception such as Edrita now practises are not the way for him to achieve his aims.

While some critics see truth as possible only in action, Fritz Martini has argued that not even action can contain truth, but that only a character such as Gregor, apart from active life, can be true.[35] The distinction between action and words seems to confuse the issue, however, and the confusion is not exactly resolved by Forster when he argues that "Leon log also, indem er seine Wahrheit der Tat hinter Lüge der Tat versteckte, jene Lüge der Tat der Wahrheit der Tat dienen ließ, durch die Lüge der Tat die Wahrheit der Tat anstrebte" (p.218). Put more simply, Grillparzer shows us that the achievement of truth is difficult in ordinary life, both in action and in words. Both Seidler and Hock have pointed to Iphigenie's assertion, "ganz unbefleckt genießt sich nur das Herz", and stated that Grillparzer agrees more with the doubts expressed by Pylades "daß keiner in sich selbst, noch mit den andern / Sich rein und unverworren halten kann" (*Iphigenie auf Tauris*, 1658-59).[36] This may be a valid assessment of the difference between the two plays but, as we have already argued, Iphigenie is an extreme depiction of Goethean optimism, so that a character who falls short of those ideals should not immediately be seen in a negative light. On the contrary, Gregor, who most certainly does wish to remain untainted

by lies and deceit, is himself incapable of adhering to his own principles, for he has lied to the King and consequently failed to receive the ransom money that he needs to secure his nephew's release. Moreover his views are shown to be dangerously idealistic, impractical in ordinary life in that they lead to inactivity and excessive moral scruples. Such impracticality is mirrored in *Ein Bruderzwist in Habsburg,* in which Rudolf II also insists on the inferiority of man to the divine truth of God that is found in the truth of nature:

> Drum ist in Sternen Wahrheit, im Gestein,
> In Pflanze, Tier und Baum, im Menschen nicht.
> Und wers verstünde, still zu sein wie sie,
> Gelehrig fromm, den eignen Willen meisternd,
> Ein aufgespanntes, demutvolles Ohr,
> Ihm würde leicht ein Wort der Wahrheit kund,
> Die durch die Welten geht aus Gottes Munde.

> (411-17)

His adherence to such a belief in truth and divine order does indeed encourage Rudolf to maintain a pious and humble silence, but it also results in stagnation and a complete inability to act in a manner appropriate to the pressing and confusing political situation. Similarly, Libussa's sisters recognise that ordinary reality is a mixture of truth and lies (221), but they seek to remain in an isolated realm of truth, which Libussa justifiably leaves in order to enter a world of practical and useful activity, only to meet her death in a vain attempt to regain the realm of permanent prophetic truth (2444), which Primislaus knows has no part to play in the changing state of reality (1449).

A similar danger is also seen in Leon himself in the latter stages of the comedy. Although in the fairytale atmosphere of Act IV he is successful in telling the absolute truth, his increasing concern, if not obsession, with truth leads him to become more passive and introverted.[37] His interpretation of his mission, previously somewhat cavalier, now becomes too rigid, so that he comes to dread the inevitable confrontation with the bishop. He does not however become totally inactive and at the end admits:

> Nu, gar so rein gings freilich denn nicht ab.
> Wir haben uns gehütet wie wir konnten.
> Wahr stets und ganz war nur der Helfer: Gott!

> (1721-23)

and he himself proves the point by slipping back into lies over his true feelings for Edrita.

More importantly, however, his awareness "wie bunt, was alles wir vollführt" (1591) is echoed by Gregor's acknowledgment of "die buntverworrne Welt" (1800). Gregor accepts that Leon has done his best in the circumstances of human life and that this is the most one can hope for. In demanding absolute truth, Gregor was standing outside the human realm, for "die Wahrheit ist wirklich etwas für den Menschen Unerreichbares" (III,1082). Grillparzer was increasingly sceptical of any search for such absolute truth (IV,723), or of any belief that truth could be reduced to straightforward formulae ("Mein Vaterland", I,317). Rudolf II, despite his desire for the divine truth of nature, is at least aware of the relative and fragmentary nature of truth in real life (*Bruderzwist*, 1362). Ferdinand, by comparison, seeks to put into practice what he sees as the absolute truth of his religion and brings about the inhuman expulsion of 20,000 Protestants; Don Cäsar's search for absolute truth (1917, 1982) causes the death of Lukrezia.[38]

By the end of the comedy, however, a more balanced attitude to truth has been reached. Gregor's attitude to the truth of his own Christian beliefs ("hier ist kein Zwang" (1729)) seems symptomatic of a less rigorous approach to truth in general. He is prepared to accept the unavoidability of untruth in life, but hopes that some good can develop nevertheless:

> Das Unkraut, merk ich, rottet man nicht aus.
> Glück auf, wächst nur der Weizen etwa drüber.
>
> (1805-6)

The same view is expressed in a poem of the following year, 1839:

> Und wenn auch Unkraut wächst,
> So hütet euch vor Jäten,
> Ihr könntet im Bemühn
> Die gute Saat zertreten.
>
> (I,226)

A similar sentiment, albeit without the biblical imagery, is found in one of Goethe's maxims: "Es ist so gewiß als wunderbar, daß Wahrheit und Irrtum aus *einer* Quelle entstehen; deswegen man oft dem Irrtum nicht schaden darf, weil man zugleich der Wahrheit schadet" (Maximen, 310). Undoubtedly the supreme statement of such a belief is *Faust*, in which evil and mistakes are accepted as part of life, unavoidable even beneficial if man continues to strive for better things.

Nevertheless it is arguable even in *Faust* whether the polar opposition of good and evil is entirely resolved, and it is highly questionable whether, as Forster argues, Grillparzer's comedy shows "Aufhebung der Gegensätze in einer neuen Einheit" (p.221). As Goethe also continually stressed, man should always seek truth. People are proud of speaking what they believe to be the truth (*Wem dem, der lügt!*, 1800-1804); in his essay on censorship, Grillparzer insisted that "das Wahre" was "die Quelle alles Guten" (III,1063), elsewhere he underlined the importance of Voltaire's "Streben nach Wahrheit" (III,384) and stressed the advantages to mankind when "das Gute und Wahre eine objektive Geltung erhält" (III,1117), or when a new truth is discovered (III,248). But absolute truth is unattainable in life, even in the more rarefied spiritual realm that Gregor recommends to his nephew at the end of the comedy:

> Du wardst getäuscht im Land der Täuschung, Sohn!
> Ich weiß ein Land, das aller Wahrheit Thron;
> Wo selbst die Lüge nur ein buntes Kleid,

> Das schaffend Er genannt: Vergänglichkeit,
> Und das er umhing dem Geschlecht der Sünden,
> Daß ihre Augen nicht am Strahl erblinden.
> Willst du, so folg, wie früher war bestimmt.
>
> (1817-22)

Lies, it would seem, are to be accepted even here as an inevitable function of the transient world, and such a view of truth being unattainable is very much a theme of Classicism. Under normal circumstances the ultimate truth is overpowering, as the youth discovers to his cost in Schiller's "Das verschleierte Bild zu Saïs". For Goethe, as implicitly also for Schiller, beauty is the veil through which one may view the truth (*HA* I,152, 206). This image of the veil is used by Grillparzer in the early poem **"Der Unzufriedene"** and also in **"Irenens Wiederkehr"**, in which the young man thinks that nature "läßt Ungeschautes entschleiert mich sehn" (II,895). At the end of *Libussa*, the heroine presents her inspired view of "Wahrheit, nur verhüllt / In Gleichnis und in selbstgeschaffnes Bild" (2444-45). In the comedy the veil shrouding truth is provided by lies, which prevent man being blinded by absolute truth.

What is more important, however, is the truth man *can* achieve in this life. Just as Alphons in **Die Jüdin von Toledo** insists that "besiegter Fehl ist all des Menschen Tugend" (174), so the truth that Leon acquires in overcoming his errors in the course of the play is preferable to the more abstract and absolute notions of morality and truth on which Gregor insists at the beginning. Leon has not achieved the ideal except in one brief moment of confessing the truth to the ferryman, but equally he does not let his increasing awareness of the impossibility of truth deflect him from acting to carry out his mission, however imperfectly this may have been fulfilled. Leon accomplishes his task because he is selfless and had entered the bishop's service for noble reasons, which in turn motivate his desire to free Atalus. At the very beginning he is prepared to kneel, to make the gesture of humility that Rustan, Ottokar and Mathias make only in the final act, and which is so highly praised in Libussa's final prophecy. Like Faust, Leon makes mistakes: he is too self-confident, too naïvely sure of success, and not entirely immune to the sort of cultural snobbery that characterises Atalus. He does not fully realise the meaning of Gregor's command, but in view of Grillparzer's mistrust of absolute ideals, it is a cause of, rather than (as Angress argues) a detraction from, his success that he does not entirely follow the letter of Gregor's imperative.[39] By the time he grasps its underlying moral spirit, his operation is fully in motion, and some useful coincidences help him during his growing and potentially excessive moral concern. He realises the lies and deception in which he has been involved but at the end (1688) he challenges God to acknowledge that he, Leon, has behaved in good faith and has done the best he could. In so doing he has not slipped into inactivity, unlike Gregor, who is the man of contemplation and consequently impractical in ordinary life when the need is for action to rescue his nephew. As the gates open to reveal that the

Christians captured the town on the previous night, the apparently divine miracle is surely not a sign of God's power and man's inferiority, but a symbolic reward for Leon's human striving and inner development in the course of the play. As Škreb has pointed out, "es ist die sinnvolle menschliche Tätigkeit, die im Lustspiel den Sieg davonträgt", something that Grillparzer always praised.[40]

If it is to Leon's credit that he becomes more aware of the truth and of himself,[41] then it is equally important that he continues to behave in an honest fashion. Just as the statue of Joesph II had demanded "im Innern sei der Mensch sich selber wahr", so Leon also achieves the inner truth required of him by Gregor (384). In a variant to his penultimate speech, Gregor was to stress "des Menschen Wahrheit liegt in seiner Meinung, / Wer treu vor sich, der ist auch treu vor Gott" (II,1252). Yet such truth is not simply that of inner feelings or of behaving according to one's inner character, as some recent critics have argued.[42] In the first part of his essay "Zur Literaturgeschichte", written in the year of the Viennese revolutions, Grillparzer did indeed praise "die richtige Empfindung" as the palladium of man's development, but this must however be combined with the powers of thought and reason in order to produce "gesunder Menschenverstand". "Empfindung" by itself is "nicht unbedingt wahr" because it is still too close to man's more animal characteristics (III,719), and Edrita in the comedy is perhaps too much a creature of feeling, too easily swayed by instinct, whilst Kattwald and Galomir, much as their actions may be entirely "true" to character, are limited by being creatures of basic instincts. On the other hand, the role of the instincts must never be usurped by man's intellectual faculties:

> zu behaupten aber, daß der eine Teil der menschlichen Natur das Recht habe an die Stelle des Ganzen einzutreten ist lächerlich. Der Trieb, die Neigung, das Instinktmäßige sind ebenso göttlich als die Vernunft [. . .]

(III,719)

—the dangers of this latter kind of imbalance being seen not only in Gregor, but also in characters such as Rudolf II or the coldly virtuous Queen in **Die Jüdin von Toledo.** Leon, however, reveals an instinctive inner honesty of true human feelings, which in the course of the play is coupled with an increasing but never excessive moral reflection and spiritual self-awareness.

Such a belief in man as a creature of instinct and intellect must inevitably lead us back to our initial questions concerning the Classical elements in the comedy. On the one hand, although much of the terminology of the play— barbarity and coarseness, humanity and truth—is undoubtedly a reflection of the Classical inheritance, the content of the play nevertheless reflects a more realistic and less optimistic attitude than is found in the works of Goethe and Schiller. Although both of the major Classical writers recognise the impossibility of achieving absolute truth in life, their statements do imply a concept of truth that is entirely

positive and that is to be sought and cultivated at all times. Grillparzer is undoubtedly more aware of the problems involved in the search for truth, more aware of the dangers inherent in demanding absolute truth. The comedy subjects the notion of truth to close scrutiny and reveals ambiguities or even potential illogicalities in the term which the writers of Classicism chose to overlook in their search for an ideal harmony and totality. In particular, the ontological truth of nature's existence and man's moral devotion to truthfulness are revealed as two entirely separate or even mutually contradictory phenomena. And yet ultimately the inner truthfulness of Leon is remarkably similar to the Goethean belief in a balanced attitude to life: a mixture of thought and action, of spiritual and physical, of reason and instinctive experience, of good intentions and inevitable mistakes, whereby all extremes are to be avoided.[43]

The achievement of such a balance may be less straightforward for Grillparzer than for the writers of Classicism, as his lack of confidence in the processes of "Bildung" illustrates. Both Atalus and to a lesser extent Gregor are at times too concerned with externals, with the superficial manifestations of culture and humanity. Leon, however, is superior to such concerns, not, as he wrongly thinks at the beginning, because he is a Frank, but because of the inner qualities we have considered, qualities that are the true source of humanity. It is in this context that Leon's insistence is true: "der Mensch ist um so mehr, je mehr er Mensch", or as Grillparzer stressed on more than one occasion in words that clearly reflect Classical sentiments: "das Beste was der Mensch sein kann ist er als Mensch".[44]

Notes

1. Ernst Alker, *Franz Grillparzer. Ein Kampf um Leben und Kunst* (Marburg, 1930), p.161.

2. Ruth K. Angress, "*Weh dem, der lügt!*. Grillparzer and the avoidance of tragedy", *MLR* [*Modern Language Review*] 66 (1971), 355-64 (p.364); Herbert Seidler, "Grillparzers Lustspiel *Weh dem, der lügt!*", *Jahrbuch der Grillparzer-Gesellschaft* (3. Folge), 4 (1965), 7-29 (pp.24-25); Erich Hock, "Grillparzers Lustspiel", *Wirkendes Wort* 4 (1953-54), 12-23; W. E. Yates, *Grillparzer. A critical introduction* (Cambridge, 1972), p.211.

3. Ulrich Fülleborn, "Zwischen Wahrheit und Lüge", *Grillparzer-Forum Forchtenstein* (1972), 7-28 (p.21); Hock, op.cit., pp.20, 23.

4. Zdenko Škreb, "Das Göttliche bei Grillparzer", *GQ* [*German Quarterly*] 45 (1972), 620-28; Alfred Anzenberger, "Grillparzer und die Religion" (Diss., Vienna, 1948), pp.39, 88; Andreas Oplatka, *Aufbauform und Stilwandel in den Dramen Grillparzers* (Berne, 1970), p.72; Bernd Breitenbruch, *Ethik und Ethos bei Grillparzer* (Berlin, 1965), p.43.

5. Emil Reich, *Franz Grillparzers Dramen* (Dresden, 1909), p.202; Seidler, op.cit., p.8; W. E. Yates, op.cit., p.202; Hans-Georg Werner, "Grillparzers *Weh dem,*

der lügt! und die Tradition der ernsthaften Komödie", in *Die österreichische Literatur. Ihr Profil im 19. Jahrhundert,* ed. Herbert Zeman (Graz, 1982), pp.323-41 (Werner does in fact take Seidler to task for over-stressing the moral content of the comedy); see also Ilse Münch, *Die Tragik in Drama und Persönlichkeit Grillparzers* (Berlin, 1931), p.75.

6. Jean-Louis Bandet, "Grillparzers *Weh dem, der lügt!*", in *Das deutsche Lustspiel I,* ed. Hans Steffen (Göttingen, 1968), pp.144-65 (p.158); Angress, op.cit., p.364; Franz Forster, "Zur Problemstellung in Grillparzers *Weh dem, der lügt!*", *Sprachkunst* 13 (1982), 211-30 (p.221).

7. Fritz Martini, "*Weh dem, der lügt!* oder von der Sprache im Drama", in *Die Wissenschaft von deutscher Sprache und Dichtung,* Festschrift für Friedrich Maurer (Stuttgart, 1963), pp.438-57 (p.445); Angress, op.cit., p.357; Seidler, op.cit., p.29; see also Hans Gmür, *Dramatische und theatralische Stilelemente in Grillparzers Dramen* (Winterthur, 1956), pp.19,135.

8. Bruce Thompson, *Franz Grillparzer* (Boston, 1981), pp.74, 79; see also Martini, op.cit., p.442; George A. Wells, *The Plays of Grillparzer* (London, 1969), p.29.

9. Of the countless references to this theme, see especially *Herders sämtliche Werke,* ed. Bernhard Suphan (Berlin, 1877-1913), XIII,144, 196, XIV,209, XVII,138; Friedrich Schiller, *Sämtliche Werke,* ed. Gerhard Fricke and Herbert G. Göpfert (Munich, 1980) (henceforth referred to as "*SW*"), I,178, V,453-54, 471-72, 520-21, 742; *Goethes Werke,* Hamburger Ausgabe (Munich, 1978) (henceforth referred to as "*HA*"), X,359, XIII,170, *Faust,* 285-86, 6845-47, 9603, *Hermann und Dorothea,* VI,76-77.

10. References are to volume and page of the Hanser edition by Peter Frank and Karl Pörnbacher (4 vols, Munich, 1960-65), or, where necessary, to the "historisch-kritische Gesamtausgabe" [*Sämtliche Werke, Historisch-kritische Gesamtausgabe,*] of Sauer and Backmann (abbreviated "*HKA*").

11. See also I,262, 441; III,718-19, 943; IV,230.

12. See also *Medea,* 182-83, 561.

13. See *HKA* I/17, 284, 294, 300, 309; such an ideal picture is still presented by Jason in *Die Argonauten,* 1237 ff.

14. More extreme, it might be argued, than *Ein Bruderzwist in Habsburg,* which Thompson describes as "Grillparzer's most profoundly pessimistic work" (op.cit., p.108).

15. See also "Der Christbaum" (I,335), "Ungarn" (I,503), "Radikal und konservativ" (I,504), *Libussa,* 1141, *Des Meeres und der Liebe Wellen,* 308.

16. See also "Der Reichstag" (I,325), "An S. H. Mosenthal" (I,588), "Erinnerungen an Feuchtersleben" (IV,224); also III,698, 746, 1043, IV,132.

17. *Wallenstein,* "Prolog", 89, *Piccolomini,* 182, *Wallensteins Tod,* 2275, 3160, 3177. See also *Maria Stuart,* 255, 262, 308. Grimm lists a disproportionately large number of references from Schiller in his *Deutsches Wörterbuch* (vol, 8, column 1113ff.).

18. See especially *Die Braut von Messina,* 42, 1251, 1422, 1491, 2579, *Die Jungfrau von Orleans,* 198, 799, 2011, 3058, 3122, "Dar Spaziergang", 141, "Würde der Frauen", 8, 23, 54, "Das Lied von der Glocke", 59, 69, 213, 275, 305, 333.

19. See especially ("roh") *Torquato Tasso,* 1420, 1514, *Faust,* 944, *Wahlverwandtschaften* (*HA* VI,306), *Wilhelm Meisters Lehrjahre* (*HA* VII,89, 518) also *HA* X,490, XII,54, 376; ("wild") *Iphigenie auf Tauris,* 399, 827, 969, 1821, 1910, *Faust,* 1182, 1860, 5864, *Die natürliche Tochter,* 126, 640, 1657, *Hermann und Dorothea,* V,96, VI,62, 112, also *HA* VI,193, X,538.

20. See also I,325, 500, 503, III,712, 717, 915, 1020, 1040.

21. Heinz Politzer, *Franz Grillparzer oder das abgründige Biedermeier* (Vienna, 1972), p.294; Hock, op.cit., p.13, similarly Hock, *Franz Grillparzer. Besinnung auf Humanität* (Hamburg, 1949), pp.8, 44-45, 58. See also Friedrich Kainz, *Grillparzer als Denker* (Vienna, 1975) pp.598, 614. Kainz repeatedly uses the term "Bildung" in referring to passages where Grillparzer does not actually make use of the term (e.g., p.606).

22. Edrita's potential for development is also seen in her professed delight in goodness and beauty: "ich kann am Guten mich und Schönen freuen" (1162).

23. Hence one cannot agree entirely with Georg Scheibelreiter's assertion "daβ der Gegensatz zwischen Kultur und Barbarei nicht an der Verschiedenheit des zivilisatorischen Standards, sondern am Stande der Herzensbildung entscheidend zu messen ist": "Franz Grillparzer und Bischof Gregor von Tours", *Jahrbuch der Grillparzer-Gesellschaft* (3. Folge) 15 (1983), 65-78 (p.72).

24. Letter to Charlotte von Stein, 8/6/1787; see also letters of 15/6/1786 and 7/11/1786, diary entries on 26/9/1786, 30/9/1786, 26/10/1786, *Italienische Reise, HA* XI,103, 126, 156, 420, 498, 549, and in later years the conversations with Eckermann on 12/10/1825 and 16/12/1828.

25. *HA* XI,62, 324, 395, 549, VIII,255, IX,538, XIII,44-45, diary entries on 26/9/1786, 26/10/1786, letter to Schubarth, 24/8/1819, conversations with Eckermann on 4/1/1824, 18/10/1827.

26. See Goethe's "Epilog zu Schillers 'Glocke'", 30, *Maximen,* No.441, *Farbenlehre* (*HA* XIV,54), conversations with Eckermann, 5/6/1826, March 1832; Schiller's "Die Künstler", 64-65, "Die Worte des Wahns", also *SW* V,743, 976, letter to Körner, 9/3/1789.

27. See *SW* II,817, V,385, 755, 996, 1021, *Wallenstein*, "Prolog", 133-35, letter to Goethe, 4/4/1797, also the comments on the "menschlich wahr" qualities of Goethe's work in the letters of 7/1/1795, 2/7/1796, 3/7/1796, also I,211; *HA* IX,538, XII,49, 57, 70, 472, also Eckermann, 18/9/1823, 10/4/1829.

28. *SW* I,175, V,653-55, 796, 871, also "Das verschleierte Bild zu Saïs" and "Die Macht des Gesanges"; *HA* XII,405-406, 514, XIII,305, as also implicitly in *Faust,* in the poem "Zueignung" and the epigram "Jugendlich kommt sie vom Himmel" (I,206).

29. *HA* I,123, 370, VIII,307, XI,475, XII,406, 409-10, 507, XIII,45, XIV,54, Eckermann, 18/10/1827, 16/12/1828, letter to Schubarth, 24/8/1819.

30. See also III,406, 423, 425, 663, 746.

31. See also III,771, 882, 1117, I,86, 205, 213.

32. See also "Klage" (I,211), "Jugenderinnerungen im Grünen" (I,228).

33. Politzer, op.cit., p.259; Zdenko Škreb, *Grillparzer. Eine Einführung in das dramatische Werk* (Kronberg/Taunus, 1976), p.212; Renate Delphendahl, *Grillparzer, Lüge und Wahrheit in Wort und Bild* (Berne, 1975), p.97ff. (but cf. p.57, where the author insists "das Sprechen ist Ausdruck des Willens und das Handeln Ausdruck des Triebes").

34. Forster (p.224) also insists that there is no hint of "Sprachskepsis" in the play.

35. Martini, op.cit., p.445.

36. Seidler, op.cit., pp.24-25; Hock, "Grillparzers Lustspiel", p.19.

37. See Steppa Belloin, *"Weh dem, der lügt!* Zu Struktur und Poetik von Grillparzers Lustspiel", *Recherches Germaniques* 10 (1980), 100-12 (p.112); Reich, op.cit., p.211; Škreb, *Grillparzer,* p.209.

38. Kainz acknowledges that Grillparzer sees dangers in any "Absolutsetzung eines sittlichen Gebots" (op.cit., p.185), but quotes Don Cäsar's words as one indication of Grillparzer's demand for absolute truth (p.182)! See also Delphendahl, op.cit., p.66.

39. In the initial stages of his career as charted in the play, Faust also succeeds because of rather than in spite of the influence and interference of Mephistopheles.

40. Škreb, *Grillparzer,* p.209; see also my article *"Der arme Spielmann* and the Role of Compromise in Grillparzer's Work", *GR* [*Germanic Review*] 56 (1981), 134-39.

41. On the theme of "Selbstbewußtsein", see Delphendahl, op.cit., p.69; Škreb, *Grillparzer,* p.177.

42. See Thompson, op.cit., p.78; Hellmuth Himmel, "Die Wahrheit in Grillparzers Lustspiel *Weh dem, der lügt!"* in *Peripherie und Zentrum. Studien zur öster-reichischen Literatur,* ed. Gerlinde Weiss and Klaus Zelewitz (Salzburg, 1971), pp.87-120.

43. See in particular poems such as "Metamorphose der Tiere", "Dauer im Wechsel", "Vermächtnis", *Wilhelm Meisters Wanderjahre* (*HA* VIII,263), *Torquato Tasso,* 1704-706, *Faust,* 1110-17, *Maximen,* 1049, letter to Knebel, 8/4/1812, conversation with Müller, 29/4/1818.

44. III,1021, IV,860. See also I,252, III,706, IV,394, *Libussa,* 404, 1396-97, 2192, *Bruderzwist,* 2406, *Die Jüdin von Toledo,* 1519, 1571. The importance of the concept "Mensch" in Grillparzer's writing has often been stressed; see Margret Dietrich, "Grillparzer und die Gesellschaft seiner Zeit", in *Grillparzer-Feier der Akademie 1972* (Vienna, Cologne, Graz, 1972), pp.35-67; Reinhold Schneider, *Dämonie und Verklärung* (Vaduz, 1947), pp.329-75; Urs Helmensdorfer, *Grillparzers Bühnenkunst* (Berne, 1960), pp.112-13.

William C. Reeve (essay date 1999)

SOURCE: "The Inescapable Paternal Legacy: Act One," in *Grillparzer's* "*Libussa*": *The Tragedy of Separation,* McGill-Queen's University Press, 1999, pp. 9-57.

[*In the following excerpt, Reeve explores the first act of* Libussa, *focusing on the title character's struggle to define herself in relation to the men in her life, particularly her father, while also distancing herself from the circle of women in the play.*]

All of Grillparzer's completed posthumous plays commence with a negation: "PRIMISLAUS *an der Tür der Hütte horchend*: Bist du schon fertig? LIBUSSA *von innen*: Nein"; "GERICHTSPERSON Im Namen kaiserlicher Majestät / Ruf' ich euch zu: Laßt ab! DON CÄSAR Ich nicht, fürwahr!" (*Ein Bruderzwist* 1-2); "ISAK Bleib zurück, geh nicht in' Garten!" (*Die Jüdin* 1). In all three instances the denial, pointing to a personal conflict, whether between a man and a woman, father and son, or father and daughter, reflects on the individual level a social development threatening the stability of a well established political structure or ideology. Negation implies an attempt to distance the self from a perceived potential threat. Libussa's first utterance of the tragedy is a simple, succinct "Nein": she stands up to Primislaus, and being in control from the outset, refuses to be rushed. Moreover, the one asking the question normally occupies the inferior position, i.e., expresses a dependence upon the person being asked. In contrast, the staging establishes a visual internal/external dichotomy: the woman within the cottage to which traditional gender patterns would relegate her and to which she will return at the beginning of the fifth act and the man on the outside, a dramatic realization of the female inner versus the masculine outer orientation.[1] Primislaus's listening at the door may also convey esteem or deference. Therefore, the spectator immediately gains an inkling of a problematic relationship: although the physical staging reinforces typical sexual stereotypes, the attitudes expressed by word and gesture suggest their inversion.

Conflicting reviews and views have long characterized the fate of *Libussa* on stage and at the hands of literary critics. It has enjoyed little success with audiences—most recently Roe has alluded to "its undramatic quality which makes it one of Grillparzer's most disappointing works" (*A Century* 98)—but while the author himself conceded the weakness of the fifth act: "Im fünften Akt ist mir die Libussa nicht so geraten" (Bachmaier 734), he defended the prologue: "Das Vorspiel, [. . .] das ist auch das Beste dran. Das Vorspiel zur Libussa ist gut, ist vielleicht das Beste, was ich geschrieben hab', ist vortrefflich" (Bachmaier 733), high praise which one should take into account, given its source, i.e., Austria's greatest playwright. In an effort to explain what some commentators have judged to be thematic inconsistencies, Lorenz, turning to Grillparzer's own "schlüsselhafte Deutungen", concludes that he elected to place "den Schwerpunkt auf eine Konfliktsituation, nicht auf die Harmonie, auf den Gegensatz der Hauptfiguren, nicht auf ihren Einklang" ("Neubewertung" 33). If she is correct in her designation of conflict or opposition and their non-resolution as the focal point of *Libussa,* then one would expect the "Vorspiel" to introduce this perspective. Indeed, this theatrical exposition of psychological game-playing presents an underlying theme of separation/*Scheiden*: high from low, aristocracy from peasantry, female from male, far from near, unity from duality, meeting from parting, and life from death. Both on the basis of its visual and verbal message, the opening scene deserves closer scrutiny than it has received to date.

Commenting upon Primislaus's first monologue, Politzer observes, "Dem festen Nein der Frau entspricht ein lyrischer Erguß des Mannes, der ihn nicht eigentlich zu den Taten prädestiniert erscheinen läßt, zu denen ihn der Dichter bestimmt hatte" (309). This may be true of the tone, more spontaneous and hence more emotional than in his subsequent dialogue with Libussa,[2] but the difficulties that will emerge in their relationship already manifest themselves in his choice of words and images. His initial contact with her was acoustic, "ein Schrei" (4) indicative of her defencelessness—the demoiselle in distress—and then visual: "eines Weibes leuchtende Gewande, / Vom Strudel fortgerafft, die Nacht durchblinken" (5-6). According to Grillparzer's own assessment, Libussa is equal or even superior to Primislaus in every respect except one: perseverance or determination. "Es war die Idee, dieser Beharrlichkeit ein äußeres Gegenbild zu geben. Libussa, im Walde verirrt und von den Fluthen eines Bergstromes fortgerissen, wird von Primislaus gerettet" (Bachmaier 727-8). From the perspective of the rescuer, the steadfast figure on the shore, the image of being caught in a whirlpool and dragged along against one's will further substantiates the impression of the helpless, irresolute woman. To describe his visual perception of the heroine, he resorts to

metonymy: the clothes stand for the person who only exists as the presumed bearer of the garments. Pieces of clothing will continue to play a major role within the drama and, as signifiers, they lead an important life of their own, often functioning as concrete indicators of the unconscious realm. Primislaus's insistence upon the emanation of light—"leuchtende;" "durchblinken"—not only indicates the male tendency to idealize the female but also alludes to the richness of her attire, the first sign of the social barrier separating the two main protagonists. The retrieval of a woman from a stream is not in itself extraordinary. Her exalted status, clearly out of place in a mountain stream late at night, does attract his attention and arouse his curiosity. Hence, did the incident really happen as he perceived it: "Ist es denn wahr? und ist es wirklich so?" (2)

By continuing to dwell upon the impersonal, material aspects of Libussa's semblance in the next lines: "Ich eile hin und fasse sie [die Gewande oder Libussa?], und trage / Die süße Beute, laue Tropfen regnend, / Hierher" (7-9), he betrays himself as the man more concerned with external appearances than with the individual personality underneath. Staking his claim on her person, he unconsciously treats her as an object, thereby inadvertently disclosing through his choice of metaphor his male desire to possess her: she embodies the spoils of war, an exclusively masculine prerogative, which he has rightfully earned by wresting her from a natural enemy. When in the second act Libussa rejects the "Reiche Beute" (609) offered in homage by the miners: "Mich ekelt an der anspruchsvolle Tand" (611), the pejorative aspect of Primislaus's impulsive utterance becomes more evident. Since Mother Earth does not freely bestow her treasures, men have to remove them by doing violence to her, an environmental rape particularly noteworthy in view of the symbolic significance of the mountain, the *Bergwerk* (609) from which *Bergknappen* (p. 300) extract the minerals: "Diese immer noch zum Elementarcharakter des Gefäßes gehörende [Schutz] Funktion wird besonders deutlich im 'Berg,' der im Deutschen symbolisch mit sich bergen, sich verbergen und mit Geborgenheit ebenso wie mit Burg zusammenzustellen ist" (Neumann 57). His own words later in the second act add credence to this interpretation when he laments, "Doch nah' ich ihr, rückstattend meinen *Raub*, / Lohnt sie mit Gold die Tat, die mich beglückt" (748-9). "Raub" again invokes the martial male imagery in that it means plunder or booty, but it also signifies rape. As will become apparent, his choice of "Raub" to designate Libussa's jewel possesses a particular appropriateness.

Primislaus's account of the divestment exhibits obvious sexual overtones: "und sie erholt sich, und ich löse / Die goldnen Schuhe selbst ihr von den Füßen, / Und breit' ins Gras den schwergesognen Schleier, / Und meine Hütt' empfängt den teuern Gast" (9-12), although it is not without some ambiguity. The removal of her shoes could also signal his respect: stooping to serve her, he humbles himself. Lorenz speaks of "die Vorstellung einer Schändung der *bewußtlosen* Libussa" ("Neubewertung" 37) which

Roe interprets to mean: "Lorenz insists that Primislaus may even have raped Libussa" (*A Century* 97), but in fairness to Lorenz, the noun "Vorstellung" could simply denote the fantasy of a rape, a possibility which the symbolic message clearly supports and, according to St Matthew's gospel, to harbour lust is just as reprehensible as to seek its actual satisfaction: "But I [Christ] say unto you, That whosoever looketh on a woman to lust after her hath committed adultery with her already in his heart" (5:28). However, the text contains no direct evidence that Libussa ever lost consciousness—"sie erholt sich" does not necessarily signify a regaining of consciousness and has the contextual meaning of catching her breath—and, in any case, the removal of the wet clothing occurs after she recovers. Later Libussa asserts, "Ich half mir selbst, glaub nur! erschienst du nicht" (27), a trivializing of the danger she faced which Grillparzer would appear to have endorsed: "[Libussa] wird von Primislaus gerettet, oder vielmehr er hilft ihr die Gefahr bestehen, denn die letztere ist durchaus nicht so ernsthaft gemeint, daβ ohne seinen Beistand, Libussens Lage hilflos gewesen wäre" (Bachmaier 728). She could not have been unconscious in a whirlpool if her life was never in jeopardy. Furthermore, she does not come across as the fainting type. The description does hint at a symbolic or metaphorical rape, especially through the reference to her veil for, along with the "Hütte," it belongs to the cultural symbols of protection or containment, elementary attributes of the female vessel archetype (cf. Neumann 45). In some Middle Eastern cultures, only the husband may remove his wife's veil and view her face (cf. Rhodope's veil in Hebbel's *Gyges und sein Ring*). Since circumstances have provided Primislaus with this opportunity, this detail already anticipates his marital claim reinforced later by his removing her jewel. The "Schleier" also represents her divine heritage and mission, a symbol of the unknown, enigmatic woman in her closeness to nature. To quote Goethe's *Faust*: "Geheimnisvoll am lichten Tag / Läβt sich Natur des Schleiers nicht berauben" (672-3). In the case at hand, Libussa's veil has been brought low, desecrated in another visual image of her descent from the realm of her sisters to a man's cottage in anticipation of the domestic sphere to which she will be eventually reduced at the beginning of the last act.[3]

Primislaus's monologue concludes with yet another implied sexual fantasy: "Glückselige, ihr meiner Schwester Kleider, / Die sie getragen und mir sterbend lieβ, / Ihr werdet dieser Hohen Leib umhüllen, / Und näher sie mir zaubern, die so fern" (13-16). He envies his sister's clothes because they cover Libussa's body and thus he seeks to disguise the sexual desire she has aroused in him behind the socially admissible love he feels for his late sister. The "sie" of his final line refers to his sister but could also include Libussa, for he knows both women to be beyond his reach, his sister by the ultimate separation of death (*Scheiden*) and Libussa by her birth. His first speech of the tragedy draws heavily upon the social division he senses between himself and the woman he has saved, hence the prominence of "fern" as the last word of his monologue. The allusion to the light emanating from her clothing (cf.

the German *Durchlaucht*), the golden shoes, the veil to conceal and distinguish the noble from the common, and aristocratic superiority in body and soul ("dieser *Hohen* Leib")[4] set her apart from the ordinary. As Nietzsche was to point out later in the nineteenth century, the aristocracy claims its right to rule by its distinctiveness from "allem Niedrigen, Niedrig-Gesinnten, Gemeinen und Pöbelhaften," what he called the "Pathos der Vornehmheit und *Distanz*, [. . .] das dauernde und dominierende Gesamt—und Grundgefühl einer höheren herrschenden Art im Verhältnis zu einer niederen Art, zu einem 'Unten'" (*Zur Genealogie* 185). Primislaus knows that this woman stands above him on the social ladder and as a result of the feelings she has stirred in him, whether they be of love or, from a more cynical point of view, of desire for social advancement, or a combination of both, he faces a dilemma created by class distinction, a distance also apparent in the impersonal manner he employs to depict the rescue: "eines Weibes leuchtende Gewande" (5). The sense of excitement his soliloquy conveys intimates that despite his humble credentials, he still harbours the audacity to hope as he in retrospect confesses to Libussa in the fourth act (1610).

The audience's visual introduction to the titular heroine "*in ländlicher Tracht aus der Hütte tretend*" (p. 277) suggests an affinity with this unpretentious ambience in contrast to the sophisticated garments laid out to dry, and her initial words only serve to reinforce this impression: "Hier bin ich, und verwandelt wie du siehst. / Des Bauern Kleider hüllen minder warm nicht / Als eines Fürsten Rock; in so weit, merk' ich, / Sind sie sich gleich" (17-20). In this meeting between the two classes, she immediately appears quite openminded: in comparing the outer shells from the point of practicality, she sees no difference. Already, this scene, both in its visual and verbal content, signals the feasibility of convergence on an equal ("gleich") basis between these representatives of the nobility and peasantry,[5] but her speech also tends to underscore the social obstacles, even though it may seek on one level to deny them. Class distinction may pose less of a problem for her than it does for Primislaus: it costs her little to adopt this stance, smacking of condescension, since she occupies the dominant position. Interpreting in part the significance of Libussa's peasant dress, Lorenz maintains, "Indem Primislaus Libussa in die Bauerntracht seiner Schwester hüllte und sie der Abzeichen ihres Ranges sowie des mütterlichen Bildes aus der Spange beraubte, hat er sie ihrer Herkunft und ihrer Identität entäuβert" ("Neubewertung" 37). Lorenz is more explicit in her 1986 monograph where she states, "Er [zieht] ihr die Kleider seiner Schwester an" (*Grillparzer* 184). Her antipathy for the ploughman is readily understandable, but on occasion she allows her dislike to colour her judgement as in the above quotations. Having retrieved an unknown noble woman from the water, can he realistically be expected to leave her in her wet clothing or to have at hand an outfit more in keeping with her station in life? He merely offers her his sister's "Bauerntracht" which she exchanges for her own wet attire (minus the shoes and the veil which remain outside) within his cottage as the text indicates: "LI-

BUSSA *in ländlicher Tracht aus der Hütte tretend*: / Hier bin ich, und *verwandelt* wie du siehst" (17). She has done the dressing herself in the privacy of the cottage while Primislaus impatiently waits for her outside, as decorum would dictate, and imagines how his sister's clothes will cover, i.e., future tense ("werdet [. . .] umhüllen") her body. Her country costume does have an obvious symbolic, visual function; however, her wearing it is a matter of fortuity rather than design and whereas Primislaus may steal her jewel, he does not deprive her of the "Abzeichen ihres Ranges": he returns them to their rightful owner once they have presumably dried out: "Dein Schleier und die schimmernden Gewande, / In denen ich den Fluten dich entriß, / Hier eingebunden trägts des Pferdes Rücken" (261-3).

In his epithet to address her, Primislaus persists in drawing attention to the separating distance: "Du *Hohe*, Herrliche! / Wie zierst du diese ländlich *niedre* Tracht!" (20-1), while she has raised the possibility of ignoring it and has even expressed an outlook in keeping with his practical bent. Later in the drama he claims, "Bist du am offenbarsten wenn verhüllt / Und trägst die Krone wenn du sie verleugnest" (1771-2). From his perspective she cannot hide her royal aura, her inherent preeminence, even in a peasant outfit. Lorenz has overstated her case when she asserts: "Bereits in den scheinbar idyllischen Anfangsszenen fallen auf seiten Primislaus' Besitzgier und Mangel an Achtung vor der fremden, vornehmen Frau auf. Er möchte Libussa *sofort* zu seinesgleichen, ja Geringerem als seinesgleichen, zu einer Frau seines Standes, zu seiner Frau, seinem Eigentum, machen. [. . .] Obwohl diese [lines 25-7] und andere Worte eine Bemühung Libussas darstellen, eine Entfernung zwischen sich und den in ihr Leben eingebrochenen Fremden zu setzen, übersieht Primislaus taktlos derartige Versuche und hält seinerseits die Distanz möglichst klein" ("Neubewertung" 36-7). At the beginning of the scene, Libussa is the one to break down the barriers; Primislaus harps upon them. He faces, after all, quite a predicament: on the one hand he clearly feels physically attracted to her—she is a beautiful woman—but on the other he cannot deny his awareness of the social distance separating them. The critics have generally ignored or given only passing reference to the motif of love across the class barrier. While Florack implicitly acknowledges its importance in the early stages, she sees it as incidental later in the tragedy: "Nebensächlich jedoch wird die soziale Differenz zwischen den Antagonisten, wenn sich Primislaus im Verlauf der Handlung damit begnügt, daß Libussa seinem Weiblichkeitsideal ähnlicher wird" (242). However, the very last line of the work plays on the same separation with which **Libussa** began: "Das *Hohe* schied, sein Zeichen sei hie*nieden*" (2513). Also, Florack's view that the love interest functions "die Standesproblematik zu überdecken" (242) fails to appreciate how, from the beginning to the end, the "Standesproblematik" puts a strain on their relationship and complicates the "Liebesmotiv" and the wider social issues. The omission or deemphasizing of this

dynamic not only does Primislaus an injustice but also does not take into full account the subtle play between the sexes which Grillparzer was such a master at suggesting.

The direct allusion to his late sister and to her reincarnation through Libussa as she enters in the dead girl's attire strikes a sincere note despite the ulterior motive of the flattering comparison (24). The fact that he also mentions his recent loss in his monologue during Libussa's absence, i.e., with no one to impress, gives his words a ring of genuineness by virtue of the implied tenderness for a departed loved one and does provide an explanation for the immediacy and urgency of his pursuit of the strange woman which goes beyond the overtly sexual. After death has separated him from a close family member, he must now relinquish her again in the person his mind has cast as a surrogate.

Libussa's spontaneous response is to show gratitude and to acknowledge him as her saviour: "Auch für die Kleider Dank! du mein Erretter!" (25), but she then proceeds to minimize the significance of his heroic deed: "Wenn Rettung ja wo die Gefahr nicht groß. / Ich half mir selbst, glaub nur! erschienst du nicht" (26-7). As in her opening utterance of the play, "Nein", she declares her independence, refusing to assume the part of the helpless female. Adamantly she seeks to avoid incurring a debt, an obligation, which can easily become a form of servitude.[6] When he shows concern for her present physical well-being, she denies him again: "Ich hab' geruht, nun ruft mich ein Geschäft" (31) and refrains from going along with his solicitous attitude. Not one to be easily discouraged, Primislaus tries again to offer assistance only to be rebuffed by another "Nein" (32) and, just four lines later in the dialogue, she once more contradicts him: "Dort nicht" (36). The persistence with which she avoids any show of reliance and her constant denials, either direct or implied, may denote a strong, conscious resistance to a repressed attraction to this man. As Ehrhard has proposed, "Und nicht aus Undankbarkeit spricht sie [Libussa] so, sondern sie wehrt sich gegen eine Neigung, die ihr Retter einflößt" (506). Lorenz misses the point: "Gleich im ersten Akt ist das Verhältnis zwischen Libussa und ihrem zukünftigen Gatten feindselig und ohne jede 'Innigkeit'" ("Neubewertung" 36). Indeed, reticence—there is no evidence of hostility—frequently masks the very intimacy Lorenz would deny this scene. As Volkelt remarked back in 1888, "Die Tragödie erhält ihren Zauber erst durch das zwischen Libussa und Primislaus stattfindende Liebesspiel" (67).

The dialogue contains further indications of her apparent control of the present situation: "Du [Libussa] hast den Ort bezeichnet, der dein Ziel. / Geleiten *sollt'* ich zu drei Eichen dich" (33-4). She has already expressed her wish, if not her command, before she entered his cottage, and the "Ziel" designates a resolve; she does not normally flow with the tide. In the face of her laconic replies suggesting her fear of further involvement, he must "dig" for information. While her objective is to leave as soon as possible in order to attend to urgent domestic matters, his is somehow to guarantee a second meeting: "Und ich / Soll dort dem Ungefähr dich übergeben, / Das niemals wohl uns mehr zusammenführt?" (37-9). Ironically he anticipates Libuss's subsequent strategy since she does in fact leave their next encounter to chance: "Und überließ dem Zufall denn / Ob sie [the Wladiken] des Rätsels Lösung dennoch fänden?" (792-3), an approach which this man of practical reason finds unacceptable.[7] His choice of words, "dich übergeben", divulges a sense of ownership on his part, as if he were required to surrender a possession or renounce a valid claim (cf. his earlier use of "Beute"). Libussa's response, taking the form of a proverbial statement, both summarizes and foretells their mutual fate: "Der Menschen Wege kreuzen sich gar vielfach / Und leicht begegnet sich Getrennter Pfad" (40-1). They seem to be constantly at odds, as the path each chooses proves to be different in nature and aims, and yet on occasion the two do meet, do reach a reconciliation of sorts in their common concern for the welfare of their people (although the means or method to that end diverge) and in the attraction they feel for one another. According to Lorenz, *Libussa* is "keine Liebeshandlung [. . .] sondern der Machtkampf zweier verschieden gearteter Herrschergestalten" ("Neubewertung" 35), but a love story, given the chemistry of some physical relationships (cf. Kleist's *Penthesilea* as an extreme example), can frequently represent a struggle for dominance and an extreme reluctance to expose one's vulnerability, a lesson the eternal bachelor Grillparzer knew only too well from personal experience. "Getrennter Pfad," appearing in the emphatic final position, stresses the realization that despite occasional concurrence, their final position will be one of separation: the crossings will be few and temporary. The text would thus seem to recognize the inevitability of disjunction, whether between male and female, patriarchy and matriarchy, community and individual, or a nineteenth- and eighteenth-century political ideal. Ultimately, notwithstanding their feelings for one another, each of the main protagonists will go his/her separate way.

Libussa's aphorism may also attempt to conceal a specific interest in her interlocutor behind a generalization.[8] Despite all the disqualifications contained in "Getrennter"—divisions of sex or social status—she still holds open the prospect of a future meeting, indeed presents it as even likely ("vielfach"; "leicht"). Hence, Wolf-Cirian's analysis of Libussa's attitude does not do her full justice: "Primislaus gegenüber ist sie durchaus von herber Verschlossenheit, von ablehnender Haltung. Ihrem Sinnen ist der Mann gleichgültig, [. . .] und die Huldigung, die ihr Primislaus entgegenbringt, gleitet, ohne jeglichen Eindruck auf ihre Eitelkeit zu machen, von ihrer stolzen, gefürsteten Natur ab" (249-50). Encouraged by Libussa's concession, Primislaus exhibits bluntness or lack of tact, but also some deference when he asks for permission to sue for her hand in marriage: "Du bist kein Weib um das man werben könnte?" (42), an unambiguous expression of his honourable intentions. Since a negative interrogative normally anticipates a negative answer, what he has been consistently receiving from her, his query betrays a lack of con-

fidence: given the visible signs of social distinction, an imbalance in her favour, he solicits her counsel. In this instance she does not say no directly, opting for a milder form of denial which credits him with insight: "Du hasts erraten" (43). Anxious to know the exact cause of ineligibility, he seeks to confirm the obvious: "Und, verbeuts dein Stand, / Sinds andre Gründe, die's verbieten?" to which she replies, "Beides" (43-4). As has become the norm, he singles out the class issue, but significantly neither speaker alludes directly to his or her own personal feelings as the disqualifying factor, and she intimates that she has no or very little say in the matter, i.e., she does not enjoy the luxury of being able to follow her own inclinations. Although she acknowledges her dependence upon social conventions, her lack of control over her matrimonial destiny, a scenario partly confirmed by the tragedy, the audience already has sufficient evidence of an independent, spirited woman who does not wish to be beholden to anyone. Yet in an image which invites the spectator to interpret her words on a more symbolic level and in a prophetic vein, she commands her host, "*gedenke* deines Worts / Und *führe* mich aus dieses Waldes Schlünden / Zum Ziel meines Weges, das du kennst" (45-7). While sufficiently in control of the current situation to issue two orders, one of which reminds him that as a gentleman he must fulfil his word, she still concedes, albeit somewhat theatrically, the need for his protection and his guidance if she is to attain her goal; significantly she cannot reach it on her own. Moreover, as Primislaus's reaction makes evident—"Wohl, du gebeutst und ich muß dir gehorchen" (48)—he recognizes the obedience he owes her both as the magnanimous rescuer of the beautiful demoiselle in distress but also as an obscure peasant before an illustrious lady. Even though by rights Libussa should be in his debt—he did retrieve her from the water and provide shelter and clothing—she comes across as the dominant party.

Taking his cue from Libussa's phrase "Getrennter Pfad" (41), Primislaus now transforms the "drei Eichen" (34) into "Trennungs-Eichen" (51) repeated for emphasis (52). The number three appears as well in the three Wladiken, or the three sisters or the three belts. It expresses "sufficiency, or the growth of unity within itself", especially since it "represents the solution of the conflict posed by dualism" (Cirlot 232). *Libussa* supports this symbolic meaning since the three Wladiken form an almost indistinguishable unity, a self-serving sufficiency in the unanimity of their views while the sisters forgo this harmony, becoming a duality of sorts, i.e., Tetka/Kascha versus Libussa once the latter abandons the fold ("Der Kreis getrennt" [382]). The number three does pose a threat for Primislaus in his pursuit of the queen, as the never completely severed link to her two sisters creates an ever present tension between him and her. But above all he becomes himself the great separator who, unwittingly or by conscious design, destroys the illusion of oneness either within the self or with the natural world (cf. 2320f).

The theme of separation achieves a culmination when Primislaus alludes to the fate of Libussa's belt towards the end of the opening scene: "Des Gürtels reiche Ketten aufgesprengt / Und in zwei Stücken ein so schönes *Ganze.* / Ich samml' es dir und trag' es dienend nach, / Bis an dem Ort der *Trennung* du's erhältst" (55-8). On the most general level the belt or its later variation as a necklace reflects "das Große Runde" (Neumann) symbolizing the sheltering, protective function associated with the elementary character of the Feminine (cf. Libussa's mission to save her father). In this instance, however, the *divided* belt announces both the loss of unity within herself and the forfeiture of innocence or virginity, a message intended by the dramatist[9] and first highlighted by Dunham: "[T]he belt, while symbolizing family solidarity and the life of contemplation, stands also for chastity" (37).[10] This convergence of two paths: "Der Menschen Wege kreuzen sich gar vielfach" (40), a crossroads in Libussa's life, will have far-reaching repercussions and implications as subsequently visualized by Kascha: "Sie ist in jener Lagen einer, / sprichts mir, / Aus denen Glück und Unglück gleich entsteht, / Am *Scheideweg* von Seligkeit und Jammer" (282-4), another play on separation occasioned by "des Vaters Scheiden" (887). Thus the "Ort der Trennung" will mark not only a temporary parting from Primislaus but also a more permanent parting from a whole way of life: "Nur vorwärts führt das Leben," she will come to realize, "rückwärts nie" (386).

As soon as Libussa leaves the stage to retrieve her basket, Primislaus takes advantage of her absence to ensure a reunion: "Ich will ein *Zeichen* nehmen meiner Tat, / Daran ich sie, sie mich dereinst erkennt, / Denn sie verhehlt, ich seh's, mit Fleiß ihr edles Selbst" (65-7). Later in the first act, one of Kascha's aphorisms: "Die Liebe knüpft sich gern an feste *Zeichen*" (377), intended as a criticism of Libussa, describes more accurately Primislaus's attitude, his insistence upon a concrete sign in response to the basic insecurity of a lover in the initial stages of a relationship and his/her need for a tangible guarantee. Despite Libussa's endeavour to minimize her deliverance at his hands, he persists in seeing it as granting him some right over her. Not only is he determined to remind her of this debt to him, but he also desires to retain a token as a means to discover her identity. His choice of her jewel: "Das [Kleinod] lös ich los und wahre mirs als Pfand" (71) achieves these objectives, but its forced removal from her belt conjures up the image of a rape, "Raub."[11] Tradition depicts a woman's virginity as her most precious and most carefully guarded jewel (cf. Rhodope's diamond in *Gyges und sein Ring*). His act therefore signals his intention to "deflower" her and secure his claim.[12] In an effort to downplay his offence, he stresses the jewel's relatively minor material merit but does concede its human worth: "wohl nicht reich zumeist, / Allein beprägt mit Bildern und mit Sprüchen" (69-70). One can assume that the images and sayings possess a personal significance for its owner. From a practical point of view the jewel also provides the means to ascertain both her name and "Stamm und Haus und Stand" (72), a threefold reinforcement of her social ranking, his constant topic, if not obsession, throughout this episode. One should also bear in mind that the opportunity to steal the jewel only arises because Libussa has returned

to his cottage to recover "*ein Körbchen mit Kräutern*" (p. 279) symptomatic of her close connection to the natural world and of her practical concern for the physical welfare of her father, information to which the audience gains access in the next scene (81-4). Her gesture comes to reinforce our perception of her pragmatic orientation as intimated earlier in her comparison of peasant and noble attire (18-20).[13]

As this sequence concludes, she issues another command: "So komm!" (74) and moves towards his horse while he follows, "*Libussas Gewande tragend*" (p. 279). In this final visual image, he shows reverence by serving her, but by depriving her of her jewel, he demonstrates that he has a mind of his own. Already this "Vorspiel" bears evidence of the strong, individual wills of each of the main protagonists despite the limitations imposed by their respective sexual or social status: Libussa, as a semidivine princess, is supposed to remain aloof from mortal concerns and contacts, while Primislaus, as a humble farmer from the lowest social order, should know his place. A test of wills has begun, what Roe has fittingly called "an elaborate game, in which two equally proud individuals refuse to be the first to show any sign of weakness" (*Introduction* 227).

There are some striking correspondences between this first scene from *Libussa* and the opening episode of Kleist's *Prinz Friedrich von Homburg* where the titular hero describes his experience in the garden. The two expositions depend upon the tension between dream and reality: Primislaus's description of his state of mind: "Und wie ein Träumender nach seines Traums Entschwinden, / Frag' ich mich selbst: wie wars? und weiß mich nicht zu finden" (62-3) approximates Homburg's upon his regaining consciousness: "Ich weiß nicht, [. . .] wo ich bin" (111). Griesmayer, in his analysis of the meaning of Primislaus's rescue of Libussa, maintains, "Das Traumhafte wird zum Anstoß, es zu verwirklichen [. . .] In diesem Streben nach Verwirklichung und Versicherung liegt die Bedeutung dieses Bildes [the deliverance from the stream]. Aus ihr wird sich alles künftige Handeln Primislaus' erklären" (265). One could, of course, make the same claim for the dream sequence as it relates to Homburg's subsequent aspirations and actions, although Grillparzer's ploughman emerges as much more securely anchored in reality. In both instances the dramas associate female allurement with light in a nocturnal, wet setting: "Und weil die Nacht so lieblich mich umfing, / Mit blondem Haar [an allusion to the moonlight shining through the trees], von Wohlgeruch ganz triefend [i.e., dripping]" (*Prinz Friedrich* 120-1), all of which suggests the Eros-Thanatos theme. The two works thus convey an underlying drive for sexual union: "So legt ich hier in ihren [night's] Schoß mich nieder" (*Prinz Friedrich,* 123); "Glückselige, ihr meiner Schwester Kleider, / Die sie getragen und mir sterbend ließ, / Ihr werdet dieser Hohen Leib umhüllen" (13-15). Lacan's theory regarding the woman's meeting with the phallus, i.e., the law of the father, comes to mind: "The round, worshipped maternal body hides the disturbing darkness of the subject's origins and the wound that both penetration [presumably Primislaus had to reach down into the whirlpool to remove Libussa] and birth [immersion symbolizes a rebirth] leave behind on the virgin-whole-body of the woman. The woman does not come out unscathed from the encounter with the phallus [. . .] as it takes possession of her body ["Ich eile hin und fasse sie"] in order to deflorate [the removal of her jewel] and impregnate her" (Benvenuto/Kennedy 193).

As a final parallel, Homburg and Primislaus, having forcefully removed a token, plan to use it to discover the identity of the woman who appeared to them in a dreamlike situation: "Das lös' ich los und wahre mirs als *Pfand*, / Das Namen mir enthüllt" (71-2); "Ein *Pfand* [the glove] schon warfst du [das Glück], im Vorüberschweben, / Aus deinem Füllhorn lächelnd mir [Homburg] herab [he actually snatched it away himself]" (359-60), and which they conceal next to their hearts as a sign of emotional commitment: "*Er [Homburg] nimmt den Handschuh aus dem Kollett*" (p. 644); "*Er [Primislaus] steckt das Kleinod in den Busen*" (p. 279).

Although critics and audiences alike in the nineteenth century maligned the garden sequence in *Prinz Friedrich* and Hebbel even recommended its deletion, our own century has come to appreciate its theatrical excellence and the dramatist's skill in introducing the basic motivations operative in the remainder of the play. Similarly, **Libussa**'s "Vorspiel", called by its creator "vielleicht das Beste, was [er] geschrieben [hat]," presents all the tragedy's major themes, including a power struggle and a love interest, captured in a visually effective and psychologically suggestive manner. Just as *Prinz Friedrich* returns to the garden to play out its last scene, **Libussa** looks back to its beginning in the concluding line which is made up of motifs introduced and developed in the first scene: "Das Hohe schied, sein Zeichen [the belts] sei hienieden" (2513).

A short interlude, a continuation of the exposition to fill in more background for the audience, introduces Wlasta: "*Dann kommt Wlasta mit einem Jagdspieße bewaffnet*" (p. 279). Whereas the opening scene presented a woman in traditional peasant dress emerging from a cottage, the symbol of female domesticity, the drama now highlights an Amazon, an aggressive, more masculine orientation in contrast to the usual feminine stereotype. This contributes to a blurring of the two well defined gender spheres, for according to the anthropologist Sanday, "Sexual separation for whatever reason creates two worlds—one male and one female—each consisting of a system of meaning and a program of behavior, almost like separate and distinct cultures. The male world focuses on such exclusively male activities as warfare and hunting" (109-10). By way of explanation Sanday proposes: "If there is a basic difference between sexes, other than the differences associated with human reproductivity, it is that women as a group have not willingly faced death in violent conflict. This fact, perhaps more than any other, explains why men have sometimes become the dominating sex" (210). Wlasta's initial stage appearance as a hunter thus calls the strict conventional sense of gender division into question.

WLASTA: Und nirgends Menschen?—Doch! Hier eine
Hütte.
An die Türe schlagend: Ihr drin im Hause!—
Keine Antwort?
Nachdem sie die Türe geöffnet: Leer!

(75-7)

Her first words are indicative of a blunt directness and her actions—she does not knock at the door; she strikes it and then proceeds to open it herself—and give the impression of an assertiveness more in keeping with expected male behaviour.

For the first time the audience hears Libussa's name; Dobromila juxtaposes it with her social status as "Fürstin" (80-1), a verbal confirmation of the underlying assumption of the "Vorspiel." In addition she justifies her mistress's absence from her usual environment and sets up an important association: "Einsam ging sie, / Nach Kräutern suchend für den kranken Vater" (81-2). Although Politzer concludes that Grillparzer had no knowledge of Johann Jakob Bachofen's *Das Mutterrecht,* published in 1861 (309-10), the playwright's inclusion of these details points to his awareness of the customary basis for the matriarchy. "If prior matriarchies did exist," Sanday observes, "they were probably a consequence of the evolution of plant domestication from the plant-gathering activities of women. This would have given women economic and ritual centrality and, hence, a primary voice in decision making. . . . To conclude, the ascribed basis for female power and authority in the secular domain is found in a ritual orientation to plants, the earth, maternity and fertility" (120). The very decision to seek a practical cure for her father's illness denotes in advance her suitability to succeed him by assuming "das Amt der Hüterin des Vaterlandes" (Bachmaier 739) and conveys a predisposition for the *vita activa* before her meeting with Primislaus: "So zeigt sie sich vorausbestimmt, die unnütze Beschaulichkeit aufzugzeben, um ins thätige Leben einzutreten" (Ehrhard 496).[14]

With another sudden change in locale to the sisters' castle at Budesch, the dramatist exploits the stars as a means of prophecy and as a subtle device to transmit an underlying sociopolitical message.[15] Florack has provided an excellent interpretation of the meaning behind the various constellations (247-8) to which I would only add two further considerations. The lines, "Die Krone sinkt am Himmel und der Adler / Lenkt nach den Bergen seinen müden Flug" (99-100), may predict the death of Krokus, especially in the reference to the crown, but they may also connote the inevitable decline of an exhausted upper class ("Adler"). The vitality and cunning necessary to rule have passed on to another class embodied by Primislaus: "Die kluge Schlange droht mit fahlem Blinken" (114). Secondly, the observation, "Und auf dem Pfad der königlichen Sterne / Folgt namenloses Volk zu weiter Ferne" (115-6), may allude to the habitual dependence of the people upon the aristocracy for leadership. Being of an inferior order of life—"Fuchs, Fisch und Eidechs drängen / Die niedre Form dem edlen Vogel nach" (112-3)—the lower classes still need direction from above, a view expressed, needless to say, by a partisan of the governing hierarchy.

Grillparzer's attitude towards the *Adel* as revealed in *Libussa* is problematic. The titular heroine and her sisters belong to the nobility, but one could also construe their status as prophets or seers living aloof from normal human intercourse as a metaphor for the isolation of the artist. On the other hand, the Wladiken, who now make their noisy entry, provide a comic contrast to the three sisters: "Die Wladiken, böhmische Fürsten, die den aristokratischen Standpunkt kompromiβlos vertreten und deshalb die Unterschiede von Adel und Bürger erhalten wissen wollen, fungieren in ihrer Dreizahl als satirisches Pendant zu Libussa und ihren beiden Schwestern" (Bachmaier 740). Reminiscent of Wlasta in the previous sequence, Domaslav, the first to be heard, authoritatively demands, "Wo sind die Fürstinnen? Bring mich vor sie!" (125). Obviously accustomed to having their own way, they show no hesitation to resort to the typical male expedient, force: "Sie müssen uns vernehmen, sei's mit Zwang" (132). Another of Domaslav's assertions inadvertently exposes their true priority: "Doch frommt es uns, es frommt dem ganzen Land" (129). What comes first in this spontaneous utterance is their own self-interest, then, as an afterthought, the good of the country. In their arrogance and egotism they associate their own well-being with that of the nation and, when thwarted, resort to sexist disparagement: "der Grund genügt, / Daβ man den Schlummer stört, in dem ein Weib sich wiegt" (141-2). In the exchange with these caricatures—each allegedly embodies one quality (cf. 664-6)—Dobra easily gains the upper hand as she put the intruders in their place: "Am Tor der Einsicht tobt und lärmt der Wilde, / Hört er am liebsten doch der eignen Worte Klang" (133-4), a truism expressed here at the expense of a self-centred aristocracy. She goes on to vindicate her mistresses: "Sie schlummern nicht, doch wenn in Schlaf versenket, / Ihr Träumen acht' ich mehr als was ihr Andern denket" (143-4). As a woman defending women, she posits their access to a higher spiritual dimension, but she also implies a preference for the unconscious over the conscious realm. Grillparzer portrays the revelation of psychological truth more in the former than in the latter since the self prefers to conceal and distort rather than confront an unpleasant reality. In this respect he anticipated his fellow Viennese, Freud, by more than half a century.

As if to confirm Dobra's evaluation, the two sisters now enter already apprised of their father's fate and of Libussa's future decision to forsake their exalted sphere of meditation: "Ihr Platz ist dunkel in den sonn'gen Kreisen" (152). In the subsequent dialogue between Kascha and Tetka, the dramatist deals with the potential power of the human mind—its aptitude to will its own health but also its illness—and raises the issue of the extent to which we exercise control over our own mental lives. Tetka very perceptively observes that attitude or placebos can make a difference in the healing process, demonstrating Grillparzer's awareness of psychosomatic phenomena:

> Wenn du den Kranken mit dem Besten tränkest,
> Er stirbt, hält er für Gift was du gebracht.

> Als Krücke mag es sein daβ sie [Kascha's medical
>   skills] noch leiste
> Für schwache Seelen, die am Willen krank,
> In Wahrheit hilft doch nur der Geist dem Geiste,
> Er ist der Arzt, das Bette und der Trank.
>
> (169-74)

In other words a person cannot be cured unless he or she really wants to be cured.

The sisters then turn to the consequences of Krokus's death for themselves:

> KASCHA: Nun aber ist er tot, wir sind verwaist.
> TETKA: Bist du verwaist? ich nicht. Ich seh' ihn noch,
>   Nicht wie zuletzt in seiner Schwachheit Banden.
>   Ehrwürd'ger Greis, war Greis er immer doch,
>   Ehrwürd'ger Greis, war Greis er immer doch,
>   Mir ist er als ein Jüngling auferstanden.
>
> (179-83)

Both women acknowledge a dependency upon the father, while Kascha confirms his continued presence beyond the grave. Parents embody the child's first object choices, but the relationship between father and daughter can be particularly strong as implied in this instance. According to Freud, "betrachten sich die Frauen als infantil geschädigt, ohne ihre Schuld um ein Stück verkürzt und zurückgesetzt, und die Erbitterung so mancher Tochter gegen ihre Mutter hat zur letzten Wurzel den Vorwurf, daβ sie sie als Weib anstatt als Mann zur Welt gebracht hat" ("Einige Charaktertypen," 10: 235). The text rarely mentions the mother of the three daughters, but by contrast, their father, although not a participating dramatic character, still represents a force to be reckoned with. In "normal" development, the parent becomes a prototype transferred to other people; however, for Kascha and Tetka who remain cloistered in their castle, the father retains his dominant function. As a venerable old man, a personification of wisdom but also of traditional authority, he commanded their respect and even after death he still has considerable power over their respective destinies (the belts). His passing only appears to end his control, for as Tetka concedes, her mind has resurrected him in the shape of a young man, i.e., he has usurped the role of husband/mate. She has not really progressed beyond the ideal-prototype stage. In Libussa's case, one could argue that once she left the protective walls of the domestic stronghold, Primislaus merely took over where the father left off. The night of their meeting significantly marked Krokus's "Scheiden" (887).

The two sisters conduct this whole conversation as if the others present did not exist, a sign that they dwell in another world and have access to a different dimension: "Wir haben es gewuβt, bevor es noch geschah" (186). As an additional indication of their self-centredness, Kascha and Tetka actually resent their father's involvement in politics, his commitment to others, and would have preferred him to have devoted himself fully to his daughters (190-2). Social responsibilities took precedence over domestic obligations—he neglected his family—and even contributed to his early death: "Weil euer Trutz vergällt ihm jeden Tag, / Gab er dem Kummer sich und welkte hin, erlag" (193-4). The drama thus introduces the problem of leadership very early on, proposing that the defiance and recalcitrance of the ruled take their toll upon the personal life of the ruler. In both *Libussa* and *Ein Bruderzwist* the thankless task of governing proves fatal for its practitioners and in *Die Jüdin* the representatives of the state eliminate the royal concubine in an effort to bring the king back from personal indulgence to his social and political duty.

In response to Tetka's complaint, Domaslav pleads, "Laβt das uns nicht entgelten, hohe Frauen, / Belohnt, mit dem wir nahn, das kindliche Vertrauen, / Vollendet was begann des Vaters hohes Haupt" (197-9). Speaking as an aristocrat, he implies that the desired leader should act as a father to his subjects. This model, typical of eighteenth-century thought, portrays the people as helpless children in need of care and direction, incapable of managing their own affairs, and hence prepared to trust their political fate to a caring parent. The wording deserves particular note since "das kindliche Vertrauen" will become the publicly proclaimed foundation of Libussa's regime at the end of this act: "In Zukunft herrscht nur Eines hier im Land: / Das kindliche Vertraun" (444-5). The fact that the overt villains of the tale, the Wladiken, exploit the same principle in seeking a female substitute for Krokus, one whom they plan to manipulate to serve their own selfish ends, casts a shadow upon its later reiteration in the mouth of the central character. Although Libussa's perception of how she will transform childlike trust into beneficial social reforms devised by her, from which all will benefit equally, runs counter to the intent of the Wladiken, far from representing "den Geist der bewuβten Demokratie" (Lorenz, "Neubewertung" 42), her political ideal owes much to her own class and its fear of the masses.[16] When Domaslav proceeds to vindicate the sisters' incumbency, the eventual divergences manifest themselves: "Ihr stammet, wissen wir, von höhern Mächten, / Wir sind ein dunkles Volk, unkundig in den Rechten; / Der *Stab*, der in Fürst Krokus Händen lag, / Wer, als sein eignes *Blut*, zu halten ihn vermag?" (202-5). Aristocratic prejudice claims the divine right of the upper class to rule, symbolized in the images of light in antithesis to the dark, ignorant lower class and justified by the preservation of a pure line of descent. "Hinweise auf 'Zucht,' 'edles Blut' und 'hohe Geburt' und überhaupt die Vorstellung der Aristokratie als einer erblichen Klasse—alle diese Dinge sind Ausdruck des aristokratischen Anspruchs auf ihre biologische Besonderheit" (Kautsky 12). Whereas Libussa also sets herself apart, she does not place as much store in these noble values and clearly has no use for "Rechte" and the rod. The latter fills a double function: it announces the life-and-death jurisdiction of the monarch, his ability to protect—Thomas Hobbes defines political power in terms of the leader's competence in this area: "The Obligation of Subjects to the Sovereign, is understood to last as long, and no longer, than the power lasteth by which he is able to protect them" (114)—but closely related to this consideration, the "Stab," a phallic symbol, also reifies the ultimate and absolute au-

thority of the father figure here extended to the social model of the monarchy. Patriarchal practice has designated sexual prowess as a mark of the male's worthiness to hold office. For instance, the king from *Die Jüdin* expresses his desire to dominate Rahel sexually by drawing an implied parallel between himself and the gentile Persian king Ahasverus who took Esther to wife and protected her people: "Von Ahasverus, der den *Herrscherstab* / Ausstreckte über Esther, die sein Weib / Und selber Jüdin, Schutzgott war den Ihren" (499-501). Domaslav, by stressing the rod in Krokus's hand, may well be betraying his wish to reign through one of the daughters, for the phallus denotes what the mother lacks in the relationship between parents and their children. If one is to believe Freud or his later defender, Lacan, "sexual difference can only be the consequence of a division, without this division it would cease to exist. But it must exist because no human being can become a subject outside the division into two sexes. One must take up a position as either a man or a woman" (Mitchell 6). From the drama's male perspective, the sisters will always lack that which confers the right to rule.

When offered the Bohemian crown, Kascha reacts by outlining her realm, the traditionally female sphere of nature. Drawn to the organic world which continually evolves but lacks awareness, she repudiates the conscious level of advanced organisms such as human beings, because "Des Lebend'gen Dasein ist Tod" (212), or as Freud put it equally succinctly, "Das Ziel alles Lebens ist der Tod" ("Jenseits des Lustprinzips" 3: 248). With our knowledge of death's inevitability, we are from the outset mere "Leichen" (213). Unwilling to renounce the power her affinity to nature provides—"Was Natur vermag und kann / Ist mir willig untertan" (209-10)—she refuses to leave her inner orientation: "Geht zu Andern mit euern Reichen, / Was ist mir gemein mit Euch?" (214-5) and thus substantiates an anthropological finding: "In societies where the forces of nature are sacralized ['Schloβ der Schwester'], . . . there is a reciprocal flow between the power of nature and the power inherent in women" (Sanday 4-5). Tetka also rejects the offer, but in order to preserve or pursue oneness in the face of the disintegration of the subject: "Was sein soll ist nur Eins, / Was sein kann ist ein Vieles, / Ich aber will sein einig und Eins" (217-19). At Lacan's mirror stage (the sisters' province as the *vita contemplativa*), the ego gains the impression of being autonomous and whole; however, this is only an illusion and the individual will persist in seeking an imaginary completeness throughout life, but in vain, since fragmentation or separation, the underlying message of *Libussa,* characterizes human existence (Benvenuto/Kennedy 61). Tetka wants to deny by an act of will the divisive nature of the "Real Order" which Lacan links to the dimensions of death and sexuality, the domain out there. Both sisters seek to avoid any contact with the external world: "Mein sonnig Reich strahlt hellres Licht, / Von mir! Ich mag eure Krone nicht!" (224-5), preferring to live in splendid isolation in their castle, excluded from any foreign disturbances. As commented upon earlier, Kascha disclaims death and, as for sexuality, Tetka has resurrected her father and transformed him into a young man, an unconscious surrogate, indicative of Krokus's continuing dictatorial influence over his female offspring.

Lorenz interprets "Wells', p. 153, geringschätziges Abtun der geistigen Tätigkeit der Schwestern: 'Libussa's love for man raises her above the selfishness of her sisters'" as an example of "sexistisch[e] Vorurteile," a judgment which strikes me as patently unfair and not supported by the text. The sisters come across as condescending, arrogant, and totally caught up with themselves: "Was ist *mir* gemein mit Euch?" (215) or "*Mein* sonnig Reich strahlt hellres Licht, / Von *mir*! Ich mag eure Krone nicht!" (224-5) and prove indifferent to the welfare of the people: "ʟᴀᴘᴀᴋ So laßt ihr uns denn hilflos und verwaist!" (226). This line echoes Kascha's earlier utterance: "Nun aber ist er [Krokus] tot, wir sind verwaist" (179). The sisters are able to overcome their loss—they see their father's death only as it relates to themselves—by resorting to the imaginary dimension, to the prototype of the typical narcissistic relationship of the child before the mirror captivated by its own image, and by shunning the unpleasantness of the external world: "Nutzen und Vorteil zählen, / Aus Wahrheit und Lüge wählen, / Recht erdenken das kein Recht, / Dafür sucht einen Sündenknecht" (220-3).[17] Whereas Krokus's death actually orphaned the sisters, Lapak's exclamation (226) assumes the parental model of the monarchy discussed previously. Krokus, as a signifier of a social system, embodied a means of signification for his subjects. Indeed, they prove unable to function adequately unless the semiotic order is upheld and a new symbolic head appointed.

This scene concludes fittingly with the sisters and their entourage forming a closed circle and donning their black veils after having condescendingly sent away the Wladiken and the people to satisfy their common material needs, "Speis' und Trank," "was sie am meisten lockt" (234-5).

> Nun aber ihr!
> Stellt euch ringsum, senkt eure düstern Schleier,
> Und feiert still und trauernd das Gedächtnis
> Des edlen Manns, der unsern Kreis verließ.
> Nacht um uns und Dunkel,
> Damit in uns es Licht!
>
> (238-43)

Both words and gestures show their concerted bid to blot out the Real Order: they retreat to an introspective, solipsistic realm of inner light in order to deal with the darkness of death. While Krokus may have died, he has not really left their domain, for as we shall ascertain, they still wear his chastity belts as a sign of his continuing control despite his physical absence. This episode also contains accents of the Lord's address to the archangels in the "Prolog im Himmel" from Goethe's *Faust*:

> Doch ihr, die echten Göttersöhne,
> Erfreut euch der lebendig reichen Schöne! . . .
> Und was in schwankender Erscheinung schwebt,
> Befestigt mit dauernden Gedanken.
>
> (344-5; 348-9)

The Lord discriminates between the spiritual, ideal level embodied by a lofty coterie of archangels and the material, real world represented by Mephistopheles. A similar degree of aloofness, an attempt to ignore "wie sich die Menschen plagen" (*Faust* 280) by indulging in metaphysical meditation characterizes both works.

The dramatist has set up the next scene as a contrast. Even though a common darkness ("*Es ist noch dunkel*" [p. 286]) connects the two scenes, the specific visual figuration projects a very different message: "*Primislaus tritt auf, ein weißes Roß am Zügel führend, auf dem Libussa sitzt*" (p. 286). The audience's last view of the two sisters had them trying to exclude physical reality; Libussa now appears in peasant dress in the company of a man and obviously involved in life. "Von ihren theoretisch-spekulativen Schwestern hebt sich Libussa durch ihren praktischen Sinn ab. Sie läßt sich mit der Welt ein" (Geißler, 116). Whereas the sisters veiled themselves (p. 286), she moves openly in the world. (Her veil is part of the bundle on the horse's back.) Primislaus, walking as she rides, pays homage to her—she is literally more exalted (*altus* equals high; cf. his opening salutation: "Du *Hohe*, Herrliche!" [20])—but he leads the way or retains control. Historians have hypothesized that the association of the aristocracy with height to signal social distinction may be derived from the nobleman's affiliation with the horse, which he alone could afford and from whose back he could talk down to the peasant. The aristocrat is the "Er*ober*er" and the peasants "ihm *unter*worfen" (Kautsky, 12). One can ascertain this close rapport between the upper class and the horse in the words used to designate the highborn knight: *eques, Ritter, chevalier, caballero* or cavalier (Kautsky 8). These considerations add to the complications and the extraordinary nature of the budding liaison between Libussa and Primislaus, for in this case the *Ritter* is a female aristocrat and a *Bauer* owns the palfrey. These stage directions also prefigure their relationship in the fifth act: although he portrays himself as her agent and defers to her (1952-8), in actual fact, he supplies the real political direction, (1959-61), institutes a specific policy or goal, and runs the country while she has become a figurehead.

Accentuating his obedience to her word, he once more attempts to elicit the merest vestige of interest on her part as a consequence of her increased obligation to him. As usual, Libussa is curt: "Sei drum bedankt" (246), but again this may signal an effort to disguise her emotional involvement by a terse, businesslike response: she hides behind formality. The audience has just witnessed a scene that ended with the mourning of a "Scheiden," the separation of the living from the dead, and Primislaus raises another variation of the same theme when he asks, "Nun soll ich von dir *scheiden*, dich verlassen, / Dich nie mehr wiedersehn vielleicht?" (247-8); indeed, he resorts to this same verb four times in this episode, three of which occur in the emphatic final position. While this obvious harping upon parting conveys the urgency of his desire to maintain some connection with this unknown woman, it also reflects the general note of separation and disintegration—death being the ultimate dissolution—typical of the tragedy as a whole. In this particular context, a well known French expression comes to mind, one which also ties in with the previous incident: "Partir, c'est mourir un peu." The poem by Edmond Harancourt from which the line is taken goes on to claim, "C'est mourir à ce qu'on aime. / On laisse un peu de soi-même / En toute heure et dans tout lieu."[18] The idea of leaving something of one's self both in the literal (jewel/horse) and figurative sense plays a significant part for both Libussa and Primislaus. The "vielleicht" he tacks on to the end of his question indicates that he is "clutching at straws," anxious for her to make a small concession, anything to keep his hopes alive. During courtship at least, the female enjoys some influence since she can always decline the male's suit.

Libussa shows a willingness to humour him with her succinct concession, "Vielleicht" (248), as it does leave open the possibility of a future reunion. Her response thus emboldens Primislaus to pose his question a second time: "Du bist kein Weib um das man werben könnte?" (249), further proof of his "Beharrlichkeit." He stubbornly persists in his attempt to establish a physical link, maintaining that he would always recognize her, even in the dark—an indirect form of flattery—but "would she recognize him?" (252) On the basis of his acquaintance with her up to this point, he remains understandably unsure of her feelings towards him and thus requests a sign: "Im Dunkel fand ich dich, im Dunkel scheid' ich. / Gib mir ein Zeichen dran du mich erkennst / Wenn ich dich wiederseh'" (253-5). Coming as it does upon the heels of his renewed campaign to obtain permission to court her, this speech underscores by repetition the ominous *Liebestod* prelude to their relationship with its accent upon night and "Scheiden." As both Freud and Lacan point out, "Desire persists as an effect of a primordial absence [the failure of the child to find complete satisfaction] and it therefore indicates that . . . there is something fundamentally impossible about satisfaction itself" (Mitchell, 6). Therefore, the text's persistent allusions to separation, absence, or division suggest the illusory nature of the romantic belief that one sex could ever complement or fulfil the other, the insight of a dramatist who studied women closely but avoided any lasting connection.

Primislaus is the one to insist upon a visible token of commitment, if only implied—in fact the audience knows that he has already acquired his "Zeichen" by stealth—while Libussa fails to see the need: "Es ist nicht nötig" (255). Ostensibly a suitable keepsake will promote her remembrance of him, should their paths cross again, but in practice he wants something concrete as a hold over her, as a reminder of her indebtedness to him. *Die Jüdin* contains a parallel; only the gender roles are reversed. Both Primislaus and Rahel go against the specific will of his/her partner: Libussa declines to provide a memento and the king insists Rahel return the painting. The instigators want to preserve a link to guarantee the eventual resumption of an incipient relationship and to this end choose an object (*Kleinod/Bild*) symbolic of their sexual control over the

queen/king. When Primislaus tries to discover her future reaction to the scenario he has intentionally stagemanaged by stealing her jewel, he does not receive the reassuring response for which he has been fishing: "Bring es hierher, ich werde darnach senden / Und lös' es gern um Gold und jeden Preis" (258-9). She cannot be said to encourage his advances, as she insultingly offers to pay for his services. Out of wounded pride that she could misjudge him so, he retorts abruptly, "Für mich ist Gold kein Preis. So laß uns scheiden!" (260). This is the first of several misunderstandings that cloud their association since both protagonists set little *personal* store by material wealth.[19] His exclamation: "So laß uns scheiden!" registers what he assumes to be an incompatibility, i.e., he can have little respect for someone who covets gold, the *Geldsackgesinnung* more typical of the nineteenth-century middle class, "des Bürgers Hand, des Krämers, Mäklers, / Der allen Wert abwägt nach Goldgewicht" (*Bruderzwist* 1239-40). She underestimates him by supposing he can be bought with gold and likewise he misreads her by assuming she holds wealth in high esteem. The play illustrates how easily misconceptions can arise in the initial stages of a courtship where both parties, being particularly sensitive and thus readily hurt, evince a reluctance to expose their true feelings, to render themselves vulnerable; hence the issue of finding common ground becomes all the more difficult.

Attention now focuses once more upon her belt:

> Nur eine Kette noch, es war dein Gürtel,
> Der unter meiner Retterhand zerstückt,
> Doch füg' ich neu die goldnen Hakenglieder,
> Neig mir dein Haupt und trag den neuen Schmuck.
> *Libussa senkt ihr Haupt, er hängt ihr die Kette um den Hals.*
>
> (264-7)

Primislaus transforms her "Gürtel," symbolic of chastity, into a "Kette." It broke when he seized her—his formulation "Retterhand" again draws attention to his heroic deed—and therefore foreshadows her eventual loss of virginity to him; however, in a figurative sense she has already forgone her innocence because this chance encounter has removed her from her accustomed environment, a change manifested in her peasant costume. He has fashioned the new modification of the belt, a chain, and appropriately so, for he bears much of the responsibility for her becoming a ruler. She will be tied to a new earthly function and its obligations, i.e., the chains of office. Viewed as a "Gnadenkette," a symbol of terrestrial authority, it provides an omen that she will accept the Bohemian crown. When he commands her to lower her head to receive the belt in its new form, she obeys,[20] a visual demonstration of a symbolic subjugation and a sign of her sexual dependence upon him. (The "Kette" performs the identical function in *Die Jüdin*.) In many male-dominated societies, a woman's chastity belongs to the man as the jealously guarded property of the father, the ownership of which he passes on to the husband. (Even today the father gives his daughter in marriage.)

The casting of Libussa in the role of the victim continues in an exchange which, however brief in terms of her participation, still suggests a degree of "Innigkeit" which Lorenz finds lacking in their relationship:

> PRIMISLAUS: So zier' ich dich du Schöne, Hehre, Hohe;
>   Für wen? ich weiβ nicht; ists doch nicht
>   für mich.
>   Und so leb wohl!
> LIBUSSA: Auch du!
>
>   (268-70)

He views his gesture as a mark of his respect, what Griesmeyer calls "[d]as ehrfürchtige Bild des Hohen" (265) (the adjectives "Hehre, Hohe" again highlight the class distinction), but his description also strongly implies the adorning of a sacrificial lamb (another anticipation of the fifth act), here the dressing of a woman before her wedding. The fact that the embellishment is designed to please a man—he regrets not being that fortunate male—again signals her dependent status, i.e., he decorates her not for her own sake but rather for someone else. The anonymous consort remains the main player even if Primislaus cannot be that individual.

His final speech of the scene reminds the audience that all of this takes place at a crossroad, a "Scheideweg von Seligkeit und Jammer" (284), to use Kascha's prophetic phrase from the next sequence:

>   Nur noch drei Schritte.
> Dort teilt, von selber kennbar, sich der Weg
> Und leicht gelangst du wieder zu den Deinen,
> Wenn du den Waldpfad rechts nur sorglich meidest,
> Die du, ein Märchen, kamst, und eine Wahrheit
>   scheidest.
> *Das Pferd leitend*:
> Vertrau dem Pferd, es trägt dich gut und sicher. *Beide ab.*
>
>   (270-75)

Scheiden in the form of *Entscheiden* signifies a decision and the image of the "Scheideweg" has from the earliest times denoted the need to choose one of two options—in the case of Hercules, for instance, either virtue or pleasure[21]—and the choice inevitably proves to be both far reaching and irrevocable. In a very real sense this has already occurred, as the crucial decisions in Libussa's life have been made without her awareness. Her own caring personality is partly to blame: it brought her down into the world to save her father, and Primislaus's unsolicited intrusion and his theft of the jewel will have serious repercussions: she can no longer return "zu den Deinen." The warning to avoid the "Waldpfad" comes too late. The first scene opened in an "*Offn[em] Platz im Walde*" (p. 277), and Primislaus's cottage from which she emerged stands in close proximity to "dieses Waldes Schlünden" (46). Already wearing the attire of this ambience, she has conceded how comfortable she feels in it. She came to him as if from a fairy-tale, i.e., such providential intervention or her rich dress as a fairy queen belongs to the supernatural realm of her remote sisters. The tragedy may be regarded as an ironic, self-reflective text, one consciously singling out its own implausibility, the fantastical dimension or the folklore sources of the tale: the peasant and the princess, the miraculous rescue from the water (Melusine in reverse). But the mythical has become real for him, has become a flesh-and-blood person whom he desires and on whom he wishes to stake a claim. Two lines from *Die Jüdin* play on the same tension and cast additional light on Primislaus's enigmatic pronouncement: in speaking of the Jewish tradition as recorded in the Old Testament, Alphons mentions, "Samt all der Märchenwelt, die Wahrheit auch / Von Kain und Abel, von Rebekkas Klugheit" (495-6). Fairy-tales or myths have yielded a rich store of universal truths or archetypes for literary and psychological enquiry. And finally the gesture of leading the horse and her mounted departure illustrate his continuing control over her fate—the palfrey becomes an extension of Primislaus and his bond to her—and raises the issue of trust: she should have faith in his intent to care for her and should rely on his directions, a further foreshadowing of the last act. Trust or its absence will indeed become an obstacle to their relationship since he has already abused her confidence.

When in the subsequent scene Kascha gives evidence of her sibyllic gift by her reference to Libussa at the crossroads, she also provides evidence of being privy to specific details of the meeting between her sister and Primislaus: "Horch! Spricht ein Mann?" (285); "Allein sie ist begleitet" (286). This device informs the audience that the two scenes are not sequential, but take place simultaneously, thereby enhancing the contrast between them. It is no accident that the text consistently relates the two sisters to their castle, a well established metaphor for a woman's virginity.[22] While the Wladiken and the people force ("*dringen . . . herein*" [p. 282]) their way into the "Vorhof," they never gain admittance to the inner sanctum.

Libussa now reappears: "*Sie hat einen weißen Mantel übergeworfen und ein Federbarett auf dem Kopfe. Wlasta und Dobromila gewaffnet hinter ihr*" (p. 288). Sensing the inappropriateness of her dress, she mantles it. Her conscious desire is to return to her sisters, but under the surface lies indisputable proof that another way of life has touched her. Kascha's visionary eye saw her involved with a man and, interestingly enough, the outward semblance of this entry evokes typically masculine features: the cap with its feather, a notorious phallic symbol associated with the rake, and two armed servants suggest the dominant, aggressive male. She sends the horse back "zu den drei Eichen" (300), instructing the servant to reimburse its owner if he will accept payment; in other words, she still tries to discharge her obligation. But of particular interest is her amazingly succinct summary of what has transpired in her two scenes with the ploughman: "Im Wald verirrt, nicht Wegesspur, noch Führer, / Ein Gießbach wollte sich das Ansehn geben / Als sei er fürchterlich. Da kam mir Hilfe" (305-7). She clearly downplays its importance. "Die Demut," Politzer maintains, "die sie am Ende den Menschen predigen will, ist zu Beginn die Sache dieser Libussa nicht" (309). He assumes that the danger she faced was genuine: "das Sturzwasser, das ihr beinahe den Garaus gemacht hätte" (309). Although unwilling to admit it, she might well have been in jeopardy, but we do not know this with any certainty, especially in view of the dramatist's own comments cited earlier. One could also interpret her account as dictated by modesty: she does not wish to play for effect by overstating the seriousness of the threat. However, what is striking is her failure to furnish any details about her helper and "Führer." Instead she employs an impersonal construction to conceal male assistance which would doubtlessly raise eyebrows in this miniature matriarchy. According to her formulation, the source of help need not even have been a person.

Once Libussa obtains confirmation of Krokus's death, she completes the exposition by filling in the remaining details as to why she left her dying father's side:

> In all der Zeit
> Als ich an seinem Bette saß und wachte,
> Da schwebte vor den Augen des Gemüts,
> Hatt' *ichs* gehört nun, oder wußt' *ichs* sonst,
> Das Bild mir einer Blume, weiß und klein,
> Mit siebenspalt'gem Kelch und schmalen Blättern;
> Die gib dem Vater, *sprachs,* und er genest.
>
> (309-15)

Later in the tragedy in response to Primislaus's riddle, she will assert in words equally applicable to the present anecdote, "Das ist nun wohl des Ostens Blumensprache, / Die träumend redet mit geschloßnem Mund" (1294-5). Female wisdom, "Sophia-Weibliche," achieves, according to Neumann, "als Blüte die höchste sichtbare Form seiner Entfaltung" and remains, in contrast to male abstraction, "an die irdische Grundlage der Wirklichkeit gebunden" (305). At the bed of her father, the eyes of the mind disclosed the truth of the unconscious,[23] the realm of the Other—hence the three instances of the impersonal pronoun "es." This reverie, availing itself of "Blumensprache," focuses on the little white flower with its open, seven-petalled calyx surrounded by narrow leaves. The vessel, cup, or chalice denotes one of the most widespread manifestations of the female archetype, "das alles enthaltende Große Runde" (Neumann, 205). "Von Anbeginn an und bis zu den spätesten Stadien der Entwicklung finden wir dieses archetypische Symbol als Inbegriff des Weiblichen. Die symbolische Grundgleichung Weib = Körper = Gefäß entspricht der vielleicht elementarsten Grunderfahrung der Menschheit vom Weiblichen, in der das Weibliche sich selber erlebt, in der es aber auch vom Männlichen erlebt wird" (Neumann, 51). As Neumann goes on to explain, the experience of woman as the containing vessel has an obvious source: "Die Frau als Körpergefäß ist der natürliche Ausdruck der Erfahrung, daß das Weibliche das Kind in sich trägt, und daß der Mann im Sexualakt 'in' sie 'eingeht'" (Neumann, 54). Libussa's imagery drawn from the unconscious, "die Mutter aller Dinge" (Neumann, 204), features other attributes of the Great Mother. Since the

"Kelch" is an open vessel, it "verbindet den Elementarcharakter des Enthaltens mit dem des Nährens. Dadurch, daß die Symbole dieser Reihe [i.e., Gefäß, Schale, Becher, *Kelch,* Gral] ihrer Natur und Form nach . . . offen sind . . . , ist die Natur des *Gebens,* Spendens und Darreichens betont" (Neumann 57-8). Libussa's nourishing role, later captured in her self-portrait as the gardener—"Was euch die Gärtnerin mit nächster Sorge, / Verteilend hilfreich Naß und Wärm' und Schatten, / Kann nützlich sein, das ist euch ja gewiß" (600-602)—manifests itself already in her desire to minister to her father and to *give* him the means to recover: "Die [the flower] *gib* dem Vater, sprachs, und er genest" (315). "[D]as Lebenselixier [behält] den Charakter des Natursymbols, und das 'höchste Gut' tritt auf als Unsterblichkeits-Kraut [cf. *Libussa kommt zurück, ein Körbchen mit Kräutern tragend"* (p. 279)] oder—Frucht, als Rauschtrank oder als Lebenswasser, als Edelstein oder als Perle, als *Blüte* oder als Kern" (Neumann, 69). Even the location of the sought-for elixir intimates the realm of "die Große Mutter," i.e., "In feuchten *Gründen"* (316) and "Das Tal von Budesch" (317). "Teile dieses Bezirkes [i.e., "Bauch" and "Schoß der Erde"] sind . . . die Symbole von Schlucht, Schlund und Abgrund ebenso wie von *Tal* und *Tiefe,* die in unzähligen Riten und Mythen die Rolle des Schoßes der zu befruchtenden Erdregion spielen" (Neumann 55-6). The number seven also shares this symbolism since it represents the "perfect order, a complete period or cycle" (Cirlot 233) and an important relationship of "Mond-Symbolik" to the underworld: "Mond-Sieben, die archetypische Beziehung zur Erd- und Fruchtbarkeitsgöttin" (Neumann 158). In other words Libussa offers herself vicariously to her father through the blossom which dwells "In feuchten Gründen" (316). This same image with a more explicit but equally illicit sexual connotation occurs in *Die Jüdin* during the king's imaginative invention of a hypothetical seduction: "Und Blumenkelche duften süßen Rausch / Bis nun der günst'ge Augenblick erscheint" (461-2),[24] a scenario replete with erotic allusions. Moreover, folk tradition depicts a woman's chastity as her flower (cf. *Jungfernkranz*) and to deflower a girl is to rob her of her virginity. It follows that Libussa may well be voicing the forbidden urge to sleep with her father—she later confesses that she has sought in vain to find his equal for her mate: "Allein zu Lieb' und Ehe braucht es Zwei; / Und, sag' ichs nur, mein Vater, euer Fürst, / War mir des Mannes ein so würdig Bild, / Daß ich vergebens seines Gleichen suche" (656-9). Therefore, the subsequent reference to "die unfreiwill'ge Schuld" (320) in the same speech in which the white flower surfaces could also bear upon the guilt she feels at this unconscious sexual fantasy: she may even consider her culpable desire as having led to the punishment of his death. Lorenz posits the source of her guilt in her meeting with Primislaus, a delay which may have cost her father's life (38), while Politzer proposes: "Diese Schuld besteht aber nicht darin, daß sie suchte, sondern daß sie sich finden ließ. Ein Etwas in ihr weiß und ahnt auch, daß das Bild des toten Vaters mit dem des vitalen Pflügers in Konflikt geraten ist" (310). It is not so much a conflict as a succession since the latter usurps the vacant role of the former as ruler and possessor of her virginity (jewel).

The text includes a number of possible phallic allusions in support of male dominance. Relatively early in the play, Domaslav, a speaker with a decided sexist outlook, announces the people's need to have a leader who can bear the "Stab, der in Fürst Krokus Händen lag" (204). This sexual symbolism ties in significantly with the general thesis of separation. According to the Freudian/Lacanian model, initially during the phallic phase, the male and female child share the identical sexual history: both have a masculine orientation—the first object of their desire is the mother—and both essential they possess the phallus which the mother wants. The advent of the castration complex "'makes' the girl a girl and the boy a boy, in a division that is both essential and precarious" (Mitchell, 7). The forbidding agent, the one who by his presence as the bearer of the phallus, gives rise to the differentiation and thus separates the sexes into those who have and those who do not have the phallus,[25] is the father, the embodiment of the law. Eagleton summarizes: "The little girl, perceiving that she is inferior because 'castrated,' turns in disillusionment from her similarly 'castrated' mother to the project of seducing the father; but since the project is doomed, she must finally turn back reluctantly to the mother, effect an identification with her, assume her feminine gender role, and unconsciously substitute for the penis which she envies but can never possess a baby, which she desires to receive from the father" (155-6). This same idea of the phallus as the separator underlines the opening speech from Kleist's *Penthesilea*, another nineteenth-century mythical drama dealing with an alleged[26] matriarchy:

> Wenn Mars entrüstet, oder Delius,
> Den Stecken nicht ergreift, der Wolkenrüttler.
> Mit Donnerkeilen nicht dazwischen wettert:
> Tot sinken die Verbißnen heut noch nieder,
> Des einen Zahn im Schlund des anderen.
>
> (7-11)

In Odysseus's assessment the male and female armies will destroy one another unless the masculine gods of the patriarchy intervene. This violent mediation, whether through the rods of Mars or Apollo or the thunderbolts of Zeus, seeks to reestablish male ascendancy through the signifier of masculine sexual superiority and distinction: the phallus. It must restore what the male speaker cannot comprehend—indistinguishable Greek and Amazon warriors locked in mortal combat—to the patriarchal norm by imposing masculine authority. A related but less overtly violent solution holds true for **Libussa** as well.

No sooner does Kascha excuse one of the sisters: "Sag Zwei'n" (325) from the passive task of mourning their father's death than Libussa immediately jumps to the conclusion of a more specific exclusion: "Warum? Wen schließest du nur aus?" (325). Since she instinctively views herself as singled out, her oversensitive reaction points to a bad conscience and, like the concealed clothing, draws attention to what she herself has characterized as "die unfreiwill'ge Schuld" (320): her unavoidable dependence upon a man and her unconscious attraction to him. I generally concur with Wolf-Cirian's analysis: "Libussa, aber, die wahre Tochter ihres irdischen Vaters, stand *immer* im Gegensatz zu ihren Schwestern und empfand diesen wohl oft als stillschweigenden Vorwurf—daher ihr gereiztes Auffahren, als sie sich aus dem Bunde der Schwestern ausgeschlossen wähnte" (251), but fail to detect on what grounds she assumes Libussa "always" stood in opposition to Tetka and Kascha as the text relates only the one previous incident indicative of an attitude contrary to that of her sisters. Once Kascha outlines the specific nature of the separating obligation: "Die, welcher obliegt mehr als ihn Beklagen: / Zu folgen ihm in seiner harten Pflicht" (326-7), the drama has predisposed the audience to cast Libussa as the ideal successor, for her "actions speak louder than words" and her two sisters have already eliminated themselves by their supercilious repudiation of the crown. Even though Libussa's immediate reaction is to decline: "Nehmt ihrs, ich nicht!" (331), this could be construed as an emotional response again dictated by guilty feelings: she has betrayed her loyalty to her father and has sensed being drawn to human society in the person of Primislaus. In addition, one should compare this spontaneous, emotional refusal to those of Kascha and Tetka, which are more extensive, with considerable preamble, giving the impression of a well considered decision (207f).

This episode verifies the extent to which the father continues to exert authority over his daughters even after death: "Doch sähe gern der Vater unvollendet / Was er für dieses dunkle Volk getan? / Und heißt es sein Gedächtnis hoch nicht ehren, / Fortsetzen, wenn auch schwach, was er begann?" (332-5). Here he embodies a sentimental influence: the force of tradition or the burden of obligation to one's parents. One of the daughters cannot escape the unavoidable duty of upholding her father's heritage, and in this sense Libussa becomes his victim at the conscious level as well. "When their major role is to discipline and control, fathers are not unlike supreme beings. They are distant, controlling figures who are removed from biological processes [such as death]" (Sanday 64). This appeal to Krokus's memory does have an effect: "Laßt denn das Los entscheiden" (336), a return to another variation on the *Scheiden* motif. As remarked earlier, *Entscheiden* also implies a division, i.e., the necessity to decide between alternatives, a theme reinforced by Kascha's proposal to allow fate or chance, "das Los," to make the determination (*losen* means "eine vom Menschen unabhängige *Entscheidung* zu erzielen" [*Duden Etymologie* 409]). Her choice of expression may also recall the identical word, but with a different root, used by Primislaus in the opening scene to announce the most portentous separation of the tragedy: "Das [Kleinod] lös' ich los und wahre mirs als Pfand"

(71)—a case of a retrospectively ironic play on words. Both instances of the "los" / "Los" have the potential to sever Libussa's ties to her sisters' realm.

The separation theme continues with Kascha's long speech describing the origin of the belts. "Am Jahrestag von unsrer Mutter *Scheiden*" (339), the father resolved to commemorate her passing by creating the bands featuring the image of both parents: "Ein kostbar Kleinod mit der Eltern Bild" (340). Hence the jewel may be said to reflect the tension between male and female, active and passive, real and ideal, or "Wahrheit" and "Märchen." Another "Scheiden," the death of the father, has brought about the current political crisis, one which requires a decision, *Entscheidung*. But one could argue that yet another "Scheiden" (260), Libussa's parting from Primislaus as she unknowingly stood at a "Scheideweg" (284) between two modes of life, has already made the choice: circumstances largely beyond her control have separated her from her jewel (71), her innocence, and any solidarity with her sisters. The recognition that Krokus had three belts made for three daughters looks back to Lessing's parable of the three rings and poses the question: who wears the true belt, i.e., who best incarnates the will of the father?

Krokus may have conceived of the three belts as an efficient means of keeping his daughters chaste:

> Die Gürtel nun, des Vaters letzte Gabe
> Und geistiges Vermächtnis noch dazu—
> Sprach er doch ja: so oft ihr sie vereint,
> Will ich im Geist bei euch sein und mit Rat—
> Laßt legen uns in diese Opferschale.
>
> (346-50)

Since the belts are only effective if united, the father can thus keep his harem to himself and exclude any other male intruder. To stake his claim, Primislaus transformed the belt, a circle which he broke,[27] into a chain which he placed about Libussa's neck, and as a mark of her subservience, she had to lower her head to receive it. While the belt, a "letzte Gabe," does possess a material existence, as a symbol of a spiritual or intellectual legacy, it also dominates the daughters' minds. Indeed, by the terms of Krokus's testament, to assure continuity they would have to stay together, remain pure, and refuse to permit anyone to come between them. The phrase "mit Rat" further implies their reliance upon the paternal figure: because he intends to counsel them from beyond the grave, they will become a mere extension of his will, having very little, if any, independence. Kascha's formulation may contain another intertextual allusion, this time to the Bible. To prepare the disciples for his departure, Christ declares: "Denn wo zwei oder drei versammelt sind in meinem Namen, da bin ich mitten unter ihnen" (Matthäus 18:20). Just as Christ proved obedient to his father unto death in the garden of Gethsemane, Kascha proposes putting their belts which bear their respective names upon the "Opferschale." In a figurative sense they are to be sacrificed—their virginity represents their most treasured possession—to a god, the memory of their father. As a final manifestation of male tyranny over the female, the text reunites the three belts only at the end of the tragedy to legitimize the reinstatement of the patriarchy through Primislaus after Libussa's self-immolation for the good of the nation.[28] Krokus or the father reasserts his male dominance via his surrogate, the ploughman. Ironically, Kascha inadvertently foretells this development when, in working out the details as to how she plans to conduct the draw, she concludes, "Der Dritten Gürtel wird zum Diadem. / Sie folgt, ob ungern, in die Fürstenwohnung" (354-5). Both sisters obviously prefer remaining in their present domain to the undesirable occupation of governing in the real world with its petty concerns. It is an obligation entailing dependence ("folgen") and domesticity and therefore undertaken with great reluctance only because of what their father expects of them.

At the prospect of the proposed lottery, Libussa removes her *"Barett und Mantel"* to expose her *"Bauerntracht"* (p. 290). Before she may have intentionally hidden her dress but now, at this crucial juncture, she unconsciously reveals what lies beneath and thus may divulge her concealed desire. The abrupt change in visual image also conveys a new orientation: the feathered cap and cloak projected a male tendency while the peasant attire, originating with Primislaus's sister, suggests the domestic, subservient female role, a suitable alteration in view of Kascha's preceding description of the father's despotic regulation of his female offspring. While Tetka draws attention to the strangeness of the costume,[29] Libussa's defensive reaction testifies to the dramatist's remarkable skill at intimating the secret workings of the mind:

> LIBUSSA: *sich betrachtend*: Sonderbar?
> Vergaß ichs doch beinah! Je, gute Tetka,
> Der Zufall kommt und meldet sich nicht an,
> Auftauchend ist er da; und wohl uns, wenn
>　　beim *Scheiden*
> Er äußerlich verändert nur uns läßt.
> Das Kleid ist warm, und also lieb' ich es.
>
> (357-62)

She personifies chance as a male agent who appears without warning—fortuitously or conveniently "Zufall" is masculine—and therefore once more disguises Primislaus's participation in an abstract, impersonal form. Lacan refers to such veiled language as "parole pleine," the symbolic discourse of the unconscious, in this example, the verbal means to present her meeting and her unconscious/conscious attraction to her rescuer. Her image projects a surprisingly assertive portrait of chance/Primislaus—she is still unaware of the theft—while she generally occupied the dominant position in their dialogue and depreciated the extent of her indebtedness to him: she voiced her wishes, if not commands, and he reluctantly obeyed. *Auftauchen* means literally to rise to the surface and thus invokes her sudden emergence from the whirlpool through Primislaus's interference, but in her current formulation, the roles seem to have been reversed—the "er" is the one suddenly to resurface according to strict grammatical usage. However, the audience, in light of its knowledge, is more inclined to interpret the "Auftauchend" as relating directly to the speaker. Also, for the first time, she herself mentions "Scheiden," an echo of Primislaus's leitmotif from their final parting scene where he resorted to it four times (247; 253; 260; 274—a variation, "Trennung," of the same theme occurs four times in the opening scene). Although she couches her thought in a distancing, impersonal proverbial framework, the reappearance of "Scheiden" here reminds the spectator of a very specific separation and invokes Primislaus's continuing presence at the back of her mind.

Unwittingly she concedes that the confrontation with a man and the subsequent parting did in fact touch her deeply. Even though she endeavours to insinuate that the experience had no lasting effect, that there was no emotional commitment on her part, she then goes on to concede that the peasant outfit gives her warmth and that she loves it—the peasant Primislaus earlier expressed the desire to be the clothes that cover her body (13-15)—and by extension this attitude betrays some affection for the man who gave the dress to her. As she later acknowledges, the warmth of the coat, far from remaining "aüβerlich," penetrates "bis zur tiefsten Brust" (403), the seat of human emotion in contrast to the cold, stellar, spiritual regions inhabited by her sisters. The "wohl uns" implies a certain urgency and while she alleges to be unaffected *within* her person, the oblique indications contained in her verbal images and her physical semblance undermine her position by advancing a different message. Moreover, her reference to "Scheiden" in the final position tends to recall Primislaus's parting line: "Die du, ein Märchen, kamst, und eine Wahrheit *scheidest*" (274). A separation evincing the truth cannot but effect the parties involved. Libussa has evolved and her own view of herself is beginning to undergo a transformation. Prior to making this speech, she looks at herself in a new role: "LIBUSSA *sich betrachtend*" (p. 290). She once wore these clothes, feeling comfortable in them and forgetting their existence. The attractive young man from Kleist's essay, "Über das Marionettentheater," comes to mind. After he gazes upon himself in a mirror, he acquires awareness of himself and forfeits his grace, his unconscious unity with nature (2: 243-4). Likewise, as Libussa is about to discover, she cannot return to her original state of innocence.

When the women remove their respective belts, Libussa's sisters, noticing the changes, are curious to learn the details: "Doch wie—?" (363); however, she avoids disclosing any further information.

> LIBUSSA: *das Geschmeide vom Halse nehmend*:
>   Hier ist mein Gürtel.
> TETKA: *ihren Gürtel ablösend*: Hier der meine.
> KASCHA: *Libussens Geschmeide nehmend*:
>   Am Hals?
> LIBUSSA: Und doch er selbst, wie ich dieselbe.
> KASCHA: Das ist dein Gürtel nicht.
> LIBUSSA: Wie wäre das?

> KASCHA: Die Ketten wohl; allein der Mutter Bildnis,
>   Das Mittelkleinod fehlt mit deinem Namen,
>   O Unbesonnene!
>
>   (363-8)

Kasha directs attention to her belt around her neck, the unusual location proclaiming subjugation (a dog or slave collar) and, according to another tradition, pointing to the very nature of her servitude. In Book III of the *Argonautica*, Apollonius Rhodius portrays how passion for Jason gradually invades the unsuspecting Medea through the neck: "[E]ver within anguish tortured her, a smouldering fire through her frame, and about her fine nerves and deep down beneath the nape of the neck where the pain enters keenest, whenever the unwearied Loves direct against the heart their shafts of agony" (247).[30] The object actually testifies against her, exposes the truth of the unconscious and proves her wrong in her claim not to have changed. Since she met Primislaus, she is not the same, and this is graphically verified by her costume and the position of the belt (cf. Roe, *Introduction* 225). Kascha then focuses on the loss of the mother's image and Libussa's name (a person's essence), both of which were inscribed upon the missing jewel. The latter supposedly depicts both parents ("mit der Eltern Bild" [340]) but tellingly Kascha specifies only two female representations which now rest in the hands of a new male.

This incident touches on an issue conducive to the more or less universal subjugation of women, specifically purity versus pollution. Through her association with Primislaus, Libussa has metaphorically forfeited her virginal immaculateness and, contaminated by this contact, she may not return to the undefiled realm of her sisters. The demand for female purity requiring menstruating women in some societies to be ostracized from the rest of the community and thus seriously restricting female activities, obliges Libussa in this instance to enter the real world of male politics. Kascha and Tetka exploit the same dichotomy to justify their self-imposed isolation from crass male concerns (234-5). "Purity beliefs seem to be particularly attractive to women, who very often elaborate the norms concerned with purity, the rules for strict dress and demeanour, modesty, cleanliness, and prudishness, which they use as a device for contrasting their world and the men's world—establishing grounds for order and status among themselves" (Rosaldo 38).

At this precise moment when Kascha makes an issue of the lost stone and Libussa replies in righteous indignation: "Was schmähst du mich?" (368), further evidence of a guilty conscience, Dobromila returns to report her lack of success in finding "jenen Mann" (370). The timing reinforces the enormous influence "that man" has had and will continue to have on Libussa, as she herself begins to recognize: "*Vor sich hin*: Das hat mir Der getan!" (372). On this occasion she states the male gender directly but only to herself and confirms how he has compromised her more than he ever intended. Since his reminder (65-6) will be indirectly responsible for bringing her down into the real world where she will eventually become a "Weib um das man werben könnte" (249), he unwittingly achieves his objective by a fortuitous combination of circumstances. The subsequent exchange only serves to emphasize male domination: "KASCHA Die Nacht im Wald, in Bauerntracht gehüllt, / Verloren deines Vaters Angedenken. / LIBUSSA Mein Vater lebt, ein Lebender, in mir, / So lang ich atme lebt auch sein Gedächtnis" (373-6). Now the gem becomes a memorial to the father rather than to the mother in whose memory Krokus ostensibly fashioned it. Reminiscent of Tetka's earlier remark—"Mir ist er [Krokus] als ein Jüngling auferstanden" (183)—Libussa's confirmation of her father's tyrannical power over her, even after his death, is truer than she realizes. More so than her two sisters, she cannot really lead her own life. In a manner anticipating Kafka's characters, she is guilty, "die unfreiwill'ge Schuld" (320), no matter what she does and despite her best intentions, for she cannot escape the Law, the realm of the father, "des Vaters strenge Rechte" (427). In fact she regards herself as his reincarnation, an ironically accurate assessment, as she will accept his office and comes closest to him in her active, more socially responsible attitude.

To ensure healthy heterosexuality Freud considered it normal for the female child to transfer to her father her initial attachment to her mother: "Aber am Ende der Entwicklung soll der Mann-Vater das neue Liebesobjekt geworden sein, d.h. dem Geschlechtswechsel des Weibes muß ein Wechsel im Geschlecht des Objekts entsprechen" ("Weibliche Sexualität 278). This identification with the father increases her sense of individuation and independence: "Most psychoanalytic and social theorists claim that the mother inevitably represents to her daughter (and son) regression, passivity, dependence, and lack of orientation to reality, whereas the father represents progression, activity, independence, and reality orientation" (Chodorow, 65), the paternal values present to some degree in Libussa relative to her sisters. Consistent with this argument, her mother receives only passing reference throughout the tragedy. At the same time this male orientation may well damage her confidence in her own femininity. The third act will afford numerous signs of the heroine's lack of faith in her ability as a woman to attract Primislaus (cf. 1249).

Libussa's claim, "Mit Einem Wort löst' ich die Rätsel leicht, / Doch würdet ihrs entstellen und verkehren" (379-80), comes across as childish and overly defensive, i.e., I could explain everything but you wouldn't understand, the typical excuse of an adolescent. Anticipating their disapproval, she secretly appreciates how compromising a full revelation of her adventure would seem to her sisters and, as already noted, she has consistently skirted any direct, public reference to her male rescuer. The fear of misrepresentation could just as easily be a cover for genuine misgivings about her own emotional involvement with Primislaus. Only her heart knows for sure, but it will keep its counsel to itself: "Drum halt nur was du weißt, mein sichres Herz!" (381). Can it be trusted? Libussa's dramatic predecessors call into serious doubt the reliability of feel-

ings to judge objectively in such matters. Sappho, Medea, or Hero all delude themselves on an irrational level: the heart is anything but "sicher."

Another pretender has broken the protective ring raised by Krokus to safeguard his harem: "Der Kreis getrennt. Du kannst mit uns nicht losen" (382). Primislaus, the one to harp upon trennen in the opening scene (41; 51; 52; 58) has without specific intent, separated Libussa from any vestige of a unified self and from what her sisters embody. Her petulant reaction to exclusion again appears in a childish light: "Nicht losen? Und wer weiß, ob ichs auch will? / Ein Schritt aus dem Gewohnten, merk' ich wohl, / Er zieht unhaltsam hin auf neue Bahnen, / Nur vorwärts führt das Leben, rückwärts nie" (383-6). In other words, if you won't let me, it doesn't matter since I didn't want to in the first place. Out of wounded pride she is obviously attempting to save face. She took the initial step away from the usual routine when she opted to leave the castle, to descend to the valley, and thus to precipitate the chain of events in which Primislaus came to play such a key role. The universal application she abstracts from her experience conveys the recognition that for good or bad we can only move forward. There is no sense in trying to restore the past and its way of life, although one need not necessarily enthuse about the new political, social and commercial developments change brings in its wake.

As a generalization on the function of will in Grillparzer's works, Papst has observed, "Man is still, as for Schiller, a creature with the distinctive characteristic of willing, but he no longer wills in accordance with genuine moral choice; he wills what he must will, what he is driven to will" (109). Libussa's rationalizations offer a case in point:

> Ich soll nicht losen? Und ich *will* es nicht.
> Wo sind die Männer aus der Czechen Rat?
> Den Vater *will* ich ehren durch die Tat,
> Mögt ihr das Los mit dumpfen Brüten fragen:
> Ich *will* sein Amt und seine Krone tragen.

> (387-91)

Does she really speak for herself or on behalf of her father or does he speak through her? Have not conditions largely created by Primislaus forced her to adopt this stance to salvage her dignity?[31] Four times in the same speech she insists upon her will, her independence to make a decision. Such emphatic insistence begs another question: whom is she really trying to convince? At first she expresses doubt as to whether or not this is her intent: "ob ichs auch will" (383), but only four lines later, she declares, "Und ich will es nicht" (387). Then she maintains that her will is to honour her father by taking over his function. In the cleverly constructed verse: "Den Vater will ich ehren durch die Tat" (389), the father and the deed, traditionally associated with the male, occupy the initial and final emphatic positions respectively while the ego remains caught in the middle. Since at the conscious level she wants to make her dead father proud of her, she will assume *his* office and *his* crown. This formulation strongly implies that she has no intention of ruling in her own right, but as a surrogate, whereas in reality she later contrasts her rule with that of her father, the sign of a rebellion against paternal authority. By progressive stages Grillparzer shows how she gradually convinces herself and claims credit for a decision largely determined by outside pressures: her father's legacy, Primislaus's intervention, and her sisters' disapproval. To quote a relevant line from *Die Jüdin*, "Und unser Wille will oft weil er muß" (428).

The deed, traditionally a male monopoly, she sets opposite her sisters' *vita contemplativa* which she denigrates with the phrase "mit dumpfen Brüten" (390). The latter means to sit on eggs, to incubate or to brood, pejorative connotations to characterize dull, stifling meditation. In this game of "one-upmanship," she now insults her siblings and, partly out of pique, puts down their major preoccupation. The irrationalism underlying this quarrel bears the responsibility in the first instance for her electing to accept the crown while the more ideal motivation, "an irresistible impulse of love [for her people], awoken in her by her encounter with Primislaus" (Papst 113), may simply constitute a rationalization or afterthought. When Kascha allows that her insult may have prompted her sister's petulant reaction: "Wenn ich gekränkt dich mit zu raschem Wort" (393), Libussa nevertheless resolves to abide by her resolve: "Mein Wort ein Fels" (395).

She now consciously distances herself from her sisters: "Denk' ich von heut / Mich wieder hier in *eurer* stillen Wohnung" (396-7), i.e., your dwelling, not mine, and rejects their way of life as being empty, monotonous and remote from human interchange to which she now feels attracted: "Mit Menschen Mensch sein dünkt von heut mir Lust, / Des Mitgefühles Pulse fühl' ich schlagen, / Drum will ich dieser Menschen Krone tragen" (404-6), quite a change of heart from her first impulse: "Nehmt ihrs, ich nicht!" (331). Once more she declares her will but fails to appreciate how circumstances have conspired to induce her to reach this determination. Hence I cannot agree with Politzer's designation, "die freiwillige Fürstin," nor with his contention: "ihr Wunsch geht nach 'Mit'gefühl, wobei das Objekt dieses neu erwachten Gefühls keineswegs der Erwecker, Primislaus, ist, sondern eine Abstraktion, 'diese Menschen,' deren Krone zu tragen sie sich herabläßt" (311). If Primislaus could arouse this emotion, he would also be in part its recipient, as the many underlying signs would seem to indicate: her love of "diese Menschen" could just as easily represent a socially acceptable, anonymous proxy to conceal her affection for "den Menschen" Primislaus, given her lack of contact with other mortals from the outside world. Politzer goes on to argue: "Daß sie in denselben Zeilen gleich zweimal sagen muß, 'mir dünkt,' deutet auf den Abstand zwischen ihr und der Wirklichkeit" (311-2); nonetheless, she felt drawn to the real order when she displayed "Mitgefühl" with her father, a mark of her worthiness to rule, and risked exposing her vulnerability by leaving the safety of the castle. The text does establish distance "zwischen ihr und der Wirklichkeit," but on what basis does she make her value judg-

ments? What has provided Libussa in her ignorance of human affairs, i.e., "Mit Menschen Mensch sein," with a gauge by which to reject her past and look forward to the future? One must posit Primislaus's agency here, however indirect, concretely manifested on stage through the peasant costume, his gift to her, to which she herself alludes with sensual relish: "Dies Kleid es reibt die Haut mit dichtern Fäden / Und weckt die Wärme bis zur tiefsten Brust" (402-3).[32]

After the Wladiken reenter and Domaslav enquires, "Und welche will—?" (411), Libussa retorts, "Hier ist von Wollen nicht" (411), even though she has dwelt upon exercising her will, indeed five times, and now seeks to deny it: "Von Müssen ist die Rede und von Pflicht" (412). This implies the Kantian moral position—absolute obedience to "Pflicht," adherence to an intellectual obligation, to the exclusion of "Neigung," the disavowal of any natural drive or personal interest. She would seem to negate the Schillerian solution of "Neigung zur Pflicht," i.e., freely choosing to do one's moral duty, as for example in Homburg's speech before the assembled court: "Ruhig! Es ist mein unbeugsamer *Wille*! / Ich *will* das heilige Gesetz des Kriegs / Das ich verletzt, im Angesicht des Heers, / Durch einen *freien* Tod verherrlichen!" (*Prinz Friedrich* 1149-52). Whereas her sisters were prepared to let fate decide by drawing lots, she rejects a haphazard selection and, contradicting herself, expresses her will by freely accepting the responsibility: "Und da nun Eine muß aus unsrer Zahl, / So *will* ich und begebe mich der Wahl" (413-4). Grillparzer has nonetheless made it clear that a subjective "Wollen," in which personal interests have a significant share, plays its part not only at the conscious but at the unconscious level as well where emotions such as petulance, pride, and passion influence the will. In her refusal to leave the choice to chance, one out of *three,* she ironically mirrors a similar reluctance in Primislaus: "Und ich / Soll dort [*drei* Eichen] dem Ungefähr dich übergeben, / Das niemals wohl uns mehr zusammenführt?" (37-9). A ruler may strive to eliminate accident in order to build on a more secure, permanent basis,[33] but chance in the form of Primislaus's direct and indirect intervention at several crucial stages (cf. 359-61) has had a discernible effect upon events to date and has contributed to her reaching her current determination. Both Libussa and Homburg rebel against someone (her sisters; the Elector) by "going one better." Put in an embarrassing situation, they endeavour to extricate themselves by "turning the tables" on their accusers and voluntarily assuming the nobler role in an attempt to restore a public image sullied in the eyes of their peers.

In outlining her credentials for the task at hand, Libussa exhibits a vacillating attitude which casts some doubt upon the conviction Lorenz attributes to her: "Dem väterlich-männlichen Staat will sie das Beispiel eines mütterlich-weiblichen entgegensetzen, nicht aus Mangel an autoritativer Stärke, sondern aus Überzeugung" ("Neubewertung" 38-9). The drama includes several signs of her shaken confidence in herself: she admits to a lack of maturity and defers to her sisters' goodness and wisdom (415-6). Since she raises these issues herself, she both anticipates possible criticism and feels the need to defend herself in advance. Tetka and Kascha, being the embodiment of "Hohes" (417), deserve veneration while she, concerned with "irdisch niedres Tun" (418) does not. In this instance, however, she puts her sisters up in order to put them down, suggesting that she has a more practical grasp on reality than her contemplative siblings (a claim borne out by the tragedy) and thus is the more suitable candidate.[34] But perhaps most tellingly, she again acknowledges her dependence upon her father: "Wenn nun des Vaters Geist auf mir beruht, / So fügt sichs wie es kann und, hoff' ich, gut" (421-2). Wanting to follow his spirit, she allows for the possibility of error and of not being able to fill his shoes.

The "Überzeugung" of which Lorenz speaks comes more to the fore once Libussa begins to differentiate her understanding of her rule from that of her father: "Es hielt euch fest des Vaters strenge Rechte / Und beugt' euch in heilsam weises Joch" (427-8). "Freud always insisted that it was the presence or absence of the phallus and *nothing else* [Mitchell's emphasis] that marked the distinction between the sexes" (Mitchell 6) and the father, as the bearer of the phallus, has the authority to lay down the Law, indeed personifies it. Truth, especially when of a disturbing nature, seeks to express itself through the unconscious despite the efforts of the conscious self either to disregard or misconstrue it. "While conscious knowledge is ignorant, the apparently unknown knowledge in the unconscious speaks. It says what it knows, while the subject does not know it" (Benvenuto/Kennedy 166-7). It is therefore no accident that Libussa attempts to deny the paternal law as epitomized in phallic images:

> Ich bin ein Weib und, ob ich es vermöchte,
> So widert mir die starre Härte doch.
> Wollt ihr nun mein als einer Frau gedenken,
> Lenksam dem Zaum, so daß kein Stachel not,
> Will freudig ich die Ruhmesbahn euch lenken,
> Ein überhörtes wär' mein letzt' Gebot.
>
> (429-34)

She insists on her femaleness, in Lacan's view, a lack or omission (*Scheiden*), depicts her regime as necessarily dissimilar, and makes her pronouncements out of self-consciousness of her sex and its perceived limitations in anticipation of the later criticism levelled at her administration. She is on the defensive from the outset. Her concessional clause, "ob ich es [to rule like a man] vermöchte" implies: I could elect to govern in a male manner but I have chosen not to—a "choice" which looks back to her alleged free decision to accept the crown. Now she finds distasteful "die starre Härte" and repudiates the "Stachel," *paroles pleines* intimating the phallus,[35] the real legitimization of her father's rule and his tyrannical control over her. In light of the fact that only eight lines earlier she wished that her father's spirit would lie upon her, she betrays an ambivalent attitude to the male symbol of power: desire/dread, attraction/repulsion. Even if she had it, she would not use it, thus making a virtue out of a necessity.

Since it should come as no surprise that a text depicting a battle of the sexes contains several phallic symbols, there would seem to be some justification for dealing briefly with the concept of penis envy. In Freud's reconstruction of childhood, he claimed that all children, regardless of gender, fault their mother for various self-centred reasons (cf. "Weibliche Sexualität" 283), but the female offspring has to come to terms with a particularly devastating discovery: "Daß sie [the mother] dem Kind kein richtiges Genitale mitgegeben, d.h. es als Weib geboren hat" ("Weibliche Sexualität" 283). Rejecting her mother, the daughter turns to her father. Rarely does Libussa mention her mother (only three times) while she openly and frequently acknowledges her love, admiration, and devotion to her father (sixteen times).

The women's movement obviously could not condone Freud's belief in "die Überlegenheit des Mannes" ("Weibliche Sexualität" 279), his explanation of female psychology as derived essentially from "die Wirkungen des Kastrationskomplexes" ("Weibliche Sexualität" 279), or his generally low opinion of women. Whereas he drew most of his conclusions regarding them from the central function of the phallus, an aspect which Lacan was to adopt, many psychoanalysts now regard these deductions as "ideological mistakes" attributable to his culture and times, but "still allow that his clinical observations of penis envy might be correct" (Chodorow 52). Undertaking to make Freud's theories more compatible with feminist views, Clara Thompson has "stressed the fact that the actual envy of the penis, as such, is not as important in the psychology of women as their envy of the position of the male in society. This position of privilege and alleged superiority is symbolized by the possession of a penis. The owner of this badge of power has special opportunities while those without have more limited possibilities" (51). This more sociological, political revision of Freud provides insight into Libussa's underlying frustration vis-à-vis the male world as embodied by her father, the Wladiken and Primislaus and into her several attempts to downplay or denigrate the phallus in its various guises as prick, rod, hook, or ploughshare.

Politically oriented commentators such as Florack and Lorenz, both of whom see *Libussa* as a reflection of the social and political climate around the 1848 revolution, place considerable emphasis upon this speech. Lorenz, for instance, comments, "Libussa plant, den hierarchischen Staat in einen brüderlichen zu verwandeln" ("Neubewertung" 39), to create a "[d]emokratisch" society ("Neubewertung" 41) with the "Abschaffung von Klassenunterschieden" ("Neubewertung" 39) a position about which Florack harbours justifiable reservations: "Doch wenn Libussas Herrschaft nun 'demokratisch' und dem 'Humanitätsideal der bürgerlichen Aufklärung' verpflichtet genannt wird, übersehen selbst solche Analysen, wie sehr das von Libussa Propagierte und im Stück positiv Gewertete einer Bestätigung ständischer Ordnung gleichkommt" (240). Whether it be in Krokus's patriarchy or in her proposed matriarchy, the basic hierarchy, still firmly entrenched, promotes a distinct *separation* between the ruler and the ruled, "Denn für Libussa gibt es bei aller humanen, brüderlichen Zuwendung doch eine Art Hierarchie" (Geißler 123). Both styles of governing cast the people metaphorically as dependent animals, either to pull the carriage or to bear the rider. The major difference lies only in how the master will treat the animal. In the case of Krokus's tenure, the beast had to place its neck in a yoke, thus forfeiting all personal freedom, i.e., the subjugation (*sub-jugum; Unter-jochung*—under the yoke) of the masses, while for Libussa, the people correspond to a horse responsive to the reins, i.e., still subservient but subject to a kinder, gentler rider who desires to avoid the goad or spur. Libussa will remain true to this model of the benevolent dictator till the end when in her concluding vision she summarizes the nature of her regime by paraphrasing the Christian simile of the good shepherd: "Gehütet hab' ich euch dem Hirten gleich, / Der seine Lämmer treibt auf frische Weide" (2314-5; cf. John 10:11). As a matriarchal figure she intends to function as the "Great Mother" to her immature children: "Dieser 'Größe' des Weiblichen entspricht, daß das Enthaltene, Geschützte und Genährte, Gewärmte und Festgehaltene immer ein Kleines, Wehrloses, ein Anhängendes und auf Leben und Tod dem Großen Weiblichen Ausgeliefertes ist. Nirgends vielleicht ist es so evident, daß ein Menschliches als 'Großes' erfahren werden muß, wie bei der Mutter. Jeder Blick auf einen Säugling und auf ein Kind [cf. the opening of the second act] wiederholt und bestätigt ihre Erscheinung als 'Große Mutter' und als 'Großes Weibliches'" (Neumann 54). But in both Libussa's metaphors, the aristocratic leader takes advantage of the animal either as a means of conveyance or as a source of food and clothing so that the horse or lamb serves the upper class and supports its way of life.

In her defence one should bear in mind that since she wants to be thought of as a woman (431), she takes for granted that her people will act as they have been conditioned to behave towards a woman, that is to say, with love and respect. According to Machiavelli, she makes the mistake of seeking to govern on the basis of love rather than fear (Krokus): "Men have . . . less hesitation in doing an injury to a ruler who inspires affection than one who inspires fear. Affection is a tie like duty which, such is the worthlessness of men, is easily broken by selfish interest; but fear arises out of the imminence of punishment ["Stachel"], and will last a lifetime" (89). She assumes the people will prove amenable to her view of community and will naturally do the right thing by following her example. "Um ihre Unterthanen zu beherrschen, ruft sie deren gute Instinkte an, die, ihrer Überzeugung nach, über die bösen siegen müssen" (Ehrhard 498). By projecting her own ideal of goodness onto others, she sets herself up for a major disappointment. But as her implied threat (434) makes clear, she is not above using emotional blackmail: if you don't live up to my expectations, I'll resign. Since she alone will determine what lies in her people's best interest,[36] she really wants a well trained, tame people that she can lead to its own welfare without any resistance. As Neumann has shown, "das Große Weibliche" is not above

using "den 'Liebesentzug' als Instrument seiner Macht, als Mittel, seine Herrschaft als 'Große Mutter' zu verewigen, um das Geborene nicht zu seiner Selbständigkeit kommen zu lassen" (76).

In the final lines following her description of her model administration, the "Scheiden" motif makes an ominous return: "So wie ich ungern nur von hinnen *scheide*, / Lenkt' ich zurück dann meinen müden Lauf / Und träte bittend zwischen diese Beide; / Ihr nähmet, Schwestern, mich doch wieder auf?" (435-8). She admits her reluctance to leave the secure ethos of her sisters. The use of "Scheiden," recalling its many repetitions by Primislaus at their parting, reminds the audience of his continuing influence at this very moment and reaffirms her loss of "ein so schönes Ganze" (56) as another contradiction emerges. Whereas she asserted earlier in the scene, "Nur vorwärts führt das Leben, rückwärts nie" (386), she is now attempting to keep an escape route open, a retrogressive one, in the event of failure—we learn later that when opposition arises, she does in fact send Wlasta to enquire if her sisters will take her back (1140f). Even before she begins to exercise her rule, she jeopardizes it by allowing for the possibility of defeat and again exposes her lack of confidence. According to the subtext, the symbolic language of the unconscious, this low self-esteem may stem from another lack, that of the phallus.[37]

No sooner does Domaslav offer his class's fealty and that of their subjects than Libussa vehemently rejects and forbids the use of the word "Untertanen" (442): "Dies letzte Wort, es sei von euch verbannt, / In Zukunft herrscht nur Eines hier im Land: / Das kindliche Vertraun" (443-5). With this declaration she seemingly puts herself at odds with a noble society that assumes the privilege to have power over others by its god-given genetic superiority. The basis of her administration, childlike trust, supposes a confidence in the goodness, generosity, and wisdom of the ruler, which leads one to submit voluntarily to the gentle reins of her rule. If one loves someone as a child loves its mother, then one can accept that person as a parent and believe the he or she will always act in one's best interest. This must be seen in contrast to fear as the motivating force: "Der Stab, der in Fürst Krokus Händen lag" (204); one behaves in a certain way because one wishes to avoid the punishment contingent upon failure to comply, the more dependable political expediency if one is to believe Machiavelli. Both scenarios, however, have in common the immaturity of the child, its need to be directed and cared for, a reflection of the dramatist's basic distrust of the masses and democracy: "Erträglich ist der Mensch als Einzelner, / Im Haufen steht die Tierwelt gar zu nah" (*Bruderzwist* 1479-80). As commented upon previously, the negative depiction of an aristocracy availing itself of the same metaphor already discredits in part the feasibility of "das kindliche Vertrauen" (198) as a basis for governing, since it can also serve as a camouflage for self-interest.

In the same speech Libussa raises the real issue: "Und nennt ihrs Macht, / Nennt ihr ein Opfer das sich selbst gebracht, / Die Willkür, die sich allzu frei geschienen / Und, eigner Herrschaft bang, beschloβ zu dienen" (445-8). Ultimately the issue is power and how one rationalizes its tenure by a class or an individual from a particular class. (*Ein Bruderzwist* offers the same political message: "Die Macht ist was sie wollen" [1231].) She leaves the reference to a sacrifice impersonal so that it could refer either to herself or her subjects: she willingly agrees to renounce her personal happiness to assure the welfare of her people, just as they in turn forfeit their political independence by placing their destiny confidently in her hands.[38] "Willkür," meaning arbitrary, if not despotic, rule, would be more characteristic of the aristocracy where there are no controls on the regime other than the good will of the leader. Whereas the nobility once reigned "allzu frei," without being accountable to anyone but itself, it now adopts through her a *noblesse oblige* posture, Frederick the Great's or Joseph II's stance of service to one's country.[39] However, little has really changed since the head of state still answers only to his/her conscience. The phrase "eigner Herrschaft bang," in the sense of fearful *for* its own rule, may allude to the movement within the nobility itself to reform, the so-called "inner revolution," to eliminate the social injustices and bad political practice which made the French Revolution possible. (Arnim and Eichendorff recognized that their class had gone too far and had alienated the people by corrupt, self-serving, arbitrary practices.) Again one could regard Libussa's political manifesto as symptomatic of the author's own conservative attitude: his fear of the masses and their demagogues on the one hand and his resentment of the upper class and their privileges on the other. His compromise in the interest of "Ordnung" would seem to point to an enlightened monarch who would deny self-interest and govern in the name of the common good. In support of this position, Rudolf uses the same metaphors to characterize how he views his relationship to his subjects: "Die Zeit ist schlimm, / Die solche Kinder nährt und braucht des Zügels. / Der Lenker findet sich, wohl auch der Zaum" (*Bruderzwist* 1343-5).[40]

Both the dictatorial and impractical nature of her projected regime surface in her final lines: "Wollt ihr als Brüder leben, eines Sinns, / So nennt mich eure Fürstin und ich bins; / Doch sollt' ich Zwei'n ein zweifach Recht erdenken, / Wollt' eher ich an euch euch selbst als Sklaven schenken" (449-52). While the concepts of universal fraternity and equality, the rejection of a double standard, signal the liberal influence of the French Revolution (Lorenz, "Neubewertung" 39), Libussa nonetheless envisions a uniformity or conformity of mind, i.e., a harmony of attitude synonymous with her own outlook, and as the next act will verify, her desire for unity fails to accommodate the practical demands and diversity of the real world. To achieve her goal she is not above resorting yet again to emotional blackmail: "Allein vergäβt ihr was uns Allen frommt, / . . . / Da Diese hier [her sisters] den Rücktritt mir versagen, / So ging' ich hin es meinem Vater klagen" (454-6). In fact her sisters did not explicitly forbid her return: "Wenn du's noch kannst, von Irdischem umnachtet" (439), for they foresaw the potential problem in her, while she chooses to blame them. What she is saying amounts

to, in Politzer's apt formulation, a "Selbstmorddrohung" (313): if you don't meet my ideal expectations and live together in harmonious brotherhood, I will die and my death will be upon your head—both a threat and a prophecy as it turns out. If this experiment, the matriarchy, fails, it will destroy her; she will have no one to turn to since her sisters have repudiated her. By implication she here closely associates her own death with that of her father—the mother is once more conspicuous by her absence—and by so doing she again combines Eros and Thanatos.

Critics have interpreted the Libussa of the first act as being forceful and resolute in contrast to the last act, but the text does furnish several indications of a lack of confidence in herself and a dependence upon a heritage in which her late father's influence still holds sway. Her commands to her followers: "Ihr Mädchen mir voraus, und stoβt ins Horn, / Bis jetzt mir nächst, steht billig ihr nun vorn" (459-60), while anticipating the central role of females in her administration, also suggest that she needs her warrior women to shield her (cf. the fourth act) and that she still counts upon her past life for support. "Und so, gehobnen Haupts, mit furchtlos offnen Blicken, / Entgegen kühn den kommenden Geschicken" (461-2). As if to contradict this verbally bold exit, her sisters and their attendants have the final say, a not particularly reassuring appraisal: "Ich [Tetka] bedaure sie, / Sie wirds bereun, und früher als sie denkt" (464-5). In addition, whereas she proposes marching fearlessly towards whatever the fates have in store, their emissaries, the stars, announce a different message: "Die Jungfrau blinkt, doch nein, / Ich irrte mich, es ist des Löwen Macht, / Der auf sein Böhmen schaut" (475-7). The lion, belonging to "den Tieren der Sonne [i.e., the male god]" (Neumann 207) and hence signifying masculine sexuality, is in the ascendant (Primislaus), not the virgin (Libussa) who has symbolically lost her virginity to the lion.[41] Similarly, in the last line of the act: "dem Tag weicht die Nacht!" (478), the female night succumbs to the masculine day. These two ominously mantic nocturnal images reinforce what the text has implied more or less consistently throughout the first act: the dominance of the male (father/suitor) over the female (mother/daughter).

Act one opens upon a scene of spatial disjunction, the female inside the cottage and the male outside, an arrangement indicative of the opposition between an inner and outer orientation. At first sight, Libussa would seem to be in charge: she insists upon her independence and refuses to acknowledge a debt of gratitude or at least downplays its significance. Continually denying Primislaus, she issues the orders and he reluctantly obeys. When he privately speaks of his female guest as an object and stakes his claim to her person, he exposes his patriarchal bias. There are, however, indications of a lack of confidence in both of these strong willed protagonists. Libussa does not feel comfortable in her new role as monarch as she attempts to keep an escape route open and actually allows for her own eventual failure. Primislaus likewise shows signs of insecurity, but in his case they stem from his preoccupation with the social discrepancy which puts him at a distinct disadvantage.

The basic problem comes down to the issue of *Scheiden* in its many manifestations. The separation between an aristocrat and a ploughman, between high and low, the dramatist captures in the contrast between *Schleier* and *Bauerntracht*: the aloof, secret, ideal realm of the sisters, the *vita contemplativa,* versus the intimate, open, natural world of the peasant, the *vita activa.* Although Primislaus feels drawn to Libussa the woman, Libussa the queen raises a seemingly insurmountable social barrier and hence the *Standesproblematik* does put considerable pressure on their relationship by complicating the love interest. As "Getrennt[e]" (41) their paths and ultimate destinations may frequently diverge, but they still have much in common, above all a mutual physical attraction. The love story, a struggle for dominance, illustrates the sensitivity of lovers in the early stages of a liaison, as disclosed in their extreme reluctance to expose their vulnerability, another source of alienation leading to several misunderstandings.

A major portion of the first act concentrates upon the leave-taking/*Scheiden* between Libussa and her rescuer, what turns out to be a parting from a whole way of life, a separation which takes place during the night at the passing/*Scheiden* of Krokus. Therefore, the love interest develops concurrently with the death of the nonappearing major player, while the heroine wears the clothing of a dearly beloved, departed sister, an ominous confluence of love and death. Such references to absence or division point to the illusory nature of the romantic belief that one sex could ever fulfil the other, for while Eros strives for union—"In keinem anderen Falle [auf der Höhe eines Liebesverhältnisses] verrät der Eros so deutlich den Kern seines Wesens, die Absicht, aus mehreren eines zu machen . . . ." (*Das Unbehagen* 237)—Thanatos seeks disintegration: "Infolge dieser primären Feindseligkeit [i.e., "Aggressionsneigung" attributable to Thanatos] der Menschen gegeneinander ist die Kulturgesellschaft beständig vom Zerfall bedroht" (*Das Unbehagen* 241).

A crucial *Entscheidung* at a "Scheideweg" (284) brings about a far-reaching separation for Libussa. Once she resolved to descend to the valley in aid of her father and leave the secure ethos of her sisters' domain, she set a process in motion whereby, without her knowledge, her father's legacy, Primislaus's intervention, and her sisters' disapproval largely determine all the irreversible life choices made during this act. Her "Vaters Scheiden" (887) gives rise to the current political crisis and the need for an *Entscheidung* through "losen" (382), i.e., allowing fate to decide among three alternatives, a scenario culminating in Libussa's severing her ties to Kascha and Tetka: "Der Kreis getrennt" (382).

The two central male characters, Krokus and his successor, Primislaus, share the role of the separator. As the bearer of the "Stab" (204) or "Stachel" (432), Krokus enjoyed the male right to rule by virtue of his sexual authority. The phallus separates male from female, ruler from ruled. Unconsciously Libussa betrays the desire to offer herself, her flower, to him. At the anniversary of his wife's

death/"Scheiden" (339), he gave each of his three daughters what amounts to a chastity belt as a means to isolate them from normal human intercourse and thus to keep them to himself. His memory, the burden of obligation and tradition, dominates Libussa (375-6) and is instrumental in her decision to accept his crown. However, the text also suggests some sexual ambiguity in terms of strict gender stereotypes, since Libussa appears in male attire (p. 288) followed by armed Amazons. Furthermore her public proclamation also implies a limited rebellion against "des Vaters strenge Rechte" (427), the rule of the phallus, as she outlines the kinder, gentler disposition of her proposed autocratic regime in which she hopes to perform a maternal function vis-à-vis obedient, grateful children. In other words she perpetuates the separation practised by her father while vindicating her rule as being based upon voluntary submission to and trust in her benevolent wisdom.

Taking over where Krokus left off, Primislaus separates Libussa from her jewel, a symbolic rape, and, so doing, bears the indirect responsibility for bringing her down permanently to the real world and removing her from the circle of her sisters. He also parts the chain, "ein so schönes Ganze" (56), shattering the illusion of harmony within herself and threatening her sense of identity with nature. Whereas the first act initiates the contest of wills so integral to the dramatic interest of the next three acts, it also intimates the foregone conclusion. Primislaus's final portentous gesture of the opening act is to place the chain about Libussa's neck: *"Libussa senkt ihr Haupt, er hängt ihr die Kette um den Hals"* (p. 287), a symbolic subjugation to signal the inevitable dominance of the male (father/suitor/husband) over the female (mother/daughter/wife) as substantiated in the last act.

Notes

1. Cf. Sanday 110-11.

2. Yates overlooks this change in mood when he claims, "In his wooing of Libussa, as in his political attitudes, Primislaus is the voice of calculating intellect" (257-8).

3. Cf. "Versteht man den zerbrochenen, des zentralen Kleinods beraubten Gürtel und den unbrauchbar gewordenen Schleier als symbolisch für den Verlust der jungfräulichen Unberührtheit einer intellektuell und rangsmäßig höheren Frau an einen niederen Mann, so tritt zu dem Motiv der Schändung auch das der Degradierung" (Lorenz, "Neubewertung" 37).

4. Kautsky points out how aristocratic racism led its adherents to define noble features as good and beautiful while the conquered people were considered inferior and ugly: "Hinweise auf 'Zucht,' 'edles Blut' und 'hohe Geburt' und überhaupt die Vorstellung der Aristokratie als einer erblichen Klasse—alle diese Dinge sind Ausdruck des aristokratischen Anspruchs auf ihre biologische Besonderheit" (12).

5. As a ploughman Primislaus belongs to the lower class, but clearly he is not an average poor farmer

(cf. 1006-1014), and many of the views he expresses, especially in the last act, have more to do with the middle-class economic and political values of the nineteenth century. Cf. Florack 238-54.

6. Cf. "[B]enefits oblige; and obligation is thraldome; and unrequitable obligation, perpetual thraldome" (Thomas Hobbes 162).

7. Cf. "Dem Zufall dank' ich [Primislaus] nichts, noch eines Menschen Gnade" (1377). Several *allegedly* rationally oriented male rulers of the nineteenth century see chance as inimical to their rule and thus strive through careful planning to eliminate its influence, usually to no avail. For example, the Elector from Kleist's *Prinz Friedrich von Homburg* declares publicly, "Doch wär er [der Sieg] zehnmal größer, das entschuldigt / Den nicht, durch den der *Zufall* mir ihn schenkt: / Mehr Schlachten noch, als die, hab ich zu kämpfen, / Und will, daß dem *Gesetz* Gehorsam sei" (1: 731-4). Subsequent references to this play will appear in the text. The Elector's insistence upon the law also anticipates Primislaus's position.

8. Cf. "Obgleich sie sichs nicht gestehen will, fühlt sie eine Neigung zu dem Mann, der sie gerettet hat" (Ehrhard 497). Grillparzer demonstrates his insight and skill as a psychologist of love by the subtlety with which he suggests the incipient attraction felt by both parties.

9. Early in Grillparzer's conception of the tragedy, he viewed the belt in this fashion: "SCHWESTERN Weh, weh! Verletzt das Zeichen jungfräulicher Zucht!" (Quoted in Bachmaier 721).

10. See also Politzer 314 and Lorenz, "Neubewertung" 37.

11. Cf. "When she refuses to reveal her identity, he steals a jewel from the chain she wears around her waist and keeps it as a reminder of the encounter. Certain critics have chosen to see this as symbolic of Libussa's loss of virginity the night before, but if that is the case, then her behaviour shows none of the signs that reveal the change in Hero's character after her first night with Leander" (Roe, *An Introduction* 225). First of all, Primislaus never asks for her name; she never offers to supply it. He never reveals his identity; she never requests it. According to a folk tradition, to know a person's name is to have power over him/her. Secondly it is not just *a* jewel but *the* jewel with a strong personal value which he recognizes and which he plans to exploit as a means to ensure a reunion and to remind her of her debt to him. Finally, although no actual rape took place—the text makes this clear—all the signs of a symbolic violation, a loss of innocence, are present.

12. In view of Primislaus's two references to her body, the removal of her veil and her superior attractiveness vis-à-vis his sister, a rather blunt quotation from Lacan comes to mind: "The 'beauty' of [a woman's] body is the veil covering her genitals" (quoted in Benvenuto/Kennedy 193).

13. As an indication that Primislaus has had an effect on Libussa, Roe points out, "She almost forgets the herbs that were the reason for her expedition" (Introduction 225).

14. One of Dobromila's sententious observations deserves some comment: "Ach, die Künst, / Sie endet auch, oft eh man noch am Ende" (88-9). While it refers specifically to the sisters' secret practices, taken out of context, it could just as easily relate to the dramatist's fear of losing his talent with the approach of old age, the apprehension that his inspiration was abandoning him.

15. Grillparzer employs the same device in *Ein Bruderzwist* with a similar message (398f).

16. Hence I am in partial agreement with Florack's view: "Doch wenn Libussas Herrschaft nun 'demokratisch' und dem 'Humanitätsideal der bürgerlichen Aufklärung' verpflichtet genannt wird, übersehen selbst solche Analysen, wie sehr das von Libussa Propagierte und im Stück positiv Gewertete einer Bestätigung ständischer Ordnung gleichkommt" (240). I say "partial" because aspects of Libussa's position are in fact indebted to the "Humanitätsideal der bürgerlichen Aufklärung" such as her faith in the essential goodness of the individual: "Der Mensch ist gut" (2458).

17. Tetka does provide additional evidence of her prophetic gift as she here outlines quite accurately the emerging values of the nineteenth-century commercial middle class as championed by Primislaus.

18. Quoted in Dupré (ed.), *Encyclopédie des Citations* 153.

19. Unlike Klesel, who does not deny his desire to line his pockets "von den Schätzen dieser ird' schen Welt" (2502), Primislaus does not seek to acquire wealth for his own individual benefit but sees it rather as a useful tool to improve the material lot of the people: "LIBUSSA So achtest du das Gold? PRIMISLAUS Ich nicht, doch Andre, / Und Andern eben bieten wir es dar. / So schafft uns Tausch was hier noch etwa fehlt" (2054-6). Beriger recognized this back in 1927: "Reichtum und Macht, die Ottokar verlocken, begehrt [Primislaus] nicht" (122). However, Beriger failed to appreciate the cunning tactics employed by the ploughman to extend his power over Libussa.

20. Hock detects a more practical ulterior motive in this gesture: "Schlau verbirgt er das Fehlen des Gliedes mit dem Umhängen der Kette" (455).

21. Keller parodies the motif of the "Jüngling am Scheidewege" in *Kleider machen Leute,* where Strapinski must decide between "Glück, Genuß und Verschuldung" or "Arbeit, Entbehrung, Armut, Dunkelheit . . . aber auch ein gutes Gewissen" (435). Robert

Frost's poem "The Road Not Taken" would be a more contemporary interpretation.

22. Other examples include the soldiers' chorus from *Faust* (884-902), Schiller's *Maria Stuart* (2: 1083-85) or Kleist's *Die Marquise von O . . .* (2: 114).

23. Cf. "Was dieses 'es' ist, das da spricht, wird nicht verraten; aber es ist vag und weitgespannt genug, um uns glauben zu lassen, daß die Blume mit dem folklorischen siebenfältigen Kelch ihrem Unbewußtsein entwachsen ist" (Politzer 309-10).

24. As a further example Kleist uses a simile with a similar implied erotic message in *Das Käthchen von Heilbronn* where Strahl comments in reference to the heroine's complete surrender to himself: "Mir, dessen Blick du da liegst, wie die Rose, / Die ihren jungen Kelch dem Licht [Strahl, meaning a ray of light, is a phallic symbol] erschloß?" (470-1). I have dealt with this symbolism more extensively in *Kleist's Aristocratic Heritage*, pp. 25-6 and pp. 114-15.

25. The phallic phase concludes with the sight of the penis which has an immediate effect upon the girl: "She makes her judgment and her decision in a flash. She has seen it and known that she is without it and wants to have it" (quoted in Lacan, *Feminine Sexuality* 102).

26. This proviso is necessary since the Amazons acknowledge as their head of state the male god Mars; indeed, they refer to themselves as "Mars' reine Töchter" (2602). Krokus, I shall argue, performs a comparable function in *Libussa*.

27. Similarly Wotan places a ring of fire, a male element, around his daughter Brünnhilde to protect her from unwanted suitors.

28. Cf. "Eine deutliche Anspielung auf Passion und Opfer Christi beschließt das Drama" (Florack 252).

29. Cf. "Das Kleid, die Bauerntracht, symbolisiert die Berührung mit dem wahren Leben, das da außerhalb der Ringmauern des Schlosses brandet: eine fremde Macht nimmt von ihr Besitz und scheidet sie immer mehr von ihren Schwestern" (Wolf-Cirian 251).

30. Cf. "Brannte nicht in dem Kusse, der er auf meinen entblößten Nacken drückte, die ganze Fackel der Liebe?" Heinrich Wilhelm von Gerstenberg (quoted in Grimm 13: 241).

31. Politzer also sees her as reacting to outside pressures: "Das Fehlen des Kleinods in Libussas Gürtel macht sie dann zur Ausgestoßenen, die in einer ebenso stolzen wie irrationalen Reflexbewegung die Krone als Zeichen ihres Andersseins akzeptiert. Als Symbol aber schließt das fehlende Juwel nicht nur das Anderssein, sondern auch den Identitätsverlust Libussas mit sich ein" (315). One could argue, however, that her father has largely determined her identity, although she does show evidence of having a more independent will than her two sisters.

32. Cf. "Durch die erste Begegnung mit Primislaus ist das ganze Wesen Libussas so erregt, erwärmt, von süßen Vorahnungen eines neuen Lebens erfüllt, daß sie wesentlich aus dieser Stimmung heraus den Entschluß faßt, nach der Krone zu greifen" (Volkelt 67); or, as Ehrhardt has put it, "Ihr Zusammentreffen mit der Menschheit, die ihr im Primislaus' Gestalt erschien, macht sie geneigt, den Bitten der Wladiken Gehör zu schenken, daß des Fürsten Krokus Macht auf eine seiner Töchter übergehe" (497).

33. Cf. "Den Sieg nicht mag ich [Kurfürst], der, ein Kind des Zufalls, / Mir von der Bank fällt; das Gesetz will ich, / Die Mutter meiner Krone, aufrecht halten, / Die ein Geschlecht von Siegen mir erzeugt!" (*Prinz Friedrich* 1566-9).

34. Libussa's statement, "Doch handelt sichs um irdisch niedres Tun, / Wo zu viel Einsicht schädlich dem Vollbringen. / Fernsichtigkeit geht fehl in nahen Dingen" (418-20), could readily serve as a summary of Rudolf's dilemma in *Ein Bruderzwist*.

35. Cf. "[F]or Lacan all of our discourse is in a sense a slip of the tongue: if the process of language is as slippery and ambiguous as he suggests, we can never mean precisely what we say and never say precisely what we mean" (Eagleton 169). Grimm's *Wörterbuch* implies this sexual undercurrent when it alludes to "hitzige stacheln des fleisches, der geilheit" (17: 388).

36. Florack reaches essentially the same conclusion but as a result of her analysis of the second act: "Libussas Staat [beruht] doch darauf, daß ihr Wille als Norm akzeptiert wird" (246). Although Libussa claims in theory to have based her rule on "Vernunft" (979), Geißler calls it "ihre Art Vernunft" (118), for what it really amounts to is an intuitiveness or spontaneity based more on inspiration, instinct, or feeling. Beriger, in my view, comes closer, when he calls her reign a "Gefühlsherrschaft" (114).

37. "Following Freud, Lacan maintained that sexual difference is inscribed in language only in relation to the phallus; the other sex is such, only because it does not have the phallus" (Benvenuto/Kennedy 189).

38. But as Gisela Stein and before her Emil Reich (1898) observed, benevolent monarchy can easily become self-serving tyranny: "that idyllic regime, where the best thing is done more because it meets the wishes of the princess than because it really is the best, bears the germ of the worst despotism within it in case of a change in the ruler's sentiments" (Stein 167-8).

39. Cf. "Daß Libussa als erste Dienerin ihres Staats den 'Typus des idealen aufgeklärten Fürsten' repräsentiert, bemerkt [Gerd] Müller zu Recht" (Florack 245).

40. Many commentators have remarked on the similarities between Libussa and Rudolf II. One of the earli-

est comparisons of the two reluctant rulers occurs in Volkelt's 1888 study (61).

41. Cf. "*Jungfrau /*Libussa zugeordnetes Sternzeichen" and "*Lowen]* Wappentier Böhmens, Primislaus zugeordnet" (Bachmaier 749).

Works Cited

Alker, Ernst. *Franz Grillparzer: Ein Kampf um Leben und Kunst. Beiträge zur deutschen Literaturwissenschaft,* 36. Marburg: N.G. Elwert 1930.

Arendt, Hannah. "The Crisis in Culture: its Social and its Political Significance." In *Between Past and Future: Six Exercises in Political Thought,* 197-226. London: Faber and Faber 1961.

Bachmaier, Helmut. "Kommentar" to *Franz Grillparzer. Werke,* ed. H. Bachmaier. Vol. 3. Frankfurt am Main: Deutscher Klassiker 1987.

Bachofen, Johann Jakob. *Das Mutterrecht.* In *Gesammelte Werke,* ed. Karl Mueli. Vol. 2. Basel: Benno Schwabe 1948.

Backmann, Reinhold. "Grillparzers *Libussa.*" *Jahrbuch der Grillparzer-Gesellschaft* (Neue Folge) 2 (1942): 22-47.

Bakan, David. *The Duality of Human Existence.* Chicago: Rand McNally 1966.

Beauvoir, Simone de. *Le deuxième sexe.* Paris: Gallimard 1949.

Benvenuto, Brice and Kennedy, Roger. *The Works of Jacques Lacan. An Introduction.* New York: St. Martin 1986.

Beriger, Leonard. *Grillparzers Persönlichkeit in seinem Werk.* Zurich, Leipzig: Münster-Presse 1928.

Bible. King James Version. London, New York: Eyre and Spottiswoode, Harper & Brothers, no date.

Borchmeyer, Dieter. "Franz Grillparzer: *Die Jüdin von Toledo.*" In *Deutsche Dramen,* ed. Harro Müller-Michaels, 200-238. Vol. 1 and 2. Königstein: Athenäum 1981.

Brecht, Bertolt. *Gesammelte Werke in 20 Bänden.* Frankfurt am Main: Suhrkamp 1967.

Büchner, Georg. *Sämtliche Werke und Briefe,* ed. Werner R. Lehmann, Vol. 1. Munich: Hanser 1979.

Chodorow, Nancy. "Family Structure and Feminine Personality." In *Women, Culture and Society,* ed. Michelle Zimbalist Rosaldo and Louise Lamphere, 43-66. Stanford: Stanford U.P. 1974.

Cirlot, J. E. *A Dictionary of Symbols.* New York: Vail-Ballou 1981.

Collier, Jane Fishburne. "Women in Politics." In *Women, Culture and Society,* ed. Michelle Zimbalist Rosaldo and Louise Lamphere, 89-96. Stanford: Stanford U.P. 1974.

Dotzler, Bernard J. "'Seht doch wie ihr vor Eifer schäumet . . .' Zum männlichen Diskurs über Weiblichkeit um 1800." *Jahrbuch der deutschen Schillergesellschaft* 30 (1986): 339-82.

Duden. Etymologie, ed. Paul Grebe. Vol. 7. Mannheim: Duden 1963.

Dunham, T. C. "The Circle Image in Grillparzer's *Libussa.*" *Germanic Review* 36 (1961): 125-36.

Dupré, P. (ed.). *Encyclopédie des Citations.* Paris: Editions de Trévice 1959.

Eagleton, Terry. *Literary Theory. An Introduction.* Minneapolis: University of Minnesota Press 1987.

Ehrhard, August. *Franz Grillparzer. Sein Leben und seine Werke.* Munich: C. H. Beck'sche Verlagsbuchhandlung 1902.

Fichte, Johann Gottlieb. *Grundlage des Naturrechts nach Principien der Wissenschaftslehre. Zweiter Theil oder angewandtes Naturrecht.* In J. G. Fichte. *Gesamtausgabe der Bayerischen Akademie.* Vols. 1, 4, ed. Reinhard Lauth and Hans Gliwitzky. Stuttgart: Friedrich Fromm 1970.

Florack, Ruth. "Nachruf auf die Landesmutter oder Vom unaufhaltsamen Aufstieg des Bürgerkönigs." In *Gerettete Ordnung. Grillparzers Dramen,* ed. Bernhard Budde and Ulrich Schmidt, 238-54. Frankfurt am Main, New York, Paris: Lang 1987.

Freud, Sigmund. "Das Ich und das Es." *Studienausgabe,* 273-330. Vol. 3. Frankfurt am Main: Fischer 1977.

———"Jenseits des Lustprinzips." *Studienausgabe,* 213-72. Vol. 3. Frankfurt am Main: Fischer 1977.

———"Über die weibliche Sexualität." *Studienausgabe,* 273-92. Vol. 5. Frankfurt am Main: Fischer 1977.

———*Das Unbehagen in der Kultur. Studienausgabe,* 191-270. Vol. 9. Frankfurt am Main: Fischer 1977.

———"Einige Charaktertypen aus der psychoanalytischen Arbeit." *Studienausgabe,* 229-53. Vol. 10. Frankfurt am Main: Fischer 1977.

Geißler, Rolf. *Ein Dichter der letzten Dinge. Grillparzer heute.* Vienna: Braumüller 1987.

Goethe, Johann Wolfgang von. *Faust.* In *Goethes Werke,* ed. Erich Trunz. Vol. 3. Hamburg: Christian Wegner 1962.

Griesmeyer, Norbert. *Das Bild des Partners in Grillparzers Dramen. Studien zum Verhältnis ihrer sprachkünstlerischen Gestaltung.* Wiener Arbeiten zur deutschen Literatur 3. Stuttgart, Vienna: Wilhelm Braumüller 1972.

Grillparzer, Franz. *Sämtliche Werke. Ausgewählte Briefe, Gespräche, Berichte.* Ed. Peter Frank and Karl Pörnbacher. 4 vols. Munich: Hanser 1964.

———*Werke.* ed. Helmut Bachmaier. Vols. 2 and 3. Frankfurt am Main: Deutscher Klassiker 1987.

Grimm, Jacob and Wilhelm. *Deutsches Wörterbuch.* 33 vols. Munich: DTV 1984.

Harancourt, Edmond. Poem quoted in Dupré, P. (ed.), *Encyclopédie des Citations*.

Hegel, Georg W. F. *Grundlinien der Philosophie des Rechts oder Naturrecht und Staatswissenschaft im Grundrisse*. In *Werke*, ed. Eva Moldenhauer and Karl Markus Michel. Vol. 7. Frankfurt am Main: Suhrkamp 1986.

Hesse, Hermann. *Der Steppenwolf*. Frankfurt am Main: Suhrkamp 1969.

Hobbes, Thomas. *Leviathan*. Harmondsworth: Penguin 1968.

Hock, Erich. "Grillparzer. *Libussa*." In *Das deutsche Drama vom Barock bis zur Gegenwart*, ed. Benno von Wiese, 451-74. Vol. 1. Düsseldorf: Bagel 1958.

Hoffmann, Volker. "Elisa und Robert oder das Weib und der Mann, wie sie sein sollten. Anmerkungen zur Geschlechtercharakteristik der Goethezeit." In *Klassik und Moderne. Die Weimarer Klassik als historisches Ereignis und Herausforderung im kulturgeschichtlichen Prozeß*. Walter Müller-Seidel zum 65. Geburtstag. ed, Karl Richter and Jörg Schönert, 80-97. Stuttgart: Metzler 1983.

Jeffrey, David Lyle (general editor). *A Dictionary of Biblical Tradition in English Literature*. Grand Rapids, Michigan: William B. Eerdmans Publishing Co. 1992.

Kaiser, Joachim. *Grillparzers dramatischer Stil*. Munich: Hanser 1961.

Kautsky, John H. "Funktionen und Werte des Adels." In *Legitimationskrisen des deutschen Adels 1200-1800*, ed. Uwe Hohendahl and Paul Michael Lützeler, 1-16. Stuttgart: Metzler 1979.

Keller, Gottfried. *Gottfried Keller. Werke*, ed. Jonas Fränkel and Karl Helbling. Vol. 1. Zurich: Atlantis 1951.

Kleist, Heinrich von. *Sämtliche Werke und Briefe*, ed. Helmut Sembdner. 2 vols. Munich: Hanser 1984.

Lacan, Jacques. *Feminine Sexuality. Jacques Lacan and the école freudienne*, ed. Juliet Mitchell and Jacqueline Rose, trans. Jacqueline Rose. London and Basingstoke: Macmillan 1982.

Lessing, Gotthold Ephraim. *Nathan der Weise*. In *Sämtliche Schriften*, ed. Karl Lachmann, vol. 3. Stuttgart: G. J. Göschen'sche Verlagshandlung 1887.

Lorenz, Dagmar C. G. "Grillparzers *Libussa*: Eine Neubewertung." *Jahrbuch der Grillparzer-Gesellschaft* 14/3 (1980): 33-47.

————"Frau und Weiblichkeit bei Grillparzer." In *Der widerspenstigen Zähmung*. ed. Sylvia Wallinger and Monika Jonas, 201-16. Innsbruck: Institut für Germanistik 1986.

————*Grillparzer. Dichter des sozialen Konflikts*. Vienna, Cologne, Graz: Hermann Böhlaus Nachf. 1986.

Luban, David. "Some Greek Trials: Order and Justice in Homer, Hesiod, Aeschylus and Plato." *Tennessee Law Review* 54 (1987): 279-325.

Machiavelli, Niccolò. *The Ruler (II Principe)*. Trans. Peter Rodd. London: The Bodley Head 1954.

Mitchell, Juliet. "Introduction I" to *Feminine Sexuality. Jacques Lacan and the école freudienne*, ed. Juliet Mitchell and Jacqueline Rose. London and Basingstoke: Macmillan 1982.

Müller, Gerd. "Bürgerlichkeit und Patriotismus: Grillparzers *Libussa* und die österreichischen Ereignisse von 1848." In *Für und wider eine österreichische Literatur*, ed. Kurt Bartsch, Dietmar Goltschnigg and Gerhard Melzer, 17-31. Königstein/Taunus: Athenäum 1982.

Munch, Ilse. *Die Tragik in Drama und Persönlichkeit Franz Grillparzers*. Berlin: Junker 1931.

Nadler, Josef. *Franz Grillparzer*. Vaduz: Liechtenstein Verlag 1948.

Nehring, Wolfgang. "Tun und Nichttun bei Grillparzer. Eine Problematik des Biedermeier." In *"Was nützt der Glaube ohne Werke . . ." Studien zu Franz Grillparzer anläßlich seines 200. Geburtstages*, ed. August Obermeyer, 31-47. Dunedin: University of Otago 1992.

Neumann, Erich. *Die große Mutter*. Olten and Freiburg im Breisgau: Walter-Verlag 1977.

Nietzsche, Friedrich. *Zur Genealogie der Moral*. In *Werke in zwei Bänden*, ed. Karl Schlechta. Vol. 2. Munich: Hanser 1967.

Österreich zu Zeit Joseph II. Katalog des Nö. Landesmuseums. Vienna 1980.

Ortner, Sherry B. "Is Female to Male as Nature is to Culture?" In *Woman, Culture and Society*, ed. Michelle Zimbalist Rosaldo and Louise Lamphere, 67-87. Stanford: Stanford U.P. 1974.

Papst, Edmund E. "Franz Grillparzer." In *German Men of Letters*. ed. Alex Natan, 99-120. Vol. 1. London: Oswald Wolff 1965.

Politzer, Heinz. *Franz Grillparzer oder Das abgründige Biedermeier*. Vienna, Munich, Zurich: Fritz Molden 1972.

Pörnbacher, Karl. ed. *Franz Grillparzer, Dichter über ihre Dichtungen*. Munich: Heimerau 1970.

Reeve, William C. "Proportion and Disproportion in Grillparzer's *Der arme Spielmann*." *Germanic Review* 53 (1978): 41-49.

————*Kleist's Aristocratic Heritage and "Das Käthchen von Heilbronn."* Montreal & Kingston: McGill-Queen's U.P. 1991.

————*The Federfuchser/Penpusher from Lessing to Grillparzer*. Montreal & Kingston: McGill-Queen's U.P. 1995.

————"On Feathers, Sex and Related Matters in Kleist's Works." *Colloquia Germanica* 28 (1995): 127-146.

Reich, Emil. *Franz Grillparzers Dramen*. Dresden: Pierson 1894.

Rhodius, Apollonius. *The Argonautica* with an English translation by R.C. Seaton. London: William Heinemann; Cambridge, Mass.: Harvard U. P. 1967.

Roe, Ian F. *An Introduction to the Major Works of Franz Grillparzer.* Lewiston, Lampeter: Mellen 1991.

———*Franz Grillparzer: A Century of Criticism.* Columbia S.C.: Camden House 1995.

Rosaldo, Michelle Zimbalist and Lamphere, Louise, eds. *Woman, Culture, and Society,* Stanford: Stanford U.P. 1974.

Rosaldo, Michelle Zimbalist. "Woman, Culture, and Society: A Theoretical Overview." In *Woman, Culture, and Society,* ed. Michelle Zimbalist Rosaldo and Louise Lamphere, 17-42. Stanford: Stanford U.P. 1974.

Rose, Jacqueline. "Introduction ɪɪ" to *Feminine Sexuality. Jacques Lacan and the école freudienne,* ed. Juliet Mitchell and Jacqueline Rose. London and Basingstoke: Macmillan 1982.

Rousseau, Jean-Jacques. *Discours sur l'origine et les fondements de l'inégalité parmi les hommes.* In *Œuvres Complètes.* Vol. 3. Paris: Gallimard 1964.

Ruitenbeek, Hendrik M. ed., *Psychoanalysis and Female Sexuality.* New Haven, Conn.: New Haven College & U.P. 1966.

Sanday, Peggy Reeves. *Female Power and Male Dominance: On the Origins of Sexual Inequality.* Cambridge: Cambridge U.P. 1981.

Schäble, Gunter. *Franz Grillparzer.* Velber bei Hanover: Friedrich 1967.

Schiller, Friedrich von. *Maria Stuart.* In *Sämtliche Werke.* Vol. 2. Darmstadt: Wissenschaftliche Buchgesellschaft 1981.

Seidler, Herber. *Studien zu Grillparzer und Stifter.* Vienna, Cologne, Graz: Böhlau 1970.

Škreb, Zdenko. "Franz Grillparzers *Libussa.* Versuch einer Deutung." *Jahrbuch der Grillparzer-Gesellschaft* 6, No. 3 (1967): 75-93.

Sophocles, *Antigone* In *Greek Drama for Everyman.* Trans. F. L. Lucas. London: J. M. Dent 1954.

Stein, Gisela. *The Inspiration Motif in the Works of Franz Grillparzer. With Special Consideration of "Libussa."* The Hague: Martinus Nijhoff 1955.

Thompson, Clara. "Some Effects of the Derogatory Attitude Toward Female Sexuality." In *Psychoanalysis and Female Sexuality,* ed. Hendrik M. Ruitenbeek, 51-60. New Haven, Conn.: New Haven College & University Press 1966.

Volkelt, Johannes. *Grillparzer als Dichter des Tragischen.* Nördlingen: Beck 1988.

Wangermann, Ernst. "Grillparzer und das Nachleben des Josephinismus." In *Öffentliche Vorträge 1991. Franz Grill-*

parzer, 55-73. Vienna: Österreichische Akademie der Wissenschaften 1992.

Wells, George A. *The Plays of Grillparzer.* London, Oxford: Pergamon 1969.

Wiese, Benno von. *Die deutsche Tragödie von Lessing bis Hebbel.* Stuttgart, Berlin: Hoffmann und Campe 1952.

Wittkowski, Wolfgang. "Motiv und Strukturprinzip der Schwelle in Grillparzers *Jüdin von Toledo.*" *Modern Austrian Literature* 28 (1995): 105-45.

Wolf-Cirian, Francis. *Grillparzers Frauengestalten.* Stuttgart, Berlin: J. G. Cott'sche Buchhandlung Nachfolger 1908.

Woolf, Virginia. *A Room of One's Own.* San Diego, New York, London: Harcourt Brace Jovanovich 1957.

Yates, W. E. *Grillparzer. A Critical Introduction.* Cambridge: Cambridge U.P. 1972.

FURTHER READING

Criticism

Birrell, Gordon. "Time, Timelessness, and Music in Grillparzer's *Spielmann.*" *German Quarterly* 57, No. 4 (Fall 1984): 558-75.
> Discusses the internal logic of the fiddler's music in the context of his inability to experience time.

Burkhard, Arthur. *Franz Grillparzer in England and America.* Wien, Austria: Bergland Verlag, 1961, 82 p.
> Comments on English translations of Grillparzer's works and on the opinions of his works cited by various English and American critics.

Burkhard, Marianne. "Love, Creativity, and Female Role: Grillparzer's *Sappho* and Staël's *Corinne* between Art and Cultural Norm." *Jahrbuch fur Internationale Germanistik* 16, No. 2 (1984): 128-46.
> Argues that both *Corinne* and *Sappho* examine the position of the woman poet in society.

Hitchman, Sybil. *The World as Theatre in the Works of Franz Grillparzer.* Berne, Switzerland: Peter Lang, 1979, 246 p.
> Suggests that Grillparzer viewed all life and society as a theater and that his characters are not naturalistic, but rather actors who play to an audience in each particular work.

Lenz, Harold F. H. *Franz Grillparzer's Political Ideas and "Die Jüdin von Toledo."* New York: published privately, 1938, 96 p.
> Terms *Die Jüdin* Grillparzer's "most misunderstood" play and points out that it typifies his main political

theme—the struggle between individual rights and the interests of the state.

Nolte, Fred O. "Grillparzer." In *Grillparzer, Lessing, and Goethe in the Perspective of European Literature*, pp. 29-96. Lancaster, Penn.: Lancaster Press, 1938.

Discusses Grillparzer's role in the development of German drama in the nineteenth century, noting that his aim was "to combine as intimately as possible the genuinely theatrical with the truly poetic."

Pizer, John. "The Disintegration of Libussa." *Germanic Review* 73, No. 2 (Spring 1998): 145-60.

Demonstrates that, in the course of exploring the theme of matriarchy giving way to patriarchy in *Libussa*, the main character loses her integrity and identity.

Pollak. Gustav. "Grillparzer's Originality as Critic." In *International Perspective in Criticism: Goethe, Grillparzer, Sainte-Beuve, Lowell*, pp. 24-38. Port Washington, N.Y.: Kennikat Press, 1914.

Focuses on Grillparzer as literary critic.

Reeve, William C. "'In the beginning . . .': The Opening Scene of Grillparzer's *Die Jüdin von Toledo*." *Modern Austrian Literature* 31, No. 1 (1998): 1-19.

Explores biblical references in the first act of *Die Jüdin* and traces their significance for the remainder of the play.

Roe, Ian F. "Grillparzer and the Language of Quietism." *German Life and Letters* 44, No. 3 (1991): 221-35.

Posits that Grillparzer viewed quietism and solitude as an ideal in his early writings, but that he revised his thinking later, admitting that a quiet, withdrawn life offered him no satisfaction, and could even be "a potential source of inhumanity."

———. *Franz Grillparzer: A Century of Criticism.* Columbia, S.C.: Camden House, 1995, 172 p.

Presents a comprehensive overview of major trends in Grillparzer criticism, discussing individual works in groups.

Thompson, Bruce and Mark Ward, eds. *Essays on Grillparzer.* Hull, England: Hull University, 1978, 92 p.

Collection of essays treating various themes in Grillparzer.

Ward, Mark G. "Some Notes on Grillparzer's *Köning Ottokar* and the 'Entfernte Ähnlichkeit.'" *German Life and Letters* 34, No. 2 (1981): 214-22.

Investigates the role of Napoleon in *Köning Ottokar*.

———. "Reflections and Refractions: An Aspect of the Structure of Grillparzer's *Köning Ottokars Glück und Ende*." *Forum for Modern Language Studies* 25, No. 3 (July 1989): 209-24.

Discusses Grillparzer's problems in dealing with historical material in the writing of *Köning Ottokars Glück und Ende*.

———. "The Structure of Grillparzer's Thought." *German Life and Letters* 44, No. 3 (1991): 236-52.

Explores how Grillparzer interpreted and reflected the events of his time in his dramas.

Wells. G. A. "Grillparzer on the Thinking Process." *Modern Austrian Literature* 19, No. 2 (1986): 1-14.

Maintains that Grillparzer did not agree with commonly held views of eighteenth- and nineteenth-century dramatists regarding the role of tragedy. Unlike them, Grillparzer felt that tragedy exposes the frailty of human beings, rather than their grandeur.

Additional coverage of Grillparzer's life and career is contained in the following sources published by the Gale Group: *Dictionary of Literary Biography,* **Vol. 133; and** *Drama Criticism,* **Vol. 14.**

Francisco de Paula Martínez de la Rosa
1787-1862

(Full name Francisco de Paula Martínez de la Rosa Berdejo Gómez y Arroyo) Spanish statesman, playwright, poet, historian, essayist, novelist, and children's writer.

INTRODUCTION

An early supporter of the Spanish constitution of 1812 and a minister of Spain, Martínez de la Rosa was a noted playwright whose play *La conjuración de Venecia* (1830; *Tragedy of the Conspiracy of Venice*) is traditionally viewed as the first expression of Romanticism in Spanish theater. A revolutionary in his youth, Martínez de la Rosa was imprisoned and later exiled, but nevertheless developed a moderate political view and advocated constitutional monarchy. The theme of political moderation, along with Martínez de la Rosa's moralism and neoclassical manner, figure prominently in his collected writings, which in addition to drama, include significant works of poetry and history. As premier of Spain, he is remembered for his skilled oratory and signing of a treaty to suppress the North African slave trade. As a writer, he is said to occupy a transitional place in Spanish literature, illustrated principally by his historical tragedies, which are thought to represent the shift from eighteenth-century classicism to early Romanticism in Spain.

BIOGRAPHICAL INFORMATION

Martínez de la Rosa was born in 1787 into a wealthy and established bourgeois family of Granada, Spain. His father encouraged him in the study of science, languages, and classical literature, and the precocious Martínez de la Rosa excelled as a student. He received a doctorate in civil law in 1804 and was subsequently awarded a professorship in moral philosophy at the University of Granada. Martínez de la Rosa began writing while obtaining his university degree, often responding through poetry to the turbulent period of Spanish history in which he lived. In 1808 Napoleonic France invaded Spain and Martínez de la Rosa became part of the literary and political resistance. As an active member of the revolutionary constitutionalists at this time, he was sent on a mission to Cádiz to secure weapons for his cause. The following year, in response to a literary contest held by the Central Junta to memorialize Spanish victories against France, Martínez de la Rosa wrote the poem "Zaragoza," first published in London in 1811. Soon, however, French troops pushed the Spanish back as far as Cádiz and Martínez de la Rosa decided to depart for England, where he was later engaged in both diplomatic and literary activities. After returning to Cádiz in 1811, he continued his involvement in revolutionary politics. His first play, the comedy *Lo que puede un empleo,* was performed in Cádiz while the city was under siege in 1812. By the time the attack had ceased, he had produced another play, *La viuda de Padilla* (first printed in 1814; *The Widow of Padilla*). 1813 saw his election to the governing Cortes as deputy from Granada. The ensuing coup d'état of Ferdinand VII, which restored the former absolute monarch to power, signaled a dramatic shift in Martínez de la Rosa's career. As a leader of the constitutional government he was accused of treason by Ferdinand and sentenced to prison, first in Madrid and later for a ten-year term at the North African Peñón de la Gomera. While in the penal colony, Martínez de la Rosa began his *Poética y anotaciones* (1827) and numerous other works. A victory by the constitutionalists in Spain prompted his early release from prison in 1820. His political views having shifted from revolutionary to moderate following his incarceration, Martínez de la Rosa was appointed prime minister by Ferdinand in 1822, but the fell out of favor with both the newly-strengthened king and with his former liberal allies by the following year and was forced to flee to France. Exiled in Paris for the next eight years, Martínez de la Rosa wrote what were to become his most enduring literary works, including his *La conjuración de Venecia.* He was able to return to Madrid by 1830, and re-established himself both as a statesman and a successful writer. The mid-1830s witnessed the high point of his influence as premier of Spain. He also continued to write and publish, focusing increasingly on history, notably in his ten-volume study of European history *El espíritu del siglo* (1835-51; *Spirit of the Age*). Martínez de la Rosa left politics in 1840, withdrawing to Paris in order to pursue his writing, although he was recalled briefly to diplomatic service in 1848 as ambassador to Italy. He died in Madrid in 1862.

MAJOR WORKS

Composed while Martínez de la Rosa was in political exile, the drama *La conjuración de Venecia* features a brooding and pessimistic protagonist, Rugiero, who becomes involved in a conspiracy to overthrow the Venetian Doge in 1310. The coup, conducted in the midst of Carnival, culminates in his arrest. Brought to trial, the Romantic hero discovers his captor to be his lost father, and when sentenced to execution goes peacefully to his death. *Aben-Humeya ou La Révolte des Maures sous Philip II* (1830) depicts a 1568 rebellion against the Spanish government of Philip II. Its protagonist, Aben Humeya, a member of the old royal family, seizes power only to fall victim to a subsequent coup. Martínez de la Rosa's remaining tragedies include three more historical dramas, *La viuda de Padilla, Morayma* (1827), and *Amor de padre* (1848), all of which share a similar formula to that of the above works, presenting failed revolutions, fallen heroes, and tragic lovers. *Edipo* (1828) is a classical drama based upon Sophocles's *Oedipus Rex,* while the topical political satire *Lo que puede un empleo* is representative of the playwright's comedies. First collected in his *Poesías* (1833), Martínez de la Rosa's early poetry is generally political in nature, commemorating contemporary historical events, such as the Spanish victory at Salamanca and the War of Granada. His long didactic poem, *Poética,* repeats the tenets of neoclassical poetic theory while defending the merits of Spanish national literature. Principal among his historical works, *El espíritu del siglo* considers the foundations of government in Europe from the Roman Era to the end of the eighteenth century, with particular focus on the causes of French Revolution. In it, Martínez de la Rosa expresses a political theme of moderation achieved through a proper balance of political freedom and civil order. Other non-fictional works include the picaresque historical biography *Hernán Pérez del Pulgar el de las hazañas* (1834), and *Bosquejo histórico de la política de España desde los tiempos de los Reyes Católicos hasta nuestros días* (1857), an examination of Spanish history. In addition to his better known dramatic, poetic, and historical writings, Martínez de la Rosa also wrote a three-volume novel, *Doña Isabel de Solís, Reina de Granada* (1837-46), and a collection of moral tales, poems, and fables for children entitled *Libro de los niños* (1839; *Book for Children*).

CRITICAL RECEPTION

During his lifetime, Martínez de la Rosa distinguished himself as a writer primarily through his dramatic works. Among them, the popular classical tragedy *La viuda de Padilla,* which critics consider to be representative of his early plays, has, like many of Martínez de la Rosa's other writings, since been largely dismissed as lacking any enduring literary merit. His best known play, *La conjuración de Venecia,* was a considerable success when first performed and while many subsequent commentators have admired its incipient Romanticism, a number of modern critics have tended to view the drama as essentially a neoclassical work, culled from various sources and exhibiting only a few Romantic elements. The lengthy *Poética y anotaciones* has provided additional evidence of Martínez de la Rosa's neoclassicism, though some scholars have pointed out the significant nationalist qualities of the work. Additionally, the historical romance *Doña Isabel de Solís* was both a critical and a popular failure, and has generally failed to elicit critical interest. Commentators have found in Martínez de la Rosa's non-fictional writings, however, considerable intrinsic value, especially in the ambitious *El espíritu del siglo.* Most acknowledge, nonetheless, that his historical studies have been largely superseded by the work of other, less politically motivated historians, both in terms of style and acuity. Overall, modern critical consensus has generally regarded Martínez de la Rosa as neither an innovator in drama, nor a pioneer of Romanticism in Spain, but rather an erudite and prolific writer who synthesized his works from a vast knowledge of classical and modern literature.

PRINCIPAL WORKS

Odas a los atributos de Dios que brillan en la Sacrosanta Encaristía (poetry) 1805

"La revolución actual de España" (essay) 1810

Zaragoza (poetry) 1811

Lo que puede un empleo (play) 1812

La viuda de Padilla [*The Widow of Padilla*] (play) 1814

Poética y anotaciones (poetry and criticism) 1827

Obras literarias. 5 vols. (dramas, poetry, and prose) 1827-30

Edipo (play) 1828

Aben-Humeya ou La Révolte des Maures sous Philippe II [also published as *Abén Humeya o la Rebelión de los Moriscos*] (play) 1830

La conjuración de Venecia [*Tragedy of the Conspiracy of Venice*] (play) 1830

Los celos infundados o el marido en la chimenea (play) 1833

Poesías (poetry) 1833

Hernán Pérez del Pulgar el de las hazañas [*Life of Pérez del Pulgar*] (history) 1834

El espíritu del siglo. [*Spirit of the Age*] 10 vols. (history) 1835-51

Doña Isabel de Solís, Reina de Granada. 3 vols. (novel) 1837-46

†*Obras literarias.* 4 vols. (dramas, poetry, and prose) 1838

Libro de los niños [*Book for Children*] (children's literature) 1839

‡*Obras dramáticas* (play) 1843

Obras completas (play, poetry, history, and novel) 1844-45

Amor de padre (play) 1848

El parricida (play) 1856

Bosquejo histórico de la política de España desde los tiempos de los Reyes Católicos hasta nuestros días. 2 vols. (history) 1857

Obras de Don Francisco Martínez de la Rosa. 9 vols. (play, poetry, history, novel, and essay) 1964

*In addition to previously published works, this edition of the *Obras literarias* contains *Apéndices sobre la literatura española, La niña en casa y la madre en la máscara, Morayma, Edipo, Epístola a los Pisones,* and *Apuntes sobre el drama histórico.*

†Comprised of the works from the 1827-30 edition plus Martínez de la Rosa's poetry and the dramas *Lo que puede un empleo* and *Los celos infundados.*

‡Contains all plays to 1843 as well as the dramas *El español en Venecia* and *La boda y el duelo.*

CRITICISM

James Kennedy (essay date 1852)

SOURCE: "Francisco Martínez de la Rosa," in *Modern Poets and Poetry of Spain,* Longman, Brown, Green, and Longmans, 1852, pp. 169-82.

[*In the following excerpt, Kennedy recounts the life of Martínez de la Rosa and briefly examines his principal writings.*]

Throughout the civilized world, and even beyond it, this eminent statesman has long been heard of, as one who, while devoting his life faithfully to promote the welfare of his own country, had exerted himself no less assiduously for the general interests of mankind. As an orator, a statesman and a political writer, he has thus obtained a deservedly high European reputation, due to his services and merits. In Spain he is further known as one of the first literary characters of whom his country has to boast, and as a dramatist and lyric poet of a very superior order.

Martinez de la Rosa was born the 10th March, 1789, at Granada, where also he received his education, completing it at the University in that city. Before the age of twenty he had gone through the usual course of study in the ancient and some of the modern languages, in philosophy, mathematics, canon and civil law, with such success as to have been enabled to undertake a professorship of philosophy there, perfecting himself in the art of oratory, in which his natural talents already had become manifest, as they soon afterwards gave him the means of greater distinction. From those pursuits he was called away, in 1808, on the occurrence of the French invasion, to take an active part in the struggle for national independence, into which he entered with youthful ardour, by public declamations, and by writing in a periodical instituted to maintain it.

As the French arms advanced victoriously, Martinez de la Rosa, with others of the party who had been most conspicuous in their opposition to them, had to take refuge in Cadiz. He was first employed to proceed to Gibraltar, as his future colleague, the Conde de Toreno, had been sent to London, to obtain a cessation of hostilities, in the war then yet existing between England and Spain, and concert measures of alliance against the French. In this mission he had the desired success, having further obtained from the governor of Gibraltar arms and ammunition, which enabled the Spanish forces under Castanios to march and obtain, at Bailen, the memorable triumph of the 19th July, 1808. In consequence of this victory, the French had to evacuate Madrid, and the Central Junta was formed, superseding the first actors in the conflict. On this, Martinez de la Rosa took advantage of the circumstances to go to England, and observe there himself, says his biographer, the celebrated Pacheco, "in its birthplace, where it was natural, complete and necessary, that representative system, which the spirit of reform wished to bring over for the people of the Continent." Wolf says he had there a diplomatic commission, adding, that he took advantage of it "to familiarize himself with the English constitution, for which he always had a great predilection."

Whether he had public duties entrusted to him or not, Martinez de la Rosa seems then to have stayed some time in London, studying the workings of the parliamentary system, the good fruits of which he, as Mirabeau had before him, found in his legislative career. There he printed, in 1811, his poem, *Zaragoza,* written in competition for the prize offered by the Central Junta, in celebration of the defence of that city in 1809, and there also he wrote several other poems. The one of Zaragoza seems not to have been reprinted in Spain till the publication of his collected poems in Madrid in 1833, and no adjudication ever was made on the compositions prepared at the suggestion of the Junta, but it is stated that the judges had unanimously agreed to confer on him the premium offered in the name of the nation.

In 1811 the French armies had driven the assertors of national independence from all the other principal parts of Spain to Cadiz, and there the Cortes were convoked to meet. There then, Martinez de la Rosa returned, and though not yet of the age required by law to be chosen a Deputy, he took part in all the deliberations of the national councils, and was appointed Secretary to the commission on the freedom of the press. Meanwhile the siege of Cadiz was commenced by the French and pressed unremittingly; but the spirit of the defenders did not fail them. Martinez de la Rosa and Quintana continued their literary labours, and the former produced a comedy and a tragedy, both of which were received with much favour. The latter continues a favourite on the stage, on a subject well chosen from Spanish history, and entitled the **Widow of Padilla.** To use his own words, "It was represented, for the first time, in July 1812, and in days so unfortunate, that it could not be produced even in the theatre at Cadiz, on account of the great danger from the bombs of the enemy, which had nearly caused, a little before, the destruction of the building, crowded at the time with a numerous audience. For this reason they had to erect a theatre of wood in another part of the city, at a distance from where the French artillery had directed their aim."

Shortly after this the siege was raised, and the French having again evacuated Madrid, the Cortes were convoked to assemble there, when Martinez de la Rosa was elected Deputy for his native city. He had throughout the struggle joined the most active members of the liberal party, Arguelles, Quintana and others, who, all honourable and patriotic characters, had acted in perfect sincerity in forming the Constitution of 1812, as it was called, which they hoped would secure the future freedom of the country.

In this, however, they found themselves mistaken; the representative system had scarcely time to develope its advantages, when it was overthrown entirely on the return of Ferdinand to Spain, who, by his decree of the 4th of May, 1814, annulled the Constitution, and dissolved the Cortes. Had he been contented with this, as in re-assumption of the regal authority exercised by his predecessors, the liberal party might have had only to lament the abrupt termination of their hopes. But, unfortunately, proceedings still more arbitrary were commenced against their leaders individually, of a nature unknown, even in Spain, till then, and in comparison with which the rule of the Prince of the Peace was a pattern of toleration. As those leaders had not been guilty of any act which could make them amenable to any legal tribunal, Ferdinand VII. took on himself to pass the sentences he chose to inflict on them for the opinions they had held, and the conduct they had pursued, in the momentous struggle for national independence, resulting in his restoration. The partisans of the Absolute King wished to extort from Martinez de la Rosa a retractation of the opinions he had maintained; but they miscalculated his character. He refused to listen to their overtures, and he was sentenced to ten years' imprisonment in the penal settlement of Gomera in Africa.

In 1820 a reaction took place, and the constitutional party again obtained possession of the government. Martinez de la Rosa had then passed six years of unjust imprisonment,

when he was recalled to Spain, and was received, in his native city, with triumphal arches erected to welcome him, and other tokens of public respect and rejoicing. At the first election of deputies afterwards for the Cortes, he was sent with that character from Granada, but his sentiments on public affairs had become considerably modified. Others of the liberal party had returned from exile or imprisonment with exasperated feelings; but Martinez de la Rosa had employed his time more philosophically, in considering the means that should be adopted, to use his own expression, "for resolving the problem, most important for the human race, how to unite order with liberty." Avoiding all extreme opinions, he gave his support to the ministry he found existing and their successors, as the means of preserving order, until they fell under the combination of unworthy jealousies among their own party, and the constant attacks of those holding the extreme opinions of democracy and absolutism.

On the 1st March, 1821, Martinez de la Rosa was called on to form a ministry, which duty he finally undertook, though he had at first strenuously declined it. He had good reason to decline it, as the king himself was throughout that period plotting against his own ministers and government, to re-establish himself in absolute power. At the end of June, Martinez de la Rosa found himself under the necessity of tendering his resignation, and insisting upon its being accepted, though both the king and the council at first refused to do so. The moderate course which he wished to follow pleased neither party; and even he, who had suffered six years of unjust imprisonment in the popular cause, was now looked on as a traitor by the people, and ran great risk of being murdered in a public commotion raised in the city. Had he chosen to take a more decisive part, either on the one side or the other, the weight of his character would no doubt have given it the preponderance. As it was, the question was decided by the invasion of the French under the Duc d'Angoulême, who restored Ferdinand VII. to his former authority.

When the French entered Spain, the constitutionalist government had retired to Seville; but Martinez de la Rosa had been obliged, from illness, to remain at Madrid. There being called upon to give in his adhesion to the authority imposed by foreign arms on the nation, he declined to do so, and thought himself fortunate in having no severer penalty to suffer thereupon, than to have his passport given him to go from Spain, while others had to suffer so much more severely. He then retired to Paris, where he resided eight years, paying occasional visits to Italy, and though not proscribed directly as an exile, yet he was not allowed to return to his country.

During those eight years he devoted his leisure to literary pursuits, and composed most of those works on which his fame must permanently rest; such as his poem, **Arte Poetica**; his very beautiful **'Ode on the Death of the Duchess de Frias,'** and several plays; among them the **Tragedy of the Conspiracy of Venice,** considered the best of all he had written. Thus occupied in endeavouring to make future generations wiser and better, Martinez de la Rosa gained increased respect at home with his increased reputation abroad; and on the moderating of the first angry party-feelings in Spain, was at the end of eight years allowed to return to Granada.

The events of 1830 had produced the effect in Spain of milder councils being adopted in the government, which prevailed still more on the Queen Christina assuming power, first on the illness of the king, and afterwards as Regent on his death in 1833. Martinez de la Rosa had then been permitted to return to Madrid, and in this latter year he published the first collection of his poems, dedicating himself to writing at the same time his *Life of Perez del Pulgar,* one of the old warriors of Spain, and other works. From these labours he was then called to undertake again the duties of government. The existing ministry formed under a former line of policy, was not suitable to the exigences of the times, rendered still more pressing now by the pretensions of Don Carlos to the throne. It was necessary to oppose those pretensions, by obtaining the zealous aid of the constitutional party; and Martinez de la Rosa was chosen as the leader, embodying in himself the characteristics of moderation and just principles, to form a ministry.

It does not become a foreigner, least of all in a purely literary work, to enter in judgement on any questions of a political nature. The best-intentioned persons in the world may take different views of the same question, under the same emergences, and the wisdom of any particular measure is not always to be judged of by the result. In the conflicts of contending parties, the most unscrupulous and daring may often succeed, where wiser and better men may fail. Of Martinez de la Rosa, his biographer has observed, that "he was one of those men who would not conspire even for good ends unlawfully; and that if he could not obtain what he wished by just means, he would cross his arms, and leave the rest to Providence." The events of those years present much ground for regret for all parties, and it is a truly honourable consideration for such a one as Martinez de la Rosa, that, acting according to the best of his judgement on many very difficult occasions, he might have been compelled to yield to force and violence, without any imputation on his probity or statesmanship.

But if it be beyond our consideration of duty to enter on questions of internal polity, there are two others, connected with his administration, to which we may venture to refer, as to be judged of by those great principles of right and justice, which are applicable to all times and all countries, and become thus fairly subject to commendation or censure, as affecting the general interests of mankind.

Though Martinez de la Rosa had been one of the principal actors among those who had established the Constitution of 1812, for which also he suffered as a prisoner and an exile, he learned soon to perceive that it required considerable modifications in a country like Spain, where the people were not fully prepared to receive it. One of his

first measures then was to promulgate what might be termed a new Constitution, called the Estatuto Real, the general wisdom and propriety of which may be admitted, or at least not disputed, while one part of it may be pronounced indefensible. This was in the design to subvert the ancient rights of the Basque people, by amalgamating their provinces into the kingdom, without obtaining or asking their assent. This was a measure unjust in itself; and because unjust, also impolitic; leading to a long-protracted struggle, in which the whole force of Spain being employed, army after army was destroyed, and general after general disgraced, by a comparatively inconsiderable number of undisciplined peasantry. When England sought to incorporate the Parliaments of Scotland and Ireland into that of the United Kingdom, it was sought by what might be called legal, though not always honourable means. On the same principle, the consent of the Basques ought to have been obtained by the Spanish government, rather than the attempt made, furtively or forcibly, to deprive them of their ancient privileges.

On another great question affecting humanity, it is pleasing to consider Martinez de la Rosa among the foremost characters of the age, in attempting the suppression of the slave trade with Africa. In 1817 a treaty was made between England and Spain to suppress this traffic, which, after the experience of a few years, it was found necessary to make more stringent. Propositions to this effect were therefore made year after year to successive Spanish governments by the British, but in vain, until in 1835 Lord Palmerston was successful enough to find in him a minister of Spain, who had the courage to consent to those suggestions. The treaty of that year was then entered into, and signed on the part of the two countries, by Sir George Villiers, now Earl of Clarendon, and Martinez de la Rosa, which has had the desired effect of preventing the trade being protected by the Spanish flag. But this able statesman has done still more, to entitle him to the respect of all who look with interest on this important question. One of the stipulations of the treaty declared that a penal law should be passed in Spain, in accordance with it, to punish all Spanish subjects found infringing it. This stipulation no other Spanish minister could be found to fulfil; and after the lapse of ten years, having again come into power, it was left for him in good faith to accomplish the engagement he had previously undertaken. Accordingly in 1845, he passed a law, answering the purposes required, which received the approbation of the British government, and which seems to have been so far effective in its application.

Great, undoubtedly, is the praise due to those philanthropic statesmen, who, even at the Congress of Vienna, agreed to protect the liberty of Africa. But much greater must be acknowledged due to one who, unsupported almost in his own country, having to oppose himself to a strong colonial interest, and the cry they raised against him of acting in subservience to a foreign power, yet had the moral courage to follow the dictates of justice and humanity, on behalf of an injured race, notwithstanding all the enmity he had to encounter in so doing.

In 1836 Martinez de la Rosa had to yield his place in the government to other hands; and in 1840 he thought proper to retire again to Paris, engaging himself in those literary pursuits from which he had latterly been estranged. It is not our province to follow his political course, through the different public questions on which he had to act. During the four intermediate years various ministries were formed, to some of which he had to give an honourable support, to others as honourable an opposition; but the Regency of Espartero he avoided to acknowledge. When this fell under the attack of Narvaez, he came forward again into public life, and accepted office for a short time in the government; but seemed resolved to take the first opportunity of giving up the post of active exertion for one of more private character, though of no less public utility. Accordingly, on the accession of Pius IX. to the Papacy, he was appointed Ambassador to Rome, which important office he still continues to hold, for the advantage of the Roman Catholic church itself, as well as of his own country, in the several questions that have come since under discussion, subject to his intervention.

As a politician, Martinez de la Rosa has been conspicuous for constant rectitude and consistency of principles. "Not even in moments of the utmost defamation," says his biographer, "has a word been ever raised against his purity of conduct, nor have his greatest enemies ever permitted themselves to impugn in the least his intentions." As an orator, he has had few to equal him in his time, none to surpass him; but his eloquence has been modelled by his character to persuade and defend rather than attack; and thus, if not abounding in brilliant sallies, it has been found of more essential service to the cause of good government.

Beyond the *History of Perez del Pulgar,* Martinez de la Rosa has written several other works in prose, one of which, the latest, entitled *Spirit of the Age,* is in fact, so far as yet published, a History of the French Revolution, preceded by a few general observations on political questions. It has already advanced to six volumes, and becoming a political and philosophical history of contemporaneous events, may be extended to the utmost limits. A novel which he wrote earlier in life, *Donna de Solis,* is acknowledged a failure, as showing "that no man, however eminent, can write successfully on all kinds of subjects."

The principal literary success which Martinez de la Rosa has had, seems to have been as a dramatist; but into those works it would be impossible to enter, to treat them with justice, except by making them a prominent subject of consideration. His poems, published as before stated in 1833, contain compositions in various styles, from the light Anacreontic to the project of an Epic Poem on the Wars of Granada, of which, however, he has only published fragments. Besides a translation of Horace's 'Art of Poetry,' he has also given the world an *Ars Poetica,* for the benefit of his own countrymen, which he has enriched with many excellent notes and criticisms.

Some of the rules laid down in this *Ars Poetica* are well worthy of study, as giving room for reflection, for carrying their suggestions even further than he has done. Thus,

while insisting on the young poet depending on the excellency of his ear for the melody of verse, instead of having to count the syllables for the requisite purpose, he observes, that as the ancients regulated their metres by time, making so many long or short feet of equivalent measure, of which the judgement must depend on the cadence, so in the verses of the best Spanish poets, there are often some lines containing three or four more syllables than others, to which they form the counterpart, and which are read in the same measure, with increased pleasure for the variation.

The same observation may apply to English verse, though perhaps not so fully. Many of our syllables containing shortly sounded vowels, such as a Hebrew scholar might call Sheva and its compounds, pronounced distinctly, but two in the time of an ordinary syllable, may be found to give an elegance to the line, which would sound faulty with only one of them. But we may go further, and observe, that as in music the melody may be continued by the pause, instead of a note in the bar, so in a line, a pause with one or more long syllables may have the effect of a syllable, instead of the sound or foot to make up the measure. Readers of poetry will not require to be reminded of instances of this adaptation of sounds, and if they notice any such lines in these translations, they will perceive that they have been written in accordance with the precepts referred to.

It must be acknowledged, that in the generality of his poems, Martinez de la Rosa has not risen to any such height of sublimity or fancy as to give him a place in the superior class of poets. But one of the latest critical writers, Ferrer del Rio, who has given a more disparaging estimate of his poetical talents than justice might award, pronounces the 'Epistle to the Duke de Frias' as a composition for which "judges the most grave and least complaisant might place him on the top of Parnassus." The 'Remembrance of Spain,' Del Rio declares to be poor in images, without feeling or depth, but with much of pastoral innocency. The 'Return to Spain' is, according to him, a mere itinerary of his travels, more than an expression of pleasure on escaping from past evil. But in the 'Epistle to the Duke de Frias,' he finds "true-felt inspiration, an appropriate expression, and a plan well traced out,"—"without vagueness or artificial labour, but with phrases that soften and ideas that satisfy the mind," becoming the subject.

Another anonymous critic finds the writer dwelling too much on the remembrance of his own sorrows, instead of offering consolation to the mourner, and some incongruity in felicitating him on having witnessed the last pangs of mortality. But these topics, on such an occasion, are true to nature. Grief is apt to be egotistical, and the mind cannot but dwell on the subject in which it is absorbed. Nor is the other a less natural suggestion; and thus we may observe, that the great master of antiquity represents the sweetest of his characters lamenting that she had not been by the side of her lord at such a time, as the height of her misfortune, to receive his last embrace. . . .

In this **'Epistle to the Duke de Frias,'** Martinez de la Rosa has also introduced, as a fit consideration in his grief, the same topic of the instability of earthly things, which "the Roman friend of Rome's least mortal mind" offered him on a similar occasion of sympathy. But it also seems a favourite subject of our poet's thoughts at all times, as befitting the philosopher and the scholar, to dwell on the passing nature of worldly greatness, and so lead the mind to higher suggestions than those of the present moment. These ideas he has carried further in another work he has published, **Book for Children,** in which, like many other eminent characters, who have given the aid of their talents to the development of juvenile minds, he has inculcated lessons of virtue, and the instinct of good taste, with the feelings of patriotism and religion, as the basis of moral well-being.

Martinez de la Rosa published his works in a collected form first, in five volumes, 1827-30, at Paris, where they have been again lately reprinted. Besides these, there have been two editions in Spain, one at Madrid and the other at Barcelona. From Her Catholic Majesty he has received the decoration of the Golden Fleece, the highest order of Spain, besides other similar honours. But the world at large will consider his greatest honour to consist in having raised himself from mediocrity of station, by his talents and exertions, to the high position he has attained "without stain or reproach," while, by his literary works, he has enabled all mankind to become benefited by his genius, and interested in his fame.

James Francis Shearer (essay date 1941)

SOURCE: "The *Poética*: Motivation and Purpose, Dates and Circumstances of Composition of its Various Parts," in *The* Poética *and Apendices of Martínez de la Rosa: Their Genesis, Sources and Significance for Spanish Literary History and Criticism,* Princeton University, 1941, pp. 10-32.

[*In the following excerpt, Shearer discusses Martínez de la Rosa's motivation for composing his defense of poetry while analyzing the aesthetic principles and nationalistic character of his* Poética.]

The motivation of any important literary or critical work and the circumstances and date of its composition are necessarily of great interest since these facts frequently contribute much to a fuller understanding of the author's ideology and particular point of view. The **Poética** of Martínez de la Rosa offers no exception to this rule. Frequently an author's own statements coupled with an abundance of historical data will leave no room for doubt in regard to such facts. In the case of the **Poética** such information is not entirely lacking. However, these data do not completely elucidate the matter and for this reason we propose to clarify it to such an extent as available information will allow.

There exist two trustworthy means of approach to the problem of determining the motivation of this work. In the first place we have Martínez de la Rosa's own statements as to why he wrote the **Poética,** its *Anotaciones* and *Apéndices*. In the second instance we have the conclusions to be deduced from a study of the author's life and work as a whole, with particular emphasis on the period before 1820, since it would be unreasonable to imagine that there existed no connections between that and a work bulking as large as does the **Poética** in his literary and critical output.

Martínez de la Rosa's own statements as to his avowed purposes in writing the **Poética** and its closely correlated *Anotaciones* and *Apéndices* are to be found principally in the *Advertencia* which contains certain definite indications as to the aims of the work.[1] It is advisable to quote at some length from this section since the material is particularly revealing as regards both Martínez de la Rosa himself and the work we are considering. After commenting on the lack of a Spanish didactic poem comparable in scope to the *Art Poétique* of Boileau, Martínez de la Rosa says:

> Y esta falta, sumamente reparable en una literatura tan rica como la española, indica al mismo tiempo el motivo y el fin de esta obra. . . . Por defectuosa que sea, acarreará la ventaja de allanar a otros el camino para empresa tan difícil; siendo ademas muy útil a los jóvenes aplicados encontrar reunidos en una sola obra los preceptos esparcidos en muchas, y frecuentemente sin método ni orden.
>
> Me he ceñido a no emplear en el Poema sino ejemplos tomados de autores griegos y latinos o de poetas castellanos, para despertar en los jóvenes la afición a la literatura clásica de los antiguos y a la de su propia nación . . . y aunque alguna vez acaeciere que me equivoque, creo que en general producirá esta obra el provecho de inclinar a los jóvenes a no seguir a ciegas el voto común, sino preferir examinar las obras por si mismos.
>
> Insensiblemente se me ha ido un paso tras otro en campo tan vasto y ameno, estimulándome a proseguir el que siempre tenía presente la falta que hace en España un *curso de literatura,* en que se apliquen a nuestras obras célebres, tanto en prosa como en verso, los principios y reglas del arte de escribir.[2]

From the above material six major aims stand forth clearly: a) Martínez de la Rosa would give Spain a didactic poem which would compare favorably with the *Art Poétique.* b) Though he should not succeed in producing such a work, his efforts would at least have paved the way for his followers. c) The work admittedly will be a compilation of precepts from many sources. d) It will limit itself, as regards illustrative material, to the works of Greek, Latin and Spanish authors. e) It will, it is hoped, help young students to form independent judgements in literary matters. f) It will aim to at least partially fill the need of a *curso de literatura.*

When we consider the indirect testimony which bears upon the motivation of the **Poética,** we find in Martínez education and known interests two valid reasons why he could logically have been expected to give a formal and theoretical expression to his literary creed. The first of these motives derives from the particular nature of his youthful education and a keen interest in pedagogical reforms. His biographers reveal[3] that as a young professor at the University of Granada, this interest manifested itself in many ways: in reports on methodology and in active participation on committees for the selection of more appropriate university texts.[4] We are not referring here to the routine interest that we should expect Martínez, a university professor, to have in educational matters. We have in mind, rather, an active interest in these affairs which went beyond that which he would naturally have as a concomitant to his professional duties. This is, in fact, one of the most striking characteristics of his early life and activities.

A second and more obvious reason why one might have expected Martínez de la Rosa to codify his literary principles derives from the nature of these principles themselves. Although we shall have occasion to see in him a certain eclecticism and many instances where his conciliatory approach to critical problems tends to soften the rigor of various neo-classic tenets, it must be pointed out that he remained, throughout his life, essentially a classicist and doctrinaire.[5] Such an assertion is not invalidated by certain inconsistencies which occur at intervals during his career. These are the Romantic dramas *Aben Humeya* (1830); *La conjuración de Venecia* (1830); his *Apuntes sobre el drama histórico* (1830); the historical drama, *Amor de padre* (1849) and the comedia, *El español en Venecia* (1861). The specific relationships of these writings to the work under discussion will be considered subsequently. It may be pointed out, however, that the apparent change of front seen in the above works indicates, more than anything else, Martínez' great receptivity to different influences and currents of thought about him. This receptivity (we do not propose to term it essentially eclecticism since we interpret this word to imply a more thorough assimilation of ideas than is evident in Martínez de la Rosa) was characteristic, as we shall see, of his political as well as his literary life.[6]

There is ample evidence besides that to be found in the *Poética,* of Martínez' basal devotion to the principles and critical ideals of neo-classicism. An admirer and emulator of Leandro Fernández de Moratín[7], a very competent translator of Horace[8], already the author of one classical tragedy, *La viuda de Padilla* (1812) and the future author of another, *Edipo* (1828) it is not surprising that Martínez de la Rosa, conversant as he was through his education with neo-classic doctrine, should have given it, in 1827, his own interpretation and elaboration in an *Ars poetica.*

Martínez de la Rosa's literary position has an interesting and pertinent parallel in his political ideology for the same period.[9] Until 1820 his political principles are characterized by "somewhat radical democratic tendencies and a naively doctrinaire constitutionalism".[10] It is after the above date that his more moderate approach to political problems becomes apparent. M. Sarrailh sums up his adherence to

fixed principles during this early, formative period, in the following manner:

> Une première question à résoudre, et dont l'importance apparaitra mieux dans la suite de ce travail, consiste à rechercher quelle idée de la politique se faisait Martínez, au début de sa vie publique. Pour l'instant, ce n'est pas la forme de gouvernement dont il se fera le champion que nos tachons de déterminer. La question est antérieure à celle-là. Martínez croit-il que la politique est une science aux principes rigidement liés les uns aux autres, ou, au contraire, un art qui tient compte de l'experience. L'homme d'état peut-il, comme le professeur de logique ou le mathématicien, poser des axiomes et en déduire rigoureusement les applications practiques ou, inversement, est-il un observateur qui ne prend une mesure générale qu'après en avoir découvert la nécessité dans une multitude de cas. Martínez, dans ses années de jeunesse, adopte la première position, celle du logicien: attitude naturelle à un débutant.[11]

The above discussion establishes, we believe, four motives for the writing of the *Poética.* These we have seen to be: a) Martinez' education, which instilled in him a profound admiration for classical literature. b) His marked interest in pedagogical problems. c) His evident adherence to the principles of classicism as shown by his emulation of Moratín and his translation of Horace. d) His doctrinairism as revealed in his political ideology for the early years of his life plus a later receptivity and moderation.

The aims of the *Poética,* as stated by Martínez, and the deductions to be drawn from his education, interests, literary and critical affiliations all combine to demonstrate that the writing of such a work was entirely consistent with his ideology for the early period of his life. We are convinced, however, that the importance of the work, indeed its essential purpose, transcends that of what we might call the traditional *ars poetica.* Such a conviction, we feel, is inescapable for various reasons. Menéndez y Pelayo has called the *Poética* "la llave que cierra el período abierto por la Poética de Luzán."[12] It can indeed be said that the work, considered simply as a body of neo-classic doctrine, represents, no less than another of the same period, the *Poética* of Pérez del Camino (1829), "el testamento de una escuela que se empeñó en sobrevivirse."[13] The period of nearly a hundred years that had elapsed between the reintroduction of Aristotelian doctrines with the *Poética* of Luzán and the work of Martínez de la Rosa, had seen the issues of neo-classicism fought out on every front. R. E. Pellissier has demonstrated that the program of neo-classic indoctrination was completed with the *Comedia nueva* of Moratín. Through the medium of this work, the theories of neo-classicism were presented to the lower classes. Pellissier says:

> After his first theatrical success, Moratín came to realize that the writing of more didactic or satirical verse was the veriest carrying of coals to Newcastle. He saw clearly that what could be obtained from the middle class of Spanish society was already obtained and that the urgent problem before him was the more complete

conversion of the pit which had already fallen away from patronizing plays of an exclusively Spanish character.[14]

Thus a further, formal presentation of neo-classic theories as late as 1827 would seem almost anachronistic. In other words, while the work is a logical product of its author for the reasons already enumerated, as a purely theoretical body of doctrine its importance, either as an inculcative medium in its own time, or viewed in retrospect and in chronological relation to analogous works, scarcely transcends that of a literary curiosity.

We have already had occasion to indicate[15] the scant regard that critics have had for the **Poética,** considered as another theoretical expression of neo-classic principles. Such an attitude, we would be the first to admit, is not unjustified. It is our opinion, however, that the **Poética** cannot, as it has been, be fairly judged apart from its closely corelated *Anotaciones* and *Apéndices.* When Martínez de la Rosa, in the *Advertencia* to the work, expressed the hope that he might, in some measure, remedy the lack in Spain, of a *curso de literatura,* we are convinced that this hope was the essential motivation for the subsequent elaboration of the **Poética** through its copious *Anotaciones* and *Apéndices.* These give the work its real importance and this importance transcends unquestionably either a desire to imitate the *Art Poétique* of Boileau or what is a corollary of this desire, the attempt at this time to infuse new life into a body of threadbare doctrine and further inculcate neo-classic principles into a, by now, recalcitrant Spanish public.

An examination of the **Poética,** *Anotaciones* and *Apéndices* reveals additional aspects of Martínez de la Rosa's essential purpose in writing the work. Taking as a starting point the fact that a more comprehensive purpose was being served than that of producing another *ars poetica* and keeping in mind that this purpose was to be accomplished along the general lines of a *curso de literatura,* there are revealed certain characteristics which stamp this work as an expression of patriotism of the highest order. The patriotic impulse to which we refer leads Martínez de la Rosa, in the course of the *Anotaciones* and *Apéndices,* to develop a spirited defense and apology for the Spanish national literature. At first blush there might seem to be a contradiction in such an assertion. There is really no such contradiction, however, for Martínez the neo-classicist will indeed be seen to defend many aspects of the national literature through the medium of a clearly defined apologistic-conciliatory approach. The rather trite assertion that he was the champion of the *juste milieu* in both politics and literature takes on more meaning when we see how he attempts to harmonize the excesses of the national dramatists with the doctrines of neo-classicism. The **Poética** with its *Apéndices,* and especially in the *Apéndices,* is the first statement of the *moderado* position.

We shall presently examine in detail the nationalistic character of this work but in the immediate connection and as an indication of the patriotic purpose, we may well quote again from the *Advertencia:*

> Me he ceñido a no emplear en el poema sino ejemplos tomados de autores griegos y latinos o de poetas castellanos. . . . Unicamente en las notas he citado alguna que otra vez autores extrangeros, o por creerlo conveniente para ofrecer algun cotejo o contraste, o por parecerme que la materia misma lo requería.[16]

Here we have a definite indication of the nationalistic preoccupation which will be continually evident throughout the work. We observe too the indication that the **Poética** will constitute a continuation of the Classic-Spanish tradition rather than any other.[17] These considerations and others complementary to them will be treated in the course of our subsequent analyses.

In regard to the circumstances of composition of the **Poética** and its supplementary material, Martínez de la Rosa does not indicate conclusively in the *Advertencia,* nor elsewhere, much that we should like to know in this respect. Apparently, however, the **Poética** and its accompanying *Anotaciones* and *Apéndices* was begun while the author was a political exile at Peñón de la Gomera.

Rebello da Silva states, without documentary corroboration, that the work was begun there and implies that the *Anotaciones* were also written at that time.[18] Sarrailh follows Rebello da Silva and states, without any proof, that the work was commenced during this imprisonment to later be enlarged and annotated during Martinez' stay in Paris.[19] A. L. Owen assigns the **Poética** without explanation, to the period corresponding to that of the Paris exile.[20] Fernández y González, although he mentions the **Poética** and the translation of Horace, assigns no date for their composition.[21]

Several circumstances make it reasonable to conclude that the work was begun in Africa and subsequently annotated and revised in preparation for the publication of the author's **Obras literarias.** These same circumstances, therefore, make M. Sarrailh's hypothesis the most acceptable. First of all, certain statements by Martínez de la Rosa himself lend a considerable weight to this hypothesis. In the *Advertencia* to the above-mentioned translation of Horace, it is shown that without doubt this work was at least commenced at Peñón de la Gomera.[22] This fact lends credence to the assumption that in the leisure of his exile he might logically have turned for mental recreation to the composition of a work of an analogous nature. In the *Advertencia* to the **Poética** Martínez says, anent the wish that he might have written a complete *curso de literatura:*

> Esta empresa exigiría, para desempeñarla medianamente, un caudal bien provisto de conocimientos y mayor copia de materiales a la mano de la que puede hallarse cuando se escribe en país extrangero; y como estas circunstancias son también aplicables, hasta cierto punto, a la obra que presento al público, son otras tantas razones que aumentan mi temor y desconfianza.[23]

Further indications that the *Anotaciones* and *Apéndices* were completed in Paris are to be found in these sections themselves.[24] Further, it may be suggested that the *Oedipus rex* of Sophocles, used as the chief illustrative material in the *Anotaciones* dealing with the tragedy, may have been connected in time with the **Edipo** (1828) of Martínez, which we know was written in Paris.[25]

. . . . .

ANALYSIS OF POETICA AND ANOTACIONES

The **Poética** proper is a didactic poem in six cantos (the metrical form of which is the *silva*) devoted, like the *Epistola* of Horace, to the general thesis that poetry is an art and as such is subject to definitely prescribed rules. The poem falls naturally into two divisions. The first of these, comprising Cantos I-III (De las reglas generales de composición, De la locución poética, De la versificación), treats of the mechanics of poetry. The second, comprising Cantos IV-VI (De la índole propia de varias composiciones, De la tragedia y de la comedia, De la epopeya, Conclusión), is concerned with the theory, practice and history of poetry, the illustrative material bearing on Greek and Latin classic writers or on Spanish authors and works.

The poem itself occupies but seventy-four of the four hundred and eighty-two pages of Vol. I of the author's **Obras literarias,** the remainder of the volume being given over to the *Anotaciones*. The entire second volume (pp. 1-533) is taken up with the six *Apéndices*. The *Anotaciones* are not notes in the general sense of the word. They are more exactly extended literary and critical disquisitions, and the poem itself, becomes complementary to them and to the *Apéndices* rather than vice versa. This is true not only in a purely quantitative but also in a functional sense.

The essential unity of the work as a whole and the merely introductory or prefatory character of the poem itself will be amply evidenced in the following analysis, which, purely for the purposes of convenience, will be divided into two chapters, one dealing with the poem and its *Anotaciones,* and the other with the *Apéndices*. The complete and systematic listing of contents will be found in the Tabular Analyses.

Canto I: De las reglas generales de composición. ANALYSIS OF CONTENTS: a) Lines 1-50, Introduction-Necessary regard for precepts—Rôles of imagination and creative genius. b) Lines 50-96, Rôle of good taste—Its characteristics. c) Lines 96-154, Observations on the historical development of Greek, Roman, Italian and Spanish poetry—The remarkable simplicity of Greek poetry—The eternal qualities of beauty revealed in this poetry. d) Lines 155-169, Resumé of Spanish poetry from the *Cid* to Quintana and Cienfuegos. e) Lines 170-355, Considerations on unity, variety, and the judicious use of details.[26]

This canto of the **Poética** and the *Anotaciones* thereto (text, **Obras lit.,** Vol. I, pp. 7-19; *Anotaciones, idem,* pp. 83-95) may well be grouped with Cantos V and VI and their accompanying *Anotaciones*, since of the six cantos of the **Poética** the above three are the most general and theoretical in approach and the most classical as regards

sources, the theories therein expounded being traceable, in the main, to Aristotle and Horace. This general, theoretical treatment is the rule throughout the **Poética** in all those cases where there is to be a subsequent consideration of the material, with specific application to Spanish literature, in the *Apéndices* (viz. Epic, Tragedy, Comedy). The absence here of the ordinarily pronounced nationalistic focus is seen in the fact that this canto contains, in common with Canto VI, a comparatively small amount of quoted, Spanish illustrative material. There are, furthermore, no quotations from foreign critical and literary works; passing mention of only three foreign writers (Dante, Petrarch, Boileau); references to forty-nine and ten classical writers.

Reference to the Tabular Analyses will show that with the exception of certain material on good taste taken from Capmany and Arteaga, literary-historical material from the Marqués de Santillana and some minor considerations on the use of details in poetry from B. L. de Argensola, the balance of the material has its source in Aristotle and Horace. This is unquestionably the case as regards theories stated explicitly enough to be traced. Here, as elsewhere, it is to be pointed out that there is a vast residium of literary doctrine of too general a nature to be confidently assigned to any specific source.

Although this canto is one of the least significant for purposes of revealing certain aspects of Martínez de la Rosa's nationalistic and conciliatory attitude, it may nevertheless be said to emphasize an important aspect of the **Poética** as a whole. This is the establishment of a Classical-Spanish alignment in theory and practise as opposed specifically to a French-Spanish alignment. This emphasis on the continuation of the classical ideal in poetry as opposed to any intermediary interpretation of this ideal is to be seen, first of all, in the large number of references to Greek and Latin writers. Secondly, the doctrines set forth in this canto are commonplaces in neo-classic criticism and originate in the treatises of Aristotle and Horace. To the extent that corroborative authorities are used, these are wholly Spanish. Finally, it is significant to note that lines 96-169 contain historical sketches of Greek, Roman, Italian and Spanish poetry while a similar treatment of French poetry is lacking.

The *Anotaciones* take the form of a running commentary on the excellencies of various classical writers, the most notable deviation from this arrangement being the resumé of Spanish poetry from the *Cid* to Quintana and Cienfuegos.[27] If this canto and its *Anotaciones* can be said to have one dominant theme, this is the insistence upon the all-important rôle of good taste as the final arbiter in poetic composition.

Canto II: De la locución poética. ANALYSIS OF CONTENTS: a) Lines 1-41, Connections between clarity of conception and ease of expression—Simplicity as the essential quality of sublimity. b) Lines 42-81, Ennoblement of words—Usage to be the judge in their choice—Archaisms—Ennoblement of words through judicious linking. c) Lines 82-122, Differences between speech of poetry and prose—The inspired poet—Poetic frenzy a necessity—Avoidance of the *mot propre*. d) Lines 122-191, Rôle of syntax—Particular advantages of Spanish syntax—Limitations on poetic liberty and license—Gallicisms. e) Lines 199-201, Necessity for poetry to be pleasing to the ear. f) Lines 202-225, Praise of the Castilian tongue as a poetic vehicle.

Canto II is one of the comparatively short cantos of the *Poética*. In common with Canto I, the theories here set forth are commonplaces of neo-classicism traceable in the main, to Horace. While such a similarity exists between these first two cantos as regards the text of the poem, this similarity does not extend to the *Anotaciones*. In fact a most striking dissimilarity in this regard is apparent in Canto II, for here, in place of the more or less routine observations on Greek and Latin poetry which characterize the preceding section, we find *Anotaciones* which are overwhelmingly Spanish in application.

The nationalistic focus of this canto is most apparent in the illustrative material. The Tabular Analyses show that there are one hundred and five quotations from thirty-two different Spanish writers (both literary and critical) and that these quotations total eight hundred and forty-eight lines. In addition there are passing references to twenty more Spanish writers in the *Anotaciones*. On the other hand not a single foreign writer nor critical authority is quoted in this section and but six figure in passing references.

It may be asserted that this canto and its *Anotaciones* points clearly to the following two cantos (III, Versificación; IV, De la índole propia de varias composiciones) which are among the most thoroughly Spanish in content of all six in the *Poética*. In this sense it may be considered a preparatory canto, looking to the increasingly nationalistic approach which will be thoroughly developed in the next two cantos.

Canto III: De la versificación. ANALYSIS OF CONTENTS: a) Lines 1-14, Introductory analogy between the poet's use of words and the sculptor's use of marble. b) Lines 15-29, Syllable counting as distinguished from true poetry. c) Lines 30-80, Cadence. d) Lines 81-117, Harmony. e) Lines 118-155, Poetic facility as it is distinguished from carelessness—Need for much polishing. f) Lines 156-162, Function and need of the critic. g) Lines 163-222, Union of pleasant sound and reason—Thought never to be sacrificed to sound—Words which add nothing to the thought detract from it—Poetry never to be strained.

Canto III and its *Anotaciones* may be said to continue the preparatory work of the preceding canto, pointing as they both do to Canto IV and showing the increasingly nationalistic focus of the *Poética*. The text of this canto contains routine observations on versification. *Anotación* 1 is a digest of common metrical terms and a discussion of Greek and Latin prosody. This consideration of classical poetic practice serves as an introduction to Martinez' thesis that

the Romance Languages also have a sort of prosody. Then there follows a very detailed discussion of Spanish prosody and the balance of the *Anotaciones* constitute a treatise on Spanish versification.

The illustrative material is almost wholly Spanish or classical. There are two hundred and eighty lines of directly quoted material and this canto shows the greatest array of quotations from Spanish critics (sixty-two lines from five critics). No foreign literary or critical quotations appear here but there are seven lines from classical literary works.

Of particular interest in this canto is Martínez' determination to accord all possible dignity to the Romance Languages, and especially to Spanish, as regards a prosody comparable to the classical prosody.

Canto IV: De la índole propia de varias composiciones. ANALYSIS OF CONTENTS: a) Lines 1-21, Introduction—Poetry an art, genius necessary. b) Lines 22-41, Mixture of genres—Rules are not enough—Poet must study the models. c) Lines 42-74, The eclogue. d) Lines 75-83, The idyl. e) Lines 84-126, The elegy. f) Lines 126-137, The Pindaric ode. g) Lines 138-144, The heroic ode. h) Lines 145-158, The moral ode. i) Lines 159-170, The Anachreontic ode. j) Lines 171, 178, The letrilla. k) Lines 179-209, The *romance*. l) Lines 210-217, The song. m) Lines 218-224, The epigram. n) Lines 225-233, The madrigal. o) Lines 234-242, The sonnet. p) Lines 243-271, The apologue. q) Lines 272-302, The satire. r) Lines 303-326, The muse of knowledge teaches all men to be poets—She gives the necessary doctrines. s) Lines 327-350, Didactic poetry.

Canto IV is one of the longest cantos of the entire *Poética*. From the foregoing analysis of its contents, it can be seen that with the exception of three sections (a, b, r) the whole canto is devoted to considerations of different verse forms. The pains taken by Martiínez in the demarcation of the exact limits of these forms reveals the characteristic fondness of the neo-classicists for hair-splitting distinctions in poetic types. This canto is the major contribution of the *Poética* with regard to non-dramatic verse forms.

The *Anotaciones* are strikingly Spanish in flavor. With the single exception of two lines from Boileau there are no foreign literary or critical quotations in the illustrative material. Fifteen lines are quoted from three classical writers. As a demonstration of the distinctly nationalistic complexion of Canto IV and its *Anotaciones,* we note the truly imposing total of three thousand, five hundred and eighty-nine lines of directly quoted material from Spanish literary works and in addition twenty-nine lines of corroborative testimony from Spanish critical treatises. A comparison of the different cantos in the Tabular Analyses will readily reveal that Canto IV overshadows all others in this respect.

In this canto there occurs further evidence in support of our contention that Martínez wished to stress the existence of a link between Greek and Latin poets and the Spanish writers. A close examination of the first four cantos shows that this relationship is most completely demonstrated in the last of these. It will be recalled that Canto I and its *Anotaciones* was made up of generalities and took the form of a running commentary on the excellencies of classical literature. Cantos II and III are increasingly Spanish in nature, a fact that is especially apparent in the *Anotaciones* and finally Canto IV shows, more completely than any of the preceding, how Spanish poetry is to be measured by and be a continuation of classical practice and precept. One or two examples will illustrate this method of approach.

In his discussion of the epigram Martínez says:

> De los Latinos tenemos la colección completa de Marcial. . . . España puede lisonjearse, no solo de haber dado el ser al mencionado poeta latino, sino de haber ostentado en todas épocas el ingenio vivo y agudo de sus naturales, muy apto para esta clase de composición; en la cual se distinguieron mucho, entre los antiguos poetas, Baltasar de Alcázar y Salvador Polo de Medina, y entre los modernos, el erudito Don Juan de Iriarte y el ameno D. José Iglesias.[28]

In his discussion of the ode he says:

> Hay una oda de Francisco de la Torre en que se descubre el designio de imitar a Horacio, a la par de muchas bellezas. . . . Rioja era digno de imitar a Horacio; y así lo hizo, manifestando como él su indignación contra la temeraria osadía del hombre, en su *Oda a la riqueza*. . . . Entre los modernos se percibe en las poesías del maestro Fr. Diego González su afición a Horacio. . . .

The above examples are typical of the manner in which, in these *Anotaciones*, the classical prototypes of each poetic form are discussed, after which Martínez passes at once to an examination of what Spanish poets have accomplished in each genre.

Canto V: De la tragedia y de la comedia. ANALYSIS OF CONTENTS: a) Lines 1-16, General aims of the tragedy. b) Lines 17-107, Unities of time, place and action. c) Lines 108-130, Parts of the tragedy to be acted and those to be related. d) Lines 131-152, Exposition—Need for crescendo in plot. e) Lines 153-161, Denouement. f) Lines 162-172, Analysis of *Oedipus rex*. g) Lines 173-180, Power of destiny over human actions must be shown in the tragedy. h) Lines 181-210, One protagonist—Other characters. i) Lines 211-260, Language, style and versification. j) Lines 261-271, Aims of the comedy. k) Lines 272-299, Ideal model—Presentation of comic characters. l) Lines 300-314, Unities—Plot—Exposition—Denouement. m) Lines 315-388, Delineation of character—Style—Locution—Versification. n) Lines 389-396, Indulgence for Spanish genius.

Canto V is to be distinguished from the other cantos of the *Poética* by the fact that the nationalistic focus, characteristic of the work as a whole and of certain cantos (III, IV) in particular is almost negligible here. This canto can be most aptly described as a highly theoretical and objective treatment of the tragedy and comedy with special consideration for classical doctrine and its interpretation by French and Italian dramatists and preceptists. We have already spoken[30] and shall have occasion to speak again[31] of the distribution made by Martínez of his remarks on the tragedy and comedy (and the *comedia*) in the *Poética* and *Apéndices*. There may well be stated at this point what we consider to be the most plausible reasons for this arrangement. In the first place, such a distribution of the material was the most natural because of the lack, in a strictly formal (i. e. neo-classical) sense, of the tragedy and comedy in Spanish literature. Martínez himself readily recognizes such a situation. Since the status of the drama constituted the most controversial point in the whole literary dispute (1737-1827) and since, furthermore, Martínez would wish to present a resumé of the already generally accepted neo-classical doctrine governing the tragedy and the comedy, this sort of historical summation could best and most logically be given in close connection with the *Poética* itself. This is exactly what we have in the *Anotaciones* to Canto V. Finally, the logic of such an arrangement is seen in the fact that having considered these two genres in an historical and theoretical sense in the *Anotaciones*, he has better prepared the way for a practical discussion in the *Apéndices*, not only of what few bona fide examples there are of these types in Spanish literature but by virtue of this introduction is more nearly in a position to evaluate them and whatever deviations must be considered along with them, chiefly the *comedia*.

Here, as elsewhere in the *Poética* and *Anotaciones*, much is to be gathered from an examination of the quoted, illustrative material. In the case of this canto we find but twelve lines from two Spanish critics as opposed to one hundred and twenty-five lines from seven French and Italian critics (principally from Corneille, Voltaire and Metastasio). In addition it should be pointed out that this section contains literary quotations from the largest number of foreign authors of any canto in the *Poética*. Though quantitatively a greater number of lines are quoted from Spanish literary works, the Tabular Analyses show that this material comes from but two Spanish writers, Cervantes and la Hoz.

The classical theories of Aristotle and Horace are the points of departure in this canto but as we have indicated they are examined in the light of foreign interpretations rather than Spanish. Notwithstanding this faithful adherence to the classical doctrines of Aristotle and Horace and the close attention paid to foreign interpretations of these theories, it is interesting to note certain instances in which Martínez shows a deviation from them. Among the most noteworthy of these are the following indications of a more moderate critical approach

a) Each nation can best determine the material length of the tragedy to suit its own needs. This is an attitude completely in keeping with his nationalistic viewpoint. b) Martínez follows Corneille's tendency to allow some laxity in regard to the unity of time. Some of the action can be supposed to have transpired during the entre'actes. c) He would also allow considerable indulgence in regard to the unity of place. Scenes can best be changed, however, during the entre'actes. d) Martínez does not follow the French commentators of Aristotle and proscribe death and blood on the stage. He simply insists that there be no horrible scenes. e) Although Aristotle had recommended sad endings as the most effective, a tragedy cannot be condemned simply because it ends happily.[32] f) He shows a general indulgence in the matter of the application of all rules to dramatic works. In this regard he quotes Geoffroy: "Es preciso absolutamente prestarse a la ilusión teatral y no exigir una verisimilitud más severa, que haría casi imposible la práctica del arte."[33] Martínez himself says in this connection:

> Sea dicho todo esto, no en menoscabo de la admiración que merecen los que han levantado la tragedia al más alto punto de perfección; sino como prueba de la templanza con que deben aplicarse las reglas, cuando son poquísimas las obras de los mejores maestros que no hayan menester indulgencia.[34]

Martínez de la Rosa's nationalistic and conciliatory approach is seen further in his belief that the tragedy should have the number of acts most in keeping with national custom. Since the Spanish people were accustomed to *comedias* in three acts, there is no reason why they cannot have tragedies in three acts also. We have noted his attempt to reconcile the extreme opinions regarding the unities of time and place. Furthermore, he is opposed to the stereotyped use of the monologue between the principle actor and a confidant as a means of presenting the exposition. He insists upon a more natural device and suggests that the exposition be woven into the action itself. The ancients' belief in the power of fate can be, he believes, adapted to the use of the modern tragedy through the people's belief in omens, native superstitions etc. Finally, he presents a spirited defense of Spanish versification as being admirably suited to the tragedy.

He shows a true neo-classic conception of the comedy as an "escuela de costumbres." He says:

> La comedia se propone por medio de una acción, diestramente imitada en la escena, presentar bajo aspecto ridículo los vicios y faltas morales de los hombres, para alejarlos de caer en otros parecidos. Así se ve que su fin es el más importante; pues con el incentivo de una diversión inocente y sin más armas que la donosa burla, no menos intenta que influir en la mejora de las costumbres.[35]

His treatment of the comedy may be termed summary. After insistence on the use of the ideal model and a comparison of the *Aulularia* of Plautus, *L'Avare* of Molière and *El castigo de la miseria* of Juan de la Hoz, his remarks on the unities, dramatic imitation, characters, language, style and locution are little more than analogies to like technique in the tragedy.

A slightly more nationalistic note is to be seen at the end of his discussion when he recommends for the Spanish

comedy the assonanced eight syllable *romance* meter. This choice is supported, he declares, because it conforms most nearly with Aristotle's preference for the iambic.

Canto VI: De la epopeya—Conclusión. ANALYSIS OF CONTENTS: a) Lines 1-10, General characteristics of the epic. b) Lines 10-51, Circumscribing the subject—Exposition—Length. c) Lines 52-68, Unity of action. d) Lines 69-81, The inspired epic poet. e) Lines 82-95, Use of truth and fiction. f) Lines 96-106, The necessity for crescendo in the epic. g) Lines 107-141, Grandeur in the epic subject. h) Lines 142-215, Means of elaboration. i) Lines 216-292, Characters—Achilles as a principle character. j) Lines 293-303, *Deus ex machina*. k) Lines 304-346, Mythological characters. l) Lines 347-355, Metaphysical abstractions. m) Lines 356-413, Style and versification.

As has been indicated[36], this canto is one of the most general and theoretical in approach of all the cantos of the *Poética*. In common with cantos I and V there is less emphasis on the application of doctrine to Spanish literature. The focus of the canto and its *Anotaciones* is clearly on the classical epic as is to be seen from the running comment on the *Iliad* which appears throughout the latter section. Martínez takes Homer's poem as his critical point of departure and weaves into his discussion of it, pertinent comparisons to other classical, French and Italian epics.

His remarks on the Spanish epic are limited to those on the *Canto épico* of Moratín and passing references to Ercilla, Balbuena and Lope as competent versifiers. The *Anotaciones* become more Spanish in tone toward the end in his discussion of the Spanish verse form most suitable for the epic.[37] Martínez decides in favor of the *octava*.

This canto and its *Anotaciones* are distinguished by the fact that they contain the smallest amount of quoted material of any of the cantos of the *Poética*. The Tabular Analyses show that on the basis of this modicum of critical references and quoted material, the sources are classical and Spanish. It should be pointed out that Martínez does not follow Boileau in condemning Christianity as a useful literary element in the epic. He insists rather that it can be used to great advantage if it is used with discretion. In an attempt to adapt useful devices from the old epic to modern usage, he suggests, in place of the *deus ex machina*, material based on the peoples' belief in signs, omens etc. In a related connection he suggests that the modern counterpart of mythology should be the marvellous aspect that can be given to natural phenomena.

The preceding examination of the *Poética* and the *Anotaciones* has revealed, it is hoped, much more than the critical opinions previously expressed on them.[38] It is much more than an anachronistic restatement of outmoded neo-classic precepts. Such a view is incomplete and misleading, stressing the poem to the exclusion of its copious *Anotaciones* and *Apéndices*. We have indicated the rôle which we feel the *Poética* plays as an introduction to Martínez' more ambitious desire of writing a nationalistic and apologistic treatise on Spanish poetry (exclusive of the lyric). This introductory rôle is manifest from the fact that many of the doctrines set forth in a general, theoretical fashion in the text of the poem, are expanded, profusely illustrated and, what is more significant in this connection, often modified, in the *Anotaciones*. It should be noted also that this elaboration is usually most detailed where it is a question of native Spanish forms.

Thus an important, general characteristic of the *Poética* and its *Anotaciones* is that the spirit of the two is predominantly Spanish. An estimate of the *Poética* by Menéndez y Pelayo must be quoted here since our investigation shows that it can be considerably clarified if not materially modified. He has claaed the *Poética* "una obra cuyos elementos son evidentemente de importación extranjera."[39]

Such a statement from such an eminent critic conveys, perhaps unintentionally, a false impression in regard to the ideological alignment of the work. Only in the superficial sense that the whole neo-classic movement was a thing "de importación extranjera" is the above statement valid. Martínez' own statements, as well as our examination of the material, shows that the ideology of the work represents more essentially a Spanish-Classical than Spanish-French, Spanish-English or Spanish-Italian alignment. The foregoing statement is not invalidated by the circumstance that many of the doctrines expounded herein happen to be common to French, English and Italian preceptists. Apursual of the Tabular Analyses will reveal that the overwhelming majority of the precepts come from Aristotle (probably via Pinciano) and Horace. No valid question could possibly be raised regarding Martínez' familiarity with this source material. It has been noted furthermore that in those cases where a French, Italian or English interpretation of a classical doctrine is accepted, Martínez, whenever possible, argues for the priority of statements on the same subject by native Spanish preceptists.

There are three sections (Cantos V, VI, Tragedy, Comedy and Epic) which seemingly belie this above-mentioned Spanish-Classical alignment. This contradiction, however, is only apparent. In these cantos on the tragedy, the comedy and the epic there is a greater display of French, Italian and English critical opinion than elsewhere in the *Poética* and *Anotaciones*. This circumstance is to be explained by the fact that here the genres in question are being treated in a general and theoretical manner. This being the case, the material presented here really constitutes an historical review of the critical opinions on the tragedy, the comedy and the epic as expounded by French, Italian and English preceptists and this does not necessarily entail Martínez' commitment to these opinions as representing practices best adapted to Spanish genius and temperament. To be added to this circumstance is the fact that in the *Apéndices,* where these genres will be treated with particular reference to Spanish literature, a great abundance of native criticisms, textual quotations and illustrative material will be brought to play. Such a procedure, in fact, dovetails perfectly with an important aspect of Martínez'

apologistic technique. It is frequently apparent that French, Italian and English opinions are stated simply to serve as a foil for Martínez, to be offset to the advantage of Spanish critics.

This patriotic, nationalistic approach is further revealed through the bulk of the quoted, illustrative material. Such statistical data have an added significance when coupled with the foregoing observations. The first four cantos of the *Poética* (and the accompanying *Anotaciones*) do not contain, by way of illustrative material, a single line from a foreign poetic composition. On the other hand they contain four thousand, six hundred and twelve lines from Spanish poetic works, representing eighty-five poets. The same four cantos are almost equally Spanish as regards critical material. In this connection, save for a single line quoted from la Harpe, there appear no foreign critical opinions, while one hundred and thirty-six lines from Spanish critics are quoted, representing thirteen authorities.

When we consider all six cantos on the basis of quotations, both literary and critical, the overwhelming preponderance of Spanish quotations becomes evident. There are in the *Anotaciones* nearly five thousand lines of quotations from Spanish literary and critical works as opposed to only one hundred and forty-six of foreign literary and critical material. Classical literary and critical quotations account for forty-four lines. That the spirit of the *Poética* and *Anotaciones* is unquestionably Spanish is proven by: a) The avowed and logical aim of the work. b) The illustrative material. c) Spanish theory and practice displayed as a continuation of the classical models rather than of the French, English or Italian. d) Martínez' patriotic, nationalistic and apologistic technique.

With regard to the contents of the *Poética* itself, there is to be noted the absence of a specific canto dealing with lyric poetry. This constitutes a significant omission when we consider the importance of this type of poetry in Spanish literature. Another fact to be stressed is that the non-technical material in the *Poética* (Cantos IV-VI) shows a predominant interest in dramatic poetry, a fact that is also characteristic of the *Apéndices*.

Notes

1. For other indications see also *Obras literarias,* Vol. II, p. 315.

2. *Loc. cit.,* Vol. I, p. 3 *et seq.*

3. Cf. Fernández y González, *op. cit.,* p. 28 and *passim*; Sarrailh, *op. cit.,* pp. 12-16.

4. In this connection Fernández y González says, *ibid.,* "No es ocasión de enumerar las nuevas comisiones que le confió el Claustro desde esta época, ni de reseñar los informes curiosos que continuamente brotaban de su pluma; baste decir, que siendo muy escasos en general los datos que se conservan en nuestro archivo de los profesores de este tiempo, no parece

medida notable en que no se muestre como promovedor o encargado el catedrático de ética."

5. Cf. F. Courtney Tarr, "An Unnoticed Political Article of Martínez de la Rosa (1812), in *Romanic Review,* XXIII (1932), p. 226.

6. See Chap. VI.

7. As revealed in his classical comedies in the Moratín manner: *La niña en casa y la madre en la máscara* (1827); *Los celos infundados* (1861); *La boda y el duelo* (1861)

8. Menéndez y Pelayo (*Ideas estéticas,* Vol 6, p. 206) says of him in this connection: "Para esta obra no debemos tener más que alabanzas. De las infinitas traducciones que hay en castellano, como en todas las lenguas cultas, de aquel código de buen gusto, ninguna es tan elegante y tan poética, aunque otras hay más literales".

9. Menéndez y Pelayo (*Estudios de critica literaria,* Vol. I, p. 261) in the course of a discussion of Martínez' changing political ideology, makes a fitting analogy to his literary activities: "No fué en verdad cálculo de interés ni de ambición el que trocó a Martínez de la Rosa en el primer moderado español; fué su propia naturaleza ecléctica, elegante y tímida (de aquella timidez que no es incompatible con el valor personal) tímida sobre todo para asustarse de las legítimas consecuencias de sus principios absolutos, y bastante cándida para asombrarse de que estallaran las tempestades. Este al fin y al cabo, fué destino constante de Martínez de la Rosa, así en política como en literatura: ser heraldo de revoluciones y asustarse luego de ellas; y de la misma manera en el arte, sin haber sido nunca romántico, abrir la puerta al romanticismo y triunfar primero en las tablas, en nombre de la nueva escuela".

10. Cf. Tarr, *op. cit.,* pp. 288-89.

11. *Op. cit.,* p. 60.

12. *Ideas estéticas,* Vol. 6, p. 207.

13. *Ibid.,* p. 185.

14. *Op. cit.,* p. 124. See also I. L. McClelland, *op. cit,* p. 1.

15. See *supra,* pp. x-xi.

16. *Obras literarias,* Vol. I, p. 4.

17. We refer to the desire of the Spanish *reformadores* to improve their nation's letters by going back to the Classics, without any intermediary sources.

18. "En el silencio de aquel destierro . . . compuso los seis cantos de su *Arte Poetica,* enrequicida con instructivas notas." *Op. cit.,* p. 69. This writer erroneously implies that the *Apéndices* to the *Poética* accompany Martínez' translation of Horace. Cf. *Ibid.*

19. *Op. cit.,* p. 19.

20. "His literary activity during this period (1823-31) was large and varied, ranging from an *Ars poetica* to the Romantic drama." A. L. Owen and J. T. Lister ed. *La conjuración de Venecia,* New York, 1920, p. XVII.

21. *Op. cit.,* p. 26.

22. "Lejos estoy de lisonjearme de haber evitado uno y otro escollo en esta traducción, a pesar del esmero con que trabajé en ella hace unos nueve años." That is to say about 1819.

23. *Loc. cit.,* p. 26.

24. "La edición más antigua que he hallado en París de esta obra, es la que existe en la biblioteca de Santa Genoveva. . . ." *Obras lit.,* Vol. II, p. 312, note 5; "Pues en varias ediciones distintas que he hallado en las bibliotecas de París . . ." *ibid.,* p. 380. "Por buena dicha di con ella, registrando obras manuscritas en la Biblioteca Real de París." *ibid.,* pp. 518-19.

25. See *infra,* p. 88, n21.

26. This canto ends (lines 335-340) with further observations on good taste which only repeat the ideas of lines 50-96.

27. Cf. *Poética,* lines 155-169 and *Anotación* 10.

28. *Anotación* 15, p. 290.

29. *Idem,* 10, p. 244.

30. See *supra,* p. 20.

31. See *infra,* pp. 39-40.

32. There are definite hints of this same moderate attitude in Luzán. Cf. his *Poética española,* Zaragoza, 1737, p. 401 and *passim.*

33. Cf. Julien Louis Geoffroy ed. *Oeuvres de Jean Racine.* Paris, 1808. 7 vols. Vol. II, p. 56, note 1.

34. *Poética,* p. 387.

35. *Ibid.,* p. 434.

36. See *supra,* p. 26.

37. *Poética,* pp. 479-482.

38. See *supra,* pp. x-xi.

39. *Ideas estéticas,* Vol. 6, p. 201.

Michael D. McGaha (essay date 1973)

SOURCE: "The 'Romanticism' of *La conjuración de Venecia,*" in *Kentucky Romance Quarterly,* Vol. 20, No. 2, 1973, pp. 235-42.

[In the following essay, McGaha suggests that the romantic qualities of Martínez de la Rosa's drama La conjuración de Venecia *are relatively slight and that the playwright was essentially a neoclassicist.]*

Francisco Martínez de la Rosa (1787-1862) is traditionally credited with having introduced Romanticism into Spain. The work which gained him this title was his play, *La conjuración de Venecia,* written during his exile in France and first published by Didot in 1830. The play was first performed in Madrid on April 23, 1834, and was immediately and overwhelmingly successful. Perhaps the first critic to realize the transcendent significance of the work was Eugenio de Ochoa, who in 1835 wrote of Martínez de la Rosa that "Este poeta tiene . . . la gloria de haber introducido *el primero* en el moderno teatro español las doctrinas del romanticismo."[1]

This distinction must have come as a surprise to Martínez de la Rosa who, though not a doctrinaire classicist, never considered himself a romantic. Once he had outgrown a period of youthful revolutionary ardor, Martínez de la Rosa became as staunch a moderate in literature as in politics, and all forms of extremism were thenceforth distasteful to him. In the *Advertencia* published in the first edition of his *Poesías,* he wrote: "Como todo partido extremo me ha parecido siempre intolerante, poco conforme a la razón y contrario al bien mismo que se propone, tal vez de esta causa provenga que me siento poco inclinado a alistarme en las banderas de los *clásicos* o de los *románticos* (ya que es preciso apellidarlos con el nombre que han tomado por señal y divisa); y que tengo como cosa asentada que unos y otros llevan razón cuando censuran las exorbitancias y demasías del partido contrario, y cabalmente incurren en el mismo defecto así que tratan de ensalzar su propio sistema."[2] The moderation of Martínez de la Rosa's literary creed was accompanied by an eclectic spirit, which allowed him to combine different and even opposed tendencies in his work. It is in this aspect of his character that Menéndez y Pelayo sees Martínez de la Rosa's superiority over his eighteenth century contemporaries: "Tuvo, aparte de esto, Martínez de la Rosa una ventaja y supremacía sobre los hombres del siglo XVIII, ventaja que no alcanzaron ni Quintana ni D. Juan Nicasio, y fue la de mayor tolerancia y espíritu más abierto a todas las innovaciones literarias. En este sentido, puede decirse que es poeta de transición, poeta ecléctico, y que con menos fantasía y menos habilidad para asimilarse lo ajeno, ocupa en nuestro Parnaso lugar parecido al de Casimiro Delavigne en Francia."[3]

The fact that Martínez de la Rosa did incorporate elements from a wide variety of authors into his work has led scholars to a painstaking search for the sources of these borrowings. In his edition of *La conjuración de Venecia,* aside from the known historical sources of the work, Jean Sarrailh has pointed out possible influences of Delavigne, Vigny, Shakespeare, Victor Hugo and Lope de Vega. All of these comparisons are interesting conjectures, but there is, of course, no positive proof that any of these authors directly influenced Martínez de la Rosa. Blanco García attributes the choice of Venice for the scene of the play to the influence of Byron, who had conferred a new literary prestige on that city by making it the setting for some of his own works.[4] At first sight, Sarrailh's selection of possible sources for the romantic elements in *La conjuración de Venecia* seems logical, since all of the authors mentioned played a significant role in the development of the romantic movement. It appears, however, that in the search for romantic antecedents of certain elements of Martínez de la Rosa's play, other, more probable sources have been completely ignored by the critics.

In 1774 Gaspar Melchor de Jovellanos achieved a notable success with a five-act play in prose called *El delincuente honrado.* This play introduced into Spain the genre known in France as the *comédie larmoyante* and in England as the sentimental drama. The play received almost unanimous approval from the neo-classical critics of the day. Except for a rather broad interpretation of the unity of place, Jovellanos' play conforms to the unities, and it is didactic in nature. Allison Peers writes of this play that: "Founded on emotion, and making continual use of coincidence, antithesis and other essentially Romantic devices, it clearly looks forward to the next century despite its outward adherence to neo-Classical standards."[5]

The plot of Jovellanos' play is as follows: Torcuato, a worthy representative of the ideals of the eighteenth-century Enlightenment, has been provoked into a duel in which he killed another man, whose wife he later married. Torcuato's best friend is arrested and accused of the crime, whereupon Torcuato nobly confesses his guilt. Since a recent royal edict has prescribed capital punishment for anyone found guilty of participating in a duel, regardless of the circumstances, Torcuato knows that he must die. The plot is further complicated by the fact that the judge discovers that Torcuato is his long-lost son. Torcuato narrowly escapes execution when, already on the gallows, he receives a royal pardon.

Martínez de la Rosa's esteem for this play is well known. In an appendix to his *Poética,* published in 1827, he wrote:

> El mérito principal de la composición de Jovellanos no consiste en el artificio y trama; sino en el excelente fondo y en las sólidas bellezas que encierra, dignas de granjearle los aplausos que recibe del público en la representación, y que no le niegan los inteligentes aun después de escrupuloso examen. Sanas ideas de moral y legislación, expresadas con nobleza y amenidad, impugnación de preocupaciones funestas, pasiones naturales y vivas, sentimientos virtuosos y tiernos, caracteres pintados con verdad y sencillez; y tantas apreciables prendas realzadas con estilo propio y urbano, y con dicción no menos pura que esmerada y fácil, recomiendan esa composición como una de las pocas, si es que no la única, que de ese género ofrezca el teatro español; ella sola bastaría, aun cuando faltasen otras pruebas, para que la posteridad formase concepto de lo que fue su autor: magistrado recto e instruido, hombre honrado y sensible, y escritor muy aventajado.[6]

After a careful comparison of *El delincuente honrado* and *La conjuración de Venecia,* it seems to me more than probable that Martínez de la Rosa modeled the principal characters and the non-historical elements of the plot (*i.e.,*

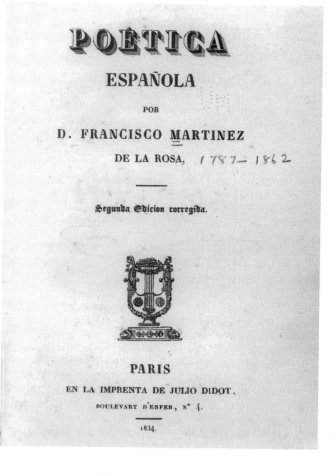

Title page of Poética, *1827.*

the love story of Rugiero and Laura) after Jovellanos' play. It has often been said that one of the innovations of *La conjuración de Venecia* was the creation of the first romantic hero of Spanish drama. Peers makes this statement, and Ángel del Río says that "La prosa cuidada . . . de Martínez de la Rosa no tiene otro atractivo que la novedad para su tiempo y el haber sabido captar en la figura de Rugiero los perfiles del héroe romántico: misterioso, valiente, pesimista, huérfano, enamorado y triste, víctima inocente de su destino trágico."[7]

Let us now examine some of these characteristics as they apply to the Torcuato of *El delincuente honrado* and the Rugiero of *La conjuración de Venecia.* Both Rugiero and Torcuato are orphans. Neither has ever known the identity of his parents. When Laura tells Rugiero that her deceased mother would surely disapprove of their clandestine union, he replies: "Tú, por lo menos, tienes el consuelo de haberla conocido, de haber pasado tu niñez a su sombra; tú recuerdas su rostro, su acento, sus caricias . . . ; a la hora de su muerte te dejó en los brazos de un padre . . . ¡Pero yo, yo, infeliz de mí, desde que abrí los ojos no he tenido en el mundo a quien volverlos! . . . Solo, huérfano, sin amparo ni abrigo . . . sin saber a quiénes debo el ser, ni

siquiera la tierra en que nací . . ."[8] Torcuato, however, expresses an even greater pessimism when he says: "El cielo me ha condenado a vivir en la adversidad. ¡Qué desdichado nací! Incierto de los autores de mi vida, he andado siempre sin patria ni hogar propio, y cuando acababa de labrarme una fortuna que me hacía cumplidamente dichoso, quiere mi mala estrella . . ."[9] Torcuato again gives expression to this feeling of personal impotence against the designs of a malevolent fate when he asks: "¿Y a dónde iré a esconder mi vida desdichada? . . . Sin patria, sin familia, prófugo y desconocido sobre la tierra, ¿dónde hallaré refugio contra la adversidad?"[10] His overwhelming pessimism is again revealed when the simple act of looking at his watch leads him to exclaim: "¡Qué tarde pasa el tiempo sobre la vida de un desdichado!"[11]

The following passage from *La conjuración de Venecia* is singled out by Sarrailh as indicative of Rugiero's pessimism, "tan característico de los héroes románticos": "Aun cuando la suerte nos fuese adversa, antes quiero perecer con las víctimas que no triunfar con los verdugos."[12] However, this noble desire for "liberty or death" is far less pessimistic than Torcuato's statement, when faced with the prospect of a permanent separation from his wife: "¡Ah, en el conflicto en que me hallo, la muerte fuera dulce a mis ojos!"[13] Both Rugiero and Torcuato are hardened against the fear of death by their stoic pessimism. Thus Rugiero asks the Tribunal: "¿Creéis que es el temor de la muerte que me hace derramar estas lágrimas? . . ."[14] And Torcuato tells Laura: "Y no creas que voy huyendo de la muerte. ¿Qué hay en ella de horrible para los desdichados?"[15]

One of the more improbable aspects of both plays is the fact that Rugiero and Torcuato are ready to die with tranquillity, after having discovered the identity of their fathers. This is particularly odd, since neither son has any cause to be grateful to his father. In both cases, the father is also the judge who has condemned his son to death. Nonetheless, Rugiero tells the Tribunal: "Yo no os pido más . . . ; nada más . . . recibir la bendición de mi padre, y entregar mi alma a Dios!"[16] And Torcuato exclaims: "¡Mi padre! . . . ¡Ay, padre mío! Después de haber pronunciado tan dulce nombre, ya no temo la muerte."[17]

Jovellanos takes full advantage of the melodramatic scene in which the father reveals his true identity. Several long, almost unbearably emotional scenes of reconciliation, marked by the father's self-recriminations and the son's generous forgiveness, ensue. Oddly enough, Martínez de la Rosa removes Rugiero's father from the scene immediately after the moment of recognition. Valbuena Prat praises him for his discretion, and considers this one of the non-romantic aspects of *La conjuración de Venecia*: "El tino con que resuelve el problema paternofilial de la obra, sin dar lugar a largas escenas lloronas de reconocimiento y efusión familiar ante la muerte cierta, sino dejando caer un velo rápidamente sobre el destino y la vida del protagonista, le da . . . una dignidad estoica diversa del pleno romanticismo."[18] Thus we are led to the paradoxical conclusion that Jovellanos' play, produced in 1774 and universally acclaimed by the neoclassical critics, is, at least in this aspect, more romantic than the work which is said to have introduced Romanticism into Spanish literature.

The heroines of both plays are called Laura. This in itself is insignificant, since Laura was a popular name for female dramatic characters in both the eighteenth and the nineteenth centuries. When we consider that the personality development of the two characters is almost identical, however, the use of the same name begins to seem more than a mere coincidence.

Both women attempt, in similar terms, to persuade their husbands not to risk their lives. The Laura of *La conjuración de Venecia* pleads: "¡No me abandones . . . , ten lástima de esta infeliz!"[19] whereas Jovellanos has his Laura say: "¿Y las lágrimas de tu esposa, hombre cruel, no podrán reprimir tus ímpetus violentos? ¿Quieres exponer mi triste vida a nuevos desconsuelos? Sosiégate, desdichado, y ten compasión de esta infeliz."[20] When their husbands are in danger, both women decide to risk their own safety and good name by revealing their guilty secrets to their fathers and seeking paternal help. Martínez de la Rosa's Laura says: "¿Quién tendrá piedad de nosotros, si nos la niega un padre!"[21] and she asks her servant, Matilde: "¿Quieres que deje perecer al esposo de mi corazón por no revelar mi secreto? . . . No, Matilde, no; es mi esposo a los ojos de Dios, y yo debo salvarle a costa de mi vida . . . ¿Qué me importa lo que digan los hombres?"[22] The Laura of *El delincuente honrado* asks, in an anguished soliloquy: "¿Y a quién acudiré con mis lágrimas? . . . Mi padre . . . ¡Ay! ¿podrá sufrir mi padre que interceda por el matador de mi esposo? . . . ¿Pero éste mismo no es mi esposo también? Sí: ya reconozco mi primera obligación."[23] Both women are ready to die with their spouses if necessary. In *La conjuración de Venecia,* Laura cries out that she will not abandon Rugiero: "No lo temas, Rugiero, no lo temas; tu Laura te salvará o morirá contigo."[24] Jovellanos' Laura informs her father that she cannot live without her husband: "Pero si vuestro corazón resiste a mis suspiros, yo iré a lanzarlos a los pies del señor don Justo; su alma piadosa se enternecerá con mis lágrimas; le ofreceré mi vida por redimir la de mi esposo, y si no pudiese salvarlo, moriremos juntos, pues yo no he de sobrevivir a su desgracia."[25]

If, in fact, *La conjuración de Venecia* was chiefly inspired by Jovellanos' play, a number of statements which have traditionally been made about Martínez de la Rosa's work must be re-examined. There can obviously be no doubt that Martínez de la Rosa incorporated certain superficially romantic elements into his play, *e.g.,* the Venetian setting, the tomb scene, the carnival atmosphere, and the use of crowds. But did he really create the first romantic hero of Spanish drama? It seems to me evident that the Torcuato of *El delincuente honrado* is every bit as much a romantic

hero as the Rugiero of *La conjuración de Venecia.* In fact, I think one might successfully claim more romantic traits for Torcuato than for Rugiero—certainly a more intense pessimism.

The only substantial deviation from neo-classicism in Martínez de la Rosa's play is his rather broad interpretation of the unities of place and time. The unity of time is perhaps more strictly observed by Jovellanos in *El delincuente honrado,* but he, too, does not hesitate to change the scene of the play between acts.

The few formal elements of Romanticism which appear in *La conjuración de Venecia* do not make of it a truly romantic play. I am confident that many of the so-called innovations of Martínez de la Rosa will eventually be recognized to have formed a part of the dramatic tradition of Spain during the eighteenth century. It is therefore a mistake to overemphasize Martínez de la Rosa's borrowings from the French and English romantics.

Francisco Martínez de la Rosa was a timid and unimaginative writer, whose chief virtue was his ability to synthesize elements taken from a wide variety of sources. If he had lived and worked in the mid-eighteenth century rather than at the crucial moment of transition from Neo-classicism to Romanticism, he would probably be scarcely remembered today. *La conjuración de Venecia* is of interest, not because of its intrinsic merit, but as a historical document. Changing sensibilities and external events conspired to make this rather mediocre play one of the milestones of Spanish literature.

Notes

1. Cited in E. Allison Peers, *A History of the Romantic Movement in Spain* (Cambridge: University Press, 1940), I, 255.

2. Francisco Martínez de la Rosa, *Obras dramáticas,* ed. Jean Sarrailh (Clásicos Castellanos; Madrid: Espasa-Calpe, S. A., 1947), p. 28.

3. Marcelino Menéndez y Pelayo, *Estudios de crítica literaria* (Madrid: Rivadeneyra, 1893), p. 243.

4. P. Francisco Blanco García, *La literatura española en el siglo XIX* (Madrid, 1909), I, p. 125.

5. Peers, *op. cit.,* I, p. 34.

6. *Obras literarias,* II, p. 508; cited by Eugenio de Ochoa, *Tesoro del teatro español desde su origen hasta nuestros días* (Paris: Garnier Frères, 1863-1899), V, p. 430.

7. Ángel del Río, *Historia de la literatura española* (New York: Holt, Rinehart and Winston, 1963), II, p. 110.

8. Martínez de la Rosa, *op. cit.,* p. 276.

9. Gaspar Melchor de Jovellanos, *El delincuente honrado,* in Ochoa, *op. cit.,* V, p. 434.

10. *Ibid.,* p. 436.

11. *Ibid.,* p. 432.

12. Martínez de la Rosa, *op. cit.,* p. 263.

13. Jovellanos, *op. cit.,* p. 433.

14. Martínez de la Rosa, *op. cit.,* p. 334.

15. Jovellanos, *op. cit.,* p. 438.

16. Martínez de la Rosa, *op. cit.,* p. 334.

17. Jovellanos, *op. cit.,* p. 447.

18. Valbuena Prat, *Historia de la literatura española* (Barcelona: Editorial Gustavo Gili, S. A., 1963), III, p. 161.

19. Martínez de la Rosa, *op. cit.,* p. 280.

20. Jovellanos, *op. cit.,* p. 439.

21. Martínez de la Rosa, *op. cit.,* p. 289.

22. *Ibid.,* p. 285.

23. Jovellanos, *op. cit.,* p. 439.

24. Martínez de la Rosa, *op. cit.,* p. 286.

25. Jovellanos, *op. cit.,* p. 443.

Robert Geraldi (essay date 1983)

SOURCE: "Francisco Martínez de la Rosa: Literary Atrophy or Creative Sagacity?" in *Hispanofila,* Vol. 27, No. 1, September, 1983, pp. 11-19.

[*In the following essay, Geraldi enumerates parallels between Martínez de la Rosa's dramas* Aben-Humeya *and* La conjuración de Venecia, *while maintaining that both plays were artistically innovative and revolutionary.*]

In reading **Aben Humeya** (1830) and **La conjuración de Venecia** (1834) by the dramatist Francisco Martínez de la Rosa, the reader becomes aware of various similarities in the two plays and may be misled to the erroneous conclusion that the author was lacking in inventive and creative powers.

It is the purpose of this article to illustrate some of these striking parallels in plot, structure, idea, characterization, situation, incident and dialogue in these dramas and offer possible reasons for these similarities and thus justify the conclusion that Martínez de la Rosa was indeed clever in developing further an original idea.

Both plays are based on historical incidents: the attempts to overthrow existing oppressive governments. Various grievances against these regimes are uttered by the two conspiratorial factions in each work. In **Aben Humeya** the

Moriscos endeavor to topple the Spanish government in 1568; in **La conjuración de Venecia** there is an attempt to overthrow the Doge of Venice in 1310.

In the event that the *coups d'état* are successful, the reestablishment of former rulers, laws and privileges is to take place. This we see in the naming of Aben Humeya as the new leader, a member of the former royal family. Although he receives the support of the majority present, there is a note of reluctance on the part of a few members to submit themselves to another ruler.

> ALFAQUÍ No basta que rompáis vuestras cadenas; es preciso que levantéis otra vez el trono de Alhamar . . . y, no lo habréis olvidado sin duda, el que destina el cielo para cimentarle de nuevo es un caudillo de sangre real y de la misma estirpe del Profeta . . .
>
> PARTAL ¡No puede ser otro sino Aben Humeya!
>
> MUCHOS MORISCOS ¡Él es! . . . ¡él es! . . .
>
> ANEN ABÓ ¡Aun no hemos desenvainado el acero, y ya buscamos a quien someternos![1]

A parallel to this is found in **La conjuración de Venecia** when one of the conspirators' Marcos Querini, states that their former laws should be revived thereby insuring a revolution that is by the people. In reality, however, this would not be a revolution for the people but rather for the ruling elite.

> Quisiera yo también, y daría mi vida por lograrlo, que se tomasen todas las precauciones para que el pueblo no sacuda el freno, y no empañe nuestra victoria con desórdenes y demasías. Ha nacido para obedecer, no para mandar; y al mismo tiempo que vea desmoronarse la obra inicua de la usurpación, debe admirar más firme y sólido el antiguo edificio de nuestras leyes. Rescatemos, sí, rescatemos de manos de infieles la herencia de nuestros mayores; mas no expongamos el bajel del Estado a las tormentas populares.[2]

Therefore, not only will previous laws and rulers be restored, but one form of tyranny will replace another. However, the two uprisings are unsuccessful.

Martínez de la Rosa did not believe that violent revolution was the answer to political problems. This was a prevalent view held by the moderate wing of the Liberal Party of which he was a member. Hence, the similar abortive outcomes in both plays.

Whereas some of the conspirators in both works urge deliberation, others desire to precipitate the rebellion immediately. In **Aben Humeya** these sentiments are echoed by Aben Farax in the cave of the Alfaquí: "¿Qué aguardamos, pues, qué aguardamos? . . ."[3] Coincidentally, the same idea is expressed in the same words by Thiépolo in **La conjuración de Venecia**: "¿Qué aguardamos, pues; qué aguardamos? . . ."[4]

These accomplices believe that their revolutionary activities are heavenly ordained and that, therefore, the work of supplanting the iniquitous yoke of the oppressors will be easily guided by the aid of Providence. In *Aben Humeya* the Alfaquí voices this idea when he says to the protagonist: "El cielo acaba de hablar por tu boca, descendiente de los Abderramanes . . . ¡Sin duda te ha escogido para ser el ministro de su venganza y el libertador de tu patria!"[5] The same belief is expressed in *La conjuración de Venecia* by Mafei when he tells his fellow conspirators: "La maldición del cielo ha caído sobre Venecia, y pide a gritos el castigo de los culpables; . . ."[6] Thus, the hand of Fate figures prominently in both dramas.

Martínez de la Rosa uses religious holidays as occasions on which to launch subversive activity. This, of course, is so the conspirators can catch their oppressors unawares and thereby greatly reduce resistance and loss of lives. The rebellion is planned by Aben Humeya for Christmas Eve when the Christians are praying in their church: "Hasta el mismo cielo parece que nos brinda con la ocasión más favorable; cabalmente esta noche celebran nuestros tiranos el nacimiento de su Dios . . ."[7] In comparison, the Ambassador of Genoa, in *La conjuración de Venecia,* sets the last day of Carnival for the *coup d'état*: "Más fácil será ahora nuestro triunfo, ya que la suerte se nos brinda propicia . . . Pasado mañana, por último día de Carnaval, . . . caerán en nuestras manos."[8] The close resemblance in wording and in the idea of divine intervention in the cited passages is also remarkable.

In both plays, Martínez de la Rosa has a conspirator express the patriotic feeling that it is better to die fighting for their country than to endure such oppressive forms of government. These words are somewhat alien to the author, a political moderate who did not relish the thought of resorting to violent means as a way of bringing about social amelioration.

The element of time also coincides in the two works. Martínez de la Rosa arranges for both *coups* to take place at twelve o'clock. In *Aben Humeya,* at this hour, the Christians will be celebrating Midnight Mass and will not be anticipating an uprising.[9] On the other hand, the hour chosen for the rebellion in *La conjuración de Venecia* is twelve o'clock noon when all thoughts will be concentrated on the merrymaking and the Carnival atmosphere, not on imminent danger.[10]

Prior to the actual clash of arms there is a festive mood as witnessed in the singing and dancing and church music in the two works. In addition, some of the intriguers wear masquerades in order to avoid detection. In *Aben Humeya* there is a multitude of people among whom are shepherds and shepherdesses singing a *villancico* about the people of Israel and the birth of the Savior.[11] This occurs also in *La conjuración de Venecia* when the disguised celebrants sing songs appropriate for the occasion. Furthermore, the *redondillas* of the pilgrims are also about the people of Israel.[12]

The organizers of the rebellions are to be considered outsiders. In *La conjuración de Venecia* the crystallizing force behind the revolution is the Ambassador of Genoa who puts his palace at the disposal of the Venetian complotters for the purpose of conspiring.[13] Although a Moslem, the Alfaquí in *Aben Humeya* should be considered an outsider also, for he is a religious ascetic who lives in a cave and thereby is out of communication with the diurnal activities of the outside world. He, too, furnishes his place of habitation to the disgruntled intrigants.[14]

Martínez de la Rosa makes use of the technique of planting spies to overhear conversations that will prove detrimental to the interlocutors. When Muley Carime and Lara are conversing they are unaware of the fact that Aben Abó and Aben Farax are listening to their conversation.[15] This same procedure is employed in *La conjuración de Venecia* when Pedro Morosini and the two spies eavesdrop on the conversation between Laura and Rugiero in the pantheon.[16]

The perception of the Moorish castle by Fátima in *Aben Humeya* and that by Laura of the pantheon, in *La conjuración de Venecia,* as something eerie and frightening, presents additional analogies. The former states that the castle is so sad and afflicts her soul so much that she would not dare traverse it alone.[17] Similarly, while waiting alone for an assignation with its sepulchres and statues which appear to be even more frightening at the midnight hour.[18] Thus, each girl is frightened by the locale and desires to escape from it.

The anxiety continues to augment as Fátima again expresses her horror of the castle and recounts the frightening tale of Abdilehí el Zagal and his decapitation for having helped the king of Castile.

> FÁTIMA En este mismo castillo vivió algún tiempo Abdilehí el Zagal, a quien maldijo el cielo por haber prestado ayuda al rey de Castilla . . . ; hasta la piedra en que solía sentarse se ha vuelto más negra que el humo . . . ; pero lo que más pavor me causa son esas manchas de sangre de que están salpicadas las paredes . . .[19]

In the pantheon, Laura also shows her fear when she alludes to the two unfortunate lovers lying in the sepulchre.

> LAURA ¡Si supieras la historia de esos esposos! . . . Se amaron muchos años, llenos de desdichas; el mismo día de sus bodas los separó la suerte, y sólo lograron reunirse en el sepulcro . . .[20]

Hence, the technique of the employment of legends lends an air of mystery and impending danger which enhances the element of intrigue.

In connection with the castle and pantheon is the employment of the sound of the wind to portend evil and catastrophe. Aben Humeya calms Zulema's anxiety when he reassures her that the sound she hears is only the wind blowing in the castle.[21] Laura, in *La conjuración de Venecia,* while talking with Rugiero, hears a noise and is persuaded by him that it is only the wind whistling through the pantheon.[22]

The conversation in **Aben Humeya** regarding the noise heard is similar to the one held by Pedro Morosini and the two spies. Close examination reveals syntactical analogies.

> ZULEMA . . . ¿Qué ruido es ése? . . .
>
> ABEN HUMEYA No es nada . . . ; tal vez el viento, que silba en ese corredor.
>
> ZULEMA Me parecía haber oído pasos . . .
>
> ABEN HUMEYA ¿Y quién pudiera venir a estas horas?
>
> ZULEMA ¡Qué sé yo! . . . Pero me parece como que oigo rumor más cerca . . .[23]

The essence of this conversation is recaptured in **La conjuración de Venecia** in the colloquy between Pedro Morosini and the spy.

> MOROSINI ¿Qué ruido es ése?
>
> ESPÍA 1.° Parece como que intentan abrir la puerta inmediata.
>
> MOROSINI ¿Quién puede ser a estas horas y en este sitio?[24]

Further analogies in phraseology are patent in **Aben Humeya** when Fátima tells her parents how she was harassed by Castilians and does not know how she was able to escape them.

> ZULEMA . . . ¿Cómo te salvaste tú sola? . . .
>
> FÁTIMA Ni aun yo misma lo sé . . .[25]

The latter expression is uttered by Laura when she relates to Matilde that she does not know what happened after the two spies attacked Rugiero.

> LAURA . . . Yo los vi con mis propios ojos salir de detrás del sepulcro, y arrojarse sobre el desdichado; pero en el mismo instante perdí la vista y el sentido . . . Mal pudiera decirte lo que haya sucedido luego; ni aun yo misma lo sé . . .[26]

Thus it is quite evident that Martínez de la Rosa was not loath to make striking incidents and phrases serve dual purposes.

The telling of a person that he has no children and that he would not understand the problems of a father is echoed in both plays. In one instance Muley Carime expresses this thought to Lara.[27] In the other, Pedro Morosini is told this by his brother Juan.[28]

Insanity is also another element shared by both dramas. In the outcome of each, the two principal female characters go insane over the tragic loss of loved ones. Zulema loses her father;[29] Laura, her husband, Rugiero.[30]

Martínez de la Rosa additionally employed ironic incidents in his plays. Aben Humeya, as the new leader, must reluctantly carry out justice and make his father-in-law commit suicide by drinking poison, for the latter has been accused of being a traitor to their cause.[31] In a parallel situation Pedro Morosini captures Rugiero and has him brought to justice for treason, which eventually leads to his execution. In the process of the trial he learns that Rugiero is his long-lost son.[32]

Both dramatic works end with the deaths of their protagonists: Aben Humeya, an innocent casualty of another conspiratorial attempt; Rugiero, equally innocent, a victim of implacable fate.

Furthermore, these two plays share a unique position which sets them apart from other Romantic dramas of the period, the fact being that they were written in prose whereas the plays of the Romantic theatre were generally in verse. This should not detract from the merits of either for they—pioneer works—plays which served as an introduction for subsequent dramas of the same genre.

It would appear to the reader unfamiliar with the totality of Martínez de la Rosa's literary output that this apparent duplication might, perhaps, suggest a lack of creative inventiveness on the part of the author. This conclusion is in error for Martínez de la Rosa was extremely prolific as evidenced by the abundance of works on a myriad of themes which include comedies and dramas in both verse and prose, historical novels, literary and political manifestoes, and lyric poetry all written under the aegis of the two literary schools of Neoclassicism and Romanticism.[33] In addition, these two plays were followed by twenty six years of literary productivity and his nomination as Director of the 'Academia Española'. Beyond the issue of his productivity brief mention must be made of Martínez de la Rosa's social and political history particularly during the period of these plays. Between the years 1823 and 1831. Martínez de la Rosa was living in exile in France. This was due to the monarchy of Fernando VII that persecuted and banished the Liberals of which Martínez de la Rosa was one. However, ever mindful that extremes in anything were odious, the author always remained a moderate in literature as well as in politics, Martínez de la Rosa sought 'el justo medio' and, therefore, used familiar historical material as the bases for his plots, adding individual touches to suit his purpose. Consequently, he did not introduce many stylistic innovations or dramatic differences from one play to the other lest he depart radically from his moderate stance and thereby alienate the theatre-going public to whom Romanticism was new. Hence, a possible reason for the many similarities in both works.

More insight is revealed into the author's possible motives for writing dramas which resemble each other if one traces the evolution of both plays. **Aben Humeya,** originally written in French when the author was living in exile in France, had its première in Paris in 1830 under the title **La revolte des Maures sous Philip II.** The play was an enormous success in France. In 1834 Martínez de la Rosa, having terminated his period of exile in France and now back in Madrid, presented the analogous **La conjuración de Venecia** in Spain with the intention of repeating his

French victory. He achieved his purpose, possible due to the utilization of the same innovative and audience-pleasing techniques as we have demonstrated. Believing that he could once again capitalize on his French success he translated into Spanish and re-introduced *La revolte des Maures sous Philip II* with the title *Aben Humeya* to the Spanish theatre in 1836. However, contrary to his expectations, this time the duplicating technique did not yield fruitful results for the play was a failure due to various reasons, some of which were, perhaps, the close similarities it bore to *La conjuración de Venecia,* high audience anticipation and, bad acting.

> The public of Madrid had already witnessed the masterpiece of Martínez, *La conjuración de Venecia,* which, together with some injudicious advertising of the present play's great Parisian success, had perhaps raised expectation too high. The representation also was marred by inferior acting.[34]

Despite their many parallels, these two dramas were radical and innovative in contrast to previous dramatic endeavor and achievement in the Neoclassical school in Spain.

In conclusion, one can see that Martínez de la Rosa was not suffering from literary atrophy as might be suggested. He was artistically sagacious to capitalize on and develop further a successful and original idea. Thus, Martínez de la Rosa was able to author two highly successful dramas. Consequently, as the author of these two works, Martínez de la Rosa deserves and maintains a distinction in Spain comparable to that of Victor Hugo in France: both writers were artistically fecund and were the first to introduce Romanticism to the theatre of their respective countries.

Notes

1. Martínez de la Rosa, "Aben Humeya," *Obras dramáticas,* ed. Jean Sarrailh (Clásicos Castellanos; Madrid: Espasa-Calpe, S. A., 1964), p. 165.

2. Martínez de la Rosa, "La conjuración de Venecia," *ibid.,* p. 259.

3. Martínez de la Rosa, "Aben Humeya," *ibid.,* p. 152.

4. Martínez de la Rosa, "La conjuración de Venecia," *ibid.,* p. 258.

5. Martínez de la Rosa, "Aben Humeya," *ibid.,* p. 164.

6. Martínez de la Rosa, "La conjuración de Venecia," *ibid.,* p. 258.

7. Martínez de la Rosa, "Aben Humeya," *ibid.,* p. 155.

8. Martínez de la Rosa, "La conjuración de Venecia," *ibid.,* pp. 261, 262.

9. Martínez de la Rosa, "Aben Humeya," *ibid.,* p. 155.

10. Martínez de la Rosa, "La conjuración de Venecia," *ibid.,* p. 308.

11. Martínez de la Rosa, "Aben Humeya," *ibid.,* p. 176.

12. Martínez de la Rosa, "La conjuración de Venecia," *ibid.,* p. 307.

13. *Ibid.,* p. 249.

14. Martínez de la Rosa, "Aben Humeya," *ibid.,* p. 156.

15. *Ibid.,* p. 186.

16. Martínez de la Rosa, "La conjuración de Venecia," *ibid.,* p. 260.

17. Martínez de la Rosa, "Aben Humeya," *ibid.,* p. 200.

18. Martínez de la Rosa, "La conjuración de Venecia," *ibid.,* p. 269.

19. Martínez de la Rosa, "Aben Humeya," *ibid.,* p. 200.

20. Martínez de la Rosa, "La conjuración de Venecia," *ibid.,* p. 274.

21. Martínez de la Rosa, "Aben Humeya," *ibid.,* p. 202.

22. Martínez de la Rosa, "La conjuración de Venecia," *ibid.,* p. 281.

23. Martínez de la Rosa, "Aben Humeya," *ibid.,* p. 202.

24. Martínez de la Rosa, "La conjuración de Venecia," *ibid.,* p. 260.

25. Martínez de la Rosa, "Aben Humeya," *ibid.,* p. 147.

26. Martínez de la Rosa, "La conjuración de Venecia," *ibid.,* p. 283.

27. Martínez de la Rosa, "Aben Humeya," *ibid.,* p. 188.

28. Martínez de la Rosa, "La conjuración de Venecia," *ibid.,* p. 297.

29. Martínez de la Rosa, "Aben Humeya," *ibid.,* p. 277.

30. Martínez de la Rosa, "La conjuración de Venecia," *ibid.,* p. 324.

31. Martínez de la Rosa, "Aben Humeya," *ibid.,* p. 216.

32. Martínez de la Rosa, "La conjuración de Venecia," *ibid.,* p. 330.

33. So prolific was Martínez de la Rosa as a writer that his collected works comprise eight volumes of the *Biblioteca de Autores Españoles.*

34. Arthur L. Owen and John Thomas Lister (eds.), *Martínez de la Rosa—La conjuración de Venecia* (New York: Benjamin H. Sanborn & Company, 1927), XXIX.

Nancy K. Mayberry (essay date 1988)

SOURCE: "More on Martínez de la Rosa's Literary Atrophy or Creative Sagacity," in *Hispanofila,* Vol. 31, No. 3, May, 1988, pp. 29-36.

[*In the following essay, Mayberry asserts that Martínez de la Rosa's tragedies display little artistic innovation, and rather rely on a formula derived from Sophocles's* Oedipus Rex.]

Martínez de la Rosa is well known to students of Spanish literature as the author of *La conjuración de Venecia,* the play that introduced Romantic drama to Spain. Somewhat less well known is his *Aben-Humeya,* the play composed in French and performed in France before being translated into Spanish and performed in Madrid in 1836. Almost totally consigned to oblivion today are his other five tragedies.[1] The purpose of this paper is to examine all of Martínez de la Rosa's tragedies, their numerous similarities, and the sources which led to the development of Martínez' tragic formula.

In an interesting article published in a recent issue of *Hispanófila,* Robert Geraldi notes the many similarities between this author's two most famous tragedies.[2] First he points out that, "In *Aben-Humeya,* the *moriscos* endeavour to topple the Spanish government in 1568; in *La conjuración de Venecia,* there is an attempt to overthrow the Doge of Venice in 1310" (p. 11). I would like to add that the three other historical tragedies follow the same formula. *La viuda de Padilla,* composed in 1812, presents the rebellion of the Castilian *comunidades* against the tyranny of Carlos V in 1522. *Morayma,* composed in 1818, depicts the Abencerrajes and Zegríes when Boabdil overthrew his father's throne; and *Amor de Padre,* composed in 1849, is the story of an aristocratic family's attempt to flee the Terror of the French Revolution. Geraldi also notes that in each of the famous plays a conspirator expresses the patriotic feeling it is better to die fighting than to endure oppressive forms of government. The same thought is expressed in the other three historical plays as well. In fact, *La viuda de Padilla* is one long debate between whether it is better to die fighting, or to surrender in the face of certain defeat. Padilla's widow urges the mob to "vencer o morir." Moryama's husband too was executed by the tyrannical faction and she challenges Boabdill to kill her as well. In *Amor de Padre,* the aristocrats determine to flee tyranny or die in the attempt. Geraldi notes that in both *Aben-Humeya* and *La conjuración de Venecia* there is one character who urges moderation and a mistrust of revolutions. The same characters appear in the other three tragedies. In the 1812 play, Laso, the figure who urges surrender rather than death, claims, "Triste él que fía en el vano favor del vulgo inquieto" (I, 42).[3] Alí in *Morayma* warns Boabdil that he has not supported Boabdil's rebellion only to see one form of tyranny replaced by another and he urges moderation. The final historical play takes place during the twenty-four hours when Robespierre and his party fell to counter-revolutionaries. That play is filled with dununciations of the irreparable harm done the country by the revolutionary mob. Finally Geraldi notes that the tragedy of *Aben-Humeya* and *La conjuración de Venecia* results from the unsuccessful attempt to escape the tyranny of the other faction. The same may be said of the other three historical tragedies. The widow of Padilla commits suicide rather than be captured by the king's besieging forces. Morayma dies of grief when Boabdil's troops kill her son while he is being helped to escape. In *Amor de Padre,* the aristocrats are caught and imprisoned, and father and son die on the guillotine. Thus, all five historical tragedies are based on actual historical rebellions, all present a patriotic love of freedom and resistance to tyranny, all urge moderation in trusting revolutionary mobs, and the tragedy of all five results from the conquest by the tyrannical faction.

The sources for this tragic formula are not difficult to find. Martínez de la Rosa lived during revolutionary times. As a youth, he had begun his literary career publishing patriotic articles denouncing Napoleon's tyranny. He was very involved in the Spanish revolt against the Napoleonic invasions of Spain and in 1810 he published an article in an English newspaper, *El Español,* entitled **"La revolución actual en España"** (IV, 369-395). It examines the roots of the revolution in Spain and proudly claims a moral and virtuous basis for it—a disinterested love of country, indignation at the betrayal of the common good, and a righteous resistance to tyranny. It was these political and philosophical ideals of Martínez de la Rosa, the patriot, politician, historian and moral philosopher, which provided the basis for his tragedy. They continued to preoccupy him the rest of his life. Although he was a prolific writer; his most ambitious writings were not drama, poetry or novel (though he did compose all these genres) but rather histories of political thought. More than thirty years of his life were spent on a monumental ten volume history of Europe entitled *Espíritu del Siglo* (V-VII). In the introduction to that work he claimed that the most important political question to be resolved in each age is "¿Cuáles son los medios para unir el orden y la libertad?" (V, 10). The question of the proper balance of political freedom and political order became Martínez' life work.

Although generally considered a moderate, Martínez began his career as a liberal. He went on revolutionary missions, including a military venture to acquire arms and ammunition for the Spanish cause against the Napoleonic invasion. In 1814 he was arrested and imprisoned by Fernando VII for his revolutionary activities. As a liberal, Martínez had hailed the return of the Spanish king from a French prison, but he was rapidly disillusioned when the king annulled the Cadiz constitution, abolished reforms and returned the country to absolute monarchy. In *Morayma,* Alí, the voice of moderation, makes the following reference to Boabdil's rebellion against the former ruler, a rebellion which Alí supported. "Quizá nosotros mismos, quizá un día lloráramos, ¡ya tarde! haber soltado al león, y sin defensa vernos a sus furores entregados" (I, 145). This was a rather daring reference to the feelings of the liberals concerning what they considered the king's betrayal of their rebellion. Martínez' mistrust of revolutions deepened even further after his studies of the French revolution while he was an exile in France. The conclusions he seems to have reached are that revolutions fail, heroes die and tyranny continues.

Historical events were not the only sources for Martínez' themes. The preface to *La viuda de Padilla* reveals another influence on Martínez' tragic formula. There he explains that in 1812 he had just finished reading the Italian

Vittorio Alfieri's tragedies and was much taken with their merit (I, 27). The Italian tragedian of the latter half of the eighteenth century was famous for his passionate political dramas which denounce tyranny and hold high the ideals of freedom. It is not surprising that the young revolutionary should have been inspired by the Italian patriot. Cadiz was under siege by the French and it recalled to the historian the siege of Toledo during the Castilian nobles' uprising in the reign of Carlos V. Another literary influence is to be found in the preface to *Morayma.* This *advertencia* was written during Martínez' exile in France while he was preparing an edition of his *Obras literarias* which appeared in 1827. There Martínez claims that it was the use of historical themes that accounts for Shakespeare's popularity in England. He therefore recommends the use of history as a means of reestablishing a Spanish national theater. No doubt Martínez had also read Stendhal's *Racine et Shakespeare* (1823), a work which came to the same conclusions.

The theme of unsuccessful revolutions is not the only constant in Martínez' historical dramas. Geraldi finds "striking parallels in plot, structure, idea, characterization, situation, incident and dialogue" (p. 10). His article lists at least eighteen similarities in the two famous tragedies. Time and space prevent the enumeration of the same and other similarities in the other three historical plays. They include parents who accuse another person of not understanding a parent's love, loyal friends who die with or for the hero or heroine, disloyal friends who betray the hero or heroine and the usual Romantic laments over the fatal star or destiny that persecutes the protagonist. I will limit myself to only those instances which became favorites with later Romantic dramatists, and for which I believe I can identify Martínez' source.

First, Geraldi notes that the heroines of both *Aben-Humeya* and *La conjuración de Venecia* are frightened by eerie surroundings in which the sound of the wind portends evil and catastrophe (p. 14). The source for this scene, I believe, is revealed by Martínez himself in his *Apéndice sobre la tragedia española* (II, 101). Martínez is much taken by Gerónimo Bermúdez's early Spanish tragedy entitled *Nise Lastimosa.* He praises a scene in which the heroine cannot be comforted by her tranquil surroundings because "nada es bastante a calmar la inquietud de doña Inés, que cada vez aparece perseguida con más angustia por tristísimos presentimientos" (II, 101). Then he quotes with approval the following dialogue.

> Bien veo que son vientos, que son sombras
> que amor me representa; mas agora
> parece que me aflija la tristeza
> más, y no sé que temo.

> (II, 101)

So enchanted was Martínez by this scene that he repeated variations of it in every tragedy from *Morayma* on, including the mention of the wind. Act V of *Morayma* opens in the Patio de los leones at night, and the stage directions

indicate that "óyese de cuando en cuando *el sordo ruido del viento.*" Morayma laments, "Este silencio, la soledad, la noche, el triste sitio el eco sordo del lejano viento con majestad terrible lisonjean mi profundo dolor" (I, 159). Geraldi notes the similar scene in *Aben-Humeya* where Fátima claims "Lo único que no puedo sufrir es este castillo . . . , no sé que tiene, tan triste y tan opaco que me acongoja el alma" and when frightened by a sound her father reassures her "no es nada . . . , tal vez el viento que silba en ese corridor" (I, 192-93). In *La conjuración de Venecia,* Laura has a similar scene in the pantheon with it sepulchres and statues. There Laura too has terrible forebodings. "Un presentimiento fatal me estrecha el corazón y ni me deja respirar siquiera . . . ni una estrella se divisa en el cielo y se oye el murmullo del viento en este canal solitario . . ." (I, 265). In the last tragedy the heroine is in the cemetery of a ruined monastery. The stage directions order the following by now too familiar scene. "Es de noche. Al principiar el acto se divisan algunos relámpagos y se oye el ruido lejano de truenos; va cesando poco a poco la tormenta, y sólo se oye de cuando en cuando *el sordo rumor del viento*" (II, 118). The heroine, like her predecessors, is frightened by the surroundings and claims "La vista de esas ruinas . . . y al otro lado esos sepulcros . . . No me quedaría aquí sola" (I, 118). These scenes were no doubt also influenced by the Romantic love of pathetic fallacy, nature in tune with the hero's mood and by the Romantic love of cemeteries, pantheons and eerie, frightening settings.

Oddly enough, even *Edipo,* Martínez' non-historical tragedy based on Sophocles' *Oedipus Rex,* also has a similar scene. In that play, it is Oedipus rather than the heroine who is overwhelmed by tragic foreboding while in a pantheon where one hears again the murmur of the wind. He narrates the incident to his friend in the following dialogue.

> Ya pisado
> del panteón el último recinto
> y el silencio, el horror, la luz escasa
> de las antorchas fúnebres, el viento
> que en las inmensas bóvedas zumbaba
> de terror religiosa me cubrían

In fact, in my opinion, it is Sophocles' *Oedipus Rex* that provides the key to many of the aspects of Martínez de la Rosa's tragic formula which most influenced the later Romantic dramatists. I refer specifically to the tragic fate theme and to the irony of the unwitting killing of a relative—in Oedipus the killing of a father by his son. We may recall that the hero of *El travador* is executed by his own brother, Don Álvaro manages to kill off all of his beloved's family and Don Juan Tenorio kills his beloved's father. Geraldi points out the irony of Aben-Humeya's causing the death of his father-in-law, and in *La conjuración de Venecia* a father causes the death of his son. I might add that in *Morayma,* a mother unwittingly causes the death of her son and the irony in *Amor de Padre* is similarly most bitter. There the hero, Eduardo, bribes a jailor to take him to another cell where he may comfort the hapless Matilde. While he is absent, guards come to take him for execution. His father steps forward when Eduardo's name is called and he substitutes for his son on the guillotine. Eduardo goes mad on realizing that he has caused his father's death and he goes happily to the guillotine rather than escape.

Madness and suicide were also a part of Martínez' tragic formula. Padilla's widow commits suicide, Morayma dies in a frenzy of grief over the death of her son, and as Geraldi notes, the female characters in the two famous tragedies also go insane over the tragic loss of loved ones. This too may have its source in Sophocles' *Oedipus* where Jocasta commits suicide upon realizing the extent of her guilt.

Much has been made over the unknown origins of the heroes in Romantic drama. Martínez' Rugiero was generally considered the first of such heroes, but Michael McGaha has convincingly demonstrated that Martínez' Rugiero was modelled on the protagonist of *El delincuente honrado*, a hero of even greater melancholy and of unknown origins. McGaha proves that many scenes and situations in *La conjuración de Venecia* are directly modelled on this sentimental eighteenth-century drama.[4] I would like to suggest that another source for Martínez' hero of unknown birth is Oedipus, for the unwitting murder results from the fact that the hero does not know his own family.

Finally, the implacable unjust fate that pursues the hero, Rugiero, is directly modelled on the Oedipus play. Martínez wrote a *Poética* while he was in France in which he studies and praises Sophocles' *Oedipus Rex* as the greatest of all tragedies. In his analysis, he points out that it was the inexorable law of an unjust fate that excites the pity and fear for Oedipus. In the *Anotaciones,* he explains that the Greek and Roman concept of fate led them to present their heroes as "Las víctimas de un destino inexorable luchando en vano contra sus decretos y arrastradas al precipicio por una fuerza superior" (II, 368). Christianity forbids such a view and Martínez de la Rosa was a devout Catholic. He explains, however, that "el común de los hombres tiene mucha propensión a creer que existe una especie de fuerza superior que los conduce casi a pesar suyo, expresando esta idea vaga con las voces de *suerte, destino, estrella, fatalidad.* Esta disposición general del pueblo le acerca, a lo menos hasta cierto punto, al estado de los antiguos; de donde nace que el poeta trágico puede aprovecharse de este sentimiento, infundado y absurdo cuanto se quiera, pero que al cabo, existe" (II, 368-9). Here then is Martínez' source for the inexorable law that brings about the undeserved death of the heroes and heroines.

This brings us to the question of whether or not Martínez de la Rosa is to be credited with creative sagacity or literary atrophy. Geraldi defends Martínez' duplication of themes, events, characters and situations on the grounds that Martínez was an extremely prolific writer of a myriad of themes written under the aegis of both Neoclassicism

and Romanticism. Martínez did indeed try his hand at almost every known form of drama. In addition to the six tragedies mentioned in this paper, he wrote six neo-classic comedies closely modelled on Moratín's plays, a golden age comedy in the style of Tirso de Molina, a historical novel in the style of Walter Scott and poetry imitating that of the eighteenth century poets. His later poetry imitated that of the Romantic poets. His creativity seems to have been a rearrangement of many scenes, situations, characters and styles based on his voluminous knowledge of Spanish, French and Italian literature.

A little noted fact about his literary production is that although he continued to write drama for some twenty-five years, Martínez never wrote another successful tragedy after *La conjuración de Venecia. Amor de Padre,* composed in 1849 was never performed in spite of repeated efforts by its author to have it staged.[5] Until now I have not mentioned his final tragic drama published in 1856 and apparently lost for over a century.[6] It is called on its title page, "un drama sentimental en dos actos," and it was so bad that Martínez de la Rosa had the good sense not to include it in the published collection of his complete works which he supervised in 1861. That play, entitled *El parricida,* is an embarrassing amalgam of almost all the situations mentioned in this paper. In it a son kills his father, hallucinates in fearful surroundings, weeps, laments and finally confesses his crime and dies in the arms of his long lost daughter. This play was in obvious imitation of the thesis drama that came into vogue after Romanticism and when Martínez de la Rosa's creative sagacity had certainly become literary atrophy.

In conclusion, an examination of Martínez de la Rosa's total tragedies reveals very few innovations. The dramatist's goal in his four historical tragedies was to provoke in the spectators the Aristotelian response of pity and fear as they witness an unsuccessful rebellion against tyranny, and heroes or heroines who die or go mad at the loss of a loved one whose death they have unwittingly caused. The latter device was no doubt inspired by Sophocles' *Oedipus* which Martínez adapted to a more Romantic mode. His final unsuccessful tragedy was one in which all the most pathetic scenes of the earlier tragedies were combined resulting in melodrama. Thus, we may conclude that Martínez' creative sagacity reached its zenith with *La conjuración de Venecia,* but quickly waned, becoming literary atrophy in his later tragedies which never again achieved the triumph of the play that introduced Romanticism to Spain.

Notes

1. They are *La Viuda de Padilla* (1812), *Morayma* (1818), *Edipo* (1828), *Amor de Padre* (1848) and *El parricida* (1856).

2. Robert Geraldi, "Francisco Martínez de la Rosa: Literary Atrophy or Creative Sagacity?," *Hispanófila,* 79 (1983), 11-19.

3. Martínez works are most readily available in volumes 148-156 of the *B.A.E., Obras de Don Fran-*

cisco Martínez de la Rosa, ed. Carlos Seco Serrano (Madrid: Ediciones Atlas, 1962), volumes I-VIII. Henceforth volumes and page numbers in the text refer to this edition.

4. Michael McGaha, "The 'Romanticism' of *La conjuración de Venecia,*" *Kentucky Romance Quarterly,* 20 (1973), 235-42.

5. See the *advertencia* to *Amor de Padre* in II, 103.

6. The play is listed in the bibliography of Palau y Dulcet, but was not studied or commented upon until a doctoral dissertation by Arsenio Alfaro, "Francisco Martínez de la Rosa (1787-1862): A Study in the Transition from Neo-Classicism to Romanticism and Ecleticism in Spanish Literature." Diss. Columbia 1964. The play is listed in the bibliography of the BAE edition of Martínez' works, but it is not included in the collection.

Robert Mayberry and Nancy K. Mayberry (essay date 1988)

SOURCE: "Histories, Essays, and Miscellaneous Writings," in *Francisco Martínez de la Rosa,* Twayne Publishers, 1988, pp. 106-21.

[*In the following excerpt, the authors survey Martínez de la Rosa's non-fictional works, including his theoretical and political writings, and particularly his ten-volume history of Europe,* El espíritu del siglo.]

Although Martínez is known to students of Spanish literature primarily as the author of the first romantic drama in Spain, his most ambitious writings were not drama, poetry, or the novel, but histories of political thought. More than thirty years of his life were spent composing a monumental history of Europe entitled *Espíritu del siglo* (*Spirit of the age*). Many other speeches, articles, and essays deal more with political than literary philosophy.[1] Time and space prevent a detailed examination of these works, which form more than half of Martínez's literary production. This chapter will therefore be limited to his major histories, together with those essays that have a direct bearing on the author's literary theories.

The author's method for the writing of history is outlined in an essay entitled **"¿Cuál es el método o sistema preferible para escribir la historia?" ("What is the preferable method or system for writing history?").**[2] First published in 1839, the essay deals approvingly with the rhetoric and literary style of the ancient Greeks, while the author condemns the dry narration of events in medieval Spanish chronicles. Similarly, he condemns the philosophical histories of the eighteenth century, which failed to deduce consequences from facts and instead molded events to fit theories. . . . Martínez believed that the historical novel was born as a reaction to the excessively philosophical histories of the preceding age, and he turned instead to

a picturesque descriptive style more appropriate to certain colorful periods. Martínez condemns the "fatalist" style of recent French historians, claiming that it contained a dangerous "destruction of morality and free will." The essay concluded that the best method of writing history is to conform the style to the subject. Weaknesses are inherent in each method—the excessive literary harangues of the classical style, and the abstract theories of the philosophical school in particular.

As in his drama and poetry, a certain evolution in theory is evident when one compares Martínez's later historical writings with his more youthful works. From a liberal, idealistic believer in the rights and inherent morality of the common people, evolves a more moderate, cautionary view in which constitutional monarchy is viewed as the best political system, leaving certain rights with the king in order to guide the less educated and to restrain the excesses of the common people.

LA REVOLUCIÓN ACTUAL DE ESPAÑA

Written during the early months of 1810 and published in numbers 8 and 10 of the London journal *El Español,* **"La revolucíon actual de España" ("The present revolution in Spain")** examines the roots of the revolution and its vicissitudes (*Obras de Martínez de la Rosa* [hereafter *O*], 4:369-95). Martínez blames a rigorous censorship of the press for giving Spaniards an imperfect knowledge of Napoleon's exploits in Europe. He proudly notes the moral and virtuous basis for the revolution—a disinterested love of country and one's fellowman, a desire for posthumous glory, an indignation at betrayal, and a subjugation of particular interests to the common good of resistance to tyranny. The properties of anarchy and despotism are listed as laziness and selfishness. Martínez is particularly grateful for England's support, both militarily and in the models that country's government provided. There is extravagant praise of the extraordinary wisdom and restraint practiced by the rebels, who submitted themselves to the rule of law and immediately chose a Central Junta in free elections, proving Spain capable of handling her own affairs. Now this government must correct political, economic, and social abuses.

This youthful essay reveals the idealistic liberal, full of fine dreams and ideals, extremely patriotic and enthusiastic. The didacticism of nearly all of Martínez's writings is evident as he attempts to point out the errors of the past and urges reforms. Although he later modified his political theories along more moderate lines, many of his basic beliefs are outlined in this essay. They are beliefs in a constitutional monarchy that corrects injustices, abolishes partiality and secrecy, and, above all, maintains a free press. The people in turn submit themselves to the rule of law, which invokes certain responsibilities and punishes those who fail to obey them. These theories reveal the influence of both French and English theorists, notably Montesquieu, Edmund Burke, and Jeremy Bentham. A constant in Martínez's theories is revealed here also—his hatred for foreign interference in Spanish affairs.

Two beliefs outlined in this essay were to change radically under the influence of later events. They were the author's Rousseau-like love for the working classes, which he calls "the healthiest in society," and his fervent love of Ferdinand, whom he views as a beloved prince whose return would correct the abuses of his predecessor and save the nation.

The style of this early work is flamboyant, filled with exclamations and the rhetorical style of the ancients, rather than the more mature polished style of the later experienced orator and statesman.

ESPÍRITU DEL SIGLO

Published in ten volumes between 1835 and 1851, *Espíritu del siglo* (*The spirit of the age*) represents Martínez de la Rosa's most ambitious endeavor. The foreword explains that it was begun in 1823 and continued intermittently until its publication. The preface, entitled "Object of This Work," briefly traces European history from the Roman Empire through the French Revolution, applying different names to each period—the spirit of crude times, the warring and religious spirit, the spirit of controversy, the mercantile spirit, and the philosophical spirit. The two most important developments in society are claimed to be representative government and trial by jury, while the most important question to be resolved in modern times is "What are the means for joining order and liberty?" (*O*, 5:10). The twelve parts are titled as follows: "Exposition of Doctrines," "Origin and Progress of the French Revolution," "Political Picture of Europe in the Time of the Constitutional Assembly," "National Legislative Assembly," "The National Convention," "The Executive Directory," "The Consulate," "The Empire," "The Restoration," "The Revolution and the Holy Alliance," "Reign of Charles X," and "The Reign of Louis Philip of Orleans."

Part 1 examines the basis of good government and evolves a concept of history based on the changing nature of social institutions. The true cause of the French Revolution is seen to be the failure of the political institutions and laws to maintain the best interests of the people in the light of the changing social organization. This included an increased educated public, (the result of the invention of the printing press), religious and political diversity, the growth of mercantilism, and a richer middle class. England's government, on the other hand, had changed with the times; the people's rights were respected and the navy protected commerce. The absolute monarchies of Europe did neither. Relying on strong armies to maintain order, the sovereigns burdened the people with high taxes, poor economy, arbitrary justice, ruinous debts, and religious persecution.

Part 2 examines the immediate causes of the French Revolution. Louis XVI is described as "wise, kind, endowed with domestic virtues, lover of the public good, but condemned by a sort of fate to pay the wicked legacy of his predecessors" (*O*, 5:60). The failure to achieve a stable government is attributed to the selfishness of those aristocrats who put their own privileges ahead of their country's need for reforms and to the weakness and hesitancy of the king. In comparing England's Bill of Rights, America's Declaration of Independence, and France's Declaration of the Rights of Man, Martínez de la Rosa admits their basic similarities, but insists on the widely differing circumstances of their history and promulgation. The French, unlike the English, were unaccustomed to any form of independence and were never trained in the duties or responsibilities that accompany freedom. Thus, although the basic theories of France's constitution were good, they could not be applied in practice, given the circumstances and institutions of France.

Martínez's preference for constitutional monarchy leads him to condemn those articles of the constitution that refused the king the right to choose his own ministers from the elected deputies, and especially the law forbidding the reelection of deputies. These two facts ended the hopes for a constitutional monarchy or a stable government. The resulting constitutional government of 1791 was a republic with a figurehead for a king, and no such government, he insists, has ever succeeded.

Part 3 examines the policies of other European nations during the time of the revolution in France. Involved with their own domestic problems, other European monarchs refused to heed the advice of the emigrants from France, failing to recognize the danger to monarchy.

Part 4 describes the time of the Legislative Assembly, calling it a bastard regimen between monarchy and republic. An invariable law of revolution, according to Martínez, is that it breeds violent passions, which in turn demand vengeance, followed by abuses. No matter how violent one party may be, another more violent party is born, and thus the French government fell into the hands of bloody revolutionaries.

Part 5 deals with the National Convention, whose members are described as "ferocious enemies of knowledge, wealth, and the merit of all classes" (*O*, 5:281). Although the government was prepared to throw everything into the battle, without concern for law, private interests, the treasury, or commerce, disunion eventually and inevitably caused their downfall. Martínez de la Rosa is particularly horrified by the cult of reason, which he claims supplanted religion, but was in reality atheism. A constant in his political philosophy is evident as he insists upon the intimate relationship between political, moral, and religious ideas. Another constant is his belief in a free press. When writers began to attack the excesses of the convention, the people slowly turned to a more moderate government to reestablish the rights of its citizens.

The final chapter of this volume summarizes the events of the three years of the convention and makes clear Martínez's belief that monarchy is the key to the social edifice. He points out, "after so much boasting had been made of liberty without limits, and absolute equality, the slave

France groaned under the most unsupportable yoke: the tyranny of a faction, with a popular assembly as accomplice and, as its instrument, the rabble" (*O,* 5:433). This represents a far cry from the ideals voiced in his first political manifesto.

Part 6 examines France's policies in the rest of Europe as new republics sprang up and numerous wars broke out. The new Director used troops against legally elected representatives of the people, thus committing political suicide, for new elections gave rise to a coalition of monarchists and constitutionalists. Martínez insists that under constitutional monarchy the king can change his ministers in the event of crisis. If that does not satisfy, he can dissolve the legislature and call new elections without harming the constitution. This represents an obvious defense of Martínez de la Rosa's own criticisms of the Spanish Constitution of 1812, which he insisted on changing when he became prime minister. In France the old constitution was abolished and a new one pronounced. This volume ends by noting that "factions disappear, the popular torrent returns again to its source, the Revolution, immense before, narrows and grows smaller and the history of a nation becomes the history of one man" (*O,* 6:111).

Part 7 examines the new consular constitution of 1799 at great length, noting the cleverness of Napoleon in keeping the greatest powers for the first consul, himself. Again Martínez points to the model English constitution as opposed to the French: Napoleon's early successes are narrated as well as the details of the Treaty of Amiens. The changes of the constitution fill the author with wonder as he notes that, in reality, the republic had become a monarchy again, but with Napoleon as king. He severely condemns that leader for his mania to interfere with the interior politics of other countries. He is particularly incensed by France's bad faith in selling Louisiana to the United States without informing Spain.

The changes in the constitution under the empire are examined in part 8. According to the author, it left the Tribunal useless, the legislative body altered, the senate holding broader powers, and almost the entire government appointed by the emperor. Napoleon's greatest error was in failing to consolidate his power in France. Instead of confronting the problem of how to maintain order with liberty, he scorned politics in favor of war, glory, and further conquests. Martínez is incensed by Spain's foolish support of Napoleon during this time, and again condemns the censorship of the press, which only published praise of Napoleon in Spain.

Several pages of this volume repeat the history outlined in the early essay on **"La revolución actual de España."** With all the benefits of hindsight, Martínez had modified his beliefs considerably. While he still feels that Ferdinand was the people's legitimate choice for monarch, he now realizes that he was also the usurper of his father's throne. The people's grasp of liberty and independence are termed "vague and confused" by contrast to the idealistic love of

country described in the first essay. Martínez is still proud of the juntas, which kept the revolution linked to law and order. Proudly and patriotically, he notes of the resistance to Napoleon in Spain marked the beginning of Bonaparte's decline. The domestic situation in France is examined as censorship of the press became more rigorous, the laws more dictatorial, and justice more arbitrary. According to Martínez, Napoleon failed to understand the "spirit of the age" and slowly lost the support of those who had welcomed him as their savior from factions and anarchy. Under Napoleon, in place of one Bastille, France now had ten, and instead of conciliatory measures, Napoleon used oppressive new laws.

This volume includes a brief history of the course of Spanish politics in the second decade. The constitution of 1812 carried out certain reforms, such as freedom of the press, abolishment of the Inquisition, and abolishment of laws permitting confiscation of private property and torture. Again Martínez defends his position on the need to reform that constitution, which too closely followed the French Constitution of 1789, forming a government that was neither monarchy nor republic. With respect to Ferdinand's sudden return to Spain, the author tells of the joy of the liberals and the consternation of those who opposed the constitution. That situation was rapidly reversed when Ferdinand condemned the members of the Cortes as rebels. Sadly, the author notes that "the idol that the nation had raised at such cost, crashed on top of them and crushed them" (*O,* 7:132).

Turning back to the history of France, Martínez notes with wonder the banishment of Napoleon and the restoration of the Bourbon monarchy: "Thus by a chain of events so singular and strange that they would be considered fiction if one had not seen and felt them, at the end of a quarter of a century, it seemed that the circle of the Revolution was going to close at the same point it started . . . and the nation founded again its last hope on a temperate monarchy which would guarantee its peace and prosperity, joining order with freedom" (*O,* 7:157).

The policies of Louis XVIII are examined in detail in part 9. Ferdinand's destruction of the constitutional reforms in Spain are narrated with disgust. Napoleon's unsuccessful bid for a restoration of the empire ended at the battle of Waterloo which, Martínez claims, decided the fate of Europe. Absolute monarchists joined in the Holy Alliance in order to provide mutual insurance against a revolutionary conflagration, but in 1820 another revolution broke out.

Part 10 explains the abuses of Ferdinand that led to the uprising by the army. The Cortes in its great desire to limit the abuses of monarchy is condemned for failing to see the weakness of the 1812 Constitution. Before continuing with Spanish history, Martínez turns to a history of the rest of Europe, explaining the fears of the Holy Alliance. Bitterly, the author notes the way in which the Cortes failed to recognize the changing times. In spite of being ill-prepared for war, it challenged the Holy Alliance. The country was exhausted, and the reforms had not had sufficient time to prove their benefits. The absolutist party continued to be obstructionist, and secret societies wreaked havoc with public confidence. Instead of fighting the invaders, as the Spaniards had done in 1808, the people, tired of liberal misrule and anarchy, accepted the French invasion.

Some years elapsed between the composition of parts 10 and 11. In a foreword, Martínez de la Rosa notes the great changes that had taken place over the nearly three decades of the whole work's composition, 1823-51. The author notes the difficulty of writing impartially of events in which he took part personally, but claims that his opinions have not changed. He is neither repentant nor embarrassed by his earlier writings begun while he was an exile and continued while he was in a high position of power.

Part 11 examines the causes for the loss of the colonies in the New World, theorizing that if Ferdinand had not been so absolute in his dealings with the American colonies, Spain would not have lost them so irrevocably. The involved history of political maneuverings in the royal house of Portugal is narrated in detail. The actions of King Ferdinand during the last ten years of his reign are soundly condemned. In France the causes of the three-day July Revolution of 1830 are examined and attributed to the repressive decrees of Charles X.

Although Martínez de la Rosa was obviously not a totally objective historian throughout this history, his remarks at the beginning of part 12 are extremely subjective, revealing a disillusioned statesman. He admits to his astonishment at the people's rejection of Louis Philip of Orleans, his brief reign being described as "a singular extraordinary epoch, unique in history . . . a prosperous happy reign such as France had never had and which ended with no one's coming to its defense; a revolution without cause ended a dynasty . . . a nation of thirty million souls found itself unexpectedly changed to a republic against its own will and without anyone's forcing it . . . the annals of the world offer no such phenomenon" (*O,* 7:75). Obviously Martínez de la Rosa failed to understand the spirit of his own age; his preference for constitutional monarchy blinded him to the need for the reforms that precipitated the 1848 revolutions.

Because Salic law forbade a female's ascension to the throne, the king had the Salic law repealed to protect his only heir—his daughter Isabel—and thus sowed the seeds for the civil war between the Carlists and the supporters of Isabel. Proudly, Martínez narrates the changes made in the 1812 constitution which, he claims, finally rectified the defects already noted. Modestly, he makes no mention of his own part in being the author of the Royal Statute instituting these constitutional reforms. Further changes were made in 1837 and 1846, of which our historian heartily approves. The last part proves how far Martínez has moved away from the young revolutionary of 1810. He condemns the revolutionary uprisings in Italy and stoutly defends the

rule of Pius IX. The many revolutions of 1848, he admits, are beyond his comprehension, since they were against a whole social order, rather than against abusive laws and governments.

Thus, at the end of his long work, Martínez de la Rosa has, like the French Revolution, completed a circle. As a young liberal he could see the abuses against his own class, but decades later he could not see the same abuses against a new industrial proletariat. Martínez could not understand this new social institution, for he was too close to the time to see this new "spirit of the age." His work ends by admitting that although a new era has begun, the author continues to affirm his unswerving belief that "morality is the key and indelible stamp of history" (*O,* 8:162).

Analysis. Although Martínez's basic political beliefs have not changed from his youthful manifesto, the style of this monumental work is much more scholarly. The sources number in the hundreds and are quoted in Spanish, French, and English, with titles of the same work at one time appearing in Spanish translation and other times in the original French or English. French sources most frequently quoted on the revolution are Mignet's *History of the Revolution,* Thiers's *History of the French Revolution,* Mme de Staël's *Considerations of the Principle Events of the French Revolution,* and Necker's *On the French Revolution and the Executive Power of the Great Estates.* English sources include Lambeth's *Introduction to the History of the Constitutional Assembly,* Cox's *Spain under the Bourbon Kings,* and Burke's *Reflections on the Revolution in France.* For the rest of Europe the principal source is Segur's *Historical and Political Picture of Europe,* the title of which is quoted now in Spanish, now in French. Other frequently quoted sources include more than fifty additional histories, memoirs of the various political figures, speeches, edicts, treaties, and letters, many of which the author states have never before been consulted.

There has been little critical comment on this history. A contemporary, Antonio Ferrer del Río, wrote in 1846 that it contained no original ideas, that its plan was enigmatic and confused, and that it relied too heavily on the French authors Thiers and Mignet.[3] Jean Sarrailh claims, however, that Martínez de la Rosa "occupies one of the first places, if not the first, in the historical production of Spain 1830-1860."[4] The style of the history is that of his prose annotations and appendixes, elegantly careful and correct, sometimes repetitive and tautological. The influence of the orator is often seen in the debate style of posing a situation, examining both sides of the question, and proposing a solution.

Most disconcerting is the mingling of two styles—an objective narration of events suddenly combined with subjective, moral pronouncements, and minisermons that reveal the moral philosopher. Examples of such occur when the author denounces political executions as murder, when he thunders at the despicable assassination of the Duke D'Enghien, and when he complains of Napoleon's illegal interference in domestic affairs of foreign nations. One subject that particularly offended the moralist views of Martínez's politics was the division of Poland, an action he repeatedly censures as immoral and despicable.

Linked to the moral pronouncements are the author's recurrent insistence on the didactic function of history. The present age must look to history to discover the sources of error and to correct past mistakes. Although expressing great belief in the cause and effect relationship in history, often the influences of a fatalistic belief are seen when circumstances beyond an individual's control are attributed to fate.

The picturesque style of **Hernán Pérez del Pulgar** is nowhere to be found in this history. The reader is often surprised by the lack of colorful description of exciting, stirring, or pathetic events. Napoleon's disastrous retreat from Moscow, so often celebrated in painting and music, is described in one colorless sentence. While moral dismay is expressed at the Reign of Terror, few details are given. The work often represents the author's citing proofs from history of his own political beliefs. Thus, he falls into the defect he himself noted in the eighteenth-century philosophical histories—the molding of events to fit theories, rather than vice versa. The failure of the republic in France is seen to be the failure to accept constitutional monarchy, wherein liberty is guaranteed by constitutional freedoms, but order is maintained by an aristocratic upper chamber restraining the excesses of the common people.

Although we are tempted to agree with Sarrailh that this view was an a priori theory applied to the revolution, in some respects it could represent the opposite. As a young revolutionary Martínez had believed in the French goals of liberty and equality. Perhaps the outcome of the revolution and, indeed, Martínez's study of it influenced his political theories and moved him to the increasingly moderate position assumed on his return to Spain. The failure of the republic in France, together with a basic mistrust of the wisdom of the common people, reinforced his rejection of a republican form of government.

"Crisis política de España en el siglo XVI"

While writing **Espírtu del Siglo** and holding important political posts in the Spanish government, Martínez published in 1838 another essay dealing with the war of the *comunidades*. This was the same subject of the sketch that accompanied **La viuda de Padilla**. Its interest again lies in showing the evolution of Martínez's political theories. Instead of a glowing defense of the just demands of the Castilian rebels and the rightness of their cause, **"Crisis política de España en el siglo XVI" ("Political crisis of Spain in the sixteenth century")** censures the ill advice of Charles's foreign advisors. Here Martínez claims that, more than a violation of freedom, it was the betrayal of the national Spanish honor by an absentee king that caused the uprising.

He carefully defends the principle of monarchy, noting that the blame fell to foreigners and newcomers, not the person of the king. Similarly, he corrects the impression

that the revolution was by the common people—rather, it was begun by nobles whose privileges were being undermined. The popular party did not have sufficient wisdom nor moderation to maintain its union with the nobility, and several nobles returned to the support of the king. It was the excesses and lack of harmony within the popular party that caused the defection of the nobles. The latter, too, paid dearly for their support of the monarch, having believed themselves strong enough to contain the king's power. Instead, the king expelled the nobility from participation in the Cortes, a step that only increased the king's power.

Clearly, Martínez mourns the failure of the nobles and common people to unite in the sixteenth century and to force a constitutional monarchy. Their failure led to the growing abuses of absolute monarchy, which came to fruition in the author's own time. Gone is the spirited defense of the justice of the people's demands and in its place is sorrowful regret at a lost opportunity, wherein the people and nobles alike failed to recognize the need for union against a common enemy and fought instead for their own privileges. Martínez's own bitter experience with politics had seen a repetition of the mistakes of the sixteenth century wherein factions fought for their own rights and failed to compromise sufficiently to maintain a strong alliance against the monarch's abuses.

Bosquejo histórico de la política de España

First published in 1857, the foreword to **Bosquejo histórico de la política de España** (Historical sketch of Spain's politics) explains that this two-volume work was also several years in composition. Having been asked to give the opening speech for a meeting of the Royal Academy of History in 1855, Martínez returned to his forgotten manuscript and abstracted from it a speech covering only the Austrian dynasty. The favorable acceptance of that history, published in 1855, encouraged him to complete the work up to the present.

Speaking of the last two reigns, he admits that "at times the pen falls from my hand and my spirit falters" (**O,** 8:165), intimidated by his fear of not being able to write impartially of events in which he took part personally. He admits to delving more deeply into those events in order to indicate the theories and political principles that motivated him to develop certain concepts of the principal events of those times. While attempting to limit the work to the politics of Spain, Martínez notes the necessity of including the influence of Spain's relationship with other nations. The foreword ends with the reaffirmation of belief in politics based on morality and "benevolence with all nations, friendship with some, intimacy with none" (**O,** 8:165).

The work traces Spanish history from the reign of the Catholic kings to the present. The principal points include Martínez's denunciation of Spanish kings whose preoccupation was with winning territory in Europe, especially

Italy. Because of her geographical position, Spain could have and should have remained neutral in the European wars that left Spain's treasury diminished and killed her sons. Similarly, because of the lack of geographical barriers, Portugal and Spain should have continued united, given their common traditions and religion. Philip II's despotism and religious intolerance first forced the Moors to rebel and later the Portuguese. Martínez further regrets the failure of nobles and commoners alike to reinstate the Cortes as a counterbalance to the king's power. Another grave error was the importation to Spain of France's Salic law forbidding the succession of the throne to females, to which Spain's tradition was diametrically opposed.

Although Martínez abhors Spain's wars in Europe, he approves the battles with England over control of Gibraltar and Menorca because of commercial and geographical needs. Each reign is examined in detail, especially in its foreign policy. Arriving at the end of the eighteenth century, Martínez is incensed with the stupidity of the Family Compact which linked France and Spain and resulted in a foolish war with England. The execution of Louis XVI in France then led to another war for Spain. The Spanish minister, royal favorite of Charles IV who treated for peace with France, won the name "the Prince of Peace," and it is by this name that Martínez consistently and bitterly refers to Godoy.

The last section of the history dealing with the nineteenth century is twice as long as the part dealing with the preceding three centuries, and in many respects it is a more detailed repetition of the last section of *Espíritu del siglo.* Interestingly, Martínez makes no mention of his own imprisonment when describing the abuses of Ferdinand VII. Spain's relationship with her colonies is examined at length, as well as the prime minister's attempt to pacify them. Only a footnote reveals that the prime minister was Martínez de la Rosa. His fall from power, the death of Alexander of Russia who had supported Ferdinand's attempts to keep the colonies, and England's recognition of their independence sounded the death knell to their recovery by either armed or peaceful means. Although Martínez advised the king to recognize the republics and to establish free trade, Ferdinand refused, "suspicious, fearful, afraid of his own shadow" (*O,* 8:361).

The final section is a more detailed repetition of the earlier history. Martínez unceasingly defends his changes in the constitution, since that of 1812 did not "suit well the fundamental principles of a monarchy" (*O,* 8:391). Of particular interest is the narration of the various revolutions of 1848 that reveal how far Martínez's political theories had changed since 1812. He is proud that the Spanish government was so firmly in control that no revolution broke out there. Although he has been unalterably opposed to Spain's involvement in European wars, he defends her interference in Italy's revolution on the grounds that it was a moral and religious duty to return the pope to his dominions and to restore European tranquillity. Reforms, he claims, could not be left to revolutionaries, but to the spiritual and temporal head of the state, the pope. Mar-

tínez is also proud of his own part in the proclamation of a concordat with the Vatican that restored to the church most of the property formerly confiscated in Spain and reestablished peaceful relations interrupted since 1834 with the Holy See. The work ends at this point, claiming that "we end this work like a traveler who at the end of a long and laborious pilgrimage, rests with good spirits at the foot of a renowned monument" (*O,* 8:417).

Analysis. As Martínez noted in the preface, the last two reigns contain a great deal of his own political philosophy. In the first edition the notes follow the work and are at least half as long as the material they annotate. The sources include those used for *Espíritu del siglo* with a rather bewildering mixture of languages. The English work by William Cox entitled *Spain Under the Bourbon Kings* is cited in English at times, at other times in French, and sometimes in Spanish. Dunham's *History of Spain* is quoted in Alcalá Galiano's Spanish translation. Additional English historians quoted include Watson's *History of the Reigns of Philip II and Philip III* and Robertson's *History of the Emperor Charles V.* French sources are numerous, including translations into French from Italian and German historians. Oddly enough, few native Spanish histories are cited with the exceptions of letters and memoirs, especially of "the Prince of Peace."

It is to be regretted that more of Martínez de la Rosa's own experiences are not narrated; he concentrates on foreign rather than domestic affairs in his own time and leaves his personal dealings to other historians. Clearly, Martínez was too close to his time to make an impartial observation of his country's politics, as he himself admitted in the preface. Rather, his own political philosophy blinds him to such problems as the queen's palace intrigues and the problem of monarchical succession. Nor does Martínez dwell on the numerous uprisings of cities and districts against Madrid's rule. Rather than an age of political progress or improved administration, this age is viewed by modern historians as an age of near anarchy and reactionary government. Martínez's work ends with a cheerfully optimistic belief that his long-held principles of constitutional monarchy have proved to be the proper form of government and have established an era of progress and prosperity for the country.

LITERARY THEORY AFTER 1830

A little-remarked facet of Martínez de la Rosa's literary production is the fact that no new plays were written after 1830 until the comedy written in the Golden Age style (for which there is no preface and no known date of composition though it was performed in 1840). His last two plays were composed after 1848, both tragedies in the sentimental vein. His literary theories during this time were presented in the forewords to the various editions of plays composed earlier, and these have already been noted. Of particular interest is the foreword to *La boda y el duelo* (1843), which demonstrates that Martínez never accepted the romantic style, especially in matters of form and in the fatalistic philosophy evident in the tragedies. His discomfiture with this philosophy has already been mentioned in connection with our discussion of "**¿Cuál es el método o sistema preferible para escribir la historia?**" and "**Del influjo de la religión cristiana en la literatura.**" The latter essay, together with "**El sentimiento religioso**" (1841), amply demonstrate the author's Catholic orthodoxy wherein man's own conscience accuses, absolves or condemns him.[5]

Space forbids a detailed examination of the numerous speeches made by our author. That Martínez never wavered from his moderate position in regards to romantic drama is evident from "**¿Cuál es la influencia del espíritu del siglo actual sobre la literatura?**" ("**What is the influence of the present spirit of the age on literature?**"). Delivered in French at the opening of the eighth congress of the Historical Institute in France (1842), this speech traced the influence of each civilization on its literature. Martínez agrees that Lope and Shakespeare were right in adapting the theater to the tastes of their age. Eighteenth-century literature is condemned for lack of piety and excessive faith in systems and theories. Certain poetic forms popular then—the eclogue, idyll, fable and pastoral—no longer correspond to the spirit of the nineteenth century. Of greatest interest are the remarks on the theater. He remarks that a cry had gone up for more freedom in drama, noting that "the public, hungry for emotions, was enchanted in the first moments by the brilliance of the talent and the attraction of novelty, but soon recovered from their surprise, and as almost always happens, *reason ended up being right.*"[6] Cautioning, as always, against excess, Martínez suggests that dramatists must practice restraint both from excessive action and movement, and from excessive simplicity in order to meet the demands of the new age. He characterizes this age as grave and serious, the result of the revolution that has left deep traces and makes the age more easily moved to tears than to laughter.

A speech delivered in 1843 shows Martínez more optimistic, caught up by the tremendous scientific advances in communication, industry, and commerce.[7] There he claims that order and freedom have joined in the nineteenth century, that civilization is progressing, and that all that remains is the necessity for moral and religious education to provide a solid foundation.

Finally, a speech in reply to Donoso Cortés's inaugural address to the Royal Academy (1847) again proves Martínez's rejection of the fatalist doctrine as he defends biblical teachings that prove men "free to act, not slaves of fate nor a vile plaything of jealous deities, but according to his own free will."[8] He admits that this interpretation is at variance with his own rendition of the Oedipus legend when he compares Sophocles' *Oedipus* to what he considers the best modern tragedy, Racine's *Athalie*. The blind Tiresias, he notes, reflects the Greek view of fate, "blind like him and implacable," while Athalie's own conscience and the prophet of the God of Israel demonstrate the Christian view of a God of providence. He continues to defend Greek literature and its paganism, rejecting Cortés's argument that only literature of Christian inspiration is worthy to be read. Again he preaches moderation in literary criticism, insisting that beauties can be found in many differing types of literature, and he quotes again his favorite Latin phrase, "ne quid nimis" (nothing in excess). This speech again proves Martínez's eclecticism and his refusal to approve or condemn any given literary style.

EL LIBRO DE LOS NIÑOS

Nowhere is Martínez's penchant for didactic moral lessons more evident than in **El libro de los niños** (*Children's Book*), a collection of maxims, poems, fables, prayers, carols, Bible stories, and moral lessons for children, published in 1839. The foreword explains that "the most important thing is that from the first words a child utters, there begin to be etched on his soul, as soft as wax, religious sentiment, the basis of morality, and firm foundation of human society" (*O*, 4:340). The project had begun as a collection of verse maxims to be put on the walls of a recently-established school, but had grown to book size with the addition of songs and longer compositions for variety's sake. The 127 two-line rhymed maxims are religious or moral in nature, extolling love of God and one's fellowman. The virtues most emphasized are truthfulness, sincerity, patriotism, courage, generosity, modesty, respect, charity, and, of course, moderation. Bible stories on Isaac and Moses again demonstrate Martínez's fondness for the theme of threatened separation of families. Hymns include adoration of the Virgin and of the cross. Prayers are given for awaking and retiring, as well as meals. Two moral tales illustrate the necessity of obeying and respecting one's parents. Little scientific lessons describe the four seasons, ending with poems illustrating God's purpose and handiwork in each season. A simplified version of the life of Fray Luis de Granada urges morality, and the collection ends with a sort of verse geography lesson on Spain.

While certainly no great work of art, this collection makes excellent use of Martínez's talent for moralizing in graceful, correct, and clear verse or prose. Menéndez y Pelayo wrote that, compared to his historical works, "His **Children's Book** is worth much more, for there even the naiveté is pleasant and appropriate to the subject; without the author's striving to appear political or philosophical, nor a profound and mysterious man."[9]

Notes

1. Martínez de la Rosa's political theories are studied by Sarrailh, *Un Homme*. Several of Martínez's political speeches are discussed in relation to Larra's criticisms by Ullman, *Mariano de Larra*.

2. *Revista de Madrid*, 2d ser., 2 (1839):531-39.

3. Ferrer del Río, *Galería de la literatura española*, 91.

4. Sarrailh, *Un Homme*, 364.

5. "El sentimiento religioso," *Revista de Madrid*, 3d ser., 2 (1841):313-22.

6. "¿Cuál es la influencia del espíritu del siglo actual sobre la literatura?" *Revista de Madrid*, 3d ser., 3

(1842):155. The same phrase is found in the foreword to *La boda y el duelo.*

7. "De la civilización en el siglo XIX," *Revista de Madrid,* 3d ser., 3 (1843):99-122.

8. "Discurso de contestación del excelentísimo Don Francisco Martínez de la Rosa a Juan Donoso Cortés," in *Discursos leídos en la Real Academia de la Lengua* (Madrid, 1847), 126.

9. Menéndez y Pelayo, *Estudios,* 4:288.

FURTHER READING

Criticism

Dendle, Brian J. "A Note on the Valencia Edition of Martínez de la Rosa's *La viuda de Padilla.*" *Bulletin of Hispanic Studies* 50, No. 1 (January 1973): 18-22.

Examines textual variants in three early editions of Martínez de la Rosa's drama *La viuda de Padilla.*

Fontanella, Lee. "Pelayo and Padilla in Reformist and Revolutionary Spain." In *Essays on Hispanic Literature in Honor of Edmund L. King,* edited by Sylvia Molloy and Luis Fernández Cifuentes, pp. 61-72. London: Tamesis Books Limited, 1983.

Refers to Martínez de la Rosa's treatment of the story of Juan de Padilla as part of a study of eighteenth- and nineteenth-century literary adaptations of Spanish legends.

Mansour, George P. "An *Abén Humeya* Problem." *Romance Notes* 8, No. 2 (Spring 1967): 213-16.

Examines the true date of composition for the first edition of Martínez de la Rosa's play *Abén-Humeya.*

Harriet Taylor Mill
1807-1858

(Born Harriet Hardy) English essayist and poet.

INTRODUCTION

Harriet Taylor Mill is best known for her influence over and possible collaboration with long-time friend and eventual husband John Stuart Mill. Their close friendship of over twenty years was controversial to their conservative contemporaries; it was considered an impropriety for a married woman and a single man to have such a close friendship and intellectual partnership. Further controversy was created after the death of both Taylor and Mill; with the publication of Mill's *Autobiography,* which described Taylor's deep involvement in his writing, the question of authorship became fodder for critical debate. While Taylor's known poems and essays center around the feminist cause and the need for equality among all people, the bulk of critical inquiry focuses on the nature of her relationship with Mill, and the extent to which she collaborated with him on his work.

BIOGRAPHICAL INFORMATION

There is little documentation on the early life of Harriet Taylor. She was born in London in 1807, and the next record of note is that she married John Taylor just after her eighteenth birthday. Taylor had three children in the first five years of her marriage, and although her marriage was not openly hostile, she was apparently unhappy. Letters to friends infer that while Taylor felt a kind of affection for her husband, his intellect was no match for her own. She did not find this match until she met John Stuart Mill in 1830, a life-altering event for both of them. The two formed an unconventional friendship that hinged on their frequent correspondence and excursions. Plagued by illness throughout her adult life, Taylor traveled frequently, and Mill was often her companion. The relationship between Taylor and Mill grew into a deep connection, and gossip ensued wherever they traveled. Despite the apparent impropriety of their friendship, they always insisted that theirs was not a sexual relationship as long as Taylor's husband was alive. Conflicted over her duty to John Taylor and her desire to be with Mill, Taylor went to Paris in 1833 to decide the fate of her marriage and her future with Mill. After deliberating for several weeks, Taylor decided to remain with her husband for appearance's sake, but to continue her close friendship with Mill. From that point to the time of John Taylor's death in 1849, the Tay-

lors carried on a marriage of convenience. Once free from her obligation to her deceased husband, Taylor married Mill in 1851. They spent much of their time together writing and discussing philosophy. When apart due to illness, the couple actively corresponded about the various projects that Mill was working on. It is through these letters that critics have gained a sense of the relationship between Mill and Taylor. Married only seven years to her intellectual companion, Taylor, after a long struggle with consumption, finally succumbed to a congestion of the lungs in 1858.

MAJOR WORKS

Little evidence indicates that Taylor wrote prior to meeting Mill; however, in 1830 two of her poems, "To the Summer Wind" and "Nature," were published in the *Monthly Repository.* She also wrote book reviews and articles that appeared in various periodicals. During their marriage, Mill wrote several feminist essays that he later attributed in his autobiography either solely or partially to Taylor, including his *Autobiography,* "The Subjection of Women," "Enfranchisement of Women," and "On Liberty." Of these, the only undisputed Taylor essay is "Enfranchisement of Women" (1851). Letters, chiefly from Taylor to Mill, but also from herself to her contemporaries, constitute the bulk of Taylor's work.

CRITICAL RECEPTION

Taylor's collaboration on Mill's writing has been controversial since the publication of his *Autobiography,* where Mill asserted that Taylor had been a major influence in all of his writing. He praised her intellect and literary ability, declaring her "a greater poet than Carlyle . . . and a greater thinker than himself," and maintained that his essays were the result of their joint efforts. In some instances he attributed most of a work's credit to her, and in the case of "Enfranchisement of Women," he gave her full credit for authorship. Upon publication, Mill's claims created a stir among critics—most claimed that Mill was exaggerating Taylor's involvement and many, such as S. E. Henshaw, vilified Taylor as having no moral scruples or femininity, and ignoring the possibility of her intelligence all together. Modern critic Jo Ellen Jacobs offers an overview of this initial criticism as well as the ensuing criticism throughout the years, beginning in 1870 and concluding with her own essay in 1994. Over time the vehement insistence against claims of collaboration has faded, and critics have realized that a dual authorship is not only possible, but is probable on most, if not all, of the essays that Mill claims as joint. Sarojini works to clear up misnomers about who wrote what essays by evaluating the writing styles of both Taylor and Mill, and then aligning those styles with their respective work. Francis Mineka, in her evaluation of Taylor's talents, offers a more balanced view of Taylor, stating that although Taylor must have contributed in part to the success of Mill, she was not the great writer and thinker that Mill asserted. Other critics, including Alice Rossi and Susan Groag Bell have studied Taylor's writing in a feminist light. While Bell examines the importance of Taylor's influence on Mill's essays and autobiography, Rossi takes the argument further, explaining the importance of Taylor's "Enfranchisement of Women," and, in turn assumes Taylor's sole authorship of the piece. Another approach that critics such as Linda Zerilli have taken has been to explore the effect that Mill's excessive praise of Taylor has caused, noting that Mill himself had unintentionally done the most damage to Taylor's credibility by naming her among the intellectual elite, a status that critics could not possibly accept. Thus, while Taylor's body of work is itself small, her influence on and participation in some of the most influential philosophical writings of the nineteenth century have secured her a controversial place in literary and philosophical critical study.

PRINCIPAL WORKS

*"Enfranchisement of Women" (essay) 1851
John Stuart Mill and Harriet Taylor: Their Correspondence and Subsequent Marriage (letters) 1951
Complete Works of Harriet Taylor Mill (essays, poems, reviews, letters) 1998

*Originally printed in the Westminster Review.

CRITICISM

S. E. Henshaw (essay date 1874)

SOURCE: "John Stuart Mill and Mrs. Taylor," in *Overland Monthly,* Vol. 13, No. 6, 1874, pp. 516-23.

[*In the following essay, Henshaw examines John Stuart Mill's* Autobiography, *focusing on Mill's excessive praise of Harriet Taylor.*]

As we lay down the deeply interesting biography of John Stuart Mill, we can not help wondering whether the volume will raise or lower him in the general regard, and what is the place that will be finally assigned him in the world of letters. His own estimate of himself can not be accepted at all. He did not know enough of children to judge his own attainments in childhood, nor enough of religion to comprehend the extent to which he was defrauded in being brought up without it, or even to see that he was defrauded at all, nor enough of women to understand Mrs. Taylor and the influence which she exerted over his life. So he underestimates the precocious acquirements of his childhood, and overestimates Mrs. Taylor by confounding that which she was to him with that which she was absolutely and to all the world; while as to Christianity, he passes it by and despises it altogether, as unworthy of serious consideration.

The great sincerity and evident honesty of the memoir, as far as it goes, can not but command respect. That he was so brilliant a scholar, and that he devoted himself as he did to the cause of human progress, challenges the utmost admiration. On the other hand, a certain self-exaltation runs through the story, which is implied, not expressed, and which assumes what it by no means actually states. One can not help feeling, also, his lack of candor in regard to his religious sentiments. That he should have kept these back through life, absolutely refusing to declare what they were when urged even by those whose interest in them was that of a constituency which he was about to represent in Parliament, and that he should have left his atheism to be learned in an autobiography published after his death, to say the least hardly savors of the heroic. Religion is, to be sure, a private affair, as he urges, but there is no question of public interest which may not infringe upon it: therefore, as no one knew better than John Stuart Mill, the request of his constituents that he should declare his religious sentiments was perfectly reasonable, especially where Church and State hold such relations as in England; and the reason which he assigned for refusing was not a reason, but an excuse. And so, when the interest of the story sufficiently abates to allow the judgment to cool, one asks one's self such questions as these: Was he, after all, a man of simple, courageous candor? Was his judgment any nearer infallibility than that of other men? Was he the true philosopher which he thought himself, and which so many believe? And—what about Mrs. Taylor?

The last question illustrates and involves most of the others; for in his association with Mrs. Taylor he found, as he himself considered it, not only his greatest happiness, but the blossom of his intellect, the perfect joy, and blessing, and crown of his existence; while she was, he thought, a creature immeasurably superior to any of the sons and daughters of men. To understand his remarkable attitude toward her, a brief survey of some of his previous life may be helpful; and to understand his life, one must go back to his father.

The elder Mill was a member of the Scotch Presbyterian Church, and was a licensed preacher in its ministry. He owed his education to the benevolence of some Christian ladies of Scotland, who paid his expenses through the Edinburgh University, from a fund raised by their exertions for the education of young men for the ministry of the Scotch Church. After receiving his license, Mr. James Mill made up his mind that he "could not believe the doctrines of that or of any other church," and so gave up preaching and religion together. The problem of evil was too much for the young student. His nature was fierce and strong, and so was the reaction which set in upon him. He found no halting-place even in deism, but fell back into the most complete, most melancholy negation. Nothing can be known; nothing of the origin of things, nothing of a God. No omnipotent being holds the world in hand; or, if omnipotent, he must be wicked to permit so much evil. Christianity is the greatest enemy to morality. The God of the Bible is a mere demon. Thus James Mill.

It was as if those ladies who gave him his education had sought to light a beneficent taper, which turned out a rocket, and flew from their hands, fizzing and hissing as it went. The consciousness that he had rewarded their kindness with a result so undesired and so wide of their intent, could not have added to his satisfaction. But, as he despised all feeling, especially of the intense sort, it is probable this did not often annoy him. This was the father who brought up and molded John Stuart Mill—training, pruning, and shaping the helpless soul of the son after a theory of his own. And had he taken his little son John Stuart at three years of age, and dislocated his spine, or broken his limbs, in the fashion of some unnatural monsters whom we read of, it would only have been an outward symbol of that which he undertook to do to the child's inner being.

The Chinese have a way of inclosing a child in a porcelain vase, leaving the head out that it may grow, while the body is dwarfed, and stunted, and made to assume the shape of its inclosing envelope. No figure is strong enough for our purpose. It is simply shocking to watch the persistent pains taken by this industrious, terrible parent to maim, cripple, and suppress the moral half of the beautiful nature on which he tried his cold-blooded psychological experiments.

One can see the grim, stern, fiercely skeptical Scotchman, with his much knowledge and his little wisdom, his worship of logic and his scorn of emotion, his narrow philosophy and his bitter hatred of Christianity, industriously laboring to stamp his own image on the helpless, pliant soul of the little innocent child. There is such pathos in the story, and in the son's unconsciousness when telling it, that one pauses, sorrowful, amazed, and indignant. Especially must they feel thus who have ever yearned over those sweet tender questionings and revealings of childhood, whereby the spirit first tries its wings and seeks to rise toward the divine. Remorselessly were these immortal promptings nipped in the bud by the elder Mill; carefully was the son kept too busy to leave room for many such. Who made the world? No one can tell. Was it God, as some say? Then, who made God? must be the next question, and so back to—no one knows what. If any God is at the head of affairs he must be either too weak to prevent evil, or too wicked to wish to prevent it. As to the Christian religion, it is a curse to mankind; as to the God of the Bible, He is a demon.

And thus the whole great subject was settled, and apparently settled forever, for John Stuart Mill. There is no evidence that he accorded Christianity importance enough ever to re-open or very earnestly to reconsider that portion of his father's instructions. He did reconsider them in other particulars, changing and in some cases reversing the lessons of childhood by the light of his maturer judgment. But to Christianity, notwithstanding the great power which it has been in the world for 2,000 years, notwithstanding that it has made rationalism itself possible, he remained to the end of his life profoundly and unphilosophically indifferent. "I looked upon it," he says, "as something which no way concerned me." Thus, despising religion, fed on heathen literature, with Socrates for his highest ideal, in a world which had no God, and only a blank, dead wall for a spiritual horizon, the child grew up, more a heathen than the heathen themselves. For they did seek after a knowledge of God, did hope in a hereafter. But this soul seems to have been utterly vacant of all such desire; utterly and persistently incurious and indifferent as to these the greatest possibilities of humanity.

There is one most singular omission in Mr. Mill's narrative. He never speaks of his mother. No most distant allusion, no most casual statement, mentions her existence. But for the necessity of the case one would be left to doubt whether he ever had a mother. The inference is inevitable—she had no hold on his affections. His young life was as bare of love for human beings as it was of faith in a Divine Being. This seems an incredible statement, but it is abundantly borne out. His father's plan of education kept him from all schools and all companions; therefore his affections were never called out toward playmates. Having been the eldest, he was made to teach his brothers and sisters, and was held responsible by his father for their progress as well as for his own—a process not apt to make him tenderly attached to them, particularly as his father was exceedingly impatient and very severe. They are dismissed from his autobiography with perhaps less mention than we have given them here; evidently they formed no part of his real life. His father was the presiding deity of his existence, and a deity who ruled by fear. The son never felt at ease in his presence, confesses that he did not love him, and was continually subject to his fierce impatience for not being able to contain and digest all the knowledge which was poured into his distended intellect. So the boy absolutely loved nobody. He had no conception of the feeling. The elder Mill's idea of education was how best to make "a reasoning machine." To this end the intellectual powers were to be stimulated, and the moral powers repressed; the affections were to be starved, and the intellect crammed. Never was a theory more thoroughly carried out. The poor child could have had as little time as temptation for the exercise of his affections. At three years of age beginning Greek, by seven he had read Herodotus, Xenophon's *Cyropædia* and *Memorials of Socrates,* some of Diogenes' *Laertius,* part of Lucian, the first six dialogues of Plato, and others; while in English he had also read Robertson, Hume, and Gibbon, Watson's *Philip II.* and *Philip III.,* Hooke's *History of Rome,* a translation of Plutarch, Millar's *Historical View of the English Government,* Mosheim's *Ecclesiastical History,* and many more.

Was there ever such a catalogue of books read by a child of seven! And those walks with his father! Fancy a little fellow of five or six years walking every morning before breakfast, and instead of a chase after butterflies, or a scamper for a wild-flower, or a run and a leap for nothing in particular—fancy such a little one carrying notes in his small hand written out from his previous day's reading, to which he occasionally refers as he converses on Mosheim's *Ecclesiastical History* or Millar's *View of the English Government*! And yet John Stuart Mill declares that his intellect in childhood was by no means remarkable, and that he accomplished nothing intellectually which could not be done by any ordinary child; which only shows how little he knew of children. At eight, he began Latin and also the instruction of his brothers and sisters. By twelve he had read nearly all the classics, and had completed, let us hope, as far as he was concerned, the education of the juniors of the family. He studied the higher mathematics; he was introduced to logic; he learned philosophy from Bentham, who was an intimate friend of his father. It was only that commercial philosophy, to be sure, which teaches that duty is to be ascertained by its consequences; which reduces right and wrong to a sum in arithmetic—"the greatest good of the greatest number;" which subjects morality to the drymeasure of expediency. A very proper philosophy, however, for a mind trained to recognize *no* standard of right and wrong, and, for such a mind, a positive advance.

The delight with which John Stuart Mill accepted it shows that he rejoiced over it as a rest for the sole of his intellectual foot. He had found a clue through the labyrinth, though a poor one. Duty as a great moral law, right and wrong as expressing a great inherent difference in moral quality, he might not attain, he could not appreciate; but it was something to have found some mode of distinguishing them. His own joy on the discovery is touching.

> "When I found scientific classification applied to the great and complex subject of Punishable Acts under the guidance of the ethical principle of Pleasurable and Painful Consequences, I felt taken up to an eminence from which I could survey a vast mental domain, and see stretching out into the distance intellectual results beyond all computation. As I proceeded farther, there seemed to be added to this intellectual clearness the most inspiring prospects of practical improvement in human affairs. When I laid down the last volume of the *Traité,* I had become a different being. The 'principle of utility,' understood as Bentham understood it, and applied in the manner in which he applied it through these three volumes, fell exactly into its place as the key-stone which held together the detached and fragmentary component parts of my knowledge and beliefs. It gave unity to my conceptions of things. I now had opinions; a creed, a doctrine, a philosophy; in one among the best senses of the word, a religion; the inculcation and diffusion of which could be made the principal outward purpose of a life. And I had grand conceptions laid before me of changes to be effected in the condition of mankind through that doctrine."

And thus it was that, at sixteen, John Stuart Mill passed from under the deadly shadow of negation. He at last "had opinions;" at last he had found something worth "inculcating and diffusing." With characteristic energy, he at once set about inculcating and diffusing it. He established the Utilitarian Society, he assisted in founding the *Westminster Review,* both exponents of Benthamism. To a person of his tastes his life at this period must have been delightful. It was full of intellectual interest, and led him into intimate association with many of the ardent and foremost young men, as well as older ones, of his day. His appointment to an office under the East India Company gave him independence, while it did not absorb too much of his time. He was a reformer, and much enjoyed the character. He read, he wrote, he debated, he was a leader among the choice spirits with whom he associated.

But suddenly a change fell on him. At twenty-one, without warning or premonition, a great, hopeless blank came over his life. A despair of existence set in. He found himself joyless, hopeless, helpless, a spiritual bankrupt. The moral portion of his nature seemed to him to have collapsed. He was capable of no feeling whatever. Everything had ceased to charm—he had nothing left to live for. For months nothing broke the dreariness which now enveloped existence. He found no relief, though he sought it carefully, and finally asked himself whether he could and would bear it much longer, returning answer to himself that he did not think he could possibly bear it more than a year. His feelings were dead, he feared, and there is something infinitely pathetic in his speculations on his condition and its causes. It was the last protest of his defrauded moral being before it should finally sink from inanition. What it needed was the bread of life. What it dumbly sought was God. But he knew of no such Being, and so he went hopelessly on. Instinct told him that his father could not help him; he knew of no one who could. But before the year expired, which he had set as his limit of endurance, he began to experience a gradual reaction and relief. Soon after, he became acquainted with Mrs. Taylor, and found in her the stimulus for his affections which carried him through the remainder of his life.

The estimation in which John Stuart Mill held Mrs. Taylor is one of the most remarkable developments of his mind and character. He first met her when he was twenty-five years of age. She was twenty-three, and the wife of Mr. Taylor. For twenty years they maintained a Platonic friendship which was "the joy and blessing of Mr. Mill's life." What it was to Mr. Taylor, does not appear; but we have hints from other quarters that it did not enhance his happiness. At the end of twenty years, Mr. Taylor died, and soon after, Mrs. Taylor and Mr. Mill were married; to be parted in seven years more, by the death of the former. She was buried in Avignon, and there Mr. Mill built a cottage, to be near her grave, and lived there much of the year; and there he, too, died and was buried.

A certain perfume of chivalry has hitherto hung about Mr. Mill, owing partly to his championship of woman-suffrage, and partly to rumors of his deep devotion to the memory of his wife. But on reading his autobiography a portion of this disappears. It is somewhat disappointing to find, on a closer view of the subject, that it was the wife of another man who for so many years was "the joy and blessing" of his existence. Of course a man who recognizes no divine sanction for marriage can not be expected to perceive any moral objection to interposing himself between a husband and wife. But to the ordinary apprehension, even looking at marriage as only a commercial bargain, such an act does not appear scrupulously honorable.

According to Mr. Mill, Mr. Taylor's fault was, that he "did not possess the intellectual and artistic tastes which would have made him a companion" for Mrs. Taylor. One would presume this to be a delicate waiving and veiling of the true reason for their separation, and so it probably is. That the true reason lay in some serious defect in Mr. Taylor's temper or morals is incompatible with Mr. Mill's patronizing eulogium of Mr. Taylor, who was, we are told, "a most upright, brave, and honorable man, of liberal opinions and good education, and a steady and affectionate friend to Mrs. Taylor, for whom she had a true esteem through life, *and whom she most deeply lamented when dead.*" Considering all the circumstances, the italicizing which we have

indulged in is not unnatural. From other sources it is stated that Mr. Taylor's life was rendered very unhappy by the association between his wife and Mr. Mill, as would have been natural, indeed, to "a most upright, brave, and honorable man." The pangs which such a man must have suffered in the course of twenty years—the restraint which an honorable, reticent gentleman must in those circumstances have imposed upon himself—can never be estimated.

His wife lived for the most part in a quiet part of the country with their young daughter, and occasionally in town with himself. Mr. Mill visited her equally in both places. It was the endeavor of all three that no scandal should arise from this intimacy. Mr. Taylor was, of course, the only one who could prevent scandal; he had but to utter one complaint, to give one ill-omened glance, and his wife's good name was gone forever.

But, although a man of such "unartistic tastes" as to be unfit to be her companion, he seems to have possessed a nobility of soul which enabled him to stand by and watch over her while he saw another preferred before him; a sort of slow fire which few husbands would endure, and which he bore with a courage and silence that command respect and sympathy. As a matter of course, Mr. Mill sets forth no such view of the affair. Perhaps he conceived that, on the highest-happiness principle, it was increasing the aggregate of bliss in the universe that a small nature of "unartistic tastes" should suffer, if thereby his larger soul found "the joy and blessing of its existence." The bland tone of superiority and patronage with which Mr. Mill tells this part of the story is beyond characterization. It finds its climax in the merit which he assumed, the great virtue which he implies, in the fact that he and Mrs. Taylor were willing that Mr. Taylor should live out his appointed days. "Ardently as I should have aspired to this complete union of our lives at any time in the course of my existence at which it had been practicable, I, as much as my wife, would far rather have foregone that privilege forever, than to have owed it to the premature death of one for whom I had the sincerest respect, and she the strongest affection."

What Mrs. Taylor really was it is difficult to decide, amid the colored lights which Mr. Mill is always burning around her, the incense of adulation in which he envelopes her. The effect is odd to take some of his complimentary sentences in this connection and translate them into plain English. "I was greatly indebted to the strength of character which enabled her to disregard the false interpretations liable to be put on the frequency of my visits to her while living generally apart from Mr. Taylor, and our occasionally traveling together," is the delicate phrasing whereby we are informed that she set at naught public opinion on a question vital to the instincts of most women. He tells us that one of the sources of her attraction for him was, "her complete emancipation from every kind of superstition"—meaning that she rejected revealed religion; "including that which attributes a pretended perfection to the order of nature and the universe"—meaning that neither did she believe in natural religion. Belief and opinion are treated in this generation with a wide and wise liberality which it would be a misfortune to diminish. But it is something new to find infidelity and atheism rated among the chief charms of a model woman.

Of Mrs. Taylor's intellectual powers, so lauded by Mr. Mill, we have but one specimen, namely, her article on the enfranchisement of women. It is a strong, thoughtful, occasionally verbose composition, not superior to many which have been given forth by American women on the same subject. But Mr. Mill protests that this production must not be considered a fair sample of her intellect. *That* must be looked for in the works supposed to be his, but which were written between them. "Not only during the years of our married life, but during the many years of confidential friendship which preceded, all my published writings were as much her work as mine." Rising with the subject, he asserts that "she contributed to them their most valuable ideas and features;" that she "continually struck out truths far in advance" of him, and that the chief of his work was to "build bridges" and "clear paths" up to her advanced position as a thinker. In much of this one can not escape the impression of a mutual-admiration partnership, to which the daughter of Mrs. Taylor was admitted in due course. It is evident by the minute instructions which Mr. Mill gives for distinguishing and disentangling the share contributed by Mrs. Mill to those joint productions, that he thinks this is a labor of discrimination which will give much employment to future critics. But when her daughter, too, is included in this literary parentage, one is in some sort bewildered. The solemn charge to whom it may concern has in it something provocative of a smile: "Whoever either now or hereafter may think of me and of the work I have done, *must never forget* that it is the product, not of one intellect and conscience, *but of three!*"

The affection which Mr. Mill evinces for his wife is most tender, and appeals to the deepest sympathies. But, reading his estimate of her immense importance as an intellectual factor in the vast product of human progress, and especially remembering how every compliment which he pays her is also a compliment to himself, sympathy gives way to surprise, and surprise to incredulity. Is this the man of letters, the logician, the philosopher, who thus discourses? Was Mrs. Taylor's indeed a greater intellect than that of Plato, or Milton, or Shakespeare? Was she greater than all these combined? Hear Mr. Mill (the italics are ours):

> "So elevated was *the general level* of her faculties, that *the highest poetry, philosophy, oratory, or art seemed trivial* by the side of her, and equal only to expressing *some small part* of her mind."

Again:

> "*Nothing* which she could have written would give an adequate idea of the *depth and compass of her mind;*" and, "If mankind continue to improve, their spiritual history *for ages to come will be the progressive working out of her thoughts and realization of her conceptions.*"

Men have been blinded by affection, and bewitched by womankind; men have sounded woman's praise abroad in prose and verse, in sense and nonsense, until, first and last, every perfection has been ascribed to the sex. But in his ascriptions to Mrs. Taylor, John Stuart Mill out-Herods them all. It was left for him, the philosopher and the logician, to claim for the woman of his heart an intellectual superiority to all other women and men combined—all poets, philosophers, orators, and artists—and place her on an elevation so high that they seem "trivial" to his vision, by the side of her. His amazing laudations of her are so exaggerated as not only to counteract themselves, but to infuse a certain doubt of his judgment as applied elsewhere. Contemplating her, he is filled with wonder, love, and praise. Her intellect seems to him little less than divine; and he falls down and worships her, casting his crown at her feet. The truth is, that Mrs. Taylor was, as he himself said, his *religion.* And here is the key to all which is strange in the phenomenon. The elder Mill had so brought up his son that no ennobling conception of God, no grand idea of immortality, no great refreshing thought of the divine and the infinite, ever fed his hungry spirit. He was forced to live on the husks of logic, on the low-diet of philosophic expediency.

And how those teachings were avenged! What would the elder Mill have said, had he lived to see his "reasoning machine" prostrate before Mrs. Taylor?—to read that the result of all his labors was to form a mind which acknowledged hers as its superior? Yes; here, we believe, is the key. John Stuart Mill revered no Creator, indulged no expectation of immortality, put no faith in the divine, prayed no prayer, and gave no thanks, from the cradle to the grave. How bare was such a life few, happily, can imagine. Nor, as we have seen, does he seem to have known the stirrings of affection for any human being, until he loved Mrs. Taylor. It was she, therefore, who first woke to life the unconscious soul within him, who first revealed to him the infinite powers which lay dormant and unsuspected in his benumbed moral being. Under her touch the torpid spiritual faculties of this ill-used, defrauded, beautiful nature began to stir at last, and the cramped spirit to rise and stretch its wings. The experience was such a surprise, such a delight, such a bewildering "joy and blessing," that to account for it he could only ascribe a wonderful superiority to her who wrought it. Was not she the being who had been able to lay hold of his inner, higher nature, and to evoke therefrom unsuspected powers and possibilities? The original instinct and reverence for the Highest and the Best awoke in his soul, to prove that it had not heretofore been dead, but sleeping. Thinking that it recognized in her this divine ideal, it gave to her its highest worship; and henceforth the starved spirit fed on its love for her as on bread from heaven.

And was it not such to him? At least it checked the marasmus which had set in from a diet of negations and expediencies, and preserved him alive for something better. And, so far, it was a boon to him; even though philosophy did have to hide its diminished head, and logic to blush, and all the sages to stir on their pedestals at the contempt cast on them by a votary hitherto so loyal. For the soul must obey its own laws; one of which is that it can be fed only by faith in something higher and better than itself. The elder Mill forbade his son thus to grow by feeding among the lilies of divine truth, and so the yearning spirit found other worship, and made of Mrs. Taylor its divinity, and of its love for her its religion. Peace be to both father and son! We may trust that the eyes of both see clearer now.

Mary Taylor (essay date 1912)

SOURCE: "Mrs. John Stuart Mill: A Vindication by Her Granddaughter," in *Nineteenth Century and After,* Vol. 71, 1912, pp. 357-63.

[*In the following essay, Taylor refutes an earlier article questioning both Harriet Taylor's intellect as well as her influence on John Stuart Mill.*]

In an article entitled 'Famous Autobiographies,' by an anonymous writer in the *Edinburgh Review* for October, certain statements have been made that must have grated upon all admirers of John Stuart Mill, accustomed as they are to pay respect to the memory of the woman whom he loved with unfailing constancy from youth to the day of his death; and also to that of his step-daughter, who, at the sacrifice of her best years, which she had desired to devote to her own chosen career, did her utmost to fill in some measure the void in his life caused by the death of Mrs. Mill, and to assist him in his great and exhausting labours for the good of humanity.

The injustice of the attack made upon Mrs. Mill's memory is shown by the comparison of her with the women of Cellini and Rousseau. That such men should be mentioned in the same breath with Mill in order to compare their love affairs with his attachment to Mrs. Taylor shows clearly the spirit in which the article is written. Cellini's revelation of himself in his autobiography has its chief interest as revealing the strangest union of artistic genius with the lowest depravity and brutality; while the insistent eulogy of the amours of Rousseau in the article alluded to is particularly offensive in connexion with the strictures made on the acknowledged pure relations which existed between Mill and Mrs. Taylor. According to the author of *Emile,* he had five children by Thérèse, each of whom he secretly consigned to the Foundling Hospital as soon as it was born. This wronged and unfortunate woman, who could neither learn to read, remember the names of the months, nor tell the time from the face of a clock, and whose deficiencies were made an occasion for jesting between him and his friends, is represented by the *Edinburgh* reviewer as the right helpmeet for Rousseau. But he overshoots the mark when he recommends to a man of distinction like Mill such a type as this for his life companion.

That Mill's literary work was 'vulgarised and enfeebled' by the Taylor influence is an accusation against his wife and step-daughter which is not supported by a single instance given. Certainly we cannot take this statement on the mere judgment of the writer, and no one capable of admiring the *Liberty* and the *Subjection of Women* will admit it to be other than an impertinence. The sentiment of the latter work was largely inspired by Mrs. John Stuart Mill's warm and far-seeing enthusiasm for the needs and claims of her sex. She at least led this strong masculine mind, already prepared by nature and education for just and noble thoughts, in that particular direction. It was impossible for him to reflect upon the subject of the disabilities of women, amounting, as he says, to 'chains riveted upon the weaker sex,' without desiring to strike a blow at those disabilities.

The remark that 'no one alive' could have rendered to such great writers as Rousseau, Goethe, and Mill any assistance in the formation and expression of their ideas is a species of intellectual arrogance and conceit of which I venture to say no man of genius would be guilty. The published letters of John Stuart Mill suffer, it appears, from the impression left upon them by Mrs. Mill and Miss Helen Taylor. This critic insists that no man of superior gifts should have a highly educated helpmeet, lest she by her 'flabby views of life'—a common result, he says, of high education among women—should exert a vulgarising influence upon him. He goes on to say: 'It is a well-established statistical fact that the average of two characters will always diverge less from the commonplace than a single character.' What is the logical deduction we are expected to make from this last observation? Apparently, that no one ought to influence any one else, lest the individuality of the person influenced should be lessened. Are not all education, literature, and social intercourse means through which characters endeavour to make their influence felt upon others?

The assertion that 'Mill's fame was made before his marriage and he never afterwards greatly increased it,' is written in utter disregard of the fact that the close intellectual friendship between Mill and Mrs. Taylor had existed for about twenty years before their marriage, which covered only a period of seven years. Unless, therefore, a great man should 'materially increase' his fame every seven years of his intellectual life, we must look for a 'vulgarising and enfeebling' feminine influence.

W. L. Courtney, in his *Life of John Stuart Mill,* says:

> *Liberty* was planned by Mill and his wife in concert . . . we cannot be wrong in attributing to her [Mrs. Mill] the parentage of one book of Mill, the *Subjection of Women.* It is true that Mill had before learned that men and women ought to be equal in legal, political, social and domestic relations. . . . But Mrs. Taylor had actually written on this point, and the warmth and fervour of Mill's denunciations of women's servitude were unmistakably caught from his wife's views on the practical disabilities entailed by the feminine position. . . . What his wife really was to Mill we shall perhaps never know. But that she was a natural and vivid force which roused the latent enthusiasm of his nature we have abundant evidence.

Any inferiority which the *Edinburgh* critic sees in those works which Mill produced after his marriage can be no proof of the deleterious influence of his wife upon his literary output, since while he was writing those books which are here acknowledged to be great he was in close touch with her, at a period when she was even more likely to be of that assistance to him which he declared she was than during the years of her increasing invalidism after their marriage.

Thérèse and Christiane, the women of Rousseau and Goethe, are contrasted for their helpfulness to those great writers with Mrs. Mill and Miss Helen Taylor in their injurious effect on Mill. The former were, we are told,

> healthy, robust-minded persons, whose outlook on life was free from trepidation or the vacillation which comes from unrealised ambitions and hopes . . . women . . . whose whole interest was in domestic life . . . whose outlook on life was simple, robust and confident.

Does this writer consider that Thérèse showed that 'interest' and that 'robust outlook on life' by submitting, albeit with grief and reluctance, to be deprived of all her children? It was necessary, Rousseau informs us, in order to save her honour. Our critic maintains that in the women of Goethe and Rousseau feminine characteristics predominated, but that highly educated women are apt to lose their femininity. Poor Thérèse! Hers are the womanly charms and outlook, yet she was not allowed the indulgence of her natural tastes; or perhaps the writer thinks that 'domestic life' for even the most 'feminine' woman means simply subservience to the man. But even he might have hesitated to allude to her 'freedom from the vacillation which comes from unrealised ambitions and hopes.' He proceeds to plead 'that Thérèse, after an association of thirty years with Rousseau, should fall in love with a stable-boy may not be creditable to her, but is powerful evidence of a vigorous vitality'; and to assert that this 'vigorous vitality' was the best thing for Rousseau, as having an 'invigorating effect' upon him. In other words, he looks upon a woman purely as an animal. While fully admitting the unsullied nature of the affection that Mill entertained for Mrs. Taylor, he leads the reader to imagine that, had this been otherwise, she might *then* have been able to compete in his estimation with Rousseau's mistress, as producing an 'invigorating effect' on the great man who honoured her with his regard.

As if in order to justify his comparison of Rousseau's love affairs with that of John Stuart Mill in favour of the former, we are informed that Rousseau 'must have been called a chaste man even had he lived in our day,' and that the charges of immorality against him are 'ridiculously feeble.' Does he suppose that his readers have not read the *Confessions of Jean Jacques Rousseau*? The candour of the author is the excuse made here for the revolting revelations of that autobiography. But this so-called candour is no virtue. It is rather a species of shamelessness, although Jean Jacques is primed with glib phrases expressive of self-disapproval while describing those episodes of his life which do not commend themselves for quotation here.[1]

Lord Morley remarks: 'Rousseau's repulsive and equivocal personality has deservedly fared ill in the esteem of the saner and more rational of those who have judged him.'

In short, if the *Edinburgh* critic considers that Rousseau 'cultivated morality and simplicity of life,' what value can praise or blame from his pen possess? Absolutely none.

In the last page of his article we are told that

> the only philosophical lesson we can learn from these lives is that—whether the talents were *good* or *bad,* large or small [the italics are mine], they were in each case drawn upon and exercised to the maximum extent of their capacity,

and we are to

> learn to strive not . . . even for what we think the public welfare, but simply to make the best of our talents, whithersoever they may lead.

What if these talents lead us, like Rousseau, to theft and lying and even worse actions? It is still our talent, good or bad, that we are exercising. Is this the only 'philosophical lesson' we can learn from the life of John Stuart Mill? To what a depth has criticism descended here!

Another proof of the deleterious influence exercised on Mill by his wife and step-daughter alleged in the *Edinburgh Review* is the asserted inferiority of the letters written by him after his marriage to those of an earlier date. Here again the fact that his intellectual friendship with Mrs. Taylor had survived the test of twenty years before he married her is conveniently ignored. That there is a 'vulgarisation and enfeeblement' in the letters that he wrote after meeting her in 1831, as compared with those he wrote before that date, every impartial critic will deny. Vulgarity is the last quality that can be attributed by a sincere and well-balanced mind to any of Mill's productions. But letters are only the by-product of a literary life, and by these, therefore, it cannot be judged. They are written not to instruct posterity, but for their immediate ends.

If the quality of Mill's correspondence after his marriage was really in any way impaired this is no more than we should expect. In middle life he was attacked by consumption. That in spite of this, and of his arduous work at the India House, he was still engaged in writing for the public is simply a marvel, when we consider that he was compelled to spend his winters in our raw climate and in the confinement of an office, and that the disease did not leave him until one lung was destroyed. This fact I have heard from my father, who was an inmate of Mill's house, after the latter had married my grandmother, until his own marriage in 1860, subsequent to her death. Mill's remaining lung was not attacked; consequently he recovered a tolerable degree of health, but his vitality was necessarily lowered. Mr. Courtney tells us that Mill's medical adviser at this time believed that general debility would probably prevent him from doing any other considerable work. The reviewer entirely ignores these considerations when attributing to the 'Taylor influence' the fact that in his judgment Mill wrote no great work after the age of thirty-nine. It is fortunate that the *Logic* and *Political Economy* were written previous to this; works requiring such a prodigious amount of thought and labour could scarcely have been produced afterwards. Works as great in moral inspiration might have been, and *were,* written at a later date. In such circumstances was it any wonder if less care and thought were spent upon his correspondence than during his younger and more vigorous years?

Besides, when a man has the satisfaction of close and constant intercourse with a chosen woman friend, capable of sharing in his great ideas and of appreciating his grand visions for the future of humanity, he may naturally feel less craving for expressing himself by means of his pen to friends of his own sex.

Finally, the amount of general correspondence Mill had to deal with had by this time increased to almost unmanageable proportions, and no friend of his would have wished him to use up the spare strength that remained after the duties alluded to had been discharged, by long philosophical letters that were not essential to his life-work. One can imagine how much those who cared for Mill must have desired that he should shorten his correspondence and increase his hours of rest.

With regard to the assertion that Mrs. Mill was not received in society, I challenge the writer to bring forward his authority for this statement. It was Mill himself who declined to see the three ladies mentioned by Bain as having expressed their opinion freely on the previous platonic affection between my grandmother and himself. It may be remarked that throughout her maturer years her health, as well as her natural tastes, had induced her to prefer a retired life. For many years before her second marriage she had suffered from consumptive tendencies, and had been obliged to winter abroad. Bain, whose opinion as an intimate friend of Mill can hardly be gainsaid on such a point, makes the following observations:

> Mill could almost always allow a visitor fifteen or twenty minutes in the course of his official day, and this was the only way he could be seen. He never went into any society, except the monthly meetings of the Political Economy Club. He was completely alienated from Mrs. Grote, while keeping up his intercourse with Grote himself, and as she was not the person to have an opinion without freely expressing it, I inferred that estrangement had reference to Mrs. Taylor. Mrs. Austin, too, I was told, *came in for the cold shoulder,* and Harriet Martineau, who had special opportunities of knowing the history of the connection, and also spoke her mind freely, was understood to be still more decisively *under the ban.* [The italics are my own.] He asked no one, so far as I know, to visit her. Grote would *most cordially have paid his respects to her,* had he known it would be agreeable; but he did not receive any intimation to that effect, and never saw her either before or after her marriage to Mill. Mrs. Grote had on

one occasion, at Mill's desire, taken her to the House of Commons to hear Grote speak. . . . During all the years of her marriage with Mill she was properly described as an invalid.

It is evident that the critic in the *Edinburgh Review* makes the assertion referred to in the last paragraph with the intention of prejudicing his readers against Mrs. John Stuart Mill. That Mill had close communion with my grandmother for so many years with perfect propriety, and the countenance of my grandfather, would speak in most people's estimation for the inherent goodness of both natures. Not so in the eyes of this writer; the credit is entirely the man's, and we are to take this at his word. 'John Stuart Mill,' he says, 'was by this same feature [his hatred of sensuality] preserved from immoral relations with Mrs. Taylor.' The insinuation that Mrs. Taylor was virtuous only because of Mill's impeccability shows that this anonymous critic, who professes to admire him, is incapable of appreciating the true greatness of either.

In answer to the statement that Mrs. Mill 'had no unusual qualities of mind or body,' I shall content myself by quoting George Mill, who, while unable to recognise the extraordinary genius attributed to her by his brother John, yet spoke of her as a 'clever and remarkable woman.' The impression she left on the mind of her bereaved husband is touchingly conveyed in his letter, dated November 28, 1858, acknowledging Mr. Grote's tribute of sympathy after her decease: 'Without any personal tie, merely to have known her as I do would have been enough to make life a blank now that she has disappeared from it. I seem to have cared for things or persons, events, opinions on the future of the world, only because she cared for them: the sole motive that remains strong enough to give any interest to life is the desire to do what she would have wished.'

Reference is made in the article under consideration to the intellectual pretensions of Mrs. Taylor and Miss Helen Taylor. That John Stuart Mill found his inspiration and delight in my grandmother's companionship during twenty-seven years speaks infinitely more for her mental qualities than these studied yet shallow reflections can detract from either her intellectual or moral reputation. In what way did Miss Helen Taylor pretend to intellectuality? Simply by giving up her life to her stepfather when her mother died. Had she left Mill alone, while pursuing her own path in life, instead of soothing him, as she knew her mother would have wished, by sharing his grief, distracting his thoughts by inducing him to travel, and assisting him with his books and correspondence and in any other way in which he desired her help, the reviewer would not then have accused her of pretending to intellectuality.

When the *Letters,* chiefly on public questions, appeared more than a year and a half ago there was a general demand in the Press for others of a more personal and domestic character. It was impossible to bring these out at the same time, as the book would have been swollen to too great dimensions. Besides, I felt that my personal editing would be required. Having many interesting letters of John Stuart Mill, and others bearing a Mill interest, I hope soon to carry out this work. As they only came into my possession in 1907, and two volumes have been already issued, it cannot be considered that there has been so far any unreasonable delay.²

Notes

1. On this subject see Francis Gribble's *Women whom Rousseau loved.*

2. In the published *Letters of John Stuart Mill* a portrait was given of Mrs. Mill, which professed to be a copy of a cameo in my possession, but which was not a good reproduction. All those copies of the *Letters* that are now being sold contain an excellent engraving (substituted for the original one) which faithfully represents the beautiful likeness. Any persons who have the *Letters of John Stuart Mill* containing the inferior engraving, page 213, may obtain, cost free, this new production of the portrait from the publishers, who will also, if desired, insert it in their copy of the *Letters* in place of the original one.

Guy Linton Diffenbaugh (essay date 1923)

SOURCE: "Mrs. Taylor Seen Through Other Eyes than John Stuart Mill's," in *Sewanee Review,* Vol. 31, No. 2, April, 1923, pp. 198-204.

[*In the following essay, Diffenbaugh examines various opinions of both the character and intellectual abilities of Harriet Taylor by her contemporaries, concluding that although she was certainly an intelligent woman, Taylor could not have been the intellectual giant that John Stuart Mill claimed she was.*]

Mill in reply to Grote's letter of sympathy on the death of Mrs. Mill writes: "If I were to attempt to express in the most moderate terms what she was, even you would hardly believe me."¹ This doubt appears to be not without foundation, for Grote on reading the lines which Mill wrote for his wife's grave remarked that "only Mill's reputation could survive this and similar displays."

Certainly Mill leaves no one in doubt as to his opinion of Mrs. Taylor. The inscription for her grave is characteristic:—

> Her great and loving heart, her noble soul, her clear, powerful, original, and comprehensive intellect, made her the guide and support, the instructor in wisdom and the example in goodness, as she was the sole earthly delight of those who had the happiness to belong to her. As earnest for all public good as she was generous and devoted to all who surrounded her, her influence has been felt in many of the greatest improvements of the age, and will be in those still to come. Were there even a few hearts and intellects like hers, this earth would already become the hoped-for heaven.

Of 'similar displays' there is a sufficiency,—the dedication written in some of the copies of the *Political Economy,* the dedication of the *Liberty,* and numerous passages of the *Autobiography.*

It appears that with a few exceptions Mrs. Taylor was esteemed highly by all those who were permitted the opportunity of associating with her. Unfortunately, according to the testimony of Grote, few had that opportunity.² Aside from Mill, probably the person who enjoyed the most intimate association with her was her first husband, Mr. Taylor. Some idea, then, of his relations with Mrs. Taylor cannot but be of value.

Carlyle describes Mr. Taylor as an "innocent dull man", but we are hastily assured from another source that he was "a man of education and even some culture, and certainly of a kindly disposition."³ Respecting his amiability Carlyle seems to agree, for he writes to Dr. Carlyle that Mr. Taylor was "a most joyous-natured man, the pink of social hospitality."⁴ His kindly disposition was, however, no substantial substitute for his lack of 'internal culture', and it appears that Mrs. Taylor, too, found him 'dull'. In all fairness to Mr. Taylor it must be remembered that constant attendance upon the wholesale drug business in Mark Lane was not conducive to creative thinking in any of the realms in which Mrs. Taylor excelled. That the Taylors were not congenial intellectually is verified by Mrs. Taylor's complaint to the Rev. W. J. Fox that she had married too young, before she had any knowledge of the world.⁵ Although Mr. Taylor could not meet his wife on common ground intellectually, yet, according to her own statement, "she felt a warm affection for him based on gratitude for his kindness to her."⁶

After the epoch-making dinner of 1831 at which Mrs. Taylor met Mill, there came 'the awakening of her heart'. The completeness of this awakening is evinced in a letter from Mrs. Taylor to Mrs. Fox in 1833:—

> Oh this being, seeming as though God had willed to show the type of the possible elevation of humanity. To be with him wholly is my ideal of the noblest fate; for of all states of mind and feeling which are lofty and large and fine, he is the companion spirit and heart's desire. We are not alike in trifles, only because I have so much more frivolity than he.⁷

Some such sentiment Mrs. Taylor confessed to her husband, assuring him, however, that although her love for Mill was stronger than her affection for him, she still did feel affection for him, based on gratitude for his kindness. The confession made, Mr. Taylor suggested a six-months' separation, to which his wife agreed and took up her residence in Paris, where, incidentally, Mill happened to be staying at the time. Although Mr. Taylor's hope that the separation would quicken his wife's affection for him proved futile, nevertheless he seems to welcome with delight her return to England to live with him as 'a friend and companion'. During a period of some fifteen years, whenever the Taylors were in London, Mill came regularly to dinner twice a week; and Mr. Taylor, 'the pink of social hospitality', dined out. Taylor died in 1849, and as crowning proof of his great affection and belief in his wife's loyalty, left her his entire fortune in trust for her sole use during her lifetime. Two years after his death, Mrs. Taylor married John Stuart Mill.

Mr. Taylor was not a *littérateur,* and probably for that reason has left no attempts to express his opinion of his wife's merits. But, as his biographer hints, no rhetorical flights could exhibit more clearly his regard for Mrs. Taylor than his conduct during the twenty years of her intimacy with Mill—conduct evincing a generosity and consideration that could have no other basis than genuine affection and respect. Had Mr. Taylor found literary expression as easy a task as did John Stuart Mill, he, too, might have written, "She was the sole earthly delight of those who had the happiness to belong to her."

In a brief discussion of Mill's relations with Mrs. Taylor, Courtney writes cautiously, "Opinions differ as to her merits."[8] This diversity of opinion is beautifully illustrated by the Mill family. James Mill strongly disapproved of her and expressed his disapproval not only to his son, but to several of his friends. Mrs. Mill, however, with motherly affection writes to her son in 1854 that she is well pleased with his marriage, "for he has chosen a lady capable of sharing in all his pursuits and [characteristically adding] appreciating his good qualities."[9] George, one of Mill's younger brothers, with a mind less hampered than his parents by any prejudices, and enjoying the prerogative of the younger brother's unrestricted critical utterances on the character of the eldest brother's wife, remarks with typical British sentiment that Mrs. Taylor was "a clever and remarkable woman but nothing like what John took her to be."[10] If the most enthusiastic expression of Mrs. Taylor's merits from the Mill family appears comparatively lacking in fervor, it must be remembered that, unlike Mr. Taylor or John Stuart Mill, it very definitely had not the happiness of belonging to her.[11]

Morley, who says much about John Stuart Mill, is extremely quiet on the subject of Mrs. Taylor. Speaking of the idealism of the *Subjection of Women* he remarks, in passing, that "much was, no doubt, due to the influence of the remarkable woman to whom he [Mill] paid such extraordinary homage."[12] Morley's rather wavering expression has no counterpart in the utterances of the Carlyles. Carlyle, whose friendship with Mill but faintly approaches Morley's intimacy with his master, seems at least to have had a greater opportunity than Morley of association with Mrs. Taylor. In 1834 Carlyle writes to his mother:—

> We have made, at least Jane has made, a most promising new acquaintance, of a Mrs. Taylor; a young, beautiful reader of mine and 'dearest friend' of Mill's who for the present seems 'all that is noble' and what not. We shall see how that wears.[13]

The acquaintanceship appears to have progressed fairly at the start, for ten days after Carlyle's letter to his mother he writes to Dr. Carlyle:—

> We dined with Mrs. (Platonica) Taylor and the Unitarian Fox (of the Repository, if you know it) one day: Mill was of the party, and the Husband.[14]

That the 'promising new acquaintance' did not wear well with the Carlyles is apparent from their later remarks. Mrs. Taylor, it seems, at first considered Mrs. Carlyle "a rustic spirit fit for rather tutoring and twirling about when the humour took her; but got taught better (to her lasting memory) before long."[15] Later Mrs. Carlyle writes that "she [Mrs. Taylor] is deemed dangerous"; to which Carlyle adds that she was worse than dangerous—she was patronizing.[16]

The summation of the Carlyles' opinion of Mrs. Taylor, and the general attitude of Mill's acquaintances, is suggested by Carlyle's remark that "the Mrs. Taylor business was becoming more and more of a questionable benefit to him [Mill] (we could see), but on that subject we were strictly silent, and he was pretty still."[17] Although Mill's reputation sustained him among his intimate friends, the opinion of his less intimate, contemporaries regarding his homage to Mrs. Taylor might well be expressed in Carlyle's comment on the *Autobiography*—that he never read anything "sillier by a man of sense, integrity, and seriousness of mind."[18]

It is, however, not so much what people say about Mrs. Taylor as what they do not say that causes the ardent admirer of Mill to begin casting about for an explanation of Mill's apparently isolated enthusiasm. That in any group of people who know a certain individual there is never an unanimous agreement as to the virtues of that individual is a truism. But when the cardinal virtue is seen in magnificent proportion by one, and faintly, if at all, by the others, those failing are apt to accept the situation with the same degree of concern as did the proverbial company of infantry whose latest recruit thought that he alone was in step on parade. Mill only, it appears, saw Mrs. Taylor's "all but unrivalled wisdom"—the basis of his extraordinary homage.

In striving to account for Mill's opinion of Mrs. Taylor's enormous intellectual capacity, and shying at the word 'infatuation', Courtney is forced in the end through lack of synonymous expressions to employ it.

> Infatuation, for infatuation it can only be when a man of Mill's intellectual eminence allows himself to describe his friend in terms of such unbounded adulation—'were I capable of interpreting to the world one half the great thoughts and noble feelings which are buried in her grave, I should be the medium of a greater benefit to it than is ever likely to arise from anything that I can write unprompted and unassisted by her all but unrivalled wisdom.[19]

That it was an intellectual infatuation, however, is apparent from this and other tributes, and he who reads them should attempt to discover with the assistance of biographer and critic the reason for the infatuation which causes Mill's many pages to "ring with the dithyrambic praise of his 'almost infallible counsellor.'"[20]

In a theory presented by Courtney lies for many people the entire solution of Mill's intellectual infatuation for Mrs. Taylor. It would seem unnecessary to remark that this infatuation had no basis in the cynical explanation that Mrs. Taylor captivated Mill by serving as an echo of his own opinions,[21] were it not that Courtney's theory, by some, is confused with it. Says Courtney:—

> When a clever woman gives expression to some of the thoughts which, in the man's case, are the results of hard thinking, he is apt to imagine that she, too, must have been through a similar mental discipline, and that there is as much behind her expression of the thought as there would be if he had made use of it. A man habitually underrates the woman's quickness of apprehension, and her delicate and intuitive insight into some of the problems with which he has been wrestling. He admires her, therefore, in proportion to the seriousness of his own logic, not in reference to her own native powers.[22]

Mill himself, had he been inquiring into the reasons for intellectual infatuation, would never have accepted this explanation; but his very rejection of it appears, at least, to account for his isolated opinion of Mrs. Taylor.

Intellectual infatuation! A "very will-o'-wispish iridescence of a creature; pale, passionate, sad-looking; a living-romance heroine of the royalest volition and questionable destiny"[23]—and Courtney bridges the chasm with a theory on the cleverness of women: "Quickness of apprehension, delicate and intuitive insight."

On one occasion, when Morley named Mrs. Taylor to Carlyle, who was the only one among his friends who knew her, Carlyle said something like this:—

> She was a woman full of unwise intellect, always asking questions about all sorts of puzzles—why, how, what for, what makes the exact difference—and Mill was good at answers.[24]

Yet in all fairness to Mrs. Taylor might it not be said that it took at least a clever person to inquire intelligently of Mill—'why, how, what for, what makes the exact difference'; and that it required a woman of remarkable mental gymnastics, at least, to assimilate Mill's answers with a degree of intelligent promptness sufficient to infatuate him mentally. "A clever and remarkable woman," says the younger brother, "but nothing like what John took her to be."

Notes

1. Letter to George Grote, Nov. 28, 1858. *Letters of John Stuart Mill.* Ed. Hugh Elliot. Vol. I, p. 213. London, 1910.

2. Bain, Alex.: *J. S. Mill: A Criticism,* p. 166. London, 1882.

3. *Letters of John Stuart Mill,* op. cit., p. xl.

4. *Letters of Thomas Carlyle.* Ed. C. E. Norton. Letter cxiii, Vol. II, p. 207. London, 1888.

5. Bain, op. cit., p. 164.

6. *Letters of Mill,* op. cit., p. xli.

7. *Ibid.*

8. Courtney, W. L.: *Life of J. S. Mill,* p. 113. London, 1889.

9. *Letters of Mill,* op. cit., p. xl.

10. Bain, *loc. cit.*

11. Mill's marriage made a decided breach between him and his family, caused apparently by his resentment of a fancied slight.

12. Morley, John: *Recollections,* Vol. I, p. 63. New York, 1919.

13. *Letters of Thomas Carlyle,* op. cit. Letter cxii, p. 200.

14. *Ibid.*

15. *Reminiscences.* Ed. J. A. Froude, p. 409. New York, 1881.

16. Courtney, op. cit., p. 113.

17. *Reminiscences,* loc. cit.

18. Letter to John Carlyle, Nov. 5, 1873.

19. Op. cit., p. 115.

20. Ibid., p. 112.

21. Bain, op. cit., p. 117.

22. Op. cit., p. 117.

23. The description of Mrs. Taylor is Carlyle's.

24. Morley, loc cit.

Francis E. Mineka (essay date 1963)

SOURCE: "The *Autobiography* and the Lady," in *University of Toronto Quarterly,* Vol. 32, No. 3, April, 1963, pp. 301-6.

[*In the following essay, Mineka explores the initial reaction to John Stuart Mill's* Autobiography *and his implications that Harriet Taylor collaborated on several of his essays.*]

The publication of John Stuart Mill's *Autobiography* in October 1873, less than six months after his death, created something of a sensation on both sides of the Atlantic. Mill's reputation and influence were still at their height, his *Logic* and his *Political Economy* were widely used college textbooks in both England and America, and his advice and opinions on a considerable range of topics were eagerly sought up until the very end of his life. Liberals everywhere had regarded him as perhaps their greatest philosopher and spokesman; most conservatives had been at least respectful. No sooner was he dead, however, than the conservatives' denigration of him became much more vocal. Abraham Hayward, a Tory antagonist of Mill's since the days of their encounters in the London Debating Society in the 1820's, in an obituary article in the *Times* raked up the old scandal about Mill's having as a youth been arrested for distributing birth-control information, and strenuous efforts were made to block a movement to erect a statue to him. The scandal thus raised was enough to convince Gladstone of the expediency of withdrawing his support, but Mill's admirers prevailed and the statue still stands in the garden east of the Temple underground station. The appearance of the *Autobiography* contributed fuel to the controversy.

Here were revealed for everyone to read details of the hitherto personally reticent Mill's background and extraordinary education, his religious scepticism, his reaction against the orthodox Benthamism of his youth, his acceptance of Socialist ideals, and his long-continued, unconventional friendship with Mrs. John Taylor which culminated in their marriage in 1851.

The *Autobiography* was reviewed in most of the leading periodicals, and the critics examined it in terms of their own political, philosophical, religious, and moral prepossessions. Many thought it a "cold" book, largely devoid of human emotion, a bloodless analysis of the development of his attitudes and convictions. One reviewer called it "one of the saddest books ever written." The absence of any mention of Mill's mother provoked disapproving comment. Politically conservative reviewers found confirmation of their worst fears of Mill's dangerous social and political opinions. Orthodox religious reviewers were even more shocked, for the extent of Mill's heterodoxy had been somewhat less clearly revealed in his writings than had his political and economic heresies; one American critic entitled his review "The Autobiography of an Atheist." Mill's extravagant tributes to his wife's intellectual abilities and to her contributions to his thought and writing were greeted generally with amused scepticism. The critic in the *British Quarterly Review* remarked dryly: "Mill had no great faith in a God. He had unbounded confidence in a goddess."

Alexander Bain, friend and disciple of Mill and his first biographer, reading the proofs of the *Autobiography* in September 1873, had been fearful that Mill's reputation would suffer seriously if his most extreme claims for his wife were not deleted. Bain wrote Helen Taylor, Mill's stepdaughter and literary executor, to urge that she cancel "those sentences where he declares her to be a greater poet than Carlyle . . . and a greater thinker than himself—and again, a greater leader than his father (or at all events an equal)." Helen Taylor refused to make the suggested deletions, though she did, with reluctance, remove praise of herself. Bain's fears proved to be exaggerated, and over the years most readers of the *Autobiography* have been inclined to view charitably the fulsome praise of Mrs. Mill as the harmless aberration of a love-blinded husband. Con-

sequently, Mill's reputation did not suffer greatly for this reason, and the *Autobiography* has long been regarded as one of his most important and influential books.

In recent years, however, new biographers of Mill have sought to restore Harriet Mill to the intellectual throne her husband had accorded her. Professor F. A. Hayek, to whom all scholars interested in Mill are indebted, in his pioneering biographical work, *John Stuart Mill and Harriet Taylor* (1951), led the way in the attempted revaluation of Harriet's influence. Though reaching the conclusion "that her influence on his thought and outlook, whatever her capacities may have been, were quite as great as Mill asserts," Hayek nevertheless exercised scholarly caution in advancing the case for Harriet; one notes that he ends his book with a quotation of Mill's extravagant praise of Helen Taylor which she had been persuaded to delete. Michael St. John Packe in his impressive and very readable *Life of John Stuart Mill* (1954) and Ruth Borchardt in her *John Stuart Mill: The Man* (1957) both went much beyond Hayek, however, in asserting the claims for Harriet. Packe went so far as to maintain that "her predominance was even more complete than [Mill] himself pronounced."

By no means all students of Mill have accepted fully the new biographers' contentions. The evidence thus far produced makes abundantly clear the predominance she exercised in Mill's private life. Almost from his first acquaintance with her in 1830 she became so much the centre of his emotional life that he became convinced she was also the centre of his intellectual life. There was clearly a community of intellectual interests between them, but the evidence to support the contention that she was the originating mind behind most of his work is far from convincing. Two recently published books have contributed substantially to our understanding of Mill and his wife; the weight of their contribution helps to tip the scales further against some of the contentions of the new biographers.

Professor Jack Stillinger's edition of the early draft of Mill's *Autobiography* is important perhaps more for its revelations about the purposes of the book, the circumstances of its composition, and the corrupt state of all hitherto published editions than it is for its revelations about Harriet, but it nevertheless adds to the evidence from which one must form a judgement of her and her influence upon Mill.

Three manuscripts of the *Autobiography* are extant; all three were sold in 1922 at the time of the first sale in England of Mill's papers. One, his own final draft for publication, was later purchased for Columbia University, and became the basis for the edition published by the Press of that university in 1924 and until now regarded as definitive. Professor Stillinger has clearly demonstrated the deficiencies of the Columbia edition, which though still the best available needs correcting and re-editing. The second manuscript sold in 1922, an error-ridden transcription made hurriedly after Mill's death, was the press copy used for the 1873 edition; this copy was acquired in 1959 by the

John Rylands Library of Manchester. The third manuscript was Mill's original draft, written in 1853 and 1854, giving an account of his life up to his marriage in 1851; this draft was bought by Professor Jacob Hollander of Johns Hopkins University, but remained virtually unknown for nearly twenty years until Professor A. W. Levi examined it with interesting results in 1941. From then on the manuscript was unavailable until 1958 when Hollander's large collection of rare works in economics was purchased from his heirs by the University of Illinois.

Professor Stillinger of that university rightly decided that this early draft was sufficiently important to deserve separate publication. Although the text is the same in many places as that of the first three-quarters of the final draft, there are enough hitherto suppressed passages (one, for example, criticizing his mother), unknown new facts, different emphases, and changes in tone to give independent value to the early draft. The difficulties of putting into print a manuscript full of cancellations, alterations, reorderings, and revisions (by both Mill and Harriet) have been very ably handled by Professor Stillinger, and the result is an important contribution to the study of Mill.

Many readers in the past have tended to overlook the fact that the defence and justification of Mill's and Harriet's unconventional friendship and eventual marriage constituted one of the main original purposes of the *Autobiography*. For Harriet, who participated actively in the planning of the book, it was perhaps the major purpose. The early draft was written at a time when the two were still smarting from the gossip which had pursued them over the years; it was also written at a time when Mill feared that his death was imminent. Evidently, his original intention was to divide the work into two parts, the pre- and the post-Harriet periods of his life. This division proved to be impracticable, partly because of the disproportionate lengths of the two periods, and a compromise revision was achieved which blurred the original sharp distinction between the two sections. Nevertheless, if Mill had died in, say 1856, the work if published would have given the concluding emphasis to the justification and glorification of his wife.

It is perhaps idle to speculate how successful the *Autobiography* could have been in that form, but it seems reasonable to doubt that it could have added as much to Mill's reputation as the final version definitely did. The early draft was more "human," less "cold"—it revealed more minor egotisms, more personal animosities, and in some instances franker evaluations of his own limitations than did the more objective version achieved by the revision and extension completed about 1870. The years after Harriet's death in 1858 did not lessen his extravagant estimate of her powers, but they did lead him to soften or omit a number of the asperities of the early draft which had been clearly inspired by his relationship with her and which she had not sought to soften when she read the manuscript. It was not by her advice that he eliminated the severe criticism of his mother found in the early draft, or his belit-

tling of his one-time friend John Roebuck, or his attack upon Sarah Austin, whom over the years he had addressed in many letters as "Dear Mütterlein."

It is understandable that Harriet had a grudge against the society that had excluded her from polite circles. As the pretty, striking young wife of a prosperous, not unintelligent though rather stolid business man, John Taylor, her circle had been limited but not without interest. Although Unitarians may still have been "a sect every where spoken against," they were intellectually, and to some extent socially, the aristocrats among the Dissenters. The Taylors entertained generously among those whom Carlyle scornfully labeled "friends of the species," reformers, Benthamites, yet substantial citizens withal. But there was a flaw in the outwardly happy marriage. Mr. Taylor shared too little Harriet's cultural and intellectual interests. Legend has it that she turned to her pastor, the liberal Unitarian preacher and editor, the Reverend William Johnson Fox, for advice, and that he was responsible for calling her attention to the twenty-four-year-old John Stuart Mill, then unknown to the general public as a writer but regarded in liberal circles as a highly promising if somewhat manufactured genius. Mill and Mrs. Taylor first met in 1830 in the Taylor home at a dinner-party also attended by Harriet Martineau and John Roebuck.

Just how rapidly the acquaintance ripened into love is not clear, but by the summer of 1832 Mill and Mrs. Taylor were exchanging agonized love letters and by September 1833 a crisis was reached in the Taylors' marriage. She went off to Paris for a trial separation from her husband, and Mill soon followed. Members of her family intervened to patch up the threatened marriage and obviate scandal. Mrs. Taylor returned to her husband's home and to a marriage henceforth only nominal. She had not, however, "renounced sight" of Mill, and their meetings were frequent, both at her home and elsewhere. From time to time they spent vacations together on the Continent, on occasion with her children and some of his younger brothers. Gossip thrived, of course, though the evidence is pretty clear that there was no sexual relationship. Mrs. Taylor succeeded in holding both her husband and her lover at arm's length.

Inevitably, Mill's attachment to Mrs. Taylor restricted his contacts in English society. Some of his friends he cut because they had advised him against continuing the relation or had participated in the gossip; others he cut because she disliked them. She herself seems to have had little capacity for friendship, especially with her own sex. Her only close woman friend was the somewhat elfin Eliza Flower, who was herself under a cloud because of her relationship with the Reverend W. J. Fox. The circle of Mill's friends narrowed over the long years before the death of John Taylor in 1849 finally made possible the marriage with Harriet in 1851, and thereafter the circle became even more circumscribed. He soon cut himself off from his mother and his brothers and sisters, because of fancied slights to his wife. Probably the greatest blot on Mill's character was his treatment, apparently with Harriet's encouragement, of his family after his marriage, as revealed in letters still extant. One is reminded of his letter in 1841 to his French friend Gustave d'Eichthal congratulating the latter upon his approaching marriage, but remarking that he could seldom congratulate heartily "an Englishman on a similar event, which, in nine cases out of ten, changes a man of any superiority very much for the worse, without making him happy." Was Mill the one in ten who won the prize?

As for society, Henry Reeve, acquainted with Mill since boyhood, identifiable as the writer of the *Edinburgh*'s hostile review of the *Autobiography* in 1874, spoke for Mrs. Grundy:

> From the moment he devoted himself exclusively to what he calls "the most valuable friendship in my life," [his ties with talented women like Mrs. Buller, Mrs. Austin, and Mrs. Grote were broken]. Whatever may have been their regard for Mill, these ladies found it impossible to countenance or receive a woman who had placed herself in so equivocal a position.

Enough is known of Mrs. Austin, Mrs. Carlyle, and Mrs. Grote, and of their tolerance for unconventionality to make one suspect that it was not their concern for Mrs. Grundy, but their not wholly unjustified dislike for Harriet that led them to put her out of countenance. She, deeply resenting her exclusion, of course attributed it to her breaking of convention in her long association with Mill during her husband's lifetime. And under her sway Mill made the justification of that association one of his major purposes in writing his autobiography.

Was he then simply deluded? Was he who was ordinarily so discerning in his analysis of men and motives so blinded when it came to appraising her? There can be no question that from the first she filled an enormous need in his emotional life. Suffering from a too exclusively intellectual education that starved the affections and led to his near nervous breakdown at twenty, he sought a friend with whom he could share his inmost thoughts and feelings and upon whom he could depend. For a time it seemed that John Sterling might be that friend, and for a while, even after Mill had met Harriet, Carlyle appeared to be a possibility. But, for good or ill, the friend he found was Mrs. Taylor: for good, in that she provided a centre of stability for his emotional and, to some extent, his intellectual life; for ill, in that she fostered the isolation from his contemporaries that had characterized his earlier life. Lover-like, in his early relation with her, he engaged in lover's flattery of her, not of her beauty but of her intellectual abilities, on which she prided herself. She was intelligent, she shared his passion for social reform, and she was at times more direct and unwavering than he in going to the heart of a social or political problem. She also had a much better sense than he did of the management of everyday, practical affairs, and after their marriage he became dependent upon her judgement in such matters. She in turn seems to have become more and more dependent upon him for her

meed of praise. One can understand a woman's acceptance of even extravagant flattery in a lover's or even a husband's letters; one finds it difficult to comprehend a wife's coolly approving for publication as her due such extraordinary tributes as Mill paid Harriet in the *Autobiography*.

Though he did make certain qualifications in his statements of indebtedness to her, as H. O. Pappe has pointed out in his short monograph *John Stuart Mill and the Harriet Taylor Myth,* the qualifications tended to be overwhelmed by the ardour of his praise. Mill was almost invariably a painstakingly correct and always honest writer, but he was often over-generous in his assessment of persons he admired. Professor Pappe soberly reviews the evidence of Harriet's scanty writings, both those published in her own life-time and those first published by Hayek, to see how reliable are the contentions of the recent biographers that she was the truly forceful, originating mind behind Mill's work, particularly in the *On Liberty, The Subjection of Women,* and the extensive revisions in the later editions of the *Political Economy*. Although Pappe sometimes too readily overlooks difficult bits of conflicting evidence, his refutation of the claims for Harriet is in the main convincing.

Harriet's early essay on toleration, advanced as the source of the *On Liberty,* Pappe rightly points out, probably owes much to Mill himself. No one, however, seems to have called attention to the essay "Remarks on Association," published in England in 1830 by the American Unitarian leader William Ellery Channing, which anticipates some of the central doctrines of the *On Liberty*. Channing was widely read by English Unitarians, and there is evidence that Mill was acquainted with his essay months before he met Harriet. As for the claim that her essay on marriage was the source of *The Subjection of Women,* Pappe properly emphasizes that Mill held feminist views before 1830. Pappe does not, however, call attention to the fact that advanced views on marriage and women's education were common in the circle about W. J. Fox and were advocated in his magazine, the *Monthly Repository*. Also, no doubt, as in the case of Milton, unhappiness in marriage had a part in shaping both Fox's and Harriet's desire to change the prevailing rules and attitudes of conventional society.

Harriet was a rebel not without cause. In Mill she found a man whose extraordinary education had shaped him also for rebellion against the social, moral, and political conventions of his time. In him she found too a man almost desperately lonely, subject to recurring periods of depression. It is perhaps small wonder that in gratitude for her braving the censure of society, for her sharing in his devotion to liberal causes, and for her strengthening of his spiritual and mental resources, he sought in his *Autobiography* to induce the world to accept his estimate of her. Neither he nor his recent biographers have convinced us that she was the originating mind behind his work, but no one can doubt her importance in Mill's inner life, the well-springs of which had been threatened by drought.

Works Cited

Jack Stillinger, ed., *The Early Draft of John Stuart Mill's Autobiography.* Urbana: University of Illinois Press. 1961. Pp. viii, 218.

H. O. Pappe, *John Stuart Mill and the Harriet Taylor Myth.* Melbourne University Press on behalf of the Australian National University (Toronto: Macmillan). 1961. Pp. x, 51.

Alice S. Rossi (essay date 1970)

SOURCE: "Sentiment and Intellect: The Story of John Stuart Mill and Harriet Taylor Mill," in *Essays on Sex Equality: John Stuart Mill and Harriet Taylor Mill,* University of Chicago Press, 1970, pp. 3-63.

[*In the following excerpt, Rossi examines the Mill/Taylor controversy from a sociological perspective, paying particular attention to the influence of the Unitarian Radicals and the Philosophical Radicals on the early stages of the couple's relationship.*]

If we could go back to the town of Avignon in the year 1860, we might take a two-mile stroll along the banks of the Rhone, through meadows and groves of mulberries, to the house in which John Stuart Mill wrote the first draft of *The Subjection of Women.* As we approached the house, we would see an oblong garden with an avenue of sycamores and mulberry trees, and at the end the small square house in which Mill lived and worked. A white stone building with a tile roof and green blinds, Mill's home commanded a view of green fields, backed by ranges of mountains. Here Mill wrote during the morning hours, passed the afternoons roaming the surrounding countryside, and spent the evenings with reading and correspondence. Close to this secluded house is the cemetery in which Mill's wife Harriet was buried two years before (1858), a quiet place John Mill visited daily.[1]

This then is the setting in which Mill wrote his major volume on women. When he finished the draft of the essay in 1861, Mill intended to keep it among his other unpublished papers, "improving it from time to time if I was able, and to publish it at the time when it should seem likely to be most useful."[2] By "useful" Mill meant politically expedient, and that time did not come for another eight years. The intervening years were very full and active ones: a prodigious amount of writing that brought to fruition a lifetime of intellectual effort, and a culmination of Mill's active political commitments in the three years (1865-68) he served as a member of the House of Commons. In 1868 Mill retired again to his home near Avignon, where he revised the manuscript of the essay on women for publication in 1869.

One hundred years have passed since *The Subjection of Women* was published, yet it stands almost alone as an intellectual analysis of the position of women and an appeal for political action to secure equality of the sexes. Nothing quite like it had been published before 1869, and nothing like it was to appear again until the publication in 1898 of Charlotte Perkins Gilman's *Women and Economics,* and another fifty years until the publication in 1951 of Simone de Beauvoir's *The Second Sex.* These three volumes are landmarks in both the long history of the women's movement for political and economic rights and the shorter history of intellectual analyses of sex roles and the relations between the sexes. All three share that rare quality of rigorous intellectual analysis combined with passionate commitment to the goal of sex equality. *The Subjection of Women* is of very special interest as the first and as the only one of the three written by a man.

Many men in the history of western intellectual thought have been deeply committed to the fight against tyranny over the minds and bodies of the powerless in nation after nation. Generations of young people have been stirred by intellectual and political battles against a host of "establishments": the church, the aristocracy, the bourgeoisie, the military-industrial complex. The subjection of peasants, slaves, religious dissenters, and workers to a variety of ruling elites has stirred liberal and radical thinkers and activists for the past two centuries. John Stuart Mill stands as the solitary male intellectual figure who devoted his efforts to tracing the analogous subjection of women. It is a measure of the snail's pace at which the movement toward sex equality has progressed that *The Subjection of Women* is typically merely cited by title by scholars of Mill, but hardly ever analyzed, summarized, or included in collections of his essays on liberty and egalitarianism.[3]

John Stuart Mill was a man of sixty-three when the essay on women was published. A man of towering intellectual importance to his contemporaries, he stands as a significant figure in the history of ideas, one who straddled the eighteenth and nineteenth centuries and anticipated the twentieth. How did this man come to write a book on women? Why had this Victorian Englishman withdrawn to a secluded village in France to live and write? When during his lifetime did he develop an interest in the position of women? To answer such questions requires an examination of the development of Mill's thought and the course of his personal life, for a long period of gestation and a complex personal history preceded the publication of *The Subjection of Women.*

A scholar need proceed no further than a reading of Mill's autobiography and the prefaces he wrote for most of his work following the 1848 publication of the *Principles of Political Economy* to encounter Harriet Taylor as a central figure in Mill's intellectual and personal life. It is doubtful that *The Subjection of Women* would ever have been written if it were not for Mill's twenty-eight-year relationship with Harriet. Hence it is not only Mill's own development, but the history of his relationship with Harriet Taylor, that must be examined if we are to understand why Mill wrote a book on women and why the book has such remarkable survival power and impact.

John Mill and Harriet Taylor were in their early twenties when they first met. Harriet was at that time a young married woman with two young children, but within a year the relationship between Mill and Mrs. Taylor was one of intellectual and spiritual intimacy. For the next twenty years, Mill continued to live at home with his mother and younger siblings, while Mrs. Taylor remained in her husband's household, yet it is clear that the unconventional relationship they enjoyed with each other was the very core of their lives. It was not until 1851, two years after her husband's death, when they were in their forties and suffering very poor health, that they married. Just seven years later, Harriet died at Avignon, and Mill bought a home near the cemetery in which she was buried. The nature of their relationship, and the exact contribution of Harriet Taylor to Mill's thought and writing, has been the subject of controversy for over a hundred years.

In an era in which sociology has confined itself to the here-and-now, and to a methodology that focuses on the quantitative analysis of survey and experimental data, it may seem strange that a sociologist like me should attempt an essentially biographical investigation into nineteenth-century historical materials. There is, however, a sociological tradition with which this is fully consistent. C. Wright Mills argued, to that minority of sociology graduate students who listened to him, that social science was basically the study of human variety, which consists of "all the social worlds in which men have lived, are living and might live."[4] Mills argued that a proper sociological perspective involves the study of biography and of history, and the intersection of the two in particular social structures. It is in keeping with this sociological tradition that I attempt a selective review of the personal lives and the work of John and Harriet Mill, with particular attention to the two distinct, though overlapping social and intellectual circles—the Philosophic Radicals and the Unitarian Radicals—in which they moved during the critical early years of their relationship.

This analysis has a further relevance to contemporary concerns about sex equality. In 1970 there are two quite distinct levels to the new renascence of concern for the position of women. One concentrates on the reformist, liberal pursuit of widening and consolidating the legal rights of women in the political and economic spheres. This activity builds on the long tradition of the women's rights movement throughout American history of the past 120 years, symbolically initiated by the Declaration of Sentiments at the Seneca Falls convention in 1848. The second, more radical approach focuses attention on the private as well as the public sector and pushes both for an analysis of human sexuality in general and for a critical examination of marriage and the family as social institutions. This approach has involved a search, romantic as well as radical, for a new vision of relations between the sexes, based on the hope that it is possible to blend physical sex, sentiment, and intellect in the husband-wife relationship. As yet few notable examples of such marriages have appeared, and so a contemporary sociologist is strongly inclined to widen

the sample of such relationships by turning backward in time to earlier, prominent examples in history. A cross-sex relationship, inside or outside marriage, in which sex and intellect, family and work, are blended, is a dream in the heart of many young women searching for liberation in 1970.

Any scholar who attempts to examine Mill's personal history faces two special difficulties, and it will be well if we confront these at the outset. One difficulty is rooted in the image Mill both wittingly and unwittingly projected of himself. For his contemporaries, as for those who read his famous autobiography, the major features of this image are Mill's high moral tone, deep commitment to intellectual effort, and rigorous rational analysis. The image is aptly caught in Gladstone's characterization of Mill as the "Saint of Rationalism." This is nowhere more apparent than in the autobiography itself, which is remarkable for its impersonality. It is so nearly a pure intellectual recital of Mill's development that John Jacob Coss could say: "In many ways it is primarily an account of the social history of England in the first three quarters of the Nineteenth Century."[5] It was because of this quality of the autobiography that Coss used the book in his philosophy courses at Columbia University, along with Plato's *Republic,* Aristotle's *Ethics,* and Bacon's *Advancement of Learning.* In a more recent commentary, Hayek made a similar observation: "Of what in the ordinary sense of the word we should call his life, of his human interests and personal relations, we learn practically nothing."[6]

Hayek's contribution to our understanding of the personal side of Mill's life was the publication of the John Mill-Harriet Taylor correspondence in 1951. Even this volume of correspondence is far from complete, for many of Mill's personal letters were destroyed during World War II while Hayek was attempting to gather them in London; others appear to have been destroyed by Helen Taylor after her stepfather's death, and a good number remain unpublished in private collections in England and America. When the first full collection of Mill's work began to issue from the University of Toronto Press in the 1950s, Hayek wrote that no other major figure of the nineteenth century has had to wait almost one hundred years before his collected works were published. In 1970 several volumes remain to be published by the Toronto press.

It is interesting that an earlier draft of the *Autobiography* has come to light only in recent years. This document has had a curious history. It was bought in London in 1922 by Jacob Harry Hollander, a professor of political economy at Johns Hopkins University, and at the time of his death in 1940 the manuscript had apparently been read by only one other person—A. W. Levi, who subsequently wrote two essays based on a psychoanalytic study of it.[7] With the rest of Hollander's library the draft was stored in a Baltimore warehouse after his death and remained there until 1958, when the University of Illinois purchased the collection. Finally, in 1961, the early draft, edited by Jack Stillinger, was published by the University of Illinois Press.[8] This earlier version is less exclusively an intellectual document than the later one. The basic draft was written by John Mill, and Harriet penciled in suggested revisions and comments. When Mill accepted her suggestions, he penned over her penciled emendations, thus permitting Stillinger to examine the written evidence of Harriet's contributions to the "life," as they referred to it in their correspondence. Stillinger's examination of the manuscript led him to comment that Mill and his wife (and to an even greater degree, Mill alone, in his subsequent rewriting in the early 1860s) had made it progressively more "public" and less "human" than it had been at the start. As a result of the long unavailability of both the early draft of the autobiography and so much of the correspondence, it is clear that a great deal of the scholarship on Mill's personal life is still to be done.

Where Harriet Taylor is concerned, the scholar's task is even more difficult. Mill himself rejected the idea that an adequate memoir could be written on her life. When the American suffragist Paulina Wright Davies asked Mill about such a possibility in 1870, he responded:

> Were it possible in a memoir to have the formation and growth of a mind like hers portrayed, to do so would be as valuable a benefit to mankind as was ever conferred by a biography. But such a psychological history is seldom possible, and in her case the materials for it do not exist. All that could be furnished is her birthplace, parentage and a few dates.[9]

A good deal more than a "few dates" remain to the scholar interested in forming a profile of Harriet Taylor Mill. It is clear that paucity of historical evidence has not prevented, and may even have stimulated, the long series of very opinionated views about her. I shall review some of these contradictory assessments and suggest my own at a later point in this essay.

A second problem for a late twentieth-century scholar is the difficulty of emphatically penetrating the mystique of Victorian morality where "passionate" relations between the sexes are concerned. Unwittingly, the reader falls in line with the Victorian writers and early twentieth-century commentators in drawing up a balance sheet of evidence of the "did they or didn't they sleep together" variety, until one impatiently calls oneself back to the perspective of our own time and place. We are dealing neither with a casual sex encounter nor with a conventional marital relationship, but with a complex and subtle mutuality of intellect and sentiment between a man and a woman. It may be that in nineteenth-century Victorian England avoidance of the physical act of adultery and adherence to the formal obligations of the marital relationship were more significant than the existence of intellectual and personal intimacy between an unmarried man and a married woman. In the mid-twentieth century the ordering of these priorities would be reversed: intimacy of sentiment and intellect in a cross-sex relationship outside the marriage is a greater threat to the marriage than adultery per se. In any event one surmises that "passion" in the lives of both John Mill

and Harriet Taylor was a sublimated and highly intellectualized emotion, and that Harriet made an apt characterization when she told Gumperz that from 1831 on, her relationship both to her husband John Taylor and to John Mill was that of "Seelenfreundin."[10] What remains of central significance to us today is the subtle and pervasive transformation that their love for each other brought about in the personal lives and in the ideas and intellectual efforts of John Mill and Harriet Taylor.

What follows is an account of Mill's life and development with special attention to the ideas on marriage, divorce, and the position of women that were current in the social and intellectual circles in which Mill and Harriet Taylor moved. At appropriate points in the unfolding chronology, I shall summarize and highlight the essays they wrote on women in 1832, 1851, and 1869. . . .

PHILOSOPHIC RADICALS AND MILL'S EMOTIONAL CRISIS (1822-29)

The formal phase of Mill's unconventional education ended in his fourteenth year when he went abroad for a year of study in France. There he lived with Jeremy Bentham's brother, Sir Samuel Bentham, and concentrated his studies on the sciences, French, and music. On his return, he began his life-long association with the East India Company, starting as a clerk directly under his father in 1822, and retiring from the company in 1858 as chief of the office of the examiner of India correspondence. Almost simultaneously with the beginning of his employment, John Mill and a group of young radicals formed the Utilitarian Society. James Mill was the intellectual and political mentor to this talented circle of politically ambitious young men, bent upon modelling themselves after the French *philosophes* of the eighteenth century. James Mill encouraged them to work toward parliamentary reform, either through active political careers or through vigorous political writing in the journals of the day. The *Westminster Review* was established in 1824 by Jeremy Bentham and his immediate followers, and within a few years this journal became the medium for the expression of the political ideas of John Mill and his Philosophic Radical associates.

This first relatively extensive social milieu of which John Mill became a part was a diverse group of radical thinkers that included both women and men, some of whom were self-educated and others Cambridge-educated. This circle included many people who were to become prominent in British politics and scholarship: George and Harriet Grote, John Roebuck, Charles Buller, Joseph Hume, William Molesworth, Sydney Smith, Charles and Sarah Austin, Francis Place, and Mill's first close friend, Eyton Tooke.[11] It is reasonable to assume that apart from his mother, the women in this social circle were among the first adult women Mill got to know well. Although George Grote served as the group's spokesman in Parliament, his wife Harriet, according to many other members of the group, served as its "tactician." From contacts with Harriet Grote during a trip to England, Charles Sumner characterized her as a "high-minded . . . masculine" woman, "one of the most remarkable women in England." Sydney Smith said she was the "queen of the radicals," and Francis Place that she *was the Philosophic Radicals.*" Her salon was the political center for deliberations about tactics during the peak of the radicals' activism in Parliament in the early- to mid-1830s. Harriet Grote was perhaps the first woman intellectual Mill had met, a living model of what women were capable of doing even in the restricted world of English politics early in the nineteenth century. Sarah Austin seems also to have been an early example to Mill of the capabilities of women. Though he later wrote of her with some asperity in the early draft of the autobiography, during these early years she was an important figure in his life whom he addressed in his letters as "liebes Mütterlein." There is no record of what Mill thought of these women when he was a very young man in the 1820s, though they may have provided content for his much later discussion, in *The Subjection of Women,* of women's administrative capacity and shrewd practical judgment of people and events.

Involvement with the Philosophic Radicals lay at the center of Mill's political life and writings for the major part of the period from 1822 to 1840. His employment at the East India Company precluded direct political participation, but he became the thinker and writer in the background of the radicals' attempt to achieve parliamentary reform in England. Some assessment of his own role and of the standard he imposed on the quality of his political writing may be read into his observation that "Journalism is to modern Europe, what political oratory was to Athens and Rome; to become what it ought, it should be wielded by the same sort of men."

Beneath the surface of Mill's busy life during the 1820s, however, a storm was brewing: Mill was attempting to define his own identity and to differentiate it from that of his father. His severe mental depression in 1826 was but the beginning of a transformation in Mill's intellectual and personal orientation. Had this crisis not developed, Mill might have been but a minor figure in English intellectual history, a mere exponent of the ideas developed by Bentham and James Mill.

Intellectual and emotional weaning from paternal influence would almost have to be severe following a childhood of such extreme domination of thought and morality as that young John Mill experienced under the tutelage of his strong-willed father. In the fall of 1826, Mill reports:

> I was in a dull state of nerves. . . . It occurred to me to put the question directly to myself: "Suppose that all your objects in life were realized; that all the changes in institutions and opinions which you are looking forward to, could be completely effected at this very instant: would this be a great joy and happiness to you?" And an irrepressible self-consciousness distinctly answered, "No!" At this my heart sank within me: the whole foundation on which my life was constructed fell down. . . . I seemed to have nothing left to live for.[12]

Characteristically, Mill attempted to cope with his depression by turning to books, hoping to find "relief from . . . those memorials of past nobleness and greatness from which I had always hitherto drawn strength and animation." This did not help, and Mill felt there was no one he could turn to for sympathy or advice: "If I had loved any one sufficiently to make confiding my beliefs a necessity, I should not have been in the condition I was." His father, of course, was "the last person" to whom he could look for help. Mill made no mention of his turmoil to his friends among the Philosophic Radicals, but his reasons for not approaching them with his difficulty seem clear: he was struggling with an experience which he thought denied crucial premises of Utilitarian theory. If he, the outstanding product of the intense education of cognitive abilities, could experience a demise of pleasurable associations and feelings toward the goals of increasing happiness for the "whole," then perhaps "the habit of analysis has a tendency to wear away the feelings." Though his life went along its usual course, Mill characterized his efforts at writing and debate as spiritless and mechanical.

The worst of his depression lifted suddenly while he was reading Marmontel's *Mémoires,* the content of which, and Mill's response, provided the major elements for Levi's psychoanalytic imputation to Mill of "death wishes" toward his father.[13] The passage describes Marmontel's father's death, the distressed position of the family, and "the sudden inspiration by which he, then a mere boy, felt and made them feel that he would be everything to them—would supply the place of all that they had lost." Mill's tension was resolved into tears with this reading. "From this moment," he relates, "my burthen grew lighter. The oppression of the thought that all feeling was dead within me, was gone. I was no longer hopeless: I was not a stock or a stone."[14]

One may or may not subscribe to the psychological thesis that Mill's crisis centered on a repressed death wish against his father and the guilt it engendered along with the dread that he would never be free of his father's domination. What matters most to the course of our present analysis is the consequence of this depression and of its lifting. In Mill's own words:

> The cultivation of the feelings became one of the cardinal points in my ethical and philosophical creed. And my thoughts and inclinations turned in an increasing degree towards whatever seemed capable of being instrumental to that object. I now began to find meaning in the things which I had read or heard about the importance of poetry and art as instruments of human culture.[15]

This implied a direct criticism of the "pure" world of rationalism at the heart of his father's ideas on education and politics. This criticism was made even more pointedly in the early draft of his autobiography, where he commented that he and his friends in the Philosophic Radicals group "had no idea of real culture. In our schemes for improving human affairs we overlooked human beings."[16] In

1827, however, these thoughts left Mill essentially alienated, at a deep personal and intellectual level, from his political associates. Restlessly he began to read from a far wider range, turning with a new responsiveness to the work of Coleridge, Carlyle, the French Saint Simonians, Comte, and Macaulay. His personal loneliness and deep alienation from the Utilitarianism of the Philosophic Radicals are reflected in a letter to John Sterling dated 15 April 1829:

> There is now no human being (with whom I can associate on terms of equality) who acknowledges a common object with me, or with whom I can co-operate even in any practical undertaking, without the feeling that I am using a man, whose purposes are different, as an instrument for the furtherance of my own.[17]

This is the personal mood that Mill was in just a year before he met the woman who was to share a wide range of "common objects" with him for the following twenty-eight years.

Unitarian Radicals and the Love in Mill's Life (1830-51)

Historical evidence is vague about the exact circumstances which first brought John Mill and Harriet Taylor together. Mill's new-found responsiveness to poetry and literature, and the long-standing interest in radical politics among Unitarians were clearly in the background of the encounter.[18] The connecting link is thought to have been William J. Fox, Unitarian minister of the South Place Chapel, whose parish included not only Harriet and her husband John, but Jeremy Bentham's leading disciples, John Bowring and Southwood Smith. Fox had himself contributed in 1826 to the Philosophic Radicals' journal, *Westminster Review*. As a voracious reader of contemporary journals, we may assume that Mill was a regular subscriber to the *Monthly Repository,* edited by William Fox since 1827, and that he was sufficiently attracted by William Fox's politics to overcome his anticlerical resistance to Fox's ministerial capacity.

Tradition has it that Mill and Harriet Taylor met at a dinner party at William Fox's home in the summer or fall of 1830, a social occasion that included two of Mill's Philosophic Radical friends, John Roebuck and George John Graham. Harriet Martineau, known personally by Fox since the early 1820s, was also a member of the party, and it was she who was very fond of telling and embroidering upon the occasion of John and Harriet's first meeting. Hayek concludes from an examination of a letter written by Eliza Flower, a close friend of Harriet's, that the relationship between John and Harriet was already intimate by the summer of 1831, a year or so after they met.[19] At the time of their meeting, Harriet was twenty-three, already married for more than four years, and the mother of two sons. Her last child, Helen, was born the following year, in July 1831.

Concern for the status of women and the relations between the sexes was no new idea in the social circle of the Unitarian Radicals in the early 1830s. Mary Wollstonecraft had herself been a Unitarian intellectual, and down through the years of the Unitarian journal, the *Monthly Repository,* there are numerous articles both friendly to and persistent in their demands for the education of women. Harriet Martineau had written one such article, "On Female Education," in 1823, in which she argued that women must be educated to be "companions to men, instead of playthings or servants." The Utilitarian *Westminster Review* had similarly been a champion for the cause of women almost from the first issue. This background makes somewhat curious Mill's later explicit denial that his views on the relations between the sexes had been adopted or learnt from Harriet. In a footnote to his autobiography he explained:

> This was so far from being the fact, that those convictions were among the earliest results of the application of my mind to political subjects, and the strength with which I held them was, as I believe, more than anything else, the originating cause of the interest she felt in me.[20]

It would be more accurate to say that the ideas on sex equality were not unique to either John Mill or Harriet Taylor. They had both absorbed much of the thinking on this issue of the two main social circles within which they moved, the Philosophic Radicals and the Unitarian Radicals.

We can probably assume that if an article appeared in a journal in 1832, the topic of that article was much discussed in the preceding year in the intellectually vigorous circles within which John and Harriet moved. It is of interest, from this point of view, to examine the content of one of William Fox's essays on women, "A Political and Social Anomaly," which appeared in the *Monthly Repository* in September 1832, for he may have aired and discussed the issues it touched upon in the group that included John Stuart Mill, Eliza Flower, Harriet and John Taylor, and William and Sarah Adams. (Sarah was Eliza's sister). Fox went some distance beyond the usual stress on merely improved education for women, to suggest quite radical ideas concerning women's potential for intellectual achievement and their right to the franchise. In an anticipation of the argument that genuine education for women might "raise them above their station," Fox, in his usual peppery fashion, replied: "All the better. They might thus shame men into something like intellectual progress." He summed up his argument thus:

> We understand not why one half of the community should have no other destiny than irremediable dependence upon the other half; as long as women have nothing in the world to look to but marriage, they cannot become qualified, in the best manner, for a married life; so long as the modes in which property is inherited, acquired and distributed, leave them in utter dependence, they can never, in that institution, treat or be treated as independent parties, making a fair and equal contract for mutual benefit. Under the present order of things, a large proportion of them must remain as they are, fools to be cajoled, toys to be sported with, slaves to be commanded, and in ignorant pride that they are so.[21]

Sometime during 1831 or early 1832, John Mill and Harriet Taylor wrote essays for each other on women and their position in marriage. Written some thirty-seven years before Mill was to express himself in print on the subject of women, these two essays are of special interest. They show an understandable emphasis on the problem of divorce and provision for the children of divorce, in light of the fact of Harriet's marriage. The manuscripts, now part of the Mill-Taylor Collection in the British Library of Political and Economic Science (London School of Economics), were first published by Hayek in 1951. They form a natural first entry in this volume which brings together the written evidence of the ideas of John Stuart Mill and Harriet Taylor on the subject of women.

There are several points of contrast between the arguments developed by John and Harriet in these two early essays. Harriet Taylor was by far the more radical in her views. Impulsive and far less intellectually disciplined than Mill, she argued that there should not be any laws on marriage, and that a woman should take responsibility for her own children, thus eliminating from the divorce question the problem of providing for the children. She also argued that since a woman would be responsible for her children's maintenance, she would think carefully about how many children she should have, instead of considering the addition of children a means for increasing "her ties to the man who feeds her." John Mill was more cautious in his reasoning. He called for a revision of marriage law and urged that since people tend to marry young, there was always a risk of an error in choice which would require divorce. To avoid what Mill considered possible demoralization through repeated mistakes, he urged a postponement of child-bearing for a long period after marriage, during which the couple could test their compatibility. Writing at a time when the control of birth was largely by continence and coitus interruptus rather than contraception, he was aware that many people would be unable to avoid pregnancies before the marital relationship was sufficiently secure, and hence that provision for children in case of divorce remained a problem. At this point Mill, perhaps thinking of the Owenite planned community experiments, almost anticipated the search among many young people in the 1960s for communal living with shared responsibility for the care of children:

> It will therefore most commonly happen that when circumstances arise which induce the parents to separate, there will be children to suffer by the separation: nor do I see how this difficulty can be entirely got over, until the habits of society allow of a regulated community of living, among persons intimately acquainted, which would prevent the necessity of a total separation between the parents even when they had ceased to be connected by any nearer tie than mutual good will, and a common interest in their children.

A second point of contrast between John and Harriet concerns the use to which women should put their improved education in the future. Again Harriet took the more radical position: if women are not to barter their persons for bread, they not only must be well educated but must be permitted to enter any occupational field they wish. Mill took the more cautious position, that a woman's goal would continue to be marriage to a man she loved; her occupation after marriage would be to "adorn and beautify life" by sharing fully and intelligently her husband's occupations and interests. This view was not moderated with the passage of time; thirty-seven years later Mill was still arguing that he saw no benefit to a wife's contributing to the income of the family, on the grounds that her work in the household and the rearing of children were her contribution to the family unit.

Despite her radical views, Harriet ended her impassioned call for great change in the status of women with a plea that John Mill become the "apostle of all the highest virtues" and teach the world the way to true equality. An awareness of counterparts in the 1960s combining fiery verbal feminism and personal dependence on a man, helps to curb critical assessment of this contrast in Harriet Taylor. Liberation of the intellect is far easier to achieve than liberation of the deeper emotions. It should also be noted than in 1832 Harriet Taylor was a largely self-educated woman, with years of intellectual growth ahead of her. By 1851 she would show no such passive submission to John Mill's leadership.

The year 1833 was a critical year in the relationship between John Mill and Harriet Taylor, and there are sufficient historical data to describe part of the turmoil they passed through. For Harriet the dilemma centered on whether and how a pattern could be established that would permit her to continue her close contact with John Mill yet fulfill her obligations to her husband. For Mill the dilemma was more complex, for he was continuing to explore the new intellectual world opened to him following his earlier mental crisis as well as trying to cope with his new personal relationship with Harriet.

It is probable that within the privacy of the social circle of the Unitarian Radicals, even more extreme views were expressed on marriage and divorce and women's education than any William Fox, William Adams, John Mill, or Harriet Taylor would and did express in public print. The degree to which the public and private views of this group of radical thinkers departed from the customary patterns of the mid-nineteenth century can be appreciated by noting the response of their contemporaries to the clearly visible attraction and close association between John Mill and Harriet Taylor. This can be illustrated by the comments of Thomas and Jane Carlyle before and after they met Harriet Taylor and the circle of Unitarian Radicals. Thomas Carlyle strikes a contemporary reader as a nineteenth-century Podhoretz, busily trying to "make it" in the world of London letters and politics by cultivating contacts with the influential people of his day. But he is by the same token a good transmitter of the gossip of the time. Before they met Harriet, Jane Carlyle wrote her husband's brother of the local gossip that Mrs. Taylor had "ogled Mill successfully so that he was desperately in love." Yet when they met

Harriet, Thomas Carlyle's sketch of her was greatly muted: he wrote his brother that "she is a living romance heroine, of the clearest insight, of the royalist volition, very interesting, of questionable destiny, not above 25." After the Carlyles were introduced to the social circle of the Unitarian Radicals, they showed both attraction to and repulsion from its members. On one occasion, Carlyle wrote:

> [The] party we had at the Taylors' was the most brisk, the cleverest (best gifted) I have been at for years: Mill, Charles Buller (one of the gayest, lightly sparkling, lovable souls in the world), Repository Fox (who hotches and laughs at least), Fonblanque, the Examiner editor, were the main men.[22]

There is clearly a conflict in Carlyle's response between the cultural values of his time and his private individual response to Harriet and her social circle. The cultural values eventually win out. In another letter Carlyle drew a more pointed contrast between the Philosophic Radicals set and that of the Unitarian Radicals, commenting on the latter as follows:

> Mill . . . is greatly occupied of late times with a set of quite opposite character, which the Austins and other friends mourn much and fear much over. It is the fairest Mrs. Taylor you have heard of, with whom, under her husband's very eyes, he is (Platonically) over head and ears in love. Round her come Fox the Socinian and a flight of really wretched looking "friends of the species," who (in writing and deed) struggle not in favour of Duty being done, but against Duty of any sort almost being required. A singular creed this. . . . Most of these people are very indignant at marriage and the like; and frequently indeed are obliged to divorce their own wives or be divorced: for though the world is already blooming (or is one day to do it) in everlasting "happiness of the greatest number" these people's own houses (I always find) are little Hells of improvidence, discord, unreason. Mill is far above all that and I think will not sink in it; however, I do wish him fairly far from it.[23]

The Carlyles did not know that 1833 was a year of personal crisis for two pairs in the set of Unitarian Radicals. William Fox, older by some twenty years than the other members of the group, had lived through an unhappy marriage for many years and had been strongly attracted to the young Eliza Flower, for whom, together with her sister Sarah, he was guardian after the death of their father. Unconventional, highly artistic, and endowed with unusual musical talent, Eliza became increasingly devoted to William, helping him in church, journal, and correspondence duties. Eliza was an intimate friend of Harriet Taylor's, and the similar complexity of their heterosexual relations probably served to bring the two men into a closer relationship. Certainly Mill confided to a greater degree in Fox than in any other man with whom he corresponded, judging from the Mill letters that have been published thus far. The fact that Fox combined so successfully the two poles of politics and art may also have encouraged Mill to unburden himself of the effects of his intellectual turmoil during these years. Early in the spring of 1833, he wrote to Fox:

> If there are any rumors that I was writing anything for the *Monthly Repository* of this month, I am sorry I cannot confirm them. I have abundance of vague intentions of writing for you, but I have been very idle of late, and in fact never have been in a state more unfit for work: from various causes, the chief of which is, I think, a growing want of interest in all the subjects which I understand, a growing sense of incapacity ever to have real knowledge of, or insight into the subject in which alone I shall ever again feel a strong interest . . . I feel so unequal to any of the higher moral and aesthetic subjects.[24]

This was rather strong language from a man who was yet to write a *System of Logic* and the *Principles of Political Economy*. Mill was probably still on a honeymoon with the world of literature, art, and poetry, unsure exactly how his own philosophic and economic views would shape up or how far they would depart from his intellectual origins in Benthamism. The *Monthly Repository* became an important outlet for Mill, in which, Mineka suggests, he tried out ideas he did not publicly espouse for more than a decade.[25] Either under pseudonyms or in unsigned articles, Mill departed considerably from orthodox Benthamite economics in the essays he wrote in the mid-1830s. In a discussion of his advocacy of a property tax instead of taxes upon consumption and industry (a position the Philosophic Radicals would share), Mill went on to show his scorn of any assumed link between the accumulation of a personal fortune and intelligence or ingenuity—a view that would have very much displeased his Benthamite associates at the time. In an article in 1833 he made a point that would have shocked any laissez faire economist and that foreshadowed the turn toward socialist thinking that Mill would take only years later:

> We hope the time is coming for more rational modes of distributing the productions of nature and of art, than this expensive and demoralizing plan of individual competition, the evils of which have risen to such enormous height.[26]

On a more personal level, Harriet and John Taylor agreed to a trial separation for approximately six months, apparently with the hope on her husband's part that she would decide to cut her tie to John Mill and return fully to him as his wife. Mill joined Harriet in Paris in the fall of 1833 for several weeks. They wrote joint letters from Paris to Eliza Flower and William Fox that give ample evidence of the quality of their relationship and the indecision that hung over them. This was also the first time the two had any long period of time for talk and mutual exploration. John Mill wrote his friend Fox:

> I am astonished when I think how much has been restrained, how much untold, unshewn and uncommunicated til now; how much which by the mere fact of its being spoken, has disappeared. . . . There will never again I believe be any obstacle to our being together entirely from the slightest doubt that the experiment would succeed with respect to ourselves. . . . And yet—all the other obstacles or rather the one obstacle being as great as ever—our futurity is still perfectly

uncertain. She has decided nothing except what has always been decided—not to renounce the liberty of sight—and it does not seem likely that anything will be decided until the end of the six months. . . . I know it is the common notion of passionate love that it sweeps away all other affections—but surely the justification of passion, and one of its greatest beauties and glories, is that in an otherwise fine character it weakens no feeling which deserves to subsist, but would naturally strengthen them all.[27]

In the same letter, Harriet enclosed one of her own to her friend Eliza:

O this being seeming as though God had willed to show the type of possible elevation of humanity. To be with him wholly is my ideal of the noblest fate for all states of mind and feeling which are lofty and large and fine; he is the companion spirit and heart desire—we are not alike in trifles only because I have so much more frivolity than he.[28]

As might be anticipated from the mood of these letters, Harriet did not renounce the liberty of seeing John Mill, and her husband agreed to such an arrangement in exchange for retaining the external formality of residing as his wife in his household. From 1834 until their marriage in 1851 (two years after the death of her husband), John Mill and Harriet Taylor continued this pattern, seeing each other for dinner at Harriet's home when John Taylor was absent, and spending frequent weekends at summer places along the English coast, as Harriet moved restlessly about from place to place with her daughter Helen. Mill continued to live at home with his mother, working at India House, tutoring his younger siblings, and writing widely on numerous political topics of the day.

Like so many Europeans of their time, both John and Harriet had numerous bouts of ill health. Much of their correspondence reported on one or another aspect of their health, but avoided the realization that both were suffering from tuberculosis. During the 1830s and 1840s Harriet took numerous trips to southern France and Italy in the search of improved health through exposure to a sunny, warm climate. Mill's employment with the East India Company limited the occasions on which he could join Harriet in the south, but he did manage many short visits during these years.

Numerous scholars of John Stuart Mill have suggested that it was a growing awareness of the gossip about his irregular relationship with Harriet Taylor that led to his radical withdrawal from social life by the mid-1840s. A closer reading suggests a rather different interpretation. If it were merely social disapproval of the John-Harriet relationship, one would expect the social set of the Philosophic Radicals to have continued intact after Mill's withdrawal from it. This was not the case, however. What seems to have occurred was a total breakup of the Philosophic Radical group as the members became politically disillusioned by parliamentary defeat and empirical refutation of their theories.

Since this larger demise of radicalism was important to the development of Mill's thinking and later intellectual effort as well as to a correction of the interpretation placed on the social withdrawal of John and Harriet during the 1840s, we might examine what happened to the radical cause during these years. The Philosophic Radicals were dedicated to the central idea that the basic cleavage in English society was between the aristocracy and the "people." Bentham's idea of "sinister interests" was narrowed by James Mill to the sinister interests of just the aristocracy or ruling elite. They saw the church and the legal profession as mere props to the aristocracy, and the universities as only subdivisions of the church. When Karl Marx was a mere boy in 1819, James Mill was writing about and teaching this rulers versus ruled thesis, arguing for example that it was aristocratic control of government which fomented war, since only in times of international hostilities could the government increase the proportion of the national wealth at its command and the proportion of the population subject to its control. Where the Philosophic Radicals differed from radical working class organizations was in their view that the cleavage between the middle class and the working classes was based merely on ignorance and fear. Political education, they thought, would cement the two classes together in opposition to the aristocracy.

The political efforts of the Philosophic Radicals centered on the attempt to effect a realignment of the Whig and Tory parties. They counted on this realignment as a necessary stage to conform with the underlying struggle between the people and the aristocracy. Counter to their expectations, however, the Tories increased in strength during the mid-1830s, the radical factions within the Tories and the Whigs showed increasing enmity rather than a consolidation of mutual interests, and the Chartists, which two members of the Philosophic Radicals (Roebuck and Place) had in fact helped to establish, showed increasing hostility toward the middle class and increasing threats of violence. By 1837 the Philosophic Radicals were in despair at their failure to achieve party realignment and were angry with the moderate reformers for not identifying themselves as Radicals. Between 1838 and 1840 they saw an increase in class consciousness and conflict and mounting evidence that the party system they thought obsolete had a good deal of life and energy left in it.

By 1840 their political hopes were dashed, and during the next few years the group gradually fell apart. If we note the shift of interest and activity among other members of the Philosophic Radicals, it becomes apparent that Mill was far from the exception. As John Mill shifted from political articles in the radical journals to work on philosophic and historical topics in the early 1840s, so the other members also turned to scholarship. George and Harriet Grote tacitly agreed not even to discuss politics; George Grote returned to his studies of Greek history and soon started a new classical journal with G. C. Lewis. Harriet Grote wrote that their interests had shifted from politics to letters, philosophy, and "projects for the rational enjoyment of our lives." By 1841 this fiery anti-aristocrat was writing her sister that she had "made a number of new acquaintances among fine folks, which I think to follow up now that Radicalism is extinct and politics no longer absorb my energies." Molesworth turned to work on his edition of Hobbes, Sarah Austin to translating German books, and her brother-in-law Charles confessed to a disappointment so bitter that he would never take an interest in politics again.

Having already wrestled (during his mental crisis of 1826-29) with the painful task of piecing together a new credo from the shambles of an older one no longer acceptable to him, John Mill may have been better prepared to cope with political disillusionment than were his Philosophical Radical friends. In any event, by 1842 he wrote that he was out of heart about public affairs and "had almost given up thinking of the subject." Hamburger suggests that "having failed as politician, he now downgraded that role and looked for improvement through philosophy." Ever the optimist, Mill tried to "fashion a role for himself as a philosopher whose task was to synthesize the various themes current in a transitional era in order to prepare for the future."[29]

These then, were the political events which preceded Mill's return to scholarship and the eventual publication of the *System of Logic* in 1843 and his *Principles of Political Economy* in 1848.

INTELLECTUAL COLLABORATION BETWEEN JOHN MILL AND HARRIET TAYLOR

Controversy has raged for more than a century on what Harriet Taylor was like in personality and intellectual capability, as it has on the nature of her relationship to Mill and her contribution to his published writings. We have already seen that in his early contacts with her, Thomas Carlyle conceded that Harriet was an interesting and romantic figure with a high degree of insight and firm purpose. Mill himself was lavish in his praise of her as a woman and as an intellectual. In the *Autobiography,* in several prefaces to his published work, and in the inscription he had carved on her tombstone in Avignon.[30] Mill was extravagant in his comparisons of Harriet with prominent intellectual and artistic figures in English history. He portrayed her as more of a poet than Carlyle, more of a thinker than himself, like Shelley in temperament and organization but his superior in thought and intellect.[31] Mill's friend and first biographer, Alexander Bain,[32] tried to prevent the publication of such excessive praise when he read the proof for the first publication of the *Autobiography* in 1873. He wrote to Mill's stepdaughter, Helen Taylor: "I venture to express the opinion that no such combination has ever been realized in the history of the human race."[33] Bain felt that Mill outraged all credibility in his descriptions of Harriet's "matchless genius." Mill's praise was retained in the published work, despite Bain's urging that it be deleted or toned down. Nine years later Bain's assessment of Harriet was that she stimulated Mill's intellectual faculties by "intelligently controverting" his ideas.[34]

William Fox was one contemporary who was warm in his feeling toward Harriet Taylor and high in his assessment of her ability, moral commitment, and devotion to Mill. When Harriet died at Avignon, Fox wrote to his daughter:

> Mrs. Mill died on the 3rd at Avignon. She would not have objected to being buried there, in the ground in which Petrarch has given a wide-world fame; and of which it might . . . be said, "A greater than Laura is here."[35]

Fox's biographer, Garnett, commented that if Petrarch's Laura was, as is usually believed, a married woman, the correspondence between the relations of the two pairs was amazing, even to their connection with Avignon, although the "field of mutual interests common to the English lovers was infinitely wider and comparison might afford no fallacious measure of Woman's progress between the 14th and 19th century."[36] A more recent scholar, Francis Mineka, shares the sympathetic view of Harriet's influence on Mill:

> However over colored by emotion his estimate of her powers may have been, there can be no doubt that she was the saving grace of his inner life. Without her, John Mill might well have been a different person, but one can doubt that he would have been as fine, as understanding or as great a man.[37]

Positive assessments of Harriet Taylor such as this have been few, and they are far outweighed by often harshly negative assessments. Many Mill scholars quote a reply Harold Laski gave Justice Holmes when the latter asked him about Harriet Taylor. Laski wrote:

> I believe that he was literally the only person who was in the least impressed by her. Mrs. Grote said briefly that she was a stupid woman. Bain said she had a knack of repeating prettily what J. S. M. said and that he told her it was wonderful; Morley told me that Louis Blanc told him he once sat for an hour with her and that she repeated to him what afterwards turned out to be an article Mill had just finished for the Edinburgh. . . . If she was what he thought, someone else at least should have given us indications.[38]

Closer to our own time, Keith Rinehart has portrayed Mill as a submissive man whose autobiography shows a movement from the "aegis of one demi-god, his father, to another, his wife."[39] Stillinger leaned heavily on the earlier negative assessments of Harriet, with no mention of the more favorable ones. He summed up his impression of her in the following way:

> Harriet of the incomparable intellect . . . was largely a product of his imagination, an idealization, according to his peculiar needs, of a clever, domineering, in some ways perverse and selfish, invalid woman.[40]

Disregarding the state of their health, the typically English search for its improvement through winters on the Mediterranean, and the fact that when they were separated they wrote almost daily to each other, Stillinger suggests that Mill "enjoyed her more as a correspondent than as a companion." Max Lerner took a curious attitude toward the relationship between the two, pointing out that Mill himself was a proper Victorian in his attitudes toward sex and that Harriet Taylor was "in all probability a frigid woman." He softens the psychological imputation of the latter by suggesting that Harriet's frigidity was a matter of principle rather than of neurosis.[41] It is not clear what the difference is between "a proper Victorian attitude" and "principled frigidity." Why not merely suggest that both John and Harriet Mill had Victorian attitudes toward sex?

No one has exceeded Diana Trilling in the harshness of her account of Harriet Taylor.[42] John Mill had characterized Harriet as his "intellectual beacon," but Mrs. Trilling suggests she had in fact "nothing more than a vestpocket flashlight of a mind . . . one of the meanest and dullest ladies in literary history, a monument of nasty self-regard, as lacking in charm as in grandeur," whose correspondence shows a "fleshless, bloodless quality" full of "injured vanity, petty egoism and ambition." Mrs. Trilling then exhibits the standard of femininity by which she assesses Harriet Taylor much more clearly than the male scholars who preceded her had done: Harriet Taylor had "no touch of true femininity, no taint of the decent female concerns which support our confidence in the intelligence of someone like Jane Carlyle."

It is difficult to see why Mrs. Trilling's confidence in the "intelligence" of a woman depends on her possession of "decent female concerns." One suspects that she means "normality" rather than "intelligence." If by a "normal" woman one means a clinging, uneducated, submissive woman of the nineteenth century, or a well-educated, supportive wife-companion of the twentieth century, then by either standard Harriet Taylor was indeed very far from "normal." For that matter, neither was John Stuart Mill a "normal" man of his age, in either personal qualities, intellectual style, or manner of relating to the woman of his life.

One must be cautious in assessing the views held of Harriet by either her male contemporaries or the scholars who read the scattered fragments of evidence from those contemporaries. Assertive women were undoubtedly an even greater irritation to Victorian men than they are to men today. In a man single-mindedness of purpose has always been considered admirable; in a woman, whether in Victorian England or contemporary America, it has usually been thought a sign of selfishness, a distasteful departure from conventional ideals of femininity. Harriet Taylor was no shrinking violet, no soft and compliant woman. She had, after all, lived against the grain of Victorian London in an unconventional liaison with John Mill for twenty years before their marriage. Under his tutelage she had a most unusual opportunity to grow intellectually, and we may assume that over the years of their collaboration, Harriet's self-confidence also grew as she tested her mettle against the strength of Mill's intellect and fund of knowledge.

One element contributing to the negative views held of Harriet was no doubt rooted in general cultural expectations of the role of women. Then as now, women who are intellectually or politically brilliant are more readily accepted by men if they are also properly feminine in their style and deportment with men. This helps to assure that there will be few women of achievement for men to "exempt" from the general category of women, since the traits associated with traditional femininity—softness, compliance, sweetness—are rarely found together with the contradictory qualities of a vigorous and questioning intellect, and a willingness to persist on a problem against conventional assumptions. The hypothesis that a mere woman was the collaborator of so logical and intellectual a thinker as Mill, much less that she influenced the development of his thought, can be expected to meet resistance in the minds of men right up to the 1970s.

There is a second approach to interpreting the contradictory assessments of Harriet Taylor that is of special sociological interest. If one links the assessment to the social circle to which the writer, friend, or scholar belonged or was intellectually and politically attuned, one begins to see the influence of social structure upon attitude and belief. The negative assessments of Harriet turn out to be held mainly by members of the Philosophic Radicals or scholars interested in that circle, whereas the positive assessments are held by those associated with the Unitarian Radicals. Significant differences existed between these two circles in theory, politics, and morality. The Philosophic Radicals represented a pole of moral righteousness, theoretical commitment to Utilitarianism, and political concern for parliamentary reform. The Unitarian Radicals, by contrast, were individually more unconventional, more artistic, and passionately committed to a wide range of political and social reforms in the area of domestic affairs and the institution of the family. One member of the Unitarian Radical set, William Bridges Adams, went so far as to criticize conventional domestic arrangements for their waste of time and energy, advocating, in 1834, the building of what we would call apartment houses, with provisions for communal kitchens and laundries.[43] This was the social set with which Harriet Taylor was personally affiliated. Mill's association with the Unitarian Radicals was seen by his political associates as a threat to his allegiance to the Utilitarian cause, and Harriet was the symbol of that association.

In keeping with this thesis, the people whom Laski cited in his letter to Holmes, all of them very critical of Harriet, belonged to the Philosophic Radical circle: Harriet Grote, Morley, Bain, Sarah Austin, John Roebuck. These were all persons who disapproved of Mill's involvement with Harriet and with the Unitarian Radicals. Carlyle, in a letter quoted earlier, specifically referred to the Austins as disapproving of Mill's attraction to the Fox social set. At the time, the early 1830s, the Philosophic Radicals knew nothing of the intellectual distance Mill had traveled from Utilitarian theory, quite on his own, following his mental crisis in 1826. They may well have attributed the subsequent changes in Mill's thinking to the influence of Harriet and her social circle rather than to the intellectual ferment within Mill himself which had begun several years before he met Harriet and the Unitarian Radicals.

Scholars are more apt to do research on people whose thinking they find attractive than on people whose thinking they dislike or disapprove. Accordingly, one observes a division among modern scholars in their opinions of Harriet which reflects the division of the Philosophic Radicals and the Unitarian Radicals themselves. Bain, Elliot, Laski, and Stillinger were primarily concerned with the development of Mill's philosophic and political thought, and they tended to view Harriet in negative terms. The more positive views were held by the scholars of the Unitarian Radicals: William Fox's biographer, Garnett, and Francis Mineka, who studied the Unitarian journal, *Monthly Repository,* through the years of Fox's editorship. Cutting across this division is the political perspective of the scholars themselves. Hayek, himself opposed to socialism (the new road to serfdom), was more likely to concede considerable influence to Harriet, since he could then interpret Mill's socialist phase as a temporary aberration due to Harriet's influence over him. Though careful to indicate that more detailed study is required, Hayek suggested that such a study would show that Mill withdrew from the more advanced (i.e., socialist) positions he took under her influence and returned in later years to views closer to those he had held in his youth.[44] The Victorian scholar Basil Willey tended to a similar interpretation of Mill's views on religion.[45] In contrast, Harold Laski, a socialist, did not wish to view Mill's socialist thinking as a product of a woman's influence and hence followed the earlier trend toward a negative view of Harriet and of her contribution to Mill's thinking.[46] The Fabian Socialists who followed Mill did not share Laski's hesitation; on the contrary, the ideal of a working intellectual partnership between the sexes became a traditional Fabian idea.

Throughout all this debate and controversy about the personal qualities of Harriet Taylor and her contribution to Mill's thought and work, there has been surprisingly little attention paid to direct historical evidence. We may forgive earlier writers who did not have access to the Mill-Taylor correspondence, but not for their neglect of the ideals John and Harriet expressed in their published work on the relations between the sexes and the status of women. None of the Mill scholars have examined the essays collected in this volume for clues to the kind of relationship John and Harriet tried to maintain in their years together. Nor has due allowance been made, in my judgment, for Mill's own intellectual toughness. Mill was not a man to be easily influenced and won over by any idea or person. He rarely lost his critical, sifting, integrative orientation to the weighing of an idea. As Mill described his own process of growth: "When I had taken in any new idea, I could not rest til I had adjusted its relation to all my old opinions."[47]

The scholars attuned to the Unitarian Radicals seem to have come closest to an appreciation of the role Harriet Taylor played in Mill's work. Garnett stands almost alone in going behind the effusive praise Mill extended to Harriet to a comparison of Mill's work before he met Harriet with that which followed. He points out, for example, that

Mill's essay on Tennyson, written shortly after he first became attracted to poetry, is probably a clear reflection of the influence of Harriet Taylor. Garnett suggests that this essay's "appreciation of other poets and discussion of the principles of poetry in general, would have been impossible to Mill" without a large contribution from Harriet Taylor.[48]

Mill refers to many of his publications from 1840 onward as "joint productions" of Harriet and himself. Again it is Garnett who points out that this claim is far more believable than it would be if Mill had included his *System of Logic* among the joint productions. This Mill did not do but expressly exempted the *Logic* from Harriet's collaboration. It is the *Principles of Political Economy* which Mill cited as their first joint effort. An examination of the Taylor-Mill correspondence and of Harriet's letters to her husband, in which she explained the postponement of her plans to go to Brighton because of intensive work on this book, supports Mill's claim that it was a joint effort.[49] Mill himself described the contribution of each to the writing of the *Political Economy*: what was abstract and purely scientific was generally his, while the more human elements and lively practical illustrations were from her. He acknowledged that his first draft of the book had no chapter on the future condition of the working class, and that the one which was finally included was "wholly an exposition of her thoughts, often in words taken from her own lips."[50] *On Liberty* Mill claimed was even more fully a joint effort:

> [It was] more directly and literally our joint production than anything else which bears my name, for there was not a sentence of it that was not several times gone through by us together, turned over in many ways, and carefully weeded of any faults, either in thought or expression, that we detected in it.[51]

It remains a puzzle why, if her contribution was so great, everything appeared under Mill's name alone. Social expediency probably ruled out such joint authorship during the long years of their unconventional relationship, and by the time they married, they may have felt that his "established" name would draw larger readership and sales than her lesser-known name. There is some evidence that Harriet was not completely satisfied with such a state of affairs. When it came time to publish the *Principles of Political Economy,* Mill wrote a footnote comment that "her dislike of publicity alone" prevented the insertion of dedications in all but the gift copies of the first edition. In actual fact, Harriet had approached her husband, John Taylor, about such a dedication, indicating pleasure at the prospect, and suggesting precedents for it in other recently published work. Taylor, however, was profoundly opposed to the idea. In a letter to Harriet he said that

> all dedications are in bad taste, that under our circumstances the proposed one would evince on both author's part as well as the lady to whom the book is to be dedicated, a want of taste and tact which I could not have believed possible. . . . The dedication will revive

recollections now forgotten and will create observations and talk that cannot but be extremely unpleasant to me.[52]

Two months later, Harriet explained to William Fox that the dedication was limited to copies given to friends "at my special request . . . my reason being that opinions carry more weight with the authority of his name alone." Hayek concluded that Harriet contributed a considerable amount to the *Political Economy* volumes and to their subsequent revision for later editions. One can imagine Harriet chafing at the social conventions that required her to remain unknown and unacknowledged by the reading public.

There is also dispute concerning the authorship of the essay entitled **"Enfranchisement of Women."** In writing to the editor of the *Westminster Review,* Mill referred to this essay as one *he* had almost ready. Yet two years before, in February 1849, Mill wrote to Harriet criticizing an article on women he had read:

> I do not think that anything that could be written would do nearly so much good on that subject, the most important of all, as the finishing of your pamphlet or little book rather, for it should be that. I do hope you are going on with it. Gone on with and finished and published it must be and next season too.[53]

From an internal analysis of this essay, a comparison with the earlier 1832 essays and Mill's later famous one in 1869, I have concluded that Harriet was the primary author of the **"Enfranchisement of Women."** The essay has a central core of analysis that is practically unconnected to its prelude and ending. It begins and ends with a discussion of the convention in Worcester, Massachusetts, which took place in the spring of 1850. The letter quoted above which refers to Harriet's "pamphlet" on women was written in 1849, before the Worcester convention. I believe the first several pages and the ending were added to Harriet's pamphlet to lend the essay some topical appeal.

What makes the case stronger for Harriet as the primary author of the essay is the content of the argument. Several positions taken in this essay are identical to those Harriet took in her earlier 1832 paper but do not agree with anything Mill himself subscribed to either in his 1832 essay or in 1869 in the *Subjection of Women*. In neither of Mill's essays did he subscribe to the view that married women should seek employment. In one essay he argued that such employment would flood the labor market and hence lower the wages paid. In the **"Enfranchisement"** essay, Harriet took this point by the horn and demolished it in the following manner:

> Even if every woman, as matters now stand, had a claim on some man for support, how infinitely preferable is it that part of the income should be the woman's earning, even if the aggregate sum were but little increased by it, rather than that she should be compelled to stand aside in order that men may be the sole earners, and the sole dispensers of what is earned. . . .

> A woman who contributes materially to the support of the family, cannot be treated in the same contemptuously tyrannical manner as one who, however she may toil as a domestic drudge, is a dependent on the man for subsistence.

In both of John Mill's essays he claimed that married women already had an occupation, the care of their homes and children, and that they should therefore devote themselves to being educated companions to their husbands rather than holding outside jobs. But in the 1851 essay Harriet argued strongly against the idea of training women to become mere "companions of men":

> The modern . . . modes of education of women abjure an education of mere show and profess to aim at solid instruction, but mean by that expression, superficial information on solid subjects. . . . High mental powers in women will be but an exceptional accident, until every career is open to them and until they as well as men, are educated for themselves and for the world, not one sex for the other.

Her conclusion was that "what is wanted for women is equal rights, equal admission to all social privileges, not a position apart, a sort of sentimental priesthood."

This was strong language for 1851, and I submit that it was written by a strong-willed and intelligent woman, Harriet Taylor. It was a far more radical position than John Mill ever espoused on the subject of women, either twenty years earlier or twenty years later.

The image of John Stuart Mill as primarily a logical rationalist can be supported if one takes into account only his autobiography and major books. As more of his correspondence becomes available, the dominant image of Mill as the Saint of Rationalism may undergo a subtle correction. A few scholars in the past twenty years have begun to balance this one-sided image of Mill as the "logic machine." The English scholar Basil Willey has paved the way for this more rounded assessment. With access to the British library collection of correspondence, Willey in his tart, brisk way made the following comment on Mill:

> What a piece of work is Mill. The steam engine radical, frightened at his own progress, whistling for the flowery meadows, his power loom prose booming out the sentiments of Rousseau or D. H. Lawrence.[54]

So too Max Lerner has struck a new note in his comments about Mill, pointing out that for all his apparatus of rationalism, Mill was a committed and incurable romantic who saw everything in more than life-size proportions, whether it was Harriet Taylor or the idea of liberty or the blind malevolence of nature. Lerner wrote:

> Here was no . . . sawdust-stuffed Victorian moralist, no prim and unctuous spokesman for a carefully ordered world. Here was rather a man of strong passions, large vision, tenacious will, powerful intellect, who used and fused all his qualities in the service of a vision of a better world for all his fellow men.[55]

Part of that vision included a new relationship between men and women, and I suspect both John and Harriet Mill would have been very responsive to the image caught in Elizabeth Barrett Browning's poem, *Aurora Leigh,* in which Aurora says:

> The world waits
> For help. Beloved, let us work so well,
> Our work shall still be better for our love
> And still our love be sweeter for our work.[56]

The mutuality suggested in these lines makes insignificant any shrewd calculus of the "how much was hers, how much his" variety in assessing the collaboration between John Mill and Harriet Taylor. Though it is couched in terms of detached scholarship, one senses in Mill scholars an unwitting desire to reject Harriet Taylor as capable of contributing in any significant way to the vigor of Mill's analysis of political and social issues unless it included some tinge of sentiment or political thought the scholar disapproved of, in which case this disliked element was seen as Harriet's influence. The upcoming generation of students and scholars, it is to be hoped, will work on less sex-biased assumptions.

BRIEF YEARS OF MARRIAGE (1851-58)

Harriet Taylor and John Mill had known each other for twenty-one years when they were finally married in the London Register's Office in April 1851. There is no better example of the manner in which they attempted to put in practice the principles they were so firmly committed to on the proper relations between the sexes, than the remarkable statement Mill wrote two months before his marriage. There is no record of what Mill did with this statement, nor of any discussion between them prior to his drafting the document, but it is so fine an example of principles put to practice that it is worth inclusion here. The necessity for drafting a personal declaration in the form of an individuated marriage "pledge" applies to our own time as it did in 1851, for legal and ecclesiastical strictures continue to be alien to the spirit in which many men and women committed to sex equality wish to join their lives:

> Being about, if I am so happy as to obtain her consent, to enter into the marriage relation with the only woman I have ever known, with whom I would have entered into that state; and the whole character of the marriage relation as constituted by law being such as both she and I entirely and conscientiously disapprove, for this among other reasons, that it confers upon one of the parties to the contract, legal power and control over the person, property, and freedom of action of the other party, independent of her own wishes and will; I, having no means of legally divesting myself of these odious powers (as I most assuredly would do if an engagement to that effect could be made legally binding on me) feel it my duty to put on record a formal protest against the existing law of marriage, in so far as conferring such powers; and a solemn promise never in any case or under any circumstances to use them. And in the event of marriage between Mrs. Taylor and me I declare it to be my will and intention, and the condi-

tion of the engagement between us, that she retains in all respects whatever the same absolute freedom of action and freedom of disposal of herself and of all that does or may at any time belong to her, as if no such marriage had taken place; and I absolutely disclaim and repudiate all pretension to have acquired any rights whatever by virtue of such marriage.

> 6 March 1851 J. S. Mill[57]

A resounding ring of liberty for individual men and women sounds in this statement of Mill's as it was again to echo from the pages of their "joint production" in the famous essay *On Liberty,* and in Harriet's essay on the **"Enfranchisement of Women"**:

> We deny the right of any portion of the species to decide for another portion . . . what is and what is not their 'proper sphere.' The proper sphere for all human beings is the largest and highest which they are able to attain to. What this is, cannot be ascertained, without complete liberty of choice.

Little is known about the first two years of their marriage, partly because they were together and it is through their correspondence that we get a view of their personal and intellectual affairs. The Mills spent the summer following their marriage in France and Belgium, returning in September to settle in Blackheath Park, at that time a rural district on the outskirts of London, from which Mill commuted by train to India House. The rural quality of the setting is caught by a contemporary description that the house faced "a wide open space of rolling meadows bounded far off by a blue outline of distant hills." Here the Mills lived a quiet and solitary life for two years, with only occasional weekend visitors such as William Fox and his daughter or foreign scholars.

Harriet's two youngest children, then in their early twenties, were members of the Blackheath Park household, and it is from their pens that Hayek provides us with the only scraps of evidence that suggest something of the personal routine of their home life. A few years later when Helen Taylor was off on a brief fling at a stage career, she wrote her mother:

> I like to think about nine o'clock that you are talking with him. I am unhappy at three because you are at dinner and I am not there to help you. I grow impatient at five because he has not come in but at six it is pleasant to think that he is making tea and you have got my letter (which he has brought home).[58]

Harriet's son Algernon provided another, little known side of their home life and of Mill's musical talent:

> Mr. Mill used, now and then, to perform on the piano, but only when asked to do so by my mother; and then he would at once sit down to the instrument, and play music entirely of his own composition, on the spur of the moment: music of a singular character . . . rich in feeling, vigour and suggestiveness. . . . When he had finished, my mother would, perhaps, enquire what had been the idea running in his mind, and which had

formed the theme of the improvisation—for such it was, and a strikingly characteristic one too.[59]

There is more evidence on the period from 1853 until Harriet's death in 1858, though for the unhappy reason that their declining health led to numerous separations as one or the other sought the relief of southern or coastal climates. Their first separation was in 1853. Far from enjoying her "more as a correspondent than as a companion," as Stillinger suggests, Mill wrote his wife:

> This is the first time since we were married my darling wife that we have been separated and I do not like it at all—but your letters are the greatest delight and as soon as I have done reading one I begin thinking how soon I shall have another.[60]

It must be noted that the Mills had had twenty-one years before their marriage in which to establish the style of their relationship. It was an intellectual and sentimental communion through discussion and written correspondence. From their own views of the place of physical sex in individual lives and the larger society, there is no reason to assume that sheer physical togetherness was as necessary to their relationship as it would be to us in our day.

Even during their most prolonged separation, when Mill was ordered out of England by his doctor (December 1854 to the summer of 1855), they were in constant contact by letter. Mill's correspondence during these months in Italy, Sicily, and Greece are not yet available in print, although Hayek has tempted us with some sample letters. They make fascinating reading, as one follows Mill on mule trips into remote parts of Sicily, or mountain climbing in Greece, all the while writing fully in a style that shows an expansion of his spirits and improvement in his health, as he visits the places of historic significance familiar to him from Greek and Latin reading in childhood. This "symbol of rationalism" often trembled with emotion in these encounters with the classical past. One sample must suffice here, from a letter Mill wrote to his wife from Naples in February 1855:

> Nothing can be more beautiful than this place . . . now in this bedroom by candlelight I am in a complete nervous state from the sensation of the beauty I am living among—while I look at it I seem to be gathering honey which I savor the whole time afterwards.[61]

Throughout the correspondence between 1853 and 1858 there was an undercurrent of urgency, a feeling that they must quickly complete their work before death claimed them. Already in 1853 Mill wrote to his wife at Sidmouth:

> We must finish the best we have got to say, and not only that, but publish it while we are alive. I do not see what living depository there is likely to be of our thoughts, or who in this weak generation that is growing up will even be capable of thoroughly mastering and assimilating your ideas, much less of re-originating them—so we must write them and print them, and then they can wait until there are again thinkers.[62]

In 1854 Mill worked on his autobiography, and there is an interesting exchange of letters with his wife about what should be said in it concerning their personal life. Mill wrote Harriet in February that on "what particularly concerns our life there is nothing yet written, except the descriptions of you and of your effect on me," prophetically ending:

> But we have to consider, which we can only do together, how much of our story it is advisable to tell, in order to make head against the representations of enemies when we shall not be alive to add anything to it. If it was not to be published for 100 years, I should say tell all, simply and without reserve. As it is there must be care taken not to put arms into the hands of the enemy.[63]

Within five days Harriet responded to this letter, in part as follows:

> This ought to be done in its genuine truth and simplicity—strong affection, intimacy of friendship, and no impropriety. It seems to me an edifying picture for those poor wretches who cannot conceive friendship but in sex—nor believe that expediency and the consideration for feelings of others can conquer sensuality. But of course this is not my reason for wishing it done. It is that every ground should be occupied by ourselves on our own subject.[64]

This Victorian concept of "reason" controlling the "lower," "base," or "animal" instincts is often present in their writings and is the one area bearing on the lives of the two sexes in which the twentieth-century reader experiences a discordant note. Radical though they may be in political and logical argument on the social and legal barriers which kept women in involuntary or voluntary captivity, these Victorians had a view of the body as an unfortunate trap of the human spirit and intellect, to be controlled, clothed, forgotten—save when its frequent illness forced attention. The liberation of women was not thought of in terms of sexual liberation of women in the modern sense at all. Helen Taylor, whose ideas one may presume were moulded by her mother and stepfather, expressed the Victorian view very pointedly in a letter written in 1870, in which she said:

> I think it probable that this particular passion will become with men, as it is already with a large number of women, completely under the control of the reason. It has become so with women because its becoming so has been the condition upon which women hoped to obtain the strongest love and admiration of men. The gratification of this passion in its highest form, therefore, has been with women conditional upon their restraining it in its lowest. It has not yet been tried what the same conditions will do for men. I believe that they will do all that we wish, nor am I alone in thinking that men are by nature capable of as thorough a control over these passions as women are. . . .[65]

The Mills espoused very advanced and radical ideas about the status of women, marriage and divorce laws, the right of women to education and the franchise, and the injustice of denying basic human rights to the female half of humanity; but in the area of human sexuality they were very much the products of their Victorian era. One might raise the question, however, whether this is not equally true in the 1970s. We have witnessed, over the decade of the 1960s, a legal revolution in the rights of women in the employment sphere, yet our literature continues to be dominated by infantile acts of physical rape in the pages of a Norman Mailer and of female-male encounters confined to genital contact in the pages of a John Updike. Young women by the score still limp away bruised in spirit from sexual encounters they initiate under the banner of sexual freedom, but with an archaic stance of "take me" that acknowledges the male as actor and themselves as objects. Women still face a long struggle to secure the right to control their own bodies through repeal of man-made laws on contraception and abortion.

So too we have not even begun to digest the implications of recent laboratory studies of human sexuality.[66] This research has now dispelled the twin Freudian ideas of lesser female sexuality and the view that vaginal orgasm is distinct from and superior to clitoral orgasm. It is doubtful, however, that these findings will be quickly reflected in the literary work of our male writers. Even further in the future is a serious coming to grips with the Masters-Johnson finding that there is greater intensity to female sexuality than male sexuality, or that the human female is often still aroused and sexually interested when her partner is sexually satisfied. It is rare for anyone to conclude from these findings, as Mary Shurfey recently did, that we can at last reject the myth of relative asexuality among women as a biological absurdity and realize that women's sexuality has been suppressed in the name of monogamy at the service of a man-centered civilization. No one has traced the implications of these research results for the structure of marriage and the family.

Fifty years of acceptance of Freudian concepts of female sexuality will not be quickly undone by one set of empirical researches on the human sexual response. Psychoanalytic theories have penetrated deep into the modern scientific and artistic consciousness. This is nowhere more apparent than in the sociological and psychological literature on sex roles and sex differences. Hence it is perhaps not surprising that it is not a social scientist but a twentieth-century playwright, Genet, who has written the most perceptive analysis of sex as a caste and its effects upon the larger society. Kate Millett has analyzed Genet's plays—*The Blacks, The Balcony,* and *The Screens*—as rationalist blasts against the most fundamental of society's follies, its view of sex as a caste structure ratified by nature. In Millett's analysis of these plays,[67] Genet considers human sexuality not only hopelessly tainted in its own sphere, but the prototype of institutionalized inequality of all other sorts—racial, political, and economic. Genet is convinced that by dividing humanity into two groups and appointing one to rule over the other by virtue of birthright, the social order has already established and ratified a system of oppression which underlies and corrupts all

other human relationships. Genet's plea is that unless we go to the very center of the sexual politic and root out the power and violence there, all our efforts at liberation will only land us again in the same primordial stews.

In her **"Enfranchisement"** essay, Harriet Mill commented that it was fitting that abolitionists, committed to the extirpation of the aristocracy of color, should join forces in the first collective protest against the "aristocracy of sex" at the 1850 convention in Worcester, Massachusetts. But if anyone had carried the idea of sex as a caste system into the intimate area of human sexuality along the lines Genet has now done, one can imagine what a feverish struggle John and Harriet would have had to fit this new set of ideas into the fabric of their thought! It is fitting in 1970 that many men who were active in the civil rights movement of the 1960s have now joined in the "second" collective protest against the same aristocracy of sex, the contemporary women's liberation movement. At the same time it is also clear that beneath the fine words of liberation, many of us are far from liberated in the deeper roots of our attitudes toward male and female sexuality.

There are so many points in the writings of the Mills that show an uncanny anticipation of things to come, so fine an ability to project beyond their own time and place, that one hesitates to assert that even the new radical perspective on human sexuality might not have been woven into their philosophy, if not their personal behavior. More than one hundred years ago, Mill and his wife must have discussed many of their ideas about solutions to social problems confronting the world. The ideas come fresh across ten decades, in such observations as the following:

> The social problem of the future we considered to be, how to unite the greatest individual liberty of action with a common ownership in the raw material of the globe, and an equal participation of all in the benefits of combined labour.[68]

This is from the draft of the *Autobiography* written in the early 1850s when Marx was working away, unknown to Mill, in the British Museum. It is a judgment that Americans, who now consume over half the raw materials of the globe although they comprise less than ten percent of the world's population, have yet to confront. Mill was looking far ahead, extrapolating from the hopes engendered in him by the revolutions of 1848, seeing beyond nationalism to a world that shared the natural wealth of the globe, a socialist world with a more equitable distribution of the world's bounty.

Or the following, from a letter to Professor Carl Heinrich Rau of Heidelberg written in 1852:

> it is to be decided whether Europe shall enter peacefully and prosperously into a better order of things, or whether the new ideas will be inaugurated by a century of war and violence like that which followed the Reformation of Luther.[69]

Again, Mill was referring to the uprising of the working class in nation after nation, anticipating increased class warfare unless men had freedom to determine their own economic and political destiny. By the 1850s Mill saw that the aristocracy had been replaced by what he called the "shopocracy," middle-class mercantile interests with no more concern for the welfare and rights of the working class than the aristocracy before them. Even before the French workers' uprising in 1848, Mill had confided to a friend in 1847:

> In England I often think that a violent revolution is very much needed, in order to give that general shake up to the torpid mind of the nation which the French Revolution gave to Continental Europe. England has never had any general break-up of old associations and hence the extreme difficulty of getting any ideas into its stupid head.[70]

It is little wonder that Hugh Elliot reported the experience of turning over numerous pages devoted to Mill's work in the Catalogue of Printed Books in the British Museum to find one headed by the entry: "Mill (John Stuart): see Anti-Christ."

Men and women in the nineteenth century may not have had our sense of the expanse of physical space, but they often show a grasp of man's place in the long sweep of history that our existentialist times lack. It is refreshing to encounter Mill in Palermo in 1855 reading Goethe, speculating about the vast accretion of knowledge since Greek times, thinking about Goethe's responsiveness to the Greek sense of symmetry, and then commenting in a letter to his wife:

> the moderns have vastly more material to reduce to order than the ancients dreamt of and the secret of harmonizing it all has not yet been discovered. It is too soon by a century or two to attempt either symmetrical reproductions in art or symmetrical characters. We all need to be blacksmiths or ballet dancers with good stout arms or legs, useful to do what we have got to do and useful to fight with at times. . . . We cannot be Apollos and Venuses just yet.[71]

A nineteenth-century man reading an eighteenth-century poet in a setting steeped in pre-Christian history, speculating about man in the twenty-first century!

A last illustration of Mill's anticipation of the future can be shown by his alertness to the connection between the status of women and the problem of population growth, a connection made only in a few isolated quarters in the social sciences of our time. In the chapter he attributed to Harriet on the future condition of the working classes in his *Political Economy,* Mill stated this connection in the following manner:

> The ideas and institutions by which the accident of sex is made the groundwork of an inequality of legal rights, and a forced dissimilarity of social functions, must ere long be recognized as the greatest hindrance to moral, social and even intellectual improvement. On the present occasion I shall only indicate, among the probable consequences of the industrial and social independence of women, a great diminution of the evil of over

population. It is by devoting one half of the human species to that exclusive function, by making it fill the entire life of one sex and interweave itself with almost all the objects of the other, that the "animal" instinct in question is nursed into the disproportionate preponderance which it has hitherto exercised in human life.[72]

When in 1848 an American reviewer of the *Political Economy* objected to Mill's ideas on population growth, Mill responded in biting fashion, linking the objections to the reviewer's nationality:

> On the population question, my difference with the reviewer is fundamental, and in the incidental reference which he makes to my assertion of equality of political rights and of social position in behalf of women, the tone assumed by him is really below contempt. But I fear that a country where institutions profess to be founded on equality, and which yet maintains the slavery of black men and of all women will be one of the last to relinquish that other servitude.[73]

In 1970 the United States exports millions of contraceptive pills and devices to Asian and Latin American countries, but it exports little education on what John Mill and Harriet Taylor understood so long ago, that freedom of choice and a wider range of life goals would undercut women's desires for a bountiful maternity. A few years after the above letter was penned, Harriet put the issue very pointedly in the **"Enfranchisement"** essay:

> Numbers of women are wives and mothers only because there is no other career open to them, no other occupation for their feelings or other activities. . . . To say women must be excluded from active life because maternity disqualifies them for it, is in fact to say that every other career should be forbidden them in order that maternity may be their only resource.

One closes a book of Mill's writings or correspondence with a nagging question: who among us in 1970 are now thinking and writing with a foresight that will speak meaningfully to our descendants in the mid-twenty-first century, as Mill so often did to us? On issue after issue our language is different from Mill's, but the problems are the same, and often we have yet to rediscover the solutions Mill proposed a century ago.

HARRIET'S DEATH AND "THE SUBJECTION OF WOMEN"

John Mill retired from the East India Company in the autumn of 1858, and the Mills took off for the south of France in October, planning to stay during the winter at Hyères, where Harriet's health had improved during a previous stay, and then to spend the spring in Italy. They never reached their destination, for a cold that Harriet had caught developed into severe lung congestion, and she died in Avignon on 3 November. Mill's own words are the best description of the aftermath of her death:

> Since then I have sought for such alleviation as my state admitted of, by the mode of life which most en-

ables me to feel her still near me. I bought a cottage as close as possible to the place where she is buried, and there her daughter (my fellow-sufferer and now my chief comfort) and I, live constantly during a great portion of the year. My objects in life are solely those which were hers; my pursuits and occupations those in which she shared, or sympathized, and which are indissolubly associated with her.[74]

In keeping with this mood, the first things that Mill published after his wife's death were the first two volumes of his collected essays, *Dissertations and Discussions,* including the **"Enfranchisement"** essay of his wife's and the volume *On Liberty* that had occupied them the previous few years. During 1860-61 Mill drafted *The Subjection of Women.* In his autobiography he explained that the essay was written at his daughter's suggestion that there might be a "written exposition of my opinions on that great question, as full and conclusive as I could make it." Concerning its content, he said:

> As ultimately published it was enriched with some important ideas of my daughter's, and passages of her writing. But in what was of my own composition, all that is most striking and profound belongs to my wife; coming from the fund of thought which had been made common to us both, by our innumerable conversations and discussions on a topic which filled so large a place in our minds.[75]

An important idea in Mill's view of the equality of the sexes is tapped in this passage: the "fund of thought made common" to Harriet and himself. Mill shied away from any direct personal account of his marital relationship, but the reader feels he was speaking from a personal basis when he described a marriage between equals toward the end of the *Subjection* essay. Although he first rejected the desirability of giving such a description (on the ground that those who can conceive such a marriage need no description, and to those who cannot conceive such a marriage, it would appear but the dream of an enthusiast), he proceeded to describe just such a relationship—a marriage between

> two persons of cultivated faculties, identical in opinions and purposes, between whom there exists that best of equality, similarity of powers and capacities with reciprocal superiority in them so that each can enjoy the luxury of looking up to the other, and can have alternately the pleasure of leading and of being led in the path of development. . . . This and this only is the ideal of marriage; . . . all opinions, customs and institutions which favor any other notion of it . . . are relics of primitive barbarism.

The idea of complementary skills and knowledge, such that each spouse can be both leader and follower, teacher and student, on a firm base of shared values and goals, reads like a description of the Mills' own marriage. There is an echo here of Mill's description of what he and his wife contributed to the analysis of the position of women. Mill acknowledged that before he became an intimate friend of Harriet's, his views on the position of women

were nothing more than an abstract principle: he saw no more reason why women should be held in legal subjection to other people than why men should. Harriet's contribution he described as follows:

> that perception of the vast practical bearings of women's disabilities which found expression in the book on the "Subjection of Women" was acquired mainly through her teaching. . . . But for her rare knowledge of human nature and comprehension of moral and social influences, I should have had a very insufficient perception of the mode in which the consequences of the inferior position of women intertwine themselves with all the evils of existing society and with all the difficulties of human improvement.[76]

Mill had a poor view of the capacity of men in his time to live out a marriage on a basis of equality. In fact he argued that the reason barriers are maintained against the liberation of women from their caste status is that "the generality of the male sex cannot yet tolerate the idea of living with an equal." John Stuart Mill clearly could and did.

There are several reasons why *The Subjection of Women* continues to be a powerfully effective essay, which people in the 1970s can find as stimulating as those who read it for the first time in the 1870s. It is grounded in basic libertarian values that ring as true today as then:

> We have had the morality of submission and the morality of chivalry and generosity: the time is ripe for morality of justice. . . . The principle of the modern movement in morals and politics is that conduct and conduct alone entitles to respect: that not what men are but what they do constitutes their claim to deference. . . . It is totally out of keeping with modern values to have ascribed statuses; . . . human beings are no longer born to their place in life; . . . individual choice is our model now.

To the generations of the twentieth century who have seen tyranny and the suppression of human liberty in all forms of government—Fascist, Communist, and democratic—John Stuart Mill's invocation of the rights of men and women to liberty and justice have a strong, continuing appeal. And to the women of the twentieth century, who have seen very little difference in the actual condition, if not the formal rights, of women under any existing form of government, *The Subjection of Women* continues to serve as a resounding affirmation of their human right to full equality and a sophisticated analysis of the obstacles that bar their way to it.

A second basic reason for the continuing relevance of the Mill essay on women is that it is not burdened with the dead weight of any of the social and psychological theories that have emerged during the hundred years separating us from the Mills: no Darwinism to encourage an unthinking expectation of unilinear progress of mankind through "natural selection" or "selective breeding"; no Freudian theory to belittle women's sexuality and encourage their acceptance as the "second sex"; no functional anthropology or sociology to justify a conservative acceptance of the status quo; no Marxist theory to encourage a narrow concentration on economic variables. What the Mills had as their guide is what we have only begun to recapture in our counterpart efforts to expand the horizons of men and women to fuller realization of their human potential: a blend of compassion and logic and a commitment to the view that liberty cannot exist in the absence of the power to use it.

The closest analogy to Mill's intellectual style is the formal structure of what is known in the behavioral sciences as functional analysis, but with this difference: Mill attempted to probe beneath the surface of social forms to find the latent function served by that form, not, however, to pinpoint its "social utility" but to identify the root cause which must be changed to effect the release of women from their subjection. Thus in analyzing chivalry and its equivalent in modern times, "consideration for women," Mill characterized it as a mask hiding the idea of servitude, the notion that women need protection or help because they are "weak." So in a passage that anticipates Genet's analysis, Mill argued that society can never be organized on merit, or depart from its imposition of the power of the strong over the weak, so long as this right of the strong rules in the family, the heart of society:

> The principle can not get hold of men's inmost sentiments until this assumption of superiority of power merely on the ascribed grounds of sex, persists. The selfish propensities, self worship of men, have their source and root in the present constitution of the relation between men and women.

So, too, Mill had a terse and firm answer to the claim that there are "natural" differences between the sexes which preclude full equality for women (by our time amplified by the thousands of psychological and sociological studies which demonstrate differences between the sexes): "No one can know the nature of the sexes as long as they have only been seen in their present relation to each other; . . . what women are is what we have required them to be." Mill left open the possibility that women qua women may have some special type of originality to contribute, though cautious to point out we have no way to predict this until women have had the freedom to develop in an autonomous way, with time to emancipate themselves from the "influence of accepted male models," and strike out on their own.

From Mill's correspondence following the publication of the *Subjection* essay, we can gain some understanding of his reasons for developing the particular arguments he does in the volume, and for excluding certain other topics. There is, for example, little or nothing in the book on marriage and divorce laws. In a letter to Professor John Nichol of Glasgow, Mill wrote:

> I thought it best not to discuss the questions of marriage and divorce along with that of the equality of women; not only from the obvious inexpediency of establishing a connection in people's minds between the equality and any particular opinions on the divorce question, but also because I do not think that the conditions of the dissolubility of marriage can be properly determined until women have an equal voice in determining them, nor until there has been experience of the marriage relation as it would exist between equals. Until then I should not like to commit myself to more than the general principle of relief from the contract in extreme cases.[77]

Mill's sense of political expediency and timing played a major role in what he felt was useful to discuss in the essay. At the time he wrote, women had no legal right to their own children, and one reader of his essay wrote to suggest that since there was an infinitely closer relationship of children to their mothers than to their fathers, the law should really reflect this reality, and if anything, give legal rights over children to women. Mill answered Mrs. Hooker:

> What you so justly say respecting the infinitely closer relationship of a child to its mother than to its father, I have learned . . . to regard as full of important consequences with regard to the future legal position of parents and children. This, however, is a portion of the truth for which the human mind will not, for some time, be sufficiently prepared to make its discussion useful.[78]

The underlying intent behind Mill's argument in the essay comes out most clearly in a letter to his friend and biographer, Alexander Bain. Mill explained that the stress he gave to the capacities of women, which occupy so large a proportion of the essay, was done for two reasons. One was that the principal objection then offered against sex equality was that women were not "fit for or capable of this, that or the other mental achievement." The second reason is perhaps as cogent in 1970 as it was in John Mill's own time:

> But there is a still stronger reason. The most important thing women have to do is to stir up the zeal of women themselves. We have to stimulate their aspirations—to bid them not despair of anything, nor think anything beyond their reach, but try their faculties against all difficulties. In no other way can the verdict of experience be fairly collected, and in no other way can we excite the enthusiasm in women which is necessary to break down the old barriers. I believe the point has now been reached at which, the higher we pitch our claims, the more disposition there will be to concede part of them. . . . Everything I hear strengthens me in the belief, which I at first entertained with a slight mixture of misgiving, that the book has come out at the right time, and that no part of it is premature.[79]

It is fitting to note the reaction to the book by an American woman famous in the history of the women's movement, Elizabeth Cady Stanton. This *enfant terrible* of the suffrage cause wrote Mill after reading the *Subjection* essay in 1869:

I lay the book down with a peace and joy I never felt before, for it is the first response from any man to show he is capable of seeing and feeling all the nice shades and degrees of woman's wrongs and the central point of her weakness and degradation.[80]

That Mill was able to achieve this is a tribute to the remarkable blend of compassion and logic both Harriet and Mill himself brought to the analysis of women and the hope for a future equality of the sexes.

When Carrie Chapman Catt wrote her foreword to an American edition of Mill's *The Subjection of Women,* she closed with a few lines that are as relevant in 1970 as they were in 1911:

> For some years the book has been out of print, and its pages have grown unfamiliar to those who should know them best. A new edition is a happy incident and its accessibility to the masses will prove of untold value to the movement.[81]

In 1911 the "movement" was the suffrage movement, still some nine years from its victory in securing the vote for American women. In 1970 the movement is much broader and its goals more diffuse, for the women's liberation movement seeks nothing short of full equality of the sexes. In this sense contemporary activists are closer to the perspective of John Mill and Harriet Taylor than of the majority of turn-of-century American suffragists. We can not tell how many years remain until our movement is victorious. The answer lies with those who read and study these pages: all the tens of thousands of women and men who seek to understand the political and ideological history of the movement to secure equality between the sexes. If these same readers carry their knowledge into a vigorous commitment to scholarship and to political action, at least one small corner of this whirling globe may know full sex equality by the close of the twentieth century.

Notes

1. The description of Mill's home and the mode of his life there during his last years come from a letter by W. T. Thornton to his friend, Henry Fawcett. See Hugh S. R. Elliot, *The Letters of John Stuart Mill* (London: Longmans, Green & Co., 1910), 1: 261-62.

2. John Jacob Coss, ed., *Autobiography of John Stuart Mill* (New York: Columbia University Press, 1924), p. 186.

3. An example of this tendency is the collection edited by Max Lerner, *Essential Works of John Stuart Mill* (New York: Bantam Books, 1961). This collection includes the *Autobiography, On Liberty, On Utilitarianism* and *The Utility of Religion.* Although Lerner makes the point that Mill's writings and ideas have a continuing relevance to the issues with which men and women in the 1960s are struggling, he makes no mention of the essay on women as sharing this continued relevance to modern issues. It seems clear from its omission from the collection, that Lerner did

not consider *The Subjection of Women* to be among the "essential" works of John Stuart Mill.

4. C. Wright Mills, *The Sociological Imagination* (New York: Oxford University Press, 1959), p. 132.

5. Coss, *Autobiography of John Stuart Mill,* p. v.

6. Friedrich A. Hayek, *John Stuart Mill and Harriet Taylor: Their Friendship and Subsequent Marriage* (Chicago: University of Chicago Press, 1951), p. 17.

7. A. W. Levi, "The Mental Crisis of John Stuart Mill," *Psychoanalytic Review,* 32, (1945): 86-101; and "The Writing of Mill's Autobiography," *Ethics,* 61, (1951): 284-96.

8. Jack Stillinger, ed., *The Early Draft of John Stuart Mill's Autobiography* (Urbana: University of Illinois Press, 1961).

9. Elizabeth Cady Stanton, Susan B. Anthony, and J. A. Gage, *History of Woman Suffrage* (New York, 1889), vol. I, pp. 219-20.

10. Hayek, *John Stuart Mill and Harriet Taylor,* pp. 56, 291.

11. An excellent analysis of the political ideology and parliamentary activities of this group, from its rise in the early 1820's to its break-up in disillusionment by 1839, is Joseph Hamburger, *Intellectuals in Politics: John Stuart Mill and the Philosophic Radicals* (New Haven: Yale University Press, 1965).

12. Coss, *Autobiography of John Stuart Mill,* p. 94.

13. Levi, "The Mental Crisis of John Stuart Mill," p. 98.

14. The brief Mill quotations in the preceding two paragraphs are from Coss, *Autobiography of John Stuart Mill,* chapter 5.

15. Ibid., p. 101.

16. Stillinger, *The Early Draft,* pp. 17, 103.

17. [Francis E. Mineka, ed., *The Earlier Letters of John Stuart Mill 1812-1848,* vol. 12 of *Collected Works of John Stuart Mill* (Toronto: University of Toronto Press, 1963)], 12:30.

18. There were close connections between the Unitarians and Utilitarians well back into the preceding century. Joseph Priestley, scientist and prominent spirit in Unitarianism, had written an essay on government in 1768 which gave Jeremy Bentham his idea of the "greatest happiness" principle, the lead idea of Utilitarianism. An excellent analysis of the political and personal ties between these two groups can be found in Francis E. Mineka, *The Dissidence of Dissent* (Chapel Hill: University of North Carolina Press, 1944).

19. Hayek, *John Stuart Mill and Harriet Taylor,* pp. 36-37. Eliza asked Harriet whether a recent article (June 1831) she had read was by Mill or Harriet, suggest-

ing Eliza was fully aware of the similarity of views between her friend Harriet and John Mill.

20. Coss, *Autobiography of John Stuart Mill,* p. 173.

21. Mineka, *The Dissidence of Dissent,* pp. 286-87.

22. Hayek, *John Stuart Mill and Harriet Taylor,* pp. 82-83.

23. Ibid., p. 82.

24. Richard Garnett, *The Life of W. J. Fox* (London: John Lane Co., 1910), p. 103.

25. Mineka, *The Dissidence of Dissent,* p. 275.

26. Ibid., p. 277.

27. Mineka, *The Earlier Letters,* 12:186-88.

28. Hayek, *John Stuart Mill and Harriet Taylor,* p. 54.

29. This section on the disillusionment of the Philosophic Radicals relies heavily on Hamburger, *Intellectuals in Politics,* pp. 242-72.

30. The inscription, which is reproduced in Hayek, *John Stuart Mill and Harriet Taylor,* p. 267, is as follows: To the beloved memory of Harriet Mill, the dearly beloved and deeply regretted wife of John Stuart Mill. Her great and loving heart, her noble soul, her clear, powerful, original, and comprehensive intellect made her the guide and support, the instructor in wisdom, and the example in goodness—as she was the sole earthly delight—of those who had the happiness to belong to her. As earnest for the public good as she was generous and devoted to all who surrounded her, her influence has been felt in many of the greatest improvements of the age and will be in those still to come. Were there but a few hearts and intellects like hers, this earth would already become the hoped-for heaven. She died, to the irreparable loss of those who survive her, at Avignon, Nov. 3, 1858.

31. See Mill's introductory comments to the "Enfranchisement of Women" in this volume for an example of this extravagant assessment.

32. Alexander Bain, *John Stuart Mill: A Criticism* (London, 1882).

33. Letter from Bain to Helen Taylor, 6 September 1873, in Stillinger, *The Early Draft,* p. 23.

34. Bain, *John Stuart Mill,* pp. 171, 173.

35. Garnett, *The Life of W. J. Fox,* p. 99.

36. Ibid., p. 155.

37. Mineka, *The Dissidence of Dissent,* pp. 274-75.

38. Stillinger, *The Early Draft,* pp. 24-25.

39. Keith Rinehart, "John Mill's Autobiography: Its Art and Appeal," *University of Kansas City Review* 19 (1953): 265-73.

40. Stillinger, *The Early Draft,* p. 27.

41. Lerner, ed., *Essential Works of John Stuart Mill,* p. xiv.

42. Diana Trilling, "Mill's Intellectual Beacon," *Partisan Review* 19 (1952): 116-20.

43. William Bridges Adams, "Housebuilding and Housekeeping," *Monthly Repository* Vol. 8 (1834); cited in Mineka, *The Dissidence of Dissent,* p. 350.

44. Hayek, *John Stuart Mill and Harriet Taylor,* p. 266.

45. Basil Willey, *Nineteenth Century Studies* (London: Chatto & Windus, 1950), pp. 141-86.

46. Max Lerner draws this distinction between Hayek and Laski in his introduction to Mill's *Autobiography, Essential Works of John Stuart Mill,* p. 6.

47. Stillinger, *The Early Draft,* p. 133.

48. Garnett, *The Life of W. J. Fox,* p. 98.

49. Late in 1847 Harriet wrote to her husband: "I do certainly look more like a ghost than a living person. . . . I think I shall not be able to go [to Brighton] before the end of next week being just now much occupied with the book." By February 1848 she is still absorbed in the manuscript: "I am so taken up with the Book which is near the last . . . that I could not leave town before the beginning of April if even then." Hayek, *John Stuart Mill and Harriet Taylor,* pp. 119, 120.

50. Coss, *Autobiography of John Stuart Mill,* p. 174.

51. Ibid., p. 176.

52. Hayek, *John Stuart Mill and Harriet Taylor,* p. 121.

53. Ibid., p. 138.

54. Willey, *Nineteenth Century Studies,* p. 161. What preceded this exclamatory assessment of Mill by Willey was a long passage from the *Political Economy* in which Mill argued for a reduction in population growth, urging that men have need for space and solitude. Mill ended the passage with a comment we in 1970 have good cause to rephrase in our own terms: "If the earth must lose that part of its pleasantness which it owes to things that the unlimited increase of wealth and population would extirpate from it, for the mere purpose of enabling it to support a larger, but not a better or a happier population, I sincerely hope, for the sake of posterity, that they will be content to be stationary, long before necessity compels them to it."

55. Lerner, *Essential Works of John Stuart Mill,* p. xxix.

56. Curious ties often link together many figures in nineteenth-century letters. Robert Browning was befriended as a young boy by Sarah Flower, and she brought some of his poetry to William Fox for his assessment. Fox was among the earliest critics to ac-

knowledge Browning's poetic talents. In later years, Browning remained in close correspondence with Fox, viewing him as his "literary father." The slim volume, *Aurora Leigh,* by his wife Elizabeth Barrett Browning, also figured in the life of one of the leading nineteenth-century American suffragists: Susan B. Anthony carried it with her everywhere, as one of her main sources of inspiration, a model of what a future woman's life might be. See Alma Lutz, *Susan B. Anthony, Rebel, Crusader, Humanitarian* (Boston: Beacon Press, 1959), pp. 74-76.

57. Elliot, *The Letters of John Stuart Mill,* 1:58.

58. Hayek, *John Stuart Mill and Harriet Taylor,* p. 183.

59. Ibid.

60. Hayek, *John Stuart Mill and Harriet Taylor,* p. 184.

61. Ibid., p. 221.

62. Ibid., p. 185.

63. Ibid., p. 194.

64. Ibid., p. 196.

65. Elliot, *The Letters of John Stuart Mill,* vol. 1, p. 241.

66. William Masters and Virginia Johnson, *Human Sexual Response* (New York: Little Brown, 1966).

67. Kate Millett, "Sexual Politics: Miller, Mailer and Genet," *New American Review,* no. 7 (1969), pp. 7-32; also Kate Millett, *Sexual Politics* (New York: Doubleday, 1970).

68. Coss, *Autobiography of John Stuart Mill,* p. 162.

69. Elliot, *The Letters of John Stuart Mill,* vol. 1, p. 170.

70. Mineka, *The Earlier Letters,* vol. 13, p. 713.

71. Hayek, *John Stuart Mill and Harriet Taylor,* pp. 225-26.

72. John Stuart Mill, *Principles of Political Economy,* ed. J. M. Robson (University of Toronto Press, 1965) 3:765-66.

73. Mineka, *The Earlier Letters,* vol. 13, p. 741.

74. Coss, *Autobiography of John Stuart Mill,* p. 170.

75. Ibid., p. 186.

76. Ibid., p. 173.

77. Elliot, *The Letters of John Stuart Mill,* vol. 2, p. 212.

78. Ibid., p. 214.

79. Ibid., p. 210.

80. Alma Lutz, *Created Equal: A Biography of Elizabeth Cady Stanton* (New York: John Day Company, 1940), pp. 171-72.

81. John Stuart Mill, *The Subjection of Women* (New York: Frederick A. Stokes, 1911), p. xv.

Susan Groag Bell (essay date 1990)

SOURCE: "The Feminization of John Stuart Mill," in *Revealing Lives: Autobiography, Biography, and Gender,* edited by Susan Groag Bell and Marilyn Yalom, State University of New York Press, 1990, pp. 81-92.

[*In the following essay, Bell explores critics' refusal to acknowledge Harriet Taylor's contribution to John Stuart Mill's writing, and offers possible reasons for this resistance.*]

The *Autobiography* of John Stuart Mill, the most famous male feminist of the nineteenth century, is inspired by a presence that has infuriated many critics—that of his wife Harriet. In Mill's words, she was "the most admirable person I had ever known" (p. 114). He insisted that his published writings were "not the work of one mind, but of the fusion of two" (p. 114), "as much her work as mine" (p. 145).[1] He attributed to Harriet "the most valuable ideas and features in these [our] joint productions—those which have been most fruitful of important results and have contributed most to the success and reputation of the works themselves." And, downplaying his own contribution, he added that his own part in them was "no greater than in any of the thoughts which I found in previous writers and made my own only by incorporating them with my own system of thought" (pp. 145-6).

Why are these statements so unpalatable to Mill scholars? Stillinger, for example, who edited various drafts of the autobiography, states that Mill's "encomiums [on Harriet] are a blemish on the work . . . we should object to such extravagances in fiction, and similarly must object to them in autobiography" (p. xvii). An examination of the circumstances in which the autobiography was composed illuminates this question and, additionally, offers a basis for analyzing Mill's pivotal stance in nineteenth-century views on women and gender.

In the first page of the *Autobiography,* Mill presented his intention to describe the story of his "intellectual and moral development;" and further, to acknowledge his debt to others, particularly to "the one to whom most of all is due" [i.e., his wife, Harriet] (p. 3). In fact, one may say that Mill offered a collective self to the world, a self joining Harriet's practical concerns and her emphasis on human connectedness to his own theoretical bent. In an important passage, totally lacking the sentimentality of which he is so often accused, he explained the exact nature of Harriet's contribution to his thought:

> I have often received praise, which in my own right I only partially deserve, for the greater practicality which is supposed to be found in my writings, compared with those of most thinkers who have been equally addicted to large generalizations. The writings in which this quality has been observed, were not the work of one mind, but of the fusion of two, one of them as preeminently practical in its judgments and perceptions of things present, as it was high and bold in its anticipations for a remote futurity.

(p. 114)

It is this concern for his debt, this intellectual debt to his wife, that deeply troubles many of his critics. One of these, H. O. Pappe, has devoted an entire book to an attempt to disprove Harriet's intellectual influence on Mill.[2]

Mill describes his mental development with shining modesty and integrity—beginning with his earliest education, when he was obliged to learn classical Greek at the age of three. However, as readers, we are also aware of the clear psychological implications of his story. Prior to Mill's involvement with Harriet, his life had been dominated by his father James Mill, portrayed by his son as a stern, driving, unloving and unforgiving man. Since the dominating presence of Mill's father has been dealt with at length by others, I do not propose to discuss this further.[3] But what of John Stuart Mill's mother? Was she indeed as absent from his psyche as the final version of the *Autobiography* would lead us to believe?

Most commentators find it easy to dismiss Mill's mother since she appears to be totally absent from the published version of the *Autobiography*. A good example of this point of view, and one of the most recent, is offered by A. O. J. Cockshut: "He [Mill] does not appear to see that he was unusual in having no discernible feeling at all about his mother. If he had disliked her, we could understand it. But not to notice her! . . . Something which Mill never mentions, and (as far as we know) never considered, becomes one of the most fascinating issues in the judgment of his work."[4] Had Cockshut taken into consideration the first draft of the manuscript, he would not have written such a sentence. Ever since 1961, when Stillinger published his edition of the early draft of Mill's *Autobiography*, we have known that at the time of composing this first draft, Mill not only thought about his mother, but actually wrote down some of his negative feelings about her.

The most telling of his observations about his mother (in the first draft) lies in the following remarks: "In an atmosphere of tenderness and affection he [my father] would have been tender and affectionate; but his ill assorted marriage . . . disabled him from making such an atmosphere."[5] And again, "a really warm-hearted mother would in the first place have made my father a totally different being, and in the second, would have made the children grow up loving and being loved. . . . I thus grew up in the absence of love and in the presence of fear."[6] Strong words—an unflinching indictment only few sons would dare to voice. And from the exchange of letters between Mill and Harriet Taylor, published in 1951, we have long known how instrumental Harriet was in editing and censoring Mill's work.[7] These letters clearly show that in order not to aggravate his mother's hurt feelings, Harriet persuaded him to erase everything he had written about her. Harriet's editing, in fact, went so far that in her distress and haste to prevent Mill's negative remarks about his mother from being published, she sometimes led him to expunge certain sections that would have shown his mother's concern for his upbringing and manners. For example, in the passage of the *Autobiography* where Mill de-

scribes how as a young boy he had been disputatious and impertinent towards adults, Harriet erased the following sentence: "My mother did tax me with it, but for her remonstrances I never had the slightest regard" (p. 21n). In other passages in the original drafts which Harriet insisted he remove, Mill had bitterly expressed his disappointment with his lack of practical knowledge of day-to-day life and his dependence on others for practical matters. "I had also the great misfortune of having, in domestic matters everything done for me," he had written, and he continued, "it would never have occurred to my mother who without misgivings of any sort worked from morning till night for her children" (p. 24).

What were the psychological pressures, conscious and unconscious, that brought Mill to write negatively about his mother and then to allow Harriet to erase all mention of her?

The autobiography was written at the beginning of Mill's and Harriet's marriage. At this time Mill was deeply angry because he felt his mother had slighted Harriet by not paying her sufficient respect. Apparently the elder Mrs. Mill and her daughters had not called upon their new daughter- and sister-in-law. Thus, in middle age, after living amiably with his mother and sisters until he was forty-five, Mill became estranged from them, and especially from his mother.

According to Bruce Mazlish, Mill defeated his father in a symbolic Oedipal drama when he married Harriet Taylor. With their marriage, Mazlish claims, Harriet replaced Mill's mother and, because of her intellectual capacities, also his father.[8] Mazlish discusses Mill's guilt feelings, when against his father's, as well as society's, standard of morality he conducted his (albeit platonic) love affair with Harriet for twenty years while her husband John Taylor was still alive. At the same time he had been "devotedly attached to his mother" as a young man, according to family friends.[9] One does not have to be a psychohistorian to understand that Mill would subsequently feel guilty toward his widowed mother when, after long years as a loyal bachelor son living in the maternal household, he left her for Harriet. The *Autobiography* emphasizes his craving to be within the orbit of a loving and demonstrative nature. Thus, however foolish or unnecessary the quarrel between Mill and his mother might have been, the break with her left him feeling guilty and unable to deal with her adequately or fairly while he was composing the autobiography.

Mill stated that his aim was to show his mental development, but he and Harriet had another concern: to assure a skeptical world that their twenty-year friendship before their marriage had been purely platonic. Since Harriet and Mill had clearly been in love, spending many days and weeks together in her small house or travelling in various parts of the Continent, with her husband's knowledge and acquiescence, a public statement was in order. Their exchange of letters in January and February of 1854 includes many suggestions as to how this should be done in the *Autobiography*. "Something must be said," Mill wrote, to "stop the mouths of enemies hereafter", and "to make head against the representation of enemies when we shall not be alive." Harriet wanted to provide an "edifying picture for those poor wretches who cannot conceive friendship but in sex."[10] In the original draft of the autobiography Mill finally wrote:

> . . . our relation at that time was one of strong affection and confidential intimacy only. For though we did not consider the ordinances of society binding on a subject so entirely personal, we did feel bound that our conduct should be such as in no degree to bring discredit on her husband nor therefore on herself; and we disdained, as every person not a slave of his animal appetites must do, the abject notion that the strongest and tenderest friendship cannot exist between a man and a woman without a sensual relation.[11]

But even the phrase "animal appetites" was later removed as it seemed to be too suggestive. No reading of the short paragraph in the final publication would let the reader suspect the agitated correspondence that had passed between these "married friends," nor their struggle over sexuality.

Setting aside the immediate personal context in which Mill composed the *Autobiography,* let us now consider the broad spectrum of ideas at the time of its composition during 1853-1854. Mill's birth and youthful development coincided with the shaping of industrial capitalism and middle-class ideology painstakingly analyzed in Davidoff and Hall's *Family Fortunes.* Davidoff and Hall suggest that this period was one of co-operation between articulate men and women, particularly in marriages concerned with building the "material, social and religious base of their identity."[12] To that extent, John Stuart and Harriet Taylor Mill fit in with the prevailing models. While their intellectual partnership soared far above that of almost all their contemporaries, and their sexual partnership was possibly equally lofty, the rest of their relationship appears to have followed the conventional pattern of masculinity and femininity of their time. In other words Mill, as the published writer and *acknowledged* "thinker," was the "doer" of the partnership, while Harriet provided the emotional stimulus and practical contribution that Mill had missed in his earlier life and deemed essential for its stability.

This pattern of a gendered partnership was based on two well developed streams in nineteenth-century Western thought that fed into Mill's *Autobiography* and provide the context of the prevailing debate on gender. One of these streams is the scientific discussion on evolution, and the other the discourse of Romanticism. Both of them, to put it crudely, allocated intellect to men, and emotional primacy to women.

By the 1860s, soon after Harriet Taylor Mill's death, a proliferation of scholarly publications by historians, anthropologists, biologists and zoologists attempted to order in a scientific manner the romantic equation of: male = intellect, female = emotion. Thus, for example, in 1861 Johann-Jakob Bachofen in his *Mutterrecht* and Sir Henry Maine in *Ancient Law* published their (by now well known) anthropological and legal histories of male-female dichotomies in which women clearly represented the non-intellectual side of humanity.[13] The French craniologist, professor of clinical physiology Paul Broca, wrote in 1861 that the "relatively small size of the female brain depends in part upon her physical inferiority and in part upon her intellectual inferiority."[14] Similarly sexist and equally racist, the 1864 English translation of the famous German Professor of Zoology, Karl Christoph Vogt, stated that "the grown up Negro partakes, as regards the intellectual faculties, of the nature of the child, the female, and the senile white [male]."[15]

I suggest that Mill's emphasis on his wife's intellectual capacity in the *Autobiography,* which such critics as Stillinger and H. O. Pappe found so exaggerated and unsettling even in the 1960s, sprang from an effort to counter this denigration of women's intellect, something Mill did quite consciously and logically in his other published works.[16] For example, he described in the *Autobiography* how Harriet translated his abstract ideas into concrete human terms:

> . . . in all that concerned the application of philosophy to the exigencies of human society and progress, I was her pupil, alike in boldness of speculation and cautiousness of practical judgment. . . . Her mind invested all ideas in a concrete shape and formed to itself a conception of how they would actually work and her knowledge of the existing feelings and conduct of mankind was so seldom at fault that the weak point in any unworkable suggestion seldom escaped her.
>
> (p. 149)

Thus Mill tried to answer the evolutionists' "scientific" approach to the problems of gender by pointing not only to Harriet's clear judgment, her loftiness of thought, but also to her common sense.

While Mill attempted to refute the contemporary scientific diminishment of women, we must not forget that he lived in the hey-day of Romanticism. Romantics, from Wordsworth in the 1790s to Ruskin in the 1860s, turned to nature as a catalyst for their emotions, generally linking women with nature as the twin founts of beauty and rapture. This Romantic sensibility is present in Mill's *Autobiography,* not only in the sections dealing with Harriet but in those that trace his intellectual development from its origins in the eighteenth-century rationalism of the Benthamite school.

Romanticism affected Mill's style in the *Autobiography,* particularly in his descriptions of Harriet. He was profoundly influenced by Wordsworth, who is presented in the *Autobiography* as Mill's psychic savior when Mill found himself in a deep depression at the age of twenty-two (pp. 88-90). Wordsworth's poems extolling nature and the primacy of the senses[17] spoke directly to the emotionally starved "reasoning machine" Mill claimed he had become (p. 66). In the *Autobiography,* Mill further tells us how continental influences—French and German nineteenth-century reaction against eighteenth-century rationalism—were "streaming in upon" him (p. 97). He was nothing if not well read, having mastered French, at fourteen when he lived for a year in the south of France (pp. 36-39), and German at the age of nineteen (p. 72). Both Rousseau[18] and Goethe,[19] whose work he knew well, expected women to be tender, loving and morally inspiring, and above all "eternally feminine" helpmeets to men. The French positivist, Auguste Comte, with whom Mill conducted a philosophical correspondence for five years, claimed that "the new doctrine [Comte's vision of a secular religion of humanity] will institute the worship of Woman. . . . Man will kneel to Woman and Woman alone."[20]

How does Mill's description of Harriet compare with this Romantic vision? Mill's extravagances on Harriet's behalf are of a piece with other romantic descriptions of womanhood. But in the *Autobiography* he emphasized—in keeping with his intention to focus on his own mental development—both his belief in women's intellectual equality with men and his androgynous theory of gender. He therefore concentrated on Harriet's intellectual performance and how it meshed with his own. Like other Romantics, he subscribed to the view that women's influence on men and children was important, but his style was quite distinct from the language of other Victorian Romantics.

On the whole, critics do not find it difficult to accept Victorian hyperbole on "woman." This is shrugged off as the "Victorian style," in keeping with Victorian religiosity and Romanticism. But Mill, the rationalist, the interpreter of utilitarianism, the author of works on political economy, must not be allowed to fall into the Romantic trap. Perhaps critics find Mill's encomiums to Harriet unacceptable because they extol her intellectual rather than her emotional contributions to his life. Mill's assertion that Harriet offered "a boundless generosity, and a lovingness ever ready to pour itself forth upon any or all human beings who were capable of giving the smallest feeling in return" (p. 113) is never commented upon or questioned by these same critics because such qualities were in keeping with the conventional view of "woman's nature."

Mill is indeed almost unique in the history of Western thought for publicly acknowledging the cooperation of a woman in his highly acclaimed philosophical publications. (We can hardly count all those prefaces "thanking the wife.") The only other that comes to mind is William Thompson, a member of the Benthamite circle, whose work was certainly known to Mill and who, when Mill was nineteen, had published a long feminist essay, which he openly attributed to his friend Anna Wheeler.[21] Even so, there is an important difference. The Thompson/Wheeler essay dealt exclusively with improving the status of women, whereas Mill attributed Harriet's joint authorship to a broader spectrum of his works—those which are ac-

knowledged as a significant contribution to the canon of economic, political and social thought. Particularly controversial is his attribution to Harriet of much of the basic thought in his popular masterpiece *On Liberty,* of which he wrote:

> The "Liberty", was more directly and literally our joint production than anything else which bears my name, for there was not a sentence of it that was not several times gone through by us together, turned over in many ways, and carefully weeded of any faults, either in thought or expression, that we detected in it. . . . The whole mode of thinking of which the book was the expression, was emphatically hers. But I also was so thoroughly imbued with it that the same thoughts naturally occurred to us both. That I was thus penetrated with it, however, I owe in a great degree to her . . . she benefitted me as much by keeping me right when I was right, as by leading me to new truths and ridding me of errors.
>
> (p. 148)

It is instructive to compare Mill's praise of Harriet with other mid-century Romantics. For example, Coventry Patmore's panegyric on his wife in the "Angel in the House" (1854): "Her disposition is devout / her countenance angelical / The best things that the best believe / are in her face so kindly writ / The faithless, seeing her, conceive / Not only heaven, but hope of it."[22] Or Jules Michelet's description of "woman" in *La Femme* (1860): "She is your nobleness, your own, so raising you above yourself. When you return from the forge, panting, fatigued with labor, she, young and fresh pours over you her youth, brings the sacred wave of life to you and makes you a god again with a kiss."[23] Or Ruskin writing "Of Queens' Gardens" in *Sesame and Lilies* (1865): "Man is eminently the doer, the creator, the discoverer, the defender. His intellect is for speculation and invention . . . but her intellect is not for invention or creation, but for sweet ordering,. . . . She must be . . . incorruptibly good; instinctively, infallibly wise."[24]

The Romantics, here represented by Patmore, Michelet and Ruskin, invoked the divine and the sublime. Women were consequently "angels" ministering to men; however, they were hardly asexual angels in their capacity to revive diminishing male sexual prowess. Clearly these writers fuse morality and sexuality. Like Patmore, Michelet and Ruskin, Mill also thought that women's contribution to civilization was essential, but it was not women's angelic nature, eroticized or not, that would raise men to new heights. Unlike that of the three cited above, Mill's is the voice of reason; he does not confuse the mystical, the religious, and the sexual. Extravagant as his praise of Harriet might have been, he did not make of her a religious idol. "She was the source of . . . what I hope to effect . . . for human improvement."(111) Mill understood her value as a force in history. He would have agreed with Fourier, who in 1808 wrote: "the extension of women's privileges is the general principle for all social progress." And, in the same vein, Mill's own father had, in 1817, called "the condition of women . . . one of the most decisive criterions of the stage of society at which [a nation has] arrived."[25] Echoing both Fourier's and his father's view of women as a barometer of historical progress, he wrote in 1868:

I am profoundly convinced that the moral and intellectual progress of the male sex runs a great risk of stopping, if not receding, as long as that of the women remains behind, and that, not only because nothing can replace the mother for the education of the child, but also, because the influence upon man himself of the character and ideas of the companion of his life cannot be insignificant; women must either push him forward or hold him back.[26]

There was, moreover, a fundamental difference between Mill and the rest of the Victorian Romantics. They believed womanly qualities to be innate; Mill, like his eighteenth-century British precursors Catharine Macaulay-Graham and Mary Wollstonecraft, understood that these qualities were conditioned.[27] As he claimed in *The Subjection of Women*:

any of the mental differences supposed to exist between women and men are but the natural effect of the differences in their education and circumstances, and indicate no radical difference, far less radical inferiority, of nature.[28]

Harriet reminded him of Shelley in that her "protests against many things that are still the established constitution of society," resulted, he believed, "not from hard intellect but from noble and elevated feeling"; yet that did not prevent her, as it had not prevented Shelley, from "piercing to the very heart and marrow of the matter . . . the essential idea or principle." (p. 112)

His editor Stillinger felt we must "cringe" at Mill's exaggerated praise of Harriet, but what Stillinger objects to so strongly is exclusively the praise of Harriet's intellect. In this, Mill stands out in contrast to practically all other male authors of his time writing about their own close female connections, or about women in general. To object to Mill's language is to read the book without placing it into the context of mid nineteenth-century male rhetoric on women. I suggest that he occasionally adopted the romantic rhetoric of his day in his description of Harriet—but applied it to the one feature of existence that he most wanted to elucidate in his autobiography: the human mind.

Unlike other major male figures writing at mid-century, however, Mill did not look for opposite poles or complementarity in male and female qualities. In his pathbreaking parliamentary speech advocating woman's suffrage in 1867, Mill put this very succinctly:

Under the idle notion that the beauties of character of the two sexes are mutually incompatible, men are afraid of manly women; but those who have considered the nature and power of social influences well know, that unless there are manly women, there will not much longer be manly men . . . the two sexes must now rise or sink together.[29]

As early as 1833 he had expressed his view of androgyny with great clarity in a letter to Carlyle:

The women, of all I have known, who possessed the highest measure of what are considered feminine qualities, have combined with them more of the highest masculine qualities than I have ever seen in any but one or two men. . . . I suspect it is the second-rate people of the two sexes that are unlike—the first-rate are alike in both . . . but then, in this respect, my position has been and is . . . "a peculiar one."[30]

What Mill considered "peculiar" here has been the ideal for many feminists throughout the nineteenth and twentieth centuries. But what did he understand by "feminine" and "masculine" qualities? I believe he associated tenderness, sympathy, and the expression of feelings, but not passivity, with the feminine; and intellectual rigor with the masculine. Harriet combined both. Throughout the *Autobiography* Mill demonstrated vividly how well Harriet integrated qualities that he considered feminine and masculine in her own person—but what about himself? What of the "feminine" in Mill? The phrase "the first rate are alike in both" is highly significant for appreciating Mill's own striving towards the "first rate," the combination of masculine and feminine as he understood it, in his own character.

Having missed love and tenderness in his childhood and youth, Mill craved and admired those qualities he believed to be feminine—sensitivity and emotional warmth. He deeply resented his father's denigration of passionate emotions (p. 31) and his father's objection to his own tendency to daydream, which the elder Mill called "inattention" (p. 24). He described in lyric terms the grounds of Ford Abbey in Devon, where he spent several years during his early adolescence as "riant and secluded, umbrageous, and full of the sound of falling waters," surroundings that he deemed to be producing "a larger and freer existence and a sort of poetic cultivation" (pp. 35-36). Retrospectively he understood the crisis of despair that he had suffered in his early twenties as caused largely by a lack of familial love and tenderness, and consequently his own inability *to* love. "If I had loved anyone sufficiently . . . I should not have been in the condition I was" (p. 81). He pulled himself out of the crisis when he began to appreciate "states of feeling" and, even more important, the fact that "thought [could be] coloured by feeling" (p. 89). He asserted that "The cultivation of feelings, became one of the cardinal points of my ethical and philosophical creed" (p. 86).

It is profoundly moving to find this man, this reasoning machine, as he called himself, struggling to nurture the growth of emotions and susceptibilities he viewed as feminine. Most importantly, his life-long commitment to justice became infused with fervent emotion. Unlike women in general (according to the received wisdom of his age), he had to *learn* to feel and to express emotion. In this endeavor, first poetry and later Harriet were undeniably his teachers.

In examining the "feminization" of John Stuart Mill, I have used the concept of the "feminine" as Mill himself conceived of it. Since Mill's writing and political activity suffused the thinking about women of his time, and even subsequently, his ideas are a part of the development of progressive thought. His "self-feminization" derived from a conscious attempt to incorporate qualities that he valued. The current discourse on "femininity" and "masculinity," while far more complex, attempts to validate these same qualities and to make them prevalent in the whole society. Our late twentieth-century debate has invented dramatically new "feminine" roles for men as infant caretakers, "house-husbands," and nurses. Men are encouraged as never before to express their tender emotions; it is now almost permissible for enlightened men to weep. Mill, then, was not only a man of his time, but a man ahead of his time, not merely politically, as we have long known, but also socially and psychologically.

Notes

1. All references in parentheses are to John Stuart Mill, *Autobiography,* edited with an introduction and notes by Jack Stillinger (Boston, MA: Houghton Mifflin, 1969).

2. H. O. Pappe, *John Stuart Mill and the Harriet Taylor Myth* (London and New York: Cambridge University Press, 1960).

3. See for example, Bruce Mazlish, *James and John Stuart Mill, Father and Son in the Nineteenth Century* (New York, NY: Basic, 1975), pp. 284-288. (A new edition exists with a New Introduction: New Brunswick, NJ: Transaction Publishers, 1988.)

4. A. O. J. Cockshut, *The Art of Autobiography in 19th and 20th Century England* (New Haven, CT: Yale University Press, 1984), p. 9.

5. Jack Stillinger, ed., *The Early Draft of John Stuart Mill's "Autobiography"* (Urbana, IL: University of Illinois Press, 1961), p. 66.

6. Ibid., p. 184.

7. F. A. Hayek, *John Stuart Mill and Harriet Taylor: Their Correspondence and Subsequent Marriage* (Chicago, IL: University of Chicago Press, 1951).

8. Bruce Mazlish, *James and John Stuart Mill, passim.*

9. Hayek, pp. 32, 33.

10. Ibid., pp. 190, 194, 196.

11. Stillinger, *The Early Draft,* p. 171.

12. Leonore Davidoff and Catherine Hall, *Family Fortunes: Men and Women of the English Middle Class 1780-1850* (Chicago, IL: University of Chicago Press, 1987).

13. Sir Henry Maine and Johann Bachofen, Documents 101 and 102 in Susan Groag Bell and Karen Offen, eds., *Women, the Family and Freedom, The Debate in Documents 1750-1950,* 2 Vols. (Stanford, CA: Stanford University Press, 1983), Vol. 1.

14. Paul Broca, "Sur le volume et la forme du cerveau suivant les individus et suivant les races," *Bulletin Société d'Anthropologie,* Paris 2: (1861) p. 153.

15. Karl Christoph Vogt, *Lectures on Man, His Place in Creation and in the History of the Earth,* Anthropological Society of London, 1864, p. 183 f.

16. See, for example, Bell and Offen, Vol. 1, Document 105 *The Subjection of Women* (1869). Also Document 135 the *Speech* in the House of Commons (1867), and Mill's correspondence with Auguste Comte, in L. Lévy-Bruhl, *Lettres inédites de John Stuart Mill à Auguste Comte* (Paris: Felix Alcan, 1899).

17. For example, William Wordsworth, "Tintern Abbey, 1798" in *Selected Poetry* (New York, NY: The Modern Library, 1950), p. 106.

18. Bell and Offen, Vol. 1, Doc. 10, pp. 43-49, Rousseau from *Émile*: "It is impossible for a woman who permits herself to be morally compromised ever to be considered virtuous . . . on the care of women depends the early education of men; and on women again, depend their mores, their passions, their tastes, their pleasures, and even their happiness."

19. Ibid., Doc. 28, p. 115 (Goethe from *Wilhelm Meister*).

20. Ibid., Doc. 63, pp. 226, Auguste Comte; and see also: Ibid., Doc. 43, p. 166 Louis Aimé-Martin: "On the maternal bosom the mind of nations reposes; their manners, prejudices, and virtues—in a word the civilization of the human race all depend upon maternal influence;" and p. 170, Joseph de Maistre: "Woman can accomplish anything by working through man's heart."

21. Ibid., Doc. 32, pp. 120-130 (Thompson/Wheeler).

22. Erna Hellerstein, Leslie Hume, and Karen M. Offen, eds., *Victorian Women, A Documentary Account of Women's Lives in Nineteenth-Century England, France and the United States* (Stanford, CA: Stanford University Press, 1981), p. 135.

23. Bell and Offen, Vol. 1, Doc. 97, p. 342 (Michelet, "Woman").

24. Ibid., Doc. 104, p. 389. (Ruskin, "Queens' Gardens").

25. Charles Fourier, *Théorie des quatre mouvements et des destinées générales* 3rd ed. (1841-1848). Originally published in 1808. Tr. Karen Offen in Bell and Offen, Vol. 1, Doc. 9, p. 41. James Mill, *The History of British India,* 2nd ed. (London: Baldwin, Craddock and Joy, 1820) p. 293, originally published 1817.

26. Cited in Mazlish, p. 329 from a letter to a Russian correspondent in 1868, from the Mill Taylor Collection 45/85; and see Bell and Offen, Vol. 1, Doc. 135,

pp. 482-88 (Mill's speech from the debate in the House of Commons, 1867).

27. Bell and Offen, Vol. 1, Doc. 11, p. 53 (Catharine Macaulay), and Doc. 12, pp. 57, 59 (Mary Wollstonecraft).

28. *The Subjection of Women,* reprinted in Alice Rossi, ed., *John Stuart Mill and Harriet Taylor Mill, Essays in Sex Equality* (Chicago, IL and London: University of Chicago Press, 1970), p. 185.

29. Bell and Offen, Vol. 1, Doc. 135, pp. 485-486 (Mill's speech to the Commons).

30. Francis E. Mineka, ed., *The Earlier Letters of John Stuart Mill, 1812-1848* (Toronto: University of Toronto Press, 1962), p. 184. (This letter was written three years after falling in love with Harriet Taylor, when Mill was twenty-seven years old.)

Leah D. Hackleman (essay date 1992)

SOURCE: "Suppressed Speech: The Language of Emotion in Harriet Taylor's *The Enfranchisement of Women,*" in *Women's Studies,* Vol. 20, No. 3-4, 1992, pp. 273-86.

[*In the following essay, Hackleman explores the impact that Harriet Taylor's "Enfranchisement of Women" had on the feminist movement.*]

> Suppressed speech gathers into a storm . . .
>
> Eliza Sharples, 1832

Histories of the early English feminist movement often locate its beginning in the middle nineteenth century with the rise of women's reform societies and trace its development to the suffrage movement of the early twentieth century. One textbook claims that "the feminist movement in England truly began in the 1850s"[1] with concerns about women's education, employment and legal status emanating from the ranks of upper middle class women. This was the time in which the Woman Question was drawing the greatest number of respondents from a multiplicity of political positions. Carol Bauer and Laurence Ritt argue in another sourcebook of nineteenth century feminist documents that "it was not a coincidence that the feminist movement arose in the late 1850's and 60's" in the wake of a surplus female population and the rise of leisured middle-class women.[2] In both instances, the writings of earlier, radical feminists are acknowledged but located solely in other social movements like the Chartist or socialist groups. While this strategy can certainly be justified, it allows only the later reformists to be categorized as part of a feminist movement.[3] To limit a discussion of women's agitation on behalf of women to the latter half of the nineteenth century is to promote a feminist movement that is homogenized and reduced to its most nonthreatening aspects.

Janice Doane and Devon Hodges argue that the need to display only one strain of the women's movement as its sum and entirety arises out of *nostalgia,* which contains the desire for fixity.[4] A polyvocal and contradictory cacophony of feminism*s* is more threatening because it becomes too varied to be contained. Feminist critics and historians can unintentionally collaborate in this nostalgia by not allowing other voices to problematize any tidy conclusions. Thus the totality of nineteenth century feminism seems to be the more conservative, reform-minded agitation of the latter half of the century.[5] The general aims of the movement were to secure legal rights for women, such as the vote and various property laws, as well as to remove major obstacles to individual emancipation. Education was a primary concern, as was the opening of the professions to middle class women.[6] Because it was an upper middle class movement, born of the ideas of the Enlightenment, the emphasis lay upon the expression of individual rights, rather than the entire restructuring—"leveling"—of English society. The women leading this movement wanted to be equal to the men of their class. For historians to present these kinds of views as the only ones within the entire century is easy because these were the ones published and debated as well as the ones drawing the most support among women. What often gets lost is any of the quieter, and more threatening, dissenting voices of the earlier parts of the century. Promoting, say, John Stuart Mill's *The Subjection of Women* as the single most important (i.e., canonized) text of the feminist movement[7] suppresses the discourse not only of the more conservative women but also the more radical.

The literary canon of the nineteenth century movement is outlined by various historians; for example the authors of *Free and Ennobled,* a textbook of source readings, write, "Three books which can properly be called classical statements of the feminist position are Mary Wollstonecraft's *Vindication of the Rights of Woman* (1792); William Thompson, *Appeal of One Half the Human Race, Women, Against the Pretensions of the Other Half, Men* (1825); John Stuart Mill, *The Subjection of Woman* (1867)" (298). The inclusion of Thompson's book here is striking because most accounts of feminist texts leap from Wollstonecraft to Mill, leaving a gap of over half a century, as though Mill's ideas were simply a natural progression of Wollstonecraft's work. In fact, Thompson comes much closer to being an ideological descendant of Wollstonecraft; in the *Appeal* he constructs a socialist feminist position based on the principles of Robert Owen and calls for a radical restructuring of society to achieve the goal of freedom for all (B. Taylor 27). Mill's text, on the other hand, argues that if women are placed in civil equality and allowed unrestricted access to the same opportunities, then ability and enterprise will determine individual success. His *laissez-faire* approach is indicative of the women's movement of his time in its promotion of individual success and cultural reform rather than a rethinking of society that would call class privilege and the patriarchal family unit into question. When authors of textbooks like *Free and Ennobled* call three such strikingly dissimilar works "statements of *the* feminist position," they disregard the historical contingency of any feminism and ignore the distinct changes in the political location and the argument of such cannonized texts (emphasis mine).

Even in otherwise remarkably insightful studies, nineteenth century feminism is relegated to the latter half of the century. For example, Denise Riley's *"Am I That Name?" Feminism and the Category of "Women" in History* puzzles out the connections between "women," "human" and "the social" in the nineteenth century, arguing that the "social" sphere becomes an extension of the domestic sphere of the eighteenth century and thus a place for women to become actors or agents in, and objects of, reform movements.[8] Because of denoting a "proper field on which female good could be exercised," "women" could be collectively defined (Riley 55). The establishment of the "social" was at the cost of displacing the "political," but Riley argues that it did serve effectively to define a sociological group—women—which could go on to demand collective political gains: "The new senses of 'women' allowed their candidacy for humanity new assault routes upon it. The older democratic appeal for equality, based on the idea of 'rights,' had cut less ice: it remained to be seen how successful the newer appeals might prove" (55). Riley demonstrates how the eighteenth century notions of a "naturalized femininity" were taken on in the next century "to be wielded as weapons of women's elevation," but Riley moves from a discussion of Madame de Staël to John Stuart Mill, Harriet Taylor and Harriet Martineau with no mention of the struggles or texts of the Owenite feminists (46). Not only does her text thus miss locating a crucial point in the history of feminist agitation but also loses an important substantiation for its argument and purpose. The documents of the Owenite feminists should be examined for their own participation in the ongoing definition of "women" during a particular historical moment.

The Owenite feminists of the 1830s and 40s argued that marriage was but another form of private property which would disappear with the establishment of egalitarian co-operative communities. Women like Anna Wheeler, Emma Martin, and Fanny Wright lectured on the intersection of gender and economic oppression, the abolition of religion, the social construction of character, and the need for a socialist revolution. Because of the Owenite insistence on the social construction of character, women were able to assert that women's apparent weaknesses were the result of "external influences" (B. Taylor 24; 30-31). At the same time, however, women were given an exalted role in the creation of the new society because they were the holders of a morality which would elevate the new world (Riley 47-48). A peculiar stance was taken in which women's "bad" characteristics were conditioned, but their "good" qualities were natural or innate. Thus the arguments revolved around the theory posited by Owenite feminist Catherine Barmby: "Woman and man are two in variety and one in equality" (B. Taylor 289).

This position—"different but equal"—had several political effects. The valuation of women increased because of their special (gendered) functions in creating the moral utopia, but the feminine qualities which generated these functions showed that woman were entirely "sexed," and thus always different from men. An outcome of this contradiction was that "women" became a group, based on the commonalities of innate femaleness, and became capable of collective demands.[9] For example, in 1843 Catherine Barmby identified one method of effecting change to be the "formation of a 'woman's society' in every city, town, and village possible" where women could "prepare each other for the mission of the apostle" (B. Taylor 392). Socialist feminists could then argue that women's oppression as women cuts across economics distinctions, thus calling the Owenite theories of economic revolution into question even as they used socialist rhetoric:

> To exemplify the state and position of the women of all classes, the men of the working class will serve me, as the men of the upper and wealthiest class are opposed to their progression, to their obtaining a knowledge of their injuries, and a desire for the redression of them, so are the men in all conditions whatever, equally as strongly influenced in crushing every thought, and every hope that may spring from it, of amelioration and good in the heart of woman; any expression of her wrongs, or any question as to their amendment.
>
> (Barmby, quoted in B. Taylor 390)

Barmby also, for example, widens the definition of revolutionary change by not only pinpointing women's economic and political situations but also their position in religion, the modes of dress and behavior, and acceptance into the "universal": "the *complete emancipation* of woman" (B. Taylor 391). Thus while the Owenite women define the functions and characters of women they also stress the need for complete, revolutionary change in all aspects of existence.

Barbara Taylor has pointed out that the changeover from revolutionary ideology to reformist practice occurred during the early 1850s (276, 278): "In place of the Owenite dream of a communal egalitarian utopia there arose a sustained, pragmatic strategy for the piecemeal reform of women's social and economic condition" (279). Though it is impossible to deduce a specific reason for this change, if indeed there is one, the outer limits of this historical and political spectrum are marked on one side by the radical Owenite feminists and on the other by the reformist Victorian feminists. Approximately in the middle stands Harriet Taylor's 1851 essay, **"The Enfranchisement of Women."** Containing an "interesting blend of standard liberal philosophy and quasi-Owenite sentiments" (B. Taylor 278) **"The Enfranchisement of Women"** can be considered, along with the Owenite writings and later feminist works, a key text in the history of feminism, since it came at a time when a dramatic shift in the political position and ideology of feminism occurred: feminism gradually undid its ties with utopian socialism and radical movements like the Chartists. Though this shift cannot be explained historically by examining Taylor's work, its role in the development of feminist strategy is important. Within her text lies the process of a rapid ideological change; it both relies on the past utopian feminist dreams and the new reformist agenda.

In "Dilemmas of Difference: Feminism, Modernity, and Postmodernism," Christine Di Stefano identifies a rationalist position as one which "takes the Englightenment view of rationality and humanism at its word and as its starting point. On this view, common respect is due to all people because they are rational."[10] Di Stefano astutely sees rationalist rhetoric as the negation of difference, in which all people are collapsed into a supposedly gender-neutral human, the "(masculine) figure of the Everyman" (Di Stefano 77). She goes on to assert that one political counterpart to this rhetorical position is liberalism—for feminists, a commitment "to equality and the elimination of gender differences" (72)—and notes that this is John Stuart Mill's strategy in *The Subjection of Women* (79 n. 3). But anti-rationalism, as a strategy,

> comes face to face with the denigration of feminized nature within rationalism and attempts to revalorize the feminine in light of this denigration. . . . Anti-rationalism celebrates the designated and feminized irrational, invoking a strong notion of difference against the genderneutral pretensions of a rationalist culture that opposes itself to nature, the body, natural contingency, and intuition.
>
> (67)

Anti-rationalism, then, becomes the valorization of gender differences in this type of feminist argument. In the early socialist writings, for instance, "'women' . . . functioned as an anti-positivist spiritual category" (Riley 47); this tendency is especially clear in Barmby's "The Demand for the Emancipation of Woman, Politically and Socially" which appeared in the Owenite *New Tracts for the Times* in 1843 (reprinted in B. Taylor 386-392). Against the threat of the elimination of gender differences, Barmby wages the battle:

> But although we would equalize, we would not identify the sexes. Such identification would be unnatural, unbeautiful, and accordant with the miserable state of the sexes among the lowest of orders. . . . In woman, sentiment; in man, intellect, variously prevail. . . .
>
> (B. Taylor 391)

Her valorization of difference also forces a confrontation with the rationalist position itself. A society based simply on reason is one to be avoided because it leaves out important feminine values: "Society should equally provide, through its institutions, that the sentiment of the woman should be strengthened by intellect, and the intellect of the man refined by sentiment" (Barmby in B. Taylor 391). The appeal to a vision of an integrated society gives a woman—and the anti-rational—a unique place in the new order. Thus Barmby's text allies the irrational with the feminine while it allies both with the revolutionary impulse to create the world anew.

"The Enfranchisement of Women," on the other hand, appears to collude entirely with rationalist arguments for change. But I would argue that in its appeals to liberal individualism, Taylor's text consciously suppresses the discourse of anti-rationalism, the language of emotion, for its political goals. Her text thus displays what Jane Tompkins calls "cultural work," "expressing and shaping the social context that produced [it]."[11] The gaps and collisions in Taylor's text, caused by its overt suppression of the irrational, expresses the uneasiness of a surrounding feminist context. But the suppression cannot be complete, because the text writes in revolutionary goals that it borrows from the earlier utopian visions. As Judith Newton and Deborah Rosenfelt argue, "The discourse suppressed tells as much as the discourse expressed, for omission throws the margins of the text's production into relief, allowing us to see the limits and the boundaries of what it posits as the real."[12] In my reading of Taylor's essay, I show that the manipulation of the discourse of rationality suppresses the language of irrationality or emotion—which then intrudes into the text at various points. With this reading, **"The Enfranchisement of Women"** becomes an historical phenomenon, mapping the changing ideological stance of feminism in the nineteenth century.

In Harriet Taylor's text, rationality is the prevailing argumentative mode: "A reason must be given why anything should be permitted to one person and interdicted to another."[13] The force of her words is directed towards those to be persuaded by appeals to their reasonableness and justice. Through this tactic, Taylor inscribes her belief that the rational mind is the place where learning and change begin. The text sets up arguments against women's emancipation that are based on prejudices or "custom" (a socialized prejudice), both of which are irrational forces; the **"Enfranchisement"** challenges and defeats these kinds of opposition but also ultimately cuts through their logical fallacies to the basic question, "whether it is right and expedient that one-half the human race should pass through life in a state of forced subordination to the other half" (23). The obviousness of the answer is a key to Taylor's rhetorical strategy. Taylor's setting herself on the side of reason relegates all arguments against women's emancipation to the realm of the irrational.

By setting up this opposition, Taylor also places her cause on the side of historical progression. If the rational mind is the one capable of learning and change, then it is also the impetus for human progress. Progression and rationality are allied to make any contradiction to her arguments seem old-fashioned or conservative as well as irrational: "For the interest, therefore, not only of women but of men, and of human improvement in the widest sense, the emancipation of women cannot stop where it is" (37). Taylor understands the freedom of women to be part of the general progress of the country coming during the nineteenth century, when "all things now tend to substitute, as the general principle of human relations, a just equality, instead of the dominion of the strongest" (13). In this "age of changes like the present," human beings are reaching their full potential as rational creatures, capable of understanding and acting against an anachronistic injustice (10). Her analysis of human character seems strikingly simple:

An uncustomary thought, on a subject which touches the greater interests of life, still startles when first presented; but if it can be kept before the mind until the impression of strangeness wears off, it obtains a hearing, and as rational a consideration as the intellect of the hearer is accustomed to bestow. . . .

(11)

The "startling idea" of women's emancipation will spread from individual to individual, lessening in shock value as it is rationally pondered. Progress and change are therefore posited as ultimately individual, when the listener is persuaded by the strength of the argument.

It is clear that Taylor uses the rhetoric of reason as a strategy to convince each of her readers individually. But this model of change also has consequences for the women's movement as a whole, clearly expressed by her references to the newborn American women's movement:

> [T]here are women, seemingly numerous, and now organized for action on the public mind, who demand equality . . . and demand it by a straightforward appeal to men's sense of justice, not plead for it with a timid deprecation of their displeasure.
>
> (4)

Her appreciative remarks about the American women serve to promote their demands and resolutions as political and rhetorical strategies to be emulated. In doing so, Taylor also breaks down the cultural stereotypes that equated women with emotion (especially hysteria) and men with reason and rationality. The demands of the U.S. women—and Taylor's own arguments—are both strictly rational and thus seemingly unquestionable—and they arise from women, not men. The text draws attention to this fact: "It is a political movement, practical in its objectives, carried on in a form which denotes an intention to persevere. And it is a movement not merely *for* women, but *by* them" (3). While women take on the rational arguments for this cause, Taylor sees men as the holders of irrational claims:

> Give [an average] man the idea that he is first in law and in opinion—that to will is his part, and hers to submit; it is absurd to suppose that this idea merely glides over his mind, without sinking into it, or having any effect on his feelings and practice.
>
> (33)

She is careful not to attribute any specific emotional reactions entirely to men or women as a "natural" function linked to biology, but as culturally conditioned responses to given situations. This allows her to make a case for the social determination of character for women, calling into question the valorization of "feminine" qualities: "[N]o inferior caste that we have heard of have [sic] been taught to regard their degradation as their honor" (38). It is the learned characteristics associated with womanhood which may, in Taylor's view, be detrimental to the movement:

> The strength of the cause lies in the support of those who are influenced by reason and principle; and to at-

tempt to recommend it by sentimentalities, absurd in reason, and inconsistent with the principle on which the movement is founded, is to place a good cause on a level with a bad one.

(42)

Here as in all her rhetoric associated with women's emancipation, Taylor posits the opposition between *reason* and *emotion,* or "nonsense" (42). Women's learned "sentimentality," when seen as a celebratory trait, is retrogressive to their emancipatory progress; appealing to these emotions in other people is likewise detrimental to the movement. If we follow her equation even further, emotion itself impedes historical progression, whether that emotion emanates from women or from men.

Taylor's rhetorical strategy can be seen as indicative of the women's movement's changing goals. Her textual pragmatism is distinctly different from the utopian idealism of the Owenite feminists, and she seems to embrace the theories of *laissez-faire* capitalism:

> Let every occupation be open to all, without favour or discouragement to any, and employment will fall into the hands of those men or women who are found by experience to be most capable of worthily exercising them.
>
> (14)

Her statements promoting reform, as I have said, rely on the devaluing of emotion, as she does not include women's desire for specific employment in her equation. Some women do work in factory jobs for less than livable wages, whether or not they want to do something else, because they do not have the skills for other employment. Her answer to this is education, and it is here that her elitism and middle class alliances are clear:

> Every improvement in [women's] education, and enlargement of their faculties, everything which renders them more qualified for any other mode of life [than marriage and motherhood], increases the number of those to whom it is an injury and an oppression to be denied the choice.
>
> (19)

Emancipation is again isolated and localized; rather than all women gaining liberty, it is reserved for the special few (to whom it *is* an affront to oppress). Though Taylor's text predates the outpouring of middle class feminist writings, it shares with them the biases of their class. But although **"The Enfranchisement of Women"** manipulates the language of reason and reform, it also poses a contradictory impulse towards utopianism. Not only does Taylor harshly criticize the impulses of "the moderate reformers" who would "maintain the old bad principles, mitigating their consequences" (29), she targets the suppositions of many feminists who "weakly attempt to combine nominal equality between men and women, with enforced distinctions in their privileges and functions" (42). That is, the biological essentialist impulse to embrace "femininity" or difference while arguing for equality is injurious for the women's movement.

Because the text's strategy is to discount entirely a biological basis for character, it breaks with—while arising from—the arguments of Owenite feminists: Taylor's essay carries through the socialists' insistence of the social construction of character but it is willing to sacrifice the notion of a natural feminine sensibility to achieve the goal of complete equality. Taylor's rationalist strategy poses a problem, however, in her construction of "women" as a political collective. As Denise Riley has pointed out, a plea for the special nature of "women" binds them into a social group (48-51). Owenite texts valued the participation of "women" in a revolution because they contained spiritual/moral qualities essential to the formation of the new world. Harriet Taylor's text, in rejecting the antirationalist position, needs to construct "women" in other ways that would make collective action a possibility. Although in her search for the origin of the "custom" of women's inferiority she resorts to biology, she is concerned with physicality rather than biologically-derived character traits: "Until very lately, the rule of physical strength was the general law of human affairs" (12). On the surface, the text seems to define "women" collectively because of their domination by men, even comparing "women" to "slaves": both groups are constructed by their domination by others. The text briefly manipulates the discourse of natural rights: since every person is owed certain personal rights and freedoms because she is human, domination is wrong because it interferes with the exercising of these rights. But rather than merely arguing for women's inclusion into the category "human" that this discourse sets up, the **"Enfranchisement,"** as part of its rationalist stand, promotes "citizen" as the category women must be entered into.

This rhetorical strategy allows Taylor to construct "women" non-biologically, as a political category by the fact of non-citizenship. Like "slaves," women do not have access to the workings of high politics or government; if their inclusion as "human" is not a reasonable argument, citizenship may be:

> Even those who do not look upon a voice in the government as a matter of personal right, nor profess principles which require that it should be extended to all, have usually traditional maxims of political justice with which it is impossible to reconcile the exclusion of all women from the common rights of citizenship.
>
> (8)

Taylor's rationalist position allows her a more concrete location for women's entry into the political sphere, and later suffragists will pick up on the argument she mentions—taxation without representation (8)—as they petition for political reforms. "Women," then, becomes an entity because of its exclusion from "citizen." She uses another group of non-citizens to analogize the deplorable situation of women: "To foreigners the law accords the privilege of claiming that half the jury should be composed of themselves; not so to women" (9). Later, she also compares "women" to "tenants" or "labourers," who cannot act fully as citizens—to benefit the public good—because they vote to please their landlords or bosses (39).

The **"Enfranchisement"**'s most complicated argument rests on this notion of citizenship as it is pitted against the domestic: because men (citizens) are now spending more time in the company of women (non-citizens)—who have been trained in "petty subjects and interests" (29)—men are in danger of falling into "the feebleness which they have so long cultivated in their companions" (28). Taylor is careful throughout to identify women's retrogressive characteristics as a result of external cultivation rather than innate qualities, and she identifies those characteristics as a threat to the public good through male citizens:

> How rarely is the wife's influence on the side of public virtue; how rarely does it do otherwise than discourage any effort of principle by which the private interests or worldly vanities of the family can be expected to suffer. Public spirit, a sense of duty toward the public good, is of all virtues, as women are now educated and situated, the most rarely to be found among them. . . .
>
> (35)

Her insistence on the social formation of character allows her to ally the rational "public good" with another sentiment or feeling, "public spirit." Men's feelings are swayed to their families rather than to citizenship: again, what impedes progress is the irrational. The text also makes women's position as non-citizens especially dangerous for liberals:

> In England, the wife's influence is usually on the illiberal and anti-popular side: this is generally the gaining side for personal interest and vanity; and what to her is the democracy or liberalism in which she has no part—which leaves her the Pariah it found her?
>
> (36)

Thus if women continue to be non-citizens, their close association with men will halt the progress of civilization towards democracy as it is worked out in state governments. Here Taylor's text takes up earlier, Hegelian arguments about the ethical sphere of women being familial and irrational (Riley 41) but complicates the strict division of the domestic and the political using the figure of the husband, who currently inhabits both worlds. It is imperative that "women" also be allowed free access to all realms of life, to be part of the category "citizen." This rhetorical strategy paves the way for reformist arguments about education, property, and the vote; it identifies a specific route to women's emancipation while it also defines "women" rationally, without resort to biology or special natures.

Throughout Taylor's text there is an equation of reason and rationality with reformist or pragmatic political objectives. Yet the suppressed speech of her work is the language of irrationality—of emotion, desire, hope, utopia. John Stuart Mill's introduction to the 1859 reprinting of Taylor's essay points toward an understanding of the strategy behind the words. He explains that the **"Enfranchisement"** was written "to promote a cause which she had deeply at heart," using arguments "appealing only to the strictest reason" in which "the strongest arguments were necessarily omitted, as being unsuited for popular effect" (2):

> Had she lived to write out all her thoughts on this great question, she would have produced something as far transcending in profundity the present Essay, as, *had she not placed a rigid restraint on her feelings,* she would have excelled it in fervid eloquence.
>
> (2; emphasis mine)

This suggests even more clearly that Taylor structured her rhetoric with a particular effect in mind. By keeping emotions textually repressed she sought to enlist a greater amount of support, still convinced that rational minds were the ones to address. Her argumentative structure also mimics the general aim of her program of pragmatic approaches. Her suppression of a discussion of feelings within the text is also a self suppression. At one point, however, her "calmly argumentative" (2) demeanor opens to reveal her own struggle: "It requires unusual moral courage as well as a disinterestedness in a woman, to express opinions favorable to women's enfranchisement, until, at least, there is some prospect of obtaining it" (40). Not only does she write her own frustrations into the margins of the text, and with them the antifeminism around her, she also shows her text arising from an emotional basis: "moral courage." Though she believes the rational mind is where learning and change originate, she shows what Mill hints at: rational arguments can be produced by the irrational feelings, which come out of an emotional engagement with society. At the same time, she produces a contradiction in an essay which has as its guiding principle the privileging of reason over emotion, and reform over revolution.

But by writing in revolutionary goals, the **"Enfranchisement"** complicates the gulf between reform and revolution. Despite strict attention to the pragmatics of women's emancipation, Taylor's text allows the socialist utopianism to intrude, positing nothing less than the overthrow of the capitalist system:

> With respect to the future, we neither believe that . . . the division of mankind into capitalists and hired labourers mainly by demand and supply, will forever, or even much longer, be the rule of the world.
>
> (21)

This supposition distinctly separates Taylor from the later middle class feminists who simply demand an equal share of the existing system. Her plan does not view reform as the goal, believing instead in reforms in law and education as a gradual approach to the real goal of complete freedom in an egalitarian world. Though not a "pure" socialist ("so long as competition is the general law of human life, it is tyranny to shut out one half of the competitors" [21]), her plans echo the communistic notions of the Owenite feminists. She analyzes the hierarchical structure underlying capitalism and all oppression as a result of difference:

> [W]e are firmly convinced that the division of mankind into two castes, one born to rule over the other, is in this case, as in all cases, an unqualified mischief . . . [which forms] a bar, almost inseparable while it lasts, to any really vital improvement, either in the character or in the social condition of the human race.
>
> (9-10)

Though Taylor has been criticized by twentieth-century feminists for her individualistic and elitist approach to women's emancipation,[14] we can see a glimmer of Taylor's own resistance to the order of the day. Her desire for a new kind of world is strong enough to seep into her generally reformist arguments and is remarkable considering her middle class origins. By portraying this understanding of the binary oppositions which form the structure of oppression ("we" versus "they") her analysis comes much closer to a revolutionary view of women's emancipation, seeing the subordinate member (women) as not equalling the higher one (men) but usurping the structure itself.

It is here in the breakdown of the "reason/emotion" oppositional structure that the context of the women's movement is inscribed. In the change from utopian idealism to reformist pragmatism the women's movement's *strategies* had undergone a tremendous upheaval. While the Owenite feminists sought to build an alternate communal society and plotted the death of the capitalist system, the Victorian women constructed a program of practical reforms to remove the obstacles to individual women's freedom. Taylor's text is historically distinct in problematizing the gap that divides these two world views. Her program of reforms working toward an ultimate goal could provide a possible linkage between nineteenth century political polarities, which ultimately revolve around questions of strategy. Reading **"The Enfranchisement of Women"** as a document in a struggle which continues to the present moment allows us to see the shifts and alliances of the feminist political program. Though marred by its elitism and class biases, it plays an important role in mapping the strategies and solutions of nineteenth century feminism. She provides the link between liberal reformist and socialist feminist impulses, for her text aims to connect reforms with what can still be termed the *dream* of a wholly new society.

Notes

1. Patricia Hollis, *Women in Public: The Women's Movement 1850-1900* (London: George Allen and Unwin, 1979) vii.

2. *Free and Ennobled: Source Readings in the Development of Victorian Feminism* (Oxford: Pergamon, 1979) 55. Hereafter cited in text.

3. I will use the term "feminism" throughout to denote a collective effort on the part of women toward social, economic and political changes benefitting women. In one sense, I am being anachronistic because "feminism" was not used until much later; I use the term, however, to denote the forms of gendered political struggle which precede our own, to see the continuity in women's efforts for change.

4. *Nostalgia and Sexual Difference* (London: Methuen, 1987) 7.

5. Of course, it is erroneous to present even this movement as univocal, since a few women continued radical critiques of English society. These voices are important, though few.

6. Barbara Taylor, *Eve and the New Jerusalem: Feminism and Socialism in the Nineteenth Century* (London: Virago, 1983) 278. Hereafter cited in text. Taylor's important study has been indispensible to my own work.

7. For example, Kate Soper, in her introduction to Harriet Taylor and John Stuart Mill's essays, praises its "excelling quality and great intrinsic power" and notes that it has "seldom . . . been rivalled." Introduction, *The Subjection of Women* by John Stuart Mill and *The Enfranchisement of Women* by Harriet Taylor Mill (London: Virago, 1983) i.

8. Denise Riley, *"Am I That Name?" Feminism and the Category of "Women" in History* (Minneapolis: Minnesota UP, 1988). Hereafter cited in text.

9. I am indebted to Riley's work for illuminating the *varied* political consequences of such "essentialist" thinking.

10. Christine Di Stefano, "Dilemmas of Difference: Feminism, Modernity, and Post-modernism" *Feminism/Postmodernism,* ed. Linda J. Nicholson (New York: Routledge, 1990) 67. Hereafter cited in text.

11. Jane Tompkins, "'But Is It Any Good?' The Institutionalization of Literary Value," *Sensational Designs: The Cultural Work of American Fiction 1790-1860* (New York: Oxford UP, 1985) 200.

12. "Introduction: Toward a Materialist-Feminist Criticism," *Feminist Criticism and Social Change: Sex, Class, and Race in Literature and Culture,* eds. Newton and Rosenfelt (New York: Methuen, 1985) xxiii.

13. Harriet Taylor Mill, *The Enfranchisement of Women,* cited in n. 7, above. When she wrote this essay, she was Harriet Taylor, and I refer to her as such throughout my paper. All page numbers refer to this edition of the essay.

14. See Soper, xii.

Works Cited

Bauer, Carol and Lawrence Ritt. *Free and Ennobled: Source Readings in the Development of Victorian Feminism.* Oxford: Pergamon P, 1979.

Belsey, Catharine. "Constructing the Subject: Deconstructing the Text." *Feminist Criticism and Social Change: Sex, Class and Race in Literature and Culture.* Eds. Judith Newton and Deborah Rosenfelt. New York: Methuen, 1985. 45-64.

Di Stefano, Christine. "Dilemmas of Difference: Feminism, Modernity, and Postmodernism." *Feminism/ Postmodernism.* Ed. Linda J. Nicholson. New York: Routledge, 1990. 63-82.

Doane, Janice and Devon Hodges. *Nostalgia and Sexual Difference.* London: Methuen, 1987.

Hollis, Patricia. *Women in Public: The Women's Movement 1850-1900.* London: George Allen and Unwin, 1979.

Newton, Judith and Deborah Rosenfelt. "Introduction: Toward a Materialist-Feminist Criticism." In Newton and Rosenfelt, above.

Riley, Denise. *"Am I That Name?" Feminism and the Category of "Women" In History.* Minneapolis: U Minnesota P, 1988.

Soper, Kate. "New Introduction." *The Subjection of Women.* John Stuart Mill. And *The Enfranchisement of Women.* Harriet Taylor Mill. London: Virago P, 1983, i-xii.

Taylor (Mill), Harriet. "The Enfranchisement of Women." London: Virago P, 1983.

Taylor, Barbara. *Eve and the New Jerusalem: Feminism and Socialism in the Nineteenth Century.* London: Virago P, 1983.

Tompkins, Jane. "'But is it Any Good?' The Institutionalization of Literary Value." *Sensational Designs: The Cultural Work of American Fiction 1790-1860.* New York: Oxford U P, 1985. 186-201.

Linda M.-G. Zerilli (essay date 1992)

SOURCE: "Constructing 'Harriet Taylor': Another Look at J. S. Mill's *Autobiography*," in *Constructions of the Self,* edited by George Levine, Rutgers University Press, 1992, pp. 191-212.

[*In the following essay, Zerilli explores Harriet Taylor's impact on John Stuart Mill's life, including the possibility that Taylor acted as a "mother-figure" to Mill.*]

> But if I were to say in what above all she is preeminent, it is her profound knowledge of human nature. To know all its depths and elevations she had only to study herself.
>
> —*John Stuart Mill*

Readers of John Stuart Mill will recognize this passage as but another expression of his homage to Harriet Taylor, a woman of exceptional character and superior intellect. "The knowledge and contemplation of her," Mill wrote, was itself the study of humankind—a study that, for him, "so inferior in nature," involved a "long course of educa-tion."[1] Mill's timeless and genderless portrait of his wife was simultaneously a rebuke of English society, of a petty world far too "insipid" to appreciate a nature as lofty and poetic as hers: "Such a woman could not be otherwise than alone in the world," lamented Mill, "especially in a world like England," where sensibility is commonly dis-missed as "madness" ("EDRL" ["Early Draft Rejected Leaves," in *Collected Works*], 618). Thus, he wrote to Thomas Carlyle, it fell to the "man of speculation," to Mill himself, to translate the intuitive truths of the artist into the language of practical politics.[2] The innovative ideas found in his writings, Mill reiterated in his *Autobiog-raphy,* "originated" not with him but Taylor; they were "emanations from her mind" (146).

In wielding the pen that affixed his name to an extensive body of writings, then, Mill claimed that he was but a me-diator between "original thinkers" such as Taylor and oth-erwise uncomprehending English readers (*Autobiography,* 146). He noted in his diary that his self-appointed task "as the interpreter of the wisdom of one whose intellect is as much profounder as is her heart nobler" was difficult if not daunting: "I do not wish that I were so much her equal as not to be her pupil, but I would gladly be more capable than I am of thoroughly appreciating and worthily repro-ducing her admirable thoughts."[3] But if Taylor was the au-thor and Mill was her scribe, this representation of intel-lectual collaboration is itself mediated by another image of his wife as the beautiful muse, whose "influence" and "prompting" inspired Mill to write on the "great questions of feeling and life" (*Correspondence,* 199). Indeed the ambiguity if not the anxiety of authorship is evident in the following diary entry, in which we find a doubled figure of woman as both the origin and the addressee of the theo-rist's language: "Neibuhr said that he wrote only for Sav-igny: so I write only for her when I do not write entirely *from* her" (*Correspondence,* 198).

I propose to examine the question of gender identity and authorship in Mill's writings and to suggest one interpreta-tion of the highly contested representations of the Mill-Taylor intellectual relationship.[4] Rather than speculating whether Mill's superlatives paint a historically realistic picture of Harriet Taylor, I am concerned both to point out how such language works against its purported claim to establish Mill's companion as a speaking subject and an intellect in her own right and to suggest possible reasons for this paradox. Specifically, I am interested in the con-struction of the written self in Mill's work as an attempted reconfiguration of sexual identity. "Harriet Taylor," as Mill portrays her in his writings, is best understood as part of his larger effort to challenge conventional gender distinc-tions by incorporating into himself a traditionally feminine sensibility—an effort, as I have argued elsewhere, that bears directly on the politics of his feminism.[5] Indeed Tay-lor, in Mill's self-representation,[6] was the preeminent fig-ure in that distinguished community of androgynous "higher natures," in whom morality and inclination coin-cided: "If all resembled you, my lovely friend," wrote Mill

in an early essay on marriage, "it would be idle to pre-scribe rules for them."[7] Unfortunately, in Mill's view, the world was populated by the "lower natures," whose de-sires, specifically sexual desires, were an obstacle to that complementary wholeness of the sexes coveted by Ro-mantic poets and embraced by Mill in his lifelong struggle to free himself from the emotional straitjacket of his fa-ther's utilitarianism.

The problem of signature and gender, however, which goes far beyond the documented disbelief with which read-ers have responded to presumably exaggerated accounts of Taylor's contribution, character, and intellect, cannot be addressed meaningfully without some attention to the haunting figure of Mill's mother, née Harriet Burrows. Al-though mention of Mrs. James Mill is missing entirely from her son's *Autobiography,* as Christine Di Stephano has written, she looms large by virtue of the "sheer excess of her absence."[8] And it is to the absent mother that "the Life" is addressed.[9] "Harriet Taylor," the central figure on the Millian narrative landscape, bears more resemblance to the maternal figure than the Christian name which they share: as a core trope in Mill's writings, Taylor is one of many substitutes for the maternal desire that his prose both evokes and manages. Notwithstanding Mill's insis-tence that his work but "fixed in writing" Taylor's unique voice, his tributes to her, I will argue, work to return her to the position of the lost maternal object, that is, to "the feminine" in language.

The mother's absence in Mill's exalted portrait of his fa-ther and of Taylor has special significance for Mill's mul-tiple self-representations as dutiful son, as political cham-pion of women, and as an androgynous "higher nature"— "Harriet Taylor Mill." Mill's explicit claim to androgyny needs to be read through its far more disturbing subtext of rememoration—a symbolic reworking of the past that cre-ates the possibility of authorship by allowing Mill to be both son and father, father and mother, male and female at once.[10] "Harriet Taylor," in short, is a self-constituting trope in Mill's written self; a trope deployed in Mill's ef-fort to master his own genealogy: both his personal gene-alogy as a son born into a nineteenth-century family orga-nized around patriarchal authority, and his intellectual genealogy as a political theorist educated according to the principles of utilitarianism.

HIS CONSTRUCTION OF THEIR UNION

"When two persons have their thoughts and speculations completely in common," wrote Mill in the *Autobiography,* "it is of little consequence in respect to the question of originality which of them holds the pen" (145). Had Mill lived a hundred years longer, he might have been sur-prised to discover just what a difference it made that he held the pen. But if Harriet Taylor has been blamed for everything that Mill's readers find inconsistent or undesir-able in his writings—ranging from his "naive socialism" to his "excessive liberalism"—the problem of distinguish-ing her contribution from that of the acknowledged author must, at least in part, be blamed on Mill himself. For if Mill was obsessed with giving Taylor her due in his writings, his tributes to her function instead fused two distinct identities into one; merged Mill into Taylor and Taylor into Mill such that later generations of readers would have difficulty in disentangling them, and, consequently, those who were hostile to the figure of "Taylor" would have little trouble in dismissing her contribution entirely.

One example of this blurring of identities is suggested by Mill's own problematic relationship to his wife's historical past. In a letter to an American feminist, Pauline Wright Davis, Mill, as F. A. Hayek writes, "emphatically denied that a proper memoir of his wife could be written":

> Were it possible in a memoir to have the formation and growth of a mind like hers portrayed, to do so would be as valuable a benefit to mankind as was ever conferred by a biography. But such a psychological history is seldom possible, and in her case the materials for it do not exist. All that could be furnished is her birth-place, parentage, and a few dates, and it seems to me that her memory is more honoured by the absence of any attempt at a biographical notice than by the presence of a most meager one. What she was, I have attempted, though most inadequately, to delineate in the remarks prefaced to her essay, as reprinted with my *Dissertations and Discussions*.[11]

Harriet Taylor Mill died at the age of fifty-one. That Mill, who knew her intimately for a period of twenty-eight years, could not provide Davis with any more biographical information than her "birth-place, parentage, and a few dates" casts more doubt on his willingness to disclose such knowledge than it convinces us of his own ignorance of Taylor's past. The gesture, however, was not unusual: Mill was notoriously secretive about his relationship with Taylor and was quick to disown those friends whom he suspected of spreading rumors about the impropriety of their long friendship before the death of Taylor's husband in July 1849 and their subsequent marriage in April 1851. Not surprisingly, then, George Makepeace Towle, who in 1869 had requested materials for a biography of Mill, received a response similar to the one sent to Davis: once again, all that could be provided were a "few dates."[12] Hence Mill's unwillingness to cooperate with the American feminist might be read as nothing more than an extension of the veil of confidentiality that has frustrated scholars in search of the "truth" of that self-proclaimed *Seelenfreundschaft*.

This reading of Mill's reply to Davis, however, begs the question of the veil itself. What, we might ask, is being concealed by the claim to ignorance? Students of Mill need not be reminded of the speculative literature that has vigorously pursued precisely this question. Perhaps the metaphor of the veil is itself misleading; for it suggests that the scholar, through persistence and close study of archival materials, might someday lift the shroud of secrecy that envelops the Mill-Taylor relationship, thereby revealing its historical "truth." This approach, however, under-

taken by those who are eager either to prove or, more often, to disprove the validity of Mill's account of his wife, founders on the problem of representation: in this case, the uncritical assumption that Mill's *Autobiography* and his personal correspondence offer the reader access to a life unmediated by language. Further, when the written is assumed to be the writing self, it matters not whether one reads Mill's words skeptically or literally; for the effect is to reduce the constitutive act of writing to a debate polarized around two possible meanings: deception or description. I suggest that if we think about the letter to Davis less as a poly intended to hide the "facts" of Taylor's past from a voyeuristic community of readers and more as a constructive strategy deployed (consciously and unconsciously) in the larger project of self-invention, Mill's curious reply to Davis is not so much a biographical ruse as it is a mode of self-presentation.

Whatever the "truth" of Mill's intentions in keeping "Taylor," and, by extension, himself, from her would-be biographers, his response to Davis is telling in yet another way that relates to the issues of writing the self noted above. For in the absence of an independent biography, we are left with Mill's personal account: a sketch of a life in which Harriet Taylor's "history" begins with her "introduction" to Mill in 1830, when he "was in his twenty-fifth and she in her twenty-third year":

> It is not to be supposed that she was, or that anyone, at the age at which I first saw her, could be all that she afterwards became. . . . Up to the time when I first saw her, her rich and powerful nature had chiefly unfolded itself according to the received type of feminine genius. . . . Married at a very early age, to a most upright, brave, and honourable man, of liberal opinions and good education, but without the intellectual or artistic tastes which would have made him a companion for her . . . ; shut out by the social disabilities of women from any adequate exercise of her highest faculties in action of the world without; her life was one of inward meditation, varied by familial intercourse with a small circle of friends, of whom only one (long since deceased) was a person of genius, or of capacities of feeling or intellect kindred with her own.
>
> (*Autobiography*, 111-112)

The movement of this passage, which locates Mill first as an outsider and then quickly establishes him as privileged soul mate, perfunctorily acknowledges Taylor's social position as the wife of another (honourable) man only to separate her through a kind of intellectual divorce. Similarly, in portraying her as the friend of dear but mentally inferior (or deceased) persons, the enigmatic figure of Taylor before 1830 is recuperated through language as a product of Mill's own life trajectory. As if she were a sleeping princess waiting to be awakened by a man of similar feeling and intellect, Taylor is introduced to the reader as part of the theorist's second birth: a reinvention of self, as will shortly become apparent, that released Mill from the prison of his ratiocinative utilitarian education.

"To be admitted into any degree of mental intercourse with a being of these qualities," Mill tells the reader, "could not but have a most beneficial influence on my development" (113). Still, it took many years "before her mental progress and mine went forward in the complete companionship they at last attained" (113). Of course, he adds, the benefit he gained from the friendship "was far greater" (113) than any that he could give her. Nevertheless, Mill qualifies, since he and Taylor developed their opinions in different ways—she through "moral intuition" and "strong feeling" and he through "study and reasoning" (113)—it is not unjust to note that in "the rapidity of her intellectual growth, her mental activity, which converted everything into knowledge, doubtless drew from me, as it did from other sources, many of its materials" (113).

In many ways, of course, the description of Taylor's emergence as a thinker in the *Autobiography* is classic Mill. The story of his education, as is often noted, carries traces of self-deprecation that suggest that the writing is not even worth the ink spilled over the selective recollections of "so uneventful a life": "I do not for a moment imagine that any part of what I have to relate can be interesting to the public as a narrative, or as being connected with myself" (3), Mill writes in his first sentences. Instead, we are told from the start, the subject at hand is not John Stuart Mill the person but John Stuart Mill the pupil: "I have thought that in an age in which education, and its improvement, are the subject of . . . study, it may be useful that there should be some record of an education which was unusual and remarkable" (3).[13] Likewise, the author, who makes no claim to originality, proposes merely to record the "debts" his "intellectual and moral development owes to other persons" (3). Some of these individuals are well known, for example, Jeremy Bentham; some are less known than they ought to be; "and the one to whom most of all is due," as it turns out, is the "one whom the world had no opportunity of knowing" (3).

The *Autobiography,* then, proposes to present this "one" to society at large—a society whose patriarchal conventions have rendered her, like all women, invisible as subjects and authors in their own right. The decision to describe "what I owe to you *intellectually,*" Mill wrote to Taylor in 1854, "is the most important to commemorate, as people are comparatively willing to suppose all the rest" (*Correspondence,* 194). The attempt to pay his "debt" to Taylor, however, raised the question of how to negotiate the pedagogical and personal aspects of the *Autobiography*: that is, how to write what Mill referred to in his letter as "the Life" and "*our* life" (194). The two, of course, were inextricably linked, since Taylor's "effect" on Mill was central to the instructive purposes of writing an autobiography; however, the problem of what constitutes a "fair representation" preoccupied Mill as he struggled to imagine himself as a reader of his own life story: "Of course one does not, in writing a life, . . . undertake to tell everything—& it will be right to put something into *this* which shall prevent any one from being able to suppose or to pretend, that we undertake to keep nothing back" (194). But Mill's concern in writing his/their life, I would argue, has less to do with concealing the "facts" of

his relationship with Taylor, noted above, than it does with a specific anxiety of authorship—with a fear of being rewritten by the reader.[14] Stated somewhat differently, what Mill called his "sacred duty of fixing in writing" (*Correspondence,* 189; see also 199) a life that would "be of use to the many" (198) was fraught with the problems of authorial control. For what was to prevent readers of the *Autobiography* from producing their own meanings for Mill's "Life," from reconstructing his written self?

To grasp the complexities of reader and author, however, as well as the positioning of "Harriet Taylor" in Mill's self-representations, we must first turn to the issues of enunciation and address encoded in the narrative structure of the very text that, as we have seen, was presumably of no interest as a personal narrative.

THE BOOK AND THE BOY

"I was born in London, on the 20th of May, 1806, and was the eldest son of James Mill, the author of the History of British India" (*Autobiography,* 4). So begins Mill's account of his life—a touching story of creation, as Bruce Mazlish has argued, in which the mother is missing. Instead, writes Mazlish, "we have the book and the boy."[15] Significantly, I would add, the *Autobiography* ends with the following: "I have written various articles in periodicals . . . , have made a small number of speeches on public occasions, especially at the meetings of the Women's Suffrage Society, have published the "Subjection of Women," . . . and have commenced the preparation of matter for future books, of which it will be time to speak more particularly if I live to finish them. Here, therefore, for the present, this Memoir may close" (185). These two passages, which frame the autobiographical account of what Mill called his "education" and his "self-education," are linked by more than the seemingly random event of his birth and the authorial need for narrative closure. John Stuart's figurative reinstatement of himself within Oedipal law, as the son of James Mill, a self-proclaimed Malthusian whose wife would bear him nine children, is itself transfigured in the final passage of "the Life," in which the son's signature is annexed to his own textual creations. Of the latter, the one that is named is the book that defended women against the "brute instinct" of male sexual desire and the debilitating demands of maternity. What began as a tribute to the father and to paternity, then, in which the pen that signs the scholarly book inscribes as well the identity of the boy, ends as a radical intervention into the field of heterosexuality and eighteenth-century gender relations. In authoring a Life that concludes by putting his name to "The Subjection of Women," Mill, as we shall see, distances himself from the project of his father—a project that stamped both sons and women as the mere *re*presentations of paternal identity—and constructs an alternative self that is intimately bound up with questions of power and sexual difference.

It is worth lingering for a moment over the very project of writing one's life. For, as noted above, the distinction between the written and the writing self is crucial to my

John Stuart Mill, 1806-1873.

reading of Mill. Since an autobiography culls its materials from the author's memory, a brief caveat on the meaning of memory is in order. Notwithstanding Mill's claim to have merely recorded the events of his past, a radical reading of the *Autobiography* must begin with the insight that, as Freud argues, memories of one's past cannot be understood as simply emerging from the multiplicity of childhood experience; instead all memories are formed in relation to the psychic needs of the present.[16] Hence re-memoration is a process in which the past is not so much recollected as it is worked over—a process in which the "I" of childhood, for example, constitutes and is constituted in relation to the "I" of the locutor. Understood in this manner, then, memory, as Patricia Spacks has written, is a means of possessing one's past,[17] of transforming it in the urgency of the present. Like Harriet Taylor, then, the personages encountered by a reader of Mill's *Life* are best understood as figures deployed in the construction of the author's subjectivity.

To substantiate these claims I return to the Oedipal issues raised in Mill's self-introduction. The "debt" to his father is repaid with interest, so to speak, by a painful presentation of self as the pedagogical utilitarian "experiment," whose seven-chapter autobiography consists of at least two devoted entirely to his father's ideas on politics, education, and social reform. More significant, however, is the manner in which John Stuart constitutes himself in rela-

tion not only to the *History of British India* but also to the closed world of books in which he was immersed until the age of fourteen. As he recollected his life, we have seen, Mill was unable, or unwilling, to distinguish his own birth from that of a book. It is not surprising, then, that the first chapter of Mill's *Life* situates him exclusively in relation to the numerous texts his father made him read. Cut off from "intercourse with other boys" (22), Mill, in short, is subjected to a rigorous educational program, which, among other things, has him learning Greek at age three under his "father's tuition." That tuition, however, was invasive for reasons that went beyond the fact that, as Mill writes, "I went through the whole process of preparing my Greek lessons in the same room and at the same table at which he (the father) was writing." Not only did he read in the presence of his father, but "as in those days Greek and English lexicons were not, . . . I was forced to have recourse to him for the meaning of every word which I did not know. This incessant interruption he, one of the most impatient of men, submitted to, and wrote under that interruption several volumes of his History and all else that he had to write during those years" (6).

Under the tutelage of James Mill, the otherwise private practice of reading is transformed into terrifying episodes in accountability in which the final meaning of texts and of language is the province of the father. In addition to his required reading, Mill mentions his "private reading" of Mitford's *Greece* only to note that "my father had put me on my guard against the Tory prejudices of this writer" (9). Similarly, after reading Latin treatises on scholastic logic, Mill tells us that he was forced to give to his father, each day, in their walks together, "a minute account of what I had read," and was required to answer his "numerous and searching questions" (12). Hence what he learned from the elder Mill, among other things, was how to dissect a bad argument with logic: a skill that forms "exact thinkers, who attach a precise meaning to words and propositions, and are not imposed on by vague, loose, or ambiguous terms" (13). The same lesson, we are told, was learned by reading Plato, whose work constrains the "man of vague generalities . . . either to express his meaning to himself in definite terms or to confess that he does not know what he is talking about" (15). Finally, the fear of using words whose meanings have not been properly defined is connected to Mill's overwhelming sense of failure as a pupil and, hence, as a son:

> I remember at some time in my thirteenth year, on my happening to use the word idea, he asked me what an idea was; and expressed some displeasure at my ineffectual efforts to define the word: I recollect also his indignation at my using the common expression that something was true in theory but required correction in practice; and how, after making me vainly strive to define the word theory, he explained its meaning, and showed the fallacy of the vulgar form of speech which I had used; leaving me fully persuaded that . . . I had shewn unparalleled ignorance.

(20)

That Mill's earliest recollections of spoken and written language are presented in terms of his subjection to his father is elaborated further in his description of the exercises in elocution, which were part of his education. Of all the things he was made to do, Mill tells us, there was nothing in which he failed so miserably as in his efforts to read aloud to his father, who "had thought much on the principles of reading." The "rules" of "modulation," Mill writes, were "strongly impressed" upon him, and he was taken "severely to task for every violation of them" (16). Thus even when Mill is speaking he is really listening; for it is his father who, in the son's account, defined not only the books to be read but also the manner in which they were to be read and discussed. But if James Mill seemed to exercise complete control over the terms of discourse, there was, Mill tells us, one sphere in which he was left to explore the fantasies of his imagination: "A voluntary exercise to which throughout my boyhood I was addicted, was what I called writing histories. . . . My father encouraged me in this useful amusement, though, as I think judiciously, he never asked to see what I wrote; so that I did not feel that in writing it I was accountable to any one, nor had the chilling sensation of being under a critical eye" (10). However, Mill notes, he later destroyed all the papers he had written "in contempt of (his) childish efforts" (10). Moreover, these exercises in youthful creativity paled in comparison to that great *History of India,* the text of which John Stuart read aloud to his father as the elder Mill corrected the proofs of his monumental manuscript in the year 1817.

The effect of an education that stressed the analytic over the poetic uses of language was to deprive Mill of those literary modes of expression he would later rediscover in his reading of Romantic poetry, specifically Wordsworth. The young Mill's sporadic attempts at self-imagining through the writing and reading of verse, he notes, were crushed by his father's derision of most English poetry. Indeed, it was more than the "spontaneous promptings" of Mill's "poetical ambition" that were destroyed by turning an exercise "begun from choice" into one "continued by command" (11). The instrumental approach of his father to language, the son recounts, was but part of his more general contempt "for passionate emotions of all sorts, and for everything which has been said or written in exaltation of them" (31). Hence, Mill wrote in a 1833 letter to Thomas Carlyle, the poet's boundless capacity for feeling, especially love, was completely lacking in himself; and consciousness of this lack only heightened the pain associated with willing what could not be willed: "I can do nothing for myself and others can do nothing for me; all the advice which can be given, . . . is, not to beat against the bars of my iron cage."[18]

Mill's measured criticism of his father and of his education bears the traces of the anxiety of authorship spoken of at the beginning of this essay. Assessing his relation to the required books, specific meanings, and circumscribed textual world of his childhood, Mill is torn between exalting and doubting the excellences of the paternal figure. On the

one hand, Mill represents himself as the product, legacy, and beneficiary of his father's efforts. This point is underscored, significantly, in a passage in which the author of the Life repeats James Mill's last words to him upon leaving his "father's house for a long absence" at age fourteen:

> I remember the very place in Hyde Park where, . . . he told me that I should find, as I got acquainted with new people, that I had been taught many things which youths of my age did not commonly know; and that many persons would be disposed . . . to compliment me upon it. . . . He wound up by saying, that whatever I knew more than others, could not be ascribed to any merit in me, but to the very unusual advantage which had fallen to my lot, of having a father who was able to teach me, and willing to give the necessary trouble and time. . . . I felt that what my father had said . . . was exactly the truth . . . and it fixed my opinion and feeling from that time forward.
>
> (22)

On the other hand, Mill also explicitly criticizes his father's method, which sacrificed, among other things, affect at the altar of reason. Some of these, more tempered, critiques are woven into the fabric of the published text, but the most damning of them are to be found in the rejected leaves of the *Autobiography.* Here we are told that James Mill's "children neither loved him, nor, with any warmth or affection anyone else" (33 n. 3); that John Stuart's "was not an education of love but of fear" (33 n. 3); and that the pedagogical consequences of utilitarianism included a form of moral (as well as physical) enervation: "I acquired a habit of leaving my responsibility as a moral agent to rest on my father, my conscience never speaking to me except by his voice" (33 n. 3).

Mill's overly punitive and severe internalization of paternal authority, however, cannot be understood apart from another representation of his father, found as well in the rejected leaves: an image of James Mill as the victim of an ill-assorted marriage and of his eldest son as the unfortunate child of an unloving mother. It is to Harriet Burrows, then, that I next turn in my reading of Mill's life story. For in naming, criticizing, and then crossing out the mother, Mill's subtext tells us something about the place of desire in his account of a life whose stated intent it was to pay back a "debt" by offering himself as an example for the reader.[19]

THE ABSENT MOTHER

Noting that Mill's autobiography represents the author's birth as analogous to that of a book only begins to unravel the meaning of his self-introduction to the reader. Retelling the tale of the author's reinscription of himself within Oedipal law acknowledges but has yet to explain the meaning of the mother's absence. Indeed, our discussion so far would seem to affirm a familiar reading of Mill as a prodigal son, whose struggle for language might be read as symptomatic of the "anxiety of influence" outlined by critics such as Harold Bloom.[20] In other words, as Marlon

Ross writes in a related context, Mill might be said to be caught in a generational "tug-of-war" with his father, in which "only the strong man wins, for only he can create himself despite the father's overriding claims of insemination, authority, and paternal possession."[21] On this reading, writing is the process through which Mill would do battle with the father who made him; but, as Bloom recognizes, any notion of conquest is illusory; for "the son wins self-possession only tentatively, if at all, in the same way that he may realize that he has made himself who he is *only* because he could not be what his father has already become."[22]

In contrast to a reading that would situate Mill, and the question of authorship, strictly in relation to paternal authority, literary and familial, feminist theories of writing and language acquisition offer a different angle from which to speculate on Mill's narrative account of his education. By focusing on the pre-Oedipal period, which precedes the child's entry into the symbolic order of language, American literary critics such as Margaret Homans and French theorists such as Julia Kristeva and Luce Irigaray have stressed the centrality of the loss (or, on Irigaray's account, the overt murder) of the mother to the emergence of the male speaking subject.[23] The abyss that separates subject and object, to which, for example, Mill alluded in his letter to Carlyle about Man's capacity to love, is that of a man and his absent mother. Following Jacques Lacan, these feminists have argued that language is founded on the figurative substitutes for the originary unmediated relationship to a pre-Oedipal maternal figure.[24] As Freud demonstrated in his account of the child's *Fort!/Da!* game, language is, among other things, a means for both mastering and replaying the mother's absence.[25] But the symbolic rendering of the lost object, as Homans puts it, which requires the absence of the object, also permits its controlled return: "What the son searches for, in searching for substitutes for the mother's forbidden body, is a series of figures, someone like his mother."[26] Figuration, then, allows the son to flee from the mother and the lost referent, the literal, with which she is identified. In our "predominant myth of language," argues Homans, "the presence of the mother's body," of the literal, would make figurative meaning unnecessary, "it would hypothetically destroy the text."[27] Thus, the "feminine" in language is the absent referent that makes possible and engenders figurative structures of literature. The "woman," writes Homans, must remain forever out of reach in order for male authors "to speculate forever on how to reach her, or to replace her with their own abstractions."[28]

This abbreviated account of language acquisition proves very useful to an exploration of the workings of the Oedipus myth in John Stuart's narrative of his childhood. For if James Mill is presented to us as an exalted, almost superhuman figure, we might well wonder about the meaning of this larger-than-life portrait in Mill's written self. From a slightly different angle, then, one could argue that the unusual description of Mill's birth, in which the mother is refused by not being represented, works not only to re-

instate the author as son but also to shore up the identity of James Mill as father: in short, to affirm paternity. The exaltation of the father figure, wrote Freud in his "Family Romances," occurs when the child realizes that *pater semper incertus est,* while the mother is *certissima.*"[29] In Mill's account, however, that affirmation is even more curious; for in what amounts to a textual self-genesis, Mill's prose works to deny as well the fact that he is not the product of writing but of coitus, not of intellect but of desire. Indeed, in the *Autobiography* language reconstructs what Freud called the intolerable fact of parental sexual intercourse to make it more acceptable to the author.

The theme of sexual desire in Mill's autobiography is often articulated in terms of the son's efforts to explain the inconsistency of his father's life and his politics, that is, the fact that the size of James Mill's family stood in flagrant contradiction to his theoretical Malthusianism. Mill himself leads the reader in this direction when he writes that his father, "with no resources but the precarious one of writing in periodicals, . . . married and had a large family; conduct than which nothing could be more opposed, both as a matter of good sense and of duty, to the opinions which, at least at a later period of life, he strenuously upheld" (*Autobiography,* 4). Accordingly, it is the father's desire that is problematic and hence male sexual desire that must be accounted for and explained. Although Mill's life story does not provide the extended critique of male sexuality found in his political writings, it does suggest at least one way of accounting for statements such as the following: Something in the "merely physical subjection to their will as an instrument, causes them (husbands) to feel a sort of disrespect and contempt towards their own wife which they do not feel towards any other woman, or any other human being."[30] For if Mill's feminism would focus on what he held to be the barbaric nature of male sexuality, the *Autobiography* situates the demon of (hetero)sexual "instinct" in relation to the author's mother—a figure whose swollen body stands as more than what Christine Di Stephano calls "a pregnant reminder of her husband's illicit desires and behavior, which had little legitimate space within the frame of his rationalist Utilitarianism."[31] What Mill's account of his birth and his childhood reconstructs and in effect denies, I would add, is not only the embarrassing fact of the father's recurring desire but also the mother's.[32]

That Mill can hardly mention sexuality without condemning it, and, with it, the men who force themselves on their wives is one of the more curious if commonly acknowledged aspects of his feminism.[33] Indeed, there is little room in Mill's theory for a notion of sexual desire that is not masculine and invasive. Human instincts, he argues, are the dangerous, natural impulses that Mill believed the progress of civilization would eventually contain, if not eradicate, through the triumph of reason and, specifically, through the rational extension of political equality to women.[34] In Mill's account, the political and economic subjection of women is the cultural product of their subjection to male sexual instinct. The image of woman in

Mill's political writings as the passive and helpless victim of male desire, however, is complicated by the *Autobiography*'s subtext, in which the acknowledged absence of gender equality in the Mill household is but a pretext for explaining the father's unfortunate situation in being married to a woman to whom "he had not, and never could have supposed that he had, the inducements of kindred intellect, tastes, or pursuits" (4 n. 2). This sentence, which follows the passage on the size of James Mill's family, quoted above, is an indirect reference to the mother; and, like all other references to the mother, it was crossed out and finally deleted from the published manuscript. The price of James Mill's marriage to such a woman, however—which included the enormous financial burdens of a large family and the "extraordinary energy which was required to lead the life which he led"—was paid not once but twice; the second time by his eldest son: "A man who, in his practice, so vigorously acted up to the principle of losing no time, was likely to adhere to the same rule in the instruction of his pupil. I have no remembrance of the time when I began to learn Greek" (5). That this passage is preceded by a reference to Mill's mother is significant. For it is the loss of the mother that is replayed in the subtext of Mill's narrative account of language acquisition, which begins with a painful memory of learning Greek under the tutelage of his father. At the same time, that the first textual trace of maternal negation, that is, the explicit because written crossing-out of the mother, occurs at a point in the manuscript where Mill acknowledges his entry into the symbolic order of language suggests as well not so much the loss as the overt murder of the mother suggested by Irigaray. It is a murder, however, fraught with ambivalence. Like the book, which, as a figurative substitution for the maternal body, allows Mill both to deny that his mother (and her desire) was necessary to his birth and to replace her with a more sanitary figure, learning Greek presupposes the mother's absence while permitting her controlled return within the symbolic order of paternal law. But this loss or murder of the mother is, as we have seen, not without its destructive consequences. What is lost with the death of mother is the unmediated communication with others, the ability to merge identities in a (pre-Oedipal) universe of feeling.

The argument about Mill's own subjection to his father comes full circle when we attend to the rejected leaves of his autobiography. But Mill's ambivalence or reluctance to "pronounce whether I was more a loser or gainer by his severity" (32) is managed in a long, deleted passage that follows—a passage in which the father is forgiven for his deficient moral relation to his children, his "lack of tenderness," for he too was unloved. "In an atmosphere of tenderness and affection," we are told, James Mill "would have been tender and affectionate":

> That rarity in England, a really warm hearted mother, would in the first place have made my father a totally different being, and in the second would have made the children grow up loving and being loved. But my mother with the very best intentions, only knew how to pass her life in drudging for them. Whatever she could

do for them she did, and they liked her, because she was kind to them, but to make herself loved, looked up to, or even obeyed, required qualities which she unfortunately did not possess.

(33)

The literature on the marriage of James and Harriet Mill agrees, for the most part, with John Stuart's assessment.[35] James Mill's attitude towards his wife is commonly portrayed as one bordering on complete indifference if not contempt. Although we know from a variety of letters, written by friends of the Mills, that James Mill played tyrant in his home, when considering John Stuart's representation of his mother, we still need to consider the complex role played by the imagination and fantasy in the construction of personal narrative.

By attending to the ways in which Mill's prose manages the loss of the mother, we can read Mill's melancholia, recounted in his famous "mental crisis" at age twenty, in terms of a loss of "narcissistic supplies" rather than strictly as an Oedipal narrative. For the superego, as Thomas Weiskel has written in his account of Wordsworth, is likewise "a precipitate of the mother as well as the father, and its displeasure may thus be manifested not only in the fantasy of castration but also in the sense of loss—of self-esteem."[36] But by telling the reader "I neither estimated myself highly nor lowly; I did not estimate myself at all" (*Autobiography*, 21), Mill seems to underscore a reading of his life in which the father is the central figure whose powerful presence prohibits any attempt at self-invention. Thus, his crisis might be read in terms of the liberating effect that the reading of Marmontel's *Memoirs* had upon the young Mill, specifically the passage that, Mill writes, "relates the father's death, the distressed position of the family, and the sudden inspiration by which he, then a mere boy, felt and made them feel that he would be everything to them—would supply the place of all they had lost" (85). Apart from the "rescue fantasy" suggested by Mill's text,[37] a strict focus on the patricidal wish in this passage overlooks the more troubling problem of self-consciousness with which Mill concludes the episode: the absence of genuine feeling, of true happiness, in a world whose "objects of human desire" had been dissolved by the "influence of analysis" (*Autobiography*, 84). Instead of searching for happiness as an object in itself, Mill writes, "Let your self-consciousness, your scrutiny, your self-interrogation exhaust themselves" on something external to it; only then will you "inhale happiness with the air you breathe, without dwelling on it or thinking about it, without either forestalling it in the imagination, or putting it to flight by fatal questioning" (86).

Mill's "cultivation of the feelings" sought an unmediated connection to others through poetry and music. That Mill identified Wordsworth as the poet whose writings made him aware of the existence of genuine feeling is significant. Although Mill may not have read *The Prelude*, in which the poet recounts the "mute dialogues" which he held with his mother as an infant, Wordsworth's poetry had a profound effect upon the author of the *Autobiography.* Indeed, in reading the "famous Ode," Mill writes, he found that "he (Wordsworth) too had had similar experience to mine" (90). Wordsworth's poetry, Mill tells us, allowed him to recapture that "real, permanent happiness in tranquil contemplation"; something of that "first freshness of youthful enjoyment of life" (90); that "sympathetic and imaginative pleasure, which could be shared in by all human beings; which had no connection with struggle or imperfection" (89); in short, a world in which language offered the (illusory) possibility of crossing the abyss between subject and object, a world without difference and separation.

Not surprisingly, then, in his essay on marriage, Mill echoed Wordsworth's longing for those lost dialogues. Motherhood, Mill insisted, is not about doing but about being: "It is not by particular effects, but imperceptibly and unconsciously that she (the mother) makes her own character pass into the child; that she makes the child love what she loves."[38] But Mill's depiction of such a blissful state, and the acts of figuration that engender it, is only possible if the illusion that we might have access to some originary ground of meaning is sustained.[39] And central to this illusion, as I now conclude, is Mill's "Harriet Taylor," that other figure whose "presence" in Mill's narrative requires her absence as subject.

Conclusion

The *Autobiography,* I have suggested, is not so much, as it represents itself, an account of Mill's education at the hands of his father. Rather, as Mary Jacobus has written of *The Prelude,* it is "an educational treatise directed at the missing mother."[40] That Mill drafted his autobiography in the years 1853-1854, years in which his mother fell gravely ill and finally passed away, may be but a crude indication of the possible links between Mill's project of writing his Life and the mother who gave him life.[41] More significant, perhaps, is that although the *Autobiography* seems to confirm the author's identity as the indebted son of the author of the "History of British India" by denying the place of the mother in creation, the text works primarily to affirm a myth of self-possession. For by reducing the debt to his father to the life of the mind, Mill's prose reconstructs what he owes to his parents (his birth) in terms that can be repaid through the act of writing itself. But if the infidelity involved in adopting intellectual positions on political questions contrary to the teachings of his father are legitimated, in part, by replacing the inner "voice" of his father with that of "Harriet Taylor," so too is the potential *refu*sion with the mother through fusion with his wife mediated by an unusual conjugal relationship—a marriage that will produce not children but books, and a relationship that will cultivate not sexual passion but elevated ideas of human community.

On 6 March 1851, shortly before his marriage to Harriet Taylor, Mill wrote a lengthy letter in which, among other things, he divested himself of the "odious powers" of any

"right" to his wife's "person" and "property" (*Correspondence,* 168). But Mill's insistence that his wife would retain "in all respects whatever the same absolute freedom of action, & freedom of disposal of herself . . . , as if no marriage had taken place" (168) needs to be squared with his desire to abnegate any separate sense of self, to "merg(e) . . . the entire being with that of another, which is the characteristic of strong passion" ("EDRL," 621-622). Mill's refusal to participate in the social practices of coverture entailed, not only a relinquishment of his claim to Taylor's body, but also an insistence that the "renunciation of any separate existence" be both "spontaneous" and "equally complete on both sides" ("EDRL," 621). He found inspiration for such union in the romantic rhetoric of androgyny, in a poetic language of inclusion that promised to reconcile the grammar of opposites that was sexual difference.

"A great mind must be androgynous," wrote Coleridge.[42] Similarly, Mill asked rhetorically in a letter to Carlyle: "Is there really any distinction between the highest masculine and the highest feminine character?"[43] The "first-rate" people of both sexes, Mill answered, seemed to combine the highest masculine and the highest feminine traits in perfect harmony.[44] By the "higher natures," Mill wrote in his essay on marriage, I mean those characters who have "the greatest capacity of feeling happiness, and of bestowing it."[45] To be both the "natural object" and the giver of "love," Mill adds, is the crux of an identity that can "promote the greatest possible happiness of all who are within the sphere of (its) influence."[46] The reference to his wife was echoed in the *Autobiography,* in a passage in which Taylor is portrayed as a woman of "boundless generosity, and a lovingness ever ready to pour itself forth upon any or all human beings who were capable of giving the smallest feeling in return" (113). But the love that Mill experienced in the presence of Taylor was more than a substitute for that which he claimed to have neither felt nor received from his mother, as some critics have suggested.[47] The link between happiness and love, which Mill drew time and again in his writings, was central to the myth of selfpossession described by Freud in his 1914 essay on narcissism. "To be their own ideal once more, in regard to sexual no less than other trends," wrote Freud, "as they were in childhood—this is what people strive to attain as their happiness."[48]

Language acquisition, as I have argued, marks indelibly the birth of the speaking subject in a universe of difference, a world in which, as Blake wrote, one may hope only for an "organized innocence"[49] but never again complete or originary innocence. But if writing signified this impossibility, so too did it offer the illusion of crossing the gap that marked human separateness. When Mill, as quoted above, writes that he is not "fit to write on anything but the outskirts of the great questions of feeling & life," he echoes Wordsworth's concern at the beginning of *The Prelude* that, as Geoffrey Hartman notes, he "cannot decide whether he is fit to be a poet on an epic scale."[50] Like Wordsworth, Mill "cannot find his theme because he already has it: himself."[51] Mill shared with the poet the weight of self-consciousness, of a passion that is "murderous to dissect."

Taylor, I have suggested, was the trope that linked the ratiocinative world of Mill's father and the repressed desires of and for his mother. To ask whether Mill's representation of "Harriet Taylor" succeeds in avoiding the dangers posed by the one-sided (female) abnegation of self is to raise the problem of androgyny as a completion of the male ego.[52] Despite Mill's concern with establishing Taylor as a subject in her own right, the *Autobiography* tells a different story—one in which Mill incorporates the "feminine" by choosing, as Freud writes, "a sexual ideal after the narcissistic type which possesses the excellences to which he (the male subject) cannot attain."[53] That Mill saw Taylor as the embodiment of "perfect disinterestedness," a rare condition that his political theory sought to attain, is of some relevance here. In a passage deleted from the published text of his autobiography, Mill wrote that his wife's "strong feeling" on the social position of women, in short, her feminism, "was the effect of principle and not of any desire on her own part to mingle in the turmoil and strife of the occupations which the dominant sex has hitherto reserved to itself" ("EDRL," 621). What is contested by Mill in this image of his wife, whose intellect he credits for his political writings, is a far more problematic idea of her as someone whose own desire for recognition through action in the world would undermine the *Autobiography*'s idealized image of Taylor as a woman of complete "unselfishness." Although the political issues raised by Mill's idealization of Taylor are far too complex to examine here, readers of the *Subjection of Women* will recognize the links between Mill's benevolent image of his wife and his rather sentimentalized notion of how female suffrage would effect a kind of cultural husbandry of patriarchal society.

To return to the question of authorship and signature with which we began—if Mill's "Harriet Taylor" is but a feminized version of himself, so too does she mark the discursive space in the *Autobiography*, between the writer and his absent mother, that cannot be crossed but the illusion of which must be sustained if the project of writing is to succeed in affirming the author's identity. "Whenever I look back at any of my own writing of two or three years previous," Mill wrote in his diary in the year of his mother's death, "they seem to me like the writing of some stranger whom I have seen and known long ago" (***Correspondence**,* 198). Although Mill accounts for this distance in terms of the gap between the "enlargement of his ideas and feelings," which he owes "to *her* (Taylor's) influence," and his inadequate "powers of execution" (198), the "stranger" that confronted Mill as reader of his own life was, perhaps, nothing other than that haunting maternal figure, one whose absence in the writing spoke powerfully to her presence in the unconscious.

Notes

1. John Stuart Mill, "Early Draft Rejected Leaves," in *Collected Works,* ed. J. M. Robinson and Jack Still-

inger (Toronto: University of Toronto Press, 1972), 1: 617. Henceforth cited in the text as "EDRL." The epigraph to this chapter is from "EDRL," 612.

2. John Stuart Mill to Thomas Carlyle, 5 July 1833, *The Earlier Letters of John Stuart Mill,* ed. Francis E. Mineka, in the *Collected Works,* 12: 163. On the same point, see John Stuart Mill, *Autobiography,* ed. Jack Stillinger (New York: Houghton Mifflin, 1969), 122. Henceforth cited in the text as *Autobiography.*

3. *John Stuart Mill and Harriet Taylor Mill, Their Correspondence and Subsequent Marriage,* ed. F. A. Hayek (Chicago: University of Chicago Press, 1951), 193. Henceforth cited in the text as *Correspondence.*

4. The recent speculative literature on Harriet Taylor's contribution to Mill's writings and her influence on his thinking is fairly consistent. Whereas earlier biographers and critics, such as Packe and Hayek, granted Taylor a legitimate, if "feminine" place in Mill's intellectual development, contemporary readers are more likely to deny Taylor any role at all or to blame her for those parts of Mill's work which seem inconsistent or problematic. For Gertrude Himmelfarb, who claims that the liberalism of *On Liberty* is far too "absolutistic and simplistic," the problem lay not with Mill but with Harriet Taylor: "This was his wife's way of thinking." See *On Liberty and Liberalism: The Case of John Stuart Mill* (New York: Alfred A. Knopf, 1974). Bernard Semmel praises Himmelfarb's "brilliantly argued" hypothesis of the two Mills: the one influenced by Taylor and the other "much sounder Mill." See *John Stuart Mill and the Pursuit of Virtue* (New Haven: Yale University Press, 1984), 5 n. 4. Alan Ryan portrays Taylor as rather spoiled and "bored" by her marriage to John Taylor: "It seems clear that Harriet was put out by the fact that her husband was no Shellyesque hero, though she aspired to be a romantic heroine." See *J. S. Mill* (London: Routledge & Kegan Paul, 1974), 49. In comparison, Michael St. Packe's portrait of Taylor as a woman who had "given up her manly ambition to . . . express herself in a more feminine way through her effect on him (Mill)" seems harmless. See Packe, *The Life of John Stuart Mill* (New York: Macmillan, 1954), 140. see also 237, 315-316, 348, and 371.

5. See Linda M.-G. Zerilli, *Images of Women in Political Theory: Agents of Culture and Chaos* (Madison: University of Wisconsin Press, 1992).

6. As I am concerned with the question of Mill's self-representation in this essay, I do not examine the letters written by Taylor to Mill, nor do I speculate on the rewriting of the *Autobiography,* some of the revisions of which are in Taylor's hand. In the face of critical hostility to Taylor, needless to say, such an analysis would be both useful and informative.

7. John Stuart Mill, "Essay on Marriage and Divorce," in *Essays on Sex Equality,* ed. Alice S. Rossi (Chicago: University of Chicago Press, 1970), 69.

8. Christine Di Stephano, "Rereading J. S. Mill: Inter-polations from the (M)Otherworld," in *Discontented Discourses: Feminism, Textual Intervention, Psycho-analysis,* ed. Marleen S. Barr and Richard Feinstein (Urbana: University of Illinois Press, 1989), 163.

9. On the importance of the maternal subtext in male writing, see Coppelia Kahn, "Excavating 'Those Dim Minoan Regions': Maternal Subtexts in Patriarchal Literature," *Diacritics* 12, no. 2 (1982): 32-41.

10. I am indebted to an essay by Gayatri Chakravorty Spivak on Wordsworth for this point. Spivak, how-ever, reads Wordsworth's myth of self-possession in terms of his refusal of paternity. See Spivak, "Sex and History in *The Prelude* (1805): Books Nine to Thirteen," *Texas Studies in Literature and Language* 23 (Fall 1981): 324-360.

11. Quoted in Hayek's introduction to the *Correspondence,* 15.

12. John Stuart Mill to George Makepeace Towle, 13 September 1869, *The Later Letters of John Stuart Mill,* ed. Francis E. Mineka, in the *Collected Works,* 17: 1641.

13. Mill would seem to extend the eighteenth-century notion that an autobiography ought to be instructive. See Patricia Spacks, *Imagining a Self: Autobiogra-phy and Novel in Eighteenth-Century England* (Cambridge: Harvard University Press, 1976).

14. On the ways in which "feminine figures seem to bear" a male author's "anxiety of authorship" and his fear of being rewritten by the reader, see Sonia Hof-kosh, "The Writer's Ravishment, Women and the Romantic Author—The Example of Byron," in *Ro-manticism and Feminism,* ed. Anne K. Mellor (Bloomington: Indiana University Press, 1988), 93-114.

15. *James and John Stuart Mill: Father and Son in the Nineteenth Century* (New York: Basic Books, 1975), 3.

16. See, "Screen Memories," *The Standard Edition of the Complete Psychological Works of Sigmund Freud,* ed. James Strachey et al. (London, 1953-66), 3: 322. On the same point, see Thomas Weiskel, *The Ro-mantic Sublime* (1976; reprint, Baltimore: The Johns Hopkins University Press, 1986), 170.

17. Spacks, *Imagining a Self,* 3.

18. John Stuart Mill to Thomas Carlyle, 9 March 1833, *The Earlier Letters of John Stuart Mill,* in *Collected Works,* 12:143.

19. It should be noted that portions of Mill's early draft were marked for deletion in the hand of Harriet Tay-lor. But Mill, of course, made the final decision on what to include in the manuscript.

20. Harold Bloom, *The Anxiety of Influence: A Theory of Poetry* (London: Oxford University Press, 1967).

21. Marlon Ross, "Romantic Quest and Conquest: Trop-ing Masculine Power in the Crisis of Poetic Iden-tity," in Mellor, *Romanticism and Feminism,* 27. Al-though Ross is critical of Bloom's patriarchal poetics, he persists, nonetheless, in reading the cultivation of a specifically feminine sensibility in terms of the Oe-dipal struggle between fathers and sons.

22. Ibid.

23. Irigaray argues that the mother ("femme-mere") is not simply lost but murdered. Irigaray contests Freud's reading of the birth of culture in his *Totem and Taboo.* See Luce Irigaray, *Le Corps-a-corps avec la mere* (Ottowa: Pleine Lune, 1981), 15-16. I am in-debted to Margaret Homans's introductory essay in her book *Bearing the Word* (Chicago: University of Chicago Press, 1986), 2, for this reference. Among numerous other writings, see especially, Homans, *Bearing the Word,* especially chap. 1; Luce Irigaray, *This Sex Which Is Not One,* trans. Catherine Porter and Carolyn Burke (Ithaca: Cornell University Press, 1985); and Julia Kristeva, *Desire in Language* (New York: Columbia University Press, 1980); and *Tales of Love,* trans. Leon S. Roudiez (New York: Colum-bia University Press, 1987).

24. See Jacques Lacan, "The Mirror Stage," "The Signi-fication of the Phallus," and "The Function and Field of Speech and Language in Psychoanalysis," espe-cially 65-68, in *Ecrits,* trans. Alan Sheridan (New York: W. W. Norton, 1977).

25. Sigmund Freud, "Beyond the Pleasure Principle," in *Standard Edition,* 18: 14-17. See Lacan's discussion of Freud in "The Function and Field of Speech," in *Ecrits,* 65.

26. Homans, *Bearing the Word,* 9.

27. Ibid., 4. Homans adds: "This possibility is always, but never more than, a threat, since literal meaning cannot be present in the text: it is always elsewhere."

28. Ibid., 2.

29. Sigmund Freud, "Family Romances," in *The Com-plete Psychological Works of Sigmund Freud* (London: The Hogarth Press, 1959), 9: 239.

30. John Stuart Mill, *Principles of Political Economy,* ed. J. M. Robson, in *Collected Works,* 3: 373. Mill is referring here to the working class.

31. Di Stephano, "Rereading J. S. Mill," 164.

32. On the problem of representing maternal desire, see Julia Kristeva, "Motherhood According to Giovanni Bellini," in *Desire in Language.*

33. On Mill's feminism, see Susan Moller Okin, *Women in Western Political Thought* (Princeton: Princeton University Press, 1979); Zillah Eisenstein, *The Radi-cal Future of Liberal Feminism* (New York: Long-man, 1981); Jennifer Ring, "Mill's *The Subjection of*

Women: The Methodological Limits of Liberal Feminism," *The Review of Politics* 47, no. 1 (January 1985): 27-44; and Julia Annas, "Mill and the Subjection of Women," *Philosophy* 52 (1977): 179-194.

34. See John Stuart Mill, *The Subjection of Women,* in *Essays on Sex Equality*; *Political Economy,* in *Collected Works,* vol. 3.

35. See Mazlish, *James and John Stuart Mill*; Packe, *The Life of John Stuart Mill*; and Josephine Kamm, *John Stuart Mill in Love* (London: Gordon & Cremonesi, 1977), 13.

36. *The Romantic Sublime,* 102. On the same point see Julia Kristeva, *Black Sun: Depression and Melancholia,* trans. Leon Roudiez (New York: Columbia University Press, 1989).

37. Sigmund Freud, "Contributions to the Psychology of Love," in *Sexuality and the Psychology of Love,* ed. Philip Reiff (New York: Collier Books, 1963), especially 56-57.

38. "Essay on Marriage," 76.

39. See Homas, *Bearing the Word,* 4.

40. Quoted in Marlon Ross, "Romantic Quest and Conquest," 51 n. 17.

41. Mill declined to be the executor of his mother's will and refused (until Taylor convinced him otherwise) to accept his share of the maternal inheritance. Mill seems unable to reach a decision on these matters without consulting his wife. Even more curious is his reluctance to claim his mother's more personal belongings, such as her furniture. See *Correspondence,* 209-211.

42. Quoted in Alan Richardson, "Romanticism and the Colonization of the Feminine," in Mellor, *Romanticism and Feminism,* 20.

43. John Stuart Mill to Thomas Carlyle, 5 October 1833, *Earlier Letters,* in *Collected Works,* 12: 184.

44. Ibid.

45. "Essay on Marriage and Divorce," 68.

46. Ibid.

47. See, for example, Kamm, *John Stuart Mill in Love,* especially chap. 2.

48. Sigmund Freud, "On Narcissism: An Introduction," 100.

49. Quoted in Geoffrey Hartman, "Romanticism and Anti-Self-Consciousness," in *Romanticism and Criticism,* ed. Harold Bloom (New York: W. W. Norton, 1970), 49.

50. Ibid., 53.

51. Ibid.

52. For a critique of the politics of androgyny in romantic thought, see Alan Richardson, "Romanticism and the Colonization of the Feminine," especially 19.

53. "On Narcissism: An Introduction," 101.

Jo Ellen Jacobs (essay date 1994)

SOURCE: "'The Lot of Gifted Ladies Is Hard': A Study of Harriet Taylor Mill Criticism," in *Hypatia: A Journal of Feminist Philosophy,* Vol. 9, No. 3, Summer, 1994, pp. 132-62.

[*In the following essay, Jacobs considers critiques written about Harriet Taylor and attempts to offer a new perspective on her life and influence on Mill.*]

Who can tell a life? How can I reconstruct the inside, not merely the shell, of another? Margaret Atwood quotes the end of Arnold Bennett's biography by Margaret Drabble:

> "Many a time, . . . reading a letter or a piece of his journal, I have wanted to shake his hand, or to thank him, to say well done. I have written this instead." "To shake his hand." I suppose this may be what we really want, when we read biographies and when we write them: some contact, some communication, some way to know and to pay tribute. . . . We play Mr. Hyde, constantly, to our various Dr. Jekylls; we supersede ourselves. We are our own broken puzzles, incomplete, scattered through time. It is up to the biographers, finally, painstakingly, imperfectly, to put us together again.
>
> (Atwood 1989, 8)

I want to shake hands with Harriet Taylor Mill. I will put the pieces of her life together in a way that will reveal a new portrait, shockingly different from the usual one presented by historians of philosophy who have cast sidelong glances at this puzzling creature in John Stuart Mill's life. I'd like to introduce you to Harriet,[1] not Mrs. John Mill.

I want to shake hands with Harriet Taylor Mill, but that larger project must begin with a history of the critiques written about her, especially in the history of philosophy. And we need to understand why she has been presented as she has. The goal of this article is to begin to uncover the answers to the question "Why has Harriet Taylor Mill appeared in the history of philosophy as she has?" I believe there are several answers, not one answer. The answers intertwine the personality and politics of Harriet, the sexism of those who wrote of her (which was a reflection of the overall status of women during the periods the commentators wrote), and misunderstandings of the means and meaning of her collaboration with JSM. [John Stuart Mill] Some of these answers were first suggested by Le Doeuf (1987), Rossi (1970), August (1975), Tulloch (1989), and Rose (1984). I extend, systematize, and collect their reasons. For example, Rossi demonstrated the sexism of individual commentators on HTM. [Harriet Taylor Mill] I show that the history of the critiques is not merely a collection of individual sexist accounts, but parallels the history of progress and backlash in women's concerns. I extend Le Doeuf's analysis of the "Héloïse complex" to the relationship between Harriet and John.

Is there anything new in this article? Yes, the issues of how collaborative writing works and of how the ignorance or refusal of philosophers to use or acknowledge collaborative writing plays an important role in most philosophers' misunderstanding of Harriet's work. Furthermore, no one has pointed out the negative mythology of women's asking questions. Women's questions threaten men's knowledge. Harriet's philosophical thinking resulted in more questions than answers. Questions are more disturbing than answers because their open-endedness disturbs the drive for conclusions. Eve's sin was to desire to eat of the fruit of the tree of knowledge. So was Harriet's.

Philosophers like to think they write a history of *ideas*—sexless, bodiless ideas. If Aristotle has been treated unfairly by certain commentators or during certain historical periods, that is the result of philosophical assumptions or misunderstandings of the commentator—a problem of ideas. We philosophers might be willing to recognize that some political prejudices, say the paranoia about a possible link between Nazism and Nietzsche, creep into the less trustworthy historical analyses, but really, don't we feel above such petty biases as sexism? If not yesterday, then clearly today, we are above the small-mindedness of judging on the basis of sex.

Disclosing the nasty pettiness of her critics will reveal not only the biases against Harriet Taylor Mill. A more general pattern of attitudes toward women thinkers is ingrained in these critiques. I will show that the history of the philosophy of John Stuart Mill reveals that the critique of Harriet centers on her personality while her ideas are ignored. The predominance of ad feminam attacks and an almost complete refusal to consider HTM's ideas makes me suspicious. First, commentators seem to ignore Harriet's ideas automatically, and then they proceed to judge her life on the basis of openly sexist criteria. The unladylike questions that Harriet was famous for and her refusal to accept the passive role assigned by society—Victorian or Anglo-American twentieth-century—are not merely personality quirks that make it difficult for commentators to be fair. The same qualities in male philosophers are universally admired. Her atheism, her ideas about women working outside the home even if they were married (and her insistence on the importance of this idea), and her views on divorce have continued to grate, but they are not openly challenged or confronted. Her "radically" pro-socialist position irritates both those who agree and those who disagree with socialism, but all agree that HTM's ideas are only important insofar as they "influence" JSM's ideas. Philosophers have asked, "How influential was HTM on JSM?" and "Was that influence positive or negative?" They had not set out to ask, "What are HTM's ideas?" or "Are these ideas important or valuable?"

Ahh, you may say, but these comments about HTM are contained in critiques of JSM's work, so obviously the focus is on his ideas. But why has there been no critical biography of HTM? Why no book-length critique of her ideas?

Before I try to answer the question of HTM's place in history, I want to outline the details of that critique. How has Harriet been drawn in the past? I will quickly sketch the raw details of her life; then I will record the slow, dreary history of Harriet as written in academic publications; and finally, I will analyze why this portrait has been drawn as it has. If you are already acquainted with the scholarship on Harriet Taylor Mill, you may want to skip directly to Part 2, "The Analysis of the HTM Criticism." If you want to refresh your memory, or want to learn the details of the history of HTM criticism, read on.

PART 1: THE HISTORY OF HTM CRITICISM

The daughter of an obstetrician, Harriet was born in 1807 and married John Taylor when she was 18. She had two children, Harry and Algernon, in the first four years of her marriage. Harriet met JSM a few months after Algernon was born. Their friendship quickly escalated into love during Harriet's pregnancy with Helen, her third and final child, who was conceived when Algernon was less than nine months old. Harriet also began her publishing career during this pregnancy. She published poems, book reviews, and articles in the *Monthly Repository*.

After a brief separation from her husband, she organized living arrangements that provided both the continuation of her intimate friendship with JSM and her formal marriage with her husband. JSM spent weekends and evenings with HTM and traveled frequently with her during the following 20 years. In the 1840s and early 1850s Harriet co-wrote a number of newspaper articles on domestic violence despite her near-invalid condition due to consumption and partial paralysis. She wrote one chapter of JSM's *Principles of Political Economy,* the **"Enfranchisement of Women"** for the *Westminster Review,* and a pamphlet on a domestic violence bill before the legislature during the same period. John Taylor died in 1849, and Harriet and JSM married in 1851. During the mid-1850s, Harriet worked with John on the manuscript that would become *On Liberty* and on his *Autobiography.* Neither were published until after her death in 1858.

CRITIQUES FROM 1870 TO 1900

Historical attitudes toward Harriet are not sympathetic. John was effusive in his praise of Harriet's intellect and sensibilities in his *Autobiography,* dedications to various works, and his tombstone for her. Historians reacted with disbelief, disgust, and disapproval.

The earliest commentators admitted some contribution by Harriet to John's work and acknowledged her own work. In 1873, Henry Richard Fox Bourne wrote, "During more than twenty years he had been aided by her talents and encouraged by her sympathy in all the work he had undertaken," and "Mrs. Mill's weak state of health seems to have hardly, repressed her powers of intellect. By her was written the celebrated essay on **'The Enfranchisement of Women'**" (Bourne 1873, 504). Mansfield Marston, also in 1873, concluded that "she must have been gifted with the rarest powers of moral and intellectual symathy [*sic*], for she awoke in Mill an admiration as passionate as it was pure. . . . After the death of her first husband, Mrs. Taylor became the wife of John Mill, and never did a philosopher find a more devoted or absorbing companion" (Marston 1873, 9-10).

But it wasn't long before a pattern that would become familiar emerged. S. E. Henshaw announced, in 1874, "What Mrs. Taylor really was it is difficult to decide, amid the colored lights which Mr. Mill is always burning around her, the incense of adulation in which he envelopes her. . . . Men have been blinded by affection, and bewitched by womankind, . . . [but] John Stuart Mill out-Herods them all" (Henshaw 1874, 521, 523). Harriet bewitched poor innocent John: "Under her touch the torpid spiritual faculties of this [John's] ill-used, defrauded, beautiful nature began to stir at last, and the cramped spirit to rise and stretch its wings" (523). According to Henshaw this bewitching was not a metaphor since Harriet's chief sins were her "infidelity and atheism" (522) which complement her erotic "torpid spiritual faculties."

The charge of bewitching would be repeated throughout the history of Harriet criticism. The earliest commentators, like Henshaw, were probably relying on Carlyle's statements about Harriet. Thomas Carlyle, a notoriously biased (not to mention misogynistic) observer, had initially thought Harriet "a living romance heroine, of the clearest insight, of the royalist volition, very interesting, of questionable destiny" (quoted in Hayek 1951, 80). However, his good opinion lasted only as long as he thought her "a young beautiful reader of mine" (81). When Harriet demonstrated that she was not a disciple of Carlyle, he reported that she was "a dangerous looking woman and engrossed with a dangerous passion." In short, she was John's "charmer" (85). Carlyle had "not seen any riddle of human life which I could so ill form a theory of" (85), but that did not stop him from assigning blame to Harriet for "charming" John. Critics and biographers continued to talk of John as "besotted," "bewitched," and "charmed" (even "Bewitched, Bothered, and Bewildered"?) by Harriet. John is seen as a naive goofus who is so innocent of women he is overwhelmed by the first one to cross his path. (Commentators ignored his intimacy with Eliza Flower, Caroline Fox, and Sarah Austin, among others.) Harriet was the evil seductress who used her magic to capture an exotic prey.

In 1882 Alexander Bain, a friend of JSM, attempts an even-handed approach to Harriet's role in John's life, but no matter how he struggles to understand John's attachment to Harriet, he simply could not overcome his traditional views of women. Overall, he seems to agree with John's younger brother, George's, assessment that Harriet was clever enough, but not as wonderful as John thought (166). Bain tries to understand what he takes to be John's misunderstanding of Harriet's worth: "Hard thinkers are most often *charmed,* not by other thinkers, but by minds of the more concrete and artistic mould" (168).[2] Bain recognizes that John might have agreed that Harriet was more concrete and artistic, but JSM would have believed these elements of her genius. John would not have agreed with his deprecation of Harriet's abilities, but Bain can't help concluding, "Such a *state of subjection* to the will of another, as he candidly avows, and glories in, cannot be received as a right state of things. It *violates our sense of due proportion in the relationship of human beings.* Still, it is but the natural outcome of his *extraordinary hallucination* as to the personal qualities of his wife" (171). He tries to understand this odd relationship without damaging Mill's reputation as a great thinker. Bain denies that Harriet is merely a parrot that echoes John's ideas, as some had suggested, or that John is egoistical enough to delight in this reiteration of his ideas (173), but Bain can find no positive explanation of John's attraction other than the vague "witchery of the other sex" (172). Bain's problem is that faced by all JSM scholars: How does one admire JSM, yet account for his "excessive" devotion to this woman?

Later in the decade, William Courtney tries his hand at explaining the "strange influence to which Mill was subjected" in his *The Life of John Stuart Mill.* This infatuation, "for *infatuation* it can only be called when a man of Mill's intellectual eminence *allows himself* to describe his friend in terms of such unbounded adulation," suggests two explanations (Courtney 1889, 115). First, women have a devious way of dressing up ideas, of making clear and distinct ideas more "picturesque." Like Comte and Descartes, JSM was an example of "philosophic weakness." A man who is engrossed in philosophy is often fascinated by "the concrete and the practical" mind of a woman. "The latter faculty is so far denied to him that he tends to *overestimate its importance.* It seems like a revelation from another world if a *woman of wit* and imagination can clothe with living and palpable flesh some of those arid skeletons among which his mind has had to make its home" (116). This tendency to overestimate imaginatively dressed ideas of women is a fault that all (male) philosophers should be wary of. (Interestingly, even in 1960, a commentator on JSM was still warning others that previous critics who have been favorable to Harriet have fallen victim to the same enchantment that JSM did and that Courtney warned of [Pappe 1960, 28]).

The second danger Courtney warned of consists of women's uncanny ability to jump ahead of logic with intuitive understanding of issues. "Clever women," unlike intelligent men, often derive their knowledge by imaginative leaps, not the "hard thinking" and "mental discipline" that men employ. "A man habitually underrates the woman's quickness of apprehension, and her delicate and intuitive insight into some of the problems with which he has been wrestling. He admires her, therefore, in proportion to the seriousness of his own logic, not in reference to her own native powers." Again, like Bain, Courtney recognizes that such an explanation had been explicitly denied by JSM himself. But JSM's insistence on the similarity of the minds of women and men "would itself support some such *delusion* as that which has been traced above. It is, at least, *a fact,* that the *feminine mind* is *surprisingly quick in assimilating and reproducing thoughts* and ideas which have been sympathetically presented to it. It can adapt itself, perhaps, with greater readiness than the average masculine intellect to a new medium" (Courtney 1889, 117-18). Again, John's example serves as a warning to other philosophers who may fall under the sway of similar feminine intuitions.

CRITIQUES FROM 1900 TO 1930

After the end of the Victorian period, especially from 1910 through the 1920s, commentators offered a more sympathetic portrait of Harriet. In *The Life of W. J. Fox,* Richard Garnett declared that "Harriet Mill occupies a position below her desert in the intellectual history of her time. This is in a measure unavoidable in the case of those who have left no tangible evidence of their power. *The lot of gifted ladies is hard*: if they write they are liable to be anathematised as 'scribbling women,' [*sic*] if they are content to guide and inspire, the reality of the invisible influence is called in question" (Garnett 1910, 97). He looks at the work performed before and after John's friendship with Harriet and decides that John "was not the victim of hallucination" although he may have had "a defective sense of proportion" (97).

Mary Taylor, following in the tradition of her aunt, Helen Taylor, and her grandmother, HTM, lambastes a critic who in the 1910s insisted "that no man of superior gifts should have a highly educated helpmeet, lest she by her 'flabby views of life'—a common result, he says, of high education among women—should exert a vulgarising influence upon him" (1912, 358). This critic had openly suggests a type of relationship between an intellectual man and his companion that seems to underlie, but remain unspoken in, many of the negative criticisms of Harriet, both before and after this time. He suggests Rousseau and his mistress as the appropriate model. However, Mary Taylor argues that the type of relationship Rousseau had is hardly the best suited for a man of genius, much less for a man of conscience: "According to the author of *Emile,* he had five children by Thérèse, each of whom he secretly consigned to the Foundling Hospital as soon as it was born. This wronged and unfortunate woman, who could neither learn to read, remember the names of the months, nor tell the time from the face of a clock, and whose deficiencies were made an occasion for jesting between him and his friends, is represented by the *Edinburgh* reviewer as the right helpmeet for Rousseau" (357). Mary Taylor notes that it is sheer ignorance to believe that geniuses could not be aided by smart women: "The remark that 'no one alive' could have rendered to such great writers as Rousseau, Goethe,

and Mill any assistance in the formation and expression of their ideas is a species of intellectual arrogance and conceit of which I venture to say no man of genius would be guilty" (358). Substitute Einstein and you will hear the same argument offered in the twentieth century for dismissing the contributions of women companions of "geniuses." Mary points to one piece of evidence in favor of Harriet's abilities overlooked by previous critics: the length of a relationship that for more than twenty years was not legally binding on either party (363).

M. Ashworth, in "The Marriage of John Stuart Mill," confirms Mary Taylor's opinion, claiming that Harriet had "a certain mental quality and critical insight what was wasted on her surroundings" prior to meeting John (Ashworth 1916, 164). Ashworth acknowledges their collaboration: "As the friendship progressed, the two got into the habit of working together. . . . She threw in extra threads—golden ones—into the web of his thoughts" (169-70).

Guy Linton Diffenbaugh, in the 1920s, examined the history of Harriet criticism and concluded, "It appears that with a few exceptions Mrs. Taylor was esteemed highly by all those who were permitted the opportunity of associating with her" (1923, 198). Yet he quotes with approval Carlyle's statement: "She was a woman full of *unwise intellect,* always asking questions about all sorts of puzzles—why, how, what for, what makes the exact difference—and Mill was good at answers" (quoted in Diffenbaugh 1923, 204). This may be one of the few astute judgments of Harriet by Carlyle, although I doubt that he understood its significance. Like many of the critics of Harriet and John to follow, Carlyle was chagrined by Harriet's penchant for asking questions. Reacting like God in the Garden to Eve's eating of the tree of the fruit of knowledge, most biographers are threatened, not delighted, by Harriet's provocative questions. Diffenbaugh tries to be impartial: "Yet in all fairness to Mrs. Taylor might it not be said that it took at least a clever person to inquire intelligently of Mill— 'why, how, what for, what makes the exact difference'; and that it required a woman of remarkable mental gymnastics, at least, to assimilate Mill's answers with a degree of intelligent promptness sufficient to infatuate him mentally" (204). Diffenbaugh sees Harriet's questions as merely "clever," and it is a cleverness designed to infatuate, but at least her "witchery" is based on some sort of intelligence in this analysis.

In Ray Strachey's *The Cause: A Short History of the Women's Movement in Great Britain,* the innuendos about Harriet are examined. "Perhaps it was the fact that she lived apart from her first husband which put her wrong with the world; perhaps she was always socially on the defensive as well as too exclusively devoted to Mill. Perhaps she cared nothing at all for other people, was unsympathetic or even unkind, impatient of stupidity and of conventions. There may have been a dozen such outward difficulties which hid her from the world, and obscured her image in the records which are to be found in the lives and letters of her day. We cannot now judge what it was that made his friends distrust her" (1928, 68). The most important evidence that these innuendos are wrong is that which had been offered by Mary Taylor a decade earlier: John's long devotion.

CRITIQUES FROM *1930 TO 1950*

In 1930, Knut Hagberg continues the line of criticism first seen in Henshaw in 1874. Harriet is a powerful but bad influence on John. It is neither her socialism nor her Unitarian tendencies that are the problem, but her atheism. Hagberg concludes that Harriet "came to have a decisive influence over Mill. Unhappily, this seems to have been anything but good." She "made him into a Radical rationalist" (Hagberg 1930, 196). It was this rationalism that led her and seduced John into agnosticism or even atheism. As soon as John was free of Harriet's influence, he turned to a Romantic mysticism. "Mill became a mystic, but only from the moment when he stood alone and detached from her to whose service he, like a medieval knight, had dedicated his life" (198). Here is an explanation that will account for both John's greatness—he had a medieval knight's dedication to his beloved—and the incorrectness of his views—which were due to Harriet's rationalism, and which were corrected upon her death.

In the 1940s Francis E. Mineka shifted the discussion from Harriet's intellectual gifts to her emotional support of John. Harriet could be praised because she offered spiritual sustenance. Harriet Taylor "was a woman of refinement and taste, interested in literature and questions of ethics and politics, but endowed with a strong emotional nature which kept her out of the bluestocking category. . . . However over-colored by emotion his estimate of her powers may have been, there can be no doubt that she was the saving grace of his inner life. Without her, John Mill might well have been a different person, but one can doubt that he would have been as fine, as understanding, or as great a man" (Mineka 1944, 273-75).

CRITIQUES IN THE *1950s*

All biographers before 1951 had based their observations on secondhand information about Harriet. Not until nearly one hundred years after Harriet's death, when F. A. Hayek published *John Stuart Mill and Harriet Taylor: Their Friendship and Subsequent Marriage* (1951), did scholars have access to some of Harriet's letters, unpublished essays, and poems. (Hayek also mentions her work on the newspaper articles listed as coauthored in John's handwritten bibliography, although no scholar to date has studied these works carefully.) Hayek notes that "apart from Mill none of those who expressed views about Harriet Taylor's qualities have really had much grounds on which to base them, except W. J. Fox, whose is also the only other voice that joins in her praise" (Hayek 1951, 15). Hayek's opinion after studying these newly available documents was that "her influence on his thought and outlook, whatever her capacities may have been, [was] quite as great as Mill asserts, but that [it] acted in a way somewhat different from what is commonly believed. Far from it having been

the sentimental it was the rationalist element in Mill's thought which was mainly strengthened by her influence" (17). The letters Hayek printed for the first time revealed the depth of Harriet's involvement in the writing published in John's name.

Diana Trilling's analysis of Harriet's writings published in Hayek's book expressed a very different opinion of Harriet. Whereas Hayek's examination of these documents revealed that Harriet's early unpublished essays "curiously anticipate[d] some of the arguments of *On Liberty*" (26), Trilling asserts that these essays and letters blow the whistle on Harriet. "Mrs. Taylor . . . [was] one of the meanest and dullest ladies in literary history, a monument of nasty self-regard, as lacking in charm as in grandeur" (Trilling 1952, 116). Harriet was "prideful, vain and mean-spirited. . . . This intellectual beacon . . . was nothing more than a vest-pocket flashlight of a mind" (120). These pronouncements became the most often repeated comments on Harriet. What evidence does Trilling point to in the letters or other documents? None. She is simply sure that "this was no woman, no real woman—the letters, full as they are of injured vanity, petty egoism and ambition, show no touch of true femininity, no taint of the decent female concerns which support our confidence in the intelligence of someone like Jane Carlyle" (119-20). Harriet's flaw is that she is not a "real woman" and shows no signs of "true femininity." Perhaps if she had gotten up before dawn the way Jane Carlyle did to quiet the chickens so her man would not be disturbed (Rose, 1984, 246-67), Trilling would have admired her more.

Michael Packe's *The Life of John Stuart Mill* was the first biography written using the new material found in the London School of Economics archives which Hayek brought to light. Whereas Trilling condemned Harriet for not being feminine enough, Packe (returning to Mineka's approach) believed that Harriet used all her feminine charms to control John. His portrait of Harriet is almost a cartoon of the 1950s view of women. She was a "handsome sprat" that another man could use "to catch an exceptional mackerel" (Packe 1954, 128). Packe decided that at first Harriet had ambitions of her own to write, for example, when she published the reviews, articles and poems in the *Monthly Repository* during the early 1830s. "Harriet, not yet aware of the august mouthpiece she was soon to gain, had a great ambition to become a writer like Harriet Martineau" (131-32). But after a spat with John during which he hadn't done any significant work, her true feminine side surfaced and she finally behaved herself. Harriet gave up her "manful ambition" in order to be of use to John, to "express herself in a more feminine way through her effect on him. . . . Harriet Taylor's influence on Mill at this time was soft and womanly. She soothed him in anxiety; she worried about his health. She afforded him emotional release. In this respect she was completely adequate (237).[3]

According to Packe, however, as Harriet's beauty evaporated, so did her soft, womanly support. "She was now 34. Her beauty had begun to fade, and, as a result of her nervous disorder, the early vivacity of her quick emphatic temperament became more and more tempestuous" (289). Now Packe's language about Harriet changes. Harriet "insisted on" John changing the *Principles of Political Economy.* "She demanded a complete reversal of his economic treatise in its most essential feature. And she obtained it . . . he was forced to give way" (313). In short, "Harriet's astounding, almost hypnotic control of Mill's mind was not confined to reversing the direction of his economic theory" (315). Oddly, despite these passages, Packe denies that Harriet's influence should be reduced to her "charm[ing] and bewitch[ing] his mind," (316) as other critics put it. He believes that her influence went even further: "The influence she had gradually extended over him now ended in complete ascendancy, and his further writings were not the work of one mind, but of the fusion of two. . . . Her predominance was even more complete than he himself pronounced" (316). John was not only emotionally seduced by Harriet, he was intellectually coerced as well. "Mill ceased to make distinction between Harriet's mind and his. In little things as well as great, he followed where she led" (370). Packe acknowledged the intellectual contributions of Harriet but only by exaggerating her power over John. Instead of contributing to their mutual work, Harriet is seen as dominating John's work. Instead of partnership, Packe sees a matriarchy.

Ruth Borchard wrote *John Stuart Mill: the Man* in 1957. Borchard's Harriet was a "forceful, domineering personality" who "overpowered" John "by her intensely feminine atmosphere" (Borchard 1957, 38, 46). John necessarily obeyed Harriet (55). Harriet's "morbid inclinations" result in an interest in domestic violence, as witnessed by the newspaper articles. "She induced Mill to publish articles against such offenses. . . . This preoccupation with, and passionate railing against, [domestic violence] denote that some primitive spring in Harriet herself was touched. A trace of masochism is part of a normal woman's psychology; it fits her for the job of childbirth. But Harriet's . . . hungry interest in sadistic treatment of women . . . point[s] to a deep-seated masochism unfitting her for normal physical love" (66-67).[4]

What more can one say? Borchard argued that Harriet "had successfully taken his [JSM's] father's place in his life" (72). The charge that Harriet played a man's role in John's life while he played the woman's role is repeated throughout the history of scholarship on the two. Always the assumptions underlying the analysis are that if John wasn't in charge, wasn't dominant, then Harriet must have been; and that roles must be defined along gender lines. Borchard attributes power to Harriet, but only a domineering kind of power that can then be held responsible for all the ideas in John's philosophy that Borchard disapproves of, for example, his socialism. She claims: "Her influence on Mill can hardly be over-estimated. Whatever influence Mill exerted in his own time and over English history must be equally ascribed to Harriet. And the strong impetus given by his books towards socialism and the present welfare state must certainly be attributed more to Harriet

than to Mill himself" (99). Would Joseph McCarthy have thought Harriet such a communist that he would have asked her to testify before the House Un-American Affairs Committee? At least Borchard is cleared—along with John. The villain is Harriet.

A couple of small articles in the 1950s tried to balance this picture of Harriet. L. Robbins, in a review of Packe's book, points out Harriet's good sense in her reaction to John's correspondence with Comte (Robbins 1957, 250-9). Maurice Cranston describes Harriet as "a beautiful, forceful, aspiring woman, living like the heroine of a play by Ibsen, in an atmosphere which thwarted her and curbed her spirit, in which she felt a lack of intellectual culture and of visionary ardour" (Cranston 1959, 385). Cranston describes a partnership between them, or what he calls "a marriage of minds," which is unusual among philosophers. However, neither of these were adequate ammunition against the two 1950s biographies of John.

CRITIQUES IN THE *1960s*

Although in the 1950s Harriet was drawn as a sort of intellectual vamp, she did appear as powerful (even if the power was a malicious, unhealthy sort). As unbelievable as it will sound after having read the last couple of pages, the writers in the 1950s were considered supporters of Harriet. In fact, they were criticized for portraying Harriet as too important. In 1960 H. O. Pappe's *John Stuart Mill and the Harriet Taylor Myth,* a 48-page monograph that has always received more attention than it deserves, was published. Pappe chastises previous writers on John and Harriet for presenting Harriet as too powerful. He praises Borchard because "[b]eing a woman, she is not overpowered by Harriet's *anima* (as were, I believe, Hayek and Packe). She has enough feminine earthiness to see through some of Harriet's aspirations and devices" (Pappe 1960, 28). Pappe goes on to claim that Borchard herself "does not go far enough in tracing Harriet's masochism" (29). Pappe believes Harriet is not very smart (22) and did not influence John's ideas in any significant way (19, 46). He suggests that all previous scholars have gotten it wrong; instead of Harriet influencing John it was the other way around.

The following year, Jack Stillinger published *The Early Draft of John Stuart Mill's Autobiography.* The draft of JSM's autobiography that had been buried in various libraries and unavailable to scholars was now unveiled. This early draft displays the suggested changes made by Harriet as well as the acceptance of those changes by John. Here we can see their mutual work on this one manuscript—a manuscript that, as an autobiography, should be more exclusively in one person's voice than any other. Stillinger's assessment? "Her alterations in the early draft show her to have had some sense of style and propriety of tone, but they do not confirm Mill's estimate of her intellectual qualities" (Stillinger 1961, 25). He quoted the infamous Trilling article approvingly and signed on to the psychological theory first presented in Borchard that Harriet replaced John's father (28).

In the 1960s, only Gertrude Himmelfarb would argue in a short article that would later develop into a book that Harriet was influential, but again, as in the 1950s biographies, the influence was negative. Himmelfarb claims that John's move toward socialism—the worst idea John had, according to Himmelfarb—was all Harriet's doing.[5]

Aside from one short, virtually undocumented biography by John Ellery (1964),[6] the other biographers in the next several years would try a new approach to Harriet: ignore her. Joseph Hamburger's *Intellectuals in Politics: John Stuart Mill and The Philosophic Radicals* (1965), has only three passing references to Harriet in a book devoted to the period in which Harriet and John were beginning their intimate acquaintance and in which Harriet played a distinct role in John's life. Alan Ryan doesn't even mention Harriet in the index of his biography (1970).

Two "defenders" of Harriet during the sixties offered only lukewarm support. Mineka reiterated his claim from the forties that Harriet was an emotional, not an intellectual, contributor to John's life and work (1963, 306).[7] John Robson, in "Harriet Taylor and John Stuart Mill: Artist and Scientist," says there are two approaches to Harriet, that of the 1950s, that is, that Harriet dominated John, and that of the 1960s, that is, that Harriet contributed little to John's work. Robson adopts the hypothesis that "the relation between Mill and Harriet, it seems likely, was that common, if not invariable, in marriages between members of the *intelligentsia*: frequent discussion, mutual enlightenment, considerable independence in thought, and—the pattern is now changing—subordination of the wife's ambitions to the husband's" (Robson 1966, 171). In his investigation of this hypothesis, Robson focuses on the question of Harriet's specific contributions to John's work by examining her writing. This is a milestone in HTM scholarship. One hundred and eight years after her death, someone finally considers Harriet's writing (even if it is only two paragraphs long!). Mind you, it is only to discover whether or not she contributed to John, not to consider simply what she had to say. But, at least Harriet's work is finally studied.

Robson's conclusions are a bit confusing. Although he says Harriet's early essays and her **"Enfranchisement of Women"** "can be seen as forerunners of Mill's *Subjection of Women* and *On Liberty* "(171), his overall assessment is that she didn't influence him, in fact the opposite occurred (172). How can her essays be forerunners of two important works, if "there is no strong indication of influence"? In Robson's study of John's comments on Harriet's share in the work, the reason for the confusion becomes clearer. Using a passage from the last chapter of the *Logic*, Robson casts Harriet as the Artist, and John as the Scientist. Although John believes the Artist's role is fundamental, Robson believes that "the division of labour is rather unusual" (178). Interestingly, this view of woman as the "dreamer," the emotional one; and man as the logical "scientist" is one of the "backward" views of John's that Harriet fought against. That this statement of John's would

one day be used to classify her, especially without John's generous affirmation of the importance of such attributes, would have rankled both of them. Robson is willing to declare that Harriet was the more practical of the two: "The persuasion of others, and the practicability of programmes, both derive from experience and habitual recognition of conflicts and contingencies . . . there is no reason to doubt that Harriet Taylor, whose approach as poet and prophetess was more concrete than abstract, also influenced him in this direction" (181). His final pronouncement on Harriet's role is that Harriet encouraged John's "many-sidedness," but "the theoretical groundwork is Mill's . . . She was not, in any meaningful sense, the 'joint author' of his works" (186). Underlying this analysis is the echo of William Courtney's warning about women's clever kind of knowledge that "leaps ahead of logic" mixed with Mineka's assessment that Harriet provided emotional but not intellectual support. Although this analysis is more careful than most, the prize of male scholarship, the text, is still John's sole possession. Harriet can only dream, support, and suggest.

CRITIQUES IN THE 1970S

What a breath of fresh air it was when, in 1970, Alice Rossi edited *Essays on Sex Equality* by John Stuart Mill and Harriet Taylor. According to Rossi, the resistance to the acceptance of Harriet's contribution to John's ideas is due to three factors: the fight between Philosophical Radicals and Unitarian Radicals (Rossi 1970, 36), the commentator's attitude toward socialism (38), and plain old sexism (45). I will discuss these and other reasons for the currents in Harriet scholarship in Part 2.

Rossi believes, as I do, that Harriet's works need to be studied in order to make an accurate assessment of her work or her influence on John. "None of the Mill scholars have examined the essays collected in this volume for clues to the kind of relationship John and Harriet tried to maintain in their years together. Nor has due allowance been made, in my judgment, for Mill's own intellectual toughness. Mill was not a man to be easily influenced and won over by an idea or person" (Rossi 1970, 39). As is clear from the quotations I've offered throughout this history, Harriet is seen either as noninfluential or as important only because she seduces John into bad ideas. "Though it is couched in terms of detached scholarship, one senses in Mill scholars an unwitting desire to reject Harriet Taylor as capable of contributing in any significant way to the vigor of Mill's analysis of political and social issues unless it included some tinge of sentiment or political thought the scholar disapproved of, in which case this disliked element was seen as Harriet's influence" (Rossi 1970, 44-45).

Virginia Held, in a review of Rossi's introduction to *Essays on Sex Equality,* supports this approach to Harriet. Held recognizes an important point about Harriet scholarship: "As for Harriet Taylor's coldness, it is more in the eye of the critic than implicit in the evidence" (Held 1971, 406). Max Lerner's pronouncement that "we know [Harriet] was a frigid woman" (in the introduction to *The Essential Works of John Stuart Mill*, quoted in Held 1971, 405) is rejected in favor of this analysis of Harriet's relationship to John and her husband: "She tried to arrive at a reasonable solution that would cause the least pain to all concerned" (Held 1971, 406). What a difference between these new critics and everyone who has written on Harriet before! A couple of years later, the first academic study of John's *The Subjection of Women* was published (Tatalovich 1973). Although this is one text we know Harriet was not involved in writing (it was written after her death), Tatalovich is able to see her influence. Harriet showed John the mental capabilities of a woman and their partnership served as a basis for his description of "the benefits of a marriage [based] on equality" (Tatalovich 1973, 288).

In the 1970s for the first time, a biography of John was written that began to understand the relationship between John and Harriet. Eugene August's *John Stuart Mill: A Mind at Large* (1975), was an important contribution. Instead of Harriet's domination of John, on the one hand, or her insignificance, on the other hand, their work is presented as a partnership. Not the simple partnership of equals in every way, but the partnership of a woman with a good mind but little training because of the educational and social background she had to endure and a man who had both a great mind and extraordinary training. August lets John explain the problem: "Deficiency of education has cut off women from the great traditions of thought and art. Even when a woman hits upon a lucky insight, it is frequently lost, Mill points out (waxing autobiographical again), for want of a husband or friend to evaluate and publicize it. 'Who can tell,' he wonders, 'how many of the most original thoughts put forth by male writers, belong to a woman by suggestion, to themselves only by verifying and working out? If I may judge by may own case, a very large proportion indeed'" (Mill, quoted in August 1975, 218). August sketches a new picture of the Mills's life together: "John's creative energies underwent an astonishing renewal during the collaboration with Harriet. No longer was it *his* genius; it was *their* genius" (August 1975, 136; original emphases).

Have scholars since the early seventies continued to expand and explore the "new" portrait of Harriet? Unfortunately, the backlash began even by the mid-1970s. Three major studies of John, Gertrude Himmelfarb's *On Liberty and Liberalism: The Case of John Stuart Mill* (1974); Bruce Mazlish's *James and John Stuart Mill: Father and Son in the Nineteenth Century* (1975); and Josephine Kamm's *John Stuart Mill in Love* (1977) all return to the view of Harriet found in the fifties and sixties.

Himmelfarb's book, like her article from a decade earlier, argues that all the bad ideas John had, his leanings toward socialism in *Principles of Political Economy* and all of *On Liberty*, were Harriet's doings. Even though Himmelfarb realizes that "the closer any collaboration, the less evidence of it there is likely to be. And a marital collaboration is, of course, the hardest to document" (Himmelfarb

1974, 239); the simplistic ideas and paranoid attitudes she finds in *On Liberty* must be Harriet's (259). The similarities between Harriet's early unpublished essays on tolerance and the ideas in *On Liberty* are taken as evidence for John's corruption. But, as we have seen in other commentators, Himmelfarb still will not attribute authorship to Harriet of the sacred text. John may have been overwhelmed by Harriet's dumb ideas, but the text—the words on the page that really count—is John's. John was "'thoroughly imbued' with a mode of thought that was 'emphatically hers'," but he still owns the text (267). We're back to "Bewitched, Bothered, and Bewildered."

Bruce Mazlish takes a Freudian tack. John chose Harriet not because she was intelligent or provocative but because her name was Harriet. Harriet? you say? Yes, because John's mother and a sister were named Harriet. Mazlish proposes that because Harriet had the same name as John's mother, but had the personality of his father, by loving her John could "possess not only his mother, but his father as well" (Mazlish 1975, 284). And he's not joking. It is John's "bisexuality" that allowed him to be attracted to such a manly woman as Harriet (329). Given the Freudian flavor of this study, it will be no surprise to discover that Harriet is not particularly well thought of. John didn't need Harriet to do the work he did, even though Harriet was not an idiot. (She was an above-average 23-year-old "girl" [307].) Harriet may have a sensitive heart, but she still had "hypnotic power" over John. Mazlish repeats a story about a chair hanging over a cliff that John and his friends visited in Ireland. The folklore declared that whoever had the courage to sit in the chair would rule the house. Neither John nor his friends sat, thus symbolizing an important characteristic of John: he wasn't a "real man," or, as Mazlish puts it, "Conjugal male preeminence was not a prominent trait in his relation to Harriet. Rather, the reverse was true, and willed as such by Mill himself" (309). "The Mill-Taylor relation was almost a parody of the patriarchal family, but with Harriet commanding and Mill obeying" (308). Just as we've seen in Packe and others, the assumption is always that someone must control, must dominate a relationship. Since it is clear John didn't, Harriet must have. Real sharing of power is not even conceived as an option.

Josephine Kamm's contribution, *John Stuart Mill in Love*, is merely a rehashing of the fifties approach. She virtually repeats Borchard when she says that Harriet's concern with domestic violence is an expression of Harriet's masochism (Kamm 1977, 42). Back is Harriet's rule over John (83). Kamm grudgingly respects Harriet only because she must have been strong in order to force John to acquiesce to her ideas. "What was remarkable was that this largely self-educated woman could, and did, speak and correspond with him on equal terms and, when she felt strongly enough, force him to accept her ideas" (39).

CRITIQUES FROM 1980 TO PRESENT

In 1989, Gail Tulloch published the first book-length study of John's views on sexual equality. Although Harriet's name does not appear in the title, Tulloch does include, for the first time in history, a preliminary study of Harriet's essays on equality, including her **"Enfranchisement of Women."** Tulloch's "judgement is that Harriet Taylor's influence was clearly considerable" (1989, 72). This careful study of John's work and Harriet's in relation to John's is a very important contribution. Tulloch concludes the section on Harriet with the following: "Harriet's position is thus both more consistent in itself and a better guide to practice. It is also consistent with Mill's emphasis on social equality, and is what he too should have said" (99). I only wish she had written the book on Harriet's work primarily instead of secondarily.

Phyllis Rose's *Parallel Lives: Five Victorian Marriages* (1984) is a delightful, provocative study of power relations in the marriages of the Dickenses, Ruskins, Carlyles, and Mills and the common-law marriage of George Lewes and George Eliot (Marianne Evans). Although I admire this book enormously, Rose's attitude toward Harriet and John vacillates. On the one hand, John is a man "with strongly egalitarian politics," yet he is "still subject to domination by [a shrew]" (Rose 1984, 15). Rose says that "Harriet made the decisions. Harriet ran the show. A female autocrat merely replaced the usual male" (137). On the other hand, just the page before, she says, "The Mills were embarked upon a great experiment, something new in the history of relations between men and women—a true marriage of equals. But so unusual was this situation that for Harriet to be anywhere near equal she had to be 'more than equal.' Think of it as a domestic case of affirmative action. To achieve equality, more power had to go to Harriet, in compensation for the inequality of their conditions" (136). "They were a perfect intellectual team" because Harriet "was the executive. She made decisions. . . . She cut crudely, perhaps, but emphatically and practically to important matters." John's mind needed direction, and Harriet was willing and capable of providing direction. John's mind "initiated nothing. He was like an automaton which functioned perfectly when set on course, but could not set its own course or turn itself on. So Harriet, spontaneous, imperious, intellectually passionate, without self-doubt, put the logic machine into motion. She was his starter button. . . . She served as the part of himself that cared" (132, 131). Was this a "perfect intellectual team" or the domination of a good man by a shrew?

Alan Ryan, in "Sense and Sensibility in Mill's Political Thought" (1991) may clarify the attitude toward intellectual history that allows us to sympathize with Rose's ambiguity. He says, "Generosity and flexibility can be aimed at and with luck achieved; a God-like perspective in which all times and places are equally transparent cannot" (Ryan 1991, 122). Harriet and John's relationship was neither simple nor straightforward. It was a mixture of dependency and independence which can only be grasped through a generous shaking of the hand that is offered in letters, essays, manuscripts, and other scraps of information left as a trail through the woods of their lives. Without the trail everyone will get lost in his or her own historical, sociological, and philosophical prejudices. What is

needed is to present all of Harriet Taylor Mill's words for the first time, to allow her to speak. When that happens, each of us can listen and try to put together at least one plausible map through the woods.

PART 2. ANALYSIS OF *HTM* CRITICISM

Why have critics been so hard on Harriet? There are a number of reasons. First are the three outlined by Alice Rossi: the fight between Philosophical Radicals and Unitarian Radicals; the commentator's attitude toward socialism; and sexism. Philosophical Radicals, such as Bentham, James Mill, George Grote, and others, believed in the reform of the legal system. They believed that the greatest division in society was that between the aristocracy and "the people." The Unitarian Radicals, including William Fox and Harriet Martineau were more concerned with personal and social reforms and were more skeptical of legislative reform. They were more socially unconventional. They acknowledged a deep division between the working classes and middle classes as well as that between the middle classes and the aristocracy. Although the groups overlapped, a certain tension remained between them. Harriet was a Unitarian when she met John and contributed to the Unitarian publication *The Monthly Repository*. John had been moving away from the Philosophical Radicals since his mental crisis in which he questioned all possibility of real advancement of society. Those who liked JSM and were ardent Philosophical Radicals blamed HTM for John's move away from his roots. Those who sympathized with the Unitarian Radicals were kinder in recounting Harriet's influence on John. Not only did this difference of opinion occur among actual participants in these groups but also among the scholars of these groups. As Rossi demonstrates so clearly, Garnett and Mineka, who studied the Unitarians, were the most sympathetic critics of HTM. Laski, Rinehard, Stillinger, Lerner, and Trilling, who specialized in the Philosophical Radicals, were harsher in their critiques (Rossi 1970, 33-34).

Rossi also uncovers another source of the dislike of Harriet: the critic's opinion of socialism. If, like Hayek (1951), (and later Himmelfarb [1965] and even Borchard [1957]—although these commentators are not mentioned by Rossi) a critic disapproves of socialism, Harriet is seen as powerful and is thus blamed for John's move toward socialism. Critics of socialism "could then interpret Mill's socialist phase as a temporary aberration due to Harriet's influence over him." Most socialists, however, did not approve of Harriet's influence. For example, "Laski, a socialist, did not wish to view Mill's socialist thinking as a product of a woman's influence and hence followed the earlier trend toward a negative view of Harriet and of her contribution to Mill's thinking" (38). So either way, Harriet lost out. If critics didn't like socialism, it was all Harriet's fault that John leaned that way; if critics liked socialism, they weren't about to attribute it to a mere woman's influence. So Harriet was strong and evil, or weak and good. Not a happy choice.

Finally, Rossi points to the overall sexism in critics' treatment of Harriet. The history I have included here is far more extensive than the one Rossi includes, but it only re-inforces the obvious bias in HTM scholarship. "Assertive women were undoubtedly an even greater irritation to Victorian men than they are to men today. Harriet Taylor was no shrinking violet, no soft and compliant woman" (Rossi 1970, 35-6). The numerous references to Harriet's masochism because she was interested in domestic violence, frigidity because she chose not to have sex with John, or the persistent attempts to portray Harriet as stupid, incompetent, or aggressive support Rossi's observation.

Looking at the history of Harriet criticism as a whole, I see a pattern that Rossi overlooked. Who are the sensitive critics of HTM? Richard Garnett and Mary Taylor in the 1910s; Diffenbaugh and Ray Strachey in the 1920s; Francis Mineka in the 1940s; Hayek in the early 1950s; Rossi, Virginia Held, and Eugene August in the 1970s. A quick comparison of these dates with a history of feminism shows a clear parallel. The 1910-1920s, 1940s, and 1970s were periods of growth for women's rights. The thirties, fifties and eighties were backlash periods. The history of criticism of Harriet is a history in miniature of women during the past one hundred years. Historians of philosophy are more influenced by the prevailing societal attitudes than most would like to admit. Philosophers like to think of themselves as "above" all that. The pattern in the critiques of Harriet demonstrates otherwise.

Even with the individual and general sexism in the history of philosophy, HTM would probably not have drawn quite so much ire if she had just "behaved herself." Historians haven't been so nasty to Jane Carlyle, Elizabeth Barrett Browning, or Sarah Austin, for example. But Harriet refused to play the role of a traditional Victorian subservient "lady." She asked questions that irritated and provoked nearly everyone but JSM.[8] Ladies don't ask such impertinent questions as, "How do you know?" "Why?" "What is the difference?" Intellectual curiosity was not an acceptable attribute in Victorian women, or in their more modern sisters. Jane Eyre wreaks havoc on others and on herself by asking dangerous questions such as, "Who is the woman in the attic?" or "What should I do?" or "What do I want?" The responses to Jane's questions—denial, subterfuge, lies, expressions of confusion and anxiety—demonstrate the danger others perceive in her questions. Questioners are always disruptive, as Socrates' death testifies, but women's questions are particularly threatening. They remind us of that source of all evil: Eve. Eve, with her unholy passion to know, to eat of the tree of the fruit of knowledge, is the mythological baggage that haunts our minds like the madwoman in the attic. Jane and Eve and Harriet don't have knowledge. They just have a passion to know. They know they don't know, so they ask. Unlike the fictional Jane Eyre, Harriet Taylor is not forced to starve or find a position as a schoolteacher, she is merely ostracized by both contemporaries and historians for her "unwise intellect."

Harriet's insistence on asking questions is the sign of her philosophizing. She wonders. Aristotle says that philosophy begins in wonder. That "radical lack which the Other

cannot complete," as Le Doeuf puts it, "forms the true starting point of philosophy" (1987, 188). Men have a difficult time accepting women who cannot be completed by men's existence alone—a woman who won't give up questioning either his ideas or those of others, a woman who asks "why, how, what for, what makes the exact difference" (Carlyle, in Diffenbaugh 1923, 204). Much of Harriet's philosophizing was verbal, not written. In her letters and in John's there are many references to their mutual desire to be together again so they can talk about the issues that concerned them. She writes, "I confess I prefer an aristocracy of men & women together to an aristocracy of men only—for I think the last is far more sure to last—but all this we have often said. . . . If you think this can be done & were to do it before Sat^y we could talk it over together" (II/322).[9] And again, "I have so much to say to you that no one but you could understand" (L/28). And yet again, "I have so very much to say which must wait" (L/30). Harriet writes to John, "I am ready to stand by my opinions but not to hear them travestied, & mixed up with what appears to me opinions founded on no principles & arguments so weak that I should dread for the furtherance of my anti religious opinions the imputation that they do not admit of being better defended. The fool ought to be sharply set down by *reasons*—but he is such an *excessive fool* & so lost in self sufficiency that he will cavil & prate say what you will" (original emphases). Later in the same letter she writes, "I was excessively amused by the top paragraph in the Daily News from Paris saying that Proudhon moved that the fiction of the acknowledgement of the being of a God sh^d be erased. It does one good to find one man who dares to open his mouth & say what he thinks on that subject. It did me good, & I need something for the spirits. . . . Adio caro carissimo till Sat^y when we shall talk over all these things" (L/8). This is the letter of a person who asks, challenges, critiques, and loves to talk about issues: it is the letter of a philosopher, not merely an admirer of a philosopher.

In addition to her "exasperating" questions, Harriet was strong, aggressive, and practical. She writes to her daughter about a recent journey: "The fact is we always get the last seats in the railway carriage, as I cannot run on quick, & if he goes on he never succeeds, I always find him running up and down & looking lost in astonishment, so I have given up trying to get any seats but those that are left" (LIII/12). To a man who could not clothe himself until he was ten years old, who, as an adult, was shocked to discover that the house required more coal in winter than summer, and who couldn't accomplish the difficult task of finding a seat for himself and his wife on a train by himself, Harriet was a savior. Her practical, no-nonsense ability to undertake daily life was a godsend. But to contemporaries and historians of philosophy who don't appreciate these characteristics, she was pushy, domineering, and vexatious. Harriet understood the finances of a newspaper purchase (XXVIII/174), could negotiate the details of publishing a book (XXVIII/178), and figured out that the gold rush in California might mean an increased need for the drugs her husband sold (XXVIII/225). Harriet had a type of practical knowledge that not only JSM but many "thinkers" since have lacked. These absentminded professors are more often than not males, and each has someone, more often than not a woman, in his life who buys and prepares food, sees that the toilet is cleaned, and calls the dentist. Harriet had a practical wisdom which she asserted. I believe there is an assumption among too many philosophers that "real" philosophers, deep thinkers, are so devoted to the life of the mind that to attend to "trivial" practical affairs would take away from their intellectual pursuits. To them, being absentminded is not a vice, but a virtue; it is proof that you are serious. Harriet's practical wisdom, conversely, is proof that she is not a serious thinker. She was a nice helper for JSM, tending to his everyday needs, but clearly not a philosopher. Real philosophers don't know how to grab a seat on the train or know who to call to catch a rat.

Furthermore, Harriet gets angry, even at the child prodigy, the famous philosopher, John Stuart Mill. She writes to him: "I am not one to 'create chimeras about nothing'— you should know enough about the effects of petty annoyances to know that they are wearing & depressing not only to body but to mind—these, on account of our relation, I have & you have not. . . . I am not a fool & I should laugh at, or very much dislike the thought, that you sh^d make your 'life obscure insignificant & useless' pour les beaux yeux" (L/7). Historians of philosophy have not taken well to such expressions of anger against one of their own. HTM refuses to take John's reputation seriously: "Good heaven have you at last arrived at fearing to be *'obscure & insignificant'*! What *can* I say to that but 'by all means pursue your brilliant and important career'. . . . Good God what has the love of two equals to do with making obscure & insignificant. If ever you *could* be obscure & insignificant you *are* so whatever happens & certainly a person who did not feel contempt at the very idea the words create is not one to brave the world" (L/6; HTM's emphases). Sometimes her critique of him is less angry, but no less forceful, as when she chides him about his wishy-washy attitude toward Comte. She writes to him, "I now & then find a generous defect in your mind or yr method—such is your liability to take an over large *measure* of people—having to draw in afterwards—a proceeding more needful than pleasant" (II/327; HTM's emphasis). Although she is using good sense in her critique of Mill's attitude toward Comte, her lack of respect rankles historians of philosophy. As I will show below, she refuses to play the student to the "great philosopher." JSM apparently came to his senses: too many historians of philosophy have not.

To complicate matters even more, Harriet combined her potent personality with radical views about marriage, religion, and socialism. Harriet's ideas were more extreme (and more advanced) than even John's on a number of issues. She noted the discriminatory nature of the marriage contract, "the only contract ever heard of, of which a necessary condition in the contracting parties was, that one should be entirely ignorant of the nature and terms of the contract. For owing to the voting of chastity as the greatest virtue of women, the fact that a woman knew what she undertook would be considered just reason for preventing her undertaking it" (Box III/77). Harriet argues that women must be emancipated "from their present degraded slavery to the *necessity* of marriage, or to modes of earning their living which (with the sole exception of artists) consist only of poorly paid & hardly worked occupations, all the professions, mercantile clerical legal & medical, as well as all government posts being monopolized by men. . . . The great practical ability of women which is now wasted on worthless trifles or sunk in the stupidities called *love* would tell with most 'productive' effect on the business of life" (XXVII/40; HTM's emphases). She believed that women should be able to work outside the home even if they were married and that if women had access to education and professions, they would choose for themselves whether or not to have children and how many they would have. Her views on divorce were also more revolutionary than JSM's. Both the left and the right criticized Harriet's views and life on this subject. Those on the right thought she was a loose woman because she abandoned her husband for a liaison with John. Those on the left thought it unnecessary prudery on Harriet's part not to live openly with John, not to go to bed with him, and to give in to conventionality by marrying him only after her husband died. Furthermore, Harriet was an atheist. John was too, but an atheist woman has been much harder for others to swallow than a man with the same beliefs. From Henshaw in 1874 on, Harriet's religious beliefs have been a source of irritation. Finally, her interest in the 1848 French revolution and her pro-socialism continue, as I pointed out above, to be interpreted as part of her seductively ruinous effect on John (according to critics on the right) or as nothing but her insipid ineffectiveness (according to critics on the left). Although I suspect that these ideas are the source of some of the unpleasantness in the HTM critiques, none of the critics attacks or even mentions these ideas directly. They just hover like a fog behind the ad feminam attacks.

So far I've reiterated Rossi's three reasons for the negative views of Harriet, noted the parallel between the periods of progress and backlash in the women's movement and periods when Harriet is treated negatively and positively in the history of philosophy, and discussed Harriet's character traits—her penchant for asking questions, her practical wisdom, and her radical ideas. All of these are partial answers to the question I am pursuing. To these I now add our lack of understanding of women partners of "famous" philosophers. Michèle Le Doeuf in "Women and Philosophy" describes a pattern of such relationships as the "Héloïse complex." She notes that Hipparchia, Héloïse, and Elisabeth (Descartes' correspondent) "had one thing in common: they all experienced great passions, and their relationship with philosophy existed only through their love for a man, a particular philosopher" (Le Doeuf 1987, 184-85). Their love of philosophy was intertwined with their love of the man who made philosophy available to them. This transference is not unusual among students and teachers, but it is particularly troublesome for women because until recently women have had no access to philosophy except through the mediation of a man. Universities have not been open to women until this century. "The 'godfather' relationship has opened up the whole field of philosophy to the disciple's desire, whilst women's transference relationships to the theoretical have only opened up to them the field of their idol's own philosophy" (Le Doeuf 1987, 187). Whereas the institution of the university provided support for the scholar who became disillusioned with a particular teacher or philosophical position, "the women amateurs . . . have been bound to the dual relationship, because a dual relationship does not produce the dynamics that enable one to leave it" (187).

In *Hipparchia's Choice: An Essay Concerning Women, Philosophy, Etc.,* Le Doeuf adds to her characterization of the Héloïse complex. Not only does Abelard desire the admiration of Héloïse, but he also requires the admiration of the scholarly world. He "wants not only to produce philosophy but also to be a philosopher" (Le Doeuf 1991, 164). Sartre and Beauvoir fit the general pattern, but Beauvoir may have escaped it by producing philosophy without "posing" as a philosopher (165). I believe that, like Simone de Beauvoir, Harriet may have escaped the Héloïse complex by doing philosophy without seeing herself as a philosopher. During a period in which Harriet must have felt very vulnerable, that is, during her husband's final illness, she writes to JSM, "The certainty of being really of use & quite indispensable to him (or to any one) gives me a quantity of strength and life—. . . . Take care of yourself for the world's sake" (XXIX/250-51). Although her prime reference is John Taylor, she implies that she has partially assumed the Héloïse role in regard to JSM. She wants to be of "use" to him, so that he can produce something "for the world's sake." After all, she had only written some newspaper pieces about domestic violence and some poems and reviews. And parts of books under JSM's name. But she does not remain in this role for long.

In general her letters make it clear that she acts as a partner with JSM, not as his admirer or student. In private she and John both knew she philosophized and wrote of their verbal discussions and work on manuscripts. Her few surviving letters are most often used to condemn her. Harriet's letters to her husband, John Taylor, tell of her work on manuscripts with John Mill and sometimes ask that manuscripts of her own be sent to her. About the initial work on *Principles of Political Economy*, Harriet writes to her husband, "I do certainly look more like a ghost [than] a living person, but I dare say I shall soon recover some better looks when we get to Brighton. I think I shall not be able to go before the end of next week being just now much occupied with the book" (XXVIII/170). "The book on The Principles of Political Economy which has been the work of all this winter is now nearly ready and will be published in ten days" (XXVIII/179). Harriet directs her husband to send manuscripts that she left in London because "I am very busy writing for the printers & want to get some scraps out of that" (XXVIII/152). She is actively involved in all of their collaborative work: "I think the words

which I have put the pencil through are better omitted—but they might with a little alteration be placed at the end? The *reason* I should give to Capt S. if a reason is asked, is that the way in which you are mentioned in the letters is calculated to give an erroneous impression of you. . . . The words I have added at the end do not go quite right but you will make them do so" (L/25; HTM's emphasis). Concerning a point of contention between them on an idea, JSM writes "But we shall have all these questions out together & they will all require to be entered into to a certain depth, at least in the new book which I am so glad you look forward to as I do with so much interest" (21 March 1849).[10] The text does not always reflect Harriet's suggestions; for example, John writes, "I think I agree in all your remarks & have adopted them almost all—but I do not see the possibility of bringing in the first two pages (from the preceding chapter)—I see no place which they would fit" (14 March 1854). Some revisions can be done simply by John, but meatier matters require the contribution of both. John writes, "One page I keep for consideration when I can shew it to you. It is about the qualities of English work people, & of the english generally. It is not at all as I would write it now, but I do not in reality, know how to write it" (19 February 1857).

These types of letters, and John's public proclamations that she philosophized (which no one believes no matter how many times he says it) are the evidence to show her as an uppity woman—one who pretends to do what no woman can—namely, philosophize. HTM may be more dangerous than Simone de Beauvoir, because John celebrated her philosophical activities. He openly acknowledged her philosophical contributions. He didn't pretend that he was the great philosopher and that she just wrote "feminist" (read that as "philosophically unimportant") works. Harriet got angry with some of John's ideas and revealed that in letters she did not destroy. Not Lou Salomé, not Simone de Beauvoir, not even Clotilde is treated with as much venom in the history of philosophy as Harriet was. It is Camille Claudel whose name rises to my mind. She too suffered, perhaps even more than Harriet. Again, why? Because she, like Harriet, had the audacity to move from model/supporter/helper/caregiver to sculptor? Women can't sculpt and women can't philosophize?

In addition to the peculiar relationship between women and men philosophers, our inability to penetrate the individual examples of the multiple kinds of collaboration that occurs between husbands and wives, lovers, colleagues, partners, and so on, contributes to our misreading of Harriet. We don't have a vocabulary for sharing work. We don't have enough paradigms or carefully examined particulars to show us how it is typically done, what is usual and what is not. Throughout the history of Harriet, the assumption underlying the analysis was always that someone was in control. The question was only, Who? Who controlled their lives? Who controlled their writing? The critics' understanding of collaboration, especially the collaboration of women partners of "geniuses," reminds me of a doctor's understanding of medicine in the Middle Ages—the shocking ignorance is pitiable. We are only beginning to understand and appreciate men's and women's ways of knowing (to sort out the similarities, differences, and complementaries where they exist). John was convinced that Harriet's ways of understanding complemented and furthered his own. Why doesn't anyone believe him?

One answer was pointed out by Phyllis Rose: "The world does not take kindly to a successful collaboration between a married couple. When John Lennon insisted on making records with Yoko Ono, he was accused of deifying an inferior artist, and she was accused of destroying a great artistic unit." It doesn't matter whether the star is male or female. The same incredulity occurred with Joan Sutherland and Barbara Streisand. "What is at work here seems to be a collective jealousy. The public, whose relationship with any celebrity (writer, philosopher, or film star) is partly erotic, resents another person's coming between it and the object of it attention" (Rose 1984, 132). I can't help smiling just thinking of John Stuart Mill and John Lennon in the same breath, but I believe this accounts for some of the nastiness in the comments on Harriet in JSM scholarship.

The particular problem of those in the shadows of the famous is part of the overall problem in understanding collaboration, especially collaborative writing.[11] Our acceptance of collaboration has developed since the Renaissance. Dante's Beatrice and Petrarch's Laura were merely emotional inspiration for their famous lovers, or at least that's how the story goes. Descartes and Princess Elizabeth debated his work, but he didn't claim, or she assert, a share in the work. During John and Harriet's period, women in partnership were beginning to be recognized for their contribution of ideas as well as emotional support. Comte claimed that his lover, Clotilde, was the source of his ideas. John disagrees and, according to August, "regrets only that Clotilde lacked the intellect Comte attributed to her. Were she really so perceptive . . . , she would have curbed her lover's rage for authoritarian order, as Harriet had done for [JSM] during the thirties and forties" (August 1975, 187). Eliza Flower and Sarah Austin did their own quiet work behind the lights of their husband's or lover's fame. Jane Carlyle vented her frustrated intellect in her letters.

Only after Harriet and John could biographers see a couple as truly sharing work. One couple, Sidney and Beatrice Webb (who were inspired in part by the ideas of HTM and JSM) enjoyed what Harriet and John did not: a reputation for shared ideas. This is how a biographer, Mary Agnes Hamilton, tells their story.

> Almost impossible, nowadays, to think of Sidney and Beatrice Webb except as a couple. It is not only that they have written, together, books in which no one can detach what belongs to one from what belongs to the other. They talk, if you meet them, in the dual, almost always. . . . When they say "we," the listener knows, no matter who uses it, that the number is right; the

thinking is, somehow,—he does not know quite how—a joint process. . . . They are in fact, and have been, for forty years, the brightest example of what she has called a "double-star personality, the light of one being indistinguishable from that of the other." The effective fusion of two shining minds has, indeed, worked, as he suggested to her in the days before it took place, not as a mere sum in addition . . . one and one, side by side, in a proper integrated relationship, makes not two but eleven.

> (Hamilton n.d., 1-2)

A double star. We still have trouble imagining such a constellation. Albert and Mileva Maric Einstein. Simone de Beauvoir and Sartre. Hillary and Bill Clinton. JSM and HTM assert for all couples who share the intellectual work that it doesn't matter who holds the pen, who types the page, or who holds the office—both should share the credit. Rose describes the relationship of Harriet and John thus:

> Both had been made lonely by exceptional intelligence, and they rejoiced in each other like two giants, two midgets, or any two people who have feared their oddness would prevent them from ever knowing close companionship. They were a happy couple, discussing everything, sharing everything. Most important, they shared his work—or what posterity called his work, despite Mill's insistence that virtually everything published in his name was Harriet's as much as his. Mill believed that when two people together probe every subject of interest, when they hold all thoughts and speculations in common, whatever writings may result are joint products. The one who has contributed the least to composition may have contributed the most to thought. It is of little consequence which of them holds the pen.

> (Rose 1984, 127-28)

The problem of collaborative work is particularly tricky when it comes to collaborative writing. In *Singular Texts/Plural Authors: Perspectives on Collaborative Writing* (1990), Lisa Ede and Andrea Lunsford discuss a number of different types and contexts of collaborative writing. The study of collaborative writing is still quite new. It is very difficult to explain the elaborate dance of writing, thinking, talking, arguing, discussing, rewriting, pondering, revising, writing out, writing down, and writing over which constitutes collaboration. Each collaboration is different: each is peculiar to those involved with that work of collaboration. Because philosophers have rarely written collaboratively or assigned collaborative projects in their classes, they remain embarrassingly ignorant of the silliness of asking, "who contributed what?"

Why haven't philosophers written collaboratively or acknowledged it when they did on the sly? Le Doeuf's recognition of the assumption of a pedagogy of the "master 'who knows' and the pupil 'who does not yet know'" suggests an answer. If we believe, as Socrates did, that the search for knowledge is necessarily a social enterprise, a work of collaboration, a revolution would occur. "If the subject of the enterprise is no longer a person, or better still, if each person involved in the enterprise is no longer in the position of being the subject of the enterprise but in that of being a worker, engaged in and committed to an enterprise which is seen from the outset as collective, it seems to me that the relationship to knowledge—and to gaps in knowledge—can be transformed. Here again, it is hard to describe the revolution that would be effected by a collective form of philosophical work *and* be a recognition of the fact that, in any case, the enterprise cannot be reduced to personal initiatives" (Le Doeuf 1987, 207; original emphasis).

HTM and JSM performed this revolutionary act. They created work that was "seen from the outset as collective." In the first years of their acquaintance, Harriet wrote an essay defending the necessity for collaboration in the search for truth: "We would have the Truth, and if possible all the Truth. . . . But we would never lose sight of the important fact that what is truth to one mind is often not truth to another." Language cannot capture the shades of meaning that color the truth. "To an honest mind what a lesson of tolerance is included in this knowledge." We must learn to find "something that is admirable in all, something to interest and respect in each. . . . As the study of the mind of others is the only way in which effectually to improve our own" (Box III/78).

Later, they even wrote a book defending the belief that knowledge is more likely to be gained in the interchange, debate, and struggle of those collaborating in learning. In *On Liberty* the passionate commitment to collaborative learning pours over the reader: "Truth, in the great practical concerns of life, is so much a question of the reconciling and combining of opposites that very few have minds sufficiently capacious and impartial to make the adjustment with an approach to correctness, and it has to be made by the rough process of a struggle between combatants fighting under hostile banners" (Mill 1859, 110-11). "There is always hope when people are forced to listen to both sides; it is when they attend only to one that errors harden into prejudices, and truth itself ceases to have the effect of truth by being exaggerated into falsehood" (115). Harriet Taylor Mill and John Stuart Mill recognized that they needed each other. They believed in doing philosophy the way Le Doeuf describes: "'I do not do everything on my own,' . . . I am a tributary to a collective discourse and knowledge, which have done more towards producing me than I shall contribute in continuing to produce them; and replace the mystery with a recognition of the necessarily incomplete character of all theorization" (Le Doeuf 1987, 208).

I agree with Le Doeuf that "The future of women's struggle for access to the philosophical will be played out somewhere in the field of plural work" (Le Doeuf 1987, 208). If we recognize HTM's contributions to philosophy, we will find at least one example of how philosophical work can be done. But that is a big "if."

Why is Harriet treated with so much nastiness? She asked too many questions thus challenging male assumptions of knowledge and thereby exemplifying Eve's passion to know and giving rise to those anxieties buried in the myth. Her practicality makes it easy for those with very important things on their mind, a.k.a. philosophers, to doubt her ability to think about anything other than practical matters. Her views were so radical that they were easier to ignore than to critique. Harriet's friends, the Unitarian Radicals, also got her into trouble with supporters and historians of their rivals, the Philosophical Radicals. The blatant sexism of commentators, which mirrors the sexism of the period in which the critiques were written, adds to the unfairness of the treatment of her. Her collaboration with a philosopher has been misunderstood for a number of reasons, not the least of which is that philosophers like to think of themselves as Romantic geniuses on a lonely pursuit of a type of knowledge that they have and students don't, instead of as a team of thinkers who collaborate in a search for knowledge which will never be complete. All of these reasons overlap as they contort our attempts to understand what Harriet thought.

How to tell a life? First we need to listen to Harriet. It is time to put her words together for the first time. Until now, Harriet's published works (or her published works that have been republished) have been scattered in a variety of sources.[12] Some of her letters and private manuscripts have never been published, and those that have are often buried in biographies of JSM. Next, we need to overcome our fear of the intentional fallacy and explore the intertwining of life and ideas. Furthermore, we need to compare and contrast Harriet's and John's work where it is distinct, and acknowledge collaboration when it is deserved. Finally, we need to use some of the new paradigms discovered by feminist scholars in the last twenty years so that we can properly shake hands with Harriet Taylor Mill.

Notes

1. I will be using either the first names or initials of Harriet Taylor Mill and John Stuart Mill in contrast to the usage in all of the scholarship in which John is regularly referred to as "Mill," while Harriet Taylor Mill is usually simply "Harriet," an unequal use of names which smacks of sexism.

2. Unless otherwise noted, all emphases in quotations have been added.

3. See also similar passages: "Perhaps, as is often the feminine way, she took a less tragic view of the affair, having a better notion than either of the men how it might be expected to turn out" (Packe 1954, 143); "During the years of Mill's activity as an editor and politician, Harriet's share in his work was commonplace and feminine. . . . Although she played no open part in the business decisions, everything was submitted to her judgment" (236); and, "Her passionate and downright sympathy with the oppressed, her robust and practical common sense, two qualities more commonly found together in women than in men, made her feel that the condition of the poor was far more miserable than she had at first supposed" (312). Other examples are abundant.

4. According to Susan Faludi, during the backlash years of the 1980s, the term masochism is associated again with women: in *Being a Woman,* "Masochism is just the naturally feminine 'desire to endure pain rather than inflict it; to relinquish control rather than seize it.' And so, [Grant] concludes, 'In this sense, certainly, most women are indeed masochistic'." Even the psychiatric community reestablishes masochistic personality disorder, almost always a problem of women, as a disease (Grant, in Faludi 1991, 344, 357).

5. It was Harriet's charms, "not the charm of common ownership to which Mill had succumbed" (Himmelfarb 1965, 26, 28-9).

6. Ellery continues the condemnation of Harriet: "Harriet Taylor seems to have had a penchant for expressing her views on the slightest provocation, and she seemingly was driven by ambitions to have them immortalized in print. . . . The force of her personality established her power over him, and she was very much aware of the fact" (Ellery 1964, 37).

7. "Harriet was a rebel not without cause. . . . Neither he nor his recent biographers have convinced us that she was the originating mind behind his work, but no one can doubt her importance in Mill's inner life, the well-springs of which had been threatened by drought" (Mineka 1963, 306).

8. See Diffenbaugh's (1923) critique above.

9. I will cite the letters by the volume and number or Box number and item number of the Mill/Taylor Collection assigned by the British Library of Political and Economic Science of the London School of Economics where they are collected.

10. This letter and the other quoted in this paragraph are located in the Sterling Library at Yale. They are included in an appendix to the *Principles of Political Economy* volume in *The Collected Works of John Stuart Mill.*

11. My unpublished "The Newspaper Writings of Harriet Taylor Mill and John Stuart Mill: The Means and Meaning of Their Collaboration," explores the importance of collaboration in the philosophizing of HTM and JSM much more thoroughly.

12. The best source of HTM's work is Hayek (1951). Hayek included the majority of letters that have been collected in the London School of Economics. Some letters not included in Hayek are found in Borchard (1957), Packe (1954), and Mazlish's (1975) biographies. Harriet's early essays on marriage and toleration appear in Hayek (1951) and in Rossi (1970). "The Enfranchisement of Women" appears in Rossi (1970). The newspaper articles appear in the *Collected Works of John Stuart Mill,* vols. 24 and 25. Harriet's chapter in the *Principles of Political Economy,* is published under JSM's name, as is *On Liberty.* I am currently working on a book that will publish all of Harriet's work for the first time.

Works Cited

Ashworth, M. 1916. The marriage of John Stuart Mill. *Englishwoman* 30: 159-72.

Atwood, Margaret. 1989. Biographobia: Some personal reflections on the act of biography. In *Nineteenth-century lives: Essays presented to Jerome Hamilton Buckley,* ed. Lawrence S. Lockridge, John Maynard, and Donald D. Stone. Cambridge: Cambridge University Press.

August, Eugene. 1975. *John Stuart Mill: A mind at large.* New York: Charles Scribner's Sons.

Bain, Alexander. 1882. *John Stuart Mill: A criticism with personal recollections.* London: Longmans, Green & Co.

Borchard, Ruth. 1957. *John Stuart Mill: The man.* London: Watts.

Bourne, Henry Richard Fox. 1873. John Stuart Mill: A sketch of his life. *Examiner* 17: 582-86.

Courtney, William. 1889. *The life of John Stuart Mill.* London: Walter Scott.

Cranston, Maurice. 1959. Mr. and Mrs. Mill on liberty. *The Listener* 62: 385-86.

Diffenbaugh, Guy Linton. 1923. Mrs. Taylor seen through other eyes than Mill's. *Sewanee Review* 31: 198-204.

Ede, Lisa, and Andrea Lunsford. 1990. *Singular texts/plural authors: Perspectives on collaborative writing.* Carbondale: Southern Illinois University Press.

Ellery, John B. 1964. *John Stuart Mill.* New York: Twayne.

Elliot, Hugh S. R., ed. 1910. *The Letters of John Stuart Mill.* Vol. 1. New York: Longmans, Green and Co.

Faludi, Susan. 1991. *Backlash: The undeclared war against American women.* New York: Crown.

Garnett, Richard. 1910. *The life of W. J. Fox.* London: John Lane at Bodley Head.

Hagberg, Knut. 1930. *Personalities and powers.* Trans. Elizabeth Sprigge and Claude Napier. London: John Lane at Bodley Head.

Hamburger, Joseph. 1965. *Intellectuals in politics: John Stuart Mill and the philosophic radicals.* New Haven: Yale University Press.

Hamilton, Mary Agnes. N. d. [c.1932]. *Sidney and Beatrice Webb: A study in contemporary biography.* London: Sampson Low, Marston.

Hayek, F. A. 1951. *John Stuart Mill and Harriet Taylor: Their friendship and subsequent marriage.* New York: Augustus M. Kelley.

Held, Virginia. 1971. Justice and Harriet Taylor. *The Nation* (October 25): 405-6.

Henshaw, S. E. 1874. John Stuart Mill and Mrs. Taylor. *Overland Monthly* 13: 516-23.

Himmelfarb, Gertrude. 1965. The two Mills. *The New Leader* 10 (May): 26, 28-29.

———. 1974. *On liberty and liberalism: The case of John Stuart Mill.* New York: Alfred A. Knopf.

Kamm, Josephine. 1977. *John Stuart Mill in love.* London: Gordon & Cremonesi.

Le Doeuf, Michèle. 1987. Women and Philosophy. In *French feminist thought,* ed. Toril Moi, Oxford: Basil Blackwell.

———. 1991. *Hipparchia's choice: An essay concerning women, philosophy, etc.* Trans. Trista Selous. Oxford: Basil Blackwell.

Marston, Mansfield. 1873. *The life of John Stuart Mill: politician and philosopher, critic and metaphysician.* London: F. Farrah.

Mazlish, Bruce. 1975. *James and John Stuart Mill: Father and son in the nineteenth century.* New York: Basic Books.

Mill, John Stuart. 1982. *On Liberty.* Gertrude Himmelfarb, ed. New York: Penguin Books.

Mill-Taylor Collection. British Library of Political and Economic Science of the London School of Economics.

Mineka, Francis E. 1944. *The dissidence of dissent: "The Monthly Repository," 1806-1838.* Chapel Hill, NC: University of North Carolina Press.

Mineka, Francis E. 1963. The *Autobiography* and the lady. *University of Toronto Quarterly* 32: 301-6.

Packe, Michael St. John. 1954. *The life of John Stuart Mill.* New York: Macmillan.

Pappe, H. O. 1960. *John Stuart Mill and the Harriet Taylor myth.* Melbourne: Melbourne University Press.

Priestley, F. E. L. and J. M. Robson, eds. *The collected works of John Stuart Mill.* Toronto: University of Toronto Press.

Robbins, L. 1957. Packe on Mill. *Economics* 24 (August): 250-59. Also published in *John Stuart Mill: Critical assessments,* vol. 4, ed. John Cunningham Wood. London: Routledge, 1988.

Robson, John. 1966. Harriet Taylor and John Stuart Mill: Artist and scientist. *Queen's Quarterly* 73: 167-86.

Rose, Phyllis. 1984. *Parallel lives: Five Victorian marriages.* New York: Vintage.

Rossi, Alice S., ed. 1970. *Essays on sex equality,* by John Stuart Mill and Harriet Taylor Mill. Chicago: The University of Chicago Press.

Ryan, Alan. 1970. *John Stuart Mill.* New York: Pantheon.

———. 1991. Sense and sensibility in Mill's political thought. In *A cultivated mind: Essays on J. S. Mill presented to John M. Robson,* ed. Michael Laine. Toronto: University of Toronto Press.

Stillinger, Jack, ed. 1961. *The early draft of John Stuart Mill's "Autobiography."* Urbana: University of Illinois Press.

Strachey, Ray. 1928. *The cause: A short history of the women's movement in Great Britain.* Portway: Cedric Chivers.

Tatalovich, A. 1973. John Stuart Mill: *The subjection of women*: An analysis. *Southern Quarterly* 12 (1): 87-105. Also published in *John Stuart Mill: Critical assessments,* vol. 4, ed. John Cunningham Wood. London: Routledge, 1988.

Taylor, Mary. 1912. Mrs. John Stuart Mill: A vindication by her granddaughter. *Nineteenth Century and after* 71: 357-63.

Trilling, Diana. 1952. Mill's intellectual beacon. *Partisan Review* 19: 115-16, 118-120.

Tulloch, Gail. 1989. *Mill and sexual equality.* Boulder, CO: Lynne Rienner.

Sarojini (essay date 1996)

SOURCE: "Better Deal for the Better Half: Mill and Harriet Taylor on the Subjection of Women," in *Women's Writing: Text and Context,* edited by Jasbir Jain, Rawat Publications, 1996, pp. 56-63.

[*In the following essay, Sarojini offers a comparison of the essential views that Harriet Taylor and John Stuart Mill held concerning men and women, marriage and divorce.*]

In the English speaking world the feminist movement might be said to have begun with the publication of Mary Wollstonecraft's *Vindication of the Rights of Women* in 1792. It made very little impact on its contemporaries, partly because it was so obviously a child of the French Revolution, and partly because of its impassioned style. It aroused more derision than sympathy. Moreover a woman crusading for women is less persuasive than a male champion for the women's cause. The male voices, however, were rare and solitary. In 1825 William Thomson in his "Appeal of one half of the human race" contended that there would be no progress until women were given equal opportunities for education and equal political rights. In the mid 19th century John Stuart Mill lent the weight of his philosophical authority to the cause of feminism. His famous treatise *On the Subjection of Women* (1869) is a clear, cool-headed, well argued plea that compelled the reader to wonder that so self-evident a cause should need a champion. Written in his characteristic manner, he presented his views with cogency and comprehensives. His essay provides the women's movement with a philosophic rationale and is a landmark in the long history of women's struggle for political, legal and economic rights.

Mill's interest in the woman question goes back to the "very earliest period when I had formed any opinions at all on social and political matters" (*Subjection* 125). He was reprimanded at the age of seventeen for scattering tracts through the streets of London which advocated birth control. But Mill's commitment to women's issues acquired a new dimension after he met Harriet Taylor in 1830, as he tells us in his autobiography:

> What is true is, that until I knew her, the opinion was in my mind, little more than an abstract principle. . . . But that perception of the vast practical bearings of women's disabilities, which found expression in the book on the "Subjection of Women" was acquired mainly through her teaching.
>
> (*Autobiography* 207)

In 1832 just at the outset of their friendship, Mill and Harriet wrote essays on "Marriage and Divorce", a subject of mutual interest. It arose out of Harriet's intellectual incompatibility with her husband. These essays throw some light on Mill's preoccupation with the feminist cause which later led to his writing of *The Subjection of Women.* Taking into account the prevalent civil disabilities of married women, wherein a woman was entirely dependent for her social position on her marital status, Mill felt that the indissolubility of marriage was a boon to women. He strongly felt that divorce would be of no use to women so long as society was based on inequality. In fact the indissolubility of marriage served as a safeguard for a woman in such a society. Hence, he held that before dealing with divorce one must first consider the question of marriage. "Determine whether marriage is to be a relation between two equal beings or between a superior and an inferior, between a protector and a dependent, and all other doubts will easily be resolved" (*Essays* 73).

He aptly pointed out that everything finally centered on the debate on the status of women in society and pleaded in all earnestness for the equality of the sexes and improved education for women to release them from their dependence on men. But he was reluctant to advise women to become career oriented:

> It is not desirable to burthen the labour market with a double number of competitors. In a healthy state of things, the husband would be able by his single exertions to earn all that is necessary for both . . . it will be for the happiness of both that her occupation should rather be to adorn and beautify it (life).
>
> (*Essays* 74-75)

Compared to Mill, Harriet is more radical in her views which she expressed in her essay **"Enfranchisement of Women"** written in 1850. She argues at length against the domestication of women. She categorically states that education and social indoctrination are responsible for such a notion. Women are wives and mothers only because there is no other career open to them. On grounds of maternity they are excluded from active life: "There is no inherent reason or necessity that all women should voluntarily choose to devote their lives to one animal function and its consequences (*Essays,* 104). She demolishes the argument that equal employment opportunities for women would create unemployment. She pointed out that in order to alleviate the unemployment problem, child labour needed legislative regulation. That would also protect children from exploitation. Withholding women's right to employment was not a solution to the problem. Harriet strongly believed that a woman's contribution to the family income would raise her status from the position of a servant to that of a partner:

> A woman who contributes materially to the support of the family, cannot be treated in the same contemptuously tyrannical manner as one, who, however she may toil as a domestic drudge, is a dependent on the man for subsistence.
>
> (*Essays* 105)

If Harriet is more radical in her views, Mill is more rational in his approach. Having resolved the issue of the status of women, he considers marriage as an institution. Marriage, he states, is a necessary social institution for no man is complete without a woman. However, he advocates free choice in marriage. It should not be a necessity for a woman. Nor should she be expected to cling to a marriage which is better dissolved. Given the equality of the sexes, he feels, divorce will be in the interest of both the parties. These were ideas, indeed, much ahead of his time. He was aware that his advocacy of divorce would create complex social problems. The innocent children of such broken marriages would be the greatest suffers. To counteract such a danger, Mill suggested delay in having children till both partners had tested their compatibility. His advocacy of birth control was bound to meet with stiff resistance in an age when contraceptives were taboo. Hence provision for children remained a problem. He suggested communal living as a solution.

Harriet, however, differed with Mill on the question of children. She strongly felt that a woman ought to take entire responsibility of her own children. Instead of regarding children as a means of binding her to the man who feeds her, she should think carefully how many children she should have. Harriet's demand for a mother's legal rights over the children points to the increased responsibilities of women that the equality of the sexes entails. Rights cannot be demanded without accepting corresponding duties. Harriet understood that freedom of choice and a wider range of life goals would undercut women's desire for a bountiful maternity. She was adamant in her demand of complete equality in every sphere of life and equal admission to all social privileges.

What characterized Mill's involvement with women's disabilities was that he ceased to look upon the rights merely as an abstract theory. He made them a living principle of action. Particularly after Harriet's death Mill imbued with a passionate fervour to keep her memory alive, drafted *The Subjection of Women* (1861) at the suggestion of his daughter. In keeping with his mood he dedicated the treatise to his wife with whom he had shared these views. Right at the start Mill pointed out that the primary object of the treatise was to explain the grounds of his belief in women's rights.

Before writing *The Subjection of Women* Mill was well aware of the enormous cultural resistance he was working against in advocating an anti-patriarchal doctrine. He set about it courageously and persuasively, presenting each issue in its historical perspective, demolishing every counter argument with logical reasonings. Mill's approach consisted of two enquiries, viz., investigation of historical facts and analysis of human nature. The historical perspective led him to examine whether the long survival and widespread existence of male dominance provides an argument in its favour. In the course of his analysis he examined the social organization of early man, the origin of law and the evolution and development of present institutions. To him the inquiry indisputably proved that the belief in the subordination of women was purely hypothetical. Just because from the dawn of history every woman was found in a state of bondage to some man, it does not follow that she should continue to be so. All laws based on despotism and muscular strength have been abolished or are in the process of being replaced. The continued fight against slavery and colour prejudice is proof enough of erroneous laws having persisted owing to the force of custom. The peculiar character of the modern world is:

> That human beings are no longer born to their place in life, and chained down by an inexorable bond to the place they are born to, but are free to employ their faculties, and such favourable chances as offered, to achieve the lot which may appear to them as most desirable.

> (*Subjection* 143)

Hence women's subordination is a breach of the fundamental law, "a single relic of an old world of thought and practice exploded in everything else, but retained in the one thing of most universal interest (*Subjection* 146). Justice and expediency demand that due to the fatality of birth, higher social functions ought not to be closed to half the human race.

Analysis of human nature was the other course Mill followed to examine the belief in the superiority of men over women. He firmly believed in the power of society to mould human nature. A person's character, Mill believed, resulted not only from innate qualities but from environment and education, Mill's central argument in *The Subjection of Women* was based on the assumption that it was an irrepressible tendency of human beings to usurp power over their fellowmen in the absence of proper laws and restraints imposed by society or institutions. Mill pointed out that the unlimited power given to husbands over their wives evokes the latent tendency of selfishness in husbands and offers them a licence for cruelty and despotism. Under the prevalent law, Mill declares, wives could be forced to endure the worst forms of slavery and bondage known to history. Unlike most other slaves, a wife could be put on duty all hours of the day or night, she had no legal means of findings redress from a tyrannical husband. Worst of all she could not refuse her master but had to submit to being made the instrument of an animal function against her wish.

Mill refutes the assumption of women's inferiority with a number of arguments. He holds that with the right type of education, training and opportunity, women would do as well as men in any profession. By means of social indoctrination, men had successfully held women in subjection for centuries. There was no scientific proof of their intellectual inferiority. He asserted that the domestic and social circumstances in which women lived sufficiently explained almost all the differences between man and woman, including the sentimental myth of woman's moral superiority.

Mill's attack on the prevalent laws of marriage was directed to bring out the inhumanity of the situation. Society has appointed marriage to be the destination of all women. Foul means are employed in its execution. Girls are bartered or disposed of, without their consent, in marriage, treated as personal property by their husbands, compelled to obey them and in general treated as slaves. A wife is not allowed to own property or have legal right over her children. If she leaves her husband she can take nothing with her. If the husband chooses, he can compel her to return by law or by physical force. Mill points out the dangers of such despotism and draws attention to the serious results of the abuse of this institution. He gives constructive suggestions for the division of rights and duties in a marriage based on individual abilities and mutual consent. No laws can be constructed on an unequal foundation. The reciprocity of relationship which binds men and women can only result in personal and social pleasures. He goes on to describe the ideal relationship in a marriage:

> What marriage may be in the case of two persons of cultivated faculties, identical in opinion and purposes, between whom exists that best kind of equality, similarity of powers and capacities with reciprocal superiority over them—so that each can enjoy the luxury of looking up to the other, and can have alternately the pleasure of leading and of being led in the path of development . . . I maintain with the profoundest conviction that this, and this only, is the ideal of marriage.

> (*Subjection* 235)

In *The Subjection of Women* Mill revolutionized the traditional concept of a wife. He has rescued her from the prevailing glorification of female submissiveness and demolished the myth of "delicacy" and "femininity" which meant a total dependence upon a husband. He envisaged a completely new relationship based on equality which would lead to a greater fulfilment of man's quest for wholeness. Both in precept and example, Mill was a fully liberated man.

Mill's battle has been won because he demanded identifiable goals—the vote, education, right to property, divorce and employment. But the more difficult battle is still on—the mysterious inflexibility of the male mind towards women. There is still a considerable residue of the mental cliches which regards men as persons but women as merely women.

Works Cited

Mill, J. S. *Autobiography.* Oxford University Press, 1944.

Mill, J. S. *The Subjection of Women, Essays on Sex Equality: John Stuart Mill and Harriet Taylor,* ed. Alice Ross, University of Chicago Press, 1970.

Mill J. S. "Early Essay on Marriage and Divorce", *Essays on Sex Equality,* ed. Alice Ross.

Taylor, Harriet. "Enfranchisement of Women", *Essays on Sex Equality,* ed. Alice Ross.

FURTHER READING

Biography

Hayek, F. A. "On Marriage and Divorce." In *Midway* 16, (Autumn 1963): 100-26.

Includes a brief background on Harriet Taylor and John Mill's relationship, and two essays, one written from Taylor to Mill and one from Mill to Taylor, both on the subject of marriage and divorce.

Criticism

Allen, Virginia. "On Liberty and Logic: The Collaboration of Harriet Taylor and John Stuart Mill." In *Listening to Their Voices: The Rhetorical Activities of Historical Women,"* pp. 42-68. Columbia, South Carolina: University of South Carolina Press, 1997.

Discusses the strong likelihood that Harriet Taylor and John Mill collaborated on much of Mill's writing, citing letters and Mill's autobiography for evidence, and points to the misogynistic attitude of some critics as the reason for a general undervaluing of Taylor's talents.

Cranston, Maurice. "Mr. and Mrs. Mill on Liberty." In *The Listener* 62, No. 1589, (1959): 385-86.

Examines Harriet Taylor's influence on John Mill's *On Liberty,* and concludes that her influence was significant.

Rossi, Alice S. "Sentiment and Intellect: The Story of John Stuart Mill and Harriet Taylor Mill." In *Midway* 10, No. 4, (Spring 1970): 29-51.

Reviews the history of the Taylor/Mill relationship, and examines varied critical opinions of Taylor in the context of this relationship.

Stillinger, Jack. "Who Wrote J. S. Mill's Autobiography?" In *Victorian Studies* 27, No. 1, (Autumn 1983): 7-23.

Discusses the composition and revision of John Stuart Mill's *Autobiography,* looking at the collaborative influences of the work, and focuses on Harriet Taylor's influence in particular.

Alfred de Vigny
1797-1863

(Full name Alfred Victor de Vigny) French poet, play-wright, short story writer, and novelist.

For further information on Vigny's life and career, see *NCLC*, Volume 7.

INTRODUCTION

A leader of the early French Romantic movement, Vigny is considered one of the finest poets of the nineteenth century. He is best known for the philosophical poems of his *Les destinées: Poèmes philosophiques* (1864), which feature a study of the artist's spiritual disaffection in modern society. Vigny is additionally recognized for his historical novel *Cinq-Mars* (1826), his play *Chatterton* (1835)—which is numbered among the most profoundly influential Romantic dramas—and for his short works of prose fiction. Though rarely accorded the acclaim granted to his contemporaries Victor Hugo, Alfred de Musset, and others, Vigny is praised for the technical virtuosity, philosophical content, and imagery of his poetry.

BIOGRAPHICAL INFORMATION

Vigny was born at Laches in the Touraine region of France to aristocratic parents who, though once wealthy, had suffered financially following the French Revolution. The family moved to Paris, where Vigny was raised among the survivors of the *ancien régime* of pre-Revolutionary France. In 1814, he followed family tradition by joining the Royal Guard, and served for thirteen years. Near the end of his military service, he married Lydia Bunbury, the daughter of a rich and eccentric Englishman who disapproved of Vigny and promptly disinherited her. The marriage rapidly disintegrated, and Vigny subsequently became involved with several other women. Meanwhile, he had begun his literary career, establishing his early reputation with *Poèmes antiques et modernes* in 1826. The same year he also published his novel *Cinq-Mars; ou, Une conjuration sous Louis XIII* (*Cinq-Mars; or, A Conspiracy under Louis XIII*) to immediate popular success. Shortly thereafter, Vigny developed an interest in the theater when, in 1827, he saw the performances of an English Shakespearean troupe in Paris. He translated several of Shakespeare's plays into French, including *Othello,* which was produced as *Le more de Venise* at the Comédie-française in 1829. While he continued to write fiction, poetry, and dramas, after more than a decade of disillusionment with politics, failed love affairs, and lack of recognition as a

writer, Vigny withdrew from Parisian society in 1835. In 1845 he was elected to the prestigious literary Académie française, having been denied membership on several previous attempts. Three years later, Vigny retreated to the family home at Charente, where he lived quietly until his death in 1863.

MAJOR WORKS

Poèmes antiques et modernes includes the ten verses of his earlier *Poëmes* (1822) and *Éloa; ou, La soeur des anges, mystère,* (1824) containing a total of twenty-one poems divided into three groups: mystical, ancient, and modern. With this collection Vigny championed the *poème,* which he defined as an epic or dramatic composition in verse crystallized around a particular philosophical idea. Characterized by their stoical pessimism, compact form, and visual imagery, Vigny's *poèmes* explore themes such as God's indifference to humanity, women's deceit, inexorable fate, and the poet's alienation from the world. Based upon historical events, his novel *Cinq-Mars* depicts life in the court of the seventeenth-century French monarch Louis XIII. Vigny's didactic purpose in the work was to demonstrate that the king's chief minister, Duc Armand du Richelieu, contributed to the downfall of the French monarchy by weakening the aristocracy. In his collections of shorter prose works, *Les consultations du Docteur Noir: Stello; ou, Les diables bleus, Première consultation* (1832; *Stello: A Session with Doctor Noir*), *Servitude et grandeur militaires* (1835; *The Military Necessity*), and *Daphné (Deuxième consultation du Docteur Noir)* (1913), Vigny defended those he considered to be the outcasts of society: the poet, the soldier, and the visionary. *Stello* takes the form of a dialogue between Stello, a poet symbolizing the imagination and generous spirit of the creative artist, and Docteur Noir, an embodiment of rational intellect, who recounts the stories of three poets—Thomas Chatterton, Nicolas Gilbert, and André Chénier—and examines the poet's relationship to authority. *The Military Necessity,* similar in form and thought to *Stello,* consists of three stories unified by the author's personal comments on the soldier as a victim of society. In the work, Vigny describes the struggle between a soldier's conscience and the exigencies of war; he also contends that the soldier's greatness lies in his dignified and passive obedience to authority. Vigny's third collection, which was to detail the sufferings of the religious prophet, contains only one story, *Daphné.* A dramatic adaptation of a short tale earlier published in *Stello, Chatterton* depicts the tragic love story of an English poet eventually driven to suicide by an unappreciative and materialistic society. Although classical in its taut construction, simple plot, and restrained emotion, the drama offers its attack on society, moral examination of the artist's soul, and impassioned defense of emotion in the Romantic mode. In the poems of his posthumously published *Les destinées,* Vigny refined and developed thoughts already present in earlier works, including his ambivalent feelings toward women and nature, the role of the poet in an increasingly mechanized world, and the ruptured relationship between humanity and its creator—the governing idea of the collection. Composed between 1839 and 1863, the eleven poems of *Les destinées* trace Vigny's departure from an attitude of stoical resignation in the early works to his rejection of Christian fatalism and renewed confidence in the human spirit, particularly in his last poem, "L'esprit pur."

CRITICAL RECEPTION

Despite the popular success of *Cinq-Mars* upon publication—which can be attributed in part to the current vogue of the historical novel at the time, prompted by the successful writings of Sir Walter Scott—the work has generally been denigrated by critics who have found his characters flat and his historical thesis untenable. In regard to Vigny's later fiction, commentators have praised the improved literary technique in his story collections *Stello* and *The Military Necessity,* and have admired the simple and effective plots of these tales. However, some critics have observed that by combining didactic intent with storytelling, Vigny often sacrificed coherent narrative to the dictates of his philosophical ideas. Generally, critics have considered the poems of Vigny's *Les destinées* his greatest poetic achievement, though some have viewed their quality as uneven. Still, many commentators have praised the technical skill of his finest and most frequently studied poems: "La maison du berger," "La mort du loup," "Le mont des oliviers," "La bouteille à la mer," and "L'esprit pur." Although *Les destinées* confirmed Vigny's reputation as the philosopher of Romantic poetry, it has since been associated with his efforts to develop a coherent doctrine of preexisting ideas rather than with the introduction of any innovative thoughts. Finally, in relation to his influence as a dramatist, critics have acknowledged that the success of Vigny's translation of Shakespeare's *Othello* had a tremendous impact on subsequent French drama. In addition, his preface to the published version of *Le more de Venise* has been regarded as one of the most important manifestos of the nineteenth-century French theater. Additionally, his tragedy *Chatterton* has been regarded as his most influential artistic exploit, though the work itself is infrequently studied.

PRINCIPAL WORKS

Poëmes (poetry) 1822

Éloa; ou, La soeur des anges, mystère (poetry) 1824

Cinq-Mars; ou, Une conjuration sous Louis XIII [*Cinq-Mars; or, A Conspiracy under Louis XIII*; also translated as *The Conspirators* and *The Spider and the Fly*] (novel) 1826

Poëmes antiques et modernes (poetry) 1826

Le more de Venise [translator; from the drama *Othello* by William Shakespeare] (play) 1829

Le maréchale d'Ancre (play) 1831

Les consultations du Docteur Noir: Stello; ou, Les diables bleus, Première consultation [*Stello: A Session with Doctor Noir*] (short stories) 1832

Quitte pour la peur (play) 1833

Chatterton (play) 1835

Servitude et grandeur militaires [*The Military Necessity*; also published as *The Military Condition*] (short stories) 1835

Oeuvres complètes. 7 vols. (poetry, short stories, novel, and dramas) 1837-39

Théâtre complet du comte Alfred de Vigny (dramas) 1848

Les destinées: Poèmes philosophiques (poetry) 1864

Alfred de Vigny: Journal d'un poète (journal) 1867

Oeuvres complètes. 8 vols. (poetry, short stories, novel, and dramas) 1883-85

Correspondance de Alfred de Vigny, 1816-1863 (letters) 1905

*Shylock [translator; from the drama *The Merchant of Venice* by William Shakespeare] (play) 1905

Daphné (Deuxième consultation du Docteur Noir) (unfinished novel) 1913

*This work was composed in 1830.

CRITICISM

Temple Bar (essay date 1863)

SOURCE: "Alfred de Vigny: Poet," in *Temple Bar,* Vol. 9, October, 1863, pp. 500-505.

[*In the following anonymous essay, the critic reviews Vigny's career and works.*]

"Let no oration be pronounced over my tomb." Such was the expressed wish of Alfred de Vigny only a short time before his death; and it was a wish consonant with that silent reserve with which he had enshrouded himself from public notice during the last half of his life. He shuddered at the thought of cold official praises being uttered over his tomb, and would have blamed himself for sanctioning it beforehand, as a sort of posthumous indiscretion. The single and innocent vanity of which he has left a trace was the desire that military honours should be paid to his coffin. In this he was faithful to one of the dearest, the liveliest, and the most constant instincts of his character. The illustrious writer, the soldierly Academician, only asked that his young comrades of the army should follow to the cemetery the old Captain of Infantry: the single sound which he permitted around his grave was the muffled voice of the drums veiled in crape.

Alfred Victor, Count de Vigny, was born at Loches, in Touraine, on the 27th of March 1799, of a family of soldiers who originally came from Beauce. His father had distinguished himself in the Seven Years' War; his mother was the granddaughter of Admiral Baraudin, and cousin of Bougainville. Whilst still young De Vigny came to Paris, and entered, towards the close of the First Empire, the institution of M. Hix. Here he caught from his comrades that passion for war which then inflamed the youth, and more especially the students, of France. He dreamed of epaulettes, shakos, waving plumes, drawn swords, fights, and massacres. To withdraw him from this absorbing influence, his mother, who was averse to his military predilections, engaged for him at home a tutor, the Abbé Gaillard. This, however, was of no avail. Although devoting himself patiently to study, the boy De Vigny dreamed ever of combats and conquests. Hardly had he arrived at his sixteenth year when the Restoration brought back the Bourbons, and sent Napoleon to Elba. He then received a commission in the Red Musketeers of the Household of the King; and it was his misfortune to accompany Louis XVIII. in his flight from Paris. A part of the king's escort only accompanied the fugitive monarch to Ghent; and M. de Vigny was spared the ignominy of crossing the frontier. He was sent to Amiens, where he remained during the eventful Hundred Days. A return to the capital being prohibited to all those who had attended their sovereign, De Vigny was exiled thirty leagues from Paris.

In 1823 he transferred himself to the Line, in order that he might take part in the expedition, under the Duc de Vendôme, which was sent into Spain. His regiment, however, advanced no further than the valleys of the Pyrenees. This chafed his spirits; and to fill up his leisure-hours, and dissipate the *ennui* of barrack-life, he devoted himself to study and poesy. At length, becoming disenchanted with the life of a soldier, he decided, in 1828, on resigning his commission, and consecrating his future life to the muse of verse. Before this event, however, M. de Vigny had wielded the pen, and with more effect than the sword. "**Le Dryade et Symeta,**" imitations of Theocritus, he had published in 1815; in 1822 appeared, under the title of "**Livre Mystique,**" "**Livre Antique,**" "**Livre Moderne,**" "**Héléna,**" "**La Somnambule,**" "**La Fille de Jephté,**" "**La Femme Adultère,**" "**Le Bal,**" "**La Prison,**" "**La Déluge,**" "**Moïse,**" "**Dolorida,**" "**La Trappiste,**" "**La Neige,**" "**Le Cor,**" *Eloa,* which were written between the years 1824 and 1826. Alfred de Vigny was a profound reader of the Holy Scriptures, and the inspiration which he derived from the sacred writings may be traced in nearly all these poems. *Eloa* had an immediate success, and raised the author to the first rank in the new school of poetry. The legend of *Eloa* is singularly fanciful and medieval. The tear which our Saviour shed on hearing of the death of Lazarus was carried, so runs the story, to heaven, and there metamorphosed into a creature half-woman, half-angel:

"Comme l'incens qui brûle aux rayons du soleil
Le change en un feu pur, éclatant et vermeil;
On vit alors du sein de l'urne éblouissante
S'élever une forme et blanche et grandissante—
Une voix s'entendit qui disait: Eloa—
Et l'ange apparaissant répondit, Me voilà."

Being woman, she clung to earth and earthly things, and, notwithstanding the splendour with which she was surrounded, sighed for human love and sympathy. One day, strolling outside the gates of heaven, she encountered the Tempter in the form of a beautiful and ravishing youth. She at once fell in love with him, listened to his bland words, and for him abandoned the perfumed groves amidst which the angels wander. Too late she found that she had mated her Satan, the Arch-Deceiver.

In 1826 M. Alfred de Vigny appeared before the public with his great historical romance, *Cinq-Mars,* which ran through four editions in three years, and is still regarded in France as a model of this kind of fiction. The style and dramatic action of the work created universal admiration, though hyper-severe critics reproached the author with having falsified history and exalted his hero at the expense of Richelieu. In 1832 appeared *Stello, ou les Diables bleus,* and in 1835 *Servitude et Grandeur militaires.* These two works enjoyed a no less success than *Cinq-Mars,* and provoked equally bitter criticisms; the great events and the principal personages of the Republic and the Empire being, according to his stern censors, represented more by the poet than the historian. He had given too much play to his imagination, and devoted himself too little to the study of facts. Not in poetry and historic romance alone, however, did M. de Vigny shine. He made a name for himself in the drama. At the Théâtre Français a translation of

Shakespeare's *Othello* was played in 1829. This performance was the more remarkable, inasmuch as it was the first romantic drama ever put upon the stage of this privileged house. He had also in preparation *The Merchant of Venice;* but owing to the confusion caused by the Revolution of July, it was never put upon the stage. The attacks levelled against this new effort, and the praises sung in De Vigny's honour, were equally exaggerated. *La Maréchale d'Ancre,* an original piece represented in 1831, had but a doubtful triumph; in 1835, however, the poet detached from his *Stello* the episode of Chatterton, and dramatised it. This play obtained a great run, and produced a tremendous sensation. The reality of the principal character, and the general morality of the piece, which ended by a suicide, were nevertheless severely contested; some deputies of the Corps Législatif even protested in a full house against the *dénouement.* The interest of the drama itself, graceful pictures of society drawn in *Stello,* the elegance of its style, and the talent of Madame Dorval, triumphed over every criticism. *Chatterton* was reproduced, but with less sensation, in 1857.

For a long time previous to his death the noble poet had withdrawn himself from the busy world. The last twenty-eight years of his life, it may be said, were passed in a kind of meditative silence, scarcely interrupted, in 1843, by some fragments of **"Poèmes philosophiques"** published in the *Revue des Deux Mondes,*—**"Le Sauvage," "La Mort du Loup," "La Flûte,"** &c. &c., and by his speech on the occasion of his reception at the French Academy, where he replaced M. Etienne in 1846. His literary life closed, properly speaking, in 1835, when he published, nearly at the same time, *Chatterton* and *Servitude et Grandeur militaires.* Henceforth he kept himself from the crowd—far from its rude noise and wearying activity, from its baseless hopes and delusive ambitions. It is difficult, however, satisfactorily to explain the nature of his retirement—whether it was pride or discouragement, or a combination of both those feelings. He dwelt in a world of his own—narrow apropos of *the* world; broad and illimitable compared with *that* world the creation of his own genius and imagination. He thought and dreamed and lived on alone, almost in ascetic seclusion; admitting to his intimacy only a few privileged persons, tried and trusted friends, whose tastes coincided with his own, whose judgment he valued, and whose praise he honestly appreciated. He rarely quitted his studious retreat. Occasionally he issued forth; but then generally it was to vote at the Academy, which he did free from every influence of sect or party. He loved to defend within its walls what appeared to him true art—that is, art unfettered, disinterested, and independent. One of those whose cause he valiantly gained before the illustrious Assembly was precisely a writer of his intellectual calibre,—M. Ratisbonne,—whom, by a touching adoption, he has appointed the executor of his literary bequests. On the day of battle the author of *Eloa* obtained the suffrages of the Academy in favour of the translator and poet. This was one of his last academical victories. They were rare; for he never sought to acquire over his *confrères* of the Institute any undue influence,

since he regarded such influence as being rarely the sign and prize of superiority; he felt, moreover, that, when once acquired, more trouble and anxiety and care were required to retain it than would suffice to produce a good work.

There were doubtless many causes to account for his seclusion. Some of them may escape us, whilst others can only be traced by penetrating into the shade of his intimate life. Without drawing aside the veil of privacy, without entering into biographical details to search for an explanation, may not very plausible and natural grounds for the kind of life he chose be discovered in his writings? What seemed to dominate him was a horror of any thing trivial or conventional; his soul aspired after "the beautiful," "the exquisite," "the rare," "the singular." Without the folly and vanity of Don Quixote, he had a fund of chivalrous ideas and sentiments; and at an early period of life manifested a strong taste for adventure. By a fatality of circumstances, however, these chivalrous sentiments never found vent in action. This taste for adventure only met with grievous deception. He dreamed "great" things, and awoke to find himself surrounded by the "little." The disproportion he found between that passion for the ideal which exalted his soul, and the stern and mediocre reality of events in the midst of which he moved, tortured him. Scattered throughout his works we find here and there passages which reveal, or seem to reveal, to us these inner sufferings. In the first chapter of *Servitude et Grandeur militaires,* a symptom of this feeling may be traced. "I belong to that generation which, nourished with bulletins by the Empire, had always before its eyes a drawn sword; and I came to clutch it at the moment when France thrust it back into the scabbard of the Bourbons. The events which I sought became not so great as I had hoped. What was to be done?" As he proceeds, he seems to utter a cry of pain, of despair for having to remain for fourteen years of his life between the echo and the dream of battles. He was inconsolable at the hours lost in uselessly waiting for the opportunity of glory; he consumed himself, as it were, in the shade. Educated by a father who amused his childhood, already pensive, with the narratives of the Seven Years' War,—himself contemporary with the heroic struggles of Imperial France against Europe,—his early impressions were derived from the narratives of Napoleon's campaigns, which were being acted before him; and he became, even in youth, a prey to this "vision of victory." He became a soldier, hoping to realise this vision; but he grasped only an empty shadow. A permanent peace reigned over the Continent, which was thoroughly sick and weary of the bloody and protracted hostilities that had exhausted its strength and impoverished its exchequers. In the place of the field of battle there were only parades. Becoming impatient of this existence, he at length sent in his resignation, at the age of thirty; but he had scattered and dissipated, in this sterile attempt, his brightest dreams. He felt his hopes fade, his ambition blighted; and as he thrust back his sword into its scabbard, he also thrust himself back into private life, dejected and disappointed.

From the career of arms which absorbed fourteen years of his life, he carried into his private sphere something more than the incurable wound of a deceived passion. He brought to it that lively and powerful sentiment which constrained him throughout his whole existence, and became his infallible guide; he seemed to personify and also to worship the soldier's moral ideal—Honour, the *sans peur et sans reproche* of the Chevalier Bayard. From an Englishman's point of view this exalted abstraction is obscure, vague, and impalpable; and even where tangible, changeable according to the impressions of the time and the country. All-powerful as the sentiment may be in some breasts, it still requires to be defined by the double idea of human duty and of human dignity. De Vigny, however, regards it as something divine, and paid it poetic worship.

As the glory of arms was his dream in active life, so art the most pure, the most elevated, was his dream as a writer. "I have had occasion," says M. Caro, "to say elsewhere, and I repeat it with a conviction strengthened by a renewed reading of his works, that the principal feature which characterises them is the minute carefulness with which he selects his ideas, and the elegance of form in which he expresses them—in a word, his respect for human thought. He has given to his contemporaries a beautiful example of chasteness, temperance, and harmony, well worthy of being reflected upon, at a time of prodigal improvisation of immoderate *abandon,* of vulgar indiscretion, of *sans façon,* alike disregardful of art and the public. Lovable and rare is the spirit which thus respects itself in the choice of subjects, in the conscience with which it meditates upon them, and in that search and inquiry after perfection of detail which reveals the true artist. This enthusiasm for idea, this curiosity for expression, this solicitude, this instinct, this taste for the refinements of thought and style, is indeed true faith in art—the real worship of the ideal; it is, in a word, the sentiment of honour applied to letters." It bore out with exquisite fidelity the profound remark of La Bruyère, who says: "Entre toutes les différentes expressions qui peuvent rendre une seule de nos pensées, il n'y en a qu'une que soit la bonne; on ne la rencontre pas toujours en parlant ou en écrivant. Il est vrai néanmoins qu'elle existe, que tout ce que ne l'est point est faible, et ne satisfait point un homme d'esprit qui veut se faire entendre."

M. De Vigny was the last amongst the poets of the day to think of placing himself before the public. As we have said before, he shrank with nervous horror from the world; nor did he in his retirement seek the noisy applause of men. He was chary of his works no less than of himself. To use one of his own expressions, he repelled the temptation of amusing the idle by scraps of his life or the misdirection of his vocation. Many passages full of pleasant and genial irony has he levelled against those vain contemporary writers, the Dumas' and the George Sands', for example, who delight in letting the world look into their heart of hearts, laying bare their consciences, and calling upon their fellow-creatures to gaze upon the revelations of their lives. De Vigny had too much self-respect to let the light thus publicly in upon his most private thoughts, and wave to the world to come to those chambers of the soul

in which its holiest secrets shall be kept. He refused, as others did not, to exhibit his mind confused, perhaps disordered, and still encumbered with familiar *souvenirs* of the most cherished faults; he did not judge himself either sufficiently illustrious or sufficiently repentant to make his confessions in a loud voice, and to intrust a whole nation with his sins. If ever a cry breaks from him, a cry that has been drawn from his bosom by bitter experience, it is only through the medium of another that the voice is heard. Into his ideal creations alone is it that he has thrown any of his passion and his pain; and if his first occasionally betrays, like that of Byron, personal emotion, it is under a veil that he becomes emotional and that his heart beats.

Every where throughout his works he was mindful of his art. Art was subordinate to every thing. Peruse his most exquisite *morceaux,* and it will be perceived that they are never written haphazard, but that they are connected by a general conception, they are instinct with one motive. The dominant idea in **Cinq-Mars** is the end of the Monarchy, prepared by the great revolutionary Richelieu; **Stello** is the true mission of the poet and the artist; whilst **Servitude et Grandeur militaire** is a consistent denunciation of that demoralising institution, a permanent army.

Bearing in mind, then, what we have said, it is easy to understand why M. de Vigny condemned the last thirty years of his life to a sort of exile from the world. In the fine, exquisite, passionate, nervous temperament of the poet, ardent in the pursuit of the ideal and of glory, but rendered vulnerable by these very qualities, may be found many causes which would make a contact with the public exceedingly painful. Popularity, that noisy part of glory, he never sought; but the glory which he obtained was subdued as the reflection of the light in an alabaster lamp. By his fortunate flight from the world M. de Vigny was able to preserve pure and intact that which would otherwise, perhaps, have been compromised, and its lustre diminished, had he written, and written prodigally, for the world. His object was of a higher character, and the greatness he achieved he has unquestionably obtained. Amongst his own countrymen he will hold a high niche in the Temple of Fame; his memory will be cherished with the memory of Alfred de Musset, Béranger, St.-Beuve, and Victor Hugo.

Robert Nugent (essay date 1979)

SOURCE: "Vigny's *Stello* and Existential Freedom," in *Nineteenth-Century French Studies,* Vol. 8, Nos. 1-2, Fall, 1979, pp. 37-46.

[*In the following essay, Nugent interprets Vigny's* Stello *as a romantic and existential revolt against rationalism.*]

Vigny's **Stello** is significant from three points of view: biographical, literary, and philosophical. Clearly the three are interrelated; the first two have frequently been discussed. In 1831-32 Vigny went through a period of self-examination and self-questioning, going from a sense of immaturity to one of maturity.[1] This doubt and anguish found a parallel shift in Vigny's writings from a Romantic lyricist to a philosophical poet; from a historical novelist to one of ideas; from Romantic idealism to Stoic realism. The shift further reflects a contemporary dilemma between poetic idealism and social concern, between spiritualist psychology and a materialistic one resulting from an evaluation of rationalism.[2] The dilemma arose at a time of failure of political idealism (around 1830) and a persistent materialism. Both conditions of this dilemma, moreover, demand from a writer a resolution, a belief, which allows him to exist and function. Vigny's answer, in **Stello,** refuses either term. His answer is, rather, one of "no answer," a "theory of uncertainty,"[3] that is basically existential freedom and authenticity. Vigny explains and defines this position in **Stello.**

To establish precisely a link between existentialism and Romanticism is difficult except insofar as both attitudes represent an opposition to eighteenth-century rationalism.[4] The two differ, however, in their response to this rationalism: for the Romantics, sentimentalism; for the existentialists, a re-definition of freedom. Vigny, by the time he wrote **Stello,** had rejected both rationalism and sentimentalism. The remaining position tends, then, towards existentialist freedom definable in terms of anguish and nothingness.[5] In **Stello,** this sense of freedom and anguish gives, I believe, a final meaning to this "no answer," to this "theory of uncertainty," in three specific concerns. These are: (1) authenticity (how a poet seeks to maintain an inner world of self where he can freely explore his ideas); (2) alienation (a need to uphold the inner self as a criterion necessary to carry out any act); (3) revolt (the search for the self becomes revolt against society, although liberalism frequently ends—as Camus has pointed out—in conformism).

These concerns involve a problem of self-definition that goes back to Descartes's distinction between the *res extensa* and the *res cogitans*.[6] The distinction, ultimately, finds its main spokesman in Schopenhauer, who affirms the right of the self against the *res extensa* to create a world of one's own will and idea. Between Descartes and Schopenhauer the search for the authentic self becomes increasingly existential. In the words of one critic, "the romantic quest for freedom changed into an existentialist quest for an authentic self capable of being identified amid the average."[7] Further, the problem of maintaining this inner world involves authenticity faced with a Romantic dissassociation of scientific and non-scientific sensibilities (a similar split had occurred in England at the end of the seventeenth century). Romantic sensibility became anti-scientific and "sentimental" in its search for the ineffable and the meaningful; the search, because of its "disorganized" perceptions, rejects the outer world. Stello would then represent a poet who must deal with this dissassociation in ways other than scientific or sentimental, that is, existential. Stello discovers in himself the dual nature of perceptiveness, between his solitude and a phenomenal structure outside himself. He refuses, however, to choose one in favor of the other, preferring an openness of "no answer."

The dualism is essentially Romantic. The first part of **Stello** describes the problem of the Romantic self, before going on to distinguish in the "cases" of three eighteenth-century poets—Gilbert, Chatterton and Chénier—the three stages of the existential, non-answer self. The Romantic self shows, fundamentally, a dichotomy. Although Stello has been born "le plus heureusement du monde," protected by "l'étoile le plus favorable," his inner world is one of malaise and solitude.[8] His life seems dominated by a wish to fall ill. The outer world, even with *fatigues* and *chagrins,* is attractive solely because it acts as an antidote to these *funestes accès.* (p. 624) His sadness appears *imperissable*; the discovery of an authentic open existential self that can face the given world seems remote. What, then, are the remedies that can cure this sickness; what are the ways open to an individual (Stello), confronted with alienation, that can effect an authenticity of self? It is Doctor Noir's rôle to prescribe remedies and means.

He begins his consultation by pointing out the dual aspects of life: reason (*vie de raison,* close to scientific materialism) and emotions (*vie d'émotions,* suffering, sadness, disappointment). Stello has accepted the latter view (. . . *la vie de solitude est empoisonnée pour lui. . . . Il le sait mais il s'y abandonne cependant.*) (p. 624) Stello's will gives way to abulia as is true of Baudelaire's *homo duplex.* The duality also implies an inner world of sadness and suffering which approximates existential anguish. In turn, anguish leads to an apology for the rights of the inner imagination and the inner life.[9] The existentialist need to maintain this inner world becomes then a defense of authenticity and uncertainty. The question is, to what extent can Stello himself arrive at this point, where does he waver, at what moment does he remain committed more to Romantic posture than existential doubt. The difficulty is also formalistic: the novel itself is an exploration rather a novel of set design: the open literary form reflects a search for the self.

The first part of this search for self authenticity deals with escape. For Stello, as for Baudelaire later (in the second *Spleen* poem of 1857, for example), spleen leads to a desire to escape. Spleen is expressed in physical terms of revolt against physical nature—snow, rain, darkness of evening, even the overpowering presence of the sun: *J'ai le soleil en haine et la pluie en horreur.* (p. 625) Escape deepens into a metaphysical and moral malady of *ennui,* for which a symbolic form must be found (*Quelle forme symbolique pourrais-je donner jamais à cette incroyable souffrance?*) (p. 625) The need to find analogies between the inner and outer worlds reflects a shifting of *ennui* to the outer world; the effect is *nausée,* a vomiting forth of the inner psychic world, a profound need to confess. Finding analogies is also a way to escape from the eternal solitude of being a single individual in a world created by the imagination and establishing communion with others through a common, psychologically analogous (or symbolic) *nausée*. This way is uncertain (as in Sartre's *Le Mur*) and Stello is thrown back to a search for self-identity, realizable only through making the "illness" as complete and as possessive of the individual as possible. (. . . *je vous guérirai en rendant plus complet le mal qui vous tient,* counsels Docteur Noir.) (p. 630)

Stello is still working here from a Romantic viewpoint; he feels deep within himself *"une puissance, invisible et indéfinissable, toute pareille à un pressentiment de l'avenir et à une révélation des causes mystérieuses du présent."* (p. 636) He sees into the future and defines his own reason for being as prophetic aspiration.[10] His declaration shows a sense of time, and with time, structure. The evolving of time also poses a threat of losing a continued presence of self image. Vigny's concern lies, as Poulet has pointed out, in the "conversion of past into future," in prophetic thought.[11] Here Vigny differs from Proust, who is convinced that the self is lost when the past is lost. For both Vigny and Proust, however, the duration of time is a fixed center from which the self can go forth to explore its own consciousness. Stello has thus reduced even the Cartesian *res extensa* to an existential anguish. By creating a treasure house of impressions, beliefs and ideas, he also works towards creating an existential present and an existential solitude of his own making.[12]

This existential solitude involves a question of creativity. Just as a lamp which has insufficient oil splutters and goes out, so with Stello, the "inner light" (poetic ambition) goes out when the inner life-force (his authenticity) is insufficient. (p. 637) Further, Stello defends his inner life (whose elements are *volonté, amour,* and *esprit*) against a view of the outer world, one of illusion (*phénix au plumage doré*). The former is "productive" and "inspiring" (*qui féconde et appelle*), the latter "obscuring" and "repulsive" (*qui tarit et repousse*). (p. 637) The *vie intérieure* not only describes, but also is, the authentic self. Stello strives, as does Baudelaire, towards a *tonalité psychologique du moi*. Such tonality remains Romantic in two ways: the constituent parts of self-estimation (the mind that encompasses pity and devotion, a concept of love formed in oneself that proceeds towards others); deliverance from inner turmoil and distress (the world of intuitions and inner perceptions). This tonality is also existential in two ways: the search for authenticity of self resides in the work itself (pointing the way towards Mallarmé and Sartre's appreciation of *Hérodiade*); the revolt against reason (the determination of criteria or references to an outward structure, perceptible and discoverable, and therefore "real") without yielding to Romantic self-pity.

The description of this existential-Romantic dilemma is apparent when Docteur Noir relates to Stello three stories which point out the three aspects of existential freedom: that of Gilbert (the rôle of reason, especially in regard to authenticity); that of Chatterton (the creation of a world of poetry apart from the "real"); and that of Chénier (the final consideration of revolt after problems both of the inner,

authentic, existential world and of the esthetic determination of this inner world—achieved even at the cost of alienation from the "real"—have been explored).

The protest against reason is Romantic in its revolt against the seeming inevitableness of reason itself and in its apparent dominance over human life and the heart. On his death bed Gilbert cries out: *Qui m'expliquera la SOUMISSION de la raison?* He quotes St. Augustine that reason would not submit unless it judged that it should (. . . *il est donc juste qu'elle se soumette quand elle juge qu'elle le doit*). This answer perplexes Gilbert, for it appears to him that reason—even in submitting—does so only by its own will and therefore continues to dominate (*continue d'être reine*). Gilbert further quotes from Pascal's *Mémorial*. The notion implied here is that, if reason does not give way to the heart (Pascal's *le cœur a ses raisons*), no change can be effected in the inner life, no testing of experience on its own terms and eventually no creative spontaneity.[13] The search for self-identity appears an extension of Pascal's answer to Descartes, an answer which may be considered at the root of a Romantic definition of self.

The apology for the life of the heart results in social ostracism. A poet must resort to hypocrisy (*dissimulation sainte*) (p. 641); become immersed in isolation; see himself as the "stranger" against whom destiny and society have joined forces. His image of himself, moreover, is seen essentially (proceeding from God) or existentially (formed in the struggle with God).[14] The latter viewpoint can include man's struggle with his own fate, a secularization of the spiritual search, where revolt against God—taken in the sense of the absurd—becomes, in effect, the spiritual search (much as in Camus's *l'Étranger*). Vigny could pity those whom he felt to be victims of fate or prisoners of destiny.[15] Only revolt, then, *sur cette terre ingrate,* where love is *toujours menacé,* is the answer, especially in seeking authenticity. The only possible escape is apparently death, where the soul again finds *la vue et la clarté* (**"La Flûte"**). Vigny poses, before Camus does, the problem of existential authenticity: to live is equivalent to being *l'homme révolté*. Suicide, which is evidently a reasonable answer (Stoicism) or a Romantic one (the ultimate pure gesture of despair) is no answer to an existential search for the self.

Yet Vigny can see in such action (suicide) a possibility of courage, a temptation to be, through the most individualistic of acts. Chatterton, in the end, makes a choice. He takes upon himself the courage to be, in an existentialist, heroic, sense; he creates his own liberty. These heroic qualities the hero-victim finds in himself; he has, in his search for the self, defined his own world. He proceeds from Romantic alienation, especially in questions of the will. He is a prototype of the Romantic self when he brings up the question, where does the will to create, to make for the inner self a world distinguishable from the outer world, originate? How does it thus invent an alter ego, that is, an alienated ego? Chatterton writes Kitty Bell that he has freedom through the creation of his imagination as directed by the will; that he feels himself to be not of this world, but drawn on by a mysterious desire. (p. 661) Two realities stand in contrast: happiness of the inward vision and the wounded ego faced with the external world. Each represents a search for the self; each leads to an *ébranlement romantique*. The solution to this breakdown, for Chatterton, is fatalism:[16] . . . *pourquoi ai-je été créé comme je suis?* . . . *Si dans la foule il n'y a pas de place pour moi, je m'en irai.* (p. 661) The act of the will to create an inner world is extended to cover an activity in society while still maintaining a separate entity. Further, the suffering of the self in its search for its own existence can be a part of the world only insofar as the world adds to that existence. This necessary anguish does not arise when the self contributes to a definition of the outside world in accordance with external demands for action: *O funeste penchant que nous avons tous à sortir de notre vie et des conditions de notre ère,* cries out Docteur Noir.[17]

If, then, an attempt to create a self from within oneself appears doomed to failure, the question remains, how do we maintain an authentic self in the world? The answer is the story of André Chénier. The setting is the French Revolution, a time when the element of chance is most at play, when the hero is most acutely faced with a problem of defining his own existence. A constant challenge of circumstances forces the individual to elect one decision and refuse another, a time of commitment. The stake is power and a possibility of happiness through force (a problem later to be raised by Mauriac in *le pari contre Machiavel* and in the Camus's reflections on Saint-Juste). Life itself is in question: *si tout homme jouait au pouvoir, tout homme du moins jetait sa tête au jeu.* (p. 630) Does the Romantic self go so far that it should risk its own continued presence in the world? On the one hand, the always present possibility of death and the mystery of death make the self more aware of its need for courage in order to affirm its own right to define existence in its own terms. More significantly, during the Revolution, another feeling takes the place of soul, the attraction towards violence: *l'émotion continue de l'assassinat.* (p. 694) On the other hand, the presence of death can become, not a moment when the self can say *I have become* something or someone, but rather a process of struggle against an incomprehensible divinity or fate. Vigny here never becomes totally existential, because the struggle never abandons the self to its own liberty of choice. Vigny sees man as always *entraîné par le sort* (a consideration close to Sartre's criticism of Baudelaire). Vigny believes that man's *entraînement* comes from a strange desire for self-destruction. The Romantic self faced with the demands from the external world for acts of decision—apart from any absolute good or evil—can, again, frequently answer these demands only by acceptance—fatalism—or by refusal—suicide.[18] The latter is far more an act of definition than the former.[19]

Another act of defiance is, however, possible: separation, alienation, existential otherness. In its search for otherness the self asks questions: whether life holds any purpose apart from a fulfillment of its own needs; whether the closeness of death demands consolation; what to do about the destructive power that arises once the self has decided to act.[20] In **Stello** Vigny's concept of otherness remains Romantic when he points out that the use of power can be fatalistic: . . . *cette chose fatale entre toutes: LE POUVOIR.* (p. 749) Also Romantic is the belief that the self is chosen as Joshua is *l'élu du Tout Puissant.* (**"Moïse,"** I, p. 60) An extension of this fatalism and special election is guilt, especially expiatory guilt. Again, although self-discovery through an effective use of power may save society, it may also bring with it immolation: *L'innocent immolé pour le coupable sauve sa nation; donc il est juste et bon qu'il soit immolé par elle* . . . (p. 752) Yet implicitly existential otherness is there, especially in the problem of evil.

Is it wrong to defy and to act contrary to the accepted norm, since those who try to find an authentic self are, in effect, wounded by a society that rejects them. In his **Journal** (II, p. 875) Vigny cites Job, xxiv, 12: *Les âmes blessées poussent leurs cris vers le ciel.* The problem of evil, seen in a Romantic viewpoint of the self defining its relationship to the world, does not reside in a mere statement of such suffering. The self must always be in a state, as one critic has said in writing of Job, "delineating the power that acts and the passion that suffers,"[21] an existential quest. A possible answer of dualism of good and evil lies in the absoluteness of each quality cancelling out the other in order to reach a state of existential purity. It is true that a consistent duality is evident in Vigny: *l'Homme-Dieu;* the soul is death, *la Mort de l'Âme;* Satan is redeemed, *Satan racheté; la Terre punie.*

In accepting such duality the self could submit to a directive and authoritative power outside itself (this is true of Chenier). The self, however, has an existential fear of the *néant.* The Romantic self must distinguish itself from the outer world. It must also, by an act of the will, establish its own condition of becoming; . . . *employer toutes les forces de volonté à détourner sa vue des entreprises trop faciles de la vie active* (p. 802) is the final advice of Docteur Noir. Self-identity does not lie within the definable limits of action outside oneself, but in the inner world of imagination and its constructs. Stello is always to bear in mind the images of Gilbert, Chatterton, and Chénier. The final question of so making a world of one's own by a self that is identifiable only by itself and in itself is frequently unhappy. *Pourquoi?* and *Hélas!* are Stello's final words when he realizes the necessity of what he is to do and where he will find his self. The Romantic self has explored the various stages of its existence: the rights of the inner world against those of reason; the will to create its own world; the search for authenticity. The significance of this quest may be understood in the words spoken by "le Masque de Fer" in **"La Prison"**: *Du récit de mes maux vous êtes bien avide; / Pourquoi venir fouiller dans ma mémoire vide, / Où, stérile de jours, le temps dort effacé?* (I, p. 123) The Romantic self must exist, then, only in the tensions it cannot eventually cope with, cannot answer. In avowing this unanswerability to tensions it creates its search for identity; the search becomes an existential end in itself and the only possibility of freedom.

Notes

1. See Fernand Baldensperger, *Alfred de Vigny* (Paris: *La Nouvelle Revue critique*, 1929), esp. ch. IV, "Les crises de l'honneur et du cœur."

2. See Irving Massey, in his introduction to his translation of *Stello: A Session with Docteur Noir* (Montréal: McGill University Press, 1963), p. xiv, for the above description.

3. Cf. Massey, *op. cit.*, p. xxiii.

4. Cf. John Macquarrie, *Existentialism* (Philadelphia: Westminster, 1972), p. 34.

5. Cf. H. G. Schenk, *The Mind of the European Romantics* (New York: Ungar, 1967), p. 68.

6. Cf. Wylie Sypher, *Loss of Self in Modern Literature and Art* (New York: Random House, 1962), p. 20.

7. *Ibid.*, p. 29.

8. Alfred de Vigny, *Œuvres complètes*, éd. par F. Baldensperger (Paris, éd de la Pléiade, 2 vols., 1948). Quotations from *Stello* are from vol. I and are followed by page numbers. Quotations from other works are indicated by volume and page number.

9. Cf. Georges Poulet, *Studies in Human Time* (New York: Harper Torchbooks, 1959), p. 232.

10. *Je crois en moi, parce qu'il n'est dans la nature aucune beauté, aucune grandeur qui ne me cause un frisson prophétique . . .* (p. 636)

11. Poulet, *op. cit., loc. cit.*

12. Cf. the lines in "La Maison du berger": *L'Invisible est réel. Les âmes ont leur monde / Où sont accumulés d'impalpables trésors.*

13. Vigny, however, showed hostility towards Pascal in that Vigny would not accept Pascal's apology for Christian faith; Vigny could accept Pascal's suffering as a kind of self-awareness or presence of the heart. Cf. Charles G. Hill, "Vigny and Pascal," *PMLA* [*Publications of the Modern Language Association*], LXXXIII (Dec., 1958), 533-537, esp. p. 533.

14. On the importance of the *imago Dei* in contemporary literature, see John Killinger, *The Failure of Theology in Modern Literature* (New York and Nashville: Abingdon Press, 1963), pp. 59-62.

15. References to pity and compassion are frequent in Vigny. In his *Journal* Vigny writes that Docteur Noir "n'était armé que contre les idées et jamais contre les hommes pour lesquels il avait une céleste pitié." (I, p. 992) This pity derives from sympathy for men seen as prisoners of time and space. In "La Maison du berger," Vigny writes: *Mais il faut triompher du temps et de l'espace, / Arriver ou mourir.* The means

of escape from this prison are *la Rêverie, le pur enthousiasme, un Esprit pur.*

16. Other later solutions might have been possible: Baudelaire's *héroïsme de la vie moderne* (acknowledging a duality of one's own personality); Rimbaud's abandoning poetry; Mallarmé's fear of *la page blanche,* which threatens a construct of one's own creation; or even Surrealist free association (reconstruction from deep psychic remembrance between given objects of created nature and the past and present of one's own emotional life). Vigny's remedy for this fatalism rests once more on the prophetic rôle of the poet. Against the utilitarian ethic of Beckford, Chatterton replies: ". . . le poète cherche aux étoiles quelle route montre le doigt du Seigneur." (p. 677)

17. The problem is how to deal with events. In his *Journal* (II, p. 880), Vigny writes: "Le fort fait ses événements, le faible subit ceux que la destinée lui impose."

18. A possible third choice would be exile from the world and one's fellow men, evident in both Camus and Vigny. Cf. Charles G. Hill, "Camus and Vigny," *PMLA,* LXXXVII (March, 1962), 156-167, esp. p. 159.

19. On suicide and Romantic longing for self-extinction, cf. Schenk, *op. cit.*, p. 64. Vigny treated the subject of suicide at greater length in the first version of *Stello.*

20. A similar problem also arises in Vigny's novel *Cinq-Mars,* who differs—however—from *l'homme révolté* of the twentieth century in that he does not describe himself *a posteriori,* but *a priori.* Early in the novel, Cinq-Mars is reading with pleasure Descartes on innate ideas.

21. Horace M. Kallen, *The Book of Job as a Greek Tragedy* (New York: Hill and Wang, 1959), p. 43.

Barbara T. Cooper (essay date 1982)

SOURCE: "Exploitation of the Body in Vigny's *Chatterton:* The Economy of Drama and the Drama of Economics," in *Theatre Journal,* Vol. 34, No. 1, March, 1982, pp. 20-26.

[*In the following essay, Cooper explores references to the body as they contribute to an economic analysis of Chatterton.*]

In the preface he composed during the night of 29-30 June 1834 for his just completed drama, **Chatterton,** Alfred de Vigny wrote: "This is not ideology."[1] That statement was not a pro forma disclaimer of philosophical bias. Rather, it was a deliberately made and seriously intended definition of the grounds on which Vigny meant to fight for the unencumbered leisure to develop his artistic talents.[2] "Already in *Stello,* [Vigny] had proclaimed the superiority of Poetry and Imagination over philosophy and 'the mind that weighs and measures.'"[3] That Vigny must make clear he his not arguing his case on the basis of some political or philosophical doctrine tells us much about the world in which he lived and the society he was addressing.[4]

But if *Chatterton* is not an ideological drama, it is, nonetheless, a "drama of ideas" for, as Vigny stated in his preface: "The Poet was everything to me; Chatterton was just a man's name, and I have deliberately set aside some of the actual facts of his life and borrowed from it only those things which made of his fate an ever-deplorable example of noble deprivation" (p. 823). In light of this remark it should come as no surprise that *Chatterton* is, among other things, a drama of economics which gives expression to Vigny's concerns for the Poet's property, prosperity, and peace of mind.

Chatterton was not, however, the first version of the eighteenth-century English poet's life Vigny had composed. A narrative account of Chatterton's sufferings had already been published as one of a trio of fictional biographies of poets Vigny had presented in *Stello* in 1832. Explaining his decision to rework that episode in dramatic form, Vigny wrote in the preface to his play: "Many [people] have read my book and liked it as a book; but few hearts, alas! has been changed by it" (p. 813). Clearly, Vigny hoped that the theatrical version of Chatterton's story would have a greater impact on its intended audience. We shall want to consider why Vigny believed that the stage might enhance the persuasive potential of his *démonstration-plaidoyer.* Prior to that, however, we must attempt to understand why Vigny chose to dramatize the story of Chatterton's existence rather than develop the Gilbert or André Chénier episodes included in *Stello.*

We can make some sense of Vigny's choice of the Chatterton episode by examining the substantive modifications the text underwent in its transformation from short story to stage piece. Generally speaking, nearly all of the major differences between the narrative and dramatic accounts Vigny gives of Chatterton's life point to a shift away from the domain of pure politics (Dr. Noir explicitly ties each poet's fate to the political regime under which he lived[5]) toward the realm of political economics. For example, John Bell, who had played a tardy and altogether minor role in *Stello,* becomes a key figure in *Chatterton* and is transformed from a celebrated London saddlemaker into a wealthy merchant-industrialist. Dr. Noir has been replaced by an elderly Quaker who, having given all his worldly possessions to his nephews, hopes to live a life of quiet contemplation in his lodgings at Bell's country home. Kitty Bell is no longer the proprietress of a bakery and tea shop regularly frequented by the members of the nearby Houses of Parliament. A timid, reclusive woman in the play, she now spends her life in the living quarters located behind her husband's office. Finally, Chatterton's work, his suffering, and his unpaid rent are given greater promi-

nence in the play than they were in the narrative. In fact, in the drama, Chatterton has not one, but two rent bills to pay. Taken together, these revisions suggest an economic reorientation of the story's focus—a reorientation that would have been impossible had Vigny chosen either of the other poet's biographies. Neither the France of Louis XV nor that of the Revolution could provide the appropriate setting for a sustained examination of the Poet's economic condition. Only the episode set in the England of the late eighteenth century could support the kind of economic discourse Vigny seems intent on inscribing in his test.

Other modifications of the initial text are the result of the generic differences which separate the two versions of Chatterton's life. In the dramatization of his narrative, Vigny, naturally, had to sacrifice his narrator, Dr. Noir, and the frame structure of his text. But in exchange for these sacrifices, Vigny gained the "economies" of drama, "economies" that are the result of the coexistence of verbal and visual signs whose signifieds complete and complement one another. By shifting genres, Vigny could do much more than merely deplore the *noble misère* of the Poet, more than simply talk about it. He could make that misery real, tangible, visible. He could reduce the distance between the Poet and the audience by putting them in closer proximity to one another and by eliminating the mediating vision of the narrator. Indeed, the text of *Chatterton,* with its detailed descriptions of costume and set and its systematic inclusion of stage directions, suggests that Vigny's interest in the performative aspects of the drama were central to his conception of the play and its propagandistic purpose.[6]

If we are right in suggesting that Vigny chose to develop the Chatterton episode in order to highlight the "drama" of economics and recast his text in a theatrical mold to take advantage of the "economies" of drama, we must reexamine his play to determine how well *la forme* has fused with *le fond.* A close study of *Chatterton* reveals the considerable emphasis placed on the role of the body in both the dialogue and the stage directions. A number of purely literary devices establish the equation: body = instrument of production = commodity = means of exchange. But it is not left to rhetoric alone to suggest that a character's body serves as a sign of his socioeconomic status. Such things as stage position, posture, and physical appearance also help to make that point. Thus, Chatterton's status within the nascent capitalist system represented in the play is as clearly spelled out by his identification with an isolated part of the set, his visibly undernourished body, and his onstage suicide as it is by the spoken references to his weakness and his financial woes. This coupling of verbal and visual signs proves highly effective in communicating Vigny's condemnation of society's indifference and insensitivity to artistic underprivilege. In order to understand how Vigny exploits the full range of all the economies of drama to write a drama of economics, we shall need to look closer at each of these sign systems.

Among the nonverbal allusions to the body are the detailed descriptions of each protagonist's character and costume Vigny provided at the beginning of the play.[7] The careful precision of each portrait testifies to the importance Vigny attached to this aspect of his drama and to the control he wished to exercise in this domain. Interestingly, under the heading "character," Vigny specifies both the physical features and personality traits he wants to be made visible to the audience. Chatterton, for example, is described as a "Young man of eighteen, pale, with an energetic face and a weak body, worn out from sleepless nights and thinking, at once simple and elegant in his manners, timid and tender in front of Kitty Bell, friendly and kind with the Quaker, proud with the others, and on the defensive with everyone; grave and passionate in his speech and his language" (p. 824). In marked contrast to the young poet, his current landlord, John Bell, is described as a "Man of forty-five or fifty, vigorous, red-faced, swollen with ale, dark beer, and roast beef, demonstrating by the way he walks the aplomb his wealth has conferred upon him; a suspicious, dominating gaze; avaricious and jealous, brusque in his manners and making it clear with each word and gesture that he is the master" (p. 825). This intermingling of physique and personality suggests that, at least when writing this drama, Vigny subscribed to the notion—fairly typical of early nineteenth-century thinking—that there was some correlation between the physical and the spiritual sides of human nature. His systematic use of gesture and pantomime throughout the play, and most particularly in the final scenes of the drama, appears to corroborate this interpretation of Vigny's intentions.

Vigny had already used gestures and pantomime in *Stello* to add drama to Dr. Noir's account of his contacts with Chatterton. But descriptions of facial expressions, postures, and movements are never as effective or as powerful as when they are given concrete representation and, in *Chatterton,* Vigny takes full advantage of the visual impact of drama. Thus throughout the play, the posture a character assumes reveals something about his relative status in the social structure defined in the drama. It does not take long for the perceptive spectator to discover that the carriage and gestures of one group of characters (namely John Bell, Lord Talbot, and the Lord Mayor of London, Mr. Beckford) connote power while the postures of a second group of characters (Chatterton, Kitty Bell, and the Quaker) connote some form of weakness. John Bell, for example, is never seen sitting down. His erect stance is a visible symbol both of his strength and his status. Kitty Bell, the Quaker, and Chatterton, however, are often seen seated. The inherent defenselessness of the position serves as a sign of their powerlessness and adds visible depth to those purely verbal allusions to their submissive or contemplative personalities. (The Lord Mayor provides the one notable exception to the standing/sitting dichotomy outlined here. When, toward the end of the drama, Beckford regally distributes his attention and his favors from a seated position, that pose changes to one of power and dominance.)

The physical proximity of one character to another provides another clue to the nature of their relationship. Thus, the natural affinities that link Chatterton, Kitty Bell, and the Quaker are made manifest not only by their overt expressions of sympathy and concern for one another, but also by means of direct and indirect physical contacts. The Quaker, for example, has taken it upon himself to be both friend and doctor to Chatterton. His arms often go out to the young poet in gestures of both physical and emotional support and it is in the Quaker's arms that Chatterton eventually dies.[8] Separated both by social circumstance and by physical distance, Kitty Bell and Chatterton express their feelings for one another by means of contacts for which either the Quaker or Kitty's children serve as vehicles. These mediated declarations of affection are all the more eloquent for being unspoken and they contrast dramatically with the verbal and physical orders John Bell addresses to his wife. Thus, when Bell grabs Kitty's arm and orders her to her room (p. 835) or when he physically confronts her as she is about to leave the parlor (p. 890), the power structure which defines their relationship is made clearly visible and visibly different from the relationship between Chatterton and Kitty.

The preceding discussions of carriage and stage position have already provided two examples of the economic use of the body in *Chatterton.* By assigning symbolic significance as well as pictorial value to posture and physical proximity, Vigny has been able to convey several types of information with one set of signs. The dramatist also links a character's mobility to his position within the fictional power structure, equating mastery of space with the notions of control and dominance. Thus, a character's movement about the stage not only provides for those entrances and exits necessary for the forward movement of the plot, but also serves as a visual clue to his status within the late eighteenth-century society Vigny depicts in his drama.

John Bell, of course, comes and goes at will, crossing the stage in all directions and forcefully opening those doors which block his passage. The range and aggressiveness of his movements provide a clear indication of his position in the power hierarchy the play defines. Chatterton's movements are much more restricted. The poet has spent most of the past three months in his room—an elevated retreat from which he ventures forth only rarely during the course of the play and which is marked off from the rest of the set by a lengthy staircase.[9] That room, at first a symbol of Chatterton's voluntary, monastic withdrawal from society, will eventually become the poet's tomb, and his movements, already circumscribed within the area between his bare, frigid quarters and the parlor, will cease altogether.

Kitty's movements are similarly restricted and have as their poles her first floor room and the parlor. Thus, when, in the last scene of the play, she climbs the stairs to Chatterton's room, Kitty crosses an invisible barrier, thereby visibly overstepping the boundaries of her position. In the end, the almost identical limits imposed on Kitty Bell's and Chatterton's movements and the near intersection of their paths in the parlor highlight the analogous positions of the Poet and Woman in the world of this drama.

To this point, I have focused on Vigny's use of the body as a purely visual sign. We have seen how Vigny has fully profited from those "economies" of drama which allow for the simultaneous transmission of two messages from one set of signs. It now remains to see how Vigny uses the body to create a drama of economics. For this part of the study, I shall consider those purely verbal references to the body found in **Chatterton.**

Key among those allusions to the body given no visible representation on stage is a discussion in Act I, scene ii, which centers around the mutilated arm of one of John Bell's recently fired factory workers. This scene is one of particular significance for my study of the economic dimensions of **Chatterton** both because it is without parallel in **Stello** and because it clearly establishes an equivalence between men's bodies and machines. As the scene opens, John Bell harshly rejects an appeal by twenty of his factory workers to rehire one of their recently injured and summarily dismissed co-workers named Tobie. The Quaker, a long-time friend and frequent critic of Bell's, urges him to reconsider his negative decision. After all, the Quaker reminds him, "What minute of [the workers'] existence is not given to you? What drop of [their] sweat does not earn a shilling for you? You hold the town of Norton, with its houses and families, in your hand just as Charlemagne held the globe in his.—You are the absolute ruler [baron] of your feudal factory" (p. 832). Bell is unimpressed by this argument, however, for to his mind, "Everything, animate and inanimate things alike, must generate a profit [bring in money]" (p. 833). When the Quaker reminds him that Tobie has broken his arm in one of the factory's machines, Bell heartlessly retorts, "Yes, and he also broke the machine." Seeing that further discussion is pointless, the Quaker concludes, "And I am sure that in your heart you feel worse about [the damage to] the iron lever than you do about [what happened to] the flesh and blood lever: go on, your heart is made of steel just like your machines" (p. 833). This cluster of references to hands, arms, levers, and machines does more than simply reveal John Bell's cruel, miserly soul. It also makes the point that, in the world of this drama, power is based on the ownership and control of the means of production (be they men or machines) and that utility and productiveness are the key measures of worth.[10]

The poet's status within this system is made clear during a conversation between Chatterton and the Quaker in the very next scene. In response to the Quaker's assertion that constant daydreaming has destroyed Chatterton's ability to act, the young man says: "Well, what of it, if one hour of this reverie produces more work than twenty days of activity by someone else? . . . Is there nothing for man other than physical [bodily] labor, and are not the labors of the mind worthy of some pity? Is Pythagoras the God of the universe? Must I tell my burning inspirations: 'Do not come, you are useless?'" (p. 839). Chatterton goes on

to tell the Quaker of his vain attempts to engage in some kind of practical, remunerative work. But all-night vigils have so weakened the poet's body and poetry has invaded his mind to such an extent that he is no longer capable of ordinary work. "And yet, do I not have some right to the love of my fellow men, I who work for them day and night . . . ? . . . If only you knew how hard I worked!" (pp. 839-40). The context in which this discussion takes place makes it apparent that the qualification of the poet's activities as "work" and the description of his composition as "works" are more than mere conventions of language. The juxtaposition of this conversation and the preceding reflections on Tobie's broken arm underscore the similarities between the worker and the poet. Both have been mutilated, made useless by their work; both have been cast out and left to die by a society in which humanity and poetry have no place because they have no marketable value.

The notion that the body is an instrument of production whose value can be measured by its utility links these two passages to a third conversation which takes place toward the end of the drama. As was also true of the two segments just examined, this scene (III. iv) has no parallel in **Stello.** Here we learn that Chatterton had previously agreed to pay the past-due rent he owed his former landlord, a multimillionaire property owner named Skirner, with the funds he expected to receive from the sale of his writings. Should he be unable to meet that obligation, Chatterton has agreed that Skirner be given the money the College of Surgery would be willing to pay for his dead body. The terms of this contract suggest that Chatterton's body is not only a means of production. If necessary, that body can also be considered a commodity which can be exchanged for another (writings) or for cash. This is the day the promissory note falls due, and because cold and hunger have immobilized his imagination and his hand, Chatterton has no manuscript to sell. As a last resort, the poet has appealed to Mr. Beckford, the Lord Mayor of London and an acquaintance of his deceased father.

Humbling his pride and his genius more for Kitty Bell's sake than out of a desire to prolong his existence, Chatterton agrees to give up poetry (III. vi). In exchange for that promise, Beckford hands the poet a newspaper and a sealed proposal which he says will bring the young man an annual income of £100 sterling. Chatterton discovers in the newspaper an article accusing him of having plagiarized the works of a tenth-century monk. The Lord Mayor's letter offers Chatterton a job as his personal manservant. Thus denied both the fruits of his labors and his physical independence, the poet opts for suicide. After consuming sixty grains of opium, Chatterton begins shredding and burning his manuscripts, transforming both his *corps* (body) and his corpus into corpses. The poet's death, like the destruction of his writing, represents the ultimate triumph of the body over the spirit, of a mean, mercantile mentality over humane and humanitarian values. Kitty Bell's subsequent death—perhaps the most spectacular demise from a broken heart in all of French drama—lends further support to such an interpretation of Chatterton's suicide. Here, as vividly as anywhere else in the play, Vigny had taken advantage of the economies of drama to highlight the drama of economics. The highly emotional impact of the successive deaths of the sensitive poet and the sensitive woman results from Vigny's dramatic use of the body both as theatrical property and as metaphor.

Notes

1. Alfred de Vigny, "Dernière Nuit de travail, du 29 au 30 juin 1834," preface to *Chatterton* in *Oeuvres complètes,* ed. F. Baldensperger (Paris: Gallimard, Eds. de la Pléiade, 1955), I, 820. All quotations from the preface and the play will be taken from this edition. Future page references will be noted in the body of my article. All translations are my own. By "ideology" I assume Vigny, like Hayden White, from whom I borrow this definition, means "a set of prescriptions for taking a position in the present world of social praxis and acting upon it (either to change the world or to maintain it in its current state . . .)." Hayden White, *Metahistory: The Historical Imagination in Nineteenth-Century Europe* (Baltimore and London: The Johns Hopkins University Press, 1973, paperback. ed. 1975), p. 22.

2. Thus Vigny wrote in his preface: "The cause is the perpetual martyrdom and the perpetual immolation of the Poet.—The cause is the right he should have to live.—The cause is the bread no one gives him.—The cause is the suicide he is forced to commit."

3. Anne Srabian de Fabry, *Vigny: Le Rayon Intérieur ou la permanence de Stello* (Paris: La Pensée Universelle, 1978), p. 260. Translation is my own.

4. Vigny's world was one marked by a new set of economic realities and his society was one whose values have frequently been summarized in Thiers's famous formula "Get rich!". In this context, the writers' situation, like that of other groups, was substantially changed. James Smith Allen has surveyed the changed circumstances of early nineteenth-century authors' lives in his recent study of *Popular French Romanticism* (Syracuse, N.Y.: Syracuse University Press, 1981). I read his work after completing an earlier draft of this paper for presentation at the 1980 Modern Language Association convention. The information in Allen's book tends to corroborate my interpretation of *Chatterton* as a drama of economics.

5. For an example of this see *Stello,* I, 689-90 in the above-cited edition of Vigny's *Oeuvres complètes.*

6. For a corroboration of this assumption see Barry V. Daniels, "An Exemplary French Romantic Production: Alfred de Vigny's *Chatterton,*" ThS [*Theatre Survey: The American Journal of Theatre History*], 16 (1975), 65-88. For reasons which should be apparent, I cannot agree with the conclusions drawn by Laurence M. Porter as reported in the article by Fernande Bassan, "Le Drame romantique," *Nineteenth-Century French Studies* (1979), 172-3.

7. As Daniels makes clear, such detailed physical descriptions of characters could already be found in the works of Diderot and Beaumarchais as well as in the dramatic writings of Vigny's contemporaries.

8. The Quaker plays a similar role vis-à-vis Kitty, who also dies in his arms. If my interpretations of the significance of body language are valid, they suggest that all of the characters in the play, and not just Chatterton, need to be considered both as symbols and as individuals. In that event, John Bell surely must represent economic power, Lord Talbot social power, and Mr. Beckford political power (see III. v) while the Quaker incarnates tolerance and Kitty Bell love.

9. Chatterton does not come down from his room until well into the first act (I. iv). He returns to his room at the end of II. iv and stays there until III. iv. His final trip up the stairs to his room occurs at the end of III. viii, just moments before he dies. (Act I has a total of six scenes; Act II has five; and Act III has nine).

10. In the course of this same conversation Bell tells the Quaker: "A truly clever [calculating] man keeps nothing useless around him" (p. 833).

Keith Wren (essay date 1982)

SOURCE: "A Suitable Case for Treatment: Ideological Confusion in Vigny's *Cinq-Mars,*" in *Forum for Modern Language Studies,* Vol. 18, No. 4, October, 1982, pp. 335-50.

[*In the following essay, Wren critiques the political thesis of Vigny's novel* Cinq-Mars, *contending that it is weakened by the author's inability to find in Cardinal Richelieu a suitable historical persona to satisfy his view of French history.*]

In May 1837 Alfred de Vigny wrote of his novel *Cinq-Mars,* first published eleven years previously, that "il n'y a pas de livre que j'ai plus longtemps et plus sérieusement médité".[1] This opinion of the importance which the author retrospectively ascribed to the position of *Cinq-Mars* in his literary output has not, in any great measure, been echoed by critics, who tend to dismiss the novel as a heavily biased and over-subjective interpretation of historical reality. Most would subscribe without demur to the assessment of Georg Lukács:

> Vigny . . . sees history sufficiently clearly to regard the French Revolution not as an isolated, sudden event, but rather as the final consequence of the "youthful errors" of French development . . . In his novel he goes back to the time of Richelieu in order to reveal artistically the historical sources of this "error" . . . which could be made good with proper insight . . . He approaches the facts of history with a subjectivist, moral *a priori,* the content of which is precisely Legitimism.[2]

Critics would similarly accept that the most powerful influence on Vigny in terms of political theory was Montesquieu, and that Vigny's vision of the role of the aristocracy in the structure and conduct of the state derives almost in its entirety from *De l'Esprit des lois*: it is communicated to his readers in the observations and discussions of the conspirators in *Cinq-Mars*. J. Sungolowsky notes that "Montesquieu lui a enseigné qu'en opprimant la noblesse, une monarchie dégénère en un despotisme abject".[3] Vigny himself made no secret of where his sympathies lay: "J'avais . . . le désir de faire une suite de romans historiques qui serait comme l'Épopée de la Noblesse et dont *Cinq-Mars* était le commencement" (466).

This all seems perfectly straightforward. *Cinq-Mars* is the retrospective demonstration of the rightness of Montesquieu's analysis. In Lukács's terms the novel shows us where French history definitively "went wrong", and chronicles the last serious attempt by the nobility to prevent it from so doing. (It is significant in this respect that Vigny describes the subsequent Fronde as a "sanglante comédie" [207].) Yet the more carefully one examines the text of the novel, the less convinced one becomes that it is, as Lukács implies, just a straightforward threnody for the defunct second estate. On the contrary, it becomes progressively clearer that *Cinq-Mars* is ideologically confused, in that notwithstanding its *intention* to demonstrate Montesquieu's thesis, it most signally fails to do so. The source of this confusion lies not so much in the historical period which Vigny describes in the novel as in the contemporary political situation of the post-Napoleonic Bourbon restoration. Like so many of his contemporaries Vigny fell victim to the Napoleonic myth, and the internal contradictions which characterise *Cinq-Mars* reflect the conflict in the author's own mind between the traditional legitimism of his family and his own disillusionment with the restored monarchy. The purpose of this article is to distinguish the areas of ideological confusion in the novel, and to justify the contention that the Napoleonic myth is responsible for it. In order to do so, I shall first review briefly Vigny's own ideas on the practice of the historical novel, as exemplified in his *ex post facto* preface to *Cinq-Mars,* and subsequently demonstrate the existence of confusion in the novel itself in the light of the preface and of Vigny's acknowledged political credo.

This preface, entitled "Réflexions sur la vérité dans l'art", first published in 1829, when *Cinq-Mars* had reached its fourth edition, is a vital illustration of what Vigny perceived as his objective in the novel. From the first paragraph, he argues the central importance of history in the contemporary novel: "L'étude du destin général des sociétés n'est pas moins nécessaire aujourd'hui dans les écrits que l'analyse du cœur humain" (23). Such a declaration is redolent of the influence and practice of Walter Scott, but Vigny is no camp-follower, and rejects the basic structural method of the *Waverley Novels*: "je crus . . . ne pas devoir imiter les étrangers, qui dans leurs tableaux, montrent à peine à l'horizon les hommes dominants de leur histoire; je plaçai les nôtres sur le devant de la scène" (23). That such a procedure involves a highly subjective view of history Vigny is perfectly willing to acknowledge, and he stresses "la liberté que doit avoir l'imagination d'enlacer dans ses nœuds formateurs toutes les figures principales d'un siècle, et . . . de faire céder parfois la réalité des faits à l'IDÉE que chacun d'eux doit représenter aux yeux de la postérité, enfin . . . la différence que je vois entre la VÉRITÉ de l'Art et le VRAI du Fait" (24).

Vigny is here advancing two points of major significance, paralleling Hugo's better-known (and probably earlier) treatment in the *Préface de Cromwell*. The intrinsic historical fact is important only insofar as it fits the author's preconceived notion of characters and events, of which the corollary is inevitably that the author's approach is didactic rather than aesthetic, a vision of history imposed on posterity. This is the *vérité* to which the *vrai* must always be subservient. Here, indeed, it is no critical commonplace to speak of the author as God, for this is precisely the role which Vigny arrogates to himself:

> Mais à quoi bon la mémoire des faits véritables, si ce n'est à servir d'exemple de bien ou de mal? Or les exemples que présente la succession lente des événements sont épars et incomplets; il leur manque toujours un enchaînement palpable et visible, qui puisse amener sans divergence à une conclusion morale; les actes de la famille humaine sur le théâtre du monde ont sans doute un ensemble, mais le sens de cette vaste tragédie qu'elle y joue ne sera visible qu'à l'œil de Dieu
>
> (24-25).[4]

And to the eye of the poetic imagination. Vigny is in essence no different from the *philosophe* historians of the Enlightenment, whose Sisyphean endeavours to unravel the meaning of the universe he so derides.[5]

In this context, Vigny's observation that "L'HISTOIRE EST UN ROMAN DONT LE PEUPLE EST L'AUTEUR" (26), is hardly very convincing, for the lodestar of his reconstruction of history is, by his own admission, his imagination. At the most, he can be seen to make an artistic principle out of the popular tendency to see historical figures as either heroes or villains, and to adapt it to fit his own requirements:

> . . . Lorsque la MUSE vient raconter, dans ses formes passionnées, les aventures d'un personnage que je sais avoir vécu, et qu'elle recompose ses événements, selon la plus grande idée de vice ou de vertu que l'on puisse concevoir de lui . . . je ne sais pas pourquoi on serait plus difficile avec elle qu'avec cette voix des peuples qui fait subir chaque jour à chaque fait de si grandes mutations
>
> (28).

Vigny, then, argues for a subjective and didactic view of history with characterisation tailor-made to match. *Cinq-Mars*, it seems, was to be one section of tetralogy entitled *Histoire de la Noblesse*, of which Vigny indicates the broad scope in his journal (1836):

> 1. Les nobles règnent paisiblement: féodalité.—Ils se défient des Bourbons qui s'établissent cruellement.—Le roi Jean.

2. *Cinq-Mars*: Louis XIII par Richelieu décime les nobles.

3. *La Duchesse de Portsmouth*: Louis XIV les avilit dans ses antichambres, les ruine par le jeu et la vanité.

4. La Révolution les fait *parias,* ce qu'ils sont à présent.

(484)

In 1833 the project had been even vaster:

Après avoir achevé l'histoire de *la Duchesse de Portsmouth* qui sera le second degré de la décadence de la noblesse . . . je ferai un autre roman intitulé *le Soldat* qui sera la dernière partie de mon épopée,—puis un premier roman prenant le plus grand et le premier martyr sous saint Louis,—précédé d'un volume qui servira de préface à tout l'ouvrage et sera intitulé *Histoire de la grandeur et du martyre de la noblesse de France.*

(484)

The highly emotive twin reference to martyrdom confirms the closeness of Vigny's analysis to that of Montesquieu, which also warns, albeit less emphatically, of the dangers inherent in the destruction of the nobility, seen as an intermediary body between the crown and the people:

La monarchie se perd lorsqu'un prince croit qu'il montre plus sa puissance en changeant l'ordre des choses qu'en les suivant; lorsqu'il ôte les fonctions naturelles des uns pour les donner arbitrairement à d'autres . . . La monarchie se perd lorsque le prince, rapportant tout uniquement à lui, appelle l'état à sa capitale, la capitale à sa cour, et la cour à sa seule personne.[6]

Once the delicate balance between crown and nobility is upset, disaster ensues. *Cinq-Mars* is dedicated to the exemplification of the fact that "le roi et la noblesse étaient deux anciens amants qu'on avait brouillés" (Pléiade, II, 1131), and Vigny's vision of history, or rather, of where history 'went wrong' is regularly repeated throughout the novel by a series of characters all endowed with an astonishing degree of prescience. Bassompierre, Bouillon, de Thou, all intone the same refrain. De Thou urges Cinq-Mars on with these words:

Poursuivez, mon ami, ne soyez jamais découragé; parlez hautement au Roi du mérite et des malheurs de ses plus illustres amis que l'on écrase; dites-lui sans crainte que sa vieille noblesse n'a jamais conspiré contre lui . . . dites-lui que les vieilles races de France sont nées avec sa race, qu'en les frappant il remue toute la nation et que, s'il les éteint, la sienne en souffrira, qu'elle demeurera seule exposée au souffle du temps et des événements . . .

(193)

Somewhat implausibly, Vigny even puts similar words into the mouth of Richelieu himself: "Je renverse l'entourage du trône. Si, sans le savoir, je sapais ses fondements et hâtais sa chute!" (179) In other words, the entire stated purpose of the novel is to impose a highly personal view of the historical process on the reader, and it is this overtly propagandist stance adopted by Vigny that leads M. Citoleux to declare: "Ce qui empêche *Cinq-Mars* d'être le chef-d'œuvre incontesté du roman historique, c'est que, malgré son apparence objective, il est une œuvre de passion et toute personnelle."[7]

Unfortunately, Vigny's personal rancour against the destroyer of his class, combined with his avowed desire to modify the authorial approach of his model Scott, lead him into difficulty. He is overly dismissive (and not entirely accurate) in his assessment of Scott's art:

Je pensais que les romans historiques de *Walter Scott* étaient trop faciles à faire, en ce que l'action était placée dans des personnages inventés que l'on fait agir comme l'on veut, tandis qu'il passe de loin en loin à l'horizon une grande figure historique dont la présence accroît l'importance du livre et lui donne une date. Ces Rois ne représentaient ainsi qu'un chiffre, je cherchai à faire le contraire de ce travail et à renverser sa manière.

(466)

The net result of such a procedure ought to be to facilitate his propagandist objectives, if we bear in mind the curiously simplistic concept of historical characterisation advanced in the **"Réflexions"**. The reader expects the depiction of a Manichaean struggle between the forces of good and evil, embodied respectively by Cinq-Mars and his aristocratic supporters, and by Richelieu. The outcome, however, despite Vigny's apparent intentions, is rather different.

The author is, admittedly, in something of a quandary. If he wishes—as he manifestly does—to give his novel substance as a retrospective analysis of the seventeenth-century social and political situation, then he must take care not to falsify history too greatly, whilst, at the same time, avoiding the trap which converts accuracy into pedantry.[8] He thereby places himself in a position where he has to *explain* the triumph of Richelieu to the reader at the same time as conveying the idea that it represents an irreparable disaster for France. The reader should be left with a sense of tragedy at the realisation that evil, in the shape of Richelieu, has triumphed over good and that the damage to French society had been effected a century before Montesquieu ever advanced his theory. Not only does Vigny fail to achieve this objective: he falls little short of demonstrating the complete reverse.

The effect is all the more curious because Vigny loads the fictional dice against Richelieu, even before the Cardinal appears. A number of devices are used in the first six chapters of the novel to achieve this end. We note first of all the idyllic setting of the opening pages, the description of the castle of Chaumont, Cinq-Mars's ancestral home:

Des arbres noires et touffus entourent de tous côtés cet ancien manoir et, de loin, ressemblent à ces plumes qui environnaient le chapeau du roi Henri; un joli village s'étend au pied du mont, sur le bord de la rivière, et l'on dirait que ses maisons blanches sortent du sable doré; il est lié au château qui le protège par un étroit sentier qui circule dans le rocher; une chapelle est au milieu de la colline; les seigneurs descendaient et les villageois montaient à son autel: terrain d'égalité, placé comme une ville neutre entre la misère et la grandeur, qui se sont trop souvent fait la guerre.

(36-37)

This passage seems to mirror the tableau of the nobility reigning peacefully under the feudal system that was to have been depicted in the first novel of the projected tetralogy. It is paradise, but paradise is created to be lost. The theme of degeneration is now introduced by the character who—symbolically—dominates the first chapter, then disappears from the novel—Bassompierre.

After the *benedicite* has been pronounced over the meal, Bassompierre takes over. He is out-of-date even in his own time:

Il avait conservé sous ses cheveux blancs un air de vivacité et de jeunesse fort étrange à voir; ses manières nobles et polies avaient quelque chose d'une galanterie surannée comme son costume, car il portrait une fraise à la Henri IV et les manches tailladées à la manière du dernier règne, ridicule impardonnable aux yeux des *beaux* de la Cour.

(39-40)

His youthfulness is an important feature, symbolic of happier times in a more politically youthful society, before the decline into despotism set in. It assumes its full significance in the light of the subsequent descriptions of Richelieu, whose physical decay symbolises for Vigny the moral and political degeneracy of the view of society he embodies.

Vigny uses Bassompierre to refute the argument that particularist power among the feudal nobility constituted a disruptive force in the state—"Ces révoltes et ces guerres . . . n'ôtaient rien aux lois fondamentales de l'Etat et ne pouvaient pas plus renverser le trône que ne le ferait un duel" (43-44)—and as the first of the series of prophets predicting the ultimate results of Richelieu's centralising policy:

Oui, je n'en doute plus à présent, le Cardinal-duc accomplira son dessein en entier, la grande Noblesse quittera et perdra ses terres, et, cessant d'être la grande propriété, cessera d'être une puissance; la Cour n'est déjà plus qu'un palais où l'on sollicite: elle deviendra plus tard une antichambre, quand elle ne se composera plus que des gens de la suite du Roi; les grands noms commenceront par ennoblir des charges viles; mais, par une terrible réaction, ces charges finiront par avilir les grands noms. Étrangère à ses foyers, la Noblesse ne sera rien que par les emplois qu'elle aura reçus, et, si les peuples, sur lesquels elle n'aura plus d'influence, veulent se révolter . . .

(44)

The inference is clear, as are the overtones of Montesquieu:[9] Richelieu's policy leads directly to the French Revolution, as we realise even more at the end of the novel, when Corneille and Milton overhear a member of the crowd jubilantly proclaim: "Le Parlement est mort . . . les seigneurs sont morts: dansons, nous sommes les maîtres; le vieux Cardinal s'en va, il n'y a plus que le roi et nous" (404).

Bassompierre's arrest by de Launay, one of the Cardinal's minions, again symbolises the triumph of the new over the old, of evil over good. It shows that for Cinq-Mars the game is lost before it has begun, a point underlined by the series of "signs" pointing to the tragic conclusion even before he sets out on his journey. Not only is it the day of the martyrs St Gervase and St Protasius, but the assembled company at table numbers thirteen, Cinq-Mars's horse stumbles as he leaves the castle, and, at his secret rendezvous with Marie de Gonzague, the hands of the two lovers appear, by a trick of the light, red with blood.[10]

Vigny continues to marshal sympathy for Cinq-Mars's cause by showing us the effects of the Cardinal's policy in the Urbain Grandier affair. The object of this apparent digression in the novel is to stress the parallel between Grandier and Cinq-Mars in terms of their moral worth, and to prefigure the ultimate fate of the latter by the death of the former—another "sign". Both are men of superior ability whom Richelieu, "le grand niveleur" (246), cannot permit to stand in his way. It is this treatment of a man so similar to himself that sets the seal on Cinq-Mars's opposition to Richelieu, first evidenced by the unavailing attempt to rescue Bassompierre and reinforced by the revelations of the abbé Quillet.[11]

Vigny has thus carefully accumulated the evidence against Richelieu before introducing him into the novel. His intention is clearly to bias the reader in favour of Cinq-Mars's initiative to overthrow the minister, and in consequence Cinq-Mars himself benefits from an extremely flattering presentation. He is akin to the accepted stereotype of the Romantic hero, "un jeune homme d'une assez belle taille; il était pâle, ses cheveux étaient bruns, ses yeux noirs, son air triste et insouciant" (42): his first words, or thoughts, recall the idealised Satan, the rebel of *Éloa*:

"O nature, nature! se disait-il, belle nature, adieu! Bientôt mon cœur ne sera plus assez simple pour te sentir, et tu ne plairas plus qu'à mes yeux; ce cœur est déjà brûlé par une passion profonde, et le récit des intérêts des hommes y jette un trouble inconnu: il faut donc entrer dans ce labyrinthe; je m'y perdrai peut-être, mais pour Marie . . .

(44-45)[12]

Adumbrated here is the sacrifice theme, "la beauté du sacrifice de soi-même à une généreuse pensée" (24), of which Cinq-Mars and de Thou provide the two prime examples in the novel. Elevated in the reader's eyes by this selflessness and by the righteous indignation that characterises his reactions to the Bassompierre and Grandier affairs, Cinq-Mars is thus an attractive figure.

Unfortunately for the author, "he that diggeth a pit shall fall into it", and we must now ask ourselves how it comes about that Vigny, having apparently prepared his case so carefully, effectively destroys his own thesis.

Five interlinked points need to be taken into consideration: the *manque de sérieux* of the conspirators, the weakness of their leaders, the dubious motivation of Cinq-Mars, the treaty with Spain, and the role of the King. Overarching them all is the necessity for the reader to be convinced by the novelist that the destiny of France would be better served by the replacement of Richelieu at the head of the government by the conspirators in alliance with the King, in order to restore and maintain the balance of power advocated by Montesquieu, and embodied in the vision of a political "Paradise Lost" advanced by Bassompierre. This Vigny fails to do, and the novel demonstrates that his failure derives from the fact that he himself, despite multiple protestations, remains fundamentally unconvinced. Let us now consider how this is made clear by the text.

The conspiracy against Richelieu is handled by the participants with extraordinary inefficiency. It is not merely that they are careless, although this is an important factor. Gondi remarks:

> En vérité, je suis tenté de mettre mon valet de chambre aussi dans le secret; on n'a jamais vu traiter une conjuration aussi légèrement. Les grandes entreprises veulent du mystère; celle-ci serait admirable si l'on s'en donnait la peine. Notre partie est plus belle qu'aucune que j'ai lue dans l'histoire; il y aurait là de quoi renverser trois royaumes si l'on voulait, et les étourderies gâteront tout.

(278-79)

Far more serious is the fact that they are led by a group of aristocrats who, in their various ways, are totally inadequate for the roles in which they have cast themselves and who, in consequence, are clearly unable to agree on a common strategy. Evidence of this contention is provided by the anti-Richelieu riots in Paris, recounted in chapter 14: fomented by Gondi, "cette dégoûtante cohue" (213) induces only disgust in the partisans of Cinq-Mars and Gaston, and, rather than accept the mob's assistance, they help Chavigny, the Cardinal's aide, to escape. Vigny's comment is illuminating, suggesting as it does a marked lack of confidence in those of whom he supposedly approves:

> Rougissant de la supériorité du nombre et des ignobles troupes qu'ils semblaient commander, entrevoyant peut-être pour la première fois, les funestes conséquences de leurs jeux politiques et voyant quel était le limon qu'ils venaient de remuer, ils se divisèrent pour se retirer . . .

(213)

None of the leaders of the conspiracy can escape the charge of inadequacy. The nominal head, the King's brother Gaston, termed MONSIEUR (I exclude from consideration for the moment the King himself), never seriously challenges such categorisation, from the moment we first encounter him, panic-stricken by the riots, to his abject submission of which Richelieu writes the script. But the effect of his overt and consistent weakness is less insidious to Vigny's purpose than the evolution of the character of the duc de Bouillon, a peer apparently worthy of our utmost esteem:

> Le duc de Bouillon avait une chaleur d'expression et une assurance qui captivait toujours ceux qui l'entendaient: sa valeur, son coup d'œil dans les combats, la profondeur de ses vues politiques, sa connaissance des affaires d'Europe, son caractère réfléchi et décidé tout à la fois le rendaient l'un des hommes les plus capables et les plus imposants de son temps, le seul même que redoutât réellement le Cardinal-duc.

(248)

It should perhaps be stressed that this, *Vigny's* description of the man, follows on immediately from a speech in which Bouillon addresses the future King Louis XIV in terms identical to those used by Bassompierre in his opening denunciation of Richelieu. The fact that he is the author's spokesman therefore renders Bouillon's fate all the more significant. His behaviour at the time of the discovery and suppression of the conspiracy is hardly calculated to inspire confidence in him, and indeed retrospectively demolishes in the reader's eyes his validity and credibility as a conspirator: "Quant au magnifique et puissant duc de Bouillon, seigneur souverain de Sedan et général en chef des armées d'Italie, il vient d'être saisi par ses officiers au milieu de ses soldats et s'était caché dans une botte de paille" (348). Certainly Cinq-Mars's disillusioned assessment of his fellow-plotters' "pensées secrètes" seems to be borne out by the effect:

> Je les connais toutes; j'ai lu leur espérance à travers leur feinte colère; je sais qu'ils tremblent en menaçant: je sais qu'ils sont déjà prêts à faire leur paix en me livrant comme gage; mais c'est à moi de les soutenir et de décider le Roi.

(257)

In other words, they are weak, self-interested and cowardly, hardly adjectives that could be attached to Cinq-Mars himself. Or could they?

Weak and cowardly, certainly not. Events throughout the novel persistently underline Cinq-Mars's courage in the face of danger and moral strength in adversity. But the matter of self-interest merits closer examination. As we have seen, Bassompierre defines the political situation prevailing in France, the hegemony of Richelieu which the conspiracy is designed to overturn. How sincere is Cinq-Mars's own commitment to the political salvation of his country?

The answer to this question seems to be that Cinq-Mars becomes a political activist by accident. He loves Marie de Gonzague, Duchess of Mantua. But marriage to Marie can be achieved only by self-elevation, it being a case of "Tout autre qu'un monarque est indigne de moi".[13] So the midwife of Cinq-Mars's political consciousness is arrivisme: "L'amour a versé l'ambition dans mon cœur comme un poison brûlant; oui, je le sens pour la première fois, l'ambition peut être ennoblie par son but" (55). Hence Richelieu's real crime in the eyes of Cinq-Mars is to impede his social advancement: it is Richelieu's *political* stance that prevents the realisation of Cinq-Mars's *per-*

sonal objectives. Despite the interposition of the long narrative digression about Grandier, which seems to offer Cinq-Mars a more principled basis on which to found his opposition to Richelieu—"Plutôt la mort mille fois que son amitié! J'ai tout son être, et jusqu'à son nom même, en haine; il verse le sang des hommes avec la croix du Rédempteur" (171)—the accusation of self-interest remains and is substantiated by subsequent developments, notably his embarrassment when de Thou credits him with precisely that principled motivation, "ce sentiment d'amour pour la France" (192), which he *should* have demonstrated in order to rebut the accusation:

> Je ne suis pas étranger à ces idées qui vous possèdent . . . L'amour de la France, la haine vertueuse de l'ambitieux qui l'opprime et brise ses antiques mœurs avec la hache du bourreau, la ferme croyance que la vertu peut être aussi habile que le crime, voilà mes dieux, les mêmes que les vôtres. Mais, quand vous voyez un homme à genoux dans une église, lui demandez-vous quel saint ou quel ange protège et reçoit sa prière?
>
> (194)

The saint or angel in question here is clearly not St Denys but the Romantic angel Marie de Gonzague.

Even more unpardonable is the fact that it is Marie's childish impatience with delay that finally sparks off the conspirators' move against Richelieu. Cinq-Mars takes the initiative after carefully observing Marie's behaviour during the audience with the Queen: "un mouvement d'impatience de son pied lui donna l'ordre d'en finir et de régler enfin toute la conspiration" (249). He is aware that this move has doomed him, as he later admits to de Thou: "Ah! que vous me connaissez mal . . . si vous croyez que je n'aie pas vu jusqu'au fond de mon destin! Je lutte contre lui, mais il est le plus fort, je le sens; j'ai entrepris une tâche au-dessus des forces humaines, je succomberai" (257). And this ill-fated Romantic hero proceeds to explain the situation in full to his puzzled collaborator:

> Je le suis, ambitieux, mais parce que j'aime . . . Vous m'avez prêté de nobles desseins . . . de hautes conceptions politiques; elles sont belles, elles sont vastes, peut-être; mais, vous le dirai-je? ces vagues projets du perfectionnement des sociétés corrompues me semblent ramper encore bien loin au-dessous du dévouement de l'amour.
>
> (258)

It emerges, however, that Cinq-Mars's acceptance of the inevitability of his impending failure is based on the knowledge that he has acted too soon: "Tout était bien jusqu'ici; mais une barrière invisible m'arrête; il faut le rompre, cette barrière: c'est Richelieu. Je l'ai entrepris tout à l'heure devant vous, mais peut-être me suis-je trop hâté! je le crois à présent" (258). Significantly Vigny repeats this analysis of Cinq-Mars's decision a few pages later.[14]

Now whether or not this is true (and Vigny seems to contradict himself on the point later when recounting Richelieu's reactions to the conspiracy) it raises a difficult problem.[15] If Cinq-Mars believes that he has wrecked his and the conspirators' chances of success by moving too soon in order to satisfy Marie, then he has confirmed our diagnosis of his conduct throughout the novel: that is to say, he has been consistent in subordinating political to personal ends. The good of France as perceived by his fellow conspirators has fortunately coincided with the path he would in any case have had to tread to win the hand of Marie de Gonzague: "Le bonheur de l'État s'accorde avec le mien. Je le fais en passant, si je détruis le tyran du Roi" (259). Cinq-Mars is thus equally as guilty of impurity of motivation as any of the other conspirators.

We begin to realise, therefore, that despite Vigny's overt support for the *thèse nobiliaire* the examples of aristocratic resistance to Richelieu he has chosen to portray are singularly flawed. We might perhaps object that this criticism should not apply to de Thou, apparently a fine example of a man of principle. But de Thou is a profoundly apolitical figure, or, more accurately, a figure who ultimately abandons his political principles for what he perceives as a greater good. His fate—and the way in which Vigny presents it—reminds us of the celebrated lines of *Éloa*:

> Gloire dans l'Univers, dans les Temps, à celui
> Qui s'immole à jamais pour le salut d'autrui.[16]

The situation in **Cinq-Mars** is very similar. Neither Éloa's nor de Thou's sacrifice is efficacious in terms of redemption: on the contrary, the person for whom they make the sacrifice, Satan or Cinq-Mars, merely involves them in his own ruin. It is the intrinsic beauty of the sacrificial act that specifically impresses Vigny.

Intrinsic beauty or no, we should not be blinded to the *political* implications of de Thou's stance. As a man of action he is an abject failure (witness the extended quid pro quo of chapter 16), and as a man of principle he is also on rather doubtful terrain: as he himself acknowledges after having committed himself to the conspiracy: "je vais être criminel, je vais mériter la mort; mais puis-je faire autrement? Je ne dénoncerai pas ce traître, parce que ce serait aussi trahir, et qu'il est mon ami, et qu'il est malheureux" (261).[17] Political principles are thus here subordinated to personal affection. De Thou considers Cinq-Mars to be ill-advised in his conduct of the conspiracy, but stands by him, even after Cinq-Mars has signed the treaty with Spain, which makes him a traitor. From the purely human angle this is doubtless very admirable, and Vigny eagerly underlines the point: "Le sang de François-Auguste de Thou a coulé au nom d'une idée sacrée, et qui nous demeurera telle tant que la *religion de l'honneur vivra parmi nous*; c'est l'impossibilité de la dénonciation sur les lèvres de l'homme de bien" (444). Unfortunately, de Thou's human attachment is counterbalanced by his abdication of political principle, his complete subordination of his clarity of judgement to his affection for his friend, which, in a novel of this sort, designed to validate a *political* thesis, is to say the least rather regrettable, and weakens Vigny's argument still further.

Cinq-Mars's position is rendered even more untenable by the treaty with Spain. Both de Thou and Anne of Austria reject this as an instrument of policy: "Savez-vous qu'il y va de partager votre patrie? savez-vous que si vous livrez nos places fortes, on ne vous les rendra jamais? savez-vous que votre nom sera l'horreur de la postérité?" (260). The Queen's refusal to countenance the treaty, and subsequent withdrawal from the conspiracy gains piquancy from the fact that she is herself Spanish; she declares that "la patrie d'une reine est autour de son trône" (252). Such a condemnation from such a source hardly improves Cinq-Mars's moral position. But he is caught in the *engrenage*. In order for his conspiracy, based, as we have seen, primarily on self-interest, to succeed, he must become a traitor. The only mitigation of this intention de Thou can achieve is to modify Cinq-Mars's resolve to sign the treaty directly until after the favourite has seen the King. And the character of the King is such as to ensure the necessity of signature.

The King is the final element in the equation. Depicted as a dying man, whose reign is "une continuelle agonie" (122), as "ce cœur glacé qui croit désirer quelque chose" (266), he endeavours to justify his decision to hand over power to Richelieu:

> J'ai donné mon sceptre à porter à un homme que je hais, parce que j'ai cru sa main plus forte que la mienne; j'ai supporté le mal qu'il me faisait à moi-même en songeant qu'il faisait du bien à mes peuples: j'ai dévoré mes larmes pour tarir les leurs; et je vois que mon sacrifice a été plus grand même que je ne le croyais, car ils ne l'ont pas aperçu.
>
> (272-73)

But this is talk without substance. Louis's sacrifice is even more suspect than Cinq-Mars's, let alone de Thou's. Brave enough in battle, as he demonstrates during the siege of Perpignan, the King is hopelessly inadequate in all the other functions of kingship. Confronted by Richelieu's challenge to rule by himself, he proves completely unequal to the task—to the extent of being unaware, two years after the event, of the independence of Portugal and the revolt of the Catalans:

> Ce fut alors que Louis XIII se vit tout entier, et s'effraya du néant qu'il trouvait en lui-même . . . sous chaque contrée, il crut voir fumer un volcan; il lui semblait entendre les cris de détresse des rois qui l'appelaient, et les cris de fureur des peuples; il crut sentir la terre de France craquer et se fendre sous ses pieds; sa vue faible et fatiguée se troubla, sa tête malade fut saisie d'un vertige qui refoula le sang vers son cœur.
>
> (360-61)

And he yields unconditionally—as he always has—to Richelieu.

But Louis XIII is worse than weak: he is treacherous. It is only moments after lamenting to Cinq-Mars about his people's loss of confidence in him that he gives an example of precisely why this has happened, betraying the conspiracy to Joseph, the *éminence grise*. It is the monarch who effectively forces Cinq-Mars to sign the treaty with Spain:

> Le roi disait que lui-même dirigerait tout à Perpignan; et cependant Joseph, cet impur espion, sortait du cabinet des Lys! O Marie! vous l'avouerai-je? au moment où je l'ai appris, mon âme a été bouleversée; j'ai douté de tout et il m'a semblé que le centre du monde chancelait en voyant la vérité quitter le cœur d'un roi . . . Un moyen me restait, je l'ai employé . . . Le traité d'Espagne était dans ma main, je l'ai signé.
>
> (314)

What emerges from this analysis, therefore, is that Vigny's characterisation makes a mockery of his political thesis. He could hardly have made a worse case for the *thèse nobiliaire* if he had tried. A weak and treacherous monarch, presiding intermittently over a group of conspiring aristocrats suspect either from the point of view of courage or motivation, and who prove insufficient to the task, both in terms of concerted planning and adequate security—are we really asked to accept, *pace* Montesquieu, that such a grouping would be more beneficial to France than the iron rule of Richelieu? Especially when Richelieu himself is presented by Vigny in so ambivalent a way.

As I have suggested, Vigny's ostensible intention is to present the Cardinal as a summation of all those negative forces leading to the destruction in the holocaust of 1789 of "la monarchie, sans base, telle que Richelieu l'avait faite" (224). The duc de Bouillon stresses to the infant Louis XIV that Richelieu is "celui qui déracine votre trône" (247), and Richelieu himself, as we have seen, is depicted as having doubts: "M'était-il permis de jouer ainsi avec les hommes, et de les regarder comme des nombres pour accomplir une pensée, fausse peut-être?' (179). Vigny spares little effort to make him odious: after the Bassompiere and Grandier episodes, when Richelieu finally appears, his first act is to dismiss Olivier d'Entraigues from his service for the crime of writing a love-letter: this is hardly calculated to endear him to readers to whom Vigny, through the character of Cinq-Mars, has presented love as a supreme value. The same must be said of the cynical way in which he turns the death of the King's mother to his advantage, in order to maintain himself in power.

But Vigny's systematic endeavours to blacken the character of Richelieu are far from successful, for two main reasons. The first is that, however unpleasant Richelieu and his policies may seem to be, the alternative, as represented by the conspirators, is, at least in political terms, infinitely worse. Richelieu's grasp of the affairs of state, as evidenced particularly in chapters 7 and 24, is the more impressive when weighed against the impotence of Louis XIII and the inexperience of Cinq-Mars, of whom we are told that "jamais il n'avait laissé entrevoir par un seul mot la moindre aptitude à connaître les affaires publiques (302). In his hands, moreover, the other characters are puppets, whether to their advantage or their detriment. He stage-manages the King's military intervention at Perpignan whilst ensuring that "ce caprice de gloire ne dérangera pas mes immuables desseins: cette ville ne tombera pas encore, elle ne sera française pour toujours que dans deux ans; elle viendra dans mes filets seulement au jour marqué dans ma pensée" (153). He controls the conspirators in the same way as he had controlled previous conspirators: "Je les ai tous laissés nager plus de deux ans en pleine eau; à présent tirons le filet" (346), thus vindicating in retrospect Anne of Austria's warning: "il est à trois cents lieues de nous, mais son génie fatal veille à cette porte" (225). Vigny uses the image of the spider to illustrate Richelieu's dominance of events: "il dormait comme l'araignée au centre de ses filets" (207).

This impression of imperturbable overall grip is enhanced by the way in which Richelieu regulates the collapse of the conspiracy:

> Voici quelle sera ma soirée . . . à neuf heures nous réglerons les affaires de M. le Grand [Cinq-Mars]; à dix, je me ferai porter autour du jardin pour prendre l'air au clair de lune; ensuite je dormirai une heure ou deux; à minuit, le Roi viendra, et à quatre heures vous pourrez repasser pour prendre les divers ordres d'arrestations, condamnations ou autres que j'aurai à vous donner pour les provinces, Paris ou les armées de Sa Majesté.
>
> (345-46)

If this is heartless, it is at least efficient, and derives from a clear sense of purpose. Richelieu's ambition may be no more admirable and no less self-seeking a phenomenon than that of many of the conspirators, but it has the advantage of being decisive and unambiguous in its objectives:

> Bientôt le Roi succombera sous la lente maladie qui le consume; je serai régent alors, je serai roi de France moi-même; je n'aurai plus à redouter les caprices de sa faiblesse; je détruirai sans retour les races orgueilleuses de ce pays; j'y passerai un niveau terrible et la baguette de Tarquin; je serai seul sur eux tous.
>
> (178)

And yet Vigny seems to imply that, in Louis XIII's view, Richelieu has a more elevated and less egocentric perception of his role: "Il se rappela en un moment tous les services infatigables de Richelieu, son dévouement sans bornes, sa surprenante capacité, et s'étonna d'avoir voulu s'en séparer" (138). Ultimately Vigny is unclear about the real rarget of Richelieu's ambition, or at least he seems to shift his ground. At the end of the novel Corneille and Milton dismiss him as short-sighted—"il n'a voulu que régner jusqu'à la fin de sa vie" (407)—and devoid of the courage to implement his true objectives—"l'amour du pouvoir est bien puéril, et cet homme en est dévoré sans avoir la force de le saisir tout entier" (408). In fact Richelieu himself never goes as far as this, restricting himself to unfulfillable hypotheses: speaking of Louis XIII he exclaims: "Que de choses j'aurais pu faire avec ses droits

héréditaires si je les avais eus!" (114). And in the symbolic game of chess he plays with his master in the last chapter, he stops short of checkmate:

> Il venait d'avancer une *tour* qui mettait le roi de Louis XIII dans cette fausse position qu'on nomme *pat,* situation où ce roi d'ébène, sans être attaqué personnellement, ne peut cependant ni reculer ni avancer dans aucun sens. Le Cardinal, levant les yeux, regarda son adversaire et se mit à sourire d'un côté des lèvres seulement, ne pouvant s'interdire un secret rapprochement.
>
> (401)

Nonetheless, the dialogue between Corneille and Milton that terminates the novel is of considerable importance. Despite the fact that the novel bears Cinq-Mars's name, and that Richelieu is not even mentioned in the subtitle, *Une Conjuration sous Louis XIII,* the closing debate focuses almost entirely on the figure of the Cardinal, albeit in a critical vein. I think this offers a solution to the ideological inconsistency that besets the novel.

It is remarkable that Vigny finds himself compelled in his novel to extend a grudging admiration to Richelieu, who becomes a sort of anti-hero. One of the first images that Vigny uses to describe him is that of "un soleil qui donnait seul la vie et le mouvement à la France" (110). A few pages later he reappears as the "dieu de la France" (114). His pride—or vanity—is similarly superhuman—"colossal" (120). As governments in neighbouring countries go down like ninepins, Richelieu's France alone stands firm:

> La puissante unité de la monarchie était plus imposante encore par le malheur des États voisins; les révoltes de l'Angleterre et celles de l'Espagne et du Portugal faisaient admirer d'autant plus le calme dont jouissait la France; Strafford et Olivarès, renversés ou ébranlés, grandissaient l'immuable Richelieu.
>
> (206)

Even his efficiency becomes admirable in the face of the witless endeavours of his opponents: the final irony is perhaps that Cinq-Mars's renunciation of the conspiracy remains, though he does not realise it, merely a gesture. Richelieu already controls all his troops:

> Il reste donc encore seulement mes deux jeunes voisins. Ils s'imaginent avoir le camp tout entier à leurs ordres, et il ne leur demeure attaché que les Compagnies Rouges; tout le reste, étant à MONSIEUR, n'agira pas, et mes régiments les arrêteront. Cependant j'ai permis qu'on eût l'air de leur obéir.
>
> (349)

I wonder whether, in the deepest sense, *Cinq-Mars* is really a historical novel at all, let alone the funeral anthem for legitimism that Lukács would have us believe. Surely the over-documented recreation of the seventeenth century conceals a meditation on a much more recent past. There is too much in Vigny's presentation of Richelieu that could remind us of the Napoleon of Lamartine's "Bonaparte" or Hugo's "Les Deux Iles", as well as a couple of oblique references to the Emperor himself.[18] But it is only in the closing pages of the novel that we really perceive the ideas taking shape in Vigny's mind, as Corneille continues his discussion with Milton beside the statue of Henri IV:

> La reconnaissance prosterne les pauvres devant cette statue d'un bon roi; qui sait quel autre monument élèverait une autre passion auprès de celui-ci? qui sait jusqu'où l'amour de la gloire conduira notre peuple? qui sait si, au lieu même où nous sommes, ne s'élèvera pas une pyramide arrachée à l'Orient?
>
> —Ce sont les secrets de l'avenir, dit Milton; j'admire, comme vous, votre peuple passionné; mais je le crains pour lui-même; je le comprends mal aussi et je ne reconnais pas son esprit quand je le vois prodiguer son admiration à des hommes tels que celui qui vous gouverne.

(407-08)

The implication is clear. Corneille somewhat implausibly foresees the rise of Napoleon, the textual reference being to the elevation of the obelisk in the Place de la Concorde after the Egyptian campaign. Milton, in his reply, implicitly brackets Richelieu with Napoleon to the detriment of both. In this interchange we perceive the germ of the ambiguity of Vigny's attitude to the great men of history. We recall the admission in *Servitude et Grandeur Militaires* (1835) of his fascination with the achievements of the Empire:

> Vers la fin de l'Empire, je fus un lycéen distrait. La guerre était debout dans le lycée . . . Nulle méditation ne pouvait enchaîner longtemps des têtes étourdies sans cesse par les canons et les cloches des *Te Deum*! . . . Il me prit alors plus que jamais un amour vraiment désordonné de la gloire des armes; passion d'autant plus malheureuse que c'était le temps précisément où . . . la France commençait à s'en guérir.[19]

The effect of this military enthusiasm led Vigny to enlist in the Army under the Restoration, in the hope of exploits as glorious as those of the Empire: "La guerre nous semblait si bien l'état naturel de notre pays, que lorsque, échappés des classes, nous nous jetâmes dans l'Armée . . . nous ne pûmes croire au calme durable de la paix" (527). Disillusioned, he realised that he had missed his vocation:

> Ce ne fut que très tard que je m'aperçus que mes services n'étaient qu'une longue méprise, et que j'avais porté dans une vie tout active une nature toute contemplative. Mais j'avais suivi la pente de cette génération de l'Empire, née avec le siècle, et de laquelle je suis.

(527)

Yet, most importantly, the fantasy of the man of action remained:

> Bien souvant, j'ai souri de pitié sur moi-même en voyant avec quelle force une idée s'empare de nous, comme elle nous fait sa dupe, et combien il faut de temps pour l'user. La satiété même ne parvint qu'à me

faire désobéir à celle-ci, non à la détruire en moi, et ce livre aussi me prouve que je prends plaisir encore à la caresser, et que je ne serais pas éloigné d'une rechute.

(527)

In this way the paradox of *Cinq-Mars* becomes explicable. The closing dialogue of the novel is a conversation between two men who, like Vigny himself, are of "une nature toute contemplative". Commentators rather than participants, they stand apart from and superior to the political action taking place around them, their detachment prefiguring the attitude increasingly espoused by Vigny during his literary career. Yet Vigny himself never quite lost the urge to involve himself in "une vie tout active", and the hypnotic effect that the achievement of Napoleon exercised on so many of the Romantics is demonstrated, I would argue, by the treatment accorded to Richelieu in *Cinq-Mars*.[20] Both Napoleon's usurpation and Richelieu's centralisation represented political tendencies alien to the centrifugal legitimism hereditary in the Vigny family and embodied in the theory of Montesquieu. Yet insofar as Vigny aspired to be a man of action both Napoleon and Richelieu were infinitely more impressive examples of the *genre* than any legitimist. Vigny cannot find the men to fit his thesis, which falls to the ground, destroyed by its own internal contradictions and the fact that at the deepest level the author is arguing against himself. Only Corneille, the contemplative, can humiliate Richelieu. This superiority of the poet over the man of action is symbolised in the last chapter by the failure of Richelieu's play *Mirame* and the applause for Corneille as the author of *Le Cid*. In the political sphere Richelieu is all-powerful—"L'Europe muette l'écoutait par représentants" (396)—but "the mind is its own place". Only in this way can Vigny exorcise his fascination. The message of poetic solitude which characterises *Les Destinées* is here in germ, and is paradoxically much more convincingly demonstrated than the political thesis Vigny set himself to prove. The ideological confusion in *Cinq-Mars* derives from Vigny's unmitigated failure to find in history any convincing exemplification of the theory he propounds.

Notes

1. Alfred de Vigny, *Cinq-Mars,* edited by Jean Roudaut (Paris, Livre de Poche, 1970), p.466. All page references in the text will be to this edition, which has the best critical apparatus.

2. Georg Lukács, *The Historical Novel,* translated by Hannah and Stanley Mitchell (London, Merlin Press, 1962), pp. 75-76.

3. Joseph Sungolowsky, *Alfred de Vigny et le dix-huitième siècle* (Paris, Nizet, 1968), p.96.

4. This is strongly reminiscent of the passage in the *Préface de Cromwell* where Hugo argues that art "rétablit le jeu des fils de la providence sous les marionnettes humaines". See Hugo, *Préface de Cromwell,* edited by Maurice Souriau (Paris, S.F.I.L., 1897), p.264.

5. "Toutes les philosophies se sont en vain épuisées à l'expliquer, roulant sans cesse leur rocher, qui n'arrive jamais et retombe sur elles, chacune élevant son frêle édifice sur la ruine des autres et le voyant crouler à son tour" (21).

6. Montesquieu, *Œuvres Complètes,* edited by Roger Caillois (Paris, Pléiade, 1951), II, 354-55.

7. Marc Citoleux, *Alfred de Vigny* (Paris, Champion, 1924), p.144.

8. Vigny himself was conscious of this. This first edition of *Cinq-Mars,* published in March 1826, had no historical notes. For the second edition (June 1826), he changed his mind: "l'auteur s'aperçut de la nécessité d'indiquer les sources principales de son travail; et comme il avait toujours voulu remonter aux plus pures, c'est-à-dire aux manuscrits, et, à leur défaut, aux éditions contemporaines, il ajouta les renseignements les plus détaillés" (411). His original objective, however, had not been to depict "le *vrai* détaillé, mais l'œuvre épique" (411), in accordance with the terms of the subsequently published "Réflexions sur la vérité dans l'art".

9. "Le principe de la monarchie se corrompt lorsque les premières dignités sont les marques de la première servitude, lorsqu'on ôte aux grands le respect des peuples, et qu'on les rend de vils instruments du pouvoir arbitraire. Il se corrompt encore plus lorsque l'honneur a été mis en contradiction avec les honneurs, et que l'on peut être à la fois couvert d'infamie et de dignités." (II,355).

10. There are numerous other premonitory "signs" in the novel, notably Cinq-Mars's dream (103), the predictions of Jeanne de Belfiel (104, 184), the "fortune-telling" scene with sword and missal (195), and the sinister setting for the hunting party, with its vivid description of the sun as "une petite lune sanglante, enveloppée dans un linceul déchiré" (281).

11. It is Quillet who supplies Cinq-Mars with the details of the Grandier affair. Cinq-Mars's own sins against Richelieu are a secularised version of Grandier's: "Ceux d'une âme forte et d'un génie supérieur, une volonté inflexible qui a irrité la puissance contre lui, et une passion profonde qui a entraîné son cœur et lui a fait commettre le seul péché mortel que je croie pouvoir lui être reproché" (73-74).

12. Satan's lament is likewise for the loss of innocence:

> Simplicité du cœur, à qui j'ai dit adieu!
>
> Je tremble devant toi, mais pourtant je t'adore;
>
> Je suis moins criminel puisque je t'aime encore;
>
> Mais dans mon sein flétri tu ne reviendras pas!
>
> Loin de ce que j'étais, quoi! j'ai fait tant de pas!
>
> Et de moi-même à moi si grande est la distance,
>
> Que je ne comprends plus ce que dit l'innocence.

13. As the Infanta observes to her *confidante* Léonor in Corneille's *Le Cid* (line 100).

14. "Cette impatience d'en finir avec le sort qu'il voyait de si près hâta l'explosion de cette mine patiemment creusée, comme il l'avait avoué à son ami; mais sa situation était alors celle d'un homme qui, placé à côté du livre de vie, verrait tout le jour y passer la main qui doit tracer sa condemnation ou son salut." (264).

15. Cinq-Mars is the only leader of the conspiracy whom Richelieu does not dismiss out of hand as contemptible: "Il n'y a que ce petit Cinq-Mars qui ait de la suite dans les idées; tout ce qu'il a fait était conduit d'une manière surprenante: il faut lui rendre justice, il avait des dispositions." (346).

16. Alfred de Vigny, *Œuvres Complètes,* edited by Fernand Baldensperger (Paris, Pléiade, 1950), I,30. The theme of sacrifice is, of course, something of a *leitmotiv* in Vigny's poetry of this period: we find it in different guises in such poems as "Moïse", "La Fille de Jephté" and "Le Déluge".

17. Before committing himself to Cinq-Mars, de Thou reads out a passage from his father's memoirs, indicative of the fact that the position de Thou will adopt is treasonable: "Je pense donc que M. de Lignebœuf fut justement condamné à mort par le Parlement de Rouen pour n'avoir point révélé la conjuration de Catteville contre l'État." (261).

18. There is the apparently gratuitous reference to the Hundred Days at the beginning of chapter 14 (205-06), and the more important one to the Egyptian campaign (407), which I discuss below.

19. Alfred de Vigny, *Œuvres Complètes,* edited by Fernand Baldensperger (Paris, Pléiade, 1948), II,526-27. All subsequent references to *Servitude et Grandeur Militaires* are to this edition.

20. See Henri Guillemin, *Monsieur de Vigny, homme d'ordre et poète* (Paris, Gallimard, 1955), pp.11-30.

Martha Noel Evans (essay date 1983)

SOURCE: "Mirror Images in 'La Maison du berger,'" in *French Review,* Vol. 56, No. 3, February, 1983, pp. 393-99.

[In the following essay, Evans studies Vigny's poem "La Maison du berger" in the context of psychoanalytic theories of self-consciousness and reflection.]

That homely object the mirror has played over the centuries an extraordinarily rich metaphoric role. At various times a figure of human vanity, an image of the mimetic function of art, or a mythic emblem of self-consciousness, it has lately been elaborated and enriched as a metaphor of human consciousness by psychoanalysts like Jacques Lacan and Luce Irigaray. In his essay "Le Stade du miroir"[1] Lacan brilliantly condenses Hegel's description of self-consciousness and Freud's formulation of narcissism into a new mythic figure: the child before the mirror. In Lacan's view the process by which the child reaches self-consciousness always includes the splitting and projection of the self into an external image so that the self is first perceived as being *out there, in the mirror.* The formation of the Ego, one of the products of this defensive strategy, thus inextricably links visual processes with aggressive impulses.

In *Speculum de l'autre femme* (1974), Luce Irigaray develops further the meaning of this myth by asserting that the child before the mirror must of necessity be a male. His otherness, i.e., his femaleness, is aggressively split off and projected into the inverted image of the mirror self. While Irigaray insists that the predominance of vision in the formation of identity is a peculiarly male characteristic, she does share two assumptions with Lacan: first, that the processes of vision are linked with aggressivity; and second, that the phenomenology of sight will yield a general logic and geometry defining the subject's relationship to space and finally to the outside world.

Lacan says in "Le Stade du miroir," "l'image spéculaire semble être le seuil du monde visible" (p. 95). As "the threshold of the visible world," the mirror takes on, then, a central hermeneutic role in the meaning of seeing. The ancient *vanitas* and *speculum mundi* have evolved into a *psyché,* a looking glass, in which we simultaneously look *out* and *into* ourselves. The mirror has become the image of the sighted psyche.

All of this seems a long way from Romantic poetry, but the psychoanalytic mirror will serve us well as we look at Alfred de Vigny's poem **"La Maison du berger"** (1844). The very lexicon of the poem, studded as it is with mirrors and sight imagery, seems to make an appeal to the reader to see the seeing in this poem. Vigny's belief in the Romantic notions of poetry as a concentrating mirror and in the poet as Seer is well known. I would like to go beyond these beliefs in order to examine, in the light of Lacan's and Irigaray's myths, what this poetry reflects and how the Seer sees.

"La Maison du berger" is in the form of a letter addressed by the poet to his mistress, Eva, pressing her to flee the city with him. But Vigny immediately introduces a new and curious modification of the traditional ethics of Romantic pastoralism. As the poet presents it, the corruption and moral decay attendant on urban life do not depend, as one might expect, on the superficiality and dishonesty of city dwellers, but rather on the inevitable and unavoidable visibility of the individual to the gaze of anonymous lookers:

> Si ton corps, frémissant des passions secrètes,
> S'indigne des regards, timide et palpitant;

> S'il cherche à sa beauté de profondes retraites
> Pour la mieux dérober au profane insultant,
> . . . . .
> Pars courageusement, laisse toutes les villes.

(Vv. 15-18, 22)

In this passage, it seems to be the very visibility of his mistress that makes her morally vulnerable, as if she could be penetrated and possessed by these insulting looks. The poet paradoxically reveals the sadistic component of his own visual imagination and at the same time imagines the woman timidly palpitating under the powerful and oppressive gaze of the multitude. Vigny has supplanted the traditional ethics of pastoralism by another ethics inherent in what he conceives to be the power politics of vision. Eva's passion, for instance, is no more pure than the villainous desires of the city dwellers. What gives it its particular taint is its public visibility. The poet can therefore protect and purify his mistress by taking her away into hiding: "Viens y cacher l'amour et ta divine faute" (v. 47).

In this initial section of the poem, vision creates its own moral dynamics: it is a closed system, defined by extreme polarities and by either/or oppositions. To be seen is to be blinded and made powerless by the look of the other in a visual process of pre-emption and sexual debasement. The moral polarities set up here by Vigny promote *prostitution,* in its original etymological sense, to the position of major crime in urban social life: Eva is shamed by *standing forth* in the other's field of vision.

The logic and tone of the opening section lead us to expect that the proposed pastoral retreat will serve the purpose of establishing a form of interaction superior to the prostitution of city life. We expect Vigny to erect a third observation post from which he can watch both the seers and the seen. But although his physical retreat from society seems to propose this new triangular geometry to us, emotionally the poet remains within the dyadic struggle for visual mastery. His removal from society is not so much a liberation as a strategic retreat meant to enhance his position on the battlefield. Vigny does not spurn society's duel of looks but rather maneuvers in order to win it by reversing the direction of forces. He flees the self-alienation of visibility in order to achieve mastery as the Seer.

The poet's pastoral retreat is a feint, then, meant to enslave the multitudes who have enslaved him: "Du haut de nos pensers vois les cités serviles / Comme les rocs fatals de l'esclavage humain" (vv. 24-25). From his elevated position, the poet establishes his power by looking down on the multitudes, both physically and morally. He becomes "un roi de la Pensée,"[2] and his gift of poetic vision is defined in this moral scheme precisely by the dominance he achieves by being able to see without being seen.

The poet must thus be concealed, and the landscape he describes as his asylum is seen as a function of this need. By a process of emotional projection onto the visible world,

Nature is turned into a reflection of the poet's desires. The place of hiding becomes itself a process of self-concealment: "La forêt a voilé ses colonnes profondes / La montagne se cache" (vv. 33-34).

The poet hides himself in the hiding of Nature. He takes refuge in the mobile shepherd's hut. But eventually he finds his surest asylum in an unexpected place, the gaze of his mistress:

> Je verrai si tu veux, les pays de la neige,
> Ceux où l'astre amoureux dévore et resplendit,
>
> . . . . .
>
> Que m'importe le jour? Que m'importe le monde?
> Je dirai qu'ils sont beaux quand tes yeux l'auront dit.
>
> (Vv. 57-58, 62-63)

The poetic process is here expressed entirely in terms of sight and vision. It is, in fact, a strangely *silent* process, promoted only by Eva's will to see. In a wordless exchange, Eva provides the will to see while the poet furnishes the power of vision. By means of this symbiosis the poet becomes a passive instrument while maintaining his power of sight through the will of a blind other. The poet is thus safely shielded by Eva from the dangers of visibility. Her gaze becomes a mask for the poet to hide behind. And this mask has a double function: it protects the poet both from the hostile looks of others and from the responsibility of his own desire to be a Seer.

This desire, which appears here as a gift of love, reveals its root in the soil of aggressivity, affirming Lacan's assertion that altruism is always the product of a deeper wish to destroy: "le sentiment altruiste est sans promesse pour nous, qui perçons à jour l'aggressivité qui sous-tend l'action du philanthrope, de l'idéaliste . . . voire du réformateur" (p. 100).

The aggressivity underlying the will of this poetic idealist and pastoral reformer becomes extraordinarily clear in the following section of the poem. Having secured Eva as a mask, as the source of his sight, the poet unleashes a series of angry imprecations whose aggressive power produces images of hallucinatory brilliance. Vigny's poetry, which he calls elsewhere "le miroir magique de la vie" (*Journal*, II, 1192), seems rather here to turn into a carnival gallery of distorting mirrors, for everything the poet looks at becomes twisted into the grotesque shapes of corruption.

Seeing, here, is a process of laying bare, of penetrating and possessing, just as previously the gazes of the "profane insultant" violated Eva. Politicians, statesmen, even the Muse, appear to the poet as actors in the debasing drama of prostitution described earlier. As before, Vigny translates relationships of power inherent in social visibility into the language of promiscuous and sadistic sexuality. Even the virgin Muse is transformed by the poet's angry gaze into "une fille sans pudeur" singing like a street-walker "aux carrefours impurs de la cité" (vv. 155, 158).

And what corrupted her, what made her bad, was precisely her solicitation, not of sex, but of the other's look: "Dès que son œil chercha le regard des satyrs / Sa parole trembla, son serment fut suspect" (vv. 150-51).

What the poet's second look at society reveals is that things are exactly the opposite of what they first seemed to be. As in the opening section of the poem, all reality is divided into a closed system of polar opposites; gradations are banished; hierarchies denied. All aspects of human life thus fall into mutually exclusive categories: love or hate, master or slave, virgin or prostitute. Looking at the world is like looking at a mirror where every image is reversed, turned around. Vigny literalizes this process of reversal and betrayal in an image of sexual inversion. As the final instance of the debauchery of the Muse, the poet pictures her in ancient Greece, perched happily in the midst of a pederastic festival: "Un vieillard t'enivrant de son baiser jaloux / [. . .] parmi les garçons t'assit sur ses genoux" (vv. 163, 165).

What is most interesting about this economy of projection, reversal, and inversion is that the poet participates blindly in his own process of vision. While presenting himself as the pastoral poet who is "above it all," he is actually the occasion for the very depravity he reviles. His own look prostitutes the object of his gaze. So while he thought to hide from the capricious and hostile power of the other's look, he has, in fact, hidden from his own aggression. Although the angry and debasing thrusts of his look are concealed from the poet's consciousness, they become paradoxically visible everywhere in the spectacle of the outside world. The poet's anger, which he does not acknowledge as his own, seems therefore to be coming at him *from the outside*.

This blind spot, the focus of the poet's denied aggression, becomes particularly visible in Vigny's dazzling diatribe against the railroad. The railroad appears first of all as the corrupt and sexually inverted counterpart of the shepherd's hut. While the rolling hut wanders free like the "mobile pensée" (v. 251) of the female mind, the phallic railroad reduces space into a network of constricting straight lines. This coldly predictable machine re-emerges, however, in the contradictory guise of a fiery bull that eats up men and boys. In the poet's double vision the steam engine is at once a scientific apparatus and a dangerous, perverse monster:

> Sur le taureau de fer qui fume, souffle et beugle,
> L'homme a monté trop tôt. Nul ne connaît encor
> Quels orages en lui porte ce rude aveugle.
>
> . . . . .
>
> Son vieux père et ses fils, il les jette en otage
> Dans le ventre brûlant du taureau de Carthage.
>
> (Vv. 78-80, 82-83)

While the presentation of the railroad as a "chemin triste et droit" (v. 121) logically furthers the pastoral thematics of the poem, the ambivalence of Vigny's vision is overwhelmed by its own wildness. The mythical "dragon mugissant" (v. 90) devours its own impotent apparition as cold machinery, just as the monster's unseeing eye stares down the poet with the blindness of his own rage.

The poet's helplessness in the face of his own anger finally structures all knowledge in a paranoid mode. Vigny views the truth as a hostile force whose main property is to victimize him. This anguished sense of victimization, of undeserved betrayal, takes shape in the second apparition of Nature. The poet's aggression finally breaks out of its silent hiding place in Eva's gaze and speaks in the voice of a proud and punishing woman:

> "Je n'entends ni vos cris ni vos soupirs; à peine
> Je sens passer sur moi la comédie humaine
> Qui cherche en vain au ciel ses muets spectateurs,
> Je roule avec dédain sans voir et sans entendre."

(Vv. 285-88)

The split of the poet's consciousness is reified in this hallucinatory image of Nature where the actual relationship of self and other is at once proposed and denied. To the poet's bitter disappointment, Nature does not recognize him as her own; but, on the other hand, neither does the poet recognize her as his double. The poet's own blindness has made him invisible. The unseeing stare of his own image looks through him as if he were not there. The nightmare of reflexivity has been accomplished; the impalpable figure in the mirror has become the source of vision, while the Ego has dissolved into nothingness.

Significantly, this I/eye, this distanced self whom he does not recognize, is envisaged by the poet not as a "he" but as a "she," *la marâtre Nature,* an unnatural and perverse mother. What the poet has cut off from consciousness and rejected as a debasing component of his identity is therefore not only his aggression but also the female part of himself. The poet as "she" appears in two images in the poem: in the punishing but eloquent figure of Nature and in the passive, silent figure of Eva. In the last section of the poem, following the song of Nature, the themes of narcissism and split consciousness finally become explicit in the metaphor of the mirror.

Eva is described as a reflecting pool where God has forever fated narcissistic man to contemplate himself, "tourmenté de s'aimer, tourmenté de se voir" (v. 231). She thus becomes simultaneously a passive instrument of reflection and the place where the poet will inscribe his self-knowledge. Poetry, "ce fin miroir solide, étincelant et dur" (v. 200), and woman, "ce miroir d'une autre âme" (v. 234), merge in a bivalent symbol where love and vision blend in the single process of producing self-conscious poetic language. In his effort to forestall the dizzying process of self-contradiction and reversal, the poet here seeks unity as poetry looking at itself. Doubleness of vision seems at last evaded; subject and object, reflection and mirror, appear to fuse in the shining diamond of poetry's song.

But like someone trying in a quick turn to catch a glimpse of his own back, poetry's look at itself must of necessity be fleeting and oblique. In order to see as One, in order to

see the One, the poet must try to immobilize this evanescent moment of first sight: "Aimez ce que jamais on ne verra deux fois" (v. 308). What one sees only once is "true" because it does not change: it is forever fixed in its initial appearance. The truth is made One, is made pure, only by its disappearance.

Once again, the poet's effort to escape the tormenting vision of his own Otherness is not achieved through synthesis and integration but rather by a repetition of the same denial that was the original source of his alienation. The poet can no more recuperate the denied part of himself by visualizing it *out there* in a female reflection than Narcissus could be requited by his own image in a pool. Eva's very function as reflection disables her as a healer of the poet's narcissistic wound; immobilized by her imagined passivity, she is powerless to desire. Her love therefore can find expression only in regret, in mourning:

> appuyée aux branches incertaines
> Pleurant comme Diane au bord de ses fontaines
> Son amour taciturne et toujours menacé.

(Vv. 334-36)

At the end of **"La Maison du berger,"** the image of the mirror is itself split as it becomes the figure of an irreversibly divided consciousness. The aggression and dissolution inherent in self-enunciation splinter Vigny's mirror of poetry into two component parts. On the one hand, the quicksilver reflecting surface embodied in Eva, the moon-maiden, is the projection of the poet's passive femininity, of the silence and dissolution that threaten him, of the death that inhabits him. On the other hand, the poet isolates himself within the crystal covering of the mirror to become the pure, preserving Word, self-present and diamond-hard, never menaced by change or dissolution.

As a result of this final splitting, the poet remains an everlasting "pur esprit, roi du monde / [. . .] / visible Saint-Esprit,"[3] while his Other, woman, becomes the pool of banishment where the poet's frailty, his mortality, shimmers palely in the light reflected from the sun of his intellect. The female part of the mirror becomes the mercurial image of fleeting time while the male part represents the imperishable diamond of thought. He is the One, and she is the process of self-destruction that sustains his unity.

The two parts are contiguous without ever being joined, since fusion with his Other represents for Vigny a horrifying and repugnant union with his own death, with his own putrefaction. The preserving crystal and the quick-silver of mortality are separated by an infinitesimal space, the pressurized domain of fear and hostility whose purpose it is to keep death at a safe distance, *out there.*

But by exteriorizing his own death, Vigny has paradoxically and tragically cut himself off from his own vitality. In his attempt to localize his fear and anger in the outside world, he has, in fact, rendered himself defenseless against them. These feelings that threaten from within become hauntingly omnipresent without; they color all that the poet sees with a somber and heavily charged light. The triumphant figures of life and independence in **"La Maison du berger"** are persistently overshadowed by the specters of death and dependence. All expressions of love in this poem have, if I may use the term, a necrophilic halo. Nature, that sweet refuge, is also a tomb; the shepherd's hut, the symbol of Romantic revery, is called a "char nocturne" (v. 53); and the nuptial bed, erotic bower of pleasure, turns into a coffin-like "lit silencieux" (v. 56). The diamond of poetry itself becomes a dazzling and sadistic evil eye whose aggressive rays flutter fatally around the image of the mourning mistress, forever weeping, forever silent, forever dying.

Vigny experiences his relationship with the world as a duel with a persecuting Other. As the place where he can be most intensely alone and therefore most significantly in control of this duel, poetry becomes for Vigny a kind of therapeutic process of self-domination by dominating others. But this poetry, which represents for Vigny the gift of sight, is also a focus of his own blindness. The mimetic function of poetry, this "miroir magique de la vie," is thus fragmented and undermined by its function as *psyché,* the narcissistic looking-glass. The mirror of life is dismantled in **"La Maison du berger"** in a personal mythology that will persist in Vigny's poetry. The reflecting quick-silver of the world, at once beautiful and menacing, is separated from the crystal protective surface, the diamond of poetry, which will sing its invulnerability in a language blanched by its own purity and impoverished by its very unity.

Notes

1. *Ecrits* (Paris: Seuil, 1966), pp. 93-100.

2. Vigny, *Le Journal d'un poète,* in *Œuvres complètes,* Bibliothèque de la Pléiade (Paris: Gallimard, 1948), II, 1192.

3. "L'Esprit pur" (1863), vv. 50, 56.

Robin Buss (essay date 1984)

SOURCE: *Vigny: Chatterton,* Grant & Cutler Ltd., 1984, 78p.

[*In the following excerpt, Buss considers* Chatterton *as a dramatic defense of the poet and his purpose in an otherwise materialist society, and continues by assessing the influence of this "drama of ideas" on subsequent literature.*]

'La maladie est incurable', remarks the Quaker and, when Chatterton asks: 'La mienne?', replies:

> Non, celle de l'humanité.—Selon ton cœur, tu prends en bienveillante pitié ceux qui te disent: Sois un autre homme que celui que tu es;—moi, selon ma tête, je les ai en mépris, parce qu'ils veulent dire: Retire-toi de notre soleil; il n'y a pas de place pour toi.
>
> (p. 54)

But Chatterton, throughout his answer, carries on speaking quietly to Rachel: it is not the place of the mythical hero to understand his own role in the myth.

The Quaker's reply not only points to the social dimension of the drama, but shows also that its target is specifically the ruling class in society, those whose enjoyment of the sunshine incites them to exclude any individual subject to other laws than the ones they have devised for their own benefit and the maintenance of their power. Literally, the class under attack must be the industrial bourgeoisie and the aristocracy of wealth in Britain in the 1770s, represented by John Bell and Lord Beckford; but the scene between Bell and his workmen shows that Vigny was in touch with such events as the Luddite violence of the 1820s in Britain, while the development of industrialisation and the establishment after the Revolution of July 1830 in France of a régime modelled to some extent on the lines of British parliamentary democracy, convinced many of his contemporaries that his real target was the French bourgeoisie and the class, defined at the time as *l'aristocratie d'argent,* which was rapidly acknowledged to have been the main beneficiary of the change of power.

Vigny himself protested that his play should not be taken as an attack on the middle class, and what I want to demonstrate in this chapter are the sources of some of the ideas in a work which is considerably more subtle than merely a political pamphlet under the guise of a defence of poetry. What Vigny confronts in *Chatterton* is not just a materialist class but an ideology, that of the Liberal bourgeoisie of the 1820s; he confronts it, but at the same time finds himself obliged to argue his case on terms which are largely those laid down by his opponents. He is not alone in this, since the Romantic debate on literature in general, and poetry in particular, took place in the context of a view of history and culture that was formed during the eighteenth century and, though challenged from the early years of the nineteenth century, retained a considerable hold in the minds even of those who appeared to reject its conclusions.

The Romantic movement in literature and art is generally presented in grossly simplified terms, like a football match in which the new side of Romanticism is pitted against the old guard of Classicists, with their adherence to the outworn dogmas of Racinian tragedy. Of course, the contest was not simply one of Racine vs. Shakespeare and the very wide spectrum of ideas represented by the leading Romantic writers, as well as the changes in their attitudes even during the relatively short period of the decade 1820-1830 (when Hugo, for example, evolved from a reactionary right-wing political stance to a left-wing one), should make us doubt any simplified view of the debate. Moreover, the study of the literary and political press of the period will show that opposition to Romanticism did not by any means come solely from critics who would have liked to see a return to the literature of the seventeenth and eighteenth centuries. There was a body of opposition to the new movement, which may be broadly described as

'Liberal', basing its hostility to Romanticism on a broad ideology of human culture; this Liberal group was in fact highly influential in French intellectual life and its politics attracted, or came to attract, many of the young writers now associated with the Romantic movement.

For various reasons, it had become a cliché by the early 1830s that poetry was dead and that the more extravagant manifestations of Romanticism were symptoms connected with the exhaustion of the poetic impulse. Hugo, in his preface to *Marion de Lorme* acknowledges the existence of this view when he says that 'il y a des esprits, et dans le nombre fort élevé, qui disent que la poésie est morte'—though, as a poet, he naturally goes on to refute the idea. By 1831, when he was writing, even this gambit of putting up the statement in order to refute it had become something of a cliché.

Since the decade of the 1820s had seen the publication of large numbers of volumes of poetry, and a vital new movement represented by such poets as Hugo and Lamartine, the conviction that the poetic spirit was either dead or dying could only come from a particular concept of what constituted 'poetry' allied to a system of ideas that supported the view that poetry was in some way unsuited to the climate of the modern age. This view rested on two main arguments: firstly that civilisations developed along a pattern comparable to that of individual human development, from infancy to childhood, maturity and old age; and secondly, that the forms by which cultures expressed themselves also varied, certain types of poetry being more appropriate to early development, others to later stages, and other literary genres taking over as mankind progressed. I have stated this general idea in highly schematic terms, but the metaphors that derived from it and were used to express it, were in fact quite convincing and a good deal more pervasive than one might at first glance suppose. Indeed, it is not difficult to find examples even today of writers who hold to some points of this view: for example, that lyric poetry is peculiar to the work of young poets, that epic poetry is associated especially with the early stages of cultural development or that certain forms of poetry are 'outmoded' or impossible to produce in a contemporary context.

Hugo, in his preface to *Cromwell,* casually introduced the historical section of his argument in the following terms:

> Le genre humain dans son ensemble a grandi, s'est développé, a mûri comme un de nous. Il a été enfant, il a été homme, nous assistons maintenant à son imposante vieillesse.
>
> ([Hugo], p.20)

And, like most others who use the analogy, Hugo naturally sees his own time as corresponding to one of the more advanced stages of development (though some prefer to speak of 'maturity' rather than 'old age', however imposing!).

Death is what follows old age, so this analogy with human life had depressing connotations which appeared to be in direct conflict with the idea of progress and the perfectibility of man. The Liberal of the 1820s was generally optimistic about the outlook for human society and would not have accepted willingly that mankind was entering its dotage. A way out of the problem had been provided by one of the most widely-studied literary theorists of the time. Madame de Staël, in her book *De la littérature considérée dans ses rapports avec les institutions sociales* (1800), saw the doctrine of perfectibility as applying in different ways to science and art. In the case of the latter, a point was reached beyond which literature and the fine arts could not hope to progress, while science was capable of unending advance. Not that art would be condemned necessarily to decadence, but its further development would be dependent on that of the moral, philosophical and natural sciences:

> Lorsque la littérature d'imagination a atteint dans une langue le plus haut degré de perfection dont elle est susceptible, il faut que le siècle suivant appartienne à la philosophie, pour que l'esprit humain ne cesse pas de faire des progrès.
>
> ([de Staël], pp. 173-74).

This leads her to the statement that 'la poésie d'imagination ne fera plus de progrès en France' ([de Staël], p. 359).

Though the essential word here is *progrès*—Madame de Staël was not saying that there was no place at all for poetry in advanced societies—her arguments were borrowed to support the theory that poetry was a dying art and her qualification (*la poésie d'imagination*) developed as the basis of a fairly precise definition of poetry itself:

> La poésie est éminemment allégorique . . . son attribut essentiel consiste dans la faculté d'individualiser, c'est-à-dire de personnifier les sentiments et les passions de l'homme . . .'
>
> ([Ballanche], pp. 310-11)

What is interesting about this is that the much-admired critic Schlegel had written of Greek poetry that its main characteristic was that it 'donne de l'âme aux sentiments et un corps aux pensées' ([Schlegel], p. 30); and Ballanche, a few lines later in the passage quoted above, concludes: 'Ainsi la poésie des anciens est la seule vraie poésie'. Moreover Schlegel's succinct definition of the allegorical character of Greek poetry was taken up by Victor Chauvet, who wrote that ancient Greece possessed:

> . . . un climat délicieux, un sol couvert de fleurs, une religion remplissant au plus haut degré la condition de toute poésie, de prêter une âme à la matière et un corps à la pensée.
>
> (*Revue encyclopédique*, XXVII, 1825, pp. 323-24)

And yet again by Michelet when he speaks of the characteristic of the Ancients being their ability to 'prêter la vie aux êtres inanimés, prêter un corps aux choses immatérielles' ([Vico], p. xx).

The Greeks, then, in the 'infancy' of mankind, had enjoyed a peculiar aptitude for lyric poetry, and the nineteenth-century writers I have quoted were only in this following the eighteenth-century critic Denina who firmly asserted that lyric poetry in the age of Pindar had attained 'un point de majesté et d'élévation inaccessible à tout autre (âge)' ([Denina], p. 19), even though, as he went on to admit, hardly any examples of all this poetry have survived! As an anonymous writer in the *Revue encyclopédique* remarked, summing up all the elements of this particular argument:

> Il en est de la poésie pour les peuples comme des illusions de la jeunesse pour les individus: on a beau les regretter; vouloir rester sous leur empire, ce serait renoncer à l'âge mûr . . . L'idée du beau présidait à la civilisation antique; celle du vrai, du juste et de l'utile domine de plus en plus dans la société moderne. Si ses croyances étaient restées poétiques, elles ne seraient plus en harmonie avec sa raison.
>
> (XXXIX, 1828, p. 117)

The word *utile* brings us back to the context of **Chatterton** after what may at first sight appear to have been a long and irrelevant digression. But these ideas on poetry, which constituted the critical orthodoxy at the time when Vigny was writing and during the period when his thought was developing, are anything but irrelevant to a play which sets out to defend poets and poetry against the charge that they serve no useful purpose in the modern world. The quotations that I have given are necessarily only a small selection, but the interest of even the theme of Ancient Greece appears immediately if one turns, not to **Chatterton** itself, but to **Stello** and to the scene of the discussion with Lord Beckford which Vigny shortened when transferring it to the stage:

> Imagination! dit M. Beckford, toujours l'imagination au lieu du bon sens et du jugement! Pour être Poète à la façon lyrique et somnambule dont vous l'êtes, il faudrait vivre sous le ciel de Grèce, marcher avec des sandales, une chlamyde et les jambes nues, et faire danser les pierres avec la psaltérion.
>
> (pp. 137-38)

There is no obvious reason why Beckford, seeking an image to fix his idea of the perfect conditions for lyric poetry, and addressing his remarks to a poet whose imaginative world revolved around medieval Europe, should have envisaged him in Greek dress playing a psaltery; except that in Vigny's mind this vision of the ideal conditions for lyric poetry was associated with attacks from those who, like Beckford, judged poetry to be out of place in a modern age ruled by doctrines of utility.

Of course, with the evidence of the volumes of verse which flowed from the publishers year by year, not all writers on the subject imagined that the 'maturity' of society would simply kill off poetry. Beckford himself admits to having written verses in his youth but emphasises that 'un bon Anglais doit être utile au pays' (p. 96). He would have agreed with Madame de Staël when she said:

> Heureux le pays où les écrivains sont tristes, où les commerçants sont satisfaits, les riches mélancoliques et les hommes du peuple contents!.
>
> ([de Staël], p. 227)

(except, of course, for her condemnation of the rich). The view that social and political progress is bound to lead to the alienation from society of such exceptional individuals as poets and artists, was that of an anonymous writer in the *Revue encyclopédique* who saw in the United States of America a model for the society of the future:

> Ce peuple nous offre une image prophétique des temps vers lesquels s'achemine la civilisation du monde chrétien, temps prospère pour la science, pour la morale et pour la liberté publique, temps doux et calmes pour le gros du genre humain, . . . mais stériles et douloureux pour ces âmes particulières que la nature, se trompant d'époque, aura douées des besoins du génie poétique.
>
> (XLV, 1830, p. 33)

Who better than Chatterton, tormented by 'la passion de la pensée' (p.52), taking on the habit of the medieval monk Rowley, to represent a man born out of his time? It was a feeling well understood by Vigny, aristocrat and stoic, who shared with Chatterton his loathing of modern commercial civilisation.

Oddly enough, however, if there was one country which seemed to disprove the idea that industrial civilisation was unlikely to encourage the production of poetry, it was England. As L. Simond had remarked in his account of a journey to England in 1810 and 1811,

> L'enfance de la civilisation est l'âge poétique des nations, et voici pourtant un vieux peuple, riche et commerçant, froid et calculateur, plus fertile en véritables poètes depuis dix ans qu'il ne l'a jamais été . . .
>
> ([Simond], pp. 454-55)

But this neither contradicted the image of a society founded on the materialist values of money and devoted to cold science, nor did it guarantee that the poets born into such a society would achieve happiness or acceptance in it. What Vigny and other poets of his time would retain in these comments, was a definition of society and socially useful work that excluded imaginative literature and seemed to force them, with almost a scientific inevitability, into the role of social outcasts.

There were, however, some doctrines which appeared for a time to offer an alternative road. The most important of these, because of its influence on Vigny and some of the other Romantics, was Saint-Simonism, both the doctrines of Saint-Simon and the later development of these doctrines after his death in 1825.

The basis of Saint-Simon's 'New Christian' social order was its reliance on leadership by a sort of troika composed of industrialists, scientists and artists. The artists' mission was an almost priestly one, of guiding mankind towards the future (though, as was pointed out at the time, some Saint-Simonists were inclined to give artists the more prosaic role of propagandists for the new order and, had they ever gained power, would probably have been ruthlessly hostile to those who did not share and proclaim their views). What is interesting about Saint-Simonism, in the context of *Chatterton,* is that it conceded the point that artists must be found some *useful* role in modern society, instead of adopting, for example, a concept of 'art for art's sake', or a view of artists as guardians of culture, or entertainers, or those who expressed the higher aspirations of mankind, or some other non-materialist interpretation of their function. As Marguerite Thibert says:

> . . . l'évolution générale du saint-simonisme entraînait la théorie sociale de l'art qu'on y professait vers un mysticisme esthétique curieusement mitigé d'utilitarisme.
>
> ([Thibert], p. 25)

So, when Chatterton offers his answer to Lord Beckford, it is to show the poet as the one who 'lit dans les astres la route que nous montre le doigt du Seigneur' and to emphasise that 'nous sommes tous de l'équipage, et nul n'est inutile dans la manœuvre de notre glorieux navire' (p. 97), framing his defence in utilitarian terms which will not only be understood by Beckford, but which are those laid down by the Lord Mayor and his like as the only terms on which the argument can be conducted. It is significant that Vigny's image of the poet as navigator was subsequently borrowed in Saint-Simonian poetry.

By the time he came to write *Chatterton,* however, Vigny had become disillusioned with Saint-Simonism, and the reflection of his brief flirtation with Saint-Simonian doctrines comes rather from the episode in *Stello* (when he was still to some extent attracted by them), than from his convictions at the time of writing the play. Even by the last episode of *Stello* (that dealing with André Chénier), he was evidently disaffected from the idea of the new social order and had come to hold the view that all régimes were necessarily hostile to poets.

The image of the poet as the one who searches the stars for the road that society should take is strikingly similar to that offered by Shelley in his *Defence of Poetry*:

> Poets are the hierophants of an unapprehended inspiration; the mirrors of the gigantic shadows which futurity casts upon the present . . . Poets are the unacknowledged legislators of the world.
>
> ([Shelley], p. 159)

I am not the first to compare this with Chatterton's speech, but I am perhaps the first to point out that Shelley's defence was written in answer to precisely the same view of human history and civilisation that I have been discussing in this chapter. In his essay *The Four Ages of Poetry,* Shelley's friend Thomas Love Peacock had argued that human civilisation progresses through different stages and that the modern age, with its scientific and utilitarian preoccupations, is necessarily hostile to works of the imagination. In response, Shelley argued the universal validity of poetry, its leading role in society and its moral significance, even when those who produce it are themselves not outstanding for their moral qualities:

> But even whilst they deny and abjure, they are yet compelled to serve, the power which is seated on the throne of their own soul.
>
> ([Shelley], p. 159)

Vigny could not have known Shelley's work which, though written in 1821, was not published until 1840. The similarity in their concepts of the poet and his role in society (though I would not want to suggest that it is especially profound), can only come from their sensitivity to the climate of their times. In Vigny's case, he chose to depict the oppressive tendency of this society in two ways: indirectly through the person of John Bell, a philistine tyrant who persecutes his workmen and his wife; and directly, as far as poets are concerned, in Lord Beckford, a cultured and powerful man who is nonetheless fatally unequipped to appreciate Chatterton's sensitivity or his genius. What Beckford represents (most evidently in *Stello* where his opinions are developed at greater length than in the play), is not an English gentleman of the eighteenth century so much as a liberal bourgeois of Vigny's own time and country.

If Vigny seems largely to accept, at the end of *Stello,* that all political régimes will, for different reasons, prove hostile to poets, in *Chatterton* he has taken his thesis onto the public stage and made it rather more clearly a plea for positive action. It is a theme on which he expands in the **"Dernière nuit de travail"**, while fully aware of the problems he has raised. The idea of the poet which he puts forward is élitist—the contrary, for example, of the supposition underlying a modern 'poetry workshop' or the publication of anthologies of poems by schoolchildren, that anyone can write poetry. For Vigny, poets are rare and it is axiomatic that the majority will not appreciate them: 'son langage choisi n'est compris que d'un petit nombre d'hommes choisi lui-même' (p. 29). After a poet's death, perhaps, his genius will be recognised but in his lifetime he can expect only jealousy or indifference. The state, too, 'ne protège que les intérêts positifs' (p. 29). But society *can* afford to maintain men of genius, it has the means to keep them from starvation or humiliating and soul-destroying work if it chooses to make laws for their protection:

> C'est au législateur à guérir cette plaie, l'une des plus vives et des plus profondes de notre corps social; c'est à lui qu'il appartient de réaliser dans le présent une partie des jugements meilleurs de l'avenir, en assurant quelques années d'existence seulement à tout homme qui aurait donné un seul gage du talent divin.
>
> (p. 33)

But the problem of identification remains, as Vigny is well aware (p. 32).

A great deal of this discussion hinges on a particular concept of the poet, which includes in its turn a particular concept of poetry and in this idea, which has been implicit in much of our discussion of Chatterton as a character in the play, as well as in the subjects I have raised in this chapter, lies the central significance of the work. I said earlier that both Vigny and Shelley, in formulating their defence of poetry, did so largely on terms dictated by their opponents, by those who believed that poetry was quite simply incompatible with modern scientific society, in Vigny's own words, 'une société matérialiste, où le calculateur avare exploite sans pitié l'intelligence et le travail' (p. 34); a society that was also in the throes of industrialisation, taking men and women from the rural existence which had continued largely unchanged in Europe since the Middle Ages and crowding them into towns where their labour was exploited ruthlessly by the new feudal barons like John Bell: in view of this, and given Vigny's awareness of it, one might question, as men were increasingly to do as the century wore on, whether the suffering of poets (by Vigny's own definition, a minute social minority) was indeed one of the deepest wounds in society or the one that stood in greatest need of treatment.

That apart, the reason why Vigny, like Shelley, could hardly avoid accepting some of the premises on which this opposition to poetry was based, was partly that they were both intellectuals, well-read and alive to the climate of their age; and partly that the literature of the eighteenth century in both France and Britain had been predominantly hostile to what they defined as poetry. Looking back over the previous century, Vigny could hardly do otherwise than agree that its preoccupation had been with the literature of ideas rather than with that of the imagination. Another, perhaps unexpected, point of comparison between Vigny and Shelley is that they both had considerable respect for 'philosophy' (the term they would have used to describe the genre which had produced the most characteristic works of the eighteenth century): Shelley once remarked that his highest aspiration was to be a philosopher, while Vigny's poetry is outstanding for its concentration on ideas, and *Chatterton,* which he offers as a *drame de la pensée* and an example of a genre which he believes is bound eventually to find favour with the public, is a deliberate reaction against the verse dramas of Hugo. At the heart of the play, there is this contradiction of a work which sets out to define a certain idea of The Poet and to defend him against a hostile society, but does so in prose, in an intellectual framework remarkably similar to the one which it has described as being hostile to the poetic sensibility. The conflict between head and heart, the enthusiasm of Stello and the scepticism of Le Docteur Noir, the poetry of Chatterton and the philosophy of the Quaker, was one that Vigny experienced in himself and was never to resolve.

It is a conflict that belongs peculiarly to the age of Romanticism. The eighteenth century had been well aware of the demands of both reason and sensibility and had never doubted which, in a well-ordered society, should take precedence. But by the end of the century men had begun to doubt whether society was well-ordered and to question its right to subject the individual to its demands. When, in the political sphere, a man like Napoleon Bonaparte could impose his will on half of Europe, it appeared that there were individuals who stood so far above the crowd that their nature would not permit them to recognise normal or reasonable limitations; and if, in the political sphere, such individuals were not an unmixed blessing for humanity, who could deny that they had had their counterparts in literature and the arts and that we had benefitted from the genius of Shakespeare, Leonardo or Raphael? In **"La Dernière nuit de travail"**, it is the Poet as a man of genius that Vigny distinguishes from the man of letters or the great writer; and if he demands for him a consideration which society can justifiably withhold from the other two, it is because he believes in the Romantic concept of genius as a gift with privileges consistent with its rarity and ultimately so precious to society that it escapes from the usual norms. If men were able to recognise the ultimate value of genius, they would be susceptible to the argument of its immediate utility.

The problem, however, in Vigny's play is that, while asserting the beneficial long-term effects of poetic genius, he has no immediate definition of it to support this view. In fact, his definition excludes the idea of utility. The Poet is not described as a producer of poetry, but as the possessor of a poetic sensibility. As we pass from the man of letters (pp. 26-27), to the great writer (pp. 27-28) and finally to the poet (pp. 28-29), we move from the concrete production of literary works, to philosophical thought (expressed however in actual writings) and, finally, to a pure sensibility where only the phrase 'la divine forme des vers' (p. 29) even hints that its vessel might deign to overflow and communicate with the world outside. The comparison of these three portraits in **"La Dernière nuit de travail"**, when one looks at the actual language in which they are written and notes the transition from the tangible to the intangible, is quite remarkable. The productive writer is treated with moral contempt as insincere ('dépourvu d'émotions réelles', p. 26) and superficial; the great writer is defined by his relative lack of productive facility ('il marche le pas qu'il veut, sait jeter des semences à une grande profondeur, et attendre qu'elles aient germé, dans une immobilité effrayante', pp. 27-28), but is in touch with the society of his time; the poet is not a writer at all, but 'une nature', described almost entirely in metaphorical terms: the emphasis is entirely on his need to *do* nothing, on the idea that any activity other than complete subjection to the needs of his sensibility will destroy his gift (p. 30). The figure of Chatterton in the play is consistent with this view of the poet as one validated only by his inner conviction, his emotions and his imagination. It is no accident that Cocteau's *Les Enfants terribles,* the twentieth-century work which . . . owes most to **Chatterton,** is a myth of the poetic sensibility whose protagonists *live* their poetry entirely, never attempting to express it in the form of language.

The high status which Vigny accords to the poetic sensibility and the idea that poetry can be divorced not only from verse, but even from language, to become an almost abstract quality, is what more than anything makes *Chatterton* a work of its time. If I have stressed it particularly, it is because this concept of poetry, this definition of what is 'poetic', what the poet is (as opposed to what he does), still profoundly influences our own conception of poetry. Later in the nineteenth century, arguments of the kind used by Shelley and Vigny about the 'utility' of poetry were to be abandoned and their place taken by the doctrines of 'art for art's sake'. Even Vigny puts little conviction into the crowning image of poets as those who steer society towards the future, making it seem more like a witty demolition of Lord Beckford ('Qu'en dites-vous, mylord? lui donnez-vous tort? Le pilote n'est pas inutile', p. 97), rather than a serious attempt to define the social role of the artist. In the last resort, the play is a defence of the poet as the supreme individualist, escaping utilitarian definition, the last refuge of spiritual values in a society that has abandoned religion in favour of materialism and replaced its old aristocracy with an aristocracy of wealth. Against the triumph of values he cannot share, Vigny pleads on behalf of the individual and speaks as much for the mute aspirations of Kitty Bell as in justification of the poet she loves.

. . . . .

At midnight on 12 February 1835, Vigny was able to note in his journal: '*Chatterton* a réussi'. The play was a triumph. It had thirty-five performances at the Comédie Française before transferring to the Odéon, and was revived four times during Vigny's lifetime. It has established its place in the repertory of the French theatre and notable modern revivals include those at the Comédie Française in 1947, at the Théâtre de l'œuvre in 1956 and at the Théâtre de l'Athénée in 1962.

In his note 'Sur les représentations du drame . . .' (pp. 107-10), Vigny paid tribute to the actors who had ensured his play's first night success, recognising their contribution to the disclosure of the 'second drame' behind the text. I have tried to show that this 'second drame' is not only the extra dimension that the play gains in actual performance, but the contribution of the reader or the audience to the action in perceiving the true significance of Kitty's words and in interpreting the underlying meaning of the play, its debate on the nature of poetry and the place of poets or artists in the social order.

As for the performance, it owed a great deal to Marie Dorval, whose acting Vigny significantly describes as *poétique* (p. 109), showing the extension of the word to more than just the writing of poetry; and especially to her famous *dégringolade* when, at the end of the play, she collapsed and tumbled down the steps leading to Chatterton's garret. This theatrical piece of business had been kept secret by Dorval, whom Vigny had expected to stagger down the steps before falling on the last of them. It caused an outburst of enthusiasm in the audience which had already stopped the play briefly with its applause at the end of Chatterton's second monologue (p. 100). Marie Dorval was not an outstanding actress but she threw herself (literally) into the part of Kitty and did much to ensure the success of the play.

Despite its triumph, **Chatterton** did not have the immediate effect of spawning a school of *drames de la pensée*. It did lead to the creation of a prize for a poor poet by De Maillé, but this was hardly the major reform in patronage for the arts that Vigny had advocated: that had to wait for the modern state with its arts councils and, in some cases, its attempts to use writers as its clients, foreseen by early critics of Saint-Simon's plans to incorporate writers and artists into the state machine. What attracted most attention at first was not Vigny's advocacy of greater patronage for poetry, but his apparent defence of suicide by shifting responsibility for it from the individual to an unjust society. In its widest connotations, this accusation of society is probably the most modern aspect of the play. Suicide was still treated as a crime and criticism of the play's immorality in this respect, based on religious objections, was backed up by the fact that 'le bruit des pistolets solitaires' (p. 32) was heard once or twice as young poets, foiled in their literary ambitions, decided to follow Chatterton's example. But the growing acceptance of the part played by social conditions in individual acts of violence, including those against oneself, has taken some of the ground from under this criticism of Vigny's work and is one reason why some later writers saw it as 'socialist' in its general intent. The word is, however, wrongly applied: Vigny may have recognised some of the ills of industrial society and attacked them, but he did so from the standpoint of an élitist and an aristocrat, not of a proto-socialist.

In literature, the real vindication of Vigny's support for a theatre that appealed to the mind was to come towards the end of the century in the work of such writers as Ibsen, Shaw and, in France, Henry Becque and others. It is not easy to detect any direct influence of Vigny on late nineteenth-century realism and naturalism in France: the climate of **Chatterton** is distinctively that of Romanticism. But the play has retained its power to move audiences and readers, its admirers including Albert Camus who cited the play in his speech in Stockholm on receiving the Nobel Prize. The occasion was perhaps apt, since Nobel's foundation is independent of governments; but his prize is hardly awarded to writers at the start of their careers and, even if it had existed in 1770, would have done nothing for Chatterton. The fundamental problem of identifying genius at the moment when it is really in need of help, is as acute as it was in 1835.

The most profound influence of **Chatterton** is the intangible one of fixing more precisely than anyone had managed to do before a certain image of the poet and a certain idea of poetry. The feeling that the poet was a person cursed rather than blessed by an acute sensitivity had found expression in one form in Byron (or rather in the Byronic image), but was fully realised in **Chatterton** before being further defined by Verlaine in his study of the *poètes maudits*. Baudelaire experienced throughout his life the conviction that he was in some way damned and, though there were personal reasons for this in Baudelaire's case which could be attributed to causes other than his poetic genius, his feeling of damnation haunts some of the most personal and most moving of nineteenth-century poetry. Baudelaire, Verlaine and Rimbaud contributed, in their lives, to confirming an idea of the poet that Vigny had sensed in the partly mythical story of an eighteen-year-old English suicide and realised in his play which he wove around 'un nom d'homme' as much as the man himself.

In identifying poetic genius with a particular type of sensibility, Vigny had also posited the equation of poetry itself with this 'poetic' sensibility. Though a passage in his journal in 1843 asserts that poetry in verse is the only real form of poetry, it goes on to define it as 'un elixir des idées', to claim that 'le vrai poète' alone has the ability to discern these ideas and that 'la science est absolument interdit à la Poésie' ([*Journal d'un Poète*], p. 72). This drastic limitation of the field for poetry, which poets in previous centuries would not have accepted, itself derived from a definition of 'the poetic' which allowed it, despite Vigny's assertion, to be applied to a much wider field than that of mere verse. In the play, Chatterton is presented much more as the vehicle for a 'poetic' view of the world than as an author of poetry. He is a dreamer, a martyr who sympathises with the sufferings of mankind, but not a worker, even in words. From here it is only a step to the assertion that whatever a 'poet' does is 'poetic', and that the poetic sensibility may be divorced altogether from the actual production of poetic works.

It was this that led the twentieth-century poet Jean Cocteau to classify all his work, for its collected edition, as 'poetry', his plays becoming *poésie de théâtre,* his novels *poésie de roman,* etc. One of the latter, published in 1929, is *Les Enfants terribles,* a deliberate attempt to create a modern myth comparable with the tales of Classical mythology and a myth that is essentially that of the Romantic idea of poetry. Paul and Elisabeth, the 'children' of the title, are a brother and sister who create poetry in their lives: their room is the temple of a religion which is that of the poetic spirit; its atmosphere transforms those who have the sensitivity to appreciate it and who come within its orbit. Their religion has its ritual, *le jeu,* which is an abandonment of the conscious mind to a form of poetic inspiration; and its cult objects, *le trésor,* a drawer full of commonplace bits and pieces that they have collected which are transformed, like the words of poetry through metaphor, by being divorced from their everyday, functional significance and hidden in this sacred place.

Because the love between Paul and Elisabeth is incestuous, it cannot be disclosed even to the 'children' themselves, so, like the love between Kitty and Chatterton, it is revealed to the reader but not, until the final scene, to the protagonists. Adolescents at the start of the book, they remain children throughout, because their vision is essentially child-like: they are both very wise and very young, with the purity and innocence of Kitty and the 'marvellous boy'. It is Paul, above all, who controls the poetic atmosphere of the room, but not consciously: lazy, weak (both physically and morally), he needs to do nothing in order to be himself.

The novel is a tragedy and one that hinges (despite the Shakespearean intervention of Elisabeth as Lady Macbeth), like **Chatterton,** on a letter (actually, Cocteau makes it a more modern *pneumatique*) and an opiate. The tragic outcome is prepared both by the appearance of this drug and by such indications as the phrase 'Le suicide est un péché mortel' ([Cocteau], p. 52) which the children's friend Gérard discovers scrawled on a mirror. It comes, in fact, when Elisabeth discovers that Paul has fallen in love with Agathe: her jealously, her condemnation of Agathe as a bourgeoise who is 'not good enough' for Paul, and Paul's inability to express his love, are all distant echoes of **Chatterton** transformed in Cocteau's imagination and in the context of his story.

However, it is the final scene which most nearly recalls Vigny's play. Paul, discovering that Elisabeth has tricked him and deprived him of Agathe's love, takes the opiate in the room which the children have reconstructed in a new house by means of screens, highly suggestive of a stage set. As he lies dying on the bed, in a pose reminiscent of Henry Wallis's painting of the dead Chatterton, Elisabeth shoots herself and, as she falls, carries one of the screens with her in a *dégringolade* like that of Marie Dorval, 'faisant de la chambre secrète un théâtre ouvert aux spectateurs' ([Cocteau], p. 176). It is in this final moment that the children's love can be made explicit to them, and only then, when they are both on the brink of death.

Chatterton is by no means the only literary influence on a novel which, like Vigny's play, welds its sources into a single work of art quite independent of them. But the influence of **Chatterton** is there, less in the details which I have mentioned than in the concept of poetry. The children of Cocteau's novel are not, for the most part, unhappy, nor do they suffer the poverty and indignity of Vigny's hero: fate miraculously cares for them and provides the conditions in which their natures can flourish. But they flourish in silence, communicating their genius only to those who come within their immediate orbit, 'poetic' in their lives, without ever being 'poets' in any strict sense of the term. By giving such vivid expression to the concept of the poetic nature, **Chatterton** had prepared for it to be lifted away from the field of literature and given an independent existence.

In Cocteau's novel, as in Vigny's play, this 'Romantic' conception of poetic genius is contained in a work of 'Classical' simplicity. The labels 'Classical' and 'Romantic' are a convenient shorthand to describe some general tendencies in literature and art; they survive because they are useful, not because they are in any sense exact. Those who attempt to make them so usually create more problems than they solve. In the case of **Chatterton,** they have questioned whether the play can in fact be described as a 'Romantic' drama at all, in view of its restraint, its near respect of the unities, its simplicity of structure and similarities between Kitty and the heroines of Classical tragedy. It is certainly important to emphasise these features of the play which do much to establish it as a satisfying work of art and have helped to ensure its survival. But, beyond this, any debate on the precise classification of **Chatterton,** any attempt to situate it on a scale from 'Classical' to

'Romantic', is bound to be sterile. The form of the work may owe something to Vigny's knowledge of French drama of the seventeenth century, but it is dictated too by his need to convey a message and to do so in a way that will oblige the spectator or reader to concentrate on the ideas rather than the action. The spirit of **Chatterton** is unmistakably of its time, a time which, despite the revolutionary nature of its literary ideas, did not propose a clean break with the past. On the contrary, what is typically 'Romantic' about Vigny's play is that it incorporates references to the tragedies of Racine and those of Shakespeare, as well as to the 'bourgeois' drama of the eighteenth century and to melodrama. Its hero sees himself as a Stoic facing his destiny like a Roman; but he is also a monk who writes in the language of the Middle Ages, a period undergoing a revaluation in Vigny's day and, by implication, not despised in **Chatterton** as a desert of mere barbarism (which is how it was still considered by many of Vigny's contemporaries). If Chatterton's genius finds its outlet in a revival of medieval literature, then the Middle Ages must have produced work capable of inspiring genuine poetry. This cultural eclecticism, willing to accept as valid all manifestations of human culture, in any form and from any period, is the only proper context in which to view the so-called 'Classical' elements in the play.

More serious is the problem of reconciling what Vigny would have called 'mind' and 'heart', ideas and feelings. A work for the theatre which is going to realise Vigny's ambition of speaking directly to its audience and involving them in the debate on stage, must convince them of the 'reality' of the characters portrayed. The characters in **Chatterton** have been criticised on the grounds that they are one-dimensional, that we perceive them as spokesmen for certain points of view, not as living human beings. This criticism is partly justified. The Quaker's definition of the characters as *martyrs et bourreaux* is too neat and too simple to apply: he, himself, is too wise and virtuous to be credible, Chatterton is too obviously the Poet, Kitty the pure and virtuous heroine, John Bell the tyrannical husband, Beckford the self-satisfied bourgeois. Lord Talbot, admittedly, does reveal an unsuspected side to his nature on his second appearance and crosses the divide to come to Chatterton's defence, but only Kitty can be said to develop in any way during the course of the play, as we see her love for Chatterton overcoming her upbringing as a submissive and virtuous wife. Even in her case, this development is fairly slight and could be anticipated from the start. The other characters announce themselves on their first appearance and remain essentially unchanged by their experiences.

This lack of depth in the characters is perhaps a necessary consequence of Vigny's attempt to write an intellectual drama, and it leaves us with the strong impression that the figures move about the stage enclosed in their own private cages—a feeling reinforced by scenes of misunderstanding and non-communication such as that where Kitty and Chatterton speak through the intermediary of the Quaker. Having taken up their positions, the characters never really interact or respond very much to each other: at most, they reveal what is already there. The very nature of the love between Kitty and Chatterton precludes its future development and by their deaths they evade the choice that it would have imposed on them. If they had ever had to make that choice, they would perhaps have uncovered something in their natures other than these ideals of the martyred poet and the pure heroine which are all that we see of them. As it is, it is impossible to guess how they would have resolved their dilemma or what they would have become in doing so. Taking the immature solution of suicide (or the ideal one of a broken heart), they never have to face the complications of maturity.

Despite this, there are two reasons why the play remains an outstanding work of drama. The first is the language, which Vigny makes appropriate to his characters and which he uses to create an inner world of meanings and correspondences so that a refined and fairly restricted vocabulary becomes an instrument of considerable power. The second is that the play is recognisably a myth in which we can accept that the characters represent ideas outside themselves and pursue their own courses along predestined lines. This feeling of myth is aided not only by the simplicity of the language. Rather than a vast melodrama on the model of *Hernani* or *Ruy Blas,* this is a compressed work, for quartet rather than full orchestra, introducing, interweaving and recalling its insistent themes.

It would be fascinating to see it revived by an imaginative modern director. The concept of poetry that Vigny defends and his understanding of individual psychology may no longer correspond to those of our own time, but the play has an inner consistency that makes it more than an historical curiosity or a memorial to the Romantic ethos. Its author was perhaps wrong in thinking that he had pioneered a trend in drama when he wrote: 'Cette porte est ouverte à présent . . .' (p. 109); but in another sense his confidence was justified, as the artist is always justified in the realisation that he has created a work of art that will endure even when those who enjoy it have ceased to share the ideas it puts forward. This guide has attempted to show that beneath its relatively simple surface it conceals an intricate structure and in analysing this and the ideological framework of the play, I have tried also to suggest some of the many possible approaches to it.

Works Cited

1. Chatterton. *Quitte pour la peur.* Introduction by F. Germain (Paris, Garnier-Flammarion, 1968). This is the text used throughout the guide. All page references, indicated by one number in parentheses after the reference, are to this edition. All other references give the number of the work in this bibliography, in italics, followed by the page number.

2. *Chatterton.* Critical edition published by Liano Petroni (Bologna, Pàtron, 1962). A full critical edition, with an introduction and notes.

3. Chatterton. Edited by Martin B. Friedman, with an introduction by Henri Payre (Paris, Didier, 1967).

4. Chatterton. Edited by Jean Delume (Paris, Bordas, 1969). Two easily-obtainable school editions with useful notes and other material in French.

5. Journal d'un poète. Extracts edited by B. Grillet (Paris, Larousse, 1951). A text in the well-known Classiques Larousse series.

6. Lettres inédites . . . au marquis et à la marquise de la Grange (1827-1861). Published by Albert de Luppé (Paris, Conard, 1914).

7. Stello. Daphné. Edited by F. Germain (Paris, Garnier, 1970).

8. Ballanche, P. S. *Essai sur les institutions sociales dans leur rapport avec les idées nouvelles* (Paris, Didot, 1818).

9. Cocteau, Jean. *Les Enfants terribles* (Paris, Le Livre de Poche, 1977).

10. Denina, Charles. *Tableau des révolutions de la littérature ancienne et moderne.* French translation by T. de Livoy (Paris, 1767).

11. Hugo, Victor. *Préface de Cromwell suivie d'extraits d'autres préfaces dramatiques.* Edited by P. Grosclaude (Paris, Larousse, 1949).

12. Schlegel, A. W. *Cours de littérature dramatique* (Paris, Paschoud, 1814).

13. Shelley, P. B. 'A Defence of Poetry', in *Shelley's Letters and Philosophical Criticism* (London, Henry Frowde, 1909).

14. Simond, L. *Voyage d'un Français en Angleterre pendant les années 1810 et 1811* (Paris, Treuttel et Würtz, 1816).

15. Staël, Madame G. de. *De la littérature considérée dans ses rapports avec les institutions sociales.* Critical edition by P. van Tieghem (Geneva, Droz, 1959).

16. Thibert, Marguerite. *Le Rôle social de l'art d'après les Saint-Simoniens* (Paris, Librairie des Sciences Economiques et Sociales, 1927).

17. Vico, J. B. *Principes de la philosophie de l'histoire.* Translated by J. Michelet (Paris, Renouard, 1827).

J. C. Ireson (essay date 1984)

SOURCE: "Poetry," in *The French Romantics,* Vol. 1, edited by D. G. Charlton, Cambridge University Press, 1984, pp. 113-62.

[*In the following excerpt, Ireson surveys Vigny's adaptation of the short, eighteenth-century heroic poem as a vehicle for the representation of modern values.*]

Vigny's development as a poet is initially associated . . . with the renovation and advancement of an older form of poetry. His concern was principally with the *poème,* a form which, in the later eighteenth century, had been used to signify a short epic or heroic poem, and Vigny's intention was to adapt it to the ideas and style of his time. His experiments with the *poème* lasted between 1820 and 1829, during which period he also turned, more briefly, to another form, the *mystère,* probably from the examples given by Byron in *Cain* (1821) and *Heaven and Earth* (1822). Two other forms, the *élévation,* with which he experimented for a short time around 1830, and the *poème philosophique,* which preoccupied him from about 1839 to the year of his death (1863), were designed to permit the expression of ideas in a more complex way than was possible with the *poème* and the *mystère.*

It was probably his intention to form individual volumes from sequences of these individual types of poem. In the event, his first major volume of verse, ***Poèmes antiques et modernes,*** slowly built up in stages (***Poèmes,*** 1822; ***Poèmes antiques et modernes,*** 1826; ***Poèmes,*** 1829; ***Poèmes antiques et modernes,*** 1837), combined *poèmes, mystères* and *élévations,* the unity of the book being obtained from the arrangement of the pieces in a historical order, twenty in all in the 1837 edition.

Of these twenty poems, thirteen bear the subtitle *poème.* One or two, such as **"Le Cor"**, were originally written as experiments with the *ballade,* giving a lyrical tone and a medieval configuration and colouring, without too much concern for authenticity, to a heroic episode, in this case the stand of Roland and Oliver at Roncevaux. **"Madame de Soubise"**, though published as a 'poème du XVIe siecle', has all the marks of a *ballade* in the manner of Hugo: interesting stanza and metrical forms permitting both a heroic and lyrical interpretation of the subject (an event from the Saint Bartholomew massacre) and an attractive simulation of some mannerisms of the older language. The difference occurs in the intention of the poet. Vigny goes beyond historical fancy towards the sense of events and the performance of the figures involved in them.

His *poème* is a historical genre. It is relatively short, rarely exceeding 200 lines in length, and presents a concentrated episode shown in its effect on one or two figures. The figures themselves represent varied human types, ranging from men of spiritual or political power (Moïse, Charlemagne) to representatives of the code of military service and honour (Roland and Oliver, the soldier-monk of the Trappist order, the Captain of the frigate *La Sérieuse*). The list extends further, to the victims of political persecution (the prisoner in the iron mask), to women capable of tragic action through passion (Dolorida), and to beings capable of surmounting physical frailty through acts of courage (Madame de Soubise; Emma, the young 'princesse de la Gaule' of **"La Neige"**). His use of known events to provide perspectives for human action is, of course, not new, and Vigny's starting point is, typically, a familiar episode from the Scriptures (**"Moïse"**, **"La Fille** de Jephté", "**La Femme adultère**"), a historical or contemporary event ("**La Prison**", "**Le Trappiste**"), or even a *fait divers* of the period ("**Dolorida**"). His treatment of his subjects is original in the variety of the colour and tone of the episodes and in the evocation of personality in the human figures. Though some of the earlier pieces, such as "**La Neige**", subscribe to the fashion of a fairly cursory local colour, others, particularly those founded on biblical episodes, combine imaginative reconstruction with a remarkable degree of detail in allusions. The four major themes of "**Moïse**" are centred on four books of the Bible. Moïse's recall of the migration from Egypt to the promised land and the establishing of his leadership derives from twelve chapters of Exodus; his triumphs, miracles and final weariness of responsibility are presented by references to eight chapters from Numbers; his last acts and his death outside the promised land are based on seven chapters from Deuteronomy; the elegiac theme of complaint is a compound of allusions to eight chapters of the Book of Job. A similar technique, though less dominant in the poem, is found in "**La Femme adultère**". The most important features of Vigny's *poème* are found, however, elsewhere than in the external techniques. Although the control of the structure of individual pieces is impressive, their best achievement is found in the use of a spectacle to suggest important ideas concerning the human condition. The interaction of the characters and the situation in which they are found is dramatic (at times, as in "**La Prison**", Vigny uses passages of dialogue). The characters react through gesture, which takes on a ritual and symbolic significance, and through action, which shows the disproportion between the individual human will and impulses on the one hand, and the ordering of events on the other, whether these events are determined by natural or providential forces. Each figure is shown at grips with a dilemma occurring either as the consequence of an action or the working of an unseen process. Occasionally, as in "**Le Bal**", where the glamour of the ballroom is contrasted with the tribulations that inevitably lie ahead, the dilemma is left vague and inescapable. In most cases, it is a trial that engages the responsibility and courage of an individual: hence the action of Moïse in seeking to confront Jehovah, the unavailing effort of the priest to make contact with the mind of the dying prisoner in the iron mask, the tragic jealousy of Dolorida, the fate of the 'femme adultère', saved but not redeemed by the intervention of Christ in the processes of the Judaic law, the Christian love of Mme de Soubise, stronger than the fanatical conflicts of her century. Over this whole sequence of *poèmes* broods a general question concerning human responsibility and fatality: to what extent can moral strength counter the play of unpredictable forces that threaten human life?[1] The sombre picture is relieved by one thing, the presence of sexual love, which is painted in the suave tones of amorous pleasure ("**Dolorida**", "**La Femme adultère**") and shown briefly in its more innocent and elevated forms as a force able to illuminate and sublimate life ("**La Neige**", "**Madame de Soubise**").

The *poème*, as conceived by Vigny, is valuable for its power of illustrating an idea in heroic and sentimental terms, and its symbolic capacity is considerable, since the actions and speeches of the characters are left, within the context of the events, to carry the import of the larger ideas with which he is concerned. But its objectivity is also a limitation, in that it makes the elaboration of an idea more difficult, when the poet is not free to comment directly upon it. This fact may explain to some extent his early interest in the *mystère*, not so much in the form of the medieval play, as met with, for example, in Gringoire's ill-fated *mystère* in *Notre-Dame de Paris*, but in a rather more modern guise. Reference has been made to the examples given by Byron, which are written in the form of plays. Vigny's two *mystères* are narrative pieces, combining several different techniques, of which dramatic effect is one of the most striking. *Éloa* and "**Le Déluge**" figure among seven *mystères* listed on the first page of his journal, under the date 1823. The heading, *Les Mystères, Poèmes*, shows some hesitation between the two forms, but seems to indicate a decision to keep within a strictly poetic frame. "**Le Déluge**" does not differ superficially from the form of "**Moïse**" or "**La Femme adultère**" (*Éloa* has its own form, being written in three cantos, with ornamental devices such as simile). The difference is found in the nature of the ideas, which are more specifically concerned with the divine ordering of the world and divine intervention in the course of human history. The figures are divine or semi-divine beings. As in Byron's *Mysteries*, a modern and personal interpretation is given to events drawn from the Judaeo-Christian tradition. Éloa, the female angel of pity, is largely a creation of Vigny himself, though the name occurs in a passage by Klopstock quoted by Chateaubriand in *Le Génie du christianisme*. The figure of Satan is probably influenced by Milton's depiction of the fallen angel, but distorted by Vigny by the prominence given to the sensual theme in the description of the ensnaring of Éloa. Both poems depict the conflict between human virtues and supernatural power. Éloa, created by God from a tear shed by Christ over the body of Lazarus, is enslaved by Satan and becomes part of fallen creation, unable to do more than strive to console a suffering world. In their meeting in the depths of Chaos, the divine innocence of Éloa stirs Satan almost to repentance:

> Ah! si dans ce moment la Vierge eût pu l'entendre,
> Si la céleste main qu'elle eût osé lui tendre
> L'eût saisi repentant, docile à remonter . . .
> Qui sait? le mal peut-etre eût cessé d'exister.

The value of Christ's ministry in the world is ultimately in question here. The theme will appear again, in less symbolical terms, in Vigny's later poems. But at this stage his views seem dominated by a belief in a divine will, the principles and consistency of which remain concealed at all levels of creation.

"**Le Déluge**" is constructed on the account given in Genesis of the destruction of the world by the Flood as a divine punishment following the forbidden mingling of human beings and angels. The poem focuses on two beings—

Emmanuel, half man, half angel, and Sara, of human stock—who put their human love before their lives, which could be saved by separation, and perish on Mount Ararat in the last moments of the Deluge. The Flood, frequently treated in painting and in literature, offered an opportunity for original treatment of descriptive effects, for a poignant lyricism intrinsic to the situation imagined by Vigny, and for a strong message universalising the theme. The descriptive effects of the poem are conceived in the form of a violent disruption of harmony: glimpses of the last moments of the 'perfect order' of the antediluvian landscape are followed by visual shots of the destruction of this order by the storm and the Flood, and of the behaviour of animals and men in the rising of the 'implacable sea', until the moment of ironic calm signalled by the rainbow. The lyricism is in the doomed innocence expressed in the dialogue of the lovers. The message of the poet is conveyed in a speech attributed to the angel, father of Emmanuel, who interprets the divine judgment:

> La pitié du mortel n'est point celle des Cieux.
> Dieu ne fait point de pacte avec la race humaine:
> Qui créa sans amour fera périr sans haine.

By 1829, Vigny's *Poèmes antiques et modernes* had almost taken their final shape, although the title was not yet firm. The philosophical groundwork of the collection was already laid; the historical intention was apparent, but not yet developed as completely as Vigny wished. The poems were arranged as individual fragments of a sequence designed to reflect stages of moral development from the beginnings of Judaism to the formation of modern Europe. Despite the presence of **"Le Bal"**, **"Dolorida"** and **"La Frégate la Sérieuse"**, Vigny was still looking for a form which would permit a more detailed presentation of the values of the modern world. An entry in his journal dated 20 May 1829 notes the difficulty of finding suitable forms of expression for modern subjects; he appears to have been thinking about the possibility of a new form from about 1827, calling it *élévation*. Two poems of this type were written: **"Les Amants de Montmorency"** (1830) and **"Paris"** (1831). Vigny defined the *élévation*, referring to these two pieces, in a letter to Camilla Maunoir in 1838: 'partir de la peinture d'une image toute terrestre pour s'élever à des vues d'une nature plus divine'. Both were published separately and brought into the *Poèmes antiques et modernes* of 1837 as the last two poems of the collection. **"Les Amants de Montmorency"**, based on a newspaper account of the suicide pact of two lovers, is a lyrical projection of their state of mind during the last three days of their lives; it extends the theme of condemned or tragic love, to which he gives a special place in his vision of the complex forces that assail human life. **"Paris"**, in which Vigny gives a detailed elaboration of his thoughts inspired by the modern capital city, starts with the 'image toute terrestre' of Paris viewed by night from a tower by the poet and a traveller. Abandoning the narrative formulation of the *poèmes*, he constructs this *élévation* on a dialogue between himself and the companion who is unfamiliar with the city. The dialogue arises from two images suggested to the traveller by the sight of its

lamps and the smoke of its fires: a glowing wheel and a furnace. The poet develops the sense of these images. The wheel is the representation of the motive force transmitted by Paris to the nation, and of the radius of action of the capital. The idea of new things being forged is elaborated chiefly by reference to ideas. The work from which the shape of the future will emerge is the work of 'des Esprits', and the lamp is the symbol of their efforts. Vigny has in mind the action of four thinkers or schools of thought. Three of these, representing contemporary attitudes to religion (Lamennais), politics (Benjamin Constant) and doctrines of society (Saint-Simon), he sees as exponents of limited systems. Above them he places the effort of independent thinkers, presumably like himself, uncommitted and disinterested:

> Des hommes pleins d'amour, de doute et de pitié,
> Qui disaient: *Je ne sais,* des choses de la vie,
> Dont le pouvoir ou l'or ne fut jamais l'envie.

There is no more than a hint here of the values which he himself will seek to elaborate. Such elaboration will require long reflection, not only upon ideas themselves, but on the form and expression in which the ideas can take the most permanent shape.

For the present, Vigny's poetry remains a poetry of isolated ideas on moral and theological problems, and experiments with form appear to be his chief concern: 'Concevoir et méditer une pensée philosophique; trouver dans les actions humaines celle qui en est la plus évidente *preuve*; la réduire à une action simple qui se puisse graver en la mémoire et représenter en quelque sorte une statue et un monument grandiose à l'imagination des hommes, voilà où doit tendre cette poésie épique et dramatique à la fois' (*Journal d'un poète,* 20 May 1829). Nevertheless, the qualities of his poetry are already clearly established. Statuesque and grandiose according to his own formulation, his heroic verse is distinguished from near-contemporary examples such as Théveneau's *Charlemagne* (1816) and La Harpe's *Le Triomphe de la religion* (1814) by the vitality of the effects and the adjustment of technique to the formulation, without didacticism, of an individual idea. The features of that technique are to be found in the variation of tone and perspective (this is probably the dramatic intention referred to by Vigny), and the organisation of images of physical action in such a way as to evoke both a moral crisis and a significant historical moment (*Éloa,* for example, to all appearances purely symbolic in its action, also marks the destined role of the compassion brought by Christ to the world).

Note

1. A note in the *Journal d'un poète*, dated 1824, summarises Vigny's general position: 'Dieu a jeté—c'est ma croyance—la terre au milieu de l'air et l'homme au milieu de la destinée. La destinée l'enveloppe et l'emporte vers le but toujours voilé.—Le vulgaire est entraîné, les grands caractères sont ceux qui luttent'.

Patrick Craven (essay date 1986)

SOURCE: "Vigny's Post-Structuralist Novel: Writing History or the Story of Writing?" in *French Review,* Vol. 60, No. 2, December, 1986, pp. 216-21.

[*In the following essay, Craven probes the post-structuralist implications of Vigny's historical novel* Cinq-Mars *by discerning the work's concern with history as a form of fictive literature and its demonstration of meaning subverted via the medium of writing.*]

Although Vigny ranks among the major literary figures of the nineteenth century, his most ambitious prose piece, the historical novel **Cinq-Mars** remains largely neglected by contemporary criticism. Scholarly disaffection may be due in part to the author's ultra-conservative ideology as well as to his central focus on a marginal episode and an anecdotal figure of French history—the rise and fall of Louis XIII's minion, the bold Marquis de Cinq-Mars, one of the many prominent aristocratic victims of Richelieu's centralizing policies. Sainte-Beuve may well have conditioned future readers' indifferent or negative response to the novel. Although he welcomed Vigny's audacity in placing major historical figures at the forefront of the action, he did object to his turning them into virtually unrecognizable caricatures. Basically, he writes,

> M. de Vigny est resté au point de vue actuel, et n'a écrit qu'avec des souvenirs. Rien d'étonnant donc qu'il ait mis ainsi un masque par trop enluminé à ses personnages, puisqu'il ne les a vus qu'à distance. Il se complaît à nous rappeler cette fausse position, comme si elle n'éclatait pas assez d'ailleurs.[1]

Over a century later, the Marxist critic, Georg Lukács reinforced Sainte-Beuve's deprecatory assessment by further defining Vigny's "point de vue actuel" as Legitimism, and the "distance" as idealism (curiously permitting a new reading of Sainte-Beuve's "fausse position") and quickly passed on to less hostile ideological turf with Mérimée's *Chronique du règne de Charles IX.*[2]

I should like to rehabilitate **Cinq-Mars** intellectually, if not historically, by pointing out the striking resemblance between Vigny's text and contemporary critical discourse on the relationship between History and Literature, between the chain of events and the chain of signifiers. "[L]'histoire," as Roland Barthes observed, "est elle aussi une écriture,"[3] echoing Vigny's own belief that "L'HISTOIRE EST UN ROMAN DONT LE PEUPLE EST L'AUTEUR."[4] The relationship between History and Literature has been chiasmatically reversed: Literature is not so much a mere "part" of History as History is a specific type of Literature; the distinction between fiction and nonfiction has been blurred. Thus, if Sainte-Beuve's contention that Vigny distorted History by adopting a "point de vue actuel" still rings true, it is not so much because the text reflects Vigny's personal anguish over the nobility's political impotence in post-Revolutionary France as it does the writer's more abstract and philosophical concerns with the problematics of writing and the intelligibility of historical events. Although Vigny's pompous claim to a "VERITE toute belle, toute intellectuelle" may ruffle the modern reader's sensibilities, the "truth" he extracts from this obscure chapter of French history is remarkably post-structuralist in its implications.[5]

Vigny's obsession with the incessant *glissement* of the signified under the signifier, or writing as the necessary support and ineluctable subversion of meaning (outmodishly experienced, it is true, as an anguish rather than with Derridean jubilation) is attested by this excerpt from his diary:

> Du Livre—La vue des caractères de l'écriture dérange la pensée. Un mot du journal frappe l'air et trouble une suite de méditations. Un écrit ou un imprimé est donc souvent une rencontre dangereuse pour un penseur.[6]

The act of reading is somehow unrecognizable in this passage. Reading is no longer a transparency to meaning, but a vision obscured by "caractères," markings partaking of the enigmatic function of hieroglyphs or pictograms. Writing undermines the integrity of the self: "dérange la pensée," "trouble une suite de méditations." Writing is subversive: "une rencontre dangereuse pour un penseur." Like the chain of signifiers, the chain of historical events is experienced as fragmentary and discontinuous: "les exemples que présente la succession des événements sont épars et incomplets; il leur manque toujours un enchaînement palpable et visible." Like most writers, Vigny believed that a homeopathic cure for writing could be found in more writing, namely *belles lettres,* and that Art (Literature) could cure the indeterminancy of History. Vigny's claim notwithstanding, **Cinq-Mars** is a failed attempt to arrest the irresistible movement from signifier to signified. If, as Jeffrey Mehlman writes, "a text is less a monument than a battlefield," **Cinq-Mars** is the name of a losing battle to contain meaning.[7]

Cinq-Mars pits a redoubtable Minister—Richelieu—uncannily reminiscent of the "lynx-eyed" politician of Poe's (and Lacan's) well-known tale, against an idealized Cinq-Mars. The former is an indefatigable purloiner of letters, well-aware of the elusiveness of meaning as a means to power: "Sur quatre lignes de l'écriture d'un homme, on peut lui faire un procès criminel."[8] The latter is engaged in a vain struggle to preserve the monarch's independence and the privileges of his caste by taking advantage of his position as royal favorite to discredit the minister. The conflict in **Cinq-Mars** is only superficially a confrontation between proponents of oligarchy (Cinq-Mars) and those of absolutism (Richelieu), the root conflict is a struggle between two modes of communication, the dialectic between letter and voice. The text stages an exemplary psychoanalytical drama between unconscious writing (Richelieu) and the voice of consciousness (Cinq-Mars).

Significantly, Richelieu is first introduced in a chapter entitled "Le Cabinet"—Richelieu's or Vigny's?—while Cinq-Mars, "notre jeune voyageur [est'] endormi" (94). The reader is conveyed to the archbishop's palace in Narbonne, via a "rue inégale et obscure" (94) into a spacious and splendid room sheltering Richelieu's embryonic but none-theless efficient and industrious bureaucracy. Richelieu's location is thus doubly ex-centric, doubly removed from the centrality of the Court and consciousness: in an ob-scure area of a town on the nation's vulnerable southern border. Alert to the slightest irregularity in the quiet func-tioning of this nascent administration, Richelieu is busy dictating policy to his high-born pages and secretaries, their quills busily scratching away at the scrolls. The Car-dinal's crimson skullcap ("calotte rouge") is the room's lu-rid focal-point, a stark reminder of his victims' severed necks and in striking contrast with the plumed and phallic headdresses sported by Cinq-Mars's noble faction. The un-sleeping Minister's cabinet is the locus of a text-work as thoroughly transformational and expurgatory as dream-work. A vast network of spies in various disguises regu-larly supply him with

> les rapports détaillés des actions les plus minutieuses et les plus secrètes de tout personnage un peu important . . . On attachait ces rapports secrets aux dépêches du Roi, qui devaient toutes passer par les mains du Cardi-nal, et être soigneusement repliées, pour arriver au prince épurées, et telles qu'on voulait les lui faire lire.
>
> (107)

What the King reads is what the Cardinal wants him to read. Between the King (consciousness) and the nation (reality) is the impenetrable barrier of Richelieu's "car-actères."

Richelieu is both Other and author, the other author of *l'autre texte,* the surface of signifiers, the metonymic chain of language against which Cinq-Mars, the hero of Vigny's counter-text (*Cinq-Mars*) will provide the metaphoric illu-sion of depth, the illusion of the solid reality of waking life. As Other, Richelieu represents that element of the sig-nifier that is preliminary and refractory to meaning, that point in the chain where it is "en équilibre sur la limite de deux pensées" (144). As author, he is engaged in a pains-taking and unrelenting consignment of reality to writing. Richelieu, then, represents the alterity and opposition of a language the author of *Cinq-Mars* must overcome to ac-cede to readability and meaning.

Richelieu succeeds in thoroughly and completely encoding (writing) reality. When the King finally decides to wrest the power away from him in order to save Cinq-Mars and learn the truth about the latter's conspiracy with Spain to oust the troublesome minister, his inability to read forces him to capitulate to Richelieu:

> Le Roi . . . fit le tour de l'immense table et vit autant de porte-feuilles que l'on comptait alors d'empires, de royaumes et de cercles dans l'Europe; il en ouvrit un et le trouva *divisé* en cases, dont le nombre égalait celui des *subdivisions* de tout le pays auquel il était destiné. Tout était en *ordre,* mais dans un ordre effrayant pour lui, parce que chaque note ne renfermait que la quintes-sence de chaque affaire . . . et ne touchait que *le point juste des relations du moment* avec la France. Ce *la-*

conisme était à peu près aussi énigmatique pour Louis que les *lettres en chiffres* qui couvraient la table.

> (326, emphases mine)

The passage bears a striking resemblance to contemporary discourse on the nature of the relationship between lan-guage and reality. In his *Eléments de Sémiologie,* Barthes writes: "le langage, c'est en quelque sorte ce qui divise le réel."[9] Language is an order of divisions applied to the continuous flow of undifferentiated reality, hence reductive of that reality ("quintessence," "laconisme"); an order of divisions relating back to the speaker/writer himself, to his position in reality at a given time and place ("le point juste des relations du moment").

The passage also constitutes an abridged Lacanian lesson on the rhetorical functioning of the unconscious. Lacan, applying Roman Jakobson's contribution to linguistics to the field of psychoanalysis, has subsumed the various modes of unconscious movement of signifiers under the twin mechanisms of metaphor and metonymy. The uncon-scious operates a *condensation,* a metaphorical superimpo-sition of signifiers, as well as a metonymic *displacement* by contagion or contiguous attraction. Similarly, Rich-elieu's "lettres en chiffres" are condensations ("quintessence," "laconisme") and displacements ("ne touchait que le point juste des relations du moment"). The King is unable to discover the truth about Cinq-Mars and regain effective control of his realm because he is unable to decode the Minister's ciphers, just as consciousness is unable to decipher the discourse of the Other outside of analysis.

Cinq-Mars, as leader of the anti-Richelieu faction, vows to restore the King's voice—"Que votre voix s'élève" he ex-horts the King (247). In his aesthetico-political mission to impose the classic and phallic "ligne droite" of "la pensée de l'homme juste" (155), however, he finds himself faced with the thorny Boileauean issue of pleasing as well as in-forming:

> Il faudra plaire . . . Plaire! que ce mot est humiliant! Un soldat s'expose à mourir et tout est dit. Mais que de souplesse, de sacrifices de son caractère, que de com-position avec sa conscience, que de dégradations de sa pensée dans la destinée d'un courtisan.
>
> (154)

The politician and the writer are equally preoccupied with the question of *style* which does not always engrave the truth as neatly, sharply, and precisely as a soldier's sword, but involves a constant fretting over flexibility, composi-tion, and nuance ("dégradations").

In the process of restoring the Voice of Legitimism to the King, Cinq-Mars's voice, ironically, fades away. If the voice is that which makes a presence audible, perceptible, that which defines a presence in language, Cinq-Mars be-comes increasingly resistant to definition. The meaning of his tyrannicidal enterprise is lost in the ambiguities of his own ambition. His confidant, the virtuous de Thou, no longer recognizes his friend:

Voilà donc où vous en êtes venu! Vous allez faire exiler, peut-être tuer un homme, et introduire en France une armée étrangère; je vais donc vous voir assassin et traître à votre patrie! Par quels degrés êtes-vous descendu si bas?

(252)

The lucid and analytical Queen's description of him resembles nothing more than the portrait of his arch-enemy: "Ce jeune homme me semble être bien profond, bien calme dans ses ruses politiques, bien indépendant dans ses vastes résolutions, dans ses monstrueuses entreprises" (307). Finally, before the hero is carted off to the block, the odious Père Joseph, better known as *l'éminence grise,* attempts to rescue him, having recognized in him a power that could effectively displace the Cardinal's:

Vous et M. de Thou, qui vous piquez de ce que vous nommez vertu, vous avez manqué de causer la mort de cent mille homme peut-être, en masse et au grand jour, pour rien, tandis que Richelieu et moi, nous en avons fait périr beaucoup moins, en détail, et la nuit, pour fonder un grand pouvoir.

(336-37)

Le Père Joseph's reaction to Cinq-Mars's repeated denials and protestations of innocence is "Voilà encore des mots," "Voici encore des mots" (336-37). Cinq-Mars, in effect, has become a being fragmented by the very language he set out to rectify. Cinq-Mars, the hero, has turned into a text—"des mots"—whose "truth" can no longer be heard, but only "read," and the text "reads" very much like Richelieu. Whatever the "truth" of his "ligne droite" was, it has become increasingly deflected and undulant—something, in fact, very much like "writing."

It is precisely the consigning of his name to writing, the apposing of his signature to the letters comprising a treacherous pact with Spain, that does Cinq-Mars in. The Queen, who has been flirting with the idea of joining Cinq-Mars's faction, protests vehemently when the pact is mentioned: "on a osé aller jusque là sans mon consentement! déjà des accords avec l'étranger!" (288) and withdraws her support. Her outrage is echoed by de Thou who pleads with Cinq-Mars not to sign the pact. According to de Thou, the alliance with Spain would lead to the ultimate horror of French mothers "forcées d'enseigner à leurs enfants une langue étrangère" (236).

The value my reading attributes to the expression "langue étrangère" would be incidental were it a unique occurrence, but an interesting pattern emerges when the term is brought into play with crucial precedents. The textual itinerary takes us from "le berceau de la langue" where "le plus pur français" is spoken "sans lenteur, sans vitesse, sans accent" (28), to a "langue nouvelle," the language of the court which de Thou describes as une "une langue bien étrangère . . . mais que l'on peut parler noblement, . . . et qui saurait exprimer de belles et généreuses pensées" (176). Court language presents the hero with the overwhelming difficulties of pleasing ("Plaire") and its concomitant evils of flexibility, composition, and nuance—a maze of giddying turns and dangerous dead-ends much like the writer himself must negotiate in his efforts to speak out, "parle[r] hautement" (175) to his monarch, the sovereign reader. Thus, from the "berceau de la langue" to a "langue nouvelle" fraught with the dangers of ambiguity, the text drags the hero to the precipice of la "langue" truly "étrangère" (236)—the language truly alien to our origins that writing is. The signature of the pact with Spain marks the hero's entrance into the economy of purloined and purloining letters over which the Minister, this "*conquérant qui entre par la brèche*" (114), presides like a maleficent deity. Writing is making a breach in a natural barrier, much like a linguistic frontier; the subject's (Cinq-Mars) conscious voice and the unconscious written text that speaks him being separated like "dream thoughts" from "dream content:" "two versions of the same subject matter in two different languages."[10]

Despite the triumphant, even hagiographic depiction of Cinq-Mars's death, Vigny unwittingly hands over the victory to Richelieu. The novel's ultimate moment of truth, the locus of convergence of the incessant volley of presages, omens, and portents liberally strewn throughout the novel is the unifying moment of Cinq-Mars's decapitation under a resplendent sun, a sacred moment of sacrificial grandeur, replete with Vestal Virgins hieratically petrified in prayer (356). The novel's unifying moment of truth and meaning is also the very moment of its dispersion. The meaning dissolves back into the metonymic chains of History and Literature. The concluding dialogue between Pierre Corneille and Milton points to the truth of another text: the novel's "last word" is (in History's? Hugo's?") "Cromwell" (374). Unvanquished Cinq-Mars? Conquered by the very medium which sought to establish his invincibility!

Notes

1. Sainte-Beuve, *Le Globe* (8 July 1826).

2. Georg Lukács, *The Historical Novel,* trans. Hannah and Stanley Mitchell (London: Merlin Press, 1962) 75-77.

3. Roland Barthes, "Drame, Poème, Roman," in *Théorie d'ensemble* (Paris: Seuil, 1968), 27, note 1.

4. Alfred de Vigny, "Réflexions sur la vérité dans l'art," in *Œuvres complètes* (Paris: Gallimard, 1965), II, 22.

5. Vigny, "Réflexions," 21.

6. Vigny, *Le Journal d'un poète,* in *Œuvres complètes,* II, 1276.

7. Jeffrey Mehlman, *Revolution and Repetition* (Berkeley and Los Angeles: Univ. of California Press, 1977), 107.

8. Vigny, *Cinq-Mars* in *Œuvres complètes,* II, 327. All subsequent references to the novel are to this edition and will appear in the text.

9. Barthes, *Le Degré zéro de l'écriture* (Paris: Gonthier, 1964), 137.

10. Sigmund Freud, *Standard Edition*, IV, 277.

Malcolm McGoldrick (essay date 1989)

SOURCE: "Vigny's 'Le Mont des Oliviers' and Amos," in *French Studies Bulletin*, No. 32, Autumn, 1989, pp. 5-8.

[*In the following essay, McGoldrick describes the influence of the Old Testament on Vigny's poem "Le Mont des Oliviers" and, by implication, his other late poetry.*]

"Le Mont des Oliviers" is one of the best known of Vigny's poems. Vigny recounts Jesus' mental anguish in the Garden of Gethsemane, with a wealth of detail culled from the Gospels. Vigny's own footnotes to his manuscript attest to his precise and detailed knowledge of all four Gospels, and the selective use he made of them. The poem is confusing to a considerable degree because the Gospels are chronologically distorted to make Jesus enumerate actual details of his crucifixion. But critics have assumed that Vigny's Biblical borrowings were taken solely from the New Testament, and, understandably, have discounted the possibility of any borrowing from an Old Testament source. Marc Citoleux, for example, writes: 'Après 1842, par un renversement singulier . . . Vigny délaisse l'Ancien Testament au profit du Nouveau.'[1] [**"Le Mont des Oliviers"** was published in 1843]. Another critic, Vera Summers, states categorically that this is 'le seul de ses poèmes d'inspiration évangélique où des souvenirs de l'Ancien Testament ne viennent pas se mêler.'[2] Not surprisingly, therefore, the New Testament has been adduced in explanation of difficult passages in the poem. One such passage is contained in the second section. On lines 69-70 Jesus exhorts his Father: 'Eloigne ce calice impur et plus amer / Que le fiel, ou l'absinthe, ou les eaux de la mer.' This couplet's first line has been broadly understood, the second either misunderstood or ignored in numerous anthologies and editions.

Jesus' plea to remove this 'cup' is less terse than in the Synoptic Gospels (Matthew 26. 39; Mark 14. 36; Luke 22. 42). The reference is to the figurative 'cup of suffering', to which Jesus already alluded before his entry into Jerusalem, as an indirect reference to his death. Vigny's use of the phrase would appear to be linked to the differing accounts of the drink offered Jesus on the Cross. According to Matthew this was wine (or vinegar in some translations) mingled with gall (an Old Testament phrase found in Psalm 69. 22); in Mark wine mingled with myrrh, this last an analgesic. Vigny's Jesus apparently anticipates details of the ways in which his tormentors will taunt him on the Cross.

Critics have accordingly explained the couplet in the light of New Testament exegesis. From the general observation that gall (*fiel*, 'bile') is one of the humours in the body of man and beast, they have proceeded to note the metaphorical use of the term 'in the gall of bitterness' which occurs once in the New Testament, in Acts 8. 23. Vigny's commentators have also noted that wormwood (*absinthe*), a non-poisonous plant typifying grief and disaster, is also found just once in the New Testament, in Revelation 8. 10-11, where a star called 'Wormwood' falls from heaven and makes a third of the rivers and fountains so bitter that men who drink their waters die.

However, the critics have failed to point out that the linked phrase 'fiel et absinthe' is not to be found in the New Testament, but only in Deuteronomy, Jeremiah, Lamentations and Amos. Jeremiah 9. 15 and 23. 15 read 'eau de fiel' and 'absinthe', Lamentations 3. 19 'fiel' and 'absinthe'. In the translation by David Martin (which Vigny may have used because both he in **"Moïse,"** and it in Exodus 34. 35, failed to incorporate the standard misinterpretation of the verb 'sent forth beams' as 'horns' common to the Vulgate translation of the Bible used during the Middles Ages and immortalized by Michelangelo) Amos 6. 12 likewise reads: 'Les chevaux courront-ils par les rochers? ou y laboura-t-on avec des bœufs? mais vous avez changé le jugement en fiel, et le fruit de la justice en absinthe.' Amos compares the destruction of Jerusalem to the bitterness of wormwood and gall (5. 7), here used as a metaphor for sin.

Vigny's allusion in the second line of his couplet to the bitterness of the 'waters of the sea' has suffered total neglect at the hands of his critics. The phrase is surrounded by a number of dense, Biblical images of calamity. It lies between the 'cup' more bitter than 'gall or wormwood', and the 'lashes', 'crown of thorns', 'nails' to be driven into Jesus' hands, and the 'spear' that was to pierce his side in the Johannine account. These dense Biblical images suggest that 'les eaux de la mer' must also have a Biblical provenance, and be something more than a self-explanatory expression, or one common to the literary tradition. Yet nobody has ever attempted to explain it. The New Testament is of no avail. Again it is the Old Testament, and again Amos, that provides us with the key to its meaning:

> Cherchez celui qui a fait la poussinière et l'orion, qui change les plus noires ténèbres en aube du jour, et qui fait devenir le jour obscur comme la nuit; qui appelle les eaux de la mer, et les répand sur le dessus de la terre, le nom duquel est l'Eternel
>
> (5. 8).
>
> Car c'est le Seigneur, l'Eternel des armées, qui touche la terre, et elle se fond; et tous ceux qui l'habitent mènent deuil: et elle s'écroule toute comme un fleuve, et est submergé comme par le fleuve d'Egypte;
>
> Qui a bâti ses étages dans les cieux, et qui a établi ses armées sur la terre; qui appelle les eaux de la mer, et qui les répand sur le dessus de la terre: son nom est l'Eternel
>
> (9. 5-6).

The sense of Jesus' allusion to his cup being more bitter than gall or wormwood or the salinity of brine is thus expanded to comprise the destructive power of the waters of the sea poured over the land. The context makes clear that this is not a reference to the munificence of God, because the forces unleashed wreak havoc and the earth's inhabitants 'mènent deuil'. The 'eaux de la mer' can refer only to a flood, or possibly a tidal wave. Amos spoke in accents of doom about the destructive power of God to punish iniquity, and excluded the possibility of all but a remnant of Israel being saved.[3]

That both 'fiel et absinthe' and 'les eaux de la mer' are to be found in Amos allows Vigny's borrowing to be ascribed to this source. Just as Jesus' use of 'cup' in connection with the Lord's Supper is, together with 'gall and wormwood' figuratively related to the Old Testament, so too, the 'waters of the sea' fix **"Le Mont des Oliviers"** within the topographical setting of the Old Testament, and more specifically of Amos.[4] I would not claim for the borrowing more importance than it deserves—the interest of the poem and its focal point clearly lie elsewhere—but it does serve to emphasize Vigny's dense and imaginative fusion of images borrowed from both covenants, the subversive use to which he put them, and, incidentally, confounds the assumption that after 1842 he completely turned away from the Old Testament—the source of inspiration for so many of the **Poèmes antiques et modernes.**

Notes

1. Marc Citoleux, *Alfred de Vigny. Persistances classiques et affinités étrangères* (Paris, Champion, 1924), p. 370.

2. Vera A. Summers, *L'Orientalisme d'Alfred de Vigny* (Paris, Champion, 1930), p. 166. None of Vigny's more recent commentators has raised this question.

3. One other reference, Psalm 33. 7: 'Il assembla les eaux de la mer comme en un monceau' refers to God in an awe-inspiring but providential light, and can be dismissed. The only non-Biblical, non-literary provenance of the 'bitter sea' that I know of is the Babylonian creation story: 'La cosmogonie babylonienne connaît . . . le chaos aquatique, l'océan primordial, apsû et *tiamat*; le premier personnifiait l'océan doux sur lequel, plus tard, flottera la terre, *tiamat* est la mer salée et amère peuplée de monstres.' Quoted from Mircea Eliade, *Traité d'histoire des religions,* nouvelle édition revue et mise à jour (Paris, Payot, 1968), p. 167; translated as *Patterns in Comparative Religion* (Meridian Books, Cleveland and New York, World Publishing Company, 1963), p. 191. Although *Le Mont des Oliviers* is both a dense and a diffuse poem, I think it doubtful that Vigny would, *in medias res,* borrow from outside a Judeo-Christian source.

4. That Vigny used Amos elsewhere there can be no doubt. Three commentators—all of them early critics who appear to have been more in tune with form criticism in Bible Studies and in inter-textuality than their modern counterparts—have traced the influence of Amos in other poems. Edmond Estève, in his criti-

cal edition of the 'Poèmes antiques et modernes' (Paris, Hachette, 1914), p. 70, footnote 1, makes a *rapprochement* between line 216 of *Eloa* and Amos 8. 10; Vera Summers, *op. cit.,* between line 6 of *La Femme adultère* and Amos 4. 4, to which Clemenceau Le Clercq, in *L'Inspiration Biblique dans l'œuvre poétique d'Alfred de Vigny* (Anne-masse, Imprimerie Granchamp, 1937), adds a further one between line 6 of this poem and Isaiah 3. 16, describing these lines as 'ce patient travail de marqueterie' (p. 66). Referring to *Moïse,* Clemenceau Le Clercq writes: 'Le prophète pliant sous le poids de la vision qui lui est communiquée, c'est dans la tradition la plus pure de la Bible' (p. 88), and cites Jeremiah and Amos in support of this statement. Finally, although not citing Amos as source or influence, Le Clercq opposes the notion of a human holocaust in Judges—the basis for *La Fille de Jephté*—to Amos, citing chapter 5. 21-25 in support of the statement: 'Il faut se souvenir qu'à l'époque plus tardive, plus éclairée des Prophètes, les conceptions d'Israël s'étant affinées, Dieu, par la bouche de son prophète Amos, réprouve nettement l'holocauste' (pp. 55-56).

Malcolm McGoldrick (essay date 1991)

SOURCE: "The Setting in Vigny's 'La Mort du loup,'" in *Language Quarterly,* Vol. 29, Nos. 1-2, Winter, 1991, pp. 104-14.

[*In the following essay, McGoldrick views the setting, rather than the action, of Vigny's "La Mort du loup" as the source of tension in the poem.*]

Vigny's poem **"La Mort du Loup"** recounts the tracking-down of a wolf, its mate, and two cubs, by a band of hunters with a pack of dogs. The wolf is pursued, easily cornered and caught off guard, and attacked by one of the dogs. It seizes the dog, and only releases it from the clutch of its jaws after the animal lies dead. Then, mortally wounded by knife and bullet wounds, it too lies down to die. In the poem's second and third sections, Vigny uses the wolf's death to spell out his message of stoic resignation and submission to fate exemplified by the wolf. The poem becomes a fable, and the wolf is extolled as an example for mankind.

Because Vigny's critics have concentrated on the poem's moral lesson, they have paid relatively scant attention to the intrinsic merit of the setting in **"La Mort du Loup."** V. L. Saulnier and P.-G. Castex have included some descriptive notations about the setting in their critical commentaries.[1] However, they have not exhausted all the critical comment to be made about Vigny's setting, in which the atmosphere of suspense and murder is present as ". . . a dramatic and minatory prelude to the fierce and poignant action to come . . ." (Ince, 1969). In spite of the highly graphic depiction of the wolf's death, the landscape—

together with an equally poignant skyscape—constitutes the real tableau of **"La Mort du Loup."**[2] My *terminus ad quem* is line 26 of the poem, with which the descriptive part of the poem's first section ends; the confrontation with the wolves sets the action in motion immediately afterwards.

There are no peripeteia in the details of the hunting of the wolves. The poem is a *coup de main,* whose outcome—the wolf's death—is announced in the poem's title. The atmosphere of tension is built up in and through the setting, rather than by action. This is done partly through images which suggest forceful impact rather than clarification and logical meaning. The imagery that the poet uses makes the tableau assume a nightmarish quality. The tightness and sobriety of individual descriptive details is due to Vigny's use of those aspects of tension alone which have immediate impact.

For example, from the very beginning of the poem we are introduced to a world of danger:

> Les nuages couraient sur la lune enflammée
> Comme sur l'incendie onvoit fuir la fumée,

The adjective "enflammée" in line 1, which qualifies "lune", introduces a larger-than-life quality into the description, and the parallel with fire an inauspicious element. Line 2 is almost in parenthesis to line 1, the symmetry of the comparisons being underscored by repetition of the preposition "sur" and the chiasmic structure of the couplet, with its verbs "couraient" and "fuir" placed immediately before and after the medial causura in lines 1 and 2 respectively. The forcefulness of the analogy between moon and fire is all the more powerful after the moon has been described as "enflammée". The scene portrayed comprises a dark setting on which a certain coloration is superimposed. In these lines Vigny creates the conditions for the wind which, we learn later, causes the weather vane to produce its shrill cry, itself a portentous symbol of the tragedy to come. No mention is made here of the wind, as this would be inconsistent with the tone of the passage, which at this point conveys the hushed stillness of the landscape. Silence is important for both hunters and wolves. The hunters depend on it to stalk their prey. Their progress is marked by respect for it: "Nous marchions, sans parler . . .", "Rien ne bruissait . . ." The wolves also depend on silence to avoid being descried by the hunters.

Just as Vigny uses both hushed stillness and shrill sounds in his tableau, so too he uses both elements of a chiaroscuro motif. Darkness is emphasized. It is required for and linked to the atmosphere of sinisterness. Dark and sinister clouds billow like smoke above a fire, producing a tone of danger. Dark woods extend to the horizon and are traditionally associated through fairy tales with sinister events.[3] The hunters depend for the success of their dark designs on both silence and cover of dark.

In contradistinction to darkness, moonlight is evoked. Its importance in setting the scene through the simile of a fire, which in turn introduces the clouds hurrying across the sky, cannot be overstated.[4] The moonlight, like the weather vane, assumes the value of an omen. It is the visual agency which allows the poet-hunter later to espy the wolf cubs dancing in the moonlight. Because of the moonlight the hunters have to hide their shotguns which reflect the light. The hunter depends on the light of a star to interpret the animal footprints in the sand.[5] Later, the wolf cubs are silhouetted, and the gleam in the eye of the wolf or she-wolf is the first glimpse that the hunter catches of his quarry.[6] The whole death scene also depends on the hunters having enough natural light to witness the events and the expression on the wolf's face: moonlight is required for the whole chiaroscuro effect.

Just as Vigny uses both darkness and light for effect, so too he uses spatial dimension and constriction. The very barrenness of the landscape is not allowed to escape participating in the poignancy of the atmosphere: although **"La Mort du Loup"** portrays a desolate landscape of "landes" which extend as far as the horizon, we read later that ". . . les enfants du Loup se jouaient en silence, Sachant bien qu'à *deux pas, ne dormant qu'à demi,* / Se couche dans ses murs l'homme, leur ennemi" (italics in this quotation, and in following ones, are my own).

Shrill sounds and silence, the play of light and darkness, expanse and constriction, create for the reader an atmosphere of dramatic suspense. A variety of technical means also contributes to this effect. The subordinate clause in lines 6-7 intensifies the narration. Vigny frequently withholds the main clause of a sentence, holding the reader in suspense through a sometimes lengthy digression. In lines 9 and 10 bated breath is conveyed as a real impression through the break-up of the *hémistiches*: "Nous avons / écouté, // retenant / notre haleine / Et le pas / suspendu. //" The alliteration in "p" and the other surds (sounds that are uttered with the breath and not the voice) "b", and "s" in "suspendu", are reminiscent of a whisper. The logical order of sequence in the above lines would be: "le pas suspendu, nous avons écouté, retenant note haleine." In the adopted word-order, "listening" assumes priority, and "le pas suspendu" becomes almost a kind of ablative absolute. Bated breath and halted footsteps are in harmony with the hushed stillness of the setting in which they are found, with the atmosphere of which they are a part.

Suspense is once again created by the period and dash in line 10, which introduces six and a half lines of descriptive parenthesis before the action is resumed. Alliteration conveys the unnatural and awesome silence of "Ni le bois ni la plaine / Ne *p*oussaient un sou*p*ir dans les airs." Vigny's use of the plural "airs", and his general predilection for plurals and definite articles (his tableau consists of "les nuages", "la lune", "l'incendie", "la fumée", "les bois", "l'horizon") gives it an unreal quality of essence, of the ethereal rather than reality.[8] The vague effect created by the use of the definite article is of a universe of undefined shape and dimension.

In lines 10 to 16 in particular, Vigny creates both horizontal and vertical expanse:

. . .—Ni le bois ni la plaine
Ne poussaient un soupir dans les airs; seulement
La girouette en deuil criait au firmament.
Car le vent, élevé bien au-dessus des terres,
N'effleurait de ses pieds que les tours solitaires,
Et les chênes d'en bas, contre les rocs penchés,
Sur leurs coudes semblaient endormis et couchés.

Vigny places us in the midst of a wood-covered plain. The introduction of woods which stretch as far as the eye can see gives the tableau depth, yet defines its limit. Lines 12-16 depict the eeriness created by images in the physical setting which astound the reader's imagination. Solitary towers are to be found here. Once again Vigny uses the definite article and plural nouns even where this clashes with verisimilitude—the unlikelihood, for instance, of there being more than one of these towers in the midst of a desolate landscape—to impose upon the reader a deliberately unreal and nightmarish tableau. Mentioning the firmament creates both expanse and confinement.

After using the absence of wind to set the tone of stealth, Vigny here makes the wind an aural participant. This demonstrates the way in which he *creates* desolation and anguish. The verb "crier" on line 12 aptly renders the plaintive cry of the weather vane "en deuil", and creates a tone which is consonant with the setting. It adds to the value of "en deuil" by the common association both words have with bereavement. A word like "grincer" would be too technically precise and detract from the value of metaphor which both terms share: the cry of the weather vane connotes the wailing of mourners—imprecise yet suggestive.

Startling metaphors, the "pieds" referring to the undercurrents of wind which brush against the weather vane, and "coudes", the oaks nestling on their elbows, appearing "endormis et couchés", stand out in the description as glaringly incongruous. . . .

Many other stylistic and poetic properties assure the success of Vigny's attempt to create an imaginative *décor* that captivates the reader. Avoidance of a first-person narrative technique obviates a possible identification through sympathy between reader and narrator. The latter, being linked to his band of fellow hunters, mentions "nous" six times from the beginning of the narration onwards. Only from line 27 does he use the singular personal pronoun. He does, of course, elicit the reader's sympathy later, but not at this confrontational stage in the action. Nor is the specific function of the men in the setting revealed prematurely either. We are told only of ". . . les Loups voyageurs que nous *avions* traqués." The only person singled out for attention, before the perhaps inauspicious notation "*Trois* s'arrêtent" is "Le plus vieux des chasseurs", who probably conjures up an image of sagacity or shrewdness rather than one of aggression. Theirs is, admittedly, a foreboding presence, but for a long time it remains a purely minatory one. When the denouement comes about, it does so quite suddenly.

Vigny also makes effective use of assonance and explosive consonants (as well as of alliteration). He uses the conjunction "et" to give a conversational ring and the flavor of story-telling to his poem. He resorts to the historic present tense when the most crucial events in the progression of the hunt require the reader's full participation without any interval of time or tense coming between narrator and reader.

The setting in **"La Mort du Loup"** serves as more than a preparation for the tracking-down of the wolf and the unfolding of the plot. Much of the interest and enjoyment which the poem holds resides in its highly stylized setting in which all elements create tension, poignancy and a baleful atmosphere. Vigny achieves this by a masterful juxtaposition of contrasting effects: noise and silence, darkness and light, confinement and expanse, wilderness and the proximity of urban man (with their attendant values of nature and civilization), barrenness and luxuriant vegetation, prey and predator, realism and surrealism. François Germain wrote of the poem: "'**La Mort du Loup**' est moins un récit qu'une march funèbre."

Notes

1. Alfred de Vigny, *Les Destinées,* edited by Verdun L. Saulnier (Geneva and Paris: Textes littéraires français, 1963); *Les Destinées,* commentées par Pierre-Georges Castex (Paris: Société d'édition d'enseignement supérieur, 1968).

2. See J. O. Fischer (1977: 243): "Une des images les plus plastiques de Vigny, celle du loup mourant, ne présente pas un tableau réel, mais une scène théâtrale, l'image du loup stylisé en homme-héros pour préparer le parallèle final."

3. François Germain, (1962: 67-8), makes the following comment about the poem: "La vérité idéale du poème est . . . celle de l'angoisse; et dès les premiers vers elle est irrécusable. Avant même de parler de chasse, Vigny crée un paysage inquiétant qui confine au cauchemar: lune de sang, nuages qui fuient, bois noirs, végétation qui reparaît dans tous les contes populaires quand on veut perdre un enfant ou égorger une jeune princesse, un parfait décor de meurtre."

4. Norris J. Lacy (1976) comments on this simile (one of three that he treats): "It may reasonably be argued that the appearance of the moon and the clouds requires no visual clarification, but if Vigny's technique here does not clarify, it does intensify. Indeed, it not only conveys the vividness of the scene, but by moving from the serene and picturesque evocation of nature to the image of fire and smoke, it also establishes the mood and theme of the poem: violence superimposed on tranquillity."

5. I am using the *varia lectio* which appears in the new Pléiade edition of the *Oeuvres complètes,* edited by François Germain and André Jarry (I, Paris: N.R.F., Gallimard, 1986, Bibliothèque de la Pléiade, p. 74).

6. J. Castex (1948: 271-274) states as a hunter: "Pas plus que ceux des lions et des panthères, les yeux du loup ne peuvent flamboyer, car ils ne sont pas phos-

phorescents par eux-mêmes." François Germain (1962: 66-7) underlines the inconsistencies of the poem as a logical exposition of a hunt.

7. Clive Scott, in a perceptive study titled "The Designs of Prosody: Vigny's 'La Mort du Loup'" describes the 3+3+3+ trisyllabic measures in lines 9-11, in line 4, and elsewhere, as ". . . this spiritual space, the space of steadied self-collection, of undemonstrative aloofness, occupied by a sense of one's own worth and the self-justifying nature of that worth." This is in contradistinction to hemistichs of unequal measures (2+4, 4+2, 5+1, etc.) like line 12 (4+2+2+4, where the creaking weathercock is heard), which convey the sense of vicissitude. Each rhythmically different hemistich conveys a difference in focalization or point of view.

8. Germain remarks (1962:491): "L'emploi systématique . . . de l'article défini invite à concevoir un univers où se donnent rendez-vous des essences; comme si Vigny remontait d'un objet particulier à l'Objet, et l'infinie diversité du monde se réduit à quelques archétypes."

Works Cited

Castex, J. 1948. Alfred de Vigny et la chasse au loup. *Revue des Sciences Humaines.*

Fischer, J. O. 1977. *"Epoque romantique" et réalisme: Problèmes méthodologiques.* Prague: Univerzita Karolova [Université Charles IV].

Germain, François. 1962. *L'Imagination d'Alfred de Vigny.* Paris: Corti.

Ince, W. N. 1969. Some reflections on the poetry of Alfred de Vigny. *Symposium.*

Lacy, Norris J. 1976. Simile in "La Mort du Loup." *University of South Florida Language Quarterly*, Nos. 1-2.

Scott, Clive. 1990. The designs of prosody: Vigny's "La Mort du Loup." In C. Prendergast, ed., *Nineteenth-century French Poetry. Introductions to Close Readings.* Cambridge U.P.

de Vigny, Alfred. 1986. *Oeuvres complètes.* Edited by François Germain and André Jarry. I, Paris: N.R.F., Gallimard, Bibliothèque de la Pléiade.

————. 1968. *Les Destinées, commentées par Pierre-Georges Castex.* Paris: Société d'édition d'enseignement supérieur.

————. 1963. *Les Destinées.* Edited by Verdun L. Saulnier. Geneva and Paris: Textes littéraires français.

Phillip A. Duncan (essay date 1992)

SOURCE: "Alfred de Vigny's 'La Colère de Samson' and Solar Myth," in *Nineteenth Century French Studies*, Vol. 20, Nos. 3-4, Spring/Summer, 1992, pp. 478-81.

[*In the following essay, Duncan details Vigny's mythologizing of his personal feelings of feminine betrayal in the poem "La Colère de Samson."*]

The Biblical account of the Nazarite, Samson, involves three levels of narrative. While it relates the amorous adventures of Samson and the treachery of Dalilah, its central reference is to the superhuman exploits of a hero whose life echoes the epic of Hercules in a neighboring culture. Additionally, Samson and Dalilah (as well as Hercules) behave as celestial deities anthropomorphized. Alfred de Vigny's **"La Colère de Samson"** virtually suppresses the elements of gigantism and the marvelous to focus on the human passion and pathos that mask a combat of male solar and female lunar principles.

Vigny's troubled liaison with the actress Marie Dorval provoked the poem. There seems no doubt that his passion was intense and that he expected uncompromising affection in return. In this he was cruelly disappointed by Marie's bisexual divagations. No doubt Vigny's own truculence contributed to her disenchantment with a severe and self-righteous companion. Marie's betrayals, her sexual and emotional inconstancy, are an issue in Vigny's transposition of his personal experience to the context of the Samson legend; but Dalilah's relationship with Samson in the poem depends more on political, religious and profit motives. Dalilah is the agent of her people, the Philistines, who are committed to the subversion of a powerful enemy among the Hebrews. She strips Samson of the purity and strength emblematized by his unshorn hair, a mark of the zealot Nazarite. With the shearing of his hair and the implicit loss of masculinity as well as his God-given moral and physical powers, Samson is reduced to impotence and is led away to servitude and death. Dalilah betrays an implied professed love for Samson not so much for the sake of variety in pleasure, Marie's offense, but for personal gain and the benefit of the tribe.

Samson is Vigny as he sees himself—the anguished victim of feminine deceit. In Vigny's poem Samson is the ironic captive of his own love, or more accurately, passion, which is consistent with Jewish tradition that perceives him as allowing sensual pleasure to dominate his conduct. In the poem's central apostrophe Samson acknowledges that man is bred to carnal satisfaction:

> L'Homme a toujours besoin de caresse et d'amour;
> . . . . .
> Il rêvera partout à la chaleur du sein,
> Aux chansons de la nuit, aux baisers de l'aurore,
> A la lèvre de feu que sa lèvre dévore,
> Aux cheveux dénoués qui roule sur son front,
> Et les regrets du lit, en marchant, le suivront.[1]

Although he protests of woman that "c'est le plaisir qu'elle aime . . ." (l. 66), it is he, himself, who sits bound by the arms of Dalilah, symbolically a prisoner of his own lust. However, beyond his need for woman's "caresses" is Vigny/Samson's need for woman's love. Samson's strength in this text apparently derives fundamentally not from divine anointment but from his presumption of Dalilah's love:

> Eternel! Dieu des forts! vous savez que mon âme
> N'avait pour aliment que l'amour d'une femme

Puisant dans l'amour seul plus de sainte vigeur
Que mes cheveux divins n'en donnaient à mon coeur.

(ll. 81-84)

His blinding at the hands of his captors is the symbolic actualization of his refusal to recognize the truth of her indifference, "Interdire à ses yeux de voir ou de pleurer." (l. 104) It is not the loss of his "cheveux divins" that emasculates him but his final realization that Dalilah's love is false and the fact that he has further expended his powers in repressing his anger and frustration:

Toujours mettre sa force à garder sa colère
Dans son coeur offensé, comme en un sanctuaire
D'où le feu s'échappant irait tout dévoré,
Interdire à ses yeux de voir ou de pleurer,

(ll. 101-105)

What restores his strength in captivity is still another irony, his liberation from the need of Dalilah's love and from the need to contain his violent anger at his betrayal. Now "le feu s'échappant irait tout dévoré," (l. 103) and so the pillars of the temple of Dagon are thrust assunder in a cataclysmic demonstration of power restored. A solar fire bursts through the imprisoning bars of night.

While Vigny, in his poem, has personalized the human aspect of Samson and diminished his superhuman dimension, he has, simultaneously, enriched the latent allegory in this material of the rivalry between Night and Day. The poem opens with an exposition of place. In addition to suggesting a topography for the events, characteristics of the physical environment indicate the roles and something of the nature of the protagonists. The "shepherd" (Samson), heroic and solitary, (traits borrowed from the Biblical representation) is associated with lions. (l. 3) The lion's head has from ancient times been a solar icon. The halo of its mane imitates the "rays" of the sun and the tawny color is idealized as golden. Like the sun, the lion is represented as the solitary master of its realm. Hercules, the Greek Samson, with his twelve labors, is an acknowledged solar hero. In the first of his (adult) adventures he slew the lion of Nemea, skinned it and wore its head over his own so that his identity as the sun hero is clearly established in the myth. Samson, also the subject of twelve marvels, first slew a lion. His Hebrew name, "Shimshon," is derived from "Shemesh," the sun. To suggest the simultaneity of Samson, lion and the sun Vigny immediately adds in his introduction: "La nuit n'a pas calmé / La fournaise du jour dont l'air est enflammé." (ll. 3-4) Even though envelopped in darkness, an anticipation of Samson's blindness and captivity at the end of the poem, the sun's fierce heat and light and the hero's energy remain immanent.

Following the masculine statement of the first four lines—solitude, gritty sand, lions, fiery sun, male courage—the conclusion of the stanza is a feminine modulation:

Un vent léger s'élève à l'horizon et ride
Les flots de la poussière ainsi qu'un lac limpide.
Le lin blanc de la tente est bercé mollement;

L'oeuf d'autruche, allumé, veille paisiblement,
Des voyageurs voilés intérieure étoile,
Et jette longuement deux ombres sur la toile.

(ll. 5-10)

A soft wind ruffles the sand like waves on a pool and swells the sides of the tent to create the image of undulating water, a feminine essence. There is a further feminine presence in the liquid "l's" that lull these lines. Finally, to command this dark place there is an ostrich-egg lamp—a miniature moon to epitomize Artemis, lunar goddess or earth mother, who may adopt various guises. Her guise in **"La Colère de Samson"** is Dalilah, envoy of Dagon, god of vegetation and fertility, and in whose name resonates the Hebrew "laylah"—the night. In a diurnal allegory, Dalilah, sensual spirit of darkness, has seized and encompassed the regent of the day: "ses bras sont liés / aux genoux réunis du maître . . ." (ll. 12-13). The power of night has obscured the brilliant aura of solar majesty. His rays are extinguished (his head is shorn). The "rays" of his vision are destroyed in a bloody sunset and he is imprisoned in darkness where he awaits the restoration of his vigor at the return of day. Vigny has abridged the period of Samson's captivity in the poem (1) in the interests of concentrating dramatic impact, (2) because Dalilah's betrayal of Samson has purged him of his amorous servitude thus immediately restoring his moral and emotional wholeness, and (3) in order to compress the action into one nighttime to enhance the verisimilitude of one single solar cycle of decline and resurrection.

Samson's climactic destruction of the temple of Dagon and the symbolic daybreak is preceded elsewhere in the Biblical account (and alluded to in lines 94-95 of the poem) by another of his adventures which relates to his epic revenge and to his role as solar hero. Once when Samson was dallying with a prostitute in the town of Gaza, his enemies set an ambush for him. He was to be seized and killed at dawn. Somehow learning of the attack Samson forestalled it by uprooting the pillars holding the portals of the city, carrying off the entire gate assembly and installing it high on a hill near Mount Hebron. Dawn for the people of Gaza was signaled when the first rays of the sun entered the gates of the city. Samson had removed the break of day to a new location thus eliminating the trigger of the ambushers' assault. Closeted in this episode with an alter-Dalilah, he breaks out of his nocturnal confinement and brings first light where it falls naturally to high elevation by an act of great strength and violence and so reasserting his hegemony. Samson's explosive resolution of his contest with the Night—a shattering dawn which burst open the pillars of his somber prison—is an elaboration of the Gaza episode.

In the Book of Judges Samson is Shemesh humanized and martyred. Like Hercules, the Hebrew sun-hero comes to a human end and, like Hercules, is the victim of his all too human passions. Vigny knows his own weaknesses, but represents himself in his poem as a martyr of deception and betrayal. The latent allegory of the solar hero, as well as the Biblical reference, dignifies and redeems with a mythic dimension a confession of personal inadequacy.

Note

1. Alfred de Vigny, *Œuvres complètes,* Ed. Paul Vial-
laneix (Paris: Aux Editions du Seuil [L'Intégrale],
1965) 98-99. ll. 39 and 44-48.

Mark K. Jensen (essay date 1993)

SOURCE: "The Relation of History to Literature in
Vigny's Thought before the Preface to *Cinq-Mars,*" in
French Forum, Vol. 18, No. 2, May, 1993, pp. 165-83.

[*In the following essay, Jensen discusses Vigny's thoughts
on the close relationship of history and literature as represented in his historical novel* Cinq-Mars *and its apologetic
preface.*]

During the lifetime of Alfred de Vigny (1797-1863), *Cinq-
Mars, ou une conjuration sous Louis XIII*[1] was without a
doubt his most widely read work. Written in 1824-25 and
published in January 1826, the novel went through 12 or
13 separate editions; its popular success was thus about
twice that of *Stello* and *Servitude et grandeur militaires.*
In the introduction to his translation of *Cinq-Mars,* William Hazlitt (the younger) remarked: "There is no person
of any reading who has not present in his memory" the
various characters of the novel.[2] Nor was the success of
Cinq-Mars merely popular: both Louis-Philippe and
Napoléon III discussed the book's thesis with the author.[3]

Vigny's attitude toward popular success was almost always an aristocrat's disdain, and there is no doubt that its
very popularity led Vigny to scorn *Cinq-Mars,* stocked as
it was with elements of romance and melodrama calculated to appeal to a broad public. He hoped, however, that
success would bring him the renown needed to call attention to his other works, that celebrity would "faire lire les
autres"—amounting, at the time he made this remark, to
several poems (1028). He seems to have achieved this
aim. Today *Cinq-Mars* is less well-known than the *Poëmes
philosophiques* (*Les Destinées*) or than his play, *Chatterton.* The novel has nevertheless retained a modest popularity. In a recent "ideal library" which appeared in France
under the auspices of Bernard Pivot, *Cinq-Mars* was given
a place among the 25 best historical novels of all time.[4]

For the modern reader, however, appreciation of Vigny's
novel is hampered by the very licence which facilitated its
success. He plays fast and loose with the historical record,
and in ways even more transparent than Scott's in *Ivanhoe,* whose success in translation inspired the vogue of the
historical novel in France in the 1820s. Scott's practice
had been to create a fictional protagonist and associates
who find themselves in the thick of historical events, but
in *Cinq-Mars* all principal characters, including the eponymous hero, are based on individuals who actually existed.
Vigny simplifies them, however, so that they take their
substance not from events as they occurred, but from a
process of reducing motivations to clear and easily grasped

moral notions. The actions of characters are thoroughly altered to conform to these moral notions, and Vigny does
not hesitate to invent incidents which are historically impossible in order to heighten these effects. The means
characters employ to gain their ends are exaggerated to accord with their moral significance in the plot. As a result,
historical factors are neglected in favor of personal ones.
Furthermore, Vigny allegorizes settings in *Cinq-Mars* to
dramatize the significance of characters and their actions.
All these processes constitute a logic of idealization similar to that of romance in which attributes of divinity accrue to heroes and demonic qualities characterize their enemies.[5]

Vigny, however, went to some pains to evade the charge
of falsifying history. The second edition increased the
number of endnotes from six to 14, taking up more than
30 pages. Vigny's notes, one of which ostentatiously refers
to his use of manuscript sources in the Bibliothèque de
l'Arsenal,[6] seem intended to convince the reader that the
novel rested on a study of primary sources. When the
strategy of documentation failed to mollify critics, Vigny
published a third edition of *Cinq-Mars* (1827) in which all
historical notes were eliminated, only to be reinstated in a
different form from 1829 on. Ultimately, however, Vigny
felt that such indirect means of defense were inadequate.
Instead, he confronted the issues involved directly by coun-
terattacking with a manifesto-like preface which first appeared in 1829 and introduced all subsequent editions:
"Réflexions sur la vérité dans l'art."[7] Although critics
have tended to see in these maneuvers little more than embarrassed attempts to save face, what is in fact involved is
a conceptual struggle concerning the proper boundary between historical and fictional narrative. The long reign of
positivist historiography has obscured until recently what
is now increasingly clear: the boundary between history
and fiction appeared almost as problematic in the early
nineteenth century as it has begun, of late, to appear to
us.[8]

What exactly were Vigny's thoughts about the relation of
history to fiction in the period during which he wrote *Cinq-
Mars*? Unfortunately, no texts predating the novel address
this question. Vigny kept his project a secret from friends
and acquaintances until the novel was all but finished.
Henri Latouche refers to the work in a letter of October
1825, so the novel cannot have been completely unknown
to Vigny's friends, but the first reference to the novel in
his *Correspondence* is to be found in an undated letter to
his publisher, Urbain Canel. In the letter, apparently written in December 1825, Vigny insists on his desire for secrecy: "Je vous ai écrit, Monsieur, pour recommander le
secret exact de *Cinq-Mars,* je désire que personne ne jette
les yeux sur lui avant son jour et qu'on ignore même que
vous avez le premier volume."[9] Not even Victor Hugo,
perhaps Vigny's closest friend at the time, knew of the
large project which Vigny had undertaken in the summer
of 1824.

Various factors led Vigny to keep silent about the most
considerable enterprise he had undertaken as a writer: the

severity of the critical response to his long mythopoeic poem, *Eloa,* which had been savaged by the Catholic press in 1824, a fear of political repercussions from what could be read as an attack upon ministerial despotism (there is evidence that Vigny's literary ambitions had already caused problems in his army career),[10] and the wish to keep to himself what might turn out to be no more than another abortive project. In the absence of evidence that Vigny seriously considered the problem of the relation of history to fiction while writing *Cinq-Mars,* his determination to defend the novel from charges of inaccuracy has seemed to most commentators to be wrong-headed stubbornness. But is this so? From the perspective of the 1820s, the boundary between historical and fictional narrative was not as clear as it seemed to be during the long reign of what may be called positivist historiography. Restoration novelists were aware of the perennial tension between history and fiction. But they were also more aware than their positivistic successors of the essential role of the imagination in the constitution of narrative. Renewed interest during recent decades in the philosophical problems inherent in historical narrative render us somewhat more sympathetic to the choices Vigny made in *Cinq-Mars* and defended in **"Réflexions sur la vérité dans l'art."**

Cinq-Mars was far from being Vigny's first work to exploit history. His first literary attempt was a historical narrative of the Fronde inspired by reading Retz's memoirs. But it was poetry which attracted most of Vigny's literary effort. In 1815-17, he worked on three tragedies in verse, all of which had historical subjects: Roland, Julien l'Apostat, and Antoine et Cléopâtre. These he destroyed in 1832, when the great cholera epidemic which visited most parts of the globe at some time between 1817 and 1837 reached Paris, threatening the lives both of the author of *Cinq-Mars* and his wife and making the exigent poet tremble "dans la crainte des éditeurs posthumes" (Vigny, *Journal* 950). Except for the article **"Sur les œuvres complètes de Byron"** published in the December 1820 number of the Hugo brothers' *Conservateur Littéraire,* almost all of Vigny's literary work was poetry. The fact that Vigny's reputation before *Cinq-Mars* rested exclusively upon his poetic production was doubtless one more reason he relished the idea of springing upon the unsuspecting world a substantial work in prose.

It should already have been apparent, however, to one considering Vigny's corpus before 1826, that history was the main source—indeed, the almost exclusive source—for the settings for Vigny's literary imagination. In addition to scenic elements, these poems are generally narrative works, often taking their action from historical situations. Thus the first and longest piece in his first volume, *Poëmes,* published by Pélicier in March 1822, was **"Héléna,"** a poem dramatizing the contemporary Greek struggle for liberation. **"Héléna"** was followed by nine poems in three groupings which are historical in nature: **"Poëmes antiques," "Poëmes judaïques,"** and **"Poëmes modernes."** *Eloa,* published by Auguste Boulland in April 1824, employs generalized themes of Christian epic myth which Vigny presents as a mythico-historical mélange.

The practice of his competitors in the burgeoning field of the historical novel in the 1820s was not calculated to augment the scruples of historical novelists. As a recent study of the period notes, "Every year the number of Scott imitators had increased; 1825 and 1826 were not exceptions. Most imitations were poorly composed as well as too improbable and melodramatic."[11] Given the state of the genre in the 1820s, we should not exaggerate the fastidiousness with regard to accuracy which an author would have been likely to feel in planning and writing a historical novel.

Some idea of how Vigny fit the material to his loom can be grasped from miscellaneous papers pertaining to the novel's genesis. One entitled "Dates de C. Mars" takes notice of the awkward fact that the execution of Urbain Grandier preceded Cinq-Mars's arrival at court by several years.[12] But this should probably not be read as the expression of a twinge of conscience.[13] The following page of notes, whose material resemblance to the preceding one seems to make it contemporary with it, shows no special scrupulousness for historical detail. The page is entitled "rapprochemens et faits." Vigny notes that "le Bourreau s'était cassé la jambe on prit un homme de la lie du peuple pour 100 écus—qu'il soit lié à l'action qu'il accepte pour sauver C. Mars et ne le puisse pas" (Chantilly, Tome III, fol. 65). Though this idea was never incorporated into the novel, it shows how a historical detail was a point of departure for imagining dramatic connections which might heighten the interest of the narrative. In this case, the historical record offered the author a variety of possibilities. Different accounts assert that the man hired as executioner was a porter, a butcher, or a manual laborer, engaged to replace the incapacitated *bourreau* of Lyons.[14] Though the historical fee of 100 écus (Vaissière 94) was retained, Vigny chose not to introduce "un homme de la lie du peuple." Instead, he invented "Jean le Roux," a butcher who, according to his wife, is "un honnête homme" (Vigny, *Cinq-Mars,* . . . 2: 354). The possibility of involving the executioner in the plot to save Cinq-Mars is neglected, perhaps so that some gallows humor on the part of *le peuple* may, in the Shakespearean tradition, leaven the pathos of the hero's end. The wife, who is unhappy that her husband is being paid to "couper la tête à deux chrétiens," is told: "qu'est-ce que cela te fait que la viande qu'il coupe se mange ou ne se mange pas?" (Vigny, *Cinq-Mars* 354)

It was Vigny's peculiarly historical inspiration that led Emile Deschamps to consider him the master of the *poème,* then considered to be a particular genre of poem, distinct from an ode, ballad, elegy, etc.:

> Le Lyrique, l'Elégiaque et l'Epique étant les parties faibles de notre ancienne poésie . . . ., c'est de ce côté que devait se porter la vie de la poésie actuelle. Aussi M. Victor Hugo s'est-il révélé dans l'Ode, M. de Lamartine dans l'Elégie et M. Alfred de Vigny dans le Poème . . . à l'exemple de Byron, [M. de Vigny] a su renfermer la poésie épique dans des compositions d'une moyenne étendue et toutes inventées: il a su être grand sans être long.[15]

In the twentieth century psychological approaches to Vigny have certainly contributed much to our understanding of

Vigny, but an emphasis upon subjectivity has sometimes obscured the extent to which Vigny's practice was based upon his way of understanding the historical process.[16] Vigny, of course, was not alone in this interest. The historical inquisitiveness and historical-mindedness which marks the Romantic period so deeply fostered an interest in historical theories which attempted to explain the elaboration of myths.[17] Historical accounts of the literature of Romanticism have tended to focus on the cultivation of individual subjectivity and its expression in lyrical and fictional genres. But from another perspective, what underlies the revival of all three literary genres cited by Deschamps in his 1828 preface to *Etudes françaises et étrangères*—lyric, elegy, and "poème"—is the new consciousness of the historical uniqueness of societies and individuals as well as the ephemeral circumstantiality of their intersection in historical moments. Vigny, in pondering his work, sometimes thought of **Cinq-Mars** as the first volume of a "histoire de la noblesse" which he never wrote (Vigny, **Journal** 1049), sometimes as the first "chant" of "une sorte de poème épique sur la désillusion" (Vigny, **Journal** 1037) comments which are further confirmation of his historical consciousness.

We have noted that in **Cinq-Mars** a certain logic of idealization, similar to that which exaggerates character traits in romance, causes the heroes of the novel to approach the divine and its villains to approach the demonic. A similar tendency runs through Vigny's work from beginning to end. Whether it be the analytical Docteur Noir in **Stello** and **Daphné,** the suffering princess in **"Wanda,"** or the portrait Vigny paints of himself in the **"Commentaires sur les mœurs de mon temps et document pour l'histoire"** which Jean Sangnier entitled "L'Affaire de l'Académie,"[18] virtually every principal character depicted by Vigny in a narrative undergoes an imaginative transformation projecting him or her into what we exaggerate only slightly by calling the realm of the *merveilleux*. But this is exactly what is, according to Vigny, incompatible with modernity. In 1838 he noted in his journal:

> DU POEME EPIQUE.—Les deux choses impossibles à présent sont: dans l'ensemble des poèmes humains, un merveilleux qui se puisse admettre.—Dans le détail de la forme, le vers héroïque.—Le lecteur ne peut pas vivre avec lui.
>
> (Vigny, **Journal** 1095)

For these or for other reasons, the quasi-epic ambitions of Vigny and the other Romantics fell short of full attainment. But they were nonetheless a necessary part of the program of Romanticism, an inevitable accompaniment of the development of what Friedrich Meinecke dubbed *Historismus*—a term whose English equivalent, historism, has unfortunately not found general acceptance. As Meinecke put it: "The essence of historism is the substitution of a process of individualizing observation for a generalizing view of human forces in history."[19] This form of historical consciousness became much more widespread in the Romantic period. It was the French Revolution which, by its world-shattering cataclysmic power, extended beyond the intellectual élite the consciousness that old ways of thinking had been bound to particular historical periods. All the aspects of the literary movements we group under the name of Romanticism were affected by this consciousness.

In considering the role of history in Vigny's thought at this time, however, we must keep in mind the fact that history had not yet sought to become a science and thus to divorce itself from literature. This effort, inspired by Rankean ideals, would soon staff the cadre of professionalized historians called into existence by the needs of the modern university. Along with other forms of scientism, the idea of a "science of history" has of late become implausible. As a result, we are now better able to appreciate the perspective of the 1820s. Just as the last 25 years have witnessed the birth of a "new journalism" which infuses non-fictional accounts with narrative techniques which derive from the devices of fictional narrative, so in the field of history authors of historical narrative are coming to accept the literariness of their work.[20] The breach which the nineteenth century opened between history and literature seems to be healing. In Vigny's day, the breach was only on the verge of opening. Historical narrative, although distinguished from fiction, relied in narrating the past upon the same literary devices of plot, characterization, point of view, and so on, as fictional narrative, but without regarding such reliance as problematic. To borrow Schiller's terms, historians today are obliged to write historical narrative sentimentally, i.e., with full consciousness of its "artificial and contrived aspects," whereas in the early nineteenth century they could do so naively, i.e., supposing that their narratives heeded only the "simple nature" of events.[21]

As confirmation of the fact that history and literature were more closely allied in the early nineteenth century than they would be in the latter part of the century, when the positivistic influences led historians to aspire either to know the past "wie es eigentlich gewesen,"[22] or to formulate the laws which determined its events, on the model of the laws discovered by the natural sciences, we may cite the career of Leopold von Ranke, born two years before Vigny. Late in life he claimed that the novels of Walter Scott had encouraged his first historical researches, and that, after considering a career in literature, he decided to devote himself to history. In a letter to his brother in 1824, Ranke wrote: "It is certain that I was born for studies . . . less certain that I was born for the study of history; but I have for once taken it up . . . and will stick to it" (Ranke 5-6). Comparing the portraits of Louis XI and Charles the Bold in Scott's *Quentin Durward* and in Philippe de Comines, Ranke came to a conclusion diametrically opposed to Vigny's attitude: "I found by comparison that the truth was more interesting and beautiful than the romance. I turned away from it and resolved to avoid all invention and imagination in my works and to stick to facts."[23] The idea that it is possible to "avoid all invention and imagination" is the essence of what we have referred to above as the "naive" approach to historical perspective.

In France, the aim of a scientific reform of the discipline of history came later, and historical studies throughout the first half of the nineteenth century openly avowed their affiliation with literature. No French historian called for imagination and invention to be expunged from works of history. In Chateaubriand, literary imagination had an ascendancy over the historical record and, indeed, over his own experience rarely equaled in any other writer.[24] Yet it was the inspiration of Chateaubriand, as much as that of Scott, which presided over the renewal of interest in history in France. Augustin Thierry's description of being inspired to become a historian by a reading of Les Martyrs at the age of 15 is (or was) well known.[25] And unlike Ranke, who impugned his handling of historical materials, Thierry praised Walter Scott: "il y a plus de véritable histoire dans ses romans sur l'Écosse et sur l'Angleterre que dans les compilations philosophiquement fausses qui sont encore en possession de ce grand nom. . . ."[26] Even Guizot, whose works were reproached by Sainte-Beuve for being mechanical chains of events which suppressed the contingency of life and who set as his object not to narrate but to explain events, affirmed the necessity of using the literary imagination to understand history:

> But do you know also their external physiognomy? Have you before your eyes their individual features? The facts now dead once lived; unless they have become alive to you you know them not. The investigation of facts, the study of their relation, the reproduction of their form and motion, these constitute history, and every great historical work must be judged by these tests.[27]

The cohesion of history to other literary genres was, then, virtually unchallenged in France in the 1820s. However, far from feeling threatened and perceiving in this relation a weakness, as historians tend to do today, history regarded this relationship as a strength, another weapon in its rhetorical arsenal. For with the extension and deepening of historical consciousness in the aftermath of the French Revolution, history had become an aggressive intellectual force and was on the march. Reizov describes this state of affairs well:

> Jamais encore avant cette décennie, l'histoire n'avait eu une si grande importance pour la vie intellectuelle du pays. Les théories politiques et les utopies sociales étaient empreintes d'histoire, l'histoire se substituait presque aux recherches philosophiques et aux œuvres littéraires ou bien plutôt elle déterminait les méthodes des unes et des autres; la philosophie se transformait en histoire de la philosophie et en philosophie de l'histoire, le roman devenait "roman historique," la poésie ressuscitait les ballades et les vieilles légendes, les peintres, abandonnant le "naturel," peignaient des costumes anciens, et les hommes politiques s'en référait constamment à l'histoire.[28]

Because there was at this time a widespread consensus that history was moving in a particular direction and that progress was less a theory than a fact to be explained,[29] there was not a widely felt need to subject the phenom-enon of the apprehension of the historical past to critical scrutiny. Doubts about progress, of course, are a constant conservative presence in every milieu where groups with an interest in the status quo fear that change will lead to a decline in their importance, and they have a doctrinal basis in pessimistic religious doctrines that enjoyed a revival following the disappointments of the French Revolution. In esthetic circles widespread disenchantment with the results of the July Revolution of 1830 and subsequent movements for social and political change fostered growing skepticism toward the view that human society was providentially moving toward a happier future. In philosophy, the pessimism of Nietzsche (inspired in part by that of Schopenhauer) was perhaps the negation of progressivism which has had the most long-lasting influence. But as historical consciousness only became extensive in the aftermath of the French Revolution, so the crisis in progressivism has begun to become widespread only in the twentieth century. In the 1820s, such doubt was negligible. Its absence accounts for phenomena which contemporary cultural critics often find incomprehensible or else attribute to such factors as Eurocentrism or racism, like the virtual absence of any principled opposition at home to European colonialism. As Paul Bénichou has noted of the idea of progress dominating the Romantic period, "cette notion est désormais interprétée . . . non dans le sens d'une virtualité propre à l'homme et qu'il dépend de lui de réaliser—la perfectibilité selon le mot consacré—mais comme une assurance d'avenir humain inscrite dans le devenir du monde."[30]

These general observations are corroborated by the text of a review of Augustin Thierry's Histoire de la conquête de l'Angleterre par les Normands published in Le Constitutionnel of August 26, 1826. According to a survey of the press published in 1826, Le Constitutionnel was an independent paper with the largest subscription in France: between 20,000 and 21,000 subscribers.[31] The anonymous reviewer begins by observing the peculiar aptitude of the contemporary moment for historical writing, explaining this disposition itself historically:

> S'il était vrai, comme beaucoup de personnes le pensent, que le génie de la poésie et des arts fut perdu chez nous; qu'au dégré de civilisation auquel nous sommes parvenus, la force et la naïveté d'imagination nous fussent refusées, que nous fussions condamnés à juger, à critiquer, jamais à produire, il nous resterait un genre auquel notre esprit critique ne serait pas aussi mortel, et pour lequel nous conserverions encore assez de jeunesse et de puissance créatrice; ce genre, c'est l'histoire.[32]

The development of civilization has led to an advance because of which history, which was formerly written for rulers, is now written for all, and extends its interest to every place and time: ". . . tous les siècles, tous les régimes, tour-à-tour attaqués ou défendus par les partis, ont passé sous nos yeux et sont jugés" (3). This impartiality comes from the conviction that they are all stages in the progress of humanity:

> . . . nous sommes sans colère contre telle ou telle époque; nous les regardons toutes commes les divers

degrés de l'échelle ascendante que parcourt le genre humain en s'élevant vers le bien, vers le mieux. . . . Nous avons donc pour écrire l'histoire, d'abord une grande pensée philosophique, le perfectionnement croissant de l'espèce humaine, et ensuite l'impartialité dûe [sic] à cette pensée, qui nous fait considérer chaque état de l'espèce humaine comme une des variétés infinies de son développement progressif.

(3)

The writer could scarcely be clearer in expressing the view that the writing of history is a philosophical enterprise which involves the attainment of solid cognitive gains. But does this mean that the realm of the literary has been left behind? By no means:

Avec cette grande pensée philosophique et l'impartialité qui lui est inhérente, nous avons donc les conditions morales essentielles; réunirons-nous au même degré les conditions littéraires? saurons-nous, comme les grands narrateurs de l'antiquité, rendre dramatiques ou épiques les événements fournis par l'histoire?

(3)

The ancients had a literary advantage: they had not developed disciplines that dealt with "ces détails techniques sur l'organisation, les ressources industrielles et militaires des sociétés, que nous exigeons de l'historien" (3). Thus they were able to concentrate both their attention and their narratives upon the train of historical action they were describing. This is what history is: the narration of an interesting true story—and it is noteworthy that the reviewer writing in *Le Constitutionnel* exhibits what we have called the "naive" attitude toward narration, showing not the slightest suspicion that storytelling imports something which is not in the events themselves:

Les dissertations, quelque savantes, quelque profondes qu'elles soient, peuvent être d'une grande utilité, attester une grande sagacité de génie; mais elles ne sont pas de l'histoire. La véritable histoire est celle qui, au lieu de disséquer pièce à pièce une époque ou un peuple, fait naître les événements graduellement et avec ensemble, leur conserve la même succession, le même mouvement que dans la nature, reproduit en quelque sorte la vie même, et inspire cet intérêt, ces sympathies qu'on éprouve à l'aspect d'un événement réel et présent. Cette histoire, saurons-nous la faire, avec la condition imposée d'entrer dans tous les détails de l'organisation des sociétés?

(3)

What gifts are needed to write history? It is reassuring to the reviewer that exceptional literary gifts are not required—not because they falsify history, but because they participate in a genius to which few pretend:

Si, pour composer ce qu'on peut appeler une histoire narrative, il fallait du génie dramatique, s'il fallait l'art de tout mettre en action qu'ont eu Shakspeare [sic], Molière, nous douterions de nos succès en histoire; mais heureusement il ne faut que de l'universalité d'intelligence et un grand esprit d'ordre . . . compren-

dre les hommes et les choses, puis choisir, ordonner, tout cela suppose sans doute d'éminentes qualités, des qualités de premier ordre; néanmoins ce n'est pas encore le génie dramatique tel que l'ont eu Shakspeare et Molière, et c'est là ce qui nous rassure.

(3)

And what is the reason such gifts are not required? It is the writer's naive belief that the qualities which distinguish literary genius can already be found in the events the historian recounts: "Il faut qu'on se figure bien que tout est intéressant et dramatique dans la réalité; qu'il ne faut qu'être clair et savoir conserver la génération des choses, pour être éminemment intéressant, et souvent dramatique ou épique" (4). Before proceeding to his particular remarks on Thierry's work, the reviewer sums up in a manner which admirably demonstrates that he is unaware of any danger to truth resulting from the melding of history and literature. The only thing to beware of is an excess of enthusiasm:

Ainsi comprendre, choisir, ordonner, voilà le génie historique. Il ne faut pas sans doute que l'historien soit froid, il ne faut pas qu'il reste indifférent à ce qu'il raconte; mais saiton à quoi lui servira de se passionner lui-même? non pas à animer son récit de l'expression des sentiments qu'il éprouvera, Dieu l'en préserve, il déclamerait; mais à bien discerner les scènes dramatiques de son sujet, à les préparer, à y faire aboutir l'action. Ce qui le frappe fortement, il éprouve le besoin de le raconter; il s'y dirige, il se hâte d'y parvenir, et son besoin devient celui de lecteur, qui le suit et partage son impatience et son désir d'arriver. Encore une fois, ces qualités sont aussi éminentes qu'on le voudra, mais elles ne sont pas du génie dramatique, et, à notre gré, c'est là ce qui sauve l'histoire de nos jours, si elle est sauvée.

(4)

This interesting review is, in fact, an essay on the writing of history; the subsequent discussion of Thierry's work is shorter than the general remarks which precede it.

In the intellectual atmosphere which we have described, then, it is hardly surprising that when writing *Cinq-Mars* Alfred de Vigny did not experience a need to analyze more critically the distinction between history and fiction. Indeed, his initial tendency was to refuse to recognize any conflict between the two. Since his work participated in both, he was willing to take credit both for having written a satisfying novel, and for having authored a serious work of history.

Although the first edition of *Cinq-Mars* was published without a preface, there is good reason to suppose that Vigny at first contemplated composing a preface to precede the novel. In his survey of works of fiction in this period, Claude Duchet concludes that "la préface est à l'époque, pour le roman, un préambule nécessaire. Son absence est signifiante: indice de novation, de différence calculée ou d'un très bas niveau de lecture."[33] Since it goes without saying that Vigny aimed not at a low but at an exalted "niveau de lecture," the absence of a preface in the first edition of *Cinq-Mars* may be taken as a deliberate gesture: not so much of a "différence calculée" as of a *différence effacée*: by removing the preface Vigny positions himself to enjoy the dignities both of the novelist and the historian, to receive homages both as creative artist and as student of history. On the one hand, the lack of a preface seems to add to the novel's esthetic luster: ". . . l'absence de toute désignation paraît bien être pour le roman de cette époque la marque recherchée d'une certaine qualité, qui se dispense du langage mercantile de l'affiche" (Duchet 248). On the other hand, although Vigny endows his novel with a subtitle, he avoids including in it any term which suggests that the work is fictional in nature. Perhaps because his article is concerned with the affirmative signifying function of a preface (or its absence), or because he assumes that the category of "roman" is self-evidently constituted, Claude Duchet neglects to notice that the absence of a preface permits a generic equivalence, an amphibology which Vigny was willing to exploit.

In *Cinq-Mars,* Vigny's fidelity to history does not go much beyond using the names of historical figures for the principal characters of the novel. Vigny alters the most basic and objective facts of biography, the dates of birth and death. For example, Father Joseph, doubtless the character who has in the novel suffered the greatest transformation, died in 1638, a year before the real Cinq-Mars gained royal favor. Vigny could scarcely have hoped that readers would fail to notice such discrepancies. As Marie de Mantoue, Cinq-Mars's beloved, remarks in the novel: "Vous savez bien quelle est toute l'infortune d'une princesse: . . . toute la terre est avertie de son âge . . ." (Vigny, *Cinq-Mars* 45). Given Vigny's manipulation of the historical record, it may seem dubious that *Cinq-Mars* could have been classed as a work of history.

But this was indeed the case. If it was, in fact, among Vigny's aims to straddle the line between history and fiction, we have in the annual classification of new books for the *Bibliographie de la France* testimony to his success. Founded in 1811 at Napoleon's command, this annual publication collected in a single volume the periodicals which recorded at short intervals (in the 1830s and after, weekly) all books and pamphlets printed according to the law on the *dépôt légal.* The volume for 1826 classified the first two editions of *Cinq-Mars* as "HISTOIRE," under the rubric "Histoire de France."[34] In 1827, the third edition of the novel, despite the fact that Vigny stripped it of most of its trapping of notes, was again classified with works of history under the heading "Histoire de France" (*Bibliographie de la France . . . Année 1827* 277). Not until 1829, when the fourth edition was headed by the classificatorily helpful preface entitled **"Réflexions sur la vérité dans l'art,"** was the book's classification transferred to "BELLES-LETTRES" under the rubric "Romans et contes" (*Bibliographie . . . 1829* 238). This classification was continued for the editions of 1833 and 1837 (*Bibliographie . . . 1833* 224, *1837* 219). Then, in 1841, despite the notation in the main entry indicating that this

was the "8ᵉ édition, précédée de réflexions sur la vérité dans l'art" (*Bibliographie . . . 1841* 591), the novel mysteriously reverts in the *Tables* to the rubric "Histoire de France" (*Bibliographie . . . 1841* 248). The next edition, in 1846 (*Bibliographie . . . 1846* 210), appeared with "Romans et contes," where it belonged, and where subsequent editions remained.

We should not make too much of these shifts, which doubtless have more to do with gross errors committed by overworked, harried employees than with taxonomic *glissements* pregnant with signification to be delivered into the world by an intellectual sleuth operating à la Foucault.[35] Nevertheless, the fact that what seem to us obvious errors happened to a novel which did, after all, enjoy a certain celebrity, and not merely once but upon three separate occasions, confirms that a certain tenuousness existed on the frontier of history and fiction.

In conclusion, let us examine two early notes which may be attributed with some certainty to the period from 1824 and 1825 in which *Cinq-Mars* was conceived and written. Here we find Vigny affirming both the symbolic nature of a narrative work of fiction and the necessary truth-value of historical fiction.

The first text is an assertion of the philosophical utility of the inventions of the creative imagination:

> La tragédie ou le roman, en général toute œuvre d'imagination qui crée des caractères, est à la philosophie ce que l'exception est à la règle: l'imagination donne du corps aux idées et leur crée des types et des symboles vivants qui sont comme la forme palpable et la preuve d'une théorie abstraite. La philosophie peut donc puiser des armes dans cet arsenal créé par les grands hommes et des expressions, des noms qui donnent plus de netteté aux idées. Ainsi lorsqu'elle traitera du *vague des passions* en prenant pour terme *René*, elle sera comprise; de la séduction *Lovelace, Clarisse,* etc.
>
> (Vigny, ***Journal*** 880)

This passage does not specifically mention the historical novel, but Vigny reverts to the same ideas in the **"Réflexions sur la vérité dans l'art."** Although in the draft the "grands hommes" to whom he refers seem to be authors, Vigny's preface not only refers "à Lovelace et à Clarisse" (Vigny, *Cinq-Mars* 25) but it also develops the same idea of characters as symbols in the context of the historical novel:

> . . . la MUSE vient raconter, dans ses formes passionnées, les aventures d'un personnage que je sais avoir vécu . . . elle recompose ses événements, selon la plus grande idée de vice ou de vertu que l'on puisse concevoir de lui, réparant les vides, voilant les disparates de sa vie et lui rendant cette unité parfaite de conduite que nous aimons à voir représentée même dans le mal . . .
>
> (Vigny, *Cinq-Mars* 24)

According to Vigny, ancient historians believed that this was the manner of characterization which historians properly used: ". . . ils jetaient quelques figures colossales, symboles d'un grand caractère ou d'une haute pensée."[36] Consider Vigny's terms: symbols of character, and symbols of thought. Again Vigny deliberately straddles the border between history and fiction. Indeed, the preface to **Cinq-Mars** is above all the theoretical grounding of this position.

The second passage that seems to be a note toward a preface to his historical novel is to be found in the Vigny papers at Chantilly:

à mes yeux

La première des Muses est la Vérité. Si vous rencontrez la Beauté dans les arts, c'est elle. [Previous state: La Beauté dans tous les arts n'est autre chose qu'elle-même.] Il faut lui rendre un culte entier. [c'est une] [elle] [Ce Dieu] elle n'admet point de partage. je pense qu'il faut la dire même à contre-cœur. Lorsqu'il s'agit de tenter le tableau d'un siècle; [que serait-il sans ombres?] [L'historien] doit vivre dans le tems passé sans se souvenir du présent quoique [il fau] cet ouvrage historique ne soit pas l'histoire, il en procede et doit tenir d'elle la vérité des couleurs.

La pensée est [doit être] sans amour et sans haine; elle passe parmi [doit planer sur] les lieux et les âges [et] comme un voyageur étranger et dit ce qu'elle a vu; avec une indépendante impartialité—

[l'auteur n'a] [l'appro]

. . . . .

toutes les [grandes] masses historiques sont[37]

(Along with his idiosyncratic punctuation and capitalization, Vigny's corrections have all been reproduced so as to make apparent the tentativeness of the text.)[38]

Although the development of thought in this passage is rather rudimentary, its fundamental ideas are clear—truth, beauty, and historical fiction—as is its drift: that beauty and truth are compatible in the historical novel. Vigny's problem seems to be to generalize the notion of "vérité de couleur" so that it extends to the historical novel as a whole.[39] The prevailing theory of truth at this time being a correspondence theory, resemblance in details or in the portrayal of character deserved to be called "vérité." But Vigny's abortive attempt to elaborate an account of the truth of historical fiction foundered, perhaps, on the inadequacy of the naive perceptionism which, suggested by the notion of color, takes possession of the thought of the passage near the point at which it breaks off.

All the evidence, then, points to the conclusion that Vigny was willing to allow and to exploit opportunities afforded by the intermingling of historical and fictional narratives which was characteristic of the period. In a letter addressed to a poet who has not been identified, thanking him warmly for his encouraging praise of **Cinq-Mars,** we find phrasing which reflects Vigny's wish to believe that his work has both esthetic and historical merit. On the one hand, he underscores the historical value of the work by emphasizing the usefulness of **Cinq-Mars**: "j'ai tenté d'être utile à notre France, elle m'a récompensé déjà par d'honorables suffrages. . . ."[40] On the other hand, the work's merit ultimately depends upon its imaginative inspiration: "Si cet ouvrage vous a plu, c'est sans doute que vous y avez reconnu quelque chose. . . . Je l'adore comme vous et même involontairement; on ne saura jamais combien de fois la simple prose que vous louez a été la traduction d'une première pensée poétique que j'éteignais à regret . . ." (Vigny, **Correspondence** 225).

Notes

1. All editions published while Vigny was alive bear the subtitle on the title page, and it is regrettable that twentieth-century editions have not always followed this practice. Twentieth-century editorial offhandedness in regard to Vigny, of which this is a minor example, can often be linked to the editorial practices of Fernand Baldensperger, whose two editions of the complete works have, until recently, been the scholarly standard. Baldensperger's 1948-50 two-volume Pléiade edition provides the subtitle of *Cinq-Mars* only in the novel's listing in the *Table des matières* of the second volume (1395), but not on the volume's other title pages (5, 13, 27). Curiously, however, the subtitle is given on the front of the dust jacket, where the titles included in the second volume are listed. Such haphazard quirkiness characterizes Baldensperger's editorial work.

2. Vigny, *Cinq-Mars, or A Conspiracy under Louis XIII,* trans. William Hazlitt (Boston: Little, Brown, 1907) xviii.

3. Alfred de Vigny, *Journal d'un poète,* in *Œuvres complètes,* Bibliothèque de la Pléiade (Paris: Gallimard, 1948-50) 2: 921, 1342.

4. Pierre Boncenne, ed., *La Bibliothèque idéale,* rev. ed. (Paris: Albin Michel, 1989) 192, 197.

5. Northrop Frye, *Anatomy of Criticism: Four Essays* (Princeton: Princeton UP, 1957) 187.

6. Vigny, *Cinq-Mars, ou une conjuration sous Louis XIII,* 2nd ed. (Paris: Le Normant Père, 1826) 4: 468.

7. The precise dating of the preface presents certain difficulties. It appears in a version of the third edition by Urbain Canel dated 1827. In different editions the writing of the preface is dated "janvier 1826," "janvier 1829," and "1827." For an extended discussion of these difficulties, see Mark K. Jensen, "The Use, Abuse, and Perfection of History: Vigny's *Cinq-Mars* and the 'Réflexions sur la vérité dans l'art'" (diss. U of California at Berkeley, 1989) 338-53.

8. The term "positivist" is used here to refer to the attempt to commit the quest for knowledge of human affairs to a natural-scientific model. "The basic fault of every form of positivism in the social sciences is the belief that the act of interpretation can be circumvented." Peter L. Berger and Hansfried Kellner, *Sociology Reinterpreted: An Essay on Method and Vocation* (Garden City, NY: Anchor Books, 1981) 129.

9. Vigny, *Correspondence d'Alfred de Vigny,* ed. M. Ambrière, Thierry Bodin, Loïc Chotard, François Escoube, André Jarry, Roger Pierrot, and Jean Sangnier, vol. 1: *1816-juillet 1830* (Paris: PUF, 1989) 213.

10. André Jarry, "Contribution à une histoire de la carrière militaire de Vigny," *Bulletin de l'Association des Amis d'Alfred de Vigny* 5 (1972-73) 41-42.

11. Paul T. Comeau, *Diehards and Innovators: The French Romantic Struggle: 1800-1830* (New York: Peter Lang, 1988) 201.

12. Bibliothèque du Musée Condé, Chantilly, 91 G 13, fol. 64. Following a convention in the Vigny literature, I shall refer to this bound collection of miscellaneous notes as "Chantilly, Tome III."

13. In an essay entitled "From History to Hysteria: Nineteenth-Century Discourse on Loudun," Frank Paul Bowman reminds us that Vigny's novel is one of many nineteenth-century exploitations of the lurid history of Loudun that do violence to history "knowingly and unhesitatingly." *French Romanticism: Intertextual and Interdisciplinary Readings* (Baltimore and London: Johns Hopkins UP, 1990) 111.

14. P. de Vaissière, *Conjuration de Cinq-Mars* (Paris: Hachette, 1928) 109.

15. Cited in Vigny, *Morceaux choisis,* ed. René Canat, 5th ed. (Paris: Didier & Privat, 1933) 98.

16. For example, in Part I, ch. 2-3 of François Germain, *L'Imagination d'Alfred de Vigny* (Paris: José Corti, 1962) 41-88, a psychological approach makes Vigny's symbols a means of discovery not of the nature of the universe, but of himself: "si Vigny s'intéresse à l'énigme de l'univers, c'est qu'il consacre son attention à se découvrir lui-même" (87). The complexity of these symbols is due, according to Germain, not to the complexity of the world but to the complexity of his inner life.

17. Herbert J. Hunt, *The Epic in Nineteenth-Century France: A Study in Heroic and Humanitarian Poetry from "Les Martyrs" to "Les Siècles Morts"* (Oxford: Basil Blackwell, 1941).

18. Vigny, *Mémoires inédits,* ed. Jean Sangnier (Paris: Gallimard, 1958) 179-289.

19. Friedrich Meinecke, *Historism: The Rise of a New Historical Outlook,* trans. J. E. Anderson (London: Routledge & Kegan Paul, 1972) iv.

20. Simon Schama's recent work seems to me exemplary in this regard. See his *Citizens: A Chronicle of the French Revolution* (New York: Alfred A. Knopf, 1989), and *Dead Certainties: Unwarranted Speculations* (New York: Alfred A. Knopf, 1991). The critical response to Schama's latest work is ably summarized by Louis P. Masur, *William and Mary Quarterly* 49 (1992) 120-32, who notes that "for those who in recent years have given thought to the canons that govern historical writing, the question of the place of fiction in history has arrived" (123). The literature on this question is immense and can hardly be summarized here. The valuable discussions in *History and Theory,* Beiheft 25: *Knowing and Telling History: The Anglo-Saxon Debate,* ed. F. R. Ankersmit (1986) provide a useful survey of the literature. For more attention to Continental figures, see Hayden White, *The Content of the Form: Narrative Discourse and Historical Representation* (Baltimore: Johns Hopkins UP, 1987).

21. "We ascribe a naive temperament to a person if he, in his judgment of things, overlooks their artificial nature and contrived aspects and heeds only their simple nature." Schiller, *"Naive and Sentimental Poetry" and "On the Sublime": Two Essays,* trans. Julius A. Elias (New York: Frederick Ungar, 1966) 92.

22. Ranke's famous expression ("as it really was") occurs in his preface to his *History of the Latin and Teutonic Nations, 1494-1535.* (The work actually covers only the years 1494-1514, since a planned second volume was never finished.) Leopold von Ranke, *The Secret of World History: Selected Writings on the Art and Sciences of History,* ed. and trans. Roger Wines (New York: Fordham UP, 1981) 58.

23. Quoted in G. P. Gooch, *History and Historians in the Nineteenth Century* (Boston: Beacon Press, 1959) 74.

24. See Pierre Martino, "Le Voyage de Chateaubriand en Amérique: essai de mise au point, 1952," *Revue d'Histoire Littéraire de la France* 52 (1952) 149-64, pursuing the line of inquiry opened by Joseph Bédier's 1899 article.

25. In the preface to *Récits des temps mérovingiens* (Paris: Furne, Jouvet, 1866) 8-10. "Ce moment d'enthousiasme fut peut-être décisif pour ma vocation à venir . . . Voilà une dette envers l'écrivain de génie qui a ouvert et qui domine le nouveau siècle littéraire" (10).

26. Augustin Thierry, *Dix Ans d'études historiques* (Paris: Furne, Jouvet, 1866) 397. This was a review of *Ivanhoe* which appeared in the *Censeur Européen* on May 27, 1820.

27. Gooch 181-82. For an interesting discussion of Guizot's philosophy of history and its debt to literature, see Hans Kellner, *Language and Historical Representation: Getting the Story Crooked* (Madison: U of Wisconsin P, 1989) 79-101.

28. B. Reizov, *L'Historiographie romantique française: 1815-1830* (Moscow: Editions en Langues Etrangères, n.d.) 7-8.

29. See J. B. Bury, *The Idea of Progress: An Inquiry into Its Growth and Origin* (New York: Macmillan, 1932) 260-77.

30. Paul Bénichou, *Le Temps des prophètes: doctrines de l'âge romantique* (Paris: Gallimard, 1977) 381.

31. This "tableau de la presse" in *Le Constitutionnel* of August 26, 1826 is given in full in Eugène Hatin,

Bibliographie historique et critique de la presse périodique française (Paris: Firmin Didot, 1866) 355-56.

32. *Le Constitutionnel* (26 August 1826) 3. The editor, in a note, complains about the negativity of these remarks: "Ces assertions et ces suppositions sont purement gratuites. Peu de personnes pensent que le génie de la poésie et des arts soit perdu parmi nous. Béranger, Casimir Delavigne, Lamartine et quelques autres, prouvent que le génie de la poésie n'est pas éteint en France. Les arts d'imitation sont aussi cultivés avec succès; et pour ne parler que de la peinture, Gros, Gérard, Hersent, Guérin, ne soutiennent-ils pas l'honneur de l'école française? Nous n'aimons ni le faux ni le maniéré; l'immense popularité de Voltaire, le plus naturel des écrivains, en est une preuve décisive. Laissons les hommes médiocres crier à la décadence; ils ont leurs raisons pour dénigrer le siècle. Un homme d'esprit, tel que celui qui a composé l'article sur l'ouvrage de M. Thierry, devrait être moins injuste et moins tranchant."

33. Claude Duchet, "L'Illusion historique: l'enseignement des préfaces (1815-1832)," *Revue d'Histoire Littéraire de la France* 75 (1975) 249.

34. *Bibliographie de la France, ou Journal de l'imprimerie et la librairie, et des cartes géographiques, gravures, lithographes et œuvres de musique: Année 1826* (Paris: Pillet Aîné, 1826) 242.

35. A thorough study of the systems employed by the *Bibliographie de la France* would certainly be fruitful. It is interesting, for example, that in 1855 the title of the pigeonhole into which Vigny's novel falls has been renamed "Contes, nouvelles et romans français; Auteurs vivants" (*Bibliographie . . . 1855* 403).

36. Vigny, *Cinq-Mars* 24. The 1859, 1861, and 1863 editions of *Cinq-Mars* have "et d'une haute pensée"; all previous editions read "ou d'une haute pensée." There is reason to believe that this reading crept in unnoticed by Vigny along with other errors. See Appendix 1: "A Critical Edition of Vigny's 'Réflexions sur la vérité dans l'art,'" in Jensen 529-47.

37. Chantilly, Tome III, fol. 13v. Words crossed out in the manuscript have been bracketed. (A first state of the second sentence is given in brackets; Vigny has rewritten all the words except "dans les arts.")

38. The version of the text soon to be published in Alphonse Bouvet's new Pléiade edition of Vigny's prose writings, graciously communicated to me by M. Bouvet, with his notes, makes the fragment seem clearer than in fact it is. Bouvet restores the word "l'historien," which Vigny has barred in the ms. The sentence as it stands has no subject; it demands a substantive that refers to the author of a historical novel, not to a historian. Bouvet proposes 1826 as the date of this passage, but the same page recto bears a plan of the last chapter of *Cinq-Mars* with some text. Since the novel was at the printers by the end of 1825, it may be supposed this was written around the same time. There is no reason to think that it was inspired by Sainte-Beuve's article in *Le Globe* of 8 July 1826, as Bouvet suggests may have been the case.

39. As the term is used in the reviews of *Cinq-Mars* in 1826, "vérité" meant accuracy in historical details providing local color as well as an ambiance which gave to the fictional scene the feel of authenticity, and to the reader the sense of "being there." Thus, in the first comment on the novel in the press, the Catholic paper *Le Drapeau Blanc* praised the novel for its "vérité": "M. de Vigny a donné dans ce livre une scène du règne de Louis XIII; elle est rendu avec beaucoup de vérité et d'une manière fort pittoresque. Autour du célèbre cardinal se groupent les plus illustres personnages du siècle; les détails les plus minutieux de l'époque, les costumes, les conversations, les faits les plus curieux, tout est en relief, et le siècle de Louis XIII est là presque tout entier." *Le Drapeau Blanc* (9 May 1826) 2-3. *Le Courrier Français* said in its review: "La conversation se prolonge, elle est pleine de vérité, et donne la juste mesure de l'esprit de Louis XIII. C'est cette vérité qui fait vivre les ouvrages et qui doit assurer le succès de *Cinq-Mars*." *Le Courrier Français* (19 June 1826) 4. This is evidently the quality for which Vigny was praised in a review in *La Quotidienne*—a review which was, on other counts, rather severe: "[Son] talent est plein de vie; il se trouve particulièrement dans la peinture des caractères. En ceci l'auteur est historien, et toutes les actions qu'il prête à ses personnages, tous les discours qu'il leur fait tenir, sont autant d'attitudes réelles qu'ils ont prises ou qu'ils ont dû prendre. Sans doute ils n'ont rien dit de tout cela, mais d'après leur nature, on sent que lorsqu'ils parlaient, ils devaient avoir ce langage. Il résulte de cet heureux artifice que, s'il y a quelque fiction dans le drame, elle tourne tout entière à la plus grande ressemblance, à la plus vivante physionomie des acteurs." *La Quotidienne* (31 May 1826) 2.

40. Vigny, *Correspondence* 1: 225. Because this letter cites a line of poetry associated with "votre Elvire," it was formerly thought to have been addressed to Lamartine. As the editors of the *Correspondence* note, however, since the verse quoted by Vigny in his letter cannot be attributed to Lamartine, this is probably not the case.

FURTHER READING

Criticism

Bury, J. P. T. "A Glimpse of Vigny in 1830." In *French Studies Bulletin* 19 (Summer 1986): 8-10.
    Provides anecdotal evidence of a likely biographical source for Captain Renaud of Vigny's *Servitude et grandeur militaires.*

Charlton, D. G. "Prose Fiction." In *The French Romantics,* Volume 1, edited by D. G. Charlton, pp. 163-203. Cambridge: Cambridge University Press, 1984.

   Briefly mentions Vigny's *Stello* and *Servitude et grandeur militaires* within a survey of nineteenth-century French narrative fiction.

Corkran, Henriette. "A Little Girl's Recollections of Le Comte Alfred de Vigny." In *Temple Bar* 85 (April 1889): 580-83.

   A selection of notes written to the author by Vigny, as well as her memories of their time together when she was a young child and he a man in his sixties.

Denommé, Robert T. "Chatterton, Ruy Blas, Lorenzaccio: Three Tragic Heroes." In *Laurels* 61, No. 1 (Spring 1990): 55-67.

   Evaluates the historical protagonists of three Romantic dramas, including that of Vigny's *Chatterton.*

Howarth, W. D. "Drama." In *The French Romantics,* Volume 2, edited by D. G. Charlton, pp. 205-247. Cambridge: Cambridge University Press, 1984.

   Assesses Vigny as one of four major French Romantic dramatists, but considers *Chatterton* to be primarily of historical interest.

Whittaker, John. "Chênedollé's *Gladiateur* and Vigny's *Capitaine.*" In *French Studies Bulletin,* No. 57 (Winter 1995): 6-9.

   Compares the heroic mariner of Vigny's poem "La Bouteille à la mer" to the central figure of C. J. L. de Chênedollé's "Le Gladiateur mourant."

Woronzoff, Alexander. "The Pattern of Discovery in Lermontov's *Hero of Our Time* and Vigny's *Servitude et grandeur militaires.*" *Zapiski Russkoi Akademicheskoi Gruppy* 23 (1990): 51-61.

   Traces parallels between the narrative structure of Vigny's *Servitude et grandeur militaires* and that of Mikhail Lermontov's *Hero of Our Time,* observing the likely influence of the former upon the latter.

Additional coverage of de Vigny's life and career is contained in the following sources published by the Gale Group: *Dictionary of Literary Biography,* **Vols. 119 and 192;** *DISCovering Authors Modules*: *Poets*; **and** *Poetry Criticism,* **Vol. 26.**

How to Use This Index

The main references

> **Calvino, Italo**
> 1923-1985 .... CLC 5, 8, 11, 22, 33, 39,
> 73; SSC 3

list all author entries in the following Gale Literary Criticism series:

BLC = *Black Literature Criticism*
CLC = *Contemporary Literary Criticism*
CLR = *Children's Literature Review*
CMLC = *Classical and Medieval Literature Criticism*
DA = *DISCovering Authors*
DAB = *DISCovering Authors: British*
DAC = *DISCovering Authors: Canadian*
DAM = *DISCovering Authors: Modules*
　　DRAM: Dramatists Module; MST: Most-Studied Authors Module;
　　MULT: Multicultural Authors Module; NOV: Novelists Module;
　　POET: Poets Module; POP: Popular Fiction and Genre Authors Module
DC = *Drama Criticism*
HLC = *Hispanic Literature Criticism*
LC = *Literature Criticism from 1400 to 1800*
NCLC = *Nineteenth-Century Literature Criticism*
NNAL = *Native North American Literature*
PC = *Poetry Criticism*
SSC = *Short Story Criticism*
TCLC = *Twentieth-Century Literary Criticism*
WLC = *World Literature Criticism, 1500 to the Present*

The cross-references

> See also CANR 23; CA 85-88;
> obituary CA116

list all author entries in the following Gale biographical and literary sources:

AAYA = *Authors & Artists for Young Adults*
AITN = *Authors in the News*
BEST = *Bestsellers*
BW = *Black Writers*
CA = *Contemporary Authors*
CAAS = *Contemporary Authors Autobiography Series*
CABS = *Contemporary Authors Bibliographical Series*
CANR = *Contemporary Authors New Revision Series*
CAP = *Contemporary Authors Permanent Series*
CDALB = *Concise Dictionary of American Literary Biography*
CDBLB = *Concise Dictionary of British Literary Biography*
DLB = *Dictionary of Literary Biography*
DLBD = *Dictionary of Literary Biography Documentary Series*
DLBY = *Dictionary of Literary Biography Yearbook*
HW = *Hispanic Writers*
JRDA = *Junior DISCovering Authors*
MAICYA = *Major Authors and Illustrators for Children and Young Adults*
MTCW = *Major 20th-Century Writers*
SAAS = *Something about the Author Autobiography Series*
SATA = *Something about the Author*
YABC = *Yesterday's Authors of Books for Children*

Literary Criticism Series
Cumulative Author Index

Ambrose, Stephen E(dward)
1936- .... **CLC 145**
See also CA 1-4R; CANR 3, 43, 57, 83;
NCFS 2; SATA 40
Amichai, Yehuda 1924-2000 .. **CLC 9, 22, 57, 116**
See also CA 85-88; 189; CANR 46, 60, 99;
CWW 2; MTCW 1
Amichai, Yehudah
See Amichai, Yehuda
Amiel, Henri Frederic 1821-1881 .... **NCLC 4**
Amis, Kingsley (William)
1922-1995 ...... **CLC 1, 2, 3, 5, 8, 13, 40, 44, 129; DA; DAB; DAC; DAM MST, NOV**
See also AITN 2; BRWS 2; CA 9-12R; 150;
CANR 8, 28, 54; CDBLB 1945-1960;
CN; CP; DA3; DLB 15, 27, 100, 139;
DLBY 96; HGG; INT CANR-8; MTCW
1, 2; RGEL; RGSF; SFW
Amis, Martin (Louis) 1949- .... **CLC 4, 9, 38, 62, 101**
See also BEST 90:3; BRWS 4; CA 65-68;
CANR 8, 27, 54, 73, 95; CN; DA3; DLB
14, 194; INT CANR-27; MTCW 1
Ammons, A(rchie) R(andolph)
1926-2001 ...... **CLC 2, 3, 5, 8, 9, 25, 57, 108; DAM POET; PC 16**
See also AITN 1; CA 9-12R; CANR 6, 36,
51, 73; CP; CSW; DLB 5, 165; MTCW 1,
2; RGAL
Amo, Tauraatua i
See Adams, Henry (Brooks)
Amory, Thomas 1691(?)-1788 .... **LC 48**
Anand, Mulk Raj 1905- .. **CLC 23, 93; DAM NOV**
See also CA 65-68; CANR 32, 64; CN;
MTCW 1, 2; RGSF
Anatol
See Schnitzler, Arthur
Anaximander c. 611B.C.-c.
546B.C. .... **CMLC 22**
Anaya, Rudolfo A(lfonso) 1937- ... **CLC 23, 148; DAM MULT, NOV; HLC 1**
See also AAYA 20; CA 45-48; CAAS 4;
CANR 1, 32, 51; CN; DLB 82, 206; HW
1; MTCW 1, 2; NFS 12; RGAL; RGSF
Andersen, Hans Christian
1805-1875 .... **NCLC 7, 79; DA; DAB; DAC; DAM MST, POP; SSC 6; WLC**
See also CLR 6; DA3; MAICYA; RGSF;
RGWL; SATA 100; YABC 1
Anderson, C. Farley
See Mencken, H(enry) L(ouis); Nathan,
George Jean
Anderson, Jessica (Margaret) Queale
1916- .... **CLC 37**
See also CA 9-12R; CANR 4, 62; CN
Anderson, Jon (Victor) 1940- . **CLC 9; DAM POET**
See also CA 25-28R; CANR 20
Anderson, Lindsay (Gordon)
1923-1994 .... **CLC 20**
See also CA 125; 128; 146; CANR 77
Anderson, Maxwell 1888-1959 .... **TCLC 2; DAM DRAM**
See also CA 105; 152; DLB 7, 228; MTCW
2; RGAL
Anderson, Poul (William)
1926-2001 .... **CLC 15**
See also AAYA 5, 34; CA 1-4R; 181; CAAE
181; CAAS 2; CANR 2, 15, 34, 64; CLR
58; DLB 8; FANT; INT CANR-15;
MTCW 1, 2; SATA 90; SATA-Brief 39;
SATA-Essay 106; SCFW 2; SFW; SUFW
Anderson, Robert (Woodruff)
1917- .... **CLC 23; DAM DRAM**
See also AITN 1; CA 21-24R; CANR 32;
DLB 7

Anderson, Sherwood 1876-1941 ..... **TCLC 1, 10, 24; DA; DAB; DAC; DAM MST, NOV; SSC 1, 46; WLC**
See also AAYA 30; CA 104; 121; CANR
61; CDALB 1917-1929; DA3; DLB 4, 9,
86; DLBD 1; GLL 2; MTCW 1, 2; NFS
4; RGAL; RGSF; SSFS 4,10,11
Andier, Pierre
See Desnos, Robert
Andouard
See Giraudoux, Jean(-Hippolyte)
Andrade, Carlos Drummond de ..... **CLC 18**
See also Drummond de Andrade, Carlos
See also RGWL
Andrade, Mario de 1893-1945 .... **TCLC 43**
See also RGWL
Andreae, Johann V(alentin)
1586-1654 .... **LC 32**
See also DLB 164
Andreas Capellanus fl. c. 1185- .... **CMLC 45**
See also DLB 208
Andreas-Salome, Lou 1861-1937 ... **TCLC 56**
See also CA 178; DLB 66
Andress, Lesley
See Sanders, Lawrence
Andrewes, Lancelot 1555-1626 .... **LC 5**
See also DLB 151, 172
Andrews, Cicily Fairfield
See West, Rebecca
Andrews, Elton V.
See Pohl, Frederik
Andreyev, Leonid (Nikolaevich)
1871-1919 .... **TCLC 3**
See also CA 104; 185
Andric, Ivo 1892-1975 .... **CLC 8; SSC 36**
See also CA 81-84; 57-60; CANR 43, 60;
DLB 147; MTCW 1; RGSF; RGWL
Androvar
See Prado (Calvo), Pedro
Angelique, Pierre
See Bataille, Georges
Angell, Roger 1920- .... **CLC 26**
See also CA 57-60; CANR 13, 44, 70; DLB
171, 185
Angelou, Maya 1928- .... **CLC 12, 35, 64, 77; BLC 1; DA; DAB; DAC; DAM MST, MULT, POET, POP; PC 32; WLCS**
See also AAYA 7, 20; AMWS 4; BW 2, 3;
CA 65-68; CANR 19, 42, 65; CDALB;
CLR 53; CP; CPW; CSW; CWP; DA3;
DLB 38; MTCW 1, 2; NCFS 2; NFS 2;
PFS 2, 3; RGAL; SATA 49; YAW
Anna Comnena 1083-1153 .... **CMLC 25**
Annensky, Innokenty (Fyodorovich)
1856-1909 .... **TCLC 14**
See also CA 110; 155
Annunzio, Gabriele d'
See D'Annunzio, Gabriele
Anodos
See Coleridge, Mary E(lizabeth)
Anon, Charles Robert
See Pessoa, Fernando (Ant
Anouilh, Jean (Marie Lucien Pierre)
1910-1987 .... **CLC 1, 3, 8, 13, 40, 50; DAM DRAM; DC 8**
See also CA 17-20R; 123; CANR 32; DFS
9, 10; EW; GFL 1789 to the Present;
MTCW 1, 2; RGWL
Anthony, Florence
See Ai
Anthony, John
See Ciardi, John (Anthony)
Anthony, Peter
See Shaffer, Anthony (Joshua); Shaffer, Pe-
ter (Levin)
Anthony, Piers 1934- .... **CLC 35; DAM POP**
See also AAYA 11; CA 21-24R; CANR 28,
56, 73; CPW; DLB 8; FANT; MTCW 1,
2; SAAS 22; SATA 84; SFW; YAW

Anthony, Susan B(rownell)
1820-1906 .... **TCLC 84**
See also FW
Antoine, Marc
See Proust, (Valentin-Louis-George-Eug
Antoninus, Brother
See Everson, William (Oliver)
Antoninus, Marcus Aurelius
121-180 .... **CMLC 45**
See also AW
Antonioni, Michelangelo 1912- .... **CLC 20, 144**
See also CA 73-76; CANR 45, 77
Antschel, Paul 1920-1970
See Celan, Paul
See also CA 85-88; CANR 33, 61; MTCW
1
Anwar, Chairil 1922-1949 .... **TCLC 22**
See also CA 121
Anzaldua, Gloria (Evanjelina) 1942-
See also CA 175; CSW; CWP; DLB 122;
FW; HLCS 1; RGAL
Apess, William 1798-1839(?) .... **NCLC 73; DAM MULT**
See also DLB 175; NNAL
Apollinaire, Guillaume 1880-1918 .. **TCLC 3, 8, 51; DAM POET; PC 7**
See also CA 152; GFL 1789 to the Present;
MTCW 1; RGWL; WP
Appelfeld, Aharon 1932- ... **CLC 23, 47; SSC 42**
See also CA 112; 133; CANR 86; CWW 2;
RGSF
Apple, Max (Isaac) 1941- .... **CLC 9, 33**
See also CA 81-84; CANR 19, 54; DLB
130
Appleman, Philip (Dean) 1926- .... **CLC 51**
See also CA 13-16R; CAAS 18; CANR 6,
29, 56
Appleton, Lawrence
See Lovecraft, H(oward) P(hillips)
Apteryx
See Eliot, T(homas) S(tearns)
Apuleius, (Lucius Madaurensis)
125(?)-175(?) .... **CMLC 1**
See also AW; DLB 211; RGWL; SUFW
Aquin, Hubert 1929-1977 .... **CLC 15**
See also CA 105; DLB 53
Aquinas, Thomas 1224(?)-1274 ..... **CMLC 33**
See also DLB 115; EW
Aragon, Louis 1897-1982 .. **CLC 3, 22; DAM NOV, POET**
See also CA 69-72; 108; CANR 28, 71;
DLB 72; GFL 1789 to the Present; GLL
2; MTCW 1, 2; RGWL
Arany, Janos 1817-1882 .... **NCLC 34**
Aranyos, Kakay 1847-1910
See Mikszath, Kalman
Arbuthnot, John 1667-1735 .... **LC 1**
See also DLB 101
Archer, Herbert Winslow
See Mencken, H(enry) L(ouis)
Archer, Jeffrey (Howard) 1940- ...... **CLC 28; DAM POP**
See also AAYA 16; BEST 89:3; CA 77-80;
CANR 22, 52, 95; CPW; DA3; INT
CANR-22
Archer, Jules 1915- .... **CLC 12**
See also CA 9-12R; CANR 6, 69; SAAS 5;
SATA 4, 85
Archer, Lee
See Ellison, Harlan (Jay)
Archilochus c. 7th cent. B.C.- .... **CMLC 44**
See also DLB 176
Arden, John 1930- .... **CLC 6, 13, 15; DAM DRAM**
See also BRWS 2; CA 13-16R; CAAS 4;
CANR 31, 65, 67; CBD; CD; DFS 9;
DLB 13; MTCW 1

Blasco Ibanez, Vicente
1867-1928 .... **TCLC 12; DAM NOV**
See also CA 110; 131; CANR 81; DA3;
EW; HW 1, 2; MTCW 1

Blatty, William Peter 1928- .... **CLC 2; DAM POP**
See also CA 5-8R; CANR 9; HGG

Bleeck, Oliver
See Thomas, Ross (Elmore)

Blessing, Lee 1949- .... **CLC 54**
See also CAD; CD

Blight, Rose
See Greer, Germaine

Blish, James (Benjamin) 1921-1975 . **CLC 14**
See also CA 1-4R; 57-60; CANR 3; DLB
8; MTCW 1; SATA 66; SCFW 2; SFW

Bliss, Reginald
See Wells, H(erbert) G(eorge)

Blixen, Karen (Christentze Dinesen)
1885-1962
See Dinesen, Isak
See also CA 25-28; CANR 22, 50; CAP 2;
DA3; MTCW 1, 2; NCFS 2; SATA 44

Bloch, Robert (Albert) 1917-1994 ..... **CLC 33**
See also AAYA 29; CA 5-8R, 179; 146;
CAAE 179; CAAS 20; CANR 5, 78;
DA3; DLB 44; HGG; INT CANR-5;
MTCW 1; SATA 12; SATA-Obit 82; SFW;
SUFW

Blok, Alexander (Alexandrovich)
1880-1921 .... **TCLC 5; PC 21**
See also CA 104; 183; EW; RGWL

Blom, Jan
See Breytenbach, Breyten

Bloom, Harold 1930- .... **CLC 24, 103**
See also CA 13-16R; CANR 39, 75, 92;
DLB 67; MTCW 1; RGAL

Bloomfield, Aurelius
See Bourne, Randolph S(illiman)

Blount, Roy (Alton), Jr. 1941- .... **CLC 38**
See also CA 53-56; CANR 10, 28, 61;
CSW; INT CANR-28; MTCW 1, 2

Bloy, Leon 1846-1917 .... **TCLC 22**
See also CA 121; 183; DLB 123; GFL 1789
to the Present

Blume, Judy (Sussman) 1938- .. **CLC 12, 30; DAM NOV, POP**
See also AAYA 3, 26; CA 29-32R; CANR
13, 37, 66; CLR 2, 15, 69; CPW; DA3;
DLB 52; JRDA; MAICYA; MTCW 1, 2;
SATA 2, 31, 79; WYA; YAW

Blunden, Edmund (Charles)
1896-1974 .... **CLC 2, 56**
See also CA 17-18; 45-48; CANR 54; CAP
2; DLB 20, 100, 155; MTCW 1; PAB

Bly, Robert (Elwood) 1926- .... **CLC 1, 2, 5, 10, 15, 38, 128; DAM POET**
See also AMWS 4; CA 5-8R; CANR 41,
73; CP; DA3; DLB 5; MTCW 1, 2; RGAL

Boas, Franz 1858-1942 .... **TCLC 56**
See also CA 115; 181

Bobette
See Simenon, Georges (Jacques Christian)

Boccaccio, Giovanni 1313-1375 ... **CMLC 13; SSC 10**
See also RGSF; RGWL

Bochco, Steven 1943- .... **CLC 35**
See also AAYA 11; CA 124; 138

Bodel, Jean 1167(?)-1210 .... **CMLC 28**

Bodenheim, Maxwell 1892-1954 .... **TCLC 44**
See also CA 110; 187; DLB 9, 45; RGAL

Bodker, Cecil 1927- .... **CLC 21**
See also CA 73-76; CANR 13, 44; CLR 23;
MAICYA; SATA 14

Boell, Heinrich (Theodor)
1917-1985 ... **CLC 2, 3, 6, 9, 11, 15, 27, 32, 72; DA; DAB; DAC; DAM MST, NOV; SSC 23; WLC**
See also Boll, Heinrich
See also CA 21-24R; 116; CANR 24; DA3;
DLB 69; DLBY 85; EW; MTCW 1, 2

Boerne, Alfred
See Doeblin, Alfred

Boethius c. 480-c. 524 .... **CMLC 15**
See also DLB 115; RGWL

Boff, Leonardo (Genezio Darci)
1938- .... **CLC 70; DAM MULT; HLC 1**
See also CA 150; HW 2

Bogan, Louise 1897-1970 .... **CLC 4, 39, 46, 93; DAM POET; PC 12**
See also AMWS 3; CA 73-76; 25-28R;
CANR 33, 82; DLB 45, 169; MTCW 1,
2; RGAL

Bogarde, Dirk
See Van Den Bogarde, Derek Jules Gaspard
Ulric Niven

Bogosian, Eric 1953- .... **CLC 45, 141**
See also CA 138; CAD; CD

Bograd, Larry 1953- .... **CLC 35**
See also CA 93-96; CANR 57; SAAS 21;
SATA 33, 89

Boiardo, Matteo Maria 1441-1494 .... **LC 6**

Boileau-Despreaux, Nicolas 1636-1711 . **LC 3**
See also GFL Beginnings to 1789; RGWL

Bojer, Johan 1872-1959 .... **TCLC 64**
See also CA 189

Bok, Edward W. 1863-1930 .... **TCLC 101**
See also DLB 91; DLBD 16

Boland, Eavan (Aisling) 1944- .. **CLC 40, 67, 113; DAM POET**
See also BRWS 5; CA 143; CANR 61; CP;
CWP; DLB 40; FW; MTCW 2; PFS 12

Boll, Heinrich
See Boell, Heinrich (Theodor)
See also RGSF; RGWL

Bolt, Lee
See Faust, Frederick (Schiller)

Bolt, Robert (Oxton) 1924-1995 ...... **CLC 14; DAM DRAM**
See also CA 17-20R; 147; CANR 35, 67;
CBD; DFS 2; DLB 13, 233; MTCW 1

Bombal, Maria Luisa 1910-1980 ...... **SSC 37; HLCS 1**
See also CA 127; CANR 72; HW 1; RGSF

Bombet, Louis-Alexandre-Cesar
See Stendhal

Bomkauf
See Kaufman, Bob (Garnell)

Bonaventura .... **NCLC 35**
See also DLB 90

Bond, Edward 1934- .... **CLC 4, 6, 13, 23; DAM DRAM**
See also BRWS 1; CA 25-28R; CANR 38,
67; CBD; CD; DFS 3,8; DLB 13; MTCW
1

Bonham, Frank 1914-1989 .... **CLC 12**
See also AAYA 1; CA 9-12R; CANR 4, 36;
JRDA; MAICYA; SAAS 3; SATA 1, 49;
SATA-Obit 62; TCWW 2; YAW

Bonnefoy, Yves 1923- .. **CLC 9, 15, 58; DAM MST, POET**
See also CA 85-88; CANR 33, 75, 97;
CWW 2; GFL 1789 to the Present; MTCW
1, 2

Bontemps, Arna(ud Wendell)
1902-1973 ..... **CLC 1, 18; BLC 1; DAM MULT, NOV, POET**
See also BW 1; CA 1-4R; 41-44R; CANR
4, 35; CLR 6; CWRI; DA3; DLB 48, 51;
JRDA; MAICYA; MTCW 1, 2; SATA 2,
44; SATA-Obit 24; WCH; WP

Booth, Martin 1944- .... **CLC 13**
See also CA 93-96; CAAE 188; CAAS 2;
CANR 92

Booth, Philip 1925- .... **CLC 23**
See also CA 5-8R; CANR 5, 88; CP; DLBY
82

Booth, Wayne C(layson) 1921- .... **CLC 24**
See also CA 1-4R; CAAS 5; CANR 3, 43;
DLB 67

Borchert, Wolfgang 1921-1947 .... **TCLC 5**
See also CA 104; 188; DLB 69, 124

Borel, Petrus 1809-1859 .... **NCLC 41**
See also GFL 1789 to the Present

Borges, Jorge Luis 1899-1986 ... **CLC 1, 2, 3, 4, 6, 8, 9, 10, 13, 19, 44, 48, 83; DA; DAB; DAC; DAM MST, MULT; HLC 1; PC 22, 32; SSC 4, 41; WLC**
See also AAYA 26; CA 21-24R; CANR 19,
33, 75; DA3; DLB 113; DLBY 86; DNFS;
HW 1, 2; MTCW 1, 2; RGSF; RGWL;
SFW; SSFS 4,9; TCLC 109

Borowski, Tadeusz 1922-1951 .... **TCLC 9**
See also CA 106; 154; RGSF

Borrow, George (Henry)
1803-1881 .... **NCLC 9**
See also DLB 21, 55, 166

Bosch (Gavino), Juan 1909-
See also CA 151; DAM MST, MULT; DLB
145; HLCS 1; HW 1, 2

Bosman, Herman Charles
1905-1951 .... **TCLC 49**
See also Malan, Herman
See also CA 160; DLB 225; RGSF

Bosschere, Jean de 1878(?)-1953 ... **TCLC 19**
See also CA 115; 186

Boswell, James 1740-1795 .. **LC 4, 50; DA; DAB; DAC; DAM MST; WLC**
See also CDBLB 1660-1789; DLB 104, 142

Bottomley, Gordon 1874-1948 ..... **TCLC 107**
See also CA 120; 192; DLB 10

Bottoms, David 1949- .... **CLC 53**
See also CA 105; CANR 22; CSW; DLB
120; DLBY 83

Boucicault, Dion 1820-1890 .... **NCLC 41**

Boucolon, Maryse
See Cond

Bourget, Paul (Charles Joseph)
1852-1935 .... **TCLC 12**
See also CA 107; DLB 123; GFL 1789 to
the Present

Bourjaily, Vance (Nye) 1922- .... **CLC 8, 62**
See also CA 1-4R; CAAS 1; CANR 2, 72;
CN; DLB 2, 143

Bourne, Randolph S(illiman)
1886-1918 .... **TCLC 16**
See also Aurelius
See also AMW; CA 117; 155; DLB 63

Bova, Ben(jamin William) 1932- ...... **CLC 45**
See also AAYA 16; CA 5-8R; CAAS 18;
CANR 11, 56, 94; CLR 3; DLBY 81; INT
CANR-11; MAICYA; MTCW 1; SATA 6,
68; SFW

Bowen, Elizabeth (Dorothea Cole)
1899-1973 . **CLC 1, 3, 6, 11, 15, 22, 118; DAM NOV; SSC 3, 28**
See also BRWS 2; CA 17-18; 41-44R;
CANR 35; CAP 2; CDBLB 1945-1960;
DA3; DLB 15, 162; FW; HGG; MTCW
1, 2; RGSF; SSFS 5; SUFW

Bowering, George 1935- .... **CLC 15, 47**
See also CA 21-24R; CAAS 16; CANR 10;
DLB 53

Bowering, Marilyn R(uthe) 1949- .... **CLC 32**
See also CA 101; CANR 49; CP; CWP

Bowers, Edgar 1924-2000 .... **CLC 9**
See also CA 5-8R; 188; CANR 24; CP;
CSW; DLB 5

Bowie, David .... **CLC 17**
See also Jones, David Robert

Bromell, Henry 1947- .... **CLC 5**
See also CA 53-56; CANR 9

Bromfield, Louis (Brucker)
1896-1956 .... **TCLC 11**
See also CA 107; 155; DLB 4, 9, 86;
RGAL; RHW

Broner, E(sther) M(asserman)
1930- .... **CLC 19**
See also CA 17-20R; CANR 8, 25, 72; CN;
DLB 28

Bronk, William (M.) 1918-1999 .... **CLC 10**
See also CA 89-92; 177; CANR 23; CP;
DLB 165

Bronstein, Lev Davidovich
See Trotsky, Leon

Bronte, Anne 1820-1849 ..... **NCLC 4, 71, 102**
See also BRW; DA3; DLB 21, 199

Bronte, Charlotte 1816-1855 ...... **NCLC 3, 8,
33, 58; DA; DAB; DAC; DAM MST,
NOV; WLC**
See also AAYA 17; BRW; CDBLB 1832-
1890; DA3; DLB 21, 159, 199; NFS 4

Bronte, Emily (Jane) 1818-1848 ... **NCLC 16,
35; DA; DAB; DAC; DAM MST, NOV,
POET; PC 8; WLC**
See also AAYA 17; BRW; CDBLB 1832-
1890; DA3; DLB 21, 32, 199

Brontes
See Bront

Brooke, Frances 1724-1789 .... **LC 6, 48**
See also DLB 39, 99

Brooke, Henry 1703(?)-1783 .... **LC 1**
See also DLB 39

Brooke, Rupert (Chawner)
1887-1915 .... **TCLC 2, 7; DA; DAB;
DAC; DAM MST, POET; PC 24; WLC**
See also BRW; BRWS 3; CA 104; 132;
CANR 61; CDBLB 1914-1945; DLB 19;
GLL 2; MTCW 1, 2; PFS 7

Brooke-Haven, P.
See Wodehouse, P(elham) G(renville)

Brooke-Rose, Christine 1926(?)- ...... **CLC 40**
See also BRWS 4; CA 13-16R; CANR 58;
CN; DLB 14, 231; SFW

Brookner, Anita 1928- . **CLC 32, 34, 51, 136;
DAB; DAM POP**
See also BRWS 4; CA 114; 120; CANR 37,
56, 87; CN; CPW; DA3; DLB 194; DLBY
87; MTCW 1, 2

Brooks, Cleanth 1906-1994 . **CLC 24, 86, 110**
See also CA 17-20R; 145; CANR 33, 35;
CSW; DLB 63; DLBY 94; INT CANR-
35; MTCW 1, 2

Brooks, George
See Baum, L(yman) Frank

Brooks, Gwendolyn (Elizabeth)
1917-2000 .. **CLC 1, 2, 4, 5, 15, 49, 125;
BLC 1; DA; DAC; DAM MST, MULT,
POET; PC 7; WLC**
See also AAYA 20; AFAW 1, 2; AITN 1;
AMWS 3; BW 2, 3; CA 1-4R; 190; CANR
1, 27, 52, 75; CDALB 1941-1968; CLR
27; CP; CWP; DA3; DLB 5, 76, 165;
MTCW 1, 2; PFS 1, 2, 4, 6; RGAL; SATA
6; SATA-Obit 123; WP

Brooks, Mel .... **CLC 12**
See also Kaminsky, Melvin
See also AAYA 13; DLB 26

Brooks, Peter 1938- .... **CLC 34**
See also CA 45-48; CANR 1

Brooks, Van Wyck 1886-1963 .... **CLC 29**
See also CA 1-4R; CANR 6; DLB 45, 63,
103

Brophy, Brigid (Antonia)
1929-1995 .... **CLC 6, 11, 29, 105**
See also CA 5-8R; 149; CAAS 4; CANR
25, 53; CBD; CN; CWD; DA3; DLB 14;
MTCW 1, 2

Brosman, Catharine Savage 1934- ..... **CLC 9**
See also CA 61-64; CANR 21, 46

Brossard, Nicole 1943- .... **CLC 115**
See also CA 122; CAAS 16; CCA 1; CWP;
CWW 2; DLB 53; FW; GLL 2

Brother Antoninus
See Everson, William (Oliver)

The Brothers Quay
See Quay, Stephen; Quay, Timothy

Broughton, T(homas) Alan 1936- ..... **CLC 19**
See also CA 45-48; CANR 2, 23, 48

Broumas, Olga 1949- .... **CLC 10, 73**
See also CA 85-88; CANR 20, 69; CP;
CWP; GLL 2

Broun, Heywood 1888-1939 .... **TCLC 104**
See also DLB 29, 171

Brown, Alan 1950- .... **CLC 99**
See also CA 156

Brown, Charles Brockden
1771-1810 .... **NCLC 22, 74**
See also AMWS 1; CDALB 1640-1865;
DLB 37, 59, 73; FW; HGG; RGAL

Brown, Christy 1932-1981 .... **CLC 63**
See also CA 105; 104; CANR 72; DLB 14

Brown, Claude 1937- .... **CLC 30; BLC 1;
DAM MULT**
See also AAYA 7; BW 1, 3; CA 73-76;
CANR 81

Brown, Dee (Alexander) 1908- . **CLC 18, 47;
DAM POP**
See also AAYA 30; CA 13-16R; CAAS 6;
CANR 11, 45, 60; CPW; CSW; DA3;
DLBY 80; MTCW 1, 2; SATA 5, 110;
TCWW 2

Brown, George
See Wertmueller, Lina

Brown, George Douglas
1869-1902 .... **TCLC 28**
See also Douglas, George
See also CA 162

Brown, George Mackay 1921-1996 ... **CLC 5,
48, 100**
See also BRWS 6; CA 21-24R; 151; CAAS
6; CANR 12, 37, 67; CN; CP; DLB 14,
27, 139; MTCW 1; RGSF; SATA 35

Brown, (William) Larry 1951- .... **CLC 73**
See also CA 130; 134; CSW; INT 133

Brown, Moses
See Barrett, William (Christopher)

Brown, Rita Mae 1944- .... **CLC 18, 43, 79;
DAM NOV, POP**
See also CA 45-48; CANR 2, 11, 35, 62,
95; CN; CPW; CSW; DA3; FW; INT
CANR-11; MTCW 1, 2; NFS 9; RGAL

Brown, Roderick (Langmere) Haig-
See Haig-Brown, Roderick (Langmere)

Brown, Rosellen 1939- .... **CLC 32**
See also CA 77-80; CAAS 10; CANR 14,
44, 98; CN

Brown, Sterling Allen 1901-1989 ...... **CLC 1,
23, 59; BLC 1; DAM MULT, POET**
See also AFAW 1, 2; BW 1, 3; CA 85-88;
127; CANR 26; DA3; DLB 48, 51, 63;
MTCW 1, 2; RGAL; WP

Brown, Will
See Ainsworth, William Harrison

Brown, William Wells 1815-1884 ... **NCLC 2,
89; BLC 1; DAM MULT; DC 1**
See also DLB 3, 50; RGAL

Browne, (Clyde) Jackson 1948(?)- ... **CLC 21**
See also CA 120

Browning, Elizabeth Barrett
1806-1861 ...... **NCLC 1, 16, 61, 66; DA;
DAB; DAC; DAM MST, POET; PC 6;
WLC**
See also CDBLB 1832-1890; DA3; DLB
32, 199; PAB; PFS 2; WP

Browning, Robert 1812-1889 . **NCLC 19, 79;
DA; DAB; DAC; DAM MST, POET;
PC 2; WLCS**
See also BRW; CDBLB 1832-1890; DA3;
DLB 32, 163; PAB; PFS 1; RGEL; TEA;
WP; YABC 1

Browning, Tod 1882-1962 .... **CLC 16**
See also CA 141; 117

Brownson, Orestes Augustus
1803-1876 .... **NCLC 50**
See also DLB 1, 59, 73

Bruccoli, Matthew J(oseph) 1931- ... **CLC 34**
See also CA 9-12R; CANR 7, 87; DLB 103

Bruce, Lenny .... **CLC 21**
See also Schneider, Leonard Alfred

Bruin, John
See Brutus, Dennis

Brulard, Henri
See Stendhal

Brulls, Christian
See Simenon, Georges (Jacques Christian)

Brunner, John (Kilian Houston)
1934-1995 .... **CLC 8, 10; DAM POP**
See also CA 1-4R; 149; CAAS 8; CANR 2,
37; CPW; MTCW 1, 2; SCFW 2; SFW

Bruno, Giordano 1548-1600 .... **LC 27**
See also RGWL

Brutus, Dennis 1924- .... **CLC 43; BLC 1;
DAM MULT, POET; PC 24**
See also BW 2, 3; CA 49-52; CAAS 14;
CANR 2, 27, 42, 81; CP; DLB 117, 225

Bryan, C(ourtlandt) D(ixon) B(arnes)
1936- .... **CLC 29**
See also CA 73-76; CANR 13, 68; DLB
185; INT CANR-13

Bryan, Michael
See Moore, Brian
See also CCA 1

Bryan, William Jennings
1860-1925 .... **TCLC 99**

Bryant, William Cullen 1794-1878 . **NCLC 6,
46; DA; DAB; DAC; DAM MST,
POET; PC 20**
See also AMWS 1; CDALB 1640-1865;
DLB 3, 43, 59, 189; PAB; RGAL

Bryusov, Valery Yakovlevich
1873-1924 .... **TCLC 10**
See also CA 107; 155; SFW

Buchan, John 1875-1940 .... **TCLC 41; DAB;
DAM POP**
See also CA 108; 145; CMW; DLB 34, 70,
156; HGG; MTCW 1; RGEL; RHW;
YABC 2

Buchanan, George 1506-1582 .... **LC 4**
See also DLB 152

Buchanan, Robert 1841-1901 .... **TCLC 107**
See also CA 179; DLB 18, 35

Buchheim, Lothar-Guenther 1918- .... **CLC 6**
See also CA 85-88

Buchner, (Karl) Georg 1813-1837 . **NCLC 26**
See also EW; RGSF; RGWL

Buchwald, Art(hur) 1925- .... **CLC 33**
See also AITN 1; CA 5-8R; CANR 21, 67;
MTCW 1, 2; SATA 10

Buck, Pearl S(ydenstricker)
1892-1973 .... **CLC 7, 11, 18, 127; DA;
DAB; DAC; DAM MST, NOV**
See also AITN 1; AMWS 2; CA 1-4R; 41-
44R; CANR 1, 34; CDALBS; DA3; DLB
9, 102; MTCW 1, 2; RGAL; RHW; SATA
1, 25

Buckler, Ernest 1908-1984 .... **CLC 13; DAC;
DAM MST**
See also CA 11-12; 114; CAP 1; CCA 1;
DLB 68; SATA 47

Buckley, Vincent (Thomas)
1925-1988 .... **CLC 57**
See also CA 101

Cain, James M(allahan) 1892-1977 .. **CLC 3, 11, 28**
See also AITN 1; CA 17-20R; 73-76; CANR 8, 34, 61; CMW; DLB 226; MTCW 1; RGAL

Caine, Hall 1853-1931 .... **TCLC 97**
See also RHW

Caine, Mark
See Raphael, Frederic (Michael)

Calasso, Roberto 1941- .... **CLC 81**
See also CA 143; CANR 89

Calderon de la Barca, Pedro 1600-1681 .... **LC 23; DC 3; HLCS 1**
See also RGWL

Caldwell, Erskine (Preston) 1903-1987 .. **CLC 1, 8, 14, 50, 60; DAM NOV; SSC 19**
See also AITN 1; AMW; CA 1-4R; 121; CAAS 1; CANR 2, 33; DA3; DLB 9, 86; MTCW 1, 2; RGAL; RGSF

Caldwell, (Janet Miriam) Taylor (Holland) 1900-1985 .. **CLC 2, 28, 39; DAM NOV, POP**
See also CA 5-8R; 116; CANR 5; DA3; DLBD 17; RHW

Calhoun, John Caldwell 1782-1850 .... **NCLC 15**
See also DLB 3

Calisher, Hortense 1911- ..... **CLC 2, 4, 8, 38, 134; DAM NOV; SSC 15**
See also CA 1-4R; CANR 1, 22, 67; CN; DA3; DLB 2; INT CANR-22; MTCW 1, 2; RGAL; RGSF

Callaghan, Morley Edward 1903-1990 ...... **CLC 3, 14, 41, 65; DAC; DAM MST**
See also CA 9-12R; 132; CANR 33, 73; DLB 68; MTCW 1, 2; RGEL; RGSF

Callimachus c. 305B.C.-c. 240B.C. .... **CMLC 18**
See also DLB 176; RGWL

Calvin, Jean
See Calvin, John
See also GFL Beginnings to 1789

Calvin, John 1509-1564 .... **LC 37**
See also Calvin, Jean

Calvino, Italo 1923-1985 .... **CLC 5, 8, 11, 22, 33, 39, 73; DAM NOV; SSC 3**
See also CA 85-88; 116; CANR 23, 61; DLB 196; MTCW 1, 2; RGSF; RGWL; SFW; SSFS 12

Cameron, Carey 1952- .... **CLC 59**
See also CA 135

Cameron, Peter 1959- .... **CLC 44**
See also CA 125; CANR 50; DLB 234; GLL 2

Camoens, Luis Vaz de 1524(?)-1580
See also EW; HLCS 1

Camoes, Luis de 1524(?)-1580 .... **LC 62; HLCS 1; PC 31**
See also RGWL

Campana, Dino 1885-1932 .... **TCLC 20**
See also CA 117; DLB 114

Campanella, Tommaso 1568-1639 .... **LC 32**
See also RGWL

Campbell, John W(ood, Jr.) 1910-1971 .... **CLC 32**
See also CA 21-22; 29-32R; CANR 34; CAP 2; DLB 8; MTCW 1; SFW

Campbell, Joseph 1904-1987 .... **CLC 69**
See also AAYA 3; BEST 89:2; CA 1-4R; 124; CANR 3, 28, 61; DA3; MTCW 1, 2

Campbell, Maria 1940- .... **CLC 85; DAC**
See also CA 102; CANR 54; CCA 1; NNAL

Campbell, (John) Ramsey 1946- ..... **CLC 42; SSC 19**
See also CA 57-60; CANR 7; HGG; INT CANR-7; SUFW

Campbell, (Ignatius) Roy (Dunnachie) 1901-1957 .... **TCLC 5**
See also AFW; CA 104; 155; DLB 20, 225; MTCW 2

Campbell, Thomas 1777-1844 .... **NCLC 19**
See also DLB 93; 144; RGEL

Campbell, Wilfred .... **TCLC 9**
See also Campbell, William

Campbell, William 1858(?)-1918
See Campbell, Wilfred
See also CA 106; DLB 92

Campion, Jane .... **CLC 95**
See also AAYA 33; CA 138; CANR 87

Camus, Albert 1913-1960 ...... **CLC 1, 2, 4, 9, 11, 14, 32, 63, 69, 124; DA; DAB; DAC; DAM DRAM, MST, NOV; DC 2; SSC 9; WLC**
See also AAYA 36; CA 89-92; DA3; DLB 72; GFL 1789 to the Present; MTCW 1, 2; NFS 6; RGSF; RGWL; SSFS 4

Canby, Vincent 1924-2000 .... **CLC 13**
See also CA 81-84; 191

Cancale
See Desnos, Robert

Canetti, Elias 1905-1994 .. **CLC 3, 14, 25, 75, 86**
See also CA 21-24R; 146; CANR 23, 61; 79; CWW 2; DA3; DLB 85, 124; MTCW 1, 2; RGWL

Canfield, Dorothea F.
See Fisher, Dorothy (Frances) Canfield

Canfield, Dorothea Frances
See Fisher, Dorothy (Frances) Canfield

Canfield, Dorothy
See Fisher, Dorothy (Frances) Canfield

Canin, Ethan 1960- .... **CLC 55**
See also CA 131; 135

Cankar, Ivan 1876-1918 .... **TCLC 105**
See also DLB 147

Cannon, Curt
See Hunter, Evan

Cao, Lan 1961- .... **CLC 109**
See also CA 165

Cape, Judith
See Page, P(atricia) K(athleen)
See also CCA 1

Capek, Karel 1890-1938 ... **TCLC 6, 37; DA; DAB; DAC; DAM DRAM, MST, NOV; DC 1; SSC 36; WLC**
See also CA 104; 140; DA3; DFS 7, 11 !**; MTCW 1; RGSF; RGWL; SCFW 2; SFW

Capote, Truman 1924-1984 . **CLC 1, 3, 8, 13, 19, 34, 38, 58; DA; DAB; DAC; DAM MST, NOV, POP; SSC 2; WLC**
See also AMWS 3; CA 5-8R; 113; CANR 18, 62; CDALB 1941-1968; CPW; DA3; DLB 2, 185, 227; DLBY 80, 84; GLL 1; MTCW 1, 2; NCFS 2; RGAL; RGSF; SATA 91; SSFS 2

Capra, Frank 1897-1991 .... **CLC 16**
See also CA 61-64; 135

Caputo, Philip 1941- .... **CLC 32**
See also CA 73-76; CANR 40; YAW

Caragiale, Ion Luca 1852-1912 ...... **TCLC 76**
See also CA 157

Card, Orson Scott 1951- ..... **CLC 44, 47, 50; DAM POP**
See also AAYA 11; CA 102; CANR 27, 47, 73; CPW; DA3; FANT; INT CANR-27; MTCW 1, 2; NFS 5; SATA 83; SFW; YAW

Cardenal, Ernesto 1925- .... **CLC 31; DAM MULT, POET; HLC 1; PC 22**
See also CA 49-52; CANR 2, 32, 66; CWW 2; HW 1, 2; MTCW 1, 2; RGWL

Cardozo, Benjamin N(athan) 1870-1938 .... **TCLC 65**
See also CA 117; 164

Carducci, Giosue (Alessandro Giuseppe) 1835-1907 .... **TCLC 32**
See also CA 163; EW; RGWL

Carew, Thomas 1595(?)-1640 . **LC 13; PC 29**
See also DLB 126; PAB; RGEL

Carey, Ernestine Gilbreth 1908- ...... **CLC 17**
See also CA 5-8R; CANR 71; SATA 2

Carey, Peter 1943- .... **CLC 40, 55, 96**
See also CA 123; 127; CANR 53, 76; CN; INT 127; MTCW 1, 2; RGSF; SATA 94

Carleton, William 1794-1869 .... **NCLC 3**
See also DLB 159; RGEL; RGSF

Carlisle, Henry (Coffin) 1926- .... **CLC 33**
See also CA 13-16R; CANR 15, 85

Carlsen, Chris
See Holdstock, Robert P.

Carlson, Ron(ald F.) 1947- .... **CLC 54**
See also CA 105; CAAE 189; CANR 27

Carlyle, Thomas 1795-1881 .... **NCLC 22, 70; DA; DAB; DAC; DAM MST**
See also CDBLB 1789-1832; DLB 55; 144; RGEL

Carman, (William) Bliss 1861-1929 .... **TCLC 7; DAC; PC 34**
See also CA 104; 152; DLB 92; RGEL

Carnegie, Dale 1888-1955 .... **TCLC 53**

Carossa, Hans 1878-1956 .... **TCLC 48**
See also CA 170; DLB 66

Carpenter, Don(ald Richard) 1931-1995 .... **CLC 41**
See also CA 45-48; 149; CANR 1, 71

Carpenter, Edward 1844-1929 .... **TCLC 88**
See also CA 163; GLL 1

Carpentier (y Valmont), Alejo 1904-1980 ..... **CLC 8, 11, 38, 110; DAM MULT; HLC 1; SSC 35**
See also CA 65-68; 97-100; CANR 11, 70; DLB 113; HW 1, 2; LAW; RGSF; RGWL

Carr, Caleb 1955(?)- .... **CLC 86**
See also CA 147; CANR 73; DA3

Carr, Emily 1871-1945 .... **TCLC 32**
See also CA 159; DLB 68; FW; GLL 2

Carr, John Dickson 1906-1977 .... **CLC 3**
See also Fairbairn, Roger
See also CA 49-52; 69-72; CANR 3, 33, 60; CMW; MTCW 1, 2

Carr, Philippa
See Hibbert, Eleanor Alice Burford

Carr, Virginia Spencer 1929- .... **CLC 34**
See also CA 61-64; DLB 111

Carrere, Emmanuel 1957- .... **CLC 89**

Carrier, Roch 1937- .... **CLC 13, 78; DAC; DAM MST**
See also CA 130; CANR 61; CCA 1; DLB 53; SATA 105

Carroll, James P. 1943(?)- .... **CLC 38**
See also CA 81-84; CANR 73; MTCW 1

Carroll, Jim 1951- .... **CLC 35, 143**
See also AAYA 17; CA 45-48; CANR 42

Carroll, Lewis ... **NCLC 2, 53; PC 18; WLC**
See also Dodgson, Charles Lutwidge
See also AAYA 39; CDBLB 1832-1890; CLR 2, 18; DLB 18, 163, 178; DLBY 98; FANT; JRDA; NFS 7; PFS 11; RGEL

Carroll, Paul Vincent 1900-1968 ...... **CLC 10**
See also CA 9-12R; 25-28R; DLB 10; RGEL

Carruth, Hayden 1921- ..... **CLC 4, 7, 10, 18, 84; PC 10**
See also CA 9-12R; CANR 4, 38, 59; CP; DLB 5, 165; INT CANR-4; MTCW 1, 2; SATA 47

Carson, Rachel Louise 1907-1964 ... **CLC 71; DAM POP**
See also ANW; CA 77-80; CANR 35; DA3; FW; MTCW 1, 2; NCFS 1; SATA 23

Chapman, Lee
See Bradley, Marion Zimmer
See also GLL 1

Chapman, Walker
See Silverberg, Robert

Chappell, Fred (Davis) 1936- ..... **CLC 40, 78**
See also CA 5-8R; CAAS 4; CANR 8, 33, 67; CN; CP; CSW; DLB 6, 105; HGG

Char, Rene(-emile) 1907-1988 ..... **CLC 9, 11, 14, 55; DAM POET**
See also CA 13-16R; 124; CANR 32; GFL 1789 to the Present; MTCW 1, 2; RGWL

Charby, Jay
See Ellison, Harlan (Jay)

Chardin, Pierre Teilhard de
See Teilhard de Chardin, (Marie Joseph) Pierre

Charlemagne 742-814 .... **CMLC 37**

Charles I 1600-1649 .... **LC 13**

Charriere, Isabelle de 1740-1805 .. **NCLC 66**

Chartier, Emile-Auguste
See Alain

Charyn, Jerome 1937- .... **CLC 5, 8, 18**
See also CA 5-8R; CAAS 1; CANR 7, 61; CMW; CN; DLBY 83; MTCW 1

Chase, Adam
See Marlowe, Stephen

Chase, Mary (Coyle) 1907-1981 .... **DC 1**
See also CA 77-80; 105; CAD; CWD; DFS 11; DLB 228; SATA 17; SATA-Obit 29

Chase, Mary Ellen 1887-1973 .... **CLC 2**
See also CA 13-16; 41-44R; CAP 1; SATA 10

Chase, Nicholas
See Hyde, Anthony
See also CCA 1

Chateaubriand, Francois Rene de
1768-1848 .... **NCLC 3**
See also DLB 119; EW; GFL 1789 to the Present; RGWL

Chatterje, Sarat Chandra 1876-1936(?)
See Chatterji, Saratchandra
See also CA 109

Chatterji, Bankim Chandra
1838-1894 .... **NCLC 19**

Chatterji, Saratchandra .... **TCLC 13**
See also Chatterje, Sarat Chandra
See also CA 186

Chatterton, Thomas 1752-1770 ..... **LC 3, 54; DAM POET**
See also DLB 109; RGEL

Chatwin, (Charles) Bruce
1940-1989 . **CLC 28, 57, 59; DAM POP**
See also AAYA 4; BEST 90:1; BRWS 4; CA 85-88; 127; CPW; DLB 194, 204

Chaucer, Daniel
See Ford, Ford Madox
See also RHW

Chaucer, Geoffrey 1340(?)-1400 .. **LC 17, 56; DA; DAB; DAC; DAM MST, POET; PC 19; WLCS**
See also CDBLB Before 1660; DA3; DLB 146; PAB; RGEL; WP

Chavez, Denise (Elia) 1948-
See also CA 131; CANR 56, 81; DAM MULT; DLB 122; FW; HLC 1; HW 1, 2; MTCW 2

Chaviaras, Strates 1935-
See Haviaras, Stratis
See also CA 105

Chayefsky, Paddy .... **CLC 23**
See also Chayefsky, Sidney
See also CAD; DLB 7, 44; DLBY 81; RGAL

Chayefsky, Sidney 1923-1981
See Chayefsky, Paddy
See also CA 9-12R; 104; CANR 18; DAM DRAM

Chedid, Andree 1920- .... **CLC 47**
See also CA 145; CANR 95

Cheever, John 1912-1982 ..... **CLC 3, 7, 8, 11, 15, 25, 64; DA; DAB; DAC; DAM MST, NOV, POP; SSC 1, 38; WLC**
See also AMWS 1; CA 5-8R; 106; CABS 1; CANR 5, 27, 76; CDALB 1941-1968; CPW; DA3; DLB 2, 102, 227; DLBY 80, 82; INT CANR-5; MTCW 1, 2; RGAL; RGSF; SSFS 2

Cheever, Susan 1943- .... **CLC 18, 48**
See also CA 103; CANR 27, 51, 92; DLBY 82; INT CANR-27

Chekhonte, Antosha
See Chekhov, Anton (Pavlovich)

Chekhov, Anton (Pavlovich)
1860-1904 .... **TCLC 3, 10, 31, 55, 96; DA; DAB; DAC; DAM DRAM, MST; DC 9; SSC 2, 28, 41; WLC**
See also CA 104; 124; DA3; DFS 1, 5, 10, 12; EW; RGSF; RGWL; SATA 90; SSFS 5

Cheney, Lynne V. 1941- .... **CLC 70**
See also CA 89-92; CANR 58

Chernyshevsky, Nikolay Gavrilovich
1828-1889 .... **NCLC 1**
See also DLB 238

Cherry, Carolyn Janice 1942-
See Cherryh, C. J.
See also CA 65-68; CANR 10; FANT; SFW; YAW

Cherryh, C. J. .... **CLC 35**
See also Cherry, Carolyn Janice
See also AAYA 24; DLBY 80; SATA 93

Chesnutt, Charles W(addell)
1858-1932 .. **TCLC 5, 39; BLC 1; DAM MULT; SSC 7**
See also AFAW 1, 2; BW 1, 3; CA 106; 125; CANR 76; DLB 12, 50, 78; MTCW 1, 2; RGAL; RGSF; SSFS 11

Chester, Alfred 1929(?)-1971 .... **CLC 49**
See also CA 33-36R; DLB 130

Chesterton, G(ilbert) K(eith)
1874-1936 . **TCLC 1, 6, 64; DAM NOV, POET; PC 28; SSC 1, 46**
See also BRW; CA 104; 132; CANR 73; CDBLB 1914-1945; CMW; DLB 10, 19, 34, 70, 98, 149, 178; FANT; MTCW 1, 2; RGEL; RGSF; SATA 27; SUFW

Chiang, Pin-chin 1904-1986
See Ding Ling
See also CA 118

Ch'ien Chung-shu 1910- .... **CLC 22**
See also CA 130; CANR 73; MTCW 1, 2

Chikamatsu Monzaemon 1653-1724 ... **LC 66**
See also RGWL

Child, L. Maria
See Child, Lydia Maria

Child, Lydia Maria 1802-1880 .. **NCLC 6, 73**
See also DLB 1, 74; RGAL; SATA 67

Child, Mrs.
See Child, Lydia Maria

Child, Philip 1898-1978 .... **CLC 19, 68**
See also CA 13-14; CAP 1; RHW; SATA 47

Childers, (Robert) Erskine
1870-1922 .... **TCLC 65**
See also CA 113; 153; DLB 70

Childress, Alice 1920-1994 .. **CLC 12, 15, 86, 96; BLC 1; DAM DRAM, MULT, NOV; DC 4**
See also AAYA 8; BW 2, 3; CA 45-48; 146; CAD; CANR 3, 27, 50, 74; CLR 14; CWD; DA3; DFS 2,8; DLB 7, 38; JRDA; MAICYA; MTCW 1, 2; RGAL; SATA 7, 48, 81; YAW

Chin, Frank (Chew, Jr.) 1940- ...... **CLC 135; DAM MULT; DC 7**
See also CA 33-36R; CANR 71; CD; DLB 206; RGAL

Chislett, (Margaret) Anne 1943- ...... **CLC 34**
See also CA 151

Chitty, Thomas Willes 1926- .... **CLC 11**
See also Hinde, Thomas
See also CA 5-8R; CN

Chivers, Thomas Holley
1809-1858 .... **NCLC 49**
See also DLB 3; RGAL

Choi, Susan .... **CLC 119**

Chomette, Rene Lucien 1898-1981
See Clair, Rene
See also CA 103

Chomsky, (Avram) Noam 1928- ...... **CLC 132**
See also CA 17-20R; CANR 28, 62; DA3; MTCW 1, 2

Chopin, Kate . **TCLC 5, 14; DA; DAB; SSC 8; WLCS**
See also Chopin, Katherine
See also AAYA 33; AMWS 1; CDALB 1865-1917; DLB 12, 78; NFS 3; RGAL; RGSF; SSFS 2

Chopin, Katherine 1851-1904
See Chopin, Kate
See also CA 104; 122; DAC; DAM MST, NOV; DA3; FW

Chretien de Troyes c. 12th cent. - . **CMLC 10**
See also DLB 208; RGWL

Christie
See Ichikawa, Kon

Christie, Agatha (Mary Clarissa)
1890-1976 .... **CLC 1, 6, 8, 12, 39, 48, 110; DAB; DAC; DAM NOV**
See also AAYA 9; AITN 1, 2; BRWS 2; CA 17-20R; 61-64; CANR 10, 37; CDBLB 1914-1945; CMW; CPW; DA3; DFS 2; DLB 13, 77; MSW; MTCW 1, 2; NFS 8; RGEL; RHW; SATA 36; YAW

Christie, (Ann) Philippa
See Pearce, Philippa
See also CA 5-8R; CANR 4; CWRI; FANT

Christine de Pizan 1365(?)-1431(?) .... **LC 9**
See also DLB 208; RGWL

Chubb, Elmer
See Masters, Edgar Lee

Chulkov, Mikhail Dmitrievich
1743-1792 .... **LC 2**
See also DLB 150

Churchill, Caryl 1938- .... **CLC 31, 55; DC 5**
See also BRWS 4; CA 102; CANR 22, 46; CBD; CWD; DFS 12; DLB 13; FW; MTCW 1; RGEL

Churchill, Charles 1731-1764 .... **LC 3**
See also DLB 109; RGEL

Churchill, Winston (Leonard Spencer)
1874-1965 .... **TCLC 113**
See also CA 97-100; CDBLB 1890-1914; DA3; DLB 100; DLBD 16; MTCW 1, 2

Chute, Carolyn 1947- .... **CLC 39**
See also CA 123

Ciardi, John (Anthony) 1916-1986 . **CLC 10, 40, 44, 129; DAM POET**
See also CA 5-8R; 118; CAAS 2; CANR 5, 33; CLR 19; CWRI; DLB 5; DLBY 86; INT CANR-5; MAICYA; MTCW 1, 2; RGAL; SAAS 26; SATA 1, 65; SATA-Obit 46

Cibber, Colley 1671-1757 .... **LC 66**
See also DLB 84; RGEL

Cicero, Marcus Tullius
106B.C.-43B.C. .... **CMLC 3**
See also AW; DLB 211; RGWL

Cimino, Michael 1943- .... **CLC 16**
See also CA 105

Cullen, Countee 1903-1946 .... **TCLC 4, 37; BLC 1; DA; DAC; DAM MST, MULT, POET; PC 20; WLCS**
See also AFAW 2; AMWS 4; BW 1; CA 108; 124; CDALB 1917-1929; DA3; DLB 4, 48, 51; MTCW 1, 2; PFS 3; RGAL; SATA 18; WP

Cum, R.
See Crumb, R(obert)

Cummings, Bruce F(rederick) 1889-1919
See Barbellion, W. N. P.
See also CA 123

Cummings, E(dward) E(stlin)
1894-1962 .... **CLC 1, 3, 8, 12, 15, 68; DA; DAB; DAC; DAM MST, POET; PC 5; WLC**
See also AMW; CA 73-76; CANR 31; CDALB 1929-1941; DA3; DLB 4, 48; MTCW 1, 2; PAB; PFS 1, 3, 12; RGAL; WP

Cunha, Euclides (Rodrigues Pimenta) da
1866-1909 .... **TCLC 24**
See also CA 123; LAW

Cunningham, E. V.
See Fast, Howard (Melvin)

Cunningham, J(ames) V(incent)
1911-1985 .... **CLC 3, 31**
See also CA 1-4R; 115; CANR 1, 72; DLB 5

Cunningham, Julia (Woolfolk)
1916- .... **CLC 12**
See also CA 9-12R; CANR 4, 19, 36; CWRI; JRDA; MAICYA; SAAS 2; SATA 1, 26

Cunningham, Michael 1952- .... **CLC 34**
See also CA 136; CANR 96; GLL 2

Cunninghame Graham, R. B.
See Cunninghame Graham, Robert (Gallnigad) Bontine

Cunninghame Graham, Robert (Gallnigad) Bontine 1852-1936 .... **TCLC 19**
See also Graham, R(obert) B(ontine) Cunninghame
See also CA 119; 184; DLB 98

Currie, Ellen 19(?)- .... **CLC 44**

Curtin, Philip
See Lowndes, Marie Adelaide (Belloc)

Curtis, Price
See Ellison, Harlan (Jay)

Cutrate, Joe
See Spiegelman, Art

Cynewulf c. 770- .... **CMLC 23**
See also RGEL

Cyrano de Bergerac, Savinien de
1619-1655 .... **LC 65**
See also GFL Beginnings to 1789; RGWL

Czaczkes, Shmuel Yosef
See Agnon, S(hmuel) Y(osef Halevi)

Dabrowska, Maria (Szumska)
1889-1965 .... **CLC 15**
See also CA 106

Dabydeen, David 1955- .... **CLC 34**
See also BW 1; CA 125; CANR 56, 92; CN; CP

Dacey, Philip 1939- .... **CLC 51**
See also CA 37-40R; CAAS 17; CANR 14, 32, 64; CP; DLB 105

Dagerman, Stig (Halvard)
1923-1954 .... **TCLC 17**
See also CA 117; 155

D'Aguiar, Fred 1960- .... **CLC 145**
See also CA 148; CANR 83; CP; DLB 157

Dahl, Roald 1916-1990 ...... **CLC 1, 6, 18, 79; DAB; DAC; DAM MST, NOV, POP**
See also AAYA 15; BRWS 4; CA 1-4R; 133; CANR 6, 32, 37, 62; CLR 1, 7, 41; CPW; DA3; DLB 139; HGG; JRDA; MAICYA; MTCW 1, 2; RGSF; SATA 1, 26, 73; SATA-Obit 65; SSFS 4; YAW

Dahlberg, Edward 1900-1977 .. **CLC 1, 7, 14**
See also CA 9-12R; 69-72; CANR 31, 62; DLB 48; MTCW 1; RGAL

Daitch, Susan 1954- .... **CLC 103**
See also CA 161

Dale, Colin .... **TCLC 18**
See also Lawrence, T(homas) E(dward)

Dale, George E.
See Asimov, Isaac

Dalton, Roque 1935-1975(?) .... **PC 36**
See also CA 176; HLCS 1; HW 2

Daly, Elizabeth 1878-1967 .... **CLC 52**
See also CA 23-24; 25-28R; CANR 60; CAP 2; CMW

Daly, Maureen 1921- .... **CLC 17**
See also AAYA 5; CANR 37, 83; JRDA; MAICYA; SAAS 1; SATA 2; YAW

Damas, Leon-Gontran 1912-1978 .... **CLC 84**
See also BW 1; CA 125; 73-76

Dana, Richard Henry Sr.
1787-1879 .... **NCLC 53**

Daniel, Samuel 1562(?)-1619 .... **LC 24**
See also DLB 62; RGEL

Daniels, Brett
See Adler, Renata

Dannay, Frederic 1905-1982 . **CLC 11; DAM POP**
See also Queen, Ellery
See also CA 1-4R; 107; CANR 1, 39; CMW; DLB 137; MTCW 1

D'Annunzio, Gabriele 1863-1938 ... **TCLC 6, 40**
See also CA 104; 155; RGWL

Danois, N. le
See Gourmont, Remy(-Marie-Charles) de

Dante 1265-1321 .... **CMLC 3, 18, 39; DA; DAB; DAC; DAM MST, POET; PC 21; WLCS**
See also DA3; EFS 1; EW; RGWL; WP

d'Antibes, Germain
See Simenon, Georges (Jacques Christian)

Danticat, Edwidge 1969- .... **CLC 94, 139**
See also AAYA 29; CA 152; CAAE 192; CANR 73; DNFS; MTCW 1; SSFS 1; YAW

Danvers, Dennis 1947- .... **CLC 70**

Danziger, Paula 1944- .... **CLC 21**
See also AAYA 4, 36; CA 112; 115; CANR 37; CLR 20; JRDA; MAICYA; SATA 36, 63, 102; SATA-Brief 30; YAW

Da Ponte, Lorenzo 1749-1838 .... **NCLC 50**

Dario, Ruben 1867-1916 .... **TCLC 4; DAM MULT; HLC 1; PC 15**
See also CA 131; CANR 81; HW 1, 2; MTCW 1, 2; RGWL

Darley, George 1795-1846 .... **NCLC 2**
See also DLB 96; RGEL

Darrow, Clarence (Seward)
1857-1938 .... **TCLC 81**
See also CA 164

Darwin, Charles 1809-1882 .... **NCLC 57**
See also BRWS 7; DLB 57, 166; RGEL

Daryush, Elizabeth 1887-1977 ...... **CLC 6, 19**
See also CA 49-52; CANR 3, 81; DLB 20

Dasgupta, Surendranath
1887-1952 .... **TCLC 81**
See also CA 157

Dashwood, Edmee Elizabeth Monica de la Pasture 1890-1943
See Delafield, E. M.
See also CA 119; 154

Daudet, (Louis Marie) Alphonse
1840-1897 .... **NCLC 1**
See also DLB 123; GFL 1789 to the Present; RGSF

Daumal, Rene 1908-1944 .... **TCLC 14**
See also CA 114

Davenant, William 1606-1668 .... **LC 13**
See also DLB 58, 126; RGEL

Davenport, Guy (Mattison, Jr.)
1927- .... **CLC 6, 14, 38; SSC 16**
See also CA 33-36R; CANR 23, 73; CN; CSW; DLB 130

Davidson, Avram (James) 1923-1993
See Queen, Ellery
See also CA 101; 171; CANR 26; DLB 8; FANT; SFW; SUFW

Davidson, Donald (Grady)
1893-1968 .... **CLC 2, 13, 19**
See also CA 5-8R; 25-28R; CANR 4, 84; DLB 45

Davidson, Hugh
See Hamilton, Edmond

Davidson, John 1857-1909 .... **TCLC 24**
See also CA 118; DLB 19; RGEL

Davidson, Sara 1943- .... **CLC 9**
See also CA 81-84; CANR 44, 68; DLB 185

Davie, Donald (Alfred) 1922-1995 .... **CLC 5, 8, 10, 31; PC 29**
See also BRWS 6; CA 1-4R; 149; CAAS 3; CANR 1, 44; CP; DLB 27; MTCW 1; RGEL

Davies, Ray(mond Douglas) 1944- ... **CLC 21**
See also CA 116; 146; CANR 92

Davies, Rhys 1901-1978 .... **CLC 23**
See also CA 9-12R; 81-84; CANR 4; DLB 139, 191

Davies, (William) Robertson
1913-1995 .... **CLC 2, 7, 13, 25, 42, 75, 91; DA; DAB; DAC; DAM MST, NOV, POP; WLC**
See also Marchbanks, Samuel
See also BEST 89:2; CA 33-36R; 150; CANR 17, 42; CN; CPW; DA3; DLB 68; HGG; INT CANR-17; MTCW 1, 2; RGEL

Davies, Walter C.
See Kornbluth, C(yril) M.

Davies, William Henry 1871-1940 ... **TCLC 5**
See also CA 104; 179; DLB 19, 174; RGEL

Da Vinci, Leonardo 1452-1519 ..... **LC 12, 57, 60**
See also AAYA 40

Davis, Angela (Yvonne) 1944- .... **CLC 77; DAM MULT**
See also BW 2, 3; CA 57-60; CANR 10, 81; CSW; DA3; FW

Davis, B. Lynch
See Bioy Casares, Adolfo; Borges, Jorge Luis

Davis, B. Lynch
See Bioy Casares, Adolfo

Davis, Gordon
See Hunt, E(verette) Howard, (Jr.)

Davis, H(arold) L(enoir) 1896-1960 . **CLC 49**
See also ANW; CA 178; 89-92; DLB 9, 206; SATA 114

Davis, Rebecca (Blaine) Harding
1831-1910 .... **TCLC 6; SSC 38**
See also CA 104; 179; DLB 74, 239; FW; RGAL

Davis, Richard Harding
1864-1916 .... **TCLC 24**
See also CA 114; 179; DLB 12, 23, 78, 79, 189; DLBD 13; RGAL

Davison, Frank Dalby 1893-1970 ..... **CLC 15**
See also CA 116

Davison, Lawrence H.
See Lawrence, D(avid) H(erbert Richards)

Davison, Peter (Hubert) 1928- .... **CLC 28**
See also CA 9-12R; CAAS 4; CANR 3, 43, 84; CP; DLB 5

Davys, Mary 1674-1732 .... **LC 1, 46**
See also DLB 39

Dawson, Fielding 1930- .... **CLC 6**
See also CA 85-88; DLB 130

Destouches, Louis-Ferdinand
1894-1961 .... CLC 9, 15
See also Celine, Louis-Ferdinand
See also CA 85-88; CANR 28; MTCW 1

de Tolignac, Gaston
See Griffith, D(avid Lewelyn) W(ark)

Deutsch, Babette 1895-1982 .... CLC 18
See also CA 1-4R; CANR 4, 79; DLB
45; SATA 1; SATA-Obit 33

Devenant, William 1606-1649 .... LC 13

Devkota, Laxmiprasad 1909-1959 . TCLC 23
See also CA 123

De Voto, Bernard (Augustine)
1897-1955 .... TCLC 29
See also CA 113; 160; DLB 9

De Vries, Peter 1910-1993 ..... CLC 1, 2, 3, 7,
10, 28, 46; DAM NOV
See also CA 17-20R; 142; CANR 41; DLB
6; DLBY 82; MTCW 1, 2

Dewey, John 1859-1952 .... TCLC 95
See also CA 114; 170; RGAL

Dexter, John
See Bradley, Marion Zimmer
See also GLL 1

Dexter, Martin
See Faust, Frederick (Schiller)
See also TCWW 2

Dexter, Pete 1943- .. CLC 34, 55; DAM POP
See also BEST 89:2; CA 127; 131; CPW;
INT 131; MTCW 1

Diamano, Silmang
See Senghor, L

Diamond, Neil 1941- .... CLC 30
See also CA 108

Diaz del Castillo, Bernal 1496-1584 .. LC 31;
HLCS 1

di Bassetto, Corno
See Shaw, George Bernard

Dick, Philip K(indred) 1928-1982 ... CLC 10,
30, 72; DAM NOV, POP
See also AAYA 24; CA 49-52; 106; CANR
2, 16; CPW; DA3; DLB 8; MTCW 1, 2;
NFS 5; SFW

Dickens, Charles (John Huffam)
1812-1870 .... NCLC 3, 8, 18, 26, 37, 50,
86; DA; DAB; DAC; DAM MST, NOV;
SSC 17; WLC
See also AAYA 23; BRW; CDBLB 1832-
1890; CMW; DA3; DLB 21, 55, 70, 159,
166; HGG; JRDA; MAICYA; NFS 4, 5,
10; RGEL; RGSF; SATA 15; SUFW;
WCH; WYA

Dickey, James (Lafayette)
1923-1997 .... CLC 1, 2, 4, 7, 10, 15, 47,
109; DAM NOV, POET, POP
See also AITN 1, 2; AMWS 4; CA 9-12R;
156; CANR 10, 48, 61; CDALB
1968-1988; CP; CPW; CSW; DA3; DLB
5, 193; DLBD 7; DLBY 82, 93, 96, 97,
98; INT CANR-10; MTCW 1, 2; NFS 9;
PFS 6, 11; RGAL

Dickey, William 1928-1994 .... CLC 3, 28
See also CA 9-12R; 145; CANR 24, 79;
DLB 5

Dickinson, Charles 1951- .... CLC 49
See also CA 128

Dickinson, Emily (Elizabeth)
1830-1886 ..... NCLC 21, 77; DA; DAB;
DAC; DAM MST, POET; PC 1; WLC
See also AAYA 22; AMW; AMWR; CDALB
1865-1917; DA3; DLB 1; MAWW; PAB;
PFS 1, 2, 3, 4, 5, 6, 8, 10, 11; RGAL;
SATA 29; WP; WYA

Dickinson, Mrs.Herbert Ward
See Phelps, Elizabeth Stuart

Dickinson, Peter (Malcolm) 1927- .. CLC 12,
35
See also AAYA 9; CA 41-44R; CANR 31,
58, 88; CLR 29; CMW; DLB 87, 161;
JRDA; MAICYA; SATA 5, 62, 95; SFW;
WYA; YAW

Dickson, Carr
See Carr, John Dickson

Dickson, Carter
See Carr, John Dickson

Diderot, Denis 1713-1784 .... LC 26
See also GFL Beginnings to 1789; RGWL

Didion, Joan 1934- .... CLC 1, 3, 8, 14, 32,
129; DAM NOV
See also AITN 1; AMWS 4; CA 5-8R;
CANR 14, 52, 76; CDALB 1968-1988;
CN; DA3; DLB 2, 173, 185; DLBY 81,
86; MTCW 1, 2; NFS 3; RGAL; TCWW

Dietrich, Robert
See Hunt, E(verette) Howard, (Jr.)

Difusa, Pati
See Almodovar, Pedro

Dillard, Annie 1945- .. CLC 9, 60, 115; DAM
NOV
See also AAYA 6; AMWS 6; CA 49-52;
CANR 3, 43, 62, 90; DA3; DLBY 80;
MTCW 1, 2; NCFS 1; RGAL; SATA 10

Dillard, R(ichard) H(enry) W(ilde)
1937- .... CLC 5
See also CA 21-24R; CAAS 7; CANR 10;
CP; CSW; DLB 5

Dillon, Eilis 1920-1994 .... CLC 17
See also CA 9-12R, 182; 147; CAAE 182;
CAAS 3; CANR 4, 38, 78; CLR 26; MAI-
CYA; SATA 2, 74; SATA-Essay 105;
SATA-Obit 83; YAW

Dimont, Penelope
See Mortimer, Penelope (Ruth)

Dinesen, Isak .... CLC 10, 29, 95; SSC 7
See also Blixen, Karen (Christentze
Dinesen)
See also FW; HGG; MTCW 1; NFS 9;
RGSF; RGWL; SSFS 6

Ding Ling .... CLC 68
See also Chiang, Pin-chin

Diphusa, Patty
See Almodovar, Pedro

Disch, Thomas M(ichael) 1940- ... CLC 7, 36
See also AAYA 17; CA 21-24R; CAAS 4;
CANR 17, 36, 54, 89; CLR 18; CP; DA3;
DLB 8; HGG; MAICYA; MTCW 1, 2;
SAAS 15; SATA 92; SFW

Disch, Tom
See Disch, Thomas M(ichael)

d'Isly, Georges
See Simenon, Georges (Jacques Christian)

Disraeli, Benjamin 1804-1881 ... NCLC 2, 39,
79
See also DLB 21, 55; RGEL

Ditcum, Steve
See Crumb, R(obert)

Dixon, Paige
See Corcoran, Barbara (Asenath)

Dixon, Stephen 1936- .... CLC 52; SSC 16
See also CA 89-92; CANR 17, 40, 54, 91;
CN; DLB 130

Doak, Annie
See Dillard, Annie

Dobell, Sydney Thompson
1824-1874 .... NCLC 43
See also DLB 32; RGEL

Doblin, Alfred .... TCLC 13
See also Doeblin, Alfred
See also RGWL

Dobrolyubov, Nikolai Alexandrovich
1836-1861 .... NCLC 5

Dobson, Austin 1840-1921 .... TCLC 79
See also DLB 35; 144

Dobyns, Stephen 1941- .... CLC 37
See also CA 45-48; CANR 2, 18, 99; CMW;
CP

Doctorow, E(dgar) L(aurence)
1931- .... CLC 6, 11, 15, 18, 37, 44, 65,
113; DAM NOV, POP
See also AAYA 22; AITN 2; AMWS 4;
BEST 89:3; CA 45-48; CANR 2, 33, 51,
76, 97; CDALB 1968-1988; CN; CPW;
DA3; DLB 2, 28, 173; DLBY 80; MTCW
1, 2; NFS 6; RGAL; RHW

Dodgson, Charles Lutwidge 1832-1898
See Carroll, Lewis
See also CLR 2; DA; DAB; DAC; DAM
MST, NOV, POET; DA3; MAICYA;
SATA 100; YABC 2

Dodson, Owen (Vincent)
1914-1983 .... CLC 79; BLC 1; DAM
MULT
See also BW 1; CA 65-68; 110; CANR 24;
DLB 76

Doeblin, Alfred 1878-1957 .... TCLC 13
See also Doblin, Alfred
See also CA 110; 141; DLB 66

Doerr, Harriet 1910- .... CLC 34
See also CA 117; 122; CANR 47; INT 122

Domecq, H(onorio Bustos)
See Bioy Casares, Adolfo

Domecq, H(onorio) Bustos
See Bioy Casares, Adolfo; Borges, Jorge
Luis

Domini, Rey
See Lorde, Audre (Geraldine)
See also GLL 1

Dominique
See Proust, (Valentin-Louis-George-Eug

Don, A
See Stephen, SirLeslie

Donaldson, Stephen R(eeder)
1947- .... CLC 46, 138; DAM POP
See also AAYA 36; CA 89-92; CANR 13,
55, 99; CPW; FANT; INT CANR-13;
SATA 121; SFW

Donleavy, J(ames) P(atrick) 1926- .... CLC 1,
4, 6, 10, 45
See also AITN 2; CA 9-12R; CANR 24, 49,
62, 80; CD; CN; DLB 6, 173; INT CANR-
24; MTCW 1, 2; RGAL

Donne, John 1572-1631 .... LC 10, 24; DA;
DAB; DAC; DAM MST, POET; PC 1;
WLC
See also CDBLB Before 1660; DLB 121,
151; PAB; PFS 2,11; RGEL; WP

Donnell, David 1939(?)- .... CLC 34

Donoghue, P. S.
See Hunt, E(verette) Howard, (Jr.)

Donoso (Yanez), Jose 1924-1996 ... CLC 4, 8,
11, 32, 99; DAM MULT; HLC 1; SSC
34
See also CA 81-84; 155; CANR 32, 73;
DLB 113; HW 1, 2; LAW; MTCW 1, 2;
RGSF

Donovan, John 1928-1992 .... CLC 35
See also AAYA 20; CA 97-100; 137; CLR
3; MAICYA; SATA 72; SATA-Brief 29;
YAW

Don Roberto
See Cunninghame Graham, Robert
(Gallngad) Bontine

Doolittle, Hilda 1886-1961 . CLC 3, 8, 14, 31,
34, 73; DA; DAC; DAM MST, POET;
PC 5; WLC
See also H. D.
See also AMWS 1; CA 97-100; CANR 35;
DLB 4, 45; FW; GLL 1; MTCW 1, 2; PFS
6; RGAL

Dorfman, Ariel 1942- ...... CLC 48, 77; DAM
MULT; HLC 1
See also CA 124; 130; CANR 67, 70; CWW
2; DFS 4; HW 1, 2; INT 130

Einstein, Albert 1879-1955 .... **TCLC 65**
See also CA 121; 133; MTCW 1, 2
Eiseley, Loren Corey 1907-1977 .... **CLC 7**
See also AAYA 5; ANW; CA 1-4R; 73-76;
CANR 6; DLBD 17
Eisenstadt, Jill 1963- .... **CLC 50**
See also CA 140
Eisenstein, Sergei (Mikhailovich)
1898-1948 .... **TCLC 57**
See also CA 114; 149
Eisner, Simon
See Kornbluth, C(yril) M.
Ekeloef, (Bengt) Gunnar
1907-1968 ... **CLC 27; DAM POET; PC
23**
See also CA 123; 25-28R; EW
Ekelof, (Bengt) Gunnar
See Ekeloef, (Bengt) Gunnar
Ekelund, Vilhelm 1880-1949 .... **TCLC 75**
See also CA 189
Ekwensi, C. O. D.
See Ekwensi, Cyprian (Odiatu Duaka)
Ekwensi, Cyprian (Odiatu Duaka)
1921- ...... **CLC 4; BLC 1; DAM MULT**
See also AFW; BW 2, 3; CA 29-32R;
CANR 18, 42, 74; CN; CWRI; DLB 117;
MTCW 1, 2; RGEL; SATA 66
Elaine .... **TCLC 18**
See also Leverson, Ada
El Crummo
See Crumb, R(obert)
Elder, Lonne III 1931-1996 .... **DC 8**
See also BLC 1; BW 1, 3; CA 81-84; 152;
CAD; CANR 25; DAM MULT; DLB 7,
38, 44
Eleanor of Aquitaine 1122-1204 ... **CMLC 39**
Elia
See Lamb, Charles
Eliade, Mircea 1907-1986 .... **CLC 19**
See also CA 65-68; 119; CANR 30, 62;
DLB 220; MTCW 1; SFW
Eliot, A. D.
See Jewett, (Theodora) Sarah Orne
Eliot, Alice
See Jewett, (Theodora) Sarah Orne
Eliot, Dan
See Silverberg, Robert
Eliot, George 1819-1880 ...... **NCLC 4, 13, 23,
41, 49, 89; DA; DAB; DAC; DAM
MST, NOV; PC 20; WLC**
See also CDBLB 1832-1890; CN; CPW;
DA3; DLB 21, 35, 55; RGEL; RGSF;
SSFS 8
Eliot, John 1604-1690 .... **LC 5**
See also DLB 24
Eliot, T(homas) S(tearns)
1888-1965 ...... **CLC 1, 2, 3, 6, 9, 10, 13,
15, 24, 34, 41, 55, 57, 113; DA; DAB;
DAC; DAM DRAM, MST, POET; PC
5, 31; WLC**
See also AAYA 28; AMW; AMWR; BRW;
CA 5-8R; 25-28R; CANR 41; CDALB
1929-1941; DA3; DFS 4, 13; DLB 7, 10,
45, 63; DLBY 88; MTCW 1, 2; PAB; PFS
1, 7; RGAL; RGEL; WP
Elizabeth 1866-1941 .... **TCLC 41**
Elkin, Stanley L(awrence)
1930-1995 .. **CLC 4, 6, 9, 14, 27, 51, 91;
DAM NOV, POP; SSC 12**
See also AMWS 6; CA 9-12R; 148; CANR
8, 46; CN; CPW; DLB 2, 28; DLBY 80;
INT CANR-8; MTCW 1, 2; RGAL
Elledge, Scott .... **CLC 34**
Elliot, Don
See Silverberg, Robert
Elliott, Don
See Silverberg, Robert
Elliott, George P(aul) 1918-1980 .... **CLC 2**
See also CA 1-4R; 97-100; CANR 2

Elliott, Janice 1931-1995 .... **CLC 47**
See also CA 13-16R; CANR 8, 29, 84; CN;
DLB 14; SATA 119
Elliott, Sumner Locke 1917-1991 ..... **CLC 38**
See also CA 5-8R; 134; CANR 2, 21
Elliott, William
See Bradbury, Ray (Douglas)
Ellis, A. E. .... **CLC 7**
Ellis, Alice Thomas .... **CLC 40**
See also Haycraft, Anna (Margaret)
See also DLB 194; MTCW 1
Ellis, Bret Easton 1964- ..... **CLC 39, 71, 117;
DAM POP**
See also AAYA 2; CA 118; 123; CANR 51,
74; CN; CPW; DA3; HGG; INT 123;
MTCW 1; NFS 11
Ellis, (Henry) Havelock
1859-1939 .... **TCLC 14**
See also CA 109; 169; DLB 190
Ellis, Landon
See Ellison, Harlan (Jay)
Ellis, Trey 1962- .... **CLC 55**
See also CA 146; CANR 92
Ellison, Harlan (Jay) 1934- ... **CLC 1, 13, 42,
139; DAM POP; SSC 14**
See also AAYA 29; CA 5-8R; CANR 5, 46;
CPW; DLB 8; HGG; INT CANR-5;
MTCW 1, 2; SCFW 2; SFW; SUFW
Ellison, Ralph (Waldo) 1914-1994 .... **CLC 1,
3, 11, 54, 86, 114; BLC 1; DA; DAB;
DAC; DAM MST, MULT, NOV; SSC
26; WLC**
See also AAYA 19; AFAW 1, 2; AMWS 2;
BW 1, 3; CA 9-12R; 145; CANR 24, 53;
CDALB 1941-1968; CSW; DA3; DLB 2,
76, 227; DLBY 94; MTCW 1, 2; NFS 2;
RGAL; RGSF; SSFS 1, 11; YAW
Ellmann, Lucy (Elizabeth) 1956- ..... **CLC 61**
See also CA 128
Ellmann, Richard (David)
1918-1987 .... **CLC 50**
See also BEST 89:2; CA 1-4R; 122; CANR
2, 28, 61; DLB 103; DLBY 87; MTCW
1, 2
Elman, Richard (Martin)
1934-1997 .... **CLC 19**
See also CA 17-20R; 163; CAAS 3; CANR
47
Elron
See Hubbard, L(afayette) Ron(ald)
eluard, Paul .... **TCLC 7, 41**
See also Grindel, Eugene
See also GFL 1789 to the Present; RGWL
Elyot, Thomas 1490(?)-1546 .... **LC 11**
See also RGEL
Elytis, Odysseus 1911-1996 .... **CLC 15, 49,
100; DAM POET; PC 21**
See also Alepoudelis, Odysseus
See also CA 102; 151; CANR 94; CWW 2;
MTCW 1, 2; RGWL
Emecheta, (Florence Onye) Buchi
1944- .. **CLC 14, 48, 128; BLC 2; DAM
MULT**
See also AFW; BW 2, 3; CA 81-84; CANR
27, 81; CN; CWRI; DA3; DLB 117; FW;
MTCW 1, 2; NFS 12; SATA 66
Emerson, Mary Moody
1774-1863 .... **NCLC 66**
Emerson, Ralph Waldo 1803-1882 . **NCLC 1,
38, 98; DA; DAB; DAC; DAM MST,
POET; PC 18; WLC**
See also CDALB 1640-1865; DA3; DLB 1,
59, 73, 223; PFS 4; RGAL; WP
Eminescu, Mihail 1850-1889 .... **NCLC 33**
Empson, William 1906-1984 ... **CLC 3, 8, 19,
33, 34**
See also BRWS 2; CA 17-20R; 112; CANR
31, 61; DLB 20; MTCW 1, 2; RGEL

Enchi, Fumiko (Ueda) 1905-1986 ..... **CLC 31**
See also CA 129; 121; DLB 182; FW; MJW
Ende, Michael (Andreas Helmuth)
1929-1995 .... **CLC 31**
See also CA 118; 124; 149; CANR 36; CLR
14; DLB 75; MAICYA; SATA 61; SATA-
Brief 42; SATA-Obit 86
Endo, Shusaku 1923-1996 ..... **CLC 7, 14, 19,
54, 99; DAM NOV**
See also CA 29-32R; 153; CANR 21, 54;
DA3; DLB 182; MTCW 1, 2; RGSF;
RGWL
Engel, Marian 1933-1985 .... **CLC 36**
See also CA 25-28R; CANR 12; DLB 53;
FW; INT CANR-12
Engelhardt, Frederick
See Hubbard, L(afayette) Ron(ald)
Engels, Friedrich 1820-1895 .... **NCLC 85**
See also DLB 129
Enright, D(ennis) J(oseph) 1920- .. **CLC 4, 8,
31**
See also CA 1-4R; CANR 1, 42, 83; CP;
DLB 27; SATA 25
Enzensberger, Hans Magnus
1929- .... **CLC 43; PC 28**
See also CA 116; 119
Ephron, Nora 1941- .... **CLC 17, 31**
See also AAYA 35; AITN 2; CA 65-68;
CANR 12, 39, 83
Epicurus 341B.C.-270B.C. .... **CMLC 21**
See also DLB 176
Epsilon
See Betjeman, John
Epstein, Daniel Mark 1948- .... **CLC 7**
See also CA 49-52; CANR 2, 53, 90
Epstein, Jacob 1956- .... **CLC 19**
See also CA 114
Epstein, Jean 1897-1953 .... **TCLC 92**
Epstein, Joseph 1937- .... **CLC 39**
See also CA 112; 119; CANR 50, 65
Epstein, Leslie 1938- .... **CLC 27**
See also CA 73-76; CAAS 12; CANR 23,
69
Equiano, Olaudah 1745(?)-1797 .... **LC 16;
BLC 2; DAM MULT**
See also DLB 37, 50
Erasmus, Desiderius 1469(?)-1536 ...... **LC 16**
See also RGWL
Erdman, Paul E(mil) 1932- .... **CLC 25**
See also AITN 1; CA 61-64; CANR 13, 43,
84
Erdrich, Louise 1954- .... **CLC 39, 54, 120;
DAM MULT, NOV, POP**
See also AAYA 10; AMWS 4; BEST 89:1;
CA 114; CANR 41, 62; CDALBS; CN;
CP; CPW; CWP; DA3; DLB 152, 175,
206; MTCW 1; NFS 5; NNAL; RGAL;
SATA 94; TCWW 2
Erenburg, Ilya (Grigoryevich)
See Ehrenburg, Ilya (Grigoryevich)
Erickson, Stephen Michael 1950-
See Erickson, Steve
See also CA 129; SFW
Erickson, Steve .... **CLC 64**
See also Erickson, Stephen Michael
See also CANR 60, 68
Ericson, Walter
See Fast, Howard (Melvin)
Eriksson, Buntel
See Bergman, (Ernst) Ingmar
Ernaux, Annie 1940- .... **CLC 88**
See also CA 147; CANR 93
Erskine, John 1879-1951 .... **TCLC 84**
See also CA 112; 159; DLB 9, 102; FANT
Eschenbach, Wolfram von
See Wolfram von Eschenbach
Eseki, Bruno
See Mphahlele, Ezekiel

Friedman, Bruce Jay 1930- ...... **CLC 3, 5, 56**
See also CA 9-12R; CAD; CANR 25, 52;
CD; CN; DLB 2, 28; INT CANR-25

Friel, Brian 1929- .... **CLC 5, 42, 59, 115; DC 8**
See also BRWS 5; CA 21-24R; CANR 33,
69; CBD; CD; DFS 11; DLB 13; MTCW
1; RGEL

Friis-Baastad, Babbis Ellinor
1921-1970 .... **CLC 12**
See also CA 17-20R; 134; SATA 7

Frisch, Max (Rudolf) 1911-1991 ... **CLC 3, 9, 14, 18, 32, 44; DAM DRAM, NOV**
See also CA 85-88; 134; CANR 32, 74;
DLB 69, 124; EW; MTCW 1, 2; RGWL

Fromentin, Eugene (Samuel Auguste)
1820-1876 .... **NCLC 10**
See also DLB 123; GFL 1789 to the Present

Frost, Frederick
See Faust, Frederick (Schiller)
See also TCWW 2

Frost, Robert (Lee) 1874-1963 .. **CLC 1, 3, 4, 9, 10, 13, 15, 26, 34, 44; DA; DAB; DAC; DAM MST, POET; PC 1; WLC**
See also AAYA 21; AMW; AMWR; CA 89-
92; CANR 33; CDALB 1917-1929; CLR
67; DA3; DLB 54; DLBD 7; MTCW 1,
2; PAB; PFS 1, 2, 3, 4, 5, 6, 7, 10; RGAL;
SATA 14; WP; WYA

Froude, James Anthony
1818-1894 .... **NCLC 43**
See also DLB 18, 57, 144

Froy, Herald
See Waterhouse, Keith (Spencer)

Fry, Christopher 1907- .... **CLC 2, 10, 14; DAM DRAM**
See also BRWS 3; CA 17-20R; CAAS 23;
CANR 9, 30, 74; CBD; CD; CP; DLB 13;
MTCW 1, 2; RGEL; SATA 66

Frye, (Herman) Northrop
1912-1991 .... **CLC 24, 70**
See also CA 5-8R; 133; CANR 8, 37; DLB
67, 68; MTCW 1, 2; RGAL

Fuchs, Daniel 1909-1993 .... **CLC 8, 22**
See also CA 81-84; 142; CAAS 5; CANR
40; DLB 9, 26, 28; DLBY 93

Fuchs, Daniel 1934- .... **CLC 34**
See also CA 37-40R; CANR 14, 48

Fuentes, Carlos 1928- ... **CLC 3, 8, 10, 13, 22, 41, 60, 113; DA; DAB; DAC; DAM MST, MULT, NOV; HLC 1; SSC 24; WLC**
See also AAYA 4; AITN 2; CA 69-72;
CANR 10, 32, 68; CWW 2; DA3; DLB
113; DNFS; HW 1, 2; MTCW 1, 2; NFS
8; RGSF; RGWL

Fuentes, Gregorio Lopez y
See Lopez y Fuentes, Gregorio

Fuertes, Gloria 1918-1998 .... **PC 27**
See also CA 178, 180; DLB 108; HW 2;
SATA 115

Fugard, (Harold) Athol 1932- . **CLC 5, 9, 14, 25, 40, 80; DAM DRAM; DC 3**
See also AAYA 17; AFW; CA 85-88; CANR
32, 54; CD; DFS 3, 6, 10; DLB 225;
DNFS; MTCW 1; RGEL

Fugard, Sheila 1932- .... **CLC 48**
See also CA 125

Fukuyama, Francis 1952- .... **CLC 131**
See also CA 140; CANR 72

Fuller, Charles (H., Jr.) 1939- .... **CLC 25; BLC 2; DAM DRAM, MULT; DC 1**
See also BW 2; CA 108; 112; CAD; CANR
87; CD; DFS 8; DLB 38; INT CA-112;
MTCW 1

Fuller, Henry Blake 1857-1929 .... **TCLC 103**
See also CA 108; 177; DLB 12; RGAL

Fuller, John (Leopold) 1937- .... **CLC 62**
See also CA 21-24R; CANR 9, 44; CP;
DLB 40

Fuller, Margaret
See Ossoli, Sarah Margaret (Fuller)
See also AMWS 2

Fuller, Roy (Broadbent) 1912-1991 ... **CLC 4, 28**
See also BRWS 7; CA 5-8R; 135; CAAS
10; CANR 53, 83; CWRI; DLB 15, 20;
RGEL; SATA 87

Fuller, Sarah Margaret
See Ossoli, Sarah Margaret (Fuller)

Fulton, Alice 1952- .... **CLC 52**
See also CA 116; CANR 57, 88; CP; CWP;
DLB 193

Furphy, Joseph 1843-1912 .... **TCLC 25**
See also CA 163; DLB 230; RGEL

Fuson, Robert H(enderson) 1927- .... **CLC 70**
See also CA 89-92

Fussell, Paul 1924- .... **CLC 74**
See also BEST 90:1; CA 17-20R; CANR 8,
21, 35, 69; INT CANR-21; MTCW 1, 2

Futabatei, Shimei 1864-1909 .... **TCLC 44**
See also CA 162; DLB 180; MJW

Futrelle, Jacques 1875-1912 .... **TCLC 19**
See also CA 113; 155; CMW

Gaboriau, Emile 1835-1873 .... **NCLC 14**
See also CMW

Gadda, Carlo Emilio 1893-1973 .... **CLC 11**
See also CA 89-92; DLB 177

Gaddis, William 1922-1998 ... **CLC 1, 3, 6, 8, 10, 19, 43, 86**
See also AMWS 4; CA 17-20R; 172; CANR
21, 48; CN; DLB 2; MTCW 1, 2; RGAL

Gaelique, Moruen le
See Jacob, (Cyprien-)Max

Gage, Walter
See Inge, William (Motter)

Gaines, Ernest J(ames) 1933- ...... **CLC 3, 11, 18, 86; BLC 2; DAM MULT**
See also AAYA 18; AFAW 1, 2; AITN 1;
BW 2, 3; CA 9-12R; CANR 6, 24, 42, 75;
CDALB 1968-1988; CLR 62; CN; CSW;
DA3; DLB 2, 33, 152; DLBY 80; MTCW
1, 2; NFS 5, 7; RGAL; RGSF; RHW;
SATA 86; SSFS 5; YAW

Gaitskill, Mary 1954- .... **CLC 69**
See also CA 128; CANR 61

Galdos, Benito Perez
See P

Gale, Zona 1874-1938 .... **TCLC 7; DAM DRAM**
See also CA 105; 153; CANR 84; DLB 9,
78, 228; RGAL

Galeano, Eduardo (Hughes) 1940- . **CLC 72; HLCS 1**
See also CA 29-32R; CANR 13, 32, 100;
HW 1

Galiano, Juan Valera y Alcala
See Valera y Alcala-Galiano, Juan

Galilei, Galileo 1564-1642 .... **LC 45**

Gallagher, Tess 1943- ...... **CLC 18, 63; DAM POET; PC 9**
See also CA 106; CP; CWP; DLB 212

Gallant, Mavis 1922- .. **CLC 7, 18, 38; DAC; DAM MST; SSC 5**
See also CA 69-72; CANR 29, 69; CCA 1;
CN; DLB 53; MTCW 1, 2; RGEL; RGSF

Gallant, Roy A(rthur) 1924- .... **CLC 17**
See also CA 5-8R; CANR 4, 29, 54; CLR
30; MAICYA; SATA 4, 68, 110

Gallico, Paul (William) 1897-1976 ..... **CLC 2**
See also AITN 1; CA 5-8R; 69-72; CANR
23; DLB 9, 171; FANT; MAICYA; SATA
13

Gallo, Max Louis 1932- .... **CLC 95**
See also CA 85-88

Gallois, Lucien
See Desnos, Robert

Gallup, Ralph
See Whitemore, Hugh (John)

Galsworthy, John 1867-1933 .... **TCLC 1, 45; DA; DAB; DAC; DAM DRAM, MST, NOV; SSC 22; WLC**
See also CA 104; 141; CANR 75; CDBLB
1890-1914; DA3; DLB 10, 34, 98, 162;
DLBD 16; MTCW 1; RGEL; SSFS 3

Galt, John 1779-1839 .... **NCLC 1**
See also DLB 99, 116, 159; RGEL; RGSF

Galvin, James 1951- .... **CLC 38**
See also CA 108; CANR 26

Gamboa, Federico 1864-1939 .... **TCLC 36**
See also CA 167; HW 2

Gandhi, M. K.
See Gandhi, Mohandas Karamchand

Gandhi, Mahatma
See Gandhi, Mohandas Karamchand

Gandhi, Mohandas Karamchand
1869-1948 .... **TCLC 59; DAM MULT**
See also CA 121; 132; DA3; MTCW 1, 2

Gann, Ernest Kellogg 1910-1991 ..... **CLC 23**
See also AITN 1; CA 1-4R; 136; CANR 1,
83; RHW

Garber, Eric 1943(?)-
See Holleran, Andrew
See also CANR 89

Garcia, Cristina 1958- .... **CLC 76**
See also CA 141; CANR 73; DNFS; HW 2

Garcia Lorca, Federico 1898-1936 . **TCLC 1, 7, 49; DA; DAB; DAC; DAM DRAM, MST, MULT, POET; DC 2; HLC 2; PC 3; WLC**
See also CA 104; 131; CANR 81; DA3;
DFS 10; DLB 108; HW 1, 2; MTCW 1, 2

Garcia Marquez, Gabriel (Jose)
1928- .... **CLC 2, 3, 8, 10, 15, 27, 47, 55, 68; DA; DAB; DAC; DAM MST, MULT, NOV, POP; HLC 1; SSC 8; WLC**
See also AAYA 3, 33; BEST 89:1, 90:4; CA
33-36R; CANR 10, 28, 50, 75, 82; CPW;
DA3; DLB 113; DNFS; HW 1, 2; LAW;
MTCW 1, 2; NFS 1, 5, 10; RGSF; RGWL;
SSFS 1, 6

Garcilaso de la Vega, El Inca 1503-1536
See also HLCS 1

Gard, Janice
See Latham, Jean Lee

Gard, Roger Martin du
See Martin du Gard, Roger

Gardam, Jane 1928- .... **CLC 43**
See also CA 49-52; CANR 2, 18, 33, 54;
CLR 12; DLB 14, 161, 231; MAICYA;
MTCW 1; SAAS 9; SATA 39, 76; SATA-
Brief 28; YAW

Gardner, Herb(ert) 1934- .... **CLC 44**
See also CA 149; CAD; CD

Gardner, John (Champlin), Jr.
1933-1982 ...... **CLC 2, 3, 5, 7, 8, 10, 18, 28, 34; DAM NOV, POP; SSC 7**
See also AITN 1; AMWS 5; CA 65-68; 107;
CANR 33, 73; CDALBS; CPW; DA3;
DLB 2; DLBY 82; FANT; MTCW 1; NFS
3; RGAL; RGSF; SATA 40; SATA-Obit
31; SSFS 8

Gardner, John (Edmund) 1926- ...... **CLC 30; DAM POP**
See also CA 103; CANR 15, 69; CMW;
CPW; MTCW 1

Gardner, Miriam
See Bradley, Marion Zimmer
See also GLL 1

Gardner, Noel
See Kuttner, Henry

Gardons, S. S.
See Snodgrass, W(illiam) D(e Witt)
Garfield, Leon 1921-1996 .... **CLC 12**
See also AAYA 8; CA 17-20R; 152; CANR 38, 41, 78; CLR 21; DLB 161; JRDA; MAICYA; SATA 1, 32, 76; SATA-Obit 90; YAW
Garland, (Hannibal) Hamlin 1860-1940 .... **TCLC 3; SSC 18**
See also CA 104; DLB 12, 71, 78, 186; RGAL; RGSF; TCWW 2
Garneau, (Hector de) Saint-Denys 1912-1943 .... **TCLC 13**
See also CA 111; DLB 88
Garner, Alan 1934- ..... **CLC 17; DAB; DAM POP**
See also AAYA 18; CA 73-76, 178; CAAE 178; CANR 15, 64; CLR 20; CPW; DLB 161; FANT; MAICYA; MTCW 1, 2; SATA 18, 69; SATA-Essay 108; YAW
Garner, Hugh 1913-1979 .... **CLC 13**
See also Warwick, Jarvis
See also CA 69-72; CANR 31; CCA 1; DLB 68
Garnett, David 1892-1981 .... **CLC 3**
See also CA 5-8R; 103; CANR 17, 79; DLB 34; FANT; MTCW 2; RGEL; SFW
Garos, Stephanie
See Katz, Steve
Garrett, George (Palmer) 1929- .. **CLC 3, 11, 51; SSC 30**
See also AMWS 7; CA 1-4R; CAAS 5; CANR 1, 42, 67; CN; CP; CSW; DLB 2, 5, 130, 152; DLBY 83
Garrick, David 1717-1779 .... **LC 15; DAM DRAM**
See also DLB 84; RGEL
Garrigue, Jean 1914-1972 .... **CLC 2, 8**
See also CA 5-8R; 37-40R; CANR 20
Garrison, Frederick
See Sinclair, Upton (Beall)
Garro, Elena 1920(?)-1998
See also CA 131; 169; CWW 2; DLB 145; HLCS 1; HW 1
Garth, Will
See Hamilton, Edmond; Kuttner, Henry
Garvey, Marcus (Moziah, Jr.) 1887-1940 ...... **TCLC 41; BLC 2; DAM MULT**
See also BW 1; CA 120; 124; CANR 79
Gary, Romain .... **CLC 25**
See also Kacew, Romain
See also DLB 83
Gascar, Pierre .... **CLC 11**
See also Fournier, Pierre
Gascoyne, David (Emery) 1916- .... **CLC 45**
See also CA 65-68; CANR 10, 28, 54; CP; DLB 20; MTCW 1; RGEL
Gaskell, Elizabeth Cleghorn 1810-1865 .... **NCLC 5, 70, 97; DAB; DAM MST; SSC 25**
See also BRW; CDBLB 1832-1890; DLB 21, 144, 159; RGEL; RGSF
Gass, William H(oward) 1924- . **CLC 1, 2, 8, 11, 15, 39, 132; SSC 12**
See also AMWS 6; CA 17-20R; CANR 30, 71, 100; CN; DLB 2, 227; MTCW 1, 2; RGAL
Gassendi, Pierre 1592-1655 .... **LC 54**
See also GFL Beginnings to 1789
Gasset, Jose Ortega y
See Ortega y Gasset, Jose
Gates, Henry Louis, Jr. 1950- .... **CLC 65; BLCS; DAM MULT**
See also BW 2, 3; CA 109; CANR 25, 53, 75; CSW; DA3; DLB 67; MTCW 1; RGAL

Gautier, Theophile 1811-1872 .. **NCLC 1, 59; DAM POET; PC 18; SSC 20**
See also DLB 119; GFL 1789 to the Present; RGWL
Gawsworth, John
See Bates, H(erbert) E(rnest)
Gay, John 1685-1732 .. **LC 49; DAM DRAM**
See also DLB 84, 95; RGEL
Gay, Oliver
See Gogarty, Oliver St. John
Gaye, Marvin (Penze) 1939-1984 ..... **CLC 26**
See also CA 112
Gebler, Carlo (Ernest) 1954- .... **CLC 39**
See also CA 119; 133; CANR 96
Gee, Maggie (Mary) 1948- .... **CLC 57**
See also CA 130; CN; DLB 207
Gee, Maurice (Gough) 1931- .... **CLC 29**
See also CA 97-100; CANR 67; CLR 56; CN; CWRI; RGSF; SATA 46, 101
Gelbart, Larry (Simon) 1928- .... **CLC 21, 61**
See also Gelbart, Larry
See also CA 73-76; CANR 45, 94
Gelbart, Larry 1928-
See Gelbart, Larry (Simon)
See also CAD; CD
Gelber, Jack 1932- .... **CLC 1, 6, 14, 79**
See also CA 1-4R; CAD; CANR 2; DLB 7, 228
Gellhorn, Martha (Ellis) 1908-1998 .... **CLC 14, 60**
See also CA 77-80; 164; CANR 44; CN; DLBY 82, 98
Genet, Jean 1910-1986 .. **CLC 1, 2, 5, 10, 14, 44, 46; DAM DRAM**
See also CA 13-16R; CANR 18; DA3; DFS 10; DLB 72; DLBY 86; GFL 1789 to the Present; GLL 1; MTCW 1, 2; RGWL
Gent, Peter 1942- .... **CLC 29**
See also AITN 1; CA 89-92; DLBY 82
Gentile, Giovanni 1875-1944 .... **TCLC 96**
See also CA 119
Gentlewoman in New England, A
See Bradstreet, Anne
Gentlewoman in Those Parts, A
See Bradstreet, Anne
Geoffrey of Monmouth c. 1100-1155 .... **CMLC 44**
See also DLB 146
George, Jean
See George, Jean Craighead
George, Jean Craighead 1919- .... **CLC 35**
See also AAYA 8; CA 5-8R; CANR 25; CLR 1; DLB 52; JRDA; MAICYA; SATA 2, 68, 124; YAW
George, Stefan (Anton) 1868-1933 . **TCLC 2, 14**
See also CA 104; EW
Georges, Georges Martin
See Simenon, Georges (Jacques Christian)
Gerhardi, William Alexander
See Gerhardie, William Alexander
Gerhardie, William Alexander 1895-1977 .... **CLC 5**
See also CA 25-28R; 73-76; CANR 18; DLB 36; RGEL
Gerstler, Amy 1956- .... **CLC 70**
See also CA 146; CANR 99
Gertler, T. .... **CLC 134**
See also CA 116; 121
Ghalib .... **NCLC 39, 78**
See also Ghalib, Asadullah Khan
Ghalib, Asadullah Khan 1797-1869
See Ghalib
See also DAM POET; RGWL
Ghelderode, Michel de 1898-1962 ..... **CLC 6, 11; DAM DRAM; DC 15**
See also CA 85-88; CANR 40, 77

Ghiselin, Brewster 1903- .... **CLC 23**
See also CA 13-16R; CAAS 10; CANR 13; CP
Ghose, Aurabinda 1872-1950 .... **TCLC 63**
See also CA 163
Ghose, Zulfikar 1935- .... **CLC 42**
See also CA 65-68; CANR 67; CN; CP
Ghosh, Amitav 1956- .... **CLC 44**
See also CA 147; CANR 80; CN
Giacosa, Giuseppe 1847-1906 .... **TCLC 7**
See also CA 104
Gibb, Lee
See Waterhouse, Keith (Spencer)
Gibbon, Lewis Grassic .... **TCLC 4**
See also Mitchell, James Leslie
See also RGEL
Gibbons, Kaye 1960- .... **CLC 50, 88, 145; DAM POP**
See also AAYA 34; CA 151; CANR 75; CSW; DA3; MTCW 1; NFS 3; RGAL; SATA 117
Gibran, Kahlil 1883-1931 .... **TCLC 1, 9; DAM POET, POP; PC 9**
See also CA 104; 150; DA3; MTCW 2
Gibran, Khalil
See Gibran, Kahlil
Gibson, William 1914- .. **CLC 23; DA; DAB; DAC; DAM DRAM, MST**
See also CA 9-12R; CAD; CANR 9, 42, 75; CD; CN; CPW; DFS 2; DLB 7; MTCW 1; SATA 66; SCFW 2; SFW; YAW
Gibson, William (Ford) 1948- ... **CLC 39, 63; DAM POP**
See also AAYA 12; CA 126; 133; CANR 52, 90; DA3; MTCW 1
Gide, Andre (Paul Guillaume) 1869-1951 . **TCLC 5, 12, 36; DA; DAB; DAC; DAM MST, NOV; SSC 13; WLC**
See also CA 104; 124; DA3; DLB 65; EW; GFL 1789 to the Present; MTCW 1, 2; RGSF; RGWL
Gifford, Barry (Colby) 1946- .... **CLC 34**
See also CA 65-68; CANR 9, 30, 40, 90
Gilbert, Frank
See De Voto, Bernard (Augustine)
Gilbert, W(illiam) S(chwenck) 1836-1911 .... **TCLC 3; DAM DRAM, POET**
See also CA 104; 173; RGEL; SATA 36
Gilbreth, Frank B., Jr. 1911-2001 .... **CLC 17**
See also CA 9-12R; SATA 2
Gilchrist, Ellen 1935- .... **CLC 34, 48, 143; DAM POP; SSC 14**
See also CA 113; 116; CANR 41, 61; CN; CPW; CSW; DLB 130; MTCW 1, 2; RGAL; RGSF; SSFS 9
Giles, Molly 1942- .... **CLC 39**
See also CA 126; CANR 98
Gill, Eric 1882-1940 .... **TCLC 85**
Gill, Patrick
See Creasey, John
Gillette, Douglas .... **CLC 70**
Gilliam, Terry (Vance) 1940- .... **CLC 21, 141**
See also Monty Python
See also AAYA 19; CA 108; 113; CANR 35; INT 113
Gillian, Jerry
See Gilliam, Terry (Vance)
Gilliatt, Penelope (Ann Douglass) 1932-1993 .... **CLC 2, 10, 13, 53**
See also AITN 2; CA 13-16R; 141; CANR 49; DLB 14
Gilman, Charlotte (Anna) Perkins (Stetson) 1860-1935 .... **TCLC 9, 37; SSC 13**
See also CA 106; 150; DLB 221; FW; HGG; MAWW; MTCW 1; RGAL; RGSF; SFW; SSFS 1

Greer, Germaine 1939- .... **CLC 131**
See also AITN 1; CA 81-84; CANR 33, 70;
FW; MTCW 1, 2

Greer, Richard
See Silverberg, Robert

Gregor, Arthur 1923- .... **CLC 9**
See also CA 25-28R; CAAS 10; CANR 11;
CP; SATA 36

Gregor, Lee
See Pohl, Frederik

Gregory, Isabella Augusta (Persse)
1852-1932 .... **TCLC 1**
See also BRW; CA 104; 184; DLB 10;
RGEL

Gregory, J. Dennis
See Williams, John A(lfred)

Grekova, I. .... **CLC 59**

Grendon, Stephen
See Derleth, August (William)

Grenville, Kate 1950- .... **CLC 61**
See also CA 118; CANR 53, 93

Grenville, Pelham
See Wodehouse, P(elham) G(renville)

Greve, Felix Paul (Berthold Friedrich)
1879-1948
See Grove, Frederick Philip
See also CA 104; 141, 175; CANR 79;
DAC; DAM MST

Grey, Zane 1872-1939 . **TCLC 6; DAM POP**
See also CA 104; 132; DA3; DLB 212;
MTCW 1, 2; RGAL; TCWW 2

Grieg, (Johan) Nordahl (Brun)
1902-1943 .... **TCLC 10**
See also CA 107; 189

Grieve, C(hristopher) M(urray)
1892-1978 ..... **CLC 11, 19; DAM POET**
See also MacDiarmid, Hugh; Pteleon
See also CA 5-8R; 85-88; CANR 33;
MTCW 1; RGEL

Griffin, Gerald 1803-1840 .... **NCLC 7**
See also DLB 159; RGEL

Griffin, John Howard 1920-1980 ..... **CLC 68**
See also AITN 1; CA 1-4R; 101; CANR 2

Griffin, Peter 1942- .... **CLC 39**
See also CA 136

Griffith, D(avid Lewelyn) W(ark)
1875(?)-1948 .... **TCLC 68**
See also CA 119; 150; CANR 80

Griffith, Lawrence
See Griffith, D(avid Lewelyn) W(ark)

Griffiths, Trevor 1935- .... **CLC 13, 52**
See also CA 97-100; CANR 45; CBD; CD;
DLB 13

Griggs, Sutton (Elbert)
1872-1930 .... **TCLC 77**
See also CA 123; 186; DLB 50

Grigson, Geoffrey (Edward Harvey)
1905-1985 .... **CLC 7, 39**
See also CA 25-28R; 118; CANR 20, 33;
DLB 27; MTCW 1, 2

Grillparzer, Franz 1791-1872 . **NCLC 1, 102;
DC 14; SSC 37**
See also DLB 133; RGWL

Grimble, Reverend Charles James
See Eliot, T(homas) S(tearns)

Grimke, Charlotte L(ottie) Forten
1837(?)-1914
See Forten, Charlotte L.
See also BW 1; CA 117; 124; DAM MULT,
POET; DLB 239

Grimm, Jacob Ludwig Karl
1785-1863 .... **NCLC 3, 77; SSC 36**
See also Grimm and Grimm
See also DLB 90; MAICYA; RGSF;
RGWL; SATA 22; WCH

Grimm, Wilhelm Karl 1786-1859 .. **NCLC 3,
77; SSC 36**
See also Grimm and Grimm
See also DLB 90; MAICYA; RGSF;
RGWL; SATA 22; WCH

**Grimmelshausen, Hans Jakob Christoffel
von**
See Grimmelshausen, Johann Jakob Christoffel von
See also RGWL

**Grimmelshausen, Johann Jakob Christoffel
von** 1621-1676 .... **LC 6**
See also Grimmelshausen, Hans Jakob
Christoffel von
See also DLB 168

Grindel, Eugene 1895-1952
See
See also CA 104

Grisham, John 1955- .... **CLC 84; DAM POP**
See also AAYA 14; CA 138; CANR 47, 69;
CMW; CN; CPW; CSW; DA3; MTCW 2

Grossman, David 1954- .... **CLC 67**
See also CA 138; CWW 2

Grossman, Vasily (Semenovich)
1905-1964 .... **CLC 41**
See also CA 124; 130; MTCW 1

Grove, Frederick Philip .... **TCLC 4**
See also Greve, Felix Paul (Berthold
Friedrich)
See also DLB 92; RGEL

Grubb
See Crumb, R(obert)

Grumbach, Doris (Isaac) 1918- . **CLC 13, 22,
64**
See also CA 5-8R; CAAS 2; CANR 9, 42,
70; CN; INT CANR-9; MTCW 2

Grundtvig, Nicolai Frederik Severin
1783-1872 .... **NCLC 1**

Grunge
See Crumb, R(obert)

Grunwald, Lisa 1959- .... **CLC 44**
See also CA 120

Guare, John 1938- .... **CLC 8, 14, 29, 67;
DAM DRAM**
See also CA 73-76; CAD; CANR 21, 69;
CD; DFS 8, 13; DLB 7; MTCW 1, 2;
RGAL

Gubar, Susan (David) 1944- .... **CLC 145**
See also CA 108; CANR 45, 70; FW;
MTCW 1; RGAL

Gudjonsson, Halldor Kiljan 1902-1998
See Laxness, Halld
See also CA 103; 164; CWW 2

Guenter, Erich
See Eich, Guenter

Guest, Barbara 1920- .... **CLC 34**
See also CA 25-28R; CANR 11, 44, 84; CP;
CWP; DLB 5, 193

Guest, Edgar A(lbert) 1881-1959 ... **TCLC 95**
See also CA 112; 168

Guest, Judith (Ann) 1936- .... **CLC 8, 30;
DAM NOV, POP**
See also AAYA 7; CA 77-80; CANR 15,
75; DA3; INT CANR-15; MTCW 1, 2;
NFS 1

Guevara, Che .... **CLC 87; HLC 1**
See also Guevara (Serna), Ernesto

Guevara (Serna), Ernesto
1928-1967 .... **CLC 87; DAM MULT;
HLC 1**
See also Guevara, Che
See also CA 127; 111; CANR 56; HW 1

Guicciardini, Francesco 1483-1540 ..... **LC 49**

Guild, Nicholas M. 1944- .... **CLC 33**
See also CA 93-96

Guillemin, Jacques
See Sartre, Jean-Paul

Guillen, Jorge 1893-1984 .... **CLC 11; DAM
MULT, POET; HLCS 1; PC 35**
See also CA 89-92; 112; DLB 108; HW 1;
RGWL

Guillen, Nicolas (Cristobal)
1902-1989 ... **CLC 48, 79; BLC 2; DAM
MST, MULT, POET; HLC 1; PC 23**
See also BW 2; CA 116; 125; 129; CANR
84; HW 1; LAW; RGWL; WP

Guillevic, (Eugene) 1907-1997 .... **CLC 33**
See also CA 93-96; CWW 2

Guillois
See Desnos, Robert

Guillois, Valentin
See Desnos, Robert

Guimaraes Rosa, Joao 1908-1967
See also CA 175; HLCS 2; LAW; RGSF;
RGWL

Guiney, Louise Imogen
1861-1920 .... **TCLC 41**
See also CA 160; DLB 54; RGAL

Guiraldes, Ricardo (Guillermo)
1886-1927 .... **TCLC 39**
See also CA 131; HW 1; LAW; MTCW 1

Gumilev, Nikolai (Stepanovich)
1886-1921 .... **TCLC 60**
See also CA 165

Gunesekera, Romesh 1954- .... **CLC 91**
See also CA 159; CN

Gunn, Bill .... **CLC 5**
See also Gunn, William Harrison
See also DLB 38

Gunn, Thom(son William) 1929- .. **CLC 3, 6,
18, 32, 81; DAM POET; PC 26**
See also BRWS 4; CA 17-20R; CANR 9,
33; CDBLB 1960 to Present; CP; DLB
27; INT CANR-33; MTCW 1; PFS 9;
RGEL

Gunn, William Harrison 1934(?)-1989
See Gunn, Bill
See also AITN 1; BW 1, 3; CA 13-16R;
128; CANR 12, 25, 76

Gunn Allen, Paula
See Allen, Paula Gunn

Gunnars, Kristjana 1948- .... **CLC 69**
See also CA 113; CCA 1; CP; CWP; DLB
60

Gurdjieff, G(eorgei) I(vanovich)
1877(?)-1949 .... **TCLC 71**
See also CA 157

Gurganus, Allan 1947- . **CLC 70; DAM POP**
See also BEST 90:1; CA 135; CN; CPW;
CSW; GLL 1

Gurney, A(lbert) R(amsdell), Jr.
1930- ..... **CLC 32, 50, 54; DAM DRAM**
See also CA 77-80; CAD; CANR 32, 64;
CD

Gurney, Ivor (Bertie) 1890-1937 ... **TCLC 33**
See also CA 167; PAB; RGEL

Gurney, Peter
See Gurney, A(lbert) R(amsdell), Jr.

Guro, Elena 1877-1913 .... **TCLC 56**

Gustafson, James M(oody) 1925- .. **CLC 100**
See also CA 25-28R; CANR 37

Gustafson, Ralph (Barker)
1909-1995 .... **CLC 36**
See also CA 21-24R; CANR 8, 45, 84; CP;
DLB 88; RGEL

Gut, Gom
See Simenon, Georges (Jacques Christian)

Guterson, David 1956- .... **CLC 91**
See also CA 132; CANR 73; MTCW 2

Guthrie, A(lfred) B(ertram), Jr.
1901-1991 .... **CLC 23**
See also CA 57-60; 134; CANR 24; DLB
212; SATA 62; SATA-Obit 67

Guthrie, Isobel
See Grieve, C(hristopher) M(urray)

Harper, Frances Ellen
See Harper, Frances Ellen Watkins
Harper, Frances Ellen Watkins
1825-1911 ...... **TCLC 14; BLC 2; DAM MULT, POET; PC 21**
See also AFAW 1, 2; BW 1, 3; CA 111; 125; CANR 79; DLB 50, 221; RGAL
Harper, Michael S(teven) 1938- ... **CLC 7, 22**
See also AFAW 2; BW 1; CA 33-36R; CANR 24; CP; DLB 41; RGAL
Harper, Mrs. F. E. W.
See Harper, Frances Ellen Watkins
Harris, Christie (Lucy) Irwin
1907- .... **CLC 12**
See also CA 5-8R; CANR 6, 83; CLR 47; DLB 88; JRDA; MAICYA; SAAS 10; SATA 6, 74; SATA-Essay 116
Harris, Frank 1856-1931 .... **TCLC 24**
See also CA 109; 150; CANR 80; DLB 156, 197; RGEL
Harris, George Washington
1814-1869 .... **NCLC 23**
See also DLB 3, 11; RGAL
Harris, Joel Chandler 1848-1908 ... **TCLC 2; SSC 19**
See also CA 104; 137; CANR 80; CLR 49; DLB 11, 23, 42, 78, 91; MAICYA; RGSF; SATA 100; YABC 1
Harris, John (Wyndham Parkes Lucas) Beynon 1903-1969
See Wyndham, John
See also CA 102; 89-92; CANR 84; SATA 118; SFW
Harris, MacDonald .... **CLC 9**
See also Heiney, Donald (William)
Harris, Mark 1922- .... **CLC 19**
See also CA 5-8R; CANR 2, 55, 83; CN; DLB 2; DLBY 80
Harris, Norman .... **CLC 65**
Harris, (Theodore) Wilson 1921- ..... **CLC 25**
See also BW 2, 3; CA 65-68; CAAS 16; CANR 11, 27, 69; CN; CP; DLB 117; MTCW 1; RGEL
Harrison, Barbara Grizzuti 1934- . **CLC 144**
See also CA 77-80; CANR 15, 48; INT CANR-15
Harrison, Elizabeth Cavanna 1909-2001
See Cavanna, Betty
See also CA 9-12R; CANR 6, 27, 85; YAW
Harrison, Harry (Max) 1925- .... **CLC 42**
See also CA 1-4R; CANR 5, 21, 84; DLB 8; SATA 4; SCFW 2; SFW
Harrison, James (Thomas) 1937- ...... **CLC 6, 14, 33, 66, 143; SSC 19**
See also Harrison, Jim
See also CA 13-16R; CANR 8, 51, 79; CN; CP; DLBY 82; INT CANR-8
Harrison, Jim
See Harrison, James (Thomas)
See also AMWS 8; RGAL; TCWW 2
Harrison, Kathryn 1961- .... **CLC 70**
See also CA 144; CANR 68
Harrison, Tony 1937- .... **CLC 43, 129**
See also BRWS 5; CA 65-68; CANR 44, 98; CBD; CD; CP; DLB 40; MTCW 1; RGEL
Harriss, Will(ard Irvin) 1922- .... **CLC 34**
See also CA 111
Harson, Sley
See Ellison, Harlan (Jay)
Hart, Ellis
See Ellison, Harlan (Jay)
Hart, Josephine 1942(?)- .... **CLC 70; DAM POP**
See also CA 138; CANR 70; CPW
Hart, Moss 1904-1961 .... **CLC 66; DAM DRAM**
See also CA 109; 89-92; CANR 84; DFS 1; DLB 7; RGAL

Harte, (Francis) Bret(t)
1836(?)-1902 ... **TCLC 1, 25; DA; DAC; DAM MST; SSC 8; WLC**
See also AMWS 2; CA 104; 140; CANR 80; CDALB 1865-1917; DA3; DLB 12, 64, 74, 79, 186; RGAL; RGSF; SATA 26; SSFS 3
Hartley, L(eslie) P(oles) 1895-1972 ... **CLC 2, 22**
See also BRWS 7; CA 45-48; 37-40R; CANR 33; DLB 15, 139; HGG; MTCW 1, 2; RGEL; RGSF; SUFW
Hartman, Geoffrey H. 1929- .... **CLC 27**
See also CA 117; 125; CANR 79; DLB 67
Hartmann, Sadakichi 1869-1944 ... **TCLC 73**
See also CA 157; DLB 54
Hartmann von Aue c. 1170-c.
1210 .... **CMLC 15**
See also DLB 138; RGWL
Haruf, Kent 1943- .... **CLC 34**
See also CA 149; CANR 91
Harwood, Ronald 1934- .... **CLC 32; DAM DRAM, MST**
See also CA 1-4R; CANR 4, 55; CBD; CD; DLB 13
Hasegawa Tatsunosuke
See Futabatei, Shimei
Hasek, Jaroslav (Matej Frantisek)
1883-1923 .... **TCLC 4**
See also CA 104; 129; EW; MTCW 1, 2; RGSF; RGWL
Hass, Robert 1941- ... **CLC 18, 39, 99; PC 16**
See also AMWS 6; CA 111; CANR 30, 50, 71; CP; DLB 105, 206; RGAL; SATA 94
Hastings, Hudson
See Kuttner, Henry
Hastings, Selina .... **CLC 44**
Hathorne, John 1641-1717 .... **LC 38**
Hatteras, Amelia
See Mencken, H(enry) L(ouis)
Hatteras, Owen .... **TCLC 18**
See also Mencken, H(enry) L(ouis); Nathan, George Jean
Hauptmann, Gerhart (Johann Robert)
1862-1946 .... **TCLC 4; DAM DRAM; SSC 37**
See also CA 104; 153; DLB 66, 118; EW; RGSF; RGWL
Havel, Vaclav 1936- ..... **CLC 25, 58, 65, 123; DAM DRAM; DC 6**
See also CA 104; CANR 36, 63; CWW 2; DA3; DFS 10; DLB 232; MTCW 1, 2
Haviaras, Stratis .... **CLC 33**
See also Chaviaras, Strates
Hawes, Stephen 1475(?)-1529(?) .... **LC 17**
See also DLB 132; RGEL
Hawkes, John (Clendennin Burne, Jr.)
1925-1998 .. **CLC 1, 2, 3, 4, 7, 9, 14, 15, 27, 49**
See also CA 1-4R; 167; CANR 2, 47, 64; CN; DLB 2, 7, 227; DLBY 80, 98; MTCW 1, 2; RGAL
Hawking, S. W.
See Hawking, Stephen W(illiam)
Hawking, Stephen W(illiam) 1942- . **CLC 63, 105**
See also AAYA 13; BEST 89:1; CA 126; 129; CANR 48; CPW; DA3; MTCW 2
Hawkins, Anthony Hope
See Hope, Anthony
Hawthorne, Julian 1846-1934 .... **TCLC 25**
See also CA 165; HGG
Hawthorne, Nathaniel 1804-1864 ... **NCLC 2, 10, 17, 23, 39, 79, 95; DA; DAB; DAC; DAM MST, NOV; SSC 3, 29, 39; WLC**
See also AAYA 18; CDALB 1640-1865; DA3; DLB 1, 74, 223; HGG; NFS 1; RGAL; RGSF; SSFS 1, 7, 11; YABC 2

Haxton, Josephine Ayres 1921-
See Douglas, Ellen
See also CA 115; CANR 41, 83
Hayaseca y Eizaguirre, Jorge
See Echegaray (y Eizaguirre), Jose (Maria Waldo)
Hayashi, Fumiko 1904-1951 .... **TCLC 27**
See also CA 161; DLB 180
Haycraft, Anna (Margaret) 1932-
See Ellis, Alice Thomas
See also CA 122; CANR 85, 90; MTCW 2
Hayden, Robert E(arl) 1913-1980 . **CLC 5, 9, 14, 37; BLC 2; DA; DAC; DAM MST, MULT, POET; PC 6**
See also AFAW 1, 2; AMWS 2; BW 1, 3; CA 69-72; 97-100; CABS 2; CANR 24, 75, 82; CDALB 1941-1968; DLB 5, 76; MTCW 1, 2; PFS 1; RGAL; SATA 19; SATA-Obit 26; WP
Hayek, F(riedrich) A(ugust von)
1899-1992 .... **TCLC 109**
See also CA 93-96; 137; CANR 20; MTCW 1, 2
Hayford, J(oseph) E(phraim) Casely
See Casely-Hayford, J(oseph) E(phraim)
Hayman, Ronald 1932- .... **CLC 44**
See also CA 25-28R; CANR 18, 50, 88; CD; DLB 155
Hayne, Paul Hamilton 1830-1886 . **NCLC 94**
See also DLB 3, 64, 79; RGAL
Haywood, Eliza (Fowler)
1693(?)-1756 .... **LC 1, 44**
See also DLB 39; RGEL
Hazlitt, William 1778-1830 ...... **NCLC 29, 82**
See also DLB 110, 158; RGEL
Hazzard, Shirley 1931- .... **CLC 18**
See also CA 9-12R; CANR 4, 70; CN; DLBY 82; MTCW 1
Head, Bessie 1937-1986 .... **CLC 25, 67; BLC 2; DAM MULT**
See also BW 2, 3; CA 29-32R; 119; CANR 25, 82; DA3; DLB 117, 225; FW; MTCW 1, 2; RGSF; SSFS 5
Headon, (Nicky) Topper 1956(?)- ..... **CLC 30**
Heaney, Seamus (Justin) 1939- ... **CLC 5, 7, 14, 25, 37, 74, 91; DAB; DAM POET; PC 18; WLCS**
See also BRWS 2; CA 85-88; CANR 25, 48, 75, 91; CDBLB 1960 to Present; CP; DA3; DLB 40; DLBY 95; MTCW 1, 2; PAB; PFS 2, 5, 8; RGEL
Hearn, (Patricio) Lafcadio (Tessima Carlos)
1850-1904 .... **TCLC 9**
See also CA 105; 166; DLB 12, 78, 189; HGG; RGAL
Hearne, Vicki 1946- .... **CLC 56**
See also CA 139
Hearon, Shelby 1931- .... **CLC 63**
See also AITN 2; AMWS 8; CA 25-28R; CANR 18, 48; CSW
Heat-Moon, William Least .... **CLC 29**
See also Trogdon, William (Lewis)
See also AAYA 9
Hebbel, Friedrich 1813-1863 .... **NCLC 43; DAM DRAM**
See also DLB 129; RGWL
Hebert, Anne 1916-2000 .... **CLC 4, 13, 29; DAC; DAM MST, POET**
See also CA 85-88; 187; CANR 69; CCA 1; CWP; CWW 2; DA3; DLB 68; GFL 1789 to the Present; MTCW 1, 2
Hecht, Anthony (Evan) 1923- ...... **CLC 8, 13, 19; DAM POET**
See also CA 9-12R; CANR 6; CP; DLB 5, 169; PFS 6; WP
Hecht, Ben 1894-1964 .... **CLC 8**
See also CA 85-88; DFS 9; DLB 7, 9, 25, 26, 28, 86; FANT; IDFW 3, 4; RGAL; TCLC 101

Hedayat, Sadeq 1903-1951 .... **TCLC 21**
See also CA 120; RGSF

Hegel, Georg Wilhelm Friedrich
1770-1831 .... **NCLC 46**
See also DLB 90

Heidegger, Martin 1889-1976 .... **CLC 24**
See also CA 81-84; 65-68; CANR 34;
MTCW 1, 2

Heidenstam, (Carl Gustaf) Verner von
1859-1940 .... **TCLC 5**
See also CA 104

Heifner, Jack 1946- .... **CLC 11**
See also CA 105; CANR 47

Heijermans, Herman 1864-1924 .... **TCLC 24**
See also CA 123

Heilbrun, Carolyn G(old) 1926- .... **CLC 25**
See also CA 45-48; CANR 1, 28, 58, 94;
CMW; CPW; FW

Heine, Heinrich 1797-1856 .... **NCLC 4, 54;
PC 25**
See also DLB 90; RGWL

Heinemann, Larry (Curtiss) 1944- .. **CLC 50**
See also CA 110; CAAS 21; CANR 31, 81;
DLBD 9; INT CANR-31

Heiney, Donald (William) 1921-1993
See Harris, MacDonald
See also CA 1-4R; 142; CANR 3, 58; FANT

Heinlein, Robert A(nson) 1907-1988 . **CLC 1,
3, 8, 14, 26, 55; DAM POP**
See also AAYA 17; CA 1-4R; 125; CANR
1, 20, 53; CPW; DA3; DLB 8; JRDA;
MAICYA; MTCW 1, 2; RGAL; SATA 9,
69; SATA-Obit 56; SFW; SSFS 7; YAW

Helforth, John
See Doolittle, Hilda

Hellenhofferu, Vojtech Kapristian z
See Ha

Heller, Joseph 1923-1999 . **CLC 1, 3, 5, 8, 11,
36, 63; DA; DAB; DAC; DAM MST,
NOV, POP; WLC**
See also AAYA 24; AITN 1; AMWS 4; CA
5-8R; 187; CABS 1; CANR 8, 42, 66;
CN; CPW; DA3; DLB 2, 28, 227; DLBY
80; INT CANR-8; MTCW 1, 2; NFS 1;
RGAL; YAW

Hellman, Lillian (Florence)
1906-1984 .. **CLC 2, 4, 8, 14, 18, 34, 44,
52; DAM DRAM; DC 1**
See also AITN 1, 2; AMWS 1; CA 13-16R;
112; CAD; CANR 33; DA3; DFS 1, 3;
DLB 7, 228; DLBY 84; FW; MAWW;
MTCW 1, 2; RGAL

Helprin, Mark 1947- .... **CLC 7, 10, 22, 32;
DAM NOV, POP**
See also CA 81-84; CANR 47, 64;
CDALBS; CPW; DA3; DLBY 85; FANT;
MTCW 1, 2

Helvetius, Claude-Adrien 1715-1771 .. **LC 26**

Helyar, Jane Penelope Josephine 1933-
See Poole, Josephine
See also CA 21-24R; CANR 10, 26; SATA
82

Hemans, Felicia 1793-1835 ...... **NCLC 29, 71**
See also DLB 96; RGEL

Hemingway, Ernest (Miller)
1899-1961 .... **CLC 1, 3, 6, 8, 10, 13, 19,
30, 34, 39, 41, 44, 50, 61, 80; DA;
DAB; DAC; DAM MST, NOV; SSC 1,
25, 36, 40; WLC**
See also AAYA 19; AMW; AMWR; CA 77-
80; CANR 34; CDALB 1917-1929; DA3;
DLB 4, 9, 102, 210; DLBD 1, 15, 16;
DLBY 81, 87, 96, 98; MTCW 1, 2; NFS
1, 5, 6; RGAL; RGSF; SSFS 1, 6, 8, 9,
11; WYA

Hempel, Amy 1951- .... **CLC 39**
See also CA 118; 137; CANR 70; DA3;
MTCW 2; SSFS 2

Henderson, F. C.
See Mencken, H(enry) L(ouis)

Henderson, Sylvia
See Ashton-Warner, Sylvia (Constance)

Henderson, Zenna (Chlarson)
1917-1983 .... **SSC 29**
See also CA 1-4R; 133; CANR 1, 84; DLB
8; SATA 5; SFW

Henkin, Joshua .... **CLC 119**
See also CA 161

Henley, Beth .... **CLC 23; DC 6, 14**
See also Henley, Elizabeth Becker
See also CABS 3; CAD; CWD; DFS 2;
DLBY 86

Henley, Elizabeth Becker 1952-
See Henley, Beth
See also CA 107; CANR 32, 73; CD; CSW;
DAM DRAM, MST; DA3; FW; MTCW
1, 2

Henley, William Ernest 1849-1903 .. **TCLC 8**
See also CA 105; DLB 19; RGEL

Hennissart, Martha
See Lathen, Emma
See also CA 85-88; CANR 64

Henry VIII 1491-1547 .... **LC 10**
See also DLB 132

Henry, O. .... **TCLC 1, 19; SSC 5; WLC**
See also Porter, William Sydney
See also AMWS 2; RGAL; RGSF; SSFS 2

Henry, Patrick 1736-1799 .... **LC 25**

Henryson, Robert 1430(?)-1506(?) ...... **LC 20**
See also BRWS 7; DLB 146; RGEL

Henschke, Alfred
See Klabund

Hentoff, Nat(han Irving) 1925- .... **CLC 26**
See also AAYA 4; CA 1-4R; CAAS 6;
CANR 5, 25, 77; CLR 1, 52; INT CANR-
25; JRDA; MAICYA; SATA 42, 69;
SATA-Brief 27; WYA; YAW

Heppenstall, (John) Rayner
1911-1981 .... **CLC 10**
See also CA 1-4R; 103; CANR 29

Heraclitus c. 540B.C.-c. 450B.C. .... **CMLC 22**
See also DLB 176

Herbert, Frank (Patrick)
1920-1986 .... **CLC 12, 23, 35, 44, 85;
DAM POP**
See also AAYA 21; CA 53-56; 118; CANR
5, 43; CDALBS; CPW; DLB 8; INT
CANR-5; MTCW 1, 2; SATA 9, 37;
SATA-Obit 47; SCFW 2; SFW; YAW

Herbert, George 1593-1633 ..... **LC 24; DAB;
DAM POET; PC 4**
See also CDBLB Before 1660; DLB 126;
RGEL; WP

Herbert, Zbigniew 1924-1998 ..... **CLC 9, 43;
DAM POET**
See also CA 89-92; 169; CANR 36, 74;
CWW 2; DLB 232; MTCW 1

Herbst, Josephine (Frey)
1897-1969 .... **CLC 34**
See also CA 5-8R; 25-28R; DLB 9

Herder, Johann Gottfried von
1744-1803 .... **NCLC 8**
See also DLB 97

Heredia, Jose Maria 1803-1839
See also HLCS 2

Hergesheimer, Joseph 1880-1954 ... **TCLC 11**
See also CA 109; DLB 102, 9; RGAL

Herlihy, James Leo 1927-1993 .... **CLC 6**
See also CA 1-4R; 143; CAD; CANR 2

Hermogenes fl. c. 175- .... **CMLC 6**

Hernandez, Jose 1834-1886 .... **NCLC 17**
See also RGWL

Herodotus c. 484B.C.-c. 420B.C. .. **CMLC 17**
See also DLB 176; RGWL

Herrick, Robert 1591-1674 .... **LC 13; DA;
DAB; DAC; DAM MST, POP; PC 9**
See also DLB 126; RGAL; RGEL; WP

Herring, Guilles
See Somerville, Edith

Herriot, James .... **CLC 12; DAM POP**
See also Wight, James Alfred
See also AAYA 1; CA 148; CANR 40;
MTCW 2; SATA 86

Herris, Violet
See Hunt, Violet

Herrmann, Dorothy 1941- .... **CLC 44**
See also CA 107

Herrmann, Taffy
See Herrmann, Dorothy

Hersey, John (Richard) 1914-1993 .... **CLC 1,
2, 7, 9, 40, 81, 97; DAM POP**
See also AAYA 29; CA 17-20R; 140; CANR
33; CDALBS; CPW; DLB 6, 185; MTCW
1, 2; SATA 25; SATA-Obit 76

Herzen, Aleksandr Ivanovich
1812-1870 .... **NCLC 10, 61**

Herzl, Theodor 1860-1904 .... **TCLC 36**
See also CA 168

Herzog, Werner 1942- .... **CLC 16**
See also CA 89-92

Hesiod c. 8th cent. B.C.- .... **CMLC 5**
See also DLB 176; RGWL

Hesse, Hermann 1877-1962 .... **CLC 1, 2, 3, 6,
11, 17, 25, 69; DA; DAB; DAC; DAM
MST, NOV; SSC 9; WLC**
See also CA 17-18; CAP 2; DA3; DLB 66;
MTCW 1, 2; NFS 6; RGWL; SATA 50

Hewes, Cady
See De Voto, Bernard (Augustine)

Heyen, William 1940- .... **CLC 13, 18**
See also CA 33-36R; CAAS 9; CANR 98;
CP; DLB 5

Heyerdahl, Thor 1914- .... **CLC 26**
See also CA 5-8R; CANR 5, 22, 66, 73;
MTCW 1, 2; SATA 2, 52

Heym, Georg (Theodor Franz Arthur)
1887-1912 .... **TCLC 9**
See also CA 106; 181

Heym, Stefan 1913- .... **CLC 41**
See also CA 9-12R; CANR 4; CWW 2;
DLB 69

Heyse, Paul (Johann Ludwig von)
1830-1914 .... **TCLC 8**
See also CA 104; DLB 129

Heyward, (Edwin) DuBose
1885-1940 .... **TCLC 59**
See also CA 108; 157; DLB 7, 9, 45; SATA
21

Heywood, John 1497-1580 .... **LC 65**
See also RGEL

Hibbert, Eleanor Alice Burford
1906-1993 .... **CLC 7; DAM POP**
See also BEST 90:4; CA 17-20R; 140;
CANR 9, 28, 59; CMW; CPW; MTCW 2;
RHW; SATA 2; SATA-Obit 74

Hichens, Robert (Smythe)
1864-1950 .... **TCLC 64**
See also CA 162; DLB 153; HGG; RHW;
SUFW

Higgins, George V(incent)
1939-1999 .... **CLC 4, 7, 10, 18**
See also CA 77-80; 186; CAAS 5; CANR
17, 51, 89, 96; CMW; CN; DLB 2; DLBY
81, 98; INT CANR-17; MTCW 1

Higginson, Thomas Wentworth
1823-1911 .... **TCLC 36**
See also CA 162; DLB 1, 64

Higgonet, Margaret ed. .... **CLC 65**

Highet, Helen
See MacInnes, Helen (Clark)

Highsmith, (Mary) Patricia
1921-1995 .... **CLC 2, 4, 14, 42, 102;
DAM NOV, POP**
See also Morgan, Claire
See also BRWS 5; CA 1-4R; 147; CANR 1,
20, 48, 62; CMW; CPW; DA3; MSW;
MTCW 1, 2

Homer c. 8th cent. B.C.- .. **CMLC 1, 16; DA; DAB; DAC; DAM MST, POET; PC 23; WLCS**
See also DA3; DLB 176; EFS 1; RGWL; WP

Hongo, Garrett Kaoru 1951- .... **PC 23**
See also CA 133; CAAS 22; CP; DLB 120; RGAL

Honig, Edwin 1919- .... **CLC 33**
See also CA 5-8R; CAAS 8; CANR 4, 45; CP; DLB 5

Hood, Hugh (John Blagdon) 1928- . **CLC 15, 28; SSC 42**
See also CA 49-52; CAAS 17; CANR 1, 33, 87; CN; DLB 53; RGSF

Hood, Thomas 1799-1845 .... **NCLC 16**
See also DLB 96; RGEL

Hooker, (Peter) Jeremy 1941- .... **CLC 43**
See also CA 77-80; CANR 22; CP; DLB 40

hooks, bell .... **CLC 94; BLCS**
See also Watkins, Gloria Jean
See also FW; MTCW 2

Hope, A(lec) D(erwent) 1907-2000 .... **CLC 3, 51**
See also BRWS 7; CA 21-24R; 188; CANR 33, 74; MTCW 1, 2; PFS 8; RGEL

Hope, Anthony 1863-1933 .... **TCLC 83**
See also CA 157; DLB 153, 156; RGEL; RHW

Hope, Brian
See Creasey, John

Hope, Christopher (David Tully) 1944- .... **CLC 52**
See also AFW; CA 106; CANR 47; CN; DLB 225; SATA 62

Hopkins, Gerard Manley 1844-1889 .... **NCLC 17; DA; DAB; DAC; DAM MST, POET; PC 15; WLC**
See also CDBLB 1890-1914; DA3; DLB 35, 57; PAB; RGEL; WP

Hopkins, John (Richard) 1931-1998 .. **CLC 4**
See also CA 85-88; 169; CBD; CD

Hopkins, Pauline Elizabeth 1859-1930 ...... **TCLC 28; BLC 2; DAM MULT**
See also AFAW 2; BW 2, 3; CA 141; CANR 82; DLB 50

Hopkinson, Francis 1737-1791 .... **LC 25**
See also DLB 31; RGAL

Hopley-Woolrich, Cornell George 1903-1968
See Woolrich, Cornell
See also CA 13-14; CANR 58; CAP 1; CMW; DLB 226; MTCW 2

Horace 65B.C.-8B.C. .... **CMLC 39**
See also DLB 211; RGWL

Horatio
See Proust, (Valentin-Louis-George-Eug

Horgan, Paul (George Vincent O'Shaughnessy) 1903-1995 . **CLC 9, 53; DAM NOV**
See also CA 13-16R; 147; CANR 9, 35; DLB 212; DLBY 85; INT CANR-9; MTCW 1, 2; SATA 13; SATA-Obit 84; TCWW 2

Horn, Peter
See Kuttner, Henry

Hornem, Horace Esq.
See Byron, George Gordon (Noel)

Horney, Karen (Clementine Theodore Danielsen) 1885-1952 ...... **TCLC 71**
See also CA 114; 165; FW

Hornung, E(rnest) W(illiam) 1866-1921 .... **TCLC 59**
See also CA 108; 160; CMW; DLB 70

Horovitz, Israel (Arthur) 1939- ...... **CLC 56; DAM DRAM**
See also CA 33-36R; CAD; CANR 46, 59; CD; DLB 7

Horton, George Moses 1797(?)-1883(?) .... **NCLC 87**
See also DLB 50

Horvath, odon von
See Horvath, Oedoen von
See also DLB 85, 124; RGWL

Horvath, Oedoen von 1901-1938 ... **TCLC 45**
See also Horvath, odon von; von Horvath, Oedoen
See also CA 118

Horwitz, Julius 1920-1986 .... **CLC 14**
See also CA 9-12R; 119; CANR 12

Hospital, Janette Turner 1942- .... **CLC 42, 145**
See also CA 108; CANR 48; CN; RGSF

Hostos, E. M. de
See Hostos (y Bonilla), Eugenio Maria de

Hostos, Eugenio M. de
See Hostos (y Bonilla), Eugenio Maria de

Hostos, Eugenio Maria
See Hostos (y Bonilla), Eugenio Maria de

Hostos (y Bonilla), Eugenio Maria de 1839-1903 .... **TCLC 24**
See also CA 123; 131; HW 1

Houdini
See Lovecraft, H(oward) P(hillips)

Hougan, Carolyn 1943- .... **CLC 34**
See also CA 139

Household, Geoffrey (Edward West) 1900-1988 .... **CLC 11**
See also CA 77-80; 126; CANR 58; CMW; DLB 87; SATA 14; SATA-Obit 59

Housman, A(lfred) E(dward) 1859-1936 .... **TCLC 1, 10; DA; DAB; DAC; DAM MST, POET; PC 2; WLCS**
See also BRW; CA 104; 125; DA3; DLB 19; MTCW 1, 2; PAB; PFS 4, 7; RGEL; WP

Housman, Laurence 1865-1959 .... **TCLC 7**
See also CA 106; 155; DLB 10; FANT; RGEL; SATA 25

Howard, Elizabeth Jane 1923- ..... **CLC 7, 29**
See also CA 5-8R; CANR 8, 62; CN

Howard, Maureen 1930- .... **CLC 5, 14, 46**
See also CA 53-56; CANR 31, 75; CN; DLBY 83; INT CANR-31; MTCW 1, 2

Howard, Richard 1929- .... **CLC 7, 10, 47**
See also AITN 1; CA 85-88; CANR 25, 80; CP; DLB 5; INT CANR-25

Howard, Robert E(rvin) 1906-1936 .... **TCLC 8**
See also CA 105; 157; FANT; SUFW

Howard, Warren F.
See Pohl, Frederik

Howe, Fanny (Quincy) 1940- .... **CLC 47**
See also CA 117; CAAE 187; CAAS 27; CANR 70; CP; CWP; SATA-Brief 52

Howe, Irving 1920-1993 .... **CLC 85**
See also AMWS 6; CA 9-12R; 141; CANR 21, 50; DLB 67; MTCW 1, 2

Howe, Julia Ward 1819-1910 .... **TCLC 21**
See also CA 117; 191; DLB 1, 189, 235; FW

Howe, Susan 1937- .... **CLC 72**
See also AMWS 4; CA 160; CP; CWP; DLB 120; FW; RGAL

Howe, Tina 1937- .... **CLC 48**
See also CA 109; CAD; CD; CWD

Howell, James 1594(?)-1666 .... **LC 13**
See also DLB 151

Howells, W. D.
See Howells, William Dean

Howells, William D.
See Howells, William Dean

Howells, William Dean 1837-1920 .. **TCLC 7, 17, 41; SSC 36**
See also CA 104; 134; CDALB 1865-1917; DLB 12, 64, 74, 79, 189; MTCW 2; RGAL

Howes, Barbara 1914-1996 .... **CLC 15**
See also CA 9-12R; 151; CAAS 3; CANR 53; CP; SATA 5

Hrabal, Bohumil 1914-1997 .... **CLC 13, 67**
See also CA 106; 156; CAAS 12; CANR 57; CWW 2; DLB 232; RGSF

Hroswitha of Gandersheim c. 935-c. 1000 .... **CMLC 29**
See also DLB 148

Hsi, Chu 1130-1200 .... **CMLC 42**

Hsun, Lu
See Lu Hsun

Hubbard, L(afayette) Ron(ald) 1911-1986 .... **CLC 43; DAM POP**
See also CA 77-80; 118; CANR 52; CPW; DA3; FANT; MTCW 2; SFW

Huch, Ricarda (Octavia) 1864-1947 .... **TCLC 13**
See also CA 111; 189; DLB 66

Huddle, David 1942- .... **CLC 49**
See also CA 57-60; CAAS 20; CANR 89; DLB 130

Hudson, Jeffrey
See Crichton, (John) Michael

Hudson, W(illiam) H(enry) 1841-1922 .... **TCLC 29**
See also CA 115; 190; DLB 98, 153, 174; RGEL; SATA 35

Hueffer, Ford Madox
See Ford, Ford Madox

Hughart, Barry 1934- .... **CLC 39**
See also CA 137; FANT; SFW

Hughes, Colin
See Creasey, John

Hughes, David (John) 1930- .... **CLC 48**
See also CA 116; 129; CN; DLB 14

Hughes, Edward James
See Hughes, Ted
See also DAM MST, POET; DA3

Hughes, (James) Langston 1902-1967 .... **CLC 1, 5, 10, 15, 35, 44, 108; BLC 2; DA; DAB; DAC; DAM DRAM, MST, MULT, POET; DC 3; PC 1; SSC 6; WLC**
See also AAYA 12; AFAW 1, 2; AMWR 2; AMWS 1; BW 1, 3; CA 1-4R; 25-28R; CANR 1, 34, 82; CDALB 1929-1941; CLR 17; DA3; DLB 4, 7, 48, 51, 86, 228; JRDA; MAICYA; MTCW 1, 2; PAB; PFS 1, 3, 6, 10; RGAL; RGSF; SATA 4, 33; SSFS 4, 7; WCH; WP; YAW

Hughes, Richard (Arthur Warren) 1900-1976 .... **CLC 1, 11; DAM NOV**
See also CA 5-8R; 65-68; CANR 4; DLB 15, 161; MTCW 1; RGEL; SATA 8; SATA-Obit 25

Hughes, Ted 1930-1998 . **CLC 2, 4, 9, 14, 37, 119; DAB; DAC; PC 7**
See also Hughes, Edward James
See also BRWS 1; CA 1-4R; 171; CANR 1, 33, 66; CLR 3; CP; DLB 40, 161; MAICYA; MTCW 1, 2; PAB; PFS 4; RGEL; SATA 49; SATA-Brief 27; SATA-Obit 107; YAW

Hugo, Richard F(ranklin) 1923-1982 .... **CLC 6, 18, 32; DAM POET**
See also CA 49-52; 108; CANR 3; DLB 5, 206

Hugo, Victor (Marie) 1802-1885 .... **NCLC 3, 10, 21; DA; DAB; DAC; DAM DRAM, MST, NOV, POET; PC 17; WLC**
See also AAYA 28; DA3; DLB 119, 192; EFS 2; EW; GFL 1789 to the Present; NFS 5; RGWL; SATA 47

Isler, Alan (David) 1934- .... **CLC 91**
See also CA 156

Ivan IV 1530-1584 .... **LC 17**

Ivanov, Vyacheslav Ivanovich
1866-1949 .... **TCLC 33**
See also CA 122

Ivask, Ivar Vidrik 1927-1992 .... **CLC 14**
See also CA 37-40R; 139; CANR 24

Ives, Morgan
See Bradley, Marion Zimmer
See also GLL 1

Izumi Shikibu c. 973-c. 1034 .... **CMLC 33**

J .... **CLC 10, 36, 86; DAM NOV; SSC 20**
See also CA 97-100; CANR 36, 50, 74;
DA3; DLB 182; DLBY 94; MTCW 1, 2

J. R. S.
See Gogarty, Oliver St. John

Jabran, Kahlil
See Gibran, Kahlil

Jabran, Khalil
See Gibran, Kahlil

Jackson, Daniel
See Wingrove, David (John)

Jackson, Helen Hunt 1830-1885 .... **NCLC 90**
See also DLB 42, 47, 186, 189; RGAL

Jackson, Jesse 1908-1983 .... **CLC 12**
See also BW 1; CA 25-28R; 109; CANR
27; CLR 28; CWRI; MAICYA; SATA 2,
29; SATA-Obit 48

Jackson, Laura (Riding) 1901-1991
See Riding, Laura
See also CA 65-68; 135; CANR 28, 89;
DLB 48

Jackson, Sam
See Trumbo, Dalton

Jackson, Sara
See Wingrove, David (John)

Jackson, Shirley 1919-1965 . **CLC 11, 60, 87;
DA; DAC; DAM MST; SSC 9, 39;
WLC**
See also AAYA 9; CA 1-4R; 25-28R; CANR
4, 52; CDALB 1941-1968; DA3; DLB 6,
234; HGG; MTCW 2; RGAL; RGSF;
SATA 2; SSFS 1

Jacob, (Cyprien-)Max 1876-1944 .... **TCLC 6**
See also CA 104; GFL 1789 to the Present;
GLL 2; RGWL

Jacobs, Harriet A(nn)
1813(?)-1897 .... **NCLC 67**
See also AFAW 1; DLB 239; RGAL

Jacobs, Jim 1942- .... **CLC 12**
See also CA 97-100; INT 97-100

Jacobs, W(illiam) W(ymark)
1863-1943 .... **TCLC 22**
See also CA 121; 167; DLB 135; HGG;
RGEL; RGSF; SSFS 2; SUFW

Jacobsen, Jens Peter 1847-1885 .... **NCLC 34**

Jacobsen, Josephine 1908- .... **CLC 48, 102**
See also CA 33-36R; CAAS 18; CANR 23,
48; CCA 1; CP

Jacobson, Dan 1929- .... **CLC 4, 14**
See also CA 1-4R; CANR 2, 25, 66; CN;
DLB 14, 207, 225; MTCW 1; RGSF

Jacqueline
See Carpentier (y Valmont), Alejo

Jagger, Mick 1944- .... **CLC 17**

Jahiz, al- c. 780-c. 869 .... **CMLC 25**

Jakes, John (William) 1932- . **CLC 29; DAM
NOV, POP**
See also AAYA 32; BEST 89:4; CA 57-60;
CANR 10, 43, 66; CPW; CSW; DA3;
DLBY 83; FANT; INT CANR-10; MTCW
1, 2; RHW; SATA 62; SFW; TCWW 2

James I 1394-1437 .... **LC 20**
See also RGEL

James, Andrew
See Kirkup, James

James, C(yril) L(ionel) R(obert)
1901-1989 .... **CLC 33; BLCS**
See also BW 2; CA 117; 125; 128; CANR
62; DLB 125; MTCW 1

James, Daniel (Lewis) 1911-1988
See Santiago, Danny
See also CA 174; 125

James, Dynely
See Mayne, William (James Carter)

James, Henry Sr. 1811-1882 .... **NCLC 53**

James, Henry 1843-1916 ..... **TCLC 2, 11, 24,
40, 47, 64; DA; DAB; DAC; DAM
MST, NOV; SSC 8, 32; WLC**
See also CA 104; 132; CDALB 1865-1917;
DA3; DLB 12, 71, 74, 189; DLBD 13;
HGG; MTCW 1, 2; NFS 12; RGAL;
RGEL; RGSF; SSFS 9

James, M. R.
See James, Montague (Rhodes)
See also DLB 156

James, Montague (Rhodes)
1862-1936 .... **TCLC 6; SSC 16**
See also CA 104; DLB 201; HGG; RGEL;
RGSF; SUFW

James, P. D. .... **CLC 18, 46, 122**
See also White, Phyllis Dorothy James
See also BEST 90:2; BRWS 4; CDBLB
1960 to Present; DLB 87; DLBD 17

James, Philip
See Moorcock, Michael (John)

James, Samuel
See Stephens, James

James, Seumas
See Stephens, James

James, Stephen
See Stephens, James

James, William 1842-1910 .... **TCLC 15, 32**
See also AMW; CA 109; RGAL

Jameson, Anna 1794-1860 .... **NCLC 43**
See also DLB 99, 166

Jameson, Fredric 1934- .... **CLC 142**
See also DLB 67

Jami, Nur al-Din 'Abd al-Rahman
1414-1492 .... **LC 9**

Jammes, Francis 1868-1938 .... **TCLC 75**
See also GFL 1789 to the Present

Jandl, Ernst 1925-2000 .... **CLC 34**

Janowitz, Tama 1957- ... **CLC 43, 145; DAM
POP**
See also CA 106; CANR 52, 89; CN; CPW

Japrisot, Sebastien 1931- .... **CLC 90**
See also CMW

Jarrell, Randall 1914-1965 .... **CLC 1, 2, 6, 9,
13, 49; DAM POET**
See also CA 5-8R; 25-28R; CABS 2; CANR
6, 34; CDALB 1941-1968; CLR 6; CWRI;
DLB 48, 52; MAICYA; MTCW 1, 2;
PAB; PFS 2; RGAL; SATA 7

Jarry, Alfred 1873-1907 . **TCLC 2, 14; DAM
DRAM; SSC 20**
See also CA 104; 153; DA3; DFS 8; DLB
192; GFL 1789 to the Present; RGWL

Jawien, Andrzej
See John Paul II, Pope

Jaynes, Roderick
See Coen, Ethan

Jeake, Samuel, Jr.
See Aiken, Conrad (Potter)

Jean Paul 1763-1825 .... **NCLC 7**

Jefferies, (John) Richard
1848-1887 .... **NCLC 47**
See also DLB 98, 141; RGEL; SATA 16;
SFW

Jeffers, (John) Robinson 1887-1962 .. **CLC 2,
3, 11, 15, 54; DA; DAC; DAM MST,
POET; PC 17; WLC**
See also AMWS 2; CA 85-88; CANR 35;
CDALB 1917-1929; DLB 45, 212;
MTCW 1, 2; PAB; PFS 3, 4; RGAL

Jefferson, Janet
See Mencken, H(enry) L(ouis)

Jefferson, Thomas 1743-1826 . **NCLC 11, 103**
See also CDALB 1640-1865; DA3; DLB
31; RGAL

Jeffrey, Francis 1773-1850 .... **NCLC 33**
See also DLB 107

Jelakowitch, Ivan
See Heijermans, Herman

Jellicoe, (Patricia) Ann 1927- .... **CLC 27**
See also CA 85-88; CBD; CD; CWD;
CWRI; DLB 13, 233; FW

Jemyma
See Holley, Marietta

Jen, Gish .... **CLC 70**
See also Jen, Lillian

Jen, Lillian 1956(?)-
See Jen, Gish
See also CA 135; CANR 89

Jenkins, (John) Robin 1912- .... **CLC 52**
See also CA 1-4R; CANR 1; CN; DLB 14

Jennings, Elizabeth (Joan) 1926- ...... **CLC 5,
14, 131**
See also BRWS 5; CA 61-64; CAAS 5;
CANR 8, 39, 66; CP; CWP; DLB 27;
MTCW 1; SATA 66

Jennings, Waylon 1937- .... **CLC 21**

Jensen, Johannes V. 1873-1950 ...... **TCLC 41**
See also CA 170; DLB 214

Jensen, Laura (Linnea) 1948- .... **CLC 37**
See also CA 103

Jerome, Saint 345-420 .... **CMLC 30**
See also RGWL

Jerome, Jerome K(lapka)
1859-1927 .... **TCLC 23**
See also CA 119; 177; DLB 10, 34, 135;
RGEL

Jerrold, Douglas William
1803-1857 .... **NCLC 2**
See also DLB 158, 159; RGEL

Jewett, (Theodora) Sarah Orne
1849-1909 .... **TCLC 1, 22; SSC 6, 44**
See also AMW; CA 108; 127; CANR 71;
DLB 12, 74, 221; FW; MAWW; RGAL;
RGSF; SATA 15; SSFS 4

Jewsbury, Geraldine (Endsor)
1812-1880 .... **NCLC 22**
See also DLB 21

Jhabvala, Ruth Prawer 1927- . **CLC 4, 8, 29,
94, 138; DAB; DAM NOV**
See also CA 1-4R; CANR 2, 29, 51, 74, 91;
CN; DLB 139, 194; IDFW 4; INT CANR-
29; MTCW 1, 2; RGSF; RGWL; RHW

Jibran, Kahlil
See Gibran, Kahlil

Jibran, Khalil
See Gibran, Kahlil

Jiles, Paulette 1943- .... **CLC 13, 58**
See also CA 101; CANR 70; CWP

Jimenez (Mantecon), Juan Ramon
1881-1958 .... **TCLC 4; DAM MULT,
POET; HLC 1; PC 7**
See also CA 104; 131; CANR 74; DLB 134;
EW; HW 1; MTCW 1, 2; RGWL

Jimenez, Ramon
See Jim

Jimenez Mantecon, Juan
See Jim

Jin, Ha
See Jin, Xuefei

Jin, Xuefei 1956- .... **CLC 109**
See also CA 152; CANR 91

Joel, Billy .... **CLC 26**
See also Joel, William Martin

Joel, William Martin 1949-
See Joel, Billy
See also CA 108

John, Saint 107th cent. -100 .... **CMLC 27**

Kafka, Franz 1883-1924 . **TCLC 2, 6, 13, 29, 47, 53, 112; DA; DAB; DAC; DAM MST, NOV; SSC 5, 29, 35; WLC**
See also AAYA 31; CA 105; 126; DA3; DLB 81; MTCW 1, 2; NFS 7; RGSF; RGWL; SFW; SSFS 3, 7, 12

Kahanovitsch, Pinkhes
See Der Nister

Kahn, Roger 1927- .... **CLC 30**
See also CA 25-28R; CANR 44, 69; DLB 171; SATA 37

Kain, Saul
See Sassoon, Siegfried (Lorraine)

Kaiser, Georg 1878-1945 .... **TCLC 9**
See also CA 106; 190; DLB 124; RGWL

Kaledin, Sergei .... **CLC 59**

Kaletski, Alexander 1946- .... **CLC 39**
See also CA 118; 143

Kalidasa fl. c. 400-455 .... **CMLC 9; PC 22**
See also RGWL

Kallman, Chester (Simon)
1921-1975 .... **CLC 2**
See also CA 45-48; 53-56; CANR 3

Kaminsky, Melvin 1926-
See Brooks, Mel
See also CA 65-68; CANR 16

Kaminsky, Stuart M(elvin) 1934- ..... **CLC 59**
See also CA 73-76; CANR 29, 53, 89; CMW

Kandinsky, Wassily 1866-1944 .... **TCLC 92**
See also CA 118; 155

Kane, Francis
See Robbins, Harold

Kane, Henry 1918-
See Queen, Ellery
See also CA 156; CMW

Kane, Paul
See Simon, Paul (Frederick)

Kanin, Garson 1912-1999 .... **CLC 22**
See also AITN 1; CA 5-8R; 177; CAD; CANR 7, 78; DLB 7; IDFW 3, 4

Kaniuk, Yoram 1930- .... **CLC 19**
See also CA 134

Kant, Immanuel 1724-1804 ..... **NCLC 27, 67**
See also DLB 94

Kantor, MacKinlay 1904-1977 .... **CLC 7**
See also CA 61-64; 73-76; CANR 60, 63; DLB 9, 102; MTCW 2; RHW; TCWW 2

Kaplan, David Michael 1946- .... **CLC 50**
See also CA 187

Kaplan, James 1951- .... **CLC 59**
See also CA 135

Karageorge, Michael
See Anderson, Poul (William)

Karamzin, Nikolai Mikhailovich
1766-1826 .... **NCLC 3**
See also DLB 150; RGSF

Karapanou, Margarita 1946- .... **CLC 13**
See also CA 101

Karinthy, Frigyes 1887-1938 .... **TCLC 47**
See also CA 170

Karl, Frederick R(obert) 1927- .... **CLC 34**
See also CA 5-8R; CANR 3, 44

Kastel, Warren
See Silverberg, Robert

Kataev, Evgeny Petrovich 1903-1942
See Petrov, Evgeny
See also CA 120

Kataphusin
See Ruskin, John

Katz, Steve 1935- .... **CLC 47**
See also CA 25-28R; CAAS 14, 64; CANR 12; CN; DLBY 83

Kauffman, Janet 1945- .... **CLC 42**
See also CA 117; CANR 43, 84; DLBY 86

Kaufman, Bob (Garnell) 1925-1986 . **CLC 49**
See also BW 1; CA 41-44R; 118; CANR 22; DLB 16, 41

Kaufman, George S. 1889-1961 ...... **CLC 38; DAM DRAM**
See also CA 108; 93-96; DFS 1, 10; DLB 7; INT 108; MTCW 2; RGAL

Kaufman, Sue .... **CLC 3, 8**
See also Barondess, Sue K(aufman)

Kavafis, Konstantinos Petrou 1863-1933
See Cavafy, C(onstantine) P(eter)
See also CA 104

Kavan, Anna 1901-1968 .... **CLC 5, 13, 82**
See also BRWS 7; CA 5-8R; CANR 6, 57; MTCW 1; RGEL; SFW

Kavanagh, Dan
See Barnes, Julian (Patrick)

Kavanagh, Julie 1952- .... **CLC 119**
See also CA 163

Kavanagh, Patrick (Joseph)
1904-1967 .... **CLC 22; PC 33**
See also BRWS 7; CA 123; 25-28R; DLB 15, 20; MTCW 1; RGEL

Kawabata, Yasunari 1899-1972 ..... **CLC 2, 5, 9, 18, 107; DAM MULT; SSC 17**
See also CA 93-96; 33-36R; CANR 88; DLB 180; MJW; MTCW 2; RGSF; RGWL

Kaye, M(ary) M(argaret) 1909- .... **CLC 28**
See also CA 89-92; CANR 24, 60; MTCW 1, 2; RHW; SATA 62

Kaye, Mollie
See Kaye, M(ary) M(argaret)

Kaye-Smith, Sheila 1887-1956 .... **TCLC 20**
See also CA 118; DLB 36

Kaymor, Patrice Maguilene
See Senghor, L

Kazakov, Yuri Pavlovich 1927-1982 . **SSC 43**
See also CA 5-8R; CANR 36; MTCW 1; RGSF

Kazan, Elia 1909- .... **CLC 6, 16, 63**
See also CA 21-24R; CANR 32, 78

Kazantzakis, Nikos 1883(?)-1957 .... **TCLC 2, 5, 33**
See also CA 105; 132; DA3; MTCW 1, 2; RGWL

Kazin, Alfred 1915-1998 ..... **CLC 34, 38, 119**
See also AMWS 8; CA 1-4R; CAAS 7; CANR 1, 45, 79; DLB 67

Keane, Mary Nesta (Skrine) 1904-1996
See Keane, Molly
See also CA 108; 114; 151; CN; RHW

Keane, Molly .... **CLC 31**
See also Keane, Mary Nesta (Skrine)
See also INT 114

Keates, Jonathan 1946(?)- .... **CLC 34**
See also CA 163

Keaton, Buster 1895-1966 .... **CLC 20**

Keats, John 1795-1821 ...... **NCLC 8, 73; DA; DAB; DAC; DAM MST, POET; PC 1; WLC**
See also CDBLB 1789-1832; DA3; DLB 96, 110; PAB; PFS 1, 2, 3, 9; RGEL; WP

Keble, John 1792-1866 .... **NCLC 87**
See also DLB 32, 55; RGEL

Keene, Donald 1922- .... **CLC 34**
See also CA 1-4R; CANR 5

Keillor, Garrison .... **CLC 40, 115**
See also Keillor, Gary (Edward)
See also AAYA 2; BEST 89:3; DLBY 87; SATA 58

Keillor, Gary (Edward) 1942-
See Keillor, Garrison
See also CA 111; 117; CANR 36, 59; CPW; DAM POP; DA3; MTCW 1, 2

Keith, Michael
See Hubbard, L(afayette) Ron(ald)

Keller, Gottfried 1819-1890 .... **NCLC 2; SSC 26**
See also DLB 129; RGSF; RGWL

Keller, Nora Okja 1965- .... **CLC 109**
See also CA 187

Kellerman, Jonathan 1949- .. **CLC 44; DAM POP**
See also AAYA 35; BEST 90:1; CA 106; CANR 29, 51; CMW; CPW; DA3; INT CANR-29

Kelley, William Melvin 1937- .... **CLC 22**
See also BW 1; CA 77-80; CANR 27, 83; CN; DLB 33

Kellogg, Marjorie 1922- .... **CLC 2**
See also CA 81-84

Kellow, Kathleen
See Hibbert, Eleanor Alice Burford

Kelly, M(ilton) T(errence) 1947- ...... **CLC 55**
See also CA 97-100; CAAS 22; CANR 19, 43, 84; CN

Kelman, James 1946- .... **CLC 58, 86**
See also BRWS 5; CA 148; CANR 85; CN; DLB 194; RGSF

Kemal, Yashar 1923- .... **CLC 14, 29**
See also CA 89-92; CANR 44; CWW 2

Kemble, Fanny 1809-1893 .... **NCLC 18**
See also DLB 32

Kemelman, Harry 1908-1996 .... **CLC 2**
See also AITN 1; CA 9-12R; 155; CANR 6, 71; CMW; DLB 28

Kempe, Margery 1373(?)-1440(?) ... **LC 6, 56**
See also DLB 146; RGEL

Kempis, Thomas a 1380-1471 .... **LC 11**

Kendall, Henry 1839-1882 .... **NCLC 12**
See also DLB 230

Keneally, Thomas (Michael) 1935- ... **CLC 5, 8, 10, 14, 19, 27, 43, 117; DAM NOV**
See also BRWS 4; CA 85-88; CANR 10, 50, 74; CN; CPW; DA3; MTCW 1, 2; RGEL; RHW

Kennedy, Adrienne (Lita) 1931- ..... **CLC 66; BLC 2; DAM MULT; DC 5**
See also AFAW 2; BW 2, 3; CA 103; CAAS 20; CABS 3; CANR 26, 53, 82; CD; DFS 9; DLB 38; FW

Kennedy, John Pendleton
1795-1870 .... **NCLC 2**
See also DLB 3; RGAL

Kennedy, Joseph Charles 1929-
See Kennedy, X. J.
See also CA 1-4R; CANR 4, 30, 40; CP; CWRI; SATA 14, 86

Kennedy, William 1928- .. **CLC 6, 28, 34, 53; DAM NOV**
See also AAYA 1; AMWS 7; CA 85-88; CANR 14, 31, 76; DA3; DLB 143; DLBY 85; INT CANR-31; MTCW 1, 2; SATA 57

Kennedy, X. J. .... **CLC 8, 42**
See also Kennedy, Joseph Charles
See also CAAS 9; CLR 27; DLB 5; SAAS 22

Kenny, Maurice (Francis) 1929- ..... **CLC 87; DAM MULT**
See also CA 144; CAAS 22; DLB 175; NNAL

Kent, Kelvin
See Kuttner, Henry

Kenton, Maxwell
See Southern, Terry

Kenyon, Robert O.
See Kuttner, Henry

Kepler, Johannes 1571-1630 .... **LC 45**

Kerouac, Jack ..... **CLC 1, 2, 3, 5, 14, 29, 61**
See also Kerouac, Jean-Louis Lebris de
See also AAYA 25; CDALB 1941-1968; DLB 2, 16; DLBD 3; DLBY 95; GLL 1; MTCW 2; NFS 8; RGAL; WP

Kerouac, Jean-Louis Lebris de 1922-1969
See Kerouac, Jack
See also AITN 1; CA 5-8R; 25-28R; CANR 26, 54, 95; CPW; DA; DAB; DAC; DAM MST, NOV, POET, POP; DA3; MTCW 1, 2; WLC

Knowles, John 1926- . **CLC 1, 4, 10, 26; DA; DAC; DAM MST, NOV**
See also AAYA 10; CA 17-20R; CANR 40, 74, 76; CDALB 1968-1988; CN; DLB 6; MTCW 1, 2; NFS 2; RGAL; SATA 8, 89; YAW

Knox, Calvin M.
See Silverberg, Robert

Knox, John c. 1505-1572 .... **LC 37**
See also DLB 132

Knye, Cassandra
See Disch, Thomas M(ichael)

Koch, C(hristopher) J(ohn) 1932- .... **CLC 42**
See also CA 127; CANR 84; CN

Koch, Christopher
See Koch, C(hristopher) J(ohn)

Koch, Kenneth 1925- .... **CLC 5, 8, 44; DAM POET**
See also CA 1-4R; CAD; CANR 6, 36, 57, 97; CD; CP; DLB 5; INT CANR-36; MTCW 2; SATA 65; WP

Kochanowski, Jan 1530-1584 .... **LC 10**
See also RGWL

Kock, Charles Paul de 1794-1871 . **NCLC 16**

Koda Rohan
See Koda Shigeyuki

Koda Shigeyuki 1867-1947 .... **TCLC 22**
See also CA 121; 183; DLB 180

Koestler, Arthur 1905-1983 ... **CLC 1, 3, 6, 8, 15, 33**
See also BRWS 1; CA 1-4R; 109; CANR 1, 33; CDBLB 1945-1960; DLBY 83; MTCW 1, 2; RGEL

Kogawa, Joy Nozomi 1935- ..... **CLC 78, 129; DAC; DAM MST, MULT**
See also CA 101; CANR 19, 62; CN; CWP; FW; MTCW 2; NFS 3; SATA 99

Kohout, Pavel 1928- .... **CLC 13**
See also CA 45-48; CANR 3

Koizumi, Yakumo
See Hearn, (Patricio) Lafcadio (Tessima Carlos)

Kolmar, Gertrud 1894-1943 .... **TCLC 40**
See also CA 167

Komunyakaa, Yusef 1947- .... **CLC 86, 94; BLCS**
See also AFAW 2; CA 147; CANR 83; CP; CSW; DLB 120; PFS 5; RGAL

Konrad, George
See Konr
See also CWW 2

Konrad, Gyorgy 1933- .... **CLC 4, 10, 73**
See also Konrad, George
See also CA 85-88; CANR 97; CWW 2; DLB 232

Konwicki, Tadeusz 1926- .... **CLC 8, 28, 54, 117**
See also CA 101; CAAS 9; CANR 39, 59; CWW 2; DLB 232; IDFW 3; MTCW 1

Koontz, Dean R(ay) 1945- .... **CLC 78; DAM NOV, POP**
See also AAYA 9, 31; BEST 89:3, 90:2; CA 108; CANR 19, 36, 52, 95; CMW; CPW; DA3; HGG; MTCW 1; SATA 92; SFW; YAW

Kopernik, Mikolaj
See Copernicus, Nicolaus

Kopit, Arthur (Lee) 1937- ..... **CLC 1, 18, 33; DAM DRAM**
See also AITN 1; CA 81-84; CABS 3; CD; DFS 7; DLB 7; MTCW 1; RGAL

Kops, Bernard 1926- .... **CLC 4**
See also CA 5-8R; CANR 84; CBD; CN; CP; DLB 13

Kornbluth, C(yril) M. 1923-1958 .... **TCLC 8**
See also CA 105; 160; DLB 8; SFW

Korolenko, V. G.
See Korolenko, Vladimir Galaktionovich

Korolenko, Vladimir
See Korolenko, Vladimir Galaktionovich

Korolenko, Vladimir G.
See Korolenko, Vladimir Galaktionovich

Korolenko, Vladimir Galaktionovich
1853-1921 .... **TCLC 22**
See also CA 121

Korzybski, Alfred (Habdank Skarbek)
1879-1950 .... **TCLC 61**
See also CA 123; 160

Kosinski, Jerzy (Nikodem)
1933-1991 .... **CLC 1, 2, 3, 6, 10, 15, 53, 70; DAM NOV**
See also AMWS 7; CA 17-20R; 134; CANR 9, 46; DA3; DLB 2; DLBY 82; HGG; MTCW 1, 2; NFS 12; RGAL

Kostelanetz, Richard (Cory) 1940- .. **CLC 28**
See also CA 13-16R; CAAS 8; CANR 38, 77; CN; CP

Kotlowitz, Robert 1924- .... **CLC 4**
See also CA 33-36R; CANR 36

Kotzebue, August (Friedrich Ferdinand) von
1761-1819 .... **NCLC 25**
See also DLB 94

Kotzwinkle, William 1938- ..... **CLC 5, 14, 35**
See also CA 45-48; CANR 3, 44, 84; CLR 6; DLB 173; FANT; MAICYA; SATA 24, 70; SFW; YAW

Kowna, Stancy
See Szymborska, Wislawa

Kozol, Jonathan 1936- .... **CLC 17**
See also CA 61-64; CANR 16, 45, 96

Kozoll, Michael 1940(?)- .... **CLC 35**

Kramer, Kathryn 19(?)- .... **CLC 34**

Kramer, Larry 1935- .. **CLC 42; DAM POP; DC 8**
See also CA 124; 126; CANR 60; GLL 1

Krasicki, Ignacy 1735-1801 .... **NCLC 8**

Krasinski, Zygmunt 1812-1859 .... **NCLC 4**
See also RGWL

Kraus, Karl 1874-1936 .... **TCLC 5**
See also CA 104; DLB 118

Kreve (Mickevicius), Vincas
1882-1954 .... **TCLC 27**
See also CA 170; DLB 220

Kristeva, Julia 1941- .... **CLC 77, 140**
See also CA 154; CANR 99; DLB 242; FW

Kristofferson, Kris 1936- .... **CLC 26**
See also CA 104

Krizanc, John 1956- .... **CLC 57**
See also CA 187

Krleza, Miroslav 1893-1981 .... **CLC 8, 114**
See also CA 97-100; 105; CANR 50; DLB 147; RGWL

Kroetsch, Robert 1927- . **CLC 5, 23, 57, 132; DAC; DAM POET**
See also CA 17-20R; CANR 8, 38; CCA 1; CN; CP; DLB 53; MTCW 1

Kroetz, Franz
See Kroetz, Franz Xaver

Kroetz, Franz Xaver 1946- .... **CLC 41**
See also CA 130

Kroker, Arthur (W.) 1945- .... **CLC 77**
See also CA 161

Kropotkin, Peter (Alekseevich)
1842-1921 .... **TCLC 36**
See also CA 119

Krotkov, Yuri 1917-1981 .... **CLC 19**
See also CA 102

Krumb
See Crumb, R(obert)

Krumgold, Joseph (Quincy)
1908-1980 .... **CLC 12**
See also CA 9-12R; 101; CANR 7; MAICYA; SATA 1, 48; SATA-Obit 23; YAW

Krumwitz
See Crumb, R(obert)

Krutch, Joseph Wood 1893-1970 ..... **CLC 24**
See also CA 1-4R; 25-28R; CANR 4; DLB 63, 206

Krutzch, Gus
See Eliot, T(homas) S(tearns)

Krylov, Ivan Andreevich
1768(?)-1844 .... **NCLC 1**
See also DLB 150

Kubin, Alfred (Leopold Isidor)
1877-1959 .... **TCLC 23**
See also CA 112; 149; DLB 81

Kubrick, Stanley 1928-1999 .... **CLC 16**
See also AAYA 30; CA 81-84; 177; CANR 33; DLB 26; TCLC 112

Kueng, Hans 1928-
See Kung, Hans
See also CA 53-56; CANR 66; MTCW 1, 2

Kumin, Maxine (Winokur) 1925- ..... **CLC 5, 13, 28; DAM POET; PC 15**
See also AITN 2; AMWS 4; ANW; CA 1-4R; CAAS 8; CANR 1, 21, 69; CP; CWP; DA3; DLB 5; MTCW 1, 2; PAB; SATA 12

Kundera, Milan 1929- . **CLC 4, 9, 19, 32, 68, 115, 135; DAM NOV; SSC 24**
See also AAYA 2; CA 85-88; CANR 19, 52, 74; CWW 2; DA3; DLB 232; MTCW 1, 2; RGSF; SSFS 10

Kunene, Mazisi (Raymond) 1930- ... **CLC 85**
See also BW 1, 3; CA 125; CANR 81; DLB 117

Kung, Hans .... **CLC 130**
See also Kueng, Hans

Kunikida, Doppo 1869(?)-1908 ...... **TCLC 99**
See also DLB 180

Kunitz, Stanley (Jasspon) 1905- .. **CLC 6, 11, 14, 148; PC 19**
See also AMWS 3; CA 41-44R; CANR 26, 57, 98; CP; DA3; DLB 48; INT CANR-26; MTCW 1, 2; PFS 11; RGAL

Kunze, Reiner 1933- .... **CLC 10**
See also CA 93-96; CWW 2; DLB 75

Kuprin, Aleksander Ivanovich
1870-1938 .... **TCLC 5**
See also CA 104; 182

Kureishi, Hanif 1954(?)- .... **CLC 64, 135**
See also CA 139; CBD; CD; CN; DLB 194; GLL 2; IDFW 4

Kurosawa, Akira 1910-1998 .... **CLC 16, 119; DAM MULT**
See also AAYA 11; CA 101; 170; CANR 46

Kushner, Tony 1957(?)- .... **CLC 81; DAM DRAM; DC 10**
See also CA 144; CAD; CANR 74; CD; DA3; DFS 5; DLB 228; GLL 1; MTCW 2; RGAL

Kuttner, Henry 1915-1958 .... **TCLC 10**
See also CA 107; 157; DLB 8; FANT; SFW

Kuzma, Greg 1944- .... **CLC 7**
See also CA 33-36R; CANR 70

Kuzmin, Mikhail 1872(?)-1936 ...... **TCLC 40**
See also CA 170

Kyd, Thomas 1558-1594 .... **LC 22; DAM DRAM; DC 3**
See also BRW; DLB 62; RGEL; TEA

Kyprianos, Iossif
See Samarakis, Antonis

La Bruyere, Jean de 1645-1696 .... **LC 17**
See also GFL Beginnings to 1789

Lacan, Jacques (Marie Emile)
1901-1981 .... **CLC 75**
See also CA 121; 104

Laclos, Pierre Ambroise Francois
1741-1803 .... **NCLC 4, 87**
See also EW; GFL Beginnings to 1789; RGWL

Lacolere, Francois
See Aragon, Louis

Lawson, Henry (Archibald Hertzberg)
1867-1922 .... **TCLC 27; SSC 18**
See also CA 120; 181; DLB 230; RGEL;
RGSF
Lawton, Dennis
See Faust, Frederick (Schiller)
Laxness, Halldor .... **CLC 25**
See also Gudjonsson, Halldor Kiljan
See also RGWL
Layamon fl. c. 1200- .... **CMLC 10**
See also DLB 146; RGEL
Laye, Camara 1928-1980 ... **CLC 4, 38; BLC
2; DAM MULT**
See also BW 1; CA 85-88; 97-100; CANR
25; MTCW 1, 2
Layton, Irving (Peter) 1912- .... **CLC 2, 15;
DAC; DAM MST, POET**
See also CA 1-4R; CANR 2, 33, 43, 66;
CP; DLB 88; MTCW 1, 2; PFS 12; RGEL
Lazarus, Emma 1849-1887 .... **NCLC 8**
Lazarus, Felix
See Cable, George Washington
Lazarus, Henry
See Slavitt, David R(ytman)
Lea, Joan
See Neufeld, John (Arthur)
Leacock, Stephen (Butler)
1869-1944 .... **TCLC 2; DAC; DAM
MST; SSC 39**
See also CA 104; 141; CANR 80; DLB 92;
MTCW 2; RGEL; RGSF
Lear, Edward 1812-1888 .... **NCLC 3**
See also CLR 1; DLB 32, 163, 166; MAI-
CYA; RGEL; SATA 18, 100; WP
Lear, Norman (Milton) 1922- .... **CLC 12**
See also CA 73-76
Leautaud, Paul 1872-1956 .... **TCLC 83**
See also DLB 65; GFL 1789 to the Present
Leavis, F(rank) R(aymond)
1895-1978 .... **CLC 24**
See also BRW; CA 21-24R; 77-80; CANR
44; DLB 242; MTCW 1, 2; RGEL
Leavitt, David 1961- ..... **CLC 34; DAM POP**
See also CA 116; 122; CANR 50, 62; CPW;
DA3; DLB 130; GLL 1; INT 122; MTCW
2
Leblanc, Maurice (Marie Emile)
1864-1941 .... **TCLC 49**
See also CA 110; CMW
Lebowitz, Fran(ces Ann) 1951(?)- ... **CLC 11,
36**
See also CA 81-84; CANR 14, 60, 70; INT
CANR-14; MTCW 1
Lebrecht, Peter
See Tieck, (Johann) Ludwig
le Carre, John .... **CLC 3, 5, 9, 15, 28**
See also Cornwell, David (John Moore)
See also BEST 89:4; BRWS 2; CDBLB
1960 to Present; CMW; CN; CPW; DLB
87; MTCW 2; RGEL
Le Clezio, J(ean) M(arie) G(ustave)
1940- .... **CLC 31**
See also CA 116; 128; DLB 83; GFL 1789
to the Present; RGSF
Leconte de Lisle, Charles-Marie-Rene
1818-1894 .... **NCLC 29**
See also EW; GFL 1789 to the Present
Le Coq, Monsieur
See Simenon, Georges (Jacques Christian)
Leduc, Violette 1907-1972 .... **CLC 22**
See also CA 13-14; 33-36R; CANR 69;
CAP 1; GFL 1789 to the Present; GLL 1
Ledwidge, Francis 1887(?)-1917 .... **TCLC 23**
See also CA 123; DLB 20
Lee, Andrea 1953- ... **CLC 36; BLC 2; DAM
MULT**
See also BW 1, 3; CA 125; CANR 82
Lee, Andrew
See Auchincloss, Louis (Stanton)

Lee, Chang-rae 1965- .... **CLC 91**
See also CA 148; CANR 89
Lee, Don L. .... **CLC 2**
See also Madhubuti, Haki R.
Lee, George W(ashington)
1894-1976 .... **CLC 52; BLC 2; DAM
MULT**
See also BW 1; CA 125; CANR 83; DLB
51
Lee, (Nelle) Harper 1926- . **CLC 12, 60; DA;
DAB; DAC; DAM MST, NOV; WLC**
See also AAYA 13; AMWS 8; CA 13-16R;
CANR 51; CDALB 1941-1968; CSW;
DA3; DLB 6; MTCW 1, 2; NFS 2; SATA
11; WYA; YAW
Lee, Helen Elaine 1959(?)- .... **CLC 86**
See also CA 148
Lee, John .... **CLC 70**
Lee, Julian
See Latham, Jean Lee
Lee, Larry
See Lee, Lawrence
Lee, Laurie 1914-1997 .... **CLC 90; DAB;
DAM POP**
See also CA 77-80; 158; CANR 33, 73; CP;
CPW; DLB 27; MTCW 1; RGEL
Lee, Lawrence 1941-1990 .... **CLC 34**
See also CA 131; CANR 43
Lee, Li-Young 1957- .... **PC 24**
See also CA 153; CP; DLB 165; PFS 11
Lee, Manfred B(ennington)
1905-1971 .... **CLC 11**
See also Queen, Ellery
See also CA 1-4R; 29-32R; CANR 2;
CMW; DLB 137
Lee, Shelton Jackson 1957(?)- .... **CLC 105;
BLCS; DAM MULT**
See also Lee, Spike
See also BW 2, 3; CA 125; CANR 42
Lee, Spike
See Lee, Shelton Jackson
See also AAYA 4, 29
Lee, Stan 1922- .... **CLC 17**
See also AAYA 5; CA 108; 111; INT 111
Lee, Tanith 1947- .... **CLC 46**
See also AAYA 15; CA 37-40R; CANR 53;
FANT; SATA 8, 88; SFW; YAW
Lee, Vernon .... **TCLC 5; SSC 33**
See also Paget, Violet
See also DLB 57, 153, 156, 174, 178; GLL
1
Lee, William
See Burroughs, William S(eward)
See also GLL 1
Lee, Willy
See Burroughs, William S(eward)
See also GLL 1
Lee-Hamilton, Eugene (Jacob)
1845-1907 .... **TCLC 22**
See also CA 117
Leet, Judith 1935- .... **CLC 11**
See also CA 187
Le Fanu, Joseph Sheridan
1814-1873 ..... **NCLC 9, 58; DAM POP;
SSC 14**
See also CMW; DA3; DLB 21, 70, 159,
178; HGG; RGEL; RGSF; SUFW
Leffland, Ella 1931- .... **CLC 19**
See also CA 29-32R; CANR 35, 78, 82;
DLBY 84; INT CANR-35; SATA 65
Leger, Alexis
See Leger, (Marie-Rene Auguste) Alexis
Saint-Leger
**Leger, (Marie-Rene Auguste) Alexis
Saint-Leger** 1887-1975 .. **CLC 4, 11, 46;
DAM POET; PC 23**
See also Saint-John Perse
See also CA 13-16R; 61-64; CANR 43; EW;
MTCW 1

Leger, Saintleger
See Leger, (Marie-Rene Auguste) Alexis
Saint-Leger
Le Guin, Ursula K(roeber) 1929- ..... **CLC 8,
13, 22, 45, 71, 136; DAB; DAC; DAM
MST, POP; SSC 12**
See also AAYA 9, 27; AITN 1; ANW; CA
21-24R; CANR 9, 32, 52, 74; CDALB
1968-1988; CLR 3, 28; CN; CPW; DA3;
DLB 8, 52; FANT; FW; INT CANR-32;
JRDA; MAICYA; MTCW 1, 2; NFS 6, 9;
SATA 4, 52, 99; SFW; SSFS 2; SUFW;
WYA; YAW
Lehmann, Rosamond (Nina)
1901-1990 .... **CLC 5**
See also CA 77-80; 131; CANR 8, 73; DLB
15; MTCW 2; RGEL; RHW
Leiber, Fritz (Reuter, Jr.)
1910-1992 .... **CLC 25**
See also CA 45-48; 139; CANR 2, 40, 86;
DLB 8; FANT; HGG; MTCW 1, 2; SATA
45; SATA-Obit 73; SCFW 2; SFW; SUFW
Leibniz, Gottfried Wilhelm von
1646-1716 .... **LC 35**
See also DLB 168
Leimbach, Martha 1963-
See Leimbach, Marti
See also CA 130
Leimbach, Marti .... **CLC 65**
See also Leimbach, Martha
Leino, Eino .... **TCLC 24**
See also Loennbohm, Armas Eino Leopold
Leiris, Michel (Julien) 1901-1990 ..... **CLC 61**
See also CA 119; 128; 132; GFL 1789 to
the Present
Leithauser, Brad 1953- .... **CLC 27**
See also CA 107; CANR 27, 81; CP; DLB
120
Lelchuk, Alan 1938- .... **CLC 5**
See also CA 45-48; CAAS 20; CANR 1,
70; CN
Lem, Stanislaw 1921- .... **CLC 8, 15, 40**
See also CA 105; CAAS 1; CANR 32;
CWW 2; MTCW 1; SCFW 2; SFW
Lemann, Nancy 1956- .... **CLC 39**
See also CA 118; 136
Lemonnier, (Antoine Louis) Camille
1844-1913 .... **TCLC 22**
See also CA 121
Lenau, Nikolaus 1802-1850 .... **NCLC 16**
L'Engle, Madeleine (Camp Franklin)
1918- .... **CLC 12; DAM POP**
See also AAYA 28; AITN 2; CA 1-4R;
CANR 3, 21, 39, 66; CLR 1, 14, 57;
CPW; CWRI; DA3; DLB 52; JRDA;
MAICYA; MTCW 1, 2; SAAS 15; SATA
1, 27, 75; SFW; WYA; YAW
Lengyel, Jozsef 1896-1975 .... **CLC 7**
See also CA 85-88; 57-60; CANR 71;
RGSF
Lenin 1870-1924
See Lenin, V. I.
See also CA 121; 168
Lenin, V. I. .... **TCLC 67**
See also Lenin
Lennon, John (Ono) 1940-1980 .. **CLC 12, 35**
See also CA 102; SATA 114
Lennox, Charlotte Ramsay
1729(?)-1804 .... **NCLC 23**
See also DLB 39; RGEL
Lentricchia, Frank (Jr.) 1940- .... **CLC 34**
See also CA 25-28R; CANR 19
Lenz, Gunter .... **CLC 65**
Lenz, Siegfried 1926- .... **CLC 27; SSC 33**
See also CA 89-92; CANR 80; CWW 2;
DLB 75; RGSF; RGWL
Leon, David
See Jacob, (Cyprien-)Max

Little, Malcolm 1925-1965
See Malcolm X
See also BW 1, 3; CA 125; 111; CANR 82;
DA; DAB; DAC; DAM MST, MULT;
DA3; MTCW 1, 2

Littlewit, Humphrey Gent.
See Lovecraft, H(oward) P(hillips)

Litwos
See Sienkiewicz, Henryk (Adam Alexander
Pius)

Liu, E. 1857-1909 .... **TCLC 15**
See also CA 115; 190

Lively, Penelope (Margaret) 1933- .. **CLC 32,
50; DAM NOV**
See also CA 41-44R; CANR 29, 67, 79;
CLR 7; CN; CWRI; DLB 14, 161, 207;
FANT; JRDA; MAICYA; MTCW 1, 2;
SATA 7, 60, 101

Livesay, Dorothy (Kathleen)
1909-1996 . **CLC 4, 15, 79; DAC; DAM
MST, POET**
See also AITN 2; CA 25-28R; CAAS 8;
CANR 36, 67; DLB 68; FW; MTCW 1;
RGEL

Livy c. 59B.C.-c. 12 .... **CMLC 11**
See also DLB 211; RGWL

Lizardi, Jose Joaquin Fernandez de
1776-1827 .... **NCLC 30**
See also LAW

Llewellyn, Richard
See Llewellyn Lloyd, Richard Dafydd Viv-
ian
See also DLB 15

Llewellyn Lloyd, Richard Dafydd Vivian
1906-1983 .... **CLC 7, 80**
See also Llewellyn, Richard
See also CA 53-56; 111; CANR 7, 71;
SATA 11; SATA-Obit 37

Llosa, (Jorge) Mario (Pedro) Vargas
See Vargas Llosa, (Jorge) Mario (Pedro)

Lloyd, Manda
See Mander, (Mary) Jane

Lloyd Webber, Andrew 1948-
See Webber, Andrew Lloyd
See also AAYA 1; CA 116; 149; DAM
DRAM; SATA 56

Llull, Ramon c. 1235-c. 1316 .... **CMLC 12**

Lobb, Ebenezer
See Upward, Allen

Locke, Alain (Le Roy) 1886-1954 . **TCLC 43;
BLCS**
See also BW 1, 3; CA 106; 124; CANR 79;
DLB 51; RGAL

Locke, John 1632-1704 .... **LC 7, 35**
See also DLB 101; RGEL

Locke-Elliott, Sumner
See Elliott, Sumner Locke

Lockhart, John Gibson 1794-1854 .. **NCLC 6**
See also DLB 110, 116, 144

Lockridge, Ross (Franklin), Jr.
1914-1948 .... **TCLC 111**
See also CA 108; 145; CANR 79; DLB 143;
DLBY 80; RGAL; RHW

Lodge, David (John) 1935- ...... **CLC 36, 141;
DAM POP**
See also BEST 90:1; BRWS 4; CA 17-20R;
CANR 19, 53, 92; CN; CPW; DLB 14,
194; INT CANR-19; MTCW 1, 2

Lodge, Thomas 1558-1625 .... **LC 41**
See also DLB 172; RGEL

Loewinsohn, Ron(ald William)
1937- .... **CLC 52**
See also CA 25-28R; CANR 71

Logan, Jake
See Smith, Martin Cruz

Logan, John (Burton) 1923-1987 .... **CLC 5**
See also CA 77-80; 124; CANR 45; DLB 5

Lo Kuan-chung 1330(?)-1400(?) .... **LC 12**

Lombard, Nap
See Johnson, Pamela Hansford

Lomotey (editor), Kofi .... **CLC 70**

London, Jack .... **TCLC 9, 15, 39; SSC 4;
WLC**
See also London, John Griffith
See also AAYA 13; AITN 2; CDALB 1865-
1917; DLB 8, 12, 78, 212; NFS 8; RGAL;
RGSF; SATA 18; SSFS 7; TCWW 2

London, John Griffith 1876-1916
See London, Jack
See also AMW; CA 110; 119; CANR 73;
DA; DAB; DAC; DAM MST, NOV; DA3;
JRDA; MAICYA; MTCW 1, 2; SFW;
TUS; WYA; YAW

Long, Emmett
See Leonard, Elmore (John, Jr.)

Longbaugh, Harry
See Goldman, William (W.)

Longfellow, Henry Wadsworth
1807-1882 .. **NCLC 2, 45, 101, 103; DA;
DAB; DAC; DAM MST, POET; PC
30; WLCS**
See also CDALB 1640-1865; DA3; DLB 1,
59, 235; PAB; PFS 2, 7; RGAL; SATA
19; WP

Longinus c. 1st cent. - .... **CMLC 27**
See also DLB 176

Longley, Michael 1939- .... **CLC 29**
See also CA 102; CP; DLB 40

Longus fl. c. 2nd cent. - .... **CMLC 7**

Longway, A. Hugh
See Lang, Andrew

Lonnrot, Elias 1802-1884 .... **NCLC 53**
See also EFS 1

Lonsdale, Roger ed. .... **CLC 65**

Lopate, Phillip 1943- .... **CLC 29**
See also CA 97-100; CANR 88; DLBY 80;
INT 97-100

Lopez, Barry (Holstun) 1945- .... **CLC 70**
See also AAYA 9; ANW; CA 65-68; CANR
7, 23, 47, 68, 92; INT CANR-7, -23;
MTCW 1; RGAL; SATA 67

Lopez Portillo (y Pacheco), Jose
1920- .... **CLC 46**
See also CA 129; HW 1

Lopez y Fuentes, Gregorio
1897(?)-1966 .... **CLC 32**
See also CA 131; HW 1

Lorca, Federico Garcia
See Garc
See also DFS 4; RGWL; WP

Lord, Bette Bao 1938- .... **CLC 23**
See also BEST 90:3; CA 107; CANR 41,
79; INT 107; SATA 58

Lord Auch
See Bataille, Georges

Lord Byron
See Byron, George Gordon (Noel)
See also PAB; WP

Lorde, Audre (Geraldine)
1934-1992 ... **CLC 18, 71; BLC 2; DAM
MULT, POET; PC 12**
See also Domini, Rey
See also AFAW 1, 2; BW 1, 3; CA 25-28R;
142; CANR 16, 26, 46, 82; DA3; DLB
41; FW; MTCW 1, 2; RGAL

Lord Houghton
See Milnes, Richard Monckton

Lord Jeffrey
See Jeffrey, Francis

Loreaux, Nichol .... **CLC 65**

Lorenzini, Carlo 1826-1890
See Collodi, Carlo
See also MAICYA; SATA 29, 100

Lorenzo, Heberto Padilla
See Padilla (Lorenzo), Heberto

Loris
See Hofmannsthal, Hugo von

Loti, Pierre .... **TCLC 11**
See also Viaud, (Louis Marie) Julien
See also DLB 123; GFL 1789 to the Present

Lou, Henri
See Andreas-Salome, Lou

Louie, David Wong 1954- .... **CLC 70**
See also CA 139

Louis, Father M.
See Merton, Thomas

Lovecraft, H(oward) P(hillips)
1890-1937 ...... **TCLC 4, 22; DAM POP;
SSC 3**
See also AAYA 14; CA 104; 133; DA3;
HGG; MTCW 1, 2; RGAL; SFW; SUFW

Lovelace, Earl 1935- .... **CLC 51**
See also BW 2; CA 77-80; CANR 41, 72;
CD; CN; DLB 125; MTCW 1

Lovelace, Richard 1618-1657 .... **LC 24**
See also DLB 131; PAB; RGEL

Lowell, Amy 1874-1925 .... **TCLC 1, 8; DAM
POET; PC 13**
See also CA 104; 151; DLB 54, 140;
MTCW 2; RGAL

Lowell, James Russell 1819-1891 ... **NCLC 2,
90**
See also AMWS 1; CDALB 1640-1865;
DLB 1, 11, 64, 79, 189, 235; RGAL

Lowell, Robert (Traill Spence, Jr.)
1917-1977 .... **CLC 1, 2, 3, 4, 5, 8, 9, 11,
15, 37, 124; DA; DAB; DAC; DAM
MST, NOV; PC 3; WLC**
See also AMW; CA 9-12R; 73-76; CABS
2; CANR 26, 60; CDALBS; DA3; DLB
5, 169; MTCW 1, 2; PAB; PFS 6, 7;
RGAL; WP

Lowenthal, Michael (Francis)
1969- .... **CLC 119**
See also CA 150

Lowndes, Marie Adelaide (Belloc)
1868-1947 .... **TCLC 12**
See also CA 107; CMW; DLB 70; RHW

Lowry, (Clarence) Malcolm
1909-1957 .... **TCLC 6, 40; SSC 31**
See also BRWS 3; CA 105; 131; CANR 62;
CDBLB 1945-1960; DLB 15; MTCW 1,
2; RGEL

Lowry, Mina Gertrude 1882-1966
See Loy, Mina
See also CA 113

Loxsmith, John
See Brunner, John (Kilian Houston)

Loy, Mina ..... **CLC 28; DAM POET; PC 16**
See also Lowry, Mina Gertrude
See also DLB 4, 54

Loyson-Bridet
See Schwob, Marcel (Mayer Andr

Lucan 39-65 .... **CMLC 33**
See also AW; DLB 211; EFS 2; RGWL

Lucas, Craig 1951- .... **CLC 64**
See also CA 137; CAD; CANR 71; CD;
GLL 2

Lucas, E(dward) V(errall)
1868-1938 .... **TCLC 73**
See also CA 176; DLB 98, 149, 153; SATA
20

Lucas, George 1944- .... **CLC 16**
See also AAYA 1, 23; CA 77-80; CANR
30; SATA 56

Lucas, Hans
See Godard, Jean-Luc

Lucas, Victoria
See Plath, Sylvia

Lucian c. 125-c. 180 .... **CMLC 32**
See also DLB 176; RGWL

Ludlam, Charles 1943-1987 .... **CLC 46, 50**
See also CA 85-88; 122; CAD; CANR 72,
86

Marivaux, Pierre Carlet de Chamblain de
1688-1763 .... **LC 4; DC 7**
See also GFL Beginnings to 1789; RGWL

Markandaya, Kamala .... **CLC 8, 38**
See also Taylor, Kamala (Purnaiya)

Markfield, Wallace 1926- .... **CLC 8**
See also CA 69-72; CAAS 3; CN; DLB 2, 28

Markham, Edwin 1852-1940 .... **TCLC 47**
See also CA 160; DLB 54, 186; RGAL

Markham, Robert
See Amis, Kingsley (William)

Marks, J
See Highwater, Jamake (Mamake)

Marks-Highwater, J
See Highwater, Jamake (Mamake)

Markson, David M(errill) 1927- ...... **CLC 67**
See also CA 49-52; CANR 1, 91; CN

Marley, Bob .... **CLC 17**
See also Marley, Robert Nesta

Marley, Robert Nesta 1945-1981
See Marley, Bob
See also CA 107; 103

Marlowe, Christopher 1564-1593 ...... **LC 22, 47; DA; DAB; DAC; DAM DRAM, MST; DC 1; WLC**
See also CDBLB Before 1660; DA3; DFS 1,5, 13; DLB 62; RGEL

Marlowe, Stephen 1928- .... **CLC 70**
See also Queen, Ellery
See also CA 13-16R; CANR 6, 55; CMW; SFW

Marmontel, Jean-Francois 1723-1799 .. **LC 2**

Marquand, John P(hillips)
1893-1960 .... **CLC 2, 10**
See also AMW; CA 85-88; CANR 73; CMW; DLB 9, 102; MTCW 2; RGAL

Marques, Rene 1919-1979 ..... **CLC 96; DAM MULT; HLC 2**
See also CA 97-100; 85-88; CANR 78; DLB 113; HW 1, 2; RGSF

Marquez, Gabriel (Jose) Garcia
See Garc

Marquis, Don(ald Robert Perry)
1878-1937 .... **TCLC 7**
See also CA 104; 166; DLB 11, 25; RGAL

Marric, J. J.
See Creasey, John

Marryat, Frederick 1792-1848 .... **NCLC 3**
See also DLB 21, 163; RGEL

Marsden, James
See Creasey, John

Marsh, Edward 1872-1953 .... **TCLC 99**

Marsh, (Edith) Ngaio 1899-1982 .... **CLC 7, 53; DAM POP**
See also CA 9-12R; CANR 6, 58; CMW; CPW; DLB 77; MTCW 1, 2; RGEL

Marshall, Garry 1934- .... **CLC 17**
See also AAYA 3; CA 111; SATA 60

Marshall, Paule 1929- .. **CLC 27, 72; BLC 3; DAM MULT; SSC 3**
See also AFAW 1, 2; BW 2, 3; CA 77-80; CANR 25, 73; CN; DA3; DLB 33, 157, 227; MTCW 1, 2; RGAL

Marshallik
See Zangwill, Israel

Marsten, Richard
See Hunter, Evan

Marston, John 1576-1634 .... **LC 33; DAM DRAM**
See also DLB 58, 172; RGEL

Martha, Henry
See Harris, Mark

Marti (y Perez), Jose (Julian)
1853-1895 ...... **NCLC 63; DAM MULT; HLC 2**
See also HW 2; LAW; RGWL

Martial c. 40-c. 104 .... **CMLC 35; PC 10**
See also DLB 211; RGWL

Martin, Ken
See Hubbard, L(afayette) Ron(ald)

Martin, Richard
See Creasey, John

Martin, Steve 1945- .... **CLC 30**
See also CA 97-100; CANR 30, 100; MTCW 1

Martin, Valerie 1948- .... **CLC 89**
See also BEST 90:2; CA 85-88; CANR 49, 89

Martin, Violet Florence
1862-1915 .... **TCLC 51**

Martin, Webber
See Silverberg, Robert

Martindale, Patrick Victor
See White, Patrick (Victor Martindale)

Martin du Gard, Roger
1881-1958 .... **TCLC 24**
See also CA 118; CANR 94; DLB 65; GFL 1789 to the Present; RGWL

Martineau, Harriet 1802-1876 .... **NCLC 26**
See also DLB 21, 55, 159, 163, 166, 190; FW; RGEL; YABC 2

Martines, Julia
See O'Faolain, Julia

Martinez, Enrique Gonzalez
See Gonzalez Martinez, Enrique

Martinez, Jacinto Benavente y
See Benavente (y Martinez), Jacinto

Martinez de la Rosa, Francisco de Paula
1787-1862 .... **NCLC 102**

Martinez Ruiz, Jose 1873-1967
See Azorin; Ruiz, Jose Martinez
See also CA 93-96; HW 1

Martinez Sierra, Gregorio
1881-1947 .... **TCLC 6**
See also CA 115

Martinez Sierra, Maria (de la O'LeJarraga)
1874-1974 .... **TCLC 6**
See also CA 115

Martinsen, Martin
See Follett, Ken(neth Martin)

Martinson, Harry (Edmund)
1904-1978 .... **CLC 14**
See also CA 77-80; CANR 34

Marut, Ret
See Traven, B.

Marut, Robert
See Traven, B.

Marvell, Andrew 1621-1678 .. **LC 4, 43; DA; DAB; DAC; DAM MST, POET; PC 10; WLC**
See also CDBLB 1660-1789; DLB 131; PFS 5; RGEL; WP

Marx, Karl (Heinrich) 1818-1883 . **NCLC 17**
See also DLB 129

Masaoka, Shiki .... **TCLC 18**
See also Masaoka, Tsunenori

Masaoka, Tsunenori 1867-1902
See Masaoka, Shiki
See also CA 117; 191

Masefield, John (Edward)
1878-1967 ..... **CLC 11, 47; DAM POET**
See also CA 19-20; 25-28R; CANR 33; CAP 2; CDBLB 1890-1914; DLB 10, 19, 153, 160; FANT; MTCW 1, 2; PFS 5; RGEL; SATA 19

Maso, Carole 19(?)- .... **CLC 44**
See also CA 170; GLL 2; RGAL

Mason, Bobbie Ann 1940- ... **CLC 28, 43, 82; SSC 4**
See also AAYA 5; AMWS 8; CA 53-56; CANR 11, 31, 58, 83; CDALBS; CN; CSW; DA3; DLB 173; DLBY 87; INT CANR-31; MTCW 1, 2; NFS 4; RGAL; RGSF; SSFS 3,8; YAW

Mason, Ernst
See Pohl, Frederik

Mason, Hunni B.
See Sternheim, (William Adolf) Carl

Mason, Lee W.
See Malzberg, Barry N(athaniel)

Mason, Nick 1945- .... **CLC 35**

Mason, Tally
See Derleth, August (William)

Mass, Anna .... **CLC 59**

Mass, William
See Gibson, William

Massinger, Philip 1583-1640 .... **LC 70**
See also DLB 58; RGEL

Master Lao
See Lao Tzu

Masters, Edgar Lee 1868-1950 .... **TCLC 2, 25; DA; DAC; DAM MST, POET; PC 1, 36; WLCS**
See also AMWS 1; CA 104; 133; CDALB 1865-1917; DLB 54; MTCW 1, 2; RGAL; WP

Masters, Hilary 1928- .... **CLC 48**
See also CA 25-28R; CANR 13, 47, 97; CN

Mastrosimone, William 19(?)- .... **CLC 36**
See also CA 186; CAD; CD

Mathe, Albert
See Camus, Albert

Mather, Cotton 1663-1728 .... **LC 38**
See also AMWS 2; CDALB 1640-1865; DLB 24, 30, 140; RGAL

Mather, Increase 1639-1723 .... **LC 38**
See also DLB 24

Matheson, Richard (Burton) 1926- .. **CLC 37**
See also AAYA 31; CA 97-100; CANR 88, 99; DLB 8, 44; HGG; INT 97-100; SCFW 2; SFW

Mathews, Harry 1930- .... **CLC 6, 52**
See also CA 21-24R; CAAS 6; CANR 18, 40, 98; CN

Mathews, John Joseph 1894-1979 .. **CLC 84; DAM MULT**
See also CA 19-20; 142; CANR 45; CAP 2; DLB 175; NNAL

Mathias, Roland (Glyn) 1915- .... **CLC 45**
See also CA 97-100; CANR 19, 41; CP; DLB 27

Matsuo Basho 1644-1694 .... **LC 62; DAM POET; PC 3**
See also Basho, Matsuo
See also PFS 2, 7

Mattheson, Rodney
See Creasey, John

Matthews, (James) Brander
1852-1929 .... **TCLC 95**
See also DLB 71, 78; DLBD 13

Matthews, Greg 1949- .... **CLC 45**
See also CA 135

Matthews, William (Procter, III)
1942-1997 .... **CLC 40**
See also CA 29-32R; 162; CAAS 18; CANR 12, 57; CP; DLB 5

Matthias, John (Edward) 1941- .... **CLC 9**
See also CA 33-36R; CANR 56; CP

Matthiessen, F(rancis) O(tto)
1902-1950 .... **TCLC 100**
See also CA 185; DLB 63

Matthiessen, Peter 1927- ... **CLC 5, 7, 11, 32, 64; DAM NOV**
See also AAYA 6, 40; AMWS 5; BEST 90:4; CA 9-12R; CANR 21, 50, 73, 100; CN; DA3; DLB 6, 173; MTCW 1, 2; SATA 27

Maturin, Charles Robert
1780(?)-1824 .... **NCLC 6**
See also DLB 178; HGG; RGEL

Matute (Ausejo), Ana Maria 1925- .. **CLC 11**
See also CA 89-92; MTCW 1; RGSF

Maugham, W. S.
See Maugham, W(illiam) Somerset
Maugham, W(illiam) Somerset
1874-1965 ... **CLC 1, 11, 15, 67, 93; DA; DAB; DAC; DAM DRAM, MST, NOV; SSC 8; WLC**
See also BRW; CA 5-8R; 25-28R; CANR 40; CDBLB 1914-1945; CMW; DA3; DLB 10, 36, 77, 100, 162, 195; MTCW 1, 2; RGEL; RGSF; SATA 54
Maugham, William Somerset
See Maugham, W(illiam) Somerset
Maupassant, (Henri Rene Albert) Guy de
1850-1893 . **NCLC 1, 42, 83; DA; DAB; DAC; DAM MST; SSC 1; WLC**
See also DA3; DLB 123; EW; GFL 1789 to the Present; RGSF; RGWL; SSFS 4; SUFW; TWA
Maupin, Armistead 1944- ..... **CLC 95; DAM POP**
See also CA 125; 130; CANR 58; CPW; DA3; GLL 1; INT 130; MTCW 2
Maurhut, Richard
See Traven, B.
Mauriac, Claude 1914-1996 .... **CLC 9**
See also CA 89-92; 152; CWW 2; DLB 83; GFL 1789 to the Present
Mauriac, Francois (Charles)
1885-1970 .... **CLC 4, 9, 56; SSC 24**
See also CA 25-28; CAP 2; DLB 65; EW; GFL 1789 to the Present; MTCW 1, 2; RGWL
Mavor, Osborne Henry 1888-1951
See Bridie, James
See also CA 104
Maxwell, William (Keepers, Jr.)
1908-2000 .... **CLC 19**
See also CA 93-96; 189; CANR 54, 95; CN; DLBY 80; INT 93-96
May, Elaine 1932- .... **CLC 16**
See also CA 124; 142; CAD; CWD; DLB 44
Mayakovski, Vladimir (Vladimirovich)
1893-1930 .... **TCLC 4, 18**
See also Maiakovskii, Vladimir; Mayakovsky, Vladimir
See also CA 104; 158; EW; MTCW 2; SFW
Mayakovsky, Vladimir
See Mayakovski, Vladimir (Vladimirovich)
See also WP
Mayhew, Henry 1812-1887 .... **NCLC 31**
See also DLB 18, 55, 190
Mayle, Peter 1939(?)- .... **CLC 89**
See also CA 139; CANR 64
Maynard, Joyce 1953- .... **CLC 23**
See also CA 111; 129; CANR 64
Mayne, William (James Carter)
1928- .... **CLC 12**
See also AAYA 20; CA 9-12R; CANR 37, 80, 100; CLR 25; FANT; JRDA; MAICYA; SAAS 11; SATA 6, 68, 122; YAW
Mayo, Jim
See L'Amour, Louis (Dearborn)
See also TCWW 2
Maysles, Albert 1926- .... **CLC 16**
See also CA 29-32R
Maysles, David 1932-1987 .... **CLC 16**
See also CA 191
Mazer, Norma Fox 1931- .... **CLC 26**
See also AAYA 5, 36; CA 69-72; CANR 12, 32, 66; CLR 23; JRDA; MAICYA; SAAS 1; SATA 24, 67, 105; YAW
Mazzini, Guiseppe 1805-1872 .... **NCLC 34**
McAlmon, Robert (Menzies)
1895-1956 .... **TCLC 97**
See also CA 107; 168; DLB 4, 45; DLBD 15; GLL 1
McAuley, James Phillip 1917-1976 .. **CLC 45**
See also CA 97-100; RGEL

McBain, Ed
See Hunter, Evan
McBrien, William (Augustine)
1930- .... **CLC 44**
See also CA 107; CANR 90
McCabe, Patrick 1955- .... **CLC 133**
See also CA 130; CANR 50, 90; CN; DLB 194
McCaffrey, Anne (Inez) 1926- .... **CLC 17; DAM NOV, POP**
See also AAYA 6, 34; AITN 2; BEST 89:2; CA 25-28R; CANR 15, 35, 55, 96; CLR 49; CPW; DA3; DLB 8; JRDA; MAICYA; MTCW 1, 2; SAAS 11; SATA 8, 70, 116; SFW; WYA; YAW
McCall, Nathan 1955(?)- .... **CLC 86**
See also BW 3; CA 146; CANR 88
McCann, Arthur
See Campbell, John W(ood, Jr.)
McCann, Edson
See Pohl, Frederik
McCarthy, Charles, Jr. 1933-
See McCarthy, Cormac
See also CANR 42, 69; CN; CPW; CSW; DAM POP; DA3; MTCW 2
McCarthy, Cormac .... **CLC 4, 57, 59, 101**
See also McCarthy, Charles, Jr.
See also AMWS 8; CA 13-16R; CANR 10; DLB 6, 143; MTCW 2; TCWW 2
McCarthy, Mary (Therese)
1912-1989 .. **CLC 1, 3, 5, 14, 24, 39, 59; SSC 24**
See also AMW; CA 5-8R; 129; CANR 16, 50, 64; DA3; DLB 2; DLBY 81; FW; INT CANR-16; MAWW; MTCW 1, 2; RGAL
McCartney, (James) Paul 1942- . **CLC 12, 35**
See also CA 146
McCauley, Stephen (D.) 1955- .... **CLC 50**
See also CA 141
McClaren, Peter .... **CLC 70**
McClure, Michael (Thomas) 1932- ... **CLC 6, 10**
See also CA 21-24R; CAD; CANR 17, 46, 77; CD; CP; DLB 16; WP
McCorkle, Jill (Collins) 1958- .... **CLC 51**
See also CA 121; CSW; DLB 234; DLBY 87
McCourt, Frank 1930- .... **CLC 109**
See also CA 157; CANR 97; NCFS 1
McCourt, James 1941- .... **CLC 5**
See also CA 57-60; CANR 98
McCourt, Malachy 1932- .... **CLC 119**
McCoy, Horace (Stanley)
1897-1955 .... **TCLC 28**
See also CA 108; 155; CMW; DLB 9
McCrae, John 1872-1918 .... **TCLC 12**
See also CA 109; DLB 92; PFS 5
McCreigh, James
See Pohl, Frederik
McCullers, (Lula) Carson (Smith)
1917-1967 .... **CLC 1, 4, 10, 12, 48, 100; DA; DAB; DAC; DAM MST, NOV; SSC 9, 24; WLC**
See also AAYA 21; AMW; CA 5-8R; 25-28R; CABS 1, 3; CANR 18; CDALB 1941-1968; DA3; DFS 5; DLB 2, 7, 173, 228; FW; GLL 1; MAWW; MTCW 1, 2; NFS 6; RGAL; RGSF; SATA 27; SSFS 5; YAW
McCulloch, John Tyler
See Burroughs, Edgar Rice
McCullough, Colleen 1938(?)- .... **CLC 27, 107; DAM NOV, POP**
See also AAYA 36; CA 81-84; CANR 17, 46, 67, 98; CPW; DA3; MTCW 1, 2; RHW
McDermott, Alice 1953- .... **CLC 90**
See also CA 109; CANR 40, 90

McElroy, Joseph 1930- .... **CLC 5, 47**
See also CA 17-20R; CN
McEwan, Ian (Russell) 1948- .... **CLC 13, 66; DAM NOV**
See also BEST 90:4; BRWS 4; CA 61-64; CANR 14, 41, 69, 87; CN; DLB 14, 194; HGG; MTCW 1, 2; RGSF
McFadden, David 1940- .... **CLC 48**
See also CA 104; CP; DLB 60; INT 104
McFarland, Dennis 1950- .... **CLC 65**
See also CA 165
McGahern, John 1934- ... **CLC 5, 9, 48; SSC 17**
See also CA 17-20R; CANR 29, 68; CN; DLB 14, 231; MTCW 1
McGinley, Patrick (Anthony) 1937- . **CLC 41**
See also CA 120; 127; CANR 56; INT 127
McGinley, Phyllis 1905-1978 .... **CLC 14**
See also CA 9-12R; 77-80; CANR 19; CWRI; DLB 11, 48; PFS 9; SATA 2, 44; SATA-Obit 24
McGinniss, Joe 1942- .... **CLC 32**
See also AITN 2; BEST 89:2; CA 25-28R; CANR 26, 70; CPW; DLB 185; INT CANR-26
McGivern, Maureen Daly
See Daly, Maureen
McGrath, Patrick 1950- .... **CLC 55**
See also CA 136; CANR 65; CN; DLB 231; HGG
McGrath, Thomas (Matthew)
1916-1990 ..... **CLC 28, 59; DAM POET**
See also CA 9-12R; 132; CANR 6, 33, 95; MTCW 1; SATA 41; SATA-Obit 66
McGuane, Thomas (Francis III)
1939- .... **CLC 3, 7, 18, 45, 127**
See also AITN 2; CA 49-52; CANR 5, 24, 49, 94; CN; DLB 2, 212; DLBY 80; INT CANR-24; MTCW 1; TCWW 2
McGuckian, Medbh 1950- .... **CLC 48; DAM POET; PC 27**
See also BRWS 5; CA 143; CP; CWP; DLB 40
McHale, Tom 1942(?)-1982 .... **CLC 3, 5**
See also AITN 1; CA 77-80; 106
McIlvanney, William 1936- .... **CLC 42**
See also CA 25-28R; CANR 61; CMW; DLB 14, 207
McIlwraith, Maureen Mollie Hunter
See Hunter, Mollie
See also SATA 2
McInerney, Jay 1955- .... **CLC 34, 112; DAM POP**
See also AAYA 18; CA 116; 123; CANR 45, 68; CN; CPW; DA3; INT 123; MTCW 2
McIntyre, Vonda N(eel) 1948- .... **CLC 18**
See also CA 81-84; CANR 17, 34, 69; MTCW 1; SFW; YAW
McKay, Claude .... **TCLC 7, 41; BLC 3; DAB; PC 2**
See also McKay, Festus Claudius
See also AFAW 1, 2; DLB 4, 45, 51, 117; GLL 2; PAB; PFS 4; RGAL; WP
McKay, Festus Claudius 1889-1948
See McKay, Claude
See also BW 1, 3; CA 104; 124; CANR 73; DA; DAC; DAM MST, MULT, NOV, POET; MTCW 1, 2; WLC
McKuen, Rod 1933- .... **CLC 1, 3**
See also AITN 1; CA 41-44R; CANR 40
McLoughlin, R. B.
See Mencken, H(enry) L(ouis)
McLuhan, (Herbert) Marshall
1911-1980 .... **CLC 37, 83**
See also CA 9-12R; 102; CANR 12, 34, 61; DLB 88; INT CANR-12; MTCW 1, 2

Millay, E. Vincent
See Millay, Edna St. Vincent

Millay, Edna St. Vincent
1892-1950 .... **TCLC 4, 49; DA; DAB; DAC; DAM MST, POET; PC 6; WLCS**
See also Boyd, Nancy
See also CA 104; 130; CDALB 1917-1929; DA3; DLB 45; MTCW 1, 2; PAB; PFS 3; RGAL; WP

Miller, Arthur 1915- ...... **CLC 1, 2, 6, 10, 15, 26, 47, 78; DA; DAB; DAC; DAM DRAM, MST; DC 1; WLC**
See also AAYA 15; AITN 1; CA 1-4R; CABS 3; CAD; CANR 2, 30, 54, 76; CD; CDALB 1941-1968; DA3; DFS 1,3; DLB 7; MTCW 1, 2; RGAL; WYAS 1

Miller, Henry (Valentine)
1891-1980 ... **CLC 1, 2, 4, 9, 14, 43, 84; DA; DAB; DAC; DAM MST, NOV; WLC**
See also AMW; CA 9-12R; 97-100; CANR 33, 64; CDALB 1929-1941; DA3; DLB 4, 9; DLBY 80; MTCW 1, 2; RGAL

Miller, Jason 1939(?)-2001 .... **CLC 2**
See also AITN 1; CA 73-76; CAD; DFS 12; DLB 7

Miller, Sue 1943- .... **CLC 44; DAM POP**
See also BEST 90:3; CA 139; CANR 59, 91; DA3; DLB 143

Miller, Walter M(ichael, Jr.)
1923-1996 .... **CLC 4, 30**
See also CA 85-88; DLB 8; SFW

Millett, Kate 1934- .... **CLC 67**
See also AITN 1; CA 73-76; CANR 32, 53, 76; DA3; FW; GLL 1; MTCW 1, 2

Millhauser, Steven (Lewis) 1943- .... **CLC 21, 54, 109**
See also CA 110; 111; CANR 63; CN; DA3; DLB 2; FANT; INT 111; MTCW 2

Millin, Sarah Gertrude 1889-1968 ... **CLC 49**
See also CA 102; 93-96; DLB 225

Milne, A(lan) A(lexander)
1882-1956 ..... **TCLC 6, 88; DAB; DAC; DAM MST**
See also CA 104; 133; CLR 1, 26; CMW; CWRI; DA3; DLB 10, 77, 100, 160; FANT; MAICYA; MTCW 1, 2; RGEL; SATA 100; WCH; YABC 1

Milner, Ron(ald) 1938- .... **CLC 56; BLC 3; DAM MULT**
See also AITN 1; BW 1; CA 73-76; CAD; CANR 24, 81; CD; DLB 38; MTCW 1

Milnes, Richard Monckton
1809-1885 .... **NCLC 61**
See also DLB 32, 184

Milosz, Czeslaw 1911- ..... **CLC 5, 11, 22, 31, 56, 82; DAM MST, POET; PC 8; WLCS**
See also CA 81-84; CANR 23, 51, 91; CWW 2; DA3; MTCW 1, 2; RGWL

Milton, John 1608-1674 .... **LC 9, 43; DA; DAB; DAC; DAM MST, POET; PC 19, 29; WLC**
See also CDBLB 1660-1789; DA3; DLB 131, 151; EFS 1; PAB; PFS 3; RGEL; WP

Min, Anchee 1957- .... **CLC 86**
See also CA 146; CANR 94

Minehaha, Cornelius
See Wedekind, (Benjamin) Frank(lin)

Miner, Valerie 1947- .... **CLC 40**
See also CA 97-100; CANR 59; FW; GLL 2

Minimo, Duca
See D'Annunzio, Gabriele

Minot, Susan 1956- .... **CLC 44**
See also AMWS 6; CA 134; CN

Minus, Ed 1938- .... **CLC 39**
See also CA 185

Miranda, Javier
See Bioy Casares, Adolfo
See also CWW 2

Miranda, Javier
See Bioy Casares, Adolfo

Mirbeau, Octave 1848-1917 .... **TCLC 55**
See also DLB 123, 192; GFL 1789 to the Present

Miro (Ferrer), Gabriel (Francisco Victor)
1879-1930 .... **TCLC 5**
See also CA 104; 185

Misharin, Alexandr .... **CLC 59**

Mishima, Yukio ... **CLC 2, 4, 6, 9, 27; DC 1; SSC 4**
See also Hiraoka, Kimitake
See also DLB 182; GLL 1; MTCW 2; RGSF; RGWL; SSFS 5

Mistral, Frederic 1830-1914 .... **TCLC 51**
See also CA 122; GFL 1789 to the Present

Mistral, Gabriela
See Godoy Alcayaga, Lucila
See also RGWL; WP

Mistry, Rohinton 1952- .... **CLC 71; DAC**
See also CA 141; CANR 86; CCA 1; CN; SSFS 6

Mitchell, Clyde
See Ellison, Harlan (Jay); Silverberg, Robert

Mitchell, James Leslie 1901-1935
See Gibbon, Lewis Grassic
See also CA 104; 188; DLB 15

Mitchell, Joni 1943- .... **CLC 12**
See also CA 112; CCA 1

Mitchell, Joseph (Quincy)
1908-1996 .... **CLC 98**
See also CA 77-80; 152; CANR 69; CN; CSW; DLB 185; DLBY 96

Mitchell, Margaret (Munnerlyn)
1900-1949 . **TCLC 11; DAM NOV, POP**
See also AAYA 23; CA 109; 125; CANR 55, 94; CDALBS; DA3; DLB 9; MTCW 1, 2; NFS 9; RGAL; RHW; WYAS 1; YAW

Mitchell, Peggy
See Mitchell, Margaret (Munnerlyn)

Mitchell, S(ilas) Weir 1829-1914 .... **TCLC 36**
See also CA 165; DLB 202; RGAL

Mitchell, W(illiam) O(rmond)
1914-1998 .. **CLC 25; DAC; DAM MST**
See also CA 77-80; 165; CANR 15, 43; CN; DLB 88

Mitchell, William 1879-1936 .... **TCLC 81**

Mitford, Mary Russell 1787-1855 ... **NCLC 4**
See also DLB 110, 116; RGEL

Mitford, Nancy 1904-1973 .... **CLC 44**
See also CA 9-12R; DLB 191; RGEL

Miyamoto, (Chujo) Yuriko
1899-1951 .... **TCLC 37**
See also CA 170, 174; DLB 180

Miyazawa, Kenji 1896-1933 .... **TCLC 76**
See also CA 157

Mizoguchi, Kenji 1898-1956 .... **TCLC 72**
See also CA 167

Mo, Timothy (Peter) 1950(?)- ... **CLC 46, 134**
See also CA 117; CN; DLB 194; MTCW 1

Modarressi, Taghi (M.) 1931-1997 ... **CLC 44**
See also CA 121; 134; INT 134

Modiano, Patrick (Jean) 1945- .... **CLC 18**
See also CA 85-88; CANR 17, 40; CWW 2; DLB 83

Moerck, Paal
See Roelvaag, O(le) E(dvart)

Mofolo, Thomas (Mokopu)
1875(?)-1948 .. **TCLC 22; BLC 3; DAM MULT**
See also AFW; CA 121; 153; CANR 83; DLB 225; MTCW 2

Mohr, Nicholasa 1938- .... **CLC 12; DAM MULT; HLC 2**
See also AAYA 8; CA 49-52; CANR 1, 32, 64; CLR 22; DLB 145; HW 1, 2; JRDA; RGAL; SAAS 8; SATA 8, 97; SATA-Essay 113; YAW

Mojtabai, A(nn) G(race) 1938- ..... **CLC 5, 9, 15, 29**
See also CA 85-88; CANR 88

Moliere 1622-1673 .... **LC 10, 28, 64; DA; DAB; DAC; DAM DRAM, MST; DC 13; WLC**
See also DA3; DFS 13; GFL Beginnings to 1789; RGWL

Molin, Charles
See Mayne, William (James Carter)

Molina, Tirso de 1580(?)-1648 .... **DC 13**
See also Tirso de Molina
See also HLCS 2

Molnar, Ferenc 1878-1952 .. **TCLC 20; DAM DRAM**
See also CA 109; 153; CANR 83; DLB 215; RGWL

Momaday, N(avarre) Scott 1934- ...... **CLC 2, 19, 85, 95; DA; DAB; DAC; DAM MST, MULT, NOV, POP; PC 25; WLCS**
See also AAYA 11; AMWS 4; ANW; CA 25-28R; CANR 14, 34, 68; CDALBS; CN; CPW; DA3; DLB 143, 175; INT CANR-14; MTCW 1, 2; NFS 10; NNAL; PFS 2, 11; RGAL; SATA 48; SATA-Brief 30; WP; YAW

Monette, Paul 1945-1995 .... **CLC 82**
See also CA 139; 147; CN; GLL 1

Monroe, Harriet 1860-1936 .... **TCLC 12**
See also CA 109; DLB 54, 91

Monroe, Lyle
See Heinlein, Robert A(nson)

Montagu, Elizabeth 1720-1800 .... **NCLC 7**
See also FW

Montagu, Mary (Pierrepont) Wortley
1689-1762 .... **LC 9, 57; PC 16**
See also DLB 95, 101; RGEL

Montagu, W. H.
See Coleridge, Samuel Taylor

Montague, John (Patrick) 1929- ... **CLC 13, 46**
See also CA 9-12R; CANR 9, 69; CP; DLB 40; MTCW 1; PFS 12; RGEL

Montaigne, Michel (Eyquem) de
1533-1592 .... **LC 8; DA; DAB; DAC; DAM MST; WLC**
See also EW; GFL Beginnings to 1789; RGWL

Montale, Eugenio 1896-1981 ... **CLC 7, 9, 18; PC 13**
See also CA 17-20R; 104; CANR 30; DLB 114; MTCW 1; RGWL

Montesquieu, Charles-Louis de Secondat
1689-1755 .... **LC 7, 69**
See also GFL Beginnings to 1789

Montessori, Maria 1870-1952 ...... **TCLC 103**
See also CA 115; 147

Montgomery, (Robert) Bruce 1921(?)-1978
See Crispin, Edmund
See also CA 179; 104; CMW

Montgomery, L(ucy) M(aud)
1874-1942 .... **TCLC 51; DAC; DAM MST**
See also AAYA 12; CA 108; 137; CLR 8; DA3; DLBD 14; JRDA; MAICYA; MTCW 2; RGEL; SATA 100; WYA; YABC 1

Montgomery, Marion H., Jr. 1925- .... **CLC 7**
See also AITN 1; CA 1-4R; CANR 3, 48; CSW; DLB 6

Montgomery, Max
See Davenport, Guy (Mattison, Jr.)

Montherlant, Henry (Milon) de
1896-1972 ..... **CLC 8, 19; DAM DRAM**
See also CA 85-88; 37-40R; DLB 72; EW;
GFL 1789 to the Present; MTCW 1

Monty Python
See Chapman, Graham; Cleese, John
(Marwood); Gilliam, Terry (Vance); Idle,
Eric; Jones, Terence Graham Parry; Palin,
Michael (Edward)
See also AAYA 7

Moodie, Susanna (Strickland)
1803-1885 .... **NCLC 14**
See also DLB 99

Moody, Hiram F. III 1961-
See Moody, Rick
See also CA 138; CANR 64

Moody, Rick .... **CLC 147**
See also Moody, Hiram F. III

Moody, William Vaughan
1869-1910 .... **TCLC 105**
See also CA 110; 178; DLB 7, 54; RGAL

Mooney, Edward 1951-
See Mooney, Ted
See also CA 130

Mooney, Ted .... **CLC 25**
See also Mooney, Edward

Moorcock, Michael (John) 1939- ...... **CLC 5,
27, 58**
See also Bradbury, Edward P.
See also AAYA 26; CA 45-48; CAAS 5;
CANR 2, 17, 38, 64; CN; DLB 14, 231;
FANT; MTCW 1, 2; SATA 93; SFW;
SUFW

Moore, Brian 1921-1999 ... **CLC 1, 3, 5, 7, 8,
19, 32, 90; DAB; DAC; DAM MST**
See also Bryan, Michael
See also CA 1-4R; 174; CANR 1, 25, 42,
63; CCA 1; CN; FANT; MTCW 1, 2;
RGEL

Moore, Edward
See Muir, Edwin
See also RGEL

Moore, G. E. 1873-1958 .... **TCLC 89**

Moore, George Augustus
1852-1933 .... **TCLC 7; SSC 19**
See also BRW; CA 104; 177; DLB 10, 18,
57, 135; RGEL; RGSF

Moore, Lorrie .... **CLC 39, 45, 68**
See also Moore, Marie Lorena
See also DLB 234

Moore, Marianne (Craig)
1887-1972 .... **CLC 1, 2, 4, 8, 10, 13, 19,
47; DA; DAB; DAC; DAM MST,
POET; PC 4; WLCS**
See also AMW; CA 1-4R; 33-36R; CANR
3, 61; CDALB 1929-1941; DA3; DLB 45;
DLBD 7; MAWW; MTCW 1, 2; PAB;
RGAL; SATA 20; WP

Moore, Marie Lorena 1957-
See Moore, Lorrie
See also CA 116; CANR 39, 83; CN; DLB
234

Moore, Thomas 1779-1852 .... **NCLC 6**
See also DLB 96, 144; RGEL

Moorhouse, Frank 1938- .... **SSC 40**
See also CA 118; CANR 92; CN; RGSF

Mora, Pat(ricia) 1942-
See also CA 129; CANR 57, 81; CLR 58;
DAM MULT; DLB 209; HLC 2; HW 1,
2; SATA 92

Moraga, Cherrie 1952- .... **CLC 126; DAM
MULT**
See also CA 131; CANR 66; DLB 82; FW;
GLL 1; HW 1, 2

Morand, Paul 1888-1976 .... **CLC 41; SSC 22**
See also CA 184; 69-72; DLB 65

Morante, Elsa 1918-1985 .... **CLC 8, 47**
See also CA 85-88; 117; CANR 35; DLB
177; MTCW 1, 2; RGWL

Moravia, Alberto .... **CLC 2, 7, 11, 27, 46;
SSC 26**
See also Pincherle, Alberto
See also DLB 177; MTCW 2; RGSF;
RGWL

More, Hannah 1745-1833 .... **NCLC 27**
See also DLB 107, 109, 116, 158; RGEL

More, Henry 1614-1687 .... **LC 9**
See also DLB 126

More, Sir Thomas 1478-1535 .... **LC 10, 32**
See also BRWS 7; RGEL

Moreas, Jean .... **TCLC 18**
See also Papadiamantopoulos, Johannes
See also GFL 1789 to the Present

Morgan, Berry 1919- .... **CLC 6**
See also CA 49-52; DLB 6

Morgan, Claire
See Highsmith, (Mary) Patricia
See also GLL 1

Morgan, Edwin (George) 1920- .... **CLC 31**
See also CA 5-8R; CANR 3, 43, 90; CP;
DLB 27

Morgan, (George) Frederick 1922- .. **CLC 23**
See also CA 17-20R; CANR 21; CP

Morgan, Harriet
See Mencken, H(enry) L(ouis)

Morgan, Jane
See Cooper, James Fenimore

Morgan, Janet 1945- .... **CLC 39**
See also CA 65-68

Morgan, Lady 1776(?)-1859 .... **NCLC 29**
See also DLB 116, 158; RGEL

Morgan, Robin (Evonne) 1941- .... **CLC 2**
See also CA 69-72; CANR 29, 68; FW;
GLL 2; MTCW 1; SATA 80

Morgan, Scott
See Kuttner, Henry

Morgan, Seth 1949(?)-1990 .... **CLC 65**
See also CA 185; 132

**Morgenstern, Christian (Otto Josef
Wolfgang)** 1871-1914 .... **TCLC 8**
See also CA 105; 191

Morgenstern, S.
See Goldman, William (W.)

Mori, Rintaro
See Mori Ogai
See also CA 110

Moricz, Zsigmond 1879-1942 .... **TCLC 33**
See also CA 165

Morike, Eduard (Friedrich)
1804-1875 .... **NCLC 10**
See also DLB 133; RGWL

Mori Ogai 1862-1922 .... **TCLC 14**
See also CA 164; DLB 180; TWA

Moritz, Karl Philipp 1756-1793 .... **LC 2**
See also DLB 94

Morland, Peter Henry
See Faust, Frederick (Schiller)

Morley, Christopher (Darlington)
1890-1957 .... **TCLC 87**
See also CA 112; DLB 9; RGAL

Morren, Theophil
See Hofmannsthal, Hugo von

Morris, Bill 1952- .... **CLC 76**

Morris, Julian
See West, Morris L(anglo)

Morris, Steveland Judkins 1950(?)-
See Wonder, Stevie
See also CA 111

Morris, William 1834-1896 .... **NCLC 4**
See also BRW; CDBLB 1832-1890; DLB
18, 35, 57, 156, 178, 184; FANT; RGEL;
SFW; SUFW

Morris, Wright 1910-1998 .. **CLC 1, 3, 7, 18,
37**
See also CA 9-12R; 167; CANR 21, 81;
CN; DLB 2, 206; DLBY 81; MTCW 1, 2;
RGAL; TCLC 107; TCWW 2

Morrison, Arthur 1863-1945 .... **TCLC 72;
SSC 40**
See also CA 120; 157; CMW; DLB 70, 135,
197; RGEL

Morrison, Chloe Anthony Wofford
See Morrison, Toni

Morrison, James Douglas 1943-1971
See Morrison, Jim
See also CA 73-76; CANR 40

Morrison, Jim .... **CLC 17**
See also Morrison, James Douglas

Morrison, Toni 1931- . **CLC 4, 10, 22, 55, 81,
87; BLC 3; DA; DAB; DAC; DAM
MST, MULT, NOV, POP**
See also AAYA 1, 22; AFAW 1, 2; AMWS
3; BW 2, 3; CA 29-32R; CANR 27, 42,
67; CDALB 1968-1988; CN; CPW; DA3;
DLB 6, 33, 143; DLBY 81; FW; MTCW
1, 2; NFS 1, 6, 8; RGAL; RHW; SATA
57; SSFS 5; YAW

Morrison, Van 1945- .... **CLC 21**
See also CA 116; 168

Morrissy, Mary 1958- .... **CLC 99**

Mortimer, John (Clifford) 1923- ..... **CLC 28,
43; DAM DRAM, POP**
See also CA 13-16R; CANR 21, 69; CD;
CDBLB 1960 to Present; CMW; CN;
CPW; DA3; DLB 13; INT CANR-21;
MSW; MTCW 1, 2; RGEL

Mortimer, Penelope (Ruth)
1918-1999 .... **CLC 5**
See also CA 57-60; 187; CANR 45, 88; CN

Morton, Anthony
See Creasey, John

Mosca, Gaetano 1858-1941 .... **TCLC 75**

Mosher, Howard Frank 1943- .... **CLC 62**
See also CA 139; CANR 65

Mosley, Nicholas 1923- .... **CLC 43, 70**
See also CA 69-72; CANR 41, 60; CN;
DLB 14, 207

Mosley, Walter 1952- .... **CLC 97; BLCS;
DAM MULT, POP**
See also AAYA 17; BW 2; CA 142; CANR
57, 92; CMW; CPW; DA3; MTCW 2

Moss, Howard 1922-1987 ...... **CLC 7, 14, 45,
50; DAM POET**
See also CA 1-4R; 123; CANR 1, 44; DLB
5

Mossgiel, Rab
See Burns, Robert

Motion, Andrew (Peter) 1952- .... **CLC 47**
See also BRWS 7; CA 146; CANR 90; CP;
DLB 40

Motley, Willard (Francis)
1912-1965 .... **CLC 18**
See also BW 1; CA 117; 106; CANR 88;
DLB 76, 143

Motoori, Norinaga 1730-1801 .... **NCLC 45**

Mott, Michael (Charles Alston)
1930- .... **CLC 15, 34**
See also CA 5-8R; CAAS 7; CANR 7, 29

Mountain Wolf Woman 1884-1960 .. **CLC 92**
See also CA 144; CANR 90; NNAL

Moure, Erin 1955- .... **CLC 88**
See also CA 113; CP; CWP; DLB 60

Mowat, Farley (McGill) 1921- .... **CLC 26;
DAC; DAM MST**
See also AAYA 1; CA 1-4R; CANR 4, 24,
42, 68; CLR 20; CPW; DLB 68; INT
CANR-24; JRDA; MAICYA; MTCW 1,
2; SATA 3, 55; YAW

Mowatt, Anna Cora 1819-1870 ..... **NCLC 74**
See also RGAL

Moyers, Bill 1934- .... **CLC 74**
See also AITN 2; CA 61-64; CANR 31, 52

Mphahlele, Es'kia
See Mphahlele, Ezekiel
See also DLB 125, 225; RGSF; SSFS 11

Mphahlele, Ezekiel 1919- .... **CLC 25, 133;
BLC 3; DAM MULT**
See also Mphahlele, Es'kia
See also BW 2, 3; CA 81-84; CANR 26,
76; CN; DA3; DLB 225; MTCW 2; SATA
119

Mqhayi, S(amuel) E(dward) K(rune Loliwe)
1875-1945 ...... **TCLC 25; BLC 3; DAM
MULT**
See also CA 153; CANR 87

Mrozek, Slawomir 1930- .... **CLC 3, 13**
See also CA 13-16R; CAAS 10; CANR 29;
CWW 2; DLB 232; MTCW 1

Mrs. Belloc-Lowndes
See Lowndes, Marie Adelaide (Belloc)

M'Taggart, John M'Taggart Ellis
See McTaggart, John McTaggart Ellis

Mtwa, Percy (?)- .... **CLC 47**

Mueller, Lisel 1924- .... **CLC 13, 51; PC 33**
See also CA 93-96; CP; DLB 105; PFS 9

Muir, Edwin 1887-1959 .... **TCLC 2, 87**
See Moore, Edward
See also BRWS 6; CA 104; DLB 20, 100,
191; RGEL

Muir, John 1838-1914 .... **TCLC 28**
See also CA 165; DLB 186

Mujica Lainez, Manuel 1910-1984 ... **CLC 31**
See also Lainez, Manuel Mujica
See also CA 81-84; 112; CANR 32; HW 1

Mukherjee, Bharati 1940- .... **CLC 53, 115;
AAL; DAM NOV; SSC 38**
See also BEST 89:2; CA 107; CANR 45,
72; CN; DLB 60; DNFS; FW; MTCW 1,
2; RGAL; RGSF; SSFS 7

Muldoon, Paul 1951- .... **CLC 32, 72; DAM
POET**
See also BRWS 4; CA 113; 129; CANR 52,
91; CP; DLB 40; INT 129; PFS 7

Mulisch, Harry 1927- .... **CLC 42**
See also CA 9-12R; CANR 6, 26, 56

Mull, Martin 1943- .... **CLC 17**
See also CA 105

Muller, Wilhelm .... **NCLC 73**

Mulock, Dinah Maria
See Craik, Dinah Maria (Mulock)
See also RGEL

Munford, Robert 1737(?)-1783 .... **LC 5**
See also DLB 31

Mungo, Raymond 1946- .... **CLC 72**
See also CA 49-52; CANR 2

Munro, Alice 1931- .... **CLC 6, 10, 19, 50, 95;
DAC; DAM MST, NOV; SSC 3;
WLCS**
See also AITN 2; CA 33-36R; CANR 33,
53, 75; CCA 1; CN; DA3; DLB 53;
MTCW 1, 2; RGEL; RGSF; SATA 29;
SSFS 5

Munro, H(ector) H(ugh) 1870-1916
See Saki
See also CA 104; 130; CDBLB 1890-1914;
DA; DAB; DAC; DAM MST, NOV; DA3;
DLB 34, 162; MTCW 1, 2; RGEL; WLC

Murasaki, Lady
See Murasaki Shikibu

Murasaki Shikibu 978(?)-1026(?) ... **CMLC 1**
See also EFS 2; RGWL

Murdoch, (Jean) Iris 1919-1999 ... **CLC 1, 2,
3, 4, 6, 8, 11, 15, 22, 31, 51; DAB;
DAC; DAM MST, NOV**
See also BRWS 1; CA 13-16R; 179; CANR
8, 43, 68; CDBLB 1960 to Present; CN;
DA3; DLB 14, 194, 233; INT CANR-8;
MTCW 1, 2; RGEL

Murfree, Mary Noailles 1850-1922 ... **SSC 22**
See also CA 122; 176; DLB 12, 74; RGAL

Murnau, Friedrich Wilhelm
See Plumpe, Friedrich Wilhelm

Murphy, Richard 1927- .... **CLC 41**
See also BRWS 5; CA 29-32R; CP; DLB
40

Murphy, Sylvia 1937- .... **CLC 34**
See also CA 121

Murphy, Thomas (Bernard) 1935- ... **CLC 51**
See also CA 101

Murray, Albert L. 1916- .... **CLC 73**
See also BW 2; CA 49-52; CANR 26, 52,
78; CSW; DLB 38

Murray, Judith Sargent
1751-1820 .... **NCLC 63**
See also DLB 37, 200

Murray, Les(lie) A(llan) 1938- .... **CLC 40;
DAM POET**
See also BRWS 7; CA 21-24R; CANR 11,
27, 56; CP; RGEL

Murry, J. Middleton
See Murry, John Middleton

Murry, John Middleton
1889-1957 .... **TCLC 16**
See also CA 118; DLB 149

Musgrave, Susan 1951- .... **CLC 13, 54**
See also CA 69-72; CANR 45, 84; CCA 1;
CP; CWP

Musil, Robert (Edler von)
1880-1942 .... **TCLC 12, 68; SSC 18**
See also CA 109; CANR 55, 84; DLB 81,
124; EW; MTCW 2; RGSF; RGWL

Muske, Carol .... **CLC 90**
See also Muske-Dukes, Carol (Anne)

Muske-Dukes, Carol (Anne) 1945-
See Muske, Carol
See also CA 65-68; CANR 32, 70; CWP

Musset, (Louis Charles) Alfred de
1810-1857 .... **NCLC 7**
See also DLB 192; EW; GFL 1789 to the
Present; RGWL; TWA

Mussolini, Benito (Amilcare Andrea)
1883-1945 .... **TCLC 96**
See also CA 116

My Brother's Brother
See Chekhov, Anton (Pavlovich)

Myers, L(eopold) H(amilton)
1881-1944 .... **TCLC 59**
See also CA 157; DLB 15; RGEL

Myers, Walter Dean 1937- ..... **CLC 35; BLC
3; DAM MULT, NOV**
See also AAYA 4, 23; BW 2; CA 33-36R;
CANR 20, 42, 67; CLR 4, 16, 35; DLB
33; INT CANR-20; JRDA; MAICYA;
MTCW 2; SAAS 2; SATA 41, 71, 109;
SATA-Brief 27; YAW

Myers, Walter M.
See Myers, Walter Dean

Myles, Symon
See Follett, Ken(neth Martin)

Nabokov, Vladimir (Vladimirovich)
1899-1977 .... **CLC 1, 2, 3, 6, 8, 11, 15,
23, 44, 46, 64; DA; DAB; DAC; DAM
MST, NOV; SSC 11; WLC**
See also AMW; AMWR; CA 5-8R; 69-72;
CANR 20; CDALB 1941-1968; DA3;
DLB 2; DLBD 3; DLBY 80, 91; MTCW
1, 2; NFS 9; RGAL; RGSF; SSFS 6;
TCLC 108

Naevius c. 265B.C.-201B.C. .... **CMLC 37**
See also DLB 211

Nagai, Kafu .... **TCLC 51**
See also Nagai, Sokichi
See also DLB 180

Nagai, Sokichi 1879-1959
See Nagai, Kafu
See also CA 117

Nagy, Laszlo 1925-1978 .... **CLC 7**
See also CA 129; 112

Naidu, Sarojini 1879-1949 .... **TCLC 80**
See also RGEL

Naipaul, Shiva(dhar Srinivasa)
1945-1985 .... **CLC 32, 39; DAM NOV**
See also CA 110; 112; 116; CANR 33;
DA3; DLB 157; DLBY 85; MTCW 1, 2

Naipaul, V(idiadhar) S(urajprasad)
1932- .... **CLC 4, 7, 9, 13, 18, 37, 105;
DAB; DAC; DAM MST, NOV; SSC 38**
See also BRWS 1; CA 1-4R; CANR 1, 33,
51, 91; CDBLB 1960 to Present; CN;
DA3; DLB 125, 204, 206; DLBY 85;
MTCW 1, 2; RGEL; RGSF

Nakos, Lilika 1899(?)- .... **CLC 29**

Narayan, R(asipuram) K(rishnaswami)
1906-2001 .... **CLC 7, 28, 47, 121; DAM
NOV; SSC 25**
See also CA 81-84; CANR 33, 61; CN;
DA3; DNFS; MTCW 1, 2; RGEL; RGSF;
SATA 62; SSFS 5

Nash, (Fredric) Ogden 1902-1971 . **CLC 23;
DAM POET; PC 21**
See also CA 13-14; 29-32R; CANR 34, 61;
CAP 1; DLB 11; MAICYA; MTCW 1, 2;
RGAL; SATA 2, 46; TCLC 109; WP

Nashe, Thomas 1567-1601(?) .... **LC 41**
See also DLB 167; RGEL

Nathan, Daniel
See Dannay, Frederic

Nathan, George Jean 1882-1958 .... **TCLC 18**
See Hatteras, Owen
See also CA 114; 169; DLB 137

Natsume, Kinnosuke 1867-1916
See Natsume, S
See also CA 104

Natsume, Soseki .... **TCLC 2, 10**
See also Natsume, Kinnosuke
See also DLB 180; RGWL

Natti, (Mary) Lee 1919-
See Kingman, Lee
See also CA 5-8R; CANR 2

Naylor, Gloria 1950- .... **CLC 28, 52; BLC 3;
DA; DAC; DAM MST, MULT, NOV,
POP; WLCS**
See also AAYA 6, 39; AFAW 1, 2; AMWS
8; BW 2, 3; CA 107; CANR 27, 51, 74;
CN; CPW; DA3; DLB 173; FW; MTCW
1, 2; NFS 4, 7; RGAL

Neff, Debra .... **CLC 59**

Neihardt, John Gneisenau
1881-1973 .... **CLC 32**
See also CA 13-14; CANR 65; CAP 1; DLB
9, 54

Nekrasov, Nikolai Alekseevich
1821-1878 .... **NCLC 11**

Nelligan, Emile 1879-1941 .... **TCLC 14**
See also CA 114; DLB 92

Nelson, Willie 1933- .... **CLC 17**
See also CA 107

Nemerov, Howard (Stanley)
1920-1991 ..... **CLC 2, 6, 9, 36; DAM
POET; PC 24**
See also AMW; CA 1-4R; 134; CABS 2;
CANR 1, 27, 53; DLB 5, 6; DLBY 83;
INT CANR-27; MTCW 1, 2; PFS 10;
RGAL

Neruda, Pablo 1904-1973 .. **CLC 1, 2, 5, 7, 9,
28, 62; DA; DAB; DAC; DAM MST,
MULT, POET; HLC 2; PC 4; WLC**
See also CA 19-20; 45-48; CAP 2; DA3;
DNFS; HW 1; MTCW 1, 2; PFS 11;
RGWL; WP

Nerval, Gerard de 1808-1855 ... **NCLC 1, 67;
PC 13; SSC 18**
See also GFL 1789 to the Present; RGSF;
RGWL

Nervo, (Jose) Amado (Ruiz de)
1870-1919 .... **TCLC 11; HLCS 2**
See also CA 109; 131; HW 1; LAW

Nessi, Pio Baroja y
See Baroja (y Nessi), Pio

O'Brien, Flann .... **CLC 1, 4, 5, 7, 10, 47**
See also O Nuallain, Brian
See also BRWS 2; DLB 231; RGEL

O'Brien, Richard 1942- .... **CLC 17**
See also CA 124

O'Brien, (William) Tim(othy) 1946- . **CLC 7, 19, 40, 103; DAM POP**
See also AAYA 16; CA 85-88; CANR 40, 58; CDALBS; CN; CPW; DA3; DLB 152; DLBD 9; DLBY 80; MTCW 2; RGAL

Obstfelder, Sigbjoern 1866-1900 .... **TCLC 23**
See also CA 123

O'Casey, Sean 1880-1964 .... **CLC 1, 5, 9, 11, 15, 88; DAB; DAC; DAM DRAM, MST; DC 12; WLCS**
See also CANR 62; CBD; CD-BLB 1914-1945; DA3; DLB 10; MTCW 1, 2; RGEL

O'Cathasaigh, Sean
See O'Casey, Sean

Occom, Samson 1723-1792 .... **LC 60**
See also DLB 175; NNAL

Ochs, Phil(ip David) 1940-1976 .... **CLC 17**
See also CA 185; 65-68

O'Connor, Edwin (Greene)
1918-1968 .... **CLC 14**
See also CA 93-96; 25-28R

O'Connor, (Mary) Flannery
1925-1964 .... **CLC 1, 2, 3, 6, 10, 13, 15, 21, 66, 104; DA; DAB; DAC; DAM MST, NOV; SSC 1, 23; WLC**
See also AAYA 7; AMW; CA 1-4R; CANR 3, 41; CDALB 1941-1968; DA3; DLB 2, 152; DLBD 12; DLBY 80; MAWW; MTCW 1, 2; NFS 3; RGAL; RGSF; SSFS 2, 7, 10

O'Connor, Frank .... **CLC 23; SSC 5**
See also O'Donovan, Michael John
See also DLB 162; RGSF; SSFS 5

O'Dell, Scott 1898-1989 .... **CLC 30**
See also AAYA 3; CA 61-64; 129; CANR 12, 30; CLR 1, 16; DLB 52; JRDA; MAI-CYA; SATA 12, 60; YAW

Odets, Clifford 1906-1963 ..... **CLC 2, 28, 98; DAM DRAM; DC 6**
See also AMWS 2; CA 85-88; CAD; CANR 62; DFS 3; DLB 7, 26; MTCW 1, 2; RGAL

O'Doherty, Brian 1934- .... **CLC 76**
See also CA 105

O'Donnell, K. M.
See Malzberg, Barry N(athaniel)

O'Donnell, Lawrence
See Kuttner, Henry

O'Donovan, Michael John
1903-1966 .... **CLC 14**
See also O'Connor, Frank
See also CA 93-96; CANR 84

O'Faolain, Julia 1932- .... **CLC 6, 19, 47, 108**
See also CA 81-84; CAAS 2; CANR 12, 61; CN; DLB 14, 231; FW; MTCW 1; RHW

O'Faolain, Sean 1900-1991 ...... **CLC 1, 7, 14, 32, 70; SSC 13**
See also CA 61-64; 134; CANR 12, 66; DLB 15, 162; MTCW 1, 2; RGEL; RGSF

O'Flaherty, Liam 1896-1984 .... **CLC 5, 34; SSC 6**
See also CA 101; 113; CANR 35; DLB 36, 162; DLBY 84; MTCW 1, 2; RGEL; RGSF; SSFS 5

Ogilvy, Gavin
See Barrie, J(ames) M(atthew)

O'Grady, Standish (James)
1846-1928 .... **TCLC 5**
See also CA 104; 157

O'Grady, Timothy 1951- .... **CLC 59**
See also CA 138

O'Hara, Frank 1926-1966 .... **CLC 2, 5, 13, 78; DAM POET**
See also CA 9-12R; 25-28R; CANR 33; DA3; DLB 5, 16, 193; MTCW 1, 2; PFS 8; 12; RGAL; WP

O'Hara, John (Henry) 1905-1970 . **CLC 1, 2, 3, 6, 11, 42; DAM NOV; SSC 15**
See also AMW; CA 5-8R; 25-28R; CANR 31, 60; CDALB 1929-1941; DLB 9, 86; DLBD 2; MTCW 1, 2; NFS 11; RGAL; RGSF

O Hehir, Diana 1922- .... **CLC 41**
See also CA 93-96

Ohiyesa 1858-1939
See Eastman, Charles A(lexander)

Okigbo, Christopher (Ifenayichukwu)
1932-1967 ... **CLC 25, 84; BLC 3; DAM MULT, POET; PC 7**
See also AFW; BW 1, 3; CA 77-80; CANR 74; DLB 125; MTCW 1, 2; RGEL

Okri, Ben 1959- .... **CLC 87**
See also BRWS 5; BW 2, 3; CA 130; 138; CANR 65; CN; DLB 157, 231; INT 138; MTCW 2; RGEL

Olds, Sharon 1942- ... **CLC 32, 39, 85; DAM POET; PC 22**
See also CA 101; CANR 18, 41, 66, 98; CP; CPW; CWP; DLB 120; MTCW 2

Oldstyle, Jonathan
See Irving, Washington

Olesha, Iurii
See Olesha, Yuri (Karlovich)
See also RGWL

Olesha, Yuri (Karlovich) 1899-1960 .. **CLC 8**
See also Olesha, Iurii
See also CA 85-88; EW

Oliphant, Laurence 1829(?)-1888 .. **NCLC 47**
See also DLB 18, 166

Oliphant, Margaret (Oliphant Wilson)
1828-1897 .... **NCLC 11, 61; SSC 25**
See also Oliphant
See also DLB 18, 159, 190; HGG; RGEL; RGSF; SUFW

Oliver, Mary 1935- .... **CLC 19, 34, 98**
See also AMWS 7; CA 21-24R; CANR 9, 43, 84, 92; CP; CWP; DLB 5, 193

Olivier, Laurence (Kerr) 1907-1989 . **CLC 20**
See also CA 111; 150; 129

Olsen, Tillie 1912- .... **CLC 4, 13, 114; DA; DAB; DAC; DAM MST; SSC 11**
See also CA 1-4R; CANR 1, 43, 74; CDALBS; CN; DA3; DLB 28, 206; DLBY 80; FW; MTCW 1, 2; RGAL; RGSF; SSFS 1

Olson, Charles (John) 1910-1970 .. **CLC 1, 2, 5, 6, 9, 11, 29; DAM POET; PC 19**
See also AMWS 2; CA 13-16; 25-28R; CABS 2; CANR 35, 61; CAP 1; DLB 5, 16, 193; MTCW 1, 2; RGAL; WP

Olson, Toby 1937- .... **CLC 28**
See also CA 65-68; CANR 9, 31, 84; CP

Olyesha, Yuri
See Olesha, Yuri (Karlovich)

Omar Khayyam
See Khayyam, Omar
See also RGWL

Ondaatje, (Philip) Michael 1943- .... **CLC 14, 29, 51, 76; DAB; DAC; DAM MST; PC 28**
See also CA 77-80; CANR 42, 74; CN; CP; DA3; DLB 60; MTCW 2; PFS 8

Oneal, Elizabeth 1934-
See Oneal, Zibby
See also CA 106; CANR 28, 84; MAICYA; SATA 30, 82; YAW

Oneal, Zibby .... **CLC 30**
See also Oneal, Elizabeth
See also AAYA 5; CLR 13; JRDA

O'Neill, Eugene (Gladstone)
1888-1953 .... **TCLC 1, 6, 27, 49; DA; DAB; DAC; DAM DRAM, MST; WLC**
See also AITN 1; CA 110; 132; CDALB 1929-1941; DA3; DFS 9,11, 12; DLB 7; MTCW 1, 2

Onetti, Juan Carlos 1909-1994 ... **CLC 7, 10; DAM MULT, NOV; SSC 23**
See also CA 85-88; 145; CANR 32, 63; DLB 113; HW 1, 2; MTCW 1, 2; RGSF

O Nuallain, Brian 1911-1966
See O'Brien, Flann
See also CA 21-22; 25-28R; CAP 2; DLB 231; FANT

Ophuls, Max 1902-1957 .... **TCLC 79**
See also CA 113

Opie, Amelia 1769-1853 .... **NCLC 65**
See also DLB 116, 159; RGEL

Oppen, George 1908-1984 ..... **CLC 7, 13, 34; PC 35**
See also CA 13-16R; 113; CANR 8, 82; DLB 5, 165; TCLC 107

Oppenheim, E(dward) Phillips
1866-1946 .... **TCLC 45**
See also CA 111; CMW; DLB 70

Opuls, Max
See Ophuls, Max

Origen c. 185-c. 254 .... **CMLC 19**

Orlovitz, Gil 1918-1973 .... **CLC 22**
See also CA 77-80; 45-48; DLB 2, 5

Orris
See Ingelow, Jean

Ortega y Gasset, Jose 1883-1955 ... **TCLC 9; DAM MULT; HLC 2**
See also CA 106; 130; HW 1, 2; MTCW 1, 2

Ortese, Anna Maria 1914- .... **CLC 89**
See also DLB 177

Ortiz, Simon J(oseph) 1941- . **CLC 45; DAM MULT, POET; PC 17**
See also AMWS 4; CA 134; CANR 69; CP; DLB 120, 175; NNAL; PFS 4; RGAL

Orton, Joe .... **CLC 4, 13, 43; DC 3**
See also Orton, John Kingsley
See also BRWS 5; CBD; CDBLB 1960 to Present; DFS 3, 6; DLB 13; GLL 1; MTCW 2; RGEL

Orton, John Kingsley 1933-1967
See Orton, Joe
See also CA 85-88; CANR 35, 66; DAM DRAM; MTCW 1, 2

Orwell, George .... **TCLC 2, 6, 15, 31, 51; DAB; WLC**
See also Blair, Eric (Arthur)
See also CDBLB 1945-1960; CLR 68; DLB 15, 98, 195; NFS 3, 7; RGEL; SCFW 2; SFW; SSFS 4; YAW

Osborne, David
See Silverberg, Robert

Osborne, George
See Silverberg, Robert

Osborne, John (James) 1929-1994 .... **CLC 1, 2, 5, 11, 45; DA; DAB; DAC; DAM DRAM, MST; WLC**
See also BRWS 1; CA 13-16R; 147; CANR 21, 56; CDBLB 1945-1960; DFS 4; DLB 13; MTCW 1, 2; RGEL

Osborne, Lawrence 1958- .... **CLC 50**
See also CA 189

Osbourne, Lloyd 1868-1947 .... **TCLC 93**

Oshima, Nagisa 1932- .... **CLC 20**
See also CA 116; 121; CANR 78

Oskison, John Milton 1874-1947 .. **TCLC 35; DAM MULT**
See also CA 144; CANR 84; DLB 175; NNAL

Ossian c. 3rd cent. - .... **CMLC 28**
See also Macpherson, James

Ray, Satyajit 1921-1992 .. **CLC 16, 76; DAM MULT**
See also CA 114; 137

Read, Herbert Edward 1893-1968 ..... **CLC 4**
See also BRW; CA 85-88; 25-28R; DLB 20, 149; PAB; RGEL

Read, Piers Paul 1941- .... **CLC 4, 10, 25**
See also CA 21-24R; CANR 38, 86; CN; DLB 14; SATA 21

Reade, Charles 1814-1884 .... **NCLC 2, 74**
See also DLB 21; RGEL

Reade, Hamish
See Gray, Simon (James Holliday)

Reading, Peter 1946- .... **CLC 47**
See also CA 103; CANR 46, 96; CP; DLB 40

Reaney, James 1926- .. **CLC 13; DAC; DAM MST**
See also CA 41-44R; CAAS 15; CANR 42; CD; CP; DLB 68; RGEL; SATA 43

Rebreanu, Liviu 1885-1944 .... **TCLC 28**
See also CA 165; DLB 220

Rechy, John (Francisco) 1934- ...... **CLC 1, 7, 14, 18, 107; DAM MULT; HLC 2**
See also CA 5-8R; CAAS 4; CANR 6, 32, 64; CN; DLB 122; DLBY 82; HW 1, 2; INT CANR-6; RGAL

Redcam, Tom 1870-1933 .... **TCLC 25**

Reddin, Keith .... **CLC 67**
See also CAD

Redgrove, Peter (William) 1932- . **CLC 6, 41**
See also BRWS 6; CA 1-4R; CANR 3, 39, 77; CP; DLB 40

Redmon, Anne .... **CLC 22**
See also Nightingale, Anne Redmon
See also DLBY 86

Reed, Eliot
See Ambler, Eric

Reed, Ishmael 1938- .. **CLC 2, 3, 5, 6, 13, 32, 60; BLC 3; DAM MULT**
See also AFAW 1, 2; BW 2, 3; CA 21-24R; CANR 25, 48, 74; CN; CP; CSW; DA3; DLB 2, 5, 33, 169, 227; DLBD 8; MTCW 1, 2; PFS 6; RGAL; TCWW 2

Reed, John (Silas) 1887-1920 .... **TCLC 9**
See also CA 106

Reed, Lou .... **CLC 21**
See also Firbank, Louis

Reese, Lizette Woodworth 1856-1935 . **PC 29**
See also CA 180; DLB 54

Reeve, Clara 1729-1807 .... **NCLC 19**
See also DLB 39; RGEL

Reich, Wilhelm 1897-1957 .... **TCLC 57**

Reid, Christopher (John) 1949- ...... **CLC 33**
See also CA 140; CANR 89; CP; DLB 40

Reid, Desmond
See Moorcock, Michael (John)

Reid Banks, Lynne 1929-
See Banks, Lynne Reid
See also CA 1-4R; CANR 6, 22, 38, 87; CLR 24; CN; JRDA; MAICYA; SATA 22, 75, 111; YAW

Reilly, William K.
See Creasey, John

Reiner, Max
See Caldwell, (Janet Miriam) Taylor (Holland)

Reis, Ricardo
See Pessoa, Fernando (Ant

Remarque, Erich Maria 1898-1970 ... **CLC 21; DA; DAB; DAC; DAM MST, NOV**
See also AAYA 27; CA 77-80; 29-32R; DA3; DLB 56; MTCW 1, 2; NFS 4; RGWL

Remington, Frederic 1861-1909 ..... **TCLC 89**
See also CA 108; 169; DLB 12, 186, 188; SATA 41

Remizov, A.
See Remizov, Aleksei (Mikhailovich)

Remizov, A. M.
See Remizov, Aleksei (Mikhailovich)

Remizov, Aleksei (Mikhailovich)
1877-1957 .... **TCLC 27**
See also CA 125; 133

Renan, Joseph Ernest 1823-1892 .. **NCLC 26**
See also GFL 1789 to the Present

Renard, Jules 1864-1910 .... **TCLC 17**
See also CA 117; GFL 1789 to the Present

Renault, Mary .... **CLC 3, 11, 17**
See also Challans, Mary
See also DLBY 83; GLL 1; MTCW 2; RGEL; RHW

Rendell, Ruth (Barbara) 1930- . **CLC 28, 48; DAM POP**
See also Vine, Barbara
See also CA 109; CANR 32, 52, 74; CN; CPW; DLB 87; INT CANR-32; MSW; MTCW 1, 2

Renoir, Jean 1894-1979 .... **CLC 20**
See also CA 129; 85-88

Resnais, Alain 1922- .... **CLC 16**

Reverdy, Pierre 1889-1960 .... **CLC 53**
See also CA 97-100; 89-92; GFL 1789 to the Present

Rexroth, Kenneth 1905-1982 .... **CLC 1, 2, 6, 11, 22, 49, 112; DAM POET; PC 20**
See also CA 5-8R; 107; CANR 14, 34, 63; CDALB 1941-1968; DLB 16, 48, 165, 212; DLBY 82; INT CANR-14; MTCW 1, 2; RGAL

Reyes, Alfonso 1889-1959 .. **TCLC 33; HLCS 2**
See also CA 131; HW 1

Reyes y Basoalto, Ricardo Eliecer Neftali
See Neruda, Pablo

Reymont, Wladyslaw (Stanislaw)
1868(?)-1925 .... **TCLC 5**
See also CA 104

Reynolds, Jonathan 1942- .... **CLC 6, 38**
See also CA 65-68; CANR 28

Reynolds, Joshua 1723-1792 .... **LC 15**
See also DLB 104

Reynolds, Michael S(hane)
1937-2000 .... **CLC 44**
See also CA 65-68; 189; CANR 9, 89, 97

Reznikoff, Charles 1894-1976 .... **CLC 9**
See also CA 33-36; 61-64; CAP 2; DLB 28, 45; WP

Rezzori (d'Arezzo), Gregor von
1914-1998 .... **CLC 25**
See also CA 122; 136; 167

Rhine, Richard
See Silverstein, Alvin; Silverstein, Virginia B(arbara Opshelor)

Rhodes, Eugene Manlove
1869-1934 .... **TCLC 53**

Rhodius, Apollonius c. 3rd cent.
B.C.- .... **CMLC 28**
See also DLB 176

R'hoone
See Balzac, Honor

Rhys, Jean 1894(?)-1979 ...... **CLC 2, 4, 6, 14, 19, 51, 124; DAM NOV; SSC 21**
See also BRWS 2; CA 25-28R; 85-88; CANR 35, 62; CDBLB 1945-1960; DA3; DLB 36, 117, 162; DNFS; MTCW 1, 2; RGEL; RGSF; RHW

Ribeiro, Darcy 1922-1997 .... **CLC 34**
See also CA 33-36R; 156

Ribeiro, Joao Ubaldo (Osorio Pimentel)
1941- .... **CLC 10, 67**
See also CA 81-84

Ribman, Ronald (Burt) 1932- .... **CLC 7**
See also CA 21-24R; CAD; CANR 46, 80; CD

Ricci, Nino 1959- .... **CLC 70**
See also CA 137; CCA 1

Rice, Anne 1941- .. **CLC 41, 128; DAM POP**
See also Rampling, Anne
See also AAYA 9; AMWS 7; BEST 89:2; CA 65-68; CANR 12, 36, 53, 74, 100; CN; CPW; CSW; DA3; GLL 2; HGG; MTCW 2; YAW

Rice, Elmer (Leopold) 1892-1967 ...... **CLC 7, 49; DAM DRAM**
See also CA 21-22; 25-28R; CAP 2; DFS 12; DLB 4, 7; MTCW 1, 2; RGAL

Rice, Tim(othy Miles Bindon)
1944- .... **CLC 21**
See also CA 103; CANR 46; DFS 7

Rich, Adrienne (Cecile) 1929- ... **CLC 3, 6, 7, 11, 18, 36, 73, 76, 125; DAM POET; PC 5**
See also AMWS 1; CA 9-12R; CANR 20, 53, 74; CDALBS; CP; CSW; CWP; DA3; DLB 5, 67; FW; MAWW; MTCW 1, 2; PAB; RGAL; WP

Rich, Barbara
See Graves, Robert (von Ranke)

Rich, Robert
See Trumbo, Dalton
See also IDFW 3

Richard, Keith .... **CLC 17**
See also Richards, Keith

Richards, David Adams 1950- .... **CLC 59; DAC**
See also CA 93-96; CANR 60; DLB 53

Richards, I(vor) A(rmstrong)
1893-1979 .... **CLC 14, 24**
See also BRWS 2; CA 41-44R; 89-92; CANR 34, 74; DLB 27; MTCW 2; RGEL

Richards, Keith 1943-
See Richard, Keith
See also CA 107; CANR 77

Richardson, Anne
See Roiphe, Anne (Richardson)

Richardson, Dorothy Miller
1873-1957 .... **TCLC 3**
See also CA 104; 192; DLB 36; FW; RGEL

Richardson (Robertson), Ethel Florence Lindesay 1870-1946
See Richardson, Henry Handel
See also CA 105; 190; DLB 230; RHW

Richardson, Henry Handel .... **TCLC 4**
See also Richardson (Robertson), Ethel Florence Lindesay
See also DLB 197; RGEL; RGSF

Richardson, John 1796-1852 .... **NCLC 55; DAC**
See also CCA 1; DLB 99

Richardson, Samuel 1689-1761 ...... **LC 1, 44; DA; DAB; DAC; DAM MST, NOV; WLC**
See also CDBLB 1660-1789; DLB 39; RGEL

Richler, Mordecai 1931-2001 .... **CLC 3, 5, 9, 13, 18, 46, 70; DAC; DAM MST, NOV**
See also AITN 1; CA 65-68; CANR 31, 62; CCA 1; CLR 17; CWRI; DLB 53; MAICYA; MTCW 1, 2; RGEL; SATA 44, 98; SATA-Brief 27

Richter, Conrad (Michael)
1890-1968 .... **CLC 30**
See also AAYA 21; CA 5-8R; 25-28R; CANR 23; DLB 9, 212; MTCW 1, 2; RGAL; SATA 3; TCWW 2; YAW

Ricostranza, Tom
See Ellis, Trey

Riddell, Charlotte 1832-1906 .... **TCLC 40**
See also CA 165; DLB 156

Ridge, John Rollin 1827-1867 ...... **NCLC 82; DAM MULT**
See also CA 144; DLB 175; NNAL

Ridgeway, Jason
See Marlowe, Stephen
Ridgway, Keith 1965- .... CLC 119
See also CA 172
Riding, Laura .... CLC 3, 7
See also Jackson, Laura (Riding)
See also RGAL
Riefenstahl, Berta Helene Amalia 1902-
See Riefenstahl, Leni
See also CA 108
Riefenstahl, Leni .... CLC 16
See also Riefenstahl, Berta Helene Amalia
Riffe, Ernest
See Bergman, (Ernst) Ingmar
Riggs, (Rolla) Lynn 1899-1954 ..... TCLC 56;
DAM MULT
See also CA 144; DLB 175; NNAL
Riis, Jacob A(ugust) 1849-1914 ..... TCLC 80
See also CA 113; 168; DLB 23
Riley, James Whitcomb
1849-1916 .... TCLC 51; DAM POET
See also CA 118; 137; MAICYA; RGAL;
SATA 17
Riley, Tex
See Creasey, John
Rilke, Rainer Maria 1875-1926 .. TCLC 1, 6,
19; DAM POET; PC 2
See also CA 104; 132; CANR 62, 99; DA3;
DLB 81; MTCW 1, 2; RGWL; WP
Rimbaud, (Jean Nicolas) Arthur
1854-1891 . NCLC 4, 35, 82; DA; DAB;
DAC; DAM MST, POET; PC 3; WLC
See also DA3; EW; GFL 1789 to the
Present; RGWL; TWA; WP
Rinehart, Mary Roberts
1876-1958 .... TCLC 52
See also CA 108; 166; RGAL; RHW
Ringmaster, The
See Mencken, H(enry) L(ouis)
Ringwood, Gwen(dolyn Margaret) Pharis
1910-1984 .... CLC 48
See also CA 148; 112; DLB 88
Rio, Michel 19(?)- .... CLC 43
Ritsos, Giannes
See Ritsos, Yannis
Ritsos, Yannis 1909-1990 .... CLC 6, 13, 31
See also CA 77-80; 133; CANR 39, 61;
MTCW 1; RGWL
Ritter, Erika 1948(?)- .... CLC 52
See also CD; CWD
Rivera, Jose Eustasio 1889-1928 ... TCLC 35
See also CA 162; HW 1, 2
Rivera, Tomas 1935-1984
See also CA 49-52; CANR 32; DLB 82;
HLCS 2; HW 1; RGAL; TCWW 2
Rivers, Conrad Kent 1933-1968 .... CLC 1
See also BW 1; CA 85-88; DLB 41
Rivers, Elfrida
See Bradley, Marion Zimmer
See also GLL 1
Riverside, John
See Heinlein, Robert A(nson)
Rizal, Jose 1861-1896 .... NCLC 27
Roa Bastos, Augusto (Antonio)
1917- .... CLC 45; DAM MULT; HLC 2
See also CA 131; DLB 113; HW 1; LAW;
RGSF
Robbe-Grillet, Alain 1922- .... CLC 1, 2, 4, 6,
8, 10, 14, 43, 128
See also CA 9-12R; CANR 33, 65; DLB
83; GFL 1789 to the Present; IDFW 4;
MTCW 1, 2; RGWL
Robbins, Harold 1916-1997 .... CLC 5; DAM
NOV
See also CA 73-76; 162; CANR 26, 54;
DA3; MTCW 1, 2

Robbins, Thomas Eugene 1936-
See Robbins, Tom
See also CA 81-84; CANR 29, 59, 95; CN;
CPW; CSW; DAM NOV, POP; DA3;
MTCW 1, 2
Robbins, Tom .... CLC 9, 32, 64
See also Robbins, Thomas Eugene
See also AAYA 32; BEST 90:3; DLBY 80;
MTCW 2
Robbins, Trina 1938- .... CLC 21
See also CA 128
Roberts, Charles G(eorge) D(ouglas)
1860-1943 .... TCLC 8
See also CA 105; 188; CLR 33; CWRI;
DLB 92; RGEL; RGSF; SATA 88; SATA-
Brief 29
Roberts, Elizabeth Madox
1886-1941 .... TCLC 68
See also CA 111; 166; CWRI; DLB 9, 54,
102; RGAL; RHW; SATA 33; SATA-Brief
27
Roberts, Kate 1891-1985 .... CLC 15
See also CA 107; 116
Roberts, Keith (John Kingston)
1935-2000 .... CLC 14
See also CA 25-28R; CANR 46; SFW
Roberts, Kenneth (Lewis)
1885-1957 .... TCLC 23
See also CA 109; DLB 9; RGAL; RHW
Roberts, Michele (Brigitte) 1949- ..... CLC 48
See also CA 115; CANR 58; CN; DLB 231;
FW
Robertson, Ellis
See Ellison, Harlan (Jay); Silverberg, Rob-
ert
Robertson, Thomas William
1829-1871 .... NCLC 35; DAM DRAM
See also Robertson, Tom
See also EW
Robertson, Tom
See Robertson, Thomas William
See also RGEL
Robeson, Kenneth
See Dent, Lester
Robinson, Edwin Arlington
1869-1935 ..... TCLC 5, 101; DA; DAC;
DAM MST, POET; PC 1, 35
See also CA 104; 133; CDALB 1865-1917;
DLB 54; MTCW 1, 2; PAB; PFS 4;
RGAL; WP
Robinson, Henry Crabb
1775-1867 .... NCLC 15
See also DLB 107
Robinson, Jill 1936- .... CLC 10
See also CA 102; INT 102
Robinson, Kim Stanley 1952- .... CLC 34
See also AAYA 26; CA 126; CN; SATA 109;
SFW
Robinson, Lloyd
See Silverberg, Robert
Robinson, Marilynne 1944- .... CLC 25
See also CA 116; CANR 80; CN; DLB 206
Robinson, Smokey .... CLC 21
See also Robinson, William, Jr.
Robinson, William, Jr. 1940-
See Robinson, Smokey
See also CA 116
Robison, Mary 1949- .... CLC 42, 98
See also CA 113; 116; CANR 87; CN; DLB
130; INT 116; RGSF
Rod, Edouard 1857-1910 .... TCLC 52
Roddenberry, Eugene Wesley 1921-1991
See Roddenberry, Gene
See also CA 110; 135; CANR 37; SATA 45;
SATA-Obit 69
Roddenberry, Gene .... CLC 17
See also Roddenberry, Eugene Wesley
See also AAYA 5; SATA-Obit 69

Rodgers, Mary 1931- .... CLC 12
See also CA 49-52; CANR 8, 55, 90; CLR
20; CWRI; INT CANR-8; JRDA; MAI-
CYA; SATA 8
Rodgers, W(illiam) R(obert)
1909-1969 .... CLC 7
See also CA 85-88; DLB 20; RGEL
Rodman, Eric
See Silverberg, Robert
Rodman, Howard 1920(?)-1985 .... CLC 65
See also CA 118
Rodman, Maia
See Wojciechowska, Maia (Teresa)
Rodo, Jose Enrique 1871(?)-1917
See also CA 178; HLCS 2; HW 2
Rodolph, Utto
See Ouologuem, Yambo
Rodriguez, Claudio 1934-1999 .... CLC 10
See also CA 188; DLB 134
Rodriguez, Richard 1944-
See also CA 110; CANR 66; DAM MULT;
DLB 82; HLC 2; HW 1, 2
Roelvaag, O(le) E(dvart)
1876-1931 .... TCLC 17
See also Rolvaag, O(le) E(dvart)
See also CA 117; 171; DLB 9
Roethke, Theodore (Huebner)
1908-1963 .... CLC 1, 3, 8, 11, 19, 46,
101; DAM POET; PC 15
See also AMW; CA 81-84; CABS 2;
CDALB 1941-1968; DA3; DLB 5, 206;
MTCW 1, 2; PAB; PFS 3; RGAL; WP
Rogers, Samuel 1763-1855 .... NCLC 69
See also DLB 93; RGEL
Rogers, Thomas Hunton 1927- .... CLC 57
See also CA 89-92; INT 89-92
Rogers, Will(iam Penn Adair)
1879-1935 ... TCLC 8, 71; DAM MULT
See also CA 105; 144; DA3; DLB 11;
MTCW 2; NNAL
Rogin, Gilbert 1929- .... CLC 18
See also CA 65-68; CANR 15
Rohan, Koda
See Koda Shigeyuki
Rohlfs, Anna Katharine Green
See Green, Anna Katharine
Rohmer, Eric .... CLC 16
See also Scherer, Jean-Marie Maurice
Rohmer, Sax .... TCLC 28
See also Ward, Arthur Henry Sarsfield
See also DLB 70
Roiphe, Anne (Richardson) 1935- .. CLC 3, 9
See also CA 89-92; CANR 45, 73; DLBY
80; INT 89-92
Rojas, Fernando de 1475-1541 .... LC 23;
HLCS 1
See also RGWL
Rojas, Gonzalo 1917-
See also HLCS 2; HW 2
Rojas, Gonzalo 1917-
See also CA 178; HLCS 2
Rolfe, Frederick (William Serafino Austin
Lewis Mary) 1860-1913 .... TCLC 12
See also Corvo, Baron
See also CA 107; DLB 34, 156; RGEL
Rolland, Romain 1866-1944 .... TCLC 23
See also CA 118; DLB 65; GFL 1789 to the
Present; RGWL
Rolle, Richard c. 1300-c. 1349 ...... CMLC 21
See also DLB 146; RGEL
Rolvaag, O(le) E(dvart)
See Roelvaag, O(le) E(dvart)
See also DLB 212; NFS 5; RGAL
Romain Arnaud, Saint
See Aragon, Louis
Romains, Jules 1885-1972 .... CLC 7
See also CA 85-88; CANR 34; DLB 65;
GFL 1789 to the Present; MTCW 1

Romero, Jose Ruben 1890-1952 .... **TCLC 14**
See also CA 114; 131; HW 1

Ronsard, Pierre de 1524-1585 . **LC 6, 54; PC 11**
See also GFL Beginnings to 1789; RGWL

Rooke, Leon 1934- . **CLC 25, 34; DAM POP**
See also CA 25-28R; CANR 23, 53; CCA 1; CPW

Roosevelt, Franklin Delano
1882-1945 .... **TCLC 93**
See also CA 116; 173

Roosevelt, Theodore 1858-1919 ..... **TCLC 69**
See also CA 115; 170; DLB 47, 186

Roper, William 1498-1578 .... **LC 10**

Roquelaure, A. N.
See Rice, Anne

Rosa, Joao Guimaraes 1908-1967 ... **CLC 23; HLCS 1**
See also CA 89-92; DLB 113

Rose, Wendy 1948- .. **CLC 85; DAM MULT; PC 13**
See also CA 53-56; CANR 5, 51; CWP; DLB 175; NNAL; RGAL; SATA 12

Rosen, R. D.
See Rosen, Richard (Dean)

Rosen, Richard (Dean) 1949- .... **CLC 39**
See also CA 77-80; CANR 62; CMW; INT CANR-30

Rosenberg, Isaac 1890-1918 .... **TCLC 12**
See also CA 107; 188; DLB 20; PAB; RGEL

Rosenblatt, Joe .... **CLC 15**
See also Rosenblatt, Joseph

Rosenblatt, Joseph 1933-
See Rosenblatt, Joe
See also CA 89-92; CP; INT 89-92

Rosenfeld, Samuel
See Tzara, Tristan

Rosenstock, Sami
See Tzara, Tristan

Rosenstock, Samuel
See Tzara, Tristan

Rosenthal, M(acha) L(ouis)
1917-1996 .... **CLC 28**
See also CA 1-4R; 152; CAAS 6; CANR 4, 51; CP; DLB 5; SATA 59

Ross, Barnaby
See Dannay, Frederic

Ross, Bernard L.
See Follett, Ken(neth Martin)

Ross, J. H.
See Lawrence, T(homas) E(dward)

Ross, John Hume
See Lawrence, T(homas) E(dward)

Ross, Martin 1862-1915
See Martin, Violet Florence
See also DLB 135; GLL 2; RGEL; RGSF

Ross, (James) Sinclair 1908-1996 ... **CLC 13; DAC; DAM MST; SSC 24**
See also CA 73-76; CANR 81; CN; DLB 88; RGEL; RGSF; TCWW 2

Rossetti, Christina (Georgina)
1830-1894 . **NCLC 2, 50, 66; DA; DAB; DAC; DAM MST, POET; PC 7; WLC**
See also BRW; DA3; DLB 35, 163, 240; MAICYA; PFS 10; RGEL; SATA 20; WCH

Rossetti, Dante Gabriel 1828-1882 . **NCLC 4, 77; DA; DAB; DAC; DAM MST, POET; WLC**
See also CDBLB 1832-1890; DLB 35; RGEL

Rossner, Judith (Perelman) 1935- . **CLC 6, 9, 29**
See also AITN 2; BEST 90:3; CA 17-20R; CANR 18, 51, 73; CN; DLB 6; INT CANR-18; MTCW 1, 2

Rostand, Edmond (Eugene Alexis)
1868-1918 .... **TCLC 6, 37; DA; DAB; DAC; DAM DRAM, MST; DC 10**
See also CA 104; 126; DA3; DFS 1; DLB 192; MTCW 1

Roth, Henry 1906-1995 ..... **CLC 2, 6, 11, 104**
See also CA 11-12; 149; CANR 38, 63; CAP 1; CN; DA3; DLB 28; MTCW 1, 2; RGAL

Roth, (Moses) Joseph 1894-1939 ... **TCLC 33**
See also CA 160; DLB 85

Roth, Philip (Milton) 1933- ... **CLC 1, 2, 3, 4, 6, 9, 15, 22, 31, 47, 66, 86, 119; DA; DAB; DAC; DAM MST, NOV, POP; SSC 26; WLC**
See also AMWS 3; BEST 90:3; CA 1-4R; CANR 1, 22, 36, 55, 89; CDALB 1968-1988; CN; CPW 1; DA3; DLB 2, 28, 173; DLBY 82; MTCW 1, 2; RGAL; RGSF; SSFS 12

Rothenberg, Jerome 1931- .... **CLC 6, 57**
See also CA 45-48; CANR 1; CP; DLB 5, 193

Rotter, Pat ed. .... **CLC 65**

Roumain, Jacques (Jean Baptiste)
1907-1944 ...... **TCLC 19; BLC 3; DAM MULT**
See also BW 1; CA 117; 125

Rourke, Constance (Mayfield)
1885-1941 .... **TCLC 12**
See also CA 107; YABC 1

Rousseau, Jean-Baptiste 1671-1741 ...... **LC 9**

Rousseau, Jean-Jacques 1712-1778 .... **LC 14, 36; DA; DAB; DAC; DAM MST; WLC**
See also DA3; EW; GFL Beginnings to 1789; RGWL

Roussel, Raymond 1877-1933 .... **TCLC 20**
See also CA 117; GFL 1789 to the Present

Rovit, Earl (Herbert) 1927- .... **CLC 7**
See also CA 5-8R; CANR 12

Rowe, Elizabeth Singer 1674-1737 ..... **LC 44**
See also DLB 39, 95

Rowe, Nicholas 1674-1718 .... **LC 8**
See also DLB 84; RGEL

Rowlandson, Mary 1637(?)-1678 .... **LC 66**
See also DLB 24, 200; RGAL

Rowley, Ames Dorrance
See Lovecraft, H(oward) P(hillips)

Rowling, J(oanne) K. 1966(?)- .... **CLC 137**
See also AAYA 34; CA 173; CLR 66; SATA 109

Rowson, Susanna Haswell
1762(?)-1824 .... **NCLC 5, 69**
See also DLB 37, 200; RGAL

Roy, Arundhati 1960(?)- .... **CLC 109**
See also CA 163; CANR 90; DLBY 97

Roy, Gabrielle 1909-1983 .... **CLC 10, 14; DAB; DAC; DAM MST**
See also CA 53-56; 110; CANR 5, 61; CCA 1; DLB 68; MTCW 1; RGWL; SATA 104

Royko, Mike 1932-1997 .... **CLC 109**
See also CA 89-92; 157; CANR 26; CPW

Rozanov, Vassili 1856-1919 .... **TCLC 104**

Rozewicz, Tadeusz 1921- ..... **CLC 9, 23, 139; DAM POET**
See also CA 108; CANR 36, 66; CWW 2; DA3; DLB 232; MTCW 1, 2

Ruark, Gibbons 1941- .... **CLC 3**
See also CA 33-36R; CAAS 23; CANR 14, 31, 57; DLB 120

Rubens, Bernice (Ruth) 1923- .... **CLC 19, 31**
See also CA 25-28R; CANR 33, 65; CN; DLB 14, 207; MTCW 1

Rubin, Harold
See Robbins, Harold

Rudkin, (James) David 1936- .... **CLC 14**
See also CA 89-92; CBD; CD; DLB 13

Rudnik, Raphael 1933- .... **CLC 7**
See also CA 29-32R

Ruffian, M.
See Ha

Ruiz, Jose Martinez .... **CLC 11**
See also Martinez Ruiz, Jose

Rukeyser, Muriel 1913-1980 . **CLC 6, 10, 15, 27; DAM POET; PC 12**
See also AMWS 6; CA 5-8R; 93-96; CANR 26, 60; DA3; DLB 48; FW; GLL 2; MTCW 1, 2; PFS 10; RGAL; SATA-Obit 22

Rule, Jane (Vance) 1931- .... **CLC 27**
See also CA 25-28R; CAAS 18; CANR 12, 87; CN; DLB 60; FW

Rulfo, Juan 1918-1986 ...... **CLC 8, 80; DAM MULT; HLC 2; SSC 25**
See also CA 85-88; 118; CANR 26; DLB 113; HW 1, 2; MTCW 1, 2; RGSF; RGWL

Rumi, Jalal al-Din 1207-1273 .... **CMLC 20**
See also RGWL; WP

Runeberg, Johan 1804-1877 .... **NCLC 41**

Runyon, (Alfred) Damon
1884(?)-1946 .... **TCLC 10**
See also CA 107; 165; DLB 11, 86, 171; MTCW 2; RGAL

Rush, Norman 1933- .... **CLC 44**
See also CA 121; 126; INT 126

Rushdie, (Ahmed) Salman 1947- .... **CLC 23, 31, 55, 100; DAB; DAC; DAM MST, NOV, POP; WLCS**
See also BEST 89:3; BRWS 4; CA 108; 111; CANR 33, 56; CN; CPW 1; DA3; DLB 194; FANT; INT CA-111; MTCW 1, 2; RGEL; RGSF

Rushforth, Peter (Scott) 1945- .... **CLC 19**
See also CA 101

Ruskin, John 1819-1900 .... **TCLC 63**
See also CA 114; 129; CDBLB 1832-1890; DLB 55, 163, 190; RGEL; SATA 24

Russ, Joanna 1937- .... **CLC 15**
See also CA 5-28R; CANR 11, 31, 65; CN; DLB 8; FW; GLL 1; MTCW 1; SCFW 2; SFW

Russell, George William 1867-1935
See Baker, Jean H.
See also CA 104; 153; CDBLB 1890-1914; DAM POET; RGEL

Russell, Jeffrey Burton 1934- .... **CLC 70**
See also CA 25-28R; CANR 11, 28, 52

Russell, (Henry) Ken(neth Alfred)
1927- .... **CLC 16**
See also CA 105

Russell, William Martin 1947- .... **CLC 60**
See also CA 164; DLB 233

Rutherford, Mark .... **TCLC 25**
See also White, William Hale
See also DLB 18; RGEL

Ruyslinck, Ward .... **CLC 14**
See also Belser, Reimond Karel Maria de

Ryan, Cornelius (John) 1920-1974 ..... **CLC 7**
See also CA 69-72; 53-56; CANR 38

Ryan, Michael 1946- .... **CLC 65**
See also CA 49-52; DLBY 82

Ryan, Tim
See Dent, Lester

Rybakov, Anatoli (Naumovich)
1911-1998 .... **CLC 23, 53**
See also CA 126; 135; 172; SATA 79; SATA-Obit 108

Ryder, Jonathan
See Ludlum, Robert

Ryga, George 1932-1987 .... **CLC 14; DAC; DAM MST**
See also CA 101; 124; CANR 43, 90; CCA 1; DLB 60

S. H.
See Hartmann, Sadakichi

S. S.
See Sassoon, Siegfried (Lorraine)

Sarraute, Nathalie 1900-1999 .... **CLC 1, 2, 4, 8, 10, 31, 80**
See also CA 9-12R; 187; CANR 23, 66; CWW 2; DLB 83; GFL 1789 to the Present; MTCW 1, 2; RGWL

Sarton, (Eleanor) May 1912-1995 ..... **CLC 4, 14, 49, 91; DAM POET**
See also AMWS 8; CA 1-4R; 149; CANR 1, 34, 55; CN; CP; DLB 48; DLBY 81; FW; INT CANR-34; MTCW 1, 2; RGAL; SATA 36; SATA-Obit 86

Sartre, Jean-Paul 1905-1980 . **CLC 1, 4, 7, 9, 13, 18, 24, 44, 50, 52; DA; DAB; DAC; DAM DRAM, MST, NOV; DC 3; SSC 32; WLC**
See also CA 9-12R; 97-100; CANR 21; DA3; DFS 5; DLB 72; GFL 1789 to the Present; MTCW 1, 2; RGSF; RGWL; SSFS 9

Sassoon, Siegfried (Lorraine) 1886-1967 .... **CLC 36, 130; DAB; DAM MST, NOV, POET; PC 12**
See also BRW; CA 104; 25-28R; CANR 36; DLB 20, 191; DLBD 18; MTCW 1, 2; PAB; RGEL

Satterfield, Charles
See Pohl, Frederik

Satyremont
See P

Saul, John (W. III) 1942- ...... **CLC 46; DAM NOV, POP**
See also AAYA 10; BEST 90:4; CA 81-84; CANR 16, 40, 81; CPW; HGG; SATA 98

Saunders, Caleb
See Heinlein, Robert A(nson)

Saura (Atares), Carlos 1932-1998 .... **CLC 20**
See also CA 114; 131; CANR 79; HW 1

Sauser-Hall, Frederic 1887-1961 ...... **CLC 18**
See also Cendrars, Blaise
See also CA 102; 93-96; CANR 36, 62; MTCW 1

Saussure, Ferdinand de 1857-1913 .... **TCLC 49**

Savage, Catharine
See Brosman, Catharine Savage

Savage, Thomas 1915- .... **CLC 40**
See also CA 126; 132; CAAS 15; CN; INT 132; TCWW 2

Savan, Glenn (?)- .... **CLC 50**

Sayers, Dorothy L(eigh) 1893-1957 .... **TCLC 2, 15; DAM POP**
See also BRWS 3; CA 104; 119; CANR 60; CDBLB 1914-1945; CMW; DLB 10, 36, 77, 100; MTCW 1, 2; RGEL; SSFS 12

Sayers, Valerie 1952- .... **CLC 50, 122**
See also CA 134; CANR 61; CSW

Sayles, John (Thomas) 1950- . **CLC 7, 10, 14**
See also CA 57-60; CANR 41, 84; DLB 44

Scammell, Michael 1935- .... **CLC 34**
See also CA 156

Scannell, Vernon 1922- .... **CLC 49**
See also CA 5-8R; CANR 8, 24, 57; CP; CWRI; DLB 27; SATA 59

Scarlett, Susan
See Streatfeild, (Mary) Noel

Scarron 1847-1910
See Mikszath, Kalman

Schaeffer, Susan Fromberg 1941- ..... **CLC 6, 11, 22**
See also CA 49-52; CANR 18, 65; CN; DLB 28; MTCW 1, 2; SATA 22

Schary, Jill
See Robinson, Jill

Schell, Jonathan 1943- .... **CLC 35**
See also CA 73-76; CANR 12

Schelling, Friedrich Wilhelm Joseph von 1775-1854 .... **NCLC 30**
See also DLB 90

Scherer, Jean-Marie Maurice 1920-
See Rohmer, Eric
See also CA 110

Schevill, James (Erwin) 1920- .... **CLC 7**
See also CA 5-8R; CAAS 12; CAD; CD

Schiller, Friedrich von 1759-1805 .... **NCLC 39, 69; DAM DRAM; DC 12**
See also DLB 94; EW; RGWL

Schisgal, Murray (Joseph) 1926- .... **CLC 6**
See also CA 21-24R; CAD; CANR 48, 86; CD

Schlee, Ann 1934- .... **CLC 35**
See also CA 101; CANR 29, 88; SATA 44; SATA-Brief 36

Schlegel, August Wilhelm von 1767-1845 .... **NCLC 15**
See also DLB 94; RGWL

Schlegel, Friedrich 1772-1829 .... **NCLC 45**
See also DLB 90; EW; RGWL

Schlegel, Johann Elias (von) 1719(?)-1749 .... **LC 5**

Schlesinger, Arthur M(eier), Jr. 1917- .... **CLC 84**
See also AITN 1; CA 1-4R; CANR 1, 28, 58; DLB 17; INT CANR-28; MTCW 1, 2; SATA 61

Schmidt, Arno (Otto) 1914-1979 ...... **CLC 56**
See also CA 128; 109; DLB 69

Schmitz, Aron Hector 1861-1928
See Svevo, Italo
See also CA 104; 122; MTCW 1

Schnackenberg, Gjertrud (Cecelia) 1953- .... **CLC 40**
See also CA 116; CANR 100; CP; CWP; DLB 120

Schneider, Leonard Alfred 1925-1966
See Bruce, Lenny
See also CA 89-92

Schnitzler, Arthur 1862-1931 . **TCLC 4; SSC 15**
See also CA 104; DLB 81, 118; RGSF; RGWL

Schoenberg, Arnold Franz Walter 1874-1951 .... **TCLC 75**
See also CA 109; 188

Schonberg, Arnold
See Schoenberg, Arnold Franz Walter

Schopenhauer, Arthur 1788-1860 .. **NCLC 51**
See also DLB 90

Schor, Sandra (M.) 1932(?)-1990 ..... **CLC 65**
See also CA 132

Schorer, Mark 1908-1977 .... **CLC 9**
See also CA 5-8R; 73-76; CANR 7; DLB 103

Schrader, Paul (Joseph) 1946- .... **CLC 26**
See also CA 37-40R; CANR 41; DLB 44

Schreiner, Olive (Emilie Albertina) 1855-1920 .... **TCLC 9**
See also AFW; BRWS 2; CA 105; 154; DLB 18, 156, 190, 225; FW; RGEL

Schulberg, Budd (Wilson) 1914- .. **CLC 7, 48**
See also CA 25-28R; CANR 19, 87; CN; DLB 6, 26, 28; DLBY 81

Schulz, Bruno 1892-1942 .. **TCLC 5, 51; SSC 13**
See also CA 115; 123; CANR 86; MTCW 2; RGSF; RGWL

Schulz, Charles M(onroe) 1922-2000 .... **CLC 12**
See also AAYA 39; CA 9-12R; 187; CANR 6; INT CANR-6; SATA 10; SATA-Obit 118

Schumacher, E(rnst) F(riedrich) 1911-1977 .... **CLC 80**
See also CA 81-84; 73-76; CANR 34, 85

Schuyler, James Marcus 1923-1991 .. **CLC 5, 23; DAM POET**
See also CA 101; 134; DLB 5, 169; INT 101; WP

Schwartz, Delmore (David) 1913-1966 ... **CLC 2, 4, 10, 45, 87; PC 8**
See also AMWS 2; CA 17-18; 25-28R; CANR 35; CAP 2; DLB 28, 48; MTCW 1, 2; PAB; RGAL

Schwartz, Ernst
See Ozu, Yasujiro

Schwartz, John Burnham 1965- .... **CLC 59**
See also CA 132

Schwartz, Lynne Sharon 1939- .... **CLC 31**
See also CA 103; CANR 44, 89; MTCW 2

Schwartz, Muriel A.
See Eliot, T(homas) S(tearns)

Schwarz-Bart, Andre 1928- .... **CLC 2, 4**
See also CA 89-92

Schwarz-Bart, Simone 1938- . **CLC 7; BLCS**
See also BW 2; CA 97-100

Schwitters, Kurt (Hermann Edward Karl Julius) 1887-1948 .... **TCLC 95**
See also CA 158

Schwob, Marcel (Mayer Andre) 1867-1905 .... **TCLC 20**
See also CA 117; 168; DLB 123; GFL 1789 to the Present

Sciascia, Leonardo 1921-1989 .. **CLC 8, 9, 41**
See also CA 85-88; 130; CANR 35; DLB 177; MTCW 1; RGWL

Scoppettone, Sandra 1936- .... **CLC 26**
See also Early, Jack
See also AAYA 11; CA 5-8R; CANR 41, 73; GLL 1; SATA 9, 92; YAW

Scorsese, Martin 1942- .... **CLC 20, 89**
See also AAYA 38; CA 110; 114; CANR 46, 85

Scotland, Jay
See Jakes, John (William)

Scott, Duncan Campbell 1862-1947 .... **TCLC 6; DAC**
See also CA 104; 153; DLB 92; RGEL

Scott, Evelyn 1893-1963 .... **CLC 43**
See also CA 104; 112; CANR 64; DLB 9, 48; RHW

Scott, F(rancis) R(eginald) 1899-1985 .... **CLC 22**
See also CA 101; 114; CANR 87; DLB 88; INT CA-101; RGEL

Scott, Frank
See Scott, F(rancis) R(eginald)

Scott, Joan .... **CLC 65**

Scott, Joanna 1960- .... **CLC 50**
See also CA 126; CANR 53, 92

Scott, Paul (Mark) 1920-1978 .... **CLC 9, 60**
See also BRWS 1; CA 81-84; 77-80; CANR 33; DLB 14, 207; MTCW 1; RGEL; RHW

Scott, Sarah 1723-1795 .... **LC 44**
See also DLB 39

Scott, Walter 1771-1832 . **NCLC 15, 69; DA; DAB; DAC; DAM MST, NOV, POET; PC 13; SSC 32; WLC**
See also AAYA 22; BRW; CDBLB 1789-1832; DLB 93, 107, 116, 144, 159; HGG; RGEL; RGSF; SSFS 10; SUFW; YABC 2

Scribe, (Augustin) Eugene 1791-1861 ..... **NCLC 16; DAM DRAM; DC 5**
See also DLB 192; EW; GFL 1789 to the Present; RGWL

Scrum, R.
See Crumb, R(obert)

Scudery, Madeleine de 1607-1701 .. **LC 2, 58**
See also GFL Beginnings to 1789

Scum
See Crumb, R(obert)

Stribling, T(homas) S(igismund)
1881-1965 .... **CLC 23**
See also CA 189; 107; CMW; DLB 9;
RGAL

Strindberg, (Johan) August
1849-1912 .... **TCLC 1, 8, 21, 47; DA;**
DAB; DAC; DAM DRAM, MST; WLC
See also CA 104; 135; DA3; DFS 4, 9; EW;
MTCW 2; RGWL

Stringer, Arthur 1874-1950 .... **TCLC 37**
See also CA 161; DLB 92

Stringer, David
See Roberts, Keith (John Kingston)

Stroheim, Erich von 1885-1957 ..... **TCLC 71**

Strugatskii, Arkadii (Natanovich)
1925-1991 .... **CLC 27**
See also CA 106; 135; SFW

Strugatskii, Boris (Natanovich)
1933- .... **CLC 27**
See also CA 106; SFW

Strummer, Joe 1953(?)- .... **CLC 30**

Strunk, William, Jr. 1869-1946 ...... **TCLC 92**
See also CA 118; 164

Stryk, Lucien 1924- .... **PC 27**
See also CA 13-16R; CANR 10, 28, 55; CP

Stuart, Don A.
See Campbell, John W(ood, Jr.)

Stuart, Ian
See MacLean, Alistair (Stuart)

Stuart, Jesse (Hilton) 1906-1984 ... **CLC 1, 8,**
11, 14, 34; SSC 31
See also CA 5-8R; 112; CANR 31; DLB 9,
48, 102; DLBY 84; SATA 2; SATA-Obit
36

Sturgeon, Theodore (Hamilton)
1918-1985 .... **CLC 22, 39**
See also Queen, Ellery
See also CA 81-84; 116; CANR 32; DLB 8;
DLBY 85; HGG; MTCW 1, 2; SFW;
SUFW

Sturges, Preston 1898-1959 .... **TCLC 48**
See also CA 114; 149; DLB 26

Styron, William 1925- .... **CLC 1, 3, 5, 11, 15,**
60; DAM NOV, POP; SSC 25
See also BEST 90:4; CA 5-8R; CANR 6,
33, 74; CDALB 1968-1988; CN; CPW;
CSW; DA3; DLB 2, 143; DLBY 80; INT
CANR-6; MTCW 1, 2; NCFS 1; RGAL;
RHW

Su, Chien 1884-1918
See Su Man-shu
See also CA 123

Suarez Lynch, B.
See Bioy Casares, Adolfo; Borges, Jorge
Luis

Suassuna, Ariano Vilar 1927-
See also CA 178; HLCS 1; HW 2

Suckling, Sir John 1609-1642 .... **PC 30**
See also BRW; DAM POET; DLB 58, 126;
PAB; RGEL

Suckow, Ruth 1892-1960 .... **SSC 18**
See also CA 113; DLB 9, 102; RGAL;
TCWW 2

Sudermann, Hermann 1857-1928 .. **TCLC 15**
See also CA 107; DLB 118

Sue, Eugene 1804-1857 .... **NCLC 1**
See also DLB 119

Sueskind, Patrick 1949- .... **CLC 44**
See also Suskind, Patrick

Sukenick, Ronald 1932- .... **CLC 3, 4, 6, 48**
See also CA 25-28R; CAAS 8; CANR 32,
89; CN; DLB 173; DLBY 81

Suknaski, Andrew 1942- .... **CLC 19**
See also CA 101; CP; DLB 53

Sullivan, Vernon
See Vian, Boris

Sully Prudhomme, Rene-Francois-Armand
1839-1907 .... **TCLC 31**
See also GFL 1789 to the Present

Su Man-shu .... **TCLC 24**
See also Su, Chien

Summerforest, Ivy B.
See Kirkup, James

Summers, Andrew James 1942- .... **CLC 26**

Summers, Andy
See Summers, Andrew James

Summers, Hollis (Spurgeon, Jr.)
1916- .... **CLC 10**
See also CA 5-8R; CANR 3; DLB 6

Summers, (Alphonsus Joseph-Mary
Augustus) Montague
1880-1948 .... **TCLC 16**
See also CA 118; 163

Sumner, Gordon Matthew .... **CLC 26**
See also Sting

Surtees, Robert Smith 1805-1864 .. **NCLC 14**
See also DLB 21; RGEL

Susann, Jacqueline 1921-1974 .... **CLC 3**
See also AITN 1; CA 65-68; 53-56; MTCW
1, 2

Su Shi
See Su Shih
See also RGWL

Su Shih 1036-1101 .... **CMLC 15**
See also Su Shi

Suskind, Patrick
See Sueskind, Patrick
See also CA 145; CWW 2

Sutcliff, Rosemary 1920-1992 .... **CLC 26;**
DAB; DAC; DAM MST, POP
See also AAYA 10; CA 5-8R; 139; CANR
37; CLR 1, 37; CPW; JRDA; MAICYA;
RHW; SATA 6, 44, 78; SATA-Obit 73;
YAW

Sutro, Alfred 1863-1933 .... **TCLC 6**
See also CA 105; 185; DLB 10; RGEL

Sutton, Henry
See Slavitt, David R(ytman)

Suzuki, D. T.
See Suzuki, Daisetz Teitaro

Suzuki, Daisetz T.
See Suzuki, Daisetz Teitaro

Suzuki, Daisetz Teitaro
1870-1966 .... **TCLC 109**
See also CA 121; 111; MTCW 1, 2

Suzuki, Teitaro
See Suzuki, Daisetz Teitaro

Svevo, Italo .... **TCLC 2, 35; SSC 25**
See also Schmitz, Aron Hector
See also RGWL

Swados, Elizabeth (A.) 1951- .... **CLC 12**
See also CA 97-100; CANR 49; INT 97-
100

Swados, Harvey 1920-1972 .... **CLC 5**
See also CA 5-8R; 37-40R; CANR 6; DLB
2

Swan, Gladys 1934- .... **CLC 69**
See also CA 101; CANR 17, 39

Swanson, Logan
See Matheson, Richard (Burton)

Swarthout, Glendon (Fred)
1918-1992 .... **CLC 35**
See also CA 1-4R; 139; CANR 1, 47; SATA
26; TCWW 2; YAW

Sweet, Sarah C.
See Jewett, (Theodora) Sarah Orne

Swenson, May 1919-1989 ...... **CLC 4, 14, 61,**
106; DA; DAB; DAC; DAM MST,
POET; PC 14
See also AMWS 4; CA 5-8R; 130; CANR
36, 61; DLB 5; GLL 2; MTCW 1, 2;
SATA 15; WP

Swift, Augustus
See Lovecraft, H(oward) P(hillips)

Swift, Graham (Colin) 1949- ...... **CLC 41, 88**
See also BRWS 5; CA 117; 122; CANR 46,
71; CN; DLB 194; MTCW 2; RGSF

Swift, Jonathan 1667-1745 ..... **LC 1, 42; DA;**
DAB; DAC; DAM MST, NOV, POET;
PC 9; WLC
See also CDBLB 1660-1789; CLR 53;
DA3; DLB 39, 95, 101; NFS 6; RGEL;
SATA 19

Swinburne, Algernon Charles
1837-1909 .... **TCLC 8, 36; DA; DAB;**
DAC; DAM MST, POET; PC 24; WLC
See also CA 105; 140; CDBLB 1832-1890;
DA3; DLB 35, 57; PAB; RGEL

Swinfen, Ann .... **CLC 34**

Swinnerton, Frank Arthur
1884-1982 .... **CLC 31**
See also CA 108; DLB 34

Swithen, John
See King, Stephen (Edwin)

Sylvia
See Ashton-Warner, Sylvia (Constance)

Symmes, Robert Edward
See Duncan, Robert (Edward)

Symonds, John Addington
1840-1893 .... **NCLC 34**
See also DLB 57, 144

Symons, Arthur 1865-1945 .... **TCLC 11**
See also CA 107; 189; DLB 19, 57, 149;
RGEL

Symons, Julian (Gustave)
1912-1994 .... **CLC 2, 14, 32**
See also CA 49-52; 147; CAAS 3; CANR
3, 33, 59; CMW; DLB 87, 155; DLBY
92; MSW; MTCW 1

Synge, (Edmund) J(ohn) M(illington)
1871-1909 . **TCLC 6, 37; DAM DRAM;**
DC 2
See also BRW; CA 104; 141; CDBLB 1890-
1914; DLB 10, 19; RGEL

Syruc, J.
See Milosz, Czeslaw

Szirtes, George 1948- .... **CLC 46**
See also CA 109; CANR 27, 61; CP

Szymborska, Wislawa 1923- .... **CLC 99**
See also CA 154; CANR 91; CWP; CWW
2; DA3; DLB 232; DLBY 96; MTCW 2

T. O., Nik
See Annensky, Innokenty (Fyodorovich)

Tabori, George 1914- .... **CLC 19**
See also CA 49-52; CANR 4, 69; CBD; CD

Tagore, Rabindranath 1861-1941 ... **TCLC 3,**
53; DAM DRAM, POET; PC 8
See also CA 104; 120; DA3; MTCW 1, 2;
RGEL; RGSF; RGWL

Taine, Hippolyte Adolphe
1828-1893 .... **NCLC 15**
See also EW; GFL 1789 to the Present

Talese, Gay 1932- .... **CLC 37**
See also AITN 1; CA 1-4R; CANR 9, 58;
DLB 185; INT CANR-9; MTCW 1, 2

Tallent, Elizabeth (Ann) 1954- .... **CLC 45**
See also CA 117; CANR 72; DLB 130

Tally, Ted 1952- .... **CLC 42**
See also CA 120; 124; CAD; CD; INT 124

Talvik, Heiti 1904-1947 .... **TCLC 87**

Tamayo y Baus, Manuel
1829-1898 .... **NCLC 1**

Tammsaare, A(nton) H(ansen)
1878-1940 .... **TCLC 27**
See also CA 164; DLB 220

Tam'si, Tchicaya U
See Tchicaya, Gerald Felix

Tan, Amy (Ruth) 1952- . **CLC 59, 120; DAM**
MULT, NOV, POP
See also AAYA 9; BEST 89:3; CA 136;
CANR 54; CDALBS; CN; CPW 1; DA3;
DLB 173; FW; MTCW 2; NFS 1; RGAL;
SATA 75; SSFS 9; YAW

Tandem, Felix
See Spitteler, Carl (Friedrich Georg)

Thompson, Hunter S(tockton)
 1939- ... CLC 9, 17, 40, 104; DAM POP
  See also BEST 89:1; CA 17-20R; CANR
  23, 46, 74, 77; CPW; CSW; DA3; DLB
  185; MTCW 1, 2
Thompson, James Myers
  See Thompson, Jim (Myers)
Thompson, Jim (Myers)
 1906-1977(?) .... CLC 69
  See also CA 140; CMW; CPW; DLB 226
Thompson, Judith .... CLC 39
  See also CWD
Thomson, James 1700-1748 ... LC 16, 29, 40;
 DAM POET
  See also BRWS 3; DLB 95; RGEL
Thomson, James 1834-1882 .... NCLC 18;
 DAM POET
  See also DLB 35; RGEL
Thoreau, Henry David 1817-1862 .. NCLC 7,
 21, 61; DA; DAB; DAC; DAM MST;
 PC 30; WLC
  See also CDALB 1640-1865; DA3; DLB 1,
  223; RGAL
Thorndike, E. L.
  See Thorndike, Edward L(ee)
Thorndike, Edward L(ee)
 1874-1949 .... TCLC 107
  See also CA 121
Thornton, Hall
  See Silverberg, Robert
Thucydides c. 455B.C.-c. 395B.C. . CMLC 17
  See also DLB 176; RGWL
Thumboo, Edwin 1933- .... PC 30
Thurber, James (Grover)
 1894-1961 .... CLC 5, 11, 25, 125; DA;
 DAB; DAC; DAM DRAM, MST, NOV;
 SSC 1
  See also AMWS 1; CA 73-76; CANR 17,
  39; CDALB 1929-1941; CWRI; DA3;
  DLB 4, 11, 22, 102; FANT; MAICYA;
  MTCW 1, 2; RGAL; RGSF; SATA 13;
  SSFS 1, 10; SUFW
Thurman, Wallace (Henry)
 1902-1934 .... TCLC 6; BLC 3; DAM
 MULT
  See also BW 1, 3; CA 104; 124; CANR 81;
  DLB 51
Tibullus c. 54B.C.-c. 18B.C. .... CMLC 36
  See also AW; DLB 211; RGWL
Ticheburn, Cheviot
  See Ainsworth, William Harrison
Tieck, (Johann) Ludwig
 1773-1853 .... NCLC 5, 46; SSC 31
  See also DLB 90; EW; RGSF; RGWL;
  SUFW
Tiger, Derry
  See Ellison, Harlan (Jay)
Tilghman, Christopher 1948(?)- .... CLC 65
  See also CA 159; CSW
Tillich, Paul (Johannes)
 1886-1965 .... CLC 131
  See also CA 5-8R; 25-28R; CANR 33;
  MTCW 1, 2
Tillinghast, Richard (Williford)
 1940- .... CLC 29
  See also CA 29-32R; CAAS 23; CANR 26,
  51, 96; CP; CSW
Timrod, Henry 1828-1867 .... NCLC 25
  See also DLB 3; RGAL
Tindall, Gillian (Elizabeth) 1938- ...... CLC 7
  See also CA 21-24R; CANR 11, 65; CN
Tiptree, James, Jr. .... CLC 48, 50
  See Sheldon, Alice Hastings Bradley
  See also DLB 8; SFW
Tirso de Molina
  See Molina, Tirso de
  See also RGWL
Titmarsh, Michael Angelo
  See Thackeray, William Makepeace

Tocqueville, Alexis (Charles Henri Maurice
 Clerel 1805-1859 .... NCLC 7, 63
  See also EW; GFL 1789 to the Present
Tolkien, J(ohn) R(onald) R(euel)
 1892-1973 .. CLC 1, 2, 3, 8, 12, 38; DA;
 DAB; DAC; DAM MST, NOV, POP;
 WLC
  See also AAYA 10; AITN 1; BRWS 2; CA
  17-18; 45-48; CANR 36; CAP 2; CDBLB
  1914-1945; CLR 56; CPW 1; CWRI;
  DA3; DLB 15, 160; EFS 2; FANT; JRDA;
  MAICYA; MTCW 1, 2; NFS 8; RGEL;
  SATA 2, 32, 100; SATA-Obit 24; SFW;
  SUFW; WCH; WYA; YAW
Toller, Ernst 1893-1939 .... TCLC 10
  See also CA 107; 186; DLB 124; RGWL
Tolson, M. B.
  See Tolson, Melvin B(eaunorus)
Tolson, Melvin B(eaunorus)
 1898(?)-1966 .... CLC 36, 105; BLC 3;
 DAM MULT, POET
  See also AFAW 1, 2; BW 1, 3; CA 124; 89-
  92; CANR 80; DLB 48, 76; RGAL
Tolstoi, Aleksei Nikolaevich
  See Tolstoy, Alexey Nikolaevich
Tolstoi, Lev
  See Tolstoy, Leo (Nikolaevich)
  See also RGSF; RGWL
Tolstoy, Alexey Nikolaevich
 1882-1945 .... TCLC 18
  See also CA 107; 158; SFW
Tolstoy, Leo (Nikolaevich)
 1828-1910 .. TCLC 4, 11, 17, 28, 44, 79;
 DA; DAB; DAC; DAM MST, NOV;
 SSC 9, 30, 45; WLC
  See also Tolstoi, Lev
  See also CA 104; 123; DA3; DLB 238; EFS
  2; EW; IDTP; NFS 10; SATA 26; SSFS 5
Tolstoy, CountLeo
  See Tolstoy, Leo (Nikolaevich)
Tomasi di Lampedusa, Giuseppe 1896-1957
  See Lampedusa, Giuseppe (Tomasi) di
  See also CA 111
Tomlin, Lily .... CLC 17
  See also Tomlin, Mary Jean
Tomlin, Mary Jean 1939(?)-
  See Tomlin, Lily
  See also CA 117
Tomlinson, (Alfred) Charles 1927- .... CLC 2,
 4, 6, 13, 45; DAM POET; PC 17
  See also CA 5-8R; CANR 33; CP; DLB 40
Tomlinson, H(enry) M(ajor)
 1873-1958 .... TCLC 71
  See also CA 118; 161; DLB 36, 100, 195
Tonson, Jacob
  See Bennett, (Enoch) Arnold
Toole, John Kennedy 1937-1969 ..... CLC 19,
 64
  See also CA 104; DLBY 81; MTCW 2
Toomer, Jean 1892-1967 .... CLC 1, 4, 13, 22;
 BLC 3; DAM MULT; PC 7; SSC 1, 45;
 WLCS
  See also Pinchback, Eugene; Toomer, Eu-
  gene; Toomer, Eugene Pinchback; Toomer,
  Nathan Jean; Toomer, Nathan Pinchback
  See also AFAW 1, 2; AMWS 3; BW 1; CA
  85-88; CDALB 1917-1929; DA3; DLB
  45, 51; MTCW 1, 2; NFS 11; RGAL;
  RGSF; SSFS 5
Torley, Luke
  See Blish, James (Benjamin)
Tornimparte, Alessandra
  See Ginzburg, Natalia
Torre, Raoul della
  See Mencken, H(enry) L(ouis)
Torrence, Ridgely 1874-1950 .... TCLC 97
  See also DLB 54
Torrey, E(dwin) Fuller 1937- .... CLC 34
  See also CA 119; CANR 71

Torsvan, Ben Traven
  See Traven, B.
Torsvan, Benno Traven
  See Traven, B.
Torsvan, Berick Traven
  See Traven, B.
Torsvan, Berwick Traven
  See Traven, B.
Torsvan, Bruno Traven
  See Traven, B.
Torsvan, Traven
  See Traven, B.
Tourneur, Cyril 1575(?)-1626 .. LC 66; DAM
 DRAM
  See also DLB 58; RGEL
Tournier, Michel (edouard) 1924- ..... CLC 6,
 23, 36, 95
  See also CA 49-52; CANR 3, 36, 74; DLB
  83; GFL 1789 to the Present; MTCW 1,
  2; SATA 23
Tournimparte, Alessandra
  See Ginzburg, Natalia
Towers, Ivar
  See Kornbluth, C(yril) M.
Towne, Robert (Burton) 1936(?)- ..... CLC 87
  See also CA 108; DLB 44; IDFW 3
Townsend, Sue .... CLC 61
  See also Townsend, Susan Elaine
  See also AAYA 28; CBD; CWD; SATA 55,
  93; SATA-Brief 48
Townsend, Susan Elaine 1946-
  See Townsend, Sue
  See also CA 119; 127; CANR 65; CD;
  CPW; DAB; DAC; DAM MST; INT 127;
  YAW
Townshend, Peter (Dennis Blandford)
 1945- .... CLC 17, 42
  See also CA 107
Tozzi, Federigo 1883-1920 .... TCLC 31
  See also CA 160
Tracy, Don(ald Fiske) 1905-1970(?)
  See Queen, Ellery
  See also CA 1-4R; 176; CANR 2
Traill, Catharine Parr 1802-1899 .. NCLC 31
  See also DLB 99
Trakl, Georg 1887-1914 .... TCLC 5; PC 20
  See also CA 104; 165; MTCW 2; RGWL
Transtroemer, Tomas (Goesta)
 1931- .... CLC 52, 65; DAM POET
  See also CA 117; 129; CAAS 17
Transtromer, Tomas Gosta
  See Transtroemer, Tomas (Goesta)
Traven, B. 1882(?)-1969 .... CLC 8, 11
  See also CA 19-20; 25-28R; CAP 2; DLB
  9, 56; MTCW 1; RGAL
Trediakovsky, Vasilii Kirillovich
 1703-1769 .... LC 68
  See also DLB 150
Treitel, Jonathan 1959- .... CLC 70
Trelawny, Edward John
 1792-1881 .... NCLC 85
  See also DLB 110, 116, 144
Tremain, Rose 1943- .... CLC 42
  See also CA 97-100; CANR 44, 95; CN;
  DLB 14; RGSF; RHW
Tremblay, Michel 1942- .... CLC 29, 102;
 DAC; DAM MST
  See also CA 116; 128; CCA 1; CWW 2;
  DLB 60; GLL 1; MTCW 1, 2
Trevanian .... CLC 29
  See also Whitaker, Rod(ney)
Trevor, Glen
  See Hilton, James
Trevor, William .. CLC 7, 9, 14, 25, 71, 116;
 SSC 21
  See also Cox, William Trevor
  See also BRWS 4; CBD; DLB 14, 139;
  MTCW 2; RGEL; RGSF; SSFS 10

Valera y Alcala-Galiano, Juan
  1824-1905 .... **TCLC 10**
  See also CA 106
Valery, (Ambroise) Paul (Toussaint Jules)
  1871-1945 ... **TCLC 4, 15; DAM POET;**
  PC 9
  See also CA 104; 122; DA3; EW; GFL 1789
  to the Present; MTCW 1, 2; RGWL
Valle-Inclan, Ramon (Maria) del
  1866-1936 .... **TCLC 5; DAM MULT;**
  HLC 2
  See also CA 106; 153; CANR 80; DLB 134;
  EW; HW 2; RGSF; RGWL
Vallejo, Antonio Buero
  See Buero Vallejo, Antonio
Vallejo, Cesar (Abraham)
  1892-1938 .. **TCLC 3, 56; DAM MULT;**
  HLC 2
  See also CA 105; 153; HW 1; LAW; RGWL
Valles, Jules 1832-1885 .... **NCLC 71**
  See also DLB 123; GFL 1789 to the Present
Vallette, Marguerite Eymery
  1860-1953 .... **TCLC 67**
  See also CA 182; DLB 123, 192
Valle Y Pena, Ramon del
  See Valle-Incl
Van Ash, Cay 1918- .... **CLC 34**
Vanbrugh, SirJohn 1664-1726 . **LC 21; DAM**
  DRAM
  See also DLB 80; IDTP; RGEL
Van Campen, Karl
  See Campbell, John W(ood, Jr.)
Vance, Gerald
  See Silverberg, Robert
Vance, Jack .... **CLC 35**
  See also Vance, John Holbrook
  See also DLB 8; SCFW 2
Vance, John Holbrook 1916-
  See Queen, Ellery; Vance, Jack
  See also CA 29-32R; CANR 17, 65; CMW;
  FANT; MTCW 1; SFW
Van Den Bogarde, Derek Jules Gaspard
  Ulric Niven 1921-1999 .... **CLC 14**
  See also CA 77-80; 179; DLB 19
Vandenburgh, Jane .... **CLC 59**
  See also CA 168
Vanderhaeghe, Guy 1951- .... **CLC 41**
  See also CA 113; CANR 72
van der Post, Laurens (Jan)
  1906-1996 .... **CLC 5**
  See also AFW; CA 5-8R; 155; CANR 35;
  CN; DLB 204; RGEL
van de Wetering, Janwillem 1931- ... **CLC 47**
  See also CA 49-52; CANR 4, 62, 90; CMW
Van Dine, S. S. .... **TCLC 23**
  See also Wright, Willard Huntington
Van Doren, Carl (Clinton)
  1885-1950 .... **TCLC 18**
  See also CA 111; 168
Van Doren, Mark 1894-1972 .... **CLC 6, 10**
  See also CA 1-4R; 37-40R; CANR 3; DLB
  45; MTCW 1, 2; RGAL
Van Druten, John (William)
  1901-1957 .... **TCLC 2**
  See also CA 104; 161; DLB 10; RGAL
Van Duyn, Mona (Jane) 1921- ...... **CLC 3, 7,**
  63, 116; DAM POET
  See also CA 9-12R; CANR 7, 38, 60; CP;
  CWP; DLB 5
Van Dyne, Edith
  See Baum, L(yman) Frank
van Itallie, Jean-Claude 1936- .... **CLC 3**
  See also CA 45-48; CAAS 2; CAD; CANR
  1, 48; CD; DLB 7
van Ostaijen, Paul 1896-1928 .... **TCLC 33**
  See also CA 163

Van Peebles, Melvin 1932- .... **CLC 2, 20;**
  DAM MULT
  See also BW 2, 3; CA 85-88; CANR 27,
  67, 82
van Schendel, Arthur(-Francois-emile)
  1874-1946 .... **TCLC 56**
Vansittart, Peter 1920- .... **CLC 42**
  See also CA 1-4R; CANR 3, 49, 90; CN;
  RHW
Van Vechten, Carl 1880-1964 .... **CLC 33**
  See also AMWS 2; CA 183; 89-92; DLB 4,
  9, 51; RGAL
van Vogt, A(lfred) E(lton) 1912-2000 . **CLC 1**
  See also CA 21-24R; 190; CANR 28; DLB
  8; SATA 14; SATA-Obit 124; SFW
Varda, Agnes 1928- .... **CLC 16**
  See also CA 116; 122
Vargas Llosa, (Jorge) Mario (Pedro)
  1936- .... **CLC 3, 6, 9, 10, 15, 31, 42, 85;**
  DA; DAB; DAC; DAM MST, MULT,
  NOV; HLC 2
  See also CA 73-76; CANR 18, 32, 42, 67;
  DA3; DLB 145; DNFS; HW 1, 2; LAW;
  MTCW 1, 2; RGWL
Vasiliu, Gheorghe
  See Bacovia, George
  See also CA 123; 189; DLB 220
Vassa, Gustavus
  See Equiano, Olaudah
Vassilikos, Vassilis 1933- .... **CLC 4, 8**
  See also CA 81-84; CANR 75
Vaughan, Henry 1621-1695 .... **LC 27**
  See also DLB 131; PAB; RGEL
Vaughn, Stephanie .... **CLC 62**
Vazov, Ivan (Minchov) 1850-1921 . **TCLC 25**
  See also CA 121; 167; DLB 147
Veblen, Thorstein B(unde)
  1857-1929 .... **TCLC 31**
  See also AMWS 1; CA 115; 165
Vega, Lope de 1562-1635 .... **LC 23; HLCS 2**
  See also RGWL
Vendler, Helen (Hennessy) 1933- ... **CLC 138**
  See also CA 41-44R; CANR 25, 72; MTCW
  1, 2
Venison, Alfred
  See Pound, Ezra (Weston Loomis)
Verdi, Marie de
  See Mencken, H(enry) L(ouis)
Verdu, Matilde
  See Cela, Camilo Jos
Verga, Giovanni (Carmelo)
  1840-1922 .... **TCLC 3; SSC 21**
  See also CA 104; 123; EW; RGSF; RGWL
Vergil 70B.C.-19B.C. .... **CMLC 9, 40; DA;**
  DAB; DAC; DAM MST, POET; PC
  12; WLCS
  See also Virgil
  See also DA3; DLB 211; EFS 1
Verhaeren, emile (Adolphe Gustave)
  1855-1916 .... **TCLC 12**
  See also CA 109; GFL 1789 to the Present
Verlaine, Paul (Marie) 1844-1896 .. **NCLC 2,**
  51; DAM POET; PC 2, 32
  See also EW; GFL 1789 to the Present;
  RGWL
Verne, Jules (Gabriel) 1828-1905 ... **TCLC 6,**
  52
  See also AAYA 16; CA 110; 131; DA3;
  DLB 123; GFL 1789 to the Present;
  JRDA; MAICYA; RGWL; SATA 21;
  SCFW; SFW; WCH
Verus, Marcus Annius
  See Antoninus, Marcus Aurelius
Very, Jones 1813-1880 .... **NCLC 9**
  See also DLB 1; RGAL
Vesaas, Tarjei 1897-1970 .... **CLC 48**
  See also CA 190; 29-32R
Vialis, Gaston
  See Simenon, Georges (Jacques Christian)

Vian, Boris 1920-1959 .... **TCLC 9**
  See also CA 106; 164; DLB 72; GFL 1789
  to the Present; MTCW 2; RGWL
Viaud, (Louis Marie) Julien 1850-1923
  See Loti, Pierre
  See also CA 107
Vicar, Henry
  See Felsen, Henry Gregor
Vicker, Angus
  See Felsen, Henry Gregor
Vidal, Gore 1925- ...... **CLC 2, 4, 6, 8, 10, 22,**
  33, 72, 142; DAM NOV, POP
  See also Box, Edgar
  See also AITN 1; AMWS 4; BEST 90:2;
  CA 5-8R; CAD; CANR 13, 45, 65, 100;
  CD; CDALBS; CN; CPW; DA3; DFS 2;
  DLB 6, 152; INT CANR-13; MTCW 1,
  2; RGAL; RHW
Viereck, Peter (Robert Edwin)
  1916- .... **CLC 4; PC 27**
  See also CA 1-4R; CANR 1, 47; CP; DLB
  5; PFS 9
Vigny, Alfred (Victor) de
  1797-1863 . **NCLC 7, 102; DAM POET;**
  PC 26
  See also DLB 119, 192; EW; GFL 1789 to
  the Present; RGWL
Vilakazi, Benedict Wallet
  1906-1947 .... **TCLC 37**
  See also CA 168
Villa, Jose Garcia 1914-1997 .... **PC 22**
  See also AAL; CA 25-28R; CANR 12
Villarreal, Jose Antonio 1924-
  See also CA 133; CANR 93; DAM MULT;
  DLB 82; HLC 2; HW 1; RGAL
Villaurrutia, Xavier 1903-1950 ...... **TCLC 80**
  See also CA 192; HW 1
Villehardouin, Geoffroi de
  1150(?)-1218(?) .... **CMLC 38**
Villiers de l'Isle Adam, Jean Marie Mathias
  Philippe Auguste 1838-1889 ... **NCLC 3;**
  SSC 14
  See also DLB 123; GFL 1789 to the Present;
  RGSF
Villon, Francois 1431-1463(?) . **LC 62; PC 13**
  See also DLB 208; EW; RGWL
Vine, Barbara .... **CLC 50**
  See also Rendell, Ruth (Barbara)
  See also BEST 90:4
Vinge, Joan (Carol) D(ennison)
  1948- .... **CLC 30; SSC 24**
  See also AAYA 32; CA 93-96; CANR 72;
  SATA 36, 113; SFW; YAW
Viola, Herman J(oseph) 1938- .... **CLC 70**
  See also CA 61-64; CANR 8, 23, 48, 91
Violis, G.
  See Simenon, Georges (Jacques Christian)
Viramontes, Helena Maria 1954-
  See also CA 159; DLB 122; HLCS 2; HW
  2
Virgil
  See Vergil
  See also RGWL; WP
Visconti, Luchino 1906-1976 .... **CLC 16**
  See also CA 81-84; 65-68; CANR 39
Vittorini, Elio 1908-1966 .... **CLC 6, 9, 14**
  See also CA 133; 25-28R; RGWL
Vivekananda, Swami 1863-1902 .... **TCLC 88**
Vizenor, Gerald Robert 1934- .... **CLC 103;**
  DAM MULT
  See also CA 13-16R; CAAS 22; CANR 5,
  21, 44, 67; DLB 175, 227; MTCW 2;
  NNAL; TCWW 2
Vizinczey, Stephen 1933- .... **CLC 40**
  See also CA 128; CCA 1; INT 128
Vliet, R(ussell) G(ordon)
  1929-1984 .... **CLC 22**
  See also CA 37-40R; 112; CANR 18

Warner, Marina 1946- .... **CLC 59**
See also CA 65-68; CANR 21, 55; CN; DLB 194

Warner, Rex (Ernest) 1905-1986 ...... **CLC 45**
See also CA 89-92; 119; DLB 15; RGEL; RHW

Warner, Susan (Bogert)
1819-1885 .... **NCLC 31**
See also DLB 3, 42, 239

Warner, Sylvia (Constance) Ashton
See Ashton-Warner, Sylvia (Constance)

Warner, Sylvia Townsend
1893-1978 .... **CLC 7, 19; SSC 23**
See also BRWS 7; CA 61-64; 77-80; CANR 16, 60; DLB 34, 139; FANT; FW; MTCW 1, 2; RGEL; RGSF; RHW

Warren, Mercy Otis 1728-1814 ..... **NCLC 13**
See also DLB 31, 200; RGAL

Warren, Robert Penn 1905-1989 .. **CLC 1, 4, 6, 8, 10, 13, 18, 39, 53, 59; DA; DAB; DAC; DAM MST, NOV, POET; SSC 4; WLC**
See also AITN 1; CA 13-16R; 129; CANR 10, 47; CDALB 1968-1988; DLB 2, 48, 152; DLBY 80, 89; INT CANR-10; MTCW 1, 2; RGAL; RGSF; RHW; SATA 46; SATA-Obit 63; SSFS 8

Warshofsky, Isaac
See Singer, Isaac Bashevis

Warton, Thomas 1728-1790 ..... **LC 15; DAM POET**
See also DLB 104, 109; RGEL

Waruk, Kona
See Harris, (Theodore) Wilson

Warung, Price .... **TCLC 45**
See also Astley, William
See also RGEL

Warwick, Jarvis
See Garner, Hugh
See also CCA 1

Washington, Alex
See Harris, Mark

Washington, Booker T(aliaferro)
1856-1915 ...... **TCLC 10; BLC 3; DAM MULT**
See also BW 1; CA 114; 125; DA3; RGAL; SATA 28

Washington, George 1732-1799 .... **LC 25**
See also DLB 31

Wassermann, (Karl) Jakob
1873-1934 .... **TCLC 6**
See also CA 104; 163; DLB 66

Wasserstein, Wendy 1950- .. **CLC 32, 59, 90; DAM DRAM; DC 4**
See also CA 121; 129; CABS 3; CAD; CANR 53, 75; CD; CWD; DA3; DFS 5; DLB 228; FW; INT 129; MTCW 2; SATA 94

Waterhouse, Keith (Spencer) 1929- . **CLC 47**
See also CA 5-8R; CANR 38, 67; CBD; CN; DLB 13, 15; MTCW 1, 2

Waters, Frank (Joseph) 1902-1995 .. **CLC 88**
See also CA 5-8R; 149; CAAS 13; CANR 3, 18, 63; DLB 212; DLBY 86; RGAL; TCWW 2

Waters, Mary C. .... **CLC 70**

Waters, Roger 1944- .... **CLC 35**

Watkins, Frances Ellen
See Harper, Frances Ellen Watkins

Watkins, Gerrold
See Malzberg, Barry N(athaniel)

Watkins, Gloria Jean 1952(?)-
See hooks, bell
See also BW 2; CA 143; CANR 87; MTCW 2; SATA 115

Watkins, Paul 1964- .... **CLC 55**
See also CA 132; CANR 62, 98

Watkins, Vernon Phillips
1906-1967 .... **CLC 43**
See also CA 9-10; 25-28R; CAP 1; DLB 20; RGEL

Watson, Irving S.
See Mencken, H(enry) L(ouis)

Watson, John H.
See Farmer, Philip Jose

Watson, Richard F.
See Silverberg, Robert

Waugh, Auberon (Alexander)
1939-2001 .... **CLC 7**
See also CA 45-48; 192; CANR 6, 22, 92; DLB 14, 194

Waugh, Evelyn (Arthur St. John)
1903-1966 .. **CLC 1, 3, 8, 13, 19, 27, 44, 107; DA; DAB; DAC; DAM MST, NOV, POP; SSC 41; WLC**
See also BRW; CA 85-88; 25-28R; CANR 22; CDBLB 1914-1945; DA3; DLB 15, 162, 195; MTCW 1, 2; RGEL; RGSF

Waugh, Harriet 1944- .... **CLC 6**
See also CA 85-88; CANR 22

Ways, C. R.
See Blount, Roy (Alton), Jr.

Waystaff, Simon
See Swift, Jonathan

Webb, Beatrice (Martha Potter)
1858-1943 .... **TCLC 22**
See also CA 117; 162; DLB 190; FW

Webb, Charles (Richard) 1939- .... **CLC 7**
See also CA 25-28R

Webb, James H(enry), Jr. 1946- ...... **CLC 22**
See also CA 81-84

Webb, Mary Gladys (Meredith)
1881-1927 .... **TCLC 24**
See also CA 182; 123; DLB 34; FW

Webb, Mrs. Sidney
See Webb, Beatrice (Martha Potter)

Webb, Phyllis 1927- .... **CLC 18**
See also CA 104; CANR 23; CCA 1; CP; CWP; DLB 53

Webb, Sidney (James) 1859-1947 .. **TCLC 22**
See also CA 117; 163; DLB 190

Webber, Andrew Lloyd .... **CLC 21**
See also Lloyd Webber, Andrew
See also DFS 7

Weber, Lenora Mattingly
1895-1971 .... **CLC 12**
See also CA 19-20; 29-32R; CAP 1; SATA 2; SATA-Obit 26

Weber, Max 1864-1920 .... **TCLC 69**
See also CA 109; 189

Webster, John 1580(?)-1634(?) ... **LC 33; DA; DAB; DAC; DAM DRAM, MST; DC 2; WLC**
See also BRW; CDBLB Before 1660; DLB 58; IDTP; RGEL

Webster, Noah 1758-1843 .... **NCLC 30**
See also DLB 1, 37, 42, 43, 73

Wedekind, (Benjamin) Frank(lin)
1864-1918 .... **TCLC 7; DAM DRAM**
See also CA 104; 153; DLB 118; EW; RGWL

Wehr, Demaris .... **CLC 65**

Weidman, Jerome 1913-1998 .... **CLC 7**
See also AITN 2; CA 1-4R; 171; CAD; CANR 1; DLB 28

Weil, Simone (Adolphine)
1909-1943 .... **TCLC 23**
See also CA 117; 159; EW; FW; GFL 1789 to the Present; MTCW 2

Weininger, Otto 1880-1903 .... **TCLC 84**

Weinstein, Nathan
See West, Nathanael

Weinstein, Nathan von Wallenstein
See West, Nathanael

Weir, Peter (Lindsay) 1944- .... **CLC 20**
See also CA 113; 123

Weiss, Peter (Ulrich) 1916-1982 .. **CLC 3, 15, 51; DAM DRAM**
See also CA 45-48; 106; CANR 3; DFS 3; DLB 69, 124; RGWL

Weiss, Theodore (Russell) 1916- ... **CLC 3, 8, 14**
See also CA 9-12R; CAAE 189; CAAS 2; CANR 46, 94; CP; DLB 5

Welch, (Maurice) Denton
1915-1948 .... **TCLC 22**
See also CA 121; 148; RGEL

Welch, James 1940- ..... **CLC 6, 14, 52; DAM MULT, POP**
See also CA 85-88; CANR 42, 66; CN; CP; CPW; DLB 175; NNAL; RGAL; TCWW 2

Weldon, Fay 1931- . **CLC 6, 9, 11, 19, 36, 59, 122; DAM POP**
See also BRWS 4; CA 21-24R; CANR 16, 46, 63, 97; CDBLB 1960 to Present; CN; CPW; DLB 14, 194; FW; HGG; INT CANR-16; MTCW 1, 2; RGEL; RGSF

Wellek, Rene 1903-1995 .... **CLC 28**
See also CA 5-8R; 150; CAAS 7; CANR 8; DLB 63; INT CANR-8

Weller, Michael 1942- .... **CLC 10, 53**
See also CA 85-88; CAD; CD

Weller, Paul 1958- .... **CLC 26**

Wellershoff, Dieter 1925- .... **CLC 46**
See also CA 89-92; CANR 16, 37

Welles, (George) Orson 1915-1985 .. **CLC 20, 80**
See also AAYA 40; CA 93-96; 117

Wellman, John McDowell 1945-
See Wellman, Mac
See also CA 166; CD

Wellman, Mac .... **CLC 65**
See also Wellman, John McDowell; Wellman, John McDowell
See also CAD; RGAL

Wellman, Manly Wade 1903-1986 ... **CLC 49**
See also CA 1-4R; 118; CANR 6, 16, 44; FANT; SATA 6; SATA-Obit 47; SFW

Wells, Carolyn 1869(?)-1942 .... **TCLC 35**
See also CA 113; 185; CMW; DLB 11

Wells, H(erbert) G(eorge)
1866-1946 . **TCLC 6, 12, 19; DA; DAB; DAC; DAM MST, NOV; SSC 6; WLC**
See also AAYA 18; BRW; CA 110; 121; CDBLB 1914-1945; CLR 64; DA3; DLB 34, 70, 156, 178; HGG; MTCW 1, 2; RGEL; RGSF; SATA 20; SFW; SSFS 3; SUFW; WCH; YAW

Wells, Rosemary 1943- .... **CLC 12**
See also AAYA 13; CA 85-88; CANR 48; CLR 16, 69; CWRI; MAICYA; SAAS 1; SATA 18, 69, 114; YAW

Welsh, Irvine 1958- .... **CLC 144**
See also CA 173

Welty, Eudora 1909-2001 .... **CLC 1, 2, 5, 14, 22, 33, 105; DA; DAB; DAC; DAM MST, NOV; SSC 1, 27; WLC**
See also CA 9-12R; CABS 1; CANR 32, 65; CDALB 1941-1968; CN; CSW; DA3; DLB 2, 102, 143; DLBD 12; DLBY 87; HGG; MTCW 1, 2; RGAL; RGSF; RHW; SSFS 2, 10

Wen I-to 1899-1946 .... **TCLC 28**

Wentworth, Robert
See Hamilton, Edmond

Werfel, Franz (Viktor) 1890-1945 ... **TCLC 8**
See also CA 104; 161; DLB 81, 124; RGWL

Wergeland, Henrik Arnold
1808-1845 .... **NCLC 5**

Wersba, Barbara 1932- .... **CLC 30**
 See also AAYA 2, 30; CA 29-32R, 182;
 CAAE 182; CANR 16, 38; CLR 3; DLB
 52; JRDA; MAICYA; SAAS 2; SATA 1,
 58; SATA-Essay 103; YAW
Wertmueller, Lina 1928- .... **CLC 16**
 See also CA 97-100; CANR 39, 78
Wescott, Glenway 1901-1987 .. **CLC 13; SSC
35**
 See also CA 13-16R; 121; CANR 23, 70;
 DLB 4, 9, 102; RGAL
Wesker, Arnold 1932- ... **CLC 3, 5, 42; DAB;
DAM DRAM**
 See also CA 1-4R; CAAS 7; CANR 1, 33;
 CBD; CD; CDBLB 1960 to Present; DLB
 13; MTCW 1; RGEL
Wesley, Richard (Errol) 1945- .... **CLC 7**
 See also BW 1; CA 57-60; CAD; CANR
 27; CD; DLB 38
Wessel, Johan Herman 1742-1785 .... **LC 7**
West, Anthony (Panther)
 1914-1987 .... **CLC 50**
 See also CA 45-48; 124; CANR 3, 19; DLB
 15
West, C. P.
 See Wodehouse, P(elham) G(renville)
West, Cornel (Ronald) 1953- .... **CLC 134;
BLCS**
 See also CA 144; CANR 91
West, Delno C(loyde), Jr. 1936- .... **CLC 70**
 See also CA 57-60
West, Dorothy 1907-1998 .... **TCLC 108**
 See also BW 2; CA 143; 169; DLB 76
West, (Mary) Jessamyn 1902-1984 ... **CLC 7,
17**
 See also CA 9-12R; 112; CANR 27; DLB
 6; DLBY 84; MTCW 1, 2; RHW; SATA-
 Obit 37; YAW
West, Morris L(anglo) 1916-1999 ..... **CLC 6,
33**
 See also CA 5-8R; 187; CANR 24, 49, 64;
 CN; CPW; MTCW 1, 2
West, Nathanael 1903-1940 .... **TCLC 1, 14,
44; SSC 16**
 See also CA 104; 125; CDALB 1929-1941;
 DA3; DLB 4, 9, 28; MTCW 1, 2; RGAL
West, Owen
 See Koontz, Dean R(ay)
West, Paul 1930- .... **CLC 7, 14, 96**
 See also CA 13-16R; CAAS 7; CANR 22,
 53, 76, 89; CN; DLB 14; INT CANR-22;
 MTCW 2
West, Rebecca 1892-1983 ... **CLC 7, 9, 31, 50**
 See also BRWS 3; CA 5-8R; 109; CANR
 19; DLB 36; DLBY 83; FW; MTCW 1,
 2; RGEL
Westall, Robert (Atkinson)
 1929-1993 .... **CLC 17**
 See also AAYA 12; CA 69-72; 141; CANR
 18, 68; CLR 13; FANT; JRDA; MAICYA;
 SAAS 2; SATA 23, 69; SATA-Obit 75;
 WYA; YAW
Westermarck, Edward 1862-1939 . **TCLC 87**
Westlake, Donald E(dwin) 1933- .... **CLC 7,
33; DAM POP**
 See also CA 17-20R; CAAS 13; CANR 16,
 44, 65, 94; CMW; CPW; INT CANR-16;
 MTCW 2
Westmacott, Mary
 See Christie, Agatha (Mary Clarissa)
Weston, Allen
 See Norton, Andre
Wetcheek, J. L.
 See Feuchtwanger, Lion
Wetering, Janwillem van de
 See van de Wetering, Janwillem
Wetherald, Agnes Ethelwyn
 1857-1940 .... **TCLC 81**
 See also DLB 99

Wetherell, Elizabeth
 See Warner, Susan (Bogert)
Whale, James 1889-1957 .... **TCLC 63**
Whalen, Philip 1923- .... **CLC 6, 29**
 See also CA 9-12R; CANR 5, 39; CP; DLB
 16; WP
Wharton, Edith (Newbold Jones)
 1862-1937 .... **TCLC 3, 9, 27, 53; DA;
DAB; DAC; DAM MST, NOV; SSC 6;
WLC**
 See also AAYA 25; AMW; AMWR; CA
 104; 132; CDALB 1865-1917; DA3; DLB
 4, 9, 12, 78, 189; DLBD 13; HGG;
 MAWW; MTCW 1, 2; NFS 5, 11; RGAL;
 RGSF; RHW; SSFS 6, 7; SUFW
Wharton, James
 See Mencken, H(enry) L(ouis)
Wharton, William (a pseudonym) . **CLC 18,
37**
 See also CA 93-96; DLBY 80; INT 93-96
Wheatley (Peters), Phillis
 1753(?)-1784 ...... **LC 3, 50; BLC 3; DA;
DAC; DAM MST, MULT, POET; PC
3; WLC**
 See also AFAW 1, 2; CDALB 1640-1865;
 DA3; DLB 31, 50; RGAL
Wheelock, John Hall 1886-1978 .... **CLC 14**
 See also CA 13-16R; 77-80; CANR 14;
 DLB 45
White, Babington
 See Braddon, Mary Elizabeth
White, E(lwyn) B(rooks)
 1899-1985 . **CLC 10, 34, 39; DAM POP**
 See also AITN 2; AMWS 1; CA 13-16R;
 116; CANR 16, 37; CDALBS; CLR 1, 21;
 CPW; DA3; DLB 11, 22; FANT; MAI-
 CYA; MTCW 1, 2; RGAL; SATA 2, 29,
 100; SATA-Obit 44
White, Edmund (Valentine III)
 1940- .... **CLC 27, 110; DAM POP**
 See also AAYA 7; CA 45-48; CANR 3, 19,
 36, 62; CN; DA3; DLB 227; MTCW 1, 2
White, Hayden V. 1928- .... **CLC 148**
 See also CA 128
White, Patrick (Victor Martindale)
 1912-1990 ...... **CLC 3, 4, 5, 7, 9, 18, 65,
69; SSC 39**
 See also BRWS 1; CA 81-84; 132; CANR
 43; MTCW 1; RGEL; RGSF; RHW
White, Phyllis Dorothy James 1920-
 See James, P. D.
 See also CA 21-24R; CANR 17, 43, 65;
 CMW; CN; CPW; DAM POP; DA3;
 MTCW 1, 2
White, T(erence) H(anbury)
 1906-1964 .... **CLC 30**
 See also AAYA 22; CA 73-76; CANR 37;
 DLB 160; FANT; JRDA; MAICYA;
 RGEL; SATA 12; SUFW; YAW
White, Terence de Vere 1912-1994 ... **CLC 49**
 See also CA 49-52; 145; CANR 3
White, Walter
 See White, Walter F(rancis)
 See also BLC; DAM MULT
White, Walter F(rancis)
 1893-1955 .... **TCLC 15**
 See also White, Walter
 See also BW 1; CA 115; 124; DLB 51
White, William Hale 1831-1913
 See Rutherford, Mark
 See also CA 121; 189
Whitehead, Alfred North
 1861-1947 .... **TCLC 97**
 See also CA 117; 165; DLB 100
Whitehead, E(dward) A(nthony)
 1933- .... **CLC 5**
 See also CA 65-68; CANR 58; CD

Whitemore, Hugh (John) 1936- .... **CLC 37**
 See also CA 132; CANR 77; CBD; CD;
 INT CA-132
Whitman, Sarah Helen (Power)
 1803-1878 .... **NCLC 19**
 See also DLB 1
Whitman, Walt(er) 1819-1892 .. **NCLC 4, 31,
81; DA; DAB; DAC; DAM MST,
POET; PC 3; WLC**
 See also AMW; AMWR; CDALB 1640-
 1865; DA3; DLB 3, 64, 224; PAB; PFS 2,
 3; RGAL; SATA 20; WP; WYAS 1
Whitney, Phyllis A(yame) 1903- ...... **CLC 42;
DAM POP**
 See also AAYA 36; AITN 2; BEST 90:3;
 CA 1-4R; CANR 3, 25, 38, 60; CLR 59;
 CMW; CPW; DA3; JRDA; MAICYA;
 MTCW 2; RHW; SATA 1, 30; YAW
Whittemore, (Edward) Reed (Jr.)
 1919- .... **CLC 4**
 See also CA 9-12R; CAAS 8; CANR 4; CP;
 DLB 5
Whittier, John Greenleaf
 1807-1892 .... **NCLC 8, 59**
 See also AMWS 1; DLB 1; RGAL
Whittlebot, Hernia
 See Coward, No
Wicker, Thomas Grey 1926-
 See Wicker, Tom
 See also CA 65-68; CANR 21, 46
Wicker, Tom .... **CLC 7**
 See also Wicker, Thomas Grey
Wideman, John Edgar 1941- ...... **CLC 5, 34,
36, 67, 122; BLC 3; DAM MULT**
 See also AFAW 1, 2; BW 2, 3; CA 85-88;
 CANR 14, 42, 67; CN; DLB 33, 143;
 MTCW 2; RGAL; RGSF; SSFS 6, 12
Wiebe, Rudy (Henry) 1934- .. **CLC 6, 11, 14,
138; DAC; DAM MST**
 See also CA 37-40R; CANR 42, 67; CN;
 DLB 60; RHW
Wieland, Christoph Martin
 1733-1813 .... **NCLC 17**
 See also DLB 97; RGWL
Wiene, Robert 1881-1938 .... **TCLC 56**
Wieners, John 1934- .... **CLC 7**
 See also CA 13-16R; CP; DLB 16; WP
Wiesel, Elie(zer) 1928- ...... **CLC 3, 5, 11, 37;
DA; DAB; DAC; DAM MST, NOV;
WLCS**
 See also AAYA 7; AITN 1; CA 5-8R; CAAS
 4; CANR 8, 40, 65; CDALBS; DA3; DLB
 83; DLBY 87; INT CANR-8; MTCW 1,
 2; NFS 4; SATA 56; YAW
Wiggins, Marianne 1947- .... **CLC 57**
 See also BEST 89:3; CA 130; CANR 60
Wiggs, Susan .... **CLC 70**
Wight, James Alfred 1916-1995
 See Herriot, James
 See also CA 77-80; CPW; SATA 55; SATA-
 Brief 44; YAW
Wilbur, Richard (Purdy) 1921- ..... **CLC 3, 6,
9, 14, 53, 110; DA; DAB; DAC; DAM
MST, POET**
 See also AMWS 3; CA 1-4R; CABS 2;
 CANR 2, 29, 76, 93; CDALBS; CP; DLB
 5, 169; INT CANR-29; MTCW 1, 2; PAB;
 PFS 11, 12; RGAL; SATA 9, 108; WP
Wild, Peter 1940- .... **CLC 14**
 See also CA 37-40R; CP; DLB 5
Wilde, Oscar (Fingal O'Flahertie Wills)
 1854(?)-1900 .... **TCLC 1, 8, 23, 41; DA;
DAB; DAC; DAM DRAM, MST, NOV;
SSC 11; WLC**
 See also BRW; CA 104; 119; CDBLB 1890-
 1914; DA3; DFS 4, 8, 9; DLB 10, 19, 34,
 57, 141, 156, 190; FANT; RGEL; RGSF;
 SATA 24; SSFS 7; SUFW; TEA; WCH

Wilder, Billy .... **CLC 20**
See also Wilder, Samuel
See also DLB 26
Wilder, Samuel 1906-
See Wilder, Billy
See also CA 89-92
Wilder, Stephen
See Marlowe, Stephen
Wilder, Thornton (Niven)
1897-1975 .. **CLC 1, 5, 6, 10, 15, 35, 82;
DA; DAB; DAC; DAM DRAM, MST,
NOV; DC 1; WLC**
See also AAYA 29; AITN 2; AMW; CA 13-
16R; 61-64; CANR 40; CDALBS; DA3;
DFS 1, 4; DLB 4, 7, 9, 228; DLBY 97;
MTCW 1, 2; RGAL; RHW; WYAS 1
Wilding, Michael 1942- .... **CLC 73**
See also CA 104; CANR 24, 49; CN; RGSF
Wiley, Richard 1944- .... **CLC 44**
See also CA 121; 129; CANR 71
Wilhelm, Kate .... **CLC 7**
See also Wilhelm, Katie (Gertrude)
See also AAYA 20; CAAS 5; DLB 8; INT
CANR-17; SCFW 2
Wilhelm, Katie (Gertrude) 1928-
See Wilhelm, Kate
See also CA 37-40R; CANR 17, 36, 60, 94;
MTCW 1; SFW
Wilkins, Mary
See Freeman, Mary E(leanor) Wilkins
Willard, Nancy 1936- .... **CLC 7, 37**
See also CA 89-92; CANR 10, 39, 68; CLR
5; CWP; CWRI; DLB 5, 52; FANT; MAI-
CYA; MTCW 1; SATA 37, 71; SATA-
Brief 30
William of Ockham 1290-1349 ..... **CMLC 32**
Williams, Ben Ames 1889-1953 ..... **TCLC 89**
See also CA 183; DLB 102
Williams, C(harles) K(enneth)
1936- .... **CLC 33, 56, 148; DAM POET**
See also CA 37-40R; CAAS 26; CANR 57;
CP; DLB 5
Williams, Charles
See Collier, James Lincoln
Williams, Charles (Walter Stansby)
1886-1945 .... **TCLC 1, 11**
See also CA 104; 163; DLB 100, 153;
FANT; RGEL; SUFW
Williams, (George) Emlyn
1905-1987 .... **CLC 15; DAM DRAM**
See also CA 104; 123; CANR 36; DLB 10,
77; MTCW 1
Williams, Hank 1923-1953 .... **TCLC 81**
Williams, Hugo 1942- .... **CLC 42**
See also CA 17-20R; CANR 45; CP; DLB
40
Williams, J. Walker
See Wodehouse, P(elham) G(renville)
Williams, John A(lfred) 1925- ..... **CLC 5, 13;
BLC 3; DAM MULT**
See also AFAW 2; BW 2, 3; CA 53-56;
CAAS 3; CANR 6, 26, 51; CN; CSW;
DLB 2, 33; INT CANR-6; RGAL; SFW
Williams, Jonathan (Chamberlain)
1929- .... **CLC 13**
See also CA 9-12R; CAAS 12; CANR 8;
CP; DLB 5
Williams, Joy 1944- .... **CLC 31**
See also CA 41-44R; CANR 22, 48, 97
Williams, Norman 1952- .... **CLC 39**
See also CA 118
Williams, Sherley Anne 1944-1999 . **CLC 89;
BLC 3; DAM MULT, POET**
See also AFAW 2; BW 2, 3; CA 73-76; 185;
CANR 25, 82; DLB 41; INT CANR-25;
SATA 78; SATA-Obit 116
Williams, Shirley
See Williams, Sherley Anne

Williams, Tennessee 1914-1983 . **CLC 1, 2, 5,
7, 8, 11, 15, 19, 30, 39, 45, 71, 111; DA;
DAB; DAC; DAM DRAM, MST; DC
4; WLC**
See also AAYA 31; AITN 1, 2; CA 5-8R;
108; CABS 3; CAD; CANR 31; CDALB
1941-1968; DA3; DFS 1,3,7,12; DLB 7;
DLBD 4; DLBY 83; GLL 1; MTCW 1, 2;
RGAL
Williams, Thomas (Alonzo)
1926-1990 .... **CLC 14**
See also CA 1-4R; 132; CANR 2
Williams, William C.
See Williams, William Carlos
Williams, William Carlos
1883-1963 .... **CLC 1, 2, 5, 9, 13, 22, 42,
67; DA; DAB; DAC; DAM MST,
POET; PC 7; SSC 31**
See also CA 89-92; CANR 34; CDALB
1917-1929; DA3; DLB 4, 16, 54, 86;
MTCW 1, 2; PAB; PFS 1, 6, 11; RGAL;
RGSF; WP
Williamson, David (Keith) 1942- ..... **CLC 56**
See also CA 103; CANR 41; CD
Williamson, Ellen Douglas 1905-1984
See Douglas, Ellen
See also CA 17-20R; 114; CANR 39
Williamson, Jack .... **CLC 29**
See also Williamson, John Stewart
See also CAAS 8; DLB 8; SCFW 2
Williamson, John Stewart 1908-
See Williamson, Jack
See also CA 17-20R; CANR 23, 70; SFW
Willie, Frederick
See Lovecraft, H(oward) P(hillips)
Willingham, Calder (Baynard, Jr.)
1922-1995 .... **CLC 5, 51**
See also CA 5-8R; 147; CANR 3; CSW;
DLB 2, 44; IDFW 3; MTCW 1
Willis, Charles
See Clarke, Arthur C(harles)
Willy
See Colette, (Sidonie-Gabrielle)
Willy, Colette
See Colette, (Sidonie-Gabrielle)
See also GLL 1
Wilson, A(ndrew) N(orman) 1950- .. **CLC 33**
See also BRWS 6; CA 112; 122; CN; DLB
14, 155, 194; MTCW 2
Wilson, Angus (Frank Johnstone)
1913-1991 . **CLC 2, 3, 5, 25, 34; SSC 21**
See also BRWS 1; CA 5-8R; 134; CANR
21; DLB 15, 139, 155; MTCW 1, 2;
RGEL; RGSF
Wilson, August 1945- ... **CLC 39, 50, 63, 118;
BLC 3; DA; DAB; DAC; DAM
DRAM, MST, MULT; DC 2; WLCS**
See also AAYA 16; AFAW 2; AMWS 8; BW
2, 3; CA 115; 122; CAD; CANR 42, 54,
76; CD; DA3; DFS 3,7; DLB 228; MTCW
1, 2; RGAL
Wilson, Brian 1942- .... **CLC 12**
Wilson, Colin 1931- .... **CLC 3, 14**
See also CA 1-4R; CAAS 5; CANR 1, 22,
33, 77; CMW; CN; DLB 14, 194; HGG;
MTCW 1; SFW
Wilson, Dirk
See Pohl, Frederik
Wilson, Edmund 1895-1972 .. **CLC 1, 2, 3, 8,
24**
See also CA 1-4R; 37-40R; CANR 1, 46;
DLB 63; MTCW 1, 2; RGAL
Wilson, Ethel Davis (Bryant)
1888(?)-1980 .... **CLC 13; DAC; DAM
POET**
See also CA 102; DLB 68; MTCW 1;
RGEL

Wilson, Harriet E. Adams
1827(?)-1863(?) .... **NCLC 78; BLC 3;
DAM MULT**
See also DLB 50
Wilson, John 1785-1854 .... **NCLC 5**
Wilson, John (Anthony) Burgess 1917-1993
See Burgess, Anthony
See also CA 1-4R; 143; CANR 2, 46; DAC;
DAM NOV; DA3; MTCW 1, 2
Wilson, Lanford 1937- .... **CLC 7, 14, 36;
DAM DRAM**
See also CA 17-20R; CABS 3; CAD; CANR
45, 96; CD; DFS 4, 9, 12; DLB 7
Wilson, Robert M. 1944- .... **CLC 7, 9**
See also CA 49-52; CAD; CANR 2, 41; CD;
MTCW 1
Wilson, Robert McLiam 1964- .... **CLC 59**
See also CA 132
Wilson, Sloan 1920- .... **CLC 32**
See also CA 1-4R; CANR 1, 44; CN
Wilson, Snoo 1948- .... **CLC 33**
See also CA 69-72; CBD; CD
Wilson, William S(mith) 1932- .... **CLC 49**
See also CA 81-84
Wilson, (Thomas) Woodrow
1856-1924 .... **TCLC 79**
See also CA 166; DLB 47
Wilson and Warnke eds. .... **CLC 65**
Winchilsea, Anne (Kingsmill) Finch
1661-1720
See Finch, Anne
See also RGEL
Windham, Basil
See Wodehouse, P(elham) G(renville)
Wingrove, David (John) 1954- .... **CLC 68**
See also CA 133; SFW
Winnemucca, Sarah 1844-1891 .... **NCLC 79;
DAM MULT**
See also DLB 175; NNAL; RGAL
Winstanley, Gerrard 1609-1676 .... **LC 52**
Wintergreen, Jane
See Duncan, Sara Jeannette
Winters, Janet Lewis .... **CLC 41**
See also Lewis, Janet
See also DLBY 87
Winters, (Arthur) Yvor 1900-1968 .... **CLC 4,
8, 32**
See also AMWS 2; CA 11-12; 25-28R; CAP
1; DLB 48; MTCW 1; RGAL
Winterson, Jeanette 1959- .... **CLC 64; DAM
POP**
See also BRWS 4; CA 136; CANR 58; CN;
CPW; DA3; DLB 207; FANT; FW; GLL
1; MTCW 2; RHW
Winthrop, John 1588-1649 .... **LC 31**
See also DLB 24, 30
Wirth, Louis 1897-1952 .... **TCLC 92**
Wiseman, Frederick 1930- .... **CLC 20**
See also CA 159
Wister, Owen 1860-1938 .... **TCLC 21**
See also CA 108; 162; DLB 9, 78, 186;
RGAL; SATA 62; TCWW 2
Witkacy
See Witkiewicz, Stanislaw Ignacy
Witkiewicz, Stanislaw Ignacy
1885-1939 .... **TCLC 8**
See also CA 105; 162; DLB 215; RGWL;
SFW
Wittgenstein, Ludwig (Josef Johann)
1889-1951 .... **TCLC 59**
See also CA 113; 164; MTCW 2
Wittig, Monique 1935(?)- .... **CLC 22**
See also CA 116; 135; CWW 2; DLB 83;
FW; GLL 1
Wittlin, Jozef 1896-1976 .... **CLC 25**
See also CA 49-52; 65-68; CANR 3

Literary Criticism Series
Cumulative Topic Index

This index lists all topic entries in Gale's *Classical and Medieval Literature Criticism, Contemporary Literary Criticism, Literature Criticism from 1400 to 1800, Nineteenth-Century Literature Criticism,* and *Twentieth-Century Literary Criticism.*

Topic Index

NCLC Cumulative Nationality Index

AMERICAN

Alcott, Amos Bronson **1**
Alcott, Louisa May **6, 58, 83**
Alger, Horatio Jr. **8, 83**
Allston, Washington **2**
Apess, William **73**
Audubon, John James **47**
Barlow, Joel **23**
Beecher, Catharine Esther **30**
Bellamy, Edward **4, 86**
Bird, Robert Montgomery **1**
Brackenridge, Hugh Henry **7**
Brentano, Clemens (Maria) **1**
Brown, Charles Brockden **22, 74**
Brown, William Wells **2, 89**
Brownson, Orestes Augustus **50**
Bryant, William Cullen **6, 46**
Burney, Fanny **12, 54**
Calhoun, John Caldwell **15**
Channing, William Ellery **17**
Child, Lydia Maria **6, 73**
Chivers, Thomas Holley **49**
Cooke, John Esten **5**
Cooper, James Fenimore **1, 27, 54**
Crockett, David **8**
Dana, Richard Henry Sr. **53**
Delany, Martin Robinson **93**
Dickinson, Emily (Elizabeth) **21, 77**
Douglass, Frederick **7, 55**
Dunlap, William **2**
Dwight, Timothy **13**
Emerson, Mary Moody **66**
Emerson, Ralph Waldo **1, 38, 98**
Field, Eugene **3**
Foster, Hannah Webster **99**
Foster, Stephen Collins **26**
Frederic, Harold **10**
Freneau, Philip Morin **1**
Hale, Sarah Josepha (Buell) **75**
Halleck, Fitz-Greene **47**
Hamilton, Alexander **49**
Hammon, Jupiter **5**
Harris, George Washington **23**
Hawthorne, Nathaniel **2, 10, 17, 23, 39, 79, 95**
Hayne, Paul Hamilton **94**
Holmes, Oliver Wendell **14, 81**
Horton, George Moses **87**
Irving, Washington **2, 19, 95**
Jackson, Helen Hunt **90**
Jacobs, Harriet A(nn) **67**
James, Henry Sr. **53**
Jefferson, Thomas **11, 103**
Kennedy, John Pendleton **2**
Kirkland, Caroline M. **85**
Lanier, Sidney **6**
Lazarus, Emma **8**
Lincoln, Abraham **18**
Longfellow, Henry Wadsworth **2, 45, 101, 103**
Lowell, James Russell **2, 90**
Melville, Herman **3, 12, 29, 45, 49, 91, 93**

Mowatt, Anna Cora **74**
Murray, Judith Sargent **63**
Parkman, Francis Jr. **12**
Parton, Sara Payson Willis **86**
Paulding, James Kirke **2**
Pinkney, Edward **31**
Poe, Edgar Allan **1, 16, 55, 78, 94, 97**
Rowson, Susanna Haswell **5, 69**
Sedgwick, Catharine Maria **19, 98**
Shaw, Henry Wheeler **15**
Sheridan, Richard Brinsley **5, 91**
Sigourney, Lydia Howard (Huntley) **21, 87**
Simms, William Gilmore **3**
Smith, Joseph Jr. **53**
Southworth, Emma Dorothy Eliza Nevitte **26**
Stowe, Harriet (Elizabeth) Beecher **3, 50**
Taylor, Bayard **89**
Thoreau, Henry David **7, 21, 61**
Timrod, Henry **25**
Trumbull, John **30**
Truth, Sojourner **94**
Tyler, Royall **3**
Very, Jones **9**
Warner, Susan (Bogert) **31**
Warren, Mercy Otis **13**
Webster, Noah **30**
Whitman, Sarah Helen (Power) **19**
Whitman, Walt(er) **4, 31, 81**
Whittier, John Greenleaf **8, 59**
Wilson, Harriet E. Adams **78**
Winnemucca, Sarah **79**

ARGENTINIAN

Echeverria, (Jose) Esteban (Antonino) **18**
Hernández, José **17**

AUSTRALIAN

Adams, Francis **33**
Clarke, Marcus (Andrew Hislop) **19**
Gordon, Adam Lindsay **21**
Kendall, Henry **12**

AUSTRIAN

Grillparzer, Franz **1, 102**
Lenau, Nikolaus **16**
Nestroy, Johann **42**
Raimund, Ferdinand Jakob **69**
Sacher-Masoch, Leopold von **31**
Stifter, Adalbert **41**

CANADIAN

Crawford, Isabella Valancy **12**
Haliburton, Thomas Chandler **15**
Lampman, Archibald **25**
Moodie, Susanna (Strickland) **14**
Richardson, John **55**
Traill, Catharine Parr **31**

COLOMBIAN

Isaacs, Jorge Ricardo **70**

CUBAN

Martí (y Pérez), José (Julian) **63**

CZECH

Macha, Karel Hynek **46**

DANISH

Andersen, Hans Christian **7, 79**
Grundtvig, Nicolai Frederik Severin **1**
Jacobsen, Jens Peter **34**
Kierkegaard, Soren **34, 78**

ENGLISH

Ainsworth, William Harrison **13**
Arnold, Matthew **6, 29, 89**
Arnold, Thomas **18**
Austen, Jane **1, 13, 19, 33, 51, 81, 95**
Bagehot, Walter **10**
Barbauld, Anna Laetitia **50**
Barham, Richard Harris **77**
Barnes, William **75**
Beardsley, Aubrey **6**
Beckford, William **16**
Beddoes, Thomas Lovell **3**
Bentham, Jeremy **38**
Blake, William **13, 37, 57**
Borrow, George (Henry) **9**
Bowles, William Lisle **103**
Brontë, Anne **4, 71, 102**
Brontë, Charlotte **3, 8, 33, 58**
Brontë, Emily (Jane) **16, 35**
Browning, Elizabeth Barrett **1, 16, 61, 66**
Browning, Robert **19, 79**
Bulwer-Lytton, Edward (George Earle Lytton) **1, 45**
Burton, Richard F(rancis) **42**
Byron, George Gordon (Noel) **2, 12**
Carlyle, Thomas **22, 70**
Carroll, Lewis **2, 53**
Clare, John **9, 86**
Clough, Arthur Hugh **27**
Cobbett, William **49**
Coleridge, Hartley **90**
Coleridge, Samuel Taylor **9, 54, 99**
Coleridge, Sara **31**
Collins, (William) Wilkie **1, 18, 93**
Cowper, William **8, 94**
Crabbe, George **26**
Craik, Dinah Maria (Mulock) **38**
Darwin, Charles **57**
De Quincey, Thomas **4, 87**
Dickens, Charles (John Huffam) **3, 8, 18, 26, 37, 50, 86**
Disraeli, Benjamin **2, 39, 79**
Dobell, Sydney Thompson **43**
Du Maurier, George **86**
Eden, Emily **10**
Eliot, George **4, 13, 23, 41, 49, 89**
FitzGerald, Edward **9**
Forster, John **11**

481

Nationality Index

NCLC-102 Title Index

485

ISBN 0-7876-5234-2